C++ Programming: From Problem Analysis to Program Design

C++ Programming: From Problem Analysis to Program Design

D.S. Malik

Australia • Canada • Mexico • Singapore • Spain • United Kingdom • United States

C++ Programming: From Problem Analysis to Program Design

by D.S. Malik

Senior Editor:
Jennifer Muroff

Managing Editor:
Jennifer Locke

Development Editor:
Susan Gilbert, Edex

Associate Product Manager:
Janet Aras

Editorial Assistant:
Christy Urban

Production Editor:
Aimee Poirier

Associate Product Marketing Manager:
Angie Laughlin

Cover Designer:
Efrat Reis

Compositor:
GEX Publishing Services

Manufacturing Coordinator:
Alexander Schall

Printed in the United States

2 3 4 5 6 7 8 9 QUEB 06 05 04 03 02

For more information, contact Course Technology, 25 Thomson Place, Boston, Massachusetts, 02210.

Or find us on the World Wide Web at: www.course.com

ISBN 0-619-06213-4

TO

My Daughter

Shelly Malik

BRIEF

Contents

TABLE OF

Contents

Preface

Welcome to *C++ Programming: From Problem Analysis to Program Design.* Designed for a first Computer Science (CS1) C++ course, this text will provide a breath of fresh air to you and your students. The CS1 course serves as the cornerstone of the Computer Science curriculum. My primary goal is to motivate and excite all CS1 students, regardless of their level. Motivation breeds excitement for learning. Motivation and excitement are critical factors that lead to the success of the programming student. This text is a culmination and development of my classroom notes throughout more than fifty semesters of teaching successful programming to Computer Science students.

C++ Programming: From Problem Analysis to Program Design started as a collection of brief examples, exercises, and lengthy programming examples to supplement the books that were in use at our university. It soon turned into a collection large enough to develop into a text. *The approach taken in this book to present the material is, in fact, driven by the students' demand for clarity and readability.* The material was written and rewritten until students felt comfortable with it. Most of the examples in this book resulted from student interaction in the classroom.

As with any profession, practice is essential. Cooking students practice their recipes. Budding violinists practice their scales. New programmers must practice solving problems and writing code. This is not a C++ cookbook. We do not simply list the C++ syntax followed by an example, we dissect the "why" behind all the concepts. The crucial question of "why?" is answered for every topic when first introduced. This technique offers a bridge to learning C++. Students must understand the "why?" in order to be motivated to learn.

Traditionally, a C++ programming neophyte needed a working knowledge of another programming language. This book assumes no prior programming experience. However, some adequate mathematics background such as college algebra is required.

APPROACH

The programming language C++, which evolved from C, is no longer considered an industry-only language. Numerous colleges and universities use C++ for their first programming language course. C++ is a combination of structured programming and object-oriented programming, and this book addresses both types.

This book can be easily divided into two parts: structured programming and object-oriented programming. The first twelve chapters form the structured programming part; Chapters 13 through 18 form the object-oriented part. However, the first eleven chapters (except Chapter 8) are essential to move on to the object-oriented portion.

In July 1998, ANSI/ISO Standard C++ was officially approved. This book focuses on ANSI/ISO Standard C++, while at the same time provides instructions on how to write the same programs using Standard C++. Even though the syntax of Standard C++ and ANSI/ISO Standard C++ is mostly the same, Chapter 8 discusses some of the features of ANSI/ISO Standard C++ that are not available in Standard C++.

Chapter 1 briefly reviews the history of computers and programming languages. The reader can quickly skim through this chapter and become familiar with some of the hardware components and the software parts of the computer. This chapter also describes structured and object-oriented programming.

After completing Chapter 2, students become familiar with the basics of C++ and are ready to write programs that are complicated enough to do some computations. Input/output is fundamental to any programming language. It is introduced early, in Chapter 3, and is covered in detail.

Chapters 4 and 5 introduce control structures to alter the sequential flow of execution. Chapters 6 and 7 study user-defined functions. It is recommended that readers with no prior programming background spend extra time on Chapters 6 and 7. Several examples are provided to help readers understand the concepts of parameter passing and the scope of an identifier.

Chapter 8 discusses the user-defined simple data type (enumeration type), the namespace mechanism of ANSI/ISO Standard C++, and the `string` type. The earlier versions of C did not include the enumeration type. Enumeration types have a very limited use; their main purpose is to make the program readable. This book is organized such that readers can skip the section on enumeration types during the first reading without experiencing any discontinuity, and then later go through this section.

Chapters 9 and 10 describe arrays in detail. Searching and sorting algorithms are studied in Chapter 10. Chapter 11 introduces and discusses recursion.

Chapter 12 introduces records (`struct`s). The introduction of `struct`s in this book is similar to C `struct`s. In fact, this chapter can be completely skipped because this is not a prerequisite for any of the remaining chapters.

Chapter 13 begins the study of Object-Oriented Programming (OOP) and introduces classes. The first half of this chapter shows how classes are defined and used in a program. The second half of the chapter introduces abstract data types (ADT). This chapter shows how classes in C++ are a natural way to implement ADT. Chapter 14 continues with the fundamentals of Object-Oriented Design (OOD) and OOP, and discusses inheritance and compositions. It explains how classes in C++ provide a natural mechanism for OOD and how C++ supports OOP. Chapter 14 also discusses how to find objects in a given problem.

Chapter 15 studies pointers in detail. After introducing pointers and how to use them in a program, this chapter highlights the peculiarities of classes with pointer data members and how to avoid them. Chapter 15 also discusses a type of polymorphism accomplished via virtual functions.

Chapter 16 continues the study of OOD and OOP. In particular, it studies polymorphism in C++. Chapter 16 specifically discusses two types of polymorphism—overloading and templates.

Chapters 17 and 18 are devoted to the study of data structures. Discussed in detail are linked lists in Chapter 17, and stacks and queues in Chapter 18. The programming code developed in these chapters is generic. These chapters effectively use the fundamentals of OOD.

Appendix A lists the reserved words in C++. Appendix B shows the precedence and associativity of the C++ operators. Appendix C lists the ASCII (American Standard Code for Information Interchange) and EBCDIC (Extended Binary Coded Decimal Interchange Code) character sets. Appendix D lists the C++ operators that can be overloaded. Appendix E describes the naming conventions of the header files in both ANSI/ISO Standard C++ and Standard C++. Appendix F discusses some of the most widely used library routines, and includes the names of the standard C++ header files. The program in Appendix G prints the memory size for the built-in data types on your system. Appendix H gives the answers to selected exercises in the text.

Features

Every chapter in this book includes the following features. These features are both conducive to learning and enable students to learn the material at their own pace.

- Four-color interior design shows accurate C++ code and related comments.
- *Learning Objectives* offer an outline of the C++ programming concepts discussed in detail in the chapter.
- *Notes* highlight important facts about the concepts introduced in the chapter.
- More than 275 visual diagrams, both extensive and exhaustive, illustrate difficult concepts.
- Numbered *Examples* illustrate the key concepts with their relevant code. The programming code in these examples is numbered for easy reference, and is followed by a Sample Run. An explanation then follows that describes what each line in the code does.
- *Programming Examples* are complete programs featured at the end of each chapter. These examples include the accurate, concrete stages of Input, Output, Problem Analysis and Algorithm Design, and a Complete Program Listing.
- *Quick Review* offers a summary of the concepts covered in the chapter.
- *Exercises* further reinforce learning and ensure that students have, in fact, learned the material.
- *Programming Exercises* challenge students to write C++ programs with a specified outcome.

From beginning to end, the concepts are introduced at a pace that is conducive to learning. *The writing style of this book is simple and straightforward, and it parallels the teaching style of a classroom.* Before introducing a key concept, we explain why certain elements are necessary. The concepts introduced are then described using examples and small programs.

Each chapter has two types of programs. The first type are small programs that are part of the numbered Examples (*e.g.*, Example 4-1), and are used to explain key concepts. In these examples, each line of the programming code is numbered. The program, illustrated through a Sample Run, is then explained line-by-line. The rationale behind each line is discussed in detail.

This book also features numerous case studies called Programming Examples. These Programming Examples form the backbone of the book and are highlighted with an icon in the margin, such as the one shown to the left of this paragraph.

The programs are designed to be methodical and user-friendly. Each Programming Example starts with a Problem Analysis, and is then followed by the Algorithm Design. Every step of the algorithm is then coded in C++. In addition to teaching problem-solving techniques, these detailed programs show the user how to implement concepts in an actual C++ program. I strongly recommend that students study the Programming Examples very carefully in order to learn C++ effectively.

Quick Review sections at the end of each chapter reinforce learning. After reading the chapter, students can quickly walk through the highlights of the chapter and then test themselves using the ensuing Exercises. Many readers refer to the Quick Review as an easy way to review the chapter before an exam.

All source code and solutions have been written, compiled, and quality assurance tested with ANSI ISO Standard C++ and Standard C++. Programs can be compiled with Microsoft Visual C++ 6.0, Borland C++ Builder 5 command line development tool, or Metrowerks CodeWarrior.

TEACHING TOOLS

The following supplemental materials are available when this book is used in a classroom setting. All of the teaching tools available with this book are provided to the instructor on a single CD-ROM.

Electronic Instructor's Manual. The Instructor's Manual that accompanies this textbook includes:

- Additional instructional material to assist in class preparation, including suggestions for lecture topics.
- Solutions to all the end-of-chapter materials, including the Programming Exercises.

ExamView®. This textbook is accompanied by ExamView, a powerful testing software package that allows instructors to create and administer printed, computer (LAN-based), and Internet exams. ExamView includes hundreds of questions that correspond to the topics covered in this text, enabling students to generate detailed study guides that include page references for further review. These computer-based and Internet testing components allow students to take exams at their computers, and save the instructor time because each exam is graded automatically.

PowerPoint Presentations. This book comes with Microsoft PowerPoint slides for each chapter. These are included as a teaching aid for classroom presentations, either to make available to students on the network for chapter review, or to be printed for classroom distribution. Instructors can add their own slides for additional topics that they introduce to the class.

Distance Learning. Course Technology is proud to offer online courses in WebCT and Blackboard, as well as at MyCourse.com, Course Technology's own course enhancement tool, to provide the most complete and dynamic learning experience possible. When you add online content to one of your courses, you're adding a lot: self-tests, links, glossaries, and—most of all—a gateway to the 21st century's most important information resource. We hope that you will make the most of your course, both online and offline. For more information on how to bring distance learning to your course, contact your local Course Technology sales representative.

Source Code. The source code, in both ANSI/ISO Standard C++ and Standard C++ formats, is available at `www.course.com`, and is also available on the Teaching Tools CD-ROM. The input files needed to run some of the programs are also included with the source code. However, the input files should first be stored on a floppy disk in drive `A:`.

Solution files. The solution files for all programming exercises, in both ANSI/ISO C++ and Standard C++ formats, are available at `www.course.com`, and are also available on the Teaching Tools CD-ROM. The input files needed to run some of the programming exercises are also included with the solution files. However, the input files should first be stored on a floppy disk in drive `A:`.

Acknowledgements

There are many people that I must thank who, one way or another, contributed to the success of this book. First, I would like to thank Dr. William Newman for proofreading the second draft from cover to cover and spotting typos, errors, and making numerous suggestions to improve the text. I must also thank students who, during the preparation, were spontaneous in telling me if certain portions needed to be reworded for better understanding and clearer reading. I am thankful to Professors S.C. Cheng, John N. Mordeson, and Vasant Raval for constantly supporting this project. Dr. Randall L. Crist, whose office is next to mine, provided help in proofreading whenever necessary. I am thankful to Dr. Crist for reading whatever and whenever I gave him something to review. I must thank Lee I. Fenicle, Director, Office of Technology Transfer, Creighton University, for his involvement, support, and for providing encouraging words when I needed them. I am also very grateful to the anonymous reviewers who reviewed earlier versions of this book and offered many critical suggestions on how to improve it.

I owe a great deal to the following reviewers who patiently read each page of every chapter of the current version and made critical comments to improve on the book: Ahmad Abuhejleh, University of Wisconsin, River Falls; C. Michael Allen, University of North Carolina, Charlotte; Paul Ambrose, University of Wisconsin, Milwaukee; Julie Anderson, Capitol College; Carol Hannahs, University of Kentucky: and Judy Scholl,

Austin Community College. Additionally, I would like to thank the reviewers of the proposal package, James McGuffee of St. Edward's University and Thomas Murtagh of Austin Community College. The reviewers will recognize that their criticisms have not been overlooked and, in fact, made this a better book. Thanks to Development Editor Susan Gilbert for carefully editing and promptly returning each chapter. All this would not have been possible without the planning of Senior Editor Jennifer Muroff. My sincere thanks to Jennifer Muroff, as well as Aimee Poirier, Production Editor, and also to the QA department of Course Technology for carefully testing the code.

I am thankful to my parents for their blessings.

Finally, I am thankful for the support of my wife Sadhana and especially my daughter Shelly, to whom this book is dedicated. She cheered me up whenever I was overwhelmed during the writing of this book, and also for making sure that the corrections were in place. Shelly always draws special joy whenever I undertake such projects.

I welcome any comments concerning the text. Comments may be forwarded to the following e-mail address: `malik@creighton.edu`

D.S. Malik

CHAPTER

1

AN OVERVIEW OF COMPUTERS AND PROGRAMMING LANGUAGES

In this chapter, you will:

- Learn about different types of computers
- Explore the hardware and software components of a computer system
- Learn about the language of a computer
- Learn about the evolution of programming languages
- Examine high-level programming languages
- Discover what a compiler is and what it does
- Examine how a high-level language program is processed
- Learn what an algorithm is and explore problem-solving techniques
- Become aware of structured design and object-oriented design programming methodologies
- Become aware of Standard C++ and ANSI/ISO Standard C++

INTRODUCTION

Today we live in an era where information is processed almost at the speed of light. Through computers, the technological revolution is drastically changing the way we live and communicate with one another. Terms such as "the Internet," which was unfamiliar just a few years ago, are very common today. With the help of computers you can send letters to, and receive letters from, loved ones within seconds. You no longer need to send a résumé by mail to apply for a job; in many cases you can simply submit your job application via the Internet. You can watch how stocks perform in real time, and instantly buy and sell them. Kids in elementary school regularly "surf" the Internet and use computers to design their classroom projects. Students no longer type their papers on typewriters or write them by hand. Instead, they use powerful word processing software to complete their term papers. Many people maintain and balance their checkbooks on computers.

These examples are some of the ways that computers have greatly affected our daily lives. They are all made possible by the availability of different software, which are computer programs. For example, word processing software is a program that enables you to write term papers, create impressive looking résumés, and even write a book. This book, for example, was created with the help of a powerful word processor. Without software a computer is of no use. However, software is developed with the help of programming languages. The programming language C++ is especially well suited for developing software to accomplish a specific task.

Until the early 1990s, before beginning to teach a programming language course, instructors spent the first few weeks just teaching their students how to use computers. Today, by the time students graduate from high school, they know very well how to work with a computer. This book is not concerned with explaining how to use computers. Rather, it teaches you how to write programs in the language called C++. It is useful, however, to at least understand some of the basic terminology and different components of a computer before you begin programming. This chapter briefly describes the main components of a computer system, the history and evolution of computer languages, and some fundamental ideas about how to solve problems with computer programming.

A BRIEF OVERVIEW OF THE HISTORY OF COMPUTERS

In the 1950s, computers were large devices accessible only to a very few people. All work—including surgery, accounting, word processing, and calculations among other tasks—was done without the aid of computers. In the 1960s, multimillion-dollar computers emerged, and only large companies were able to afford them. These computers were very large in size, and only computer experts were allowed to use them. During the mid-1970s, computers became cheaper and smaller. By the mid-1990s, people from all walks of life were able to afford them. During the late 1990s, small computers became even less expensive and much faster. Although several categories of computers exist, such as mainframe, midsize, and micro, all computers share some basic elements.

Elements of a Computer System

A computer is an electronic device capable of performing commands. The basic commands that a computer performs are input (get data), output (display result), storage, and performance of arithmetic and logical operations.

In today's market, personal computers are sold with descriptions such as Pentium 4 Processor 1.4 GHz, 128MB RAM, 40GB HD, 19-inch SVGA monitor and come with preloaded software such as operating systems, games, encyclopedias, and application software such as word processors or money management programs. These descriptions represent two categories: hardware and software. Items such as "Pentium 4 Processor 1.4 GHz, 128MB RAM, 40GB HD, 19-inch SVGA monitor" fall into the hardware category. Items such as "operating systems, games, encyclopedias, and application software" fall into the software category. Let's look at the hardware first.

Hardware

Major hardware components include the following: central processing unit (CPU); main memory (MM), also called random access memory (RAM); input/output devices; and secondary storage. Some examples of input devices are the keyboard, mouse, and secondary storage. Examples of output devices are the screen, printer, and secondary storage. Let's look at each of these components in more detail.

Central Processing Unit

The **central processing unit (CPU)** is the brain of the computer and the single most expensive piece of hardware in your personal computer. The more powerful the CPU, the faster the computer. The CPU contains several components, including the control unit (CU), program counter (PC), instruction register (IR), arithmetic logic unit (ALU), and accumulator (ACC). Figure 1-1 shows how certain components of the CPU fit together.

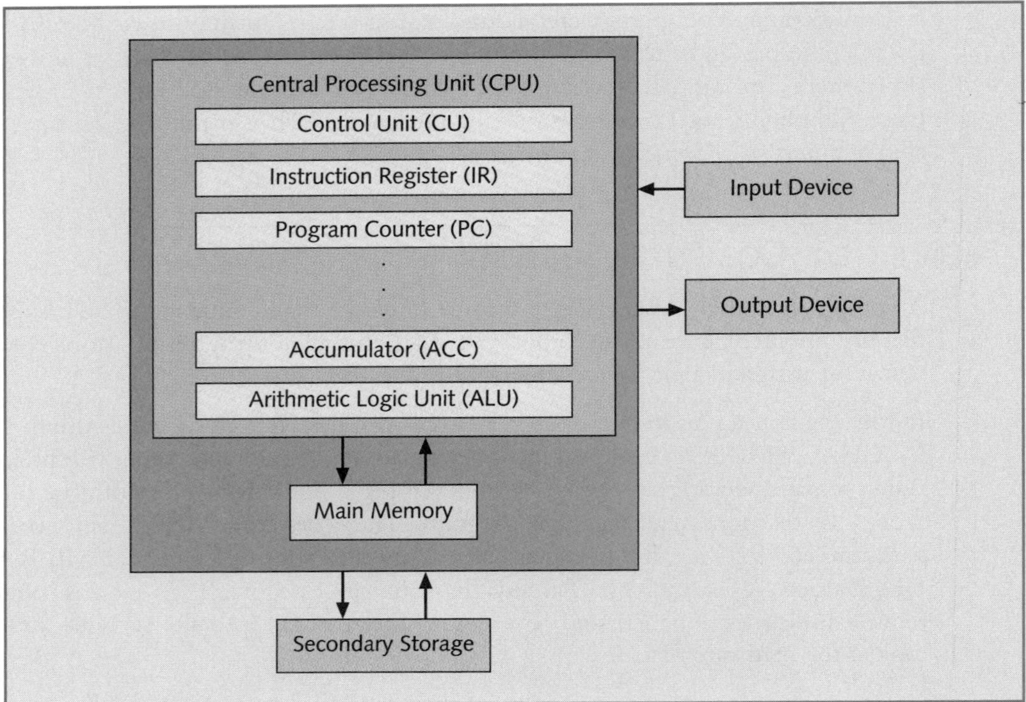

Figure 1-1 Hardware components of a computer

- Similar to the CPU, the **control unit (CU)** is the brain of the CPU. It has three main functions: fetch and decode the instructions, control the flow of information (instruction or data) in and out of main memory, and control the operation of the CPU's internal components.
- The **program counter (PC)** points to the next instruction to be executed.
- The **instruction register (IR)** holds the instruction that is currently being executed.
- The **arithmetic logic unit (ALU)** carries out all arithmetic and logical operations.
- The **accumulator (ACC)** holds the results of the operations performed by the arithmetic logic unit.

Main Memory

Main memory is directly connected to the CPU. All programs must be loaded into main memory before they can be executed. Similarly, all data must be brought into main memory before a program can manipulate it. When the computer is turned off, everything in main memory is lost for good.

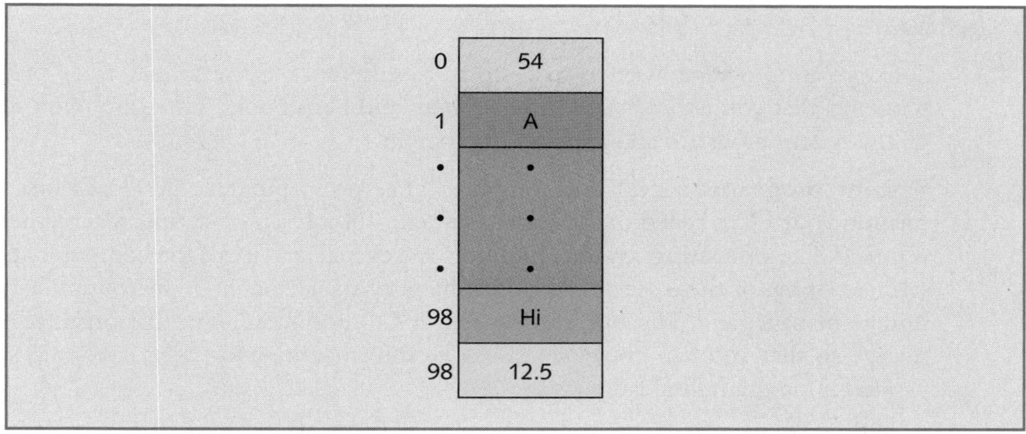

Figure 1-2 Main memory with 100 storage cells

Main memory is an ordered sequence of cells, called **memory cells**. Each cell has a unique location in main memory, called the **address** of the cell. These addresses help you access the information stored in the cell. Figure 1-2 shows main memory with 100 storage cells.

Today's computers come with main memory consisting of millions to billions of cells. Although Figure 1-2 shows data stored in cells, the content of a cell can be either a programming instruction or data.

Secondary Storage

Because programs and data must be stored in main memory before processing and because everything in main memory is lost when the computer is turned off, information stored in main memory must be transferred to some other device for permanent storage. The device that stores information permanently (unless the device becomes unusable or you change the information by rewriting it) is called **secondary storage**. To be able to transfer information from main memory to secondary storage, these components must be directly connected to each other. Examples of secondary storage are hard disks, floppy disks, Zip disks, CD-ROMs, and tapes.

Input/Output Devices

For a computer to perform a useful task, it must be able to take in data and programs and display the results of calculations. The devices that feed data and programs into computers are called **input devices**. The keyboard, mouse, and secondary storage are examples of input devices. The devices that the computer uses to display results are called **output devices**. A monitor, printer, and secondary storage are examples of output devices.

Software

Software are programs written to perform specific tasks. For example, word processors are programs that you use to write letters, papers, and even books. There are two types of programs: system programs and application programs.

System programs control the computer. The system program that loads first when you turn on your PC is called the operating system. Without an operating system, the computer is useless. The **operating system** monitors the overall activity of the computer and provides services. Some of these services include: memory management, input/output activities, and storage management. The operating system has a special program that organizes secondary storage so that you can conveniently access information. Moreover, operating systems are written in programming languages.

Application programs perform a specific task. Word processors, spreadsheets, and games are examples of application programs. All application programs are written using computer programming languages. The operating system is the program that runs application programs.

THE LANGUAGE OF A COMPUTER

When you press `A` on your keyboard and the computer displays `A` on the screen, have you ever wondered what is actually stored inside the computer's main memory? What is the language of the computer? How does it store whatever you type on the keyboard?

Remember that a computer is an electronic device. Electrical signals float inside the computer. There are two types of electrical signals: analog and digital. **Analog signals** are continuous wave forms used to represent such things as sound. Audio tapes, for example, store data in analog signals. **Digital signals** represent information with a sequence of `0`s and `1`s. A `0` represents a low voltage, and a `1` represents a high voltage. Digital signals are more reliable carriers of information than are analog signals and can be copied from one device to another with exact precision. Have you ever noticed that on a copy of an audio tape, the sound quality is not as good as that on the original tape?

Since digital signals are processed inside a computer, the language of a computer, called **machine language**, is a sequence of `0`s and `1`s. The digit `0` or `1` is called a **binary digit**, or **bit**. Sometimes a sequence of `0`s and `1`s is referred to as **binary code**.

Bit: A binary digit `0` or `1`.

A sequence of eight bits is called a **byte**. Every letter, number, or special symbol (such as `*` or `{`) on your keyboard is encoded as a sequence of bits, each having a unique representation.

The most commonly used encoding scheme on personal computers is the seven-bit American Standard Code for Information Interchange (ASCII). The ASCII data set consists of 128 characters numbered 0 through 127. That is, in the ASCII data set, the position of the first character is 0, the position of the second character is 1, and so on. In this scheme, `A` is encoded as `1000001`. In fact, `A` is the 66th character in the ASCII character code, but its position is 65 because the position of the first character is 0. Furthermore, `1000001` is the binary representation of `65`. The character `3` is encoded as `0110011`. For a complete list of the printable ASCII data set, refer to Appendix C.

Inside the computer, every character is represented as a sequence of eight bits, that is, as a byte. Because ASCII is a seven-bit code, you must add `0` to the left of the ASCII encoding of a character. Hence, inside the computer, the character `A` is represented as `01000001`, and the character `3` is represented as `00110011`.

There are other encoding schemes, such as EBCDIC (used by IBM) and Unicode, which is a more recent development. EBCDIC consists of 256 characters; Unicode consists of 65,536 characters. To store a character belonging to Unicode, you need two bytes.

THE EVOLUTION OF PROGRAMMING LANGUAGES

The most basic language of a computer, the machine language, provides program instructions in bits. Even though most computers perform the same kinds of operations, the designers of the computer may have chosen different sets of binary codes to perform the operations. Therefore, the machine language of one machine is not necessarily the same as the machine language of another machine. The only consistency among computers is that in any modern computer, all data is stored and manipulated as binary codes.

Early computers were programmed in machine language. To see how instructions are written in machine language, suppose you want to use the equation

```
wages = rate · hours
```

to calculate weekly wages. Further suppose that the binary code `100100` stands for load, `100110` stands for multiplication, and `100010` stands for store. In machine language, you might need the following sequence of instructions to calculate weekly wages:

```
100100   0000 010001
100110   0000 010010
100010   0000 010011
```

To represent the weekly wages equation in machine language, the programmer had to remember the machine language codes for various operations. Also, to manipulate data, the programmer had to remember the locations of the data in the main memory. This need to remember specific codes made programming not only very difficult, but also error-prone.

Assembly languages were developed to make the programmer's job easier. In assembly language, an instruction is an easy-to-remember form called a **mnemonic**. For example, Table 1-1 shows some examples of instructions in assembly language and their corresponding machine language code.

Table 1-1 Examples of Instructions in Assembly Language and Machine Language

Assembly Language	Machine Language
LOAD	100100
STOR	100010
MULT	100110
ADD	100101
SUB	100011

Using assembly language instructions, you can write the equation to calculate the weekly wages as follows:

```
LOAD   rate
MULT   hours
STOR   wages
```

As you can see, it is much easier to write instructions in assembly language. However, a computer cannot execute assembly language instructions directly. The instructions first have to be translated into machine language. A program called an **assembler** translates the assembly language instructions into machine language.

Assembler: A program that translates a program written in assembly language into an equivalent program in machine language.

Moving from machine language to assembly language made programming easier, but a programmer was still forced to think in terms of individual machine instructions. The next step toward making programming easier was to devise **high-level languages** that were closer to natural languages, such as English, French, German, and Spanish. Basic, FORTRAN, COBOL, Pascal, C, C++, and Java are all high-level languages. You will learn the high-level language C++ in this book.

In C++, you write the weekly wages equation as follows:

```
wages = rate * hours;
```

The instruction written in C++ is much easier to understand and is self-explanatory to a novice user who is familiar with basic arithmetic. As in the case of assembly language, however, the computer cannot directly execute instructions written in a high-level language. To run on a computer, these C++ instructions first need to be translated into machine language. A program called a **compiler** translates instructions written in high-level languages into machine code.

Compiler: A program that translates a program written in a high-level language into the equivalent machine language.

PROCESSING A HIGH-LEVEL LANGUAGE PROGRAM

Now that you have some understanding of what a machine language and a high-level language are and recognize that the computer can understand only machine language, you are ready to review the steps required to execute programs written in a high-level language. You need to carry out the following five steps, as shown in Figure 1-3, to execute a program written in a high-level language.

1. You use an editor to create (that is, type in) a program in a high-level language following the rules, or syntax, of the high-level language. This program is called the **source program**.

Source program: A program written in a high-level language.

2. You must verify that the program obeys the rules of the programming language—that is, the program is syntactically correct—and translate the program into the equivalent machine language. The compiler checks for correctness of syntax and translates a program into machine language. That is, the compiler checks the source program for syntax errors and, if no error is found, translates the program into the equivalent machine language. The equivalent machine language program is called an **object program**.

Object program: The machine language version of the high-level language program.

3. The programs that you write in a high-level language are developed using a software development kit (SDK). The SDK contains many programs that are useful in creating your program. For example, it contains the necessary code to display the results of the program and several mathematical functions to make the programmer's job somewhat easier. Therefore, if certain code is already available, you can use the available code rather than writing your own code. Once the program is developed and successfully compiled, you must still bring the code for the resources used from the SDK into your program to produce a final program that the computer can execute. This prewritten code resides in a place called the **library**. A program called a **linker** combines the object program with the programs from libraries.

Linker: A program that combines the object program with other programs provided by the SDK and used in the program to create the executable code.

4. You must next load the executable program into main memory for execution. A program called a **loader** accomplishes this task.

Loader: A program that loads an executable program into main memory.

5. The final step is to execute the program.

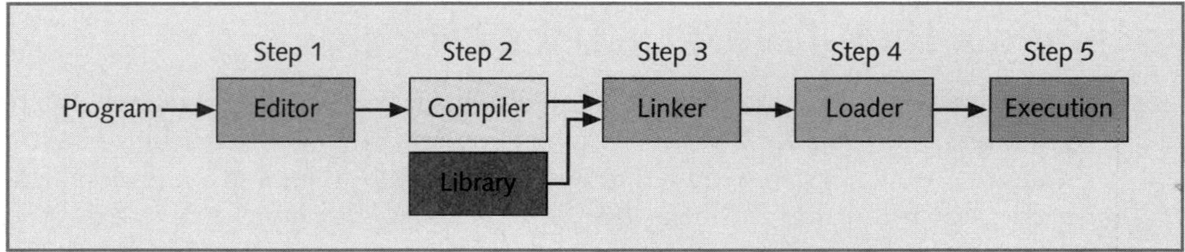

Figure 1-3 Processing a high-level language program

As a programmer, you need to be concerned with only Step 1. That is, you must learn, understand, and master the rules of the programming language to create source programs. As noted earlier, programs are developed using an SDK. Well-known SDKs used to create programs in the high-level language C++ include Visual C++ (from Microsoft), C++ Builder (from Borland), and CodeWarrior (from Metrowerks). These SDKs contain an editor to create the program, a compiler to check the program for syntax errors, a program to link the object code with the resources used from the SDK, and a program to execute the program. Furthermore, these SDKs are quite user-friendly. When you compile your program, the compiler not only identifies the syntax errors, but also typically suggests how to correct them. Moreover, with just a simple command, the object code is linked with the resources used from the SDK. The command that does the linking on Visual C++ is **Build** or **Rebuild**; on C++ Builder, it is **Build** or **Make**; and on CodeWarrior, it is **Make**. (For further clarification regarding the use of these commands, check the documentation of these SDKs.) If the program is not yet complied, each of these commands first compiles the program and then links and produces the executable code.

In general, development of a high-level language program goes through the five steps described above. A C++ program, however, goes through six steps—these five steps plus one more. This extra step takes place after Step 1, creating the source program, and before Step 2, compiling the source program. Of course, the SDK automatically takes care of this extra step. In Chapter 2, after being introduced to some basic elements of C++, you will see how a C++ program is processed. As a programmer, as noted above, you are still mainly concerned with the first step. That is, you must master the rules of C++ to create the source program.

PROGRAMMING WITH THE PROBLEM ANALYSIS–CODING–EXECUTION CYCLE

Programming is a process of problem solving. Different people use different techniques to solve problems. Some techniques are nicely outlined and easy to follow. They not only solve the problem, but also give insight into how the solution was reached. These problem-solving techniques can be easily modified if the domain of the problem changes.

To be a good problem solver and hence to become a good programmer, you must follow good problem-solving techniques. One common problem-solving technique includes analyzing a problem, outlining the problem requirements, and designing steps, called an **algorithm**, to solve the problem.

Algorithm: A step-by-step problem-solving process in which a solution is arrived at in a finite amount of time.

In the programming environment, a problem-solving process requires the following three steps:

1. Analyze the problem, outline the problem and its solution requirements, and design an algorithm to solve the problem.
2. Implement the algorithm in a programming language, such as C++, and verify that the algorithm works.
3. Maintain the program by using and modifying it if the problem domain changes.

Figure 1-4 summarizes this three-step programming process.

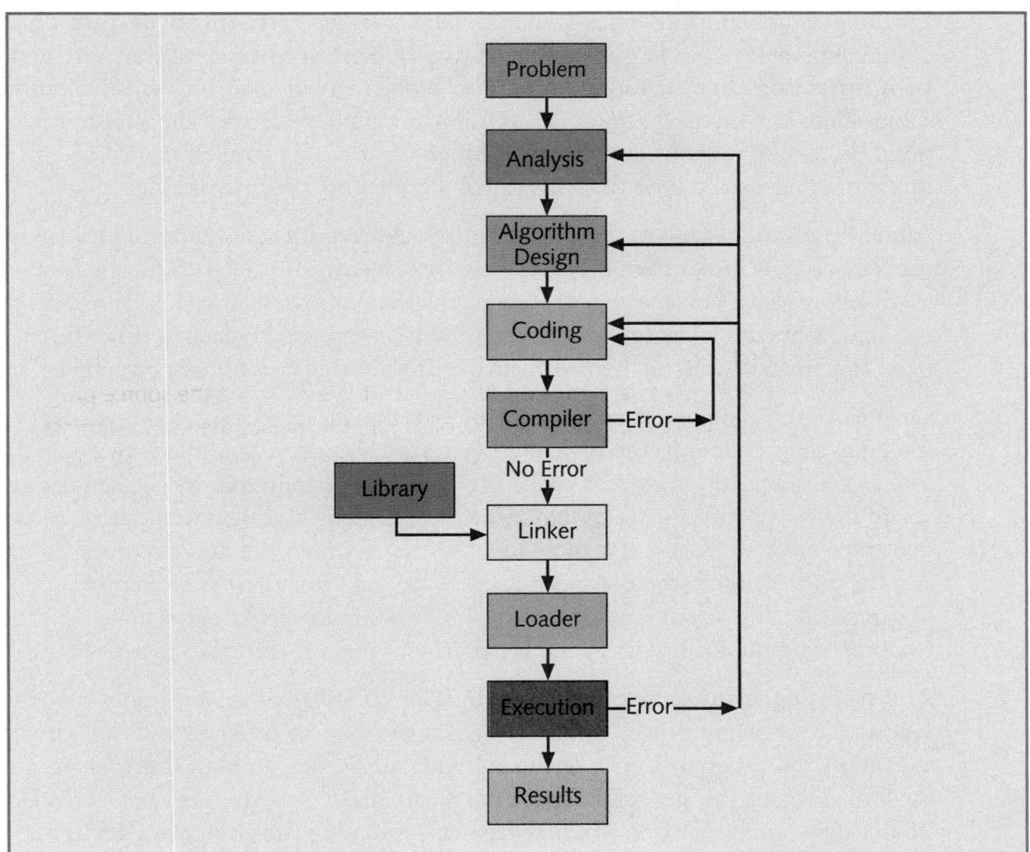

Figure 1-4 Problem analysis–coding–execution cycle

To develop a program to solve a problem, you start by analyzing the problem. You then design the algorithm; write the program instructions in a high-level language, or code the program; and enter the program into a computer system. Analyzing the problem is the first and most important step. This step requires you to do the following:

1. Thoroughly understand the problem.
2. Understand the problem requirements. Requirements can include whether the program requires interaction with the user, whether it manipulates data, whether it produces output, and what the output looks like. If the program manipulates data, the programmer must know what the data is and how it is represented. That is, you need to look at sample data. If the program produces output, you should know how the results should be generated and formatted.
3. If the problem is complex, divide the problem into subproblems and repeat Steps 1 and 2. That is, for complex problems, you need to analyze each subproblem and understand each subproblem's requirements.

Dividing a problem into smaller subproblems is called **structured design**. The structured design approach is also known as **top-down design**, **stepwise refinement**, and **modular programming**. In structured design, the problem is divided into smaller problems. Each subproblem is then analyzed, and a solution is obtained to solve the subproblem. The solutions of all subproblems are then combined to solve the overall problem. This process of implementing a structured design is called **structured programming**.

After you carefully analyze the problem, the next step is to design an algorithm to solve the problem. If you broke the problem into subproblems, you need to design an algorithm for each subproblem. Once you design an algorithm, you need to check it for correctness. You can sometimes test an algorithm's correctness by using sample data. At other times, you might need to perform some mathematical analysis to test the algorithm's correctness.

Once you have designed the algorithm and verified its correctness, the next step is to convert the equivalent code into the high-level language. You use a text editor to enter the program into a computer. You must then make sure that the program follows the language's syntax. To verify the correctness of the syntax, you run the code through a compiler. If the compiler generates error messages, you must identify the errors in the code, remove them, and then run the code through the compiler again. When all syntax errors are removed, the compiler generates the equivalent machine code, the linker links the machine code with the system's resources, and the loader places the program into main memory so that it can be executed.

The final step is to execute the program. The compiler guarantees only that the program follows the language's syntax. It does not guarantee that the program will run correctly. During execution the program might terminate abnormally due to logical errors, such as division by zero. Even if the program terminates normally, it may still generate erroneous results. Under these circumstances, you may have to reexamine the code, the algorithm, or even the problem analysis.

As you can see, you need to do a lot of work before attempting to write programming instructions. Usually, you do this work on paper using a pen or pencil. Taking this careful approach to programming has a number of advantages. It is much easier to discover errors in a program that is well analyzed and well designed. Furthermore, a thoroughly analyzed and carefully designed program is much easier to follow and modify. Even the most experienced programmers spend a considerable amount of time analyzing a problem and designing an algorithm.

Throughout this book, you will not only learn the rules of writing programs in C++, but also learn problem-solving techniques. Each chapter discusses several programming problems, each of which is clearly marked as a Programming Example. These Programming Examples teach techniques of how to analyze and solve problems and also help you understand the concepts discussed in the chapter. To gain the full benefit of this book, we recommend that you work through the Programming Examples at the end of each chapter.

Example 1-1

In this example, we design an algorithm to find the perimeter and area of a rectangle.

To find the perimeter and area of a rectangle, you need to know the rectangle's length and width. The perimeter and area of the rectangle are then given by the following formulas:

```
perimeter = 2 · (length + width)
area = length · width
```

The algorithm to find the perimeter and area of the rectangle is, therefore:

1. Get the length of the rectangle.
2. Get the width of the rectangle.
3. Find the perimeter using the following equation:

   ```
   perimeter = 2 · (length + width)
   ```

4. Find the area using the following equation:

   ```
   area = length · width
   ```

Example 1-2

In this example, we design an algorithm that calculates the monthly paycheck of a salesperson at a local department store.

Every salesperson has a base salary. The salesperson also receives a bonus at the end of each month based on the following criteria: If the salesperson has been with the store for five or less years, the bonus is $10 for each year that he or she has worked there. If the salesperson has been with the store for more than five years, the bonus is $20 for each year that he or she has worked there. The salesperson can earn an additional bonus as follows: If the total sale made by the salesperson for the month is more than $5000 but less than $10000, he or she receives a 3% commission on the sale. If the total sale made by the salesperson for the month is at least $10000, he or she receives a 6% commission on the sale.

To calculate a salesperson's monthly paycheck, you need to know the base salary, the number of years that the salesperson has been with the company, and the total sale made by the salesperson for that month. Suppose **`baseSalary`** denotes the base salary, **`noOfServiceYears`** denotes the number of years that the salesperson has been with the store, **`bonus`** denotes the bonus, **`totalSale`** denotes the total sale made by the salesperson for the month, and **`additionalBonus`** denotes the additional bonus.

You can determine the bonus as follows:

```
if(noOfServiceYears is less than or equal to five)
      bonus = 10 · noOfServiceYears
otherwise
      bonus = 20 · noOfServiceYears
```

Next, you can determine the additional bonus of the salesperson as follows:

```
if(totalSale is less than 5000)
      additionalBonus = 0
otherwise
      if(totalSale is greater than or equal to 5000 and
                        totalSale is less than 10000)
            additionalBonus = totalSale · (0.03)
      otherwise
            additionalBonus = totalSale · (0.06)
```

Following the above discussion, you can now design the algorithm to calculate a salesperson's monthly paycheck.

1. Get **`baseSalary`**.
2. Get **`noOfServiceYears`**.
3. Calculate **`bonus`** using the following formula:

   ```
   if(noOfServiceYears is less than or equal to five)

      bonus = 10 · noOfServiceYears

   otherwise

      bonus = 20 · noOfServiceYears
   ```

4. Get **`totalSale`**.

5. Calculate **additionalBonus** using the following formula:

```
if(totalSale is less than 5000)
   additionalBonus = 0
otherwise
   if(totalSale is greater than or equal to 5000 and
         totalSale is less than 10000)
         additionalBonus = totalSale · (0.03)
otherwise
      additionalBonus = totalSale · (0.06)
```

6. Calculate **payCheck** using the equation

```
payCheck = baseSalary + bonus + additionalBonus
```

OBJECT-ORIENTED PROGRAMMING

The previous section discussed the structured design programming methodology. This section briefly describes a programming methodology called object-oriented design (OOD), the use of which is very widespread.

In OOD, the first step in the problem-solving process is to identify components called objects, which form the basis of the solution, and determine how these objects interact with one another. For example, suppose you want to write a program that automates the video rental process for a local video store. The two main objects in this problem are the video and the customer.

After identifying the objects, the next step is to specify for each object the relevant data and possible operations to be performed on that data. For example, for a video object, the data might include the movie name, starring actors, producer, production company, number of copies in stock, and so on. Some of the operations on a video object might include checking the name of the movie, reducing the number of copies in stock by one after a copy is rented, and incrementing the number of copies in stock by one after a customer returns a particular video.

This illustrates that each object consists of data and operations on that data. An object combines data and operations on the data into a single unit. In OOD, the final program is a collection of interacting objects. A programming language that implements OOD is called an **object-oriented programming (OOP)** language. You will learn about the many advantages of OOD in later chapters.

Because an object consists of data and operations on that data, before you can design and use objects, you need to learn how to represent data in computer memory, how to manipulate data, and how to implement operations. In Chapter 2, you will learn the basic data types of C++ and discover how to represent and manipulate data in computer memory. Chapter 3 discusses how to input data into a C++ program and output the results generated by a C++ program.

To create operations, you write algorithms and implement them in a programming language. Because a data element in a complex program usually has many operations, to separate operations from each other and to use them effectively and in a convenient manner, you use functions to implement algorithms. After a brief introduction in Chapters 2 and 3, you will learn the details of functions in Chapters 6 and 7. Certain algorithms require that a program make decisions, a process called selection. Other algorithms might require certain statements to be repeated until certain conditions are met, a process called repetition. Still other algorithms might require both selection and repetition. You will learn about selection and repetition mechanisms, called control structures, in Chapters 4 and 5. Also, in Chapters 9 and 10, using a mechanism called an array, you will learn how to manipulate data when data items are of the same type, such as items in a list of sales figures.

Finally, to work with objects, you need to know how to combine data and operations on the data into a single unit. In C++, the mechanism that allows you to combine data and operations on the data into a single unit is called a class. You will learn how classes work, how to work with classes, and how to create classes in Chapter 13.

As you can see, you need to learn quite a few things before working with the OOD methodology. To make this learning easier and more effective, this book purposely divides control structures into two chapters (4 and 5), user-defined functions into two chapters (6 and 7), and arrays into two chapters (9 and 10).

For some problems, the structured approach to program design will be very effective. Other problems will be better addressed by OOD. For example, if a problem requires manipulating sets of numbers with mathematical functions, you might use the structured design approach and outline the steps required to obtain the solution. The C++ library supplies a wealth of functions that you can use effectively to manipulate numbers. On the other hand, if you want to write a program that would make a candy machine operational, the OOD approach is more effective. C++ was designed especially to implement OOD. Furthermore, OOD works well and is used in conjunction with structured design.

Both the structured design and OOD approaches require that you master the basic components of a programming language to be an effective programmer. In the next few chapters, you will learn the basic components of C++ required by either type of programming. After presenting the basic concepts, Chapters 2 through 12 will use the structured programming approach to solve and program particular problem solutions. From Chapter 13 onward, the book focuses on problem solving and programming with OOD.

ANSI/ISO STANDARD C++

The programming language C++ evolved from C and was designed by Bjarne Stroustrup at Bell Laboratories in the early 1980s. From the early 1980s through the early 1990s, several C++ compilers were available. Even though the fundamental features of C++ in all compilers were mostly the same, the C++ language, referred to in this book as Standard C++, was evolving in slightly different ways in different compilers. As a consequence, C++ programs were not always portable from one compiler to another.

To address this problem, in the early 1990s, a joint committee of the American National Standard Institution (ANSI) and International Standard Organization (ISO) was established to standardize the syntax of C++. In mid-1998, ANSI/ISO C++ language standards were approved. Most of today's compilers comply with this new standard.

This book focuses on the syntax of C++ as approved by ANSI/ISO, referred to as ANSI/ISO Standard C++. However, since you might come across existing code written in Standard C++ (or if you have an old compiler), the next few chapters show you what changes you would need to make in an ANSI/ISO Standard C++ program. Even though the syntax of Standard C++ and ANSI/ISO Standard C++ is largely the same, certain features are unique to ANSI/ISO Standard C++. These features are clearly identified and discussed in this book.

QUICK REVIEW

1. A computer is an electronic device capable of performing arithmetic and logical operations.
2. A computer system has two components: hardware and software.
3. The central processing unit (CPU) and the main memory are examples of hardware components.
4. The control unit (CU) controls a program's overall execution. It is one of several components of the CPU.
5. The arithmetic logic unit (ALU) is the component of the CPU that performs arithmetic and logical operations.
6. All programs must be brought into main memory before they can be executed.
7. When the power is switched off, everything in main memory is lost.
8. Secondary storage provides permanent storage for information. Hard disks, floppy disks, Zip disks, CD-ROMs, and tapes are examples of secondary storage.
9. Input to the computer is done via an input device. Two common input devices are the keyboard and the mouse.
10. The computer sends its output to an output device such as the computer screen.

11. Software is programs run by the computer.
12. The operating system monitors the overall activity of the computer and provides services.
13. The most basic language of a computer is a sequence of `0`s and `1`s called machine language. Every computer directly understands its own machine language.
14. A bit is a binary digit, `0` or `1`.
15. A byte is a sequence of eight bits.
16. Assembly language uses easy-to-remember instructions called mnemonics.
17. Assemblers are programs that translate a program written in assembly language into machine language.
18. Compilers are programs that translate a program written in a high-level language into machine code, called object code.
19. A linker links the object code with other programs provided by the software development kit (SDK) and used in the program to produce executable code.
20. In a high-level language, five steps are needed to execute a program: edit, compile, link, load, and execute.
21. A loader transfers executable code into main memory.
22. An algorithm is a step-by-step problem-solving process in which a solution is arrived at in a finite amount of time.
23. A problem-solving process has three steps: analyze the problem and design an algorithm, implement the algorithm in a programming language, and maintain the program.
24. Programs written using the structured design approach are easier to understand, easier to test and debug, and easier to modify.
25. In structured design, a problem is divided into smaller subproblems. Each subproblem is solved, and the solutions of all subproblems are then combined to solve the problem.
26. In object-oriented design (OOD), a program is a collection of interacting objects.
27. An object consists of data and operations on those data.
28. The ANSI/ISO Standard C++ syntax was approved in mid-1998.

EXERCISES

1. Mark the following statements as true or false.
   a. Assembly language is the language that uses mnemonics for its instructions.
   b. A compiler translates an assembly language program into machine code.
   c. The arithmetic logic unit performs arithmetic operations and, if an error is found, it outputs the logical errors.
   d. A loader loads the object code from main memory into the CPU for execution.

e. Development of a high-level language program includes six steps.

f. The CPU functions under the control of the control unit.

g. RAM stands for readily available memory.

h. A program written in a high-level programming language is called a source program.

i. The operating system is the first program loaded into the computer when the power is turned on.

j. The first step in the problem-solving process is to analyze the problem.

2. Name some components of the central processing unit.
3. What is the function of the control unit?
4. Name two input devices.
5. Name two output devices.
6. Why is secondary storage needed?
7. Why do you need to translate a program written in a high-level language into machine language?
8. Why would you prefer to write a program in a high-level language rather than a machine language?
9. What are the advantages of problem analysis and algorithm design over directly writing a program in a high-level language?
10. Design an algorithm to find the weighted average of four test scores. The four test scores and their respective weights are given in the following format:

```
testscore1 weight1
...
```

For example, a sample data is as follows:

```
75 0.20
95 0.35
85 0.15
65 0.30
```

11. A salesperson leaves his home every Monday and returns every Friday. He travels by company car. Each day on the road, the salesperson records the amount of gasoline put in the car. Given the starting odometer reading (that is, the odometer reading before he leaves on Monday) and the ending odometer reading (the odometer reading after he returns home on Friday), design an algorithm to find the average miles per gallon. Sample data is as follows:

```
68723 71289 15.75 16.30 10.95 20.65 30.00
```

CHAPTER

2

BASIC ELEMENTS OF C++

In this chapter, you will:

- Become familiar with the basic components of a C++ program, including functions, special symbols, and identifiers
- Explore simple data types and examine the `string` data `type`
- Discover how to use arithmetic operators
- Examine how a program evaluates arithmetic expressions
- Learn what an assignment statement is and what it does
- Discover how to input data into memory using input statements
- Become familiar with the use of increment and decrement operators
- Examine ways to output results using output statements
- Learn how to use preprocessor directives and why they are necessary
- Explore how to properly structure a program, including using comments to document a program
- Learn how to write a C++ program

In this chapter, you will learn the basics of C++. As your objective is to learn the C++ programming language, two questions naturally arise. First, what is a computer program? Second, what is programming? A **computer program** or a program is a sequence of statements whose objective is to accomplish a task. **Programming** is a process of planning and creating a program. These two definitions tell the truth, but not the whole truth, about programming. It may very well take an entire book to give a good and satisfactory definition of programming. You might gain a better grasp of the nature of programming from an analogy, so let us turn to a topic about which almost everyone has some knowledge—cooking. A recipe is also a program, and everyone with some cooking experience can agree on the following:

1. It is usually easier to follow a recipe than to create one.
2. There are good recipes and there are bad recipes.
3. Some recipes are easy to follow and some are not easy to follow.
4. Some recipes produce reliable results and some do not.
5. You must have some knowledge of how to use cooking tools to follow a recipe to completion.
6. To create new recipes, you must have much knowledge and understanding of cooking.

These same six points are also true about programming. Let us take the cooking analogy one step further. Suppose you need to teach someone how to become a chef. How would you go about it? Would you first introduce the person to good food, hoping that a taste for good food develops? Would you have the person follow recipe after recipe in the hope that some of it rubs off? Or, would you first teach the use of tools and the nature of ingredients, the foods and spices, and explain how they fit together? Just as there is disagreement about how to teach cooking, there is disagreement about how to teach programming.

Learning a programming language is like learning to become a chef or learning to play a musical instrument. All three require direct interaction with the tools. You cannot become a good chef or even a poor chef just by reading recipes. Similarly, you cannot become a player by reading books about musical instruments. The same is true of programming. You must have a fundamental knowledge of the language, and you must test your programs on the computer to make sure that each program does what it is supposed to do.

THE BASICS OF A C++ PROGRAM

A C++ program is a collection of one or more subprograms, called functions. Roughly speaking, a **subprogram** or a **function** is a collection of statements, and when it is activated, or executed, it accomplishes something. Some functions, called **predefined** or **standard** functions, are already written for us and are provided as part of the system. But to accomplish most tasks, programmers must learn to write their own functions.

Every C++ program has a function called `main`. Thus, if a C++ program has only one function, it must be the function `main`. Until Chapter 6, other than using some of the predefined functions, you will mainly deal with the function **main**. By the end of this chapter you shall have learned how to write the function **main**.

The following is an example of a C++ program. At this point you should not be concerned with the details of the program.

Example 2-1

The following is a sample C++ program.

```
#include <iostream>

using namespace std;

int main()
{
  cout<<"Welcome to C++ Programming"<<endl;
  return 0;
}
```

If you execute this program, it will print the following line on the screen:

```
Welcome to C++ Programming
```

If you have never seen a program written in a programming language, the C++ program in Example 2-1 may look like a foreign language. To make meaningful sentences in a foreign language, you must learn its alphabet, words, and grammar. The same is true of a programming language. To write meaningful programs, you must learn the programming language's special symbols, words, and syntax rules. The **syntax rules** tell you which statements (instructions) are legal, or accepted by the programming language, and which are not. You must also learn **semantic rules**, which determine the meaning of the instructions. The programming language's rules, symbols, and special words enable you to write programs to solve problems. The syntax rules determine which instructions are valid.

Programming language: A set of rules, symbols, and special words.

You can describe the syntax rules of a programming language in several ways. The language used to describe the syntax rules is called a **metalanguage**. This book uses a metalanguage called **syntax template** to describe the syntax rules. The syntax template is somewhat pictorial, and you can easily visualize it. For example, the syntax template of the function **main** is

```
int main()
{
  statement1
      .
      .
      .
  statementn
  return 0;
}
```

In a syntax template, the shading indicates the part of the definition that is optional. Furthermore, throughout this book, the syntax is enclosed in yellow boxes.

In the remainder of this section, you will learn about some of the special symbols of a C++ program. Other special symbols are introduced as other concepts are encountered in later chapters. Similarly, syntax and semantic rules are introduced and discussed throughout the book.

The smallest individual unit of a program written in any language is called a **token**. C++'s tokens are divided into special symbols, word symbols, and identifiers.

Special Symbols

Following are some of the special symbols:

```
+    -    *    /

.    ;    ?    ,

<=   !=   ==   >=
```

The first row includes mathematical symbols for addition, subtraction, multiplication, and division. The second row consists of punctuation marks taken from English grammar. Note that the comma is also a special symbol. In C++, commas are used to separate items in a list. Semicolons are used to end a C++ statement. Note that a blank, which is not shown above, is also a special symbol. You create a blank symbol by pressing the space bar (only once) on the keyboard. The third row consists of tokens made up of two characters, but which are regarded as a single symbol. No character can come between the two characters, not even a blank.

Word Symbols

A second category of tokens is word symbols. Some of the word symbols include the following:

`int, float, double, char, void, return`

Word symbols are also called **reserved words**, or **keywords**. The letters that make up a reserved word are always lowercase. Like the special symbols, each is considered to be a single symbol. Furthermore, word symbols cannot be redefined within any program; that is, they cannot be used for anything other than their intended use. For a complete list of reserved words, see Appendix A.

Throughout this book, reserved words are shown in blue.

Identifiers

A third category of tokens is identifiers. Identifiers are names of things that appear in programs, such as variables, constants, and functions. Some identifiers are predefined; others are defined by the user. All identifiers must obey C++'s rules for identifiers.

Identifier: A C++ identifier consists of letters, digits, and the underscore character (_), and must begin with a letter or underscore.

Identifiers can be made of only letters, digits, and the underscore character; no other symbols are permitted to form an identifier.

C++ is case sensitive—uppercase and lowercase letters are considered different. Thus, the identifier `NUMBER` is not the same as the identifier `number`. Similarly, the identifiers `X` and `x` are different.

In C++, identifiers can be of any length. In actuality, however, some compilers may not distinguish between identifiers that differ only beyond that system's maximum significant number of characters. (Check your system's documentation for restrictions on the length of identifiers.) For example, if only the first seven characters of the following two identifiers were distinguishable, they would be regarded as the same:

```
program1
program2
```

Two predefined identifiers that you will encounter frequently are `cout`, which is used when generating output, and `cin`, which is used to input data. Unlike reserved words, predefined identifiers can be redefined, but it would not be wise to do so.

Example 2-2

The following are legal identifiers in C++:

```
first
conversion
payRate
counter1
```

Table 2-1 shows some illegal identifiers and explains why they are illegal.

Table 2-1 Examples of Illegal Identifiers

Illegal Identifier	Description
`employee Salary`	There can be no space between `employee` and `Salary`.
`Hello!`	The exclamation mark cannot be used in an identifier.
`one+two`	The symbol + cannot be used in an identifier.
`2nd`	An identifier cannot begin with a digit.

Compiler vendors usually begin certain identifiers with an underscore (_). When the linker links the object program with the system resources provided by the software development kit (SDK), certain errors could occur. Therefore, it is advisable that you should not begin identifiers in your program with an underscore (_).

DATA TYPES

The objective of a C++ program is to manipulate data. Different programs manipulate different data. A program designed to calculate an employee's paycheck will add, subtract, multiply, and divide numbers, and some of the numbers might represent hours worked and pay rate. Similarly, a program designed to alphabetize a class list will manipulate names. You wouldn't use a program designed to perform arithmetic calculations to manipulate alphabetic characters. Furthermore, you wouldn't multiply or subtract names. Reflecting these kinds of underlying differences, C++ categorizes data into different types, and only certain operations can be performed on particular types of data. Although at first it may seem confusing, by being so type conscious, C++ has built-in checks to guard against errors.

Data type: A set of values together with a set of operations.

C++ data types fall into the following three categories and are illustrated in Figure 2-1.

1. Simple data type
2. Structured data type
3. Pointers

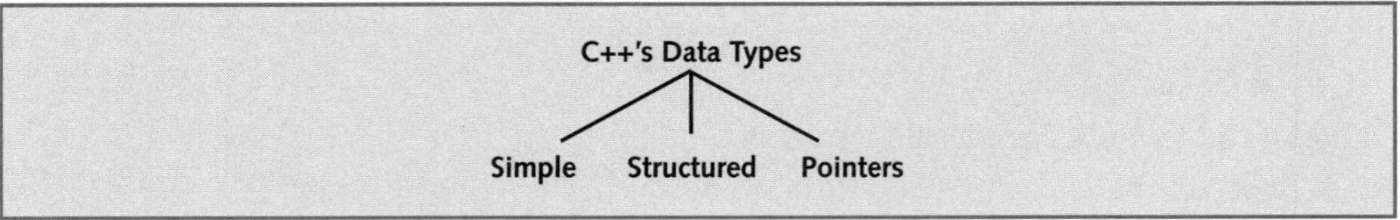

Figure 2-1 C++ data types

For the next few chapters, you will be concerned only with simple data types.

Simple Data Types

The simple data type is the fundamental data type in C++ because it becomes a building block for the structured data type, which you start learning about in Chapter 9. There are three categories of simple data:

1. **Integral**, which is a data type that deals with integers, or numbers without a decimal part
2. **Floating-point**, which is a data type that deals with decimal numbers
3. **Enumeration type**, which is a user-defined data type

Figure 2-2 illustrates these three data types.

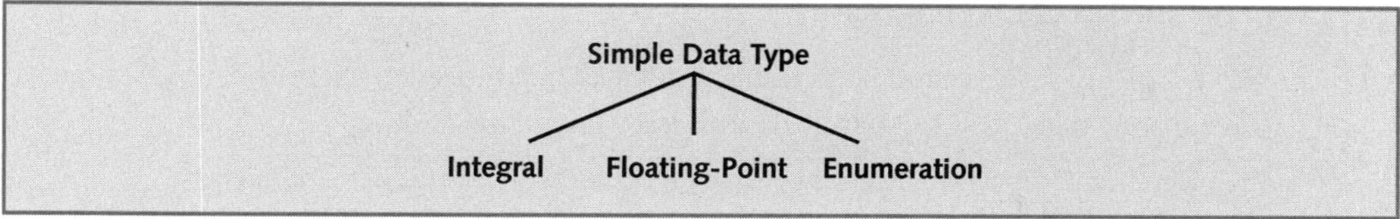

Figure 2-2 Simple data types

The enumeration type is C++'s method for allowing programmers to create their own simple data types. This data type will be discussed in Chapter 8.

Integral data types are further classified into nine categories, as shown in Figure 2-3.

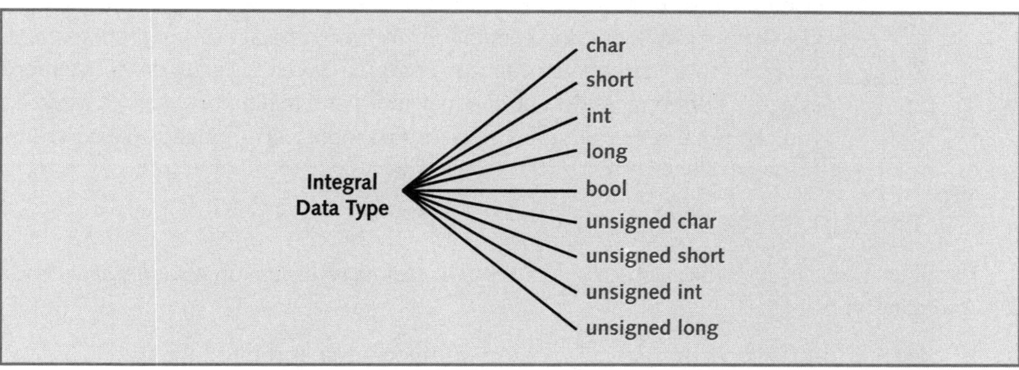

Figure 2-3 Integral data types

Why are there so many categories of the same data type? Every data type has a different set of values associated with it. For example, the `char` data type is used to represent integers between –128 and 127. The `int` data type is used to represent integers between –2147483648 and 2147483647, and the data type `short` is used to represent integers between –32768 and 32767.

Which data type you use depends how big a number your program needs to deal with. In the early days of programming, computers and main memory were very expensive. Only a small amount of memory was available to execute programs and manipulate the data. As a result, programmers had to optimize the use of memory. Because writing and making a program work is already a complicated process, not having to worry about the size of the memory makes for one less thing to think about. Thus, to effectively use memory, a programmer can look at the type of data used in a program and figure out which data type to use.

Newer programming languages have only five categories of simple data types: `integer`, `real`, `char`, `bool`, and the enumeration type. The integral data types that are used in this book are `int`, `bool`, and `char`.

Table 2-2 gives the range of possible values associated with these three data types and the size of memory allocated to manipulate these values.

Table 2-2 Values and Memory Allocation for Three Simple Data Types

Data Type	Values	Storage (in bytes)
`int`	-2147483648 to 2147483647	4
`bool`	`true` and `false`	1
`char`	-128 to 127	1

Use this table only as a guide. Different compilers may allow different ranges of values. Check your compiler's documentation. To find the exact size of the integral data types on a particular system, you can run a program given in Appendix G (Memory Size on a System). Furthermore, to find the maximum and minimum values of these data types, you can run another program given in Appendix F (The Header File `climits`).

The `int` Data Type

This section describes the `int` data type. In fact, this discussion also applies to other integral data types.

Integers in C++, as in mathematics, are numbers such as the following:

`-6728, -67, 0, 78, 36782, +763`

Note the following two rules from these examples:

1. Positive integers do not have to have a `+` sign in front of them.
2. No commas are used within an integer. Recall that in C++, commas are used for separating items in a list. So `36,782` would be interpreted as two integers: `36` and `782`.

The `bool` Data Type

The data type `bool` has only two values: `true` and `false`. Also, `true` and `false` are called the **logical (Boolean) values.** The central purpose of this data type is to manipulate logical (Boolean) expressions. An expression that evaluates to `true` or `false` is called a **logical (Boolean) expression.** Logical (Boolean) expressions will be formally defined and discussed in detail in Chapter 4. In C++, `bool`, `true`, and `false` are reserved words.

The data type `bool` is one of the newest features of C++. To be absolutely sure that you can use it, check your system's documentation to see if this data type is available on your system.

The `char` Data Type

The data type **`char`** is the smallest integral data type. In addition to dealing with small numbers (-128 to 127), the **`char`** data type is used to represent characters—that is letters, digits, and special symbols. Thus, the **`char`** data type can represent every key on your keyboard. When using the **`char`** data type, you enclose each character represented within single quotation marks. Examples of values belonging to the **`char`** data type include the following:

```
'A', 'a', '0', '*', '+', '$', '&'
```

Note that a blank space is a character and is written as `' '`, with a space between the single quotation marks.

The data type **`char`** allows only one symbol to be placed between the single quotation marks. Thus, the value **`'abc'`** is not of the type `char`. Furthermore, even though **`'!='`** and similar special symbols are considered to be one symbol, they are not regarded as possible values of the data type `char`. All the individual symbols located on the keyboard that are printable may be considered as possible values of the **`char`** data type.

Several different character data sets are currently in use. The most common are American Standard Code for Information Interchange (ASCII) and Extended Binary-Coded Decimal Interchange Code (EBCDIC). The ASCII character set has 128 values. The EBCDIC character set has 256 values and was created by IBM. Both character sets are described in Appendix C.

Each of the 128 values of the ASCII character set represents a different character. For example, the value `65` represents `'A'`, and the value `43` represents `'+'`. Thus, each character has a predefined ordering, which is called a **collating sequence**, in the set. The collating sequence is used when you compare characters. For example, the value representing `'B'` is `66`, so `'A'` is smaller than `'B'`. Similarly, `'+'` is smaller than `'A'` since `43` is smaller than `65`.

The 14th character in the ASCII character set is called the newline character and is represented as `'\n'`. (Note that the position of the newline character in the ASCII character set is `13` because the position of the first character is `0`.) Even though the newline character is a combination of two characters, it is treated as one character. Similarly, the horizontal tab character is represented in C++ as `'\t'` and the null character is represented as `'\0'` (back slash followed by zero). Furthermore, the first `32` characters in the ASCII character set are nonprintable. (See Appendix C for a description of these characters.)

Floating-Point Data Types

To deal with decimal numbers, C++ provides the floating-point data type, which we discuss in this section. To facilitate the discussion, let us review a concept from a high school or college algebra course.

You may be familiar with scientific notation. For example:

```
43872918 = 4.3872918 * 10^7       {10 to the power of seven}
.0000265 = 2.65 * 10^(-5)         {10 to the power of minus five}
47.9832 = 4.7983 * 10^1           {10 to the power of one}
```

To represent real numbers, C++ uses a form of scientific notation called **floating-point notation**. Table 2-3 shows how C++ might print a set of real numbers using one machine's interpretation of floating-point notation. In the C++ flotation-point notation, the letter `E` stands for the exponent.

Table 2-3 Examples of Real Numbers Printed in C++ Floating-Point Notation

Real Number	C++ Floating Point-Notation
75.924	7.592400E1
0.18	1.800000E-1
0.0000453	4.530000E-5
-1.482	-1.482000E0
7800.0	7.800000E3

C++ provides three data types to manipulate decimal numbers: `float`, `double`, and `long double`. As in the case of integral data types, the data types `float`, `double`, and `long double` differ in the set of values. Figure 2-4 defines these data types.

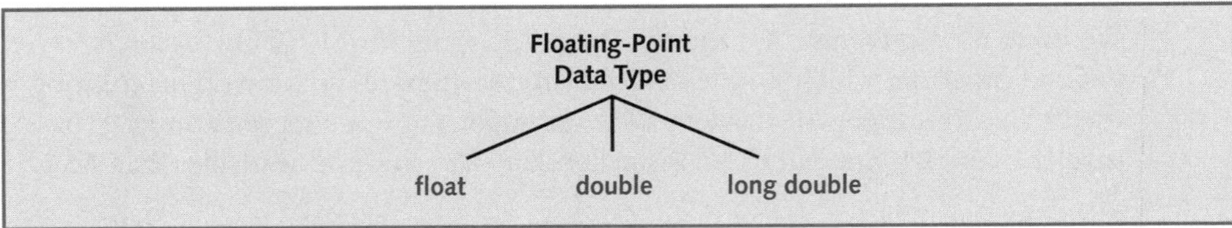

Figure 2-4 Floating-point data types

On most newer compilers, the data types `double` and `long double` are the same. Therefore, only the data types `float` and `double` are described here.

`float`: The data type `float` is used in C++ to represent any real number between `-3.4E+38` and `3.4E+38`. The memory allocated for the `float` data type is 4 bytes.

`double`: The data type `double` is used in C++ to represent any real number between `-1.7E+308` and `1.7E+308`. The memory allocated for the `double` data type is 8 bytes.

The maximum and minimum values of the data types **float** and **float** are system dependent. To find these values on a particular system, you can check your compiler's documentation or, alternatively, you can run a program given in Appendix F (The Header File **cfloat**).

Other than the set of values, there is one more difference between the data types **float** and **double**. The maximum number of significant digits—that is, the number of decimal places—in **float** values is 6 or 7. The maximum number of significant digits in values belonging to the **double** type is 15. The maximum number of significant digits is called the **precision**. Sometimes **float** values are called **single precision**, and values of the type **double** are called **double precision**. If you are dealing with decimal numbers, for the most part you need only the **float** type; if you need accuracy to more than six or seven decimal places, you can use the **double** type.

If you use the data type `float` to manipulate floating-point numbers in a program, certain compilers might give you a warning message such as `"truncation from double to float"`. To avoid such warning messages, you should use the `double` data type. For illustration purposes and to avoid such warning messages in programming examples, this book mostly uses the data type `double` to manipulate floating-point numbers.

Before leaving the discussion of data types, let us discuss one more data type—**string**.

The string Type

The data type **string** is a programmer-defined data type. It is not directly available for use in a program like the simple data types discussed earlier. To use this data type, you need to access program components from the library, which will be discussed later in this chapter. The data type **string** is a feature of ANSI/ISO Standard C++.

Prior to the ANSI/ISO C++ language standard, the standard C++ library did not provide a string data type. Compiler vendors often supplied their own programmer-defined string type, and the syntax and semantics of string operations often varied from vendor to vendor.

A **string** is a sequence of zero or more characters. Strings in C++ are enclosed in double quotation marks. A string containing no characters is called a **null** or **empty** string. The following are examples of strings. Note that `""` is the empty string.

```
"William Jacob"
"Mickey"
""
```

Every character in a string has a relative position in the string. The position of the first character is 0, the position of the second character is 1, and so on. The length of a string is the number of characters in it.

Example 2-3

String	Position of a Character in the String	Length of the String
`"William Jacob"`	Position of `'W'` is 0. Position of the first `'i'` is 1. Position of `' '` (the space) is 7. Position of `'J'` is 8. Position of `'b'` is 12.	13
`"Mickey"`	Position of `'M'` is 0. Position of `'i'` is 1. Position of `'c'` is 2. Position of `'k'` is 3. Position of `'e'` is 4. Position of `'y'` is 5.	6

When determining the length of a string, you must also count the spaces if the string contains any spaces. For example, the length of the following string is `22`.

```
"It is a beautiful day."
```

The data type `string` may not be available in Standard C++.

ARITHMETIC OPERATORS AND OPERATOR PRECEDENCE

One of the most important uses of a computer is its ability to calculate. You can use standard arithmetic operators to manipulate integral and floating-point data types. There are five arithmetic operators:

1. `+` addition
2. `-` subtraction
3. `*` multiplication
4. `/` division
5. `%` remainder (modulus operator)

You can use the operators `+`, `-`, `*`, and `/` with both integral and floating-point data types. You use `%` with only the integral data type to find the remainder in ordinary division. When you use `/` with the integral data type, it gives the quotient in ordinary division. That is, integral division truncates any fractional part; there is no rounding.

Since high school, you have been accustomed to working with arithmetic expressions such as the following:

```
3 + 4
2 + 3 * 5
5.6 + 6.2 * 3
x + 2 * 5 + 6 / y
```

In these expressions, `x` and `y` are some unknown numbers. Formally, an **arithmetic expression** is constructed by using arithmetic operators and numbers. The numbers appearing in the expression are called **operands**. Moreover, the numbers that are used to evaluate an operator are called the operands for that operator.

In the expression `3 + 4`, `3` and `4` are the operands for the operator `+`. Therefore, when `+` is evaluated, the result of the expression `3 + 4` is `7`. Note that in the expression `3 + 4`, the operator `+` has two operands. Operators that have two operands are called **binary operators**.

Operators that have only one operand are called **unary operators**. In the expression

```
–5
```

– has only one operand, which is `5`, so – acts as a unary operator. Recall that it is not necessary to put + before a positive number. Thus, in the expression

```
+27
```

`+` is a unary operator.

Unary operator: An operator that has only one operand.

Binary operator: An operator that has two operands.

In the expressions

```
3 + 4
23 - 45
```

both + and – are binary operators. Thus, – and + are both unary and binary arithmetic operators. However, as arithmetic operators, `*`, `/`, and `%` are binary and so must have two operands.

The following examples show how arithmetic operators—especially `/` and `%`—work with integral data types. As you can see from these examples, the operator `/` represents the quotient in ordinary division when used with integral data types.

Example 2-4

Arithmetic Expression	Result	Description
`2 + 5`	`7`	
`13 + 89`	`102`	
`34 – 20`	`14`	
`45 – 90`	`-45`	
`2 * 7`	`14`	
`5 / 2`	`2`	In the division `5/2`, the quotient is `2` and the remainder is `1`. Therefore, `5/2` with the integral operands evaluates to the quotient, which is `2`.

`14 / 7`	`2`	
`34 % 5`	`4`	In the division `34/5`, the quotient is `6` and the remainder is `4`. Therefore, `34%5` evaluates to the remainder, which is `4`.
`-34 % 5`	`-4`	In the division `-34 / 5`, the quotient is `-6` and the remainder is `-4`. Therefore, `-34 % 5` evaluates to the remainder, which is `-4`.
`34 % -5`	`4`	In the division `34 / -5`, the quotient is `-6` and the remainder is `4`. Therefore, `34 % -5` evaluates to the remainder, which is `4`.
`-34 % -5`	`-4`	In the division `-34 / -5`, the quotient is `6` and the remainder is `-4`. Therefore, `-34 % -5` evaluates to the remainder, which is `-4`
`4 % 6`	`4`	In the division `4/6`, the quotient is `0`, and the remainder is `4`. Therefore, `4 % 6` evaluates to the remainder, which is `4`.

Note that in the divisions `34 / 5` and `-34 /-5`, the quotients, which are `6`, are the same, but the remainders are different. In the division `34 / 5`, the remainder is `4`; in the division `-34 /-5`, the remainder is `-4`.

The following expressions show how arithmetic operators work with floating-point numbers.

Example 2-5

Expression	Result
`5.0 + 3.5`	`8.5`
`3.0 + 9.4`	`12.4`
`16.3 - 5.2`	`11.1`
`4.2 * 2.5`	`10.50`
`5.0/2.0`	`2.5`

Order of Precedence

When more than one arithmetic operator is used in an expression, C++ uses operator precedence rules to evaluate the expression. According to the order of precedence rules for arithmetic operators,

`*,   /,   %`

are at a higher level of precedence than

`+,   -`

Note that the operators `*`, `/`, and `%` have the same level of precedence. Similarly, the operators `+` and `-` have the same level of precedence.

When operators have the same level of precedence, the operations are performed from left to right. To avoid confusion, you can use parentheses to group arithmetic expressions. For example, using the order of precedence rules,


```
3*7-6+2*5/4+6
```

means the following:

```
(3 * 7) - 6 + ( ( 2 * 5) / 4 ) + 6
= 21 - 6 + (10 / 4) + 6          (Evaluate *)
= 21 - 6 + 2 + 6                 (Evaluate /)
= 15 + 2 + 6                     (Evaluate -)
= 17 + 6                         (Evaluate first +)
= 23                             (Evaluate +)
```

Note that the use of parentheses in the second example clarifies the order of precedence. You can also use parentheses to override the order of precedence rules (See, for instance, Example 2-6).

Example 2-6

In the expression

```
3+4*5
```

`*` is evaluated before `+`. Therefore, the result of this expression is `23`. On the other hand, in the expression

```
(3+4)*5
```

`+` is evaluated before `*` and the result of this expression is `35`.

Because arithmetic operators are evaluated from left to right, unless parentheses are present, the **associativity** of arithmetic operators is said to be from left to right.

(Character Arithmetic) Since the `char` data type is also an integral data type, C++ allows you to perform arithmetic operations on `char` data. You should use this ability carefully. There is a difference between the character `'8'` and the integer 8. The integer value of 8 is 8. The integer value of `'8'` is `56`, which is the ASCII collating sequence of the character `'8'`.

When evaluating arithmetic expressions, `8 + 7 = 15`, `'8'+'7' = 56 + 55`, yields `111`, and `'8'+ 7 = 56 + 7`, yields `63`. Furthermore, because '8' * '7' = 56 * 55 = 3080 and the ASCII character set has only 128 values, `'8'*'7'` is undefined in the ASCII character data set.

These examples illustrate that many things can go wrong when you are performing character arithmetic. If you must employ them, use arithmetic operations on the `char` type data with caution.

EXPRESSIONS

To this point, we have discussed only arithmetic operators. In this section, we now discuss arithmetic expressions in detail. Arithmetic expressions were introduced in the last section.

If all operands (that is, numbers) in an expression are integers, the expression is called an **integral expression.** If all operands in an expression are floating-point numbers, the expression is called a **floating-point** or **decimal expression**. An integral expression yields an integral result; a floating-point expression yields a floating-point result. Looking at some examples will help clarify these definitions.

Example 2-7

Consider the following C++ integral expressions:

```
2 + 3 * 5
3 + x – y / 7
x + 2 * (y – z) + 18
```

In these expressions, `x`, `y`, and `z` represent variables of the integer type; that is, they can hold integer values. Variables are discussed later in this chapter.

Example 2-8

Consider the following C++ floating-point expressions:

```
12.8 * 17.5 - 34.50
x * 10.5 + y - 16.2
```

Here, `x` and `y` represent variables of the floating-point type; that is, they can hold floating-point values. Variables are discussed later in this chapter.

Evaluating an integral or a floating-point expression is straightforward. As before, when operators have the same precedence, the expression is evaluated from left to right. You can always use parentheses to group operands and operators to avoid confusion.

Mixed Expressions

An expression that has operands of different data types is called a **mixed expression.** A mixed expression contains both integers and floating-point numbers. The following expressions are examples of mixed expressions:

```
2 + 3.5
6 / 4 + 3.9
5.4 * 2 – 13.6 + 18 / 2
```

In the first expression, the operand + has one integer operand and one floating-point operand. In the second expression, both operands for the operator / are integers, the first operand of + is the result of `6/4`, and the second operand of + is a floating-point number. The third example is an even more complicated mix of integers and floating-point numbers. The obvious question is: How does C++ evaluate mixed expressions?

Two rules apply when evaluating a mixed expression:

1. When evaluating an operator in a mixed expression:
   a. If the operator has the same types of operands (that is, either both integers or both floating-point numbers), the operator is evaluated according to the type of the operands. Integer operands thus yield an integer result; floating-point numbers yield a floating-point number.
   b. If the operator has both types of operands (that is, one is an integer and the other is a floating-point number), then during calculation the integer is changed to a floating-point number with the decimal part of zero and the operator is evaluated. The result is a floating-point number.
2. The entire expression is evaluated according to the precedence rules; the multiplication, division, and modulus operators are evaluated before the addition and subtraction operators. Operators having the same level of precedence are evaluated from left to right. Grouping is allowed for clarity.

From these rules, it follows that when evaluating a mixed expression, you concentrate on one operator at a time using the rules of precedence. If the operator to be evaluated has operands of the same data type, evaluate the operator using Rule 1(a). That is, an operator with integer operands will yield an integer result, and an operator with floating-point operands will yield a floating-point result. If the operator to be evaluated has one integer operand and one floating-point operand, before evaluating this operator convert the integer operand to a floating-point number with a decimal part of zero. The following examples show how to evaluate mixed expressions.

Example 2-9

Mixed Expression	Evaluation	Rule Applied
`3 / 2 + 5.0`	`= 1 + 5.0`	`3/2 = 1` (integer division; Rule 1(a))
	`= 6.0`	`(1+5.0 = 1.0+5.0` (Rule 1(b)) `= 6.0)`
`15.6 / 2 + 5`	`= 7.8 + 5`	`15.6/2 = 15.6/2.0` (Rule 1(b)) `= 7.8`
	`= 12.8`	`7.8+5 = 7.8 + 5.0` (Rule 1(b)) `= 12.8`

```
4 * 3 + 7 / 5 – 25.6     = 12 + 7 / 5 – 25.6    4*3 = 12; (Rule 1(a))
                         = 12 + 1 – 25.6        7/5 = 1 (integer division; Rule 1(a))
                         = 13 – 25.6            12 + 1 = 13; (Rule 1(a))
                         = -12.6                13–25.6 = 13.0–25.6 (Rule 1(b))
                                                        = - 12.6
```

These examples illustrate that an integer is not converted to a floating-point number unless the operator to be evaluated has one integer and one floating-point operand.

Now, consider the following examples. The values of these expressions were obtained from a C++ program. In these expressions, `x = 15`, `y = 23`, and `z = 3.75`.

Expression	Value
`x + y / z`	`21.1333`
`7 / 2 + 7.45`	`10.45`
`15 / 2 + 4 * 5 - 3.50`	`23.5`
`7 / 2 * 3.5 + 6`	`16.5`
`7.0 / 2 + 7.45`	`10.95`

Type Conversion (Casting)

In the previous section, you learned that when evaluating an arithmetic expression if the operator has mixed operands, the integer value is changed to a floating-point value with the zero decimal part. When a value of one data type is automatically changed to another data type, an **implicit type coercion** is said to have occurred. As the examples in the preceding section illustrate, if you are not careful about data types, implicit type coercion can generate unexpected results.

To avoid implicit type coercion, C++ provides for explicit type conversion through the use of a cast operator. The **cast operator**, also called **type conversion** or **type casting**, takes the following form:

```
static_cast<dataTypeName>(expression)
```

First, the **`expression`** is evaluated. Its value is then converted to a value of the type specified by **`dataTypeName`**. In C++, **`static_cast`** is a reserved word.

When converting a floating-point (decimal) number to an integer using the cast operator, you simply drop the decimal part of the floating-point number. That is, the floating-point number is truncated. The following examples show how cast operators work. Be sure you understand why the last two expressions evaluate as they do.

Example 2-10

Expression	**Evaluates to**
`static_cast<int>(7.9)`	`7`
`static_cast<int>(3.3)`	`3`
`static_cast<double>(25)`	`25.0`
`static_cast<double>(5+3)`	`= static_cast<double>(8) = 8.0`

`static_cast<double>(15)/2`	`= 15.0/2`
	(since `static_cast<double>(15) = 15.0`)
	`=15.0/2.0 = 7.5`

`static_cast<double>(15/2)`	`= static_cast<double>(7)` (since `15/2 = 7`) `= 7.0`

`static_cast<int>(7.8 +`
`static_cast<double>(15)/2)`
	`= static_cast<int>(7.8 + 7.5)`
	`= static_cast<int>(15.3)`
	`= 15`

`static_cast<int>(7.8 +`
`static_cast<double>(15/2))`
	`= static_cast<int>(7.8 + 7.0)`
	`= static_cast<int>(14.8)`
	`= 14`

Consider another series of examples. For these examples, `x = 15`, `y = 23`, and `z = 3.75`. A C++ program generated the output of the following expressions.

Expression	**Value**
`static_cast<int>(7.9 + 6.7)`	`14`
`static_cast<int>(7.9) + static_cast<int>(6.7)`	`13`
`static_cast<double>(y / x) + z`	`4.75`
`static_cast<double>(y) / x + z`	`5.28333`

In C++, the cast operator can also take the form `dataType(expression)`. This form is called C-like casting. However, `static_cast` is more stable than C-like casting.

You can also use cast operators to explicitly convert `char` data values into `int` data values, and `int` data values into `char` data values. To convert `char` data values into `int` data values, you use a collating sequence. For example, in the ASCII character set, `static_cast<int>('A')` is `65` and `static_cast<int>('8')` is `56`. Similarly, `static_cast<char>(65)` is `'A'` and `static_cast<char>(56)` is `'8'`.

Earlier in this chapter, you learned how arithmetic expressions are formed and evaluated in C++. If you want to use the value of one expression in another expression, first you must save the value of the expression. There are many reasons to save the value of an expression. Some expressions are complex and may require a considerable amount of computer time to evaluate. By calculating the values once and saving them for further use, you not only save computer time and create a program that executes more quickly, but also avoid possible typographical errors. In C++, expressions are evaluated and if the value is not saved, it is lost.

That is, unless it is saved, the value of an expression cannot be used in later calculations. In the next section, you will learn how to save the value of an expression and use it in subsequent calculations.

INPUT

As noted earlier, the main objective of C++ programs is to perform calculations and manipulate data. Recall that data must be loaded into main memory before it can be manipulated. In this section, you will learn how to put data into the computer's memory. Storing data in the computer's memory is a two-step process:

1. Instruct the computer to allocate memory.
2. Include statements in the program to put data into the allocated memory.

Allocating Memory with Constants and Variables

When you instruct the computer to allocate memory, you tell it not only what names to use for each memory location, but also what type of data to store in those memory locations. Knowing the location of data is essential, because data stored in one memory location might be needed at several places in the program. As you saw earlier, knowing what data type you have is crucial for performing accurate calculations. It is also critical to know whether your data needs to remain fixed throughout program execution or whether it should change.

Some data is special. For example, the pay rate is usually the same for all part-time employees. A conversion formula that converts inches into centimeters is fixed because `1` inch is always equal to `2.54` centimeters. When stored in memory, this type of data needs to be protected from accidental changes during program execution. In C++, you can use a **named constant** to instruct a program to mark those memory locations in which data is fixed throughout program execution.

Named constant: A memory location whose content is not allowed to change during program execution.

Certain data needs to be modified during program execution. For example, after each test, the average test score and the number of tests taken change. Similarly, after each pay increase, the employee's salary changes. This type of data must be stored in those memory cells whose contents can be modified during program execution. In C++, memory cells whose contents can be modified during program execution are called variables. More formally,

Variable: A memory location whose content may change during program execution.

To allocate memory, we use C++'s declaration statements. The syntax to declare a named constant is

```
const dataType identifier = value;
```

In C++, `const` is a reserved word.

Example 2-11

Consider the following C++ statements:

```
const double conversion = 2.54;
const int noOfStudents = 20;
const char blank = ' ';
const double payRate = 15.75;
```

The first statement tells the compiler to allocate enough memory to store a value of the type `double`, call this memory space `conversion`, and store the value `2.54` in it. Throughout a program that uses this statement, whenever the conversion formula is needed, the memory space `conversion` can be accessed. The meaning of other statements is similar.

Using a named constant to store fixed data, rather than using the data value itself, has one major advantage. When the fixed data changes, you do not need to edit the entire program and change the old value to the new value whenever the old value is used. Instead, you can make the change at just one place, recompile the program, and execute it using the new value throughout. In addition, by storing a value and referring to that memory location whenever the value is needed, you avoid typing the same value again and again and prevent accidental typos. If you misspell the name of the location, the computer will warn you through an error message, but it will not warn you if the value is mistyped.

The syntax for declaring one variable or multiple variables is

```
dataType identifier, identifier, . . .;
```

Example 2-12

Consider the following statements:

```
double amountDue;
int    counter;
char   ch;
int    x,y;
string name;
```

The first statement tells the compiler to allocate enough memory to store a value of the type `double` and call it `amountDue`. Statements 2 and 3 have similar conventions. The fourth statement tells the compiler to allocate two different memory spaces, each large enough to store a value of the type `int`; name the first memory space `x`; and name the second memory space `y`. The fifth statement tells the compiler to allocate memory space to store a string and call it `name`.

From now on, when we say "variable," we mean a variable memory location.

In C++, you must declare all identifiers before you can use them. If you refer to an identifier without declaring it, the compiler will generate an error message indicating that the identifier is not declared. Therefore, to use either a named constant or a variable, you must first declare it.

Now that data types, variables, and constants have been defined and discussed, it is possible to offer a formal definition of simple data types. A data type is called **simple** if the variable or named constant of that type can store only one value at a time. For example, if `x` is an `int` variable, at a given time only one value can be stored in `x`.

Putting Data into Variables

Now that you know how to declare variables, the next question is: How do you put data into those variables? In C++, you can place data into a variable in two ways:

1. Use C++'s assignment statement.
2. Use input (read) statements.

The Assignment Statement

The assignment statement takes the following form:

```
variable = expression;
```

In an assignment statement, the value of the **`expression`** should match the data type of the **`variable`**. The expression on the right side is evaluated, and its value is assigned to the variable (and thus to a memory location) on the left side.

A variable is said to be **initialized** the first time a value is placed in the variable.

In C++, = is called the **assignment operator**.

Example 2-13

Suppose you have the following variable declarations:

```
int I, J;
double sale;
char first;
string str;
```

Now, consider the following assignment statements:

```
I = 4;
J = 4 * 5 - 11;
sale = 0.02 * 1000;
first = 'D';
str = "It is a sunny day.";
```

For each of these statements, the computer first evaluates the expression on the right and then stores that value in a memory location named by the identifier on the left. The first statement stores the value `4` in `I`, the second statement stores `9` in `J`, the third statement stores `20.00` in `sale`, and the fourth statement stores the character `D` in `first`. The fifth statement stores the string `"It is a sunny day."` in the variable `str`.

2

A C++ statement such as:

```
I = I + 2;
```

means "evaluate whatever is in `I`, add `2` to it, and assign the new value to the memory location `I`." The expression on the right side must be evaluated first; that value is then assigned to the memory location specified by the variable on the left side. Thus, the sequence of C++ statements

```
I = 6;
I = I + 2;
```

and the statement

```
I = 8;
```

both assign `8` to `I`. In addition, the statement `I = I + 2` is meaningless if `I` has not been initialized.

You read the statement `I = 5;` as "I becomes 5" or "I gets 5." Each time a new value is assigned to `I`, the old value is erased.

Suppose that `I`, `J`, and `K` are `int` variables. The sequence of statements

```
I = 12;
I = I + 6;
J = I;
K = J / 2;
K = K / 3;
```

results in `K` having the value `3` stored in it. Tracing values through a sequence, called a **walk-through**, is a valuable tool to learn and practice. You will learn more about how to walk through a sequence of C++ statements later in this chapter.

Suppose that `x`, `y`, and `z` are `int` variables. The following is a legal statement in C++:

x = y = z;

In this statement, first the value of `z` is assigned to `y`, and then the new value of `y` is assigned to `x`. Because the assignment operator, =, is evaluated from right to left, the **associativity** of the **assignment operator** is said to be from right to left.

Now that you know how to declare variables and put data into them, you can learn how to save the value of an expression. You can then use this value in a later expression without using the expression itself, thereby answering the question raised earlier in this chapter. To save the value of an expression and use it in a later expression, do the following:

1. Declare a variable of the appropriate data type. For example, if the result of the expression is an integer, declare an `int` variable.
2. Assign the value of the expression to the variable that was declared using the assignment statement. This action saves the value of the expression into the variable.
3. Wherever the value of the expression is needed, use the variable holding the value.

The following example further illustrates this concept.

Example 2-14

Suppose that you have the following declaration:

```
int a, b, c, d;
int x, y;
```

Further suppose that you want to evaluate the expressions **-b+(b^2-4ac)** and **-b-(b^2-4ac)**, and assign the values of these expressions to **x** and **y**, respectively. Because the expression **b^2-4ac** appears in both expressions, you can first calculate the value of this expression and save its value in **d**. You can then use the value of **d** to evaluate the expressions as shown by the following statements:

```
d = b * b – 4 * a * c;
x = -b + d;
y = -b – d;
```

Earlier, you learned that if a variable is used in an expression, the expression would yield a meaningful value only if the variable has first been initialized. You also learned that after declaring a variable, you can use an assignment statement to initialize it. It is possible to initialize and declare variables at the same time. Before we discuss how to use an input (read) statement, we address this important issue.

Declaration and Initializing Variables

When a variable is declared, C++ does not automatically put a meaningful value in it. In other words, C++ does not automatically initialize variables. For example, the `int` and `double` variables are not initialized to `0`, as it happens in some programming languages. This does not mean, however, that there is no value in a variable after its declaration. When a variable is declared, memory for it is allocated.

Recall from Chapter 1 that main memory is an ordered sequence of cells, and each cell is capable of storing a value. Also, recall that the machine language is a sequence of 0s and 1s, or bits. Therefore, data in a memory cell is a sequence of bits. These bits are nothing but electrical signals, so when the computer is turned on, some of the bits are 1 and some are 0. The state of these bits depends on how the system functions. However, when you instruct the computer to store a particular value in a memory cell, the bits are set according to the data being stored.

During data manipulation, the computer takes the value stored in particular cells and performs a calculation. If you declare a variable and do not store a value in it, the memory cell still has a value—usually the value of the setting of the bits from their last use—and you have no way to know what this value is.

If you only declare a variable and do not instruct the computer to put data into the variable, the value of that variable is garbage. However, the computer does not warn us, regards whatever values are in memory as legitimate, and performs calculations using those values in memory. Using a variable in an expression without initializing it produces erroneous results. To avoid these pitfalls, C++ allows you to initialize variables while they are being declared. For example, consider the following C++ statements in which variables are first declared and then initialized:

```
int first, second;
char ch;
double x, y;

first = 13;
second = 10;
ch = ' ';
x = 12.6;
y = 123.456;
```

You can declare and initialize these variables at the same time using the following C++ statements:

```
int first = 13, second = 10;
char ch = ' ';
double x = 12.6, y = 123.456;
```

The first C++ statement declares two `int` variables, `first` and `second`, and stores `13` in `first` and `10` in `second`.

In reality, not all variables are initialized during declaration. It is the nature of the program or the programmer's choice that dictates which variables should be initialized during declaration. The key point is that all variables must be initialized before they are used.

Input (Read) Statement

In an earlier section, you learned how to put data into variables using the assignment statement. In this section, you will learn how to put data into variables from the standard input device using C++'s input (or read) statements.

In most cases, the standard input device is the keyboard.

When the computer gets the data from the keyboard, the user is said to be acting interactively.

Putting data into variables from the standard input device is accomplished via the use of `cin` and the operator >>. The syntax of `cin` together with >> is

```
cin>>variable>>variable. . .;
```

This is called an **input (read)** statement. Sometimes this is also called a `cin` statement. In C++, >> is called the **stream extraction operator**.

The input (or `cin`) statement works as follows. Suppose `miles` is a variable of the data type `double`. The statement

```
cin>>miles;
```

causes the computer to get a value, from the standard input device, of the data type `double`, and place it in the memory cell named `miles`.

By using more than one variable with `cin`, more than one value can be read at a time. Suppose `feet` and `inch` are variables of the data type `int`. A statement such as:

```
cin>>feet>>inch;
```

gets two integers from the keyboard and places them in the memory locations `feet` and `inch`, respectively.

During programming execution, if more than one value is entered in a line, these values must be separated by at least one blank or tab. Alternately, one value per line can be entered.

Remember, there are two ways to initialize a variable: by using the assignment statement and by using a read statement. Consider the following declaration:

```
int feet;
```

You can initialize the variable `feet` to a value of `35` either by using the assignment statement:

```
feet = 35;
```

or by executing the following statement and entering `35` during program execution:

```
cin>>feet;
```

If you use the assignment statement to initialize `feet`, then you are stuck with the same value each time the program runs unless you edit the source code, change the value, recompile, and run. By using an input statement each time the program runs, you are prompted to enter a value, and the value entered is stored into `feet`. Therefore, a read statement is much more versatile than an assignment statement.

Sometimes it is necessary to initialize a variable by using an assignment statement. This is especially true if the variable is used only for internal calculation and not for reading and storing data.

Recall that C++ does not automatically initialize variables when they are declared. Some variables can be initialized when they are declared, whereas others must be initialized using either an assignment statement or a read statement.

Suppose you want to store a character into a **char** variable using an input statement. During program execution, when you enter the character, you do not include the single quotes. For example, suppose that ch is a **char** variable. Consider the following input statement:

```
cin>>ch;
```

If you want to store K into ch using this statement, during program execution, you only enter K. Similarly, if you want to store a string into a variable of the type string using an input statement, during program execution, you enter only the string without the double quotes.

Example 2-15

This example further illustrates how assignment statements and input statements manipulate variables. Consider the following declarations:

```
int one, two;
double z;
char ch;
string name;
```

Also, suppose that the following statements execute in the order given.

```
1. one = 4;

2. two = 2 * one + 6;

3. z = (one + 1) / 2.0;

4. ch = 'A';

5. cin>>two;

6. cin>>z;

7. one = 2 * two + static_cast<int>(z);

8. cin>>name;

9. two = two + 1;

10. cin>>ch;

11. one = one + static_cast<int>(ch);

12. z = one - z;
```

In addition, suppose the input is

```
8 16.3 Goofy D
```

This line has four values, `8`, `16.3`, `Goofy`, and `D`, and each value is separated from the others by a blank.

Let's now determine the values of the declared variables after the last statement executes. To explicitly show how a particular statement changes the value of a variable, the values of the variables after each statement executes are shown. (In Figures 2-5 through 2-17, a question mark, ?, in a box indicates that the value in the box is unknown.)

Before statement 1 executes, all variables are uninitialized, as shown in Figure 2-5.

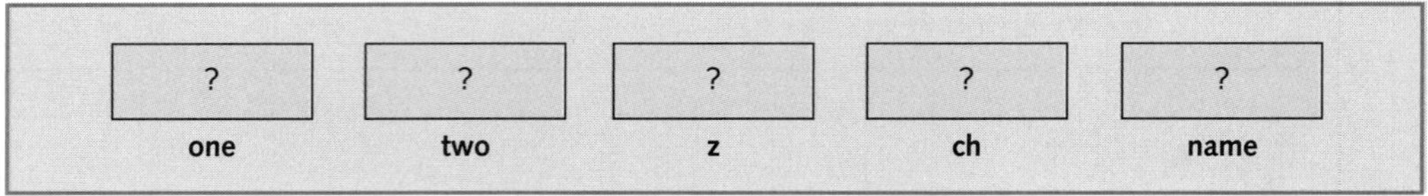

Figure 2-5 Variables before statement 1 executes

Statement 1 stores `4` into the variable named `one`. After statement 1 executes, the values of the variables are as shown in Figure 2-6.

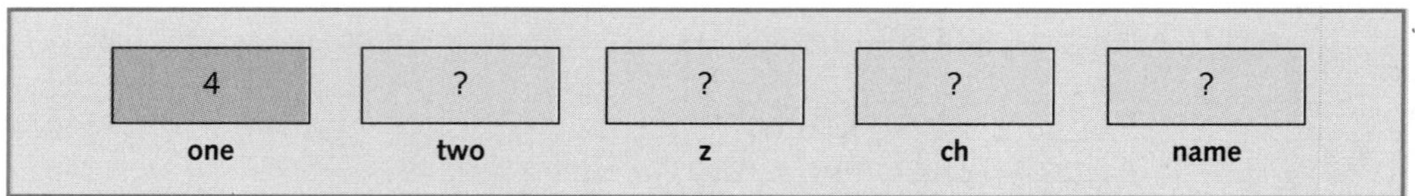

Figure 2-6 Values of `one`, `two`, `z`, `ch`, and `name` after statement 1 executes

Statement 2 first evaluates the expression `2 * one + 6` (which evaluates to `14`) and then stores the value of the expression into `two`. After statement 2 executes, the values of the variables are as shown in Figure 2-7.

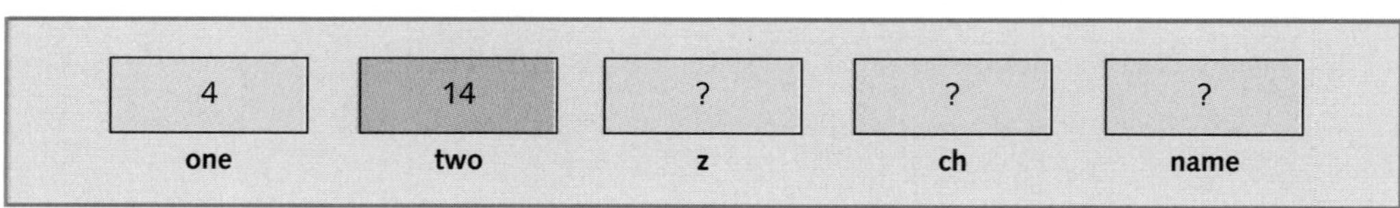

Figure 2-7 Values of `one`, `two`, `z`, `ch`, and `name` after statement 2 executes

Statement 3 first evaluates the expression `(one + 1)/2.0` (which evaluates to `2.5`) and then stores the value of the expression into `z`. After statement 3 executes, the values of the variables are as shown in Figure 2-8.

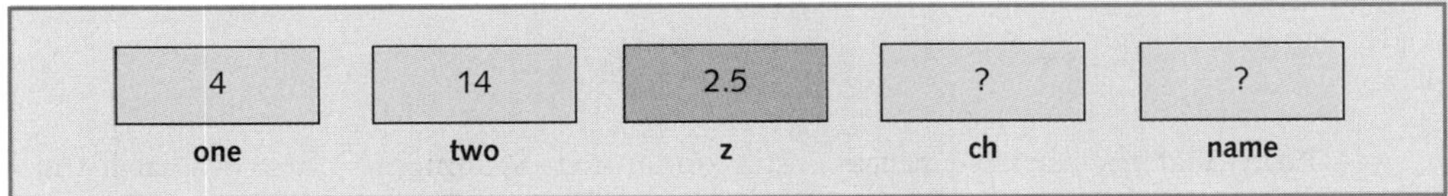

Figure 2-8 Values of `one`, `two`, `z`, `ch`, and `name` after statement 3 executes

Statement 4 stores the character `'A'` into `ch`. After statement 4 executes, the values of the variables are as shown in Figure 2-9.

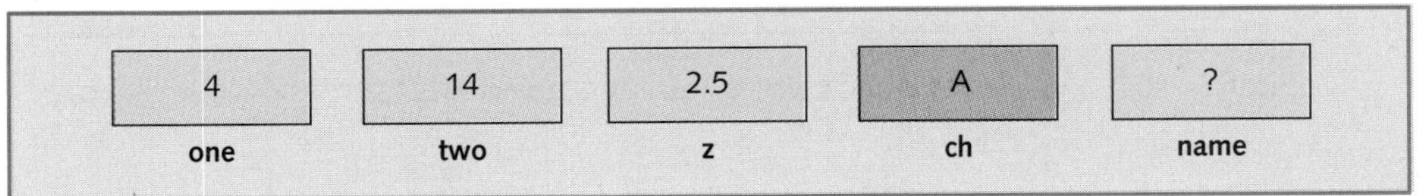

Figure 2-9 Values of `one`, `two`, `z`, `ch`, and `name` after statement 4 executes

Statement 5 reads a number from the keyboard (which is `8`) and stores the number `8` into `two`. This statement replaces the old value of `two` with this new value. After statement 5 executes, the values of the variables are as shown in Figure 2-10.

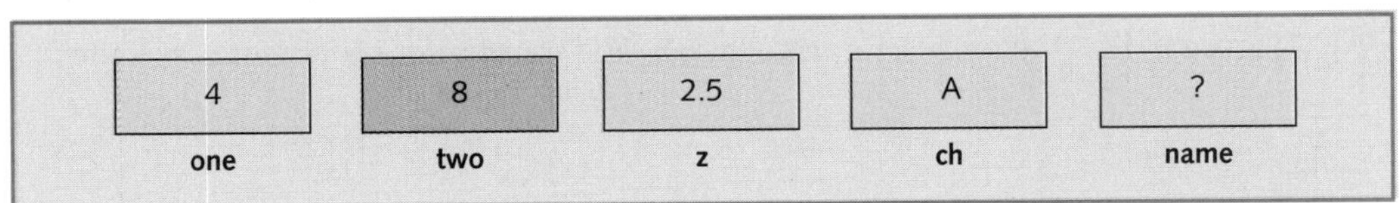

Figure 2-10 Values of `one`, `two`, `z`, `ch`, and `name` after statement 5 executes

Statement 6 reads a number from the keyboard (which is `16.3`) and stores the number into `z`. This statement replaces the old value of `z` with this new value. After statement 6 executes, the values of the variables are as shown in Figure 2-11.

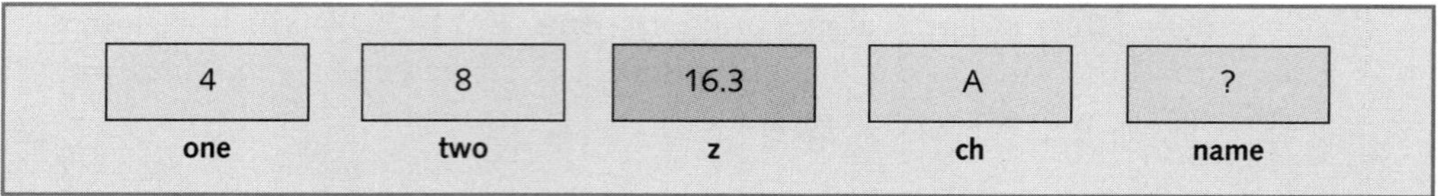

Figure 2-11 Values of one, two, z, ch, and name after statement 6 executes

Note that the variable name is still undefined. Statement 7 first evaluates the expression `2*two + static_cast<int>(z)` (which evaluates to 32) and then stores the value of the expression into one. This statement replaces the old value of one with the new value. After statement 7 executes, the values of the variables are as shown in Figure 2-12.

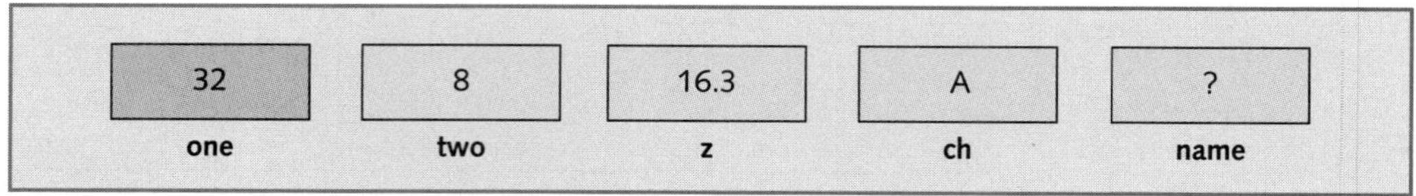

Figure 2-12 Values of one, two, z, ch, and name after statement 7 executes

Statement 8 gets the next input from the keyboard (which is Goofy) and stores it into name. After statement 8 executes, the values of the variables are as shown in Figure 2-13.

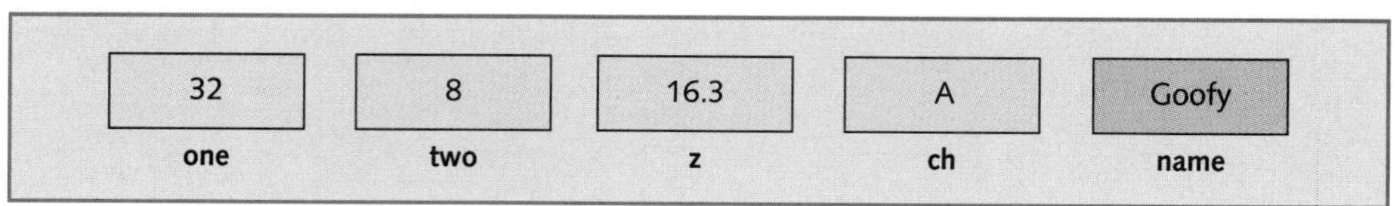

Figure 2-13 Values of one, two, z, ch, and name after statement 8 executes

Statement 9 first evaluates the expression `two + 1` (which evaluates to 9) and stores the value of this expression into two. This statement updates the value of two by incrementing the old value by 1. After statement 9 executes, the values of the variables are as shown in Figure 2-14.

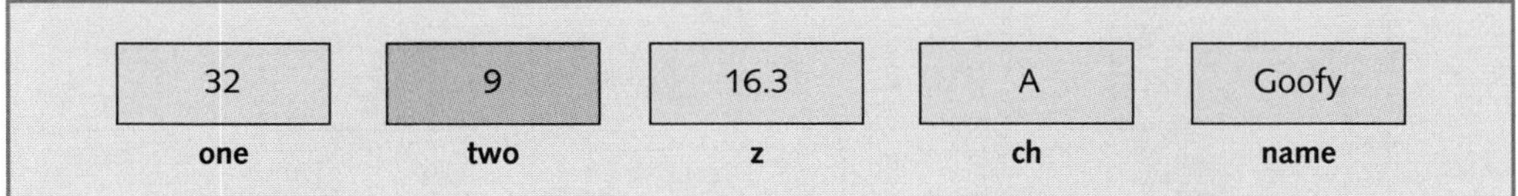

Figure 2-14 Values of one, two, z, ch, and name after statement 9 executes

Statement 10 reads the next input from the keyboard (which is D) and stores it into ch. This statement replaces the old value of ch with the new value. After statement 10 executes, the values of the variables are as shown in Figure 2-15.

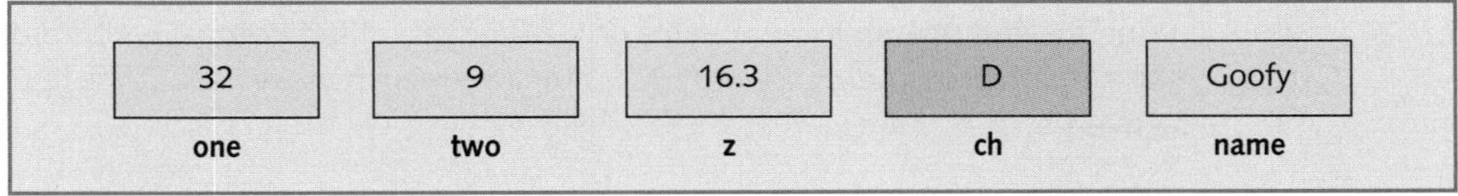

Figure 2-15 Values of one, two, z, ch, and name after statement 10 executes

Statement 11 first evaluates the expression one + static_cast<int>(ch), which is 32 + static_cast<int>('D'), which equals 32 + 68 = 100. Here static_cast<int>('D') gives the collating sequence of the character D in the ASCII character data set, which is 68. Statement 11 then stores the value of this expression into one. This statement replaces the old value of one with the new value. After statement 11 executes, the values of the variables are as shown in Figure 2-16.

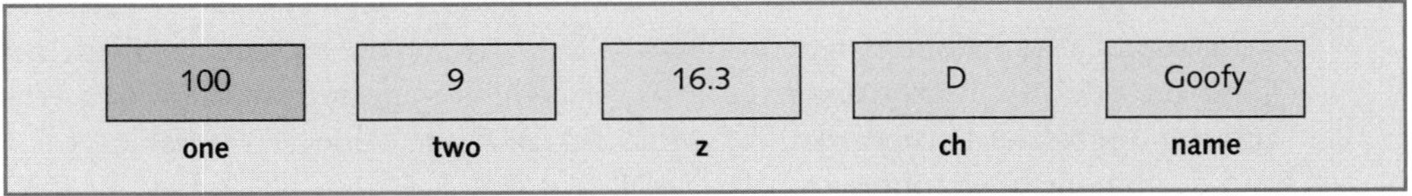

Figure 2-16 Values of one, two, z, ch, and name after statement 11 executes

Finally, statement 12 first evaluates the expression one – z (which equals 100 - 16.3 = 100.0 - 16.3 = 83.7) and then stores the value of this expression into z. The values of the variables after the last statement executes are shown in Figure 2-17.

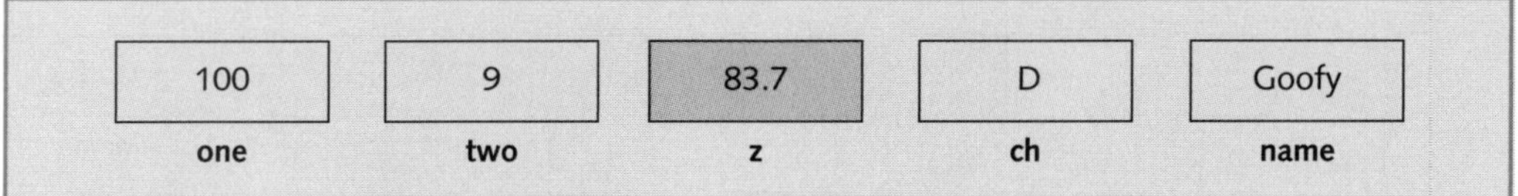

Figure 2-17 Values of one, two, z, ch, and name after statement 12 executes

When something goes wrong in a program and the results it generates are not what you expected, you should do a walk-through of the statements that assign values to your variables. Example 2-15 illustrates how to do a walk-through of your program. The walk-through is a very effective debugging technique.

If you assign the value of an expression that evaluates to a floating-point value without using the cast operator to a variable of the type `int`, the fractional part is dropped. In this case, the compiler most likely will issue a warning message about the implicit type conversion.

Increment and Decrement Operators

Now that you know how to declare a variable and enter data into a variable, in this section you will learn about two more operators: the **increment** and **decrement operators.** These operators are used frequently by C++ programmers and are useful programming tools.

Suppose `count` is an `int` variable. The statement

```
count = count + 1;
```

increments the value of `count` by `1`. To execute this assignment statement, the computer first evaluates the expression on the right, which is `count + 1`. It then assigns this value to the variable on the left, which is `count`.

As you will see in later chapters, such statements are frequently used to keep track of how many times certain things have happened. To expedite the execution of such statements, C++ provides the **increment operator**, ++, which increases the value of a variable by `1`, and the **decrement operator**, `--`, which decreases the value of a variable by `1`. Increment and decrement operators each have two forms, pre and post. The syntax of the increment operator is

Pre-increment:	`++variable`
Post-increment:	`variable++`

The syntax of the decrement operator is

Pre-decrement:	`--variable`
Post-decrement:	`variable--`

Let's look at some examples. The statement

```
++count;
```

or

```
count++;
```

increments the value of `count` by `1`. Similarly, the statement

```
--count;
```

or

```
count--;
```

decrements the value of `count` by `1`.

Because both increment and decrement operators are built into C++, the value of the variable is quickly incremented or decremented without having to use the form of an assignment statement.

As you can see from these examples, both the pre- and post-increment operators increment the value of the variable by `1`. Similarly, the pre- and post-decrement operators decrement the value of the variable by `1`. What is the difference between the pre and post forms of these operators? The difference becomes apparent when the variable using these operators is employed in an expression.

Suppose that `x` is a variable of the type `int`. If `++x` is used in an expression, first the value of `x` is incremented by `1`, and then the new value of `x` is used to evaluate the expression. On the other hand, if `x++` is used in an expression, first the current value of `x` is used in the expression, and then the value of `x` is incremented by `1`. The following example clarifies the difference between the pre- and post-increment operators.

Suppose that `x` and `y` are `int` variables. Consider the following statements:

```
x = 5;
y = ++x;
```

The first statement assigns the value `5` to `x`. To evaluate the second statement, which uses the pre-increment operator, first the value of `x` is incremented to `6`, and then this value, `6`, is assigned to `y`. After the second statement executes, both `x` and `y` have the value `6`.

Now consider the following statements:

```
x = 5;
y = x++;
```

As before, the first statement assigns `5` to `x`. In the second statement, the post-increment operator is applied to `x`. To execute the second statement, first the value of `x`, which is `5`, is used to evaluate the expression, and then the value of `x` is incremented to `6`. Finally, the value of the expression, which is `5`, is stored in `y`. After the second statement executes, the value of `x` is `6`, and the value of `y` is `5`.

The following example further illustrates how the pre and post forms of the increment operator work.

Example 2-16

Suppose `a` and `b` are `int` variables and:

```
a = 5;
b = 2 + (++a);
```

The first statement assigns `5` to `a`. To execute the second statement, first the expression `2 + (++a)` is evaluated. Because the pre-increment operator is applied to `a`, first the value of `a` is incremented to `6`. Then `2` is added to `6` to get `8`, which is then assigned to `b`. Therefore, after the second statement executes, `a` is `6` and `b` is `8`.

This book will most often use the increment and decrement operators with a variable in a stand-alone statement. That is, the variable using the increment or decrement operator will not be part of any expression.

OUTPUT

A program is of little use if it cannot display the results of calculations on an output device. Although you have seen how to put data into the computer's memory and how to manipulate that data, you have not yet learned how to make the program show the results.

The standard output device is usually the screen.

In C++, output on the standard output device is accomplished via the use of cout and the operator <<. The syntax of cout together with << is

```
cout<<expression or manipulator<<expression or manipulator...;
```

This is called an **output statement**. Sometimes this is also called a `cout` statement. In C++, << is called the **stream insertion operator**.

Generating output with `cout` statements follows two rules:

1. The expression is evaluated, and its value is printed at the current cursor position on the output device.

2. A manipulator is used to format the output. The simplest manipulator is `endl` (the last character is the letter `el`), which causes the cursor to move to the beginning of the next line.

The next example illustrates how `cout` statements work. In a `cout` statement, a string or an expression involving only one variable or a single value evaluates to itself.

When an output statement outputs `char` values, it outputs only the character without the single quotes (unless the single quotes are part of the output statement). For example, suppose `ch` is a `char` variable and `ch = 'A';`. The statement

```
cout<<ch;
```

or

```
cout<<'A';
```

outputs

```
A
```

Similarly, when an output statement outputs the value of a string, it outputs only the string without the double quotes (unless you include double quotes as part of the output).

Example 2-17

Consider the following statements. The output is shown to the right of each statement.

	Statement	**Output**
1	`cout<<29/4;`	`7`
2	`cout<<"Hello there. ";`	`Hello there.`
3	`cout<<12;`	`12`
4	`cout<<"4+7";`	`4+7`
5	`cout<<4+7;`	`11`
6	`cout<<'A';`	`A`
7	`cout<<"4 + 7 = "<<4 + 7;`	`4 + 7 = 11`
8	`cout<<2+3*5;`	`17`
9	`cout<<"Hello \nthere. ";`	`Hello` `there.`

Look at the output of statement 9. Recall that in C++, the newline character is `'\n'`; it causes the cursor to move to the beginning of the next line before printing there. Therefore, when `\n` appears in a string in an output statement, it causes the cursor to move to the beginning of the next line on the output device. This fact explains why **Hello** and **there.** are printed on separate lines.

In C++, \ is called the **escape character** and `\n` is called **newline escape sequence**.

Recall that all variables must be properly initialized; otherwise, the value stored in them may not make much sense. Also recall that C++ does not automatically initialize variables. The output of the C++ statement

```
cout<<a<<endl;
```

is meaningful provided that the variable `a` has been given a value. For example, the sequence of C++ statements

```
a = 45;
cout<<a<<endl;
```

will produce the output `45`.

Example 2-18

Consider the following statements. Assume that these statements are executed in the order given. The output, which was generated by a C++ program, appears after these statements.

```
int a, b, c, d;

a = 65 ;                                    //Line 1
b = 78 ;                                    //Line 2

cout<<29/4<<endl;                           //Line 3
cout<<3.0/2<<endl;                          //Line 4
cout<<"Hello there.\n";                     //Line 5
cout<<7<<endl;                              //Line 6
cout<<3+5<<endl;                            //Line 7
cout<<"3+5";                                //Line 8
cout<<endl;                                 //Line 9
cout<<2+3*6<<endl;                          //Line 10
cout<<"a"<<endl;                            //Line 11
cout<<a<<endl;                              //Line 12
cout<<b<<endl;                              //Line 13
cout<<c<<'\n';                              //Line 14
cout<<d;                                    //Line 15
cout<<endl;                                 //Line 16
```

In the following output, the column marked "Output of Statement at" and the line numbers are not part of the output. The line numbers are shown in this column to make it easy to see which output corresponds to which statement.

	Output of Statement at
`7`	`Line 3`
`1.5`	`Line 4`
`Hello there.`	`Line 5`
`7`	`Line 6`
`8`	`Line 7`
`3+5`	`Line 8`
`20`	`Line 10`
`a`	`Line 11`
`65`	`Line 12`
`78`	`Line 13`
`6749684`	`Line 14`
`4203005`	`Line 15`

For the most part, the output is straightforward. Look at the output of the statements at Lines 7, 8, 9, and 10. The statement at Line 7 outputs the result of `3+5`, which is `8`, and moves the cursor to the beginning of next line. The statement at Line 8 outputs the string `3+5`. Note that the statement at Line 8 consists only of the string `3+5`. Therefore, after printing `3+5`, the cursor stays positioned after `5`; it does not move to the beginning of the next line.

The output statement at Line 9 contains only the manipulator **`endl`**, which moves the cursor to the beginning of the next line. Therefore, when the statement at Line 10 executes, the output starts at the beginning of the line. Note that in this output, the column "Output of Statement at" does not contain Line 9. This is due to the fact that the statement at Line 9 does not produce any printable output. It simply moves the cursor to the beginning of the next line. Next, the statement at Line 10 outputs the result of the expression `2+3*6`, which is `20`. The manipulator **`endl`** then moves the cursor to the beginning of the next line.

Look carefully at the output of the statements at Lines 14 and 15 again. Note that the variables **`c`** and **`d`** are not properly initialized. Therefore, the printed values of **`c`** and **`d`**—`6749684` on Line 14 and `4203005` on Line 15, respectively—are meaningless. If you executed these statements on your system, you might get different values for **`c`** and **`d`**.

Outputting or accessing the value of a variable in an expression does not destroy or modify the contents of the variable.

Let us now take a close look at the newline character, `'\n'`. Consider the following C++ statements:

```
cout<<"Hello there.";
cout<<"My name is Goofy.";
```

If these statements are executed in sequence, the output is

```
Hello there.My name is Goofy.
```

Now consider the following C++ statements:

```
cout<<"Hello there.\n";
cout<<"My name is Goofy.";
```

The output of these C++ statements is

```
Hello there.
My name is Goofy.
```

When `\n` is encountered in the string, the cursor is positioned at the beginning of the next line. Note also that `\n` may appear anywhere in the string. For example, the output of the statement

```
cout<<"Hello \nthere. \nMy name is Goofy.";
```

is

```
Hello
there.
My name is Goofy.
```

Also, note that the output of the statement

```
cout<<'\n';
```

is the same as the output of the statement

```
cout<<"\n";
```

which is equivalent to the output of the statement

```
cout<<endl;
```

Thus, the output of the sequence of statements

```
cout<<"Hello there.\n";
cout<<"My name is Goofy.";
```

is equivalent to the output of the sequence of statements

```
cout<<"Hello there."<<endl;
cout<<"My name is Goofy.";
```

Example 2-19

Consider the following C++ statements:

```
cout<<"Hello there.\nMy name is Goofy.";
```

or

```
cout<<"Hello there.";
cout<<"\nMy name is Goofy.";
```

or

```
cout<<"Hello there.";
cout<<endl<<"My name is Goofy.";
```

In each case, the output of the statements is

```
Hello there.
My name is Goofy.
```


Example 2-20

The output of the C++ statements

```
cout<<"Count...\n....1\n.....2\n......3";
```

or

```
cout<<"Count..."<<endl<<"....1"<<endl
    <<"....2"<<endl<<"......3";
```

is

```
Count...
....1
.....2
......3
```

Example 2-21

Suppose that you want to output the following sentence in one line as part of a message:

```
It is sunny, warm, and not a windy day. Let us go golfing.
```

Obviously, you will use a `cout` statement to produce this output. However, in the programming code, this statement may not fit in one line as part of the `cout` statement. Of course, you can use multiple `cout` statements as follows:

```
cout<<"It is sunny, warm, and not a windy day. ";
cout<<"Let us go golfing."<<endl;
```

Note the semicolon at the end of the first statement and the identifier `cout` at the beginning of the second statement. Also, note that there is no manipulator `endl` at the end of the first statement. Here two `cout` statements are used to output the sentence in one line. Equivalently, you can use the following `cout` statement to output this sentence:

```
cout<<"It is sunny, warm, and not a windy day. "
    <<"Let us go golfing."<<endl;
```

In this statement, note that there is no semicolon at the end of the first line and the identifier `cout` does not appear at the beginning of the second line. Because there is no semicolon at the end of the first line, this `cout` statement continues at the second line. Also, note the double quotation marks at the beginning and end of the sentences on each line. The string is broken into two strings, but both strings are part of the same `cout` statement.

If a string appearing in a **cout** statement is long and you want to output the string in one line, you can break the string in a **cout** statement by using either of the above two methods. However, the following statement would be incorrect:

```
cout<<"It is sunny, warm, and not a windy day.   //illegal
       Let us go golfing."<<endl;
```

In other words, the return (or Enter) key on your keyboard cannot be part of the string. That is, in programming code, a string cannot be broken into more than one line by using the return (Enter) key on your keyboard.

Recall that the newline character is `\n`, which causes the cursor to move to the beginning of the next line. There are many escape sequences in C++, which allow you to control the output. Table 2-4 lists some of the commonly used escape sequences.

Table 2-4 Commonly Used Escape Sequences

	Escape Sequence	Description
`\n`	Newline	Cursor moves to the beginning of the next line
`\t`	Tab	Cursor moves to the next tab stop
`\b`	Backspace	Cursor moves one space to the left
`\r`	Return	Cursor moves to the beginning of the current line (not the next line)
`\\`	Backslash	Backslash is printed
`\'`	Single quotation	Single quotation mark is printed
`\"`	Double quotation	Double quotation mark is printed

The following example shows the effect of some of these escape sequences.

Example 2-22

The output of the statement

```
cout<<"The newline escape sequence is \\n"<<endl;
```

is

```
The newline escape sequence is \n
```

The output of the statement

```
cout<<"The tab character is represented as \'\\t\'"<<endl;
```

is

```
The tab character is represented as '\t'
```

The output of the statement

```
cout<<"The string \"Sunny\" contains five characters\n";
```

is

```
The string "Sunny" contains five characters
```

To use `cin` and `cout` in a program, you must include a certain header file. The next section explains what this header file is, how to include a header file in a program, and why you need header files in a program. Chapter 3 will provide a full explanation of what, in fact, `cin` and `cout` are.

PREPROCESSOR DIRECTIVES

Only a small number of operations, such as arithmetic and assignment operations, are explicitly defined in C++. Many of the functions and symbols needed to run a C++ program are provided as a collection of libraries. Every library has a name and is referred to by a header file. For example, in ANSI/ISO Standard C++, the descriptions of the functions needed to perform input/output (I/O) are contained in the header file **`iostream`**. Similarly, in ANSI/ISO Standard C++, the descriptions of some very useful mathematical functions, such as power, absolute, and sine, are contained in the header file **`cmath`**. If you want to use I/O or math functions, you need to tell the computer where to find the necessary code. You use preprocessor directives and the names of header files to tell the computer the locations of the code provided in libraries. Preprocessor directives are processed by a program called a **preprocessor**.

Preprocessor directives are commands supplied to the preprocessor that cause the preprocessor to modify the text of a C++ program before it is complied. All preprocessor commands begin with `#`. There are no semicolons at the end of preprocessor commands because they are not C++ statements. To use a header file in a C++ program, use the preprocessor directive `include`.

The general syntax to include a header file (provided by the SDK) in a C++ program is:

```
#include <headerFileName>
```

For example, the following statement includes the header file **`iostream`** in a C++ program:

```
#include <iostream>
```

Preprocessor directives to include header files are placed as the first line of a program so that the identifiers declared in those header files can be used throughout the program. (Recall that in C++, identifiers must be declared before they can be used.)

Certain header files are required to be provided as part of the ANSI/ISO Standard C++. Appendix F describes some of the commonly used header files. Individual programmers can also create their own header files. In Chapter 13, you will learn how to create your own header files and then include them in a C++ program.

In Standard C++, header files have the file extension **.h**. (In ANSI/ISO Standard C++, header files do not have any file extension.) For example, in Standard C++, the descriptions of the functions needed to perform I/O are contained in the header file **iostream.h**. The name of the Standard C++ header file containing useful mathematical functions is **math.h**. Thus, to include the header file **iostream.h** in a Standard C++ program, you need the following statement:

```
#include <iostream.h>
```

For the naming conventions of header files in ANSI/ISO Standard C++ and Standard C++, see Appendix E.

The preprocessor commands are processed by the preprocessor before the program goes through the compiler. Thus, a C++ program goes through six steps, as shown in Figure 2-18: edit, preprocess, compile, link, load, and execute.

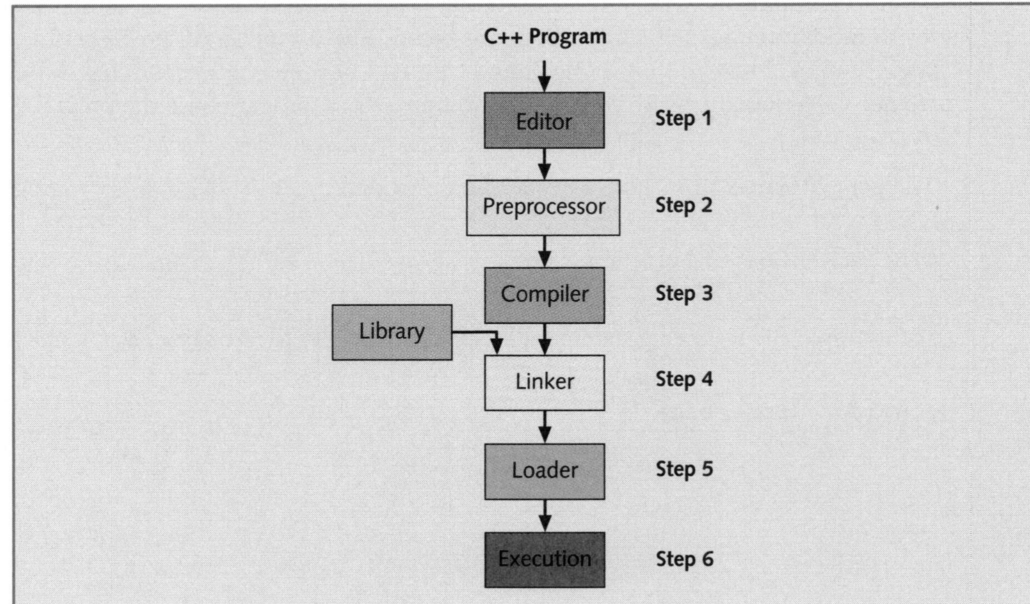

Figure 2-18 Processing a C++ program

From Figure 2-18, we can conclude that a C++ system has three basic components: the program development environment, the C++ language, and the C++ library. All three components are integral parts of the C++ system. The program development environment consists of the six steps shown in Figure 2-18. You will be learning the C++ language throughout the book, and we will discuss components of the C++ library as we need them.

2

Using `cin` and `cout` in a Program and `namespace`

Earlier you learned that both **cin** and **cout** are predefined identifiers. In ANSI/ISO Standard C++, these identifiers are declared in the header file **iostream**, but within a **namespace**. The name of this **namespace** is **std**. (The **namespace** mechanism will be formally defined and discussed in detail in Chapter 8. For now, you need to know only how to use **cin** and **cout**, and, in fact, any other identifier from the header file **iostream**.)

There are several ways you can use an identifier declared in the namespace **std**. One way to use **cin** and **cout** is to refer them as **std::cin** and **std::cout** throughout the program. Another option is to include the following statement in your program:

```
using namespace std;
```

This statement appears after the statement **#include <iostream>**. You can then refer to **cin** and **cout** without using the prefix **std::**. To simplify the use of **cin** and **cout**, this book uses the second form. That is, to use **cin** and **cout** in a program, the programs will contain the following two statements:

```
#include <iostream>
using namespace std;
```

In C++, **namespace** and **using** are reserved words.

The **namespace** mechanism is a feature of ANSI/ISO Standard C++. As you learn more C++ programming, you will become aware of other header files. For example, the header file **cmath** contains the specifications of many useful mathematical functions. Similarly, the header file **iomanip** contains the specifications of many useful functions and manipulators that help you format your output in a specific manner. However, just like the identifiers in the header file **iostream**, the identifiers in ANSI/ISO Standard C++ header files are declared within a **namespace**.

The name of the **namespace** in each of these header files is **std**. Therefore, whenever certain features of a header file in ANSI/ISO Standard C++ are discussed, this book will refer to the identifiers without the prefix **std::**. Moreover, in programs, to simplify the accessing of identifiers, the statement **using namespace std;** will be included. Also, if a program uses multiple header files, only one such **using** statement is needed. This using statement typically appears after all header files.

In Standard C++, **cin** and **cout** are declared in the header file **iostream.h**. Therefore, in Standard C++, to use **cin** and **cout** in a program, you must include the following statement:

```
#include <iostream.h>
```

Using the `string` Data Type in a Program

Recall that the `string` data type is a programmer-defined data type and is not directly available for use in a program. To use the `string` data type, you need to access its definition from the header file `string`. Therefore, to use the `string` data type in a program, you must include the following preprocessor directive:

```
#include <string>
```

Some compilers may not allow you to use the data type `string` with Standard C++ style header files—that is, header files with the extension `.h`. In other words, if you use the `string` data type in your program, the other header files that you use must be ANSI/ISO Standard C++ header files—that is, header files without the `.h` file extension. In such cases, to use `cin`, `cout`, and the `string` data type, your program must include the following preprocessor directives and statement (check your compiler's documentation):

```
#include <iostream>
#include <string>
using namespace std;
```

In the programming examples at the end of this chapter, you will see C++ code using both Standard C++ and ANSI/ISO Standard C++. In all remaining chapters except Chapter 8, the programming code will use ANSI/ISO Standard C++ style header files. The next few chapters indicate the corresponding header files in Standard C++ as needed. At the Web site corresponding to this book, the programming code is shown in both Standard C++ and ANSI/ISO Standard C++ formats.

PROGRAM STYLE AND FORM

In previous sections, you learned enough C++ concepts to write meaningful programs. Before beginning to write such programs, however, you need to learn the proper structure of a program, among other things. Using the proper structure for a C++ program makes it easier to understand and subsequently modify the program. There is nothing more frustrating than trying to follow, and perhaps modify, a program that is syntactically correct, but has no structure.

Every C++ program is divided into two parts: the preprocessor directives and the program. The preprocessor directives are commands that direct the preprocessor to modify the C++ program before compilation. The program contains statements that accomplish some meaningful results. Taken together, the preprocessor directives and program statements constitute the C++ **source code**. To be useful, this source code must be saved in a file that has the file extension `.cpp`.

When the program is compiled, the compiler generates the object code, which is saved in a file with the file extension `.obj`. When the object code is linked with system resources, the executable code is produced and saved in a file with the file extension `.exe`. The name of the file containing the object code and the name of the file containing the executable code are the same as the name of the file containing the source code. For example, if the source code is located in a file named `firstProg.cpp`, the name of the file containing the object code is `firstProg.obj`, and the name of the file containing the executable code is `firstProg.exe`.

The extensions as given above—that is, `.cpp`, `.obj`, and `.exe`—are system dependent. To be absolutely sure, check your system's or SDK's documentation.

In addition, every C++ program must satisfy certain rules of the language. A C++ program must contain the function `main`. It must also follow the syntax rules, which, like grammar rules, tell what is right and what is wrong, and what is legal and what is illegal in the language. Other rules serve the purpose of giving precise meaning to the language; that is, they support the language's semantics. The ensuing sections are designed to help you learn how to put the C++ programming elements you have learned so far together to create a functioning program. These sections cover the function `main`; syntax; the use of blanks; the use of semicolons, brackets, and commas; semantics; form and style; documentation, including comments and naming identifiers; and prompt lines.

The Function `main`

Recall that every C++ program must have the function `main`. The basic parts of the function `main` are the heading and the body of the function. The heading has the following form:

```
typeOfFunction main(argument list)
```

For example, the statement

```
int main(void)
```

means that the function `main` returns a value of the `int` data type, and it has no arguments. It is not necessary to put the word `void` in parentheses, but the parentheses are still required. Thus, the following statement is equivalent to the preceding statement:

```
int main()
```

In C++, `void` is a reserved word.

The body of the function must be enclosed between curly braces (`{` and `}`), and contain two types of statements:

- Declaration statements
- Executable statements

Declaration statements are used to declare things such as variables. In C++, variables or identifiers can be declared anywhere in the program, but they must be declared before they can be used.

Example 2-23

The following statements are examples of variable declarations:

```
int  a, b, c;
double  x, y;
```

Executable statements perform calculations, manipulate data, create output, accept input, and so on. Some executable statements that you have encountered so far are the assignment, input, and output statements.

Example 2-24

The following statements are examples of executable statements:

```
a = 4;                    //assignment statement
cin>>b;                   //input statement
cout<<a<<endl<<b<<endl;   //output statement
```

The function `main` used in this book has the following syntax:

```
int main()
{
  statement1
       .
       .
       .
  statementn
  return 0;
}
```

In the syntax of the function `main`, each of the statements (`statement1`,..., `statementn`) is usually either a declarative statement or an executable statement. The statement `return 0;` must be included in the function `main` and must be the last statement. If the statement `return 0;` is misplaced in the body of the function `main`, the results generated by the program may not be to your liking. The meaning of the statement `return 0;` will be discussed in Chapter 6. In C++, `return` is a reserved word.

Syntax

The syntax rules of a language tell what is legal and what is not legal. Errors in syntax are detected during compilation. For example, consider the following C++ statements:

```
int x;          //Line 1
int y           //Line 2:syntax error
double z;       //Line 3

y = w + x;      //Line 4:syntax error
```

When these statements are compiled, a compilation error will occur at Line 2 because the semicolon is missing after the declaration of the variable `y`. A second compilation error will occur at Line 4 because the identifier `w` is used but has not been declared.

As discussed in Chapter 1, you enter a program into the computer by using an editor. When the program is typed, errors are almost unavoidable. Therefore, when the program is compiled, you are most likely to see syntax errors. It is quite possible that a syntax error at a particular place might lead to syntax errors in several subsequent statements. It is very common for the omission of a single character to cause four or five error messages. However, when the first syntax error is removed and the program is recompiled, subsequent syntax errors caused by this syntax error may disappear. As you become more familiar and experienced with C++, you will learn how to quickly spot and fix syntax errors. Also, compilers not only discover syntax errors, but also hint and sometimes tell the user where the syntax errors are and how to fix them.

Use of Blanks

In C++, you use one or more blanks to separate numbers when data is input. Blanks are also used to separate reserved words and identifiers from each other and from other symbols. Blanks must never appear within a reserved word or identifier.

Use of Semicolons, Brackets, and Commas

All C++ statements must end with a semicolon. The semicolon is also called a **statement terminator**.

Note that brackets, `{` and `}`, are not C++ statements in and of themselves, even though they often appear on a line with no other code. You might regard brackets as delimiters, because they enclose the body of a function and set it off from other parts of the program. Brackets have other uses, which will be explained later.

Recall that commas are used to separate items in a list. For example, you use commas when you declare more than one variable following a data type.

Semantics

The set of rules that gives meaning to a language is called **semantics**. For example, the order-of-precedence rules for arithmetic operators are semantic rules.

If a program contains syntax errors, the compiler will warn you. What happens when a program contains semantic errors? It is quite possible to eradicate all syntax errors in a program and still not have it run. And if it runs, it may not do what you meant it to do. For example, the following two lines of code are both syntactically correct expressions, but they have different meanings:

```
2 + 3 * 5
```

and

```
(2 + 3) * 5
```

If you substitute one of these lines of code for the other in a program, you will not get the same results—even though the numbers are the same, the semantics are different. You will learn about semantics throughout this book.

Form and Style

You might be thinking that C++ has too many rules. However, in practice, the rules give C++ a great degree of freedom. For example, consider the following two ways of declaring variables:

```
int feet, inch;
double x, y;
```

and

```
int feet,inches;double x,y;
```

The computer would have no difficulty understanding either of these formats, but the first form is easier to read and follow. Of course, the omission of a single comma or semicolon in either format may lead to all sorts of strange error messages.

What about blank spaces? Where are they significant and where are they meaningless? Consider the following two statements:

```
int a,b,c;
```

and

```
int    a,   b,   c;
```

Both of these declarations mean the same thing. Here the blanks between the identifiers in the second statement are meaningless. On the other hand, consider the following statement:

```
inta,b,c;
```

This statement contains a syntax error. The lack of a blank between the `t` in `int` and the identifier `a` changes the reserved word `int` and the identifier `a` into a new identifier, `inta`.

The clarity of the rules of syntax and semantics frees you to adopt formats that are pleasing to you and easier to understand.

Documentation

The programs that you write should be clear not only to you, but also to anyone else. Therefore, you must properly document your programs. A well-documented program is easier to understand and modify, even a long time after you originally wrote it. You use comments to document programs. Comments should appear in a program to explain the purpose of the program, identify who wrote it, and explain the purpose of particular statements.

Comments

C++ has two types of comments: single line comments and multiple line comments. **Single line comments** begin with // anywhere in the line. Everything encountered on that line after // is ignored by the compiler. **Multiple line comments** are enclosed between /* and */. The compiler ignores anything that appears between /* and */.

2

You can insert certain comments at the top of a program to give a brief explanation of the program and information about the programmer. You can also include comments before each key step to give a brief description of what that step accomplishes.

In this book, in the programming code, the comments are shown in green color.

Naming Identifiers

When naming identifiers, choose names that are self-documenting. For example, consider the following two sets of statements:

```
const double a = 2.54;      //conversion constant
double x;                   //variable to hold centimeters
double y;                   //variable to hold inches

x = y * a;
```

and

```
const double conversion = 2.54;
double centimeters;
double inches;

centimeters = inches * conversion;
```

As you can see, self-documenting identifiers can make comments less necessary.

Consider the self-documenting identifier `inchperfoot` This identifier is called a **run-together-word**. In using self-documenting identifiers, you may inadvertently include run-together-words, which may lessen the clarity of your documentation. You can make run-together-words easier to understand by either capitalizing the beginning of each new word or by inserting an underscore just before a new word. For example, you could use either `inchPerFoot` or `inch_per_foot` to create a clearer identifier.

Prompt Lines

Part of good documentation is the use of clearly written prompts so that users will know what to do when they interact with a program. There is nothing more frustrating than sitting in front of a running program and not having the foggiest notion of whether to enter something or what to enter. **Prompt lines** are executable statements that inform the user what to do. For example, consider the following C++ statements, in which `num` is an `int` variable:

```
cout<<"Please enter a number between 1 and 10 and"
    <<" press the return key"<<endl;
cin>>num;
```

When these two statements execute in the order given, first the **cout** statement causes the following line of text to appear on the screen:

```
Please enter a number between 1 and 10 and press the return key
```

After seeing this line, users know that they must enter a number and press the return key. If the program contained only the second statement, users would have no idea that they must enter a number, and the computer would wait forever for the input. The preceding **cout** statement is an example of a prompt line.

In a program, whenever input is needed from users, you must include the necessary prompt lines. Furthermore, these prompt lines should include as much information as possible about what input is acceptable. For example, the preceding prompt line not only tells the user to input a number, but also informs the user that the number should be between 1 and 10.

More on Assignment Statements

The assignment statements you have seen so far are called **simple assignment statements**. In certain cases, you can use special assignment statements called **compound assignment statements** to write simple assignment statements in a more concise notation. For arithmetic operators, C++ defines the compound assignment operator as follows, where **op** is any of the arithmetic operators:

```
op=
```

Using the compound assignment operator, you can rewrite the simple assignment statement

```
variable = variable op (expression);
```

as

```
variable op= expression;
```

Thus, the compound assignment statement allows you to write simple assignment statements in a concise fashion by combining an arithmetic operator with the assignment operator.

Example 2-25

This example shows several compound assignment statements that are equivalent to simple assignment statements.

Simple Assignment Statement	Compound Assignment Statement
`I = I + 5;`	`I += 5;`
`counter = counter + 1;`	`counter += 1;`
`sum = sum + number;`	`sum += number;`
`amount = amount*(interest + 1);`	`amount *= interest + 1;`
`x = x / ( y + 5);`	`x /= y + 5;`

Any compound assignment statement can be converted into a simple assignment statement. However, a simple assignment statement may not be (easily) converted to a compound assignment statement. For example, consider the following simple assignment statement:

```
x = x * y + z – 5;
```

To write this statement as a compound assignment statement, the variable `x` must be a common factor in the right side, which is not the case. Therefore, you cannot immediately convert this statement into a compound assignment statement. In fact, the equivalent compound assignment statement is

```
x *= y + (z - 5)/x;
```

which is more complicated than the simple assignment statement.

In programming code, this book typically uses only the compound operator +=. That is, using the compound operator +=, statements such as `a = a + b;` are written as `a += b;`.

Programming Example: Convert Length

Write a program that takes as input given lengths expressed in feet and inches. The program should then convert and output the lengths in centimeters. Assume that the given lengths in feet and inches are integers.

Input Length in feet and inches.

Output Equivalent length in centimeters.

Problem Analysis and Algorithm Design

The lengths are given in feet and inches, and you need to find the equivalent length in centimeters. One inch is equal to `2.54` centimeters. The first thing the program needs to do is convert the length given in feet and inches to all inches. Then you can use the conversion formula, `1` inch `= 2.54` centimeters, to find the equivalent length in centimeters. To convert the length from feet and inches to inches, you multiply the number of feet by `12`, as `1` foot is equal to `12` inches, and add the given inches.

For example, suppose the input is `5` feet and `7` inches. You then find the total inches as follows:

```
totalInches  = (12 * feet) + inches
             = 12 * 5 + 7
             = 67
```

You can then apply the conversion formula, 1 inch = 2.54 centimeters, to find the length in centimeters.

```
centimeters  = totalInches * 2.54
             = 67 * 2.54
             = 170.18
```

Based on this analysis of the problem, you can design an algorithm as follows:

1. Get the length in feet and inches.
2. Convert the length into total inches.
3. Convert total inches into centimeters.
4. Output centimeters.

Variables The input for the program is two numbers: one for feet and one for inches. Thus, you need two variables: one to store feet and the other to store inches. Because the program will first convert the given length into inches, you need another variable to store the total inches. You also need a variable to store the equivalent length in centimeters. In summary, you need the following variables:

```
int feet;              //variable to hold given feet
int inches;            //variable to hold given inches
int totalInches;       //variable to hold total inches
double centimeters;    //variable to hold length in centimeters
```

Named Constant To calculate the equivalent length in centimeters, you need to multiply the total inches by 2.54. Instead of using the value 2.54 directly in the program, you will declare this value as a named constant. Similarly, to find the total inches, you need to multiply the feet by 12 and add the inches. Instead of using 12 directly in the program, you will also declare this value as a named constant. Using a named constant makes it easier to modify the program later.

```
const double conversion = 2.54;
const int inchesPerFoot = 12;
```

Main Algorithm

1. Prompt the user for the input. (Without a prompt line, the user will be staring at a blank screen and will not know what to do.)
2. Get the data.
3. Echo the input—that is, output what the program read as input. (Without this step, after the program has executed, you will not know what the input was.)
4. Find the length in inches.

5. Output the length in inches.
6. Convert the length to centimeters.
7. Output the length in centimeters.

Putting It Together Now that the problem has been analyzed and the algorithm has been designed, the next step is to translate the algorithm into C++ code. Because this is the first complete C++ program you are writing, let's review the necessary steps in sequence.

The program will begin with comments that document its purpose and functionality. As there is both input to this program (the length in feet and inches) and output (the equivalent length in centimeters), you will be using system resources for input/output. In other words, the program will use input statements to get data into the program and output statements to print the results. Because the data will be entered from the keyboard and the output will be displayed on the screen, the program must include the header file `iostream`. Thus, the first statement of the program, after the comments as described above, will be the preprocessor directive to include this header file.

This program requires two types of memory locations for data manipulation: named constants and variables. Named constants are usually placed before the function `main` so that they can be used throughout the program.

This program has only one function, the function `main`, which will contain all of the programming instructions in its body. In addition, the program needs variables to manipulate data, and these variables will be declared in the body of the function `main`. The reasons for declaring variables in the body of the function `main` are explained in Chapter 7. The body of the function `main` will also contain the C++ statements that implement the algorithm. Therefore, the body of the function `main` has the following form:

```
int main()
{
    declare variables
    statements
    return 0;
}
```

To write the complete length conversion program, follow these steps:

1. Begin the program with comments for documentation.
2. Include header files, if any are used in the program.
3. Declare named constants, if any.
4. Write the definition of the function `main`.

Complete Program Listing in ANSI/ISO Standard C++

```
//********************************************************
//   Program Convert: this program converts measurements
// in feet and inches into centimeters using the
// approximation that 1 inch is equal to
// 2.54 centimeters.
//********************************************************

      //header file
#include <iostream>
using namespace std;

      //named constants
const double conversion = 2.54;
const int inchesPerFoot = 12;

int main()
{
      //declare variables
   int feet;
   int inches;
   int totalInches;
   double centimeter;

      //Statements: Step 1 - Step 7
   cout<<"Enter two integers, one for feet, "
       <<"one for inches: ";                          //Step 1
   cin>>feet>>inches;                                 //Step 2
   cout<<endl;
   cout<<"The numbers you entered are "<<feet
       <<" for feet "<<"and" <<inches
       <<" for inches. "<<endl;                       //Step 3

   totalInches = inchesPerFoot * feet + inches;       //Step 4
   cout<<endl;
   cout<<"The total number of inches = "
       <<totalInches<<endl;                           //Step 5
   centimeter = conversion * totalInches;             //Step 6
   cout<<"The number of centimeters = "
       <<centimeter<<endl;                            //Step 7
   return 0;
}
```

Sample Run: In this sample run, the user input is shaded.

```
Enter two integers, one for feet, one for inches: 15 7
The numbers you entered are 15 for feet and 7 for inches.
The total number of inches = 187
The number of centimeters = 474.98
```

Complete Program Listing in Standard C++

```
//********************************************************
//   Program Convert: this program converts measurements
// in feet and inches into centimeters using the
// approximation that 1 inch is equal to
// 2.54 centimeters.
//********************************************************

#include <iostream.h>

     //named constants
const double conversion = 2.54;
const int inchesPerFoot = 12;

int main()
{
     //declare variables
   int feet;
   int inches;
   int totalInches;
   double centimeter;

     //Statements: Step 1 - Step 7
   cout<<"Enter two integers, one for feet, "
       <<"one for inches: ";                          //Step 1
   cin>>feet>>inches;                                 //Step 2
   cout<<endl;
   cout<<"The numbers you entered are "<<feet
       <<" for feet "<<"and "<<inches
       <<" for inches. "<<endl;                       //Step 3

   totalInches = inchesPerFoot * feet + inches; //Step 4
   cout<<endl;
   cout<<"The total number of inches = "
       <<totalInches<<endl;                           //Step 5
   centimeter = conversion * totalInches;             //Step 6
   cout<<"The number of centimeters = "
       <<centimeter<<endl;                            //Step 7
   return 0;
}
```

PROGRAMMING EXAMPLE: MAKE CHANGE

Write a program that takes as input any change expressed in cents. It should then compute the number of half-dollars, quarters, dimes, nickels, and pennies to be returned, returning as many half-dollars as possible, then quarters, dimes, nickels, and pennies, in that order. For example, `483` cents should be returned as `9` half-dollars, `1` quarter, `1` nickel, and `3` pennies.

Input Change in cents.

Output Equivalent change in half-dollars, quarters, dimes, nickels, and pennies.

Problem Analysis and Algorithm Design

Suppose the given change is `646` cents. To find the number of half-dollars, you divide `646` by `50`, the value of a half-dollar, and find the quotient, which is `12`, and the remainder, which is `46`. The quotient, `12`, is the number of half-dollars, and the remainder, `46`, is the remaining change.

Next, divide the remaining change by `25`, to find the number of quarters. Since the remaining change is `46`, division by `25` gives the quotient `1`, which is the number of quarters, and a remainder of `21`, which is the remaining change. This process continues for dimes and nickels. To calculate the reminder in an integer division, you use the mod operator, `%`.

Applying this discussion to `646` cents yields the following calculations:

1. Change = `646`
2. Number of half-dollars = `646/50 = 12`
3. Remaining change = `646 % 50 = 46`
4. Number of quarters = `46 / 25 = 1`
5. Remaining change = `46 % 25 = 21`
6. Number of dimes = `21 / 10 = 2`
7. Remaining change = `21 % 10 = 1`
8. Number of nickels = `1 / 5 = 0`
9. Number of pennies = remaining change = `1 % 5 = 1`

This discussion translates into the following algorithm:

1. Get the change in cents.
2. Find the number of half-dollars.
3. Calculate the remaining change.
4. Find the number of quarters.
5. Calculate the remaining change.

6. Find the number of dimes.
7. Calculate the remaining change.
8. Find the number of nickels.
9. Calculate the remaining change.
10. The remaining change is the number of pennies.

Variables From the previous discussion and algorithm, it appears that the program will need variables to hold the number of half-dollars, quarters, and so on. However, the numbers of half-dollars, quarters, and so on are not used in later calculations, so the program can simply output these values without saving each of them in a variable. The only thing that keeps changing is the change, so the program actually needs only one variable:

```
int change;
```

Named Constants To calculate the equivalent change, the program performs calculations using the values of a half-dollar, which is `50`; a quarter, which is `25`; a dime, which is `10`; and a nickel, which is `5`. Because these data are special and the program uses these values more than once, it makes sense to declare them as named constants. Using named constants also simplifies later modification of the program.

```
const int Halfdollar = 50;
const int Quarter   = 25;
const int Dime = 10;
const int Nickel = 5;
```

Main Algorithm

1. Prompt the user for input.
2. Get input.
3. Echo the input by displaying the entered change on the screen.
4. Compute and print the number of half-dollars.
5. Calculate the remaining change.
6. Compute and print the number of quarters.
7. Calculate the remaining change.
8. Compute and print the number of dimes.
9. Calculate the remaining change.
10. Compute and print the number of nickels.
11. Calculate the remaining change.
12. Print the remaining change.

Complete Program Listing

```
// ****************************************************
// Program Make Change: Given any amount of change
// expressed in cents, this program computes the number
// of half-dollars, quarters, dimes, nickels, and
// pennies to be returned, returning as many
// half-dollars as possible, then quarters, dimes,
// nickels, and pennies in that order.
//****************************************************
     //header file
#include <iostream>
using namespace std;

     //named constants
const int Halfdollar = 50;
const int Quarter  = 25;
const int Dime = 10;
const int Nickel = 5;

int main()
{
      //declare variable
    int change;

      //Statements: Step 1 – Step 12
    cout<<"Enter change in cents: ";                     //Step 1
    cin>>change;                                         //Step 2
    cout<<endl;
    cout<<"The change you entered is "<<change<<endl;   //Step 3

    cout<<"The number of half-dollars to be returned "
        <<"are "<<change / Halfdollar<<endl;             //Step 4
    change = change % Halfdollar;                        //Step 5

    cout<<"The number of quarters to be returned are "
        <<change / Quarter<<endl;                        //Step 6
    change = change % Quarter;                           //Step 7
    cout<<"The number of dimes to be returned are "
        <<change / Dime<<endl;                           //Step 8
    change = change % Dime;                              //Step 9

    cout<<"The number of nickels to be returned are "
        <<change / Nickel<<endl;                         //Step 10
    change = change % Nickel;                            //Step 11

    cout<<"The number of pennies to be returned are "
        <<change<<endl;                                  //Step 12
    return 0;
}
```

Sample Run: In this sample run, the user input is shaded.

```
Enter change in cents: 583
The change you entered is 583
The number of half-dollars to be returned are 11
The number of quarters to be returned are 1
The number of dimes to be returned are 0
The number of nickels to be returned are 1
The number of pennies to be returned are 3
```

To write the Make Change program using Standard C++ header files, replace the statements

```
#include <iostream>

using namespace std;
```

with

```
#include <iostream.h>
```

QUICK REVIEW

1. A C++ program is a collection of functions.
2. Every C++ program has a function called `main`.
3. In C++, identifiers are names of things.
4. A C++ identifier consists of letters, digits, and underscores, and must begin with a letter or underscore.
5. Reserved words cannot be used as identifiers in a program.
6. All reserved words in C++ consist of lowercase letters (see Appendix A).
7. The most common character sets are ASCII, which has 128 values, and EBCDIC, which has 256 values.
8. The collating sequence of a character is its preset number in the character data set.
9. The arithmetic operators in C++ are addition (+), subtraction (-), multiplication (*), division (/), and modulus (%).
10. The modulus operator, %, takes only integer operands.
11. Arithmetic expressions are evaluated using the precedence rules and the associativity of the arithmetic operators.
12. All operands in an integral expression, or integer expression, are integers, and all operands in a floating-point expression are decimal numbers.
13. A mixed expression is an expression that consists of both integers and decimal numbers.
14. When evaluating an operator in an expression, an integer is converted to a floating-point number, with a decimal part of zero, only if the operator has mixed operands.

15. You can use the cast operator to explicitly convert values from one data type to another.
16. During program execution, the contents of a named constant cannot be changed.
17. A named constant is declared by using the reserved word `const`.
18. A named constant is initialized when it is declared.
19. All variables must be declared before they can be used.
20. C++ does not automatically initialize variables.
21. Every variable has a name, a value, a data type, and a size.
22. When a new value is assigned to a variable, the old value is destroyed.
23. Only an assignment statement or an input (read) statement can change the value of a variable.
24. Outputting or accessing the value of a variable in an expression does not destroy or modify the contents of the variable.
25. In C++, >> is called the stream extraction operator.
26. Input from the standard input device is accomplished by using `cin` and the stream extraction operator >>.
27. When data is input in a program, the data items, such as numbers, are usually separated by blanks, lines, or tabs.
28. In C++, << is called the stream insertion operator.
29. Output of the program to the standard output device is accomplished by using `cout` and the stream insertion operator <<.
30. In ANSI/ISO Standard C++, to use `cin` and `cout`, the program must include the header file `iostream` and either include the statement `using namespace std;` or refer to these identifiers as `std::cin` and `std::cout`
31. The manipulator `endl` positions the cursor at the beginning of the next line on an output device.
32. The character\ is called the escape character.
33. The sequence`\n` is called the newline escape sequence.
34. All preprocessor commands start with the symbol `#`.
35. The preprocessor commands are processed by the preprocessor before the program goes through the compiler.
36. The preprocessor command **#include <iostream>** instructs the preprocessor to include the header file `iostream` in the program.
37. All C++ statements end with a semicolon. The semicolon in C++ is called the statement terminator.
38. A C++ system has three components: environment, language, and the standard libraries.
39. Standard libraries are not part of the C++ language. They contain functions to perform operations such as mathematical operations.
40. A file containing a C++ program usually ends with the extension `.cpp`.

41. A single line comment starts with the pair of symbols `//`anywhere in the line.
42. Multiline comments are enclosed between `/*` and `*/`.
43. The compiler skips comments.
44. Prompt lines are executable statements that tell the user what to do.
45. The arithmetic compound assignment operator has the form **`op=`**, where **`op`** is any arithmetic operator.
46. For arithmetic operators, the compound assignment statement has the form **`variable op= expression;`**, which is equivalent to the statement **`variable = variable op (expression);`**, where **`op`** is any arithmetic operator.

EXERCISES

1. Mark the following statements as true or false.
   a. An identifier can be any sequence of digits and letters.
   b. In C++, there is no difference between a reserved word and a predefined identifier.
   c. A C++ identifier can start with a digit.
   d. The operands of the modulus operator must be integers.
   e. If `a = 4;` and `b = 3;`, then after the statement `a = b;` the value of `b` is still `3`.
   f. In the statement **`cin>>y;`** **`y`** can only be a variable of the type **`int`** or **`double`**.
   g. In a **`cout`** statement, the newline character may be a part of the string.
   h. The following is a legal C++ program:

   ```
   int main()
   {
           return 0;
   }
   ```

   i. In a mixed expression, all operands are converted to floating-point numbers.
   j. Suppose `x = 5`. After the statement `y = x++;` executes, `y` is `5` and `x` is `6`.
   k. Suppose `a = 5`. After the statement `++a;` executes, the value of `a` is still `5` because the value of the expression is not saved in another variable.
2. Which of the following are valid C++ identifiers?
   a. `RS6S6`
   b. `MIX-UP`
   c. `STOP!`
   d. `exam1`
   e. `September1Lecture`

f. `2May`

g. `Mike's`

h. `First Exam`

i. `J`

j. `Three`

3. Which of the following is a reserved word in C++?

    a. `int`

    b. `long`

    c. `Char`

    d. `CHAR`

    e. `Float`

    f. `Double`

4. Circle the best answer.

    a. The value of `15/2` is:

        (i) `7` (ii) `7.5` (iii) `7 1/2` (iv) `0.75` (v) none of these

    b. The value of `18/3` is:

        (i) `6` (ii) `0.167` (iii) `6.0` (iv) none of these

    c. The value of `22 % 7` is:

        (i) `3` (ii) `1` (iii) `3.142` (iv) `22/7`

    d. The value of `5 % 7` is:

        (i) `0` (ii) `2` (iii) `5` (iv) undefined

    e. The value of `17.0 / 4` is:

        (i) `4` (ii) `4.25` (iii) `4 1/4` (iv) undefined

    f. The value of `5 - 3.0 + 2` is:

        (i) `0` (ii) `0.0` (iii) `4` (iv) `4.0`

    g. The value of `7 - 5 * 2 + 1` is:

        (i) `–2` (ii) `5` (iii) `6` (iv) none of these

    h. The value of `15.0 / 3.0 + 2.0` is:

        (i) `3` (ii) `3.0` (iii) `5` (iv) none of these

5. If `x=5`, `y=6`, `z=4`, and `w=3.5`, evaluate each of the following statements, if possible. If it is not possible, state the reason.

    a. `(x + z) % y`

    b. `(x + y) % w`

    c. `(y + w) % x`

d. `(x + y ) * w`

e. `(x % y) % z`

f. `(y % z) % x`

g. `(x * z) % y`

h. `((x * y) * w) * z`

6. Given

```
int n, m, l;
double x, y;
```

Which of the following assignments are valid? If an assignment is not valid, state the reason. When not given, assume that each variable is declared.

a. `n = m = 5;`

b. `m = l = 2 * n;`

c. `n = 5; m = 2 + 6; n = 6 / 3;`

d. `m + n = l;`

e. `x = 2 * n + 5.3;`

f. `l + 1 = n;`

g. `x / y = x * y;`

h. `m = n % l;`

i. `n = x % 5;`

j. `x = x + 5;`

k. `n = 3 + 4.6`

7. Do a walk-through to find the value assigned to `e`. Assume that all variables are properly declared.

```
a = 3;
b = 4;
c = (a % b) * 6;
d = c / b;
e = (a+b+c+d)/4;
```

8. Which of the following variable declarations are correct? If a variable declaration is not correct, give the reason(s) and provide the correct variable declaration.

```
n = 12;                 //Line 1
char letter = ;         //Line 2
int one = 5, two;       //Line 3
double x, y, z;         //Line 4
```

9. Which of the following are valid C++ assignment statements? Assume that `I`, `x`, and `percent` are `double` variables.

   a. `I = I + 5;`

   b. `x + 2 = x;`

   c. `x = 2.5 * x;`

   d. `percent = 10%.`

10. Write C++ statements that accomplish the following.

    a. Declares `int` variables `x` and `y`.

    b. Initializes an `int` variable `x` to `10` and a `char` variable `ch` to `'B'`.

    c. Updates the value of an `int` variable `x` by adding `5` to it.

    d. Sets the value of a `double` variable `z` to `25.3`.

    e. Copies the content of an `int` variable `y` into an `int` variable `z`.

    f. Swaps the contents of the `int` variables `x` and `y`. (Declare additional variables, if necessary.)

    g. Outputs the content of a variable `x` and an expression `2*x+5-y`, where `x` and `y` are `double` variables.

    h. Declares a `char` variable `grade` and sets the value of `grade` to `'A'`.

    i. Declares `int` variables to store four integers.

    j. Copies the value of a `double` variable `z` to the nearest integer into an `int` variable `x`.

11. Write each of the following as a C++ expression.

    a. `–10` times `a`

    b. The character that represents `8`

    c. `(`b^2`-4ac)/2a`

    d. `(–b + (`b^2`-4ac))/2a`

12. Suppose `x`, `y`, `z`, and `w` are `int` variables. What value is assigned to each of these variables after the last statement executes?

```
x = 5; z = 3;
y = x – z;
z = 2 * y + 3;
w = x – 2 * y + z;
z = w – x;
w++;
```

13. Suppose `x`, `y`, and `z` are `int` variables and `w` and `t` are `double` variables. What value is assigned to each of these variables after the last statement executes?

```
x = 17;
y = 15;
x = x + y / 4;
z = x % 3 + 4;
w = 17 / 3 + 6.5;
t = x / 4.0 + 15 % 4 - 3.5;
```

14. Suppose `x`, `y`, and `z` are `int` variables and `x = 2`, `y = 5`, and `z = 6`. What is the output of each of the following statements?

    a. `cout<<"x = "<<x<<", y = "<<y<<", z = "<<z<<endl;`

    b. `cout<<"x + y = "<<x + y<<endl;`

    c. `cout<<"Sum of "<<x<<" and "<<z<<" is "<<x+z<<endl;`

    d. `cout<<"z / x = "<<z / x<<endl;`

    e. `cout<<" 2 times "<<x<<" = "<<2*x<<endl;`

15. What is the output of the following statements? Suppose `a` and `b` are `int` variables, `c` is a `double` variable, and `a = 13`, `b = 5`, and `c = 17.5`.

	Output
a. `cout<<a + b - c<<endl;`	________
b. `cout<< 15 / 2 + c <<endl;`	________
c. `cout<<a / static_cast<double>(b) + 2 * c <<endl;`	________
d. `cout<< 14 % 3 + 6.3 + b / a<<endl;`	________
e. `cout<<static_cast<int>(c)%5 + a - b<<endl;`	________
f. `cout<< 13.5 / 2 + 4.0 * 3.5 + 18<<endl;`	________

16. How do you print the carriage return?

17. Which of the following are correct C++ statements?

    a. `cout<<"Hello There!"<<endl;`

    b.
    ```
    cout<<"Hello";
        <<" There!"<<endl;
    ```

    c.
    ```
    cout<<"Hello"
        <<" There!"<<endl;
    ```

    d. `cout<<'Hello There!'<<endl;`

18. The following two programs have syntax mistakes. Correct them. On each successive line, assume that any preceding error has been corrected.

a.

```
#include <iostream>
const int  prime=11,213;
const rate = 15.6
int main ()
{
    int i, x, y, w;
    x = 7;
    y = 3;
    x = x + w;
    prime = x + prime;
    cout<<prime<<endl;
    wages = rate * 36.75;
    cout<<"Wages = "<<wages<<endl;
    return 0;
}
```

b.

```
const char = Blank = ' ';
const int  one 5;

int main (
{
    int a, b, cc;

    a = one + 5;
    b = a + blank;
    cc := a + one * 2;
    a + cc = b;
    one = b + c;
    cout<<"a = "<<a<<", b = "<<b<<", cc = "<<cc<<endl;

    return 0;
}
```

19. Write equivalent compound statements if possible.

a. `x = 2*x`

b. `x = x+y-2;`

c. `sum = sum + num;`

d. `z = z * x + 2 * z;`

e. `y = y / (x + 5);`

20. Write the following compound statements as equivalent simple statements.

    a. `x += 5 – z;`

    b. `y *= 2 * x + 5 – z;`

    c. `w += 2 * z + 4;`

    d. `x -= z + y – t;`

    e. `sum += num;`

21. Suppose `a`, `b`, and `c` are `int` variables and `a = 5` and `b = 6`. What value is assigned to each variable after each statement executes? If a variable is undefined at a particular statement, report `UND (undefined)`.

	a	b	c
`a = (b++) + 3;`	____	____	____
`c = 2 * a + (++b);`	____	____	____
`b = 2 * (++c) – (a++);`	____	____	____

22. Suppose `a`, `b`, and `sum` are `int` variables and `c` is a `double` variable. What value is assigned to each variable after each statement executes? Suppose `a = 3`, `b = 5`, and `c = 14.1`.

	a	b	c	sum
`sum = a + b + c;`	____	____	____	____
`c /= a;`	____	____	____	____
`b += c – a;`	____	____	____	____
`a *= 2 * b + c;`	____	____	____	____

23. What is printed by the following program? Suppose the input is

    `20 15`

```
#include <iostream>
using namespace std;
const int NUM = 10;
const double x = 20.5;
int main()
{
   int a, b;
   double z;
   char grade;

   a = 25;
   cout<<"a = "<<a<<endl;
   cout<<"Enter two integers : ";
   cin>>a>>b;
   cout<<endl;
   cout<<"The numbers you entered are "
       <<a<<" and "<<b<<endl;
   z = x + 2 * a – b;
```

```
    cout<<"z = "<<z<<endl;
    grade = 'A';
    cout<<"Your grade is "<<grade<<endl;

    a = 2 * NUM + z;
    cout<<"The value of a = "<<a<<endl;
    return 0;
}
```

24. What type of input does the following program require, and in what order does the input need to be provided?

```
#include <iostream>
using namespace std;
int main()
{
  int x,y;
  char ch;
  cin>>x;
  cin>>ch>>y;
  return 0;
}
```

PROGRAMMING EXERCISES

1. Write a program that produces the following output:

```
**********************************
*     Programming Assignment 1    *
*      Computer Programming I     *
*        Author: Duffy Ducky      *
*   Due Date: Thursday, Jan. 24   *
**********************************
```

2. Write a program that produces the following output:

```
CCCCCCCCC          ++                ++
CC                 ++                ++
CC           ++++++++++++++    ++++++++++++++
CC           ++++++++++++++    ++++++++++++++
CC                 ++                ++
CCCCCCCCC          ++                ++
```

3. Write a program that prompts the user to input a decimal number and outputs the number rounded to the nearest integer.

4. Write a program that prompts the user to input the length and width of a rectangle and then prints the rectangle's area and perimeter.

5. Write a program that prompts the user to enter five test scores and then prints the average test score.
6. Write a program that prints the following pattern:

```
  *
 * *
* * *
```

7. Write a program that prints the following banner:

```
**************************
**************************
********* WELCOME *********
==========================
==========================
*********   HOME   *********
**************************
**************************
```

8. Write a program that prompts the user to input five decimal numbers. The program should then add the five decimal numbers, convert the sum to the nearest integer, and print the result.
9. Write a program that does the following:
   a. Prompts the user to input five decimal numbers.
   b. Prints the five decimal numbers.
   c. Converts each decimal number to the nearest integer.
   d. Adds the five integers.
   e. Prints the sum and average of the five integers.
10. Write a program that prompts the user to input a length expressed in centimeters. The program should then convert the length to inches to the nearest inch and output the length expressed in yards, feet, and inches, in that order. For example, `123` inches would be output as

    `3 yard(s), 1 feet (foot), and 3 inch(es)`

    It should not be output as

    `2 yard(s) 4 feet (foot) 3 inch(es),`

    or

    `10 feet (foot) 3 inch(es),`

    or

    `10.25 feet (foot).`

CHAPTER

3

INPUT/OUTPUT

In this chapter, you will:

- Learn what a stream is and examine input and output streams
- Explore how to read data from the standard input device
- Learn how to use predefined functions in a program
- Explore how to use the input stream functions `get`, `ignore`, `fill`, `putback`, and `peek`
- Become familiar with input failure
- Learn how to write data to the standard output device
- Discover how to use manipulators in a program to format output
- Learn how to perform input and output operations with the string data type
- Become familiar with file input and output

In Chapter 2, you were introduced to some of C++'s input/output (I/O) instructions, which get data into a program and print the results on the screen. You used **`cin`** and the extraction operator >> to get data from the keyboard, and **`cout`** and the insertion operator << to send output to the screen. Because I/O operations are fundamental to any programming language, in this chapter you will learn about C++'s I/O operations in more detail. First, you will learn about functions that extract input from the standard input device and send output to the standard output device. You will then learn how to format output using manipulators. In addition, you will learn about the limitations of the I/O operations associated with the standard input/output devices and extend these operations to other devices.

I/O STREAMS AND STANDARD I/O DEVICES

A program performs three basic operations: it gets data into the program, it manipulates the data, and it outputs the results. In Chapter 2, you learned how to manipulate numeric data using arithmetic operations. In later chapters, you will learn how to manipulate non-numeric data. Because writing programs for I/O is quite complex, C++ offers extensive support for I/O operations by providing substantial I/O operations, some of which you encountered in Chapter 2. In this chapter, you will learn about various I/O operations that can greatly enhance the flexibility of your programs.

In C++, I/O is a sequence of bytes, called a **stream of bytes**, from the source to the destination. The bytes are usually characters, unless the program requires other types of information such as a graphic image or digital speech. Therefore, a **stream** is a sequence of characters from the source to the destination. There are two types of streams: input streams and output streams.

Input stream: A sequence of characters from an input device to the computer.

Output stream: A sequence of characters from the computer to an output device.

Recall that the standard input device is usually the keyboard, and the standard output device is usually the screen. To receive data from the keyboard and send output to the screen, every C++ program must use the header file `iostream`. This header file contains, among other things, the definitions of two data types, `istream` (input stream) and `ostream` (output stream). The header file also contains two variable declarations, one for `cin` (pronounced "see-in"), which stands for **common input**, and one for `cout` (pronounced "see-out"), which stands for **common output**. These variable declarations are similar to the following C++ statements:

```
istream cin;
ostream cout;
```

To use `cin` and `cout`, every C++ program must use the preprocessor directive:

```
#include <iostream>
```

From Chapter 2, recall that you have been using the statement `using namespace std;` in addition to including the header file `iostream` to use `cin` and `cout`. Without the statement `using namespace std;`, you refer to these identifiers as `std::cin` and `std::cout`. In Chapter 8, you will learn about the meaning of the statement `using namespace std;` in detail.

Variables of the type `istream` are called **input stream variables**; variables of the type `ostream` are called **output stream variables**. A **stream variable** is either an input stream variable or an output stream variable.

Because `cin` and `cout` are already defined and have specific meanings, to avoid confusion you should never redefine them in programs.

The variable `cin` has access to operators and functions that can be used to extract data from the standard input device. You have briefly used the extraction operator >> to input data from the standard input device. The next section describes in detail how the operator >> works. In the following sections, you will learn how to use the functions `get`, `ignore`, `peek`, and `putback` to input data in a specific manner.

3

cin and the Extraction Operator >>

In Chapter 2, you saw how to input data from the standard input device by using `cin` and the extraction operator >>. Consider the following C++ statement:

```
cin>>payRate;
```

When the computer executes this statement, it inputs the next number typed on the keyboard and stores this number in the variable `payRate`. Therefore, if `payRate` is a variable of the `double` data type, and the user types `15.50`, the value stored in `payRate` after this statement executes is `15.50`.

The extraction operator >> is binary and thus takes two operands. The left-side operand must be an input stream variable such as `cin`. Because the purpose of an input statement is to read and store values in a memory location, and because only variables refer to memory locations, the right-side operand is a variable.

The extraction operator >> is defined only for putting data into variables of simple data types. Therefore, the right-side operand of the extraction operator >> is a variable of the simple data type. However, C++ allows the programmer to extend the definition of the extraction operator >> so that data can also be put into other types of variables by using an input statement. You will learn this mechanism in Chapter 16.

The syntax of an input statement using `cin` and the extraction operator >> is

```
cin>>variable>>variable...;
```

As you see in the preceding syntax, a single `cin` statement can read more than one data item by using the operator >> several times. Every occurrence of >> extracts the next data item from the input stream. For example, you can read both `payRate` and `hoursWorked` via a single `cin` statement by using the following code:

```
cin>>payRate>>hoursWorked;
```

There is no difference between the preceding `cin` statement and the following two `cin` statements. Which form of `cin` statement you use is a matter of convenience and style.

```
cin>>payRate;
cin>>hoursWorked;
```

How does the extraction operator >> work? When scanning for the next input, >> skips all whitespace characters. **Whitespace characters** consist of blanks and certain nonprintable characters, such as tabs and the newline character. Thus, whether you separate the input data by lines or blanks, the extraction operator >> simply finds the next input data in the input stream. For example, suppose that **payRate** and **hoursWorked** are variables of the **double** data type. Consider the following input statement:

```
cin>>payRate>>hoursWorked;
```

Whether the input is

```
15.50 48.30
```

or

```
15.50	48.30
```

or

```
15.50
48.30
```

the preceding input statement would store `15.50` in **payRate** and `48.30` in **hoursWorked**. Note that the first input is separated by a blank, the second input is separated by a tab, and the third input is separated by a line.

Now suppose that the input is `2`. How does the extraction operator >> distinguish between the character `2` and the number `2`? The right-side operand of the extraction operator >> makes this distinction. If the right-side operand is a variable of the data type **char**, the input `2` is treated as the character `2` and, in this case, the ASCII value of `2` is stored. If the right-side operand is a variable of the data type **int** or **double**, the input `2` is treated as the number `2`.

Next, consider the input `25` and the statement

```
cin>>a;
```

where **a** is a variable of some simple data type. If **a** is of the data type **char**, only the single character `2` is stored in **a**. If **a** is of the data type **int**, `25` is stored in **a**. If **a** is of the data type **double**, the input `25` is converted to the decimal number `25.0`. Table 3-1 summarizes this discussion by showing the valid input for a variable of the simple data type.

Table 3-1 Valid Input for a Variable of the Simple Data Type

Data Type of a	Valid Input for a
`char`	One printable character except the blank.
`int`	An integer, possibly preceded by a (+ or –) sign.
`double`	A decimal number, possibly preceded by a (+ or –) sign. If the actual data input is an integer, the input is converted to a decimal number with the zero decimal part.

When reading data into a **char** variable, after skipping any leading whitespace characters, the extraction operator >> finds and stores only the next character; reading stops after a single character. To read data into an **int** or **double** variable, after skipping all leading whitespace characters and reading the plus or minus sign (if any), the extraction operator >> reads the digits of the number, including the decimal point for floating-point variables, and stops when it finds a whitespace character or a character other than a digit.

Example 3-1

Suppose you have the following variable declarations:

```
int a,b;
double z;
char ch, ch1, ch2;
```

The following statements show how the extraction operator >> works.

	Statement	**Input**	**Value Stored in Memory**
1	`cin>>ch;`	`A`	`ch='A'`
2	`cin>>ch;`	`AB`	`ch='A', 'B' is held for later input`
3	`cin>>a;`	`48`	`a=48`
4	`cin>>a;`	`46.35`	`a=46, .35 is held for later input`
5	`cin>>z;`	`74.35`	`z=74.35`
6	`cin>>z;`	`39`	`z=39.0`
7	`cin>>z>>a;`	`65.78 38`	`z=65.78, a=38`
8	`cin>>a>>b;`	`4 60`	`a=4, b=60`
9	`cin>>a>>ch>>z;`	`57 A 26.9`	`a=57, ch='A', z=26.9`
10	`cin>>a>>ch>>z;`	`57   A` `26.9`	`a=57, ch='A', z=26.9`

11	`cin>>a>>ch>>z;`	`57`
		`A`
		`26.9`
			`a=57, ch='A', z=26.9`

12	`cin>>a>>ch>>z;`	`57A26.9`	`a=57, ch='A', z=26.9`
13	`cin>>z>>ch>>a;`	`36.78B34`	`z=36.78, ch='B', a=34`
14	`cin>>z>>ch>>a;`	`36.78` `B34`	`z=36.78, ch='B', a=34`
15	`cin>>a>>b>>z;`	`11 34`	`a=11, b=34, computer waits for the next number`
16	`cin>>a>>z;`	`46 32.4 68`	`a=46, z=32.4, 68 is held for later input`
17	`cin>>ch>>a;`	`256`	`ch='2', a=56`
18	`cin>>a>>ch;`	`256`	`a=256, computer waits for the input value for ch`
19	`cin>>ch1>>ch2;`	`A B`	`ch1 = 'A', ch2 = 'B'`

In statement 1, the extraction operator >> extracts and stores the character `'A'` from the input stream and stores it in the variable `ch`. In statement 2, the extraction operator >> extracts the character `'A'` from the input stream and stores it in the variable `ch`, and the value `'B'` is held in the input stream for later input.

Similarly in statement 16, the value `68` is held for later input. In statement 15, `11` is stored in `a`, and `34` is stored in `b`, but the input stream does not have enough input data to fill each variable. In this case, the computer waits (and waits, and waits,...) for the next input to be entered. The computer does not continue to execute until the next value is entered.

In statement 4, the extraction operator >> extracts `46` from the input stream and stores this value in `a`. Note that because `a` is an **`int`** variable and the character after `46` is `.` (which is non-numeric), only `46` is extracted from the input stream; as a result, reading stops at `.` and `.35` is held for later input. In statement 5, the extraction operator >> extracts `74.35` from the input stream and stores this value in `z`.

In statement 6, `z` is a variable of the **`double`** data type and the input `39` is an integer. Therefore, `39` is converted to the decimal number `39.0` and the value stored in `z` is `39.0`.

In statement 7, the first right-side operand of the extraction operator >> is a **`double`** variable and the second right-side operand is an **`int`** variable. Therefore, in statement 7, first the value `65.78` is extracted from the input stream and stored in `z`. The extraction operator then skips the blank after `65.78`, and the value `38` is extracted and stored in `a`. Statement 8 works similarly.

Note that for statements 9 through 12, the input statement is the same; however, the data is entered differently. For statement 9, data is entered on the same line separated by blanks. For statement 10, data is entered on two lines; the first two input values are separated by two blank spaces and the third input is on the next line. For statement 11, all three input values are separated by lines and for statement 12, all three input values are on the same line, but there is no space between them. Note that the second input is a non-numeric character. These statements work as follows.

In statement 9, first the extraction operator >> extracts `57` from the input stream and stores it in `a`. The extraction operator >> then skips the blank after `57`, and extracts and stores the character `'A'` in `ch`. Next, the extraction operator >> skips the blank after `A`, and extracts and stores the value `26.9` in `z` from the input stream.

In statement 10, first the extraction operator >> extracts `57` from the input stream and stores this value in `a`. The extraction operator >> then skips the two blank spaces after `57`, extracts the character `'A'` from the input stream, and stores it in `ch`. Next, the extraction operator >> skips the newline character `'\n'` after `A`, extracts `26.9` from the input stream, and stores it in `z`.

In statement 11, first the extraction operator >> extracts `57` from the input stream, and stores it in `a`. The extraction operator >> then skips the newline character `'\n'` after `57`, extracts the character `'A'` from the input stream, and stores it in `ch`. Next, the extraction operator >> skips the newline character `'\n'` after `A`, extracts `26.9` from the input stream, and stores it in `z`.

Statements 9, 10, and 11 illustrate that regardless of whether the input is separated by blanks or by lines, the extraction operator >> always finds the next input.

In statement 12, first the extraction operator >> extracts `57` from the input stream and stores it in `a`. Then the extraction operator >> extracts the character `'A'` from the input stream and stores it in `ch`. Next, `26.9` is extracted and stored in `z`.

In statement 13, because the first right-side operand of >> is `z`, which is a **`double`** variable, `36.78` is extracted from the input stream and the value `36.78` is stored in `z`. Next, `'B'` is extracted and stored in `ch`. Finally, `34` is extracted and stored in `a`. Statement 14 works similarly.

In statement 17, the first right-side operand of the extraction operator >> is a **`char`** variable, so the first non-whitespace character, `'2'`, is extracted from the input stream. The character `'2'` is stored in the variable `ch`. The next right-side operand of the extraction operator >> is an **`int`** variable, so the next input value, `56`, is extracted and stored in `a`.

In statement 18, the first right-side operator of the extraction operator >> is an **`int`** variable, so the first data item, `256`, is extracted from the input stream and stored in `a`. Now the computer waits for the next data item for the variable `ch`.

In statement 19, `'A'` is stored in `ch1`. The extraction operator >> then skips the blank, and `'B'` is stored in `ch2`.

Recall that, during program execution, when entering character data such as letters, you do not enter the single quotes around the character.

What happens if the input stream has more data items than required by the program? After the program terminates, any values left in the input stream are discarded. When you enter data for processing, the data values should correspond to the data types of the variables in the input statement. Recall that, when entering a number for a **`double`** variable, it is not necessary for the input number to have a decimal part. If the input number is an integer and has no decimal part, it is converted to a decimal value. The computer, however, does not tolerate any other kind of mismatch. For example, entering a **`char`** value into an **`int`** or **`double`** variable causes serious errors, called **input failure**. Input failure is discussed later in this chapter.

What happens when you try to read a non-numeric character into an **`int`** variable? Example 3-5, (given later in this chapter) illustrates this situation.

The extraction operator, when scanning for the next input in the input stream, skips whitespace characters such as blanks and the newline character. However, there are situations when these characters must also be stored and processed. For example, if you are processing text in a line-by-line fashion, you must know where in the input stream the newline character is located. Without identifying the position of the newline character, the program would not know where one line ends and another begins. The next few sections teach you how to input data into a program using the input functions such as `get`, `ignore`, `putback`, and `peek`. These functions are associated with the data type `istream` and are called **`istream` member functions**. I/O functions such as `get` are typically called **stream member functions** or **stream functions**.

Before you can learn about the input functions `get`, `ignore`, `putback`, `peek`, and other I/O functions that are used in this chapter, you need to understand what a function is and how it works. You will study functions in detail, and learn how to write your own, in Chapters 6 and 7.

USING PREDEFINED FUNCTIONS IN A PROGRAM

As noted in Chapter 2, a function, also called a subprogram, is a set of instructions. When a function executes, it accomplishes something. The function `main`, which you worked with in Chapter 2, executes automatically when you run a program. Other functions execute only when they are activated—that is, called. C++ comes with a wealth of functions, called **predefined functions**, that are already defined. In the following sections, you will learn how to use stream functions to perform a specific I/O operation. In this section, you will not learn how to write your own functions, but you will learn how to use some predefined functions that are provided as part of the C++ system.

Recall from Chapter 2 that predefined functions are organized as a collection of libraries, called header files. A particular header file may contain several functions. Therefore, to use a particular function, you need to know the name of the function and a few other things, which are described shortly.

A very useful function, `pow`, called the power function, can be used to calculate x^y in a program. That is, `pow(x,y)`= x^y. For example, `pow(2,3)` = 2^3 = 8 and `pow(4, 0.5)` = $4^{0.5} = \sqrt{4} = 2$. The numbers `x` and `y` that you use in the function `pow` are called the **arguments** or **parameters** of the function `pow`. For example, in `pow(2,3)`, the parameters are 2 and 3.

An expression such as `pow(2,3)` is called a **function call**, which causes the code attached to the function `pow` to execute and, in this case, computes 2^3. The header file `cmath` contains the specification of the function `pow`.

To use a predefined function in a program, you need to know the name of the header file containing the specification of the function and include that header file in the program. In addition, you need to know the name of the function, the number of parameters the function takes, and the type of each parameter. You must also be aware of what the function is going to do. For example, to use the function `pow`, you must include the header file `cmath`. The function `pow` has two parameters, both of which are numbers. The function calculates the first parameter to the power of the second parameter.

Because I/O is fundamental to any programming language, and because writing instructions to perform a specific I/O operation is not a job for everyone, every programming language provides a set of useful functions to perform specific I/O operations. In the remainder of this chapter, you will learn how to use some of these functions in a program. As a programmer, you must pay close attention to how these functions are used so that you can get the most out of them. The first function you will learn about here is the function `get`.

cin and the get Function

As you have seen, the extraction operator skips all leading whitespace characters when scanning for the next input value. Consider the variable declarations

```
char ch1, ch2;
int num;
```

and the input

```
A 25
```

Now consider the following statement

```
cin>>ch1>>ch2>>num;
```

When the computer executes this statement, `'A'` is stored in `ch1`, the blank is skipped by the extraction operator >>, the character `'2'` is stored in `ch2`, and `5` is stored in `num`. However, what if you intended to store `'A'` in `ch1`, the `blank` in `ch2`, and `25` in `num`? It is clear that you cannot use the extraction operator >> to input this data.

As stated earlier, sometimes you need to process the entire input, including whitespace characters, such as blanks and the newline character. For example, suppose you want to process the entered data on a line-by-line basis. Because the extraction operator >> skips the newline character, and unless the program captures the newline character, the computer does not know where one line ends and the next starts.

The variable `cin` can access the stream function `get`, which is used to read character data. The `get` function inputs the very next character, including whitespace characters, from the input stream and stores it in the memory location indicated by its argument. The function `get` comes in many forms. Let us discuss the one that is used to read a character.

The syntax of `cin`, together with the `get` function to read a character, follows:

```
cin.get(varChar);
```

In the `cin.get` statement, `varChar` is a `char` variable. `varChar`, which appears in parentheses following the function name, is called the **argument** or **parameter** of the function. The effect of the preceding statement would be to store the next input character in the variable `varChar`.

Now consider the following input again:

```
A 25
```

To store `'A'` in `ch1`, the `blank` in `ch2`, and `25` in `num`, you can effectively use the `get` function as follows:

```
cin.get(ch1);
cin.get(ch2);
cin>>num;
```

Because this form of the **get** function has only one argument and reads only one character, and you need to read two characters from the input stream, you need to call this function twice. Notice that you cannot use the **get** function to read data into the variable **num**, because **num** is an **int** variable. The preceding form of the **get** function reads values of only the **char** data type.

The preceding set of **cin.get** statements is equivalent to the following statements:

```
cin>>ch1;
cin.get(ch2);
cin>>num;
```

The function get has other forms, one of which you will study in Chapter 9. For the next few chapters, you need only the form of the function get introduced here.

cin and the ignore Function

When you want to process only partial data (say, within a line), you can use the stream function **ignore** to discard a portion of the input. The syntax to use the function **ignore** is:

```
cin.ignore(intExp, chExp);
```

Here **intExp** is an integer expression yielding an integer value, and **chExp** is a **char** expression yielding a **char** value. In fact, the value of the expression **intExp** specifies the maximum number of characters to be ignored in a line.

Suppose **intExp** yields a value, say **100**. This statement says to ignore the next 100 characters, or ignore the input until it encounters the character specified by **chExp**, whichever comes first. To be specific, consider the following statement:

```
cin.ignore(100,'\n');
```

When this statement executes, it ignores either the next 100 characters or all characters until the newline character is found, whichever comes first. For example, if the next 120 characters do not contain the newline character, then only the first 100 characters are discarded and the next input data is the character **101**. However, if the 75th character is the newline character, then the first 75 characters are discarded and the next input data is the 76th character. Similarly, the execution of the statement

```
cin.ignore(100,'A');
```

results in ignoring the first 100 characters or all characters until the character **'A'** is found, whichever comes first.

Example 3-2

Consider the declaration

```
int a, b;
```

and the input

```
25 67 89 43 72
12 78 34
```

Now consider the following statements:

```
cin>>a;
cin.ignore(100,'\n');
cin>>b;
```

The first statement, `cin>>a;`, stores `25` in `a`. The second statement, `cin.ignore(100,'\n');`, discards all of the remaining numbers in the first line. The third statement, `cin>>b;`, stores `12` (from the next line) in `b`.

Example 3-3

Consider the declaration

```
char ch1,ch2;
```

and the input

```
Hello there. My name is Mickey.
```

Now consider the following statements:

```
cin>>ch1;
cin.ignore(100,'.');
cin>>ch2;
```

The first statement, `cin>>ch1;`, stores `'H'` in `ch1`. The second statement, `cin.ignore(100,'.' );`, results in discarding all characters until `.` (period). The third statement, `cin>>ch2;`, stores the character `'M'` (from the same line) in `ch2`. (Remember that the extraction operator >> skips all leading whitespace characters. Thus, the extraction operator >> skips the space after `.` (period) and stores `'M'` in `ch2`.)

The `putback` and `peek` Functions

Suppose you are processing data that is a mixture of numbers and characters. Moreover, the numbers must be read and processed as numbers. You have also looked at many sets of sample data and cannot determine whether the next input is a character or a number. You could read the entire data set character-by-character and check whether a certain character is a digit. If a digit is found, you could then read the remaining digits of the number and somehow convert these characters into numbers. This programming code would be somewhat complex. Fortunately, C++ provides two very useful stream functions that can be used effectively in these types of situations.

The stream function **putback** lets you put the last character extracted from the input stream by the **get** function back into the input stream. The stream function **peek** looks into the input stream and tells you what the next character is without removing it from the input stream. By using these functions, after determining that the next input is a number, you can read it as a number. You do not have to read the digits of the number as characters and then convert these characters to that number.

The syntax to use the function **putback** is:

```
istreamVar.putback(ch);
```

Here **istreamVar** is an input stream variable, such as **cin**, and **ch** is a **char** variable.

The **peek** function returns the next character from the input stream, but does not remove the character from that stream. In other words, the function **peek** looks into the input stream and checks the identity of the next input character. Moreover, after checking the next input character in the input stream, it can store this character in a designated memory location without removing it from the input stream. That is, when you use the **peek** function, the next input character stays the same, even though you now know what it is.

The syntax to use the function **peek** is:

```
ch = istreamVar.peek();
```

Here **istreamVar** is an input stream variable, such as **cin**, and **ch** is a **char** variable.

Notice how the function **peek** is used. First, the function **peek** is used in an assignment statement. It is not a stand-alone statement like **get**, **ignore**, and **putback**. Second, the function **peek** has empty parentheses. Until you become comfortable with using a function and learn how to write one, pay close attention to how to use a predefined function.

The following example illustrates how to use the **peek** and **putback** functions.

Example 3-4

```
//Functions peek and putback

#include <iostream>
using namespace std;

int main()
{
    char ch;
```

```
    cout<<"Line 1: Enter a string: ";           //Line 1
    cin.get(ch);                                 //Line 2
    cout<<endl;                                  //Line 3
    cout<<"Line 4: After first cin.get(ch); "
        <<"ch = "<<ch<<endl;                     //Line 4

    cin.get(ch);                                 //Line 5
    cout<<"Line 6: After second cin.get(ch); "
        <<"ch = "<<ch<<endl;                     //Line 6

    cin.putback(ch);                             //Line 7
    cin.get(ch);                                 //Line 8
    cout<<"Line 9: After putback and then "
        <<"cin.get(ch); ch = "<<ch<<endl;        //Line 9

    ch = cin.peek();                             //Line 10
    cout<<"Line 11: After cin.peek(); ch = "
        <<ch<<endl;                              //Line 11

    cin.get(ch);                                 //Line 12
    cout<<"Line 13: After cin.get(ch); ch = "
        <<ch<<endl;                              //Line 13
    return 0;
}
```

Sample Run: In this sample run, the user input is shaded.

```
Line 1: Enter a string: abcd

Line 4: After first cin.get(ch); ch = a
Line 6: After second cin.get(ch); ch = b
Line 9: After putback and then cin.get(ch); ch = b
Line 11: After cin.peek(); ch = c
Line 13: After cin.get(ch); ch = c
```

The user input, `abcd`, allows you to see the effect of the functions `get`, `putback`, and `peek` in the preceding program. The statement at Line 1 prompts the user to enter a string. At Line 2, the statement `cin.get(ch);` extracts the first character from the input stream and stores it in the variable `ch`. So after Line 2 executes, the value of `ch` is `'a'`.

The `cout` statement at Line 4 outputs the value of `ch`. The statement `cin.get(ch);` at Line 5 extracts the next character from the input stream, which is `'b'`, and stores it in `ch`. At this point, the value of `ch` is `'b'`.

The `cout` statement at Line 6 outputs the value of `ch`. The `cin.putback(ch);` statement at Line 7 puts the previous character extracted by the `get` function, which is `'b'`, back into the input stream. Therefore, the next character to be extracted from the input stream is `'b'`.

The `cin.get(ch);` statement at Line 8 extracts the next character from the input stream, which is still `'b'`, and stores it in `ch`. Now the value of `ch` is `'b'`. The `cout` statement at Line 9 outputs the value of `ch` as `'b'`.

At Line 10, the statement `ch=cin.peek();` checks the next character in the input stream, which is `'c'`, and stores it in `ch`. The value of `ch` is now `'c'`. The `cout` statement at Line 11 outputs the value of `ch`. The `cin.get(ch);` statement at Line 12 extracts the next character from the input stream and stores it in `ch`. The `cout` statement at Line 13 outputs the value of `ch`, which is still `'c'`.

Note that the statement `ch=cin.peek();` at Line 10 did not remove the character `'c'` from the input stream; it merely peeked into the input stream. The output of Lines 11 and 13 demonstrate this functionality.

The Dot Notation Between I/O Stream Variables and I/O Functions: A Precaution

In the preceding sections, you learned how to manipulate an input stream to get data into a program. You also learned how to use the functions `get`, `ignore`, `peek`, and `putback`. It is important that you use these functions exactly as shown. For example, to use the `get` function, the text showed statements such as the following:

```
cin.get(ch);
```

Omitting the dot—that is, the period between the variable `cin` and the function name `get`—results in a syntax error. For example, in the statement

```
cin.get(ch);
```

`cin` and `get` are two separate identifiers separated by a dot. In the statement

```
cinget(ch);
```

`cinget` becomes a new identifier. If you used `cinget(ch);` in a program, the compiler would try to resolve an undeclared identifier, which would generate an error. Similarly, missing parentheses, as in `cin.getch;`, result in a syntax error. Also remember that you must use the input functions together with an input stream variable. If you try to use any of the input functions alone—that is, without the input stream variable—the compiler might generate an error message such as "undeclared identifier." For example, the statement `get(ch);` could result in a syntax error.

As you can see, several functions are associated with an `istream` variable, each doing a specific job. Recall that the functions `get`, `ignore`, and so on are *members* of the data type `istream`. Called the **dot notation**, the dot separates the input stream variable name from the member, or function, name. In fact, in C++, the dot is an operator called the **member access operator**.

C++ has a special name for the data types `istream` and `ostream`. The data types `istream` and `ostream` are called **classes**. The variables `cin` and `cout` also have special names, called **objects**. Therefore, `cin` is called an **`input stream` object**, and `cout` is called an **`output stream` object**. In fact, stream variables are called **stream objects**. You will learn these concepts in Chapter 13.

INPUT FAILURE

Many things can go wrong during program execution. A program that is syntactically correct might produce incorrect results. For example, suppose that a part-time employee's paycheck is calculated by using the following formula:

```
wages = payRate * hoursWorked;
```

If you accidentally type + in place of *, the calculated wages would be incorrect, even though the statement containing a + is syntactically correct.

What about an attempt to read invalid data? For example, what would happen if you tried to input a letter into an `int` variable? If the input data did not match the corresponding variables, the program would run into problems. For example, trying to read a letter into an `int` or `double` variable would result in an **input failure**. Consider the following statements

```
int a, b, c;
double x;
```

If the input is

```
W 54
```

then the statement

```
cin>>a>>b;
```

would result in an input failure, because you are trying to input the character `'W'` into the `int` variable `a`. If the input were

```
35 67.93 48 78
```

then the input statement

```
cin>>a>>x>>b;
```

would result in storing `35` in `a`, `67.93` in `x`, and `48` in `b`.

Now consider the following read statement with the previous input (the input with three values):

```
cin>>a>>b>>c;
```

This statement stores `35` in `a` and `67` in `b`. The reading stops at `.` (the decimal point). Because the next variable `c` is of the data type `int`, the computer tries to read `.` into `c`, which is an error. The input stream then enters a state called the **fail state**.

What actually happens when the input stream enters the fail state? Once an input stream enters a fail state, all further I/O statements using that stream are ignored. Unfortunately, the program quietly continues to execute with whatever values are stored in variables and produce incorrect results. The program in Example 3-5 illustrates an input failure. This program on your system may produce different results.

Example 3-5

```
//Input Failure program
#include <iostream>
using namespace std;

int main()
{
    int a = 10;                                         //Line 1
    int b = 20;                                         //Line 2
    int c = 30;                                         //Line 3
    int d = 40;                                         //Line 4

    cout<<"Line 5: Enter four integers: ";              //Line 5
    cin>>a>>b>>c>>d;                                    //Line 6
    cout<<endl;                                         //Line 7
    cout<<"Line 8: The numbers you entered are:"
        <<endl;                                         //Line 8
    cout<<"Line 9: a = "<<a<<", b = "<<b
        <<", c = "<<c<<", d = "<<d<<endl;               //Line 9
    return 0;
}
```

Sample Runs: In these sample runs, the user input is shaded.

Sample Run 1

```
Line 5: Enter four integers: 34 K 67 28

Line 8: The numbers you entered are:
Line 9: a = 34, b = 20, c = 30, d = 40
```

The statements at Lines 1, 2, 3, and 4 declare and initialize the variables `a`, `b`, `c`, and `d` to `10`, `20`, `30`, and `40`, respectively. The statement at Line 5 prompts the user to enter four integers; the statement at Line 6 inputs these four integers into variables `a`, `b`, `c`, and `d`.

In this sample run, the second input value is the character `'K'`. The `cin` statement tries to input this character into the variable `b`. However, because `b` is an `int` variable, the input stream enters the fail state. Note that the values of `b`, `c`, and `d` are unchanged, as shown by the output of the statement at Line 9. (If you run this program using standard C++ style header files, you may get different values for `b`, `c`, and `d` at Line 9.)

Sample Run 2

```
Line 5: Enter four integers: 37 653.89 23 76

Line 8: The numbers you entered are:
Line 9: a = 37, b = 653, c = 30, d = 40
```

In this sample run, the `cin` statement at Line 6 inputs `37` into `a`, and `653` into `b`, and then tries to input the decimal point into `c`. Because `c` is an `int` variable, the decimal point is regarded as a character, so the input stream enters the fail state. In this sample run, the values of `c` and `d` are unchanged, as shown by the output of the statement at Line 9. (If you run this program using standard C++ style header files, you may get different values for `c` and `d` at Line 9.)

The `clear` Function

When an input stream enters the fail state, the system ignores all further I/O using that stream. You can use the stream function `clear` to restore the input stream to a working state.

The syntax to use the function `clear` is:

```
istreamVar.clear();
```

Here `istreamVar` is an input stream variable, such as `cin`.

After using the function `clear` to return the input stream to a working state, you still need to clear the rest of the garbage from the input stream. This can be accomplished by using the function `ignore`. Example 3-6 illustrates this situation.

Example 3-6

```
//Input failure and the clear function
#include <iostream>
using namespace std;

int main()
{
    int a = 23;                                      //Line 1
    int b = 34;                                      //Line 2

    cout<<"Line 3: Enter a number followed"
        <<" by a character: ";                       //Line 3
    cin>>a>>b;                                       //Line 4
    cout<<endl<<"Line 5: a = "<<a
        <<", b = "<<b<<endl;                         //Line 5

    cin.clear();               //Restore input stream; Line 6

    cin.ignore(200,'\n');         //Clear the buffer; Line 7
```

```
    cout<<"Line 8: Enter two numbers: ";            //Line 8
    cin>>a>>b;                                       //Line 9
    cout<<endl<<"Line 10: a = "<<a
        <<", b = "<<b<<endl;                         //Line 10

        return 0;
}
```

Sample Run: In this sample run, the user input is shaded.

```
Line 3: Enter a number followed by a character: 78 d

Line 5: a = 78, b = 34
Line 8: Enter two numbers: 65 88

Line 10: a = 65, b = 88
```

The statements at Lines 1 and 2 declare and initialize the variables `a` and `b` to `23` and `34`, respectively. The statement at Line 3 prompts the user to enter a number followed by a character; the statement at Line 4 inputs this number into the variable `a` and then tries to input the character into the variable `b`. Because `b` is an `int` variable, an attempt to input a character into `b` causes the input stream to enter the fail state. The value of `b` is unchanged, as shown by the output of the statement at Line 5.

The statement at Line 6 restores the input stream by using the function `clear`, and the statement at Line 7 ignores the rest of the input. The statement at Line 8 again prompts the user to input two numbers; the statement at Line 9 inputs these two numbers into `a` and `b`. Next, the statement at Line 10 outputs the values of `a` and `b`. (If you run this program using standard C++ style header files, you may get different values for `b` at Line 5.)

OUTPUT AND FORMATTING OUTPUT

Other than writing efficient programs, generating the desired output is one of a programmer's highest priorities. Chapter 2 briefly introduced the process involved in generating output on the standard output device. More precisely, you learned how to use the insertion operator and the manipulator `endl` to display results on the standard output device.

However, there is lot more to output than just displaying results. Sometimes floating-point numbers must be output in a specific way. For example, a paycheck must be printed to two decimal places, whereas the results of a scientific experiment might require the output of floating-point numbers to six, seven, or perhaps even ten decimal places. Also, you might like to align the numbers in specific columns or fill the empty space between strings and numbers with a character other than the blank. For example, in preparing the table of contents, the space between the section heading and the page number might need to be filled with dots or dashes. In this section, you will learn about various output functions and manipulators that will allow you to format your output in a desired way.

Recall that the syntax of **cout** when used together with the insertion operator << is

```
cout<<expression or manipulator<<expression or manipulator...;
```


Here **expression** is evaluated, its value is printed, and **manipulator** is used to format the output. The simplest manipulator that you have used so far is **endl**, which is used to move the cursor to the beginning of the next line.

Other output manipulators that are of our interest include: **setprecision**, **fixed**, **showpoint**, and **setw**. The next few sections describe these manipulators.

setprecision

You use the manipulator **setprecision** to control the output of floating-point numbers. The default output of floating-point numbers is scientific notation. Some software development kits (SDKs) might use a maximum of six decimal places for the default output of floating-point numbers. However, when an employee's paycheck is printed, the desired output is a maximum of two decimal places. To print floating-point output to two decimal places, you use the **setprecision** manipulator to set the precision to 2.

The general syntax of the **setprecision** manipulator is

```
setprecision(n)
```

where **n** is the number of decimal places.

You use the **setprecision** manipulator with **cout** and the extraction operator. For example, the statement

```
cout<<setprecision(2);
```

formats the output of decimal numbers to two decimal places, until a similar subsequent statement changes the precision. Notice that the number of decimal places, or the precision value, is passed as an argument to **setprecision**.

To use the manipulator **setprecision**, the program must include the header file **iomanip**. Thus, the following include statement is required:

```
#include <iomanip>
```

fixed

To further control the output of floating-point numbers, you can use other manipulators. To output floating-point numbers in a fixed decimal format, you use the manipulator **fixed**. The following statement sets the output of floating-point numbers in a fixed decimal format on the standard output device:

```
cout<<fixed;
```

After the preceding statement executes, all floating-point numbers are displayed in the fixed-decimal format until the manipulator **`fixed`** is disabled. You can disable the manipulator **`fixed`** by using the stream member function **`unsetf`**. For example, to disable the manipulator **`fixed`** on the standard output device, you use the following statement:

```
cout.unsetf(ios::fixed);
```

After the manipulator **`fixed`** is disabled, the output of the floating-point numbers return to their default settings. The manipulator **`scientific`** is used to output floating-point numbers in scientific format.

showpoint

Suppose that the decimal part of a decimal number is zero. In this case, when you instruct the computer to output the decimal number in a fixed decimal format, the output may not show the decimal point and the decimal part. To force the output to show the decimal point and trailing zeros, you use the manipulator **`showpoint`**. The following statement sets the output of decimal numbers with a decimal point and trailing zeros on the standard input device:

```
cout<<showpoint;
```

Of course, the following statement sets the output of a floating-point number in a fixed decimal format with the decimal point and trailing zeros on the standard output device:

```
cout<<fixed<<showpoint;
```

Example 3-7

The following program illustrates how to use the manipulators **`setprecision`**, **`fixed`**, and **`showpoint`**.

```
//Example: setprecision, fixed, showpoint

#include <iostream>
#include <iomanip>

using namespace std;

int main()
{
   double x,y,z;

   x = 15.674;                                       //Line 1
   y = 235.73;                                       //Line 2
   z = 9525.9864;                                    //Line 3

   cout<<fixed<<showpoint;                           //Line 4

   cout<<setprecision(2)
       <<"Line 5: setprecision(2)"<<endl;            //Line 5
```

```
   cout<<"Line 6: x = "<<x<<endl;                          //Line 6
   cout<<"Line 7: y = "<<y<<endl;                          //Line 7
   cout<<"Line 8: z = "<<z<<endl;                          //Line 8

   cout<<setprecision(3)
       <<"Line 9: setprecision(3)"<<endl;                  //Line 9
   cout<<"Line 10: x = "<<x<<endl;                         //Line 10
   cout<<"Line 11: y = "<<y<<endl;                         //Line 11
   cout<<"Line 12: z = "<<z<<endl;                         //Line 12

   cout<<setprecision(4)
       <<"Line 13: setprecision(4)"<<endl;                 //Line 13
   cout<<"Line 14: x = "<<x<<endl;                         //Line 14
   cout<<"Line 15: y = "<<y<<endl;                         //Line 15
   cout<<"Line 16: z = "<<z<<endl;                         //Line 16

   cout<<"Line 17: "
       <<setprecision(3)<<x<<"  "
       <<setprecision(2)<<y<<"  "
       <<setprecision(4)<<z<<endl;                         //Line 17

   return 0;
}
```

Output:

```
Line 5: setprecision(2)
Line 6: x = 15.67
Line 7: y = 235.73
Line 8: z = 9525.99
Line 9: setprecision(3)
Line 10: x = 15.674
Line 11: y = 235.730
Line 12: z = 9525.986
Line 13: setprecision(4)
Line 14: x = 15.6740
Line 15: y = 235.7300
Line 16: z = 9525.9864
Line 17: 15.674  235.73  9525.9864
```

The statements at Lines 1, 2, and 3 initialize `x`, `y`, and `z` to `15.674`, `235.73`, and `9525.9864`, respectively. The statement at Line 4 sets the output of floating-point numbers in a fixed decimal format with a decimal point and trailing zeros. The statement at Line 5 sets the output of floating-point numbers to two decimal places.

The statements at Lines 6, 7, and 8 output the values of `x`, `y`, and `z` to two decimal places. Note that the printed value of `z` at Line 8 is rounded. The statement at Line 9 sets the output of floating-point numbers to three decimal places; the statements at Lines 10, 11, and 12 output the values of `x`, `y`, and `z` to three decimal places. Note that the value of `y`, at Line 11, is output to three decimal places. Because the number stored in **y** has only two decimal places, a **0** is printed as the third decimal place.

The statement at Line 13 sets the output of floating-point numbers to four decimal places; the statements at Lines 14, 15, and 16 output the values of **x**, **y** , and **z** to four decimal places. Note that at Line 14, the printed value of **x** contains a **0** in the fourth decimal place. The printed value of **y**, at Line 15, contains a **0** in the third and fourth decimal places.

The statement at Line 17 first sets the output of floating-point numbers to three decimal places and then outputs the value of **x** to three decimal places. After printing the value of **x**, the statement at Line 17 sets the output of floating-point numbers to two decimal places and then outputs the value of **y** to two decimal places. Next, it sets the output of floating-point numbers to four decimal places and then outputs the value of **z** to four decimal places.

You can also use the stream function **setf** to set **fixed**, **scientific**, and **showpoint**. In this case, **fixed**, **scientific**, and **showpoint** are referred to as **ios::fixed**, **ios::scientific**, and **ios::showpoint**, respectively, and are called formatting flags. Both the flags **ios::fixed** and **ios::scientific** are part of **ios::floatfield**, which is a data type in C++. When setting the fixed or scientific flag, to ensure that only either the **ios::fixed** or **ios::scientific** flag is set, you must pass **ios::floatfield** as a second argument to the function **setf**. The following statement illustrates how to set the flag **ios::fixed** to output floating-point numbers in a fixed decimal format on the standard output device:

```
cout.setf(ios::fixed, ios::floatfield);
```

Similarly, the following statement sets the flag **ios::showpoint** to output floating-point numbers with a decimal point and trailing zeros on the standard output device:

```
cout.setf(ios::showpoint);
```

C++ also provides the manipulator **setiosflags**, which you can use to set the flags **ios::fixed**, **ios::scientific**, and **ios::showpoint**. To use the manipulator **setiosflags**, the program must include the header file **iomanip**.

The following statement illustrates how to use the manipulator **setiosflags** to set the flags **ios::fixed** and **ios::showpoint** on the standard output device:

```
cout<<setiosflags(ios::fixed);
cout<<setiosflags(ios::showpoint);
```

You can specify more than one flag in the manipulator **setiosflags** by separating the flags with the symbol **|**. The following statement sets both the flags **ios::fixed** and **ios::showpoint** on the standard output device:

```
cout<<setiosflags(ios::fixed | ios::showpoint);
```

In ANSI/ISO Standard C++, `fixed`, `scientific`, and `showpoint` are available as both manipulators and flags. However, on some compilers in Standard C++, they are available only as flags. If this is the case and you are using Standard C++, you need to set them by using either the function `setf` or the manipulator `setiosflags`.

setw

The manipulator **setw** is used to output the value of an expression in specific columns. The value of the expression can be either a string or a number. The statement **setw(n)** outputs the value of the next expression in **n** columns. The output is right-justified. Thus, if you specify the number of columns to be 8, for example, and the output requires only 4 columns, the first four columns are left blank. Furthermore, if the number of columns specified is less than the number of columns required by the output, the output automatically expands to the required number of columns; the output is not truncated. For example, if **x** is an **int** variable, the following statement outputs the value of **x** in five columns on the standard output device:

```
cout<<setw(5)<<x<<endl;
```

To use the manipulator **setw**, the program must include the header file **iomanip**. Thus, the following include statement is required:

```
#include <iomanip>
```

Unlike **setprecision**, which controls the output of all floating-point numbers until it is reset, **setw** controls the output of only the next expression.

Example 3-8

The following program illustrates how the manipulator **setw** works.

```
//Example: setw

#include <iostream>
#include <iomanip>

using namespace std;

int main()
{
      int x = 19;                                //Line 1
      int a = 345;                               //Line 2
      double y = 76.384;                         //Line 3

      cout<<fixed<<showpoint;                    //Line 4

      cout<<"12345678901234567890"<<endl;        //Line 5
```

```
    cout<<setw(5)<<x<<endl;                        //Line 6
    cout<<setw(5)<<a<<setw(5)<<"Hi"
        <<setw(5)<<x<<endl<<endl;                  //Line 7

    cout<<setprecision(2);                         //Line 8
    cout<<setw(6)<<a<<setw(6)<<y
        <<setw(6)<<x<<endl;                        //Line 9
    cout<<setw(6)<<x<<setw(6)<<a
        <<setw(6)<<y<<endl<<endl;                  //Line 10

    cout<<setw(5)<<a<<x<<endl;                     //Line 11
    cout<<setw(2)<<a<<setw(4)<<x<<endl;            //Line 12
    return 0;
}
```

Output:

```
12345678901234567890
   19
  345   Hi   19

   345 76.38    19
    19   345 76.38

  34519
345  19
```

The statements at Lines 1, 2, and 3 declare the variables **x**, **a**, and **y** and initialize these variables to **19**, **345**, and **76.384**, respectively. The statement at Line 4 sets the output of floating-point numbers in a fixed decimal format with a decimal point and trailing zeros. The output of the statement at Line 5 shows the column positions when the specific values are printed; it is the first line of output.

The statement at Line 6 outputs the value of **x** in five columns. Because **x** has only two digits, only two columns are needed to output its value. Therefore, the first three columns are left blank in the second line of output. The statement at Line 7 outputs the value of **a** in the first five columns, the string **"Hi"** in the next five columns, and then the value of **x** in the following five columns. Because the string **"Hi"** contains only two characters, and five columns are set to output these two characters, the first three columns are left blank. See the third line of output. The fourth line of output is blank because the manipulator **endl** appears twice in the statement at Line 7.

The statement at Line 8 sets the output of floating-point numbers to two decimal places. The statement at Line 9 outputs the values of **a** in the first six columns, **y** in the next six columns, and **x** in the following six columns, creating the fifth line of output. The output of the statement at Line 10 (which is the sixth line of output) is similar to the output of the statement at

Line 9. Notice how the numbers are nicely aligned in the outputs of the statements at Lines 9 and 10. The seventh line of output is blank because the manipulator **endl** appears twice in the statement at Line 10.

The statement at Line 11 outputs first the value of **a** in five columns and then the value of **x**. Note that the manipulator **setw** in the statement at Line 11 controls only the output of **a**. Thus, after the value of **a** is printed, the value of **x** is printed at the current cursor position (see the eighth line of output).

In the **cout** statement at Line 12, only two columns are assigned to output the value of **a**. However, the value of **a** has three digits, so the output is expanded to three columns. The value of **x** is then printed in four columns. Because the value of **x** contains only two digits, only two columns are required to output the value of **x**. Therefore, because four columns are allocated to output the value of **x**, the first two columns are left blank (see the ninth line of output).

ADDITIONAL OUTPUT FORMATTING TOOLS

In the previous section, you learned how to use the manipulators **setprecision**, **fixed**, and **showpoint** to control the output of floating-point numbers, and how to use the manipulator **setw** to display the output in specific columns. Even though these manipulators are adequate to produce an elegant report, in some situations you may want to do more. In this section, you will learn additional formatting tools that give you more control over your output.

fill and setfill

Recall that, in the manipulator **setw**, if the number of columns specified exceeds the number of columns required by the expression, the output of the expression is right-justified and the unused columns to the left are filled with spaces. The output stream variables have access to a function called **fill** and a manipulator called **setfill** that allow you to fill the unused columns with a character other than a space.

The syntax to use the function **fill** is

```
ostreamVar.fill(ch);
```

where **ostreamVar** is an output stream variable and **ch** is a character. For example, the statement

```
cout.fill('*');
```

sets the fill character to `'*'` on the standard output device.

The syntax to use the manipulator **setfill** is

```
ostreamVar<<setfill(ch);
```

where `ostreamVar` is an output stream variable and `ch` is a character. For example, the statement

```
cout<<setfill('#');
```

sets the fill character to `'#'` on the standard output device.

To use the manipulator `setfill`, the program must include the header file `iomanip`.

If you use the `fill` function to set the filling character, it must be a stand-alone statement. The manipulator `setfill` is part of an output statement. The following examples illustrate the use of the function `fill` and the manipulator `setfill`.

Example 3-9

The following program illustrates the effect of using `fill` and `setfill` in a program.

```
//Example: fill and setfill

#include <iostream>
#include <iomanip>

using namespace std;


int main()
{
      int x = 15;                                   //Line 1
      int y = 7634;                                 //Line 2

      cout<<"12345678901234567890"<<endl;           //Line 3
      cout<<setw(5)<<x<<setw(7)<<y
          <<setw(8)<<"Warm"<<endl;                  //Line 4

      cout.fill('*');                               //Line 5
      cout<<setw(5)<<x<<setw(7)<<y
          <<setw(8)<<"Warm"<<endl;                  //Line 6

      cout<<setw(5)<<x<<setw(7)<<setfill('#')
          <<y<<setw(8)<<"Warm"<<endl;               //Line 7

      cout<<setw(5)<<setfill('@')<<x
          <<setw(7)<<setfill('#')<<y
          <<setw(8)<<setfill('^')<<"Warm"
          <<endl;                                   //Line 8

      cout.fill(' ');                               //Line 9
      cout<<setw(5)<<x<<setw(7)<<y
          <<setw(8)<<"Warm"<<endl;                  //Line 10
      return 0;
}
```

Output:

```
12345678901234567890
   15   7634    Warm
***15***7634****Warm
***15###7634####Warm
@@@15###7634^^^^Warm
   15   7634    Warm
```

The statements at Lines 1 and 2 declare and initialize the variables **x** and **y** to **15** and **7634**, respectively. The output of the statement at Line 3—the first line of output—shows the column position when the subsequent statements output the values of the variables. The statement at Line 4 outputs the value of **x** in five columns, the value of **y** in seven columns, and the string **"Warm"** in eight columns. In this statement, the filling character is the blank character, as shown in the second line of output.

The statement at Line 5 sets the filling character to *****. The statement at Line 6 outputs the value of **x** in five columns, the value of **y** in seven columns, and the string **"Warm"** in eight columns. Because **x** is a two-digit number and five columns are assigned to output its value, the first three columns are unused by **x** and are, therefore, filled by the filling character *****. To print the value of **y**, seven columns are assigned; **y** is a four-digit number, however, so the filling character fills the first three columns. Similarly, to print the value of the string **"Warm"**, eight columns are assigned; the string **"Warm"** has only four characters, so the filling character fills the first four columns. See the third line of output.

The output of the statement at Line 7—the fourth line of output—is similar to the output of the statement at Line 6, except that the filling character for **y** and the string **"Warm"** is **#**. In the output of the statement at Line 8 (the fifth line of output), the filling character for **x** is **@**, the filling character for **y** is **#**, and the filling character for the string **"Warm"** is **^**. The manipulator **setfill** sets these filling characters.

The statement at Line 9 sets the filling character to blank. The statement at Line 10 outputs the values of **x**, **y**, and the string **"Warm"** using the filling character blank, as shown in the sixth line of output.

The `left` and `right` Manipulators

Recall that, if the number of columns specified in the **setw** manipulator exceeds the number of columns required by the next expression, the output is right-justified. Sometimes you might want the output to be left-justified. To left-justify the output, you use the manipulator **left**.

The syntax to set the manipulator **left** is

```
ostreamVar<<left;
```

where `ostreamVar` is an output stream variable. For example, the following statement sets the output to be left-justified on the standard output device:

```
cout<<left;
```

You can disable the manipulator `left` by using the stream function `unsetf`. The syntax to disable the manipulator `left` is

```
ostreamVar.unsetf(ios::left);
```

where `ostreamVar` is an output stream variable. Disabling the manipulator `left` returns the output to the settings of the default output format. For example, the following statement disables the manipulator `left` on the standard output device:

```
cout.unsetf(ios::left);
```

The syntax to set the manipulator `right` is

```
ostreamVar<<right;
```

where `ostreamVar` is an output stream variable. For example, the following statement sets the output to be right-justified on the standard output device:

```
cout<<right;
```

Example 3-10

The following program illustrates the effect of the manipulators `left` and `right`.

```
//Example: left justification

#include <iostream>
#include <iomanip>

using namespace std;


int main()
{
      int x = 15;                                         //Line 1
      int y = 7634;                                       //Line 2

      cout<<left;                                         //Line 3

      cout<<"12345678901234567890"<<endl;                 //Line 4
      cout<<setw(5)<<x<<setw(7)<<y
          <<setw(8)<<"Warm"<<endl;                        //Line 5
```

```
    cout.fill('*');                                  //Line 6

    cout<<setw(5)<<x<<setw(7)<<y
        <<setw(8)<<"Warm"<<endl;                     //Line 7

    cout<<setw(5)<<x<<setw(7)<<setfill('#')<<y
        <<setw(8)<<"Warm"<<endl;                     //Line 8


    cout<<setw(5)<<setfill('@')<<x
        <<setw(7)<<setfill('#')<<y
        <<setw(8)<<setfill('^')<<"Warm"<<endl;       //Line 9


    cout.unsetf(ios::left);                          //Line 10
    cout.fill(' ');                                  //Line 11

    cout<<setw(5)<<x<<setw(7)<<y
        <<setw(8)<<"Warm"<<endl;                     //Line 12
    return 0;
}
```

Output:

```
12345678901234567890
15   7634   Warm
15***7634***Warm****
15***7634###Warm####
15@@@7634###Warm^^^^
   15   7634    Warm
```

The output of this program is the same as the output of Example 3-9. The only difference here is that for the statements at Lines 4 through 9, the output is left-justified. You are encouraged to do a walk-through of this program.

You can also use the stream function `setf` to set `left` and `right`. In this case, `left` and `right` are referred to as `ios::left` and `ios::right`, respectively, and are called formatting flags. Both the flags `ios::left` and `ios::right` are part of `ios::adjustfield`, which is a data type in C++. To ensure that only one of the flags `ios::left` or `ios::right` is set, `ios::adjustfield` is also passed as a second argument to the function `setf`.

The syntax to set the flag `left` is

```
ostreamVar.setf(ios::left,ios::adjustfield);
```

where **ostreamVar** is an output stream variable. For example, the following statement sets the output to be left-justified on the standard output device:

```
cout.setf(ios::left,ios::adjustfield);
```

The stream function **unsetf** can be used to disable the flag **ios::left**. The syntax to disable the flag **ios::left** is

```
ostreamVar.unsetf(ios::left);
```

where **ostreamVar** is an output stream variable. Disabling the flag **ios::left** returns the output to the default for most settings.

You can also use the stream manipulator **setiosflags** to set the flags **ios::left** and **ios::right**. For example, the following statement sets the flag **ios::left** on the standard output device:

```
cout<<setiosflags(ios::left);
```

The following statement uses the manipulator `setiosflags` to set the flags `ios::fixed`, `ios::showpoint`, and `ios::left` on the standard output device:

```
cout<<setiosflags(ios::fixed | ios::showpoint | ios::left);
```

In Standard C++, on some compilers the manipulators `left` and `right` are available only as formatting flags. Therefore, you must set `left` and `right` by using either the function `setf` or the manipulator `setiosflags`. Check your compiler's documentation for more information.

The flush Function

Both the manipulator **endl** and the newline escape sequence **'\n'** position the cursor at the beginning of the next line on the output device. However, the manipulator **endl** also has another use.

When a program sends output to an output device, the output first goes to the buffer in the computer. Whenever the buffer becomes full, the output is sent to the output device. However, as soon as the manipulator **endl** is encountered, the output from the buffer is sent to the output device immediately, even if the buffer is not full. Therefore, the manipulator **endl** positions the cursor at the beginning of the next line on an output device and helps clear the buffer.

It is quite possible that sometimes you may not see the entire output. This is due to the fact that when the program terminates, the buffer at that time may not be full.

In C++, you can use the function **flush** to clear the buffer, even if the buffer is not full. In contrast to the manipulator **endl**, the function **flush** does not move the cursor to the beginning of the next line.

The syntax to use the **flush** function is:

```
ostreamVar.flush();
```


where **ostreamVar** is an output stream variable, such as **cout**.

Just like **endl**, the function **flush** can be used as a manipulator. In such a case, **flush** is used in an output statement without the parentheses. For example, the following statement sends the output from the buffer to the standard output device:

```
cout<<flush;
```

Example 3-11

Consider the following statements in which **num** is an **int** variable:

```
cout<<"Enter an integer: " ;        //Line 1
cin>>num;                           //Line 2
cout<<endl;                         //Line 3
```

The statement at Line 1 outputs the following text: **Enter an integer:**. After outputting this line, the cursor stays positioned after the colon. Recall that the output of the statement at Line 1 first goes to the buffer. If the buffer is not full, this line of text might not be displayed, in which case the user would have no idea of what to do next.You could put the manipulator **endl** at the end of the statement at Line 1. However, by doing so, after printing the line of text, the cursor is positioned at the beginning of the next line. The user is, thus, prompted to enter the number in the following line, which is sometimes not very appealing. On the other hand, suppose that the statement at Line 1 is replaced by the following statement:

```
cout<<"Enter an integer: "<<flush;       //Line 1
```

In this case, the line of text, **Enter an integer:**, is displayed on the standard output device even if the buffer is not full. Moreover, after outputting the line of text, the cursor stays positioned after the colon; the user will then enter the number after the colon.

This chapter discusses several stream functions and stream manipulators. To use stream functions such as `get`, `ignore`, `fill`, `clear`, and `setf` in a program, the program must include the header file `iostream`. There are two types of manipulators: those with parameters and those without parameters. Manipulators with parameters are called **parameterized stream manipulators.**

For example, manipulators such as `setprecision`, `setw`, `setfill`, and `setiosflags` are parameterized. On the other hand, manipulators such as `endl`, `fixed`, `scientific`, `showpoint`, and `left` are without parameters. Because `flush` can also be used as a manipulator without any arguments, `flush` is a manipulator without parameters, too.

To use a parameterized stream manipulator—that is, a stream manipulator with parameters—in a program, you must include the header file `iomanip`. Manipulators without parameters are part of the `iostream` header file and, therefore, do not require inclusion of the header file `iomanip`.

Input/Output and the `string` Type

You can use an input stream variable, such as **`cin`**, and the extraction operator >> to read a string into a variable of the data type **`string`**. For example, if the input is the string **`"Shelly"`**, the following code stores this input into the **`string`** variable **`name`**:

```
string name; //declaration
cin>>name;   //input statement
```

Recall that the extraction operator skips any leading whitespace characters and that reading stops at a whitespace character. As a consequence, you cannot use the extraction operator to read strings that contain blanks. For example, suppose that the variable **`name`** is defined as noted above. If the input is

```
Alice Wonderland
```

the value of the variable **`name`** after the following statement executes is **`"Alice"`**:

```
cin>>name;
```

To read a string containing blanks, you can use the function **`getline`**. The syntax to use the function **`getline`** is

```
getline(istreamVar, strVar);
```

where **`istreamVar`** is an input stream variable and **`strVar`** is a variable of the type **`string`**. The reading is delimited by the newline character, **`'\n'`**.

The function **`getline`** reads until it reaches the end of the current line. The newline character is also read but not stored in the **`string`** variable.

Consider the following statement:

```
string myString;
```

If the input is 29 characters,

```
bbbbHello there. How are you?
```

where b represents a blank, after the statement

```
getline(cin,myString);
```

the value of `myString` is

```
myString = "    Hello there. How are you?"
```

All 29 characters, including the first four blanks, are stored into `myString`.

Similarly, you can use an output stream variable, such as `cout`, and the insertion operator << to output the contents of a variable of the data type `string`.

FILE INPUT/OUTPUT

The previous sections discussed in some detail how to get input from the keyboard (standard input device) and send output to the screen (standard output device). However, getting input from the keyboard and sending output to the screen has several limitations. Receiving data in a program from the keyboard is comfortable as long as the amount of input is very small. Sending output to the screen works well if the amount of data is small (no longer than the size of the screen), and you do not want to distribute the output in a printed format to others.

If the amount of input data is large, however, it is inefficient to type it at the keyboard each time you run a program. In addition to the inconvenience of typing large amounts of data, typing can generate errors, and unintentional typos cause erroneous results. You must have some way to get data into the program from other sources. By using alternative sources of data, you can prepare the data before running a program, and the program can access the data each time it runs.

Suppose you want to present the output of a program in a meeting. Distributing printed copies of the program output is a better approach than showing the output on a screen. For example, you might give a printed report to each member of a committee before an important meeting. Furthermore, output must sometimes be saved so that the output produced by one program can be used as an input to other programs.

This section discusses how to obtain data from other input devices, such as a disk (that is, secondary storage), and how to save the output to a disk. C++ allows a program to get data directly from, and save output directly to, secondary storage. A program can use the file I/O and read data from or write data to a file. Formally, a file is defined as follows:

File: An area in secondary storage used to hold information.

The standard I/O header file, `iostream`, contains data types and variables that are used only for input from the standard input device and output to the standard output device. In addition,

C++ provides a header file called `fstream`, which is used for file I/O. Among other things, the `fstream` header file contains the definitions of two data types: `ifstream`, which means input file stream and is similar to `istream`, and `ofstream`, which means output file stream and is similar to `ostream`.

The variables `cin` and `cout` are already defined and associated with the standard input/output devices. In addition, >>, `get`, `ignore`, `putback`, `peek`, and so on can be used with `cin`; <<, `fill`, `setfill`, and so on can be used with `cout`. These same operators and functions are also available for file I/O, but the header file `fstream` does not declare variables to use them. You must declare variables called **file stream variables**, which include `ifstream` variables for input and `ofstream` variables for output. You then use these variables together with >>, <<, or other functions for I/O. Remember that C++ does not automatically initialize user-defined variables. Once you declare the `fstream` variables, you must associate these file variables with the input/output sources.

File I/O is a five-step process:

1. Include the header file `fstream` in the program.
2. Declare file stream variables.
3. Associate the file stream variables with the input/output sources.
4. Use the file stream variables with >>, <<, or other input/output functions.
5. Close the files.

We will now describe these five steps in detail. A skeleton program then shows how the steps might appear in a program.

Step 1 requires that the header file `fstream` be included in the program. The following statement accomplishes this task:

```
#include <fstream>
```

Step 2 requires you to declare file stream variables. Consider the following statements:

```
ifstream inData;
ofstream outData;
```

The first statement declares `inData` to be an input file stream variable. The second statement declares `outData` to be an output file stream variable.

Step 3 requires you to associate file stream variables with the input/output sources. This step is called **opening the files**. The stream member function `open` is used to open files. The general syntax for opening a file is

```
fileStreamVariable.open(sourceName, fileOpeningMode);
```

Here `fileStreamVariable` is a file stream variable, `sourceName` is the name of the input/output file, and `fileOpeningMode` specifies the mode in which the file is to be opened. The file-opening mode is shaded, indicating that it is an optional part of the syntax definition. For **ifstream** variables, the default file-opening mode is for inputting data. For **ofstream** variables, the default file-opening mode is for outputting data. Table 3-2 lists various file-opening modes.

Table 3-2 File-Opening Modes

File-Opening Mode	Description
ios::in	Opens the file for input. This is the default for ifstream variables.
ios::out	Opens the file for output. This is the default for ofstream variables.
ios::nocreate	If the file does not exist, the open operation fails.
ios::app	If the file exists, adds the output at the end of the file (append). If the file does not exist, creates an empty file.
ios::ate	Opens the file for output and moves to the end of the file. Output may be written anywhere in the file.
ios::trunc	If the file exists, the contents will be deleted (truncated).
ios::noreplace	If the file exists, the open operation fails.

Suppose you include the declaration from Step 2 in a program. Further suppose that the input data is stored in a file called **prog.dat** on a floppy disk in drive A:, and you want to save the output in a file called **prog.out** on a floppy disk in drive A:. The following statements associate **inData** with **prog.dat** and **outData** with **prog.out**. That is, the file **prog.dat** is opened for inputting data and the file **prog.out** is opened for outputting data.

```
inData.open("A:prog.dat");  //open input file
outData.open("A:prog.out"); //open output file
```

Step 4 typically works as follows. You use the file stream variables with >>, <<, or other input/output functions. The syntax for using >> or << with file stream variables is exactly the same as the syntax for using **cin** and **cout**. Instead of using **cin** and **cout**, however, you use the file stream variable names that were declared. For example, the statement

```
inData>>payRate;
```

reads the data from the file **prog.dat** and stores it in the variable **payRate**. The statement

```
outData<<"The paycheck is: $"<<pay<<endl;
```

stores the output—**The paycheck is: $565.78**—in the file **prog.out**. This statement assumes that the pay was calculated as **565.78**.

Once the I/O is complete, Step 5 requires closing the files. Closing a file means that the file stream variables are disassociated from the storage area, and the file stream variables are freed. Once these variables are freed, they can be reused for other file I/O. You close files by using the stream function **close**. For example, assuming the program includes the declarations listed in Steps 2 and 3, the statements for closing the files are

```
inData.close();
outData.close();
```

On some systems, it is not necessary to close the files. When the program terminates, the files are closed automatically. Nevertheless, it is a good practice to close the files yourself. Also, if you want to use the same file stream variable to open another file, you must close the first file opened with that file stream variable.

In skeleton form, a program that uses file I/O is usually of the following form:

```
#include <fstream>
//Add additional header files you use
using namespace std;

int main()
{
   //Declare file stream variables such as the following
   ifstream inData;
   ofstream outData;
   ...
    //Open files
   inData.open("A:prog.dat"); //open input file
   outData.open("A:prog.out"); //open output file
   //Code for data manipulation

   //Close files
   inData.close();
   outData.close();
   return 0;
}
```

Step 3 requires the file to be opened for file I/O. Opening a file associates a file stream variable declared in the program with a physical file at the source, such as a disk. In the case of an input file, the file must exist before the **open** statement executes. If the file does not exist, the **open** statement fails and the input stream enters the fail state. An output file does not have to exist before it is opened; if the output file does not exist, the computer prepares an empty file for output. If the designated output file already exists, by default the old contents are erased when the file is opened.

In the preceding section, you learned how to use the function open to a open a file for inputting data into a program and then storing the program's output. Suppose that a program tries to open a file for inputting data, but the input file does not exist. The open statement fails and the input stream enters the fail state. In this situation, some systems will automatically create an empty file for inputting data, thereby preventing the open statement from failing.

To prevent the system from creating an empty input file, you must include `ios::nocreate` as a second argument in the open statement. The second argument, `ios::nocreate`, ensures that the open operation will fail if the input file does not exist. For example, assuming that the preceding declaration was made, the following statement opens the file `prog.dat` for inputting data. If this file does not exist, the open operation will fail.

```
inData.open("A:prog.dat",ios::nocreate);
```

PROGRAMMING EXAMPLE: MOVIE TICKET SALE AND DONATION TO CHARITY

A movie in a local theater is in great demand. To help a local charity, the theater owner has decided to donate a portion of the gross amount generated from the movie to the charity. This example designs and implements a program that prompts the user to input the movie name, adult ticket price, child ticket price, number of adult tickets sold, number of child tickets sold, and percentage of the gross amount to be donated to the charity. The output of the program is as follows.

```
-*-*-*-*-*-*-*-*-*-*-*-*-*-*-*-*-*-*-*-*-*-*-*-*-*-*-*-*-*
Movie Name: ....................... Duckey Goes to Mars
Number of Tickets Sold: ...........        2650
Gross Amount: ..................... $ 9150.00
Percentage of Gross Amount Donated:       10.00%
Amount Donated: ................... $  915.00
Net Sale: ......................... $ 8235.00
```

Note that the first column is left-justified, the numbers in the right column are right-justified, and the decimal numbers are output with two decimal places.

Input The input to the program consists of the movie name, adult ticket price, child ticket price, number of adult tickets sold, number of child tickets sold, and percentage of the gross amount to be donated to the charity.

Output The output is as shown above.

Problem Analysis and Algorithm Design

To calculate the amount donated to the local charity and the net sale, you first need to determine the gross amount. To calculate the gross amount, you multiply the number of adult tickets sold by the price of an adult ticket, multiply the number of child tickets sold by the price of a child ticket, and then add these two numbers. That is,

```
grossAmount = adultTicketPrice * noOfAdultTicketsSold
            + childTicketPrice * noOfChildTicketsSold;
```

Next, you determine the percentage of the amount donated to the charity, and then calculate the net sale amount by subtracting the amount donated from the gross amount. The formulas to calculate the amount donated and the net sale amount are given below. This analysis leads to the following algorithm:

1. Get the movie name.
2. Get the price of an adult ticket price.
3. Get the price of a child ticket price.
4. Get the number of adult tickets sold.
5. Get the number of child tickets sold.
6. Get the percentage of the gross amount donated to the charity.
7. Calculate the gross amount using the following formula:

   ```
   grossAmount = adultTicketPrice * noOfAdultTicketsSold
                 + childTicketPrice * noOfChildTicketsSold;
   ```
8. Calculate the amount donated to the charity using the following formula:

   ```
   amountDonated = grossAmount * percentDonation / 100;
   ```
9. Calculate the net sale amount using the following formula:

   ```
   netSale = grossAmount – amountDonated;
   ```

Variables From the preceding discussion, it follows that you need variables to store the movie name, adult ticket price, child ticket price, number of adult tickets sold, number of child tickets sold, percentage of the gross amount donated to the charity, gross amount, amount donated, and net sale amount. Therefore, the following variables are needed:

```
string      movieName;
double      adultTicketPrice;
double      childTicketPrice;
int         noOfAdultTicketsSold;
int         noOfChildTicketsSold;
double      percentDonation;
double      grossAmount;
double      amountDonated;
double      netSaleAmount;
```

Because `movieName` is declared as a variable of the type `string`, you need to include the header file `string`. Therefore, the program needs, among others, the following include statement:

```
#include <string>
```

Formatting Output In the output, the first column is left-justified and the numbers in the second column are right-justified. Therefore, when printing a value in the first column, the manipulator `left` is used; before printing a value in the second column, the manipulator `right` is used. The empty space between the first and second columns is filled with dots; the program uses the manipulator `setfill` to accomplish this goal. In the lines showing the gross amount, amount donated, and net sale amount, the space between the $ sign and the number is filled with blank spaces. Therefore, before printing the dollar sign, the program uses the manipulator `setfill` to set the filling character to blank. The following statements accomplish the desired output:

```
cout<<"-*-*-*-*-*-*-*-*-*-*-*-*-*-*-*"
    <<"-*-*-*-*-*-*-*-*-*-*-*-*-*-*"<<endl;
cout<<setfill('.')<<left<<setw(35)<<"Movie Name: "
    <<right<<" "<<movieName<<endl;
cout<<left<<setw(35)<<"Number of Tickets Sold: "
    <<setfill(' ')<<right<<setw(10)
    <<noOfAdultTicketsSold + noOfChildTicketsSold
    <<endl;
cout<<setfill('.')<<left<<setw(35)<<"Gross Amount: "
    <<setfill(' ')<<right<<" $"
    <<setw(8)<<grossAmount<<endl;
cout<<setfill('.')<<left<<setw(35)
    <<"Percentage of Gross Amount Donated: "
    <<setfill(' ')<<right
    <<setw(9)<<percentDonation<<'%'<<endl;
cout<<setfill('.')<<left<<setw(35)<<"Amount Donated: "
    <<setfill(' ')<<right<<" $"
    <<setw(8)<<amountDonated<<endl;
cout<<setfill('.')<<left<<setw(35)<<"Net Sale: "
    <<setfill(' ')<<right<<" $"
    <<setw(8)<<netSaleAmount<<endl;
```

Main Algorithm Following the preceding discussion, we have the main algorithm:

1. Declare the variables.
2. Set the output of the floating-point numbers to two decimal places in a fixed decimal format with a decimal point and trailing zeros. Therefore, you need to include the header file `iomanip`.
3. Prompt the user to enter a movie name.

4. Input (read) the movie name. Because the name of a movie might contain more than one word (and, therefore, might contain blanks), the program uses the function `getline` to input the movie name. Moreover, because the function `getline` also reads the newline character, after entering the movie name on a line, you need to press the Enter key twice.
5. Prompt the user to enter the price of an adult ticket.
6. Input (read) the price of an adult ticket.
7. Prompt the user to enter the price of a child ticket.
8. Input (read) the price of a child ticket.
9. Prompt the user to enter the number of adult tickets sold.
10. Input (read) the number of adult tickets sold.
11. Prompt the user to enter the number of child tickets sold.
12. Input (read) the number of child tickets sold.
13. Prompt the user to enter the percentage of the gross amount donated.
14. Input (read) the percentage of the gross amount donated.
15. Calculate the gross amount.
16. Calculate the amount donated.
17. Calculate the net sale amount.
18. Output the results.

Complete Program Listing

```
#include <iostream>
#include <iomanip>
#include <string>

using namespace std;

int main()
{
            //Step 1
  string movieName;
  double adultTicketPrice;
  double childTicketPrice;
  int noOfAdultTicketsSold;
  int noOfChildTicketsSold;
  double percentDonation;
  double grossAmount;
  double amountDonated;
  double netSaleAmount;
```

```
cout<<fixed<<showpoint<<setprecision(2);                    //Step 2

cout<<"Enter movie name: "<<flush;                          //Step 3
getline(cin,movieName);                                     //Step 4
cout<<endl;

cout<<"Enter the price of an adult ticket: "<<flush;        //Step 5
cin>>adultTicketPrice;                                      //Step 6
cout<<endl;

cout<<"Enter the price of a child ticket: "<<flush;         //Step 7
cin>>childTicketPrice;                                      //Step 8
cout<<endl;

cout<<"Enter number of adult tickets sold: "<<flush;        //Step 9
cin>>noOfAdultTicketsSold;                                  //Step 10
cout<<endl;

cout<<"Enter number of child tickets sold: "<<flush;        //Step 11
cin>>noOfChildTicketsSold;                                  //Step 12
cout<<endl;

cout<<"Enter the percentage of donation: "<<flush;          //Step 13
cin>>percentDonation;                                       //Step 14
cout<<endl<<endl;

grossAmount = adultTicketPrice * noOfAdultTicketsSold +     //Step 15
              childTicketPrice * noOfChildTicketsSold;

amountDonated = grossAmount * percentDonation / 100;        //Step 16
netSaleAmount = grossAmount - amountDonated;                //Step 17

                //Step 18: Output results
cout<<"-*-*-*-*-*-*-*-*-*-*-*-*-*-*-*-*"
    <<"-*-*-*-*-*-*-*-*-*-*-*-*-*-*"<<endl;
cout<<setfill('.')<<left<<setw(35)<<"Movie Name: "
    <<right<<" "<<movieName<<endl;
cout<<left<<setw(35)<<"Number of Tickets Sold: "
    <<setfill(' ')<<right<<setw(10)
    <<noOfAdultTicketsSold + noOfChildTicketsSold
    <<endl;
cout<<setfill('.')<<left<<setw(35)<<"Gross Amount: "
    <<setfill(' ')<<right<<" $"
    <<setw(8)<<grossAmount<<endl;
```

```
cout<<setfill('.')<<left<<setw(35)
    <<"Percentage of Gross Amount Donated: "
      <<setfill(' ')<<right
      <<setw(9)<<percentDonation<<'%'<<endl;
  cout<<setfill('.')<<left<<setw(35)<<"Amount Donated: "
      <<setfill(' ')<<right<<" $"
      <<setw(8)<<amountDonated<<endl;
  cout<<setfill('.')<<left<<setw(35)<<"Net Sale: "
      <<setfill(' ')<<right<<" $"
      <<setw(8)<<netSaleAmount<<endl;

  return 0;
}
```

Sample Run: In this sample run, the user input is shaded.

```
Enter movie name: Duckey Goes to Mars


Enter the price of an adult ticket: 4.50

Enter the price of a child ticket: 3.00

Enter number of adult tickets sold: 800

Enter number of child tickets sold: 1850

Enter the percentage of donation: 10


-*-*-*-*-*-*-*-*-*-*-*-*-*-*-*-*-*-*-*-*-*-*-*-*-*-*-*-*-*-*-*-*-*-*-*-*-*
Movie Name: ....................... Duckey Goes to Mars
Number of Tickets Sold: ..........      2650
Gross Amount: ..................... $ 9150.00
Percentage of Gross Amount Donated:     10.00%
Amount Donated: ................... $  915.00
Net Sale: ......................... $ 8235.00
```

In this output, the first six lines get the necessary data to generate the last six lines of the output as required.

PROGRAMMING EXAMPLE: STUDENT GRADE

Write a program that reads a student ID followed by five test scores. The program should output the student ID, the five test scores, and the average test score. Output the average test score with two decimal places. Assume that the student ID is a character.

The data to be read is stored in a file called `test.txt`, and the file is stored on a floppy disk in drive A:. The output should be stored in a file called `testavg.out`, and the output file should be stored on the floppy disk in drive A:.

Input A file containing the student ID and the five test scores.

Output The student ID, the five test scores, and the average of the five test scores, saved to a file.

Problem Analysis and Algorithm Design

To find the average of the five test scores, you add the five test scores and divide the sum by `5`. The input data is in the following form: the student ID followed by the five test scores. Therefore, you must read the student ID first and then read the five test scores. This problem analysis translates into the following algorithm:

1. Read the student ID and the five test scores.
2. Output the student ID and the five test scores.
3. Calculate the average.
4. Output the average.

You output the average test score in the fixed decimal format with two decimal places.

Variables The program needs to read a student ID and five test scores. Therefore, you need one variable to store the student ID and five variables to store the five test scores. To find the average, you must add the five test scores and then divide the sum by `5`. Thus, you need a variable to store the average test score. Furthermore, because the input data is in a file, you need an `ifstream` variable to open the input file. Because the program output will be stored in a file, you need an `ofstream` variable to open the output file. The program, therefore, needs at least the following variables:

```
ifstream inFile;     //input file stream variable
ofstream outFile;    //output file stream variable

int test1, test2, test3, test4, test5; //variables to
                                  //read five test scores
double average;      //variable to store average test score
char studentId;      //variable to store student ID
```

Based on the preceding discussion, you can now write the main algorithm.

Main Algorithm

1. Declare the variables.
2. Open the input file.
3. Open the output file.
4. To output the floating-point numbers in a fixed decimal format with a decimal point and trailing zeros, set the manipulators **`fixed`** and **`showpoint`**. Also, to output the floating-point numbers with two decimal places, set the precision to two decimal places.
5. Read the student ID.
6. Output the student ID.
7. Read the five test scores.
8. Output the five test scores.
9. Find the average test score.
10. Output the average test score.
11. Close the input and output files.

Because this program reads data from a file and outputs data to a file, it must include the header file `fstream`. Because the program outputs the average test score to two decimal places, you need to set the precision to two decimal places. Therefore, the program uses the manipulator **`setprecision`**, which in turn requires you to include the header file `iomanip`. The program also includes the header file `iostream` to print a message on the screen so that you will not stare at a blank screen while the program executes.

Complete Program Listing

```
//Program to calculate average test score
#include <iostream>
#include <fstream>
#include <iomanip>
using namespace std;

int main()
{
            //Declare variables; Step 1
      ifstream inFile;  //input file stream variable
      ofstream outFile; //output file stream variable

      int test1, test2, test3, test4, test5;
      double average;
      char studentId;
```

```
    inFile.open("a:test.txt");                          //Step 2
    outFile.open("a:testavg.out");                      //Step 3

    outFile<<fixed<<showpoint;                          //Step 4
    outFile<<setprecision(2);                           //Step 4

    cout<<"Processing data"<<endl;
    inFile>>studentId;                                  //Step 5
    outFile<<"Student ID: "<<studentId
           <<endl;                                      //Step 6
    inFile>>test1>>test2>>test3
          >>test4>>test5;                               //Step 7
    outFile<<"Test scores: "<<setw(4)<<test1
           <<setw(4)<<test2<<setw(4)<<test3
           <<setw(4)<<test4
           <<setw(4)<<test5<<endl;                      //Step 8
    average = static_cast<double>(test1+test2+test3+
                        test4+test5)/5.0;               //Step 9
    outFile<<"Average test score: "<<setw(6)
           <<average<<endl;                             //Step 10

    inFile.close();                                     //Step 11
    outFile.close();                                    //Step 11
    return 0;
}
```

Sample Run

Input File (contents of the file `a:test.txt`):

```
T 87 89 65 37 98
```

Output File (contents of the file `a:testavg.out`):

```
Student ID: T
Test scores:   87  89  65  37  98
Average test score:  75.20
```

NOTE

To write this program in Standard C++, replace the statements

```
#include <iostream>
#include <fstream>
#include <iomanip>
using namespace std;
```

with

```
#include <iostream.h>
#include <fstream.h>
#include <iomanip.h>
```

You might also have to replace the statement

```
outFile<<fixed<<showpoint;
```

with

```
outFile.setf(ios::fixed,ios::floatfield);
outFile.setf(ios::showpoint);
```

QUICK REVIEW

1. A stream in C++ is an infinite sequence of characters from a source to a destination.
2. An input stream is a stream from a source to a computer.
3. An output stream is a stream from a computer to a destination.
4. `cin`, which stands for common input, is an input stream object, typically initialized to the standard input device, which is the keyboard.
5. `cout`, which stands for common output, is an output stream object, typically initialized to the standard output device, which is the screen.
6. When the binary operator >> is used with an input stream object, such as `cin`, it is called the stream extraction operator. The left-side operand of >> must be an input stream variable, such as `cin`; the right-side operand must be a variable.
7. When the binary operator << is used with an output stream object, such as `cout`, it is called the stream insertion operator. The left-side operand of << must be an output stream variable, such as `cout`, and the right-side operand of << must be an expression or a manipulator.
8. When inputting data into a variable, the operator >> skips all leading whitespace characters.
9. To use `cin` and `cout`, the program must include the header file `iostream`.
10. The function `get` is used to read data on a character-by-character basis and does not skip any whitespace characters.
11. The function `ignore` is used to skip data in a line.
12. The function `putback` puts the last character retrieved by the function `get` back into the input stream.
13. The function `peek` returns the next character from the input stream, but does not remove the character from the input stream.

14. Attempting to read invalid data into a variable causes the input stream to enter the fail state.
15. Once an input failure has occurred, you use the function **clear** to restore the input stream to a working state.
16. The manipulator **setprecision** formats the output of floating-point numbers to a specified number of decimal places.
17. The manipulator **fixed** outputs floating-point numbers in the fixed decimal format.
18. The manipulator **showpoint** outputs floating-point numbers with a decimal point and trailing zeros.
19. The manipulator **setw** formats the output of an expression in a specific number of columns; the default output is right-justified.
20. If the number of columns specified in the argument of **setw** is less than the number of columns needed to print the value of the expression, the output is not truncated and the output of the expression expands to the required number of columns.
21. To use the stream functions **get**, **ignore**, **putback**, **peek**, **fill**, **clear**, **setf**, and **unsetf** for standard I/O, the program must include the header file **iostream**.
22. To use the manipulators **setprecision**, **setw**, **setfill**, and **setiosflags**, the program must include the header file **iomanip**.
23. The header file **fstream** contains the definitions of **ifstream** and **ofstream**.
24. For file I/O, you must use the statement **#include <fstream>** to include the header file **fstream** in the program. You must also do the following: declare variables of the type **ifstream** for file input and of the type **ofstream** for file output; use open statements to open input and output files; and use <<, >>, **get**, **ignore**, **peek**, **putback**, or **clear** with file stream variables.
25. To close a file as indicated by the **ifstream** variable **inFile**, you use the statement **inFile.close();**. To close a file as indicated by the **ofstream** variable **outFile**, you use the statement **outFile.close();**.

3

EXERCISES

1. Mark the following statements as true or false.
   a. The extraction operator >> skips all leading whitespace characters when searching for the next data in the input stream.
   b. In the statement **cin>>x;**, x must be a variable.
   c. The statement **cin>>x>>y;** requires the input values for x and y to appear on the same line.
   d. The statement **cin>>num;** is equivalent to the statement **num>>cin;**.

e. You generate the newline character by pressing the Enter (return key) on the keyboard.

f. The function **ignore** is used to skip certain input in a line.

2. Suppose **x** and **y** are **int** variables and **ch** is a **char** variable. Consider the following input:

```
5 28 36
```

What value (if any) is assigned to **x**, **y**, and **ch** after each of following statements executes? (Use the same input for each statement.)

a. `cin>>x>>y>>ch;`

b. `cin>>ch>>x>>y;`

c. `cin>>x>>ch>>y;`

d.
```
cin>>x>>y;
cin.get(ch);
```

3. Suppose **x** and **y** are **int** variables and **ch** is a **char** variable. Assume the following input data:

```
13 28 D
14 E 98
A B 56
```

What value (if any) is assigned to **x**, **y**, and **ch** after each of following statements executes? (Use the same input for each statement.)

a.
```
cin>>x>>y;
cin.ignore(50,'\n');
cin>>ch;
```

b.
```
cin>>x;
cin.ignore(50,'\n');
cin>>y;
cin.ignore(50,'\n');
cin.get(ch);
```

c.
```
cin>>y;
cin.ignore(50,'\n');
cin>>x>>ch;
```

d.
```
cin.get(ch);
cin.ignore(50,'\n');
cin>>x;
cin.ignore(50,'E');
cin>>y;
```

4. Given the input

```
46 A 49
```

and the C++ code

```
int x = 10, y = 18;
char z = 'A';
cin>>x>>y>>z;
cout<<x<<" "<<y<<" "<<z;
```

what is the output?

5. Write a C++ statement that uses the manipulator **setfill** to output a line containing 35 stars, as in the following line:

```
***********************************
```

6. The following program is supposed to read two numbers from a file named **input.dat**, and write the sum of the numbers to a file named **output.dat**. However, it fails to do so. Rewrite the program so that it accomplishes what it is intended to do.

```
#include <iostream>
#include <fstream>
using namespace std;
int main()
{
    int num1, num2;
    ifstream infile;

    outfile.open("output.dat");
    infile>>num1>>num2;
    outfile<<"Sum = "<<num1+num2<<endl;
    return 0;
}
```

7. What may cause an input stream to enter the fail state? What happens when an input stream enters the fail state?

8. A program reads data from a file called **inputFile.dat** and, after doing some calculations, writes the results to a file called **outFile.dat**. Answer the following questions:

   a. After the program executes, what are the contents of the file **inputFile.dat**?

   b. After the program executes, what are the contents of the file **outFile.dat** if this file was empty before the program executed?

   c. After the program executes, what are the contents of the file **outFile.dat** if this file contained 100 numbers before the program executed?

   d. What would happen if the file **outFile.dat** did not exist before the program executed?

PROGRAMMING EXERCISES

1. Consider the following incomplete C++ program.

```
#include <iostream>

int main()
{
   ...
}
```

   a. Write a statement that includes the header file `fstream` in this program.
   b. Write statements that declare `inFile` to be a variable of the type `ifstream` and `outFile` to be a variable of the type `ofstream`.
   c. The program will read data from the file `inData.txt` and write output to the file `outData.dat`. Write statements to open both these files, associate `inFile` with `inData.txt`, and associate `outFile` with `outData.dat`.
   d. Suppose that the file `inData.txt` contains the following data:

```
56 38
A
7 8
```

   Write statements so that after the program executes, the contents of the file `outData.dat` are as shown below. If necessary, declare additional variables. Your statements should be general enough so that if the content of the input file changes and the program is run again (without editing and recompiling), it outputs the appropriate results.

```
Sum of 56 and 38 = 94.
The character that comes after A in the ASCII set is B.
The product of 7 and 8 = 56.
```

   e. Write statements that close the input and output files.
   f. Write a C++ program that tests the statements in parts a–e.
2. Write a program that prompts the user to enter a decimal number and then outputs this number rounded to two decimal places.
3. The manager of a football stadium wants you to write a program that calculates the total ticket sales after each game. There are four types of tickets—box, sideline, premium, and general admission. After each game, data is stored in a file in the following form:

```
ticketPrice   numberOfTicketsSold
...
```

   Sample data are shown below:

```
250 5750
100 28000
 50 35750
 25 18750
```

The first line indicates that the ticket price is $250 and that 5750 tickets were sold at that price. Output the number of tickets sold and the total sale amount. Format your output with two decimal places.

4. Write a program to calculate the property tax. Property tax is calculated on 92% of the assessed value of the property. For example, if the assessed value is $100000, the property tax is on $92000. Assume that the property tax rate is $1.05 for each $100 of the assessed value. Your program should prompt the user to enter the assessed value of the property. Store the output in a file in the following format. (Here is a sample output.)

```
Assessed Value:                    100000.00
Taxable Amount:                     92000.00
Tax Rate for each $100.00:              1.05
Property Tax:                         966.00
```

Format your output to have two decimal places. (Note that the left column is left-justified and the right column is right-justified.)

5. Write a program that converts a temperature from degrees Fahrenheit to degrees centigrade. The formula for converting the temperature from degrees Fahrenheit to degrees centigrade is

```
C = (5/9) (F – 32)
```

Your program should prompt the user to enter a temperature given in degrees Fahrenheit. The program should output the temperature both in degrees Fahrenheit and degrees centigrade.

6. Write a program that calculates and prints the monthly paycheck for an employee. The net pay is calculated after taking the following deductions:

```
Federal Income Tax: 15%
State Tax:      3.5%
Social Security Tax: 5.75%
Medicare/Medicaid Tax:     2.75%
Pension Plan:  5%
Health Insurance:    $75.00
```

Your program should prompt the user to input the gross amount and the employee name. The output will be stored in a file. Format your output to have two decimal places. A sample output follows:

```
Bill Robinson
Gross Amount: ........... $3575.00
Federal Tax: ............ $ 536.25
State Tax: .............. $ 125.13
Social Security Tax: ..... $ 205.56
Medicare/Medicaid Tax: ... $   98.31
Pension Plan: ........... $ 178.75
Health Insurance: ....... $   75.00
Net Pay: ................ $2356.00
```

Note that the first column is left-justified and the right column is right-justified.

CHAPTER

4

CONTROL STRUCTURES I (Selection)

In this chapter, you will:

- Learn about control structures
- Examine relational and logical operators
- Explore how to form and evaluate logical (Boolean) expressions
- Discover how to use the selection control structures `if`, `if...else`, and `switch` in a program
- Learn to use the `assert` function to terminate a program

Chapter 2 defined a program as a sequence of statements whose objective is to accomplish some task. The programs you have examined so far were simple and straightforward. In executing programs, the computer starts at the first executable statement and executes the statements in order until it comes to the end. In this chapter and Chapter 5, you will learn how to tell a computer that it does not have to follow a simple sequential order of statements; it can also make decisions and repeat certain statements over and over until certain conditions are met.

CONTROL STRUCTURES

A computer can process a program in one of three ways: in sequence; selectively by making a choice, which is also called a branch; or repetitively by executing a statement over and over, using a structure called a loop (as shown in Figure 4-1). The programming examples in Chapters 2 and 3 included simple sequential programs. With such a program, the computer starts at the beginning and follows the statements in order. No choices are made; there is no repetition. Control structures provide alternatives to sequential program execution and are used to alter the sequential flow of execution. The two most common control structures are selection and repetition. In selection, the program executes particular statements depending on some condition(s). In repetition, the program repeats particular statements a certain number of times depending on some condition(s).

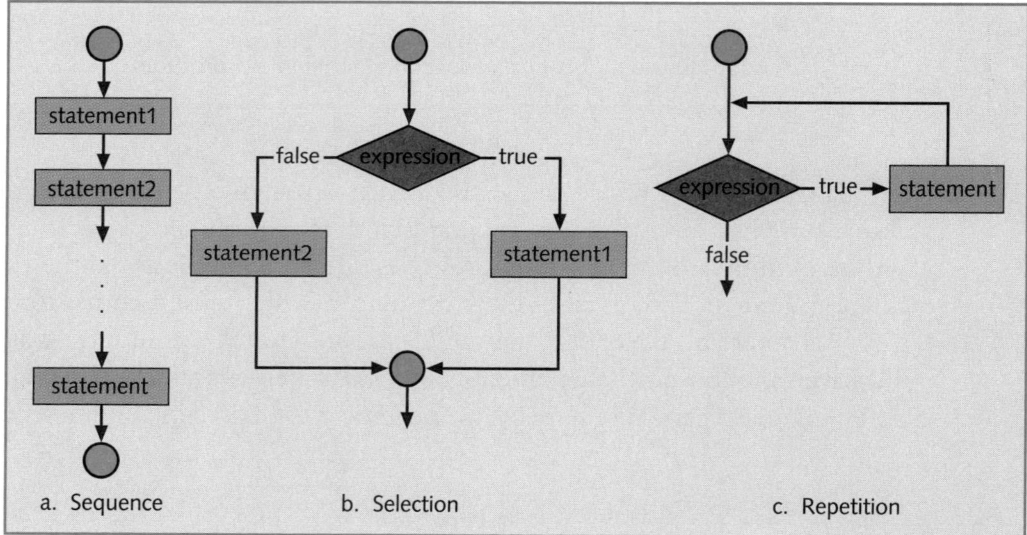

Figure 4-1 Flow of execution

Before you can learn about selection and repetition, you must understand the nature of conditional statements and how to use them. Consider the following three statements:

1.
```
if(score is greater than or equal to 90)
    grade is A
```
2.
```
if(hours worked are less than or equal to 40)
    wages = rate * hours
otherwise
    wages = (rate * 40) + 1.5 * (rate * (hours - 40))
```
3.
```
if(temperature is greater than 70 degrees and it is not
    raining)
        recommended activity is golfing
```


These statements are examples of conditional statements. You can see that certain statements are to be executed only if certain conditions are met. A condition is met if it evaluates to `true`. For example, in statement 1,

```
score is greater than or equal to 90
```

is `true` if the value of `score` is greater than or equal to `90`; it is `false` otherwise. For example, if the value of `score` is `95`, the statement evaluates to `true`. Similarly, if the value of `score` is `86`, the statement evaluates to `false`.

It would be useful if the computer could recognize these types of statements to be true for appropriate values. Furthermore, in certain situations, the truth or falsity of a statement could depend on more than one condition. For example, in statement 3, both `temperature is greater than 70 degrees` and `it is not raining` must be true for the recommended activity to be `golfing`.

As you can see from these examples, to make decisions and repeat statements, the computer must be able to react to conditions that exist when the program executes. The next few sections discuss how to represent and evaluate conditional statements in C++.

RELATIONAL OPERATORS

To make decisions, you must be able to express conditions and make comparisons. For example, the interest rate and service charges on a checking account might depend on the balance at the end of the month. If the balance is less than some minimum balance, not only is the interest rate lower, but there is also usually a service charge. Therefore, to determine the interest rate, you must be able to state the minimum balance (a condition) and compare the account balance with the minimum balance. The premium on an insurance policy is also determined by stating conditions and making comparisons. For example, to determine an insurance premium, you must be able to check the smoking status of the policyholder. Nonsmokers (the condition) receive lower premiums than smokers. Both of these examples involve comparing items. Certain items are compared for equality against a particular condition; others are compared for inequality—greater than or less than—against a particular condition.

In C++, a condition is represented by a logical (Boolean) expression. An expression that has a value of either `true` or `false` is called **a logical (Boolean) expression**. Moreover, `true` and `false` are **logical (Boolean) values**. Suppose `I` and `J` are integers. Consider the expression:

```
I > J
```

If this expression is a logical expression, it will have the value `true` if the value of `I` is greater than the value of `J`; otherwise, it will have the value `false`. You can think of the symbol > as an operator that (in this case) takes integer operands and yields a logical result. Here, the symbol > is similar to the operators + and – that yield integer or real results. In fact, the symbol > is called a relational operator because the value of `I > J` is `true` only when the relationship "greater than" holds between `I` and `J`. A **relational operator** allows you to make comparisons in a program.

C++ includes six relational operators that allow you to state conditions and make comparisons. Table 4-1 lists the relational operators.

Table 4-1 Relational Operators in C++

Operator	Description
==	equal to
!=	not equal to
<	less than
<=	less than or equal to
>	greater than
>=	greater than or equal to

In C++, the symbol ==, which consists of two equal signs, is called the **equality operator**. Recall that the symbol = is called the assignment operator. Remember that the equality operator, ==, determines whether two expressions are equal, whereas the assignment operator, =, assigns the value of an expression to a variable.

Each of the relational operators is a binary operator; that is, it requires two operands. Because the result of a comparison is `true` or `false`, expressions using these operators evaluate to `true` or `false`.

Relational Operators and Simple Data Types

You can use the relational operators with all three simple data types. For example, the following expressions use both integers and real numbers:

Expression	**Meaning**	**Value**
8 < 15	8 is less than 15	true
6 != 6	6 is not equal to 6	false
2.5 > 5.8	2.5 is greater than 5.8	false
5.9 <= 7.5	5.9 is less than or equal to 7.5	true

It is important to remember that the comparison of real numbers for equality is usually machine-dependent. It is quite possible that on a particular machine

```
6.8 + 3.1 == 2.7 + 7.2
```

will evaluate to false.

For char values, whether an expression using relational operators evaluates to true or false depends on a machine's collating sequence. Table 4-2 shows how expressions using the ASCII data set are evaluated.

Table 4-2 Evaluating Expressions Using Relational Operators and the ASCII Collating Sequence

Expression	Value of Expression	Explanation
' ' < 'a'	true	The ASCII value of ' ' is 32, and the ASCII value of 'a' is 97. Because 32 < 97 is true, it follows that ' ' < 'a' is true.
'R' > 'T'	false	The ASCII value of 'R' is 82, and the ASCII value of 'T' is 84. Because 82 > 84 is false, it follows that 'R' > 'T' is false.
'+' < '*'	false	The ASCII value of '+' is 43, and the ASCII value of '*' is 42. Because 43 < 42 is false, it follows that '+' < '*' is false.
'6' <= '>'	true	The ASCII value of '6' is 54, and the ASCII value of '>' is 62. Because 54 <= 62 is true, it follows that '6' <= '>' is true.

Comparing values of different data types may produce unpredictable results. For example, the following expression compares an integer and a character:

```
8 < '5'
```

Because the results are unpredictable, you should not use comparisons involving different data types in your programs. In the preceding expression, on a particular machine, 8 would be compared with the collating sequence of '5', which is 53. That is, 8 is compared with 53.

Expressions such as `4 < 6` and `'R' > 'T'` are examples of **logical (Boolean) expressions**. When C++ evaluates a logical expression, it returns an integer value of `1` if the logical expression evaluates to `true`; it returns an integer value of `0` otherwise. In C++, any nonzero value is treated as `true`.

Chapter 2 introduced the data type `bool`. Recall that the data type `bool` has two values, `true` and `false`. In C++, `true` and `false` are reserved words. The identifier `true` is set to `1`, and the identifier `false` is set to `0`. Even though the value of a logical expression is `1` if the logical expression evaluates to `true` and `0` otherwise, for readability, whenever logical expressions are used, the identifiers `true` and `false` will be used here as the value of the logical expression.

Relational Operators and the `string` Type

The relational operators can be applied to variables of the type `string`. Variables of the type `string` are compared character-by-character, starting with the first character and using the ASCII collating sequence. The character-by-character comparison continues until either a mismatch is found or the last characters have been compared and are equal. Consider the following declarations:

```
string str1 = "Hello";
string str2 = "Hi";
string str3 = "Air";
string str4 = "Bill";
string str5 = "Big";
```

Using these variable declarations, Table 4-3 shows how various logical expressions are evaluated.

Table 4-3 Evaluating Logical Expressions with String Variables

Expression	Value
`str1 < str2`	`true`
`str1 > "Hen"`	`false`
`str3 < "An"`	`true`
`str1 == "hello "`	`false`
`str3 <= str4`	`true`

If two strings of different lengths are compared and the character-by-character comparison is equal until it reaches the last character of the shorter string, the shorter string is evaluated as less than the larger string. For example,

Expression	**Value**
`str4 >= "Billy"`	`false`
`str5 <= "Bigger"`	`true`

LOGICAL (BOOLEAN) OPERATORS AND LOGICAL EXPRESSIONS

This section describes how to form and evaluate logical expressions that are combinations of other logical expressions. **Logical (Boolean) operators** enable you to combine logical expressions. C++ has three logical (Boolean) operators, as shown in Table 4-4.

4

Table 4-4 Logical (Boolean) Operators in C++

Operator	Description
`!`	`not`
`&&`	`and`
`||`	`or`

Logical operators take only logical values as operands and yield only logical values as results. The operator `!` is unary, so it has only one operand. The operators `&&` and `||` are binary operators. Tables 4-5, 4-6, and 4-7 define these operators.

Table 4-5 defines the operator ! (not). Table 4-5 shows that when you use the `!` operator, `!true` is `false` and `!false` is `true`. Putting `!` in front of a logical expression reverses the value of that logical expression.

Table 4-5 The ! (not) Operator

Expression	!(Expression)
`true (nonzero)`	`false (0)`
`false (0)`	`true (1)`

Example 4-1

Expression	Value	Explanation
`!('A' > 'B')`	`true`	Because `'A' > 'B'` is `false`, `!('A' > 'B')` is `true`.
`!(6 <= 7)`	`false`	Because `6 <= 7` is `true`, `!(6 <= 7)` is `false`.

Table 4-6 defines the operator `&&` (and). From this table, it follows that `Expression1&&Expression2` is `true` if and only if both `Expression1` and `Expression2` are `true`; otherwise `Expression1&&Expression2` evaluates to `false`.

Table 4-6 The `&&` (and) Operator

Expression1	Expression2	Expression1 && Expression2
`true (nonzero)`	`true (nonzero)`	`true (1)`
`true (nonzero)`	`false (0)`	`false (0)`
`false (0)`	`true (nonzero)`	`false (0)`
`false (0)`	`false (0)`	`false (0)`

Example 4-2

Expression	Value	Explanation
`(14 >= 5) && ('A' < 'B')`	`true`	Because `(14 >= 5)` is `true`, `('A' < 'B')` is `true`, and `true && true` is `true`, the expression evaluates to `true`.
`(24 >= 35) && ('A' < 'B')`	`false`	Because `(24 >= 35)` is `false`, `('A' < 'B')` is `true`, and `false && true` is `false`, the expression evaluates to `false`.

Table 4-7 defines the operator `||` (or). From this table, it follows that `Expression1||Expression2` is `true` if and only if at least one of the expressions, `Expression1` or `Expression2`, is `true`; otherwise, `Expression1||Expression2` evaluates to `false`.

Table 4-7 The `||` (or) Operator

Expression1	Expression2	Expression1 || Expression2
`true (nonzero)`	`true (nonzero)`	`true (1)`
`true (nonzero)`	`false (0)`	`true (1)`
`false (0)`	`true (nonzero)`	`true (1)`
`false (0)`	`false (0)`	`false (0)`

Example 4-3

Expression	Value	Explanation
`(14 >= 5) || ('A' > 'B')`	`true`	Because `(14 >= 5)` is `true`, `('A' < 'B')` is `false`, and `true || false` is `true`, the expression evaluates to `true`.

<table>
<tr><td>(24 >= 35) || ('A' > 'B')</td><td>false</td><td>Because (24 >= 35) is false, ('A' > 'B') is false, and false || false is false, the expression evaluates to false.</td></tr>
<tr><td>('A' <= 'a') || (7 != 7)</td><td>true</td><td>Because ('A' <= 'a') is true, (7 != 7) is false, and true || false is true, the expression evaluates to true.</td></tr>
</table>

Order of Precedence

Complex logical expressions can be difficult to evaluate. Consider the following logical expression:

```
11 > 5 || 6 < 15 && 7 >= 8.
```

This logical expression yields different results depending on whether `||` or `&&` is evaluated first. If `||` is evaluated first, it evaluates to `false`. If `&&` is evaluated first, it evaluates to `true`.

To work with complex logical expressions, there must be some priority scheme for determining which operators to evaluate first. Because an expression might contain arithmetic, relational, and logical operators, as in the expression `5 + 3 <= 9 && 2 > 3`, an order of precedence of all C++ operators needs to be established. Table 4-8 shows the order of precedence of some C++ operators, including the arithmetic, relational, and logical operators. (See Appendix B for the precedence of all C++ operators.)

Table 4-8 Precedence of Operators

<table>
<tr><th>Operators</th><th>Precedence</th></tr>
<tr><td>!, +, - (unary operators)</td><td>first</td></tr>
<tr><td>*, /, %</td><td>second</td></tr>
<tr><td>+, -</td><td>third</td></tr>
<tr><td><, <=, >=, ></td><td>fourth</td></tr>
<tr><td>==, !=</td><td>fifth</td></tr>
<tr><td>&&</td><td>sixth</td></tr>
<tr><td>||</td><td>seventh</td></tr>
<tr><td>= (assignment operator)</td><td>last</td></tr>
</table>

In C++, `&` and `|` are also operators. The meaning of these operators is very different from the meaning of `&&` and `||`. Using `&` in place of `&&`, as might result from a typographical error, would produce very strange results. Similarly, using `|` in place of `||` would produce very strange results.

Using the precedence rules given in Table 4-8 in an expression, relational and logical operators are evaluated from left to right. Because relational and logical operators are evaluated from left to right, the **associativity** of these operators is said to be from left to right.

Example 4-4 illustrates how logical expressions consisting of variables are evaluated.

Example 4-4

Suppose you have the following declarations:

```
bool found = true;
bool flag = false;
int num = 1;
double x = 5.2;
double y = 3.4;
int a = 5, b = 8;
int n = 20;
char ch = 'B';
```

Consider the following expressions:

Expression	Value	Explanation
`!found`	`false`	Because `found` is `true`, `!found` is `false`.
`x > 4.0`	`true`	Because `x` is `5.2` and `5.2 > 4.0` is `true`, the expression `x > 4.0` evaluates to `true`.
`!num`	`false`	Because `num` is `1`, which is nonzero, `num` is `true` and so `!num` is `false`.
`!found && (x >= 0)`	`false`	In this expression, `!found` is `false`. Also, because `x` is `5.2` and `5.2 >= 0` is `true`, `x >= 0` is `true`. Therefore, the value of the expression `!found && (x >= 0)` is `false && true`, which evaluates to `false`.
`!(found && (x >= 0))`	`false`	In this expression, `found && (x >= 0)` is `true && true`, which evaluates to `true`. Therefore, the value of the expression `!(found && (x >= 0))` is `!true`, which evaluates to `false`.
`x + y <= 20.5`	`true`	Because `x + y = 5.2 + 3.4 = 8.6` and `8.6 <= 20.5`, it follows that `x + y <= 20.5` evaluates to `true`.
`(n >= 0) && (n <= 100)`	`true`	Here `n` is `20`. Because `20 >= 0` is `true`, `n >= 0` is `true`. Also, because `20 <= 100` is `true`, `n <= 100` is `true`. Therefore, the value of the expression `(n >= 0) && (n <= 100)` is `true && true`, which evaluates to `true`.

`('A' <= ch && ch <= 'Z')`	`true`	In this expression, the value of `ch` is `'B'`. Because `'A' <= 'B'` is `true`, `'A' <= ch` evaluates to `true`. Also, because `'B' <= 'Z'` is `true`, `ch <= 'Z'` evaluates to `true`. Therefore, the value of the expression `('A' <= ch && ch <= 'Z')` is `true && true`, which evaluates to `true`.
`(a + 2 <= b) && !flag`	`true`	Now `a + 2 = 5 + 2 = 7` and `b` is `8`. Because `7 < 8` is `true`, the expression `a + 2 < b` evaluates to `true`. Also, because `flag` is `false`, `!flag` is `true`. Therefore, the value of the expression `(a + 2 <= b) && !flag` is `true && true`, which evaluates to `true`.

You can also write a C++ program to evaluate the logical expressions given in Example 4-4, as shown in Example 4-5.

Example 4-5

The following program evaluates and outputs the values of the logical expressions given in Example 4-4. Note that if a logical expression evaluates to `true`, the corresponding output is `1`; if the logical expression evaluates to `false`, the corresponding output is `0`, as shown in the output at the end of the program. Recall that if the value of a logical expression is `true`, it evaluates to `1`, and if the value of the logical expression is `false`, it evaluates to `0`.

```
//Chapter 4: Logical operators

#include <iostream>

using namespace std;

int main()
{
   bool found = true;
   bool flag = false;
   int num = 1;
   double x = 5.2;
   double y = 3.4;
   int a = 5, b = 8;
   int n = 20;
   char ch = 'B';

   cout<<"Line 1: !found evaluates to "
       <<!found<<endl;                              //Line 1
   cout<<"Line 2: x > 4.0 evaluates to "
       <<(x > 4.0)<<endl;                           //Line 2
   cout<<"Line 3: !num evaluates to "
       <<!num<<endl;                                //Line 3
```

```
    cout<<"Line 4: !found && (x >= 0) evaluates to "
        <<(!found && (x >= 0))<<endl;                    //Line 4
    cout<<"Line 5: !(found && (x >= 0)) evaluates to "
        <<(!(found && (x >= 0)))<<endl;                  //Line 5
    cout<<"Line 6: x + y <= 20.5 evaluates to "
        <<(x + y <= 20.5)<<endl;                         //Line 6
    cout<<"Line 7: (n >= 0) && (n <= 100) evaluates to "
        <<((n >= 0) && (n <= 100))<<endl;                //Line 7
    cout<<"Line 8: ('A' <= ch && ch <= 'Z') evaluates to "
        <<('A' <= ch && ch <= 'Z')<<endl;                //Line 8
    cout<<"Line 9: (a + 2 <= b) && !flag evaluates to "
        <<((a + 2 <= b) && !flag)<<endl;                 //Line 9

    return 0;
}
```

Output:

```
Line 1: !found evaluates to 0
Line 2: x > 4.0 evaluates to 1
Line 3: !num evaluates to 0
Line 4: !found && (x >= 0) evaluates to 0
Line 5: !(found && (x >= 0)) evaluates to 0
Line 6: x + y <= 20.5 evaluates to 1
Line 7: (n >= 0) && (n <= 100) evaluates to 1
Line 8: ('A' <= ch && ch <= 'Z') evaluates to 1
Line 9: (a + 2 <= b) && !flag evaluates to 1
```

You can insert parentheses into an expression to clarify its meaning. You can also use parentheses to override the precedence of operators. Using the standard order of precedence, the expression

```
11 > 5 || 6 < 15 && 7 >= 8
```

is equivalent to

```
11 > 5 || (6 < 15 && 7 >= 8)
```

In this expression, `11 > 5` is `true`, `6 < 15` is `true`, and `7 >= 8` is `false`. Substitute these values in the expression `11 > 5 || (6 < 15 && 7 >= 8)` to get `true || (true && false) = true || false = true`. Therefore, the expression `11 > 5 || (6 < 15 && 7 >= 8)` evaluates to `true`.

Example 4-6

Evaluate the following expression:

```
(17 < 4 * 3 + 5) || (8 * 2 == 4 * 4) && !(3 + 3 == 6)
```

Now,

```
    (17 < 4*3+5) || (8*2 == 4*4) && !(3+3 == 6)
=   (17 < 12+5) || (16 == 16) && !(6 == 6)
=   (17 < 17) || true && !(true)
=   false || true && false
=   false || false  (Because true && false is false)
=   false
```

Therefore, the value of the original logical expression is false—that is, 0.

Short-Circuit Evaluation

Logical expressions in C++ are evaluated using a highly efficient algorithm. This algorithm is illustrated with the help of the following statements:

1. (x > y) || (x == 5)
2. (a == b) && (x >= 7)

In the first statement, the two operands of the operator || are the expressions (x > y) and (x == 5). This expression evaluates to true if either the operand (x > y) is true or the operand (x == 5) is true. With short-circuit evaluation, the computer evaluates the logical expression from left to right. As soon as the value of the entire logical expression is known, the evaluation stops. For example, in statement 1, if the operand (x > y) evaluates to true, then the entire expression evaluates to true because true || true is true and true || false is true. Therefore, the value of the operand (x == 5) has no bearing on the final outcome.

Similarly, in statement 2, the two operands of the operator && are (a == b) and (x >= 7). Now, if the operand (a == b) evaluates to false, then the entire expression evaluates to false because false && true is false and false && false is false.

Short-circuit evaluation (of a logical expression): A process in which the computer evaluates a logical expression from left to right and stops as soon as the value of the expression is known.

Example 4-7

Consider the following expressions:

1. (5 >= 3) || (x = = 5)
2. (2 == 3) && (x >= 7)

In statement 1, because (5 >= 3) is true and the logical operator used in the expression is ||, the expression evaluates to true. The computer does not evaluate (x == 5). Similarly, in statement 2, because (2 == 3) is false and the logical operator used in the expression is &&, the expression evaluates to false. The computer does not evaluate (x >= 7).

In C++, logical (Boolean) expressions can be manipulated or processed in either of two ways: by using `int` variables or by using `bool` variables. The following sections describe these methods.

The `int` Data Type and Logical (Boolean) Expressions

Earlier versions of C++ did not provide built-in data types that had logical (or Boolean) values, which are **true** and **false**. Because logical expressions evaluate to either `1` or `0`, the value of a logical expression was stored in a variable of the data type `int`. Therefore, you can use the `int` data type to manipulate logical (Boolean) expressions.

Recall that nonzero values are treated as `true`. Now, consider the declarations

```
int legalAge;
int age;
```

and the assignment statement

```
legalAge = 21;
```

If you regard `legalAge` as a logical variable, the value of `legalAge` assigned by this statement is `true`.

The assignment statement

```
legalAge = (age >= 21);
```

assigns the value `1` to `legalAge` if the value of `age` is greater than or equal to `21`. The statement assigns the value `0` if the value of `age` is less than `21`.

The `bool` Data Type and Logical (Boolean) Expressions

More recent versions of C++ contain a built-in data type, `bool`, that has the logical (Boolean) values `true` and `false`. Therefore, you can manipulate logical (Boolean) expressions using the `bool` data type. Recall that in C++, `bool`, `true`, and `false` are reserved words. In addition, the identifier `true` has the value `1`, and the identifier `false` has the value `0`. Now, consider the following declaration:

```
bool legalAge;
int age;
```

The statement

```
legalAge = true;
```

sets the value of the variable `legalAge` to `true`. The statement

```
legalAge = (age >= 21);
```

assigns the value `true` to `legalAge` if the value of `age` is greater than or equal to `21`. This statement assigns the value `false` to `legalAge` if the value of `age` is less than `21`. For example, if the value of `age` is `25`, the value assigned to `legalAge` is `true`—that is, `1`. Similarly, if the value of `age` is `16`, the value assigned to `legalAge` is `false`—that is, `0`.

From the preceding sections, it follows that you can use either an `int` variable or a `bool` variable to store the value of a logical expression. For the purpose of clarity, this book uses `bool` variables to store the values of logical expressions.

Sometimes logical expressions do not behave as you might expect. Suppose, for example, that `num` is an `int` variable. Further suppose that you want to write a logical expression that evaluates to `true` if the value of `num` is between `0` and `10`, including `0` and `10`, and that evaluates to `false` otherwise. The following expression appears to represent a comparison of `0`, `num`, and `10` that will yield the desired result:


```
0 <= num <= 10
```

Although this statement is a legal C++ expression, you will not get the result you might expect. Does this expression evaluate to `true` if the value of `num` is between `0` and `10`? What happens if the value of `num` is greater than `10`? Suppose that `num = 5`. Then

```
  0 <= num <= 10
= 0 <= 5 <= 10
= (0 <= 5) <= 10        (Because relational operators are evaluated from left to right)
= 1 <= 10               (Because 0 <= 5 is true, 0 <= 5 evaluates to 1)
= 1 (true)
```

Now suppose that `num = 20`. Then

```
  0 <= num <= 10
= 0 <= 20 <= 10
= (0 <= 20) <= 10       (Because relational operators are evaluated from left to right)
= 1 <= 10               (Because 0 <= 20 is true, 0 <= 20 evaluates to 1)
= 1 (true)
```

Clearly, this answer is incorrect. Because `num` is `20`, it is not between `0` and `10`, and `0 <= 20 <= 10` should not evaluate to `true`. Note that this expression will always evaluate to `true`, no matter what `num` is. This is due to the fact that the expression `0 <= num` evaluates to either `0` or `1`, and `0 <= 10` is `true` and `1 <= 10` is `true`. So what is wrong with the expression `0 <= num <= 10`? It is missing the logical operator `&&`. The correct way to write this expression in C++ is

```
0 <= num && num <= 10
```

You must take care when formulating logical expressions. When creating a complex logical expression, you must use the proper logical operators.

SELECTION: if AND if...else

Although there are only two logical values, `true` and `false`, they turn out to be extremely useful because they permit programs to incorporate decision making that alters the processing flow. The remainder of this chapter discusses ways to incorporate decisions into a program. In C++, there are two selections, or branch control structures: `if` statements and the `switch` structure. This section discusses how `if` and `if...else` statements can be used to create one-way selection, two-way selection, and multiple selections. The `switch` structure is discussed later in this chapter.

One-Way Selection

A bank would like to send a notice to a customer if her or his checking account balance falls below the required minimum balance. That is, if the checking account balance is below the required minimum balance, it should send a notice to the customer; otherwise, it should do nothing. Similarly, if the policyholder of an insurance policy is a nonsmoker, the company would like to apply a 10% discount to the policy premium. Both of these examples involve one-way selection. In C++, one-way selections are incorporated using the `if` statement. The syntax of one-way selection is

```
if(expression)
   statement
```

Note the elements of this syntax. It begins with the reserved word `if`, followed by an `expression` contained within parentheses, followed by a `statement`. The `expression` is sometimes called a **decision maker** because it decides whether to execute the `statement` that follows it. The `expression` is usually a logical expression. If the value of the `expression` is `true`, the `statement` executes. If the value is `false`, the `statement` does not execute and the computer goes on to the next statement in the program. The `statement` following the `expression` is sometimes called the **action statement**. Figure 4-2 shows the flow of execution of the `if` statement (one-way selection).

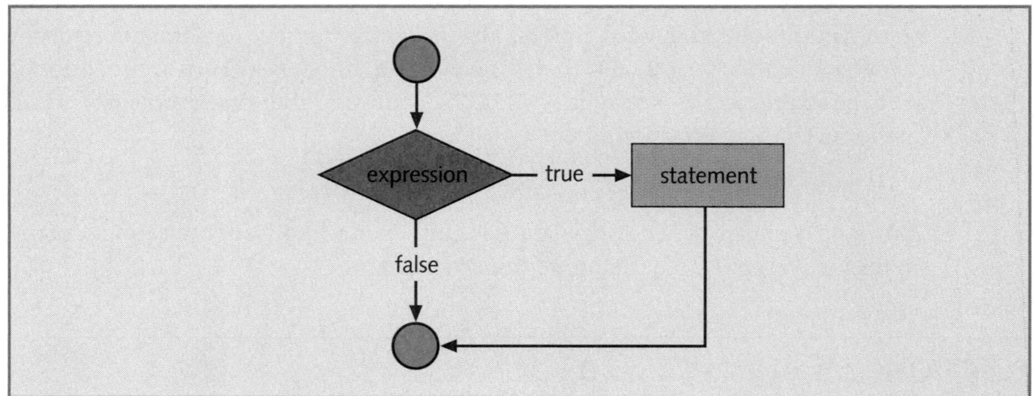

Figure 4-2 One-way selection

Example 4-8

```
if(score >= 90)
   grade = 'A';
```

In this code, if the expression `(score >= 90)` evaluates to `true`, the assignment statement, `grade = 'A';`, executes. If the expression evaluates to `false`, the statements (if any) following the `if` structure execute. For example, if the value of `score` is `95`, the value assigned to the variable `grade` is `A`.

Example 4-9

The following C++ program finds the absolute value of an integer.

```
#include <iostream>
using namespace std;

int main ()
{
   int number;

   cout<<"Please enter an integer--> ";        //Line 1
   cin>>number;                                 //Line 2
   if(number < 0)                               //Line 3
     number = -number;                          //Line 4

   cout<<endl<<"The absolute value is "
       <<number<<endl;                          //Line 5
   return 0;
}
```

Sample Run In this sample run, the user input is shaded.

```
Please enter an integer--> -6734

The absolute value is 6734
```

The statement at Line 1 prompts the user to enter an integer; the statement at Line 2 inputs the number into the variable `number`. The statement at Line 3 checks whether `number` is negative. If `number` is negative, the statement at Line 4 changes `number` to a positive number. The statement at Line 5 outputs `number`, which is the absolute value of the original number.

Example 4-10

Consider the following statement:

```
if score >= 90      //syntax error
      grade = 'A';
```

This statement illustrates an incorrect version of an **if** statement. The parentheses around the logical expression are missing, which is a syntax error.

Putting a semicolon after the parentheses following the **expression** in an **if** statement (that is, before the **statement**) is a semantic error. If the semicolon immediately follows the closing parenthesis, the **if** statement will operate on the empty statement.

Example 4-11

Consider the following C++ statements:

```
if(score >= 90);              //Line 1
      grade = 'A';            //Line 2
```

This statement represents a one-way selection. Because there is a semicolon at the end of the expression (see Line 1), the **if** statement terminates at Line 1, the action of the **if** statement is null, and the statement at Line 2 is not part of the **if** statement at Line 1. Hence the statement at Line 2 executes regardless of how the **if** statement evaluates.

Two-Way Selection

In the previous section, you learned how to implement one-way selections in a program. There are many situations in which you must choose between two alternatives. For example, if a part-time employee works overtime, the paycheck is calculated using the overtime payment formula; otherwise, the paycheck is calculated using the regular formula. This is an example of two-way selection. To choose between two alternatives—that is, to implement two-way selections—C++ provides the **if...else** statement. Two-way selection uses the following syntax:

```
if(expression)
   statement1
else
   statement2
```

Take a moment to examine this syntax. It begins with the reserved word **if**, followed by a logical expression contained within parentheses, followed by a statement, followed by the reserved word **else**, followed by a second statement. Statements 1 and 2 are any valid C++ statements. In a two-way selection, if the value of the **expression** is **true**, **statement1** executes. If the value of the **expression** is **false**, **statement2** executes. Figure 4-3 shows the flow of execution of the **if...else** statement (two-way selection).

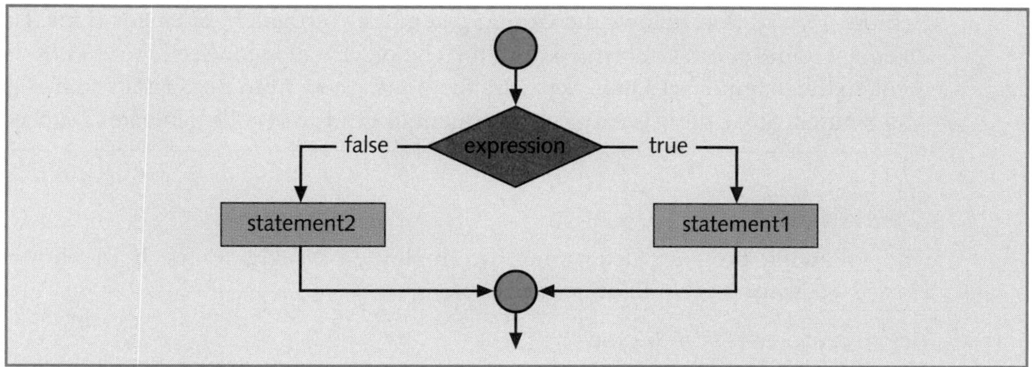

Figure 4-3 Two-way selection

Example 4-12

Consider the following statements:

```
if(hours > 40.0)                                //Line 1
   wages = 40.0 * rate +
           1.5 * rate * (hours - 40.0);         //Line 2
else                                            //Line 3
   wages = hours * rate;                        //Line 4
```

If the value of the variable **hours** is greater than **40.0**, then the **wages** include overtime payment. Suppose that **hours** is **50**. The expression in the **if** statement at Line 1 evaluates to **true**, so the statement at Line 2 executes. On the other hand, if **hours** is **30**, or any number less than or equal to **40**, the expression in the **if** statement at Line 1 evaluates to **false**. In this case, the program skips the statement at Line 2 and executes the statement at Line 4—that is, the statement following the reserved word **else** executes.

In a two-way selection statement, putting a semicolon after the **expression** and before **statement1** creates a syntax error. If the **if** statement ends with a semicolon, **statement1** is no longer part of the **if** statement, and the **else** part of the **if...else** statement stands all by itself. There is no stand-alone **else** statement in C++. That is, it cannot be separated from the **if** statement.

Example 4-13

The following statements show an example of a syntax error:

```
if(hours > 40.0);                               //Line 1
   wages = 40.0 * rate +
            1.5 * rate * (hours - 40.0);        //Line 2
else                                            //Line 3
   wages = hours * rate;                        //Line 4
```

Because a semicolon follows the closing parenthesis of the **if** statement (Line 1), the **else** statement stands alone. The semicolon at the end of **if** statement (see Line 1) ends the **if** statement, so the statement at Line 2 separates the **else** clause from the **if** statement. That is, **else** is all by itself. Since there is no **else** statement in C++, this code generates a syntax error.

Example 4-14

The following program determines an employee's weekly wages. If the **hours** worked exceed **40**, **wages** include overtime payment.

```
//Program: Weekly wages
#include <iostream>
#include <iomanip>
using namespace std;

int main()
{
  double wages, rate, hours;

  cout<<fixed<<showpoint<<setprecision(2);                //Line 1
  cout<<"Line 2: Enter working hours and rate: ";         //Line 2
  cin>>hours>>rate;                                       //Line 3

  if(hours > 40.0)                                        //Line 4
    wages = 40.0 * rate +
            1.5 * rate * (hours - 40.0);                  //Line 5
  else                                                    //Line 6
    wages = hours * rate;                                 //Line 7

  cout<<endl;                                             //Line 8
  cout<<"Line 9: The wages are $"<< wages<<endl;          //Line 9

  return 0;
}
```

Sample Run In this sample run, the user input is shaded.

```
Line 2: Enter working hours and rate: 56.45 12.50

Line 9: The wages are $808.44
```

The statement at Line 1 sets the output of the floating-point numbers in a fixed decimal format, with a decimal point, trailing zeros, and two decimal places. The statement at Line 2 prompts the user to input the number of hours worked and the pay rate. The statement at Line 3 inputs these values into the variables **hours** and **rate**, respectively. The statement at Line 4 checks whether the value of the variable **hours** is greater than **40.0**. If **hours** is greater than **40.0**, then the wages are calculated by the statement at Line 5, which includes overtime payment. Otherwise, the wages are calculated by the statement at Line 7. The statement at Line 9 outputs the wages.

Let us now consider more examples of **if** statements and examine some of the semantic errors that can occur.

Example 4-15

Consider the following statements:

```
if(score >= 90)
      grade = 'A';
      cout<<"The grade is "<<grade<<endl;
```

These statements contain a semantic error. The `if` statement acts on only one statement, which is `grade = 'A';`. The `cout` statement executes regardless of whether `(score >= 90)` is `true` or `false`.

Example 4-16 illustrates another common mistake.

Example 4-16

Consider the following statements:

```
if(score >= 60)
      cout<<"Passing"<<endl;
      cout<<"Failing"<<endl;
```

If the expression `(score >= 60)`evaluates to `false`, the output would be `Failing`. That is, this set of statements performs the same action as an `else` statement. It will execute the second `cout` statement rather than the first. For example, if the value of `score` is `50`, these statements will output the following line:

```
Failing
```

However, if the expression `score >= 60` evaluates to `true`, the program will write both statements, giving a very unsatisfactory result. For example, if the value of `score` is `70`, these statements will output the following lines:

```
Passing

Failing
```

The correct code to print `Passing` or `Failing`, depending on the value of `score`, is

```
if(score >= 60)
      cout<<"Passing"<<endl;
else
      cout<<"Failing"<<endl;
```

4

Compound (Block of) Statements

The `if` and `if...else` structures control only one statement at a time. Suppose, however, that you want to execute more than one statement if the `expression` in an `if` or `if...else` statement evaluates to `true`. To permit more complex statements, C++ provides a structure called a **compound statement** or a **block of statements**. A compound statement takes the following form:

```
{
  statement1
  statement2
      .
      .
      .
  statementn
}
```

That is, a compound statement consists of a sequence of statements enclosed in curly braces, `{` and `}`. In an `if` or `if...else` structure, a compound statement functions as if it were a single statement. Thus, instead of having a simple two-way selection similar to the following code,

```
if(age > 18)
      cout<<"Eligible to vote."<<endl;
else
      cout<<"Not eligible to vote."<<endl;
```

you could include compound statements, similar to the following code:

```
if(age > 18)
{
      cout<<" Eligible to vote."<<endl;
      cout<<" No longer a minor."<<endl;
}
else
{
      cout<<"Not eligible to vote."<<endl;
      cout<<"Still a minor."<<endl;
}
```

The compound statement is very useful and will be used in most of the ensuing structured statements in this chapter.

Multiple Selections: Nested `if`

In the previous sections, you learned how to implement one-way and two-way selections in a program. Some problems require the implementation of more than two alternatives. For example, suppose that if the checking account balance is more than \$50000, the interest rate is 7%; if the balance is between \$25000 and \$49999.99, the interest rate is 5%; if the balance is between $1000 and $24999.99, the interest rate is 3%; otherwise, the interest rate is 0%. This particular problem has four alternatives—that is, multiple selection paths. You can include multiple selection paths in a program by using an **if...else** structure, if the action statement itself is an **if** or **if...else** statement. When one control statement is located within another, it is said to be **nested**.

Assume that all variables are properly declared, and consider the following statements:


```
if(score >= 90)                               //Line 1
   cout<<"The grade is A"<<endl;              //Line 2
else                                          //Line 3
   if(score >= 80)                            //Line 4
      cout<<"The grade is B"<<endl;           //Line 5
   else                                       //Line 6
      if(score >= 70)                         //Line 7
         cout<<"The grade is C"<<endl;        //Line 8
      else                                    //Line 9
         if(score >= 60)                      //Line 10
            cout<<"The grade is D"<<endl;     //Line 11
         else                                 //Line 12
            cout<<"The grade is F"<<endl;     //Line 13
```

These statements illustrate how to incorporate multiple selections using a nested **if...else** structure.

A nested **if...else** structure demands the answer to an important question: How do you know which **else** is paired with which **if**? Recall that in C++ there is no stand-alone **else** statement. Every **else** must be paired with an **if**. The rule to pair an **else** with an **if** is as follows:

Pairing an else with an if: In a nested **if** statement, C++ associates an **else** with the most recent incomplete **if**—that is, the most recent **if** that has not been paired with an **else**.

Using this rule, in the preceding example, the **else** at Line 3 is paired with the **if** at Line 1. The **else** at Line 6 is paired with the **if** at Line 4. The **else** at Line 9 is paired with the **if** at Line 7, and the **else** at Line 12 is paired with the **if** at Line 10.

To avoid excessive indentation, some programmers prefer to write the preceding code as follows:

```
if(score >= 90)
   cout<<"The grade is A"<<endl;
else if(score >= 80)
        cout<<"The grade is B"<<endl;
else if(score >= 70)
        cout<<"The grade is C"<<endl;
else if(score >= 60)
        cout<<"The grade is D"<<endl;
else
        cout<<"The grade is F"<<endl;
```

The following examples will help you to see the various ways in which you can use nested **if** structures to implement multiple selection.

Example 4-17

Assume that all variables are properly declared, and consider the following statements:

```
if(temperature >= 50)                           //Line 1
   if(temperature >= 80)                        //Line 2
      cout<<"Good day for swimming."<<endl;     //Line 3
   else                                         //Line 4
      cout<<"Good day for golfing."<<endl;      //Line 5
else                                            //Line 6
   cout<<"Good day to play tennis."<<endl;      //Line 7
```

In this C++ code, the **else** at Line 4 is paired with the **if** at Line 2, and the **else** at Line 6 is paired with the **if** at Line 1. Note that the **else** at Line 4 cannot be paired with the **if** at Line 1. If you pair the **else** at Line 4 with the **if** at Line 1, the **if** at Line 2 becomes the action statement part of the **if** at Line 1, leaving the **else** at Line 6 dangling. Also, the statements on Lines 2 though 5 form the statement part of the **if** at Line 1.

Example 4-18

Assume that all variables are properly declared, and consider the following statements:

```
if(temperature >= 70)                           //Line 1
   if(temperature >= 80)                        //Line 2
      cout<<"Good day for swimming."<<endl;     //Line 3
   else                                         //Line 4
      cout<<"Good day for golfing."<<endl;      //Line 5
```

In this code, the **else** at Line 4 is paired with the **if** at Line 2. Note that for the **else** at Line 4, the most recent incomplete **if** is the **if** at Line 2. In this code, the **if** at Line 1 has no **else** and is a one-way selection.

Example 4-19

Assume that all variables are properly declared, and consider the following statements:

```
if(GPA >= 2.0)                                      //Line 1
   if(GPA >= 3.9)                                   //Line 2
      cout<<"Dean\'s Honor List."<<endl;            //Line 3
else                                                //Line 4
   cout<<"Current GPA below graduation requirement. "
       <<"\nSee your academic advisor."<<endl;      //Line 5
```

This code is very awkward. Following the rule of pairing an **else** with an **if**, the **else** at Line 4 is paired with the **if** at Line 2. However, this pairing produces a very unsatisfactory result. Suppose that **GPA** is **3.8**. The **expression** in the **if** at Line 1 evaluates to **true**, and the statement part of the **if**, which is an **if...else** structure, executes. Because **GPA** is **3.8**, the **expression** in the **if** at Line 2 evaluates to **false**, and the **else** associated with this **if** executes, producing the following output:

```
Current GPA below graduation requirement.
See your academic advisor.
```


However, a student with a **GPA** of **3.8** would graduate with some type of honor. In fact, the code intended to print the message

```
Current GPA below graduation requirement.
See your academic advisor.
```

only if the **GPA** is less than **2.0**, and the message

```
Dean's Honor List.
```

if the **GPA** is greater than or equal to **3.9**. To achieve that result, the **else** at Line 4 needs to be paired with the **if** at Line 1. To pair the **else** at Line 4 with the **if** at Line 1, you need to use a compound statement as follows:

```
if(GPA >= 2.0)                                              //Line 1
{
   if(GPA >= 3.9)                                           //Line 2
      cout<<"Dean\'s Honor List."<<endl;                    //Line 3
}
else                                                        //Line 4
   cout<<"Current GPA below graduation requirement. "
       <<"\nSee your academic advisor."<<endl;              //Line 5
```

In cases such as this one, the general rule is that you cannot look inside a block (that is, inside the braces) to pair an **else** with an **if**. The **else** at Line 4 cannot be paired with the **if** at Line 2 because the **if** statement at Line 2 is enclosed within braces, and the **else** at Line 4 cannot look inside those braces. Therefore, the **else** at Line 4 is paired with the **if** at Line 1.

Comparing if...else Statements with a Series of if Statements

Consider the following C++ program segments, all of which accomplish the same task.

(a)

```
if(month == 1)                                              //Line 1
   cout<<"January"<<endl;                                   //Line 2
else if(month == 2)                                         //Line 3
        cout<<"February"<<endl;                             //Line 4
else if(month == 3)                                         //Line 5
        cout<<"March"<<endl;                                //Line 6
else if(month == 4)                                         //Line 7
        cout<<"April"<<endl;                                //Line 8
```

```
else if(month == 5)                                       //Line 9
        cout<<"May"<<endl;                                //Line 10
else if(month == 6)                                       //Line 11
        cout<<"June"<<endl;                               //Line 12
```

(b)

```
if(month == 1)
   cout<<"January"<<endl;
if(month == 2)
   cout<<"February"<<endl;
if(month == 3)
   cout<<"March"<<endl;
if(month == 4)
   cout<<"April"<<endl;
if(month == 5)
   cout<<"May"<<endl;
if(month == 6)
   cout<<"June"<<endl;
```

Program segment (a) is written as a sequence of **`if...else`** statements; program segment (b) is written as a series of `if` statements. Both program segments accomplish the same thing. If `month` is `3`, then both program segments output `March`. If `month` is `1`, then in program segment (a), the expression in the `if` statement at Line 1 evaluates to `true`. The statement (at Line 2) associated with this `if` then executes; the rest of the structure, which is the `else` of this `if` statement, is skipped; and the remaining `if` statements are not evaluated. In program segment (b), the computer has to evaluate the expression in each `if` statement because there is no `else` statement. As a consequence, program segment (b) executes more slowly than does program segment (a).

Using Pseudocode to Develop, Test, and Debug a Program

There are several ways to develop a program. One method involves using an informal mixture of C++ and ordinary language, called **pseudocode** or just **pseudo**. Sometimes pseudo provides a useful means to outline and refine a program before putting it into formal C++ code. When you are constructing programs that involve complex nested control structures, pseudo can help you quickly develop the correct structure of the program and avoid making common errors.

One useful program segment determines the larger of two integers. If `x` and `y` are integers, using pseudo you can quickly write the following:

```
a. if (x > y) then
         x is larger
b. if (y > x) then
         y is larger
```

If the statement in (a) is **true**, then **x** is larger. If the statement in (b) is **true**, then **y** is larger. However, for this code to work in concert to determine the larger of two integers, the computer needs to evaluate both expressions,

`(x > y)` and `(y > x)`

even if the first statement is **true**. Evaluating both expressions is a waste of computer time. Let's rewrite this pseudo as follows:


```
if(x > y) then
    x is larger
else
    y is larger
```

Here, only one condition needs to be evaluated. This code looks okay, so let's put it into C++.

```
#include <iostream>
using namespace std;

int main()
{
      if (x > y)
```

Once you begin translating the pseudo into a C++ program, you should immediately notice that there is no place to store the value of **x** or **y**. The variables were not declared, which is a very common oversight, especially for new programmers. If you examine the pseudo, you will see that the program needs three variables, and you might as well make them self-documenting.

```
#include <iostream>
using namespace std;

int main()
{
     int num1, num2, larger;         //Line 1

     if(num1 > num2);                //Line 2; error
         larger = num1;              //Line 3
     else                            //Line 4
         larger = num2;              //Line 5

     return 0;
}
```

Compiling this program will result in the identification of a common syntax error (at Line 2). Recall that a semicolon cannot appear after the **expression** in the **if...else** statement. However, even if you corrected this syntax error, the program still would not give satisfactory results because it tries to use identifiers that have no values. The variables have not been initialized, which is another common error. In addition, because there are no output statements, you would not be able to see the results of the program.

Because there are so many mistakes in the program, you should try a walk-through to see whether it works at all. You should always use a wide range of values in a walk-through to evaluate the program under as many different circumstances as possible. For example, does this program work if one number is zero, if one number is negative and the other number is positive, if both numbers are negative, or if both numbers are the same? Examining the program, you can see that it does not check whether the two numbers are equal. Taking all of these points into account, you can rewrite the program as follows:

```
//Program: Compare Numbers
//This program compares two integers and finds the largest.

#include <iostream>
using namespace std;

int main()
{
   int num1, num2, larger;

   cout<<"Enter any two integers: ";
   cin>>num1>>num2;
   cout<<endl;

   cout<<"The two integers entered are "<<num1
       <<" and "<<num2<<endl;

   if(num1 > num2)
   {
       larger = num1;
       cout<<"The larger number is "<<larger<<endl;
   }
   else if(num2 > num1)
        {
           larger = num2;
           cout<<"The larger number is "<<larger<<endl;
        }
   else
           cout<<"Both numbers are equal."<<endl;
   return 0;
}
```

Sample Run In this sample run, the user input is shaded.

```
Enter any two integers: 78 90
The two integers entered are 78 and 90
The larger number is 90
```

One thing you can learn from the preceding program is that you must first develop a program using paper and pencil. Although a program that is first written on a piece of paper is not guaranteed to run successfully on the first try, this step is still a good starting point. On paper, it is easier to spot errors and improve the program, especially with large programs.

Input Failure and the `if` Statement

In Chapter 3, you saw that an attempt to read invalid data causes the input stream to enter a fail state. Once an input stream enters a fail state, all subsequent input statements associated with that input stream are ignored, and the computer continues to execute the program, which produces erroneous results. You can use `if` statements to check the status of an input stream variable and, if the input stream enters the fail state, include instructions that stop program execution.

In addition to reading invalid data, other events can cause an input stream to enter the fail state. Two additional common causes of input failure are the following:

- Attempting to open an input file that does not exist
- Attempting to read beyond the end of an input file

One way to address these causes of input failure is to check the status of the input stream variable. You can check the status of the input stream variable by using it as the logical expression in an `if` statement. When the input stream variable is used as an expression in an `if` statement, it evaluates to `true` if the last input succeeded and to `false` if the last input failed.

The statement

```
if(cin)
  cout<<"Input is OK."<<endl;
```

prints

```
Input is OK.
```

if the last input from the standard input device succeeded. Similarly, if `infile` is an `ifstream` variable, the statement:

```
if(!infile)
  cout<<"Input failed."<<endl;
```

prints

```
Input failed.
```

if the last input associated with the stream variable `infile` failed.

Suppose an input stream variable tries to open a file for inputting data into a program. If the input file does not exist, you can use the value of the input stream variable, in conjunction with the `return` statement, to terminate the program, as discussed next.

Recall that the last statement included in the function `main` is

```
return 0;
```

This statement returns a value of `0` to the operating system when the program terminates. A value of `0` indicates that the program terminated normally and that no error occurred during program execution. Values of the type `int` other than `0` can also be returned to the operating system via the **return** statement. The return of any value other than 0, however, indicates that something went wrong during program execution.

The **return** statement can appear anywhere in the program. Whenever a **return** statement executes, it immediately exits the function in which it appears. In the case of the function **main**, the program terminates when the **return** statement executes. You can use these properties of the **return** statement to terminate the function **main** whenever the input stream fails. This technique is especially useful when a program tries to open an input file. Consider the following statements:

```
ifstream infile;
infile.open("a:inputdat.dat");   //open inputdat.dat file

if(!infile)
{
   cout<<"Cannot open input file. "
       <<"The program terminates."<<endl;
   return 1;
}
```

Suppose that the file **inputdat.dat** does not exist. The operation to open this file fails, causing the input stream to enter the fail state. As a logical expression, the file stream variable **infile** then evaluates to **false**. Because **infile** evaluates to **false**, the expression **!infile** (in the **if** statement) evaluates to **true**, and the body of the **if** statement executes. The message

```
Cannot open input file. The program terminates.
```

is printed on the screen, and the **return** statement terminates the program by returning a value of 1 to the operating system.

Recall that some systems might require you to pass **ios::nocreate** as a second argument to the open statement so as to cause the open operation to fail if the input file does not exist. In this case, the open statement takes the following form:

```
infile.open("a:inputdat.dat", ios::nocreate);
```

Let's now use the code that responds to input failure by including these features in the Student Grade Programming Example from Chapter 3. Recall that this program calculates the average test score based on data from an input file and then outputs the results to another file. The following programming code is the same as the code from Chapter 3, except that it includes statements to exit the program if the input file does not exist:

```
//Program: Average test score

#include <iostream>
#include <fstream>
#include <iomanip>

using namespace std;
```

```
int main()
{
      ifstream inFile;  //input file stream variable
      ofstream outFile; //output file stream variable

      int test1, test2, test3, test4, test5;
      double average;
      char studentId;

      inFile.open("a:test.txt"); //open input file

      if(!inFile)
      {
         cout<<"Cannot open input file. "
             <<"The program terminates."<<endl;
         return 1;
      }

      outFile.open("a:testavg.out"); //open output file

      outFile<<fixed<<showpoint;
      outFile<<setprecision(2);

      cout<<"Processing data"<<endl;

      inFile>>studentId;

      outFile<<"Student Id: "<<studentId<<endl;

      inFile>>test1>>test2>>test3>>test4>>test5;

      outFile<<"Test scores: "<<setw(4)<<test1
             <<setw(4)<<test2<<setw(4)<<test3
             <<setw(4)<<test4<<setw(4)<<test5<<endl;

      average = static_cast<double>(test1 + test2 +
                          test3 + test4 + test5) / 5.0;

      outFile<<"Average test score: "<<setw(6)
             <<average<<endl;

      inFile.close();
      outFile.close();
      return 0;
}
```

To rewrite this program using Standard C++ style header files, replace the statements:

```
#include <iostream>
#include <fstream>
#include <iomanip>
using namespace std;
```

with

```
#include <iostream.h>
#include <fstream.h>
#include <iomanip.h>
```

Also, you might have to set the manipulators `fixed` and `showpoint` using either the function `setf` or the manipulator `setiosflags`. (See Chapter 3 for further details.)

Confusion Between the Equality Operator (==) and the Assignment Operator (=)

Recall that if the decision-making expression in the `if` statement evaluates to `true`, the `statement` part of the `if` statement executes. In addition, the `expression` is usually a logical expression. However, C++ allows you to use *any* expression that can be evaluated to either `true` or `false` as an `expression` in the `if` statement. Consider the following statement:

```
if(x = 5)
   cout<<"The value is five."<<endl;
```

The `expression`—that is, the decision maker—in the `if` statement is `x = 5`. The expression `x = 5` is called an assignment expression because the operator = appears in the expression and there is no semicolon at the end of this expression.

This expression is evaluated as follows. First, the right side of the operator = is evaluated, which evaluates to `5`. The value `5` is then assigned to `x`. Moreover, the value `5`—that is, the new value of `x`—also becomes the value of the expression in the `if` statement—that is, the value of the assignment expression. Because `5` is nonzero, the expression in the `if` statement evaluates to `true`, so the statement part of the `if` statement outputs: `The value is five.`

No matter how experienced a programmer is, almost everyone makes the mistake of using = in place of == at one time or another. One reason why these two operators are often confused is that most programming languages use = as an equality operator. Thus, experience with other programming languages can create confusion. Another reason why the assignment operator is used instead of the equality operator is not being careful when typing the program.

Despite the fact that an assignment expression can be used as an expression, using the assignment operator in place of the equality operator can cause serious problems in a program. For example, suppose that the discount on a car insurance policy is based on the insured's driving record. A driving record of `1` means that the driver is accident-free and receives a `25%` discount on the policy. The statement

```
if(drivingCode == 1)
   cout<<"The discount on the policy is 25%."<<endl;
```

outputs

```
The discount on the policy is 25%.
```

only if the value of `drivingCode` is `1`. However, the statement

```
if(drivingCode = 1)
   cout<<"The discount on the policy is 25%."<<endl;
```

always outputs

```
The discount on the policy is 25%.
```


because the right side of the assignment expression evaluates to `1`, which is nonzero and so evaluates to `true`. Therefore, the expression in the `if` statement evaluates to `true`, outputting the following line of text: `The discount on the policy is 25%.`. Also, the value `1` is assigned to the variable `drivingCode`. Suppose that before the `if` statement executes, the value of the variable `drivingCode` is `4`. After the `if` statement executes, not only is the output wrong, but the new value also replaces the old driving code.

The appearance of = in place of == resembles a *silent killer*. It is not a syntax error, so the compiler does not warn you of an error. Rather, it is a logical error.

Using = in place of == can cause serious problems, especially if it happens in a looping statement. Chapter 5 discusses looping structures.

The appearance of the equality operator in place of the assignment operator can also cause errors in a program. For example, suppose `x`, `y`, and `z` are `int` variables. The statement

```
x = y + z;
```

assigns the value of the expression `y + z` to `x`. The statement

```
x == y + z;
```

compares the value of the expression `y + z` with the value of `x`; the value of `x` remains the same, however. If somewhere else in the program you are counting on the value of `x` being `y + z`, a logic error will occur, the program output will be incorrect, and you will receive no warning of this situation from the compiler. The compiler provides feedback only about syntax errors, not logic errors. For this reason, you must use extra care when working with the equality operator and the assignment operator.

The Conditional Operator (? :)

The reader can skip this section without any discontinuation.

Certain `if...else` statements can be written in a more concise way by using C++'s conditional operator. The **conditional operator**, written as **?:**, is a **ternary operator**, which means that it takes three arguments. The syntax for using the conditional operator is

```
expression1 ? expression2 : expression3
```

This type of statement is called a **conditional expression**. The conditional expression is evaluated as follows: If `expression1` evaluates to a nonzero integer (that is, to `true`), the result of the conditional expression is `expression2`. Otherwise, the result of the conditional expression is `expression3`.

Consider the following statements:

```
if(a >= b)
   max = a;
else
   max = b;
```

You can use the conditional operator to simplify the writing of this `if...else` statement as follows:

```
max = (a >= b) ? a : b;
```

`switch` STRUCTURES

Recall that there are two selection, or branch, structures in C++. The first selection structure, which is implemented with if and if...else statements, usually requires the evaluation of a (logical) expression. The second selection structure, which does not require the evaluation of a logical expression, is called the switch structure. C++'s switch structure gives the computer the power to choose from among many alternatives.

The general syntax of the `switch` statement is

```
switch(expression)
{
case value1: statements1
             break;
case value2: statements2
             break;
          ...
case valuen: statementsn
             break;
default: statements
}
```

In C++, `switch`, `case`, `break`, and `default` are reserved words. In a `switch` structure, first the `expression` is evaluated. The value of the `expression` is then used to perform the actions specified in the statements that follow the reserved word **case**. Recall that, in a syntax template, shading indicates an optional part of the definition.

Although it need not be, the **expression** is usually an identifier. Whether it is an identifier or an expression, the value of the identifier or the expression can be only integral. The **expression** is sometimes called the **selector**. Its value determines which statement is selected for execution. A particular **case** value should appear only once. One or more statements may follow a **case** label, so you do not need to use braces to turn multiple statements into a single compound statement. The **break** statement may or may not appear after each statement. Figure 4-4 shows the flow of execution of the **switch** statement.

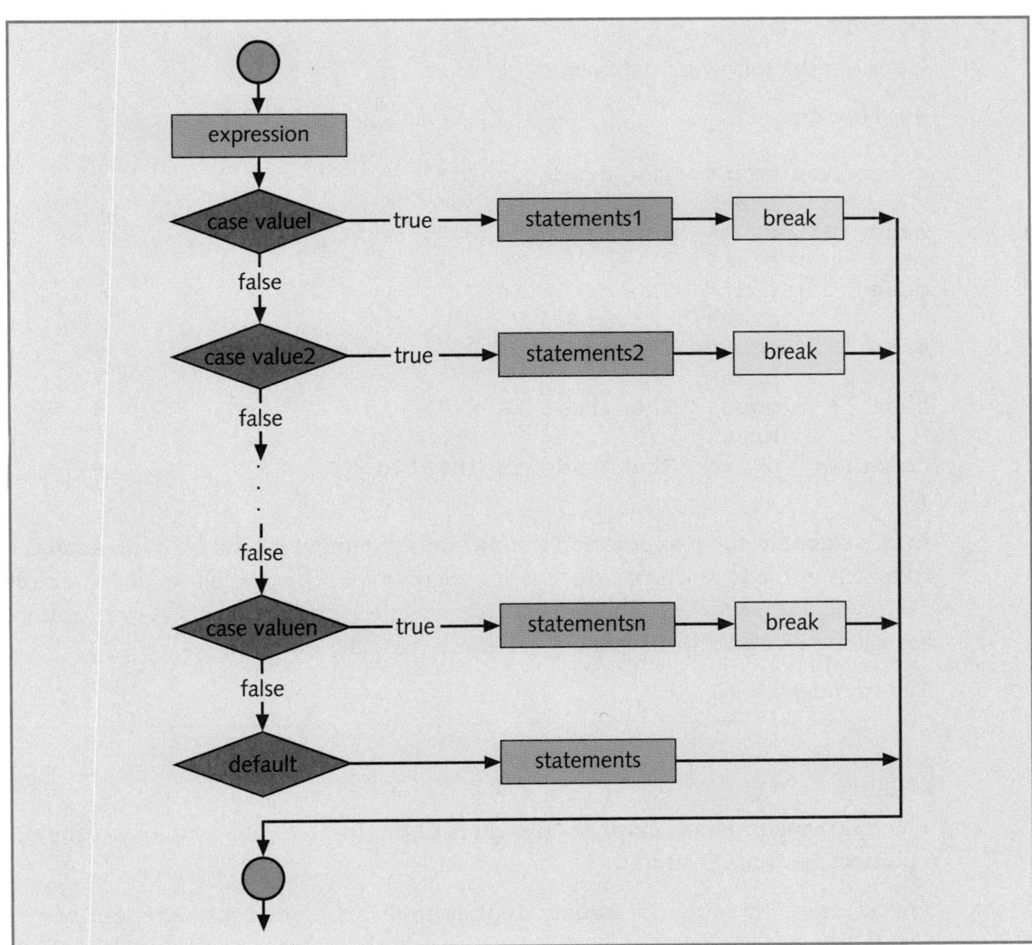

Figure 4-4 switch statement

The **switch** statement executes according to the following rules:

1. When the value of the **expression** is matched against a **case** value (also called a label), the statements execute until either a **break** statement is found or the end of the **switch** structure is reached.
2. If the value of the **expression** does not match any of the **case** values, the statements following the **default** label execute. If the **switch** structure has no **default** label, and if the value of the **expression** does not match any of the **case** values, the entire **switch** statement is skipped.
3. A **break** statement causes an immediate *exit* from the **switch** structure.

Example 4-20

Consider the following statements:

```
switch(grade)
{
case 'A': cout<<"The grade is A.";
          break;
case 'B': cout<<"The grade is B.";
          break;
case 'C': cout<<"The grade is C.";
          break;
case 'D': cout<<"The grade is D.";
          break;
case 'F': cout<<"The grade is F.";
          break;
default:  cout<<"The grade is invalid.";
}
```

In this example, the expression in the **switch** statement is a variable identifier. The variable **grade** is of the type **char**, which is an integral type. The possible values of **grade** are **'A'**, **'B'**, **'C'**, **'D'**, and **'F'**. Each **case** label specifies a different action to take, depending on the value of **grade**. If the value of **grade** is **'A'**, the output is

```
The grade is A.
```

Example 4-21

The following program illustrates the effect of the **break** statement. It asks the user to input a number between 0 and 10.

```
//Program: Effect of break statements in a switch structure
#include <iostream>
using namespace std;
```

```
int main()
{
   int a;

   cout<<"Enter an integer between 0 and 10: ";  //Line 1
   cin>>a;                                        //Line 2

   cout<<"\nThe number you entered is "<<a<<endl;//Line 3

   switch(a)                                      //Line 4
   {
   case 0:                                        //Line 5
   case 1: cout<<"Hello ";                        //Line 6
   case 2: cout<<"there. ";                       //Line 7
   case 3: cout<<"I am ";                         //Line 8
   case 4: cout<<"Mickey."<<endl;                 //Line 9
           break;                                 //Line 10
   case 5: cout<<"How ";                          //Line 11
   case 6:                                        //Line 12
   case 7:                                        //Line 13
   case 8: cout<<"are you?"<<endl;                //Line 14
           break;                                 //Line 15
   case 9: break;                                 //Line 16
   case 10: cout<<"Have a nice day."<<endl;       //Line 17
            break;                                //Line 18
   default: cout<<"Sorry number is out of "
                <<"range."<<endl;                 //Line 19
   }
   cout<<"Out of switch structure."<<endl;        //Line 20

   return 0;
}
```

Sample Runs

These outputs were obtained by executing the preceding program several times. In each of these outputs, the user input is shaded.

Sample Run 1:

```
Enter an integer between 0 and 10: 0

The number you entered is 0
Hello there. I am Mickey.
Out of switch structure.
```

Sample Run 2:

```
Enter an integer between 0 and 10: 1

The number you entered is 1
Hello there. I am Mickey.
Out of switch structure.
```

Sample Run 3:

```
Enter an integer between 0 and 10: 3

The number you entered is 3
I am Mickey.
Out of switch structure.
```

Sample Run 4:

```
Enter an integer between 0 and 10: 4

The number you entered is 4
Mickey.
Out of switch structure.
```

Sample Run 5:

```
Enter an integer between 0 and 10: 5

The number you entered is 5
How are you?
Out of switch structure.
```

Sample Run 6:

```
Enter an integer between 0 and 10: 7

The number you entered is 7
are you?
Out of switch structure.
```

Sample Run 7:

```
Enter an integer between 0 and 10: 9

The number you entered is 9
Out of switch structure.
```

Sample Run 8:

```
Enter an integer between 0 and 10: 10

The number you entered is 10
Have a nice day.
Out of switch structure.
```

Sample Run 9:

```
Enter an integer between 0 and 10: 11

The number you entered is 11
Sorry number is out of range.
Out of switch structure.
```

A walk-through of this program, using certain values of the `switch` expression, `a`, can help you understand how the `break` statement functions. If the value of `a` is `0`, the value of the `switch` expression matches the `case` value `0`. All statements following `case 0:` execute until a `break` statement appears.

The first **break** statement appears at Line 10, just before the **case** value of 5. Even though the value of the **switch** expression does not match any of **case** values (that is, 1, 2, 3, or 4), the statements following these values execute.

When the value of the **switch** expression matches a **case** value, *all* statements execute until a **break** is encountered, and the program skips all **case** labels in between. Similarly, if the value of a is 3, it matches the **case** value of 3 and the statements following this label execute until the **break** statement is encountered at Line 10. If the value of a is 9, it matches the **case** value of 9. In this situation, the action is empty, because only the **break** statement, at Line 16, follows the **case** value of 9.

4

Example 4-22

Although a **switch** structure's **case** values (labels) are limited, the **switch** statement **expression** can be as complex as necessary. For example, consider the following **switch** statement:

```
switch(score / 10)
{
case 0: case 1: case 2:
case 3: case 4: case 5:   grade = 'F';
                          break;
case 6: grade = 'D';
        break;
case 7: grade = 'C';
        break;
case 8: grade = 'B';
        break;
case 9: case 10: grade = 'A';
                 break;
default: cout<<" Invalid test score."<<endl;
}
```

Assume that score is an **int** variable with values between 0 and 100. If score is 75, then score/10 = 75 / 10 = 7 and the grade assigned is 'C'. If the value of score is between 0 and 59, then the grade is 'F'. Now if score is between 0 and 59, score /10 is 0, 1, 2, 3, 4, or 5; each of these values corresponds to the grade 'F'.

Therefore, in this **switch** structure, the action statements of **case** 0, **case** 1, **case** 2, **case** 3, **case** 4, and **case** 5 are all the same. Rather than write the statement grade = 'F'; followed by the **break** statement for each of the **case** values of 0, 1, 2, 3, 4, and 5, you can simplify the programming code by first specifying all of the case values (as shown in the preceding code) and then specifying the desired action statement. The **case** values of 9 and 10 follow similar conventions.

In addition to being a variable identifier or a complex expression, the **switch** expression can evaluate to a logical value. Consider the following statements:

```
switch(age >= 18)
{
case 1: cout<<"Old enough to be drafted."<<endl;
        cout<<"Old enough to vote."<<endl;
        break;
case 0: cout<<"Not old enough to be drafted."<<endl;
        cout<<"Not old enough to vote."<<endl;
}
```

If the value of `age` is `25`, the expression `age >= 18` evaluates to `1`—that is, **true**. If the **expression** evaluates to `1`, the statements following the **case** label `1` execute. If the value of `age` is `14`, the expression `age >= 18` evaluates to `0`—that is, **false**—and the statements following the **case** label `0` execute.

You can use **true** and **false**, instead of `1` and `0`, respectively, in the case labels, and rewrite the preceding **switch** statement as follows:

```
switch(age >= 18)
{
case true:  cout<<"Old enough to be drafted."<<endl;
            cout<<"Old enough to vote."<<endl;
            break;
case false:  cout<<"Not old enough to be drafted."<<endl;
             cout<<"Not old enough to vote."<<endl;
}
```

As you can see from the preceding examples, the **switch** statement is an elegant way to implement multiple selections. You will see the use of a **switch** statement in the programming example at the end of this chapter. Even though no fixed rules exist that can be applied to decide whether to use an **if...else** structure or a **switch** structure to implement multiple selections, the following considerations should be remembered. If multiple selections involve a range of values, you should use either an **if...else** structure or a **switch** structure, wherein you convert each range to a finite set of values.

For instance, in Example 4-22, the value of `grade` depends on the value of `score`. If `score` is between `0` and `59`, `grade` is `'F'`. Because `score` is an **int** variable, 60 values correspond to the grade of `'F'`. If you list all 60 values as **case** values, the **switch** statement could be very long. However, dividing by 10 reduces these 60 values to only 6 values: `0`, `1`, `2`, `3`, `4`, and `5`.

If the range of values consists of infinitely many values and you cannot reduce them to a set containing a finite number of values, you must use the **if...else** structure. For example, if `score` happens to be a **double** variable, the number of values between `0` and `60` is infinite. However, you can use the expression `static_cast<int>(score) / 10` and still reduce these infinitely many values to just six values.

TERMINATING A PROGRAM WITH THE assert FUNCTION

Certain types of errors that are very difficult to catch can occur in a program. For example, division by zero can be difficult to catch using any of the programming techniques you have examined so far. C++ includes a predefined function, **assert**, that is useful in stopping program execution when certain elusive errors occur. In the case of division by zero, you can use the **assert** function to ensure that a program terminates with an appropriate error message indicating the type of error and the program location where the error occurred.

Consider the following statements:

```
int numerator;
int denominator;
int quotient;
double hours;
double rate;
double wages;
char ch;
```

1. `quotient = numerator / denominator;`

2. `if(hours > 0 && ( 0 < rate && rate <= 15.50))`
   `    wages = rate * hours;`

3. `if('A' <= ch && ch <= 'B')`

In the first statement, if the **denominator** is 0, logically you should not perform the division. During execution, however, the computer would try to perform the division. If the **denominator** is 0, the program would terminate with an error message stating that an illegal operation has occurred.

The second statement is designed to compute **wages** only if **hours** is greater than 0 and **rate** is positive and less than or equal to 15.50. The third statement is designed to execute certain statements only if **ch** is an uppercase letter.

For all of these statements (for that matter, in any situation in which certain conditions must be met), if conditions are not met, it would be useful to halt program execution with a message indicating where in the program an error occurred. You could handle these types of situations by including output and return statements in your program. However, C++ provides an effective method to halt a program if required conditions are not met through the **assert** function.

The syntax to use the **assert** function is

```
assert(expression);
```

Here **expression** is any logical expression. If **expression** evaluates to **true**, the next statement executes. If **expression** evaluates to **false**, the program terminates and indicates where in the program the error occurred.

The specification of the **assert** function is found in the header file **cassert**. Therefore, for a program to use the **assert** function, it must include the following statement:

```
#include <cassert>
```

The name of the header file containing the specification of the function **assert** in Standard C++ is **assert.h**.

A statement using the **assert** function is sometimes called an **assert** statement.

Returning to the preceding statements, you can rewrite statement 1 (**quotient = numerator / denominator;**) using the **assert** function. Because **quotient** should be calculated only if **denominator** is nonzero, you include an **assert** statement before the assignment statement as follows:

```
assert(denominator);
quotient = numerator / denominator;
```

Now, if **denominator** is 0, the **assert** statement halts the execution of the program with an error message similar to the following:

```
Assertion failed: denominator, file c:\temp\assert
function\assertfunction.cpp, line 20
```

This error message indicates that the assertion of **denominator** failed. The error message also gives the name of the file containing the source code and the line number where the assertion failed.

You can also rewrite statement 2 using an assertion statement as follows:

```
assert(hours > 0 && (0 < rate && rate <= 15.50));
if(hours > 0 && (0 < rate && rate <= 15.50))
      wages = rate * hours;
```

If the **expression** in the **assert** statement fails, the program terminates with an error message similar to the following:

```
Assertion failed: hours > 0 && (0 < rate && rate <= 15.50), file
c:\temp\assertfunction\assertfunction.cpp, line 26
```

During program development and testing, the **assert** statement is very useful for enforcing programming constraints. As you can see, the **assert** statement not only halts the program, but also identifies the expression where the assertion failed, the name of the file containing the source code, and the line number where the assertion failed.

Although **assert** statements are useful during program development, after a program has been developed and put into use, if an **assert** statement fails for some reason, an end user would have no idea what the error means. Therefore, after you have developed and tested a program, you should remove or disable the **assert** statements. In a very large program, it could be tedious, and perhaps impossible, to remove all of the **assert** statements you used during development. In addition, if you plan to modify a program in the future, you might like to keep the `assert` statements. Therefore, the logical choice is to keep these statements, but to disable them. You can disable `assert` statements by using the following preprocessor directive:

```
#define NDEBUG
```

This preprocessor directive `#define` NDEBUG must be placed *before* the directive `#include <cassert>`.

PROGRAMMING EXAMPLE: CABLE COMPANY BILLING

This programming example demonstrates a program that calculates a customer's bill for a local cable company. There are two types of customers: residential and business. There are two rates for calculating a cable bill: one for residential customers and one for business customers. For residential customers, the following rates apply:

- Bill processing fee: `$4.50`
- Basic service fee: `$20.50`
- Premium channels: `$7.50` per channel.

For business customers, the following rates apply:

- Bill processing fee: `$15.00`
- Basic service fee: `$75.00` for first `10` connections; `$5.00` for each additional connection
- Premium channels: `$50.00` per channel for any number of connections.

The program should ask the user for an account number (an integer) and a customer code. Assume that `R` or `r` stands for a residential customer, and `B` or `b` stands for a business customer.

Input The customer's account number, customer code, number of premium channels to which the user subscribes, and, in the case of business customers, number of basic service connections.

Output Customer's account number and the billing amount.

Problem Analysis and Algorithm Design

The purpose of this program is to calculate and print the billing amount. To calculate the billing amount, you need to know the customer for whom the billing amount is calculated (whether the customer is residential or business) and the number of premium channels to which the customer subscribes. In the case of a business customer, you need to know the number of basic service connections and the number of premium channels. Other data needed to calculate the bill, such as bill processing fees and the cost of a premium channel, are known quantities. The program should print the billing amount to two decimal places, which is standard for monetary amounts. This problem analysis translates into the following algorithm:

1. Set the precision to two decimal places.
2. Prompt the user for the account number and customer type.
3. Determine the number of premium channels and basic service connections, compute the bill, and print the bill based on the customer type:
   a. If the customer type is `R` or `r`,
      (i) Prompt the user for the number of premium channels.
      (ii) Compute the bill.
      (iii) Print the bill.
   b. If the customer type is `B` or `b`,
      (i) Prompt the user for the number of basic service connections and number of premium channels.
      (ii) Compute the bill.
      (iii) Print the bill.

Variables Because the program will ask the user to input the customer account number, customer code, number of premium channels, and number of basic service connections, you need variables to store all of this information. Also, because the program will calculate the billing amount, you need a variable to store the billing amount. Thus, the program needs at least the following variables to compute and print the bill:

```
int    accountNumber;   //variable to store the customer's
                         //account number
char   customerType;     //variable to store the customer code
int    numberOfPremiumChannels; //variable to store the number
                                //of premium channels to which the
                                //customer subscribes
int    numberOfBasicServiceConnections; //variable to store the
                    //number of basic service connections
                   //to which the customer subscribes
double amountDue;   //variable to store the billing amount
```

Named Constants As you can see, the bill processing fees, the cost of a basic service connection, and the cost of a premium channel are fixed, and these values are needed to compute the bill. Although these values are constants in the program, they can change with little warning. To simplify the process of modifying the program later, instead of using these values directly in the program, you should declare them as named constants. Based on the problem analysis, you need to declare the following named constants:

```
      //Named constants – residential customers
const double rBillProcessingFee = 4.50;
```

```
const double rBasicServiceCost = 20.50;
const double rCostOfaPremiumChannel = 7.50;
      //Named constants - business customers
const double bBillProcessingFee = 15.00;
const double bBasicServiceCost = 75.00;
const double bBasicConnectionCost = 5.00;
const double bCostOfaPremiumChannel = 50.00;
```

Formulas The program uses a number of formulas to compute the billing amount. To compute the residential bill, you need to know only the number of premium channels to which the user subscribes. The following statement calculates the billing amount for a residential customer:

```
amountDue = rBilllProcessingFee + rBasicServiceCost +
            numberOfPremiumChannels * rCostOfaPremiumChannel;
```

To compute the business bill, you need to know the number of basic service connections and the number of premium channels to which the user subscribes. If the number of basic service connections is less than or equal to 10, the cost of basic service connections is fixed. If the number of basic service connections exceeds 10, you must add the cost for each connection over 10. The following statement calculates the business billing amount:

```
if(numberOfBasicServiceConnections <= 10)
  amountDue = bBillProcessingFee + bBasicServiceCost +
              numberOfPremiumChannels * bCostOfaPremiumChannel;
else
  amountDue = bBillProcessingFee + bBasicServiceCost +
              (numberOfBasicServiceConnections - 10) *
              bBasicConnectionCost +
              numberOfPremiumChannels * bCostOfaPremiumChannel;
```

Main Algorithm

Based on the preceding discussion, you can now write the main algorithm.

1. To output floating-point numbers in a fixed decimal format with a decimal point and trailing zeros, set the manipulators `fixed` and `showpoint`. Also, to output floating-point numbers with two decimal places, set the precision to two decimal places. Recall that to use these manipulators, the program must include the header file `iomanip`.
2. Prompt the user to enter the account number.
3. Get the customer account number.
4. Prompt the user to enter the customer code.
5. Get the customer code.

6. If the customer code is `r` or `R`,
   a. Prompt the user to enter the number of premium channels.
   b. Get the number of premium channels.
   c. Calculate the billing amount.
   d. Print the account number and the billing amount.
7. If the customer code is `b` or `B`,
   a. Prompt the user to enter the number of basic service connections.
   b. Get the number of basic service connections.
   c. Prompt the user to enter the number of premium channels.
   d. Get the number of premium channels.
   e. Calculate the billing amount.
   f. Print the account number and the billing amount.
8. If the customer code is something other than `r`, `R`, `b`, or `B`, output an error message.

For Steps 6 and 7, the program uses a **`switch`** statement to calculate the bill for the desired customer.

Complete Program Listing

```
#include <iostream>
#include <iomanip>
using namespace std;

      //Named constants – residential customers
const double rBillProcessingFee = 4.50;
const double rBasicServiceCost = 20.50;
const double rCostOfaPremiumChannel = 7.50;

      //Named constants – business customers
const double bBillProcessingFee = 15.00;
const double bBasicServiceCost = 75.00;
const double bBasicConnectionCost = 5.00;
const double bCostOfaPremiumChannel = 50.00;

int main()
{
            //Variable declaration
   int    accountNumber;
   char   customerType;
   int    numberOfPremiumChannels;
   int    noOfBasicServiceConnections;
   double amountDue;
```

```
cout<<fixed<<showpoint;                                 //Step 1
cout<<setprecision(2);                                  //Step 1

cout<<"This program computes a cable bill."<<endl;

cout<<"Enter account number: ";                         //Step 2
cin>>accountNumber;                                     //Step 3
cout<<endl;

cout<<"Enter customer type: R or r (Residential), "
    <<"B or b(Business):  ";                            //Step 4
cin>>customerType;                                      //Step 5
cout<<endl;

switch(customerType)
{
case 'r':                                               //Step 6
case 'R': cout<<"Enter the number"
              <<" of premium channels: ";               //Step 6a
          cin>>numberOfPremiumChannels;                 //Step 6b
          cout<<endl;
          amountDue = rBillProcessingFee +              //Step 6c
                      rBasicServiceCost +
                      numberOfPremiumChannels *
                      rCostOfaPremiumChannel;

          cout<<"Account number = "<<accountNumber
              <<endl;                                   //Step 6d
          cout<<"Amount due = $"<<amountDue
              <<endl;                                   //Step 6d
          break;
case 'b':                                               //Step 7
case 'B': cout<<"Enter the number of basic "
              <<"service connections: ";                //Step 7a
          cin>>noOfBasicServiceConnections;             //Step 7b
          cout<<endl;
          cout<<"Enter the number"
              <<" of premium channels: ";               //Step 7c
          cin>>numberOfPremiumChannels;                 //Step 7d
          cout<<endl;

          if(noOfBasicServiceConnections <= 10)         //Step 7e
               amountDue =  bBillProcessingFee +
                            bBasicServiceCost +
                            numberOfPremiumChannels *
                            bCostOfaPremiumChannel;
          else
```

```
                    amountDue =  bBillProcessingFee +
                                 bBasicServiceCost +
                                 (noOfBasicServiceConnections - 10)
                                 * bBasicConnectionCost +
                                 numberOfPremiumChannels *
                                 bCostOfaPremiumChannel;

               cout<<"Account number = "
                   <<accountNumber<<endl;                  //Step 7f
               cout<<"Amount due = $"<<amountDue
                   <<endl;
               break;
    default: cout<<"Invalid customer type." <<endl;    //Step 8
    }//end switch
    return 0;
}
```

Sample Run In this sample run, the user input is shaded.

```
This program computes a cable bill.
Enter account number: 12345

Enter customer type: R or r (Residential), B or b (Business): b
Enter the number of basic service connections: 16
Enter the number of premium channels: 8

Account number = 12345
Amount due = $520.00
```

Quick Review

1. Control structures alter the normal flow of control.
2. The two most common control structures are selection and repetition.
3. Selection structures incorporate decisions in a program.
4. The relational operators are == (equality), < (less than), <= (less than or equal to), > (greater than), >= (greater than or equal to), and != (not equal to).
5. Including a space between the relational operators ==, <=, >=, and ! = creates a syntax error.
6. Characters are compared using a machine's collating sequence.
7. Logical expressions evaluate to `1` (or a nonzero value) or `0`. The logical value `1` (or any nonzero value) is treated as `true`; the logical value `0` is treated as `false`.
8. In C++, `int` variables can be used to store the value of a logical expression.
9. In C++, `bool` variables can be used to store the value of a logical expression.

10. In C++, the logical operators are `!` (not), `&&` (and), and `||` (or).
11. In C++, there are two selection structures.
12. One-way selection takes the following form:

```
if(expression)
    statement
```

If **expression** is **true**, the **statement** executes; otherwise, the computer executes the statement following the `if` statement.

13. Two-way selection takes the following form:

```
if(expression)
    statement1
else
    statement2
```

If **expression** is **true**, then **statement1** executes; otherwise, **statement2** executes.

14. The expression in an `if` or `if...else` structure is usually a logical expression.
15. Including a semicolon before the **statement** in a one-way selection creates a semantic error. In this case, the action of the `if` statement is empty.
16. Including a semicolon before **statement1** in a two-way selection creates a syntax error.
17. There is no **else** statement in C++. Every **else** has a related `if`.
18. An **else** is paired with the most recent `if` that has not been paired with any other **else**.
19. A sequence of statements enclosed between braces, { and }, is called a compound statement or block of statements. A compound statement is treated as a single statement.
20. You can use the input stream variable in an `if` statement to determine the state of the input stream.
21. Using the assignment operator in place of the equality operator creates a semantic error. It can cause serious errors in the program.
22. The **switch** structure is used to handle multiway selection.
23. The execution of a **break** statement in a **switch** statement immediately exits the **switch** structure.
24. If certain conditions are not met in a program, the program can be terminated using the **assert** function.

EXERCISES

1. Mark the following statements as true or false.
    a. The result of a logical expression cannot be assigned to an `int` variable.
    b. In a one-way selection, if a semicolon is placed after the expression in an `if` statement, the expression in the `if` statement is always **true**.

c. Every `if` statement must have a corresponding `else`.

d. The expression in the `if` statement

```
if(score = 30)
   grade = 'A';
```

always evaluates to `true`.

e. The expression

```
(ch >= 'A' && ch <= 'Z')
```

evaluates to `false` if either `ch < 'A'` or `ch >= 'Z'`.

f. Suppose input is `5`. The output of the code

```
cin>>num;
if(num > 5)
  cout<<num;
  num = 0;
else
  cout<<"Num is zero";
```

is: `Num is zero`

g. The expression in a `switch` statement should evaluate to a value of the simple data type.

h. The expression `!(x > 0)` is `true` only if `x` is a negative number.

i. In C++, both `!` and `!=` are logical operators.

j. The order in which statements execute in a program is called the flow of control.

2. Circle the best answer.

a.
```
if(6 < 2*5)
   cout<<"Hello";
   cout<<" There";
```

outputs the following:

(i) `Hello There` (ii) `Hello` (iii) `Hello`
`There` (iv) `There`

b.
```
if('a' > 'b' || 66 > static_cast<int>('A'))
       cout<<"#*#";
```

outputs the following:

(i) `#*#` (ii) `#`
`*`
`#` (iii) `*` (iv) none of these

c.
```
if(7 <= 7)
    cout<<6-9*2/6;
```

outputs the following:

(i) `-1` (ii) `3` (iii) `3.0` (iv) none of these

d.
```
if(7 < 8)
{
     cout<<"2 4 6 8"<<endl;
     cout<<"1 3 5 7<<endl;
}
```

outputs the following:

(i) `2 4 6 8`
`1 3 5 7` (ii) `1 3 5 7` (iii) none of these

e.
```
if(5 < 3)
    cout<<"*";
else
    if(7 == 8)
       cout<<"&";
else
       cout<<"$";
```

outputs the following:

(i) `*` (ii) `&` (iii) `$` (iv) none of these

3. What is the output of the following C++ code?

```
x = 100;
y = 200;
if(x > 100 && y <= 200)
   cout<<x<<" "<<y<<" "<<x+y<<endl;
else
   cout<<x<<" "<<y<<" "<<2*x-y<<endl;
```

4. Write C++ statements that output `Male` if the gender is `'M'`, `Female` if the gender is `'F'`, and `invalid gender` otherwise.

5. Correct the following code so that it prints the correct message.

```
if(score >= 60)
  cout<<"You pass."<<endl;
else;
  cout<<"You fail."<<endl;
```

6. State whether the following are valid **switch** statements. If not, explain why. Assume that `n` and `digit` are `int` variables.

a.
```
switch(n <= 2)
{
case 0: cout<<"Draw.";
        break;
case 1: cout<<"Win.";
        break;
case 2: cout<<"Lose.";
        break;
}
```

b.
```
switch (digit / 4)
{
case 0, case 1: cout<<"low.";
                break;
case 1, case 2: cout<<"middle.";
          break;
case 3: cout<<"high.";
}
```

c.
```
switch(n % 6)
{
 case 1: case 2: case 3: case 4: case 5: cout<< n;
                                          break;
 case 0: cout<<endl;
         break;
}
```

d.
```
switch (n % 10)
{
case 2: case 4: case 6: case 8: cout<<"Even";
                                break;
case 1: case 3: case 5: case 7: cout<<"Odd";
                                break;
}
```

7. Suppose the input is 5. What is the value of **alpha** after the following C++ code executes?

```
cin>>alpha;
switch(alpha)
{
case 1:
case 2: alpha = alpha + 2;
        break;
case 4: alpha++;
case 5: alpha = 2 * alpha;
case 6: alpha = alpha + 5;
        break;
default: alpha--;
}
```

8. Suppose the input is 3. What is the value of **beta** after the following C++ code executes?

```
cin>>beta;
switch(beta)
{
case 3: beta = beta + 3;
case 1: beta++;  break;
case 5: beta = beta + 5;
case 4: beta = beta + 4;
}
```

9. Suppose the input is 6. What is the value of a after the following C++ code executes?

```
cin>>a;
if(a > 0)
   switch(a)
   {
   case 1: a = a + 3;
   case 3: a++;
           break;
   case 6: a = a + 6;
   case 8: a = a * 8;
           break;
   default: a--;
   }
else
      a = a + 2;
```

10. In the following code, correct any errors that would prevent the program from compiling or running.

```
include <iostream>

main ()
{
        int a,b;
        bool found;
        cout<<"Enter two integers: ;
        cin>>a>>b;

        if  a > a*b  &&  10 < b
              found = 2* a > b;
        else
        {
              found = 2 * a < b;
              if found
                 a = 3;
                 c = 15;
              if b
              {
                    b = 0;
                    a = 1;
              }
}
```

11. The following program contains errors. Correct them so that the program will run and output `w = 21`.

```
#include <iostream>
using namespace std;
const int one = 5
main  ()
{
        int  x, y, w, z;
        z = 9;

        if z > 10
              x = 12;  y = 5,    w = x + y + one;
        else
              x = 12;  y = 4,    w = x + y + one;
        cout<<"w = "<<w;
}
```

PROGRAMMING EXERCISES

1. Write a program that prompts the user to input a number. The program should then output the number and a message saying whether the number is positive, negative, or zero.
2. Write a program that prompts the user to input three numbers. The program should then output the numbers in ascending order.

3. Write a program that prompts the user to input a number between `0` and `35`. If the number is less than or equal to `9`, the program should output the number; otherwise, it should output `A` for `10`, `B` for `11`, `C` for `12`, ..., and `Z` for `35`. (*Hint:* Use the cast operator, `static_cast<char>()`, for numbers `>= 10`.)
4. The cost of an international call from New York to Paris is calculated as follows: Connection fee, \$1.99; \$2.00 for the first three minutes; and \$0.45 for each additional minute. Write a program that prompts the user to enter the number of minutes the call lasted and outputs the amount due. Format your output with two decimal places.
5. In a right triangle, the square of the length of one side is equal to the sum of the squares of the lengths of other two sides. Write a program that prompts the user to enter the lengths of three sides of a triangle and then outputs a message indicating whether the triangle is a right triangle.
6. The roots of the quadratic equation $ax^2 + bx + c = 0, a \neq 0$ are given by the following formula:

$$\frac{-b \pm \sqrt{b^2 - 4ac}}{2a}$$

In this formula, the term $b^2 - 4ac$ is called the discriminant. If $b^2 - 4ac = 0$, then the equation has a single (repeated) root. If $b^2 - 4ac > 0$, the equation has two real roots. If $b^2 - 4ac < 0$, the equation has two complex roots. Write a program that prompts the user to input the value of a (the coefficient of x^2), b (the coefficients of x), and c (the constant term), and outputs the type of roots of the equation. Furthermore, if $b^2 - 4ac \geq 0$, the program should output the roots of the quadratic equation. (*Hint:* Use the function `pow` from the header file `cmath` to calculate the square root. Chapter 3 explains how the function `pow` is used.)

7. Write a program that prompts the user to input the x-y coordinate of a point in a Cartesian plane. The program should then output a message indicating whether the point is the origin, is located on the x (or y) axis, or appears in a particular quadrant. For example:

```
(0,0) is the origin

(4,0) is on the x-axis

(0,-3) is on the y-axis

(-2,3) is in the second quadrant
```

8. Write a program that mimics a calculator. The program should take as input two integers and the operation to be performed. It should then output the numbers, the operator, and the result. (For division, if the denominator is zero, output an appropriate message.) Some sample outputs follow:

```
3 + 4 = 7
13 * 5 = 65
```

9. Redo Exercise 8 to handle floating-point numbers. (Format your output to two decimal places.)

10. A bank in your town updates its customers' accounts at the end of each month. The bank offers two types of accounts: savings and checking. Every customer must maintain a minimum balance. If a customer's balance falls below the minimum balance, there is a service charge of $10.00 for savings accounts and $25.00 for checking accounts. If the balance at the end of the month is at least the minimum balance, the account receives interest as follows:

    a. Savings accounts receive 4% interest.

    b. Checking accounts with balances of up to $5000 more than the minimum balance receive 3% interest; otherwise, the interest is 5%.

    Write a program that reads a customer's account number (**int** type), account type (**char**; **s** for savings, **c** for checking), minimum balance that the account should maintain, and current balance. The program should then output the account number, account type, current balance, and an appropriate message. Test your program by running it five times, using the following data:

```
46728 S 1000 2700
87324 C 1500 7689
79873 S 1000 800
89832 C 2000 3000
98322 C 1000 750
```

11. Write a program that implements the algorithm given in Example 1-2 (Chapter 1), which determines the monthly wages of a salesperson.

12. Write a program that calculates and prints the bill for a cellular telephone company. The company offers two types of service: regular and premium. Its rates vary depending on the type of service. The rates are computed as follows:

    Regular service: $10.00 plus first 50 minutes are free. Charges for over 50 minutes are $0.20 per minute.

    Premium service: $25.00 plus:

    a. For calls made from 6:00 A.M. to 6:00 P.M., the first 75 minutes are free; charges for over 75 minutes are $0.10 per minute

    b. For calls made from 6:00 P.M. to 6:00 A.M., the first 100 minutes are free; charges for over 100 minutes are $0.05 per minute.

    Your program should prompt the user to enter an account number, a service code (type **char**), and the number of minutes the service was used. A service code of **r** or **R** means regular service; a service code of **p** or **P** means premium service. Treat any other character as an error. Your program should output the account number, type of service, number of minutes the telephone service was used, and the amount due from the user.

    For the premium service, the customer may be using the service during the day and the night. Therefore, to calculate the bill, you must ask the user to input the number of minutes the service was used during the day and the number of minutes the service was used during the night.

CHAPTER

5

CONTROL STRUCTURES II (Repetition)

In this chapter, you will:

- Learn about repetition (looping) control structures
- Explore how to construct and use count-controlled, sentinel-controlled, flag-controlled, and EOF-controlled repetition structures
- Examine break and continue statements
- Discover how to form and use nested control structures

In Chapter 4, you saw how decisions are incorporated in programs. In this chapter, you learn how repetitions are incorporated in programs.

WHY IS REPETITION NEEDED?

Suppose you want to add five numbers to find their average. From what you have learned so far, you know that you could proceed as follows. (Assume that all variables are properly declared.)

```
cin>>num1>>num2>>num3>>num4>>num5;   //read five numbers
sum = num1+num2+num3+num4+num5;      //add the numbers
average = sum/5;                     //find the average
```

But suppose you want to add and average 100, or 1000, or more numbers. You would have to declare that many variables, and list them again in **cin** statements and, perhaps, again in the output statements. This takes an exorbitant amount of space and time. Also, if you want to run this program again with different values, or with a different number of values, you have to rewrite the program.

Suppose you want to add the following numbers:

```
5 3 7 9 4
```

Consider the following statements, in which **sum** and **num** are variables of type **int**.

1. `sum = 0;`
2. `cin>>num;`
3. `sum = sum + num;`

The first statement initializes **sum** to `0`. Let us execute statements 2 and 3. Statement 2 stores `5` in **num**; statement 3 updates the value of **sum** by adding **num** to it. After statement 3, the value of **sum** is `5`.

Let us repeat statements 2 and 3. After statement 2 (after the programming code reads the next number),

```
num = 3
```

After statement 3,

```
sum = sum + num = 5 + 3 = 8
```

At this point, **sum** contains the sum of the first two numbers. Let us again repeat statements 2 and 3 (third time). After statement 2 (after the programming code reads the next number),

```
num = 7
```

After statement 3,

```
sum = sum + num = 8 + 7 = 15
```

Now **sum** contains the sum of the first three numbers. If you repeat statements 2 and 3 two more times, **sum** will contain the sum of all five numbers.

If you want to add 10 numbers, you can repeat statements 2 and 3 ten times. And if you want to add 100 numbers, you can repeat statements 2 and 3 one hundred times. In either case, you do not have to declare any additional variables as you did in the first code. You can use this C++ code to add any set of numbers, whereas the earlier code requires you to drastically change the code.

There are many other situations where it is necessary to repeat a set of statements. For example, for each student in a class, the formula for determining the course grade is the same. C++ has three repetition, or looping, structures that let you repeat statements over and over until certain conditions are met. This chapter introduces all three looping (repetition) structures. The next section discusses the first repetition structure, called the `while` loop.

THE while LOOPING (REPETITION) STRUCTURE

In the previous section, you saw that sometimes it is necessary to repeat a set of statements several times. One way to repeat a set of statements is to type the set of statements in the program over and over. For example, if you want to repeat a set of statements 100 times, you type the set of statements 100 times in the program. However, this solution of repeating a set of statements is impractical, if not impossible. Fortunately, there is a better way to repeat a set of statements. As noted earlier, C++ has three repetition, or looping, structures that allow you to repeat a set of statements until certain conditions are met. This section discusses the first looping structure, called a `while` **loop**.

The general form of the `while` statement is

```
while(expression)
    statement
```

In C++, `while` is a reserved word. Of course, the `statement` can be either a simple or compound statement. The `expression` acts as a **decision maker** and is usually a logical expression. The `statement` is called the body of the loop. Note that the parentheses around the `expression` are part of the syntax. Figure 5-1 shows the flow of execution of a `while` loop.

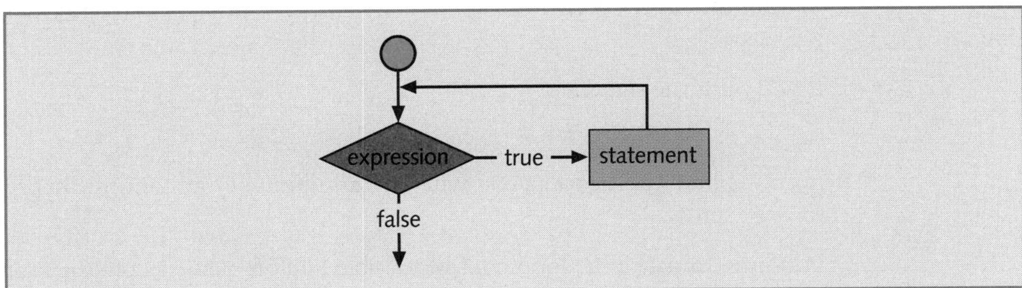

Figure 5-1 `while` loop

The expression provides an entry condition. If it initially evaluates to true, the statement executes. The loop condition—the expression—is then reevaluated. If it again evaluates to true, the statement executes again. The statement (body of the loop) continues to execute until the expression is no longer true. A loop that continues to execute endlessly is called an **infinite loop**. To avoid an infinite loop, make sure that the loop's body contains statement(s) that assure that the exit condition—the expression in the while statement—will eventually be false.

Example 5-1

Consider the following C++ program segment.

```
i = 0;                  //Line 1
while(i <= 20)          //Line 2
{
   cout<<i<<" ";        //Line 3
   i = i + 5;           //Line 4
   }
```

Output:

```
0 5 10 15 20
```

At Line 1, the variable i is set to 0. The expression in the while statement (at Line 2), i <= 20, is evaluated. Since the expression i <= 20 evaluates to true, the body of the while loop executes next. The body of the while loop consists of the statements at Lines 3 and 4. The statement at Line 3 outputs the value of i, which is 0. The statement at Line 4 changes the value of i to 5. After executing the statements at Lines 3 and 4, the expression in the while loop (at Line 2) is evaluated again. Since i is 5, the expression i <= 20 evaluates to true and the body of the while loop executes again. This process of evaluating the expression and executing the body of the while loop continues until the expression, i <= 20 (at Line 2), no longer evaluates to true.

The variable i (Line 2) in the expression is called the **loop control variable**.

Note the following from the preceding example:

a. Within the loop i becomes 25, but is not printed because the entry condition is false.

b. If you omit the statement

   ```
   i = i + 5;
   ```

   from the body of the loop, you will have an infinite loop, continually printing rows of zeros.

c. You must initialize the loop control variable i before you execute the loop. If the statement

   ```
   i = 0;
   ```

   (at Line 1) is omitted, the loop may not execute at all. (Recall that variables in C++ are not automatically initialized.)

d. In the above program segment, if the two statements in the body of the loop are interchanged, it may drastically alter the result. For example, consider the following statements:

```
i = 0;

while(i <= 20)
{
  i = i + 5;
  cout<<i<<" ";
}
```


Here the output is

```
5 10 15 20 25
```

Typically this would be a semantic error because you rarely want a condition to be true for `i <= 20`, and yet produce results for `i > 20`.

Example 5-2

Consider the following C++ program segment:

```
i = 20;                 //Line 1
while(i < 20)           //Line 2
{
   cout<<i<<" ";        //Line 3
   i = i + 5;           //Line 4
}
```

It is easy to overlook the difference between this example and Example 5-1. At Line 1, `i` is set to `20`. Since `i` is `20`, the expression `i < 20` in the **`while`** statement (Line 2) evaluates to **`false`**. Since initially the loop entry condition, `i < 20`, is **`false`**, the body of the **`while`** loop never executes. Hence, no values are output and the value of `i` remains `20`.

When a program needs to be tested again and again on certain data, or if the program will operate on a large amount of data, using the keyboard to enter data is not ideal. In such situations, you can store data on an external device such as a disk and instruct the program to read the data from the device. For simplicity, assume that the data is stored on a disk (floppy or hard) and is free of errors or otherwise not defective. This situation has four cases, as described in the next four sections.

Case 1: Counter-Controlled `while` Loops

Suppose you know exactly how many pieces of data (or entries) need to be read. In this case, the **`while`** loop assumes the form of a **counter-controlled while loop**. Suppose the file has

N data items. You can set up a counter (initialized to 0 before the while statement) to track how many items have been read. Before executing the body of the while statement, the counter is compared with N. If counter < N, the body of the while statement executes. The body of the loop continues to execute until the value of counter >= N. Thus, inside the body of the while statement, the value of the counter increments after it reads a new item. In this case, the while loop might look like the following:

```
counter = 0;
while(counter < N)
{
        .
        .
        .
        counter++;
        .
        .
        .
}
```

The value of N (the number of items in the file) can be determined in any of several ways. The program can prompt you to specify the number of items in the file, and a cin statement can read the value. Alternatively, you can specify the first item in the file as the number of items in the file, so that you need not remember the number of input values (items). This is useful if someone other than the programmer enters the data. Consider the following example.

Example 5-3

Suppose the input is

```
12 8 9 2 3 90 38 56 8 23 89 7 2 8 3 8
```

The first number, 12, specifies the number of values in the data set. Suppose you want to add these numbers and find their average. Note that only 12 values are read; the others are discarded. The complete program is as follows:

```
//Program: AVG1
#include <iostream>
using namespace std;

int  main()
{
      int limit;      //store the number of items
                      //in the list
      int number;     //variable to store the number
      int sum;        //variable to store the sum
      int counter;    //loop control variable
```

```
        cout<<"Line 1: Enter data for processing"
            <<endl;                                //Line 1
        cin>>limit;                                //Line 2

        sum = 0;                                   //Line 3
        counter = 0;                               //Line 4

        while(counter < limit)                     //Line 5
        {
              cin>>number;                         //Line 6
              sum = sum + number;                  //Line 7
              counter++;                           //Line 8
        }

        cout<<"Line 9: The sum of "<<limit
            <<" numbers = "<<sum<<endl;            //Line 9

        if(counter != 0)                           //Line 10
            cout<<"Line 11: The average = "
                <<sum / counter<<endl;             //Line 11
        else                                       //Line 12
            cout<<"Line 13: No input."<<endl;      //Line 13

        return 0;
}
```

Sample Run: In this sample run, the user input is shaded.

```
Line 1: Enter data for processing
12 8 9 2 3 90 38 56 8 23 89 7 2 8 3 8
Line 9: The sum of 12 numbers = 335
Line 11: The average = 27
```

This program works as follows. The statement at Line 1 prompts the user to input data for processing. The statement at Line 2 reads the first item from the input data and stores it in the variable `limit`. The value of `limit` indicates the number of items in the list. The statements at Lines 3 and 4 initialize the variables `sum` and `counter` to `0`. The `while` statement at Line 5 checks the value of `counter` to determine how many items have been read. If `counter` is less than `limit`, the `while` loop proceeds for the next iteration. The statement at Line 6 reads the next number and stores it in the variable `number`. The statement at Line 7 updates the value of `sum` by adding the value of `number` to the previous value, and the statement at Line 8 increments the value of `counter` by 1. The statement at Line 9 outputs the sum of the numbers; the statements at Lines 10–13 output the average.

Note that `sum` is initialized to `zero` at Line 3 in this program. At Line 7, after reading a number at Line 6, the program adds it to the sum of all the numbers scanned before the current number. The first number read will be added to zero (since `sum` is initialized to `zero`), giving the correct sum of the first number. To find the average, divide `sum` by `counter`. If `counter` is `0`, then dividing by zero will terminate the program and you get an error message. Therefore, before dividing `sum` by `counter`, you must check whether or not `counter` is `0`.

Case 2: Sentinel-Controlled `while` Loops

You do not always know how many pieces of data (or entries) need to be read, but you may know that the last entry is a special value, called a **sentinel**. In this case, you read the first item before the `while` statement. If this item does not equal the sentinel, the body of the `while` statement executes. The `while` loop continues to execute as long as the program has not read the sentinel. Such a `while` loop is called a **sentinel-controlled while loop**. In this case a `while` loop might look like the following:

```
cin>>variable;
while(variable != sentinel)
{
      .
      .
      .
      cin>> variable;
      .
      .
      .
}
```

Example 5-4

Suppose you want to read some positive integers and average them, but you do not have a preset number of data items in mind. Suppose the number –`999` marks the end of the data. You can proceed as follows.

```
//Program:  AVG2
#include <iostream>
using namespace std;

const int SENTINEL = -999;

int main()
{
      int number;       //variable to store the number
      int sum = 0;      //variable to store the sum
      int count = 0;    //variable to store the total
```

```
        cout<<"Line 1: Enter numbers ending with "
            <<SENTINEL<<endl;                           //Line 1
        cin>>number;                                    //Line 2
        while(number != SENTINEL)                       //Line 3
        {
            sum = sum + number;                         //Line 4
            count++;                                    //Line 5
            cin>>number;                                //Line 6
        }

        cout<<"Line 7: The sum of "<<count
            <<" numbers is "<<sum<<endl;                //Line 7

        if(count != 0)                                  //Line 8
            cout<<"Line 9: The average is  "
                <<sum / count<<endl;                    //Line 9
        else                                            //Line 10
            cout<<"Line 11: No input."<<endl;           //Line 11

        return 0;
}
```


Sample Run: In this sample run, the user input is shaded.

```
Line 1: Enter numbers ending with -999
34 23 9 45 78 0 77  8 3 5 -999
Line 7: The sum of 10 numbers is 282
Line 9: The average is  28
```

This program works as follows. The statement at Line 1 prompts the user to enter numbers ending with **-999**. The statement at Line 2 reads the first number and stores it in **number**. The **while** statement at Line 3 checks whether **number** is not equal to **SENTINEL**. If **number** is not equal to **SENTINEL**, the body of the **while** loop executes. The statement at Line 4 updates the value of **sum** by adding **number** to it. The statement at Line 5 increments the value of **count** by **1**; the statement at Line 6 reads and stores the next number into **number**. The statements at Lines 4–6 repeat until the program reads the **SENTINEL**. The statement at Line 7 outputs the sum of the numbers, and the statements at Lines 8–10 output the average of the numbers.

To further understand how this program works, do a walk-through of the program using the following data:

```
89 23 64 78 23 09 45 78 34

0 34 87 23 8 3 5 –999
```

Next, consider another example of a sentinel-controlled `while` loop. In this example, the user is prompted to enter the value to be processed. If the user wants to stop the program, he or she can enter the sentinel.

Example 5-5 Telephone Digits

The following program reads the letter codes `A to Z` and prints the corresponding telephone digit. This program uses a sentinel-controlled `while` loop. To stop the program, the user is prompted for the sentinel. This is also an example of a nested control structure, where `if...else`, `switch`, and the `while` loop are nested.

```
//*********************************************************
// Program:  Telephone Digits
// This is an example of a sentinel-controlled loop. This
// program converts uppercase letters to their
// corresponding telephone digits.
//*********************************************************


#include <iostream>
using namespace std;

int main()
{
   char letter;                                          //Line 1

   cout<<"This program converts uppercase "
       <<"letters to their corresponding "
       <<"telephone digits."<<endl;                      //Line 2
   cout<<"To stop the program enter Q or Z."<<endl;      //Line 3
   cout<<"Enter a letter--> ";                           //Line 4
   cin>>letter;                                          //Line 5

   cout<<endl;                                           //Line 6

   while(letter != 'Q' && letter != 'Z' )                //Line 7
   {
      cout<<"The letter you entered is ---> "
          <<letter<<endl;                                //Line 8
      cout<<"The corresponding telephone "
          <<"digit is --> ";                             //Line 9
      if(letter >= 'A' && letter <= 'Z')                 //Line 10
        switch(letter)                                   //Line 11
        {
         case 'A': case 'B': case 'C': cout<<"2\n";      //Line 12
                                       break;            //Line 13
         case 'D': case 'E': case 'F': cout<<"3\n";      //Line 14
                                       break;            //Line 15
         case 'G': case 'H': case 'I': cout<<"4\n";      //Line 16
                                       break;            //Line 17
         case 'J': case 'K': case 'L': cout<<"5\n";      //Line 18
                                       break;            //Line 19
         case 'M': case 'N': case 'O': cout<<"6\n";      //Line 20
                                       break;            //Line 21
```

```
            case 'P': case 'R': case 'S': cout<<"7\n"; //Line 22
                                          break;       //Line 23
            case 'T': case 'U': case 'V': cout<<"8\n"; //Line 24
                                          break;       //Line 25
            case 'W': case 'X': case 'Y': cout<<"9\n"; //Line 26
           }
        else                                           //Line 27
              cout<<"You entered a bad letter."<<endl; //Line 28

        cout<<"\nEnter another uppercase letter to be"
            <<" \nconverted to the corresponding "
            <<"telephone digits."<<endl<<endl;         //Line 29
        cout<<"To stop the program enter Q or Z."
            <<endl<<endl;                              //Line 30
        cout<<"Enter a letter--> ";                    //Line 31
        cin>>letter;                                   //Line 32
        cout<<endl;                                    //Line 33
    }//end while

    return 0;
}
```

Sample Run: In this sample run, the user input is shaded.

```
This program converts uppercase letters to their
corresponding telephone digits.
To stop the program enter Q or Z.
Enter a letter--> A
The letter you entered is ---> A
The corresponding telephone digit is --> 2

Enter another uppercase letter to be
converted to the corresponding telephone digits.

To stop the program enter Q or Z.

Enter a letter--> D
The letter you entered is ---> D
The corresponding telephone digit is --> 3

Enter another uppercase letter to be
converted to the corresponding telephone digits.

To stop the program enter Q or Z.

Enter a letter--> Q
```

This program works as follows. The statements at Lines 2 and 3 tell the user what to do. The statement at Line 4 prompts the user to input a letter, and the statement at Line 5 reads and stores the letter into the variable `letter`. The `while` loop at Line 7 checks that the letter is neither `Q` nor `Z`. If the letter entered by the user is neither `Q` nor `Z`, the body of the `while` loop executes. The statement at Line 8 outputs the letter entered by the user. The **if** statement at Line 10 checks whether the letter entered by the user is uppercase. The statement part of the **if** statement is the **switch** statement (Line 11). If the letter entered by the user is uppercase, the **expression** in the **if** statement (at Line 10) evaluates to **true** and the **switch** statement executes. If the letter entered by the user is not uppercase, the **else** (Line 27) executes. The statements at Lines 12–26 determine the corresponding telephone digit.

Once the current letter is processed, the statements at Lines 29 and 30 again inform the user what to do next. The statement at Line 31 prompts the user to enter a letter; the statement at Line 32 reads and stores the letter into the variable `letter`. (Note that the statement at Line 29 is similar to the statement at Line 2 and that the statements at Lines 30–33 are the same as the statements at Lines 3–6.) After the statement at Line 33 (at the end of the **while** loop) executes, the control goes back to the top of the **while** loop and the same process begins again. When the user enters either `Q` or `Z`, the program terminates.

In the program in Example 5-5, you can write the statements between Lines 10 and 28 using just a **switch** structure. (See Programming Exercise 4 at the end of this chapter.)

Case 3: Flag-Controlled while Loops

A **flag-controlled while loop** uses a Boolean variable to control the loop. Suppose `found` is a Boolean variable. The flag-controlled **while** loop takes the following form:

```
found = false;

while(!found)
{
    .
    .
    .
    if(expression)
       found = true;
    .
    .
    .
}
```

The variable `found`, which is used to control the execution of the **while** loop, is called a flag variable.

Case 4: EOF-Controlled while Loops

If the data file is frequently altered (for example, if data is frequently added or deleted), it's best not to read the data with a sentinel value. Someone might accidentally erase the sentinel value or add data past the sentinel, especially if the programmer and data entry person are different people. Also, the programmer sometimes does not know what the sentinel is. In such situations, you can use an **EOF-(End Of File) controlled while loop**.

Until now, we have used an input stream variable, such as **cin**, and the extraction operator, >>, to read and store data into variables. However, the input stream variable can also return a value after reading data:

1. If the program has reached the end of the input data, the input stream variable returns the logical value **false**.
2. If the program reads any faulty data (such as a **char** value into an **int** variable), the input stream enters into the fail state. Once a stream enters the fail state, any further I/O operations using that stream are considered to be null operations; that is, they have no effect. Unfortunately, the computer does not halt the program or give any error messages. It just continues executing the program, silently ignoring each additional attempt to use that stream. In this case, the input stream variable returns the value **false**.
3. In cases other than (1) and (2), the input stream variable returns the logical value **true**.

5

You can use the value returned by the input stream variable to determine whether the program has reached the end of the input data. Since the input stream variable returns the logical value **true** or **false**, in a **while** loop, it can be considered a logical expression.

The following is an example of an **EOF**-controlled **while** loop.

```
cin>>variable;
while(cin)
{
        .
        .
        .
        cin>>variable;
        .
        .
        .
}
```

The eof Function

In addition to checking the value of an input stream variable, such as **cin**, to determine whether the end of the file has been reached, C++ provides a function that you can use with an input stream variable to determine the end-of-file status. This function is called **eof**. Like the I/O functions—such as **get**, **ignore**, and **peek**, discussed in Chapter 3—the function **eof** is a member of the data type **istream**.

The syntax to use the function **eof** is

```
istreamVar.eof()
```

where **istreamVar** is an input stream variable, such as **cin**.

Suppose you have the declaration

```
ifstream infile;
```

Further suppose that you opened a file using the variable **`infile`**. Consider the expression:

```
infile.eof()
```

This is a logical (Boolean) expression. The value of this expression is **`true`** if the program has read past the end of the input file, **`infile`**; otherwise, the value of this expression is **`false`**.

This method of determining the end-of-file status (that is, using the function **`eof`**) works best if the input is text. The earlier method of determining the end-of-file status works best if the input consists of numeric data.

Suppose you have the declaration

```
ifstream  infile;
char ch;

infile.open("inputDat.dat");
```

The following **`while`** loop continues to execute as long as the program has not reached the end of the file.

```
infile.get(ch);
while(!infile.eof())
{
	cout<<ch;
	infile.get(ch);
}
```

As long as the program has not reached the end of the input file, the expression

```
infile.eof()
```

is **`false`** and so the expression

```
!infile.eof()
```

in the **`while`** statement is **`true`**. When the program reads past the end of the input file, the expression

```
infile.eof()
```

becomes **`true`** and so the expression

```
!infile.eof()
```

in the **`while`** statement becomes **`false`** and the loop terminates.

In the DOS environment, the end-of-file marker is entered using `ctrl+z` (hold the ctrl key and press `z`). In the UNIX environment, the end-of-file marker is entered using `ctr+d` (hold the `ctrl` key and press `d`).

PROGRAMMING EXAMPLE: CHECKING ACCOUNT BALANCE

A local bank in your town is looking for someone to write a program that calculates a customer's checking account balance at the end of each month. The data is stored in a file in the following form:

```
467343 23750.40
W 250.00
D 1200
W 75.00
I 120.74
.
.
.
```

The first line of data shows the account number followed by the account balance at the beginning of the month. Thereafter each line has two entries: the transaction code and the transaction amount. The transaction code `W` or `w` means withdrawal, `D` or `d` means deposit, and `I` or `i` means interest paid by the bank. The program updates the balance after each transaction. During the month, if at any time the balance goes below $1000.00, a $25.00 service fee is charged. The program prints the following information: account number, balance at the beginning of the month, balance at the end of the month, interest paid by the bank, total amount of deposit, number of deposits, total amount of withdrawal, number of withdrawals, and service charge if any.

Input A file consisting of data in the above format.

Output The output is of the following form:

```
Account Number: 467343
Beginning Balance: $23750.40
Ending Balance: $24611.49

Interest Paid: $366.24

Amount Deposited: $2230.50
Number of Deposits: 3

Amount Withdrawn: $1735.65
Number of Withdrawals: 6
```

Problem Analysis and Algorithm Design

The first entry in the input file is the account number and the beginning balance. Therefore the program first reads the account number and the beginning balance. Thereafter, each entry in the file is of the following form:

```
transactionCode transactionAmount
```

To determine the account balance at the end of the month, you need to process each entry that contains the transaction code and transaction amount. Begin with the starting balance and then update the account balance after processing each entry. If the transaction code is `D`, `d`, `I`, or `i`, the transaction amount is added to the account balance. If the transaction code is `W` or `w`, the transaction amount is subtracted from the balance. Since the program also outputs the number of withdrawals and deposits, you need to keep separate counts of withdrawals and deposits. This discussion translates into the following algorithm:

1. Declare the variables.
2. Initialize the variables.
3. Get the account number and beginning balance.
4. Get the transaction code and transaction amount.
5. Analyze the transaction code and update the appropriate variables.
6. Repeat Steps 4 and 5 until there is no more data.
7. Print the result.

Variables The program outputs the account number, beginning balance, balance at the end of the month, interest paid, amount deposited, number of deposits, amount withdrawn, number of withdrawals, and service charge if any. You need variables to store all this information. So far you need the following variables:

```
acctNumber          //variable to store the account number
beginningBalance    //variable to store the beginning balance
accountBalance      //variable to store the account balance at
                    //the end of the month
amountDeposited     //variable to store total amount deposited
numberOfDeposits    //variable to store the number of deposits
amountWithdrawn     //variable to store total amount withdrawn
numberOfWithdrawals //variable to store number of withdrawals
interestPaid        //variable to store interest amount paid
```

Since the program reads the data from a file and the output is stored in a file, the program needs both input and output stream variables. After the first line, the data in each line is the transaction code and the transaction amount; the program needs a variable to store this information.

Whenever the account balance goes below the minimum balance, a service charge for that month is applied. After each withdrawal, you need to check the account balance. If the balance goes below the minimum after a withdrawal, a service charge is applied. You can potentially have several withdrawals in a month; once the account balance goes below the minimum, a subsequent deposit might bring the balance above the minimum, and another withdrawal might again reduce it below the minimum. However, the service charge is applied only once.

To implement this idea, the program uses a Boolean variable, `isServiceCharged`, which is initialized to `false` and set to `true` whenever the account balance goes below the minimum. Before applying a service charge, the program checks the value of the variable `isServiceCharged`. If the account balance is less than the minimum and `isServiceCharged` is `false`, a service charge is applied. The program needs the following variables:

```
int      acctNumber;
double   beginningBalance;
double   accountBalance;

double   amountDeposited;
int      numberOfDeposits;

double   amountWithdrawn;
int      numberOfWithdrawals;

double   interestPaid;

char     transactionCode;
double   transactionAmount;

bool     isServiceCharged;

ifstream infile;   //input file stream variable
ofstream outfile;  //output file stream variable
```

Named Constants Since the minimum account balance and the service charge amount are fixed, the program uses two named constants to store them:

```
const double minimumBalance = 1000.00;
const double serviceCharge = 25.00;
```

Problem Analysis and Algorithm Design (continued)

Since this program is more complex than previous ones, before writing the main algorithm, the above seven steps are described more fully here.

1. **Declare the variables.** Declare variables as discussed previously.
2. **Initialize the variables.** After each deposit, the total amount deposited is updated and the number of deposits is incremented by `1`. Before the first deposit, the total amount deposited is `0`, and the number of withdrawals is `0`. Therefore, the variables `amountDeposited` and `numberOfDeposits` must be initialized to `0`.

Similarly, the variables `amountWithdrawn`, `numberOfWithdrawals`, and `interestPaid` must be initialized to `0`. Also, as discussed previously, the variable `isServicedCharged` is initialized to `false`. Of course, you can initialize these variables when you declare them.

Before the first deposit, withdrawal, or interest paid, the account balance is the same as the beginning balance. Therefore, after reading the beginning balance in the variable `beginningBalance` from the file, you need to initialize the variable `accountBalance` to the value of the variable `beginningBalance`.

Since the data will be read from a file, you need to open the input file. If the input file does not exist, output an appropriate message and terminate the program. Since the output will be stored in a file, you need to open the output file. Suppose the input data is in the file `Ch5_money.txt` on a floppy disk in drive A:. Also suppose that the output will be stored in the file `Ch5_money.out` on a floppy disk in drive A:. The following code opens the files:

```
infile.open("a:Ch5_money.txt"); //open the input file

if(!infile)
{
   cout<<"Cannot open input file"<<endl;
   cout<<"Program terminates!!!"<<endl;
   return 1;
}

outfile.open("a:Ch5_money.out"); //open the output file
```

3. **Get the account number and starting balance.** This is accomplished by the following input statement:

```
infile>>acctNumber>>beginningBalance;
```

4. **Get the transaction code and transaction amount.** This is accomplished by the following input statement:

```
infile>>transactionCode>>transactionAmount;
```

5. **Analyze the transaction code and update the appropriate variables.** If the `transactionCode` is `'D'` or `'d'`, update `accountBalance` by adding `transactionAmount`, update `amountDeposited` by adding `transactionAmount`, and increment `numberOfDeposits`. If the `transactionCode` is `'I'` or `'i'`, update `accountBalance` by adding `transactionAmount` and update `interestPaid` by adding `transactionAmount`. If the `transactionCode` is `'W'` or `'w'`, update `accountBalance` by subtracting `transactionAmount`, update `amountWithdrawn` by adding `transactionAmount`, increment `numberOfWithdrawals`, and if the account balance is below the minimum and service charges have not been applied, subtract the service charge from the

account balance and mark the service charges as having been applied. The following switch statement accomplishes this task.

```
switch(transactionCode)
{
case 'D':
case 'd': accountBalance = accountBalance
                           + transactionAmount;
          amountDeposited = amountDeposited
                            + transactionAmount;
          numberOfDeposits++;
          break;
case 'I':
case 'i': accountBalance = accountBalance
                           + transactionAmount;
          interestPaid = interestPaid
                         + transactionAmount;
          break;
case 'W':
case 'w': accountBalance = accountBalance
                           - transactionAmount;
          amountWithdrawn = amountWithdrawn
                            + transactionAmount;
          numberOfWithdrawals++;

          if((accountBalance < minimumBalance)
                           && (!isServiceCharged))
          {
            accountBalance = accountBalance
                             - serviceCharge;
            isServiceCharged = true;
          }
          break;

default: cout<<"Invalid transaction code"<<endl;
} //end switch
```

6. **Repeat Steps 4 and 5 until there is no more data.** Since the number of entries in the input file is not known, the program needs an EOF-controlled `while` loop.
7. **Print the result.** This is accomplished by using output statements.

Pursuant to the above discussion, following is the main algorithm.

Main Algorithm

1. Declare and initialize the variables.
2. Open the input file.

3. If the input file does not exist, exit the program.
4. Open the output file.
5. To output floating-point numbers in a fixed decimal format with the decimal point and trailing zero, set the manipulators **`fixed`** and **`showpoint`**. To output floating-point numbers to two decimal places, set the precision to two decimal places.
6. Read `accountNumber` and `beginningBalance`.
7. Set `accountBalance` to `beginningBalance`.
8. Read `transactionCode` and `transactionAmount`.
9. While (not end of input file)
   a. If `transactionCode is 'D'`
      i. Add `transactionAmount` to `accountBalance`
      ii. Increment `numberOfDeposits`
   b. If `transactionCode is 'I'`
      i. Add `transactionAmount` to `accountBalance`
      ii. Add `transactionAmount` to `interestPaid`
   c. If `transactionCode is 'W'`
      i. Subtract `transactionAmount` from `accountBalance`
      ii. Increment `numberOfWithDrawals`
      iii. If `(accountBalance < minimumBalance && !isServicedCharged)`
         1. Subtract `serviceCharge` from `accountBalance`
         2. Set `isServiceCharged` to `true`
   d. If `transactionCode` is other than `'D'`, `'d'`, `'I'`, `'i'`, `'W'`, or `'w'`, output an error message.
10. Output the results.

Since the data will be read from an input file, you must include the header file **`fstream`**. Since you will use the manipulator **`setprecision`**, you must also include the header file **`iomanip`**. If the input file does not exist, an appropriate message on the screen will be displayed, so the header file **`iostream`** is also included.

Complete Program Listing

```
//*********************************************************
// Program -- Checking Account Balance
// This program calculates a customer's checking account
// balance at the end of the month.
//*********************************************************
```

```
#include <iostream>
#include <fstream>
#include <iomanip>

using namespace std;

const double minimumBalance = 1000.00;
const double serviceCharge = 25.00;

int main()
{
      //Declare and initialize variables          //Step 1
   int acctNumber;
   double beginningBalance;
   double accountBalance;

   double amountDeposited = 0.0;
   int numberOfDeposits = 0;

   double amountWithdrawn = 0.0;
   int numberOfWithdrawals = 0;

   double interestPaid = 0.0;

   char transactionCode;
   double transactionAmount;

   bool isServiceCharged = false;

   ifstream infile;
   ofstream outfile;

   infile.open("a:Ch5_money.txt");                 //Step 2

   if(!infile)                                     //Step 3
   {
       cout<<"Cannot open input file"<<endl;
       cout<<"Program terminates!!!"<<endl;
       return 1;
   }

   outfile.open("a:Ch5_money.out");                //Step 4

   outfile<<fixed<<showpoint;                      //Step 5
   outfile<<setprecision(2);                       //Step 5

   cout<<"Processing data"<<endl;
```

```
infile>>acctNumber>>beginningBalance;          //Step 6

accountBalance = beginningBalance;             //Step 7

infile>>transactionCode>>transactionAmount;    //Step 8

while(infile)                                  //Step 9
{
    switch(transactionCode)
    {
    case 'D':                                  //Step 9.a
    case 'd': accountBalance = accountBalance
                                + transactionAmount;
              amountDeposited = amountDeposited
                                 + transactionAmount;
              numberOfDeposits++;
              break;
    case 'I':                                  //Step 9.b
    case 'i': accountBalance = accountBalance
                                + transactionAmount;
              interestPaid = interestPaid
                              + transactionAmount;
              break;
    case 'W':                                  //Step 9.c
    case 'w': accountBalance = accountBalance
                                - transactionAmount;
              amountWithdrawn = amountWithdrawn
                                 + transactionAmount;
              numberOfWithdrawals++;

              if((accountBalance < minimumBalance)
                              && (!isServiceCharged))
              {
                accountBalance = accountBalance
                                  - serviceCharge;
                isServiceCharged = true;
              }
              break;

    default: cout<<"Invalid transaction code"<<endl;
    } //end switch

    infile>> transactionCode>>transactionAmount;
}//end while

          //Output Results                      //Step 10
outfile<<"Account Number: "<<acctNumber<<endl;
outfile<<"Beginning Balance: $"<<beginningBalance<<endl;
```

```
  outfile<<"Ending Balance: $"<<accountBalance
         <<endl<<endl;
  outfile<<"Interest Paid: $"<<interestPaid<<endl<<endl;
  outfile<<"Amount Deposited: $"<<amountDeposited<<endl;
  outfile<<"Number of Deposits: "<<numberOfDeposits
         <<endl<<endl;
  outfile<<"Amount Withdrawn: $"<<amountWithdrawn<<endl;
  outfile<<"Number of Withdrawals: "<<numberOfWithdrawals
         <<endl<<endl;

  if(isServiceCharged)
      outfile<<"Service Charge: $"<<serviceCharge<<endl;

  return 0;
}
```

Sample Run: (Contents of the output file `A:Ch5_money.out`)

```
Account Number: 467343
Beginning Balance: $23750.40
Ending Balance: $24611.49

Interest Paid: $366.24

Amount Deposited: $2230.50
Number of Deposits: 3

Amount Withdrawn: $1735.65
Number of Withdrawals: 6
```

Input File: (`A:Ch5_money.txt`)

```
467343 23750.40
W 250.00
D 1200.00
W 75.00
I 120.74
W 375.00
D 580.00
I 245.50
W 400.00
W 600.00
D 450.50
W 35.65
```

NOTE To write this program using Standard C++ style header files, replace the statements

```
#include <iostream>
#include <fstream>
#include <iomanip>
using namespace std;
```

with

```
#include <iostream.h>
#include <fstream.h>
#include <iomanip.h>
```

You also might have to replace the statement

```
outp<<fixed<<showpoint;
```

with

```
outp.setf(ios::fixed, ios::floatfield);
outp.setf(ios::showpoint);
```

Programming Example: Fibonacci Number

So far, you have seen several examples of loops. A `while` loop is used mainly to read data, although it has other uses. In C++, `while` loops are used when certain statement(s) need to be executed repeatedly until certain conditions are met. Following is a program that uses a `while` loop to find a **Fibonacci number**.

Consider the following sequence of numbers:

1, 1, 2, 3, 5, 8, 13, 21, 34, ...

Given the first two numbers of the sequence (say a_1 and a_2), the nth number a_n , n >= 3, of this sequence is given by

$$a_n = a_{n-1} + a_{n-2}$$

Thus

$$\begin{aligned} a_3 &= a_2 + a_1 \\ &= 1 + 1 \\ &= 2, \\ a_4 &= a_3 + a_2 \\ &= 1 + 2 \\ &= 3, \end{aligned}$$

and so on.

Such a sequence is called a **Fibonacci sequence**. In the preceding sequence, $a_2 = 1$ and $a_1 = 1$. However, given any first two numbers, using this process, you can determine the nth number, a_n, n >= 3, of the sequence. The number determined this way is called the **nth Fibonacci number**. Suppose $a_2 = 6$ and $a_1 = 3$.

Then

$a_3 = a_2 + a_1 = 6 + 3 = 9$; $a_4 = a_3 + a_2 = 9 + 6 = 15$.

Next, we write a program that determines the nth Fibonacci number given the first two numbers.

Input The first two Fibonacci numbers and the desired Fibonacci number.

Output The nth Fibonacci number.

Problem Analysis and Algorithm Design

To find a_{10}, the tenth Fibonacci number of a sequence, you must first find a_9 and a_8, which requires you to find a_7 and a_6 and so on. Therefore, to find a_{10}, you must first find $a_3, a_4, a_5, \ldots, a_9$. This discussion translates into the following algorithm:

1. Get the first two Fibonacci numbers.
2. Get the desired Fibonacci number. That is, get the position, n, of the Fibonacci number in the sequence.
3. Calculate the next Fibonacci number by adding the previous two elements of the Fibonacci sequence.
4. Repeat Step 2 until the nth Fibonacci number is found.
5. Output the nth Fibonacci number.

Variables Since the last two numbers must be known in order to find the current Fibonacci number, you need the following variables: two variables—say, `previous1` and `previous2`—to hold the previous two numbers of the Fibonacci sequence; and one variable—say, `current`—to hold the current Fibonacci number. The number of times that Step 2 of the algorithm repeats depends on the position of the Fibonacci number you are calculating. For example, if you want to calculate the 10th Fibonacci number, you must execute Step 3 eight times. (Remember—the user gives the first two numbers of the Fibonacci sequence.) Therefore, you need a variable to store the number of times that Step 3 should execute. You also need a variable to track the number of times that Step 3 has executed the loop control variable. You therefore need five variables for the data manipulation:

```
int previous1;      //variable to store the first
                    //Fibonacci number
int previous2,      //variable to store the second
                    //Fibonacci number
int current;        //variable to store the current
                    //Fibonacci number
int counter;        //loop control variable
int nthFibonacci;   //variable to store the desired
                    //Fibonacci number
```

To calculate the third Fibonacci number, add the values of `previous1` and `previous2` and store the result in `current`. To calculate the fourth Fibonacci number, add the value of the second Fibonacci number (that is, `previous2`) and the value of the third Fibonacci number (that is, `current`). Thus, when the fourth Fibonacci number is calculated, you no longer need the first Fibonacci number. Instead of declaring additional variables, which could be too many, after calculating a Fibonacci number to determine the next Fibonacci number, `current` becomes `previous2` and `previous2` becomes `previous1`. Therefore, you can again use the variable `current` to store the next Fibonacci number. This process is repeated until the desired Fibonacci number is calculated. Initially, `previous1` and `prevous2` are the first two elements of the sequence, supplied by the user. From the preceding discussion, it follows that you need five variables.

Main Algorithm

1. Prompt the user for the first two numbers—that is, `previous1` and `previous2`.
2. Read (input) the first two numbers into `previous1` and `previous2`.
3. Output the first two Fibonacci numbers. (Echo input.)
4. Prompt the user for the desired Fibonacci number.
5. Read the desired Fibonacci number into `nthFibonacci`.
6. Since you already know the first two Fibonacci numbers of the sequence, start by determining the third Fibonacci number. Initialize `counter` to `3`, so as to keep track of the calculated Fibonacci numbers.
7. Calculate the next Fibonacci number, as follows.

   ```
   current = previous2 + previous1;
   ```
8. Assign the value of `previous2` to `previous1`.
9. Assign the value of `current` to `previous2`.
10. Increment counter.
11. Repeat Steps 7–10 until the Fibonacci number you want is calculated.

    The following `while` loop executes Steps 7–10 and determines the `nthFibonacci` number.

    ```
    while(counter <= nthFibonacci)
    {
        current = previous2 + previous1;
        previous1 = previous2;
        previous2 = current;
        counter++;
    }
    ```
12. Output the `nthFibonacci` number, which is `current`.

Complete Program Listing

```
//Program: nth Fibonacci number

#include <iostream>
using namespace std;

int main()
{
        //Declare variables
    int previous1;
    int previous2;
    int current;
    int counter;
    int nthFibonacci;

    cout<<"Enter the first two Fibonacci "
        <<"numbers -> ";                            //Step 1
    cin>>previous1>>previous2;                      //Step 2
    cout<<"\nThe first two Fibonacci numbers "
        <<"are "<<previous1<<" and "<<previous2;    //Step 3
    cout<<"\nEnter the desired Fibonacci "
        <<"number to be determined ->";             //Step 4
    cin>>nthFibonacci;                              //Step 5

    counter = 3;                                    //Step 6

            //Steps 7-10
    while(counter <= nthFibonacci)
    {
        current = previous2 + previous1;            //Step 8
        previous1 = previous2;                      //Step 8
        previous2 = current;                        //Step 9
        counter++;                                  //Step 10
    }

    cout<<"\n\nThe "<<nthFibonacci
        <<"th Fibonacci number is: "<<current
        <<endl;                                      //Step 12

    return 0;
}//end main
```

Sample Runs: In these sample runs, the user input is shaded. (This program was executed three times.)

Sample Run 1:

```
Enter the first two Fibonacci numbers -> 12 16
The first two Fibonacci numbers are 12 and 16
Enter the desired Fibonacci number to be determined -> 10

The 10th Fibonacci number is 796.
```

Sample Run 2:

```
Enter the first two Fibonacci numbers -> 1 1
The first two Fibonacci numbers are 1 and 1
Enter the desired Fibonacci number to be determined -> 15

The 15th Fibonacci number is 610.
```

Sample Run 3:

```
Enter the first two Fibonacci numbers -> 20 25
The first two Fibonacci numbers are 20 and 25
Enter the desired Fibonacci number to be determined -> 10

The 10th Fibonacci number is 1270.
```

THE `for` LOOPING (REPETITION) STRUCTURE

The `while` loop discussed in the previous section is general enough to implement most forms of repetitions. The C++ `for` looping structure discussed here is a specialized form of the `while` loop. Its primary purpose is to simplify the writing of count-controlled loops. For this reason, the `for` loop is typically called a **counted** or **indexed** `for` loop.

The general form of the `for` statement is

```
for(initial statement; loop condition; update statement)
   statement
```

The `initial statement`, `loop condition`, and `update statement` (called `for` loop **control statements**) enclosed within the parentheses control the body (`statement`) of the `for` statement. Figure 5-2 shows the flow of execution of a `for` loop.

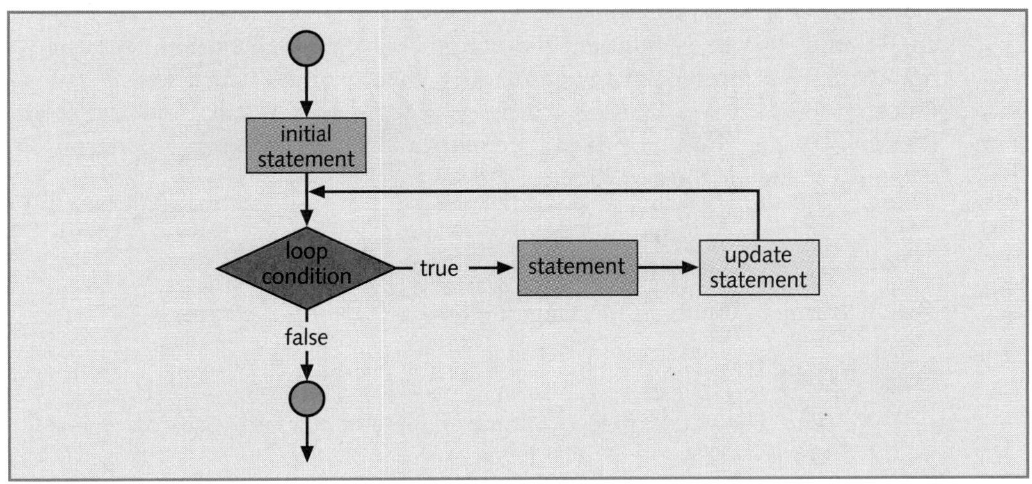

Figure 5-2 for loop

5

The for loop executes as follows:

1. The **initial statement** executes.
2. The **loop condition** is evaluated. If the **loop condition** evaluates to true
   i. Execute the for loop **statement**.
   ii. Execute the **update statement** (the third expression in the parentheses).
3. Repeat Step 2 until the **loop condition** evaluates to false.

The **initial statement** usually initializes a variable (called the for loop control, or indexed, variable).

In C++, for is a reserved word.

As the name implies, the initial statement in the for loop is the first statement to execute; it executes only once.

Example 5-6

The following for loop prints the first 10 positive integers:

```
for(i = 1; i <= 10; i++)
    cout<<i<<" ";
```

The `initial statement`, `i = 1;`, initializes the `int` variable `i` to `1`. Next, the loop condition, `i <= 10`, is evaluated. Since `1 <= 10` is `true`, the print statement executes and outputs `1`. The `update statement`, `i++`, then executes which sets the value of `i` to `2`. Once again, the `loop condition` is evaluated, which is still `true` and so on. When `i` becomes `11`, the `loop condition` evaluates to `false`, the `for` loop terminates, and the statement following the `for` loop executes.

A `for` loop can have either a simple or compound statement.

The following examples further illustrate how a `for` loop executes.

Example 5-7

1. The following `for` loop outputs the line of text and a star (on separate lines) five times:

```
for(i = 1; i <= 5; i++)
{
   cout<<"Output a line of stars."<<endl;
   cout<<"*"<<endl;
}
```

2. Consider the following `for` loop:

```
for(i = 1; i <= 5; i++)
   cout<<"Output a line of stars."<<endl;
   cout<<"*"<<endl;
```

   This loop outputs the line of text five times and the star only once. Note that the `for` loop controls only the first `cout` statement because the two `cout` statements are not made into a compound statement. Therefore, the first `cout` statement executes five times because the `for` loop executes five times. After the `for` loop executes, the second `cout` statement executes only once.

3. The following `for` loop executes five empty statements:

```
for(i = 1; i <= 5; i++);   //Line 1
   cout<<"*"<<endl;        //Line 2
```

   The semicolon at the end of the `for` statement (before the `cout` statement, Line 1) terminates the `for` loop. The action of this `for` loop is empty.

The preceding examples show that care is required in getting a `for` loop to perform the desired action.

The following are some comments on `for` loops:

- If the loop condition is initially `false`, the loop body does not execute.
- The update expression, when executed, changes the value of the loop control variable (initialized by the initial expression), which eventually sets the value of the

loop condition to **false**. The **for** loop executes indefinitely if the loop condition is always **true**.

- C++ allows you to use fractional values for loop control variables of the **double** type (or any real data type). Because different computers can give these loop control variables different results, you should avoid using such variables.
- A semicolon at the end of the **for** statement (just before the body of the loop) is a semantic error. In this case, the action of the **for** loop is empty.
- In the **for** statement, if the `loop condition` is omitted, it is assumed to be **true**.
- In a **for** statement, you can omit all three statements—`initial statement`, `loop condition`, and `update statement`. The following is a legal **for** loop:

```
for(;;)
   cout<<"Hello"<<endl;
```


Following are more examples of **for** loops.

Example 5-8

1. You can count backward using a **for** loop if the **for** loop control expressions are set correctly. For example, consider the following **for** loop:

   ```
   for(i = 10; i >= 1; i--)
      cout<<" "<<i;
   ```

   The output is

   ```
   10 9 8 7 6 5 4 3 2 1
   ```

   In this **for** loop, the variable `i` is initialized to `10`. After each iteration of the loop, `i` is decremented by 1. The loop continues to execute as long as `i >= 1`.

2. You can increment (or decrement) the loop control variable by any fixed number. In the following **for** loop, the variable is initialized to `1`; at the end of the **for** loop, `i` is incremented by `2`. This **for** loop outputs the first `10` positive odd integers.

   ```
   for(i = 1; i <= 20; i = i + 2)
      cout<<"  "<<i;
   ```

Example 5-9

Consider the following examples, where `i` is an int variable.

1. ```
   for(i = 10; i <= 9; i++)
      cout<<i<<" ";
   ```
   ```

In this `for` loop, the initial statement sets `i` to `10`. Since initially the loop condition (`i <= 9`) is `false`, nothing happens.

2. ```
   for(i = 9; i >= 10; i--)
       cout<<i<<" ";
   ```

   In this `for` loop, the initial statement sets `i` to `9`. Since initially the loop condition `(i >= 10)` is `false`, nothing happens.

3. ```
   for(i = 10; i <= 10; i++)
       cout<<i<<" ";
   ```

   In this `for` loop, the `cout` statement executes once.

4. ```
   for(i = 1; i <= 10; i++);
       cout<<i<<" ";
   ```

   This `for` loop has no effect on the `cout` statement. The semicolon at the end of the `for` statement terminates the `for` loop; the action of the `for` loop is thus empty. The `cout` statement is all by itself and executes only once.

5. ```
   for(i = 1; ; i++)
       cout<<i<<" ";
   ```

   In this `for` loop, since the `loop condition` is omitted from the `for` statement, the `loop condition` is always `true`. This is an infinite loop.

Example 5-10

In this example, a `for` loop reads five numbers and finds their sum and average. Consider the following program code, in which `i`, `newNum`, `sum`, and `average` are `int` variables.

```
sum = 0;
for(i = 1; i <= 5; i++)
{
   cin>>newNum;
   sum = sum + newNum;
}

average = sum / 5;
cout<<"The sum is "<<sum<<endl;
cout<<"The average is "<<average<<endl;
```

In the preceding `for` loop, after reading a `newNum`, this value is added to the previously calculated (partial) `sum` of all the numbers read before the current number. The variable `sum` is initialized to `0` before the `for` loop. Thus, after the program reads the first number and adds it to the value of `sum`, the variable `sum` holds the correct `sum` of the first number.

In the following C++ program, we recommend that you walk through each step.

Example 5-11

The following C++ program finds the sum of the first `n` positive integers.

```
//Program: Sum first n positive integers
//This program finds the sum of the first n positive integers.

#include <iostream>
using namespace std;

int main()
{
   int counter;      //loop control variable
   int sum;          //variable to store the sum of the numbers
   int N;            //variable to store the number of
                     //first positive integers to be added

   cout<<"Line 1: Enter the number of positive "
       <<"integers to be added:"<<endl;             //Line 1
   cin>>N;                                          //Line 2
   sum = 0;                                         //Line 3

   for(counter = 1; counter <= N; counter++)        //Line 4
       sum = sum + counter;                         //Line 5

   cout<<"Line 6: The sum of the first "<<N
       <<" positive integers is "<<sum<<endl;       //Line 6

   return 0;
}
```

Sample Run: In this sample run, the user input is shaded.

```
Line 1: Enter the number of positive integers to be added:100
Line 6: The sum of the first 100 positive integers is 5050
```

The statement at Line 1 prompts the user to enter the number of first positive integers to be added. The statement at Line 2 stores the number entered by the user in `N` and the statement at Line 3 initializes `sum` to `0`. The `for` loop at Line 4 executes `N` times. In the `for` loop, `counter` is initialized to `1` and is incremented by `1` after each iteration of the loop. Therefore `counter` ranges from `1` to `N`. Each time through the loop, the value of `counter` is added to `sum`. The variable `sum` was initialized to `0`, `counter` ranges from `1` to `N`, and the current value of `counter` is added to the value of `sum`. Therefore, after the `for` loop executes, `sum` contains the sum of the first `N` values, which in the sample run is `100` positive integers.

Recall that putting one control structure statement inside another is called **nesting**. The following programming example demonstrates a simple instance of nesting, which also nicely demonstrates counting.

PROGRAMMING EXAMPLE: CLASSIFY NUMBERS

This program reads a given set of integers and then prints the number of odd and even integers. It also outputs the number of zeros.

The program reads 20 integers, but you can easily modify it to read any set of numbers. In fact, you can modify the program so that it first prompts the user to specify how many integers are to be read.

Input 20 integers—positive, negative, or zeros.

Output The number of zeros, even numbers, and odd numbers.

Problem Analysis and Algorithm Design

After reading a number you need to check whether it is even or odd. Suppose the value is stored in `number`. Divide `number` by `2` and check the remainder. If the remainder is zero, `number` is even. Increment the even count and then check whether `number` is zero. If it is, increment the zero count. If the remainder is not zero, increment the odd count.

The program uses a `switch` statement to decide whether `number` is odd or even. Suppose that `number` is odd. Dividing by `2` gives the remainder `1` if `number` is positive and the remainder `-1` if negative. If `number` is even, dividing by `2` gives the remainder `0` whether `number` is positive or negative. You can use the mod operator, `%`, to find the remainder. For example,

```
6 % 2 = 0, -4 % 2 = 0, -7 % 2 = -1, 15 % 2 = 1.
```

Repeat the preceding process of analyzing a number for each number in the list.

This discussion translates into the following algorithm:

1. For each number in the list
   a. Get the number.
   b. Analyze the number.
   c. Increment the appropriate count.
2. Print the results.

Variables Since you want to count the number of zeros, even numbers, and odd numbers, you need three variables of type `int`—say `zeros`, `evens`, and `odds`, to track the counts. You also need a variable—say, `number`—to read and store the number to be analyzed and another variable—say, counter—to count the numbers analyzed. You need the following variables in the program:

```
int counter;          //loop control variable
int number;           //variable to store the number read
int zeros;            //variable to store the zero count
int evens;            //variable to store the even count
int odds;             //variable to store the odd count
```

Clearly, you must initialize the variables zeros, evens, and odds to zero. You can initialize these variables when you declare them.

Main Algorithm

1. Initialize the variables.
2. Prompt the user to enter 20 numbers.
3. For each number in the list
   a. Read the number.
   b. Output the number (echo input).
   c. If the number is even
      {
        i. Increment the even count.
        ii. If the number is zero, increment the zero count.
      }
      otherwise
        Increment the odd count
4. Print the results.

Before writing the C++ program, let us describe Steps 1–4 in more detail. It will be much easier for you to then write the instructions in C++.

1. Initialize the variables. You can initialize the variables **zeros**, **evens**, and **odds** when you declare them.
2. Use an output statement to prompt the user to enter 20 numbers.
3. For Step 3, you can use a **for** loop to process and analyze the 20 numbers. In pseudocode, this step is written as follows:

```
for(counter = 1; counter <= 20; counter++)
{
    read the number;
    output number;
    switch(number % 2)     //check the remainder
    {
       case 0:  increment even count;
                if(number == 0)
                    increment zero count;
                break;
```

```
            case 1: case -1: increment odd count;
        }//end switch
    }//end for
```

4. Print the result. Output the value of the variables **zeros**, **evens**, and **odds**.

Complete Program Listing

```
//********************************************************
// Program: Counts zeros, odds, and evens
// This program counts the number of odd and even numbers.
// The program also counts the number of zeros.
//********************************************************

#include <iostream>
#include <iomanip>

using namespace std;

const int N = 20;

int main ()
{
        //Declare variables
    int counter;     //loop control variable
    int number;      //variable to store the new number

    int zeros = 0;                                 //Step1
    int odds = 0;                                  //Step1
    int evens = 0;                                 //Step1

    cout<<"Please enter "<<N<<" integers, "
        <<"positive, negative, or zeros."
        <<endl;                                    //Step 2

    cout<<"The numbers you entered are --> "<<endl;

    for(counter = 1; counter <= N; counter++)     //Step 3
    {
       cin>>number;                                //Step 3a
       cout<<setw(5)<< number;                     //Step 3b

                //Step 3c
       switch(number % 2)
       {
       case 0: evens++;
               if(number == 0)
```

```
                zeros++;
            break;
        case 1:
        case -1: odds++;
       } //end switch
    } //end for

    cout<<endl;
                                //Step 4
    cout<<"There are "<<evens<<" evens, "
        <<"which also includes "<<zeros<<" zeros"<<endl;
    cout<<"Total number of odds are: "<<odds<<endl;

    return 0;
}
```

Sample Run: In this sample run, the user input is shaded.

```
Please enter 20 integers, positive, negative, or zeros.
The numbers you entered are -->
0 0 -2 -3 -5 6 7 8 0 3 0 -23 -8 0 2 9 0 12 67 54
    0    0   -2   -3   -5    6    7    8    0    3    0
-23   -8    0    2    9    0   12   67   54
There are 13 evens, which also includes 6 zeros
Total number of odds are: 7
```

We recommend that you do a walk-through of this program using the above sample input.

THE do...while LOOPING (REPETITION) STRUCTURE

This section describes the third type of looping or repetition structure called a `do...while` loop. The general form of a `do...while` statement is as follows:

```
do
  statement
while(expression);
```

Of course, `statement` can be either a simple or compound statement. If it is a compound statement, enclose it between braces. Figure 5-3 shows the flow of execution of a `do...while` loop.

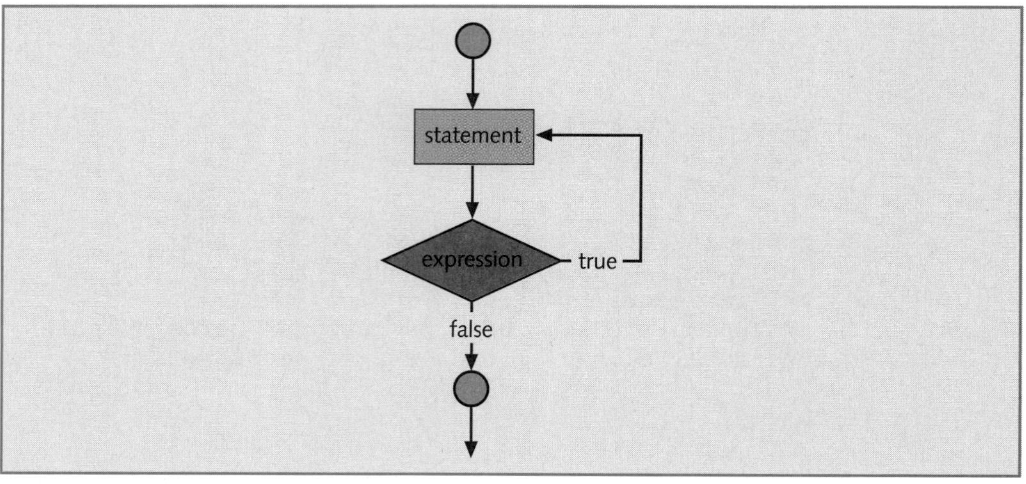

Figure 5-3 do...while loop

In C++, do is a reserved word.

The **statement** executes first, and then the **expression** is evaluated. If the **expression** evaluates to true, the **statement** executes again. As long as the **expression** in a do...while statement is true, the **statement** executes. To avoid an infinite loop, you must, once again, make sure that the loop body contains a statement that ultimately makes the **expression** false and assures that it exits properly.

Example 5-12

```
i = 0;
do
{
   cout<<i<<" ";
   i = i + 5;
}
while(i <= 20);
```

The output of this code is

```
0 5 10 15 20
```

After the value 20 is output, the statement

```
i = i + 5;
```

changes the value of i to 25 and so i <= 20 becomes false, which halts the loop.

Because the **while** and **for** loops both have entry conditions, these loops may never activate. The **do...while** loop, on the other hand, has an exit condition and therefore always goes through at least once.

Example 5-13

Consider the following two loops:

(a)

```
i = 11;
while(i <= 10)
{
    cout<<i<<"  ";
    i = i + 5;
}
```

(b)

```
i = 11;
do
{
  cout<<i<<"  ";
  i = i + 5;
}
while(i <= 10);
```

In (a), the **while** loop produces nothing. In (b), the **do...while** loop outputs the number 11.

The **do...while** loop is useful when it does not make sense to check a condition until after the action occurs. For example, it is suitable when the action is to read data that is then checked against the exit condition, as in monitoring devices used in hospitals. The following program illustrates this idea.

Example 5-14

```
//*******************************************************
//  Program: Warning Message
//  This program reads a value and prints a warning
//  message, or rings a bell, when a value falls outside
//  a given range.
//*******************************************************

#include <iostream>
using namespace std;

const int low = 60;
const int high = 100;
```

```
int main ()
{
   int pressure;

   do
       cin>>pressure;
   while((pressure > low) && (pressure < high));

   cout<<"Help"<<endl;

   return 0;
}
```

All three loops have their place in C++. You can usually replace one with another, but it's often awkward. For example, you can rewrite the `while` loop in program **AVG2** (see Example 5-4) as a `do...while` loop. To do so, however, takes the awkward form

```
if(number != -999)
  do
  {
      .
      .
      .
  }
  while(number != -999);
```

That is,

```
if(expression)
  do
    action
  while(expression);
```

replaces the simpler

```
while(expression)
   action
```

BREAK AND CONTINUE STATEMENTS

A `break` and `continue` statement alters the flow of control. The `break` statement, when executed in a `switch` structure, provides an immediate exit from the `switch` structure. Similarly, you can use the `break` statement in `while`, `for`, and `do...while` loops. When the `break` statement executes in a repetition structure, it immediately exits from these structures. The `break` statement is typically used for two purposes:

1. To exit early from a loop
2. To skip the remainder of the `switch` structure

After the **break** statement executes, the program continues to execute with the first statement after the structure.

The use of a **break** statement in a loop can eliminate the use of certain (flag) variables. The following C++ code segment helps illustrate this idea. (Assume that all variables are properly declared.)

```
sum = 0;
cin>>num;
isNegative = false;

while(cin && !isNegative)
{
   if(num < 0)    //if the number is negative, terminate the loop
   {
       cout<<"Negative number found in the data"<<endl;
       isNegative = true;
   }
   else
   {
       sum = sum + num;
       cin>>num;
   }
}
```


This **while** loop is supposed to find the sum of a set of positive numbers. If the data set contains a negative number, the loop terminates with an appropriate error message. This **while** loop uses the flag variable **isNegative** to accomplish the desired result. The variable **isNegative** is initialized to **false** before the **while** loop. Before adding **num** to **sum**, check whether num is negative. If **num** is negative, an error message appears on the screen and **isNegative** is set to **true**. In the next iteration, when the expression in the **while** statement is evaluated, it evaluates to **false** since **!isNegative** is **false**. (Note that since **isNegative** is **true**, **!isNegative** is **false**).

The following **while** loop is written without using the variable **isNegative**:

```
sum = 0;
cin>>num;

while(cin)
{
   if(num < 0)    //if the number is negative, terminate the loop
   {
      cout<<"Negative number found in the data"<<endl;
      break;
   }

   sum = sum + num;
   cin>>num;
}
```

In this form of the `while` loop, when a negative number is found, the expression in the `if` statement evaluates to `true`; after printing an appropriate message, the `break` statement terminates the loop. (After executing the `break` statement in a loop, the remaining statements in the loop are discarded.)

The `continue` statement is used in `while`, `for`, and `do...while` structures. When the `continue` statement is executed in a loop, it skips the remaining statements in the loop and proceeds with the next iteration of the loop. In a `while` and `do...while` structure, the `expression` (that is, the loop-continue test) is evaluated immediately after the `continue` statement. In a `for` structure, the `update statement` is executed after the `continue` statement, and then the `loop condition` (that is, the loop-continue test) executes.

If the previous program segment encountered a negative number, the `while` loop terminates. If you want to discard the negative number and read the next number rather than terminate the loop, replace the `break` statement with the `continue` statement, as shown in the following example.

```
sum = 0;
cin>>num;

while(cin)
{
   if(num < 0)
   {
      cout<<"Negative number found in the data"<<endl;
      cin>>num;
      continue;
   }

   sum = sum + num;
   cin>>num;
}
```

It was stated earlier that all three loops have their place in C++ and that one loop can often replace another. The execution of a `continue` statement, however, is where a `while` and a `do...while` structure differs from a `for` structure. When the `continue` statement is executed in a `while` or a `do...while` loop, the `update statement` may not execute. In a `for` structure, the `update statement` *always* executes.

Nested Control Structures

This section briefly reviews the control structures discussed so far in this chapter and in Chapter 4. You have seen that by putting one control structure within another, you can achieve dramatic and fruitful results. Nesting of control structures takes on new power, subtlety, and complexity. Consider the following program:

```
#include <iostream>
using namespace std;

int  main ()
{
    int  studentId, testScore, count = 0;

    cin>>studentId;
    while(studentId != -1)
    {
      count++;
      cin>>testScore;
      cout<<"Student Id = "<<studentId<<", test score = "
          <<testScore<<", and grade = ";
      if(testScore >= 90)
            cout<<"A."<<endl;
      else
         if(testScore >= 80)
            cout<<"B."<<endl;
         else
            if(testScore >= 70)
               cout<<"C."<<endl;
            else
               if(testScore >= 60)
                  cout<<"D."<<endl;
               else
                  cout<<"F."<<endl;
         cin>>studentId;
     }//end while

   cout<<endl<<"Students in class = "<< count<<endl;

   return 0;
}
```

How would this program work if you wrote it as a sequence of `if...` statements (with no `else` or as a `switch` structure) within the `while` loop?

Consider another example of nesting. Suppose you want to create the following pattern:

```
*
**
***
****
*****
```

Clearly, you want to print five lines of stars. In the first line you want to print one star, in the second line two stars, and so on. Since five lines will be printed, start with the following `for` statement:

```
for(i = 1; i <= 5 ; i++)
```

The value of `i` in the first iteration is `1`, in the second iteration it is `2`, and so on. You can use the value of `i` as the limiting condition in another `for` loop nested within this loop to control the number of stars in a line. A little more thought produces the following code:

```
for(i = 1; i <= 5 ; i++)
{
   for(j = 1; j <= i; j++)
     cout<<"*";
   cout<<endl;
}
```

A walk-through of this code shows that the `for` loop starts with `i = 1`. When `i` is `1`, the inner `for` loop outputs one star and the cursor moves to the next line. Then `i` becomes `2`, the inner `for` loop outputs two stars, and the cursor moves to the next line, and so on. This process continues until `i` becomes `6` and the loop stops.

What pattern does this code produce if you replace the first `for` statement with the following?

```
for(i = 5; i >= 1; i--)
```

To learn more about the nesting of `for` loops, see Exercise 30 at the end of this chapter.

QUICK REVIEW

1. C++ has three looping (repetition) structures: `while`, `for`, and `do...while`.
2. The syntax of the `while` statement is

```
while(expression)
   statement
```

3. In C++, `while` is a reserved word.
4. In the `while` statement, the parentheses around the `expression`, the decision maker, are important; they mark the beginning and end of the expression.
5. The `statement` is called the body of the loop.
6. The body of the `while` loop must contain a statement that eventually sets the expression to `false`.
7. A counter-controlled `while` loop uses a counter to control the loop.
8. In a counter-controlled `while` loop, you must initialize the counter before the loop, and the body of the loop must contain a statement that changes the value of the counter variable.
9. A sentinel is a special value that marks the end of the input data. The sentinel must be similar to, yet differ from, all the data items.

10. A sentinel-controlled `while` loop uses a sentinel to control the `while` loop. The `while` loop continues to execute until the sentinel is read.
11. An EOF-controlled `while` loop continues to execute until the program detects the end-of-file marker.
12. In the DOS environment, the end-of-file marker is entered using `ctrl+z` (hold the `ctrl` key and press `z`). In the UNIX environment, the end-of-file marker is entered using `ctrl+d` (hold the `ctrl` key and press `d`).
13. A `for` loop simplifies the writing of a count-controlled `while` loop.
14. In C++, `for` is a reserved word.
15. The syntax of the `for` loop is

```
for(initialize statement; loop condition; update statement)
   statement
```

`statement` is called the body of the `for` loop.

16. Putting a semicolon at the end of the `for` loop (before the body of the `for` loop) is a semantic error. In this case, the action of the `for` loop is empty.
17. The syntax of the `do...while` statement is

```
do
      statement
while(expression);
```

The statement is called the body of the `do...while` loop.

18. The `while` and `for` loops may not execute at all, but the `do...while` loop always executes at least once.
19. Executing a `break` statement in the body of a loop immediately terminates the loop.
20. Executing a `continue` statement in the body of a loop skips the loop's remaining statements and proceeds with the next iteration.
21. When a `continue` statement executes in a `while` or `do...while` loop, the expression update statement in the body of the loop may not execute.
22. After a `continue` statement executes in a `for` loop, the update statement is the next statement executed.

EXERCISES

1. Mark the following statements as true or false.
   a. In a counter-controlled `while` loop, it is not necessary to initialize the loop control variable.

b. It is possible that the body of a `while` loop may not execute at all.

c. In an infinite while loop, the `while` expression (the decision maker) is initially false, but after the first iteration it is always true.

d. The `while` loop

```
J = 0;
while(J <= 10)
  J++;
```

terminates if `J > 10`.

e. A sentinel-controlled `while` loop is an event-controlled `while` loop whose termination depends on a special value.

f. A loop is a control structure that causes certain statements to execute over and over.

g. To read data from a file of unspecified length, an EOF-controlled loop is a good choice.

h. When a `while` loop terminates, the control first goes back to the statement just before the `while` statement, and then the control goes to the statement immediately following the `while` loop.

2. What is the output of the following C++ code?

```
count = 1;
y = 100;
while(count < 100)
{
  y = y - 1;
  count++;
}
cout<<" y = "<<y<<" and count = "<<count<<endl;
```

3. What is the output of the following C++ code?

```
num = 5;
while(num > 5)
  num = num + 2;
cout<<num<<endl;
```

4. What is the output of the following C++ code?

```
num = 1;
while(num < 10)
{
  cout<<num<<" ";
  num = num + 2;
}
```

5. When does the following `while` loop terminate?

```
ch = 'D';
while('A' <= ch && ch <= 'Z')
     ch = static_cast<char>(static_cast<int>(ch) + 1);
```

6. Suppose that the input is `38  45  71  4  -1`. What is the output of the following code? Assume all variables are properly declared.

```
cin>>sum;
cin>>num;
for(j = 1; j <= 3; j++)
{
    cin>>num;
    sum = sum + num;
}
cout<<"Sum = "<<sum<<endl;
```


7. Suppose that the input is `38  45  71  4  -1`. What is the output of the following code? Assume all variables are properly declared.

```
cin>>sum;
cin>>num;
while(num != -1)
{
    sum = sum + num;
    cin>>num;
}
cout<<"Sum = "<<sum<<endl;
```

8. Suppose that the input is `38  45  71  4  -1`. What is the output of the following code? Assume all variables are properly declared.

```
cin>>num;
sum = num;
while(num != -1)
{
    cin>>num;
    sum = sum + num;
}
cout<<"Sum = "<<sum<<endl;
```

9. Suppose that the input is `38  45  71  4  -1`. What is the output of the following code? Assume all variables are properly declared.

```
sum = 0;
cin>>num;
while(num != -1)
{
    sum = sum + num;
    cin>>num;
}
cout<<"Sum = "<<sum<<endl;
```

10. Correct the following code so that it finds the sum of 10 numbers.

```
sum = 0;
while(count < 10)
   cin>>num;
   sum = sum + num;
   count++;
```

11. What is the output of the following program?

```
#include <iostream>
using namespace std;
int main()
{
    int  x, y, z;

    x = 4;    y = 5;
    z = y + 6;

    while(((z-x) % 4) != 0)
    {
           cout<<z<<" ";
           z = z + 7;
    }

     return 0;
}
```

12. Suppose that the input is

```
58  23  46  75  98  150  12  176  145 -999
```

What is the output of the following program?

```
#include <iostream>
using namespace std;
int main()
{
   int num;
   cin>>num;
   while(num != -999)
   {
     cout<<num%25<<"  ";
     cin>>num;
   }
   return 0;
}
```

13. Given

```
for(i = 12; i <= 25; i++)
   cout<<i;
```

a. The seventh integer printed is ______________.

b. The statement produces ______________ lines of output.

c. If `i++` were changed to `i--` a compilation error would result. True or false?

14. Given that the following code is correctly inserted into a program, state its entire output as to content and form.

```
num = 0;
for(i = 1; i <= 4; i++)
{
        num = num + 10 * (i – 1);
        cout<<num<<" ";
}
```


15. Given that the following code is correctly inserted into a program, state its entire output as to content and form.

```
j = 2;
for(i = 0; i <= 5; i++)
{
        cout<<j<<" ";
        j = 2 * j + 3;
}
cout<<j<<" "<<endl;
```

16. Assume that the following code is correctly inserted into a program:

```
s = 0;
for(i = 0; i < 5; i++)
{
  s = 2 * s + i;
  cout<<s<<" ";
}
```

a. What is the final value of `s`?

(i) `11` (ii) `4` (iii) `26` (iv) none of these

b. If a semicolon is inserted after the right parentheses in the `for` loop control expressions, what is the final value of `s`?

(i) `0` (ii) `1` (iii) `2` (iv) `5` (v) none of these

c. If the `5` is replaced with a `0` in the `for` loop control expression, what is the final value of `s`?

(i) 0 (ii) 1 (iii) 2 (iv) none of these

17. State what output, if any, results in each of the following statements.

a.
```
for(i = 1; i <= 1; i++)
    cout<<"*";
```

b.
```
for(i = 2; i >= 1; i++)
cout<<"*";
```

c.
```
for(i = 1; i <= 1; i--)
cout<<"*";
```

d.
```
for(i = 12; i >= 9; i--)
cout<<"*";
```

e.
```
for(i = 0; i <= 5; i++)
cout<<"*";
```

f.
```
for(i = 1; i <= 5; i++)
{
   cout<<"*";
   i = i+1;
}
```

18. Write a `for` statement to add all multiples of 3 between 1 and 100.

19. What is the exact output of the following program?

```
#include <iostream>
using namespace std;
int main ()
{
   int counter;
   for(counter = 7; counter <= 16; counter++)
    switch(counter % 10)
    {
    case 0: cout<<", ";
            break;
    case 1: cout<<"OFTEN ";
            break;
    case 2: case 8: cout<<"IS ";
            break;
    case 3: cout<<"NOT ";
            break;
    case 4: case 9: cout<<"DONE ";
            break;
    case 5: cout<<"WELL";
            break;
    case 6: cout<<".";
            break;
    case 7: cout<<"WHAT ";
            break;
    default:cout<<"Bad number. ";
    }
    cout<<endl;
    return 0;
}
```

20. Suppose that the input is 5 3 8. What is the output of the following code? Assume all variables are properly declared.

```
cin>>a>>b>>c;
for(j = 1; j < a; j++)
{
    d = b + c;
    b = c;
    c = d;
    cout<<c<<"  ";
}
cout<<endl;
```


21. What is the output of the following C++ program segment? Assume all variables are properly declared.

```
for(j = 0; j < 8; j++)
{
    cout<<j * 25<<" - ";
    if(j != 7)
        cout<<(j + 1) * 25 - 1<<endl;
    else
        cout<<(j + 1) * 25<<endl;
}
```

22. The following program has more than five mistakes that prevent it from compiling and/or running. Correct all such mistakes.

```
#include <iostream>
using namespace std;
const int N = 2,137;

main ()
{
    int a, b, c, d:

    a := 3;
    b = 5;
    c = c + d;
    N = a + n;
    for(i = 3; i <= N; i++)
    {
      cout<<setw(5)<<i;
      i = i + 1;
    }
    return 0;
}
```

23. Which of the following apply to the **while** loop only? To the **do...while** loop only? To both?

    a. It is considered a conditional loop.

    b. The body of the loop executes at least once.

    c. The logical expression controlling the loop is evaluated before the loop is entered.

    d. The body of the loop may not execute at all.

24. How many times will each of the following loops execute? What is the output in each case?

    a.
    ```
    x = 5;   y = 50;
    do
        x = x + 10;
    while(x < y);
    cout<<x<<" "<<y;
    ```

    b.
    ```
    x = 5;   y = 80;
    do
        x = x * 2;
    while(x < y);
    cout<<x<<" "<<y;
    ```

    c.
    ```
    x = 5;   y = 20;
    do
        x = x + 2;
    while(x >= y);
    cout<<x<<" "<<y;
    ```

    d.
    ```
    x = 5;   y = 35;
    while(x < y)
        x = x + 10;
    cout<<x<<" "<<y;
    ```

    e.
    ```
    x = 5;   y = 30;
    while(x <= y)
        x = x * 2;
    cout<<x<<" "<<y;
    ```

    f.
    ```
    x = 5;   y = 30;
    while(x > y)
        x = x + 2;
    cout<<x<<" "<<y;
    ```

25. The following loop is supposed to read some numbers until it reaches a sentinel (in this case, -1). It is supposed to add all of the numbers except for the sentinel. If the data looks like

    ```
    12    5   30   48   -1
    ```

the program fails to do what it is purported to do. Correct it.

```
#include <iostream>
using namespace std;
int main()
{
   int total=0,
       count=0,
       number;
   do
   {
       cin>>number;
       total = total + number;
       count++;
   }
   while(number != -1);

   cout<<"The number of data read is "<< count<<endl;
   cout<<"The sum of the numbers entered is  "<<total<<endl;
   return 0;
}
```

26. Using the same data as in Exercise 25, the following two loops also fail. Correct them.

a.
```
cin>>number;
while(number != -1)
   total =  total + number;
   cin>>number;
   cout<<endl;
   cout<<total;
```

b.
```
cin>>number;
while(number != -1)
{
    cin>>number;
    total = total + number;
}
cout<<endl;
cout<<total;
```

27. Given the following program segment

```
for(number = 1; number <= 10; number++)
    cout<<setw(3)<<number;
```

write a `while` and a `do...while` loop that have the same output.

28. Given the following program segment

```
j = 2;
for(i = 1; i <= 5; i++);
{
   cout<<setw(4)<<j;
   j = j + 5;
}
cout<<endl;
```

write a `while` and a `do...while` loop that have the same output.

29. What is the output of the following program?

```
#include <iostream>
using namespace std;
int main()
{
        int  x, y, z;
        x = 4;    y = 5;
        z = y + 6;
        do
        {
                cout<<z<<" ";
                z = z + 7;
        }
        while(((z-x) % 4) != 0);

        return 0;
}
```

30. To learn how nested `for` loops work, do a walk-through of the following program segments and determine, in each case, the exact output.

a.
```
int i,j;
for(i = 1; i <= 5; i++)
{
        for(j = 1; j <= 5; j++)
                cout<<setw(3)<< i*j;
        cout<<endl;
}
```

b.
```
int i,j;

for(i = 1; i <= 5; i++)
{
        for(j = 1; j <= 5; j++)
                cout<<setw(3)<<i;
        cout<<endl;
}
```

c.
```
int i,j;
for(i = 1; i <= 5; i++)
{
        for(j = (i + 1); j <= 5; j++)
                cout<<setw(5)<<j;
        cout<<endl;
}
```

d.
```
int i,j;
for(i = 1; i <= 5; i++)
{
        for(j = 1; j <= i; j++)
                cout<<setw(3)<<j;
        cout<<endl;
}
```

e.
```
const int m = 10;
const int n = 10;
int i,j;

for(i = 1; i <= m; i++)
{
    for(j = 1; j <= n; j++)
            cout<<setw(3)<<m*(i-1)+j;
    cout<<endl;
}
```

f.
```
int i,j;

for(i = 1; i <= 9; i++)
{
        for(j = 1; j <= (9 - i); j++)
                cout<<" ";
        for(j = 1; j <= i; j++)
                cout<<setw(1)<<j;
        for(j = (i -1); j >= 1; j--)
                cout<<setw(1)<<j;
        cout<<endl;
}
```


PROGRAMMING EXERCISES

1. An integer is divisible by 9 if the sum of its digits is divisible by 9. Write a program that prompts the user to input an integer. The program should then output the number and a message stating whether the number is divisible by 9. It does so by first adding the digits and then checking whether the sum of the digits is divisible by 9.

2. Write a program that prompts the user to input an integer and then outputs both the individual digits of the number and the sum of the digits. For example, it should output the individual digits of `3456` as `3 4 5 6`; output the individual digits of `8030` as `8 0 3 0`; output the individual digits of `2345526` as `2 3 4 5 5 2 6`; output the individual digits of `4000` as `4 0 0 0`; and output the individual digits of `-2345` as `2 3 4 5`.
3. Write a program that prompts the user to input an integer and then outputs the number with the digits reversed. For example, if the input is `12345`, the output should be `54321`. Your program must also output `5000` as `0005` and `980` as `098`.
4. Rewrite the program of Example 5-5, Telephone Digits. Replace the statements from Line 10 to Line 28 so that it uses only a **`switch`** structure to find the digit that corresponds to an uppercase letter.
5. The program Telephone Digits outputs only telephone digits that correspond to uppercase letters. Rewrite the program so that it processes both upper- and lowercase letters and outputs the corresponding telephone digit. If the input is other than an upper- or lowercase letter, the program must output an appropriate error message.
6. Write a program that reads a set of integers, and then finds and prints the sum of the even and odd integers.
7. Write a program that prompts the user to input a positive integer. It should then output a message indicating whether the number is a prime number. (*Note*: An even number is prime if it is 2. An odd integer is prime if it is not divisible by any odd integer less than or equal to the square root of the number.)
8. Write a program that uses a **`while`** loop to perform the following steps:
   a. Prompt the user to input two integers: `firstNum` and `secondNum` (`firstNum` must be less than `secondNum`).
   b. Output all odd numbers between `firstNum` and `secondNum`.
   c. Output the sum of all even numbers between `firstNum` and `secondNum`.
   d. Output the numbers and their square between 1 and 10.
   e. Output the sum of the square of odd numbers between `firstNum` and `secondNum`.
   f. Output all uppercase letters.
9. Redo Exercise 8 using a **`for`** loop.
10. Redo Exercise 8 using a **`do...while`** loop.
11. For research purposes and to better help students, the admissions office of your local university wants to know how well female and male students perform in certain courses. You receive a file that contains female and male student GPAs for certain courses. Due to confidentiality, the letter code `f` is used for female students and `m` for male students. Every file entry consists of a letter code followed by a GPA. Each line has one entry. The number of entries in the file is unknown. Write a program that computes and outputs the average GPA for both female and male students. Format your results to two decimal places.

12. If interest is compounded annually, it grows as follows. Suppose `P0` is the initial amount and `INT` is the interest rate per year. If `P1`, `P2`, and `P3` is the balance at the end of first, second, and third year, respectively, then

```
P1 = P0 + P0*INT = P0*(1+INT)
P2 = P1 + P1*INT = P1*(1+INT) = P0*(1+INT)*(1+INT)
   = P0*(1+INT)²
P3 = P2 + P2*INT = P2*(1+INT) = P0*(1+INT)*(1+INT)*(1+INT)
   = P0*(1+INT)³
```

and so on.

When money is deposited in an IRA account it is usually sheltered from taxes until the money is withdrawn after the age of 59. Suppose that someone dear to you opened such an account for you on your sixteenth birthday at 10% interest and that he or she forgot about it (so no money was added or withdrawn). On your sixtieth birthday, you are notified about this account by some fortune hunters. The money has been compounded annually at the 10% rate. Write a program that reads an initial amount and computes the total in the account on your sixtieth birthday.

You decide to leave the money in for another year. Starting from your sixty-first birthday, you decide to withdraw each year's interest income. In other words, you withdraw the interest and leave the rest of the money untouched. How much income per month for the rest of your life would you have?

Design your program to accept any integer input. Test it with initial investments of: $1700, $3600, and $8500.

(*Note*: Use a loop to compute the amount at your sixtieth birthday. Do not use the predefined function `pow`.)

The program should do all the computing needed, and output all the relevant data as follows:

The initial investment was $________. The total amount accumulated after ________ years, if $________ is allowed to compound with an interest of 10.00%, comes to $________.

The total amount accumulated after ________ (years + 1) years, if $ ________ is allowed to compound with an interest of 10%, comes to $________.

The interest earned during this year is $________. If interest is withdrawn each year thereafter, my income is $________ per month.

CHAPTER

6

USER-DEFINED FUNCTIONS I

In this chapter, you will:

- Learn about standard (predefined) functions and discover how to use them in a program
- Learn about user-defined functions
- Examine value-returning functions, including actual and formal parameters
- Explore how to construct and use a value-returning, user-defined function in a program

In Chapter 2, you learned that a C++ program is a collection of functions. One such function is `main`. The programs in Chapters 1 through 5 use only the function `main`; the programming instructions are packed into one function. This technique, however, is good only for short programs. For large programs, it is not practical (although possible) to put the entire programming instructions into one function, as you will soon discover. You must learn to break the problem into manageable pieces. This chapter first discusses the functions previously defined and then discusses user-defined functions.

Let us imagine an automobile factory. When an automobile is manufactured, it is not made from basic raw materials; it is put together from previously manufactured parts. Some parts are made by the company itself, others by different companies.

Functions are like building blocks. They let you divide complicated programs into manageable pieces. They have other advantages, too:

1. While working on one function, you can focus on just that part of the program and construct it, debug it, and perfect it.
2. Different people can work on different functions simultaneously.
3. If a function is needed in more than one place in a program, or in different programs, you can write it once and use it many times.

Functions are often called modules. They are like miniature programs; you can put them together to form a larger program. When user-defined functions are discussed, you will see that this is the case. This ability is less apparent with predefined functions because their programming code is not available to us. However, since predefined functions are already written for us, you will learn these first so that you can use them when needed. To use a predefined function in your programs, you need to know only how to use it.

STANDARD (PREDEFINED) FUNCTIONS

In college algebra, you learned that a function can be considered a rule or correspondence between values, called the function's arguments, and the unique value of the function associated with the arguments. Thus, if `f(x) = 2x + 5`, then

`f(1) = 7, f(2) = 9, and f(3) = 11`

where `1`, `2`, and `3` are arguments of `f`, and `7`, `9`, and `11` are the corresponding values of the function `f`.

In C++, the concept of a function is very similar. There are **predefined functions**, sometimes called **standard functions,** and there are **user-defined functions**. This section deals with only the former. Some of the pre-defined mathematical functions are `abs(x)`, `sqrt(x)`, and `pow(x,y)`.

The *power* function, `pow(x,y)`, calculates x^y; that is, the value of `pow(x,y)` $= x^y$. For example, `pow(2,3) = 8.0` and `pow(2.5,3) = 15.625`. Since the value of `pow(x,y)` is of the type `double`, we say that the function `pow` is of the type `double` or that the function pow returns a value of the type double. Moreover, x and y are called the **parameters** (or **arguments**) of the function pow. Function pow has two parameters.

The *square root* function, sqrt(x), calculates the non-negative square root of x for x >= 0.0. For example, sqrt(2.25) is 1.5. The function sqrt is of the type double and has only one parameter.

The *floor* function, floor, calculates the largest whole number that is not greater than x. For example, floor(48.79) is 48.0. The function floor is of the type double and has only one parameter.

In C++, predefined functions are organized into separate libraries. For example, the header file iostream contains I/O functions, and the header file cmath contains math functions. Table 6-1 lists some of the predefined functions, the name of the header file in which each function's specification can be found, the data type of the parameters, and the function type. The function type is the data type of the final value returned by the function. (For a list of additional predefined functions, see Appendix F. For the names of the Standard C++ header files, see Appendix E or the note after Example 6-1).

Table 6-1 Predefined Functions

Function	Standard Header File	Purpose	Parameter(s) Type	Result
abs(x)	<cstdlib>	Returns the absolute value of its argument: abs(-7) = 7	int	int
ceil(x)	<cmath>	Returns the smallest whole number that is not less than x: ceil(56.34) = 57.0	double	double
cos(x)	<cmath>	Returns the cosine of angle x: cos(0.0) = 1.0	double (radians)	double
exp(x)	<cmath>	Returns e^x, where e = 2.718: exp(1.0) = 2.71828	double	double
fabs(x)	<cmath>	Returns the absolute value of its argument: fabs(-5.67) = 5.67	double	double
floor(x)	<cmath>	Returns the largest whole number that is not greater than x: floor(45.67) = 45.00	double	double
pow(x,y)	<cmath>	Returns x^y; if x is negative, y must be a whole number: pow(0.16, 0.5) = 0.4	double	double
tolower(x)	<cctype>	Returns the lowercase value of x if x is uppercase; otherwise, returns x	int	int
toupper(x)	<cctype>	Returns the uppercase value of x if x is lowercase; otherwise, returns x	int	int

To use predefined functions in a program, you must include the header file that contains the function's specification via the include statement. For example, to use the function **pow**, the program must include

```
#include <cmath>
```

In Standard C++, the header file containing the specifications of the math functions is `math.h`.

Example 6-1

This example shows you how to use some of the predefined functions.

```
//How to use predefined functions
#include <iostream>

#include <cmath>

#include <cctype>

#include <cstdlib>

using namespace std;

int main()
{
      int   x;
      double  u,v;

      cout<<"Line 1: Uppercase a is "
          <<static_cast<char>(toupper('a'))
          <<endl;                                    //Line 1
      u = 4.2;                                       //Line 2
      v = 3.0;                                       //Line 3
      cout<<"Line 4: "<<u<<" to the power of "
          <<v<<" = "<<pow(u,v)<<endl;                //Line 4
      cout<<"Line 5: 5 to the power of 4 = "
          <<pow(5,4)<<endl;                          //Line 5
      u = u + pow(3,3);                              //Line 6
      cout<<"Line 7: u = "<<u<<endl;                 //Line 7
      x = -15;                                       //Line 8
      cout<<"Line 9: Absolute value of "<<x
          <<" = "<<abs(x)<<endl;                     //Line 9
      return 0;
}
```

Output:

```
Line 1: Uppercase a is A
Line 4: 4.2 to the power of 3 = 74.088
Line 5: 5 to the power of 4 = 625
Line 7: u = 31.2
Line 9: Absolute value of -15 = 15
```

This program works as follows. The statement at Line 1 outputs the uppercase letter that corresponds to `'a'`, which is `A`. Note that the function `toupper` returns an `int` value. Therefore, the value of the expression `toupper('a')` is `65`, which is the ASCII value of `'A'`. To print `A` rather than `65`, you need to apply the `cast` operator as shown in the statement at Line 1. In the statement at Line 4, the function `pow` is used to output u^{v}. In C++ terminology, it is said that the function `pow` is called with the parameters `u` and `v`. In this case, the values of `u` and `v` are passed to the function `pow`. The other statements have similar meanings.

To write this program using Standard C++ header files, replace the statements

```
#include <iostream>
#include <cmath>
#include <cctype>
#include <cstdlib>
using namespace std;
```

with

```
#include <iostream.h>
#include <math.h>
#include <ctype.h>
#include <stdlib.h>
```

USER-DEFINED FUNCTIONS

Using functions in a program greatly enhances the program's readability because, as Example 6-1 illustrates, it reduces the complexity of the function `main`. Also, once you write and properly debug a function, you can use it in the program (or different programs) again and again without having to rewrite the same code repeatedly. For instance, in Example 6-1, the function `pow` is used more than once.

Since C++ does not provide every function that you will ever need, and designers cannot possibly know a user's specific needs, you must learn to write your own functions.

User-defined functions in C++ are classified into two categories:

- Functions that have a data type, called **value-returning functions**
- Functions that do not have a data type, called **void functions**

The remainder of this chapter discusses value-returning functions. Many of the concepts discussed in regard to value-returning functions also apply to void functions. Chapter 7 describes void functions.

VALUE-RETURNING FUNCTIONS

The previous section introduced some predefined C++ functions such as `pow`, `abs`, `islower`, and `toupper`. These are examples of value-returning functions. To use these functions in your programs, you must know the name of the header file that contains the functions' specification. You need to include this header file in your program using the include statement and know the following items:

1. The name of the function
2. The number of **parameters**, if any
3. The data type of each parameter
4. The data type of the value computed (that is, the value returned) by the function, called the type of the function

Since the value returned by a value-returning function is unique, the natural thing for you to do is to use the value in one of three ways:

- Save the value for further calculation.
- Use the value in some calculation.
- Print the value.

This suggests that a value-returning function is used in either an assignment statement or an output statement such as `cout`. That is, a value-returning function is used (called) in an expression.

Before we look at the syntax of a user-defined value-returning function, let us review the things associated with such functions. In addition to the four properties described previously, one more thing is associated with functions (both value-returning and void):

5. The code required to accomplish the task

The first four properties form what is called the **heading** of the function (also called the **function header**); the fifth property is called the **body** of the function. Together, these five properties form what is called the **definition** of the function. For example, for the function `abs`, the heading might look like

```
int abs(int number)
```

Similarly, the function abs might have the following definition:

```
int abs(int number)
{
      if(number < 0)
         number = -number;

      return number;
}
```

The variable declared in the heading of the function abs is called the **formal parameter** of the function abs. Thus, the formal parameter of abs is number.

The program in Example 6-1 contains several statements that use the function pow. That is, in C++ terminology, the function pow is called several times. Later in this chapter, we discuss what happens when a function is called.

Suppose that the heading of the function pow is

```
double pow(double base, double exponent)
```

From the heading of the function pow, it follows that the formal parameters of pow are base and exponent. Consider the following statements:

```
double u = 2.5;
double v = 3.0;
double x, y, w;

x = pow(u, v);                //Line 1
y = pow(2.0,3.2);             //Line 2
w = pow(u,7);                 //Line 3
```

In Line 1, the function pow is called with the parameters u and v. In this case, the values of u and v are passed to the function pow. In fact, the value of u is copied into base and the value of v is copied into exponent. The variables u and v that appear in the call to the function pow in Line 1 are called actual parameters of that call. In Line 2, the function pow is called with parameters 2.0 and 3.2. In this call, the value 2.0 is copied into base and 3.2 is copied into exponent. Moreover, in this call of the function pow, the actual parameters are 2.0 and 3.2, respectively. Similarly, in Line 3, the actual parameters of the function pow are u and 7, the value of u is copied into base, and 7.0 is copied into exponent.

We can now formally present two definitions:

Formal Parameter: A variable declared in the function heading.

Actual Parameter: A variable or expression listed in a call to a function.

For predefined functions, you need to be concerned only with the first four properties. Software companies do not give out the actual source code, which is the body of the function. Otherwise, software costs would be exorbitant.

Syntax: Value-Returning Function

The syntax of a value-returning function is

```
functionType functionName(formal parameter list)
{
      statements
}
```

In this syntax template, **functionType** is the type of value that the function returns. This type is also called the data type of the value-returning function. Moreover, statements enclosed between curly braces form the body of the function.

Syntax: Formal Parameter List

The syntax of the formal parameter list is

```
dataType identifier, dataType identifier,...
```

Function Call

The syntax to call a value-returning function is

```
functionName(actual parameter list)
```

Syntax: Actual Parameter List

The syntax of the actual parameter list is

```
expression or variable, expression or variable, ...
```

Thus, to call a value-returning function, you use its name, with the actual parameters (if any) in parentheses.

A function's formal parameter list can be empty. However, if the formal parameter list is empty, the parentheses are still needed. The function heading of the value-returning function thus takes, if the parameter list is empty, either of the following forms:

```
functionType functionName()
```

or

```
functionType functionName(void)
```

If the formal parameter list is empty, in a function call the actual parameter is also empty. In this case (that is, an empty formal parameter list), in a function call the empty parentheses are still needed. Thus, a call to a value-returning function with an empty formal parameter list is

```
functionName()
```

In a function call, the number of actual parameters, together with their data types, must match with the formal parameters in the order given. That is, actual and formal parameters have a one-to-one correspondence. (Chapter 7 discusses functions with default parameters.)

As stated previously, a value-returning function is called in an expression. The expression can be part of either an assignment statement or an output statement. A function call in a program causes the body of the called function to execute.

The `return` Statement

Once a value-returning function computes the value, the function returns this value via the **`return`** statement; in other words, it passes this value outside the function via the **`return`** statement.

Syntax: `return` Statement

The **`return`** statement has the following syntax:

```
return expr;
```

where **`expr`** is a variable, constant value, or expression. The **`expr`** is evaluated and its value is returned. The data type of the value that **`expr`** computes must match the function type.

In C++, **`return`** is a reserved word.

When a **`return`** statement executes in a function, the function immediately terminates and the control goes back to the caller. Thus, when a **`return`** statement executes in the function `main`, the program terminates.

To put the ideas in this discussion to work, let us write a function that determines the larger of two numbers. Since the function compares two numbers, it follows that this function has two parameters and that both parameters are numbers. Let us assume that the data type of these numbers is floating-point (decimal)—say **`double`**. Since the larger number is of the type **`double`**, the function's data type is also **`double`**. Let us name this function `larger`. The only thing you need to complete this function is the body of the function. Thus, following the syntax of a function, you can write this function as follows:

```
double larger(double x, double y)
{
   double max;
```

```
    if(x >= y)
      max = x;
    else
      max = y;

    return max;
}
```

You can also write this function as follows:

```
double larger(double x, double y)
{
    if(x >= y)
      return x;
    else
      return y;
}
```

The first form of the function `larger` requires that you use an additional variable `max` (called a **local declaration**, where `max` is a variable local to the function `larger`); the second form does not.

1. In the function definition, `x` and `y` are formal parameters.
2. The `return` statement can appear anywhere in the function. Recall that once a `return` statement executes, all subsequent statements are skipped. Thus, it's a good idea to return the value as soon as it is computed.

Now that the function `larger` is written, the following C++ code illustrates how to use it in the function `main`.

```
int main()
{
   double one, two, maxNum;                              //Line 1

   cout<<"Larger of 5 and 6 is "
       <<larger(5,6)<<endl;                              //Line 2
   cout<<"Enter two numbers: ";                          //Line 3
   cin>>one>>two;                                        //Line 4
   cout<<endl;                                           //Line 5
   cout<<"Larger of "<<one<<" and "<<two
       <<" is "<<larger(one,two)<<endl;                  //Line 6
   cout<<"Larger of "<<one<<" and 29 is "
       <<larger(one,29)<<endl;                           //Line 7
   maxNum = larger(38.45, 56.78);                        //Line 8
   cout<<"maxNum = "<<maxNum<<endl;                      //Line 9

   return 0;
}
```

1. The expression `larger(5,6)`, at Line 2, is a function call, and 5 and 6 are actual parameters.
2. The expression `larger(one,two)`, at Line 6, is a function call. Here, `one` and `two` are actual parameters.
3. The expression `larger(one,29)`, at Line 7, is also a function call. Here, `one` and `29` are actual parameters.
4. The expression `larger(38.45, 56.78);` at Line 8 is a function call. In this call, the actual parameters are `38.45` and `56.78`. In this statement, the value returned by the function `larger` is assigned to the variable `maxNum`.

In a function call, you specify only the actual parameter, not its data type.

Once a function is written, you can use it anywhere in the program. The function **`larger`** compares two numbers and returns the larger of the two. Let us now write another function that uses this function to determine the largest of three numbers. We call this function **`compareThree`**.

```
double compareThree(double x, double y, double z)
{
   return larger(x,larger(y,z));
}
```

In the definition of the function **`compareThree`**, first the larger of **`y`** and **`z`** is determined which is then compared with **`x`**. Finally, the **`return`** statement returns the largest number. Moreover, in the function heading, **`x`**, **`y`**, and **`z`** are formal parameters.

Function Prototype

Now that you have some idea of how to write and use functions in a program, the next obvious question relates to the order in which user-defined functions should appear in a program. For example, do you place the function **`larger`** before or after the function **`main`**? Should **`larger`** be placed before **`compareThree`** or after it? Following the rule that you must declare an identifier before you can use it, and that knowing the function **`main`** uses the identifier **`larger`**, logically you must place **`larger`** before **`main`**.

In reality, C++ programmers customarily place the function **`main`** before all other user-defined functions. This organization could produce a compilation error because functions are compiled in the order in which they appear in the program. For example, if the function **`main`** is placed before the function **`larger`**, the identifier **`larger`** is undefined when the function **`main`** is compiled. To work around this problem of undeclared identifiers, we place **function prototypes** before any function definition (including the definition of **`main`**).

Function Prototype: The function heading without the body of the function.

Syntax: Function Prototype

The general syntax of the function prototype of a value-returning function is

```
functionType functionName(parameter list);
```

(Note that the function prototype ends with a semicolon.)

For the function `larger`, the prototype is

```
double larger(double x, double y);
```

When writing the function prototype, you do not have to specify the variable name in the parameter list. However, you must specify the data type of each parameter.

You can rewrite the function prototype of the function `larger` as follows:

```
double larger(double, double);
```

Final Program

You now know enough to write the entire program, compile it, and run it. The following program uses the functions `larger`, `compareThree`, and `main` to determine the larger/largest of two or three numbers.

```
//Program: Largest of three numbers
#include <iostream>
using namespace std;

double larger(double x, double y);
double compareThree(double x, double y, double z);

int main()
{
   double one, two;                                    //Line 1

   cout<<"Line 2: Larger of 5 and 10 is "
       <<larger(5,10)<<endl;                           //Line 2
   cout<<"Line 3: Enter two numbers: ";                //Line 3
    cin>>one>>two;                                     //Line 4
   cout<<endl;                                         //Line 5

   cout<<"Line 6: Larger of "<<one<<" and "
       <<two<<" is "<<larger(one,two)<<endl;           //Line 6
   cout<<"Line 7: Largest of 23, 34, and 12 is "
       <<compareThree(23,34,12)<<endl;                 //Line 7

   return 0;
}
```

```
double larger(double x, double y)
{
   if(x >= y)
      return x;
   else
      return y;
}

double compareThree (double x, double y, double z)
{
   return larger(x,larger(y,z));
}
```

Sample Run: In this sample run, the user input is shaded.

```
Line 2: Larger of 5 and 10 is 10
Line 3: Enter two numbers: 25 73
Line 6: Larger of 25 and 73 is 73
Line 7: Largest of 23, 34, and 12 is 34
```

6

In this program, the function prototypes of the functions `larger` and `compareThree` appear before their function definitions. Therefore, the definition of the functions `larger` and `compareThree` can appear in any order.

Recall that in a value-returning function the `return` statement returns the value. Consider the following `return` statement:

```
return x, y;//only the value of y will be returned
```

This is a legal `return` statement. You might think that this `return` statement is returning the values of `x` and `y`. However, this is not the case. Remember, a `return` statement returns only one value, even if the `return` statement contains more than one expression. If a `return` statement contains more than one expression, only the value of the last expression is returned. Therefore, in the case of the above `return` statement, the value of `y` is returned. The following program further illustrates this concept.

```
//A value returned by a return statement
//This program illustrates that a value-returning function
//returns only one value, even if the return statement
//contains more than one expression.


#include <iostream>

using namespace std;

int funcRet1();
```

```
int funcRet2();
int funcRet3();
int funcRet4(int z);

int main()
{
       int num = 4;
       cout<<"Line 1: Value returned by funcRet1: "
           <<funcRet1()<<endl;                              //Line 1
       cout<<"Line 2: Value returned by funcRet2: "
           <<funcRet2()<<endl;                              //Line 2
       cout<<"Line 3: Value returned by funcRet3: "
           <<funcRet3()<<endl;                              //Line 3
       cout<<"Line 4: Value returned by funcRet4: "
           <<funcRet4(num)<<endl;                           //Line 4
       return 0;
}

int funcRet1()
{
       return 23, 45;  //Only 45 is returned
}

int funcRet2()
{
       int x = 5;
       int y = 6;

       return x, y; //Only the value of y is returned
}

int funcRet3()
{
       int x = 5;
       int y = 6;

       return 37, y, 2 * x;  //Only the value of 2 * x is returned
}


int funcRet4(int z)
{
int a = 2;
int b = 3;

  return 2 * a + b, z + b; //Only the value of z + b is returned
}
```

Output:

```
Line 1: Value returned by funcRet1: 45
Line 2: Value returned by funcRet2: 6
Line 3: Value returned by funcRet3: 10
Line 4: Value returned by funcRet4: 7
```

Following is an example of a function that returns a Boolean value.

Example 6-2. Palindrome Number

In this example, a function, **isNumPalindrome**, is designed that returns **true** if an integer is a palindrome and **false** otherwise. An integer is a **palindrome** if it reads forward and backward in the same way. For example, the integers 5, 44, 434, 1881, and 789656987 are all palindromes.

Suppose num is an integer. If num < 10, it is a palindrome and so the function should return **true**. Suppose num >= 10. To determine whether num is a palindrome, first compare the first and the last digits of num. If the first and the last digits of num are not the same, it is not a palindrome and so the function should return **false**. If the first and the last digits of num are the same, remove the first and the last digits of num and repeat this process on the new number which is obtained from num after removing the first and the last digits of num. Repeat this process as long as the number is >= 10.

For example, suppose that the input is 18281. Because the first and last digits of 18281 are the same, remove the first and last digits to get the number 828. Repeat this process of comparing the first and last digits on 828. Once again, the first and last digits are the same. After removing the first and last digits of 828, the resulting number is 2, which is less than 10. Thus, 18281 is a palindrome.

To remove the first and last digits of num, you first need to find the highest power of 10 that divides num, call it pwr. The highest power of 10 that divides 18281 is 4, that is, pwr = 4. Now 18281 % 10^{pwr} = 8281, and so the first digit is removed. Also, since 8281 / 10 = 828, the last digit is removed. Therefore, to remove the first digit, you can use the mod operator, where the divisor is 10^{pwr}. To remove the last digit, divide the number by 10. You then decrement pwr by 2 for the next iteration. The following algorithm implements this discussion.

1. If num < 10, it is a palindrome and so the function should return **true**.
2. Suppose num is an integer and num >= 10. To see if num is a palindrome,
   a. Find the highest power of 10 that divides num and call it pwr. For example, the highest power of 10 that divides 434 is 2; the highest power of 10 that divides 789656987 is 8.
   b. While num is greater than or equal to 10, compare the first and last digit of num.
      b.1. If the first and last digits of num are not the same, num is not a palindrome. Return **false**.

b.2. If the first and the last digits of **num** are the same,

b.2.1. Remove the first and last digits of **num**.

b.2.2. Decrement **pwr** by **2**.

c. Return **true**.

The following function implements this algorithm:

```
bool isNumPalindrome(int num)
{
  int pwr = 0;

  if(num < 10)                                          //Step 1
      return true;
  else                                                  //Step 2
  {

    while (num / static_cast<int>(pow(10,pwr)) >= 10) //Step 2.a
      pwr++;

    while(num >= 10)                                    //Step 2.b
    {
      if((num / static_cast<int>(pow(10,pwr))) != (num % 10))
           return false;                                //Step 2.b.1
      else                                              //Step 2.b.2
      {
        num = num % static_cast<int>(pow(10,pwr)); //Step 2.b.2.1
        num = num / 10;                            //Step 2.b.2.1
        pwr = pwr - 2;                             //Step 2.b.2.2
      }
    }//end while

    return true;
  }//end else
}
```

In the definition of the function `isNumPalindrome`, the function `pow` from the header file `cmath` is used to find the highest power of `10` that divides the number. Therefore, make sure to include the header file `cmath` in your program.

Flow of Execution

As stated earlier, a C++ program is a collection of functions. Recall that functions can appear in any order. The only thing that you have to remember is that you must declare an identifier before you can use it. The program is compiled by the compiler sequentially from beginning to end. Thus, if the function **main** appears before other user-defined functions, it is compiled first. However, if **main** appears at the end (or middle) of the program, all functions whose definitions (not prototypes) appear before the function `main` are compiled before the function `main` in the order they are placed.

Function prototypes appear before any function definition, so the compiler translates these first. The compiler can then correctly translate a function call. However, when the program executes, the first statement in the function `main` always executes first, regardless of where in the program the function `main` is placed. Other functions execute only when they are called.

A function call statement transfers control to the first statement in the body of the function. In general, after the last statement of the called function executes, control is passed back to the point immediately following the function call. A value-returning function returns a value. Therefore, for value-returning functions, after executing the function when the control goes back to the caller, the value that the function returns replaces the function call statement. The execution continues at the point immediately following the function call.

PROGRAMMING EXAMPLE: LARGEST NUMBER

In this programming example, the function `larger` is used to determine the largest number from a set of numbers. For the purpose of illustration, this program determines the largest number from a set of 10 numbers. You can easily enhance this program to accommodate any set of numbers.

Input A set of 10 numbers.

Output The largest of 10 numbers.

Problem Analysis and Algorithm Design

Suppose that the input data is

```
15 20 7 8 28 21 43 12 35 3
```

Read the first number of the data set. Since this is the only number read to this point, you may assume that it is the largest number so far and call it `max`. Read the second number and call it `num`. Now compare `max` and `num`, and store the larger number into `max`. Now `max` contains the larger of the first two numbers. Read the third number. Compare it with `max` and store the larger number into `max`. At this point, `max` contains the largest of the first three numbers. Read the next number, compare it with `max`, and store the larger into `max`. Repeat this process for each remaining number in the data set. Eventually, `max` will contain the largest number in the data set. This discussion translates into the following algorithm:

1. Read the first number. Since this is the only number that you have read so far, it is the largest number so far. Save it in a variable called `max`.

2. For each remaining number in the list,
   a. Read the next number. Store it in a variable called **num**.
   b. Compare **num** and **max**. If **max < num**, then **num** is the new largest number and so update the value of **max** by copying **num** into **max**. If **max >= num**, discard **num**; that is, do nothing.
3. Because **max** now contains the largest number, print it.

To find the larger of two numbers, the program uses the function **larger**.

Complete Program Listing

```
//Program: Largest
#include <iostream>
using namespace std;

double larger(double x, double y);

int main()
{
   double num; //variable to hold the current number
   double max; //variable to hold the larger number
   int count;  //loop control variable

   cout<<"Enter 10 numbers."<<endl;
   cin>>num;                                          //Step 1
   max = num;                                         //Step 1

   for(count = 1; count < 10; count++)                //Step 2
   {
      cin>>num;                                       //Step 2a
      max = larger(max, num);                         //Step 2b
   }

   cout<<"The largest number is "<<max<<endl;  //Step 3

   return 0;
}//end main

double larger(double x, double y)
{
   if(x >= y)
      return x;
   else
      return y;
}
```

Sample Run: In this sample run, the user input is shaded.

```
Enter 10 numbers.
10 56 73 42 22 67 88 26 62 11
The largest number is 88
```

PROGRAMMING EXAMPLE: CABLE COMPANY

Chapter 4 contains a program to calculate the bill for a cable company. In that program, all of the programming instructions are packed in the function `main`. Here, we rewrite the same program using user-defined functions, further illustrating structured programming. The problem analysis phase shows how to divide a complex problem into smaller subproblems. It also shows that while solving a particular subproblem, you can focus only on that part of the problem.

Input to and output of the program are the same as before.

Problem Analysis and Algorithm Design

Since there are two types of customers, residential and business, the program contains two separate functions: one to calculate the bill for residential customers and one to calculate the bill for business customers. Both functions calculate the billing amount and then return the billing amount to the function `main`. The function `main` prints the amount due. Let us call the function that calculates the residential bill **`residential`** and the function that calculates the business bill **`business`**. The formulas to calculate the bills are the same as before.

As in Chapter 4, data such as the residential bill processing fee, the cost of residential basic service connection, and so on are special. Therefore, these are declared as named constants.

Function `residential` To compute the residential bill, you need to know the number of premium channels to which the customer subscribes. Based on the number of premium channels, you can calculate the billing amount. After calculating the billing amount, the function returns the billing amount using the **`return`** statement. The following four steps describe this function:

a. Prompt the user for the number of premium channels.
b. Read the number of premium channels.
c. Calculate the bill.
d. Return the amount due.

This function contains the statements to prompt the user to enter the number of premium channels (Step a) as well as to read the number of premium channels (Step b). Other items needed to calculate the billing amount, such as the cost of basic service connection and bill processing fees, are defined as named constants (before the definition of the function `main`). Therefore, to calculate the billing amount, this function does not need to get any value from the function `main`. This function, therefore, has no parameters.

Local Variables (Function `residential`) From the previous discussion, it follows that the function `residential` requires variables to store both the number of premium channels and the billing amount. This function needs only two local variables to calculate the billing amount:

```
int    noOfPChannels; //number of premium channels
double bAmount;       //billing amount
```

The definition of the function `residential` can now be written as follows:

```
double residential()
{
   int    noOfPChannels;
   double bAmount;

   cout<<"Enter the number of premium "
       <<"channels used : ";                        //Step a
   cin>>noOfPChannels;                              //Step b

   bAmount= rBillProcessingFee +                    //Step c
            rBasicServiceCost +
            noOfPChannels * rCostOfAPremiumChannel;

   return bAmount;                                  //Step d
}
```

Function `business` To compute the business bill, you need to know the number of both the basic service connections and premium channels to which the customer subscribes. Then, based on these numbers, you can calculate the billing amount. The billing amount is then returned using the `return` statement. The following six steps describe this function:

a. Prompt the user for the number of basic service connections.
b. Read the number of basic service connections.
c. Prompt the user for the number of premium channels.
d. Read the number of premium channels.
e. Calculate the bill.
f. Return the amount due.

This function contains the statements to prompt the user to enter the number of basic service connections and premium channels (Steps a and c). The function also contains statements to input the number of basic service connections and premium channels (Steps b and d). Other items needed to calculate the billing amount, such as the cost of basic service connection and bill processing fees, are defined as named constants (before the definition of the function `main`). It follows that to calculate the billing amount this function does not need to get any value from the function `main`. Therefore, it has no parameters.

Local Variables (Function `business`) From the preceding discussion, it follows that the function `business` requires variables to store the number of both basic service connections and premium channels as well as the billing amount. In fact, this function needs only three local variables to calculate the billing amount:

```
int  noOfBasicServiceConnections;
int  noOfPChannels;  //number of premium channels
double bAmount;      //billing amount
```

The definition of the function `business` can now be written as follows:

```
double business()
{
   int  noOfBasicServiceConnections;
   int  noOfPChannels;
   double bAmount;

   cout<<"Enter the number of basic "
       <<"service connections: ";                   //Step a
   cin>>noOfBasicServiceConnections;                //Step b

   cout<<"Enter the number of premium "
       <<"channels used :";                         //Step c
   cin>>noOfPChannels;                              //Step d

   if(noOfBasicServiceConnections <= 10)            //Step e
     bAmount = bBillProcessingFee + bBasicServiceCost +
               noOfPChannels * bCostOfAPremiumChannel;
   else
     bAmount = bBillProcessingFee + bBasicServiceCost +
               (noOfBasicServiceConnections -10) *
               bBasicConnectionCost +
               noOfPChannels * bCostOfAPremiumChannel;

   return bAmount;                                  //Step f
}
```

Main Algorithm (Function main)

1. To output floating-point numbers in a fixed decimal format with the decimal point and trailing zeros, set the manipulators **fixed** and **showpoint**.
2. To output floating-point numbers to two decimal places, set the precision to two decimal places.
3. Prompt the user for the account number.
4. Get the account number.
5. Prompt the user to enter the customer type.
6. Get the customer type.
7. a. If the customer type is R or r,
      i. Call the function **residential** to calculate the bill.
      ii. Print the bill.
   b. If the customer type is B or b,
      i. Call the function **business** to calculate the bill.
      ii. Print the bill.
   c. If the customer type is other than R, r, B, or b, it is an invalid customer type.

Complete Program Listing

```
//Cable company billing program
#include <iostream>
#include <iomanip>
using namespace std;

     //named constants; residential customers
const double rBillProcessingFee = 4.50;
const double rBasicServiceCost = 20.50;
const double rCostOfAPremiumChannel = 7.50;

     //named constants; business customers
const double bBillProcessingFee = 15.00;
const double bBasicServiceCost = 75.00;
const double bBasicConnectionCost = 5.00;
const double bCostOfAPremiumChannel = 50.00;

double residential();  //Function prototype
double business();     //Function prototype

int main()
{
     //declare variables
   int   accountNumber;
```

```
    char  customerType;
    double amountDue;

    cout<<fixed<<showpoint;                          //Step 1
    cout<<setprecision(2);                           //Step 2

    cout<<"This program computes a cable bill."
        <<endl;
    cout<<"Enter account number: ";                  //Step 3
    cin>>accountNumber;                              //Step 4
    cout<<endl;

    cout<<"Enter customer type: R, r "
        <<"(Residential), B, b (Business): "; //Step 5
    cin>>customerType;                               //Step 6

    switch(customerType)                             //Step 7
    {
       case 'r':                                     //Step 7a
       case 'R': amountDue = residential();          //Step 7a.i
                 cout<<"Account number = "
                     <<accountNumber<<endl;          //Step 7a.ii
                 cout<<"Amount due = $"
                     <<amountDue<<endl;              //Step 7a.ii
                 break;
       case 'b':                                     //Step 7b
       case 'B': amountDue = business();             //Step 7b.i
                 cout<<"Account number = "
                     <<accountNumber<<endl;          //Step 7b.ii
                 cout<<"Amount due = $"
                     <<amountDue<<endl;              //Step 7b.ii
                 break;
       default: cout<<"Invalid customer type."
                    <<endl;                          //Step 7c
    }

    return 0;
}

double residential()
{
    int    noOfPChannels; //number of premium channels
    double bAmount;       //billing Amount

    cout<<"Enter the number of premium "
        <<"channels used: ";
    cin>>noOfPChannels;
```

```
   bAmount = rBillProcessingFee +
             rBasicServiceCost +
             noOfPChannels * rCostOfAPremiumChannel;

   return bAmount;
}

double business()
{
   int  noOfBasicServiceConnections;
   int  noOfPChannels;  //number of premium channels
   double bAmount;      //billing Amount

   cout<<"Enter the number of basic "
       <<"service connections: ";
   cin>>noOfBasicServiceConnections;

   cout<<"Enter the number of premium "
       <<"channels used: ";
   cin>>noOfPChannels;

   if(noOfBasicServiceConnections <= 10)
      bAmount = bBillProcessingFee + bBasicServiceCost +
                noOfPChannels * bCostOfAPremiumChannel;
   else
      bAmount = bBillProcessingFee + bBasicServiceCost +
                (noOfBasicServiceConnections -10) *
                bBasicConnectionCost +
                noOfPChannels * bCostOfAPremiumChannel;
   return bAmount;
}
```

Sample Run: In this sample run, the user input is shaded.

```
This program computes a cable bill.
Enter account number: 21341

Enter customer type: R (Residential), B (Business): B
Enter the number of basic service connections: 25
Enter the number of premium channels used: 9
Account number = 21341
Amount due = $615.00
```

NOTE

To write this program using Standard C++ header files, replace the statements

```
#include <iostream>
#include <iomanip>
using namespace std;
```

with

```
#include <iostream.h>
#include <iomanip.h>
```

Also, you might have to replace the statement

```
cout<<fixed<<showpoint;
```

with

```
cout.setf(ios::fixed, ios::floatfield);
cout.setf(ios::showpoint);
```


Quick Review

1. Functions are like miniature programs and are called modules.
2. Functions enable you to divide a program into manageable tasks.
3. The C++ system provides the standard (predefined) functions.
4. To use a standard function, you must:
   (i) Know the name of the header file that contains the function's specification,
   (ii) Include that header file in the program, and
   (iii) Know the name and type of the function, and number and types of the parameters (arguments).
5. There are two types of user-defined functions: value-returning functions and void functions.
6. Variables defined in a function heading are called formal parameters.
7. Expressions, variables, or constant values used in a function call are called actual parameters.
8. In a function call, the number of actual parameters and their types must match with the formal parameters in the order given.
9. To call a function, use its name together with the actual parameter list.
10. A value-returning function returns a value. Therefore, a value-returning function is used (called) in either an expression or an output statement.

11. The general syntax of a user-defined function is

```
functionType  functionName(formal parameter list)
{
      statements
}
```

12. The line `functionType functionName(formal parameter list)` is called the function heading (or function header). Statements enclosed between braces `{` and `}` are called the body of the function.
13. The function heading and the body of the function are called the definition of the function.
14. If a function has no parameters, you still need the empty parentheses in both the function heading and the function call.
15. You can specify an empty formal parameter list by using either empty parentheses or the word **`void`** between parentheses.
16. A value-returning function returns its value via the **`return`** statement.
17. A function can have more than one **`return`** statement. However, whenever a **`return`** statement executes in a function, the remaining statements are skipped and the function exits.
18. A **`return`** statement returns only one value.
19. A function prototype is the function heading without the body of the function; the function prototype ends with the semicolon.
20. A function prototype announces the function type, as well as the type and number of parameters, used in the function.
21. In a function prototype, the names of the variables in the formal parameter list are optional.
22. Function prototypes help the compiler correctly translate each function call.
23. In a program, function prototypes are placed before every function definition, including the definition of the function `main`.
24. When you use function prototypes, user-defined functions can appear in any order in the program.
25. When the program executes, the execution always begins with the first statement in the function `main`.
26. User-defined functions execute only when they are called.
27. A call to a function transfers control from the caller to the called function.
28. In a function call statement, you specify only the actual parameters, not their data type or the function type.
29. When a function exits, the control goes back to the caller.

EXERCISES

1. Mark the following statements as true or false.
   a. To use a standard function in a program, you need to know only what the name of the function is and how to use it.
   b. A value-returning function returns only one value.
   c. Parameters allow you to use different values each time the function is called.
   d. When a `return` statement executes in a user-defined function, the function immediately exits.
   e. A value-returning function returns only integer values.
2. What is the output of the following C++ program? (Note that the function `sqrt` returns the square root of its argument. For example, `sqrt(16.0) = 4.0`.The specification of the function `sqrt` is in the header file `cmath`.)

```
#include <iostream>
#include <cmath>
using namespace std;

int main()
{
   int counter;

   for(counter = 1; counter <= 100; counter++)
         if(pow(floor(sqrt(counter)),2) == counter)
               cout<<counter<<" ";
   cout<<endl;
   return 0;
}
```

3. Which of the following function headings are valid? If they are invalid, explain why.
   a. `one(int a, int b)`
   b. `int thisone(char x)`
   c. `char another(int a, b)`
   d. `double yetanother`
4. Consider the following statements

```
double num1, num2, num3;
int int1, int2, int3;
int value;

num1 = 5.0; num2 = 6.0; num3 = 3.0;
int1 = 4; int2 = 7; int3 = 8;
```

and the function prototype

```
double cube(double a, double b, double c);
```

6

Which of the following statements are valid? If they are invalid, explain why.

a. `value = cube (num1, 15.0, num3);`

b. `cout<<cube(num1, num3, num2);`

c. `cout<<cube(6.0, 8.0, 10.5);`

d. `cout<<num1<<num3;`

e. `cout<<cube(num1, num3);`

f. `value = cube(num1, int2, num3);`

g. `value = cube(7, 8, 9);`

5. Consider the following functions:

```
int secret(int x)
{
        int i, j;

        i = 2 * x;
        if (i > 10)
           j = x / 2;
        else
           j = x / 3;

        return j-1;
}

int another(int a, int b)
{
        int i , j;

        j = 0;
        for(i = a; i <= b; i++)
            j = j + i;

        return j;
}
```

What is the output of each of the following program segments?

a.
```
x = 10;
cout<<secret(x)<<endl;
```

b.
```
x = 5; y = 8;
cout<<another(x,y)<<endl;
```

c.
```
x = 10; k = secret(x);
cout<<x<<" "<<k<<" "<<another(x,k)<<endl;
```

d.
```
x = 5; y = 8;
cout<<another(y,x)<<endl;
```

6. Consider the following function prototypes:

```
int test(int, char, double, int);
double two(double, double);
char three(int, int, char, double);
```

Answer the following questions.

a. How many parameters does the function `test` have? What is the type of the function `test` ?
b. How many parameters does function `two` have? What is the type of function `two`?
c. How many parameters does function `three` have? What is the type of function `three` ?
d. How many actual parameters are needed to call the function `test`? What is the type of each parameter, and in what order should you use these parameters in a call to the function `test`?
e. Write a C++ statement that prints the value returned by the function `test` with the actual parameters `5`, `5`, `7.3`, and `'z'`.
f. Write a C++ statement that prints the value returned by function `two` with the actual parameters `17.5` and `18.3`, respectively.
g. Write a C++ statement that prints the next character returned by function `three`. (Use your own actual parameters.)

7. Consider the following function:

```
int mystery(int x, double y, char ch)
{
    int u;
    if('A' <= ch && ch <= 'R')
        return(2 * x + static_cast<int>(y));
    else
        return(static_cast<int>(2*y)-x);
}
```

What is the output of the following C++ statements?

a. `cout<<mystery(5,4.3,'B')<<endl;`
b. `cout<<mystery(4,9.7,'v')<<endl;`
c. `cout<<2*mystery(6,3.9,'D')<<endl;`

8. Consider the following function:

```
int secret(int one)
{
    int I;
    int prod = 1;

    for(I = 1; I <= 3; I++)
          prod = prod * one;
    return prod;
}
```

a. What is the output of the following C++ statements?

   i. `cout<<secret(5)<<endl;`

   ii. `cout<<2 * secret(6)<<endl;`

b. What does the function **secret** do?

9. Show the output of the following program.

```
#include <iostream>
using namespace std;
int mystry(int);
int main()
{
   int n;

   for(n = 1; n <= 5; n++)
      cout<<mystry(n)<<endl;
   return 0;
}

int mystry(int k)
{
   int x, y;

   y = k;
   for(x = 1; x <= (k - 1); x++)
         y = y * (k - x);
   return y;
}
```

10. Show the output of the following program.

```
#include <iostream>
using namespace std;

bool strange(int);

int main()
{
   int num = 0;

   while(num <= 29)
   {
      if(strange(num))
            cout<<"True"<<endl;
      else
            cout<<"False"<<endl;
      num = num + 4;
   }
   return 0;
}
```

```
bool strange(int n)
{
   if(n % 2 == 0 && n % 3 == 0)
         return true;
   else
         return false;
}
```

PROGRAMMING EXERCISES

1. Write a program that uses the function `isNumPalindrome` given in Example 6-2 (Palindrome Number). Test your program on the following numbers: `10`, `34`, `22`, `333`, `678`, `67876`, `44444`, and `123454321`.
2. Write a value-returning function, `isVowel`, that returns the value `true` if a given character is a vowel and otherwise returns `false`.
3. Write a program that prompts the user to input a sequence of characters and outputs the number of vowels. (Use the function `isVowel` written in Programming Exercise 2.)
4. Consider the following program:

```
#include <iostream>
using namespace std;

int one(int x, int y);
double two(int x, double a);

int main()
{
   int num;
   double dec;
    .
    .
    .
   return 0;
}

int one(int x, int y)
{
    .
    .
    .
}
```

```
double two(int x, double a)
{
   int first;
   double z;
     .
     .
     .
}
```

a. Write the definition of function `one` so that it returns the sum of `x` and `y` if `x` is greater than `y`; otherwise, it should return `x` minus `2` times `y`.

b. Write the definition of function `two` as follows.

   i. Read a number and store it in `z`.

   ii. Update the value of `z` by adding the value of `a` to its previous value.

   iii. Assign the variable `first` the value returned by function `one` with parameters `6` and `8`.

   iv. Update the value of `first` by adding the value of `x` to its previous value.

   v. If the value of `z` is more than twice the value of `first`, return `z`; otherwise, return `2` times `first` minus `z`.

c. Write a C++ program that tests parts a and b. (Declare additional variables in the function `main`, if necessary.)

5. Write a function, `reverseDigit`, that takes an integer as a parameter and returns the number with its digits reversed. For example, the value of `reverseDigit(12345)` is `54321`.

6. The following formula gives the distance between two points (x_1, y_1) and (x_2, y_2) in the Cartesian plane:

$$\sqrt{(x_2-x_1)^2+(y_2-y_1)^2}$$

Given the center and a point on the circle, you can use this formula to find the radius of the circle. Write a program that prompts the user to enter the center and a point on the circle. The program should then output the circle's radius, diameter, circumference, and area. Your program must have at least the following functions:

a. `distance`: This function takes as its parameters four numbers that represent two points in the plane and returns the distance between them.

b. `radius`: This function takes as its parameters four numbers that represent the center and a point on the circle, calls the function `distance` to find the radius of the circle, and returns the circle's radius.

c. `circumference`: This function takes as its parameter a number that represents the radius of the circle and returns the circle's circumference. (If r is the radius, the circumference is $2\pi r$.)

d. `area`: This function takes as its parameter a number that represents the radius of the circle and returns the circle's area. (If r is the radius, the area is πr^2.)

Assume that $\pi = 3.1416$.

7. If P is the population on the first day of the year, B is the birth rate, and D is the death rate, the estimated population at the end of the year is given by the formula

$$P+\frac{B*P}{100}-\frac{D*P}{100}$$

The population growth rate is given by the formula

$$B-D$$

Write a program that prompts the user to enter the starting population, birth and death rates, and `n`, the number of years. The program should then calculate and print the estimated population after `n` years. Your program must consist of the following functions:

a. `growthRate`: This function takes as its parameters the birth and death rates, and it returns the population growth rate.

b. `estimatedPopulation`: This function takes as its parameters the current population, population growth rate, and `n`, the number of years. It returns the estimated population after `n` years.

Your program should not accept a negative birth rate, negative death rate, or a population less than 2.

8. Rewrite the program in Programming Exercise 12 of Chapter 4 (cell phone company) so that it uses the following functions to calculate the billing amount. (In this programming exercise, do not output the number of minutes during which the service is used.)

a. `regularBill`: This function calculates and returns the billing amount for regular service.

b. `premiumBill`: This function calculates and returns the billing amount for premium service.

CHAPTER

7

USER-DEFINED FUNCTIONS II

In this chapter, you will:

- Learn how to construct and use void functions in a program
- Discover the difference between value and reference parameters
- Explore reference parameters and value-returning functions
- Learn about the scope of an identifier
- Examine the difference between local and global identifiers
- Discover static variables
- Learn function overloading
- Explore functions with default parameters

In Chapter 6, you learned how to use value-returning functions. In this chapter, you will explore user-defined functions in general and especially those C++ functions that do not have a data type, called **void functions**.

VOID FUNCTIONS

Void functions and value-returning functions have similar structures. Both have a heading part and a statement part. You can place user-defined void functions either before or after the function `main`. However, the program execution always begins with the first statement in the function `main`. If you place user-defined void functions after the function `main`, you should place the function prototype before the function `main`. Because a void function does not have a data type, `functionType` in the heading part and the `return` statement in the body of the void function are meaningless. However, in a void function, you can use the `return` statement without any value; it is typically used to exit the function early. Like value-returning functions, void functions may or may not have formal parameters.

Because void functions do not have a data type, they are not used (that is, called) in an expression. A call to a void function is a stand-alone statement. Thus, to call a void function, you use the function name together with the actual parameters (if any) in a stand-alone statement.

Void Functions Without Parameters

This section discusses void functions that do not have formal parameters.

Function Definition

The general form (syntax) of the void function without parameters is as follows:

```
void functionName(void)
{
    statements
}
```

The word `void` inside the parentheses is optional. In C++, `void` is a reserved word.

Like a variable name, a function name should be descriptive, so be sure to use meaningful names when naming functions.

Function Call

The function call has the following syntax:

```
functionName();
```

Because these functions do not have parameters, no value can be passed to them (unless you use global variables, defined later in this chapter). Such functions are thus good only for displaying information about the program or printing statements. Consider the following program.

Example 7-1

Suppose you want to print the following banner to announce the annual spring sale. See a similar exercise in Chapter 2, Programming Exercise 7).

```
******************************
******************************
********** Annual   ***********
******************************
******************************
******* Spring Sale **********
******************************
******************************
```


The banner starts with two lines of stars. After printing the line containing the text `Annual`, you need to print another two lines of stars. After printing the line containing the text `Spring Sale`, you need to print two more lines of stars. You can write a function that prints two lines of stars and call it whenever you need it. The complete program looks like this:

```
#include <iostream>
using namespace std;

void printStars(void);
int main()
{
  printStars();                                           //Line 1
  cout<<"********** Annual   ***********"<<endl;          //Line 2
  printStars();                                           //Line 3
  cout<<"******* Spring Sale **********"<<endl;           //Line 4
  printStars();                                           //Line 5
  return 0;
}

void printStars(void)
{
     cout<<"******************************"<<endl;
     cout<<"******************************"<<endl;
}
```

Output:

```
******************************
******************************
********** Annual   ***********
******************************
******************************
******* Spring Sale **********
******************************
******************************
```

In Line 1, the function **printStars** is called and it outputs the first two lines of the output. The statement in Line 2 outputs the line of stars containing the text **Annual**, which is the third line of the output. In Line 3, the function **printStars** is called again and it outputs the next two lines of the output. The statement in Line 4 then outputs the line of stars containing the text **Spring Sale**, which is the sixth line of the output. In Line 5, the function **printStars** is called again and it outputs the last two lines of the output.

The statement **printStars();** in the function **main** is a function call.

In the previous program, you can replace the function **printStars** with the following function:

```
void printStars(void)
{
   int stars, lines;

   for(lines = 1; lines <= 2; lines++)     //Line 1
   {
     for(stars = 1; stars <= 30; stars++) //Line 2
         cout<<"*";                       //Line 3
     cout<<endl;                          //Line 4
   }
}
```

In this function definition, the outer **for** loop (Line 1) executes twice. For each iteration of the outer **for** loop (Line 1), the inner **for** loop (Line 2) executes 30 times, each time printing 30 stars in a line. The statement at Line 3 prints each star. The **cout** statement at Line 4 positions the cursor at the beginning of the next line on the standard output device. Because the outer **for** loop executes twice, this function outputs two lines of stars with 30 stars in each line.

You would agree that the definition of the function **printStar** using **for** loops to output 2 lines of stars with 30 stars in each line is much easier to modify than the definition of **printStar** given earlier. If you need to output 5 lines of stars instead of 2 lines, for instance, you can replace the number `2` (in the first **for** loop, Line 1) with the number `5`. Similarly, if you need to output `40` stars instead of `30` stars in each line, you can replace the number `30` (in the second **for** loop, Line 2) with the number `40`. Furthermore, as you will soon discover, the definition of the function **printStar** using **for** loops is much easier to modify in order to establish the communication links with the calling function (such as the function **main**) and to do different things each time the function **printStar** is called.

In the previous program, the function **printStars** always prints two lines of stars, with 30 stars in each line. Now suppose that you want to print the following pattern (a triangle of stars):

You could write a function similar to the function **printStars**. However, if you need to extend this pattern to 20 lines, the function **printStars** will have 20 lines. Every time you call the function **printStars**, it prints the same number of lines; the function **printStars** is inflexible. However, if you can somehow tell the function **printStars** how many lines to print, you can enhance its flexibility considerably. A communication link must exist between the calling function and the called function.

7

Void Functions with Parameters

The previous section discussed void functions without parameters and pointed out the limitations of such functions. In particular, you learned that no information can be passed in and out of void functions without parameters. The communication link between the calling function and the called function is established by using parameters. This section discusses void functions with parameters.

Function Definition

The function definition of void functions with parameters has the following syntax:

```
void functionName(formal parameter list)
{
     statements
}
```

Formal Parameter List

The formal parameter list has the following syntax:

```
dataType& variable, dataType& variable, ...
```

You must specify both the data type and the variable name in the formal parameter list. The symbol & after **dataType** has a special meaning; it is used only for certain formal parameters and is discussed later in this chapter.

Function Call

The function call has the following syntax:

```
functionName(actual parameter list);
```

Actual Parameter List

The actual parameter list has the following syntax:

```
expression or variable, expression or variable, ...
```

As with value-returning functions, in a function call the number of actual parameters together with their data types must match the formal parameters in the order given. Actual and formal parameters have a one-to-one correspondence. A function call results in the execution of the body of the called function. (Functions with default parameters are discussed at the end of this chapter.)

Example 7-2

```
void funexp(int a, double b, char c, int& x)
{
    .
    .
    .
}
```

The function `funexp` has four parameters.

Parameters provide a communication link between the calling function (such as `main`) and the called function. They enable functions to manipulate different data each time they are called. In general, there are two types of formal parameters: **value parameters** and **reference parameters**.

Value parameter: A formal parameter that receives a copy of the content of the corresponding actual parameter.

Reference parameter: A formal parameter that receives the location (memory address) of the corresponding actual parameter.

When you attach `&` after the `dataType` in the formal parameter list of a function, the variable following that `dataType` becomes a reference parameter.

Example 7-3

```
void expfun(int one, int& two, char three, double& four);
```

The function **`expfun`** has four parameters: (1) `one`, a value parameter of the type `int`; (2) `two`, a reference parameter of the type `int`; (3) `three`, a value parameter of the type `char`, and (4) `four`, a reference parameter of the type `double`.

Before considering examples of void functions with parameters, let us make the following observation about value and reference parameters. From the definition of value parameters, it follows that if a formal parameter is a value parameter, the value of the corresponding actual parameter is copied into the formal parameter. That is, the value parameter has its own copy of the data. Therefore, during program execution, the value parameter manipulates the data stored in its own memory space. After copying the data, the value parameter has no connection with the actual parameter.

On the other hand, if a formal parameter is a reference parameter, it receives the address of the corresponding actual parameter. That is, a reference parameter stores the address of the corresponding actual parameter. During program execution to manipulate the data, the address stored in the reference parameter directs it to the memory space of the corresponding actual parameter. In other words, during program execution, the reference parameter manipulates the data stored in the memory space of the corresponding actual parameter. Any changes that a reference parameter makes to its data immediately changes the value of the corresponding actual parameter. Examples 7-5 and 7-6 explicitly show how value and reference parameters work during program execution. Note that the examples in Chapter 6 use only value parameters.

Let us now write the C++ program to print the pattern (triangle of stars) given in the previous section.

Example 7-4

The following C++ program prints a triangle of stars:

```
//Program: Print a triangle of stars
#include <iostream>
using namespace std;

void printStars(int blanks, int starsInLine);

int main()
{
   int numberOfLines;
   int counter;
   int numberOfBlanks;

   cout<<"Enter the number of star lines (1 to 20)"
       <<" to be printed--> ";                        //Line 1
   cin>>numberOfLines;                                //Line 2
```

```
    while(numberOfLines <=0 || numberOfLines > 20)         //Line 3
    {
      cout<<"Number of star lines should be "
          <<"between 1 and 20"<<endl;                      //Line 4
      cout<<"Enter the number of star lines "
          <<"(1 to 20) to be printed-> ";                  //Line 5
      cin>>numberOfLines;                                  //Line 6
    }

    cout<<endl<<endl;                                      //Line 7
    numberOfBlanks = 30;                                   //Line 8

    for(counter = 1; counter <= numberOfLines; counter++)  //Line 9
    {
      printStars(numberOfBlanks, counter);                 //Line 10
      numberOfBlanks--;                                    //Line 11
    }

   return 0;                                               //Line 12
}

void printStars(int blanks, int starsInLine)
{
  int count;

  for(count = 1; count <= blanks; count++)                 //Line 13
     cout<<" ";                                            //Line 14

  for(count = 1; count <= starsInLine; count++)            //Line 15
     cout<<" *";                                           //Line 16

  cout<<endl;
}
```

Sample Run: In this sample run, the user input is shaded.

```
Enter the number of star lines (1 to 20) to be printed-> 15


                *
               * *
              * * *
             * * * *
            * * * * *
           * * * * * *
          * * * * * * *
         * * * * * * * *
        * * * * * * * * *
       * * * * * * * * * *
      * * * * * * * * * * *
     * * * * * * * * * * * *
    * * * * * * * * * * * * *
   * * * * * * * * * * * * * *
  * * * * * * * * * * * * * * *
```

In this program, the statement (see Line 10)

```
printStars(numberOfBlanks, counter);
```

in the function `main` is a function call. The identifier `numberOfBlanks` and `counter` are actual parameters.

The function `printStars` works as follows. The function `printStars` has two parameters. Whenever the function `printStars` executes, it outputs a line of stars with a certain number of blanks before the stars. The number of blanks and the number of stars in a line are passed as parameters to the function `printStars`. The first parameter, `blanks`, tells how many blanks to print; the second parameter, `starsInLine`, tells how many stars to print in a line. If the value of the parameter `blanks` is `30`, for instance, then the first `for` loop (Line 13) in the function `printStars` executes 30 times and prints 30 blanks. Also, because you want to print spaces between the stars, every iteration of the second `for` loop (Line 15) in the function `printStars` prints `' *'` (Line 16)—that is, a blank followed by a star.

7

In the function `main`, the user is first asked to specify how many lines of stars to print (Line 1). (In this program, the user is restricted to 20 lines because a triangular grid of up to 20 lines fits nicely on the screen.) Because the program is restricted to only 20 lines, the `while` loop at Lines 3–6 ensures that the program prints only the triangular grid of stars if the number of lines is between 1 and 20.

The `for` loop (Line 9) in the function `main` calls the function `printStars` (Line 10). Every iteration of this `for` loop specifies the number of blanks followed by the number of stars to print in a line, using the variables `numberOfBlanks` and `counter`. Every call of the function `printStars` receives one fewer blank and one more star than the previous call. For example, the first iteration of the `for` loop in the function `main` specifies `30` blanks and `1` star (which are passed as parameters, `numberOfBlanks` and `counter`, to the function `printStars`). The `for` loop then:

- Decrements the number of blanks by 1. This is done by executing the following statement at Line 11:

  ```
  numberOfBlanks--;
  ```

- At the end of the `for` loop, the number of stars is incremented by 1 for the next iteration. This is done by executing the update statement, `counter++` (Line 9), in the `for` statement, which increments the value of the variable `counter` by `1`.

In other words, the second call of the function `printStars` receives `29` blanks and `2` stars as parameters.

Reference Parameters

After copying data, a value parameter has no connection with the actual parameter, so value parameters cannot pass any result back to the calling function. When the function executes, any changes made to the formal parameters do not in any way affect the actual parameters. The actual parameter has no knowledge of what is happening to the formal parameter. Thus, value parameters cannot pass information outside the function. Value parameters provide only a one-way link between actual parameters and formal parameters. Hence, functions with only value parameters have limitations. On the other hand, since a reference parameter receives the address (that is, memory location of the actual parameter), reference parameters can pass one or more values from a function and can change the value of the actual parameter.

Reference parameters are useful in three situations:

- When you want to return more than one value from a function
- When the value of the actual parameter needs to be changed
- When passing the address would save memory space and time relative to copying a large amount of data.

The first two situations are illustrated throughout this book. Chapters 9 and 13 discuss the third situation when arrays and classes are introduced.

Recall that, when you attach `&` after the **`dataType`** in the formal parameter list of a function, the variable following that **`dataType`** becomes a reference parameter.

(Constant Reference Parameters) You can declare a reference (formal) parameter as a constant by using the keyword `const`. Chapter 13 discusses constant reference parameters. Until then, the reference parameters that you use will be non-constant as defined in this chapter. From the definition of a reference parameter, it follows that a constant value or an expression cannot be passed to a non-constant reference parameter. So if a formal parameter is a non-constant reference parameter, then during a function call its corresponding actual parameter must be a variable.

Example 7-5

Consider the following program. Given a course score (a value between `0` and `100`), it determines a student's course grade. This program has three functions: **`main`**, **`getScore`**, and **`printGrade`**. These three functions are described as follows.

1. `main`
   a. Get the course score.
   b. Print the course grade.
2. `getScore`
   a. Prompt the user for the input.
   b. Get the input.
   c. Print the course score.
3. `printGrade`
   a. Calculate the course grade.
   b. Print the course grade.

The complete program is as follows.

```
//Program: Compute grade.
//This program reads a course score and prints the
//associated course grade.

#include <iostream>
using namespace std;
void getScore(int& score);
void printGrade(int score);

int main ()
{
   int courseScore;

   cout<<"Line 1: Based on the course score, this program "
       <<"computes the course grade."<<endl;             //Line 1

   getScore(courseScore);                                //Line 2
   printGrade(courseScore);                              //Line 3
   return 0;
}

void getScore(int& score)
{
   cout<<"Line 4: Enter course score—> ";                //Line 4
   cin>>score;                                           //Line 5
   cout<<endl<<"Line 6: Course score is "
       <<score<<endl;                                    //Line 6
}

void printGrade(int score)
{
   cout<<"Line 7: Your grade for the course is ";        //Line 7

   if(score >= 90)                                       //Line 8
      cout<<"A"<<endl;
   else if(score >= 80)
           cout<<"B"<<endl;
   else if(score >= 70)
           cout<<"C"<<endl;
   else if(score >= 60)
           cout<<"D"<<endl;
   else
          cout<<"F"<<endl;
 }
```

Sample Run: In this sample run, the user input is shaded.

```
Line 1: Based on the course score, this program computes the course grade.
Line 4: Enter course score—> 85

Line 6: Course score is 85
Line 7: Your grade for the course is B
```

This program works as follows. The program starts to execute at Line 1, which prints the first line of the output (see the Sample Run). The statement in Line 2 calls the function `getScore` with the actual parameter `courseScore` (a variable declared in `main`). Because the formal parameter `score` of the function `getScore` is a reference parameter, the address (that is, the memory location of the variable `courseScore`) passes to `score`. Thus, both `score` and `courseScore` refer to the same memory location, which is `courseScore`. Any changes that `score` makes immediately change the value of `courseScore`.

Control is then transferred to the function `getScore`, and the statement in Line 4 executes, printing the second line of output (see the Sample Run). This statement prompts the user to enter the course `score`. The statement in Line 5 reads and stores the value entered by the user (`85` in the Sample Run) in `score`, which is actually `courseScore` (because `score` is a reference parameter). Thus, at this point, the value of the variables `score` and `courseScore` is `85`. Next, the statement in Line 6 outputs the value of `score` as shown by the third line of the sample output. After Line 6 executes, control goes back to the function `main`.

The statement in Line 3 executes next. It is a function call to the function `printGrade` with the actual parameter `courseScore`. Because the formal parameter `score` of the function `printScore` is a value parameter, the parameter `score` receives the value of the corresponding actual parameter `courseScore`. Thus, the value of `score` is `85`. After copying the value of `courseScore` into `score`, no communication exists between `score` and `courseScore`. Now the program executes the statement in Line 7, which outputs the fourth line (see the statement marked Line 7 in the Sample Run). The `if...else` statement in Line 8 determines and outputs the grade for the course. Because the output statement in Line 7 does not contain the newline character or the manipulator `endl`, the output of the `if...else` statement is part of the fourth line of the output (see the Sample Run). After the `if...else` statement executes, control goes back to the function `main`. Because the next statement to execute in the function `main` is the last statement of the function `main`, the program terminates.

In this program, the function `main` first calls the function `getScore` to get the course score from the user. The function `main` then calls the function `printGrade` to calculate and print the grade based on the course score. The course score is retrieved by the function `getScore`, and later this course score is used by the function `printGrade`. Because the value retrieved by the `getScore` function is used later in the program, the function `getScore` must pass this value outside. Thus, the formal parameter that holds this value must be a reference parameter.

Following is a summary of the properties of value and reference parameters.

Value and Reference Parameters and Memory Allocation

When a function is called, memory for its formal parameters and variables declared in the body of the function (called **local variables**) is allocated in the function data area. Recall that, in the case of a value parameter, the value of the actual parameter is copied into the memory cell of its corresponding formal parameter. In the case of a reference parameter, the address of the actual parameter passes to the formal parameter. That is, the content of the formal parameter is an address. During data manipulation, the content of the formal parameter directs the computer to manipulate the data of the memory cell indicated by its content. Thus, in the case of a reference parameter, both the actual and formal parameters refer to the same memory location. Consequently, during program execution, changes made by the formal parameter permanently change the value of the actual parameter.

Stream variables (for example, `ifstream` and `ofstream`) should be passed by reference to a function. After opening the input/output file or after reading and/or outputting data, the state of the input and/or output stream can then be passed outside the function.

Because parameter passing is fundamental to any programming language, Examples 7-6 through 7-8 further illustrate this concept. Each covers a different scenario.

Example 7-6

The following program shows how value and reference parameters work:

```
//Example 7-6: Reference and value parameters

#include <iostream>
using namespace std;

void funOne(int a, int& b, char v);
void funTwo(int& x, int y, char& w);

int main()
{
   int num1, num2;
   char ch;

   num1 = 10;                                               //Line 1
   num2 = 15;                                               //Line 2
   ch = 'A';                                                //Line 3

   cout<<"Line 4: Inside main: num1 = "<<num1
       <<", num2 = "<<num2<<", and ch = "<<ch<<endl;        //Line 4

   funOne(num1, num2, ch);                                  //Line 5
```

```
    cout<<"Line 6: After funOne: num1 = "<<num1
        <<", num2 = "<<num2<<", and ch = "<<ch<<endl;      //Line 6

    funTwo(num2, 25, ch);                                   //Line 7

    cout<<"Line 8: After funTwo: num1 = "<<num1
        <<", num2 = "<<num2<<", and ch = "<<ch<<endl;      //Line 8

return 0;
}

void funOne(int a, int& b, char v)
{
    int one;

    one = a;                                                //Line 9
    a++;                                                    //Line 10
    b = b * 2;                                              //Line 11
    v = 'B';                                                //Line 12

    cout<<"Line 13: Inside funOne: a = "<<a<<", b = "<<b
        <<", v = "<<v<<", and one = "<<one<<endl;          //Line 13
}

void funTwo(int& x, int y, char& w)
{
    x++;                                                    //Line 14
    y = y * 2;                                              //Line 15
    w = 'G';                                                //Line 16
    cout<<"Line 17: Inside funTwo: x = "<<x
        <<", y = "<<y <<", and w = "<<w<<endl;             //Line 17

}
```

Output:

```
Line 4: Inside main: num1 = 10, num2 = 15, and ch = A
Line 13: Inside funOne: a = 11, b = 30, v = B, and one = 10
Line 6: After funOne: num1 = 10, num2 = 30, and ch = A
Line 17: Inside funTwo: x = 31, y = 50, and w = G
Line 8: After funTwo: num1 = 10, num2 = 31, and ch = G
```

Let us walk through this program. The lines are numbered for easy reference, and the values of the variables are shown before and/or after each statement executes.

Just before Line 1 executes, memory is allocated only for the variables of the function `main`; this memory is not initialized. After Line 3 executes, the variables are as shown in Figure 7-1.

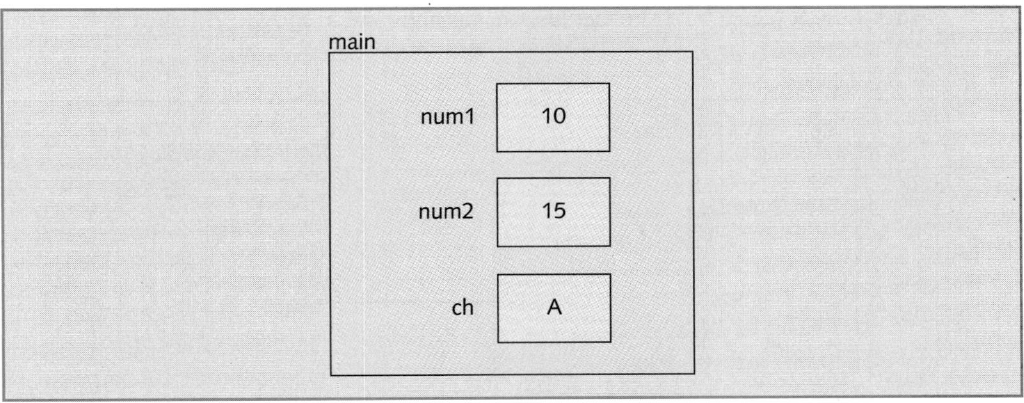

Figure 7-1 Values of the variables after Line 3 executes

Line 4 produces the following output:

```
Line 4: Inside main: num1 = 10, num2 = 15, and ch = A
```

The statement in Line 5 is a function call to the function **funOne**. Now function **funOne** has three parameters and one local variable. Memory for the parameters and the local variable of function **funOne** is allocated. Because the formal parameter b is a reference parameter, it receives the address (memory location) of the corresponding actual parameter, which is **num2**. The other two formal parameters are value parameters, so they copy the values of their corresponding actual parameters. Just before Line 9 executes, the variables are as shown in Figure 7-2.

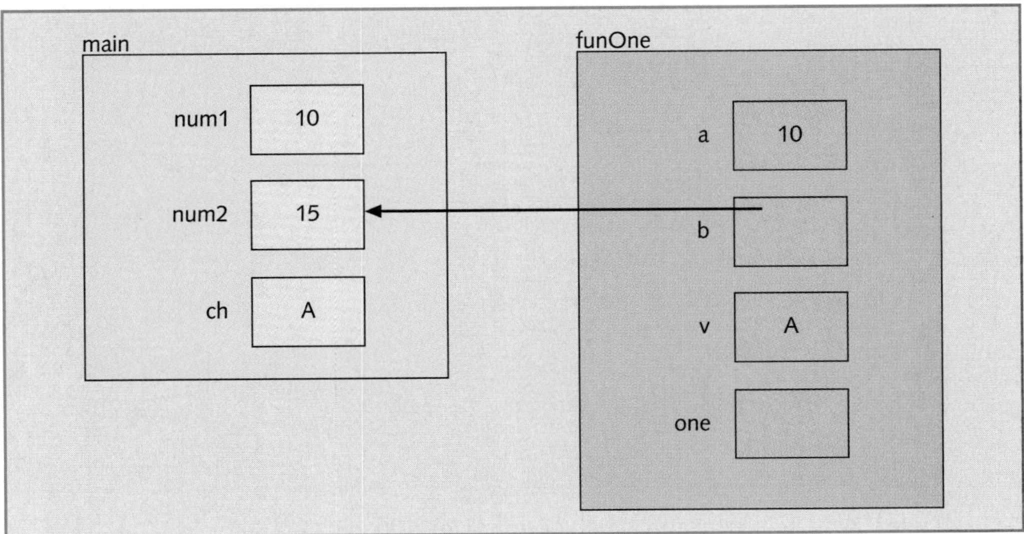

Figure 7-2 Values of the variables just before Line 9 executes

After Line 9 (`one = a;`) executes, the variables are as shown in Figure 7-3.

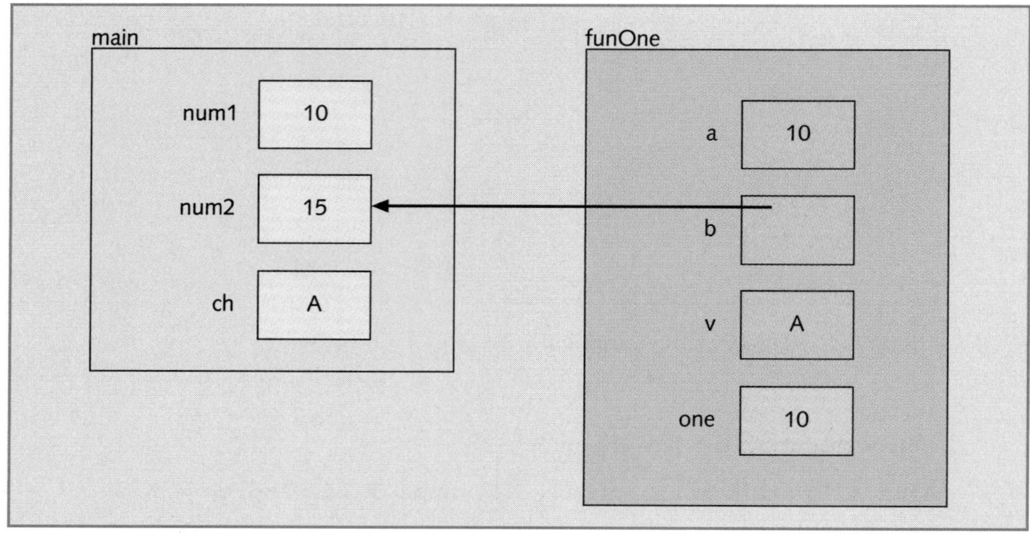

Figure 7-3 Values of the variables after Line 9 executes

After Line 10 (`a++;`) executes, the variables are as shown in Figure 7-4.

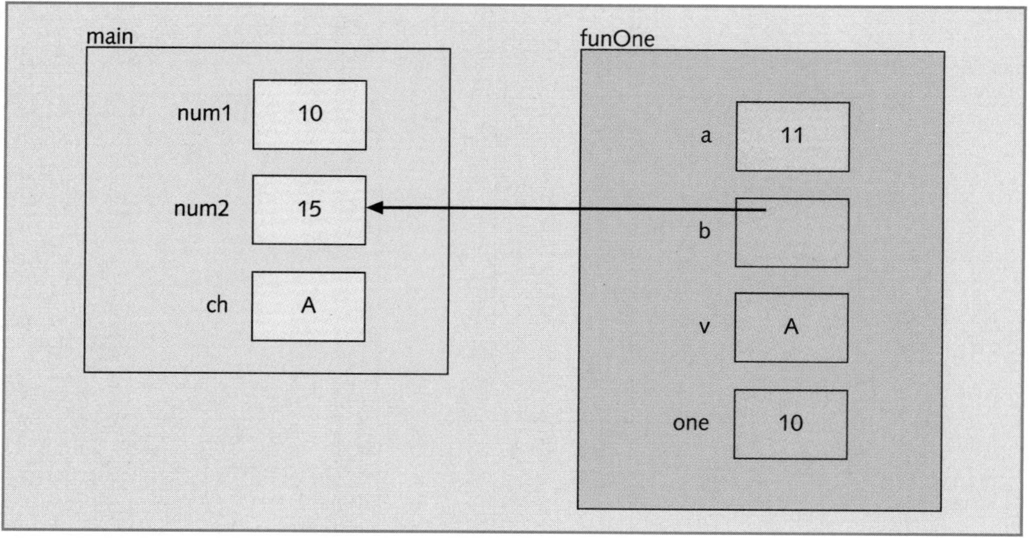

Figure 7-4 Values of the variables after Line 10 executes

After Line 11 (`b = b * 2;`) executes, the variables are as shown in Figure 7-5. (Note that the variable `b` changed the value of `num2`.)

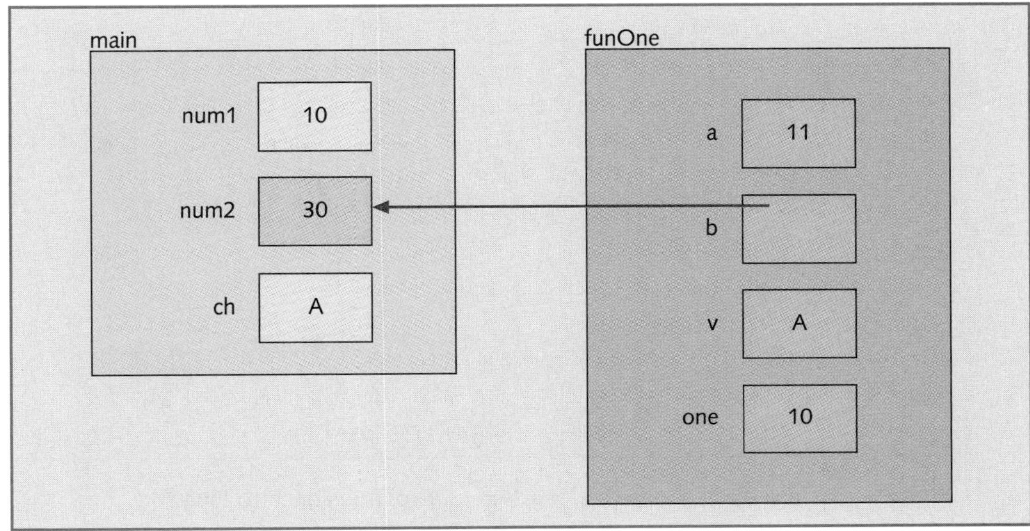

Figure 7-5 Values of the variables after Line 11 executes

After Line 12 (`v = 'B';`) executes, the variables are as shown in Figure 7-6.

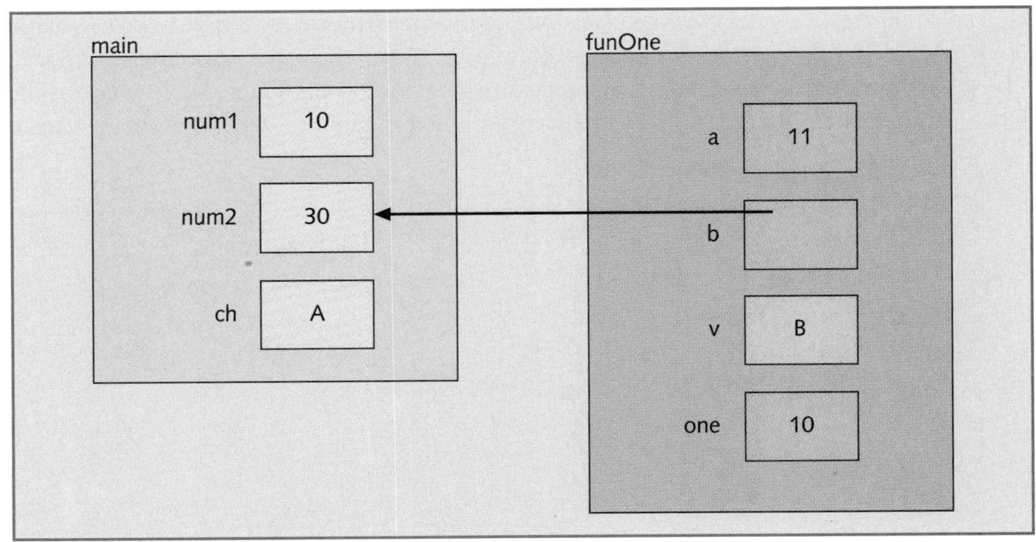

Figure 7-6 Values of the variables after Line 12 executes

Line 13 produces the following output:

```
Line 13: Inside funOne: a = 11, b = 30, v = B, and one = 10
```

After Line 13 executes, control goes back to Line 6 and the memory allocated for the variables of function `funOne` is deallocated. Figure 7-7 shows the values of the variables of the function `main`.

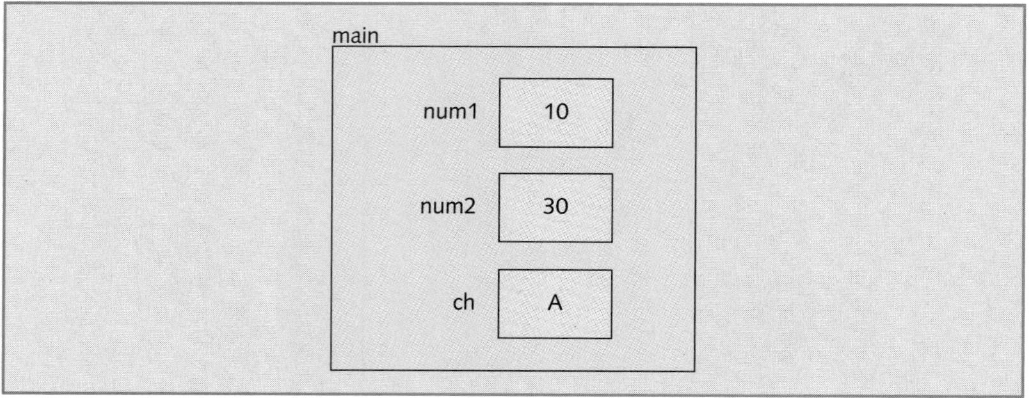

Figure 7-7 Values of the variables when control goes back to Line 6

Line 6 produces the following output:

```
Line 6: After funOne: num1 = 10, num2 = 30, and ch = A
```

The statement in Line 7 is a function call to the function `funTwo`. Now `funTwo` has three parameters: `x`, `y`, and `w`. Also, `x` and `w` are reference parameters and `y` is a value parameter. Thus, `x` receives the address of its corresponding actual parameter, which is `num2`, and `w` receives the address of its corresponding actual parameter, which is `ch`. The variable `y` copies the value `25` into its memory cell. We have the picture shown in Figure 7-8 before Line 14 executes.

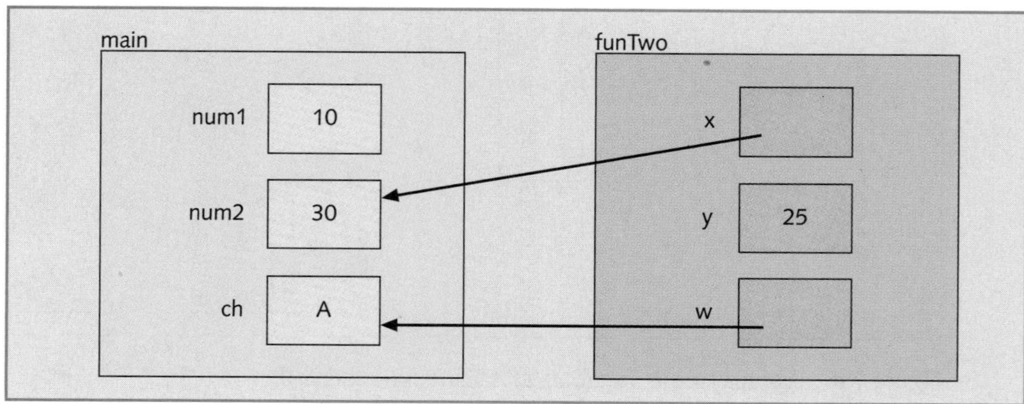

Figure 7-8 Values of the variables before Line 14 executes

After Line 14 (`x++;`) executes, the variables are as shown in Figure 7-9. (Note that the variable `x` changed the value of `num2`.)

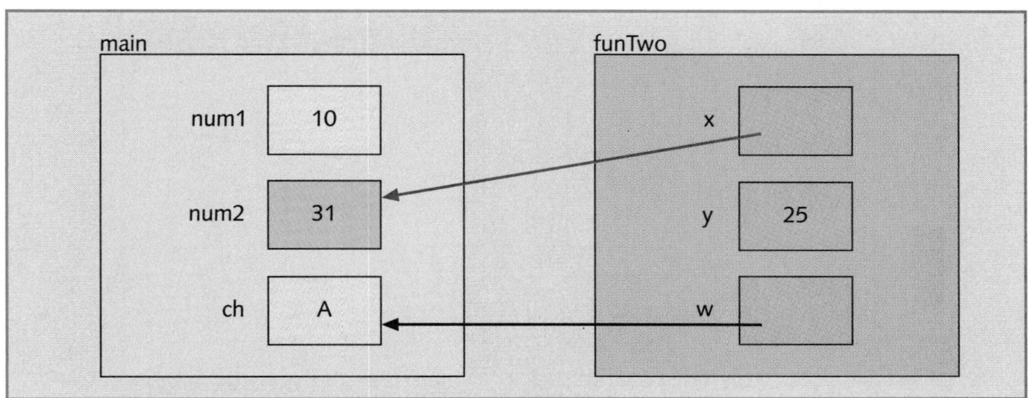

Figure 7-9 Values of the variables after Line 14 executes

After Line 15 (`y = y * 2;`) executes, the variables are as shown in Figure 7-10.

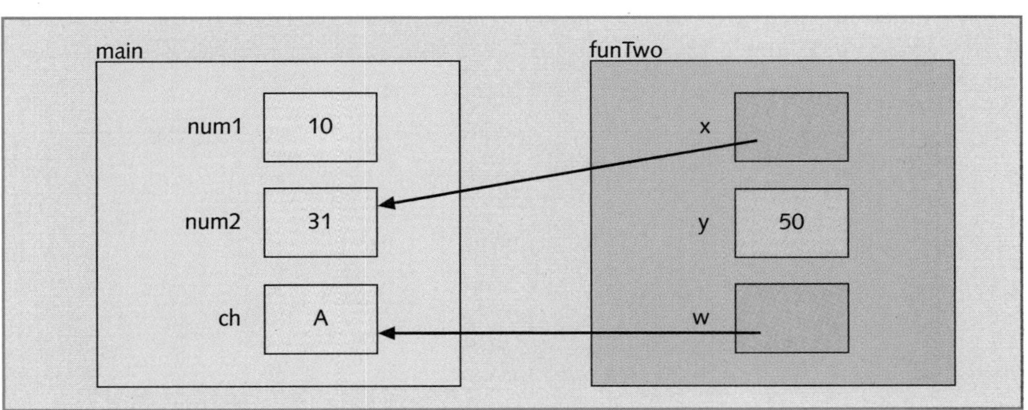

Figure 7-10 Values of the variables after Line 15 executes

After Line 16 (`w = 'G';`) executes, the variables are as shown in Figure 7-11. (Note that the variable `w` changed the value of `ch`.)

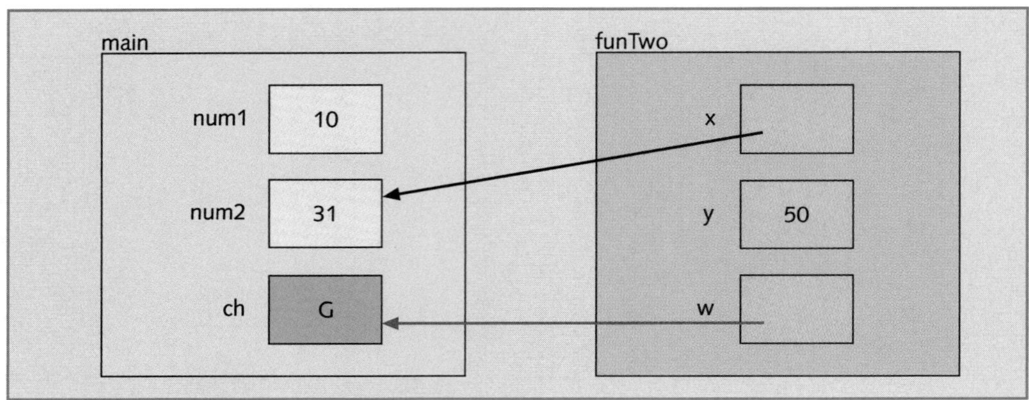

Figure 7-11 Values of the variables after Line 16 executes

Line 17 produces the following output:

```
Line 17: Inside funTwo: x = 31, y = 50, and w = G
```

After Line 17 executes, control goes to Line 8. The memory allocated for the variables of function **funTwo** is deallocated. The values of the variables of the function **main** are as shown in Figure 7-12.

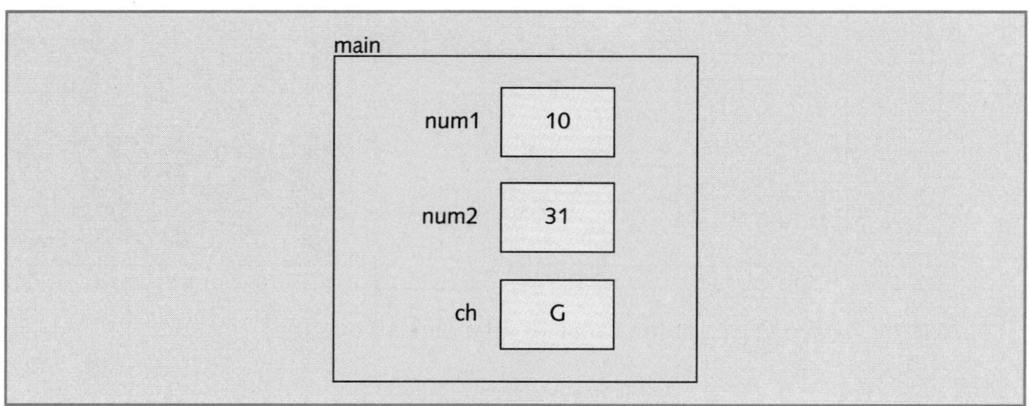

Figure 7-12 Values of the variables when control goes to Line 8

Line 8 produces the following output:

```
Line 8: After funTwo: num1 = 10, num2 = 31, and ch = G
```

After Line 8 executes, the program terminates.

Example 7-7

This example also shows how reference parameters manipulate actual parameters.

```
//Example 7-7: Reference and value parameters
//Program: Makes You Think.

#include <iostream>
using namespace std;

void addFirst(int& first, int& second);
void doubleFirst(int one, int two);
void squareFirst(int& ref, int val);

int main ()
{
   int num = 5;

   cout<<"Line 1: Inside main:  num = "<<num<<endl;     //Line 1

   addFirst(num,num);                                   //Line 2
   cout<<"Line 3: Inside main after addFirst:"
       <<"  num = " <<num<<endl;                        //Line 3

   doubleFirst(num,num);                                //Line 4
   cout<<"Line 5: Inside main after "
       <<"doubleFirst:  num = "<<num<<endl;             //Line 5

   squareFirst(num,num);                                //Line 6
   cout<<"Line 7: Inside main after "
       <<"squareFirst:  num = "<<num<<endl;             //Line 7

   return 0;
}

void addFirst(int& first, int& second)
{
   cout<<"Line 8: Inside addFirst:  first = "<<first
       <<", second = "<<second<<endl;                   //Line 8

   first = first + 2;                                   //Line 9

   cout<<"Line 10: Inside addFirst:  first = "<<first
       <<", second = "<<second<<endl;                   //Line 10

   second = second * 2;                                 //Line 11

   cout<<"Line 12: Inside addFirst:  first = "<<first
      <<", second = "<<second<<endl;                    //Line 12
}
```

```
void doubleFirst(int one, int two)
{
   cout<<"Line 13: Inside doubleFirst:  one = "<<one
       <<", two = "<<two<<endl;                        //Line 13

   one = one * 2;                                      //Line 14

   cout<<"Line 15: Inside doubleFirst:  one = "<<one
       <<", two = "<<two<<endl;                        //Line 15

   two = two + 2;                                      //Line 16

   cout<<"Line 17: Inside doubleFirst:  one = "<<one
       <<", two = "<<two<<endl;                        //Line 17
}

void squareFirst(int& ref, int val)
{
   cout<<"Line 18: Inside squareFirst: ref = "
       <<ref <<", val = "<< val<<endl;                 //Line 18

   ref = ref * ref;                                    //Line 19

   cout<<"Line 20: Inside squareFirst: ref = "
       <<ref <<", val = "<< val<<endl;                 //Line 20

   val = val + 2;                                      //Line 21

   cout<<"Line 22: Inside squareFirst: ref = "
       <<ref <<", val = "<< val<<endl;                 //Line 22
}
```

Output:

```
Line 1: Inside main:  num = 5
Line 8: Inside addFirst:  first = 5, second = 5
Line 10: Inside addFirst:  first = 7, second = 7
Line 12: Inside addFirst:  first = 14, second = 14
Line 3: Inside main after addFirst:  num = 14
Line 13: Inside doubleFirst:  one = 14, two = 14
Line 15: Inside doubleFirst:  one = 28, two = 14
Line 17: Inside doubleFirst:  one = 28, two = 16
Line 5: Inside main after doubleFirst:  num = 14
Line 18: Inside squareFirst: ref = 14, val = 14
Line 20: Inside squareFirst: ref = 196, val = 14
Line 22: Inside squareFirst: ref = 196, val = 16
Line 7: Inside main after squareFirst:  num = 196
```

Both parameters of the function **addFirst** are reference parameters, and both parameters of the function **doubleFirst** are value parameters. The statement

```
addFirst(num,num);
```

in the function **main** (Line 2) passes the reference of **num** to both of the formal parameters **first** and **second** of the function **addFirst** because the corresponding actual parameters for both formal parameters are the same. That is, the variables **first** and **second** refer to the same memory location, which is **num**. Figure 7-13 illustrates this situation.

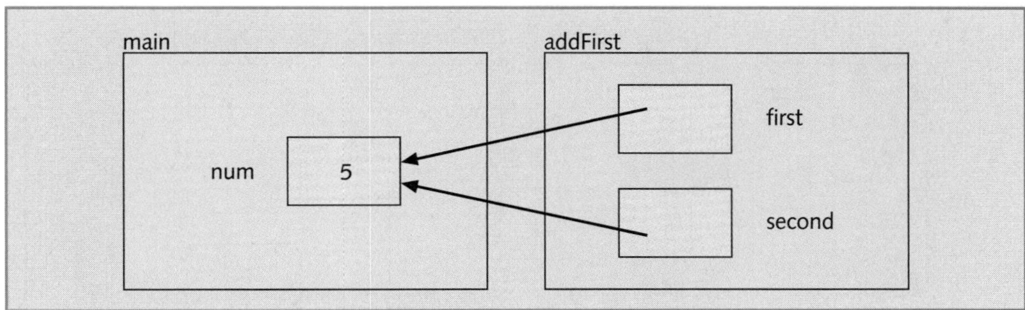

Figure 7-13 Parameters of the function **addFirst**

7

Any changes that **first** makes to its value immediately change the value of **second** and **num**. Similarly, any changes that **second** makes to its value immediately change **first** and **num**, because all three variables refer to the same memory location. (Note that **num** was initialized to 5.)

The formal parameters of the function **doubleFirst** are value parameters. So the statement

```
doubleFirst(num,num);
```

in the function **main** (Line 4) copies the value of **num** into **one** and **two** because the corresponding actual parameters for both formal parameters are the same. Figure 7-14 illustrates this scenario.

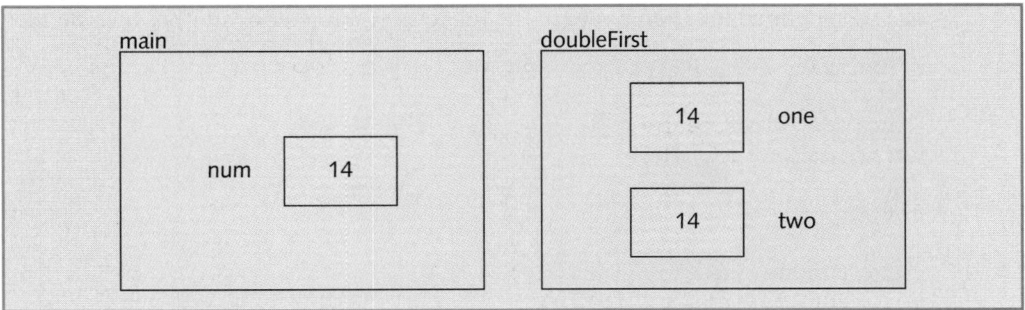

Figure 7-14 Parameters of the function **doubleFirst**

Because both **one** and **two** are value parameters, any changes that **one** makes to its value do not affect the values of **two** and **num**. Similarly, any changes that **two** makes to its value do not affect **one** and **num**. (Note that the value of **num** before the function **doubleFirst** executes is 14.)

The formal parameter **ref** of the function **squareFirst** is a reference parameter, and the formal parameter **val** is a value parameter. The variable **ref** receives the address of its corresponding actual parameter, which is **num**, and the variable **val** copies the value of its corresponding actual parameter, which is also **num**. Thus, both **num** and **ref** refer to the same memory location, which is **num**. Figure 7-15 illustrates this situation.

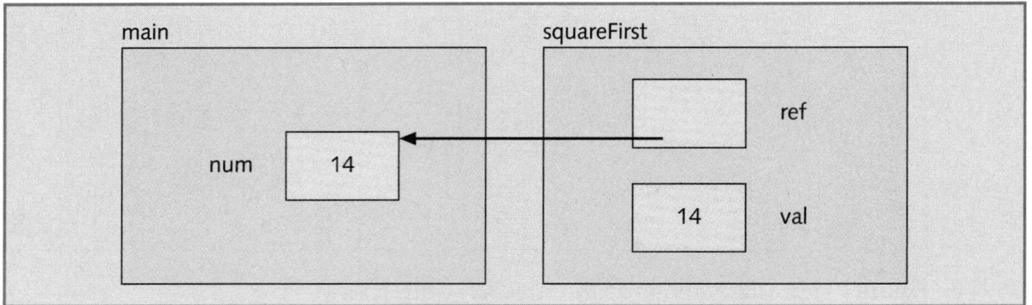

Figure 7-15 Parameters of the function **squareFirst**

Any changes that **ref** makes immediately change **num**. Any changes made by **val** do not affect **num**. (Note that the value of **num** before the function **squareFirst** executes is **14**.)

We recommend that you walk through the program in Example 7-7. The lines are numbered for easy reference. The output shows the order in which the statements execute.

Example 7-8

This example shows how a variable declared outside of any function (or block) behaves. It also shows how reference parameters affect actual parameters, when the reference parameter of a user-defined function passes to the reference parameter of another user-defined function.

```
//Example 7-8: Reference and value parameters

#include <iostream>
using namespace std;

int t;

void funOne(int& a, int& x);
void funTwo(int& u, int v);

int main()
{
   int num1, num2;

   num1 = 10;                                          //Line 1
   num2 = 20;                                          //Line 2
   t = 15;                                             //Line 3
```

```
   cout<<"Line 4: In main: num1 = "<<num1<<", num2 = "
       <<num2<<", and t = "<<t <<endl;                    //Line 4

   funOne(num1, t);                                       //Line 5
   cout<<"Line 6: In main after funOne: "<<"num1 = "
       <<num1<<", num2 = "<<num2<<", and t = "<<t
       <<endl;                                            //Line 6

   funTwo(num2, num1);                                    //Line 7
   cout<<"Line 8: In main after funTwo: "<<"num1 = "
       <<num1<<", num2 = "<<num2<<", and t = "
       <<t<<endl;                                         //Line 8
   return 0;                                              //Line 9
}

void funOne(int& a, int& x)
{
   int z;
   z = a + x;                                             //Line 10

   cout<<"Line 11: In funOne: a = "<<a<<", x = "<<x
       <<", z = "<<z<<", and t = "<<t<<endl;              //Line 11

   x = x + 5;                                             //Line 12
   cout<<"Line 13: In funOne: a = "<<a<<", x = "<<x
       <<", z = "<<z<<", and t = "<<t<<endl;              //Line 13

   a = a + 12;                                            //Line 14
   cout<<"Line 15: In funOne: a = "<<a<<", x = "<<x
       <<", z = "<<z<<", and t = "<<t<<endl;              //Line 15

   t = t + 13;                                            //Line 16
   cout<<"Line 17: In funOne: a = "<<a<<", x = "<<x
       <<", z = "<<z<<", and t = "<<t<<endl;              //Line 17

}

void funTwo(int& u, int v)
{
   int aTwo;

   aTwo = u;                                              //Line 18
   cout<<"Line 19: In funTwo: u = "<<u<<", v = "<<v
       <<", aTwo = "<<aTwo<<", and t = "<<t<<endl;        //Line 19

   funOne(aTwo,u);                                        //Line 20
   cout<<"Line 21: In funTwo after funOne:"<< " u = "
       <<u<<", v = "<<v<<", aTwo = "<<aTwo
       <<", and t = "<<t<<endl;                           //Line 21
```

```
    u = u +13;                                            //Line 22
    cout<<"Line 23: In funTwo: u = "<<u<<", v = "<<v
        <<", aTwo = "<<aTwo<<", and t = "<<t<<endl;       //Line 23

    t = 2 * t;                                            //Line 24
    cout<<"Line 25: In funTwo: u = "<<u<<", v = "<<v
        <<", aTwo = "<<aTwo<<", and t = "<<t<<endl;       //Line 25

}
```

Output:

```
Line 4: In main: num1 = 10, num2 = 20, and t = 15
Line 11: In funOne: a = 10, x = 15, z = 25, and t = 15
Line 13: In funOne: a = 10, x = 20, z = 25, and t = 20
Line 15: In funOne: a = 22, x = 20, z = 25, and t = 20
Line 17: In funOne: a = 22, x = 33, z = 25, and t = 33
Line 6: In main after funOne: num1 = 22, num2 = 20, and t = 33
Line 19: In funTwo: u = 20, v = 22, aTwo = 20, and t = 33
Line 11: In funOne: a = 20, x = 20, z = 40, and t = 33
Line 13: In funOne: a = 20, x = 25, z = 40, and t = 33
Line 15: In funOne: a = 32, x = 25, z = 40, and t = 33
Line 17: In funOne: a = 32, x = 25, z = 40, and t = 46
Line 21: In funTwo after funOne: u = 25, v = 22, aTwo = 32, and t = 46
Line 23: In funTwo: u = 38, v = 22, aTwo = 32, and t = 46
Line 25: In funTwo: u = 38, v = 22, aTwo = 32, and t = 92
Line 8: In main after funTwo: num1 = 22, num2 = 38, and t = 92
```

This program has a variable `t` that is declared before the definition of any function. Because none of the functions has an identifier `t`, the variable `t` is accessible anywhere in the program. Also, the program consists of two void functions: `funOne`, which has two formal parameters, both of which are reference parameters; and `funTwo`, which has one reference and one value parameter.

In Line 5, the function `main` calls the function `funOne`, and the actual parameters passed to `funOne` are `num1` and `t`. Thus, `a`, the formal parameter of `funOne`, receives the address of `num1`, and `x` receives the address of `t`. Any changes that `a` makes to its value immediately change `num1`, and any changes that `x` makes immediately change `t`. Because `t` can be directly accessed anywhere in the program, in Line 16 the function `funOne` changes the value of `t` by using `t` itself (see the output of Line 17). Thus, you can manipulate the value of `t` by using either a reference parameter or `t` itself.

In Line 7, the function `main` calls the function `funTwo` and passes `num2` and `num1` as actual parameters. Now `num2` is passed to `u`, which is a reference parameter—that is, `u` receives the address of `num2`. Thus, `u` and `num2` refer to the same memory location, which is `num2`. Because `num1` is passed to `v` and `v` is a value parameter, `v` copies the contents of `num1`.

In Line 20, the function **funTwo** calls the function **funOne**. The actual parameters passed to **funOne** are **aTwo** (local variable of **funTwo**) and **u** (a formal parameter of **funTwo**). Because both parameters **a** and **x** of **funOne** are reference parameters, both **a** and **x** receive the addresses of their corresponding actual parameters. Now the parameter **u** of **funTwo** is passed to **x**. Because **u** itself is a reference parameter and points to **num2**, both **u** and **x** point to **num2**. Any change made by **x** changes the value of **num2**. Thus, **u**, **x**, and **num2** refer to the same memory location, which is **num2**.

Once again, the output shows the order in which the statements are executed.

Reference Parameters and Value-Returning Functions

7

In Chapter 6, in the discussion on value-returning functions, you learned how to use value parameters only. You can also use reference parameters in a value-returning function, although this approach is not recommended. By definition, a value-returning function returns a single value; this value is returned via the **return** statement. If a function needs to return more than one value, you should change it to a **void** function and use the appropriate reference parameters to return the values.

Scope of an Identifier

The previous sections and Chapter 6 presented several examples of programs with user-defined functions. Identifiers are declared in a function heading, within a block, or outside a block. A question naturally arises: Are you allowed to access any identifier anywhere in the program? The answer is no. Certain rules exist that you must follow to access an identifier. The **scope** of an identifier refers to where in the program an identifier is accessible (visible). Recall that an identifier is the name of something in C++ such as a variable or function name. This section examines the scope of an identifier. First, we define the following two terms, which are widely used in the literature:

Local identifier: Identifiers declared within a function (or block).

Local identifiers are not accessible outside of the function (block).

Global identifier: Identifiers declared outside of every function definition.

Also, C++ does not allow the nesting of functions. That is, you cannot include the definition of one function in the body of another function.

In general, the following rules apply when an identifier is accessed.

1. Global identifiers (such as variables) are accessible by a function or a block if
   a. The identifier is declared before the function definition (block),
   b. The function name is different from the identifier,

c. All parameters of the function have names different than the name of the identifier, and

d. All local identifiers (such as local variables) have names different than the name of the identifier.

2. **(Nested Block)** An identifier declared within a block is accessible

a. Only within the block from the point at which it is declared until the end of the block, and

b. By those blocks that are nested within that block if the nested block does not have an identifier with the same name as that of the outside block (the block that encloses the nested block.)

3. The scope of a function name is similar to the scope of an identifier declared outside any block. That is, the scope of a function name is the same as the scope of a global variable.

Before considering an example to explain these scope rules, first note the scope of the identifier declared in the **`for`** statement. C++ allows the programmer to declare a variable in the initialization statement of the **`for`** statement. For example, the following **`for`** statement

```
for(int count = 1; count < 10; count++)
    cout<<count<<endl;
```

declares the variable `count` and initializes it to `1`. The scope of the variable `count` is limited to only the body of the **`for`** loop.

This scope rule for the variable declared in a **`for`** statement may not apply to Standard C++. In Standard C++, the scope of the variable declared in the `initialize` statement may extend from the point at which it is declared until the end of the block that immediately surrounds this **`for`** statement. (To be absolutely sure, check your compiler's documentation.)

The following C++ program helps illustrate the scope rules:

```
#include <iostream>
using namespace std;

const double rate = 10.50;
int z;
double t;

void one(int x, char y);
void two(int a, int b, char x);
void three(int one, double y, int z);

int main()
{
```

```
    int num, first;
    double x, y, z;
    char name, last;
      .
      .
      .
    return 0;
}

void one(int x, char y)
{
      .
      .
      .
}

int w;

void two(int a, int b, char x)
{
   int count;
      .
      .
      .
}

void three(int one, double y, int z)
{
   char ch;
   int a;
      .
      .
      .
   //Block four
   {
     int x;
     char a;
      .
      .
   }//end Block four
      .
      .
      .
}
```

Table 7-1 summarizes the scope (visibility) of the identifiers.

7

Table 7-1 Scope (Visibility) of the Identifiers

Identifier	Visibility in one	Visibility in two	Visibility in three	Visibility in Block four	Visibility in main
rate (before main)	Y	Y	Y	Y	Y
z (before main)	Y	Y	N	N	N
t (before main)	Y	Y	Y	Y	Y
main	Y	Y	Y	Y	Y
local variables of main	N	N	N	N	Y
one (function name)	Y	Y	N	N	Y
x (one's formal parameter)	Y	N	N	N	N
y (one's formal parameter)	Y	N	N	N	N
w (before function two)	N	Y	Y	Y	N
two (function name)	Y	Y	Y	Y	Y
a (two's formal parameter)	N	Y	N	N	N
b (two's formal parameter)	N	Y	N	N	N
x (two's formal parameter)	N	Y	N	N	N
local variables of two	N	Y	N	N	N
three (function name)	Y	Y	Y	Y	Y
one (three's formal parameter)	N	N	Y	Y	N
y (three's formal parameter)	N	N	Y	Y	N
z (three's formal parameter)	N	N	Y	Y	N
ch (three's local variable)	N	N	Y	Y	N
a (three's local variable)	N	N	Y	N	N
x (Block four's local variable)	N	N	N	Y	N
a (Block four's local variable)	N	N	N	Y	N

Note that function **three** cannot call function **one**, because function **three** has a formal parameter named **one**. Similarly, the block marked **four** in function **three** cannot use the **int** variable **a**, which is declared in function **three**, because block **four** has an identifier named **a**.

1. In Chapter 2, it was stated that C++ does not automatically initialize variables. However, some compilers initialize global variables to their default values. For example, if a global variable is of the type **int**, **char**, or **double**, it is initialized to zero.

2. In C++, **::** is called the **scope resolution operator**. By using the scope resolution operator, a global variable declared before the definition of a function (block) can be accessed by the function (or block) even if the function (or block) has an

identifier with the same name as the variable. For example, in the preceding example, by using the scope resolution operator, the function `main` can refer to the global variable `z` as `::z`. Similarly, suppose that a global variable `t` is declared before the definition of the function—say, `funExample`. Then `funExample` can access the variable `t` using the scope resolution operator even if `funExample` has an identifier `t`. Using the scope resolution operator, `funExample` refers to the variable `t` as `::t`. Also, in the preceding example, using the scope resolution operator, function `three` can call function `one`.

3. C++ provides a way to access a global variable declared after the definition of a function. In this case, the function must not contain any identifier with the same name as the global variable. In the preceding example, the global variable `w` is declared after the definition of function `one`. Now the function `one` does not contain any identifier named `w`. Therefore, `w` can be accessed by function `one` if you declare `w` as an **external variable** inside `one`. To declare `w` as an external variable inside function `one`, the function `one` must contain the following statement:

```
extern int w;
```

In C++, `extern` is a reserved word. The word `extern` in the above statement announces that `w` is a global variable declared elsewhere. Thus, when function one is called, no memory for `w`, as declared inside `one`, is allocated. In C++, external declaration also has another use, but it is not discussed in this book.

7

SIDE EFFECTS OF GLOBAL VARIABLES

A C++ program can contain global variables. Using global variables, however, has side effects. Any function that uses global variables is not independent and typically cannot be used in more than one program. Also, if more than one function uses the same global variable and something goes wrong, it is difficult to discover what went wrong and where. Problems caused by global variables in one area of a program might be misunderstood as problems caused in another area. We strongly recommend that you do not use global variables; instead, use the appropriate parameters.

STATIC AND AUTOMATIC VARIABLES

The variables discussed so far have followed two simple rules:

1. Memory for global variables remains allocated as long as the program executes.
2. Memory for a variable declared within a block is allocated at block entry and deallocated at block exit. For example, memory for the formal parameters and local variables of a function is allocated when the function is called and deallocated when the function exits.

A variable for which memory is allocated at block entry and deallocated at block exit is called an **automatic variable**. A variable for which memory remains allocated as long as the program executes is called a **static variable**. Global variables are static variables and, by default, variables declared within a block are automatic variables. You can declare a static variable within a block by using the reserved word **static**. The syntax for declaring a static variable is

```
static dataType identifier;
```

The statement

```
static int x;
```

declares **x** to be a static variable of the type **int**.

Static variables declared within a block are local to the block, and their scope is the same as that of any other local identifier of that block.

Static variables are usually initialized when they are declared. The statement

```
static int x = 0;
```

declares **x** to be a static variable of the type **int** and initializes **x** to 0.

Example 7-9

The following program shows how static variables behave:

```
//Program: Static and automatic variables
#include <iostream>
using namespace std;

void test();

int main()
{
      int count;

      for(count = 1; count <= 5; count++)
          test();

      return 0;
}

void test()
{
   static int x = 0;
   int y = 10;

   x = x + 2;
   y = y + 1;
```

```
   cout<<"Inside test x = "<<x<<" and y = "
       <<y <<endl;
}
```

Output:

```
Inside test x = 2 and y = 11
Inside test x = 4 and y = 11
Inside test x = 6 and y = 11
Inside test x = 8 and y = 11
Inside test x = 10 and y = 11
```

In the function `test`, `x` is a `static` variable initialized to `0`, and `y` is an automatic variable initialized to `10`. The function `main` calls the function `test` five times. Memory for the variable `y` is allocated every time the function `test` is called and deallocated when the function exits. Thus, every time the function `test` is called, it prints the same value for `y`. However, because `x` is a static variable, memory for `x` remains allocated as long as the program executes. The variable `x` is initialized once to `0`. The subsequent calls of the function `test` use the current value of `x`.

Because memory for static variables remains allocated between function calls, static variables allow you to use the value of a variable from one function call to another function call. Even though you can use global variables if you want to use certain values from one function call to another, the local scope of a static variable prevents other functions from manipulating its value.

Before we look at some programming examples, another concept about functions is worth mentioning: function overloading.

FUNCTION OVERLOADING: AN INTRODUCTION

This section is not needed until Chapter 14, so it can be skipped without any discontinuation until Chapter 14.

In C++, several functions can have the same name. In C++ terminology, this concept is called overloading a function name. Therefore, overloading a function refers to the creation of several functions with the same name. However, if several functions have the same name, every function must have a different set of parameters. The types of parameters determine which function to execute.

Suppose you need to write a function that determines the larger of two items. Both items can be integers, floating-point numbers, characters, or strings. You could write several functions as follows:

```
int largerInt(int x, int y);
char largerChar(char first, char second);
double largerDouble(double u, double v);
string largerString(string first, string second);
```

The function `largerInt` determines the larger of two integers, the function `largerChar` determines the larger of two characters, and so on. All of these functions perform similar operations. Instead of giving different names to these functions, you can use the same name—say, `larger`—for each function; that is, you can overload the function `larger`. Thus, you can write the previous function prototypes simply as

```
int larger(int x, int y);
char larger(char first, char second);
double larger(double u, double v);
string larger(string first, string second);
```

If the call is `larger(5,3)`, for example, the first function executes. If the call is `larger('A', '9')`, the second function executes, and so on.

Function overloading is used when you have the same action for different sets of data. Of course, for function overloading to work, you must give the definition of each function.

FUNCTIONS WITH DEFAULT PARAMETERS

This section is not needed until Chapter 13.

This section discusses functions with default parameters. Recall that when a function is called, the number of actual and formal parameters must be the same. C++ relaxes this condition for functions with default parameters. You specify the value of a default parameter when the function name appears for the first time, such as in the prototype. In general, the following rules apply for functions with default parameters:

- If you do not specify the value of a default parameter, the default value is used for that parameter.
- All of the default parameters must be the rightmost parameters of the function.
- Suppose a function has more than one default parameter. In a function call, if a value to a default parameter is not specified, then you must omit all of the arguments to its right.
- Default values can be constants, global variables, or function calls.
- The caller has the option of specifying a value other than the default for any default parameter.
- You cannot assign a constant value as a default value to a reference parameter.

Consider the following function prototype:

```
void funcExp(int x, int y, double t, char z = 'A', int u = 67,
             char v = 'G', double w = 78.34);
```

The function **funcExp** has seven parameters. The parameters z, u, v, and w are default parameters. If no values are specified for z, u, v, and w in a call to the function **funcExp**, their default values are used.

Suppose you have the following statements:

```
int a, b;
char ch;
double d;
```

The following function calls are legal:

1. `funcExp(a, b, d);`
2. `funcExp(a, 15, 34.6,'B', 87, ch);`
3. `funcExp(b, a, 14.56,'D');`

In statement 1, the default values of z, u, v, and w are used. In statement 2, the default value of z is replaced by 'B', the default value of u is replaced by 87, the default value of v is replaced by the value of ch, and the default value of w is used. In statement 3, the default value of z is replaced by 'D', and the default values of u, v, and w are used.

The following function calls are illegal:

1. `funcExp(a, 15, 34.6, 46.7);`
2. `funcExp(b, 25, 48.76, 'D', 4567, 78.34);`

In statement 1, because the value of z is omitted, all other default values must be omitted. In statement 2, because the value of v is omitted, the value of w should be omitted, too.

The following are illegal function prototypes with default parameters.

1. `void funcOne(int x, double z = 23.45, char ch, int u = 45);`
2. `int funcTwo(int length = 1, int width, int height = 1);`
3. `void funcThree(int x, int& y = 16, double z = 34);`

In statement 1, because the second parameter z is a default parameter, all other parameters after z must be default parameters. In statement 2, because the first parameter is a default parameter, all parameters must be the default values. In statement 3, a constant value cannot be assigned to y because y is a reference parameter.

Example 7-10 further illustrates functions with default parameters.

Example 7-10

```
#include <iostream>
#include <iomanip>
using namespace std;

int volume(int l = 1, int w = 1, int h = 1);
void funcOne(int& x, double y = 12.34, char z = 'B');
int main()
```

```
{
      int a = 23;
      double b = 48.78;
      char ch = 'M';

      cout<<fixed<<showpoint;
      cout<<setprecision(2);

      cout<<"Line 1: a = "<<a<<", b = "<<b
          <<", ch = "<<ch<<endl;                       //Line 1
      cout<<"Line 2: Volume = "<<volume()<<endl;       //Line 2
      cout<<"Line 3: Volume = "<<volume(5,4)<<endl;    //Line 3
      cout<<"Line 4: Volume = "<<volume(34)<<endl;     //Line 4
      cout<<"Line 5: Volume = "<<volume(6,4,5)<<endl;  //Line 5
      funcOne(a);                                      //Line 6
      funcOne(a, 42.68);                               //Line 7
      funcOne(a, 34.65,'Q');                           //Line 8
      cout<<"Line 9: a = "<<a<<", b = "<<b
          <<", ch = "<<ch<<endl;                       //Line 9
      return 0;
}

int volume(int l, int w, int h)
{
      return l * w * h;                                //Line 10
}

void funcOne(int& x, double y, char z)
{
   x = 2 * x;                                          //Line 11
   cout<<"Line 12: x = "<<x<<", y = " <<y
       <<", z = "<<z<<endl;                            //Line 12
}
```

Output:

```
Line 1: a = 23, b = 48.78, ch = M
Line 2: Volume = 1
Line 3: Volume = 20
Line 4: Volume = 34
Line 5: Volume = 120
Line 12: x = 46, y = 12.34, z = B
Line 12: x = 92, y = 42.68, z = B
Line 12: x = 184, y = 34.65, z = Q
Line 9: a = 184, b = 48.78, ch = M
```

In this book, the definition of the function `main` is placed before the definition of user-defined functions. You must therefore specify the default value for a parameter in the function prototype. Also, you should specify the default value in the function prototype only (not in the function definition).

PROGRAMMING EXAMPLE: CLASSIFY NUMBERS

In this example, using functions we rewrite the program that determines the number of odds and evens from a given list of integers. This program was first written in Chapter 5.

The main algorithm remains the same:

1. Initialize the variables, `zeros`, `odds`, and `evens` to `0`.
2. Read a number.
3. If the number is even, increment the even count, and if the number is also zero, increment the zero count; else increment the odd count.
4. Repeat Steps 2 and 3 for each number in the list.

The main parts of the program are initialize the variables; read and classify the numbers; and then output the results. To simplify the function `main` and further illustrate parameter passing, the program includes

- A function, `initialize`, to initialize the variables, such as `zeros`, `odds`, and `evens`.
- A function, `getNumber`, to get the number.
- A function, `classifyNumber`, to determine whether the number is odd or even (and whether it is also zero). This function also increments the appropriate count.
- A function, `printResults`, to print the results.

Let us now describe each of these functions.

`initialize` The function `initialize` initializes variables to their initial values. The variables that we need to initialize are `zeros`, `odds`, and `evens`. As before, their initial values are all zero. Clearly, this function has three parameters. Because the values of the formal parameters initializing these variables must be passed outside the function, these formal parameters must be reference parameters. Essentially this function is

```
void initialize(int& zeroCount, int& oddCount, int& evenCount)
{
      zeroCount = 0;
      oddCount = 0;
      evenCount = 0;
}
```

`getNumber` The function `getNumber` reads a number and then passes this number to the function `main`. Because you need to pass only one number, this function has only one parameter. The formal parameter of this function must be a reference parameter because the number read is passed outside the function. Essentially this function is

```
void getNumber(int& num)
{
```

```
        cin>>num;
}
```

You can also write the function **getNumber** as a value-returning function. See the note at the end of this programming example.

classifyNumber The function **classifyNumber** determines whether the number is odd or even, and, if the number is even, it also checks whether the number is zero. It also updates the values of some of the variables, **zeros**, **odds**, and **evens**. This function needs to know the number to be analyzed. Therefore, the number to be analyzed must be passed as a parameter. Because this function also increments the appropriate count, the variables (that is, **zeros**, **odds**, and **evens** declared in **main**) holding the counts must be passed as parameters to this function. Thus, this function has four parameters.

Because the number will only be analyzed, you need to pass only its value. Thus, the formal parameter corresponding to this variable is a value parameter. After analyzing the number, this function increments the values of some of the variables, **zeros**, **odds**, and **evens**. Therefore, the formal parameters corresponding to these variables must be reference parameters. The algorithm to analyze the number and increment the appropriate count is the same as before. The definition of this function is

```
void classifyNumber(int num, int& zeroCount, int& oddCount,
                    int& evenCount)
{
   switch(num % 2)
   {
      case 0: evenCount++;          //update even count
              if(num == 0)          //number is also zero
                 zeroCount++;       //update zero count
              break;
      case 1:
      case -1: oddCount++;          //update odd count
   } //end switch
}
```

printResults The function **printResults** prints the final results. To print the results (that is, the number of zeros, odds, and evens), this function must have access to the values of the variables, **zeros**, **odds**, and **evens**, declared in the function **main**. Therefore, this function has three parameters. Because this function prints only the values of the variables, the formal parameters are value parameters. The definition of this function is

```
void printResults(int zeroCount, int oddCount, int evenCount)
{
    cout<<"There are "<<evenCount<<" evens, "
        <<"which also includes "<<zeroCount<<" zeros"<<endl;
```

```
    cout<<"Total number of odds are: "<<oddCount<<endl;
}
```

We now give the main algorithm and show how the function `main` calls these functions.

Main Algorithm

1. Call the function `initialize` to initialize the variables.
2. Prompt the user to enter 20 numbers.
3. For each number in the list
   a. Call the function `getNumber` to read a number.
   b. Output the number.
   c. Call the function `classifyNumber` to classify the number and increment the appropriate count.
4. Call the function `printResults` to print the final results.

Complete Program Listing

```
//Program: Classify Numbers
//This program counts the number of zeros, odd, and even numbers

#include <iostream>
#include <iomanip>
using namespace std;

const int N = 20;

     //function prototypes
void initialize(int& zeroCount, int& oddCount, int& evenCount);
void getNumber(int& num);
void classifyNumber(int num, int& zeroCount, int& oddCount,
                    int& evenCount);
void printResults(int zeroCount, int oddCount, int evenCount);

int main ()
{
     //variable declaration
   int counter; //loop control variable
   int number;  //stores a number
   int zeros;   //stores the number of zeros
   int odds;    //stores the number of odd integers
   int evens;   //stores the number of even integers

   initialize(zeros, odds, evens);                          //Step 1

   cout<<"Please enter "<<N<<" integers."
       <<endl;                                              //Step 2
```

```
    cout<<"The numbers you entered are--> "<<endl;

    for (counter = 1; counter <= N; counter++)          //Step 3
    {
       getNumber(number);                                //Step 3a

       cout<<setw(3)<<number;                            //Step 3b
       classifyNumber(number,zeros,odds,evens);          //Step 3c
    }// end for loop

    cout<<endl;
    printResults(zeros, odds, evens);                    //Step 4
    return 0;
}

void initialize(int& zeroCount, int& oddCount, int& evenCount)
{
       zeroCount = 0;
       oddCount = 0;
       evenCount = 0;
}

void getNumber(int& num)
{
       cin>>num;
}

void classifyNumber(int num, int& zeroCount, int& oddCount,
                    int& evenCount)
{
    switch(num % 2)
    {
    case 0: evenCount++;
            if(num == 0)
               zeroCount++;
            break;
    case 1:
    case -1: oddCount++;
    } //end switch
}

void printResults(int zeroCount, int oddCount, int evenCount)
{
     cout<<"There are "<<evenCount<<" evens, "
         <<"which also includes "<<zeroCount<<" zeros"<<endl;
     cout<<"Total number of odds are: "<<oddCount<<endl;
}
```

Sample Run: In this sample run, the user input is shaded.

```
Please enter 20 integers.
The numbers you entered are—>
0 0 12 23 45 7 -2 -8 -3 -9 4 0 1 0 -7 23 -24 0 0 12
  0   0 12 23 45   7 -2 -8 -3 -9   4   0   1   0 -7 23 -24   0   0 12
There are 12 evens, which also includes 6 zeros
Total number of odds are: 8
```

In this program, because the data is assumed to be input from the standard input device (the keyboard) and the function `getNumber` returns only one value, you can also write the function `getNumber` as a value-returning function. If written as a value-returning function, the definition of the function `getNumber` is

```
int getNumber()
{
    int num;
    cin>>num;
    return num;
}
```

In this case, the statement (function call)

```
getNumber(number);
```

in the function main should be replaced by the statement

```
number = getNumber();
```

Of course, you also need to change the function prototype.

PROGRAMMING EXAMPLE: DATA COMPARISON

This programming example illustrates:

- How to read data from more than one file in the same program
- How to send output to a file
- How to generate bar graphs
- With the help of functions and parameter passing, how to use the same program segment on different (but similar) sets of data
- How to use structured design to solve a problem and how to perform parameter passing

This program is broken into two parts. First, you learn how to read data from more than one file. Second, you learn how to generate bar graphs.

Two groups of students at a local university are enrolled in certain special courses during the summer semester. The courses are offered for the first time and are taught by different teachers. At the end of the semester, both groups are given the same tests for the same courses and their scores are recorded in separate files. The data in each file is in the following form:

```
courseNo  score1, score2, ..., scoreN –999
courseNo  score1, score2, ..., scoreM –999
.
.
.
```

Let us write a program that finds the average course score for each course for each group. The output is of the following form:

```
Course#     Group#     Course Average
   A           1            80.50
               2            82.75
   B           1            78.00
               2            75.35
```

Input Because data for the two groups are recorded in separate files, the input data appears in two separate files.

Output As shown above.

Problem Analysis and Algorithm Design

Reading input data from both files is straightforward. Suppose the data is stored in the file `a:group1.txt` for group 1 and in the file `a:group2.txt` for group 2. After processing the data for one group, we can process the data for the second group for the same course, and continue until we run out of data. Processing data for each course is similar and is a two-step process:

1. a. Sum the scores for the course.
   b. Count the number of students in the course.
   c. Divide the total score by the number of students to find the course average.
2. Output the results.

We are comparing only the averages of the corresponding courses in each group, and the data in each file is ordered according to course ID. To ensure that only the averages of the corresponding courses are compared, we compare the course IDs for each group. If the corresponding course IDs are not the same, we output an error message and terminate the program.

This discussion suggests that we should write a function, `calculateAverage`, to find the course average. We should also write another function, `printResult`, to output the data in the form given. By passing the appropriate parameters, we can use the same functions, `calculateAverage` and `printResult`, to process each course's data for both groups. (In the second part of the program, we modify the function `printResult`.)

The preceding discussion translates into the following algorithm:

1. Initialize the variables.
2. Get the course IDs for group 1 and group 2.
3. If the course IDs are different, print an error message and exit the program.
4. Calculate the course average for group 1 and group 2.
5. Print the results in the form given above.
6. Repeat Steps 2–6 for each course.
7. Print the final results.

Variables (Function `main`) The preceding discussion suggests that the program needs the following variables for data manipulation in the function `main`:

```
char courseId1;           //course ID for group 1
char courseId2;           //course ID for group 2

int numberOfCourses;      //to find the average for each group

double avg1;              //average for a course in group 1
double avg2;              //average for a course in group 2

double avgGroup1;         //average group 1
double avgGroup2;         //average group 2
ifstream group1;          //input stream variable for group 1
ifstream group2;          //input stream variable for group 2
ofstream outfile;         //output stream variable
```

Next, we discuss the functions `calculateAverage` and `printResult`. Then we will put the function `main` together.

`calculateAverage` This function calculates the average for a course. Because the input is stored in a file and the input file is opened in the function `main`, we must pass the `ifstream` variable associated with the input file to this function. Furthermore, after calculating the course average, this function must pass the course average to the function `main`. Therefore, this function has two parameters, and both parameters must be reference parameters.

To find the course average, we must first find the sum of all scores for the course and the number of students who took the course, and then divide the sum by the number of students. Thus, we need a variable to find the sum of the scores, a variable to find the number of students, and a variable to read and store a score. Of course, we must initialize the variables to find the sum and the number of students to zero.

Local Variables (Function `calculateAverage`) In the previous discussion of data manipulation, we identified three variables for the function `calculateAverage`:

```
double totalScore;    //to store the sum of scores
int numberOfStudent; //to store the number of students
int score;            //to read and store a course score
```

The above discussion translates into the following algorithm for the function `calculateAverage`:

a. Declare variables.
b. Initialize `totalScore` to `0.0`.
c. Initialize `numberOfStudent` to `0`.
d. Get the (next) course score.
e. Update `totalScore` by adding the course score read in step d.
f. Increment `numberOfstudent` by 1.
g. Repeat Steps d, e, and f until the course score is equal to `-999`.
h. `courseAvg = totalScore / numberOfStudent;`

A `while` loop is used to repeat steps d, e, and f.

We are now ready to write the definition of the function `calculateAverage`.

```
void calculateAverage(ifstream& inp, double& courseAvg)
{
    double totalScore = 0.0;                          //Steps a and b
    int numberOfStudent = 0;                          //Steps a and c
    int score;                                        //Step a

    inp>>score;                                       //Step d
    while(score != -999)
    {
          totalScore = totalScore + score;            //Step e
          numberOfStudent++;                          //Step f
          inp>>score;                                 //step d
    }//end while
    courseAvg = totalScore / numberOfStudent;         //Step h
}//end calculate Average
```

`printResult` The function `printResult` prints the group's course ID, group number, and course average. The output is stored in a file. So we must pass four parameters to this function: the `ofstream` variable associated with the output file, the group number, the course ID, and the course average for the group. The `ofstream` variable must be passed by reference. Because the function uses only the values of the other variables, the remaining three parameters should be value parameters. Also, from the output, it is clear that we print the course ID only before group 1. In pseudocode, the algorithm is

```
if(group number == 1)
   print course ID
else
   print a blank

print group number and course average
```

The definition of the function `printResult` follows:

```
void printResult(ofstream& outp, char courseID, int groupNo,
                 double avg)
{
   if(groupNo == 1)
         outp<<"   "<<courseId<<"    ";
   else
         outp<<"        ";
   outp<<setw(8)<<groupNo<<setw(15)<<avg<<endl;
}//end printResult
```

Now that we have designed and defined the functions `calculateAverage` and `printResults`, we can describe the algorithm for the function `main`. Before outlining the algorithm, however, we note the following: It is quite possible that in both input files the data is ordered according to the course IDs, but one file might have fewer courses than the other. We do not discover this error until after we have processed both files and discover that one file has unprocessed data. Make sure to check for this error before printing the final answer—that is, the average for group 1 and group 2.

Main Algorithm: Function `main`

1. Declare the variables (local declaration).
2. Open the input files.
3. Print a message if you are unable to open a file and terminate the program.
4. Open the output file.
5. To output floating-point numbers in a fixed decimal format with the decimal point and trailing zeros, set the manipulators `fixed` and `showpoint`. Also, to output floating-point numbers to two decimal places, set the precision to two decimal places.

6. Initialize the course average for group 1 to `0.0`.
7. Initialize the course average for group 2 to `0.0`.
8. Initialize the number of courses to `0`.
9. Print the heading.
10. Get the course `ID`, `courseId1`, for group 1.
11. Get the course `ID`, `courseId2`, for group 2.
12. For each course in group 1 and group 2

    a. if(courseId1 != courseId2)
    ```
    {
        cout<<"Data error: Course IDs do not match.\n");
        return 1;
    }
    ```
    b. `else`
    `{`
       i. Calculate the course average for group 1 (call the function `calculateAverage` and pass the appropriate parameters).
       ii. Calculate the course average for group 2 (call the function `calculateAverage` and pass the appropriate parameters).
       iii. Print the results for group 1 (call the function `printResults` and pass the appropriate parameters).
       iv. Print the results for group 2 (call the function `printResults` and pass the appropriate parameters).
       v. Update the average for group 1.
       vi. Update the average for group 2.
       vii. Increment the number of courses.

    `}`
    c. Get the course ID, `courseId1`, for group 1.
    d. Get the course ID, `courseId2`, for group 2.
13. a. if not_end_of_file on group 1 and end_of_file on group 2
    print "Ran out of data for group 2 before group 1"
    b. else
    if end_of_file on group 1 and not_end_of_file on group 2
    print "Ran out of data for group 1 before group 2"
    c. else
    print the average of group 1 and group 2.
14. Close the input and output files.

Complete Program Listing

```
//Program: Comparison of class averages

#include <iostream>
#include <iomanip>
#include <fstream>
using namespace std;

 //function prototypes
void calculateAverage(ifstream& inp, double& courseAvg);
void printResult(ofstream& outp, char courseId,
                 int groupNo, double avg);

int main ()
{
                                                     //Step 1
   char courseId1;         //course ID for group 1
   char courseId2;         //course ID for group 2
   int numberOfCourses;
   double avg1;            //average for a course in group 1
   double avg2;            //average for a course in group 2
   double avgGroup1;       //average group 1
   double avgGroup2;       //average group 2
   ifstream group1;        //input stream variable for group 1
   ifstream group2;        //input stream variable for group 2
   ofstream outfile;       //output stream variable

   group1.open("a:group1.txt");                      //Step 2
   group2.open("a:group2.txt");                      //Step 2

   if(!group1 || !group2)                            //Step 3
   {
      cout<<"Unable to open files."<<endl;
      return 1;
   }

   outfile.open("a:student.out");                    //Step 4

   outfile<<fixed<<showpoint;                        //Step 5
   outfile<<setprecision(2);                         //Step 5

   avgGroup1 = 0.0;                                  //Step 6
   avgGroup2 = 0.0;                                  //Step 7

   numberOfCourses = 0;                              //Step 8

      //print heading: Step 9
   outfile<<"Course No   Group No    Course Average"<<endl;
```

```
    group1>>courseId1;                                        //Step 10
    group2>>courseId2;                                        //Step 11

    while(group1 && group2)                                   //Step 12
    {
       if(courseId1 != courseId2)                             //Step 12a
       {
          cout<<"Data error: Course IDs do not match."<<endl;
          cout<<"Program terminates."<<endl;
          return 1;
       }
       else                                                   //Step 12b
       {
          calculateAverage(group1, avg1);                     //Step 12b.i
          calculateAverage(group2, avg2);                     //Step 12b.ii
          printResult(outfile,courseId1,1,avg1);              //Step 12b.iii
          printResult(outfile,courseId2,2,avg2);              //Step 12b.iv
          avgGroup1 = avgGroup1 + avg1;                       //Step 12b.v
          avgGroup2 = avgGroup2 + avg2;                       //Step 12b.vi
          outfile<<endl;
          numberOfCourses++;                                  //Step 12b.vii
       }

       group1>>courseId1;                                     //Step 12c
       group2>>courseId2;                                     //Step 12d
    } //end while

    if(group1 && !group2)                                     //Step 13a
        cout<<"Ran out of data for group 2 before group 1."<<endl;
    else                                                      //Step 13b
      if (!group1 && group2)
         cout<<"Ran out of data for group 1 before group 2."<<endl;
      else                                                    //Step 13c
      {

         outfile<<"Avg for group 1: "
                <<avgGroup1 / numberOfCourses<<endl;
         outfile<<"Avg for group 2: "
                <<avgGroup2 / numberOfCourses<<endl;
      }
    group1.close();                                           //Step 14
    group2.close();                                           //Step 14
    outfile.close();                                          //Step 14

    return 0;
}
void calculateAverage(ifstream& inp, double& courseAvg)
{
```

```
   double totalScore = 0.0;
   int numberOfStudent = 0;
   int score;

   inp>>score;
   while(score != -999)
   {
      totalScore = totalScore + score;
      numberOfStudent++;
      inp>>score;
   }//end while
   courseAvg = totalScore / numberOfStudent;
}//end calculate Average

void printResult(ofstream& outp, char courseId,
                 int groupNo, double avg)
{
   if(groupNo == 1)
        outp<<"   "<<courseId<<"    ";
   else
        outp<<"         ";
   outp<<setw(8)<<groupNo<<setw(15)<<avg<<endl;
}
```

Sample Output

```
Course No   Group No    Course Average
   A           1           62.40
               2           61.13
   B           1           67.91
               2           53.30
   C           1           54.59
               2           57.38
   D           1           65.71
               2           64.29
   E           1           71.80
               2           90.00
Avg for group 1: 64.48
Avg for group 2: 65.22
```

Input Data Group 1

```
A 80 100 50 10 32 90 89 100 23 50 -999
B 80 90 80 94 90 34 23 63 23 80 90 -999
C 10 30 20 10 90 50 89 23 90 68 90 10 60 90 73 35 90 -999
D 34 80 45 89 90 23 90 12 34 90 84 100 90 59 -999
E 100 83 93 20 63 -999
```

Input Data Group 2

```
A 20 75 40 25 80 89 100 60 -999
B 80 50 70 19 10 18 80 90 90 26 -999
C 100 30 20 40 90 50 18 90 90 45 90 80 70 30 35 40 -999
D 80 85 45 92 10 90 24 90 23 65 72 90 34 100 -999
E 95 100 88 98 69 -999
```

Bar Graph

In the business world, company executives often like to see results in some visual form, such as bar graphs. Many currently available software packages can analyze data in several forms and then display the results in some visual form such as bar graphs or pie charts. The second part of this program aims to display the results found earlier in the form of bar graphs as shown below:

```
Course          Course Average
 ID      0    10   20   30   40   50   60   70   80   90   100
         |....|....|....|....|....|....|....|....|....|....|

 A       ***************
         ############
 B       *************
         #####################
Group 1 -- ****
Group 2 -- #####
```

Each symbol (* or #) in the bar graph represents 2 points. If a course average is less than 2, no symbol is printed.

Because the output is in the form of a bar graph, we need to modify the function `printResult`.

`printBar` The function `printBar` prints the course ID and the bar graph representing the average for a course. The output is stored in a file. So we must pass four parameters to this function: the `ofstream` variable associated with the output file, the group number (to print * or #), the course ID, and the course average for the department. To print the bar graph, we can use a loop to print a symbol for each two points. If the average is, `78.45`, for example, we must print `39` symbols to represent this average. To find the number of symbols to print, we can use integer division as follows.

```
numberOfSymbols = static_cast<int>(average)/2;
```

For example, `static_cast<int>(78.45)/2 = 78/2 = 39`.

Following this discussion, the definition of the function `printResult` is

```
void printResult(ofstream& outp, char courseId,
                 int groupNo, double avg)
{
```

```
int noOfSymbols;
   int count;

   if(groupNo == 1)
       outp<<setw(3)<<courseId<<"     ";
   else
       outp<<"       ";

   noOfSymbols = static_cast<int>(avg)/2;

   if(groupNo == 1)
     for(count = 1; count <= noOfSymbols; count++)
        outp<<"*";
   else
     for(count = 1; count <= noOfSymbols; count++)
        outp<<"#";
   outp<<endl;
}//end printResults
```

We also include a function, `printHeading`, to print the first two lines of the output. The definition of this function is

```
void printHeading(ofstream& outp)
{
   outp<<"Course          Course Average"<<endl;
   outp<<" ID     0    10    20    30    40    50    60    70"
       <<"    80    90    100"<<endl;
   outp<<"        |....|....|....|....|....|....|....|"
       <<"....|....|....|"<<endl;
}//end printHeading
```

If you replace the function `printResult` in the preceding program, include the function `printHeading`, include the statements to output — `Group 1 -- ****` and `Group 2 -- ####` — and rerun the program, the output for the previous data is as follows.

Sample Output:

```
Course          Course Average
 ID     0    10    20    30    40    50    60    70    80    90    100
        |....|....|....|....|....|....|....|....|....|....|
  A     ******************************
        #############################
  B     ********************************
        #########################
  C     **************************
        ############################
```

```
  D    *********************************
       #################################
  E    ************************************
       #############################################

Group 1 -- ****
Group 2 -- ####
Avg for group 1: 64.48
Avg for group 2: 65.22
```

Compare both outputs. Which one do you think is better?

QUICK REVIEW

1. A function that does not have a data type is called a void function.
2. A return statement without any value can be used in a void function. If a return statement is used in a void function, it is typically used to exit the function early.
3. The heading of a void function starts with the word void.
4. In C++, `void` is a reserved word.
5. A void function may or may not have parameters.
6. A call to a void function is a stand-alone statement.
7. To call a void function, you use the function name together with the actual parameters in a stand-alone statement.
8. There are two types of formal parameters: value parameters and reference parameters.
9. A value parameter receives a copy of its corresponding actual parameter.
10. A reference parameter receives the address (memory location) of its corresponding actual parameter.
11. The corresponding actual parameter of a value parameter is an expression, a variable, or a constant value.
12. A constant value cannot be passed to a reference parameter.
13. The corresponding actual parameter of a reference parameter must be a variable.
14. When you include & after the data type of a formal parameter, the formal parameter becomes a reference parameter.
15. The stream variables should be passed by reference to a function.
16. If a formal parameter needs to change the value of an actual parameter, in the function heading you must declare this formal parameter as a reference parameter.

17. The scope of an identifier refers to those parts of the program where it is accessible.
18. Variables declared within a function (or block) are called local variables.
19. Variables declared outside of every function definition (and block) are called global variables.
20. The scope of a function name is the same as the scope of an identifier declared outside of any block.
21. See the scope rules in this chapter (section, Scope of an Identifier).
22. C++ does not allow the nesting of function definitions.
23. An automatic variable is a variable for which memory is allocated on function (or block) entry and deallocated on function (or block) exit.
24. A static variable is a variable for which memory remains allocated throughout the execution of the program.
25. By default, global variables are static variables.
26. In C++, a function can be overloaded.
27. If a function is overloaded, all functions with the same name must have different sets of parameters.
28. C++ allows functions to have default parameters.
29. If you do not specify the value of a default parameter, the default value is used for that parameter.
30. All of the default parameters must be the rightmost parameters of the function.
31. Suppose a function has more than one default parameter. In a function call, if a value to a default parameter is not specified, then you must omit all arguments to its right.
32. Default values can be constants, global variables, or function calls.
33. The calling function has the option of specifying a value other than the default for any default parameter.
34. You cannot assign a constant value as a default value to a reference parameter.

EXERCISES

1. Mark the following statements as true or false.
   a. A function that changes the value of a reference parameter also changes the value of the actual parameter.
   b. A variable name cannot be passed to a value parameter.
   c. If a C++ function does not use parameters, parentheses around the empty parameter list are still needed.
   d. In C++, the names of the corresponding formal and actual parameters must be the same.

e. Whenever the value of a reference parameter changes, the value of the actual parameter changes.

f. In C++, function definitions can be nested; that is, the definition of one function can be enclosed in the body of another function.

g. Using global variables in a program is a better programming style than using local variables because extra variables can be avoided.

h. In a program, global constants are as dangerous as global variables.

i. The memory for a static variable remains allocated between function calls.

2. Consider the programming code given below. Identify the following:

a. Function prototype, function heading, function body, and function definitions.

b. Function call statements, formal parameters, and actual parameters.

c. Value parameters and reference parameters.

d. Local variables and global variables.

```
#include <iostream>
using namespace std;

int one;
void hello(int&, double, char);

int main()
{
   int x;
   double y;
   char z;
   .
   .
   .
   hello(x,y,z);
   .
   .
   hello(x, y-3.5, 'S');
   .
   .
   .
}

void hello(int& first, double second, char ch)
{
   int num;
   double y;
   int u ;
   .
   .
   .
}
```

3. a. Explain the difference between an actual and a formal parameter.
   b. Explain the difference between a value and a reference parameter.
   c. Explain the difference between a local and a global variable.
4. What is the output of the following program?

```
#include <iostream>
#include <iomanip>
using namespace std;
void test(int first, int& second);
int main ()
{
      int num;

      num = 5;
      test(24, num);
      cout<<num<<endl;
      test(num, num);
      cout<<num<<endl;
      test(num*num, num);
      cout<<num<<endl;
      test(num+num, num);
      cout<<num<<endl;

      return 0;
}

void test(int first, int& second)
{
    int third;

    third = first + second * second + 2;
    first = second - first;
    second = 2 * second;
    cout<<first<<"  "<<second<<"  "
        <<third<<endl;
}
```

5. Assume the following input values:

```
7 3 6 4
2 6 3 5
```

Show the output of the following program:

```
#include <iostream>
using namespace std;
void goofy(int& , int& , int , int& );
int main()
{
   int first, second, third, fourth;

   first = 3; second = 4; third = 20; fourth = 78;
   cout<<first<<"  "<<second<<"  "<<third<<"  "<<fourth<<endl;
```

```
    goofy(first, second, third, fourth);
    cout<<first<<"  "<<second<<"  "<<third<<"  "<<fourth<<endl;
    fourth = first * second + third - fourth;
    goofy(fourth, third, first, second);
    cout<<first<<"  "<<second<<"  "<<third<<"  "<<fourth<<endl;
    return 0;
}
    void goofy(int& a, int& b, int c, int& d)
{
    cin>>a>>b>>c>>d;
    c = a * b + d - c;
    c = 2 * c;
}
```

6. What is the output of the following program?

```
#include <iostream>
using namespace std;
int x;
void mickey(int&, int);
void minnie(int, int&);
int main()
{
    int first;
    int second = 5;

    x = 6;
    mickey(first, second);
    cout<<first<<" "<<second<<" "<<x<<endl;
    minnie(first, second);
    cout<<first<<" "<<second<<" "<<x<<endl;
    return 0;
}

void mickey(int& a, int b)
{
    int first;

    first = b + 12;
    a = 2 * b;
    b = first + 4;
}

void minnie(int u, int& v)
{
    int second;

    second = x;
    v = second + 4;
    x = u + v;
}
```

7. In the following program, number the marked statements to show the order in which they will execute (the logical order of execution).

```
      #include <iostream>
      using namespace std;

      void func(int val1, int val2);
      int main()
      {
              int num1, num2;
______        cout<<"Please enter two integers.\n";
______        cin>>num1>>num2;
______        func (num1, num2);
______        cout<<" The two integers are "<<num1<<", "<<num2<<endl;
______        return 0;
      }

      void func (int val1, int val2)
      {
              int val3, val4;
______        val3 = val1 + val2;
______        val4 = val1 * val2;
______        cout<<"The sum and product are "<<val3<<" and "<<val4;
      }
```


8. What is the output of the following code fragment? (Note: `alpha` and `beta` are `int` variables.)

```
alpha = 5;
beta = 10;
if(beta >= 10)
{
    int alpha = 10;
    beta = beta + alpha;
    cout<<alpha<<' '<<beta<<endl;
}
cout<<alpha<<' '<<beta<<endl;
```

9. Show the output of the program in Example 7-8 if you replace Line 7 with the following line:

```
funTwo(t,num1);
```

Show the values of the variables after each statement executes.

10. Consider the following program. What is its exact output? Show the values of the variables after each line executes, as in Example 7-6.

```
#include <iostream>
using namespace std;
void funOne(int& a);
int main()
{
  int num1, num2;
```

```
    num1 = 10;                                          //Line 1

    num2 = 20;                                          //Line 2

    cout<<"Line 3: In main: num1 = "<<num1
        <<", num2 = "<<num2<<endl;                      //Line 3
    funOne(num1);                                       //Line 4
    cout<<"Line 5: In main after funOne: num1 = "
        <<num1<<", num2 = "<<num2<<endl;                //Line 5
    return 0;                                           //Line 6
}

void funOne(int& a)
{
    int x = 12;
    int z;

    z = a + x;                                          //Line 7

    cout<<"Line 8: In funOne: a = "<<a<<", x = "<<x
        <<", and z = "<<z<<endl;                        //Line 8

    x = x + 5;                                          //Line 9

    cout<<"Line 10: In funOne: a = "<<a<<", x = "<<x
        <<", and z = "<<z<<endl;                        //Line 10
    a = a + 8;                                          //Line 11

    cout<<"Line 12: In funOne: a = "<<a<<", x = "<<x
        <<", and z = "<<z<<endl;                        //Line 12
  }
```

11. Consider the following function prototype:

```
void testDefaultParam(int a, int b = 7, char z = '*');
```

Which of the following function calls is correct?

(i) `testDefaultParam(5);`

(ii) `testDefaultParam(5,8);`

(iii) `testDefaultParam(6, '#');`

(iv) `testDefaultParam(0,0, '*');`

12. Consider the following function definition:

```
void defaultParam(int u, int v = 5, double z = 3.2)
{
    int a;
    u = u + static_cast<int>(2 * v + z);
    a = u + v * z;
```

```
    cout<<"a = "<<a<<endl;
}
```

What is the output of the following function calls?

(i) `defaultParam(6);`

(ii) `defaultParam(3,4);`

(iii) `defaultParam(3, 0, 2.8);`

PROGRAMMING EXERCISES

1. Consider the definition of the function **main**:

```
int main()
{
    int x, y;
    char z;
    double rate, hours;
    double amount;
      .
      .
      .
}
```

Write the following definitions.

a. Write the definition of the function **initialize** that initializes **x** and **y** to **0** and **z** to the blank character.

b. Write the definition of the function **getHoursRate** that prompts the user to input the hours worked and rate per hour to initialize the variables **hours** and **rate** of the function **main**.

c. Write the definition of the value-returning function **payCheck** that calculates and returns the amount to be paid to an employee based on the hours worked and rate per hour. The hours worked and rate per hour are stored in the variables **hours** and **rate**, respectively, of the function **main**. The formula for calculating the amount to be paid is as follows: for the first 40 hours, the rate is the given rate; for hours over 40, the rate is 1.5 times the given rate.

d. Write the definition of the function **printCheck** that prints the hours worked, rate per hour, and the amount due.

e. Write the definition of the function **funcOne** that prompts the user to input a number. The function then changes the value of **x** to 2 times the old value of **x** plus the value of **y** minus the value entered by the user.

f. Write the definition of the function **nextChar** that sets the value of **z** to the next character stored in **z**.

g. Write the definition of a function **main** that tests each of these functions.

2. The function `printGrade` of Example 7-5 is written as a **`void`** function to compute and output the course grade. The course score is passed as a parameter to the function `printGrade`. Rewrite the function `printGrade` as a value-returning function so that it computes and returns the course grade. (The course grade must be output in the function `main`.) Also, change the name of the function to `calculateGrade`.
3. In this exercise, you are to modify the Programming Example Classify Numbers in this chapter. As written, the program inputs data from the standard input device (keyboard) and outputs results on the standard output device (screen). The program can process only 20 numbers. Rewrite the program to incorporate the following requirements.
   a. Data to the program is input from a file of an unspecified length; that is, the program does not know in advance how many numbers are in the file.
   b. Save the output of the program in a file.
   c. Modify the function `getNumber` so that it reads a number from the input file (opened in the function `main`), outputs the number to the output file (opened in the function `main`), and sends the number read to the function `main`. Print only 10 numbers per line.
   d. Have the program find the sum and average of the numbers.
   e. Modify the function `printResult` so that it outputs the final results to the output file (opened in the function `main`). Other than outputting the appropriate counts, this new definition of the function `printResult` should also output the sum and average of the numbers.
4. Rewrite the program developed in programming Exercise 11 in Chapter 5, so that the function `main` is merely a collection of function calls. Your program should use the following functions.
   a. Function `openFiles`: This function opens the input and output files, and sets the output of the floating-point numbers to two decimal places in a fixed decimal format with a decimal point and trailing zeros.
   b. Function `initialize`: This function initializes variables such as `countFemale`, `countMale`, `sumFemaleGPA`, and `sumMaleGPA`.
   c. Function `sumGrades`: This function finds the sum of female and male students' GPAs.
   d. Function `averageGrade`: This function finds the average GPA for female and male students.
   e. Function `printResults`: This function outputs the relevant results.
   f. There can be no global variables. Use the appropriate parameters to pass information in and out of functions.
5. Write a program that prints the day number of the year, given the date in the form month-day-year. For example, if the input is 1-1-02, the day number is 1; if the input is 12-25-02, the day number is 359. The program should check for a leap year. A year is a leap year if it is divisible by 4 but not divisible by 100. For example, 1992 and

2008 are divisible by 4, but not by 100. A year that is divisible by 100 is a leap year if it is also divisible by 400. For example, 1600 and 2000 are divisible by 400. However, 1800 is not a leap year because 1800 is not divisible by 400.

6. Write a program that reads a student's name together with his or her test scores. The program should then compute the average test score for each student and assign the appropriate grade. The grade scale is as follows: `90-100, A; 80-89, B; 70-79, C; 60-69, D; 0-59, F.`

   Your program must use the following functions.

   a. A void function, `calculateAverage`, to determine the average of the five test scores for each student. Use a loop to read and sum the five test scores. (This function does not output the average test score. That task must be done in the function `main`.)

   b. A value-returning function, `calculateGrade`, to determine and return each student's grade. (This function does not output the grade. That task must be done in the function `main`.)

   Test your program on the following data. Read the data from a file and send the output to a file. Do not use any global variables. Use the appropriate parameters to pass values in and out of functions.

```
A 75 83 77 91 76
B 80 90 95 93 48
C 78 81 11 90 73
D 92 83 30 69 87
E 23 45 96 38 59
F 60 85 45 39 67
G 27 31 52 74 83
H 93 94 89 77 97
I 79 85 28 93 82
J 85 72 49 75 63
```

Sample Output:

The output should be of the following form: (Fill the last two columns and the last line showing the class average.)

```
Student  Test1  Test2  Test3  Test4  Test5  Average  Grade
   A       75     83     77     91     76
   B       80     90     95     93     48
   C       78     81     11     90     73
   D       92     83     30     69     87
   E       23     45     96     38     59
   F       60     85     45     39     67
```

```
G        27      31      52      74      83
H        93      94      89      77      97
I        79      85      28      93      82
J        85      72      49      75      63
Class Average =
```

7. Write a program to process text files. The program should read a text file and output the data in the file as is. The program should also output the number of words, number of lines, and number of paragraphs. (When you create the input file, insert a blank line between paragraphs (see d).)

   You must write and use the following functions.

   a. `initialize`: This function initializes all variables of the function `main`.

   b. `processBlank`: This function reads and writes blanks. Whenever it hits a nonblank (except whitespace characters), it increments the number of words in a line. The number of words in a line is set back to zero in the function `updateCount`. The function exits after processing blanks.

   c. `copyText`: This function reads and writes nonblank characters. Whenever it hits a blank, it exits.

   d. `updateCount`: This function takes place at the end of each line. It updates the total word count, increments the number of lines, and sets the number of words on a line back to zero. If there are no words in a line, it increments the number of paragraphs. One blank line (between paragraphs) is used to distinguish paragraphs and should not be counted with the number of lines.

   e. `printTotal`: This function outputs the number of words, number of lines, and number of paragraphs.

   Your program should read data from a file and send output to a file. Do not use any global variables. Use the appropriate parameters to pass values in and out of functions. Test your program using the function `main` that looks like

```
int main()
{
      variables declaration
      open files

      read a character
      while (not end of file)
      {
         while(not end of line)
         {
            processBlank(parameters);
            copyText(parameters);
         }
```

```
        updateCount(parameters);
        read a character;
        .
        .
    }
    printTotal(parameters);
    close files;
    return 0;
}
```

CHAPTER

8

USER-DEFINED SIMPLE DATA TYPES, NAMESPACES, AND THE `string` TYPE

In this chapter, you will:

- Learn how to create and manipulate your own simple data type—called the enumeration type
- Become aware of the `typedef` statement
- Learn about the `namespace` mechanism
- Explore the `string` data type, and learn how to use the various `string` functions to manipulate strings

In Chapter 2, you learned that C++'s simple data type is divided into three categories: integral, floating-point, and `enum`. In subsequent chapters, you worked mainly with integral and floating-point data types. In this chapter, you will learn about the `enum` type. Moreover, the statement `using namespace std;` (discussed in Chapter 2) is used in every C++ program that uses ANSI/ISO Standard C++ style header files. The second half of this chapter examines the purpose of this statement. In fact, you will learn what is the `namespace` mechanism. You will also learn about the `string` type and many useful functions that you can use to effectively manipulate strings.

ENUMERATION TYPE

Chapter 2 defined a data type as a set of values together with a set of operations on them. For example, the int data type consists of integers from -2,147,483,648 to 2,147,483,647 and the set of operations on these numbers—namely, the arithmetic operations (+, -, *, /, and %). Because the main objective of a program is to manipulate data, the concept of a data type becomes fundamental to any programming language. By providing data types, you specify what values are legal and tell the user what kinds of operations are allowed on those values. The system thus provides you with built-in checks against errors.

The data types that you have worked with until now were mostly int, bool, char, and double. Even though these data types are sufficient to solve just about any problem, situations occur when these data types are not adequate to solve a particular problem. C++ provides a mechanism for users to create their own data types, which greatly enhances the flexibility of the programming language.

In this section, you will learn how to create your own simple data types, known as the enumeration type. In ensuing chapters, you will learn more advanced techniques to create complex data types.

To define an **enumeration type**, you need the following items:

- A name for the data type
- A set of values for the data type
- A set of operations on the values

C++ lets you define a new simple data type wherein you specify its name and values, but not the operations. Preventing users from creating their own operations avoids potential system failures.

The values that you specify for the data type must be identifiers.

The syntax for enumeration type is

```
enum typeName{value1, value2, ...};
```

where value1, value2, ... are identifiers called **enumerators**. In C++, enum is a reserved word.

By listing all of the values between the braces, you also specify an ordering between the values. That is, value1 < value2 < value3 <.... Thus, the enumeration type is an ordered set of values. Moreover, the default value assigned to these enumerators starts at 0. That is, the default value assigned to value1 is 0, the default value assigned to value2 is 1, and so on. (You can assign different values—other than the default values—for the enumerators when you define the enumeration type.)

Example 8-1

The statement

```
enum colors{brown, blue, red, green, yellow};
```

defines a new data type, called `colors`, and the values belonging to this data type are `brown`, `blue`, `red`, `green`, and `yellow`.

Example 8-2

The statement

```
enum standing{freshman, sophomore, junior, senior};
```

defines `standing` to be an enumeration type. The values belonging to `standing` are `freshman`, `sophomore`, `junior`, and `senior`.

Example 8-3

Consider the following statements:

```
enum grades{'A', 'B', 'C', 'D', 'F'}; //Illegal enumeration type

enum places{1st, 2nd, 3rd, 4th};     //Illegal enumeration type
```

These are illegal enumeration types because none of the values is an identifier. The following, however, are legal enumeration types:

```
enum grades{A, B, C, D, F};
enum places{first, second, third, fourth};
```

If a value has already been used in one enumeration type, it cannot be used by any other enumeration type in the same block. The same rules apply to enumeration types declared outside of any blocks. Example 8-4 illustrates this concept.

Example 8-4

Consider the following statements:

```
enum mathStudent{John, Bill, Cindy, Lisa, Ron};

enum compStudent{Susan, Cathy, John, William}; //Illegal
```

Suppose that these statements are in the same program in the same block. The second enumeration type, `compStudent`, is not allowed because the value `John` was used in the previous enumeration type `mathStudent`.

Declaring Variables

Once a data type is defined, you can declare variables of that type. The syntax for declaring variables of an **enum** type is the same as before:

```
dataType identifier, identifier,...;
```

The statement

```
enum sports{basketball, football, hockey, baseball, soccer,
            volleyball};
```

defines an enumeration type, called `sports`. The statement

```
sports popularSport, mySport;
```

declares `popularSport` and `mySport` to be variables of the type `sports`.

Assignment

Once a variable is declared, you can store values in it. Assuming the previous declaration, the statement

```
popularSport = football;
```

stores `football` in `popularSport`. The statement

```
mySport = popularSport;
```

copies the value of `popularSport` into `mySport`.

Operations on Enumeration Types

No arithmetic operations are allowed on the enumeration type. So the following statements are illegal:

```
mySport = popularSport + 2;          //Illegal
popularSport = football + soccer;    //Illegal
popularSport = popularSport * 2;     //Illegal
```

Also, the increment and decrement operations are not allowed on enumeration types. So the following statements are illegal:

```
popularSport++; //Illegal
popularSport--; //Illegal
```

Suppose you want to increment the value of `popularSport` by `1`. You can use the cast operator as follows:

```
popularSport = static_cast<sports>(popularSport + 1);
```

When the type name is used, the compiler assumes that the user understands what he or she is doing. Thus, the above statement is compiled, and during execution it advances the value of `popularSport` to the next value in the list. Consider the following statements:

```
popularSport = football;
popularSport = static_cast<sports>(popularSport + 1);
```

After the second statement, the value of `popularSport` is `hockey`. Similarly, the statements

```
popularSport = football;
popularSport = static_cast<sports>(popularSport - 1);
```

result in storing `basketball` in `popularSport`.

Relational Operators

Because an enumeration is an ordered set of values, the relational operators can be used with the enumeration type. Once again, suppose you have the enumeration type `sports` and the variables `popularSport` and `mySport` as defined earlier. Then,

8

```
football <= soccer is true
hockey > basketball is true
baseball < football is false
```

Suppose that

```
popularSport = soccer;
mySport = volleyball;
```

Then,

```
popularSport < mySport is true
```

Enumeration Types and Loops

Recall that the enumeration type is an integral type and that, using the cast operator (that is, type name), you can increment, decrement, and compare the values of the enumeration type. Therefore, you can use these enumeration types in loops. Suppose `mySport` is a variable as declared earlier. Consider the following `for` loop:

```
for(mySport = basketball; mySport <= soccer;
                          mySport = static_cast<sports>(mySport+1))
...
```

This `for` loop executes 5 times.

Using enumeration types in loops increases the readability of the program.

Input/Output of Enumeration Types

Because input and output are defined only for built-in data types such as `int`, `char`, `double`, and so on, the enumeration type can be neither input nor output (directly). However, you can input and output enumeration indirectly. Example 8-5 illustrates this concept.

Example 8-5

Suppose you have the following statements:

```
enum courses{algebra, basic, pascal, cpp, philosophy, analysis,
             chemistry, history};
courses registered;
```

The first statement defines an enumeration type **courses**; the second declares a variable **registered** of the type **courses**. You can read (that is, input) the enumeration type with the help of the **char** data type. Note that you can distinguish between some of the values in the enumeration type **courses** just by reading the first character and others by reading the first two characters. For example, you can distinguish between **algebra** and **basic** just by reading the first character; you can distinguish between **algebra** and **analysis** by reading the first two characters. To read these values from, say, the keyboard, you read two characters and then use a selection structure to assign the value to the variable **registered**. Thus, you need to declare two variables of the type **char**.

```
char ch1,ch2;
cin>>ch1>>ch2; //read two characters
```

The following **switch** statement assigns the appropriate value to the variable **registered**:

```
switch(ch1)
{
case 'a': if(ch2 == 'l')
             registered = algebra;
          else
             registered = analysis;
          break;
case 'b': registered = basic;
          break;
case 'c': if(ch2 == 'h')
            registered = chemistry;
          else
            registered = cpp;
          break;
case 'h': registered = history;
          break;
case 'p': if(ch2 == 'a')
             registered = pascal;
          else
             registered = philosophy;
          break;
default: cout<<"Illegal input."<<endl;
}
```

Similarly, you can output the enumeration type indirectly:

```
switch(registered)
{
case algebra: cout<<"algebra";
              break;
case analysis: cout<<"analysis";
               break;
case basic: cout<<"basic";
            break;
case chemistry: cout<<"chemistry";
                break;
case cpp: cout<<"cpp";
          break;
case history: cout<<"history";
              break;
case pascal: cout<<"pascal";
             break;
case philosophy: cout<<"philosophy";
}
```

8

If you try to output the value of an enumerator directly, the computer will output the value assigned to the enumerator. For example, suppose that `registered = algebra;`. The following statement will output the value 0 because the (default) value assigned to `algebra` is 0:

```
cout<<registered<<endl;
```

Similarly, the following statement will output 4:

```
cout<<philosophy<<endl;
```

Functions and Enumeration Types

You can pass the enumeration type as a parameter to functions just like any other simple data type—that is, by either value or reference. Also, just like any other simple data type, a function can return a value of the enumeration type. Using this facility, you can use functions to input and output enumeration types.

The following function inputs data from the keyboard and returns a value of the enumeration type. Assume that the enumeration type `courses` is defined as before.

```
courses readCourses()
{
      courses registered;
      char ch1, ch2;

      cout<<"Enter the first two letters of the course: "<<endl;
      cin>>ch1>>ch2;
```

```
    switch(ch1)
    {
    case 'a': if(ch2 == 'l')
                 registered = algebra;
              else
                 registered = analysis;
              break;
    case 'b': registered = basic;
              break;
    case 'c': if(ch2 == 'h')
                 registered = chemistry;
              else
                  registered = cpp;
              break;
    case 'h': registered = history;
              break;
    case 'p': if(ch2 == 'a')
                 registered = pascal;
              else
                 registered = philosophy;
              break;
    default: cout<<"Illegal input."<<endl;
    }//end switch

    return registered;
}
```

The following function outputs an enumeration type value.

```
void printEnum(courses registered)
{
      switch(registered)
      {
      case algebra: cout<<"algebra";
                    break;
      case analysis: cout<<"analysis";
                     break;
      case basic: cout<<"basic";
                  break;
      case chemistry: cout<<"chemistry";
                      break;
      case cpp: cout<<"cpp";
                break;
      case history: cout<<"history";
                    break;
      case pascal: cout<<"pascal";
                   break;
      case philosophy:  cout<<"philosophy";
      }//end switch
}//end printEnum
```

Declaring Variables When Defining the Enumeration Type

In previous sections, you first defined an enumeration type and then declared variables of that type. C++ allows you to combine these two steps into one. That is, you can declare variables of an enumeration type when you define an enumeration type. For example, the statement

```
enum grades{A, B, C, D, F} courseGrade;
```

defines an enumeration type `grades` and declares a variable `courseGrade` of the type `grades`.

Similarly, the statement

```
enum coins{penny, nickel, dime, halfDollar, dollar} change, usCoins;
```

defines an enumeration type `coins` and declares two variables, `change` and `usCoins`, of the type `coins`.

Anonymous Data Types

A data type wherein you directly specify values in the variable declaration with no type name is called an **anonymous type**. The following statement creates an anonymous type:

```
enum {basketball, football, baseball, hockey} mySport;
```

This statement specifies the values and declares a variable `mySport`, but no name is given to the data type.

Creating an anonymous type, however, has drawbacks. First, because there is no name for the type, you cannot pass an anonymous type as a parameter to a function and a function cannot return an anonymous type value. Second, values used in one anonymous type can be used in another anonymous type, but variables of those types are treated differently. Consider the following statements:

```
enum {English, French, Spanish, German, Russian} languages;
enum {English, French, Spanish, German, Russian} foreignLanguages;
```

Even though the variables `languages` and `foreignLanguages` have the same values, the compiler treats them as variables of different types. The following statement is, therefore, illegal:

```
languages = foreignLanguages; //Illegal
```

Even though these facilities are available, use them with care. To avoid confusion, first define an enumeration type and then declare the variables.

We now describe the `typedef` statement in C++.

The `typedef` Statement

In C++, you can create synonyms or aliases to a previously defined data type by using the `typedef` statement. The general syntax of the `typedef` statement is

```
typedef existingTypeName newTypeName;
```

In C++, `typedef` is a reserved word. Note that the `typedef` statement does not create any new data type; it creates only an alias to an existing data type.

Example 8-6

The statement

```
typedef int integer;
```

creates an alias, `integer`, for the data type `int`. Similarly, the statement

```
typedef double real;
```

creates an alias, `real`, for the data type `double`. The statement

```
typedef double decimal;
```

creates an alias, `decimal`, for the data type `double`.

Using the `typedef` statement, you can create your own Boolean data type as shown in Example 8-7.

Example 8-7

From Chapter 4, recall that logical (Boolean) expressions in C++ evaluate to `1` or `0`, which are, in fact, `int` values. As a logical value, `1` represents `true` and `0` represents `false`. Consider the following statements:

```
typedef int Boolean;          //Line 1
const Boolean True = 1;       //Line 2
const Boolean False = 0;      //Line 3

Boolean flag;                 //Line 4
```

The statement at Line 1 creates an alias, `Boolean`, for the data type `int`. The statements at Lines 2 and 3 declare the named constants `True` and `False` and initialize them to `1` and `0`, respectively. The statement at Line 4 declares `flag` to be a variable of the type `Boolean`. Because `flag` is a variable of the type `Boolean`, the following statement is legal:

```
flag = True;
```

PROGRAMMING EXAMPLE: THE GAME OF ROCK, PAPER, AND SCISSORS

Everyone is familiar with the game of rock, paper, and scissors. Children often play this game. This game has two players, each of whom chooses one of the three objects: rock, paper, or scissors. If player 1 chooses rock and player 2 chooses paper, player 2 wins the game because paper covers the rock. The game is played according to the following rules:

- If both players choose the same object, this play is a tie.
- If one player chooses rock and the other chooses scissors, the player choosing the rock wins this play because the rock breaks the scissors.
- If one player chooses rock and the other chooses paper, the player choosing the paper wins this play because the paper covers the rock.
- If one player chooses scissors and the other chooses paper, the player choosing the scissors wins this play because the scissors cut the paper.

Write an interactive program that allows two people to play this game.

Input This program has two types of input:

- The users' responses to play the game
- The players' choices

Output The players' choices and the winner of each play. After the game is over, the total number of plays and the number of times that each player won should be output as well.

Problem Analysis and Algorithm Design

Two players play this game. Players enter their choices via the keyboard. Each player enters `R` or `r` for Rock, `P` or `p` for Paper, or `S` or `s` for Scissors. While the first player enters a choice, the second player looks elsewhere. Once both entries are in, if the entries are valid, the program outputs the players' choices and declares the winner of the play. The game continues until one of the players decides to quit the game. After the game ends, the program outputs the total number of plays and the number of times that each player won. This discussion translates into the following algorithm:

1. Provide a brief explanation of the game and how it is played.
2. Ask the users if they want to play the game.
3. Get plays for both players.
4. If the plays are valid, output the plays and the winner.
5. Update the total game count and winner count.
6. Repeat Steps 2–5, while the users agree to play the game.
7. Output the number of plays and times that each player won.

We will use the enumeration type to describe the objects.

```
enum objectType{Rock, Paper, Scissors};
```

Variables (Function main) It is clear that you need the following variables in the function main.

```
int    gameCount;    //to count the number of games played
int    winCount1;    //to count the number of games won by player 1
int    winCount2;    //to count the number of games won by player 2
int    gamewinner;   //to store the winner of a game
char   response;     //to get the user's response to play the game
char   selection1;   //player1's selection
char   selection2;   //player2's selection
objectType  play1;   //player1's selection
objectType  play2;   //player2's selection
```

This program is divided into the following functions, which the ensuing sections describe in detail.

- **displayRules**: This function displays some brief information about the game and its rules.
- **validSelection**: This function checks whether a player's selection is valid. The only valid selections are R, r, P, p, S, and s.
- **retrievePlay**: Because enumeration types cannot be read directly, this function converts the entered choice (R, r, P, p, S, or s) and returns the appropriate object type.
- **gameResult**: This function outputs the players' choices and the winner of the game.
- **convertEnum**: This function is called by the function gameResult to output the enumeration type values.
- **winningObject**: This function determines and returns the winning object.
- **displayResults**: After the game is over, this function displays the final results.

Function displayRules This function has no parameters. It consists only of output statements to explain the game and rules of play. Essentially, this function's definition is

```
void displayRules()
{
   cout<<"  Welcome to the game of Rock, Paper, and Scissors."<<endl;
   cout<<"  This is a game for two players. For each game, each"<<endl;
   cout<<" player selects one of the objects, Rock, Paper, or"
       <<" Scissors."<<endl;
   cout<<" The rules for winning the game are: "<<endl;
   cout<<"1. If both players select the same object, it is a"
       <<" tie."<<endl;
```

```
   cout<<"2. Rock breaks Scissors: So the player who selects Rock"
       <<" wins."<<endl;
   cout<<"3. Paper covers Rock: So the player who selects Paper"
       <<" wins."<<endl;
   cout<<"4. Scissors cut Paper: So the player who selects Scissors"
       <<" wins."<<endl<<endl;
   cout<<"Enter R or r to select Rock, P or p to select Paper, and "
       <<"S or s to select Scissors."<<endl;
}//end displayRules
```

Function `validSelection` This function checks whether a player's selection is valid.

```
if selection is 'R' or 'r' or 'S' or 's' or 'P' or 'p', then
  it is a valid selection;
otherwise the selection is invalid.
```

Let's use a `switch` statement to check for the valid selection. The definition of this function is

```
bool validSelection(char selection)
{
    switch(selection)
    {
     case 'R': case 'r':
     case 'S': case 's':
     case 'P': case 'p': return true;
     default: return false;
    }
}//end validSelection
```

Function `retrievePlay` Because the enumeration type cannot be read directly, this function converts the entered choice (`R`, `r`, `P`, `p`, `S`, or `s`) and returns the appropriate object type. This function thus has one parameter of the type `char`. It is a value-returning function and it returns a value of the type `objectType`. In pseudocode, the algorithm of this function is

```
if selection is 'R' or 'r'
      return Rock;
if selection is 'P' or 'p'
      return Paper;
if selection is 'S' or 's'
      return  Scissors;
```

The definition of the function `retrievePlay` is

```
objectType retrievePlay(char selection)
{
   objectType object;
```

```
    switch(selection)
    {
    case 'R': case 'r': object = Rock;
                        break;
    case 'P': case 'p': object = Paper;
                        break;
    case 'S': case 's': object = Scissors;
    }
    return object;
}//end retrievePlay
```

Function gameResult This function decides whether a game is a tie or which player is the winner. It outputs the players' selections and the winner of the game. Clearly, this function has three parameters: player 1's choice, player 2's choice, and a parameter to return the winner. In pseudocode, this function is

```
a. if player1 and player2 have the same selection, then
   this is a tie game
b. else
   {
      1. Determine the winning object. (Call function winningObject)
      2. Output each player's choice.
      3. Determine the winning player.
      4. Return the winning player via a reference parameter to the
         function main so that the function main can update the
         winning player's win count.
   }
```

The definition of this function is

```
void gameResult(objectType play1, objectType play2, int& winner)
{
   objectType winnerObject;

   if(play1 == play2)                                      //Step a
   {
     winner = 0;
     cout<<"Both players selected ";
     convertEnum(play1);
     cout<<". This game is a tie."<<endl;
   }
   else                                                    //Step b
   {
      winnerObject = winningObject(play1, play2);          //Step b1

               //Output each player's choice; Step b2
      cout<<"Player 1 selected ";
      convertEnum(play1);
```

```
      cout<<" and player 2 selected ";
      convertEnum(play2);
      cout<<". ";

         //Decide the winner; Step b3
      if(play1 == winnerObject)
          winner = 1;                                     //Step b4
      else
         if(play2 == winnerObject)
            winner = 2;                                   //Step b4

        //Output winner
      cout<<"Player "<<winner<<" wins this game."<<endl;
   }
}//end gameResult
```

Function convertEnum Because enumeration types cannot be output directly, let's write the function `convertEnum` to output objects of the `enum` type `objectType`. This function has one parameter of the type `objectType`. It outputs the string that corresponds to the `objectType`. In pseudocode, this function is

```
if object is Rock
  output "Rock"
if object is Paper
  output "Paper"
if object is Scissors
  output "Scissors"
```

The definition of the function `convertNum` is

```
void convertEnum(objectType object)
{
   switch(object)
   {
   case Rock:  cout<<"Rock";
               break;
   case Paper: cout<<"Paper";
               break;
   case Scissors: cout<<"Scissors";
   }
}//end convertEnum
```

Function winningObject To decide the winner of the game, you look at the players' selections and then at the rules of the game. For example, if one player chooses `Rock` and another chooses `Paper`, the player who chose `Paper` wins. In other words, the winning object is `Paper`. The function `winningObject`, given two objects, decides and returns the winning object. Clearly, this function has two parameters of the type `objectType` and the value returned by this function is also of the type `objectType`. The definition of this function is

```
objectType winningObject(objectType play1, objectType play2)
{
    if((play1 == Rock && play2 == Scissors)
        || (play2 == Rock && play1 == Scissors))
        return Rock;
    else
        if((play1 == Rock && play2 == Paper)
          || (play2 == Rock && play1 == Paper))
          return Paper;
        else
          return Scissors;

}
```

Function `displayResults` After the game is over, this function outputs the final results—that is, the total number of plays and the number of plays won by each player. The total number of plays is stored in the variable `gameCount`, the number of plays by player 1 is stored in the variable `winCount1`, and the number of plays won by player 2 is stored in the variable `winCount2`. This function has three parameters corresponding to these three variables. Essentially, the definition of this function is

```
void displayResults(int gCount, int wCount1, int wCount2)
{
   cout<<"The total number of plays: "<<gCount<<endl;
   cout<<"The number of plays won by player 1: "<<wCount1<<endl;
   cout<<"The number of plays won by player 2: "<<wCount2<<endl;
}//end displayResults
```

We are now ready to write the algorithm for the function `main`.

Main Algorithm

1. Declare the variables.
2. Initialize the variables.
3. Display the rules.
4. Prompt the users to play the game.
5. Get the users' responses to play the game.
6. `while`(response is yes)

   {

   a. Prompt player 1 to make a selection.

   b. Get the play for player 1.

   c. Prompt player 2 to make a selection.

d. Get the play for player 2.
e. If both plays are legal
   {
   i. Increment the total game count.
   ii. Declare the winner of the game.
   iii. Increment the winner's game win count by 1.
   }
f. Prompt the users to determine whether they want to play again.
g. Get the players' responses.
   }
7. Output the game results.

Complete Program Listing

```
#include <iostream>

using namespace std;

enum objectType{Rock, Paper, Scissors};

   //function prototypes
void displayRules();
objectType retrievePlay(char selection);
bool validSelection(char selection);
void convertEnum(objectType object);
objectType winningObject(objectType play1, objectType play2);
void gameResult(objectType play1, objectType play2, int& winner);
void displayResults(int gCount, int wCount1, int wCount2);

int main()
{
       //Step 1
   int    gameCount; //to count the number of games played
   int    winCount1; //to count the number of games won by player 1
   int    winCount2; //to count the number of games won by player 2
   int    gamewinner;
   char   response;  //to get the user's response to play the game
   char   selection1;
   char   selection2;
   objectType   play1;  //player1's selection
   objectType   play2;  //player2's selection

      //Initialize variables; Step 2
   gameCount = 0;
```

```
    winCount1 = 0;
    winCount2 = 0;

    displayRules();                                             //Step 3

    cout<<"Enter Y/y to play the game: ";                       //Step 4
    cin>>response;                                              //Step 5
    cout<<endl;

    while(response == 'Y' || response == 'y')                   //Step 6
    {
      cout<<"Player 1 enter your choice: ";                     //Step 6a
      cin>>selection1;                                          //Step 6b
      cout<<endl;

      cout<<"Player 2 enter your choice: ";                     //Step 6c
      cin>>selection2;                                          //Step 6d
      cout<<endl;
                                                                //Step 6e
      if(validSelection(selection1) && validSelection(selection2))
      {
         play1 = retrievePlay(selection1);
         play2 = retrievePlay(selection2);
         gameCount++;                                           //Step 6e.i
         gameResult(play1,play2,gamewinner);                    //Step 6e.ii
         if(gamewinner == 1)                                    //Step 6e.iii
            winCount1++;
         else
            if(gamewinner == 2)
               winCount2++;
      }//end if
      cout<<"Enter Y/y to play the game: ";                     //Step 6f
      cin>>response;                                            //Step 6g
      cout<<endl;
    }//end while

    displayResults(gameCount, winCount1, winCount2);            //Step 7

    return 0;
}//end main

void displayRules()
{
   cout<<"  Welcome to the game of Rock, Paper, and Scissors."<<endl;
   cout<<"  This is a game for two players. For each game, each"<<endl;
   cout<<" player selects one of the objects, Rock, Paper, or"
       <<" Scissors."<<endl;
```

```
   cout<<" The rules for winning the game are: "<<endl;
   cout<<"1. If both players select the same object, it is a"
       <<" tie."<<endl;
   cout<<"2. Rock breaks Scissors: So the player who selects Rock"
       <<" wins."<<endl;
   cout<<"3. Paper covers Rock: So the player who selects Paper"
       <<" wins."<<endl;
   cout<<"4. Scissors cut Paper: So the player who selects Scissors"
       <<" wins."<<endl<<endl;
   cout<<"Enter R or r to select Rock, P or p to select Paper, and "
       <<"S or s to select Scissors."<<endl;
}

bool validSelection(char selection)
{
   switch(selection)
   {
   case 'R': case 'r':
   case 'S': case 's':
   case 'P': case 'p': return true;
   default: return false;
   }
}

objectType retrievePlay(char selection)
{
      objectType object;

      switch(selection)
      {
      case 'R': case 'r': object = Rock;
                          break;
      case 'P': case 'p': object = Paper;
                          break;
      case 'S': case 's': object = Scissors;
      }
      return object;
}

void convertEnum(objectType object)
{
   switch(object)
   {
   case Rock: cout<<"Rock";
              break;
   case Paper: cout<<"Paper";
               break;
   case Scissors: cout<<"Scissors";
   }
```

```
}

objectType winningObject(objectType play1, objectType play2)
{
    if((play1 == Rock && play2 == Scissors)
         || (play2 == Rock && play1 == Scissors))
        return Rock;
    else
       if((play1 == Rock && play2 == Paper)
           || (play2 == Rock && play1 == Paper))
          return Paper;
       else
          return Scissors;

}

void gameResult(objectType play1, objectType play2, int& winner)
{
   objectType winnerObject;

   if(play1 == play2)
   {
        winner = 0;
        cout<<"Both players selected ";
        convertEnum(play1);
        cout<<". This game is a tie."<<endl;
   }
   else
   {
      winnerObject = winningObject(play1, play2);

           //Output each player's choice
      cout<<"Player 1 selected ";
      convertEnum(play1);
      cout<<" and player 2 selected ";
      convertEnum(play2);
      cout<<". ";

         //Decide the winner
      if(play1 == winnerObject)
          winner = 1;
          else
          if(play2 == winnerObject)
              winner = 2;

           //Output the winner
      cout<<"Player "<<winner<<" wins this game."<<endl;
   }
}
```

```
void displayResults(int gCount, int wCount1, int wCount2)
{
   cout<<"The total number of plays: "<<gCount<<endl;
   cout<<"The number of plays won by player 1: "<<wCount1<<endl;
   cout<<"The number of plays won by player 2: "<<wCount2<<endl;
}
```

NAMESPACES

In July 1998, ANSI/ISO Standard C++ was officially approved. Most recent compilers are also compatible with ANSI/ISO Standard C++. (To be absolutely sure, check your compiler's documentation.) The two standards are virtually the same. The ANSI/ISO Standard C++ language has some features that are not available in Standard C++, which the remainder of this chapter addresses. In subsequent chapters, unless specified otherwise, the C++ syntax applies to both standards. First we discuss the **namespace** mechanism of the ANSI/ISO Standard C++, which was introduced in Chapter 2.

When a header file, such as `iostream`, is included in a program, the global identifiers in the header file also become global identifiers in the program. Therefore, if a global identifier in a program has the same name as one of the global identifiers in the header file, the compiler generates a syntax error (such as "identifier redefined"). The same problem can occur if a program uses third-party libraries. To overcome this problem, third-party vendors begin their global identifiers with a special symbol. In Chapter 2, you learned that because compiler vendors begin their global identifier names with an underscore (_), to avoid linking errors you should not begin identifier names in your program with an underscore (_).

ANSI/ISO Standard C++ tries to solve this problem of overlapping global identifier names with the **namespace** mechanism.

The general syntax of the statement **namespace** is

```
namespace namespace_name
{
   members
}
```

where a **member** is usually a named constant, variable declaration, function, or another **namespace**. Note that **namespace_name** is a C++ identifier.

In C++, **namespace** is a reserved word.

Example 8-8

The statement

```
namespace globalType
{
   const int n = 10;
   const double rate = 7.50;
   int count = 0;
   void printResult();
}
```

defines `globalType` to be a `namespace` with four members: named constants `n` and `rate`, the variable `count`, and the function `printResult`.

The scope of a `namespace` member is local to the `namespace`. You can usually access a `namespace` member outside the `namespace` in one of two ways, as described below.

The general syntax for accessing a `namespace` member is

```
namespace_name::identifier
```

For example, to access the member `rate` of the `namespace` `globalType`, the following statement is required:

```
globalType::rate
```

To access the member `printResult` (which is a function), the following statement is required:

```
globalType::printResult();
```

Recall that, in C++, `::` is called the scope resolution operator. Thus, to access a member of a `namespace`, you use the `namespace_name`, followed by the scope resolution operator, followed by the member name. That is, you attach the name of the `namespace_name` and the scope resolution operator before the member name.

To simplify the accessing of a `namespace` member, ANSI/ISO Standard C++ provides the use of the statement `using`. The syntax to use the statement `using` is as follows.

(a) To simplify the accessing of all `namespace` members:

```
using namespace namespace_name;
```

(b) To simplify the accessing of a specific `namespace` member:

```
using namespace_name::identifier;
```

For example, the `using` statement

```
using namespace globalType;
```

simplifies the accessing of all members of the `namespace globalType`. The statement

```
using globalType::rate;
```

simplifies the accessing of the member `rate` of the `namespace globalType`.

In C++, `using` is a reserved word.

You typically put the `using` statement after the `namespace` declaration. For the `namespace globalType`, for example, you usually write the code as follows:

```
namespace globalType
{
   const int n = 10;
   const double rate = 7.50;
   int count = 0;
   void printResult();
}

using namespace globalType;
```

After the `using` statement, to access a `namespace` member you do not have to put the `namespace_name` and the scope resolution operator before the `namespace` member. However, if a `namespace` member and a global identifier in a program have the same name, to access this `namespace` member in the program, the `namespace_name` and the scope resolution operator must precede the `namespace` member. Similarly, if a `namespace` member and an identifier in a block have the same name, to access this `namespace` member in the block, the `namespace_name` and the scope resolution operator must precede the `namespace` member.

Examples 8-9 through 8-12 help clarify the use of the `namespace` mechanism.

Example 8-9

Consider the following C++ code.

```
#include <iostream>
using namespace std;
.
.
.
int main()
{
      .
      .
      .
```

```
}
.
.
.
```

In this example, you can refer to the global identifiers of the header file **iostream**, such as **cin**, **cout**, and **endl**, without using the prefix **std::** before the identifier name. The obvious restriction is that the block (or function) that refers to the global identifier (of the header file **iostream**) must not contain any identifier with the same name as this global identifier.

Example 8-10

Consider the following C++ code.

```
#include <cmath>

int main()
{
    double x = 15.3;
    double y;

    y = std::pow(x,2);
    .
    .
    .
}
```

This example accesses the function **pow** of the header file **cmath**.

Example 8-11

Consider the following C++ code.

```
#include <iostream>
.
.
.
int main()
{
    using namespace std;
    .
    .
    .
}
.
.
.
```

In this example, the function **main** can refer to the global identifiers of the header file **iostream** without using the prefix **std::** before the identifier name. The **using** statement appears inside the function **main**. Therefore, other functions (if any) should use the prefix **std::** before the name of the global identifier of the header file **iostream** unless the function has a similar **using** statement.

Example 8-12

Consider the following C++ code.

```
#include <iostream>
using namespace std;       //Line 1

int t;                     //Line 2
double u;                  //Line 3

namespace exp
{
   int x;                  //Line 4
   char t;                 //Line 5
   double u;               //Line 6
   void printResult();     //Line 7
}

using namespace exp;

int main()
{
   int one;                //Line 8
   double t;               //Line 9
   double three;           //Line 10

      .
      .
      .
}

void exp::printResult() //Definition of the function printResult
{
      .
      .
      .
}
```

In this C++ program:

1. To refer to the variable **t** at Line 2 in **main**, use the scope resolution operator (that is, refer to **t** as **::t**) because the function **main** has a variable named **t** (declared at Line 5).

2. To refer to the member `t` (declared at Line 5) of the `namespace exp` in `main`, use the prefix `exp::` with `t` (that is, refer to `t` as `exp::t`) because there is a global variable named `t` (declared at Line 2) and a variable named `t` in `main`.
3. To refer to the member `u` (declared at Line 6) of the `namespace exp` in `main`, use the prefix `exp::` with `u` (that is, refer to `u` as `exp::u`) because there is a global variable named `u` (declared at Line 3).
4. You can reference the member `x` (declared at Line 4) of the `namespace exp` in `main` as either `x` or `exp::x` because there is no global identifier named `x` and the function `main` does not contain any identifier named `x`.
5. The definition of a function that is a member of a `namespace`, such as `printResult`, is usually written outside the `namespace` as in the preceding program. To write the definition of the function `printResult`, the name of the function in the function heading can be either `printResult` or `exp::printResult` (because no other global identifier is named `printResult`).

The identifiers in the system-provided header files such as `iostream`, `cmath`, and `iomanip` are defined in the `namespace std`. For this reason, to simplify the accessing of identifiers from these header files, we have been using the following statement in the programs that we write:

```
using namespace std;
```

THE string TYPE

In Chapter 2, you were introduced to the data type `string`. Recall that, prior to the ANSI/ISO C++ language standard, the Standard C++ library did not provide a `string` data type. Compiler vendors often supplied their own programmer-defined `string` type, and the syntax and semantics of string operations often varied from vendor to vendor.

The data type `string` is a programmer-defined type and is not part of the C++ language; the C++ standard library supplies it. Before using the data type `string`, the program must include the header file `string`, as shown below.

```
#include <string>
```

Recall that, in C++, a string is a sequence of zero or more characters, and strings are enclosed in double quotation marks.

The statement

```
string name = "William Jacob";
```

declares `name` to be a `string` variable and initializes `name` to `"William Jacob"`. The position of the first character, `W`, in `name` is `0`; the position of the second character, `i`, is `1`; and so on. That is, the position of the first character in a `string` variable starts with `0`, not `1`.

The variable **name** can store (just about) any size string.

Chapter 3 discussed I/O operations on the **string** type; Chapter 4 explained relational operations on the **string** type. We recommend that you revisit Chapters 3 and 4 and review the I/O and relational operations on the **string** type.

Other operators, such as the binary operator **+** (to allow the string concatenation operation) and the array index (subscript) operator **[]**, have also been defined for the data type **string**. Let's see how these operators work on the **string** data type.

Suppose you have the following declarations:

```
string str1, str2, str3;
```

The statement

```
str1 = "Hello There";
```

stores the string **"Hello There"** in **str1**. The statement

```
str2 = str1;
```

copies the value of **str1** into **str2**.

If **str1 = "Sunny"**, the statement

```
str2 = str1 + " Day";
```

stores the string **"Sunny Day"** into **str2**.

Suppose **str1 = "Hello"** and **str2 = "There"**. The statement

```
str3 = str1 + " " + str2;
```

stores **"Hello There"** into **str3**. This statement is equivalent to the statement

```
str3 = str1 + ' ' + str2;
```

Also, the statement

```
str1 = str1 + " Mickey";
```

updates the value of **str1** by appending the string **"Mickey"** to its old value. Therefore, the new value of **str1** is **"Hello Mickey"**.

For the operator + to work with the **string** data type, one of the operands of + must be a **string** variable. For example, the following statements will not work:

```
str1 = "Hello " + "there!"; //Illegal
str2 = "Sunny Day" + '!';   //Illegal
```

If **str1 = "Hello there"**, the statement

```
str1[6] = 'T';
```

replaces the character **t** with the character **T**. Recall that the position of the first character in a **string** variable is **0**. Therefore, because **t** is the seventh character in **str1**, its position is **6**.

In C++, `[ ]` is called the **array subscript operator**.

As illustrated previously, using the array subscript operator together with the position of the character, you can access an individual character within a string.

Example 8-13

The following program shows the effect of the preceding statements.

```
//Example string operations

#include <iostream>
#include <string>

using namespace std;

int main()
{
    string name = "William Jacob";                    //Line 1
    string str1, str2, str3, str4;                    //Line 2

    cout<<"Line 3: Name = "<<name<<endl;              //Line 3

    str1 = "Hello There";                             //Line 4
    cout<<"Line 5: str1 = "<<str1<<endl;              //Line 5

    str2 = str1;                                      //Line 6
    cout<<"Line 7: str2 = "<<str2<<endl;              //Line 7

    str1 = "Sunny";                                   //Line 8
    str2 = str1 + " Day";                             //Line 9
    cout<<"Line 10: str2 = "<<str2<<endl;             //Line 10

    str1 = "Hello";                                   //Line 11
    str2 = "There";                                   //Line 12
    str3 = str1 + " " + str2;                         //Line 13
    cout<<"Line 14: str3 = "<<str3<<endl;             //Line 14

    str3 = str1 + ' ' + str2;                         //Line 15
    cout<<"Line 16: str3 = "<<str3<<endl;             //Line 16

    str1 = str1 + " Mickey";                          //Line 17
    cout<<"Line 18: str1 = "<<str1<<endl;             //Line 18

    str1 = "Hello there";                             //Line 19
    cout<<"Line 20: str1[6] = "<<str1[6]<<endl;       //Line 20

    str1[6] = 'T';                                    //Line 21
    cout<<"Line 22: str1 = "<<str1<<endl;             //Line 22
```

```
    //string input operations
   cout<<"Line 23: Enter a string with "
       <<"no blanks: ";                                //Line 23
   cin>>str1;                                          //Line 24
   char ch;                                            //Line 25
   cin.get(ch);          //read the newline character; Line 26
   cout<<endl;                                         //Line 27

   cout<<"Line 28: The string you entered = "<<str1
       <<endl;                                         //Line 28

   cout<<"Line 29: Enter a sentence: ";                //Line 29
   getline(cin,str2);                                  //Line 30
   cout<<endl;                                         //Line 31
   cout<<"Line 32: The sentence is: "<<str2<<endl;     //Line 32

   return 0;
}
```


Sample Run: In the following sample run, the user input is shaded.

```
Line 3: Name = William Jacob
Line 5: str1 = Hello There
Line 7: str2 = Hello There
Line 10: str2 = Sunny Day
Line 14: str3 = Hello There
Line 16: str3 = Hello There
Line 18: str1 = Hello Mickey
Line 20: str1[6] = t
Line 22: str1 = Hello There
Line 23: Enter a string with no blanks: Programming

Line 28: The string you entered = Programming
Line 29: Enter a sentence: Testing string operations


Line 32: The sentence is: Testing string operations
```

After inputting data for Line 29, you must press the Enter key twice. Recall that the `getline` function also reads the newline character.

The preceding output is self-explanatory, and its unraveling is left as an exercise for you.

Additional `string` Operations

The data type `string` contains several other functions for string manipulation. The five in which we are interested—`length`, `size`, `find`, `substr`, and `swap`—are described in the next five sections.

The data type **string** has a data type, **string::size_type**, and a named constant, **string::npos**, associated with it.

string::size_type	An unsigned integral (data) type
string::npos	The maximum value of the (data) type **string::size_type**, a number such as **4294967295** on many machines

The length Function

The **length** function returns the number of characters currently in the string. The value returned is an unsigned integer. The syntax to call the **length** function is

```
strVar.length()
```

where **strVar** is a variable of the type **string**. The **length** function has no arguments.

Be careful with the syntax of the **length** function. The dot (period) between the **strVar** and length is crucial; it separates the name of the string variable and the word **length**. Moreover, because **length** is a function with no arguments, you still need the empty parentheses. Also, because **length** is a value-returning function, the function call must appear in an expression.

Consider the following statements.

```
string firstName;
string name;
string str;

firstName = "Elizabeth";
name = firstName + " Jones";
str = "It is sunny.";
```

Statement	**Effect**
`cout<<firstName.length()<<endl;`	`Outputs 9`
`cout<<name.length()<<endl;`	`Outputs 15`
`cout<<str.length()<<endl;`	`outputs 12`

Because the function **length** returns an unsigned integer, the value returned can be stored in an integer variable. Also, because the data type **string** has the data type **string::size_type** associated with it, the variable to hold the value returned by the **length** function is usually of this type. This prevents you from guessing whether the value returned is of the type unsigned **int** or unsigned **long**.

Suppose you have the previous declaration and the statement:

```
string::size_type len;
```

Statement	**Effect**
`len = firstName.length();`	The value of `len` is `9`
`len = name.length();`	The value of `len` is `15`
`len = str.length();`	The value of `len` is `12`

Example 8-14

The following program illustrates the use of the `length` function.

```
//Example length function

#include <iostream>
#include <string>

using namespace std;

int main()
{
   string name, firstName;                              //Line 1
   string str;                                          //Line 2
   string::size_type len;                               //Line 3

   firstName = "Elizabeth";                             //Line 4
   name = firstName + " Jones";                         //Line 5
   str = "It is sunny and warm.";                       //Line 6

   cout<<"Line 7: Length of \""<<firstName
       <<"\" = "<<firstName.length()<<endl;             //Line 7

   cout<<"Line 8: Length of \""<<name
       <<"\" = "<<name.length()<<endl;                  //Line 8

   cout<<"Line 9: Length of \""<<str
       <<"\" = "<<str.length()<<endl;                   //Line 9

   len = firstName.length();                            //Line 10
   cout<<"Line 11: len = "<<len<<endl;                  //Line 11

   len = name.length();                                 //Line 12
   cout<<"Line 13: len = "<<len<<endl;                  //Line 13

   len = str.length();                                  //Line 14
   cout<<"Line 15: len = "<<len<<endl;                  //Line 15

   return 0;
}
```

Output:

```
Line 7: Length of "Elizabeth" = 9
Line 8: Length of "Elizabeth Jones" = 15
Line 9: Length of "It is sunny and warm." = 21
Line 11: len = 9
Line 13: len = 15
Line 15: len = 21
```

The output of this program is self-explanatory. The details are left as an exercise for you.

The `size` Function

Some people prefer to use the word **size** instead of the word **length**. Thus, to accommodate both terms, the **string** type provides a function named **size** that returns the same value as does the function **length**. The syntax to call the function **size** is

```
strVar.size()
```

where **strVar** is a variable of the type **string**. Like the function **length**, the function **size** has no arguments.

The `find` Function

The **find** function searches a string to find the first occurrence of a particular substring and returns an unsigned integer value (of the type **string::size_type**), giving the result of the search. The syntax to call the function **find** is

```
strVar.find(strExp)
```

where **strVar** is a string variable and **strExp** is a string expression evaluating to a string. The string expression, **strExp**, can also be a character. If the search is successful, the function **find** returns the position in **strVar** where the match begins. For the search to be successful, the match must be exact. If the search is unsuccessful, the function returns the special value **string::npos** ("not a position within the string"). (This value is suitable for "not a valid position" because the string operations do not let any string become this long.) Because the function **find** returns an unsigned integer, the returned value can be stored in an integer variable (usually of the type **string::size_type**).

Suppose **str1** and **str2** are of the type **string**. The following are valid calls to the function **find**:

```
str1.find(str2)
str1.find("the")
str1.find('a')
str1.find(str2 + "xyz")
str1.find(str2 + 'b')
```

Consider the following statements:

```
string   sentence;
string   str;
string::size_type position;

sentence = "It is cloudy and warm.";
str = "cloudy";
```

Statement	**Effect**
`cout<<sentence.find("is")<<endl;`	Outputs 3
`cout<<sentence.find("and")<<endl;`	Outputs 13
`cout<<sentence.find('s')<<endl;`	Outputs 4
`cout<<sentence.find('i')<<endl;`	Outputs 3
`cout<<sentence.find(str)<<endl;`	Outputs 6
`cout<<sentence.find("the")<<endl;`	Outputs the value of `string::nops`
`position = sentence.find("warm");`	Assigns 17 to `position`

Note that the search is case sensitive. Therefore, the position of `i` (lowercase `i`) in the string `sentence` is 3.

Example 8-15

The following program illustrates how to use the `string` function `find`.

```
//Example find function

#include <iostream>
#include <string>

using namespace std;

int main()
{
   string    sentence, str;                                 //Line 1
   string::size_type position;                              //Line 2

   sentence = "It is cloudy and warm.";                     //Line 3
   str = "cloudy";                                          //Line 4

   cout<<"Line 5: Position of \"is\" in \""<<sentence
       <<"\" = "<<sentence.find("is")<<endl;                //Line 5

   cout<<"Line 6: Position of \"and\" in \""<<sentence
       <<"\" = "<<sentence.find("and")<<endl;               //Line 6

   cout<<"Line 7: Position of 's' in \""
       <<sentence<<"\" = "<<sentence.find('s')<<endl;       //Line 7

   cout<<"Line 8: Position of 'i' in \""
       <<sentence<<"\" = "<<sentence.find('i')<<endl        //Line 8
```

```
    cout<<"Line 9: Position of \""<<str<<"\" in \""
        <<sentence<<"\" = "<<sentence.find(str)<<endl;     //Line 9

    cout<<"Line 10: Position of \"the\" in \""<<sentence
        <<"\" = "<<sentence.find("the")<<endl;             //Line 10

    position = sentence.find("warm");                      //Line 11
    cout<<"Line 12: "<<"Position = "<<position<<endl;      //Line 12

    return 0;
}
```

Output:

```
Line 5: Position of "is" in "It is cloudy and warm." = 3
Line 6: Position of "and" in "It is cloudy and warm." = 13
Line 7: Position of 's' in "It is cloudy and warm." = 4
Line 8: Position of 'i' in "It is cloudy and warm." = 3
Line 9: Position of "cloudy" in "It is cloudy and warm." = 6
Line 10: Position of "the" in "It is cloudy and warm." = 4294967295
Line 12: Position = 17
```

The output of this program is self-explanatory. The details are left as an exercise for you.

The `substr` Function

The **substr** function returns a particular substring of a string. The syntax to call the function **substr** is

```
strVar.substr(expr1,expr2)
```

where **expr1** and **expr2** are expressions evaluating to unsigned integers. The expression **expr1** specifies a position within the string (starting position of the substring); the expression **expr2** specifies the length of the substring to be returned.

Consider the following statements:

```
string   sentence;
string   str;

sentence = "It is cloudy and warm.";
```

Statement	Effect
`cout<<sentence.substr(0,5)<<endl;`	Outputs: `It is`
`cout<<sentence.substr(6,6)<<endl;`	Outputs: `cloudy`
`cout<<sentence.substr(6,16)<<endl;`	Outputs: `cloudy and warm.`
`cout<<sentence.substr(3,6)<<endl;`	Outputs: `is clo`
`str = sentence.substr(0,8);`	`str = "It is cl"`
`str = sentence.substr(2,10);`	`str = " is cloudy"`

Example 8-16

The following program illustrates how to use the **string** function **substr**.

```
//Example substr function

#include <iostream>
#include <string>

using namespace std;

int main()
{
   string  sentence;                                    //Line 1
   string  str;                                         //Line 2

   sentence = "It is cloudy and warm.";                 //Line 3

   cout<<"Line 4: substr(0,5) in \""<<sentence
       <<"\" = \""<<sentence.substr(0,5)<<"\""<<endl; //Line 4

   cout<<"Line 5: substr(6,6) in \""<<sentence
       <<"\" = \""<<sentence.substr(6,6)<<"\""<<endl; //Line 5

   cout<<"Line 6: substr(6,16) in \""<<sentence
       <<"\" = "<<endl<<"        \""
       <<sentence.substr(6,16)<<"\""<<endl;             //Line 6

   cout<<"Line 7: substr(3,6) in \""<<sentence
       <<"\" = \""<<sentence.substr(3,6)<<"\""<<endl; //Line 7

   str = sentence.substr(0,8);                          //Line 8
   cout<<"Line 9: "<<"str = \""<<str<<"\""<<endl;       //Line 9

   str = sentence.substr(2,10);                         //Line 10
   cout<<"Line 11: "<<"str = \""<<str<<"\""<<endl;      //Line 11

   return 0;
}
```

Output:

```
Line 4: substr(0,5) in "It is cloudy and warm." = "It is"
Line 5: substr(6,6) in "It is cloudy and warm." = "cloudy"
Line 6: substr(6,16) in "It is cloudy and warm." =
        "cloudy and warm."
Line 7: substr(3,6) in "It is cloudy and warm." = "is clo"
Line 9: str = "It is cl"
Line 11: str = " is cloudy"
```

The output of this program is self-explanatory. The details are left as an exercise for you.

The swap Function

The **swap** function is used to swap—that is, interchange—the contents of two string variables. The syntax to use the **swap** function is

```
strVar1.swap(strVar2);
```

where **strVar1** and **strVar2** are **string** variables. After this statement executes, the contents of **strVar1** and **strVar2** are swapped.

Suppose you have the following statements:

```
string str1 = "Warm";
string str2 = "Cold";
```

After the following statement executes, the value of **str1** is **"Cold"** and the value of **str2** is **"Warm"**.

```
str1.swap(str2);
```

Additional **string** functions such as **empty**, **clear**, **erase**, **insert**, and **replace** are provided in Appendix F (The Header File **string**).

PROGRAMMING EXAMPLE: PIG LATIN STRINGS

In this programming example, we write a program that prompts the user to input a string and then outputs the string in the pig Latin form. The rules for converting a string into pig Latin form are as follows:

1. If the string begins with a vowel, add the string **"-way"** at the end of the string. For example, the pig Latin form of the string **"eye"** is **"eye-way"**.
2. If the string does not begin with a vowel, first add **"-"** at the end of the string. Then rotate the string one character at a time; that is, move the first character of the string to the end of the string until the first character of the string becomes a vowel. Then add the string **"ay"** at the end. For example, the pig Latin form of the string **"There"** is **"ere-Thay"**.
3. Strings such as **"by"** contain no vowels. In cases like this, the letter **y** can be considered a vowel. So, for this program the vowels are **a**, **e**, **i**, **o**, **u**, **y**, **A**, **E**, **I**, **O**, **U**, and **Y**. Therefore, the pig Latin form of **"by"** is **"y-bay"**.
4. Strings such as **"1234"** contain no vowels. The pig Latin form of the string **"1234"** is **"1234-way"**. That is, the pig Latin form of a string that has no vowels in it is the string followed by the string **"-way"**.

Input Input to the program is a string.

Output Output of the program is the string in the pig Latin form.

Problem Analysis and Algorithm Design

Suppose that `str` denotes a string. To convert `str` into pig Latin, check the first character, `str[0]`, of `str`. If `str[0]` is a vowel, add `"-way"` at the end of `str`—that is, `str = str + "-way"`.

Suppose that the first character of `str`, `str[0]`, is not a vowel. First add `"-"` at the end of the string. Then remove the first character of `str` from `str` and put it at end of `str`. Now the second character of `str` becomes the first character of `str`. This process of checking the first character of `str` and moving it to the end of `str` if the first character of `str` is not a vowel is repeated until either the first character of `str` is a vowel or all characters of `str` are processed, in which case `str` does not contain any vowels.

In this program, we write a function `isVowel`, to determine whether a character is a vowel; a function `rotate`, to move the first character of `str` to the end of `str`; and a function `pigLatinString`, to find the pig Latin form of `str`. The previous discussion translates into the following algorithm:

1. Get `str`.
2. Find the pig Latin form of `str` by using the function `pigLatinString`.
3. Output the pig Latin form of `str`.

Before writing the main algorithm, each of these functions is described in detail.

Function `isVowel` This function takes a character as a parameter and returns `true` if the character is a vowel, and `false` otherwise. The definition of the function `isVowel` is

```
bool isVowel(char ch)
{
   switch(ch)
   {
   case 'A': case 'E':
   case 'I': case 'O':
   case 'U': case 'Y':
   case 'a': case 'e':
   case 'i': case 'o':
   case 'u': case 'y': return true;
   default: return false;
   }
}
```

Function `rotate` This function takes a string as a parameter, removes the first character of the string, and places it at the end of the string. This is done by extracting the substring starting at position `1` (which is the second character) until the end of the string, and then adding the first character of the string. The new string is returned as the value of this function. Essentially, the definition of the function **rotate** is

```
string rotate(string pStr)
{
   int len = pStr.length();

   string rStr;

   rStr = pStr.substr(1,len - 1) + pStr[0];

   return rStr;
}
```

Function pigLatinString This function takes a string, **pStr**, as a parameter and returns the pig Latin form of **pStr**. Suppose **pStr** denotes the string to be converted to its pig Latin form. There are three possible cases: **pStr[0]** is a vowel; **pStr** contains a vowel and the first character of **pStr** is not a vowel; or **pStr** contains no vowels. Suppose that **pStr[0]** is not a vowel. Move the first character of **pStr** to the end of **pStr**. This process is repeated until either the first character of **pStr** has become a vowel or all characters of **pStr** are checked, in which case **pStr** does not contain any vowels. This discussion translates into the following algorithm:

1. If **pStr[0]** is a vowel, add **"-way"** at the end of **pStr**.
2. Suppose **pStr[0]** is not a vowel.
3. Move the first character of **pStr** to the end of **pStr**. The second character of **pStr** becomes the first character of **pStr**. Now **pStr** may or may not contain a vowel. We use a Boolean variable, **foundVowel**, which is set to **true** if **pStr** contains a vowel and **false** otherwise.
   a. Suppose that **len** denotes the length of **pStr**.
   b. Initialize **foundVowel** to **false**.
   c. If **pStr[0]** is not a vowel, move **pStr[0]** to the end of **pStr** by calling the function **rotate**.
   d. Repeat Step b until either the first character of **pStr** becomes a vowel or all characters of **pStr** have been checked.
4. Convert **pStr** into the pig Latin form.
5. Return **pStr**.

The definition of the function **pigLatinString** is

```
string pigLatinString(string pStr)
{
   int len;

   bool foundVowel;

   int counter;

   if(isVowel(pStr[0]))                                    //Step 1
      pStr = pStr + "-way";
   else                                                    //Step 2
   {
      pStr = pStr + '-';
      pStr = rotate(pStr);                                 //Step 3

      len = pStr.length();                                 //Step 3.a
      foundVowel = false;                                  //Step 3.b

      for(counter = 1; counter < len - 1; counter++)      //Step 3.d
          if(isVowel(pStr[0]))
          {
             foundVowel = true;
             break;
          }
          else                                             //Step 3.c
              pStr = rotate(pStr);

          if(!foundVowel)                                  //Step 4
              pStr = pStr.substr(1,len) + "-way";
          else
              pStr = pStr + "ay";
   }

   return pStr;                                            //Step 5
}
```

Main Algorithm

1. Get the string.
2. Call the function **pigLatinString** to find the pig Latin form of the string.
3. Output the pig Latin form of the string.

Complete Program Listing

```
#include <iostream>
#include <string>

using namespace std;

bool isVowel(char ch);
string rotate(string pStr);
string pigLatinString(string pStr);

int main()
{
   string str;

   cout<<"Enter a string: ";
   cin>>str;
   cout<<endl;

   cout<<"The pig Latin form of "<<str<<" is: "
       <<pigLatinString(str)<<endl;

   return 0;
}


bool isVowel(char ch)
{
   switch(ch)
   {
   case 'A': case 'E':
   case 'I': case 'O':
   case 'U': case 'Y':
   case 'a': case 'e':
   case 'i': case 'o':
   case 'u': case 'y': return true;
   default: return false;
   }
}

string rotate(string pStr)
{
   int len = pStr.length();

   string rStr;

   rStr = pStr.substr(1,len - 1) + pStr[0];
```

```
    return rStr;
}
string pigLatinString(string pStr)
{
    int len;

    bool foundVowel;

    int counter;

    if(isVowel(pStr[0]))                                    //Step 1
       pStr = pStr + "-way";
    else                                                    //Step 2
    {
       pStr = pStr + '-';
       pStr = rotate(pStr);                                 //Step 3

       len = pStr.length();                                 //Step 3.a
       foundVowel = false;                                  //Step 3.b

       for(counter = 1; counter < len - 1; counter++)       //Step 3.d
           if(isVowel(pStr[0]))
           {
              foundVowel = true;
              break;
           }
           else                                             //Step 3.c
              pStr = rotate(pStr);

    if(!foundVowel)                                         //Step 4
        pStr = pStr.substr(1,len) + "-way";
    else
        pStr = pStr + "ay";
    }

    return pStr;                                            //Step 5
}
```

Sample Runs In these sample runs, the user input is shaded.

Sample Run 1:

```
Enter a string: eye

The pig Latin form of eye is: eye-way
```

Sample Run 2:

```
Enter a string: There

The pig Latin form of There is: ere-Thay
```

Sample Run 3:

```
Enter a string: why

The pig Latin form of why is: y-whay
```

Sample Run 4:

```
Enter a string: 123456

The pig Latin form of 123456 is: 123456-way
```

QUICK REVIEW

1. An enumeration type is a set of ordered values.
2. C++'s reserve word **enum** is used to create an enumeration type.
3. The syntax of **enum** is

   `enum typeName{value1, value2,...};`

   where `value1, value2,...` are identifiers, and `value1<value2<....`
4. No arithmetic operations are allowed on the enumeration type.
5. Relational operators can be used with **enum** values.
6. Enumeration type values cannot be input or output directly.
7. Enumeration types can be passed as parameters to functions either by value or by reference.
8. A function can return a value of the enumeration type.
9. An anonymous type is one where a variable's values are specified without any type name.
10. C++'s reserved word **typedef** is used to create synonyms or aliases to previously defined data types.
11. Anonymous types cannot be passed as parameters to functions.
12. The **namespace** mechanism is a feature of ANSI/ISO Standard C++.
13. A **namespace** member is usually a named constant, variable, function, or another **namespace**.

14. The scope of a `namespace` member is local to the `namespace`.
15. One way to access a `namespace` member outside the `namespace` is to precede the `namespace` member name with the `namespace` name and scope resolution operator.
16. In C++, `namespace` is a reserved word.
17. To use the `namespace` mechanism, the program must include the ANSI/ISO Standard C++ header files—that is, the header files without the extension `h`.
18. The `using` statement simplifies the accessing of `namespace` members.
19. In C++, `using` is a reserved word.
20. The keyword `namespace` must appear in the `using` statement.
21. When accessing a `namespace` member without the `using` statement, the `namespace` name and the scope resolution operator must precede the name of the `namespace` member.
22. To use an identifier declared in the standard header files without the `namespace` name, after including all the necessary header files, the following statement must appear in the program:

    ```
    using namespace std;
    ```
23. A string is a sequence of zero or more characters.
24. Strings in C++ are enclosed in double quotation marks.
25. To use the type `string`, the program must include the header file `string`. The other header files used in the program should be ANSI/ISO Standard C++ style header files.
26. The assignment operator can be used with the `string` type.
27. The operator `+` can be used to concatenate two values of the type `string`. For the operator `+` to work with the `string` data type, one of the operands of `+` must be a `string` variable.
28. Relational operators can be applied to the `string` type.
29. In a string, the position of the first character is `0`, the position of the second character is `1`, and so on.
30. The length of a string is the number of characters in the string.
31. In C++, `[]` is called the array subscript operator.
32. To access an individual character within a string, use the array subscript operator together with the position of the character.
33. The function `length` returns the number of characters currently in the string. The syntax to call the function `length` is

    ```
    strVar.length()
    ```

    where `strVar` is a variable of the type `string`.

34. The function **size** returns the number of characters currently in the string. The syntax to call the function **size** is

```
strVar.size()
```

where **strVar** is a variable of the type **string**. The function **size** works in the same way as the **length** function does.

35. The function **find** searches a string to find the first occurrence of a particular substring and returns an unsigned integer value (of the type **string::size_type**) giving the result of the search. The syntax to call the function **find** is

```
strVar.find(strExp)
```

where **strVar** is a string variable and **strExp** is a string expression evaluating to a string.

36. The argument of the function **find** (that is, **strExp**) can also be a character.

37. If the search is successful, the function **find** returns the position in **strVar** where the match begins. If the search is unsuccessful, the function **find** returns the **npos** value.

38. The function **substr** returns a particular substring of a string. The syntax to call the function **substr** is

```
strVar.substr(expr1,expr2)
```

where **expr1** and **expr2** are expressions evaluating to unsigned integers. The expression **expr1** specifies a position within the string (the starting position of the substring); the expression **expr2** specifies the length of the substring to be returned.

39. The function **swap** is used to swap the contents of two string variables. The syntax to use the function **swap** is

```
strVar1.swap(strVar2);
```

where **strVar1** and **strVar2** are string variables. This statement swaps the values of **strVar1** and **strVar2**.

EXERCISES

1. Mark the following statements as true or false.
   a. The following is a valid C++ enumeration type:

   ```
   enum romanNumerals{I, V, X, L, C, D, M};
   ```

   b. Given the declaration:

   ```
   enum cars{Ford, GM, Toyota, Honda};
   cars domesticCars = Ford;
   ```

   the statement

   ```
   domesticCars = domesticCars + 1;
   ```

   sets the value of **domesticCars** to **GM**.
   c. A function can return a value of an enumeration type.
   d. You can input the value of an enumeration type directly from a standard input device.

e. The only arithmetic operations allowed on the enumeration type are increment and decrement.

f. The values in the domain of an enumeration type are called enumerators.

g. The following are legal C++ statements in the same block of a C++ program:

```
enum mathStudent{Bill, John, Lisa, Ron, Cindy, Shelly};
enum historyStudent{Amanda, Bob, Jack, Tom, Susan};
```

h. The following statement creates an anonymous type:

```
enum {A, B, C, D, F} studentGrade;
```

i. You can use the `namespace` mechanism with header files with the extension `h`.

j. Suppose `str = "ABCD";`. After the statement `str[1] = 'a';`, the value of `str` is `"aBCD"`.

k. Suppose `str = "abcd"`. After the statement

```
str = str + "ABCD";
```

the value of `str` is `"ABCD"`.

2. Write C++ statements that do the following:

   a. Define an `enum` type, `bookType`, with the values `Math`, `CSC`, `English`, `History`, `Physics`, and `Philosophy`.

   b. Declare a variable `book` of the type `bookType`.

   c. Assign `Math` to the variable `book`.

   d. Advance `book` to the next value in the list.

   e. Output the value of the variable `book`.

3. Given

```
enum currencyType{Dollar, Pound, Frank, Lira, Mark};
currencyType currency;
```

which of the following statements are valid?

a. `currency = Dollar;`

b. `cin>>currency;`

c. `currency = currencyType(currency + 1);`

d.
```
for(currency = Dollar; currency <= Mark; currency++)
        cout<<"*";
```

4. Given:

```
enum cropType{wheat, corn, rye, barley, oats};
cropType  crop;
```

circle the correct answer.

a. `static_cast<int>(wheat) is 0`   `(i) true`   `(ii) false`

b. `static_cast<cropType>(static_cast<int>(wheat) - 1) is wheat`
`(i) true`   `(ii) false`

c. `rye > wheat`   `(i) true`   `(ii) false`

d.
```
for(crop = wheat; crop <= oats; ++crop)
        cout<<"*";
    outputs: *****                              (i) true     (ii) false
```

5. What is wrong with the following program?

```
   #include <iostream>                           //Line 1
   int main()                                    //Line 2

   {
   cout<<"Hello World! "<<endl;                  //Line 3
   return 0;                                     //Line 4
}
```

6. What is wrong with the following program?

```
#include <iostream.h>                            //Line 1

using namespace std;                             //Line 2

int main()                                       //Line 3
{
   int x = 0;                                    //Line 4
   cout<<"x = "<<x<<endl;                        //Line 5
   return 0;                                     //Line 6
}
```

7. What is wrong with the following program?

```
#include <iostream>                              //Line 1


namespace aaa                                    //Line 2
{
     const int x = 0;                            //Line 3
     double y;                                   //Line 4
}

using namespace std;                             //Line 5

int main()                                       //Line 6
{
     y = 34.50;                                  //Line 7
```

```
    cout<<"x = "<<x<<", y = "<<y<<endl;    //Line 8
    return 0;                              //Line 9
}
```

8. What is wrong with the following program?

```
#include <iostream>   //Line 1
#include <cmath>      //Line 2

using std;            //Line 3

int main()            //Line 4
{
    return 0;         //Line 5
}
```

9. What is the output of the following program?

```
#include <iostream>
#include <string>

using namespace std;

int main()
{
   string str1 = "Amusement Park";
   string str2 = "Going to";
   string str3 = "the";
   string str;

   cout<<str2 + ' '+  str3 + ' ' + str1<<endl;
   cout<<str1.length()<<endl;
   cout<<str1.find('P')<<endl;
   cout<<str1.substr(1,5)<<endl;

   str = "ABCDEFGHIJK";
   cout<<str<<endl;
   cout<<str.length()<<endl;

   str[0] = 'a';
   str[2] = 'd';

   cout<<str<<endl;
   return 0;
}
```

Programming Exercises

1. a. Define an enumeration type, `triangleType`, that has the values `scalene`, `isosceles`, `equilateral`, and `noTriangle`.

   b. Write a function, `triangleShape`, that takes as parameters three numbers, each of which represents the length of a side of the triangle. The function should return the shape of the triangle. (*Note*: In a triangle, the sum of the lengths of any two sides is greater than the length of the third side.)

   c. Write a program that prompts the user to input the length of the sides of a triangle and outputs the shape of the triangle.

2. Redo Programming Exercise 12 of Chapter 4 (cell phone company) so that all of the named constants are defined in a `namespace`.

3. The Programming Example Pig Latin Strings converts a string into the pig Latin form, but it processes only one word. Rewrite the program so that it can be used to process a text of unspecified length. If a word ends with a punctuation mark, in the pig Latin form put the punctuation at the end of the string. For example, the pig Latin form of `Hello` is `ello-Hay`. Assume that the text contains the following punctuation marks: `,` (comma), `.` (period), `?` (question mark), `;` (semicolon), and `:` (colon).

4. Write a program that can be used to calculate the federal tax. The tax is calculated as follows: For single people, the standard exemption is $4000; for married people, the standard exemption is $7000. A person can also put up to 6% of his or her gross income in a pension plan. The tax rates are as follows: If the taxable income is

   - Between $0 and $15000, the tax rate is 15%
   - Between $15001 and $40000, the tax is $2250 plus 25% of the taxable income over $15000
   - Over $40,000, the tax is $8460 plus 35% of the taxable income over $40000

   Prompt the user to enter the following information:

   - Marital status
   - If the martial status is "married," ask for the number of children under the age of 14
   - Gross salary (If the marital status is "married" and both spouses have income, enter the combined salary.)
   - Percentage of gross income contributed to a pension fund.

   Your program must consist of at least the following functions:

   a. Function `getData`: This function asks the user to enter the relevant data.

   b. Function `taxAmount`: This function computes and returns the tax owed.

   To calculate the taxable income, subtract the sum of the standard exemption, the amount contributed to a pension plan, and the personal exemption, which is $1500 per person.

5. A set of integers a, b, and c is called a Pythagorean triple if $a^2 + b^2 = c^2$. For example, the integers 3, 4, and 5 form a Pythagorean triple because $3^2 + 4^2 = 5^2$. To find Pythagorean triples, use the following formula. Let m and n be integers. If $a = m^2 - n^2$, $b = 2mn$, and $c = m^2 + n^2$, then a, b, and c are a Pythagorean triple. Write a program that prompts the user to enter values for m and n and outputs the Pythagorean triple corresponding to m and n.
6. **(Fraction Calculator)** Write a program that lets the user perform arithmetic operations on fractions. Fractions are of the form a/b, where a and b are integers and $b \neq 0$. Your program must be menu driven, allowing the user to select the operation (`+`, `-`, `*`, or `/`) and input the numerator and denominator of each fraction. Furthermore, your program must consist of at least the following functions:
   a. Function `menu`: This function informs the user about the program's purpose, explains how to enter data, and allows the user to select the operation.
   b. Function `addFractions`: This function takes as parameters four integers representing the numerators and denominators of two fractions, adds the fractions, and returns the numerator and denominator of the result.
   c. Function `subtractFractions`: This function takes as parameters four integers representing the numerators and denominators of two fractions, subtracts the fractions, and returns the numerator and denominator of the result.
   d. Function `multiplyFractions`: This function takes as parameters four integers representing the numerators and denominators of two fractions, multiplies the fractions, and returns the numerators and denominators of the result.
   e. Function `divideFractions`: This function takes as parameters four integers representing the numerators and denominators of two fractions, divides the fractions, and returns the numerator and denominator of the result.

   Some sample outputs are

   ```
   3 / 4 + 2 / 5 = 23 / 20
   2 / 3 * 3 / 5 = 6 / 15
   ```

   Your answer need not be in the lowest terms.

CHAPTER

9

ARRAYS AND STRINGS

In this chapter, you will:

- Learn about arrays
- Explore how to declare and manipulate data into arrays
- Understand the meaning of "array index out of bounds"
- Become familiar with the restrictions on array processing
- Discover how to pass an array as a parameter to a function
- Learn about C-strings
- Examine the use of string functions to process C-strings
- Discover how to input data in—and output data from—a C-string
- Learn about parallel arrays

In previous chapters, you worked with simple data types. In Chapter 2, you learned that C++ data types fall into three categories. One of these categories is the structured data type. Chapter 9 and the next few chapters focus on structured data types.

Recall that a data type is called **simple** if variables of that type can store only one value at a time. In contrast, in a **structured data type**, each data item is a collection of other data items. Simple data types are building blocks of structured data types. The first structured data type that we will discuss is, as the name of this chapter indicates, an array. Chapters 12 and 13 discuss other structured types.

Before formally defining an array, let us consider the following problem. We want to write a C++ program that reads five numbers, finds their sum, and prints the numbers in reverse order.

In Chapter 5, you learned how to read numbers, print them, and find the sum. The difference here is that we want to print the numbers in reverse order. So we cannot print the first four numbers until we have printed the fifth, and so on. This means that we need to store all the numbers before we start printing them in reverse order. From what we have learned so far, the following program accomplishes this task.

```
//Program to read five numbers, find their sum, and print the
//numbers in reverse order.

#include <iostream>
using namespace std;

int main()
{
   int  item0, item1, item2, item3, item4;
   int sum;

   cout<<"Enter five integers: ";
   cin>>item0>>item1>>item2>>item3>>item4;
   cout<<endl;

   sum = item0 + item1 + item2 + item3 + item4;

   cout<<"The sum of the numbers = "<<sum<<endl;
   cout<<"The numbers in reverse order are: ";
   cout<<item4<<" "<<item3<<" "<<item2<<" "
       <<item1<<" "<<item0<<endl;

   return 0;
}
```

This program works fine. However, if you need to read 100 (or more) numbers and print them in reverse order, you would have to declare 100 variables and have to write many `cin` and `cout` statements. Thus, for large amounts of data, this type of program is not desirable.

Note the following in the preceding program:

1. Five variables must be declared because the numbers are to be printed in reverse order.
2. All variables are of the type `int`—that is, of the same data type.

3. The way in which these variables are declared indicates that the variables to store these numbers have the same name except the last character, which is a number.

Statement 1 tells you that you have to declare five variables. Statement 3 tells you that it would be convenient if you could somehow put the last character, which is a number, into a counter variable and use one **`for`** loop to count from `0` to `4` for reading and another **`for`** loop to count from `4` to `0` for printing. Finally, because all variables are of the same type, you should be able to specify how many variables must be declared—and their data type—with a simpler statement than the one we used earlier.

The data structure that lets you do all of these things in C++ is called an array.

ARRAYS

An **array** is a collection of a fixed number of components wherein all of the components are of the same data type. A **one-dimensional array** is an array in which the components are arranged in a list form. The remainder of this chapter discusses only one-dimensional arrays. (Chapter 10 discusses two- or more dimensional arrays.)

9

The general form of declaring a one-dimensional array is

```
dataType arrayName[intExp];
```

where **`intExp`** is any expression that evaluates to a positive integer. Also, **`intExp`** specifies the number of components in the array.

Example 9-1

The statement

```
int num[5];
```

declares an array `num` of `5` components. Each component is of the type **`int`**. The components are `num[0]`, `num[1]`, `num[2]`, `num[3]`, and `num[4]`. Figure 9-1 illustrates the array `num`.

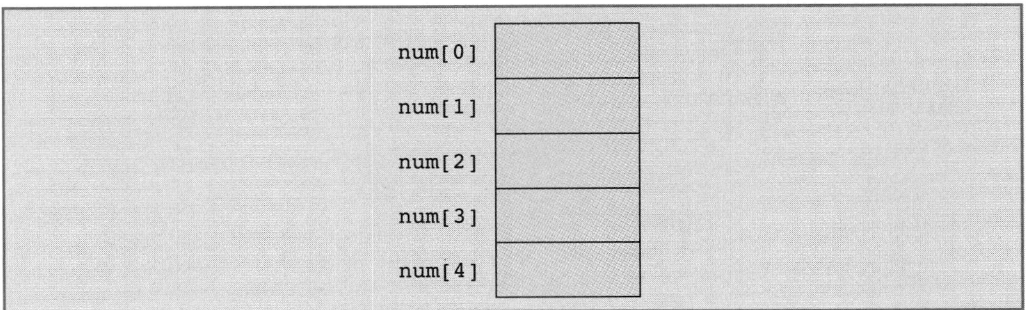

Figure 9-1 Array num

Accessing Array Components

The general form (syntax) used for accessing an array component is

```
arrayName[indexExp]
```

where **indexExp**, called **index**, is any expression whose value is a non-negative integer. The index value specifies the position of the component in the array.

In C++, [ ] is an operator, called the **array subscripting operator**. Moreover, in C++, the array index starts at 0.

Consider the following statement:

```
int list[10];
```

This statement declares an array list of 10 components. The components are list[0], list[1], ..., list[9]. In other words, we have declared 10 variables. (See Figure 9-2.)

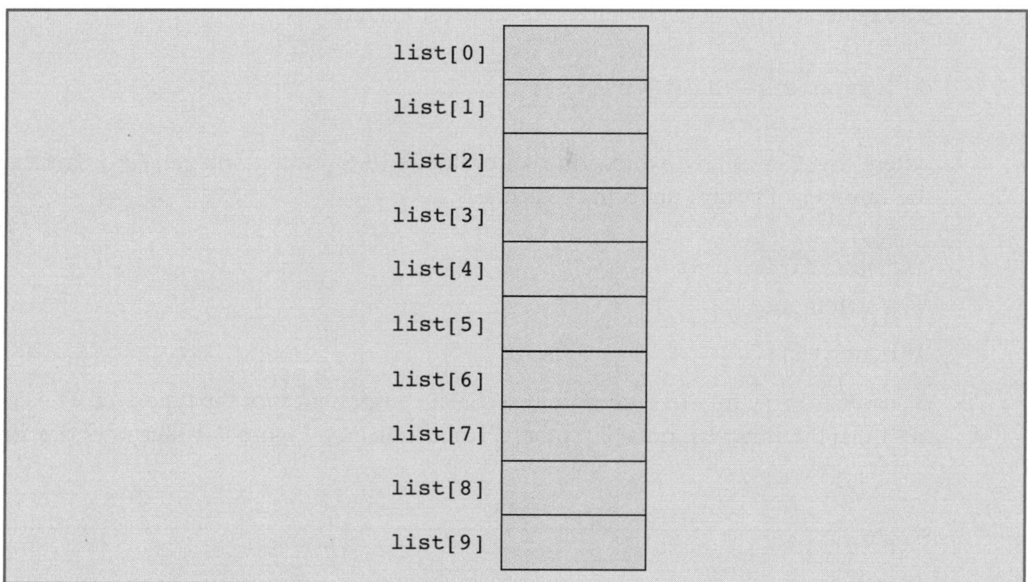

Figure 9-2 Array list

The assignment statement

```
list[5] = 34;
```

stores 34 in list[5], which is the sixth component of the array list. (See Figure 9-3.)

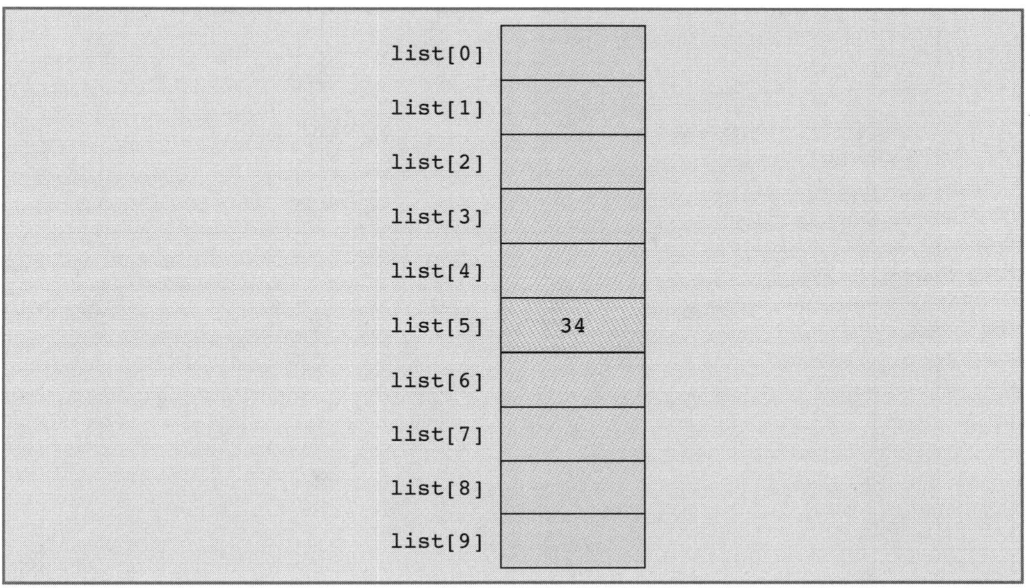

Figure 9-3 Array `list` after the statement `list[5] = 34;` executes

Suppose `i` is an `int` variable. Then the assignment statement

```
list[3] = 63;
```

is equivalent to the assignment statements

```
i = 3;
list[i] = 63;
```

If `i` is `4`, then the assignment statement

```
list[2*i-3] = 58;
```

stores `58` in `list[5]`, because `2*i-3` evaluates to `5`. The index expression is evaluated first, giving the position of the component in the array.

Next, consider the following statements:

```
list[3] = 10;
list[6] = 35;
list[5] = list[3]+list[6];
```

The first statement stores `10` in `list[3]`, the second statement stores `35` in `list[6]`, and the third statement adds the contents of `list[3]` and `list[6]` and stores the result in `list[5]`. (See Figure 9-4.)

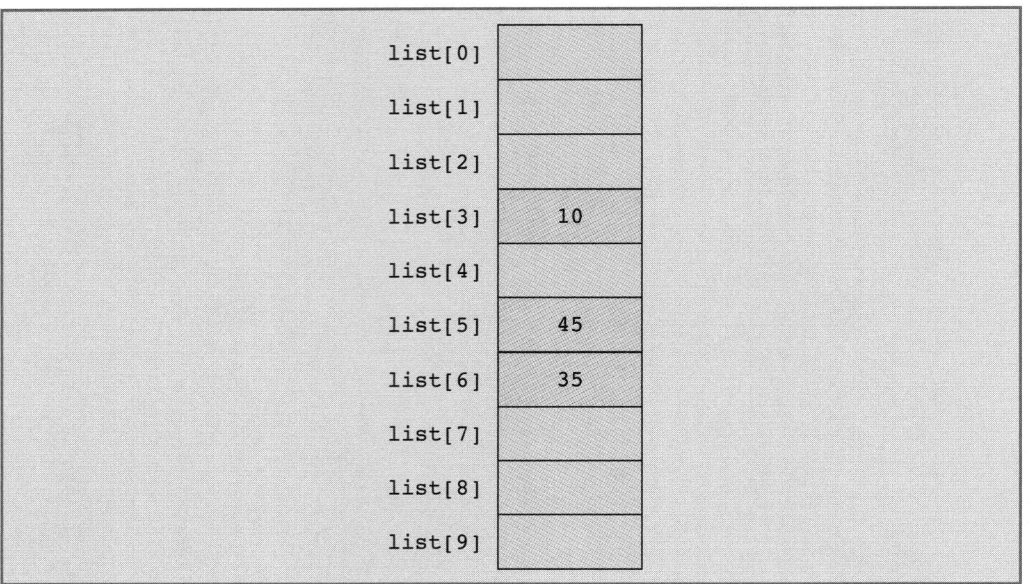

Figure 9-4 Array `list` after the statements `list[3] = 10;`, `list[6] = 35;`, and `list[5] = list[3]+list[6];` execute

Example 9-2

You can also declare arrays as follows:

```
const int arraySize = 10;

int list[arraySize];
```

That is, you can first declare a named constant and then use the value of the named constant to declare an array and specify its size.

NOTE

When you declare an array, its size must be known. For example, you cannot do the following:

```
int arraySize;                                  //Line 1

cout<<"Enter the size of the array: ";          //Line 2
cin>>arraySize;                                 //Line 3
cout<<endl;                                     //Line 4

int list[arraySize];                            //Line 5; not allowed
```

The statement in Line 2 asks the user to enter the size of the array when the program executes. The statement in Line 3 inputs the size of the array into `arraySize`. When the compiler compiles Line 1, the value of the variable `arraySize` is unknown. Therefore, during compilation, the value of the variable `arraySize` is unknown. Thus, when the compiler compiles Line 5, the size of the array is unknown and the compiler will not know how much memory space to allocate for the array. In Chapter 15, you will learn how to specify the size of an array during program execution and then declare an array of that size using pointers. Arrays that are created during program execution using pointers are called **dynamic arrays**. For now, whenever you declare an array, its size must be known.

Processing One-Dimensional Arrays

Some of the basic operations performed on a one-dimensional array are: initialize, input data, output data stored in an array, and find the largest and/or smallest element. Moreover, if the data is numeric, find the sum and average of the elements of the array. Each of these operations requires the ability to step through the elements of the array. Stepping through the elements of an array is easily accomplished by using a loop. For example, suppose that we have the following statements:

```
int list[100];     //list is an array of the size 100
int i;
```

The following **`for`** loop steps through each element of the array `list` starting at the first element of `list`.

```
for(i = 0; i < 100; i++)     //Line 1
    process list[i]          //Line 2
```

If processing `list` requires inputting data into `list`, the statement in Line 2 takes the form of an input statement, such as the `cin` statement. For example, the following statements read 100 numbers from the keyboard and store the numbers in `list`.

```
for(i = 0; i < 100; i++)
    cin>>list[i];
```

Similarly, if processing `list` requires outputting data, then the statement in Line 2 takes the form of an output statement. Example 9-3 further illustrates how to process one-dimensional arrays.

Example 9-3

This example shows how loops are used to process arrays. The following declaration is used throughout this example:

```
double sale[10];
int index;
double largestSale, sum, average;
```

The first statement declares an array `sale` of `10` components with each component being of the type `double`. The meaning of the other statements is clear.

a. **Initializing an array:** The following loop initializes every component of the array `sale` to `0.0`.

```
for(index = 0; index < 10; index++)
    sale[index] = 0.0;
```

b. **Reading data in an array:** The following loop inputs data in the array `sale`. For simplicity, we assume that the data is entered at the keyboard.

```
for(index = 0; index < 10; index++)
    cin>>sale[index];
```

c. **Printing an array:** The following loop outputs the array `sale`. For simplicity, we assume that the output goes to the screen.

```
for(index = 0; index < 10; index++)
    cout<<sale[index]<<" ";
```

d. **Finding the sum and average of an array:** Because the array `sale`, as its name implies, represents certain sales data, it is natural to find the total sale and average sale amounts. The following C++ code finds the sum of the elements of the array `sale` and the average sale amount:

```
sum = 0;
for(index = 0; index < 10; index++)
    sum = sum + sale[index];

average = sum / 10;
```

e. **Largest element in the array:** We now discuss the algorithm to find the largest element in an array—that is, the array component with the largest value. However, in general, the user is more interested in determining the location of the largest element in the array. Of course, if you know the location (that is, the index of the largest element in the array), you can easily determine the value of the largest element in the array. So let us describe the algorithm to determine the index of the largest element in an array—in particular, the index of the largest sale amount in the array `sale`.

We assume that `maxIndex` will contain the index of the largest element in the array `sale`. The general algorithm is quite straightforward. Initially, we assume that the first element in the list is the largest element and so `maxIndex` is initialized to `0`. We then compare the element pointed to by **maxIndex** with every element in the list. Whenever we find an element in the array larger than the element pointed to by **maxIndex**, we update **maxIndex** so that it points to the new larger element. The algorithm is as follows:

```
maxIndex = 0;
for(index = 1; index < 10; index++)
   if(sale[maxIndex] < sale[index])
          maxIndex = index;

largestSale = sale[maxIndex];
```

Let us demonstrate the way in which this algorithm works with the help of an example. Suppose the array **sale** is as given in Figure 9-5.

	[0]	[1]	[2]	[3]	[4]	[5]	[6]	[7]	[8]	[9]
sale	12.50	8.35	19.60	25.00	14.00	39.43	35.90	98.23	66.65	35.64

Figure 9-5 Array sale

Here we determine the largest element in the array **sale**. Before the **for** loop begins, **maxIndex** is initialized to 0 and the **for** loop initializes **index** to 1. In the following, we show the values of **maxIndex**, **index**, and certain array elements during each iteration of the **for** loop:

index	maxIndex	sale[maxIndex]	sale[index]	sale[maxIndex] < sale[index]
1	0	12.50	8.35	12.50 < 8.35 is **false**
2	0	12.50	19.60	12.50 < 19.60 is **true;** maxIndex = 2
3	2	19.60	25.00	19.60 < 25.00 is **true;** maxIndex = 3
4	3	25.00	14.00	25.00 < 14.00 is **false**
5	3	25.00	39.43	25.00 < 39.43 is **true;** maxIndex = 5
6	5	39.43	35.90	39.43 < 35.90 is **false**
7	5	39.43	98.23	39.43 < 98.23 is **true;** maxIndex = 7
8	7	98.23	66.25	98.23 < 66.65 is **false**
9	7	98.23	35.64	98.23 < 35.64 is **false**

After the **for** loop executes, **maxIndex = 7**, giving the index of the largest element in the array **sale**. Thus, **largestSale = sale[maxIndex] = 98.23**.

You can write an algorithm to find the smallest element in the array that is similar to the algorithm for finding the largest element in an array. (See Programming Exercise 2 at the end of this chapter.)

Now that you know how to declare and process arrays, we can rewrite the program that was discussed in the beginning of this chapter. Recall that this program reads five numbers, finds the sum, and prints the numbers in reverse order.

Example 9-4

```
//Program to read five numbers, find their sum, and
//print the numbers in reverse order.

#include <iostream>
using namespace std;

int main()
{
      int item[5];  //declare an array item of five components
      int sum;
      int counter;

      cout<<"Enter five numbers."<<endl;

      sum = 0;

      for(counter = 0; counter < 5; counter++)
      {
          cin>>item[counter];
          sum = sum + item[counter];
      }

          cout<<"The sum of the numbers is: "<<sum<<endl;
          cout<<"The numbers in reverse order are: ";

         //print the numbers in reverse order
      for(counter = 4; counter >= 0; counter--)
          cout<<item[counter]<<" ";

      cout<<endl;

      return 0;
}
```

Sample Run: In this sample run, the user input is shaded.

```
Enter five numbers.
12 76 34 52 89
The sum of the numbers is: 263
The numbers in reverse order are: 89  52  34  76  12
```

Array Index Out of Bounds

Consider the following declaration:

```
double num[10];
int  i;
```

The component `num[i]` is valid, that is, `i` is a valid index, if `i = 0, 1, 2, 3, 4, 5, 6, 7, 8, or 9`.

The index—say, `index`—of an array is **in bounds** if `index >= 0` and `index <= arraySize - 1`. If either `index < 0` or `index > arraySize - 1`, then we say that the index is **out of bounds**.

Unfortunately, in C++, there is no guard against out-of-bounds indices. Thus, C++ does not check whether the index value is within range—that is, between `0` and `arraySize - 1`. If the index goes out of bounds and the program tries to access the component specified by the index, then whatever memory location is indicated by the index is accessed. This situation can result in altering or accessing the data of a memory location that you never intended. Consequently, if during execution the index goes out of bounds, several strange things can happen. It is solely the programmer's responsibility to make sure that the index is within bounds.

A loop such as the following can set the index out of bounds:

```
for(i = 0; i <= 10; i++)
    list[i] = 0;
```

Here we assume that `list` is an array of `10` components. When `i` becomes `10`, the loop test condition `i <= 10` evaluates to `true` and the body of the loop executes, which results in storing `0` in `list[10]`. Logically, `list[10]` does not exist.

Array Initialization During Declaration

Like any other simple variable, an array can also be initialized while it is being declared. For example, the following C++ statement declares an array, `list`, of five components and initializes these components.

```
double sales[5] = {12.25, 32.50, 16.90, 23, 45.68};
```

The values are placed between braces and separated by commas. Here `sales[0] = 12.25`, `sales[1] = 32.50`, `sales[2] = 16.90`, `sales[3] = 23.00`, and `sales[4] = 45.68`.

When initializing arrays while declaring them, it is not necessary to specify the size of the array. The size of the array is determined by the number of initial values in the braces. However, you must include the brackets following the array name. The previous statement is, therefore, equivalent to

```
double sales[] = {12.25, 32.50, 16.90, 23, 45.68};
```

Although it is not necessary to specify the size of the array if it is initialized during declaration, it is a good practice to do so.

Partial Initialization of Arrays During Declaration

When you declare and initialize an array simultaneously, you do not need to initialize all components of the array. This procedure is called **partial initialization of an array during declaration**. However, if you partially initialize an array during declaration, you must exercise some caution. The following examples help explain what happens when you declare and partially initialize an array.

The statement

```
int list[10] = {0};
```

declares `list` to be an array of `10` components and initializes all components to `0`. The statement

```
int list[10] = {8,5,12};
```

declares `list` to be an array of `10` components, initializes `list[0]` to `8`, `list[1]` to `5`, `list[2]` to `12`, and all other components to `0`. Thus, if all values are not specified in the initialization statement, the array components for which the values are not specified are initialized to `0`. Note that here the size of the array in the declaration statement does matter. For example, the statement

```
int list[] = {5,6,3};
```

declares `list` to be an array of `3` components and initializes `list[0]` to `5`, `list[1]` to `6`, and `list[2]` to `3`. In contrast, the statement

```
int list[25]= {4,7};
```

declares `list` to be an array of `25` components. The first two components are initialized to `4` and `7`, respectively, and all other components are initialized to `0`.

Some Restrictions on Array Processing

Suppose `x` and `y` are two arrays of the same type and size, say `25`. Further suppose that array `x` has been initialized, and now you want to copy array `x` into array `y`. The following statement is illegal:

```
y = x;   //illegal
```

To copy one array into another array, you must copy it component-wise—that is, one component at a time. This can be done using a loop like the following:

```
for(j = 0; j < 25; j++)
    y[j] = x[j];
```

Similarly, comparing arrays—reading data into an array and printing the contents of an array—must be done component-wise. The following statements are, therefore, illegal:

```
cin>>x;          //illegal
cout<<y;         //illegal
if(x <= y)       //illegal
 .
 .
 .
```

Thus, C++ does not allow aggregate operations on an array. An **aggregate operation** on an array is any operation that manipulates the entire array as a single unit.

Arrays as Parameters to Functions

Now that you have seen how to work with arrays, a question naturally arises: How are arrays passed as parameters to functions?

By reference only: In C++, arrays are passed by reference only.

Because arrays are passed by reference only, you do not use the symbol `&` when declaring an array as a formal parameter.

9

When declaring a one-dimensional array as a formal parameter, the size of the array is usually omitted. If you specify the size of the one-dimensional array when it is declared as a formal parameter, it is ignored by the compiler.

The following function takes as an argument any **int** array:

```
void initialize(int list[])
{
   int count;
   for(count = 0; count < 5; count++)
         list[count] = 0;
}
```

Because the **for** loop inside the function executes 5 times, this function correctly initializes any **int** array of size 5 to 0. Thus, if the size of the array changes, another function needs to be written. However, if you add another formal parameter (say, **size**) in the function heading, use the value of **size** to control the **for** loop iterations (that is, use **size** instead of 5), and pass the name of the actual array together with its **size** during the call, then you can use the same function for an array of any size. Let us rewrite this function as follows:

```
void initialize(int list[], int size)
{
   int count;
   for(count = 0; count < size; count++)
       list[count] = 0;
}
```

The first parameter of the function **initialize** is an **int** array of any size. When the function **initialize** is called, the size of the actual array is passed as the second parameter of the function **initialize**.

Constant Arrays as Formal Parameters

Recall that when a formal parameter is a reference parameter, then whenever the formal parameter changes, the actual parameter changes as well. However, even though an array is always passed by reference, you can still prevent the function from changing the actual parameter. You do so by using the reserved word **const** in the declaration of the formal parameter. Consider the following function:

```
void example(int x[], const int y[], int sizeX, int sizeY)
{
    .
    .
    .
}
```

Here the function **example** can modify the array **x**, but not the array **y**. Any attempt to change **y** results in a compile-time error. It is a good programming practice to declare an array to be constant as a formal parameter if you do not want the function to modify the array.

Example 9-5

This example shows how to write functions for array processing and declare an array as a formal parameter.

```
        //Function to initialize an array to 0
void initializeArray(int x[], int sizeX)
{
       int counter;

       for(counter = 0; counter < sizeX; counter++)
           x[counter] = 0;
}
        //Function to read data and store it in an array
void fillArray(int x[], int sizeX)
{
       int counter;

       for(counter = 0; counter < sizeX; counter++)
           cin>>x[counter];
}
        //Function to print the array
void printArray(const int x[], int sizeX)
{
       int counter;
```

```
        for(counter = 0; counter < sizeX; counter++)
            cout<<x[counter]<<" ";
}

        //Function to find and return the sum of an array
int sumArray(const int x[], int sizeX)
{
        int counter;
        int sum = 0;

        for(counter = 0; counter < sizeX; counter++)
            sum = sum + x[counter];

        return sum;
}

        //Function to find and return the index of the
        //largest element of an array
int indexLargestElement(const int x[], int sizeX)
{
        int counter;

        int maxIndex = 0; //Assume first element is the largest

        for(counter = 1; counter < sizeX; counter++)
            if(x[maxIndex] < x[counter])
               maxIndex = counter;

        return maxIndex;
}

          //Function to copy one array into another array
void copyArray(const int x[], int y[], int length)
{
          int counter;

          for(counter = 0; counter < length; counter++)
              y[counter] = x[counter];
}
```

Note that for the function **copyArray** to work correctly, the array **y** must be at least as large as the array **x**.

Base Address of an Array

The **base address** of an array is the address (that is, memory location) of the first array component. For example, if `list` is a one-dimensional array, then the base address of `list` is the address of the component `list[0]`.

When you pass an array as a parameter, the base address of the actual array is passed to the formal parameter.

9

If you allow arrays to be passed by value, the computer has to allocate memory for the components of the formal parameter as well as copy the contents of the actual array into the corresponding formal parameter. If the array size is large, this process wastes not only memory, but also a lot of computer time in copying the data.

Functions Cannot Return a Value of the Type Array

C++ does not allow functions to return a value of the type `array`. The functions `sumArray` and `largestElement` described earlier return values of the type `int`.

Example 9-6

The following program illustrates how arrays are passed as actual parameters in a function call.

```
//Arrays as parameters to functions

#include <iostream>

using namespace std;

const int arraySize = 10;

void initializeArray(int x[], int sizeX);
void fillArray(int x[], int sizeX);
void printArray(const int x[], int sizeX);
int sumArray(const int x[], int sizeX);
int indexLargestElement(const int x[], int sizeX);
void copyArray(const int x[], int y[], int length);


int main()
{
  int listA[arraySize] = {0};                         //Line 1
  int listB[arraySize];                               //Line 2

  cout<<"Line 1: listA elements: ";                   //Line 3
  printArray(listA, arraySize);                       //Line 4
  cout<<endl;                                         //Line 5

  initializeArray(listB,arraySize);                   //Line 6

  cout<<"Line 7: ListB elements: ";                   //Line 7
  printArray(listB, arraySize);                       //Line 8
  cout<<endl<<endl;                                   //Line 9

  cout<<"Line 10: Enter "<<arraySize
      <<" integers: ";                                //Line 10
  fillArray(listA, arraySize);                        //Line 11
  cout<<endl;                                         //Line 12
```

```
  cout<<"Line 13: After filling listA the elements are:"
      <<endl;                                          //Line 13
  printArray(listA, arraySize);                        //Line 14
  cout<<endl<<endl;                                    //Line 15

  cout<<"Line 16: Sum of the elements of listA is: "
      <<sumArray(listA, arraySize)<<endl<<endl;        //Line 16
  cout<<"Line 17: Location of the largest element in listA is: "
      <<indexLargestElement(listA, arraySize) + 1
      <<endl;                                          //Line 17
  cout<<"Line 18: Largest element in listA is: "
      <<listA[indexLargestElement(listA, arraySize)]
      <<endl<<endl;                                    //Line 18

  copyArray(listA, listB, arraySize);                  //Line 19
  cout<<"Line 20: After copying the elements of "
      <<"listA into listB"<<endl
      <<"         listB elements are: ";               //Line 20
  printArray(listB, arraySize);                        //Line 21
  cout<<endl;                                          //Line 22

  return 0;
}

//Place the definition of the functions initializeArray, fillArray,
//and so on here. Example 9-5 gives the definitions of these
//functions.
```

Sample Run: In this sample run, the user input is shaded.

```
Line 1: listA elements: 0 0 0 0 0 0 0 0 0 0
Line 7: ListB elements: 0 0 0 0 0 0 0 0 0 0

Line 10: Enter 10 integers: 33 77 25 63 56 48 98 39 5 12

Line 13: After filling listA the elements are:
33 77 25 63 56 48 98 39 5 12

Line 16: Sum of the elements of listA is: 456

Line 17: Location of the largest element in listA is: 7
Line 18: Largest element in listA is: 98

Line 20: After copying the elements of listA into listB
         listB elements are: 33 77 25 63 56 48 98 39 5 12
```

The output of this program is straightforward. The statement in Line 1 declares an array `listA` of 10 components and initializes each component of `listA` to `0`. The statement in Line 2 declares an array `listB` of 10 components. The statement in Line 4 calls the function `printArray` and outputs the values stored in `listA`. The statement in Line 11 calls the function `fillArray` to input data into array `listA`. The statement in Line 16 calls the function `sumArray` and outputs the sum of all elements of `listA`. Similarly, the statement in Line 18 outputs the value of the largest element in `listA`.

The sections Enumeration Type and The `typedef` Statement in Chapter 8 are required for this section.

Integral Data Type and Array Indices

Other than integers, C++ allows any integral type to be used as an array index. This flexibility can greatly enhance the program's readability. Consider the following statements:

```
enum paintType{Green, Red, Blue, Brown, White, Orange, Yellow};
double paintSale[7];
paintType paint;
```

The following loop initializes the array `paintSale` to `0`:

```
for(paint = Green; paint <= Yellow;
                  paint = static_cast<paintType>(paint + 1))
   paintSale[paint] = 0.0;
```

The following statement updates the sale amount of `Red` paint:

```
paintSale[Red] = paintSale[Red] + 75.69;
```

As you can see, the above code is much easier to follow than the code that used integers for the index. For this reason, you should use the enumeration type for the array index or other integral data type wherever possible.

Other Ways to Declare Arrays

Suppose that a class has 20 students and you need to keep track of their scores. Because the number of students can change from semester to semester, instead of specifying the size of the array while declaring it, you can declare the array as follows:

```
const int noOfStudents = 20;
int testscore[noOfStudents];
```

Other forms used to declare arrays are

```
const int size = 50;                                     //Line 1
typedef double list[size];                               //Line 2

list a;                                                  //Line 3
list mylist;                                             //Line 4
```

The statement in Line 2 defines a data type `list`, which is an array of `50` components of the type `double`. The statements in Lines 3 and 4 declare two variables, `a` and `mylist`. Both are arrays of `50` components of the type `double`. Of course, these statements are equivalent to

```
double a[50];
double mylist[50];
```

C-STRINGS (CHARACTER ARRAYS)

Until now, we have avoided discussing character arrays for a simple reason: Character arrays are of special interest and you process them differently than you process other arrays. C++ provides many (predefined) functions that you can use with character arrays.

Character array: An array whose components are of the type `char`.

Recall that the most widely used character sets are ASCII and EBCDIC. The first character in the ASCII character set is the null character, which is nonprintable. Also recall that in C++, the null character is represented as `'\0'`, a backslash followed by a zero.

The statement

```
ch = '\0';
```

stores the null character in `ch`, where `ch` is a `char` variable.

As you will see, the null character plays an important role in processing character arrays. Because the collating sequence of the null character is `0`, the null character is less than any other character in the `char` data set.

The most commonly used term for character arrays is C-strings. However, there is a subtle difference between the two. Recall that a string is a sequence of zero or more characters and strings are enclosed in double quotation marks. In C++, C-strings are null terminated; that is, the last character in a C-string is always the null character. A character array might not contain the null character, but the last character in the C-string is always the null character. As you will see, the null character should not appear anywhere in the C-string except the last position. Also, C-strings are stored in (one-dimensional) character arrays.

Throughout this section, unless otherwise stated, by a "string" we mean a C-string. The following are examples of strings:

```
"John L. Johnson"
"Hello there."
```

From the definition of strings, it is clear that there is a difference between `'A'` and `"A"`. The first one is character `A`; the second is string `A`. Because strings are null terminated, `"A"` represents two characters: `'A'` and `'\0'`. Similarly, `"Hello"` represents six characters: `'H'`, `'e'`, `'l'`, `'l'`, `'o'`, and `'\0'`. To store `'A'` we need only one memory cell of the type `char`; to store `"A"`, we need two memory cells of the type `char`—one for `'A'` and one for `'\0'`. Similarly, to store the string `"Hello"` in computer memory, we need six memory cells of the type `char`.

Consider the following statement:

```
char name[16];
```

This statement declares an array `name` of `16` components of the type `char`. Because strings are null terminated and `name` has `16` components, the largest string that can be stored in `name` is of length `15`. If you store a string of length `10` in `name`, the first `11` components of `name` are used and the last `5` are left unused.

The statement

```
char name[16] = {'J', 'o', 'h', 'n', '\0'};
```

declares an array `name` containing `16` components of the type `char` and stores the string `"John"` in it. During `char` array variable declaration, C++ allows the string notation to be used in the initialization statement. The above statement is, therefore, equivalent to

```
char name[16] = "John";            //Line A
```

Recall that the size of an array can be omitted if the array is initialized during the declaration. The statement

```
char name[] = "John";              //Line B
```

declares a string variable `name` of a length large enough—in this case, `5`—and stores `"John"` in it. There is a difference between the last two statements: Both statements store `"John"` in `name`, but the size of `name` in first statement in Line A is `16`, and the size of `name` in the statement in Line B is `5`.

Most rules that apply to other arrays also apply to character arrays. Consider the following statement:

```
char studentName[26];
```

Suppose you want to store `"Lisa L. Johnson"` in `studentName`. Because aggregate operations, such as assignment and comparison, are not allowed on arrays, the following statement is not legal:

```
studentName = "Lisa L. Johnson"; //Illegal
```

C++ provides a set of functions that can be used for string manipulation. The header file `cstring` describes these functions. We often use three of these functions: `strcpy` (string copy, to copy a string into a string variable—that is, assignment); `strcmp` (string comparison, to compare strings); and `strlen` (string length, to find the length of a string). Table 9-1 summarizes these functions.

Table 9-1 `strcpy`, `strcmp`, and `strlen` **functions**

Function	Effect
`strcpy(s1,s2)`	Copies string `s2` into string variable `s1` The length of `s1` should be at least as large as `s2`
`strcmp(s1,s2)`	Returns a value < `0` if `s1` is less than `s2` Returns `0` if `s1` and `s2` are the same Returns a value > `0` if `s1` is greater than `s2`
`strlen(s)`	Returns the length of the string `s`, excluding the null character

To use these functions, the program must include the header file **`cstring`** via the **`include`** statement. That is, the following statement must be included in the program:

```
#include <cstring>
```

String Comparison

In C++, strings are compared character-by-character using the system's collating sequence. Let us assume that you use the ASCII character set.

1. The string **`"Air"`** is less than the string **`"Boat"`** because the first character of **`"Air"`** is less than the first character of **`"Boat"`**.
2. The string **`"Air"`** is less than the string **`"An"`** because the first character of both strings are the same, but the second character **`'i'`** of **`"Air"`** is less than the second character **`'n'`** of **`"An"`**.
3. The string **`"Bill"`** is less than the string **`"Billy"`** because the first four characters of **`"Bill"`** and **`"Billy"`** are the same, but the fifth character of **`"Bill"`**, which is **`'\0'`** (the null character), is less than the fifth character of **`"Billy"`**, which is **`'y'`**. (Recall that C-strings in C++ are null terminated.)
4. The string **`"Hello"`** is less than **`"hello"`** because the first character **`'H'`** of the string **`"Hello"`** is less than the first character **`'h'`** of the string **`"hello"`**.

As you can see, the function **`strcmp`** compares its first string argument with its second string argument character-by-character.

Example 9-7

Suppose you have the following statements:

```
char studentName[21];
char myname[16];
char yourname[16];
```

The following statements show how string functions work:

Statement	Effect
`strcpy(myname,"John Robinson");`	`myname = John Robinson`
`strlen("John Robinson");`	Returns `13`, the length of the string `"John Robinson"`
`int len;` `len = strlen("Sunny Day");`	Stores `9` into `len`
`strcpy(yourname, "Lisa Miller");` `strcpy(studentName, yourname);`	`yourname = Lisa Miller` `studentName = Lisa Miller`
`strcmp("Bill", "Lisa");`	Returns a value < `0`

`strcpy(yourname, "Kathy Brown");`
`strcpy(myname, "Mark G. Clark");`
`strcmp(myname, yourname);`
	`yourname = Kathy Brown`
	`myname = Mark G. Clark`
	Returns a value > `0`

In this chapter, we define a `C`-string to be a sequence of zero or more characters. `C`-strings are enclosed in double quotation marks. We also said that `C`-strings are null terminated, so the `C`-string `"Hello"` has six characters even though only five are enclosed in double quotation marks. Therefore, to store the `C`-string `"Hello"` in computer memory, you must use a character array of size `6`. The length of a `C`-string is the number of actual characters enclosed in double quotation marks, for example the length of the string `"Hello"` is `5`. Thus, in a logical sense a `C`-string is a sequence of zero or more characters, but in the physical sense (that is, to store the `C`-string in computer memory), a `C`-string has at least one character. Because the length of the string is the actual number of characters enclosed in double quotation marks, we define a `C`-string to be a sequence of zero or more characters. However, you must remember that the null character stored in computer memory at the end of the `C`-string plays a key role when we compare `C`-strings, especially `C`-strings such as `"Bill"` and `"Billy"`.

Reading and Writing Strings

As mentioned earlier, most rules that apply to arrays apply to strings as well. Aggregate operations such as assignment and comparison are not allowed on arrays. Even the input/output of arrays is done component-wise. However, the one place where C++ allows aggregate operations on arrays is the input and output of strings (that is, character arrays).

We will use the following declaration for our discussion:

```
char name[31];
```

String Input

Because aggregate operations are allowed for string input, the statement

```
cin>>name;
```

stores the next input string into **name**. The length of the input string must be less than or equal to 30. If the length of the input string is 4, the computer stores the four characters that we input and the null character '\0'. If the length of the input string is more than 30, then because there is no check on the array index bounds, the computer continues storing the string in whatever memory cells follow **name**. This process can cause serious problems because data in the adjacent memory cells will be corrupted.

Recall that the extraction operator, >>, skips all leading whitespace characters and stops reading data into the current variable as soon as it finds the first whitespace character or invalid data. As a result, strings that contain blanks cannot be read using the extraction operator, >>. For example, if a first name and last name are separated by blanks, they cannot be read into **name**.

How do you input strings with blanks in a character array? Once again, the function **get** comes to our rescue. Recall that the function **get** is used to read character data. In the past, the form of the function **get** that you used (Chapter 3) read only a single character. However, the function **get** can also be used to read strings. To read strings, you use the form of the function **get** that has two parameters. The first parameter is a string variable; the second parameter specifies how many characters to read in the string variable.

To read strings, the general form (syntax) of the **get** function, together with an input stream variable such as **cin**, is

```
cin.get(str,m+1);
```

This statement stores the next **m** characters, or all characters until the newline character '\n' is found, in **str**. The newline character is not stored in **str**. If the input string has fewer than **m** characters, then the reading stops at the newline character.

Consider the following statements:

```
char str[31];
cin.get(str,31);
```

If the input is

```
William T. Johnson
```

then **"William T. Johnson"** is stored in **str**. If the input is

```
Hello there. My name is Mickey Mouse.
```

then the string "Hello there. My name is Mickey" is stored in **str**.

Now suppose that we have the statements

```
char str1[26];
char str2[26];
char discard;
```

and two lines of input

```
Summer is warm.
Winter will be cold.
```

Further suppose that we want to store the first string in `str1` and the second string in `str2`. Both `str1` and `str2` can store strings that are up to `25` in length. Because the number of characters in the first line is `15`, the reading stops at `'\n'`. You must read and discard the newline character at the end of the first line to store the second line in `str2`. The following sequence of statements stores the first line in `str1` and the second line in `str2`:

```
cin.get(str1,26);
cin.get(discard);
cin.get(str2,26);
```

String Output

The output of strings is another place where aggregate operations on arrays are allowed. You can output strings by using an output stream variable, such as `cout`, together with the insertion operator, <<. For example, the statement

```
cout<<name;
```

outputs the contents of `name` on the screen. The insertion operator, <<, continues to write the contents of `name` until it finds the null character. Thus, if the length of `name` is `4`, the above statement outputs only four characters. If `name` does not contain the null character, then you will see strange output because the insertion operator continues to output data from memory adjacent to `name` until `'\0'` is found.

Specifying Input/Output Files at Execution Time

In Chapter 3, you learned how to read data from a file. In subsequent chapters, the name of the input file was included in the `open` statement. By doing so, the program always received data from the same input file. In real-world applications, the data may actually be collected at several locations and stored in separate files. Also, for comparison purposes, someone might want to process each file separately and then store the output in separate files. To accomplish this task efficiently, the user would prefer to specify the name of the input and/or output file at execution time rather than in the programming code. C++ allows the user to specify the names of the input/output files at execution time.

Consider the following statements:

```
ifstream infile;
ofstream outfile;

char fileName[51];        //assume file name is at most
                          //50 characters long
```

The following statements prompt and allow the user to specify the input and output files at execution time:

```
cout<<"Enter the input file name: ";
cin>>fileName;

infile.open(fileName);    //open the input file
.
.
.
cout<<"Enter the output file name: ";
cin>>fileName;

outfile.open(fileName);  //open the output file
```

9

The `string` Type and Input/Output Files

In Chapter 8, we discussed the data type `string`. We now want to point out that values (that is, strings) of the type `string` are not null terminated. Variables of the type `string` can also be used to read and store the names of input/output files. However, the argument to the function `open` must be a null-terminated string—that is, a C-string. Therefore, if we use a variable of the type `string` to read the name of an input/output file and then use this variable to open a file, the value of the variable must (first) be converted to a C-string (that is, a null-terminated string). The header file `string` contains the function `c_str`, which converts a value of the type `string` to a null-terminated character array (that is, C-string). The syntax to use the function `c_str` is

```
strVar.c_str()
```

where `strVar` is a variable of the type `string`.

The following statements illustrate how to use variables of the type `string` to read the names of input/output files during program execution and open those files:

```
ifstream infile;
string   fileName;

cout<<"Enter the input file name: ";
cin>>fileName;

infile.open(fileName.c_str());    //open the input file
```

Of course, you must also include the header file `string` in the program. The output file has similar conventions.

Parallel Arrays

Two (or more) arrays are called **parallel** if their corresponding components hold related information.

Suppose you need to keep track of students' course grades, together with their ID numbers, so that grades can be posted at the end of the semester. Further suppose that there are `50` students in a class and their IDs are `5` digits long. Because there are `50` students, you need `50` variables to store the students' IDs and `50` variables to store their grades. You can declare two arrays: `studentId` of the type `int` and `courseGrade` of the type `char`. Each array has `50` components. Furthermore, `studentId[0]` and `courseGrade[0]` will store the ID and course grade of the first student, `studentId[1]` and `courseGrade[1]` will store the ID and course grade of the second student, and so on.

The statements

```
int studentId[50];
char courseGrade[50];
```

declare these two arrays.

Programming Example: Code Detection

When a message is transmitted in secret code over a transmission channel, it is usually transmitted as a sequence of bits, that is, `0`s and `1`s. Due to noise in the transmission channel, the transmitted message may become corrupted. That is, the message received at the destination is not the same as the message transmitted; some of the bits may have been changed. There are several techniques to check the validity of the transmitted message at the destination. One technique is to transmit the same message twice. At the destination, both copies of the message are compared bit by bit. If the corresponding bits are the same, the message received is error-free.

Let's write a program to check whether the message received at the destination is error-free. For simplicity, assume that the secret code representing the message is a sequence of digits (`0` to `9`) and the maximum length of the message is `250` digits. Also, the first number in the message is the length of the message. For example, if the secret code is

```
7 9 2 7 8 3 5 6
```

then the message is `7` digits long, and it is transmitted twice.

The previous message is transmitted as

```
7 9 2 7 8 3 5 6 7 9 2 7 8 3 5 6
```

Input A file containing the secret code and its copy.

Output The secret code, its copy, and a message—if the received code is error-free—in the following form:

```
Code Digit   Code Digit Copy
      9              9
      2              2
      7              7
      8              8
      3              3
      5              5
      6              6
Message transmitted OK.
```

Problem Analysis and Algorithm Design

Because we have to compare the corresponding digits of the secret code and its copy, you first read the secret code and store it in an array. Then you read the first digit of the copy and compare it with the first digit of the secret code, and so on. If any corresponding digits are not the same, you indicate this fact by printing a message next to the digits. Because the maximum length of the message is `250`, you use an array of `250` components. The first number in the secret code, and in the copy of the secret code, indicates the length of the code. This discussion translates into the following algorithm:

1. Open the input and output files.
2. If the input file does not exist, exit the program.
3. Read the length of the secret code.
4. If the length of the secret code is greater than `250`, terminate the program because the maximum length of the code in this program is `250`.
5. Read and store the secret code into an array.
6. Read the length of the copy.
7. If the length of the secret code and its copy are the same, compare the codes; otherwise, print an error message.

To simplify the function `main`, let us write a function, `readCode`, to read the secret code and another function, `compareCode`, to compare the codes. Next, we describe these two functions.

`readCode` This function first reads the length of the secret code. If the length of the secret code is greater than `250`, a Boolean variable `lengthCodeOk`, which is a reference parameter, is set to `false` and the function terminates. The value of `lengthCodeOk` is passed to the calling function to indicate whether the secret code was read successfully. If the length of the code is less than `250`, the `readCode` function reads and stores the secret code into an array. Because the input is stored into a file and the file was opened in the function `main`, the input stream variable corresponding to the input file must be passed as a parameter to this function. Furthermore, after reading the length of the secret code and the code itself, the `readCode` function must pass these values to the function `main`. Therefore, this function has four parameters: an input file stream variable, an array to store the secret code, the length of the code, and the `bool` parameter `lengthCodeOk`. The definition of the function `readCode` is as follows:

```
void readCode(ifstream& infile, int list[], int& length,
              bool& lenCodeOk)
{
    int count;

    lenCodeOk = true;

    infile>>length;   //get the length of the secret code
    if(length > maxCodeSize)
    {
       lenCodeOk = false;
       return;
    }

    for(count = 0; count < length; count++) //get the secret code
       infile>>list[count];
}
```

`compareCode` This function compares the secret code with its copy. Therefore, it must have access to the array containing the secret code and the length of the secret code. The copy of the secret code and its length are stored in the input file. Thus, the input stream variable corresponding to the input file must be passed as a parameter to this function. Also, the `compareCode` function compares the secret code with the copy and prints an appropriate message. Because the output will be stored in a file, the output stream variable corresponding to the output file must also be passed as a parameter to this function. Therefore, the function has four parameters: an input file stream variable, an output file stream variable, the array containing the secret code, and the length of the secret code. This discussion translates into the following algorithm for the function `compareCode`.

a. Declare the variables.
b. Set a `bool` variable `codeOk` to `true`.
c. Read the length of the copy of the secret code.
d. If the length of the secret code and its copy are not the same, output an appropriate error message and terminate the function.

e. For each digit in the input file
   e.1. Read the next digit of the copy of the secret code.
   e.2. Output the corresponding digits from the secret code and its copy.
   e.3. If the corresponding digits are not the same, output an error message and set the **bool** variable **codeOk** to **false**.

f. If the **bool** variable **codeOk** is **true**
   Output a message indicating that the secret code was transmitted correctly.
   else
   Output an error message.

Following this algorithm, the definition of the function **compareCode** is

```
void compareCode(ifstream& infile, ofstream& outfile,
                 int list[], int length)
{
        //Step a
  int length2;
  int digit;
  bool codeOk;

  int count;

  codeOk = true;                                          //Step b

  infile>>length2;                                        //Step c

  if(length != length2) //compare the lengths of the codes; Step d
  {
      cout<<"The original code and its copy are not of"
          <<" the same length."<<endl;
      return;
  }
  outfile<<"Code Digit    Code Digit Copy"<<endl;

  for(count = 0; count < length; count++)                 //Step e
  {
      infile>>digit;                                      //Step e.1
      outfile<<setw(7)<<list[count]<<setw(20)<<digit;  //Step e.2
      if(digit != list[count])                            //Step e.3
      {
          outfile<<"         code digit not the same"<<endl;
          codeOk = false;                                 //Step e.3
      }
      else
```

```
            outfile<<endl;
    }

    if(codeOk)                                          //Step f
        outfile<<"Message transmitted OK."<<endl;
    else
        outfile<<"Error in transmission. Retransmit!!"<<endl;
}
```

Following is the algorithm for the function **main**.

Main Algorithm

1. Declare the variables.
2. Open the files.
3. Call the function **readCode** to read the secret code.
4. If (length of the secret code <= 250)
   Call the function **compareCode** to compare the codes.
   else
   Output an appropriate error message.

Complete Program Listing

```
//Program: Check Code
#include <iostream>
#include <fstream>
#include <iomanip>
using namespace std;

const int maxCodeSize = 250;

void readCode(ifstream& infile, int list[],
              int& length, bool& lenCodeOk);
void compareCode(ifstream& infile, ofstream& outfile,
                 int list[], int length);
int main()
{
            //Step 1
   int codeArray[maxCodeSize];    //array to store the secret code
   int codeLength;              //variable to store the length
                                //of the secret code
   bool lengthCodeOk;         //variable to indicate if the length of the
                              //secret code is less than or equal to 250
   ifstream incode;           //input file stream variable
   ofstream outcode;          //output file stream variable
   char inputfile[25];        //variable to store the name of the
                              //input file
```

```
    char outputfile[25]; //variable to store the name of the
                         //output file

    cout<<"Enter the input file name: ";
    cin>>inputfile;
    cout<<endl;
                         //Step 2
    incode.open(inputfile);
    if(!incode)
    {
       cout<<"Cannot open the input file."<<endl;
       return 1;
    }

    cout<<"Enter the output file name: ";
    cin>>outputfile;
    cout<<endl;

    outcode.open(outputfile);

    readCode(incode, codeArray, codeLength, lengthCodeOk); //Step 3

    if(lengthCodeOk)                                     //Step 4
       compareCode(incode, outcode, codeArray, codeLength);
    else
       cout<<"Length of the secret code must be <= "
           <<maxCodeSize<<<<endl;                        //Step 5

    incode.close();
    outcode.close();

    return 0;
}

void readCode(ifstream& infile, int list[], int& length,
              bool& lenCodeOk)
{
    int count;

    lenCodeOk = true;

    infile>>length;  //get the length of the secret code
    if(length > maxCodeSize)
    {
       lenCodeOk = false;
       return;
    }
```

```
   for(count = 0; count < length; count++) //get the secret code
      infile>>list[count];
}

void compareCode(ifstream& infile, ofstream& outfile,
                 int list[], int length)
{
   int length2;
   int digit;
   bool codeOk;
   int count;

   codeOk = true;

   infile>>length2;

   if(length != length2)
   {
      cout<<"The original code and its copy are not of"
          <<" the same length."<<endl;
      return;
   }

   outfile<<"Code Digit    Code Digit Copy"<<endl;
   for(count = 0; count < length; count++)
   {
      infile>>digit;
      outfile<<setw(7)<<list[count]<<setw(20)<<digit;
      if(digit != list[count])
      {
            outfile<<"          code digit not the same"<<endl;
            codeOk = false;
      }
      else
            outfile<<endl;
   }

   if(codeOk)
      outfile<<"Message transmitted OK."<<endl;
   else
      outfile<<"Error in transmission. Retransmit!!"<<endl;
}
```

Sample Run: In this sample run, the user input is shaded.

```
Enter the input file name: a:Ch9_SecretCodeData.txt

Enter the output file name: a:Ch9_SecretCodeOut.txt
```

Input File Data: (a:Ch9_SecretCodeData.txt)

```
7 9 2 7 8 3 5 6 7 9 2 7 8 3 5 6
```

Output File Data: (a:Ch9_SecretCodeOut.txt)

```
Code Digit    Code Digit Copy
     9                9
     2                2
     7                7
     8                8
     3                3
     5                5
     6                6
Message transmitted OK.
```

PROGRAMMING EXAMPLE: TEXT PROCESSING

(Line and letter count) Let us now write a program that reads a given text, outputs the text as is, and also prints the number of lines and the number of times each letter appears in the text. An uppercase letter and a lowercase letter are treated as being the same; that is, they are tallied together.

Because there are 26 letters, we use an array of `26` components to perform the letter count. We also need a variable to store the line count.

The text is stored in a file, which we will call `textin.txt` (and is on a floppy drive, which we will assume is `a`). The output will be stored in a file, which we will call `textout.out`.

Input A file containing the text to be processed.

Output A file containing the text, number of lines, and the number of times a letter appears in the text.

Problem Analysis and Algorithm Design

Based on the desired output, it is clear that we must output the text as is. That is, if the text contains any whitespace characters, they must be output as well. Furthermore, we must count the number of lines in the text. Therefore, we must know where the line ends, which means that we must trap the newline character. This requirement suggests that we cannot use the extraction operator to process the input file. Because we also need to perform the letter count, we use the `get` function to read the text.

Let us first describe the variables that are necessary to develop the program. This will simplify the discussion that follows.

Variables (Function `main`) We need to store the letter count and the line count. Therefore, we need a variable to store the line count and 26 variables to perform the letter count. We will use an array of `26` components to perform the letter count. We also need a variable to read and store each character in turn, because the input file is to be read character by character. Because data is to be read from an input file and output is to be saved in a file, we need an input stream variable to open the input file and an output stream variable to open the output file. These statements indicate that the function **`main`** needs (at least) the following variables:

```
int         lineCount;         //variable to store the line count
int         letterCount[26];   //array to store the letter count
char        ch;                //variable to read a character
ifstream    infile;            //input file stream variable
ofstream    outfile;           //output file stream variable
```

In this declaration, `letterCount[0]` stores the `A` count, `letterCount[1]` stores the `B` count, and so on. Clearly, the variable `lineCount` and the array `letterCount` must be initialized to `0`.

The algorithm for this program is

1. Declare the variables.
2. Open the input and output files.
3. Initialize the variables.
4. While there is more data in the input file
   - 4.1 For each character in a line
     - 4.1.1 Read and write the character.
     - 4.1.2 Increment the appropriate letter count.
   - 4.2 Increment the line count.
5. Output the line count and letter counts.
6. Close the files.

To simplify the function `main`, we divide it into four functions:

- Function `initialize`
- Function `copyText`
- Function `characterCount`
- Function `writeTotal`

The following sections describe each of these functions in detail. Then, with the help of these functions, we describe the algorithm for the function `main`.

initialize This function initializes the variable `lineCount` and the array `letterCount` to `0`. It therefore has two parameters: one corresponding to the variable `lineCount` and one corresponding to the array `letterCount`. Clearly, the parameter corresponding to `lineCount` must be a reference parameter. The definition of this function is

```
void initialize(int& lc, int list[])
{
      int j;
      lc = 0;

      for(j = 0; j < 26; j++)
          list[j] = 0;
}
```

copyText This function reads a line and outputs the line. Whenever a nonblank character is found, it calls the function `characterCount` to update the letter count. Clearly, this function has four parameters: an input file stream variable, an output file stream variable, a `char` variable, and the array to update the letter count.

Note that the `copyText` function does not perform the letter count, but we still pass the array `letterCount` to it. We take this step because this function calls the function `characterCount`, which needs the array `letterCount` to update the appropriate letter count. Therefore, we must pass the array `letterCount` to the `copyText` function so that it can pass the array to the function `characterCount`.

```
void copyText(ifstream& intext, ofstream& outtext, char& ch,
              int list[])
{
      while(ch != '\n')               //Process the entire line
      {
        outtext<<ch;                  //Output the character
        characterCount(ch,list);      //Call function character count
        intext.get(ch);               //Read the next character
      }
      outtext<<ch;                    //Output the newline character
}
```

characterCount This function increments the letter count. To increment the appropriate letter count, it must know what the letter is. Therefore, the `characterCount` function has two parameters: a `char` variable and the array to update the letter count. In pseudocode, this function is

a. Convert the letter to uppercase.

b. Find the index of the array corresponding to this letter.

c. If the index is valid, increment the appropriate count. At this step, we must ensure that the character is a letter. We are counting only letters, so other characters—such as commas, hyphens, and periods—are ignored.

Following this algorithm, the definition of this function is

```
void characterCount(char ch, int list[])
{
       int index;

       ch = toupper(ch);                             //Step a
       index = static_cast<int>(ch) - 65;            //Step b
       if(0 <= index && index < 26)                  //Step c
          list[index]++;
}
```

`writeTotal` This function outputs the line count and the letter count. It has three parameters: the output file stream variable, the line count, and the array to output the letter count. The definition of this function is

```
void writeTotal(ofstream& outtext, int lc, int list[])
{
      int index;

      outtext<<"The number of lines = "<<lc<<endl;
      for(index = 0; index < 26; index++)
          outtext<<static_cast<char>(index+65)<<" count = "
                 <<list[index]<<endl;
}
```

We now describe the algorithm for the function `main`.

Main Algorithm

1. Declare the variables.
2. Open the input and output files.
3. If the input file does not exist, exit the program.
4. Open the output file.
5. Initialize the variables, such as `lineCount` and the array `letterCount`.
6. Read the first character.
7. while (not end of input file)
   7.1 Process the next line; call the function `copyText`.
   7.2 Increment the line count. (Increment the variable `lineCount`.)
   7.3 Read the next character.
8. Output the line count and letter counts. Call the function `writeTotal`.
9. Close the files.

Complete Program Listing

```
//Program: Line and letter count
#include <iostream>
#include <fstream>
#include <cctype>

using namespace std;

void initialize(int& lc, int list[]);
void copyText(ifstream& intext, ofstream& outtext, char& ch,
              int list[]);
void characterCount(char ch, int list[]);
void writeTotal(ofstream& outtext, int lc, int list[]);

int main()
{
                //Step 1; Declare variables
      int         lineCount;
      int         letterCount[26];
      char        ch;
      ifstream    infile;
      ofstream    outfile;

      infile.open("a:textin.txt");                         //Step 2


      if(!infile)                                          //Step 3
      {
         cout<<"Cannot open input file."<<endl;
         return 1;
      }

      outfile.open("a:textout.out");                       //Step 4

      initialize(lineCount, letterCount);                  //Step 5

      infile.get(ch);                                      //Step 6
      while(infile)                                        //Step 7
      {
          copyText(infile,outfile,ch,letterCount);         //step 7.1
          lineCount++;                                     //Step 7.2
          infile.get(ch);                                  //Step 7.3
      }

      writeTotal(outfile,lineCount,letterCount);           //Step 8
      infile.close();                                      //Step 9
      outfile.close();                                     //Step 9
```

```
      return 0;
}

void initialize(int& lc, int list[])
{
      int j;
      lc = 0;

      for(j = 0; j < 26; j++)
          list[j] = 0;
}

void copyText(ifstream& intext, ofstream& outtext, char& ch,
              int list[])
{
    while(ch != '\n')            //Process the entire line
    {
      outtext<<ch;               //Output the character
      characterCount(ch,list);   //Call function character count
      intext.get(ch);            //Read the next character
    }
    outtext<<ch;                 //Output the newline character
}

void characterCount(char ch, int list[])
{
      int index;

      ch = toupper(ch);                                   //Step a
      index = static_cast<int> (ch) - 65;                 //Step b
      if(0 <= index && index < 26)                        //Step c
         list[index]++;
}

void writeTotal(ofstream& outtext, int lc, int list[])
{
      int index;

      outtext<<endl<<endl;
      outtext<<"The number of lines = "<<lc<<endl;
      for(index = 0; index < 26; index++)
          outtext<<static_cast<char>(index+65)<<" count = "
                 <<list[index]<<endl;
}
```

QUICK REVIEW

1. A data type is simple if variables of that type can hold only one value at a time.
2. In a structured data type, each data item is a collection of other data items.
3. An array is a structured data type with a fixed number of components. Every component is of the same type, and components are accessed using their relative positions in the array.
4. Elements of a one-dimensional array are arranged in the form of a list.
5. There is no check on array index out of bounds.
6. In C++, an array index starts with `0`.
7. An array index can be any expression that evaluates to a non-negative integer. The value of the index must always be less than the size of the array.
8. There are no aggregate operations on arrays, except for the input/output of character arrays (`C`-strings).
9. Arrays can be initialized during their declaration. If there are fewer initial values than the array size, the excess elements are initialized to `0`.
10. The base address of an array is the address of the first array component. For example, if `list` is a one-dimensional array, the base address of `list` is the address of `list[0]`.
11. When declaring a one-dimensional array as a formal parameter, you usually omit the array size. If you specify the size of a one-dimensional array, in the formal parameter declaration, the compiler will ignore it.
12. In a function call statement, when passing an array as an actual parameter, you use only its name.
13. As parameters to functions, arrays are passed by reference only.
14. Because as parameters arrays are passed by reference only, when declaring an array as a formal parameter you do not use the symbol `&` after the data type.
15. A function cannot return a value of the type `array`.
16. Although as parameters arrays are passed by reference, when declaring an array as a formal parameter, using the reserved word `const` before the data type prevents the function from modifying the array.
17. Individual array components can be passed as parameters to functions.
18. In C++, a string is any sequence of characters enclosed between double quotation marks.
19. In C++, `C`-strings are null terminated.
20. In C++, the null character is represented as `'\0'`.
21. In the ASCII character set, the collating sequence of the null character is `0`.
22. `C`-strings are stored in character arrays.
23. Character arrays can be initialized during declaration using string notation.

24. Input and output of C-strings is the only place where C++ allows aggregate operations.
25. The header file `cstring` contains the specifications of functions that can be used for C-string manipulation.
26. Commonly used C-string manipulation functions include: `strcpy` (string copy), `strcmp` (string comparision), and `strlen` (string length).
27. C-strings are compared character by character.
28. Because strings are stored in arrays, individual characters in the string can be accessed using array component access notation.
29. Parallel arrays are used to hold related information.

EXERCISES

1. Mark the following statements as true or false.
   a. A `double` type is an example of a simple data type.
   b. A one-dimensional array is an example of a structured data type.
   c. Arrays can be passed as parameters to a function either by value or by reference.
   d. A function can return a value of the type `array`.
   e. The size of an array is determined at compile time.
   f. The only allowable aggregate operations on `int` arrays are the increment and decrement operations.
   g. Given the declaration

      ```
      int list[10];
      ```

      the statement

      ```
      list[5] = list[3]+list[2];
      ```

      updates the content of the fifth component of the array `list`.
   h. If an array index goes out of bounds, the program terminates in an error.
   i. In C++, some aggregate operations are allowed for strings.
   j. The declaration

      ```
      char name[16] = "John K. Miller";
      ```

      declares `name` to be an array of 15 characters because the string `"John K. Miller"` has only 14 characters.
   k. The declaration

      ```
      char str = "Sunny Day";
      ```

      declares `str` to be a string of an unspecified length.

2. Given the declaration

```
char string15[16];
```

mark the following statements as valid or invalid. If a statement is invalid, explain why.

a. `strcpy(string15, "Hello there");`

b. `strlen(string15);`

c. `string15 = "Jacksonville";`

d. `cin>>string15;`

e. `cout<<string15;`

f.

```
if(string15 >= "Nice day")
     cout<<string15;
```

g. `string15[6] = 't';`

3. Given the declaration

```
char str1[15];
char str2[15] = "Good day";
```

mark the following statements as valid or invalid. If a statement is invalid, explain why.

a. `str1 = str2;`

b.

```
if(str1 == str2)
   cout<<" Both strings are of the same length."<<endl;
```

c.

```
if(strlen(str1) >= strlen(str2))
     str1 = str2;
```

d.

```
if(strcmp(str1,str2) < 0)
     cout<<"str1 is less than str2."<<endl;
```

4. Given the declaration

```
char name[8] = "Shelly";
```

mark the following statements as "Yes" if they output `Shelly`; otherwise, mark the statement as "No" and explain why it does not output `Shelly`.

a. `cout<<name;`

b.

```
for(int j = 0; j < 6; j++)
      cout<<name[j];
```

c.

```
int j = 0;
while(name[j] != '\0')
     cout<<name[j++];
```

d.

```
int j = 0;
while(j < 8)
     cout<<name[j++];
```

5. Given the declaration

```
char str1[21];
char str2[21];
```

   a. Write a C++ statement that stores `"Sunny Day"` in `str1`.
   b. Write a C++ statement that stores the length of `str1` into an `int` variable `length`.
   c. Write a C++ statement that copies the value of `name` into `str2`.
   d. Write C++ code that outputs `str1` if `str1` is less than or equal to `str2`, and otherwise outputs `str2`.

6. Write C++ statements to do the following.
   a. Declare an array `alpha` of `15` components of the type `int`.
   b. Output the value of the tenth component of the array `alpha`.
   c. Set the value of the fifth component of the array `alpha` to `35`.
   d. Set the value of the ninth component of the array `alpha` to the sum of the sixth and thirteenth components of the array `alpha`.
   e. Set the value of the fourth component of the array `alpha` to three times the value of the eighth component minus `57`.
   f. Output `alpha` so that five components per line are printed.

7. Consider the function headings

```
void funcOne(int alpha[], int size);
int funcSum(int x, int y);
void funcTwo(const int alpha[], int beta[]);
```

   and the declarations

```
    int list[50];
    int Alist[60];
    int num;
```

   write C++ statements that do the following:
   a. Call the function `funcOne` with the actual parameters, `list` and `50`, respectively.
   b. Print the value returned by the function `funcSum` with the actual parameters, `50` and the fourth component of `list`, respectively.
   c. Print the value returned by the function `funcSum` with the actual parameters, the thirtieth and tenth components of `list`, respectively.
   d. Call the function `funcTwo` with the actual parameters, `list` and `Alist`, respectively.

8. Suppose `list` is an array of five components of the type `int`. What is stored in `list` after the following C++ code executes?

```
for(I = 0; I < 5; I++)
{
    list[I] = 2 * I + 5;
    if(I % 2 == 0)
        list[I] = list[I] - 3;
}
```

9. Suppose `list` is an array of six components of the type `int`. What is stored in `list` after the following C++ code executes?

```
list[0] = 5;
for(I = 1; I < 6; I++)
{
    list[I] = I * I + 5;
    if(I > 2)
        list[I] = 2 * list[I] - list[I-1];
}
```

10. Assume the following declarations:

```
char name[21];
char yourName[21];
char studentName[31];
```

Mark the following statements as valid or invalid. If a statement is invalid, explain why.

a. `cin>>name;`

b `cout<<studentName;`

c. `yourName[0] = '\0';`

d. `yourName = studentName;`

e.
```
if(yourName == name)
        studentName = name;
```

f. `int x = strcmp(yourName,studentName);`

g. `strcpy(studentName,Name);`

h.
```
for(int j = 0; j < 21; j++)
        cout<<name[j];
```

9

11. What is the output of the following program?

```
#include <iostream>
using namespace std;
int main()
{
   int count;
   int alpha[5];

   alpha[0] = 5;
   for(count = 1; count < 5; count++)
   {
         alpha[count] = 5 * count + 10;
         alpha[count - 1] = alpha[count] - 4;
   }
   cout<<"List elements: ";
   for(count = 0; count < 5; count++)
         cout<<alpha[count]<<" ";
   cout<<endl;
   return 0;
}
```

12. What is the output of the following program?

```
#include <iostream>
using namespace std;

int main()
{
   int j;
   int one[5];
   int two[10];

   for(j = 0; j < 5; j++)
      one[j] = 5 * j + 3;
   cout<<"One contains: ";
   for(j = 0; j < 5; j++)
      cout<<one[j]<<" ";
   cout<<endl;
   for(j = 0; j < 5; j++)
   {
      two[j] = 2 * one[j] - 1;
      two[j + 5] = one[4 - j] + two [j];
   }
   cout<<"Two contains: ";
   for(j = 0; j < 10; j++)
      cout<<two[j]<<" ";
   cout<<endl;
   return 0;
}
```

PROGRAMMING EXERCISES

1. Write a C++ program that declares an array `alpha` of `50` components of the type `double`. Initialize the array so that the first 25 components are equal to the square of the index variable and the last 25 components are equal to three times the index variable. Output the array so that 10 elements per line are printed.
2. Write a C++ function, `smallestIndex`, that takes as parameters an `int` array and its size, and returns the index of the smallest element in the array. Also, write a program to test your function.
3. Write a program that reads a file consisting of students' test scores in the range `0–200`. It should then determine the number of students having scores in each of the following ranges: `0–24`, `25–49`, `50–74`, `75–99`, `100–124`, `125–149`, `150–174`, and `175–200`. Output the score ranges and the number of students. (Run your program with the following input data: `76`, `89`, `150`, `135`, `200`, `76`, `12`, `100`, `150`, `28`, `178`, `189`, `167`, `200`, `175`, `150`, `87`, `99`, `129`, `149`, `176`, `200`, `87`, `35`, `157`, `189`.)
4. In a gymnastics or diving competition, each contestant's score is calculated by dropping the lowest and highest scores received and then adding the remaining scores. Write a program that allows the user to enter eight judges' scores and outputs the points received by the contestant. Format your output with two decimal places. (A judge awards points between `1` and `10`, with `1` being the lowest and `10` being the highest.) For example, if the scores are `9.2`, `9.3`, `9.0`, `9.9`, `9.5`, `9.5`, `9.6`, and `9.8`, the contestant receives a total of `56.90` points.
5. Write a program that prompts the user to input a string and outputs the string in uppercase letters. (Use a character array to store the string.)
6. The history teacher at your school needs help in grading a True/False test. The students' IDs and test answers are stored in a file. The first entry in the file contains answers to the test in the form

   ```
   TFFTFFTTTTFFTFTFTFTT
   ```

   Every other entry in the file is the student ID, followed by a blank, followed by the student's response. For example, the entry

   ```
   ABC54301 TFTFTFTT TFTFTFFTTFT
   ```

   indicates that the student ID is ABC54301 and the answer to question 1 is True, the answer to question 2 is False, and so on. This student did not answer question 9. The exam has 20 questions, and the class has more than 150 students. Each correct answer is awarded two points, each wrong answer gets –1 point, and no answer gets 0 points. Write a program that processes the test data. The output should be: the student's ID, followed by the answers, followed by the test score, followed by the test grade. Assume the following grade scale: `90%–100%`, `A`; `80%–89.99%`, `B`; `70%–79.99%`, `C`; `60%–69.99%`, `D`; and `0%–59.99%`, `F`.

7. Write a program that allows the user to enter the last names of five candidates in a local election and the votes received by each candidate. The program should then output each candidate's name, votes received by that candidate, and the percentage of the total votes received by the candidate. Your program should also output the winner of the election. A sample output is

```
Candidate  Votes Received  % of Total Votes
Johnson          5000           25.91
Miller           4000           20.72
Duffy            6000           31.09
Robinson         2500           12.95
Ashtony          1800            9.33
Total           19300
The Winner of the Election is Duffy.
```

8. Write a program that allows the user to enter the students' names followed by their test score and outputs the: (assume that maximum number of students in the class is 50)
   (i) Class average
   (ii) Names of all students whose test scores are below the class average with an appropriate message
   (iii) Highest test score and the names of all students having the highest score

CHAPTER

10

ARRAYS II

Applications and Extensions

In this chapter, you will:

- Learn how to implement the sequential search algorithm
- Explore how to sort an array using the selection sort algorithm
- Learn how to implement the binary search algorithm
- Discover how to manipulate data in a two-dimensional array
- Learn about multidimensional arrays

Chapter 9 introduced arrays, a structured data type. When the data values are all of the same type, arrays are a convenient way to store and process them. You can effectively use loops for input/output, initialization, and other operations. Moreover, you can pass the entire set of values as a parameter with a single statement. The next section continues our discussion of one-dimensional arrays and shows you how to use them effectively for list processing. We then examine two-dimensional and multidimensional arrays.

LIST PROCESSING

A **list** is a set of values of the same type. Because all values are of the same type, a convenient place to store a list is in an array, and particularly in a one-dimensional array. The size of a list is the number of elements in the list. Because the size of a list can increase and decrease, the array you use to store the list should be declared as the maximum size of the list.

Basic operations performed on a list include the following:

1. Search the list for a given item.
2. Sort the list.
3. Insert an item in the list.
4. Delete an item from the list.

The following sections discuss the searching and sorting algorithms.

Searching

Searching a list for a given item is one of the most common operations performed on a list. To search the list, you need three pieces of information:

1. The list—that is, the array containing the list.
2. The length of the list.
3. The item for which you are searching.

After the search is completed,

4. If the item is found, then report "success" and the location where the item was found.
5. If the item is not found, then report "failure."

To accommodate 4 and 5, we will write a value-returning function as follows: If the search item is found in the list, the function returns the location in the list where the search item is found; otherwise, it returns `-1`, indicating an unsuccessful search. From this output, it is clear that the value-returning function we will write has three parameters:

1. The array, `list`, containing the list.
2. The length of the list, `listLength`. (Note that `listLength <= arraySize`).
3. The item, `searchItem`, for which you are searching.

The search algorithm described here is called the **sequential search** or **linear search**. As the name implies, it sequentially searches the array starting with the first array component. It compares the `searchItem` with the element in the array (that is, `list`) and continues the search until either it finds the item or no more data is left in the `list` to be compared with the `searchItem`.

Consider the list of seven elements shown in Figure 10-1.

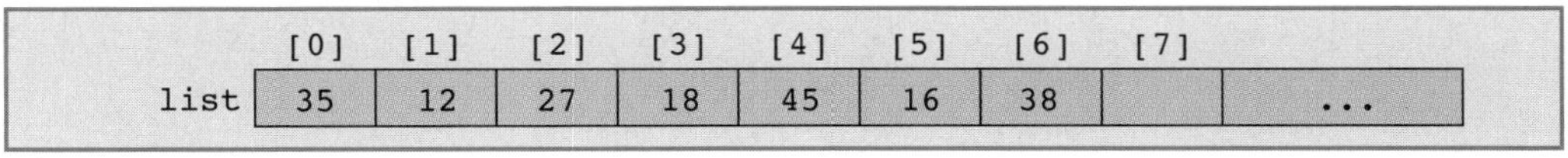

	[0]	[1]	[2]	[3]	[4]	[5]	[6]	[7]	
list	35	12	27	18	45	16	38		...

Figure 10-1 List of seven elements

Suppose that you want to determine whether `27` is in the list. The sequential search works as follows: First, you compare `27` with `list[0]`—that is, compare `27` with `35`. Because `list[0]` $\neq$ `27`, you then compare `27` with `list[1]` (that is, with `12`, the second item in the list). Because `list[1]` $\neq$ `27`, you compare `27` with the next element in the list—that is, compare `27` with `list[2]`. Because `list[2] = 27`, the search stops. This is a successful search.

Let us now search for `10`. As before, the search starts with the first element in the list—that is, at `list[0]`. This time the search item, which is `10`, is compared with every item in the list. Eventually, no more data is left in the list to compare with the search item. This is an unsuccessful search.

It now follows that, as soon as you find an element in the list that is equal to the search item, you must stop the search and report "success." (In this case you usually also tell the location in the list where the search item was found.) Otherwise, after the search item is compared with every element in the list, you must stop the search and report "failure."

Suppose that the name of the array containing the list elements is `list`. The previous discussion translates into the following algorithm for the sequential search:

```
found is set to false;
for(loc = 0; loc < length; loc++)
    if (list[loc] is equal to searchItem)
    {
        found is set to true
        exit loop
    }
if(found)
   return loc;
else
   return -1;
```

The following function performs a sequential search on a list. To be specific, and for illustration purposes, we assume that the list elements are of the type `int`.

```
int seqSearch(const int list[], int listLength, int searchItem)
{
      int loc;
      bool found = false;

      for(loc = 0; loc < listLength; loc++)
          if(list[loc] == searchItem)
          {
             found = true;
             break;
          }

      if(found)
         return loc;
      else
         return -1;
}
```

If the function `seqSearch` returns a value greater than or equal to `0`, it is a successful search; otherwise, it is an unsuccessful search.

As you can see from this algorithm, you start the search by comparing `searchItem` with the first element in the `list`. If `searchItem` is equal to the first element in the `list`, you exit the loop; otherwise, `loc` is incremented by `1` to point to the next element in the `list`. You then compare `searchItem` with the next element in the `list`, and so on.

Suppose that you have a list with 1000 elements (see Figure 10-2). If the search item is the second item in the list, the sequential search makes `2` **key** (also called **item**) comparisons to determine whether the search item is in the list. Similarly, if the search item is the 900th item in the list, the sequential search makes 900 key comparisons to determine whether the search item is in the list. If the search item is not in the list, the sequential search makes 1000 key comparisons.

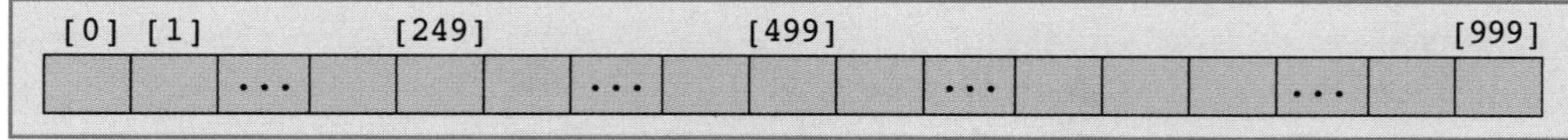

Figure 10-2 List of 1000 elements

Therefore, if `searchItem` is always at the bottom of the `list`, it will take many comparisons to find `searchItem`. Also, if `searchItem` is not in the `list`, then we compare `searchItem` with every element in the `list`. A sequential search is therefore not very efficient for large lists. In fact, it can be proved that, on average, the number of comparisons (key comparisons—not index comparisons) made by the sequential search is equal to half the size of the list. So, for a list size of 1000, on average, the sequential search makes about 500 key comparisons.

The preceding search algorithm does not assume that the list is sorted. If the list is sorted, then you can somewhat improve the search algorithm. Next, we discuss how to sort a list.

Sorting a List: Selection Sort

Many sorting algorithms are available in the literature. The sorting algorithm discussed here is called the **selection sort**.

As the name implies, in the selection sort we rearrange the list by selecting an element in the list and moving it to its proper position. This algorithm finds the location of the smallest element in the unsorted portion of the list, and moves it to the top of the unsorted portion of the list. The first time we locate the smallest item in the entire list, the second time we locate the smallest item in the list starting from the second element in the list, and so on.

As an example, suppose that you have the list shown in Figure 10-3.

	[0]	[1]	[2]	[3]	[4]	[5]	[6]	[7]	[8]	[9]
list	16	30	24	7	25	62	45	5	65	50

Figure 10-3 List of 10 elements

Initially, the entire list is unsorted. So we find the smallest item in the list, which is at position 7, as shown in Figure 10-4.

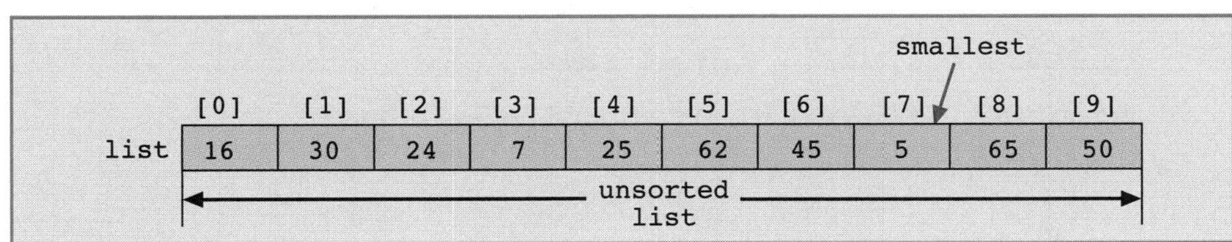

Figure 10-4 Smallest element of unsorted list

Because this is the smallest item, it must be moved to position 0. We therefore swap 16 (that is, `list[0]`) with 5 (that is, `list[7]`), as shown in Figure 10-5.

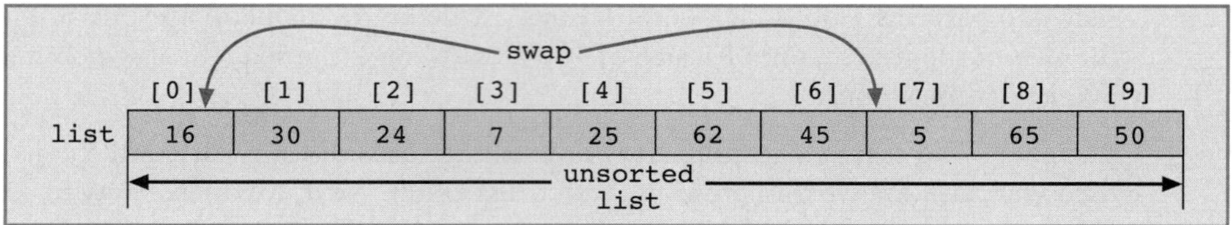

Figure 10-5 Swap elements `list[0]` and `list[7]`

After swapping these elements, the resulting list is as shown in Figure 10-6.

	[0]	[1]	[2]	[3]	[4]	[5]	[6]	[7]	[8]	[9]
list	5	30	24	7	25	62	45	16	65	50

unsorted list

Figure 10-6 List after swapping `list[0]` and `list[7]`

Now the unsorted list is `list[1]...list[9]`. Next, we find the smallest element in the unsorted portion of the list. The smallest element is at position 3, as shown in Figure 10-7.

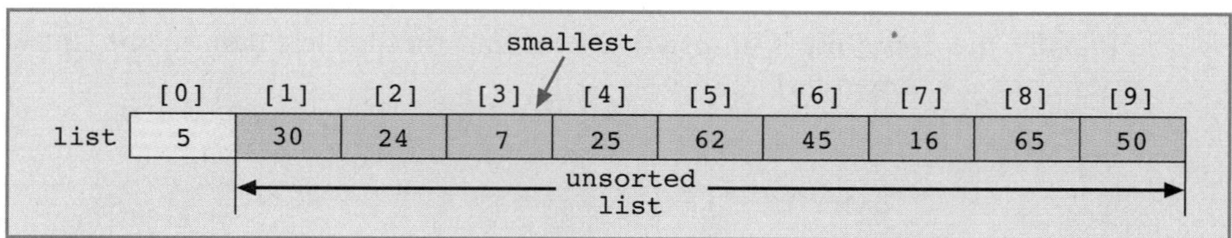

Figure 10-7 Smallest element in unsorted portion of `list`

Because the smallest element in the unsorted list is at position 3, it must be moved to position 1. That is, we swap 7 (that is, `list[3]`) with 30 (that is, `list[1]`), as shown in Figure 10-8.

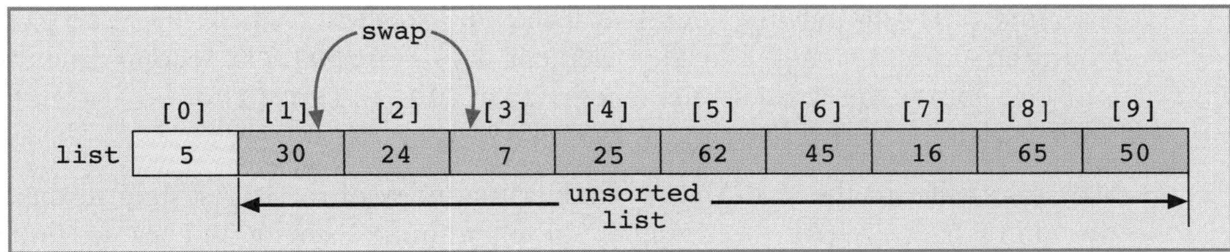

Figure 10-8 Swap `list[1]` with `list[3]`

After swapping `list[1]` with `list[3]`, the resulting list is as shown in Figure 10-9.

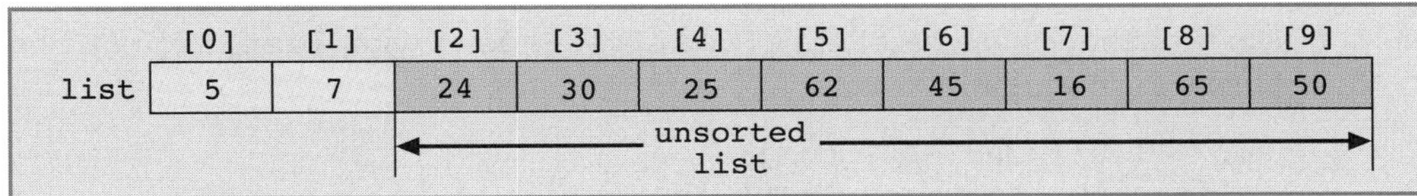

Figure 10-9 `list` after swapping `list[1]` with `list[3]`

10

Now the unsorted list is `list[2]...list[9]`. We repeat the process of finding the (position of the) smallest element in the unsorted portion of the list and moving it to the beginning of the unsorted portion of the list. The selection sort thus involves the following steps:

In the unsorted portion of the list:

a. Find the location of the smallest element.

b. Move the smallest element to the beginning of the unsorted list.

Initially, the entire list (that is, `list[0]...list[length-1]`) is the unsorted list. After executing Steps a and b once, the unsorted list is `list[1]...list[length-1]`. After executing Steps a and b a second time, the unsorted list is `list[2]...list[length-1]`, and so on. In this way, we can keep track of the unsorted portion of the list and repeat Steps a and b with the help of a **`for`** loop:

```
for(index = 0; index < length – 1; index++)
{
   a. Find the location, smallestIndex, of the smallest element in
      list[index]...list[length].
   b. Swap the smallest element with list[index]. That is, swap
      list[smallestIndex] with list[index].
}
```

The first time through the loop, we locate the smallest element in `list[0]...list[length-1]` and swap the smallest element with `list[0]`. The second time through the loop, we locate the smallest element in `list[1]...list[length-1]` and swap the smallest element with `list[1]`, and so on.

Step a is similar to the algorithm of finding the index of the largest item in the list, as discussed in Chapter 9. (Also see Chapter 9, Programming Exercise 2.) Here we find the index of the smallest item in the list. The general form of Step a is

```
smallestIndex = index; //assume first element is the smallest

for(minIndex = index + 1; minIndex < length; minIndex++)
  if(list[minIndex] < list[smallestIndex])
     smallestIndex = minIndex; //current element in the list is
                               //smaller than the smallest so
                               //far, so update smallestIndex
```

Step b swaps the contents of `list[smallestIndex]` with `list[index]`. The following statements accomplish this task:

```
temp = list[smallestIndex];
list[smallestIndex] = list[index];
list[index] = temp;
```

Before writing the selection sort function, let us apply this algorithm to sort the list shown in Figure 10-10.

	[0]	[1]	[2]	[3]	[4]	[5]
list	14	6	23	2	9	20

Figure 10-10 Unsorted list

Let us call this array containing the list elements `list`. The length of `list` is `6`; that is, `length = 6`.

Iteration 1: Sort `list[0]...list[5]`.

Step a: Find the index of the smallest element in `list[0]...list[5]`. (See Figure 10-11.)

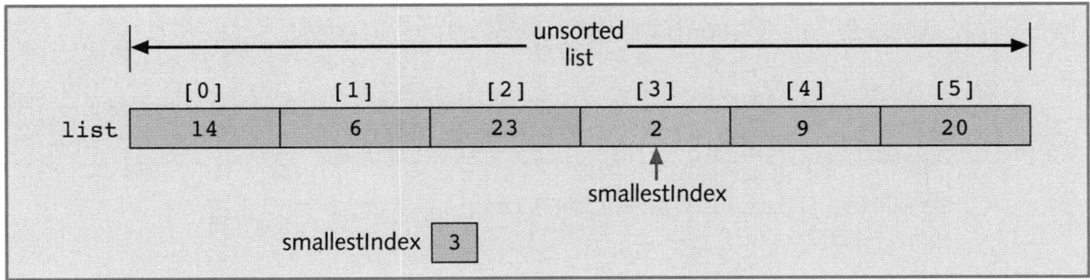

Figure 10-11 Smallest element in unsorted list is at position 3

Step b: Swap `list[smallestIndex]` with `list[index]`. That is, swap `list[3]` with `list[0]`. Figure 10-12 shows the resulting array.

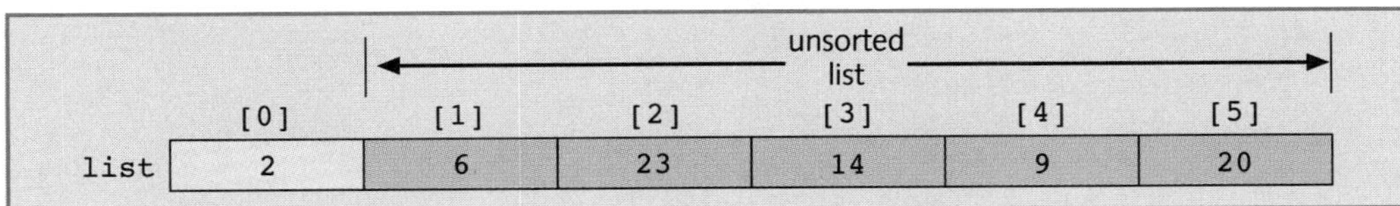

Figure 10-12 `list` after swapping `list[3]` with `list[0]`

Iteration 2: Sort `list[1]...list[5]`. Here `index = 1`.

Step a: Find the index of the smallest element in `list[1]...list[5]`. (See Figure 10-13.)

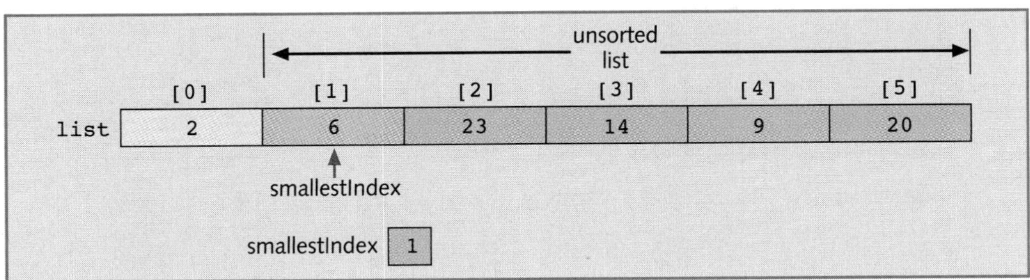

Figure 10-13 Smallest element in unsorted list is at position 1

Step b: `Swap list[smallestIndex]` with `list[index]`. That is, swap `list[1]` with `list[1]`. Figure 10-14 shows the resulting array.

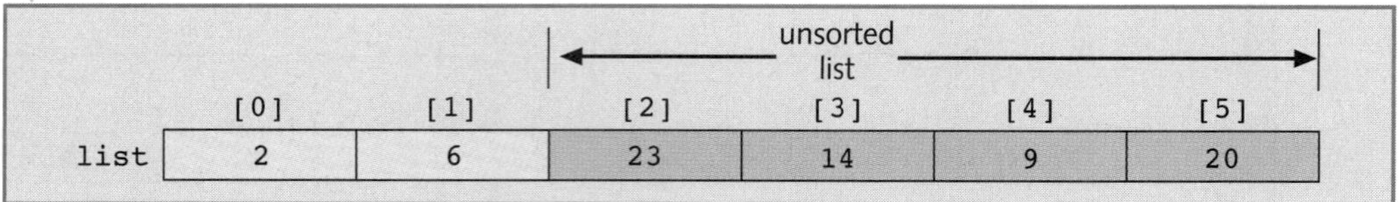

Figure 10-14 `list` after swapping `list[1]` with `list[1]`

Iteration 3: Sort `list[2]...list[5]`.

Step a: Find the index of the smallest element in `list[2]...list[5]`. (See Figure 10-15.)

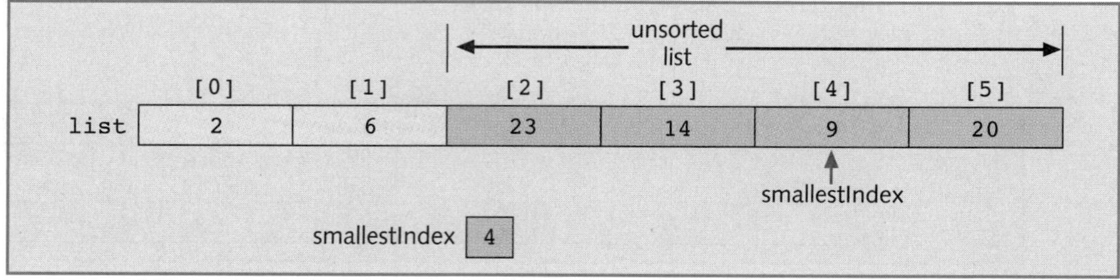

Figure 10-15 Smallest element in unsorted list is at position 4

Step b: Swap `list[smallestIndex]` with `list[index]`. That is, swap `list[4]` with `list[2]`. Figure 10-16 shows the resulting array.

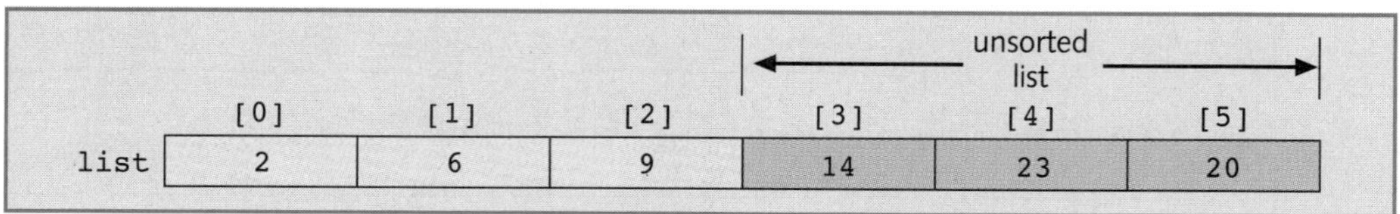

Figure 10-16 `list` after swapping `list[4]` with `list[2]`

Iteration 4: Sort `list[3]...list[5]`.

Step a: Find the index of the smallest element in `list[3]...list[5]`. (See Figure 10-17.)

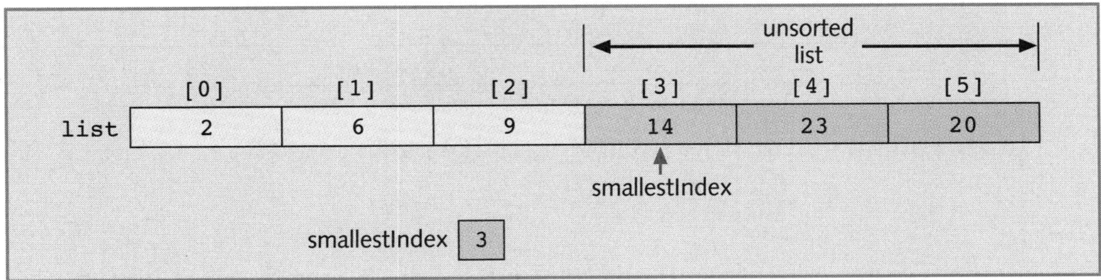

Figure 10-17 Smallest element in unsorted list is at position 3

Step b: Swap `list[smallestIndex]` with `list[index]`. That is, swap `list[3]` with `list[3]`. Figure 10-18 shows the resulting array.

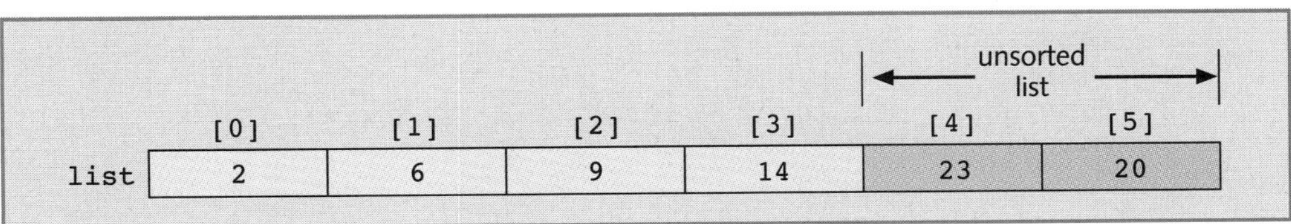

Figure 10-18 `list` after swapping `list[3]` with `list[3]`

Iteration 5: Sort `list[4]...list[5]`.

Step a: Find the index of the smallest element in `list[4]...list[5]`. (See Figure 10-19.)

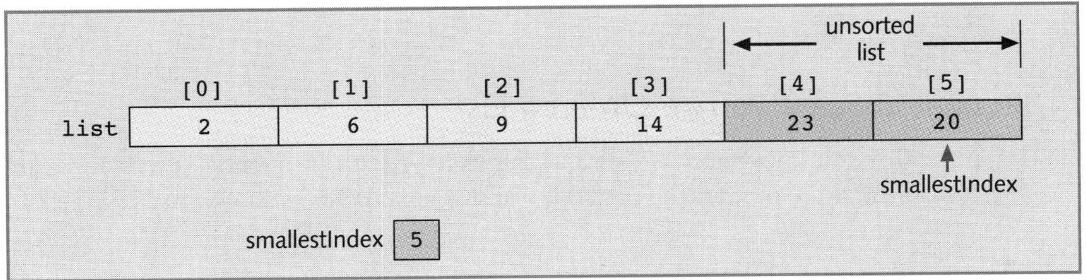

Figure 10-19 Smallest element in the unsorted list is at position 5

Step b: Swap `list[smallestIndex]` with `list[index]`. That is, swap `list[5]` with `list[4]`. Figure 10-20 shows the resulting array.

	[0]	[1]	[2]	[3]	[4]	[5]
list	2	6	9	14	20	23

Figure 10-20 `list` after swapping `list[4]` with `list[5]`

After five iterations of Steps a and b, the list is in order—that is, sorted. Note that the length of the list is 6, but we needed to repeat Steps a and b only 5 times, that is, `length - 1` times.

We can now write the function that can sort a list. Let us call this function `selectionSort`. The definition of the function `selectionSort` is

```
void selectionSort(int list[], int length)
{
   int index;
   int smallestIndex;
   int minIndex;
   int temp;

   for(index = 0; index < length – 1; index++)
   {
           //Step a
        smallestIndex = index;

        for(minIndex = index + 1; minIndex < length; minIndex++)
           if(list[minIndex] < list[smallestIndex])
              smallestIndex = minIndex;

           //Step b
        temp = list[smallestIndex];
        list[smallestIndex] = list[index];
        list[index] = temp;
   }
}
```

Sequential Search on an Ordered List

Now that you know how to sort a list, let us rewrite the sequential search and take advantage of a sorted list. Consider the sorted list of seven elements as shown in Figure 10-21.

	[0]	[1]	[2]	[3]	[4]	[5]	[6]	[7]	
list	4	12	27	38	45	53	58		...

Figure 10-21 Sorted list of seven elements

Suppose that you want to determine whether `38` is in the list. You start the search at the first element of the list. Of course, the search stops at `list[3]`. Now suppose that you want to determine whether `40` is in the list. From the description of the list, it follows that you should not search the list past `list[4]` because `list[4] >= 40`.

From these two cases, it follows that you search `list` until either you arrive at an item in the list that is greater than or equal to `searchItem` (the item for which you are searching) or `list` has no more elements left to be compared with `searchItem`. The general form of the sequential search on a sorted list is

```
found is set to false;

for(loc = 0; loc < listLength; loc++)
      if (list[loc] is greater than or equal to searchItem)
      {
            found is set to true
            exit loop
      }
```

Note that the loop stops (that is, `found` is set to `true`) if you find an element in `list` that is either greater than or equal to the item for which you are searching. Actually, `found` should be `true` only if the item is equal to some element in `list`. So you must correctly set the value of `found` outside the loop. The following statement accomplishes this task:


```
if(found)
   if(list[loc] == searchItem)
      return loc;
   else
      return -1;
else
      return -1;
```

Now we can complete the definition of the function—sequential search—to perform a search on a sorted list.

```
int seqOrderdSearch(const int list[], int listLength, int searchItem)
{
     int loc;                                       //Line 1
     bool found = false;                            //Line 2

     for(loc = 0; loc < listLength; loc++)          //Line 3
        if(list[loc] >= searchItem)                 //Line 4
        {
             found = true;                          //Line 5
             break;                                 //Line 6
        }
```

```
        if(found)                                   //Line 7
           if(list[loc] == searchItem)              //Line 8
               return loc;                          //Line 9
           else                                     //Line 10
               return -1;                           //Line 11
        else                                        //Line 12
            return -1;                              //Line 13
}
```

Let us trace this algorithm on the list shown in Figure 10-22.

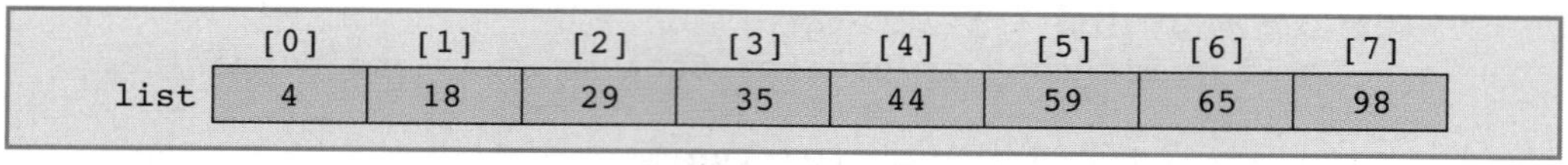

	[0]	[1]	[2]	[3]	[4]	[5]	[6]	[7]
list	4	18	29	35	44	59	65	98

Figure 10-22 Sorted list of eight elements

The length of the list is 8, so `length = 8`.

Suppose that the item for which you are searching is `35`. Therefore, `searchItem = 35`. Before the `for` loop executes, `loc = 0`, and `found = false`. Next, we trace the execution of the `for` loop, showing the values of `loc`, `found`, and certain list elements during each iteration:

Iteration	`loc`	`found`	`list[loc]`	`list[loc]>= searchItem`
1	0	`false`	4	`4 >= 35` is `false; loc = 1`
2	1	`false`	18	`18 >= 35` is `false; loc = 2`
3	2	`false`	29	`29 >= 35` is `false; loc = 3`
4	3	`false`	35	`35 >= 35` is `true; found = true`

During the fourth iteration of the `for` loop, found becomes `true` and the `break` statement exits the loop. After the `for` loop, the following statement executes:

```
if(found)                              //Line 7
   if(list[loc] == searchItem)         //Line 8
      return loc;                      //Line 9
   else                                //Line 10
      return -1;                       //Line 11
else                                   //Line 12
   return -1;                          //Line 13
```

Because `found` is `true`, the `if` statement at Line 8 executes. Because `list[loc] = 35` and `searchItem = 35`, the expression

```
list[loc] == searchItem
```

evaluates to `true` and the `return` statement at Line 9 returns the value of `loc`, which is `3`. This is a successful search.

Let us now search for `40`. That is, `searchItem = 40`. Before the `for` loop executes, `loc = 0` and `found = false`. As before, we trace the execution of the `for` loop, showing the values of `loc`, `found`, and certain list elements during each iteration:

Iteration	loc	found	list[loc]	list[loc]>= searchItem
1	0	false	4	4 >= 40 is false; loc = 1
2	1	false	18	18 >= 40 is false; loc = 2
3	2	false	29	29 >= 40 is false; loc = 3
4	3	false	35	35 >= 40 is false; found = 4
5	4	false	44	44 >= 40 is true; found = true

During the fifth iteration of the `for` loop, `found` becomes `true` and the `break` statement exits the loop. After the `for` loop, the following statements (between Lines 7 and 13) execute:

```
if(found)                           //Line 7
   if(list[loc] == searchItem)      //Line 8
      return loc;                   //Line 9
   else                             //Line 10
      return -1;                    //Line 11
else                                //Line 12
   return -1;                       //Line 13
```


Because `found` is `true`, the `if` statement at Line 8 executes. Because `list[loc] = 44` and `searchItem = 40`, the expression

```
list[loc] == searchItem
```

evaluates to `false`, the statement at Line 9 is skipped, and the `return` statement at Line 11 executes, which returns `-1`. This is an unsuccessful search.

It can be proved that to determine whether an item is in a list, a sequential search on an ordered list—on average—searches half the list. That is, for a list of 1000 elements (in the successful case), a sequential search, on average, makes 500 comparisons.

Binary Search

A sequential search performs somewhat better on a sorted list, but is still not very efficient for large lists. It typically searches about half the list. However, if the list is sorted, you can use another search algorithm, called a **binary search**. A binary search is much faster than a sequential search. The requirement to apply a binary search is that the list must be sorted.

A binary search is similar to a dictionary search. A binary search uses the "divide and conquer" technique to search the list. First, the search item is compared with the middle element of the list. If the search item is less than the middle element of the list, we restrict the search to the upper half of the list; otherwise, we search the lower half of the list.

Consider the following sorted list of `length = 12`, as shown in Figure 10-23.

	[0]	[1]	[2]	[3]	[4]	[5]	[6]	[7]	[8]	[9]	[10]	[11]
list	4	8	19	25	34	39	45	48	66	75	89	95

Figure 10-23 List of length `12`

Suppose that we want to determine whether `75` is in the list. Initially, the entire list is the search list (see Figure 10-24).

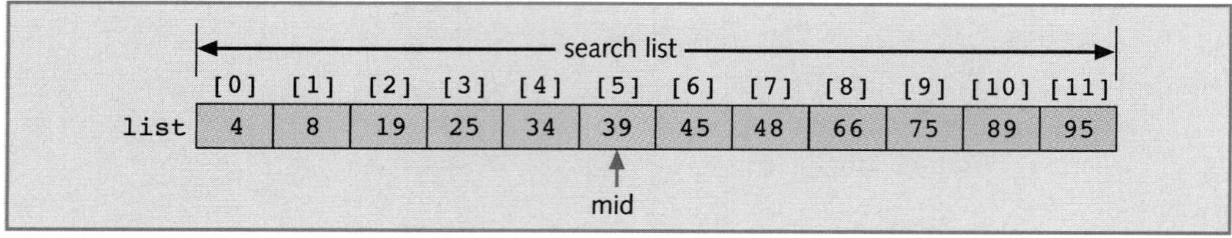

Figure 10-24 Search list, `list[0]...list[11]`

First we compare `75` with the middle element in the list, `list[5]` (which is `39`). Because `75` ≠ `list[5]` and `75 > list[5]`, we then restrict our search to the list `list[6]...list[11]`, as shown in Figure 10-25.

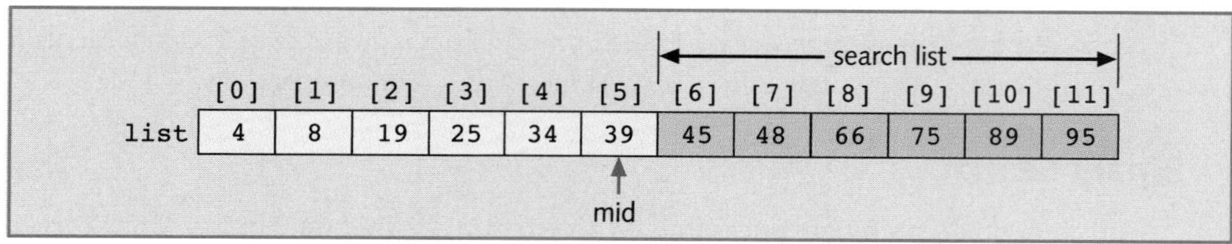

Figure 10-25 Search list, `list[6]...list[11]`

This process is repeated on the list `list[6]...list[11]`, which is a list of `length = 6`.

Because we need to frequently determine the middle element of the list, the binary search algorithm is usually implemented on array-based lists. To determine the middle element of the list, we add the starting index, `first`, and the ending index, `last`, of the search list and divide by `2` to calculate its index. That is, $\texttt{mid} = \frac{\texttt{first+last}}{2}$. Initially, `first = 0` and (because an array index in C++ starts at `0` and the length denotes the number of elements in the list) `last = listLength - 1`.

The following C++ function implements the binary search algorithm. If the item is found in the list, its location is returned. If the search item is not in the list, `- 1` is returned.

```
int binarySearch(const int list[], int listLength, int searchItem)

{
	int first = 0;
	int last = listLength - 1;
	int mid;

	bool found = false;
	while(first <= last && !found)
	{
		mid = (first + last) / 2;

		if(list[mid] == searchItem)
			found = true;
		else
		    if(list[mid] > searchItem)
		        last = mid - 1;
		    else
		        first = mid + 1;
	}

	if(found)
	    return mid;
	else
	   return -1;
}//end binarySearch
```

In the binary search algorithm, each time through the loop we make two key comparisons. The only exception is the successful case, wherein the last time through the loop only one item key comparison is made.

Next, let us walk through the binary search algorithm using the list shown in Figure 10-26.

	[0]	[1]	[2]	[3]	[4]	[5]	[6]	[7]	[8]	[9]	[10]	[11]
list	4	8	19	25	34	39	45	48	66	75	89	95

Figure 10-26 Sorted list for binary search

The size of this list is 12; that is, `listLength = 12`. Suppose that the item for which we are searching is 89; that is, `searchItem = 89`. Before the `while` loop executes, `first = 0`, `last = 11`, and `found = false`. Next, we trace the execution of the `while` loop, showing the values of `first`, `last`, `mid`, `found`, and the number of key comparisons during each iteration:

Iteration	first	last	mid	list[mid]	Number of Key Comparisons
1	0	11	5	39	2
2	6	11	8	66	2
3	9	11	10	89	1 (`found` is `true`)

The item is found at location 10 and the total number of key comparisons is 5.

Next, let us search the list for 34; that is, `searchItem = 34`. Before the `while` loop executes, `first = 0`, `last = 11`, and `found = false`. As before, we trace the execution of the `while` loop, showing the values of `first`, `last`, `mid`, `found`, and the number of key comparisons during each iteration:

Iteration	first	last	mid	list[mid]	Number of Key Comparisons
1	0	11	5	39	2
2	0	4	2	19	2
3	3	4	3	25	2
4	4	4	4	34	1 (`found` is `true`)

The item is found at location 4 and the total number of key comparisons is 7.

Let us now search for 22; that is, `searchItem = 22`. Before the `while` loop executes, `first = 0`, `last = 11`, and `found = false`. We trace the execution of the `while` loop, showing the values of `first`, `last`, `mid`, `found`, and number of key comparisons during each iteration:

Iteration	first	last	mid	list[mid]	Number of Key Comparisons
1	0	11	5	39	2
2	0	4	2	19	2
3	3	4	3	25	2
4	3	2	The loop stops (because `first > last`)		

This is an unsuccessful search. The total number of key comparisons is 6.

From these traces of the binary search algorithm, you can see that, every time you go through the loop, you cut the size of the sublist in half. That is, the size of the sublist you search the next time through the loop is about half the size of the previous sublist.

Performance of Binary Search

Suppose that `L` is a sorted list of 1000 elements and you want to determine whether `x` is in `L`. Because `L` is sorted, you can apply the binary search algorithm to search for `x`. Suppose `L` is as shown in Figure 10-27.

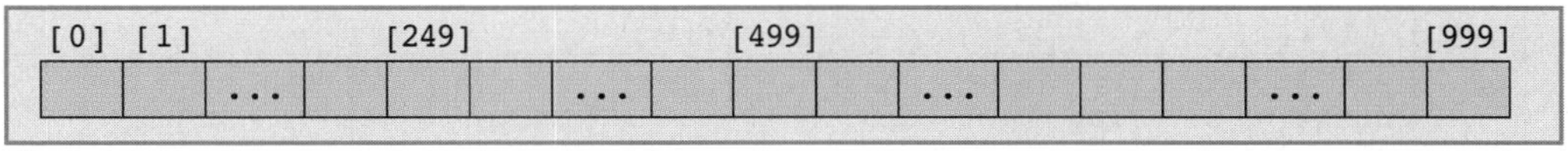

Figure 10-27 List `L`

The first iteration of the `while` loop searches for `x` in `L[0]...L[999]`, which is a list of `1000` items. This iteration of the `while` loop compares `x` with `L[499]`. (See Figure 10-28.)

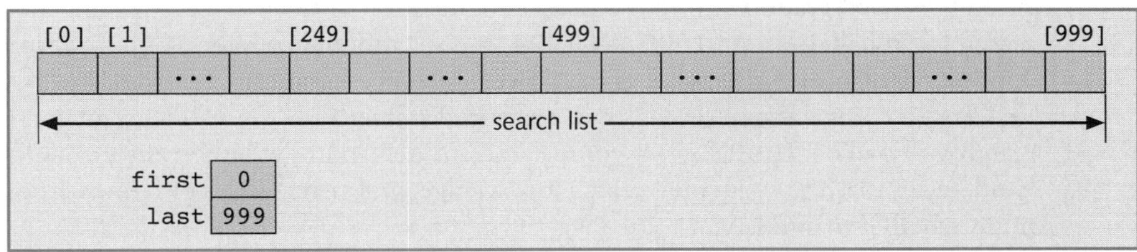

Figure 10-28 Search list

Suppose that `x ≠ L[499]`. If `x < L[499]`, the next iteration of the `while` loop looks for `x` in `L[0]...L[498]`; otherwise, the `while` loop looks for `x` in `L[500]...L[999]`. Suppose that `x < L[499]`. Then the next iteration of the `while` loop looks for `x` in `L[0]...L[498]`, which is a list of `499` items, as shown in Figure 10-29.

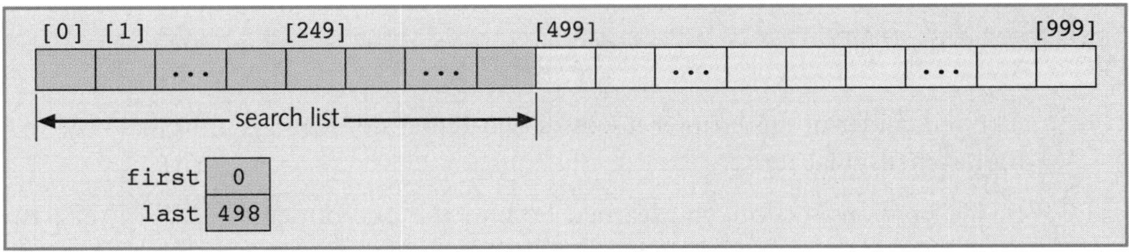

Figure 10-29 Search list after first iteration

This iteration of the `while` loop compares `x` with `L[249]`. Once again, suppose that `x ≠ L[249]`. Further suppose that `x > L[249]`. The next iteration of the `while` loop searches for `x` in `L[250]...L[498]`, which is a list of `249` items, as shown in Figure 10-30.

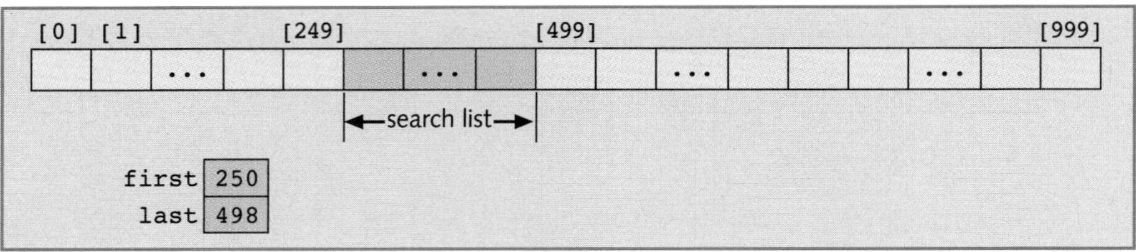

Figure 10-30 Search list after second iteration

From these observations, it follows that every iteration of the `while` loop cuts the size of the search list in half. Because `1000` $\approx$ `1024` = 2^{10}, the `while` loop will have at most 11 iterations to determine whether `x` is in `L`. Because every iteration of the `while` loop makes 2 key (item) comparisons (that is, `x` is compared twice with the elements of `L`), the binary search will make at most 22 key comparisons to determine whether `x` is in `L`. On the other hand, recall that the sequential search, on average, will make 500 key comparisons to determine whether `x` is in `L`.

To get a better idea of how fast the binary search is as compared with the sequential search, suppose that `L` is of size `1000000`. Since `1000000` $\approx$ `1048576` = 2^{20}, it follows that the `while` loop in the binary search will have at most 21 iterations to determine whether an element is in `L`. Every iteration of the `while` loop makes `2` key (that is, item) comparisons. Therefore, to determine whether an element is in `L`, the binary search makes at most 42 key comparisons. On the other hand, on average, the sequential search will make 500,000 key (item) comparisons to determine whether an element is in `L`.

In general, if `L` is a sorted list of size `n`, to determine whether an element is in `L`, the binary search makes at most $2*\log_2 n + 2$ key (item) comparisons.

Two- and Multidimensional Arrays

The remainder of this chapter discusses two-dimensional arrays as well as ways to work with multidimensional arrays.

In the previous section, you learned how to use one-dimensional arrays effectively for list processing. If the data is provided in a list form, you can use one-dimensional arrays. However, sometimes data is provided in a table form. For example, suppose that you want to keep track of how many cars of a particular color a local dealership has in stock. The dealership sells 6 types of cars in 5 different colors. Figure 10-31 shows a sample data.

inStock	[Red]	[Brown]	[Black]	[White]	[Gray]
[GM]	10	7	12	10	4
[Ford]	18	11	15	17	10
[Toyota]	12	10	9	5	12
[BMW]	16	6	13	8	3
[Nissan]	10	7	12	6	4
[Volvo]	9	4	7	12	11

Figure 10-31 Table `inStock`

You can see that the data is in a table format. The table has 30 entries, and every entry is an integer. Because all of the table entries are of the same type, you can declare a one-dimensional array of 30 components of the type **`int`**. The first 5 components of the one-dimensional array can store the data of the first row of the table, the next 5 components of the one-dimensional array can store the data of the second row of the table, and so on. In other words, you can simulate the data given in a table format in a one-dimensional array.

If you do so, the algorithms to manipulate the data in the one-dimensional array will be somewhat complicated because you must take care where one row ends and another begins. You must also correctly compute the index of a particular element. C++ simplifies the processing of manipulating data given in a table form with the use of two-dimensional arrays. This section first discusses how to declare two-dimensional arrays and then looks at ways to manipulate data in a two-dimensional array.

Two-dimensional array: A collection of a fixed number of components arranged in rows and columns (that is, in two dimensions), wherein all components are of the same type.

The syntax for declaring a two-dimensional array is

```
dataType  arrayName[intExp1][intExp2];
```

where **`intExp1`** and **`intExp2`** are expressions yielding positive integer values. The two expressions, **`intExp1`** and **`intExp2`**, specify the number of rows and the number of columns, respectively, in the array.

The statement

```
double sales[10][5];
```

declares a two-dimensional array `sales` of `10` rows and `5` columns, where every component is of the type `double`. As in the case of a one-dimensional array, the rows are numbered `0...9` and the columns are numbered `0...4`. (See Figure 10-32.)

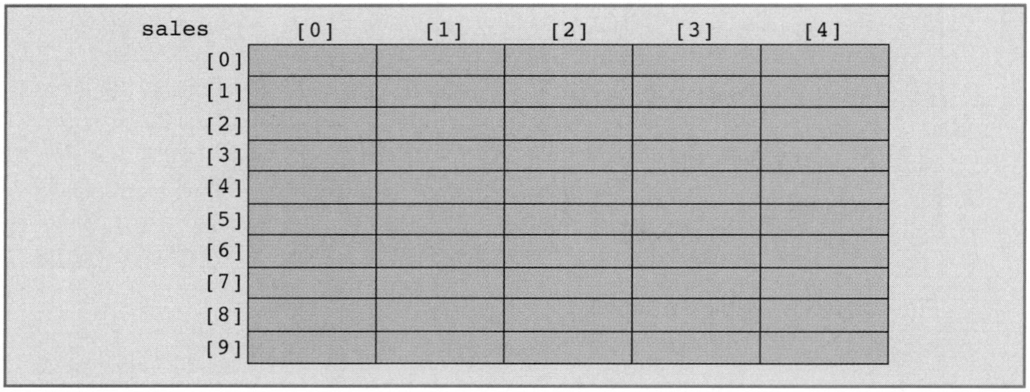

sales	[0]	[1]	[2]	[3]	[4]
[0]					
[1]					
[2]					
[3]					
[4]					
[5]					
[6]					
[7]					
[8]					
[9]					

Figure 10-32 Two-dimensional array `sales`

Accessing Array Components

To access the components of a two-dimensional array, you need a pair of indices: one for the row position and one for the column position.

The syntax to access a component of a two-dimensional array is

```
arrayName[indexExp1][indexExp2]
```

where `indexExp1` and `indexExp2` are expressions yielding non-negative integer values. `indexExp1` specifies the row position; `indexExp2` specifies the column position.

The statement

```
sales[5][3] = 25.75;
```

stores `25.75` into row number `5` and column number `3` (that is, the `6th` row and the `4th` column) of the array `sales`. (See Figure 10-33.)

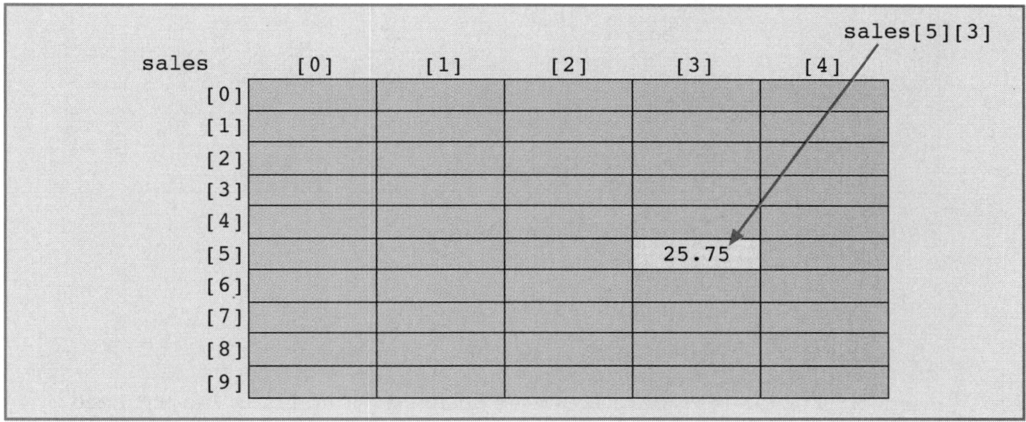

Figure 10-33 sales[5] [3]

Suppose that

```
int i = 5;
int j = 3;
```

Then the previous statement

```
sales[5][3] = 25.75;
```

is equivalent to

```
sales[i][j] = 25.75;
```

So the indices can also be variables.

Two-Dimensional Array Initialization During Declaration

Like one-dimensional arrays, two-dimensional arrays can be initialized when they are declared. The following example helps illustrate this concept.

Consider the following statement:

```
int board[4][3] = {{2, 3, 1},
                   {15, 25, 13},
                   {20,4,7},
                   {11,18,14}};
```

This statement declares `board` to be a two-dimensional array of `4` rows and `3` columns. The components of the first row are `2`, `3`, and `1`; the components of the second row are `15`, `25`, and `13`; the components of the third row are `20`, `4`, and `7`; and the components of the fourth row are `11`, `18`, and `14`, respectively. Figure 10-34 shows the array `board`.

board	[0]	[1]	[2]
[0]	2	3	1
[1]	15	25	13
[2]	20	4	7
[3]	11	18	14

Figure 10-34 Two-dimensional array `board`

To initialize a two-dimensional array when it is declared:

1. The elements of each row are enclosed within braces and separated by commas.
2. All rows are enclosed within braces.
3. For number arrays, if all components of a row are not specified, the unspecified components are initialized to `0`. In this case, at least one of the values must be given to initialize all components of a row.

Two-Dimensional Arrays and Enumeration Types

Chapter 8 is required to understand this section.

You can also use the enumeration type for array indices. Consider the following statements:

```
const int rows = 6;
const int columns = 5;

enum carType{GM, Ford, Toyota, BMW, Nissan, Volvo};
enum colorType{Red, Brown, Black, White, Gray};

int inStock[rows][columns];
```

These statements define the **`carType`** and **`colorType`** enumeration types and then define **`inStock`** as a two-dimensional array of `6` rows and `5` columns. Suppose that each row in **`inStock`** corresponds to a car type, and each column in **`inStock`** corresponds to a color type. That is, the first row corresponds to the car type **`GM`**, the second row corresponds to the car type **`Ford`**, and so on. Similarly, the first column corresponds to the color type **`Red`**, the second column corresponds to the color type **`Brown`**, and so on. Suppose further that each entry in **`inStock`** represents the number of cars of a particular type and color. (See Figure 10-35.)

inStock	[Red]	[Brown]	[Black]	[White]	[Gray]
[GM]					
[Ford]					
[Toyota]					
[BMW]					
[Nissan]					
[Volvo]					

Figure 10-35 Two-dimensional array `inStock`

The statement

```
inStock[1][3] = 15;
```

is equivalent to the following statement (see Figure 10-36):

```
inStock[Ford][White] = 15;
```


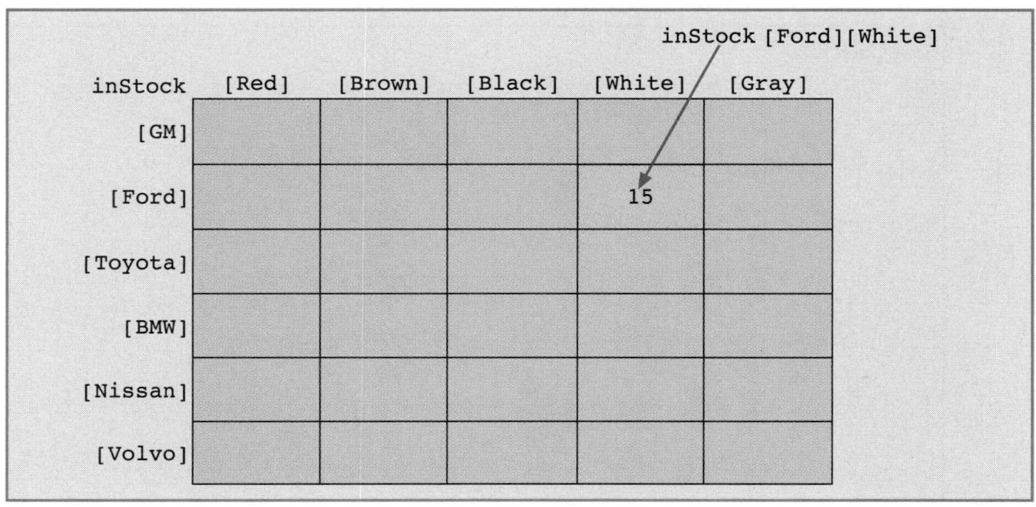

Figure 10-36 `inStock[Ford][White]`

The second statement easily conveys the message—that is, set the number of `White Ford` cars to `15`. This example illustrates that enumeration types can be used effectively to make the program readable and easy to manage.

Processing Two-Dimensional Arrays

A two-dimensional array can be processed in three ways:

1. Process the entire array.
2. Process a particular row of the array, called **row processing**.
3. Process a particular column of the array, called **column processing**.

Initializing and printing the array are examples of processing the entire two-dimensional array. Finding the largest element in a row (column) or finding the sum of a row (column) are examples of row (column) processing. We will use the following declaration for our discussion:

```
const int rows = 7;     //this can be set to any number
const int columns = 6; //this can be set to any number
int matrix[rows][columns];
int row;
int col;
int sum;
int largest;
int temp;
```

Figure 10-37 shows the array `matrix`.

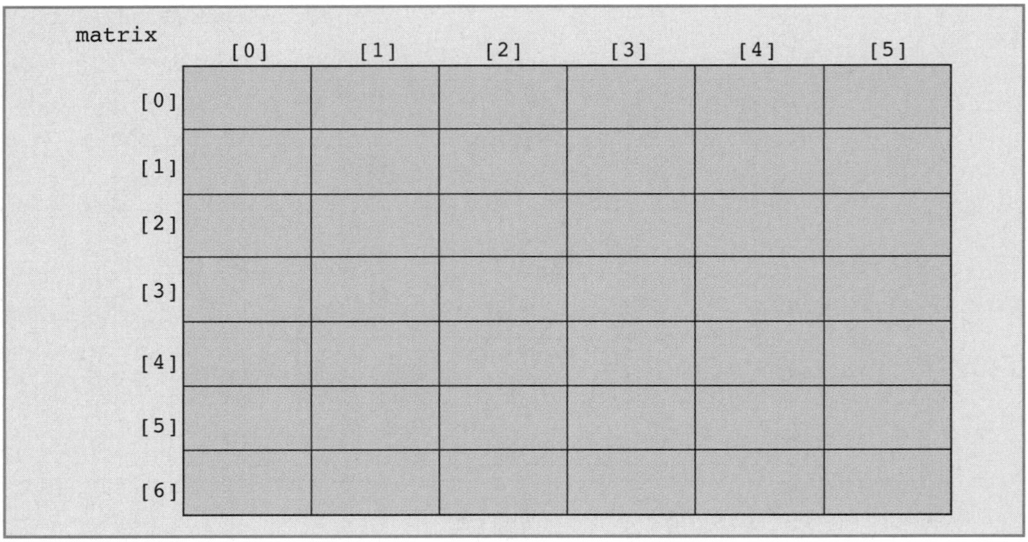

matrix	[0]	[1]	[2]	[3]	[4]	[5]
[0]						
[1]						
[2]						
[3]						
[4]						
[5]						
[6]						

Figure 10-37 Two-dimensional array `matrix`

Because the components of a two-dimensional array are of the same type, the components of any row or column are of the same type. This means that each row and each column of a two-dimensional array is a one-dimensional array. Therefore, when processing a particular row or column of a two-dimensional array, we use algorithms similar to those that process one-dimensional arrays. We further explain this concept with the help of the two-dimensional array `matrix`, as declared above.

Suppose that we want to process row number `5` of `matrix`, (or the `sixth` row of `matrix`). The components of row number `5` of `matrix` are:

```
matrix[5][0], matrix[5][1], matrix[5][2], matrix[5][3], matrix[5][4],
matrix[5][5]
```

We see that in these components the first index (the row position) is fixed at `5`. The second index (the column position) ranges from `0` to `5`. Therefore, we can use the following `for` loop to process row number `5`:

```
for(col = 0; col < columns; col++)
    process matrix[5][col]
```

Clearly, this `for` loop is equivalent to the following `for` loop:

```
row = 5;
for(col = 0; col < columns; col++)
    process matrix[row][col]
```


Similarly, suppose that we want to process column number `2` of `matrix`, that is, the `third` column of `matrix`. The components of this column are

```
matrix[0][2], matrix[1][2], matrix[2][2], matrix[3][2], matrix[4][2],
matrix[5][2], matrix[6][2]
```

Here the second index (that is, the column position) is fixed at `2`. The first index (that is, the row position) ranges from `0` to `6`. In this case, we can use the following `for` loop to process column `2` of `matrix`:

```
for(row = 0; row < rows; row++)
    process matrix[row][2]
```

Clearly, this `for` loop is equivalent to the following `for` loop:

```
col = 2;
for(row = 0; row < rows; row++)
    process matrix[row][col]
```

Next, we discuss specific processing algorithms.

Initialization

Suppose that you want to initialize row number `4` to `0`, that is the 5th row to `0`. As explained earlier, the following `for` loop initializes row number `4` to `0`:

```
row = 4;
for(col = 0; col < columns; col++)
    matrix[row][col] = 0;
```

If you want to initialize the entire `matrix` to `0`, you can also put the first index (that is, the row position) in a loop. By using the following nested `for` loops, we can initialize each component of `matrix` to `0`:

```
for(row = 0; row < rows; row++)
    for(col = 0; col < columns; col++)
        matrix[row][col] = 0;
```

Print

By using a nested `for` loop, you can output the components of `matrix`. The following nested `for` loops print the components of `matrix`, one row per line:

```
for(row = 0; row < rows; row++)
{
   for(col = 0; col < columns; col++)
       cout<<setw(5)<<matrix[row][col]<<" ";

   cout<<endl;
}
```

Input

The following `for` loop inputs data into row number `4`, that is, the 5th row of `matrix`:

```
row = 4;
for(col = 0; col < columns; col++)
    cin>>matrix[row][col];
```

As before, by putting the row number in a loop, you can input data into each component of `matrix`. The following `for` loop inputs data into each component of `matrix`:

```
for(row = 0; row < rows; row++)
    for(col = 0; col < columns; col++)
        cin>>matrix[row][col];
```

Sum by Row

The following `for` loop finds the sum of row number `4` of `matrix`; that is, it adds the components of row number `4`:

```
sum = 0;
row = 4;
for(col = 0; col < columns; col++)
    sum = sum + matrix[row][col];
```

Once again, by putting the row number in a loop, we can find the sum of each row separately. Following is the C++ code to find the sum of each individual row:

```
//Sum of each individual row
for(row = 0; row < rows; row++)
{
```

```
    sum = 0;
    for(col = 0; col < columns; col++)
        sum = sum + matrix[row][col];

    cout<<"Sum of row "<<row+1<<" = "<<sum<<endl;
}
```

Sum by Column

As in the case of sum by row, the following nested `for` loop finds the sum of each individual column:

```
//Sum of each individual column
for(col = 0; col < columns; col++)
{
    sum = 0;
    for(row = 0; row < rows; row++)
        sum = sum + matrix[row][col];

    cout<<"Sum of column "<<col+1<<" = "<<sum<<endl;
}
```

Largest Element in Each Row and Each Column

10

As stated earlier, two other possible operations on a two-dimensional array are finding the largest element in each row and each column and finding the sum of both diagonals. Next, we give the C++ code to perform these operations.

The following `for` loop determines the largest element in row number `4`:

```
row = 4;
largest = matrix[row][0]; //assume that the first element of the
                          //row is the largest
for(col = 1; col < columns; col++)
    if(largest < matrix[row][col])
       largest = matrix[row][col];
```

The following C++ code determines the largest element in each row and each column:

```
//Largest element in each row
for(row = 0; row < rows; row++)
{
    largest = matrix[row][0]; //assume that the first element
                              //of the row is the largest
    for(col = 1; col < columns; col++)
        if(largest < matrix[row][col])
           largest = matrix[row][col];

    cout<<"Largest element of row "<<row+1<<" = "<<largest<<endl;
}
```

```
//Largest element in each column
for(col = 0; col < columns; col++)
{
    largest = matrix[0][col]; //assume that the first element of
                              //the column is the largest
    for(row = 1; row < rows; row++)
       if(largest < matrix[row][col])
          largest = matrix[row][col];

    cout<<"Largest element of col "<<col+1<<" = "<<largest<<endl;
}
```

Reversing Diagonal

Suppose that **matrix** is a square array, that is, the number of rows and the number of columns are the same. Then **matrix** has a main diagonal and an opposite diagonal. To be specific, suppose that we have the following:

```
const int rows = 4;
const int columns = 4;
```

The components of the main diagonal of **matrix** are **matrix[0][0]**, **matrix[1][1]**, **matrix[2][2]**, and **matrix[3][3]**. The components of the opposite diagonal are **matrix[0][3]**, **matrix[1][2]**, **matrix[2][1]**, and **matrix[3][0]**.

We want to write a C++ code to reverse both the diagonals of **matrix**.

Assume that the array **matrix** is as shown in Figure 10-38.

matrix	[0]	[1]	[2]	[3]
[0]	1	8	10	11
[1]	34	2	12	45
[2]	0	13	3	20
[3]	14	35	56	4

Figure 10-38 Two-dimensional array **matrix**

After reversing both the diagonals, the array **matrix** is as shown in Figure 10-39.

matrix	[0]	[1]	[2]	[3]
[0]	4	8	10	14
[1]	34	3	13	45
[2]	0	12	2	20
[3]	11	35	56	1

Figure 10-39 After reversing diagonals, the array `matrix`

It is clear that, to reverse the main diagonal, we do the following:

1. Swap `matrix[0][0]` with `matrix[3][3]`.
2. Swap `matrix[1][1]` with `matrix[2][2]`.

To reverse the opposite diagonal, we do the following:

1. Swap `matrix[0][3]` with `matrix[3][0]`.
2. Swap `matrix[1][2]` with `matrix[2][1]`.

The following **for** loops reverse the diagonals:

```
//Reverse the main diagonal
for(row = 0; row < rows / 2; row++)
{
      temp = matrix[row][row];
      matrix[row][row] = matrix[rows-1-row][rows-1-row];
      matrix[rows-1-row][rows-1-row] = temp;
}
//Reverse the opposite diagonal
for(row = 0; row < rows / 2; row++)
{
      temp = matrix[row][rows-1-row];
      matrix[row][rows-1-row] = matrix[rows-1-row][row];
      matrix[rows-1-row][row] = temp;
}
```

This C++ code to reverse the diagonals of a square, two-dimensional array works for an array of any size.

Passing Two-Dimensional Arrays as Parameters to Functions

Two-dimensional arrays can be passed as parameters to a function and they are passed by reference. The base address (that is, the address of the first component of the actual parameter) is passed to the formal parameter. If `matrix` is the name of a two-dimensional array, then `matrix[0][0]` is the first component of `matrix`.

When storing a two-dimensional array in the computer's memory, C++ uses the **row order form**. That is, the first row is stored first, followed by the second row, followed by the third row, and so on.

In the case of a one-dimensional array, when declaring it as a formal parameter, we usually omit the size of the array. Because C++ stores two-dimensional arrays in row order form, to compute the address of a component correctly, the compiler must know where one row ends and the next row begins. Thus, when declaring a two-dimensional array as a formal parameter, you can omit the size of the first dimension, but not the second; that is, you must specify the number of columns.

Consider the following function definition:

```
void example(int table[][5], int rowsize)
{
    .
    .
    .
}
```

This function takes as a parameter a two-dimensional array of an unspecified number of rows, but `5` columns. During the function call, the number of columns of the actual parameter must match the number of columns of the formal parameter.

Arrays of Strings

Suppose that you need to perform an operation, such as alphabetizing a list of names. Because every name is a string, a convenient way to store the list of names is to use an array. Strings in C++ can be manipulated using either the data type `string` or character arrays (`C`-strings). Also, on some compilers, the data type `string` may not be available in Standard C++ (that is, non-ANSI/ISO Standard C++). This section illustrates both ways to manipulate a list of strings.

Arrays of Strings and the `string` Type

Processing a list of strings using the data type `string` is straightforward. Suppose that the list consists of a maximum of 100 names. You can declare an array of 100 components of the type `string` as follows:

```
string list[100];
```

Basic operations, such as assignment, comparison, and input/output, can be performed on values of the `string` type. Therefore, the data in `list` can be processed just like any one-dimensional array discussed in Chapter 9 and in the first part of this chapter.

Arrays of Strings and C-Strings (Character Arrays)

Suppose that the largest string (for example, name) in your list is 15 characters long and your list has 100 strings. You can declare a two-dimensional array of 100 rows and 16 columns as follows (see Figure 10-40):

```
char list[100][16];
```

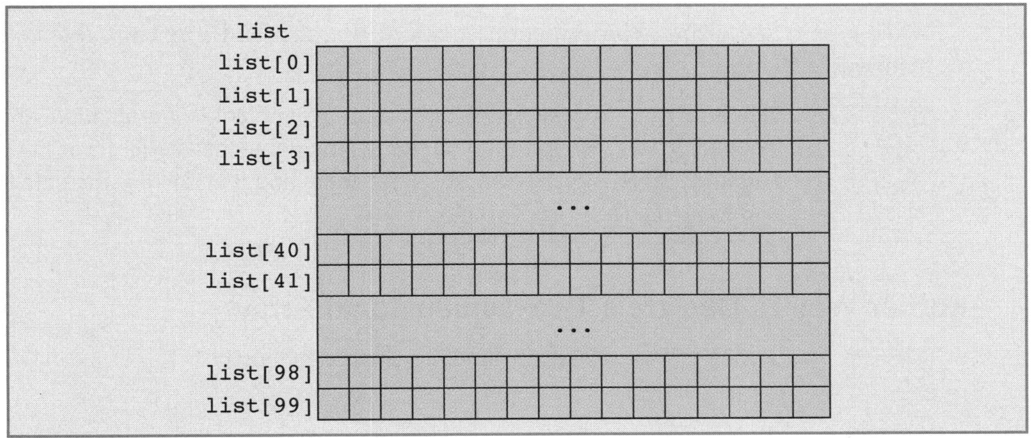

Figure 10-40 Array `list` of strings

Now `list[j]` for each `j, 0 <= j <= 99`, is a string of at most `15` characters in length. The following statement stores `"Snow White"` in `list[1]` (see Figure 10-41):

```
strcpy(list[1], "Snow White");
```

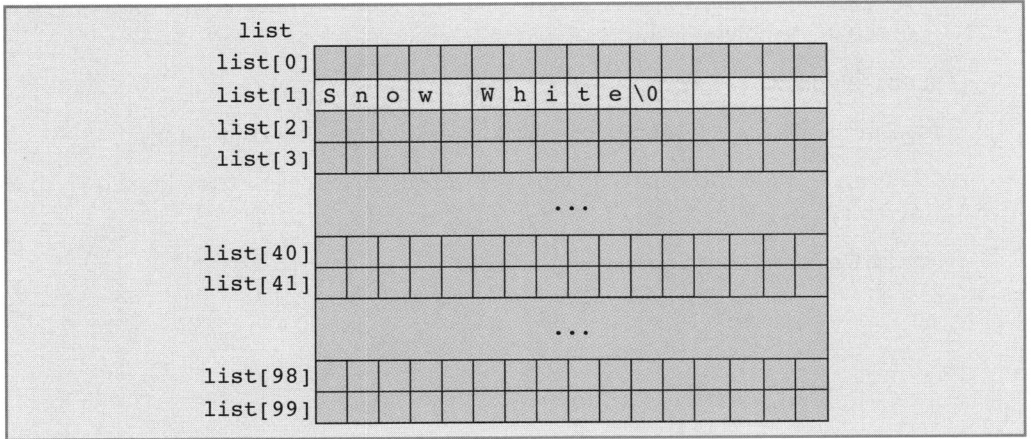

Figure 10-41 Array `list`, showing `list[1]`

Suppose that you want to read and store data in **list** and that there is one entry per line. The following **for** loop accomplishes this task:

```
for(j = 0; j < 100; j++)
    cin.get(list[j],16);
```

The following **for** loop outputs the string in each row:

```
for(j = 0; j < 100; j++)
    cout<<list[j]<<endl;
```

You can also use other string functions (such as **strcmp** and **strlen**) and **for** loops to manipulate **list**.

The data type `string` has operations such as assignment, concatenation, and relational operations defined for it. If you use Standard C++ header files and the data type `string` is available on your compiler, we recommend that you use the data type `string` to manipulate lists of strings.

Another Way to Declare a Two-Dimensional Array

This section may be skipped without any loss of continuity.

If you know the size of the tables with which the program will be working, then you can use **typedef** to first define a two-dimensional array data type and then declare variables of that type. For example, consider the following:

```
const int numberOfRows = 20;
const int numberOfColumns = 10;

typedef int tableType[numberOfRows][numberOfColumns];
```

The previous statement defines a two-dimensional array data type **tableType**. Now we can declare variables of this type. So

```
tableType matrix;
```

declares a two-dimensional array **matrix** of **20** rows and **10** columns.

You can also use this data type when declaring formal parameters, as shown in the following code:

```
void initialize(tableType table)
{
      int row;
      int col;
```

```
      for(row = 0; row < numberOfRows; row++)
         for(col = 0; col < numberOfColumns; col++)
            table[row][col] = 0;
}
```

This function takes as an argument any variable of the type **tableType**, which is a two-dimensional array, and initializes the array to 0.

By first defining a data type, you do not need to keep checking the exact number of columns when you declare a two-dimensional array as a variable or formal parameter, or when you pass an array as a parameter during a function call.

MULTIDIMENSIONAL ARRAYS

Chapter 9 defined an array as a collection of a fixed number of elements (called components) of the same type. A one-dimensional array is an array in which the elements are arranged in a list form; in a two-dimensional array, the elements are arranged in a table form. We can also define three-dimensional or larger arrays. In C++, there is no limit on the dimension of arrays. Following is the general definition of an array.

Array: A collection of a fixed number of elements (called components) arranged in n dimensions (n >= 1), called an **n-dimensional** array.

10

The general syntax for declaring an n-dimensional array is

```
dataType arrayName[intExp1][intExp2] ... [intExpn];
```

where **intExp1**, **intExp2**, **...** , and **intExpn** are constant expressions yielding positive integer values.

The syntax to access a component of an n-dimensional array is

```
arrayName[indexExp1][indexExp2] ... [indexExpn]
```

where **indexExp1**,**indexExp2**, **...**, and **indexExpn** are expressions yielding non-negative integer values. **indexExpi** gives the position of the array component in the ith dimension.

For example, the statement

```
double carDealers[10][5][7];
```

declares **carDealers** to be a three-dimensional array. The size of the first dimension is 10, the size of the second dimension is 5, and the size of the third dimension is 7. The first dimension ranges from 0 to 9, the second dimension ranges from 0 to 4, and the third dimension ranges from 0 to 6. The base address of the array **carDealers** is the address of the first array component—that is, the address of **carDealers**[0][0][0]. The total number of components in the array **carDealers** is 10*5*7 = 350.

The statement

```
carDealers[5][3][2] = 15564.75;
```

sets the value of the component `carDealers[5][3][2]` to `15564.75`.

You can use loops to process multidimensional arrays. For example, the nested **`for`** loops

```
for(i = 0; i < 10; i++)
   for(j = 0; j < 5; j++)
      for(k = 0; k < 7; k++)
          carDealers[i][j][k] = 0.0;
```

initialize the entire array to `0.0`.

When declaring a multidimensional array as a formal parameter in a function, you can omit the size of the first dimension but not the other dimensions. As parameters, multidimensional arrays are passed by reference only, and a function cannot return a value of the array type. There is no check to determine whether the array indices are within bounds.

PROGRAMMING EXAMPLE: ELECTION RESULTS

The presidential election for the student council of your local university will be held soon. For reasons related to confidentiality, the chair of the election committee wants to computerize the voting. The chair is looking for someone to write a program to analyze the data and report the winner. Let us write a program to help the election committee.

The university has four major divisions, and each division has several departments. For the purpose of the election, the four divisions are labeled as Region 1, Region 2, Region 3, and Region 4. Each department in each division manages its own voting process and directly reports the votes received by each candidate to the election committee. The voting is reported in the following form:

```
candidate_name region# number_of_votes_for_this_candidate
```

The election committee wants the output in the following tabular form:

```
          -------------Election Results-------------

Candidate                          Votes
Name         Region1   Region2   Region3   Region4    Total
---------    -------   -------   -------   -------   ------
Balto              0         0         0       272      272
Doc               25        71       156        97      349
.
.
.

Winner: ???,  Votes Received: ???
Total votes polled: ???
```

The names of the candidates in the output must be in alphabetical order.

For this program, we assume that six candidates seek the student council's president post. This program can be enhanced to include any number of candidates.

The data is provided in two files. One file, `candData.txt`, consists of the names of candidates seeking the president's post. The names of the candidates in the file are in no particular order. In the second file, `voteData.txt`, each line consists of the voting results in the following form:

```
candidateName regionNumber numberOfVotesForThisCandidate
```

That is, each line in the file `voteData.txt` consists of the candidate's name, region number, and the number of votes received by that candidate in the region. There is one entry per line. For example, the input file, containing the voting data, looks like

```
Donald 1 23
Pluto 2 56
Doc 1 25
Pluto 4 23
.
.
.
```

The first line indicates that `Donald` received `23` votes from Region `1`.

Input Two files, one containing the candidates' names and the other containing the voting data as described previously.

Output Election results in a tabular form as described previously, and the winner.

Problem Analysis and Algorithm Design

From the output, it is clear that the program must organize the voting data by region. The program must also calculate the total number of votes received by each candidate as well as the total votes cast in the election. Furthermore, the names of the candidates must appear in alphabetical order.

Because the data type of a candidate's name (which is a string) and the data type of the number of votes (which is an integer) are different, we need two separate arrays—one to hold the candidates' names and one to hold the voting data. The array to hold the names of the candidates is a one-dimensional array, and each component of this array is a string. Instead of using a single two-dimensional array to hold the voting data, we will use a two-dimensional array to hold the next four columns of the output (that is, the votes by region data) and a one-dimensional array to hold the total votes received by each candidate. These three arrays are parallel arrays (see Figure 10-42).

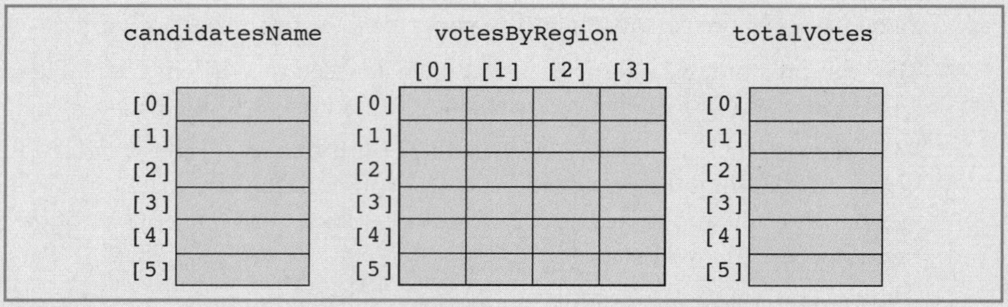

candidatesName		votesByRegion [0]	[1]	[2]	[3]	totalVotes
[0]		[0]				[0]
[1]		[1]				[1]
[2]		[2]				[2]
[3]		[3]				[3]
[4]		[4]				[4]
[5]		[5]				[5]

Figure 10-42 Parallel arrays: `candidatesNames`, `votesByRegion`, and `totalVotes`

The data in the first row of these three arrays corresponds to the candidate whose name is stored in the first row of the array `Candidate Name`, and so on. In the voting by region array, column 1 corresponds to Region 1, column 2 corresponds to Region 2, and so on. Recall that, in C++, an array index starts at `0`. Therefore, if the name of this array in the program is `votesByRegion`, then `votesByRegion[][0]` refers to the first column and thus Region 1, and so on.

For easy reference, for the rest of this discussion suppose that in the program that we are writing, the name of the candidates' names array is `candidatesName`, the name of the voting totals by region array is `votesByRegion`, and the name of the total votes array is `totalVotes`.

The first thing that we must do in this program is read the candidates' names from the input file `candData.txt` into the array `candidatesName`. Once the candidates' names are stored in the array `candidatesName`, we must sort this array.

Next, we must process the voting data. Every entry in the file `voteData.txt` contains a `candidateName`, `regionNumber`, and `votesReceivedByTheCandidate`. To process each entry, we find the appropriate entry in the array `votesByRegion` and update it by adding `votesReceivedByTheCandidate` to this entry. Therefore, it follows that array `votesByRegion` must be initialized to zero. (Processing voting data is described in detail later in this section.)

After processing the voting data, the next step is to calculate the total votes received by each candidate. This task is accomplished by adding the votes received in each region. Therefore, we must initialize the array `totalVotes` to zero. Finally, we output the results as shown earlier.

This discussion translates into the following algorithm:

1. Read the candidates' names into the array `candidatesName`.
2. Sort the array `candidatesName`.
3. Initialize the arrays `votesByRegion` and `totalVotes`.

4. Process the voting data.
5. Calculate the total votes received by each candidate.
6. Output the results.

Because the input data is provided in two separate files, in this program we must open two files. We open both input files in the function `main`.

To implement the six steps of the algorithm, this program consists of several functions, as described next.

Function `getCandidatesName` This function reads data from the input file `candData.txt` and fills the array `candidatesName`. The input file is opened in the function `main`. We see that this function has three parameters: a parameter corresponding to the input file, a parameter corresponding to the array `candidatesName`, and a parameter to pass the number of rows of the array `candidatesName`. Essentially, this function is

```
void getCandidatesName(ifstream& inp, string cNames[], int noOfRows)
{
      int i;

      for(i = 0; i < noOfRows; i++)
          inp>>cNames[i];            //read candidate_name
}
```

After a call to this function, the arrays to hold the data are as shown in Figure 10-43.

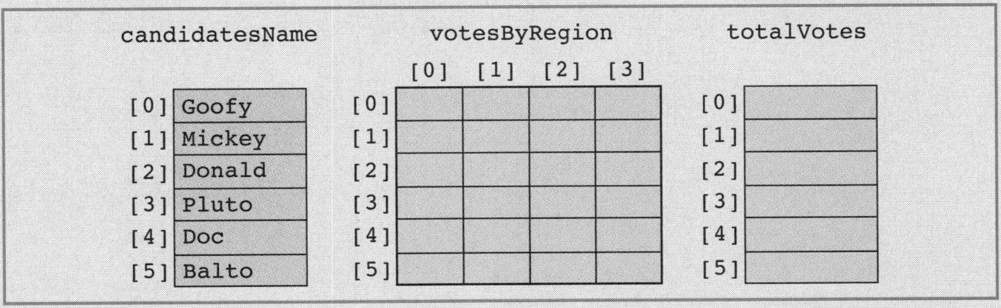

candidatesName
[0] Goofy
[1] Mickey
[2] Donald
[3] Pluto
[4] Doc
[5] Balto

votesByRegion
[0] [1] [2] [3]
[0]
[1]
[2]
[3]
[4]
[5]

totalVotes
[0]
[1]
[2]
[3]
[4]
[5]

Figure 10-43 Arrays `candidatesNames`, `votesByRegion`, and `totalVotes` after reading candidates' names

Function `sortCandidatesName` This function uses the selection sort algorithm to sort the array `candidatesName`. This function has two parameters: a parameter corresponding to the array `candidatesName` and a parameter to pass the number of rows of the array `candidatesName`. Essentially, this function is

```
void sortCandidatesName(string cNames[], int noOfRows)
{
      int i, j;
      int min;

            //selection sort
      for(i = 0; i < noOfRows - 1; i++)
      {
            min = i;

            for(j = i + 1; j < noOfRows; j++)
                  if(cNames[j] < cNames[min])
                        min = j;

            cNames[i].swap(cNames[min]);
    }
}
```

After a call to this function, the arrays are as shown in Figure 10-44.

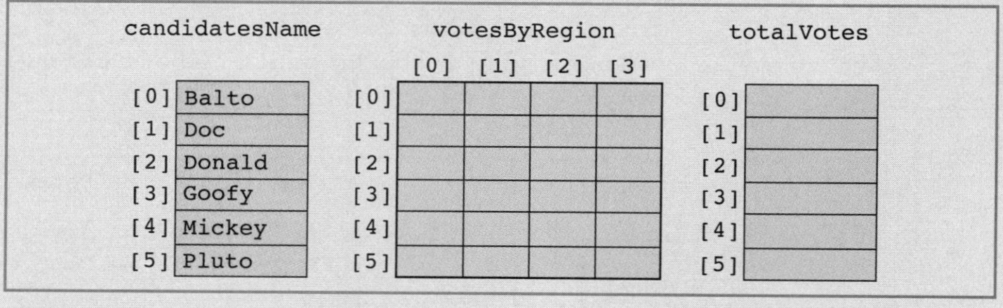

	candidatesName		votesByRegion [0]	[1]	[2]	[3]		totalVotes
[0]	Balto	[0]					[0]	
[1]	Doc	[1]					[1]	
[2]	Donald	[2]					[2]	
[3]	Goofy	[3]					[3]	
[4]	Mickey	[4]					[4]	
[5]	Pluto	[5]					[5]	

Figure 10-44 Arrays `candidatesNames`, `votesByRegion`, and `totalVotes` after sorting names

Function `initialize` The function `initialize` initializes the arrays `votesByRegion` and `totalVotes` to zero. This function must have three parameters: a parameter corresponding to the array `votesByRegion`, a parameter corresponding to the array `totalVotes`, and a parameter to pass the number of rows of the array `votesByRegion`. Note that both arrays have the same number of rows. The definition of this function is

```
void initialize(int vbRegion[][noOfRegions], int tVotes[],
                int noOfRows)
{
      int i,j;
```

```
    for(i = 0; i < noOfRows; i++)
        for(j = 0; j < noOfRegions; j++)
            vbRegion[i][j] = 0;

    for(i = 0; i < noOfRows; i++)
        tVotes[i] = 0;
}
```

After a call to this function, the arrays `votesByRegion` and `totalVotes` are as shown in Figure 10-45.

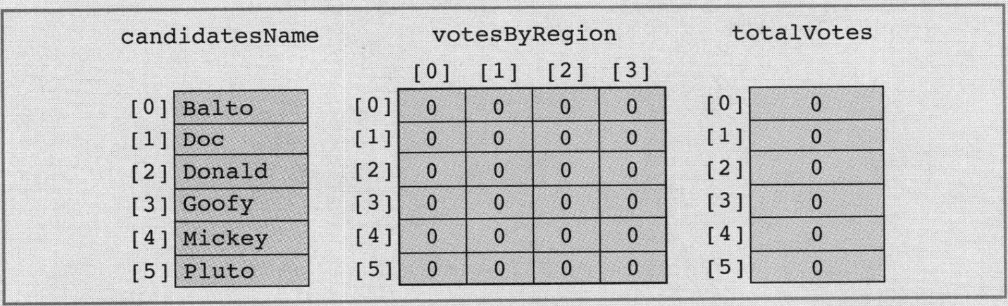

candidatesName		votesByRegion	[0]	[1]	[2]	[3]	totalVotes	
[0]	Balto	[0]	0	0	0	0	[0]	0
[1]	Doc	[1]	0	0	0	0	[1]	0
[2]	Donald	[2]	0	0	0	0	[2]	0
[3]	Goofy	[3]	0	0	0	0	[3]	0
[4]	Mickey	[4]	0	0	0	0	[4]	0
[5]	Pluto	[5]	0	0	0	0	[5]	0

Figure 10-45 Arrays `candidatesNames`, `votesByRegion`, and `totalVotes` after initialization

Process Voting Data Processing voting data is quite straightforward. Each entry in the file `voteData.txt` is in the following form

`candidateName regionNumber numberOfVotesForThisCandidate`

The general algorithm to process the voting data is shown next. For each entry in the file `voteData.txt`, we do the following:

a. Get a `candidateName`, `regionNumber`, and `numberOfVotesForTheCandidate`.
b. Find the row number in the array `candidatesName` corresponding to this candidate. This gives the corresponding row number in the array `votesByRegion` for this candidate.
c. Find the column in the array `votesByRegion` corresponding to the `regionNumber`.
d. Update the appropriate entry in the array `votesByRegion` by adding the `numberOfVotesForTheCandidate`.

Step b requires us to search the array `candidatesName` to find the location (that is, row number) of a particular candidate. Because the array `candidatesName` is sorted, we can use the binary search algorithm to find the row number corresponding to a particular candidate. Therefore, the program also includes a function, **binSearch**, to implement the binary search algorithm on the array **candidatesName**. We will write the definition of the function **binSearch** shortly. First, let us discuss how to update the array **votesByRegion**.

Suppose that the three arrays are as shown in Figure 10-46.

candidatesName

[0]	Balto
[1]	Doc
[2]	Donald
[3]	Goofy
[4]	Mickey
[5]	Pluto

votesByRegion

	[0]	[1]	[2]	[3]
[0]	0	0	50	0
[1]	10	0	56	0
[2]	76	13	0	0
[3]	0	45	0	0
[4]	80	0	78	0
[5]	100	0	0	20

totalVotes

[0]	0
[1]	0
[2]	0
[3]	0
[4]	0
[5]	0

Figure 10-46 Arrays candidatesNames, votesByRegion, and totalVotes

Further suppose that the next entry read from the input file is

```
Donald 2 35
```

We must locate the row in the grid that corresponds to this candidate. To find the row, we search the array **candidatesName** to find the row that corresponds to this name. **Donald** corresponds to row number 2 in the array **candidatesName**. (See Figure 10-47.)

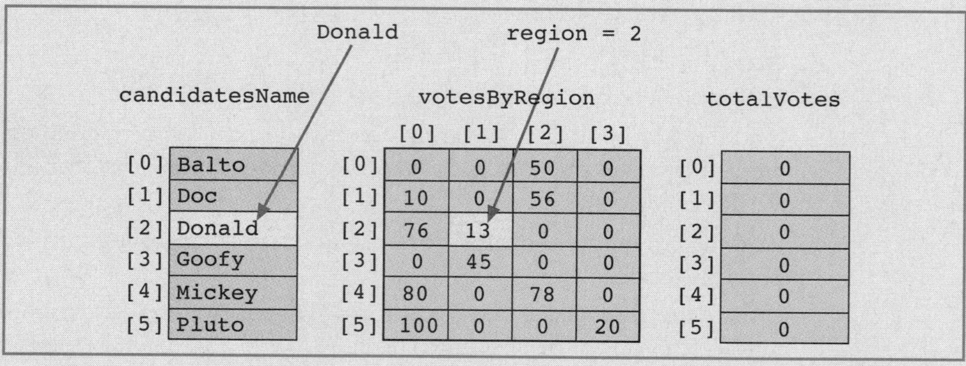

Figure 10-47 Position of Donald and region = 2

To process this entry, we access row number `2` of the array `votesByRegion`. Because `Donald` received `35` votes from Region 2, we access row `2` and column number `1` (that is, `votesByRegion[2][1]`) and update this entry by adding `35` to its previous value. The following statement accomplishes this task:

```
votesByRegion[2][1] = votesByRegion[2][1] + 35;
```

After processing this entry, the three arrays are as shown in Figure 10-48.

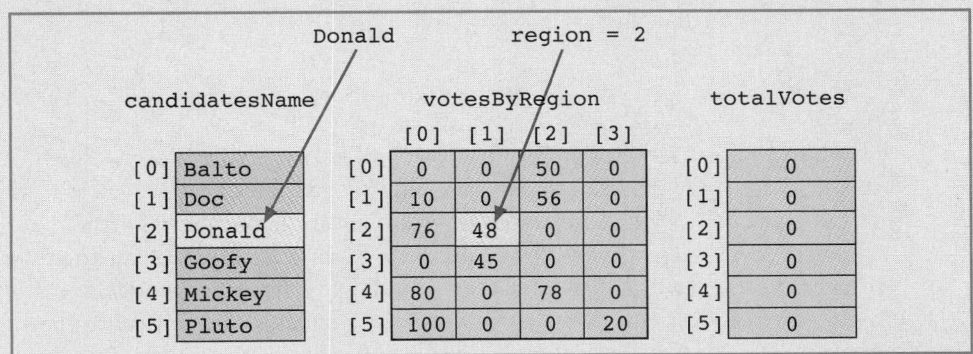

Figure 10-48 Arrays `candidatesName`, `votesByRegion`, and `totalVotes` after processing the entry `Donald 2 35`

Next, we describe the function `binSearch` and the function `processVotes` to process the voting data.

Function `binSearch` This function implements the binary search algorithm on the array `candidatesName`. It is similar to the function `binarySearch` discussed earlier in this chapter. Its definition is

```
int binSearch(string cNames[], int noOfRows, string name)
{
      int first, last, mid;
      bool found;

      first = 0;
      last = noOfRows - 1;
      found = false;

      while(!found && first <= last)
      {
            mid = (first + last) / 2;
```

```
            if(cNames[mid] == name)
                found = true;
            else
                if(cNames[mid] > name)
                    last = mid - 1;
                else
                    first = mid + 1;
        }

        if(found)
           return mid;
        else
           return -1;
}
```

Function processVotes This function processes the voting data. Clearly, it must have access to the arrays `candidatesName` and `votesByRegion`, as well as to the input file, `voteData.txt`. We also need to tell this function the number of rows in each array. Thus, the function `processVotes` has four parameters: a parameter to access the input file `voteData.txt`, a parameter corresponding to the array `candidatesName`, a parameter corresponding to the array `votesByRegion`, and a parameter to pass the number of rows in each array. The definition of this function is

```
void processVotes(ifstream& inp, string cNames[],
                  int vbRegion[][noOfRegions], int noOfRows)
{
   string candName;
   int region;
   int noOfVotes;
   int loc;

   inp>>candName>>region>>noOfVotes;                 //Step a
   while(inp)
   {
      loc = binSearch(cNames,noOfRows,candName);     //Step b
      if(loc != -1)
         vbRegion[loc][region - 1] = vbRegion[loc][region - 1]
                                     + noOfVotes;    //Steps c and d
      inp>>candName>>region>>noOfVotes;              //Step a
   }
}
```

Calculate Total Votes (Function addRegionsVote) After processing the voting data, the next step is to calculate the total votes for each candidate. Suppose after processing the voting data the arrays are as shown in Figure 10-49.

	candidatesName		votesByRegion [0]	[1]	[2]	[3]		totalVotes
[0]	Balto	[0]	0	0	0	272	[0]	0
[1]	Doc	[1]	25	71	156	97	[1]	0
[2]	Donald	[2]	110	158	0	0	[2]	0
[3]	Goofy	[3]	0	34	0	0	[3]	0
[4]	Mickey	[4]	112	141	156	89	[4]	0
[5]	Pluto	[5]	285	56	0	46	[5]	0

Figure 10-49 Arrays `candidatesName`, `votesByRegion`, and `totalVotes` after processing the voting data

After calculating the total votes received by each candidate, the three arrays are as shown in Figure 10-50.

	candidatesName		votesByRegion [0]	[1]	[2]	[3]		totalVotes
[0]	Balto	[0]	0	0	0	272	[0]	272
[1]	Doc	[1]	25	71	156	97	[1]	349
[2]	Donald	[2]	110	158	0	0	[2]	268
[3]	Goofy	[3]	0	34	0	0	[3]	34
[4]	Mickey	[4]	112	141	156	89	[4]	498
[5]	Pluto	[5]	285	56	0	46	[5]	387

Figure 10-50 Arrays `candidatesName`, `votesByRegion`, and `totalVotes` after calculating total votes received by each candidate

To calculate the total votes received by each candidate, we add the contents of each row in the `votesByRegion` array and store the sum in the corresponding row in the `totalVotes` array. This task is accomplished by the function `addRegionsVote`.

The function `addRegionsVote` calculates the number of total votes received by each candidate. This function must access the arrays `votesByRegion` and `totalVotes`. Also, we must tell this function the number of rows in each array. The function has three parameters: a parameter corresponding to the array **votesByRegion**, a parameter corresponding to the array **totalVotes**, and a parameter to pass the number of rows in each array. The definition of this function is

```
void addRegionsVote(int vbRegion[][noOfRegions], int tVotes[],
                    int noOfRows)
{
      int i,j;

      for(i = 0; i < noOfRows; i ++)
          for(j = 0; j < noOfRegions; j++)
              tVotes[i] = tVotes[i] + vbRegion[i][j];
}
```

We now describe the remaining functions required to get the desired output.

Function printHeading This function outputs the first four lines of input, so it contains certain output statements. The definition of this function is

```
void printHeading()
{
   cout<<"      --------------Election Results--------------"
      <<endl<<endl;
   cout<<"Candidate                     Votes"<<endl;
   cout<<"Name         Region1   Region2   Region3    "
      <<"Region4    Total"<<endl;
   cout<<"---------  -------    -------   -------  -------    "
      <<"------"<<endl;
}
```

Function printResults This function outputs the remaining lines of the output. Clearly, it must have access to each of the three arrays. We must also tell the function the number of rows in each array. (Note that each array has the same number of rows.) Thus, this function has four parameters. Suppose that the parameter **cName** corresponds to **candidatesName**, the parameter **vbRegion** corresponds to **votesByRegion**, and the parameter **tVotes** corresponds to **totalVotes**.

Further suppose that the variable **sumVotes** holds the number of total votes cast in the election, the variable **largestVotes** holds the largest number of votes received by a candidate, and the variable **winLoc** holds the index of the winning candidate in the array **candidatesName**. The algorithm for this function is

i. Initialize **sumVotes**, **largestVotes**, and **winLoc** to 0.

ii. For each row in each array

   a.
   ```
   if(largestVotes < tVotes[i])
   {
       largestVotes = tVotes[i];
       winLoc = i;
   }
   ```

b. `sumVotes = sumVotes + tVotes[i];`

c. Output the data from the corresponding rows of each array.

iii. Output the final lines of output.

The definition of this function is

```
void printResults(string cNames[], int vbRegion[][noOfRegions],
                  int tVotes[], int noOfRows)
{
     int i, j;
     int largestVotes = 0;                    //Step i
     int winLoc = 0;                          //Step i
     int sumVotes = 0;                        //Step i

     for(i = 0; i < noOfRows; i++)            //Step ii
     {
          if(largestVotes < tVotes[i])        //Step ii.a
          {
               largestVotes = tVotes[i];
               winLoc = i;
          }

          sumVotes = sumVotes + tVotes[i];        //Step ii.b

                    //Step ii.c
          cout<<left;                //output name left justified
          cout<<setw(9)<<cNames[i]<<"  ";
          cout<<right;
          for(j = 0; j < noOfRegions; j++)
               cout<<setw(8)<<vbRegion[i][j]<<"  ";
          cout<<setw(6)<<tVotes[i]<<endl;
     }
               //Step iii
     cout<<endl<<endl<<"Winner: "<<cNames[winLoc]
         <<",  Votes Received: "<<tVotes[winLoc]<<endl<<endl;
     cout<<"Total votes polled: "<<sumVotes<<endl;
}
```

We now give the main algorithm.

Suppose that the variables in the function `main` are

```
string candidatesName[noOfCandidates]; //array to store
                                       //candidate's name
int votesByRegion[noOfCandidates][noOfRegions]; //array to hold
                                                //voting data by region
int totalVotes[noOfCandidates];  //array to hold total votes
                                 //received by each candidate

ifstream infile;  //input file variable
```

Furthermore, suppose that the candidates' names are in the file **candData.txt** and the voting data is in the file **voteData.txt**.

Main Algorithm: Function main

1. Declare the variables.
2. Open the input file **candData.txt**.
3. If the input file does not exist, exit the program.
4. Read the data from the file **candData.txt** into the array **candidatesName**.
5. Sort the array **candidatesName**.
6. Close the file **candData.txt**.
7. Open the input file **voteData.txt**.
8. If the input file does not exist, exit the program.
9. Initialize the arrays **votesByRegion** and **totalVotes**.
10. Process the voting data and store the results in the array **votesByRegion**.
11. Calculate the number of total votes received by each candidate and store the results in the array **totalVotes**.
12. Print the heading.
13. Print the results.

Complete Program Listing

```
#include <iostream>
#include <fstream>
#include <string>
#include <iomanip>

using namespace std;

const int noOfCandidates = 6;
const int noOfRegions = 4;

void printHeading();
void initialize(int vbRegion[][noOfRegions], int tVotes[],
                int noOfRows);
void getCandidatesName(ifstream& inp, string cNames[],
                       int noOfRows);
void sortCandidatesName(string cNames[], int noOfRows);
int binSearch(string cNames[], int noOfRows, string name);
void processVotes(ifstream& inp, string cNames[],
                  int vbRegion[][noOfRegions], int noOfRows);
void addRegionsVote(int vbRegion[][noOfRegions], int tVotes[],
                    int noOfRows);

void printResults(string cNames[], int vbRegion[][noOfRegions],
                  int tVotes[], int noOfRows);
```

```
int main()
{
            //Declare variables; Step 1
   string candidatesName[noOfCandidates];
   int votesByRegion[noOfCandidates][noOfRegions];
   int totalVotes[noOfCandidates];
   ifstream infile;

   infile.open("a:candData.txt");                           //Step 2
   if(!infile)                                              //Step 3
   {
      cout<<"Input file (candData.txt) does not exit."<<endl;
      return 1;
   }

   getCandidatesName(infile, candidatesName,
                     noOfCandidates);                       //Step 4
   sortCandidatesName(candidatesName,noOfCandidates);       //Step 5

   infile.close();                                          //Step 6

   infile.open("a:voteData.txt");                           //Step 7
   if(!infile)                                              //Step 8
   {
      cout<<"Input file (voteData.txt) does not exit."<<endl;
      return 1;
   }

   initialize(votesByRegion, totalVotes, noOfCandidates); //Step 9
   processVotes(infile, candidatesName, votesByRegion,
                noOfCandidates);                            //Step 10
   addRegionsVote(votesByRegion, totalVotes,
                  noOfCandidates);                          //Step 11

   printHeading();                                          //Step 12
   printResults(candidatesName, votesByRegion,
            totalVotes, noOfCandidates);                    //Step 13

   return 0;
}

void initialize(int vbRegion[][noOfRegions], int tVotes[],
                int noOfRows)
{
     int i,j;

     for(i = 0; i < noOfRows; i++)
         for(j = 0; j < noOfRegions; j++)
             vbRegion[i][j] = 0;
```

```
    for(i = 0; i < noOfRows; i++)
        tVotes[i] = 0;
}

void getCandidatesName(ifstream& inp, string cNames[], int noOfRows)
{
    int i;

    for(i = 0; i < noOfRows; i++)
        inp>>cNames[i];
}

void sortCandidatesName(string cNames[], int noOfRows)
{
    int i, j;
    int min;

        //selection sort
    for(i = 0; i < noOfRows - 1; i++)
    {
        min = i;

        for(j = i + 1; j < noOfRows; j++)
            if(cNames[j] < cNames[min])
                min = j;

        cNames[i].swap(cNames[min]);
    }
}

int binSearch(string cNames[], int noOfRows, string name)
{
    int first, last, mid;
    bool found;
    first = 0;
    last = noOfRows - 1;
    found = false;

    while(!found && first <= last)
    {
        mid = (first + last) / 2;

        if(cNames[mid] == name)
           found = true;
        else
           if(cNames[mid] > name)
              last = mid - 1;
           else
```

```
                         first = mid + 1;
    }

    if(found)
       return mid;
    else
       return -1;
}

void processVotes(ifstream& inp, string cNames[],
                  int vbRegion[][noOfRegions], int noOfRows)
{
   string candName;
   int region;
   int noOfVotes;
   int loc;

   inp>>candName>>region>>noOfVotes;

   while(inp)
   {
     loc =  binSearch(cNames,noOfRows,candName);

     if(loc != -1)
        vbRegion[loc][region - 1] = vbRegion[loc][region - 1]
                                     + noOfVotes;
     inp>>candName>>region>>noOfVotes;
   }
}

void addRegionsVote(int vbRegion[][noOfRegions], int tVotes[],
                    int noOfRows)
{
     int i,j;

     for(i = 0; i < noOfRows; i ++)
         for(j = 0; j < noOfRegions; j++)
             tVotes[i] = tVotes[i] + vbRegion[i][j];
}

void printHeading()
{
   cout<<"      --------------Election Results--------------"
       <<endl<<endl;
   cout<<"Candidate                       Votes"<<endl;
   cout<<"Name        Region1   Region2   Region3   "
       <<"Region4    Total"<<endl;
   cout<<"---------   -------   -------   -------   -------   "
```

```
        <<"------"<<endl;
}

void printResults(string cNames[], int vbRegion[][noOfRegions],
                  int tVotes[], int noOfRows)
{
      int i, j;
      int largestVotes= 0;
      int winLoc = 0;
      int sumVotes = 0;

      for(i = 0; i < noOfRows; i++)
      {
            if(largestVotes < tVotes[i])
            {
                  largestVotes = tVotes[i];
                  winLoc = i;
            }

            sumVotes = sumVotes + tVotes[i];

            cout<<left;
            cout<<setw(9)<<cNames[i]<<"  ";
            cout<<right;
            for(j = 0; j < noOfRegions; j++)
                cout<<setw(8)<<vbRegion[i][j]<<"  ";
            cout<<setw(6)<<tVotes[i]<<endl;
      }

      cout<<endl<<endl<<"Winner: "<<cNames[winLoc]
          <<",  Votes Received: "<<tVotes[winLoc]<<endl<<endl;
      cout<<"Total votes polled: "<<sumVotes<<endl;
}
```

Sample Run:

```
      --------------Election Results--------------

Candidate                         Votes
Name        Region1   Region2   Region3   Region4    Total
---------   -------   -------   -------   -------   ------
Balto             0         0         0       272      272
Doc              25        71       156        97      349
Donald          110       158         0         0      268
Goofy             0        34         0         0       34
Mickey          112       141       156        89      498
Pluto           285        56         0        46      387
```

```
Winner: Mickey,  Votes Received: 498

Total votes polled: 1808
```

Input Files

candData.txt	**voteData.txt**
Goofy	Goofy 2 34
Mickey	Mickey 1 56
Donald	Donald 2 56
Pluto	Pluto 1 78
Doc	Doc 4 29
Balto	Balto 4 78
	Mickey 2 63
	Donald 1 23
	Pluto 2 56
	Doc 1 25
	Pluto 4 23
	Doc 4 12
	Balto 4 82
	Mickey 3 67
	Donald 2 67
	Doc 3 67
	Balto 4 23
	Mickey 1 56
	Donald 2 35
	Pluto 1 27
	Doc 2 34
	Pluto 4 23
	Mickey 4 89
	Pluto 1 23
	Doc 3 89
	Mickey 3 89
	Pluto 1 67
	Doc 2 37
	Balto 4 89
	Mickey 2 78
	Donald 1 87
	Pluto 1 90
	Doc 4 56

Quick Review

1. A list is a set of elements of the same type.
2. The length of a list is the number of elements in the list.
3. A one-dimensional array is a convenient place to store and process lists.

4. The sequential search algorithm searches a list for a given item starting with the first element in the list. It continues to compare the search item with the other elements in the list until either the item is found or the list has no more elements left to be compared with the search item.
5. On average, the sequential search searches half the list.
6. The sequential search is good only for very short lists.
7. The binary search is much faster than the sequential search.
8. The binary search requires that the list elements be in order—that is, sorted.
9. For a list of length `1024`, to determine whether an item is in the list, the binary search algorithm requires no more than 22 key comparisons.
10. The selection sort sorts the list by finding the smallest (or largest) element in the list and moving it to the beginning (end) of the list.
11. A two-dimensional array is an array in which the elements are arranged in a table form.
12. To access an element of a two-dimensional array, you need a pair of indices: one for the row position and one for the column position.
13. In a two-dimensional array, the rows are numbered `0` to `rowsize - 1` and the columns are numbered `0` to `columnsize - 1`.
14. If `matrix` is a two-dimensional array, then the base address of `matrix` is the address of the array component `matrix[0][0]`.
15. In row processing, a two-dimensional array is processed one row at a time.
16. In column processing, a two-dimensional array is processed one column at a time.
17. When declaring a two-dimensional array as a formal parameter, you can omit the size of the first dimension but not the second.
18. When a two-dimensional array is passed as an actual parameter, the number of columns of the actual and formal arrays must match.
19. C++ stores, in computer memory, two-dimensional arrays in a row order form.

EXERCISES

1. Mark the following statements as true or false.
   a. A sequential search of a list assumes that the list is in ascending order.
   b. A binary search of a list assumes that the list is in sorted order.
   c. A binary search is faster on ordered lists and slower on unordered lists.
   d. A binary search is faster on large lists, but a sequential search is faster on small lists.
   e. As parameters, two-dimensional arrays are passed either by value or by reference.

2. Consider the following list:

```
63 45 32 98 46 57 28 100
```

Using the sequential search, how many comparisons are required to determine whether the following items are in the list? (Recall that by "comparisons" we mean key comparisons, not index comparisons.)

a. `90`

b. `57`

c. `63`

d. `120`

3. Consider the following list:

```
5 12 17 35 46 65 78 85 93 110 115
```

Using the sequential search on ordered lists, how many comparisons are required to determine whether the following items are in the list? (Recall that by "comparisons" we mean key comparisons, not index comparisons.)

a. `35`

b. `60`

c. `78`

d. `120`

4. Consider the following list:

```
2 10 17 45 49 55 68 85 92 98 110
```

Using the binary search, how many key comparisons are required to determine whether the following items are in the list? Show the values of **`first`**, **`last`**, and **`middle`** and the number of key comparisons after each iteration of the loop.

a. `15`

b. `49`

c. `98`

d. `99`

5. Consider the following declarations:

```
const int carTypes = 5;
const int colorTypes = 6;

double sales[carTypes][colorTypes];
```

a. How many components does the array **`sales`** have?

b. What is the number of rows in the array **`sales`**?

c. What is the number of columns in the array **`sales`**?

d. To sum the sales by `carTypes`, what kind of processing is required?

e. To sum the sales by `colorTypes`, what kind of processing is required?

6. Write C++ statements that do the following:

   a. Declare an array `alpha` of `10` rows and `20` columns of the type `int`.

   b. Initialize the array `alpha` to `0`.

   c. Store `1` in the first row and `2` in the remaining rows.

   d. Store `5` in the first column, and make sure that the value in each remaining column is twice the value in the previous column.

   e. Print the array `alpha` one row per line.

   f. Print the array `alpha` one column per line.

7. Consider the following declaration:

```
int beta[3][3];
```

What is stored in `beta` after each of the following statements executes?

a.
```
for(i = 0; i < 3; i++)
    for(j = 0; j < 3; j++)
        beta[i][j] = 0;
```

b.
```
for(i = 0; i < 3; i++)
    for(j = 0; j < 3; j++)
        beta[i][j] = i + j;
```

c.
```
for(i = 0; i < 3; i++)
    for(j = 0; j < 3; j++)
        beta[i][j] = i * j;
```

d.
```
for(i = 0; i < 3; i++)
    for(j = 0; j < 3; j++)
        beta[i][j] =  2 * (i + j) % 4;
```

PROGRAMMING EXERCISES

1. Write a function, `remove`, that takes three parameters: an array of integers, the length of the array, and an integer (say, `removeItem`). The function should find and delete the first occurrence of `removeItem` in the array. If the value does not exist or the array is empty, output an appropriate message. (Note that after deleting the element, the array size is reduced by `1`.) Assume that the array is unsorted.

2. Write a function, `removeAt`, that takes three parameters: an array of integers, the length of the array, and an integer (say, `index`). The function should delete the array element indicated by `index`. If `index` is out of range or the array is empty, output an appropriate message. (Note that after deleting the element, the array size is reduced by `1`.) Assume that the array is unsorted.

3. Write a function, **removeAll**, that takes three parameters: an array of integers, the length of the array, and an integer (say, **removeItem**). The function should find and delete all occurrences of **removeItem** in the array. If the value does not exist or the array is empty, output an appropriate message. (Note that after deleting the element, the array size is reduced.) Assume that the array is unsorted.
4. Redo Exercises 1, 2, and 3 for a sorted array.
5. Write a function, **insertAt**, that takes four parameters: an array of integers, the length of the array, an integer (say, **insertItem**), and an integer (say, **index**). The function should insert **insertItem** in the array at the position specified by **index**. If **index** is out of range, output an appropriate message. (Note that **index** must be between **0** and **maxSize**; that is, **0 ≤ index < maxSize**.) Assume that the array is unsorted.
6. Consider the following function **main**:

```
int main()
{
    int inStock[10][4];
    int alpha[20];
    int beta[20];
    int gamma[4] = {11, 13, 15, 17};
    int delta[10] = {3, 5, 2, 6, 10, 9, 7, 11, 1, 8};

    .
    .
    .
}
```

a. Write the definition of the function **setZero** that initializes any one-dimensional array of the type **int** to **0**.

b. Write the definition of the function **inputArray** that prompts the user to input 20 numbers and stores the numbers into **alpha**.

c. Write the definition of the function **doubleArray** that initializes the elements of **beta** to two times the corresponding elements in **alpha**. Make sure that you prevent the function from modifying the elements of **alpha**.

d. Write the definition of the function **copyGamma** that sets the elements of the first row of **inStock** to **gamma** and the remaining rows of **inStock** to three times the previous row of **inStock**. Make sure that you prevent the function from modifying the elements of **gamma**.

e. Write the definition of the function **copyAlphaBeta** that stores **alpha** into the first five rows of **inStock** and **beta** into the last five rows of **inStock**. Make sure that you prevent the function from modifying the elements of **alpha** and **beta**.

f. Write the definition of the function **printArray** that prints any one-dimensional array of the type **int**. Print 15 elements per line.

g. Write the definition of the function **setInStock** that prompts the user to input the elements for the first column of **inStock**. The function should then set the elements in the remaining columns to two times the corresponding element in the previous column, minus the corresponding element in **delta**.

h. Write C++ statements that call each of the functions in parts a through g.

i. Write a C++ program that tests the function `main` and the functions discussed in parts a through g.

7. Write a program that uses a two-dimensional array to store the highest and lowest temperatures for each month of the year. The program should output the average high, average low, highest, and lowest temperatures of the year. Your program must consist of the following functions:

   a. Function `getData`: This function reads and stores data in the two-dimensional array.

   b. Function `averageHigh`: This function calculates and returns the average high temperature of the year.

   c. Function `averageLow`: This function calculates and returns the average low temperature of the year.

   d. Function `indexHighTemp`: This function returns the index of the highest high temperature in the array.

   e. Function `indexLowTemp`: This function returns the index of the lowest low temperature in the array.

   (These functions must all have the appropriate parameters.)

8. Write a program that reads in a set of positive integers and outputs how many times a particular number appears in the list. You may assume that the data set has at most 100 numbers and `-999` marks the end of the input data. The numbers must be output in increasing order. For example, for the data

```
15 40 28 62 95 15 28 13 62 65 48 95 65 62 65 95 95
```

   the output is:

```
Number    Count
13        1
15        2
28        2
40        1
48        1
62        3
65        3
95        4
```

9. **(Airplane Seating Assignment)** Write a program that can be used to assign seats for a commercial airplane. The airplane has 13 rows, with 6 seats in each row. Rows 1 and 2 are first class; the remaining rows are economy class. Also, rows 1 through 7 are nonsmoking. Your program must prompt the user to enter the following information:

   a. Ticket type (first class or economy class)

   b. For economy class, the smoking or nonsmoking section

   c. Desired seat

Output the seating plan in the following form:

```
        A    B    C    D    E    F
Row 1   *    *    X    *    X    X
Row 2   *    X    *    X    *    X
Row 3   *    *    X    X    *    X
Row 4   X    *    X    *    X    X
Row 5   *    X    *    X    *    *
Row 6   *    X    *    *    *    X
Row 7   X    *    *    *    X    X
Row 8   *    X    *    X    X    *
Row 9   X    *    X    X    *    X
Row 10  *    X    *    X    X    X
Row 11  *    *    X    *    X    *
Row 12  *    *    X    X    *    X
Row 13  *    *    *    *    X    *
```

Here, `*` indicates that the seat is available; `X` indicates that the seat is occupied. Make this a menu-driven program; show the user's choices and allow the user to make the appropriate choices.

10. **(Magic Square)**

a. Write a function `createArithmeticSeq` that prompts the user to input two numbers, `first` and `diff`. The function then creates a one-dimensional array of `16` elements ordered in an arithmetic sequence. It also outputs the arithmetic sequence. For example, if `first = 21` and `diff = 5`, the arithmetic sequence is `21 26 31 36 41 46 51 56 61 66 71 76 81 86 91 96.`

b. Write a function `matricize` that takes a one-dimensional array of 16 elements and a two-dimensional array of 4 rows and 4 columns as parameters. (Other values, such as the sizes of the arrays, must also be passed as parameters.) It puts the elements of the one-dimensional array into the two-dimensional array. For example, if A is the one-dimensional array created in part a and B is a two-dimensional array, then after putting the elements of A into B, the array B is

```
21 26 31 36
41 46 51 56
61 66 71 76
81 86 91 96
```

c. Write a function `reverseDiagonal` that reverses both the diagonals of a two-dimensional array. For example, if the two-dimensional array is as in part b, after reversing the diagonals, the two-dimensional array is

```
96 26 31 81
41 71 66 56
61 51 46 76
36 86 91 21
```

10

d. Write a function `magicCheck` that takes a one-dimensional array of size `16`, a two-dimensional array of `4` rows and `4` columns, and the sizes of the arrays as parameters. By adding all of the elements of the one-dimensional array and dividing by `4`, this function determines the `magicNumber`. The function then adds each row, each column, and each diagonal of the two-dimensional array and compares each sum with the magic number. If the sum of each row, each column, and each diagonal is equal to the `magicNumber`, the function outputs "`It is a magic square`"; otherwise, it outputs `"It is not a magic number"`. Do not print the sum of each row, each column, and the diagonals.

e. Write a function `printMatrix` that outputs the elements of a two-dimensional array, one row per line. This output should be as close to a square form as possible.

f. The functions written in parts a through e should be general enough to apply to an array of any size. (That is, the work should be done by using loops, not by merely plodding through and adding the necessary elements one at a time.) The function `magicCheck` works better if it calls two separate functions: one to add rows and columns and one to add the diagonals. (In this case, the program compares the magic number with each sum (row, column, and diagonal) in the respective function).

g. Test your functions written in parts a through e using the following function `main`:

```
const int rows = 4;
const int columns = 4;

const int listSize = 16;
...
int main()
{

      int list[listSize];
      int matrix[rows][columns];

      createArithmeticSeq(list, listSize);
      matricize(list, matrix, rows);
      printMatrix(matrix, rows);
      reverseDiagonal(matrix, rows);
      printMatrix(matrix, rows);
      magicCheck(list, matrix, listSize, rows);

      return 0;
}
```

CHAPTER

11

RECURSION

In this chapter, you will:

- Learn about recursive definitions
- Explore the base case and the general case of a recursive definition
- Discover what is a recursive algorithm
- Learn about recursive functions
- Explore how to use recursive functions to implement recursive algorithms

In previous chapters, to devise problem solutions we used the most common technique, called iteration. For certain problems, however, using the iterative technique to obtain the solution is quite complicated. This chapter introduces another problem-solving technique, called recursion, and provides several examples demonstrating how recursion works.

RECURSIVE DEFINITIONS

The process of solving a problem by reducing it to smaller versions of itself is called **recursion**. Recursion is a very powerful way to solve certain problems for which the solution would otherwise be very complicated. Let us consider a problem that is familiar to most everyone.

In mathematics, the factorial of an integer is defined as follows:

$$0! = 1 \qquad (11\text{-}1)$$

$$n! = n \times (n - 1)! \quad \text{if} \quad n > 0 \qquad (11\text{-}2)$$

In this definition, `0!` is defined to be `1`, and if n is an integer greater than `0`, first we find $(n - 1)!$ and then multiply it by n. To find $(n - 1)!$, we apply the definition again. If $(n - 1) > 0$, then we use Equation 11-2; otherwise, we use Equation 11-1. Thus, for an integer n greater than `0`, $n!$ is obtained by first finding $(n - 1)!$ (that is, $n!$ is reduced to a smaller version of itself) and then multiplying $(n - 1)!$ by n.

Let us apply this definition to find `3!`. Here $n = 3$. Because $n > 0$, we use Equation 11-2 to obtain

$$3! = 3 \times 2!$$

Next, we find `2!` Here $n = 2$. Because $n > 0$, we use Equation 11-2 to obtain

$$2! = 2 \times 1!$$

Now to find `1!`, we again use Equation 11-2 because $n = 1 > 0$. Thus

$$1! = 1 \times 0!$$

Finally, we use Equation 11-1 to find `0!`, which is `1`. Substituting `0!` into `1!` gives $1! = 1$. This gives $2! = 2 \times 1! = 2 \times 1 = 2$, which in turn gives $3! = 3 \times 2! = 3 \times 2 = 6$.

The solution in Equation 11-1 is direct—that is, the right side of the equation contains no factorial notation. The solution in Equation 11-2 is given in terms of a smaller version of itself. The definition of the factorial as given in Equations 11-1 and 11-2 is called a **recursive definition**. Equation 11-1 is called the **base case** (that is, the case for which the solution is obtained directly); Equation 11-2 is called the **general case**.

Recursive definition: A definition in which something is defined in terms of a smaller version of itself.

From the previous example (factorial), it is clear that:

1. Every recursive definition must have one (or more) base cases.
2. The general case must eventually be reduced to a base case.
3. The base case stops the recursion.

The concept of recursion in computer science works in a very similar fashion. Here we talk about recursive algorithms and recursive functions. An algorithm that finds the solution to a given problem by reducing the problem to smaller versions of itself is called a **recursive algorithm**. The recursive algorithm must have one or more base cases, and the general solution must eventually be reduced to a base case.

A function that calls itself is called a **recursive function**. That is, the body of the recursive function contains a statement that causes the same function to execute before completing the current call. Recursive algorithms are implemented using recursive functions.

Next, let us write the recursive function that implements the factorial function.

```
int fact(int num)
{
   if(num == 0)
      return 1;
   else
      return num * fact(num - 1);
}
```

Figure 11-1 traces the execution of the following statement:

```
cout<<fact(4)<<endl;
```

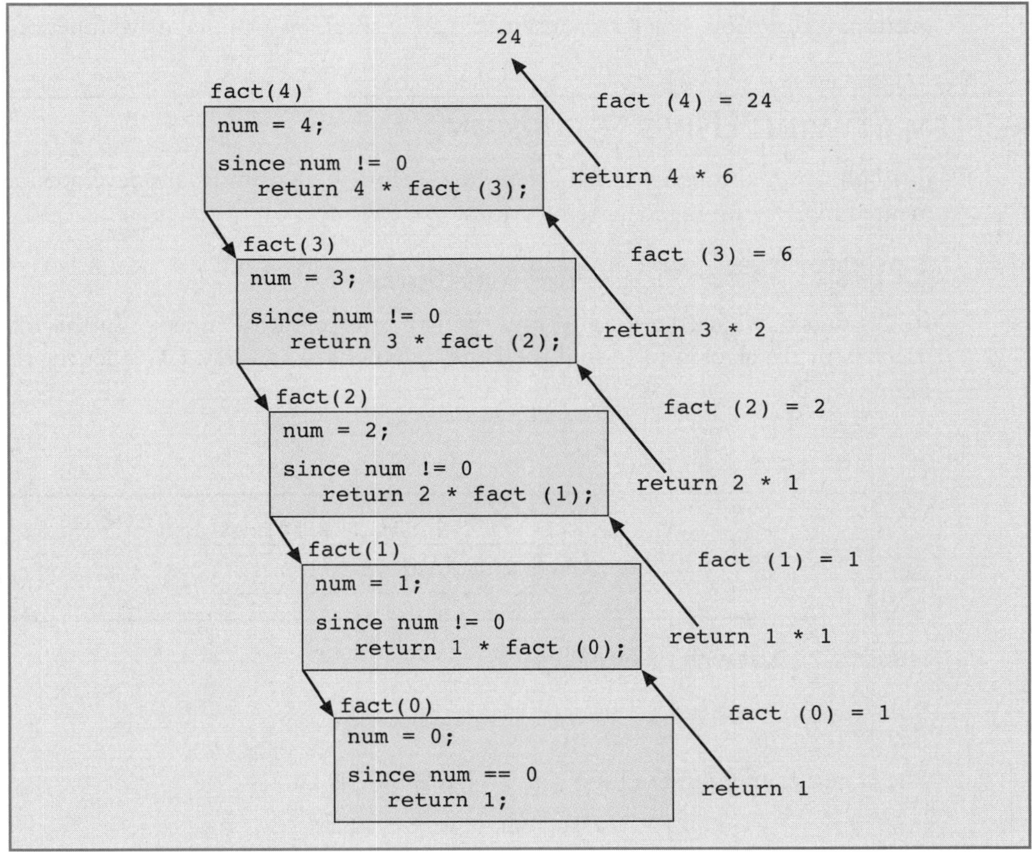

Figure 11-1 Execution of `fact (4)`

The output of the preceding `cout` statement is

```
24
```

In Figure 11-1, the down arrow represents the successive calls to the function `fact`, and the upward arrows represent the values returned to the caller, that is, the calling function.

Let us note the following from the preceding example, involving the factorial function:

- Logically, you can think of a recursive function as having infinitely many copies of itself.
- Every call to a recursive function—that is, every recursive call—has its own code and its own set of parameters and local variables.
- After completing a particular recursive call, the control goes back to the calling environment, which is the previous call. The current (recursive) call must execute completely before the control goes back to the previous call. The execution in the previous call begins from the point immediately following the recursive call.

A recursive function in which the last statement executed is the recursive call is called a **tail recursive function**. The function `fact` is an example of a tail recursive function.

PROBLEM SOLVING USING RECURSION

Examples 11-1 through 11-3 illustrate how recursive algorithms are developed and implemented in C++ using recursive functions.

Example 11-1: Largest Element in the Array

In Chapter 9, we used a loop to find the largest element in an array. In this example, we use a recursive algorithm to find the largest element in an array. Consider the list given in Figure 11-2.

	[0]	[1]	[2]	[3]	[4]	[5]	[6]
list	5	8	2	10	9	4	

Figure 11-2 List with six elements

The largest element in the list given in Figure 11-2 is `10`.

Suppose `list` is the name of the array containing the list elements. Also, suppose that `list[a]...list[b]` stands for the array elements `list[a]`, `list[a+1]`, `...`, `list[b]`. For example, `list[0]...list[5]` represents the array elements `list[0]`, `list[1]`, `list[2]`, `list[3]`, `list[4]`, and `list[5]`. Similarly, `list[1]...list[5]` represents the array elements `list[1]`, `list[2]`, `list[3]`, `list[4]`, and `list[5]`. To write a recursive algorithm to find the largest element in `list`, let us think in terms of recursion.

If `list` is of length `1`, then `list` has only one element, which is the largest element. Suppose the length of `list` is greater than `1`. To find the largest element in `list[a]...list[b]`, we first find the largest element in `list[a+1]...list[b]` and then compare this largest element with `list[a]`. That is, the largest element in `list[a]...list[b]` is given by

```
maximum(list[a], largest(list[a+1]...list[b]))
```

Let us apply this formula to find the largest element in the list shown in Figure 11-2. This list has six elements, given by `list[0]...list[5]`. Now the largest element in `list` is

```
maximum(list[0], largest(list[1]...list[5]))
```

That is, the largest element in `list` is the maximum of `list[0]` and the largest element in `list[1]...list[5]`. To find the largest element in `list[1]...list[5]`, we use the same formula again because the length of this list is greater than `1`. The largest element in `list[1]...list[5]` is then

11

```
maximum(list[1], largest(list[2]...list[5]))
```

and so on. We see that every time we use the preceding formula to find the largest element in a sublist, the length of the sublist in the next call is reduced by one. Eventually, the sublist is of length `1`, in which case the sublist contains only one element, which is the largest element in the sublist. From this point onward, we backtrack through the recursive calls. This discussion translates into the following recursive algorithm, which is presented in pseudocode:

```
if the size of the list is 1
   the only element in the list is the largest element
else
   to find the largest element in list[a]...list[b]
       a. find the largest element in list[a+1]...list[b] and call it
          max
```

```
b. compare the elements list[a] and max
    if(list[a] >= max)
        the largest element in list[a]...list[b] is list[a]
    otherwise
        the largest element in list[a]...list[b] is max
```

This algorithm translates into the following C++ function to find the largest element in an array:

```
int largest(const int list[], int lowerIndex, int upperIndex)
{
   int max;

   if(lowerIndex == upperIndex)   //size of the sublist is 1
      return list[lowerIndex];
   else
   {
     max = largest(list, lowerIndex + 1, upperIndex);
     if(list[lowerIndex] >= max)
        return list[lowerIndex];
     else
        return max;
   }
}
```

Consider the `list` given in Figure 11-3.

	[0]	[1]	[2]	[3]	[4]	[5]	[6]
list	5	10	12	8			

Figure 11-3 `list` with four elements

Let us trace the execution of the following statement:

```
cout<<largest(list,0,3);
```

Here `upperIndex = 3` and the list has four elements. Figure 11-4 traces the execution of `largest(list,0,3)`.

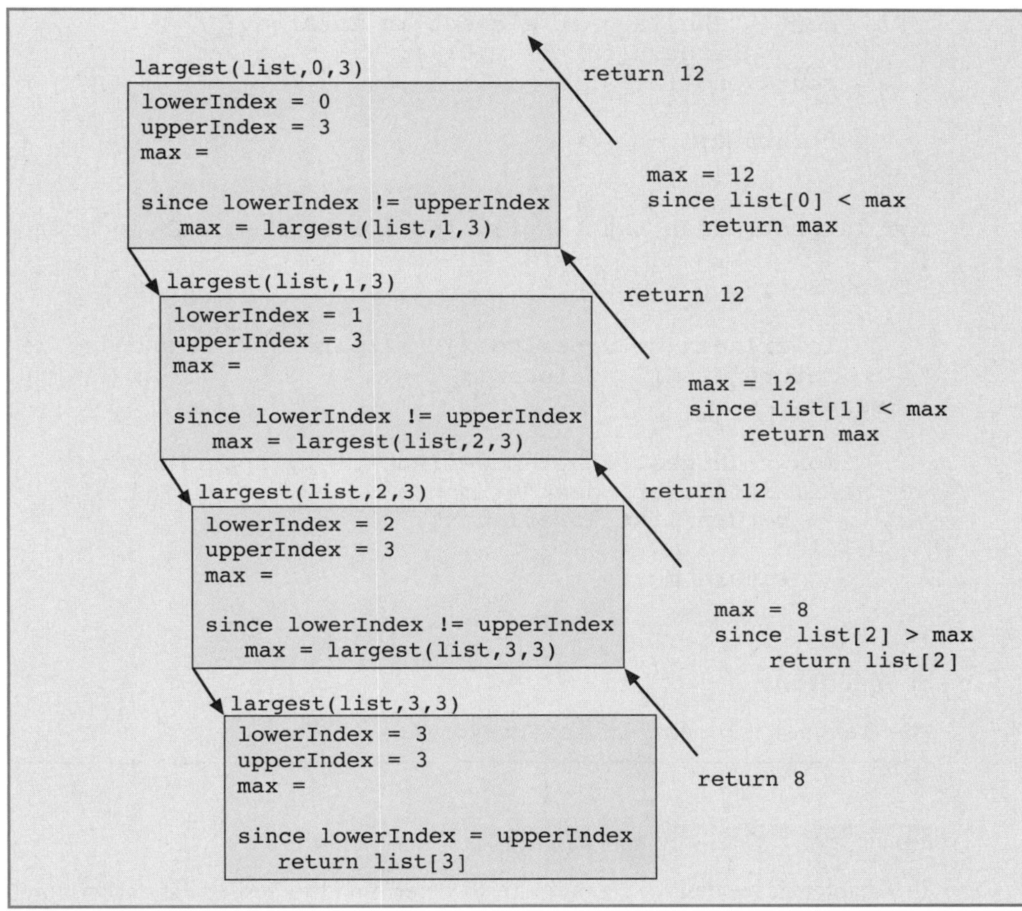

Figure 11-4 Execution of `largest (list,0,3)`

The value returned by the expression `largest(list,0,3)` is `12`, which is the largest element in `list`.

The following C++ program uses the function `largest` to determine the largest element in the list:

```
//Largest Element in an Array

#include <iostream>

using namespace std;

int largest(const int list[], int lowerIndex, int upperIndex);

int main()
{
      int intArray[10] = {23, 43, 35, 38, 67, 12, 76, 10, 34, 8};
```

```
      cout<<"The largest element in intArray: "
          <<largest(intArray,0,9);
      cout<<endl;

      return 0;
}

int largest(const int list[], int lowerIndex, int upperIndex)
{
   int max;

   if(lowerIndex == upperIndex)    //size of the sublist is 1
      return list[lowerIndex];
   else
   {
      max = largest(list, lowerIndex + 1, upperIndex);
      if(list[lowerIndex] >= max)
         return list[lowerIndex];
      else
         return max;
   }
}
```

Sample Run:

```
The largest element in intArray: 76
```

Example 11-2: Fibonacci Number

In Chapter 5, we designed a program to determine the desired Fibonacci number. In this example, we write a recursive function, **rFibNum**, to determine the desired Fibonacci number. The function **rFibNum** takes as parameters three numbers representing the first two numbers of the Fibonacci sequence and a number *n*, the desired *n*th Fibonacci number. The function **rFibNum** returns the *n*th Fibonacci number in the sequence.

Recall that the third Fibonacci number is the sum of the first two Fibonacci numbers. The fourth Fibonacci number in a sequence is the sum of the second and third Fibonacci numbers. Therefore, to calculate the fourth Fibonacci number, we add the second Fibonacci number and the third Fibonacci number (which is itself the sum of the first two Fibonacci numbers). The following recursive algorithm calculates the *n*th Fibonacci number, where *a* denotes the first Fibonacci number, *b* the second Fibonacci number, and *n* the *n*th Fibonacci number:

$$\text{rFibNum}(a,b,n) = \begin{cases} a & \text{if } n = 1 \\ b & \text{if } n = 2 \\ \text{rFibNum}(a,b,n-1) + \text{rFibNum}(a,b,n-2) & \text{if } n > 2. \end{cases} \qquad (11\text{-}3)$$

Suppose that we want to determine

`recFibNumber(2,5,4)`

Here a = `2`, b = `5`, and n = `4`. That is, we want to determine the fourth Fibonacci number of the sequence whose first number is `2` and whose second number is `5`. Because n is `4 > 2`,

1. `rFibNum(2,5,4) = rFibNum(2,5,3) + rFibNum(2,5,2)`

Next, we determine `rFibNum(2,5,3)` and `rFibNum(2,5,2)`. Let us first determine `rFibNum(2,5,3)`. Here, a = `2`, b = `5`, and n is `3`. Since n is `3`,

1.a `rFibNum(2,5,3) = rFibNum(2,5,2) + rFibNum(2,5,1)`

This statement requires us to determine `rFibNum(2,5,2)`and `rFibNum(2,5,1)`. In `rFibNum(2,5,2)`, a = `2`, b = `5`, and n = `2`. Therefore, from the definition given in Equation 11-3, it follows that

1.a.1 `rFibNum(2,5,2) = 5`

To find `rFibNum(2,5,1)`, note that a = `2`, b = `5`, and n = `1`. Therefore, by the definition given in Equation 11-3,

1.a.2 `rFibNum(2,5,1) = 2`

We substitute the values of `rFibNum(2,5,2)`and `rFibNum(2,5,1)` into (1.a) to get

`rFibNum(2,5,3) = 5 + 2 = 7`

Next, we determine `rFibNum(2,5,2)`. As in (1.a.1), `rFibNum(2,5,2) = 5`. We can substitute the values of `rFibNum(2,5,3)`and `rFibNum(2,5,2)` into (1) to get

`rFibNum(2,5,4) = 7 + 5 = 12`

The following recursive function implements this algorithm:

```
int rFibNum(int a, int b, int n)
{
  if(n == 1)
     return a;
  else if(n == 2)
          return b;
  else
     return rFibNum(a, b, n - 1) + rFibNum(a, b, n - 2);
}
```

Let us trace the execution of the following statement:

```
cout<<rFibNum(2, 3, 5)<<endl;
```

11

In this statement, the first number is 2, the second number is 3, and we want to determine the 5th Fibonacci number of the sequence. Figure 11-5 traces the execution of the expression **rFibNum(2,3,5)**. The value returned is 13, which is the 5th Fibonacci number of the sequence whose first number is 2 and whose second number is 3.

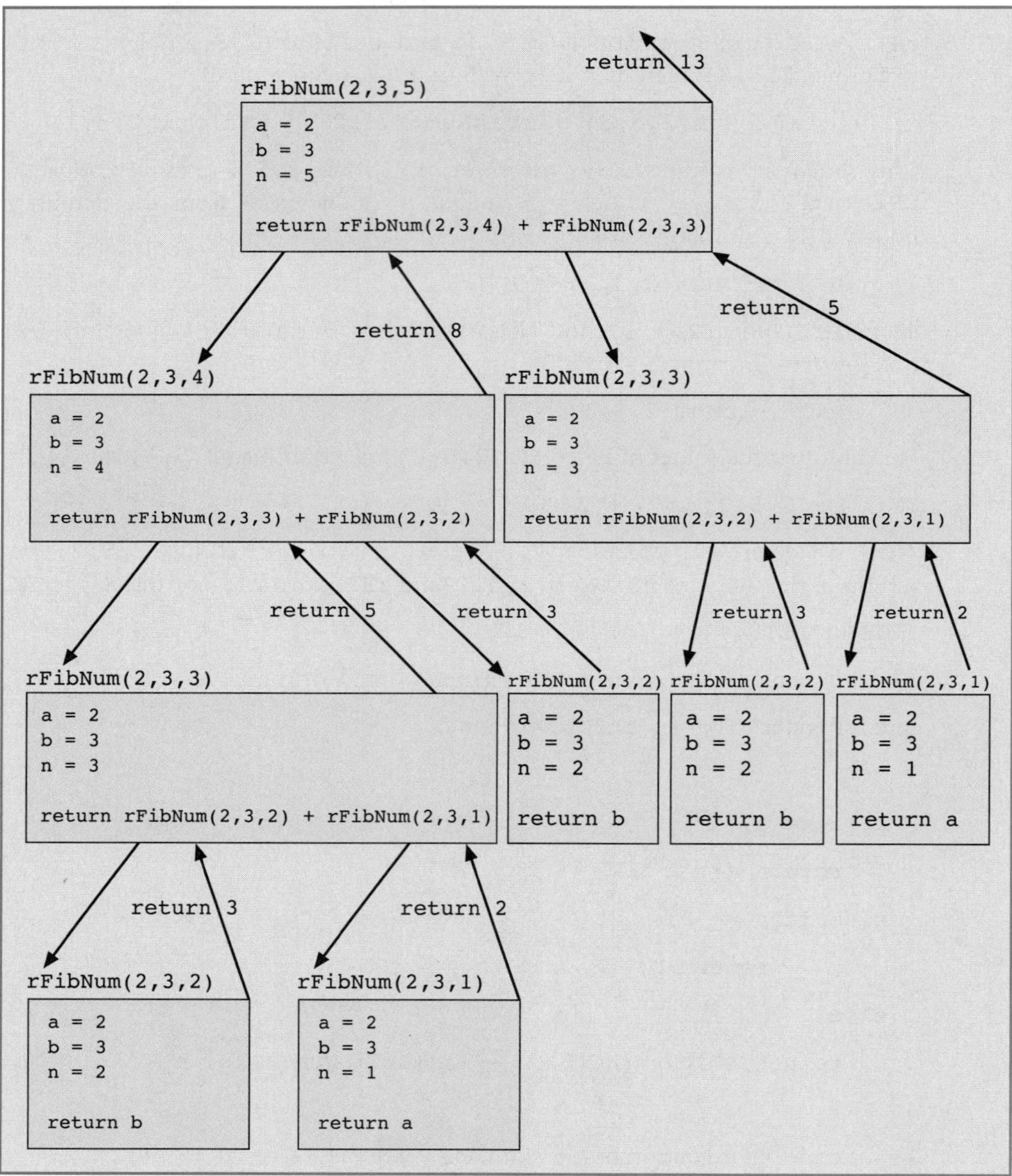

Figure 11-5 Execution of `recFibNumber(2,3,5)`

The following C++ program uses the function **rFibNum**:

```
//Chapter 11: Fibonacci Number

#include <iostream>

using namespace std;

int rFibNum(int a, int b, int n);

int main()
{
   int firstFibNum;
   int secondFibNum;
   int nth;

   cout<<"Enter first Fibonacci number: ";
   cin>>firstFibNum;
   cout<<endl;

   cout<<"Enter second Fibonacci number: ";
   cin>>secondFibNum;
   cout<<endl;

   cout<<"Enter desired Fibonacci number: ";
   cin>>nth;
   cout<<endl;

   cout<<"Fibonacci number at position "<<nth<<" is: "
       << rFibNum(firstFibNum, secondFibNum, nth)<<endl;

   return 0;
}

int rFibNum(int a, int b, int n)
{
  if(n == 1)
     return a;
  else if(n == 2)
          return b;
  else
     return rFibNum(a, b, n - 1) + rFibNum(a, b, n - 2);
}
```

Sample Runs: In these sample runs, the user input is shaded.

Sample Run 1

```
Enter first Fibonacci number: 2
```

```
Enter second Fibonacci number: 5

Enter desired Fibonacci number: 6

Fibonacci number at position 6 is: 31
```

Sample Run 2

```
Enter first Fibonacci number: 3

Enter second Fibonacci number: 4

Enter desired Fibonacci number: 6

Fibonacci number at position 6 is: 29
```

Sample Run 3

```
Enter first Fibonacci number: 12

Enter second Fibonacci number: 18

Enter desired Fibonacci number: 15

Fibonacci number at position 15 is: 9582
```

Example 11-3: Tower of Hanoi

In the nineteenth century, a game called the Tower of Hanoi became popular in Europe. This game represents work that is under way in the temple of Brahama. At the creation of the universe, priests in the temple of Brahama were supposedly given three diamond needles, with one needle containing 64 golden disks. Each golden disk is slightly smaller than the disk below it. The priests' task is to move all 64 disks from the first needle to the third needle. The rules for moving the disks are as follows:

1. Only one disk can be moved at a time.
2. The removed disk must be placed on one of the needles.
3. A larger disk cannot be placed on top of a smaller disk.

The priests were told that once they had moved all the disks from the first needle to third needle, the universe would come to an end.

Our objective is to write a program that prints the sequence of moves needed to transfer the disks from the first needle to the third needle. Figure 11-6 shows the Tower of Hanoi problem with three disks.

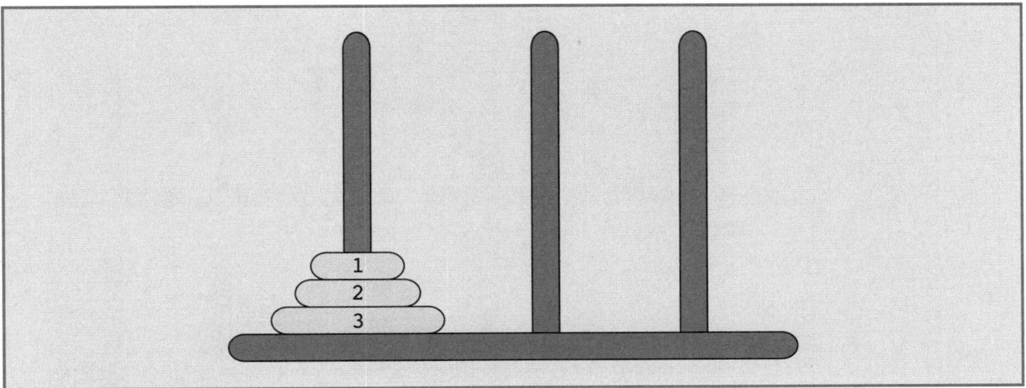

Figure 11-6 Tower of Hanoi problem with three disks

As before, we think in terms of recursion. Let us first consider the case when the first needle contains only one disk. In this case, the disk can be moved directly from needle 1 to needle 3. So let us consider the case when the first needle contains only two disks. In this case, first we move the first disk from needle 1 to needle 2, and then we move the second disk from needle 1 to needle 3. Finally, we move the first disk from needle 2 to needle 3. Next, we consider the case when the first needle contains three disks and then generalize this to the case of 64 disks (in fact, to an arbitrary number of disks).

Suppose that needle 1 contains three disks. To move disk number 3 to needle 3, the top two disks must first be moved to needle 2. Disk number 3 can then be moved from needle 1 to needle 3. To move the top two disks from needle 2 to needle 3, we use the same strategy as before. This time we use needle 1 as the intermediate needle. Figure 11-7 shows a solution to the Tower of Hanoi problem with three disks.

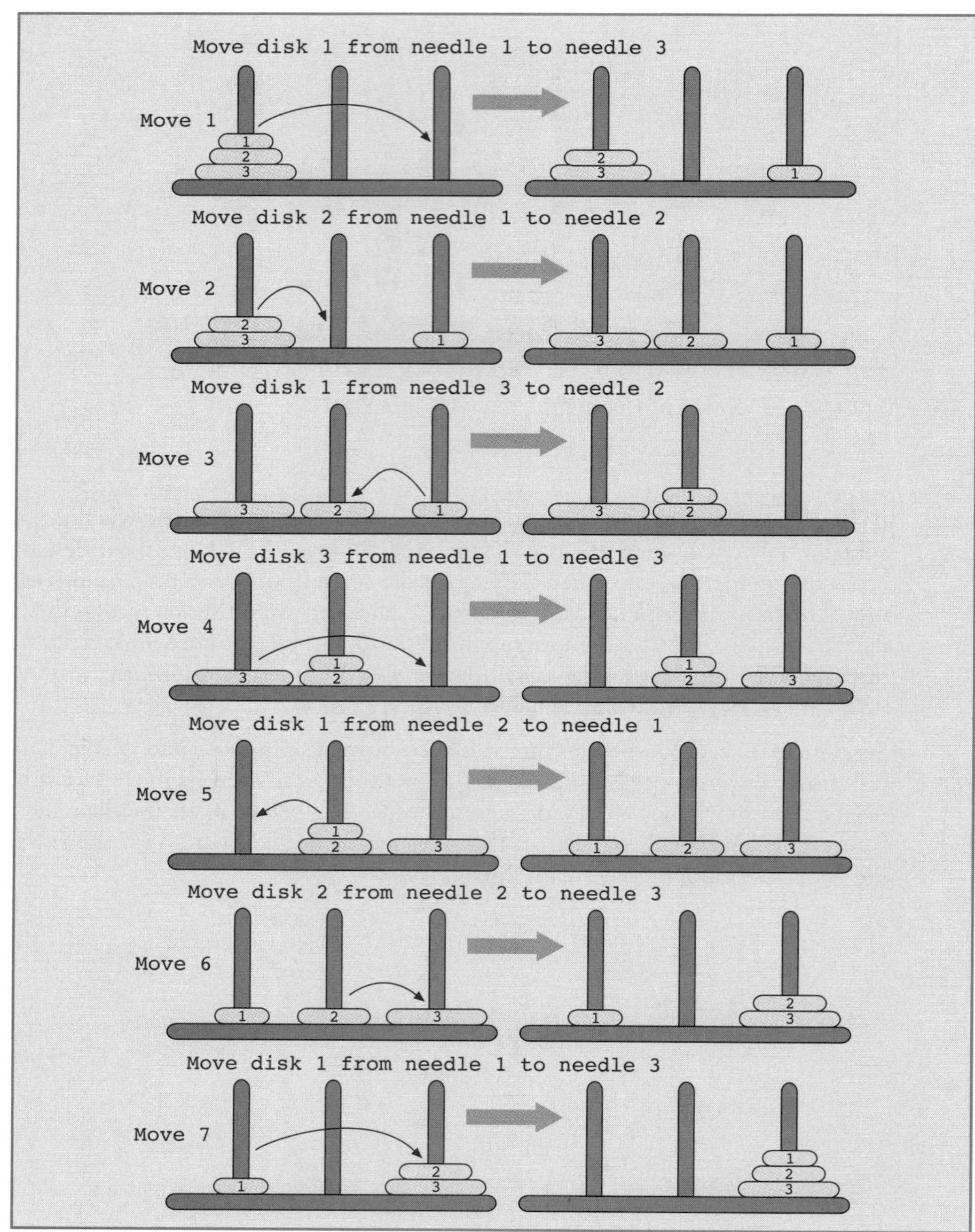

Figure 11-7 Solution of Tower of Hanoi problem with three disks

Let us now generalize this problem to the case of 64 disks. To begin, the first needle contains all 64 disks. Disk number 64 cannot be moved from needle 1 to needle 3 unless the top 63 disks are on the second needle. So first we move the top 63 disks from needle 1 to needle 2, and then we move disk number 64 from needle 1 to needle 3. Now the top 63 disks are all on needle 2. To move disk number 63 from needle 2 to needle 3, we first move the top 62 disks from needle 2 to needle 1, and then we move disk number 63 from needle 2 to needle 3. To move the remaining 62 disks, we use a similar procedure. This discussion translates into the following recursive algorithm given in pseudocode. Suppose that needle 1 contains n disks, where $n \geq 1$.

1. Move the top n - 1 disks from needle 1 to needle 2 using needle 3 as the intermediate needle.
2. Move disk number n from needle 1 to needle 3.
3. Move the top n - 1 disks from needle 2 to needle 3 using needle 1 as the intermediate needle.

This recursive algorithm translates into the following C++ function:

```
void moveDisks(int count, int needle1, int needle3, int needle2)
{
   if(count > 0)
   {
      moveDisks(count-1, needle1, needle2, needle3);
      cout<<"Move disk "<<count<<" from "<<needle1
          <<" to "<<needle3<<"."<<endl;
      moveDisks(count-1, needle2, needle3, needle1);
   }
}
```

11

Tower of Hanoi: Analysis

If needle 1 contains 3 disks, then the number of moves required to move all 3 disks from needle 1 to needle 3 is $2^3 - 1 = 7$. Similarly, if needle 1 contains 64 disks, then the number of moves required to move all 64 disks from needle 1 to needle 3 is $2^{64} - 1$. Since $2^{10} = 1024 \approx 1000 = 10^3$,

$$2^{64} = 2^4 * 2^{60} \approx 2^4 * 10^{18} = 1.6 * 10^{19}$$

The number of seconds in one year is approximately $3.2 * 10^7$. Suppose the priests move one disk per second and they do not rest. Now

$$\begin{aligned} 1.6 * 10^{19} &= 5 * 3.2 * 10^{18} = 5 * (3.2 * 10^7) * 10^{11} \\ &= (3.2 * 10^7) * (5 * 10^{11}) \end{aligned}$$

The time required to move all 64 disks from needle 1 to needle 3 is roughly $5 * 10^{11}$ years. It is estimated that our universe is about 15 billion $= 1.5 * 10^{10}$ years old. Also, $5 * 10^{11} = 50 * 10^{10} \approx 33 * (1.5 * 10^{10})$. This calculation shows that our universe would last about 33 times as long as it already has.

Assume that a computer can generate 1 billion = `10`^{9} moves per second. Then the number of moves that the computer can generate in one year is

$(3.2 * 10^7) * 10^9 = 3.2 * 10^{16}$

So the computer time required to generate 2^{64} moves is

$2^{64} \approx 1.6 * 10^{19} = 1.6 * 10^{16} * 10^3 = (3.2 * 10^{16}) * 500$

Thus, it would take about 500 years for the computer to generate 2^{64} moves at the rate of 1 billion moves per second.

RECURSION OR ITERATION?

In Chapter 5, we designed a program to determine a desired Fibonacci number. That program used a loop to perform the calculation. In other words, the programs in Chapter 5 used an iterative control structure to repeat a set of statements. More formally, **iterative control structures** use a looping structure, such as **`while`**, **`for`**, or **`do...while`**, to repeat a set of statements. In Example 11-2, we designed a recursive function to calculate a Fibonacci number. From the examples here, it follows that in recursion a set of statements is repeated by having the function call itself. Moreover, a selection control structure is used to control the repeated calls in recursion.

Similarly, in Chapter 9, we used an iterative control structure (a **`for`** loop) to determine the largest element in a list. In this chapter, we use recursion to determine the largest element in a list. In addition, this chapter began by designing a recursive function to find the factorial of a non-negative integer. Using an iterative control structure, we can also write an algorithm to find the factorial of a non-negative integer. The only reason to give a recursive solution to a factorial problem is to illustrate how recursion works.

We thus see that there are usually two ways to solve a particular problem—iteration and recursion. The obvious question is which method is better—iteration or recursion? There is no simple answer to this question. In addition to the nature of the problem, the other key factor in determining the best solution method is efficiency.

Example 7-6 (Chapter 7), while tracing the execution of the problem, showed us that whenever a function is called, memory space for its formal parameters and (automatic) local variables is allocated. When the function terminates, that memory space is then deallocated.

This chapter, while tracing the execution of recursive functions, also shows us that every (recursive) call has its own set of parameters and (automatic) local variables. That is, every (recursive) call requires the system to allocate memory space for its formal parameters and (automatic) local variables, and then deallocate the memory space when the function exits. Thus, there is overhead associated with executing a (recursive) function both in terms of memory space and computer time. Therefore, a recursive function executes more slowly than its iterative counterpart. On slower computers, especially those with limited memory space, the (slow) execution of a recursive function would be visible.

Today's computers, however, are fast and have inexpensive memory. Therefore, the execution of a recursion function is not noticeable. Keeping the power of today's computer in mind, the choice between the two alternatives—iteration or recursion—depends on the nature of the problem. Of course, for problems such as mission control systems, efficiency is absolutely critical and, therefore, the efficiency factor would dictate the solution method.

As a general rule, if you think that an iterative solution is more obvious and easier to understand than a recursive solution, use the iterative solution, which would be more efficient. On the other hand, problems exist for which the recursive solution is more obvious or easier to construct, such as the Tower of Hanoi problem. (In fact, it turns out that it is difficult to construct an iterative solution for the Tower of Hanoi problem.) Keeping the power of recursion in mind, if the definition of a problem is inherently recursive, then you should consider a recursive solution.

PROGRAMMING EXAMPLE: CONVERTING A NUMBER FROM BINARY TO DECIMAL

Chapter 1 said that the language of a computer, called machine language, is a sequence of `0`s and `1`s. When you press the key `A` on the keyboard, `01000001` is stored in the computer. Also, you know that the collating sequence of `A` in the ASCII character set is `65`. In fact, the binary representation of `A` is `01000001` and the decimal representation of `A` is `65`.

The numbering system we use is called the decimal system, or base 10 system. The numbering system that the computer uses is called the binary system, or base 2 system. In this and the next programming example, we discuss how to convert a number from base 2 to base 10 and from base 10 to base 2.

Binary to Decimal To convert a number from base 2 to base 10, we first find the weight of each bit in the binary number. The weight of each bit in the binary number is assigned from right to left. The weight of the rightmost bit is 0. The weight of the bit immediately to the left of the rightmost bit is 1, the weight of the bit immediately to the left of it is 2, and so on. Consider the binary number `1001101`. The weight of each bit is as follows:

```
weight   6  5  4  3  2  1  0
         1  0  0  1  1  0  1
```

We use the weight of each bit to find the equivalent decimal number. For each bit, we multiply the bit by `2` to the power of its weight and then we add all of the numbers. For the above binary number, the equivalent decimal number is

$$1 * 2^6 + 0 * 2^5 + 0 * 2^4 + 1 * 2^3 + 1 * 2^2 + 0 * 2^1 + 1 * 2^0$$
$$= 64 + 0 + 0 + 8 + 4 + 0 + 1$$
$$= 77$$

To write a program that converts a binary number into the equivalent decimal number, we note two things: (1) the weight of each bit in the binary number must be known, and (2) the weight is assigned from right to left. Because we do not know in advance how many bits are in the binary number, we must process the bits from right to left.

After processing a bit, we can add 1 to its weight, giving the weight of the bit immediately to the left of it. Also, each bit must be extracted from the binary number and multiplied by 2 to the power of its weight. To extract a bit, we can use the mod operator. Consider the following recursive algorithm, which is given in pseudocode:

```
if(binaryNumber > 0)
{
   bit = binaryNumber % 10;                //extract the rightmost bit
   decimal = decimal + bit * power(2, weight);
   binaryNumber = binaryNumber / 10;  //remove the rightmost bit
   weight++;
   convert the binaryNumber into decimal
}
```

This algorithm assumes that the memory locations **decimal** and **weight** have been initialized to 0 before using this algorithm. This algorithm translates to the following C++ recursive function:

```
void binToDec(int binaryNumber, int& decimal, int& weight)
{
   int bit;

   if(binaryNumber > 0)
   {
     bit = binaryNumber % 10;
     decimal = decimal + bit * static_cast<int>(pow(2, weight));
     binaryNumber = binaryNumber / 10;
     weight++;
     bintoDec(binaryNumber, decimal, weight);
   }
}
```

In this function, both **decimal** and **weight** are reference parameters. The actual parameters corresponding to these parameters are initialized to 0. After extracting the rightmost bit, this function updates the decimal number and the weight of the next bit. Suppose **decimalNumber** and **bitWeight** are **int** variables. Consider the following statements:

```
decimalNumber = 0;
bitWeight = 0;
binToDec(1101,decimalNumber,bitWeight);
```

Figure 11-8 traces the execution of the last statement. It shows the content of the variables **decimalNumber** and **bitWeight** next to each function call.

```
binToDec(1101,decimalNumber,bitWeight)
```

In Figure 11-8, each down arrow represents the successive function call. Because the last statement of the function **binToDec** is a function call, after this statement executes, nothing happens. After the statement

```
binToDec(1101,decimalNumber,bitWeight);
```

executes, the value of the variable **decimalNumber** is 13.

```
                    binToDec(1101,decimalNumber,bitWeight)
                    binaryNumber = 1101
before call         bit =
decimalNumber = 0
bitWeight = 0       since binaryNumber > 0
                      bit = 1101 % 10 = 1;
                      decimal = 0 + 1 * 2^0 = 1;
                      weight = 1;
                      binaryNumber = 1101 / 10 = 110;
                      binToDec(110,decimal,weight);

                     binToDec(110,decimal,weight)
                     binaryNumber = 110
 before call         bit =
 decimalNumber = 1
 bitWeight = 1       since binaryNumber > 0
                       bit = 110 % 10 = 0;
                       decimal = 1 + 0 * 2^1 = 1;
                       weight = 2;
                       binaryNumber = 110 / 10 = 11;
                       binToDec(11,decimal,weight);

                      binToDec(11,decimal,weight)
                      binaryNumber = 11
  before call         bit =
  decimalNumber = 1
  bitWeight = 2       since binaryNumber > 0
                        bit = 11 % 10 = 1;
                        decimal = 1 + 1 * 2^2 = 5;
                        weight = 3;
                        binaryNumber = 11 / 10 = 1;
                        binToDec(1,decimal,weight);

                       binToDec(1,decimal,weight)
                       binaryNumber = 1
   before call         bit =
   decimalNumber = 5
   bitWeight = 3       since binaryNumber > 0
                         bit = 1 % 10 = 1;
                         decimal = 5 + 1 * 2^3 = 13;
                         weight = 4;
                         binaryNumber = 1 / 10 = 0;
                         binToDec(10,decimal,weight);

                        binToDec(0,decimal,weight)
                        binaryNumber = 0
   before call          bit =
   decimalNumber = 13
   bitWeight = 4        since binaryNumber = 0
                          the if statement fails and this call exits
```

Figure 11-8 Execution of `binToDec(1101,decimalNumber,bitWeight)`

The following C++ program tests the function **binToDec**:

```
//Chapter 11: Program - Binary to Decimal

#include <iostream>
#include <cmath>

using namespace std;
void binToDec(int binaryNumber, int& decimal, int& weight);

int main()
{
    int decimalNum;
    int bitWeight;
    int binaryNum;

    decimalNum = 0;
    bitWeight = 0;
    cout<<"Enter number in binary: ";
    cin>>binaryNum;
    cout<<endl;
    binToDec(binaryNum, decimalNum, bitWeight);
    cout<<"Binary "<<binaryNum<<" = "<<decimalNum
        <<" decimal"<<endl;
    return 0;
}

void binToDec(int binaryNumber, int& decimal, int& weight)
{
   int bit;

   if(binaryNumber > 0)
   {
     bit = binaryNumber % 10;
     decimal = decimal + bit * static_cast<int>(pow(2, weight));
     binaryNumber = binaryNumber / 10;
     weight++;
     binToDec(binaryNumber, decimal, weight);
   }
}
```

Sample Run: In this sample run, the user input is shaded.

```
Enter number in binary: 11010110

Binary 11010110 = 214 decimal
```

PROGRAMMING EXAMPLE: CONVERTING A NUMBER FROM DECIMAL TO BINARY

The previous programming example discussed and designed a program to convert a number from a binary representation to a decimal format—that is, from base 2 to base 10. This programming example discusses and designs a program that uses recursion to convert a non-negative integer in decimal format—that is, base 10—into the equivalent binary number—that is, base 2. First we define some terms.

Let `x` be an integer. We call the remainder of `x` after division by `2` the **rightmost bit** of `x`.

Thus, the rightmost bit of `33` is `1` because `33 % 2` is `1`, and the rightmost bit of `28` is `0` because `28 % 2` is `0`.

We first illustrate the algorithm to convert an integer in base 10 to the equivalent number in binary format with the help of an example.

Suppose we want to find the binary representation of `35`. First, we divide `35` by `2`. The quotient is `17` and the remainder—that is, the rightmost bit of `35`—is `1`. Next, we divide `17` by `2`. The quotient is `8` and the remainder—that is, the rightmost bit of `17`—is `1`. Next, we divide `8` by `2`. The quotient is `4` and the remainder—that is, the rightmost bit of `8`—is `0`. We continue this process until the quotient becomes `0`.

The rightmost bit of `35` cannot be printed until we have printed the rightmost bit of `17`. The rightmost bit of `17` cannot be printed until we have printed the rightmost bit of `8`, and so on. Thus, the binary representation of `35` is the binary representation of `17` (that is, the quotient of `35` after division by `2`), followed by the rightmost bit of `35`.

Thus, to convert an integer `num` in base 10 into the equivalent binary number, we first convert the quotient `num/2` into an equivalent binary number, and then append the rightmost bit of `num` to the binary representation of `num/2`.

This discussion translates into the following recursive algorithm, where `binary(num)` denotes the binary representation of `num`:

1. `binary(num) = num` if `num = 0`.
2. `binary(num) = binary(num/2)` followed by `num % 2` if `num > 0`.

The following recursive function implements this algorithm:

```
void decToBin(int num, int base)
{
    if(num > 0)
    {
        decToBin(num/base, base);
        cout<<num % base;
    }
}
```

Figure 11-9 traces the execution of the following statement:

```
decToBin(13,2);
```

where `num` is `13` and `base` is `2`.

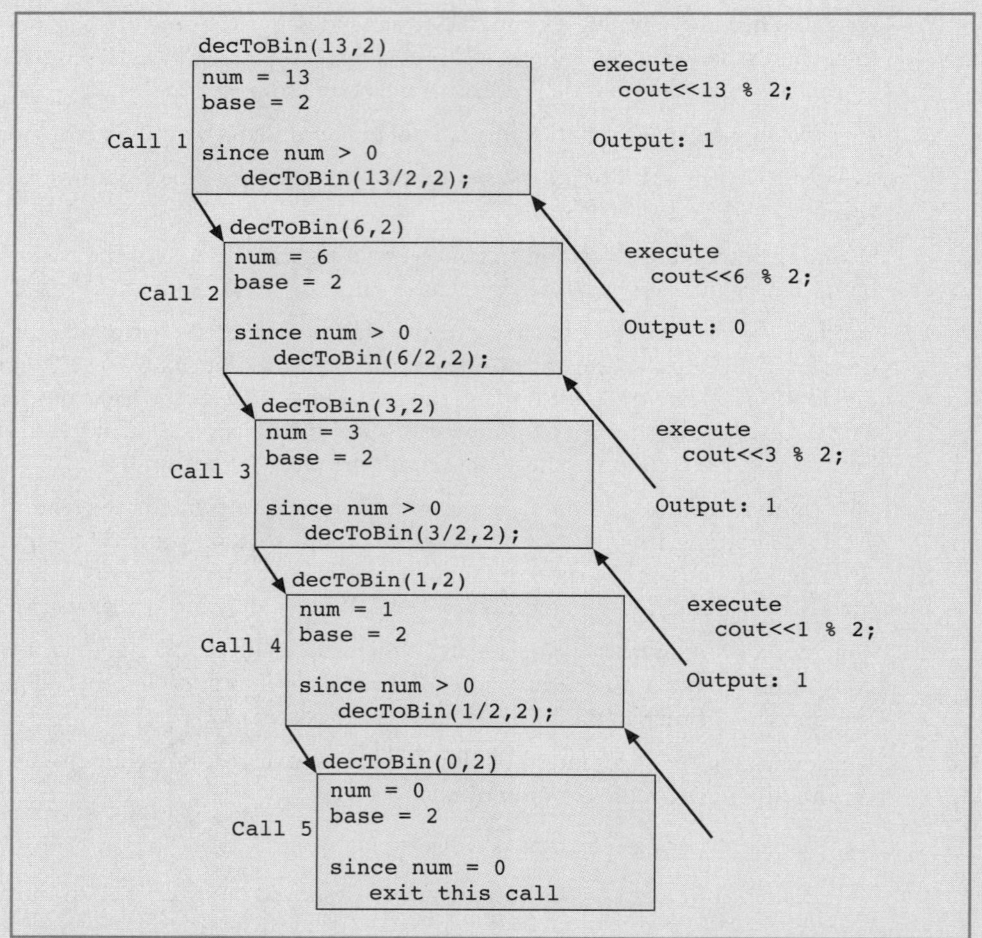

Figure 11-9 Execution of `decToBin(13,2)`

Since the `if` statement in call 5 fails, this call does not print anything. The first output is produced by call 4, which prints `1`; the second output is produced by call 3, which prints `1`; the third output is produced by call 2, which prints `0`; and the fourth output is produced by call 1, which prints `1`. Thus, the output of the statement

```
decToBin(13, 2);
```

is

```
1101
```

The following C++ program tests the function **decToBin**:

```
//Chapter 11: Program - Decimal to Binary

#include <iostream>

using namespace std;

void decToBin(int num, int base);

int main()
{
      int decimalNum;
      int base;

      base = 2;

      cout<<"Enter number in decimal: ";
      cin>>decimalNum;
      cout<<endl;
      cout<<"Decimal "<<decimalNum<<" = ";
      decToBin(decimalNum, base);
      cout<<" binary"<<endl;

      return 0;
}

void decToBin(int num, int base)
{
   if(num > 0)
   {
      decToBin(num/base, base);
      cout<<num % base;
   }
}
```

Sample Run: In this sample run, the user input is shaded.

```
Enter number in decimal: 57

Decimal 57 = 111001 binary
```

Quick Review

1. The process of solving a problem by reducing it to smaller versions of itself is called recursion.
2. A recursive definition defines the problem in terms of smaller versions of itself.
3. Every recursive definition has one or more base cases.
4. A recursive algorithm solves a problem by reducing it to smaller versions of itself.
5. Every recursive algorithm has one or more base cases.
6. The solution to the problem in a base case is obtained directly.
7. A function is called recursive if it calls itself.
8. Recursive algorithms are implemented using recursive functions.
9. Every recursive function must have one or more base cases.
10. The general solution breaks the problem into smaller versions of itself.
11. The general case must eventually be reduced to a base case.
12. The base case stops the recursion.
13. Logically, a recursive function has unlimited copies of itself. Every call to a recursive function has its own copy of the body of the function.
14. Every recursive call has its own copy of the parameters and the local variables.
15. A recursive call must execute completely before the control goes back to the previous call. The execution in the previous call begins from the point immediately following the recursive call.
16. A recursive function in which the last statement executed is the recursive call is called a tail recursive function.

Exercises

1. Mark the following statements as true or false.
   a. Every recursive definition must have one or more base cases.
   b. Every recursive function must have one or more base cases.
   c. The general case stops the recursion.
   d. In the general case, the solution to the problem is obtained directly.
   e. A recursive function always returns a value.
2. Consider the following recursive function:

```
void funcRec(int u, char v)
{
   if(u == 0)
      cout<<v;
   else if(u == 1)
```

```
            cout<<static_cast<char>(static_cast<int>(v) + 1);
    else
        funcRec(u - 1, v);
}
```

Answer the following questions.

a. Identify the base case.

b. Identify the general case.

c. What is the output of the following statement?

```
funcRec(5,'A');
```

3. Consider the following function:

```
int test(int x, int y)
{
    if(x == y)
        return x;
    else if(x > y)
            return (x + y);
    else
        return test(x + 1, y – 1);
}
```

What is the output of the following statements?

a. `cout<<test(5,10)<<endl;`

b. `cout<<test(3,9)<<endl;`

4. Consider the following function:

```
int Func(int x)
{
    if(x == 0)
        return 2;
    else if(x == 1)
            return 3;
    else
        return (Func(x – 1) + Func(x – 2));
}
```

What is the output of the following statements?

a. `cout<<Func(0)<<endl;`

b. `cout<<Func(1)<<endl;`

c. `cout<<Func(2)<<endl;`

d. `cout<<Func(5)<<endl;`

PROGRAMMING EXERCISES

1. Write a recursive function, `vowels`, that returns the number of vowels in a string. Also, write a program to test your function.
2. Write a recursive function that finds and returns the sum of the elements of an `int` array. Also, write a program to test your function.
3. A palindrome is a string that reads the same both forward and backward. For example, the strings `"madam"` and `"madam I'm adam"` are palindromes. Write a program that uses a recursive function to check whether a string is a palindrome. Your program must contain a value-returning recursive function that returns `true` if the string is a palindrome and `false` otherwise. Do not use any global variables; use appropriate parameters.
4. Write a program that uses a recursive function to print a string backward. Your program must contain a recursive function that prints the string backward. Do not use any global variables; use appropriate parameters.
5. Write a recursive function, `reverseDigits`, that takes an integer as a parameter and returns the number with the digits reversed. Also, write a program to test your function.
6. Write a recursive function, `power`, that takes as parameters two integers x and y such that x is nonzero and returns x^y. You can use the following recursive definition to calculate x^y. If $y \geq 0$,

$$power(x,y) = \begin{cases} 1 & \text{if } y = 0 \\ x & \text{if } y = 1 \\ x * power(x,y-1) & \text{if } y > 1. \end{cases}$$

If $y < 0$,

$$power(x,y) = \frac{1}{power(x,-y)}$$

Also, write a program to test your function.

7. **(Greatest Common Divisor)** Given two integers x and y, the following recursive definition determines the greatest common divisor of x and y, written $\gcd(x,y)$:

$$\gcd(x,y) = \begin{cases} x & \text{if } y = 0 \\ \gcd(y, x\%y) & \text{if } y \neq 0 \end{cases}$$

Note: In this definition, % is the mod operator.

Write a recursive function, `gcd`, that takes as parameters two integers and returns the greatest common divisor of the numbers. Also, write a program to test your function.

8. **(Recursive Sequential Search)** The sequential search algorithm given in Chapter 10 is nonrecursive. Write and implement a recursive version of the sequential search algorithm.
9. **(Recursive Binary Search)** The binary search algorithm given in Chapter 10 is nonrecursive. Write and implement a recursive version of the binary search algorithm.

10. In the Programming Example, Converting a Number from Decimal to Binary, given in this chapter, you learned how to convert a decimal number into the equivalent binary number. Two more number systems, octal (base 8) and hexadecimal (base 16), are of interest to computer scientists. In fact, in C++, you can instruct the computer to store a number in octal or hexadecimal.

    The digits in the octal number system are `0, 1, 2, 3, 4, 5, 6,` and `7`. The digits in the hexadecimal number system are `0, 1, 2, 3, 4, 5, 6, 7, 8, 9, A, B, C, D, E,` and `F`. So `A` in hexadecimal is `10` in decimal, `B` in hexadecimal is `11` in decimal, and so on.

    The algorithm to convert a positive decimal number into an equivalent number in octal (or hexadecimal) is the same as discussed for binary numbers. Here we divide the decimal number by 8 (for octal) and by 16 (for hexadecimal). Suppose a_b represents the number `a` to the base `b`. For example, 75_{10} means 75 to the base 10 (that is decimal), and 83_{16} means 83 to the base 16 (that is, hexadecimal). Then

    $753_{10} = 1361_8$
    $753_{10} = 2F1_{16}$

    The method of converting a decimal number to base 2, or 8, or 16 can be extended to any arbitrary base. Suppose you want to convert a decimal number `n` into an equivalent number in base `b`, where `b` is between `2` and `36`. You then divide the decimal number `n` by `b` as in the algorithm for converting decimal to binary.

    Note that the digits in, say base 20, are `0, 1, 2, 3, 4, 5, 6, 7, 8, 9, A, B, C, D, E, F, G, H, I,` and `J`.

    Write a program that uses a recursive function to convert a number in decimal to a given base `b`, where `b` is between `2` and `36`. Your program should prompt the user to enter the number in decimal and in the desired base.

    Test your program on the following data:

    `9098` and base `20`
    `692` and base `2`
    `753` and base `16`

CHAPTER

12

RECORDS (Structs)

In this chapter, you will:

- Learn about records (`structs`)
- Examine various operations on a `struct`
- Explore ways to manipulate data using a `struct`
- Learn about the relationship between a `struct` and functions
- Discover how arrays are used in a `struct`
- Learn how to create an array of `struct` items

In Chapters 9 and 10, you learned how to group values of the same type by using arrays. You also learned how to process data stored in an array and how to perform list operations, such as searching and sorting.

This chapter may be skipped without experiencing any discontinuation.

In this chapter, you will learn how to group related values that are of different types. C++ provides another structured data type, called `struct` (some languages use the term "record") to group related items of different types. An array is a homogeneous data structure; a `struct` is a heterogeneous data structure. The treatment of a `struct` in this chapter is similar to the treatment of a `struct` in C; a `struct` in this chapter, therefore, is a C-like `struct`. Chapter 13 introduces and discusses another structured data type, called a class.

Records (Structs)

Suppose that you want to write a program to process student data. A student record consists of, among other things, the student's name, student ID, GPA, courses taken, and course grades. Thus, various components are associated with a student. However, these components are all of different types. For example, the student's name is a string and the GPA is a floating-point number. Because these components are of different types, you cannot use an array to group all of the items associated with a student. C++ provides a structured data type called `struct` to group items of different types. Grouping components that are related, but of different types, offers several advantages. For example, a single variable can pass all components as parameters to a function.

`struct`: A collection of a fixed number of components in which the components are accessed by name. The components may be of different types.

The components of a `struct` are called the **members** of the `struct`. The general syntax of a `struct` in C++ is

```
struct structName
{
   dataType1  identifier1;
   dataType2  identifier2;
       .
       .
       .
   dataTypen  identifiern;
};
```

In C++, **struct** is a reserved word. The members of a **struct**, even though enclosed in braces (that is, they form a block), are not considered to form a compound statement. Thus, a semicolon (after the right brace) is essential to end the **struct** statement. A semicolon at the end of the **struct** definition is, therefore, a part of the syntax.

The statement

```
struct employeeType
{
   string firstName;
   string lastName;
   string address1;
   string address2;
   double salary;
   string deptID;
};
```

defines a **struct** `employeeType` with `6` members. The members `firstName`, `lastName`, `address1`, `address2`, and `deptID` are of the type `string`, and the member `salary` is of the type **double**.

Like any type definition, a **struct** is a definition, not a declaration. That is, it defines only a data type; no memory is allocated.

Once a data type is defined, you can declare variables of that type. Let us first define a **struct** type, `studentType`, and then declare variables of that type.

```
struct studentType
{
   string   firstName;
   string   lastName;
   char     courseGrade;
   int      testScore;
   int      programmingScore;
   double   GPA;
};

//variable declaration
studentType newStudent;
studentType student;
```

These statements declare two **struct** variables, `newStudent` and `student`, of the type `studentType`. The memory allocated is large enough to store `firstName`, `lastName`, `courseGrade`, `testScore`, `programmingScore`, and `GPA`. (See Figure 12-1.)

12

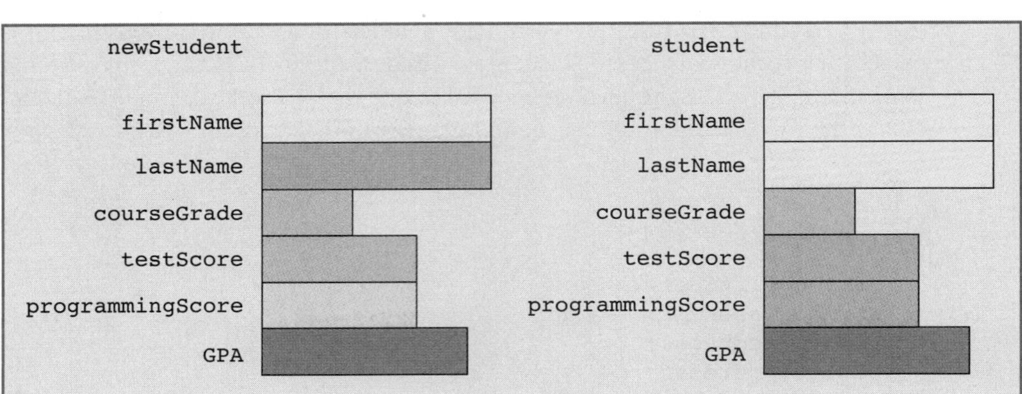

Figure 12-1 `struct` `newStudent` and `student`

Accessing `struct` Members

In arrays, you access a component by using the array name together with the relative position (index) of the component. The array name and index are separated using square brackets. To access a structure member (component), you use the **`struct`** variable name together with the member name; these names are separated by a dot (period). The syntax for accessing a **`struct`** member is

```
structVariableName.memberName
```

The `structVariableName.memberName` is just like any other variable. For example, `newStudent.courseGrade` is a variable of the type **`char`**, `newStudent.firstName` is a string variable, and so on. As a result, you can do just about anything with **`struct`** members that you normally do with variables. You can, for example, use them in assignment statements or input/output (where permitted) statements.

In C++, the dot, (`.`), is an operator, called the **member access operator**.

Suppose you want to initialize the member `GPA` of `newStudent` to `0.0`. The following statement accomplishes this task:

```
newStudent.GPA = 0.0;
```

Similarly, the statements

```
newStudent.firstName = "John";
newStudent.lastName = "Brown";
```

store `"John"` in the member `firstName` and `"Brown"` in the member `lastName` of `newStudent`.

After the preceding three assignment statements execute, `newStudent` is as shown in Figure 12-2.

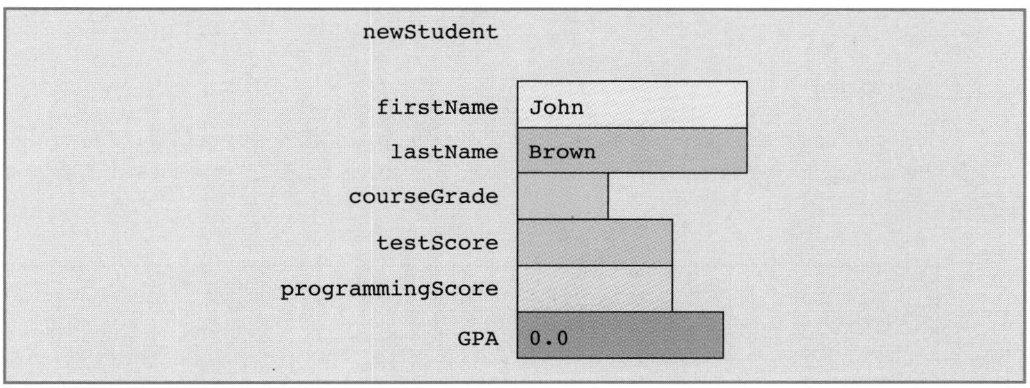

Figure 12-2 `struct` `newStudent`

The statement

```
cin>>newStudent.firstName;
```

reads the next string from the standard input device and stores it in

```
newStudent.firstName
```

The statement

```
cin>>newStudent.testScore>>newStudent.programmingScore;
```

reads two integer values from the keyboard and stores them in `newStudent.testScore` and `newStudent.programmingScore`, respectively.

Suppose that `score` is a variable of the type `int`. The statement

```
score = newStudent.testScore + newStudent.programmingScore;
```

adds the contents of `newStudent.testScore` and `newStudent.programmingScore` and stores the result in `score`.

The following statement determines the course grade and stores it in **newStudent.courseGrade**:

```
if(score >= 90)
   newStudent.courseGrade = 'A';
else if(score >= 80)
        newStudent.courseGrade = 'B';
else if(score >= 70)
        newStudent.courseGrade = 'C';
else if(score >= 60)
        newStudent.courseGrade = 'D';
else
   newStudent.courseGrade = 'F';
```

Assignment

We can assign the value of one **struct** variable to another **struct** variable of the same type by using an assignment statement. Suppose that **newStudent** is as shown in Figure 12-3.

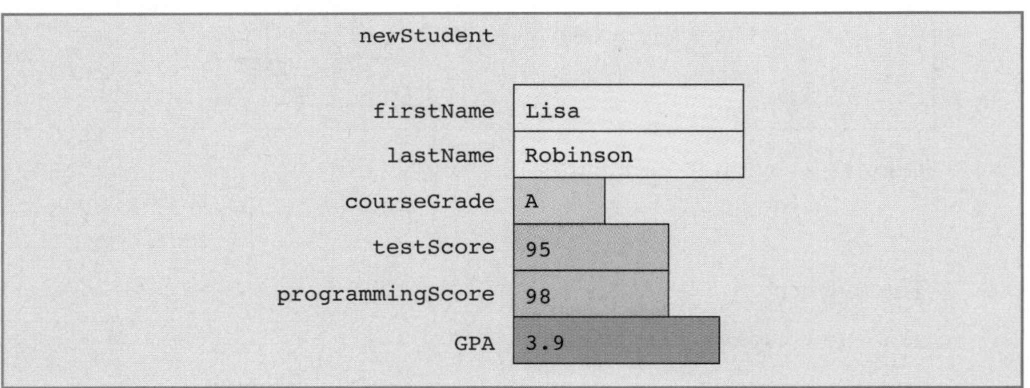

Figure 12-3 struct newStudent

The statement

```
student = newStudent;
```

copies the contents of **newStudent** into **student**. After this assignment statement executes, the values of **student** are as shown in Figure 12-4.

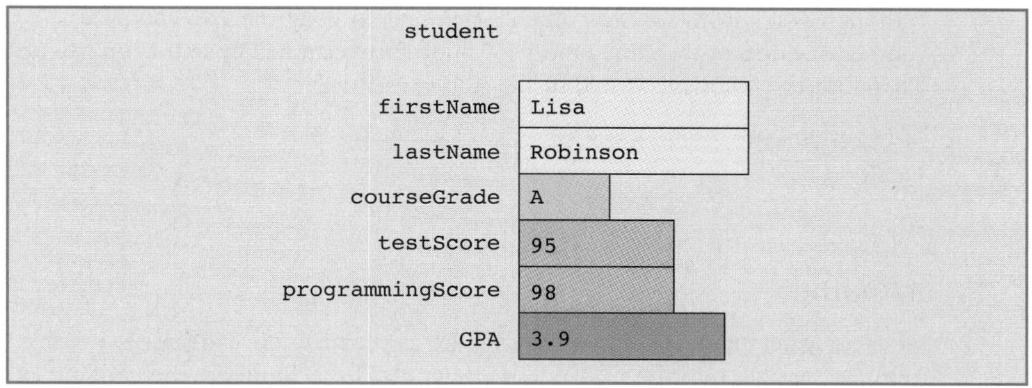

Figure 12-4 `student` after `student = newStudent`

In fact, the assignment statement

```
student = newStudent;
```

is equivalent to the following statements:

```
student.firstName = newStudent.firstName;
student.lastName = newStudent.lastName;
student.courseGrade = newStudent.courseGrade;
student.testScore = newStudent.testScore;
student.programmingScore = newStudent.programmingScore;
student.GPA = newStudent.GPA;
```

12

Comparison (Relational Operators)

To compare **struct** variables, you compare them member-wise. As with an array, no aggregate relational operations are performed on a **struct**. For example, suppose that **newStudent** and **student** are declared as shown earlier. Furthermore, suppose that you want to see whether **student** and **newStudent** refer to the same student. Now **newStudent** and **student** refer to the same student if they have the same first name and the same last name. To compare the values of **student** and **newStudent**, you must compare them member-wise, as follows:

```
if(student.firstName == newStudent.firstName &&
   student.lastName == newStudent.lastName)
.
.
.
```

Although you can use an assignment statement to copy the contents of one **struct** into another **struct** of the same type, you cannot use relational operators on **struct** variables. Therefore, the following would be illegal:

```
if(student == newStudent)    //illegal
.
.
.
```

Input/Output

No aggregate input/output operations are performed on a **struct** variable. Data in a **struct** variable must be read one member at a time. Similarly, the contents of a **struct** variable must be written one member at a time.

We have seen how to read data into a **struct** variable; let us now see how to output a **struct** variable. The statement

```
cout<<newStudent.firstName<<" "<<newStudent.lastName<<" "
    <<newStudent.courseGrade<<" "<<newStudent.testScore<<" "
    <<newStudent.programmingScore<<" "<<newStudent.GPA<<endl;
```

outputs the contents of the **struct** variable `newStudent`.

struct Variables and Functions

Recall that arrays are passed by reference only, and a function cannot return a value of the type `array`. However,

- A **struct** variable can be passed as a parameter either by value or by reference, and
- A function can return a value of the type **struct**.

The following function reads and stores a student's first name, last name, test score, programming score, and GPA. It also determines the student's course grade and stores it in the member `courseGrade`.

```
void readIn(studentType& student)
{
   int score;

   cin>>student.firstName>>student.lastName;
   cin>>student.testScore>>student.programmingScore;
   cin>>student.GPA;

   score = newStudent.testScore + newStudent.programmingScore;

   if(score >= 90)
      student.courseGrade = 'A';
   else if(score >= 80)
           student.courseGrade = 'B';
```

```
    else if(score >= 70)
         student.courseGrade = 'C';
    else if(score >= 60)
            student.courseGrade = 'D';
    else
       student.courseGrade = 'F';
}
```

The statement

```
readIn(newStudent);
```

calls the function `readIn`. The function `readIn` stores the appropriate information in the variable `newStudent`.

Similarly, we can write a function that will print the contents of a **`struct`** variable. For example, the following function outputs the contents of a **`struct`** variable of the type `studentType` on the screen:

```
void printStudent(studentType student)
{
      cout<<student.firstName<<" "<<student.lastName<<" "
          <<student.courseGrade<<" "<<student.testScore<<" "
          <<student.programmingScore<<" "<<student.GPA<<endl;
}
```

Arrays versus Structs

The previous discussion shows us that a **`struct`** and an array have similarities as well as differences. Table 12-1 summarizes this discussion.

12

Table 12-1 Arrays vs. Structs

	Aggregate Operation	Array	Struct
1	Arithmetic	No	No
2	Assignment	No	Yes
3	Input/output	No (except strings)	No
4	Comparison	No	No
5	Parameter passing	By reference only	By value or by reference
6	Function returning a value	No	Yes

Arrays in Structs

Chapter 10 discussed list-processing algorithms. A list has two things associated with it: the values (that is, elements) and the length. In the searching and sorting functions, discussed in Chapter 10, as parameters we needed to pass these two things separately to the function.

Because the values and the length are both related to a list, we can define a **struct** containing both items. We then need to pass only one parameter, not two. We illustrate this concept by rewriting the sequential search algorithm. First, we define the following **struct**:

```
const arraySize = 1000;

struct listType
{
   int listElem[arraySize];      //array containing the list
   int listLength;               //length of the list
}


int seqSearch(const listType& list, int searchItem)
{
   int loc;

   bool found = false;

   for(loc = 0; loc < list.listLength; loc++)
      if(list.listElem[loc] == searchItem)
      {
            found = true;
            break;
      }

   if(found)
      return loc;
   else
      return -1;
}
```

In this function, because **listLength** is a member of **list**, we access this by **list.listLength**. Similarly, we can access an element of **list** via **list.listElem[loc]**.

Notice that the formal parameter **list** of the function **seqSearch** is declared as a constant reference parameter. This means that **list** receives the address of the corresponding actual parameter, but **list** cannot modify the actual parameter. Constant reference parameters are discussed in detail in Chapter 13.

Likewise, we can also rewrite the sorting, binary search, and other list processing functions.

Structs in Arrays

Suppose a company has 50 full-time employees. We need to print their monthly paychecks and keep track of how much money has been paid in the year-to-date. First, let's define an employee's record.

```
struct employeeType
{
```

```
    string    firstName;
    string    lastName;
    int       personID;
    string    deptID;
    double    yearlySalary;
    double    monthlySalary
    double    yearToDatePaid;
    double    monthlyBonus;
};
```

Each employee has the following members (components): first name, last name, personal ID, department ID, yearly salary, monthly salary, year-to-date paid, and monthly bonus.

Because we have 50 employees, and the data type of each employee is the same, we can use an array of 50 components to process the employees' data.

```
employeeType employees[50];
```

This statement declares an array `employees` of `50` components of the type `employeeType`. (See Figure 12-5.) Every element of `employees` is a `struct`. For example, Figure 12-5 also shows `employees[2]`.

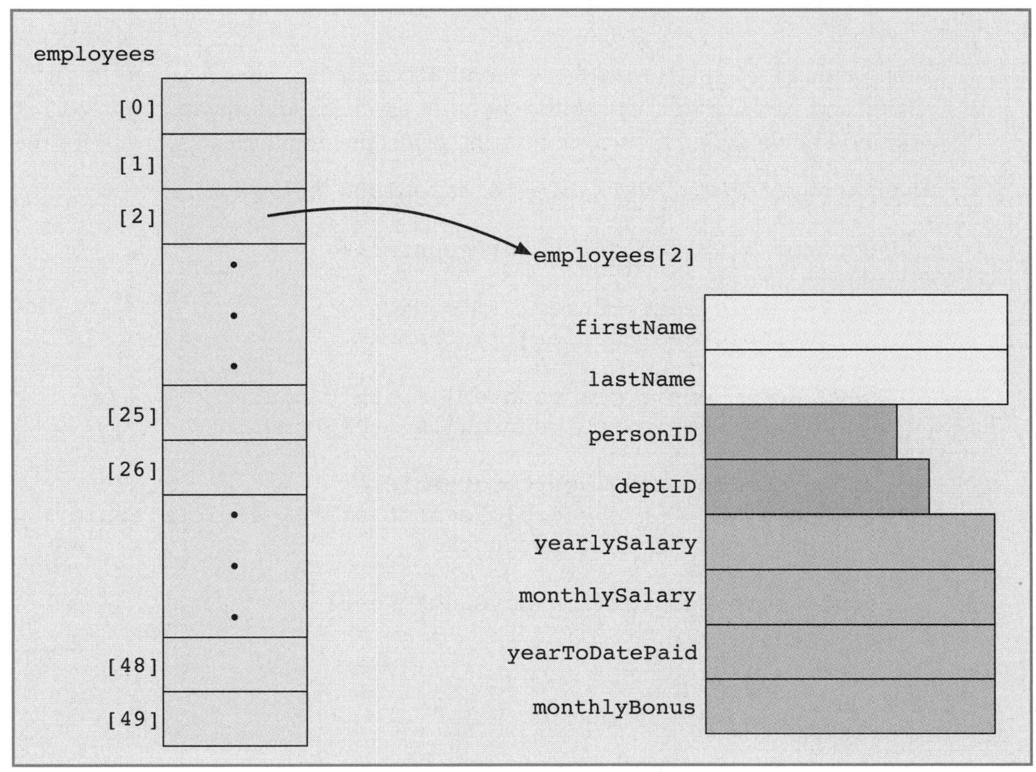

Figure 12-5 Array of `structs` `employees`

12

Suppose we also have the following declaration:

```
int counter;
```

Further suppose that every employee's (initial data) first name, last name, personal ID, department ID, and yearly salary are provided in a file. For our discussion, we assume that each employee's data is stored in a file—say, **`employee.dat`**. The following C++ code loads the data into the employees' array. We assume that initially **`yearToDatePaid`** is `0` and that the monthly bonus is determined each month based on performance.

```
ifstream infile; //input stream variable
                 //assume that employee.dat file has been opened
for(counter = 0; counter < 50; counter++)
{
    infile>>employees[counter].firstName
          >>employees[counter].lastName
          >>employees[counter].personID
          >>employees[counter].deptID
          >>employees[counter].yearlySalary;
    employees[counter].monthlySalary =
                 employees[counter].yearlySalary/12;
    employees[counter].yearToDatePaid = 0.0;
    employees[counter].monthlyBonus = 0.0;
}
```

Suppose that for a given month the monthly bonuses are already stored in each employee's record, and we have to calculate the monthly paycheck and update the **`yearToDatePaid`** amount. The following loop computes and prints the employee's paycheck for the month:

```
double payCheck; //variable to calculate the paycheck

for(counter = 0; counter < 50; counter++)
{
    cout<<employees[counter].firstName<<" "
        <<employees[counter].lastName<<" ";

    payCheck = employees[counter].monthlySalary +
               employees[counter].monthlyBonus;

    employees[counter].yearToDatePaid =
                         employees[counter].yearToDatePaid +
                         payCheck;

    cout<<setprecision(2)<<payCheck<<endl;
}
```

Structs within a struct

You have seen how the **struct** and array data structures can be mixed together to organize information. You also saw examples wherein a member of a **struct** is an array, and the array type is a **struct**. In this section, you will learn about situations where it is beneficial to organize data in a **struct** using another **struct**.

Let us consider the following employee record:

```
struct employeeType
{
    string  firstname;
    string  middlename;
    string  lastname;
    string  emplID;
    string  address1;
    string  address2;
    string  city;
    string  state;
    string  zip;
    string  hiremonth;
    string  hireday;
    string  hireyear;
    string  quitmonth;
    string  quitday;
    string  quityear;
    string  phone;
    string  cellphone;
    string  fax;
    string  pager;
    string  email;
    string  deptID;
    double  salary;
};
```


As you can see, a lot of information is packed into one **struct**. This **struct** has 22 members. Some members of this **struct** will be accessed more frequently than others, and some members are more closely related than others. Moreover, some members will have the same underlying structure. For example, the hire date and the quit date are of the type **date**. Let us reorganize this **struct** as follows:

```
struct nameType
{
      string  first;
      string  middle;
      string  last;
};


struct addressType
```

```
{
      string  address1;
      string  address2;
      string  city;
      string  state;
      string  zip;
};

struct dateType
{
      string  month;
      string  day;
      string  year;
};

struct contactType
{
      string  phone;
      string  cellphone;
      string  fax;
      string  pager;
      string  email;
};
```

We have separated the employee's name, address, and contact type into subcategories. Furthermore, we have defined a `struct dateType`. Let us rebuild the employee's record as follows:

```
struct employeeType
{
      nameType        name;
      string          emplID;
      addressType     address;
      dateType        hiredate;
      dateType        quitdate;
      contactType     contact;
      string          deptID;
      double          salary;

};
```

The information in this employee's `struct` is easier to manage then the previous one. Some of this `struct` can be reused to build another `struct`. For example, suppose that you want to define a customer's record. Every customer has a first name, last name, and middle name, as well as an address and a way to be contacted. You can, therefore, quickly put together a customer's record by using the `struct`, `nameType`, `addressType`, `contactType`, and the members specific to the customer.

Next, let us declare the variables of **employeeType** and discuss how to access its members.

```
     //variable declaration
employeeType newEmployee;
employeeType employees[100]; //declare 100 employees' records
```

The statement

```
newEmployee.salary = 45678.00;
```

sets the salary of **newEmployee** to **45678.00**. The statements

```
newEmployee.name.first = "Mary";
newEmployee.name.middle = "Beth";
newEmployee.name.last = "Simmons";
```

set the **first**, **middle**, and **last** name of **newEmployee** to **"Mary"**, **"Beth"**, and **"Simmons"**, respectively. Note that **newEmployee** has a member called **name**. We access this member via **newEmployee.name**. Note also that **newEmployee.name** is a **struct** and has three members. We apply the member access criteria to access the member **first** of the **struct newEmployee.name**. So **newEmployee.name.first** is the member where we store the first name.

The statement

```
cin>>newEmployee.name.first;
```

reads and stores a string into **newEmployee.name.first**. The statement

```
newEmployee.salary = newEmployee.salary * 1.05;
```


updates the salary of **newEmployee**.

The **for** loop

```
for(j = 0; j < 100; j++)
    cin>>employees[j].name.first>>employees[j].name.middle
       >>employees[j].name.last;
```

reads and stores the names of 100 employees in the array **employees**. Because **employees** is an array, to access a component we use the index. For example, **employees[50]** is the 51st component of the array **employees** (recall that an array index starts with **0**). Because **employees[50]** is a **struct**, we apply the member access criteria to select a particular member.

PROGRAMMING EXAMPLE: SALES DATA ANALYSIS

A company has six salespeople. Every month they go on road trips to sell the company's product. At the end of each month, the total sales for each salesperson, together with that salesperson's ID and the month, is recorded in a file. At the end of each year, the manager of the company wants to see this report in this following tabular format:

```
----------- Annual Sales Report -------------

  ID        QT1        QT2       QT3        QT4      Total
_______________________________________________________________
12345     1892.00      0.00     494.00     322.00    2708.00
32214      343.00    892.00    9023.00       0.00   10258.00
23422     1395.00   1901.00       0.00       0.00    3296.00
57373      893.00    892.00    8834.00       0.00   10619.00
35864     2882.00   1221.00       0.00    1223.00    5326.00
54654      893.00      0.00     392.00    3420.00    4705.00
Total     8298.00   4906.00   18743.00    4965.00


Max Sale by SalesPerson: ID = 57373, Amount = $10619.00
Max Sale by Quarter: Quarter = 3, Amount = $18743.00
```

In this report, `QT1` stands for quarter 1 (months 1 to 3), `QT2` for quarter 2 (months 4 to 6), `QT3` for quarter 3 (months 7 to 9), and `QT4` for quarter 4 (months 10 to 12).

The salespeople's IDs are stored in one file; the sales data is stored in another file. The sales data is in the following form:

```
salesPersonID  month  saleAmount
.
.
.
```

Furthermore, the sales data is in no particular order; it is not ordered by ID.

Let us write a program that produces the output in the specified format.

Input One file containing each salesperson's ID, and a second file containing the sales data.

Output A file containing the annual sales report in the above format.

Problem Analysis and Algorithm Design

Based on the problem's requirements, it is clear that the main components for each salesperson are the salesperson's ID, quarterly sales amount, and total annual sales amount. Because the components are of different types, we can group them with the help of a **`struct`**, defined as follows:

```
struct salesPersonRec
{
      string ID;         //salesperson's ID
      double saleByQuarter[4];  //array to store the total
                                //sales for each quarter
      double totalSale;  //salesperson's yearly sales amount
};
```

Because there are six salespeople, we use an array of 6 components, wherein each component is of the type `salesPersonRec`, defined as follows:

```
salesPersonRec salesPersonList[noOfSalesPersons];
```

where the value of `noOfSalesPersons` is `6`.

Because the program requires us to find the company's total sales for each quarter, we need an array of four components to store the data. Note that this data will be used to determine the quarter in which the maximum sales were made. Therefore, the program also needs the following array:

```
double totalSaleByQuarter[4];
```

We will refer to these variables throughout the discussion.

The array `salesPersonList` is as shown in Figure 12-6.

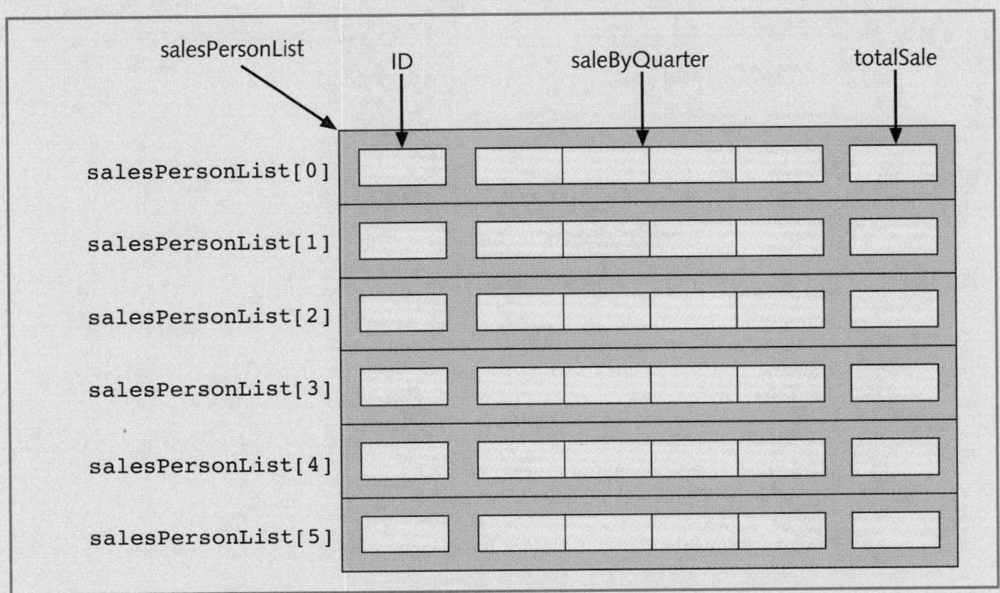

Figure 12-6 Array `salesPersonList`

The first step of the program is to read the salespeople's IDs into the array **salesPersonList** and initialize the quarterly sales and total sales for each salesperson to **0**. After this step, the array **salesPersonList** is as shown in Figure 12-7.

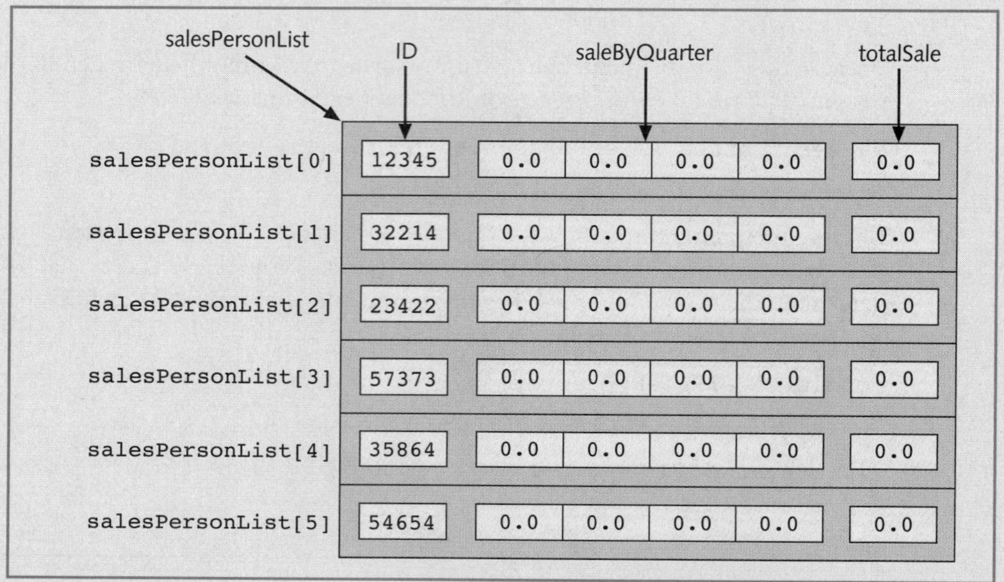

Figure 12-7 Array `salesPersonList` after initialization

The next step is to process the sales data. Processing the sales data is quite straightforward. For each entry in the file containing the sales data,

1. Read the salesperson's ID, month, and sale amount for the month.
2. Search the array **salesPersonList** to locate the component corresponding to this salesperson.
3. Determine the quarter corresponding to the month.
4. Update the sales for the quarter by adding the sale amount for the month.
   Once the sales data file is processed,
   a. Calculate the total sales by salesperson.
   b. Calculate the total sales by quarter.
   c. Print the report.

This discussion translates into the following algorithm:

1. Initialize the array `salesPersonList`.
2. Process the sales data.
3. Calculate the total sales by salesperson.
4. Calculate the total sales by quarter.
5. Print the report.
6. Calculate and print the maximum sales by salesperson.
7. Calculate and print the maximum sales by quarter.

To reduce the complexity of the main program, let us write a separate function for each of these seven steps.

Function `initialize` This function reads the salesperson's ID from the input file and stores the salesperson's ID in the array `salesPersonList`. It also initializes the quarterly sales amount and the total sales amount for each salesperson to `0`. The definition of this function is

```
void initialize(ifstream& indata, salesPersonRec list[],
                int listSize)
{
      int count;
      quarterType quarter;

      for(count = 0; count < listSize; count++)
      {
            indata>>list[count].ID; //get salesperson's ID

            for(quarter = QT1; quarter <= QT4;
                quarter = static_cast<quarterType>(quarter + 1))
                list[count].saleByQuarter[quarter] = 0.0;

            list[count].totalSale = 0.0;
      }
}
```

Function `getData` This function reads the sales data from the input file and stores the appropriate information in the array `salesPersonList`. The algorithm for this function is

1. Read the salesperson's ID, month, and sales amount for the month.
2. Search the array `salesPersonList` to locate the component corresponding to the salesperson. (Because the salespeople's IDs are not sorted, we will use a sequential search to search the array.)

3. Determine the quarter corresponding to the month.
4. Update the sales for the quarter by adding the sales amount for the month.

Suppose that the entry read is

```
57373 2 350
```

Here the salesperson's ID is `57373`, the month is `2`, and the sale amount is `350`. Suppose that the array `salesPersonList` is as shown in Figure 12-8.

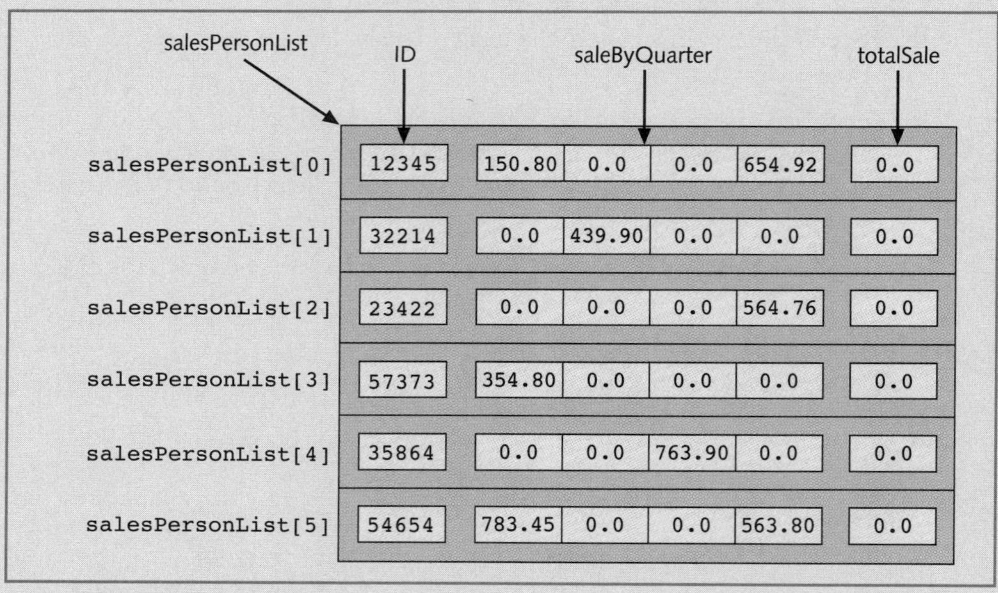

Figure 12-8 Array `salesPersonList`

Now ID `57373` corresponds to the array component `salesPersonList[3]`, and month `2` corresponds to quarter `1`. Therefore, you add `350` to `354.80` to get the new amount, `704.80`. After processing this entry, the array `salesPersonList` is as shown in Figure 12-9.

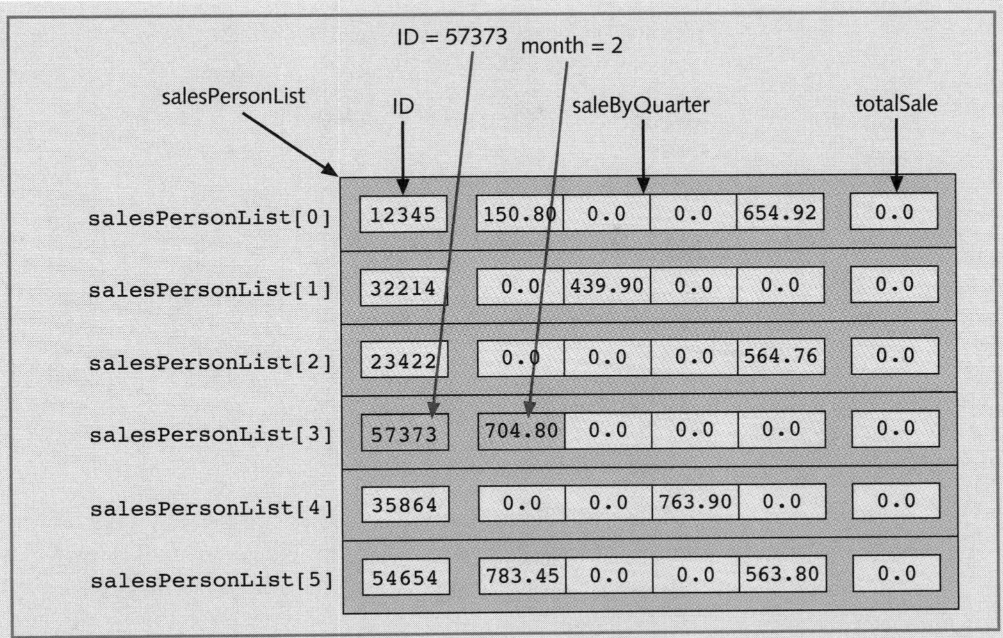

Figure 12-9 Array `salesPersonList` after processing entry `57373 2 350`

The definition of the function `getData` is

```
void getData(ifstream& infile, salesPersonRec list[],
             int listSize)
{
  int count;
  quarterType quarter;
  string sID;
  int month;
  double amount;

  infile>>sID;                                          //Step 1
  while(infile)
  {
      infile>>month>>amount;                            //Step 1

      for(count = 0; count < listSize; count++)         //Step 2

      {
         if(sID == list[count].ID)
         {
            if(1 <= month && month <= 3)                //Step 3
                 quarter = QT1;
```

```
            else if(4 <= month && month <= 6)
                    quarter = QT2;
            else if(7 <= month && month <= 9)
                     quarter = QT3;
            else
                quarter = QT4;

            list[count].saleByQuarter[quarter] += amount;  //Step 4

            break;                 //exit for loop
        }//end if
     }//end for

     infile>>sID;                                           //Step 1
  }//end while
}//end getData
```

Function `saleByQuarter` This function finds the company's total sales for each quarter. To find the total sales for each quarter, we add the sales amount of each salesperson for that quarter. Clearly, this function must have access to the array **`salesPersonList`** and the array **`totalSaleByQuarter`**. This function also needs to know the number of rows in each array. Thus, this function has three parameters. The definition of this function is

```
void saleByQuarter(salesPersonRec list[], int listSize,
                   double totalByQuarter[])
{
   quarterType quarter;
   int count;

   for(quarter = QT1; quarter <= QT4;
              quarter = static_cast<quarterType>(quarter+1))
      totalByQuarter[quarter] = 0.0;

   for(quarter = QT1; quarter <= QT4;
               quarter = static_cast<quarterType>(quarter+1))
      for(count = 0; count < listSize; count++)
         totalByQuarter[quarter] +=
                              list[count].saleByQuarter[quarter];
}
```

Function `totalSaleByPerson` This function finds each salesperson's yearly sales amount. To find an employee's yearly sales amount, we add that employee's sales amount for the four quarters. Clearly, this function must have access to the array **`salesPersonList`**. This function also needs to know the size of the array. Thus, this function has two parameters. The definition of this function is

```
void totalSaleByPerson(salesPersonRec list[], int listSize)
{
   int count;
```

```
   quarterType quarter;

   for(count = 0; count < listSize; count++) //for each salesperson
      for(quarter = QT1; quarter <= QT4;      //for each quarter
                quarter = static_cast<quarterType>(quarter + 1))
            list[count].totalSale +=
                           list[count].saleByQuarter[quarter];
}
```

Function `printReport` This function prints the annual report in the specified format. The algorithm in pseudocode is

a. Print the heading—that is, the first three lines of output.
b. Print the data for each salesperson.
c. Print the last line of the table.

Note that the next two functions will produce the final two lines of output.

Clearly, the `printReport` function must have access to the array `salesPersonList` and the array `totalSaleByQuarter`. Also, because the output will be stored in a file, this function must have access to the `ofstream` variable associated with the output file. Thus, this function has four parameters: a parameter corresponding to the array `salesPersonList`, a parameter corresponding to the array `totalSaleByQuarter`, a parameter specifying the size of the array, and a parameter corresponding to the `ofstream` variable. The definition of this function is

```
void printReport(ofstream& outfile, salesPersonRec list[],
                 int listSize, double saleByQuarter[])
{
   int count;
   quarterType quarter;
                   //Step a
   outfile<<"-----------  Annual Sales Report -------------"<<endl;
   outfile<<endl;
   outfile<<" ID          QT1         QT2       QT3        "
         <<"QT4        Total"<<endl;
   outfile<<"_______________________________________________"
         <<"_______________"<<endl;

   for(count = 0; count < listSize; count++)    //Step b
   {
      outfile<<list[count].ID<<"    ";

      for(quarter = QT1; quarter <= QT4;
               quarter = static_cast<quarterType>(quarter + 1))
         outfile<<setw(10)<<list[count].saleByQuarter[quarter];

      outfile<<setw(10)<<list[count].totalSale<<endl;
```

```
    }

    outfile<<"Total    ";                                  //Step c
    for(quarter = QT1; quarter <= QT4;
                   quarter = static_cast<quarterType>(quarter + 1))
      outfile<<setw(10)<<saleByQuarter[quarter];

    outfile<<endl<<endl<<endl;
}
```

Function `maxSaleByPerson` This function prints the name of the salesperson who produces the maximum sales amount. To identify this salesperson, we look at the total sales for each salesperson and find the largest sales amount. Because each employee's total sales is maintained in the array `salesPersonList`, this function must have access to the array `salesPersonList`. Also, because the output will be stored in a file, this function must have access to the `ofstream` variable associated with the output file. Therefore, this function has three parameters: a parameter corresponding to the array `salesPersonList`, a parameter specifying the size of this array, and a parameter corresponding to the output file.

The algorithm to find the largest sales amount is similar to the algorithm to find the largest element in an array (discussed in Chapter 9). The definition of this function is

```
void maxSaleByPerson(ofstream& outData, salesPersonRec list[],
                     int listSize)
{
    int maxIndex = 0;
    int count;

    for(count = 1; count < listSize; count++)
       if(list[maxIndex].totalSale < list[count].totalSale)
           maxIndex = count;

    outData<<"Max Sale by SalesPerson: ID = "<<list[maxIndex].ID
           <<", Amount = $"<<list[maxIndex].totalSale<<endl;
}
```

Function `maxSaleByQuarter` This function prints the quarter in which the maximum sales were made. To identify this quarter, we look at the total sales for each quarter and find the largest sales amount. Because the total sales for each quarter is in the array `totalSaleByQuarter`, this function must have access to the array `totalSaleByQuarter`. Also, because the output will be stored in a file, this function must have access to the `ofstream` variable associated with the output file. Therefore, this function has two parameters: a parameter corresponding to the array `totalSaleByQuarter` and a parameter corresponding to the output file.

The algorithm to find the largest sales amount is the same as the algorithm to find the largest element in an array (discussed in Chapter 9). The definition of this function is

```
void maxSaleByQuarter(ofstream& outData, double saleByQuarter[])
{
   quarterType quarter;
   quarterType maxIndex = QT1;

   for(quarter = QT1; quarter <= QT4;
                    quarter = static_cast<quarterType>(quarter+1))
      if(saleByQuarter[maxIndex] < saleByQuarter[quarter])
            maxIndex = quarter;

   outData<<"Max Sale by Quarter: Quarter = "
          << static_cast<int>(maxIndex) + 1
          <<", Amount = $"<<saleByQuarter[maxIndex]<<endl;
}
```

To make the program more flexible, we will prompt the user to specify the input and output files during its execution.

We are now ready to write the algorithm for the function `main`.

Main Algorithm

1. Declare the variables.
2. Prompt the user to enter the name of the file containing the salesperson's ID data.
3. Read the name of the input file.
4. Open the input file.
5. If the input file does not exist, exit the program.
6. Initialize the array `salesPersonList`. Call the function `initialize`.
7. Close the input file containing the salesperson's ID data.
8. Prompt the user to enter the name of the file containing the sales data.
9. Read the name of the input file.
10. Open the input file.
11. If the input file does not exist, exit the program.
12. Prompt the user to enter the name of the output file.
13. Read the name of the output file.
14. Open the output file.
15. To output floating-point numbers in a fixed decimal format with the decimal point and trailing zeroes, set the manipulators `fixed` and `showpoint`. Also, to output floating-point numbers to two decimal places, set the precision to two decimal places.
16. Process the sales data. Call the function `getData`.
17. Calculate the total sales by quarter. Call the function `saleByQuarter`.

18. Calculate the total sales for each salesperson. Call the function `totalSaleByPerson`.
19. Print the report in a tabular format. Call the function `printReport`.
20. Find and print the salesperson who produces the maximum sales for the year. Call the function `maxSaleByPerson`.
21. Find and print the quarter that produces the maximum sales for the year. Call the function `maxSaleByQuarter`.
22. Close the files.

Complete Program Listing

```
//Program: Sales data analysis
#include <iostream>
#include <fstream>
#include <iomanip>
#include <string>

using namespace std;

const int noOfSalesPerson = 6;

enum quarterType{QT1,QT2,QT3,QT4};

struct salesPersonRec
{
      string ID;  //salesperson's ID
      double saleByQuarter[4];
      double totalSale;
};

void initialize(ifstream& indata, salesPersonRec list[],
                int listSize);
void getData(ifstream& infile, salesPersonRec list[],
             int listSize);
void saleByQuarter(salesPersonRec list[], int listSize,
                   double totalByQuarter[]);
void totalSaleByPerson(salesPersonRec list[], int listSize);
void maxSaleByPerson(ofstream& outData, salesPersonRec list[],
                     int listSize);
void maxSaleByQuarter(ofstream& outData, double saleByQuarter[]);
void printReport(ofstream& outfile, salesPersonRec list[],
                 int listSize, double saleByQuarter[]);
int main()
{
            //Step 1
   ifstream infile;      //input file stream variable
```

```
ofstream outfile;     //output file stream variable
char inputfile[25];  //variable to hold the input file name
char outputfile[25]; //variable to hold the output file name

double totalSaleByQuarter[4]; //array to hold the
                               //sales by quarter

salesPersonRec salesPersonList[noOfSalesPerson]; //array to
                         //hold the salesperson's data
cout<<"Enter SalesPerson ID file name : ";              //Step 2
cin>>inputfile;                                          //Step 3
cout<<endl;

infile.open(inputfile);                                  //Step 4

if(!infile)                                              //Step 5
{
   cout<<"Cannot open input file."<<endl;
   return 1;
}

initialize(infile, salesPersonList, noOfSalesPerson); //Step 6

infile.close();   //reclaim input file stream variable; Step 7

cout<<"Enter sales data file name: ";                   //Step 8
cin>>inputfile;                                          //Step 9
cout<<endl;

infile.open(inputfile);                                  //Step 10

if(!infile)                                              //Step 11
{
   cout<<"Cannot open input file."<<endl;
   return 1;
}

cout<<"Enter output file name: ";                       //Step 12
cin>>outputfile;                                         //Step 13
cout<<endl;

outfile.open(outputfile);                                //Step 14

outfile<<fixed<<showpoint<<setprecision(2);             //Step 15

getData(infile, salesPersonList, noOfSalesPerson);     //Step 16
```

```
    saleByQuarter(salesPersonList, noOfSalesPerson,
                  totalSaleByQuarter);                     //Step 17
    totalSaleByPerson(salesPersonList, noOfSalesPerson);   //Step 18

    printReport(outfile, salesPersonList, noOfSalesPerson,
                totalSaleByQuarter);                       //Step 19
    maxSaleByPerson(outfile, salesPersonList,
                    noOfSalesPerson);                      //Step 20
    maxSaleByQuarter(outfile, totalSaleByQuarter);         //Step 21

    infile.close();                                        //Step 22
    outfile.close();                                       //Step 22
      return 0;
}

void initialize(ifstream& indata, salesPersonRec list[],
                int listSize)
{
    int count;
    quarterType quarter;

    for(count = 0; count < listSize; count++)
    {
       indata>>list[count].ID; //get salesperson's ID

       for(quarter = QT1; quarter <= QT4;
                quarter = static_cast<quarterType>(quarter + 1))
            list[count].saleByQuarter[quarter] = 0.0;

       list[count].totalSale = 0.0;
    }
}

void getData(ifstream& infile, salesPersonRec list[],
             int listSize)
{
    int count;
    quarterType quarter;
    string sID;
    int month;
    double amount;

    infile>>sID;  //get salesperson's ID
    while(infile)
    {
       infile>>month>>amount; //get the sales month and sales amount

       for(count = 0; count < listSize; count++)
       {
```

```
         if(sID == list[count].ID)
         {
            if(1 <= month && month <= 3)
                  quarter = QT1;
            else if(4 <= month && month <= 6)
                      quarter = QT2;
            else if(7 <= month && month <= 9)
                   quarter = QT3;
            else
                quarter = QT4;
          list[count].saleByQuarter[quarter] += amount;
          break;
       }//end if
    }//end for

    infile>>sID;
   }//end while
}//end getData

void saleByQuarter(salesPersonRec list[], int listSize,
                   double totalByQuarter[])
{
   quarterType quarter;
   int count;

   for(quarter = QT1; quarter <= QT4;
                 quarter = static_cast<quarterType>(quarter+1))
      totalByQuarter[quarter] = 0.0;

   for(quarter = QT1; quarter <= QT4;
              quarter = static_cast<quarterType>(quarter+1))
      for(count = 0; count < listSize; count++)
         totalByQuarter[quarter] +=
                        list[count].saleByQuarter[quarter];
}

void totalSaleByPerson(salesPersonRec list[], int listSize)
{
   int count;
   quarterType quarter;

   for(count = 0; count < listSize; count++)
    for(quarter = QT1; quarter <= QT4;
                 quarter = static_cast<quarterType>(quarter + 1))
        list[count].totalSale +=
                              list[count].saleByQuarter[quarter];
}
```

```
void maxSaleByPerson(ofstream& outData, salesPersonRec list[],
                     int listSize)
{
   int maxIndex = 0;
   int count;
   for(count = 1; count < listSize; count++)
      if(list[maxIndex].totalSale < list[count].totalSale)
          maxIndex = count;

   outData<<"Max Sale by SalesPerson: ID = "<<list[maxIndex].ID
          <<", Amount = $"<<list[maxIndex].totalSale<<endl;
}

void maxSaleByQuarter(ofstream& outData, double saleByQuarter[])
{
   quarterType quarter;
   quarterType maxIndex = QT1;

   for(quarter = QT1; quarter <= QT4;
                 quarter = static_cast<quarterType>(quarter+1))
      if(saleByQuarter[maxIndex] < saleByQuarter[quarter])
            maxIndex = quarter;

   outData<<"Max Sale by Quarter: Quarter = "
          <<static_cast<int>(maxIndex) + 1
          <<", Amount = $"<<saleByQuarter[maxIndex]<<endl;
}

void printReport(ofstream& outfile, salesPersonRec list[],
                 int listSize, double saleByQuarter[])
{
   int count;
   quarterType quarter;

   outfile<<"-----------  Annual Sales Report -------------"<<endl;
   outfile<<endl;
   outfile<<"  ID         QT1        QT2      QT3       "
          <<"QT4       Total"<<endl;
   outfile<<"________________________________________________"
          <<"_______________"<<endl;

   for(count = 0; count < listSize; count++)
   {
      outfile<<list[count].ID<<"   ";

      for(quarter = QT1; quarter <= QT4;
                 quarter = static_cast<quarterType>(quarter + 1))
          outfile<<setw(10)<<list[count].saleByQuarter[quarter];
```

```
        outfile<<setw(10)<<list[count].totalSale<<endl;
    }

    outfile<<"Total    ";

    for(quarter = QT1; quarter <= QT4;
            quarter = static_cast<quarterType>(quarter + 1))
        outfile<<setw(10)<<saleByQuarter[quarter];

     outfile<<endl<<endl<<endl;
}
```

Sample Run

Input File: Salespeople's IDs

```
12345
32214
23422
57373
35864
54654
```

Input File: Salespeople's Data

```
12345 1 893
32214 1 343
23422 3 903
57373 2 893
35864 5 329
54654 9 392
12345 2 999
32214 4 892
23422 4 895
23422 2 492
57373 6 892
35864 10 1223
54654 11 3420
12345 12 322
35864  5 892
54654  3 893
12345 8 494
32214 8 9023
23422 6 223
23422 4 783
57373 8 8834
35864 3 2882
```

Output File

```
-----------  Annual Sales Report -------------

  ID          QT1         QT2        QT3         QT4         Total
______________________________________________________________________
12345       1892.00      0.00     494.00      322.00      2708.00
32214        343.00    892.00    9023.00        0.00     10258.00
23422       1395.00   1901.00       0.00        0.00      3296.00
57373        893.00    892.00    8834.00        0.00     10619.00
35864       2882.00   1221.00       0.00     1223.00      5326.00
54654        893.00      0.00     392.00     3420.00      4705.00
Total       8298.00   4906.00   18743.00     4965.00


Max Sale by SalesPerson: ID = 57373, Amount = $10619.00
Max Sale by Quarter: Quarter = 3, Amount = $18743.00
```

QUICK REVIEW

1. A **struct** is a collection of a fixed number of components.
2. Components of a **struct** can be of different types.
3. The syntax of defining a **struct** is

```
struct structName
{
   dataType identifier;
   dataType identifier;
        .
        .
};
```

4. In C++, **struct** is a reserved word.
5. In C++, **struct** is a definition; no memory is allocated. Memory is allocated for the **struct** variables only when you declare them.
6. Components of a **struct** are called members of the **struct**.
7. Components of a **struct** are accessed by name.
8. Members of a **struct** are accessed by using the dot (**.**) operator. If **employeeType** is a **struct**, **employee** is a variable of the type **employeeType**, and **name** is a member of **employee**, then the expression **employee.name** accesses the member **name**. That is, **employee.name** is a variable and can be manipulated like other variables.
9. In C++, the dot (**.**) operator is called the member access operator.
10. The only built-in operations on a **struct** are the assignment and member access operations.

11. No arithmetic and relational operations are allowed on `struct`(s).
12. As a parameter to a function, a `struct` can be passed either by value or by reference.
13. A function can return a value of the type `struct`.
14. A `struct` can be a member of another `struct`.

EXERCISES

1. Mark the following statements as true or false.
   a. A `struct` is a homogenous data structure.
   b. A function cannot return a value of the type `struct`.
   c. A member of a `struct` can be another `struct`.
   d. The only allowable operations on a `struct` are assignment and member selection.
   e. An array can be a member of a `struct`.
   f. In C++, some aggregate operations are allowed on a `struct`.
   g. Because a `struct` has a finite number of components, relational operations are allowed on a `struct`.
2. Consider the following statements:

```
struct nameType
{
   string first;
   string last;
};
struct dateType
{
   int month;
   int day;
   int year;
};
struct personalInfoType
{
   nameType name;
   int pID;
   dataType dob;
};
personalInfoType person;
personalInfoType classList[100];
nameType student;
```

   Mark the following statements as valid or invalid. If a statement is invalid, explain why.

   a. `person.name.first = "William";`

   b. `cout<<person.name;`

12

c. `classList[1] = person;`

d. `classList[20].pID = 000011100;`

e. `person = classList[20];`

f. `student = person.name;`

g. `cin>>student;`

h.
```
for(int j = 0; j < 100; j++)
    classList[j].pID = 00000000;
```

i. `classList.dob.date = 1;`

j. `student = name;`

3. Consider the following statements (`nameType` is as defined in Exercise 2):

```
struct employeeType
{
   nameType name;
   int    performanceRating;
   int    pID;
   string dept;
   double salary;
};
employeeType employees[100];
employeeType newEmployee;
```

Mark the following statements as valid or invalid. If a statement is invalid, explain why.

a. `newEmployee.name = "John Smith";`

b. `cout<<newEmployee.name;`

c. `employees[35] = newEmployee;`

d.
```
if(employees[45].pID == 555334444)
    employees[45].performanceRating = 1;
```

e. `employees.salary = 0;`

4. Assume the declarations of Exercises 2 and 3. Write C++ statements that do the following.

a. Store the following information in `newEmployee`:

```
name: Mickey Doe
pID:  111111111
performanceRating: 2
dept: ACCT
salary: 34567.78
```

b. In the array `employees`, initialize each `performanceRating` to `0`.

c. Copy the information of the twentieth component of the array `employees` into `newEmployee`.

d. Update the salary of the fiftieth employee in the array `employees` by adding `5735.87` to its previous value.

PROGRAMMING EXERCISES

1. Write a program that reads students' names followed by their test scores. The program should output each student's name followed by the test scores and the relevant grade. It should also find and print the highest test score and the name of the students having the highest test score.

   Student data should be stored in a `struct` variable of the type `studentType`, which has three components: `studentName` of the type `string`, `testScore` of the type `int` (`testScore` is between `0` and `100`), and `grade` of the type `char`. Suppose that the class has 20 students. Use an array of 20 components of the type `studentType`.

   Your program must contain, at least, the following functions:

   a. A function to read the students' data into the array.

   b. A function to assign the relevant grade to each student.

   c. A function to find the highest test score.

   d. A function to print the names of the students having the highest test score.

   Your program must output each student's name in this form: last name followed by a comma, followed by a space, followed by the first name, and the name must be left-justified. Moreover, the function `main` should, other than declaring variables and opening the input and output files, be just a collection of function calls.

2. Define a `struct`, `menuItemType`, with two components: `menuItem` of the type `string` and `menuPrice` of the type `double`.

3. Write a program to help a local restaurant automate its breakfast billing system. The program should do the following:

   a. Show the customer the different breakfast items offered by the restaurant.

   b. Allow the customer to select more than one item from the menu.

   c. Calculate and print the bill.

   Assume that the restaurant offers the following breakfast items (the price of each item is shown to the right of the item):

```
Plain Egg             $1.45
Bacon and Egg         $2.45
Muffin                $0.99
French Toast          $1.99
Fruit Basket          $2.49
Cereal                $0.69
Coffee                $0.50
Tea                   $0.75
```

12

Use an array, `menuList`, of the `struct menuItemType`, as defined in Programming Exercise 2. Your program must contain the following functions:

- **Function `getData`:** This function loads the data into the array `menuList`.
- **Function `showMenu`:** This function shows the different items offered by the restaurant and tells the user how to select items.
- **Function `printCheck`:** This function calculates and prints the check. (Note that the billing amount should include a 5% tax.)

A sample output is

```
Welcome to Johnny's Restaurant
Bacon and Egg     $2.45
Muffin            $0.99
Coffee            $0.50
Tax               $0.20
Amount Due        $4.14
```

Format your output with two decimal places. The name of each item in the output must be left-justified. You may assume that the user selects only one item of a particular type.

4. Redo Exercise 3 so that the customer can select multiple orders of a particular type. A sample output in this case is

```
Welcome to Johnny's Restaurant
1 Bacon and Egg     $2.45
2 Muffins           $1.98
1 Coffee            $0.50
  Tax               $0.25
  Amount Due        $5.18
```

5. Write a program whose main function is merely a collection of variable declarations and function calls. This program reads a text and outputs the letters together with their counts, as explained in the function `printResult`, below. (There can be no global variables! All information must be passed in and out of the functions. Use a structure to store the information.) Your program must consist of at least the following functions:

   - **Function `openFile`:** Opens the input and output files. You must pass the file streams as parameters (by reference, of course). If the file does not exist, the program should print an appropriate message and exit. The program must ask the user for the names of the input and output files.
   - **Function `count`:** Counts every occurrence of capital letters `A`–`Z` and small letters `a`–`z` in the text file opened in the **function `openFile`**. This information must go into an array of structures. The array must be passed as a parameter, and the file identifier must be passed in as a parameter.
   - **Function `printResult`:** Prints the number of capital letters and small letters, as well as the percentage of capital letters for every letter `A`–`Z` and the percentage of small letters for every letter `a`–`z`. The percentages should look like this: "`25%`". This information must come from an array of structures, and this array must be passed as a parameter.

CHAPTER

13

CLASSES AND DATA ABSTRACTION

In this chapter, you will:

- Learn about classes
- Learn about `private`, `protected`, and `public` members of a class
- Explore how classes are implemented
- Examine constructors and destructors
- Learn about the abstract data type (ADT)
- Explore how classes are used to implement ADT
- Learn about information hiding
- Explore how information hiding is implemented in C++

In Chapter 12, you learned how to group data items that are of different types using a `struct`. The definition of a `struct` given in Chapter 12 is similar to the definition of a C `struct`. However, the members of a C++ `struct` can be data items as well as functions. C++ provides another structured data type, called a **class**, which is specifically designed to group data and functions. This chapter first introduces classes and explains how to use them, and then discusses the similarities and differences between a `struct` and a `class`.

Chapter 12 is not a prerequisite for this chapter. In fact, a `struct` and a `class` have similar capabilities as discussed in the section, "A `struct` versus a `class`" later in this chapter.

CLASSES

Chapter 1 introduced the problem-solving methodology called object oriented design (OOD). In OOD, the first step is to identify the components called objects; an object combines data and the operations on that data in a single unit. In C++, the mechanism that allows you to combine data and the operations on that data in a single unit is called a class. Now that you know how to store and manipulate data in computer memory and how to construct your own functions, you are ready to learn how objects are constructed. This and subsequent chapters develop and implement programs using OOD. This chapter first explains how to define a class and use it in a program.

A **class** is a collection of a fixed number of components. The components of a class are called the **members** of the class.

The general syntax for defining a class is

```
class classIdentifier
{
    classMembersList
};
```

where **`classMembersList`** consists of variable declarations and/or functions. That is, a member of a **`class`** can be either a variable (to store data) or a function.

- If a member of a class is a variable, you declare it just like any other variable. Also, in the definition of the class, you cannot initialize a variable when you declare it.
- If a member of a class is a function, you typically use the function prototype to define that member.
- If a member of a class is a function, it can (directly) access any member of the class—data members and function members. That is, when you write the definition of the member function, you can directly access any data member of the class without passing it as a parameter. The only obvious condition is that you must declare an identifier before you can use it.

In C++, **`class`** is a reserved word, and it defines only a data type; no memory is allocated. It announces the declaration of a class. Moreover, note the semicolon (**`;`**) after the right brace. The semicolon is part of the syntax. A missing semicolon, therefore, will result in a syntax error.

The members of a **`class`** are classified into three categories: **`private`**, **`public`**, and **`protected`**. This chapter mainly discusses the first two types—that is, **`private`** and **`public`**.

Following are some facts about **`public`** and **`private`** members of a class:

- By default, all members of a class are **`private`**.
- If a member of a class is **`private`**, you cannot access it outside the class. (Example 13-1 illustrates this concept.)

- A **public** member is accessible outside the **class**. (Example 13-1 illustrates this concept.)
- To make a member of a class **public**, you use the label **public** with a colon.

In C++, **private**, **protected**, and **public** are reserved words, and are called **member access specifiers**.

Suppose that we want to define a class to implement the time of day in a program. Because a clock gives the time of the day, let us call this class **clockType**. Furthermore, to represent time in computer memory we use three **int** variables: one to represent the hours, one to represent the minutes, and one to represent the seconds. We also want to perform the following operations on the time:

1. Set the time.
2. Return the time.
3. Print the time.
4. Increment the time by one second.
5. Increment the time by one minute.
6. Increment the time by one hour.
7. Compare the two times for equality.

From this discussion, it is clear that the **class clockType** has 10 members: three data members and seven function members. (See Figure 13-1.)

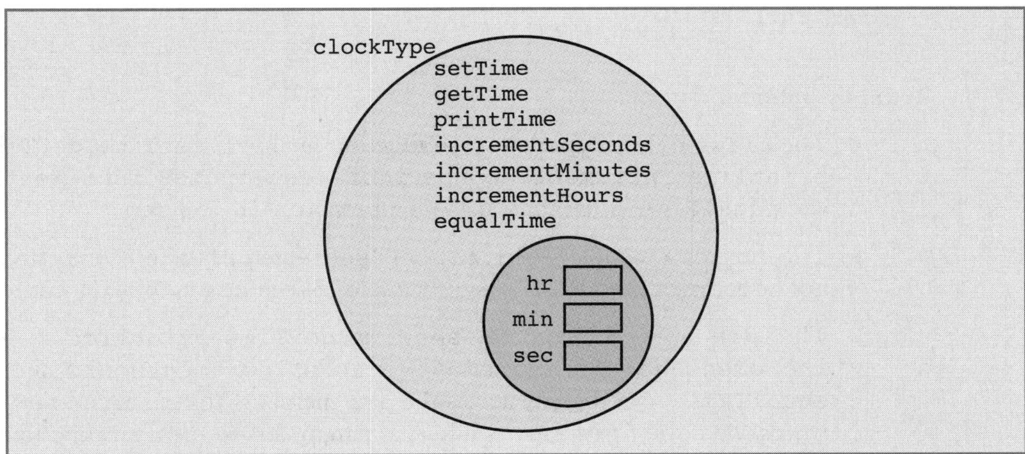

Figure 13-1 `class clockType` and its members

Some members of the **class clockType** will be **private**; others will be **public**. Deciding which member to make **public** and which to make **private** depends on the nature of the member. The general rule is that any member that needs to be accessed outside the class is declared **public**; any member that should not be accessed directly by the user should be declared **private**. For example, the user should be able to set the time and print the time. Therefore, the members that set the time and print the time should be declared **public**.

Similarly, the members to increment the time, and compare the time for equality, should be declared **public**. On the other hand, to control the *direct* manipulation of the data members **hr**, **min**, and **sec**, we will declare them **private**. Furthermore, note that if the user has direct access to the data members, member functions such as **setTime** are not needed. The second part of this chapter (beginning with the section, "Information Hiding"), teaches you why some members are **public** and others are **private**.

The following statements define the **class clockType**:

```
class clockType
{
public:
    void setTime(int, int, int);
    void getTime(int&, int&, int&);
    void printTime() const;
    void incrementSeconds();
    void incrementMinutes();
    void incrementHours();
    bool equalTime(const clockType& otherClock) const;
private:
    int hr;
    int min;
    int sec;
};
```

In this definition:

- The **class clockType** has seven function members: **setTime**, **getTime**, **printTime**, **incrementSeconds**, **incrementMinutes**, **incrementHours**, and **equalTime**. It has three data members: **hr**, **min**, and **sec**.
- The three data members—**hr**, **min**, and **sec**—are **private** to the class and cannot be accessed outside the class. (Example 13-1 illustrates this concept.)
- The seven function members—**setTime**, **getTime**, **printTime**, **incrementSeconds**, **incrementMinutes**, **incrementHours**, and **equalTime**—can directly access the data members (**hr**, **min**, and **sec**). In other words, we do not pass data members as parameters to member functions.

- In the function **equalTime**, the parameter **otherClock** is a constant reference parameter. That is, in a call to the function **equalTime**, the parameter **otherClock** receives the address of the actual parameter, but **otherClock** cannot modify the value of the actual parameter. You could have declared **otherClock** as a value parameter, but that would require **otherClock** to copy the value of the actual parameter, which could result in poor performance. (See the section "Reference Parameters and Class Objects (Variables)" later in this chapter for an explanation.)
- The word **const** at the end of the member functions **printTime** and **equalTime** specifies that these functions cannot modify the data members of a variable of the type **clockType**.

The **private** and **public** members can appear in any order. If you want, you can declare the **private** members first and then declare the **public** ones. The section "Order of **public** and **private** Members of a Class" later in this chapter discusses this issue.

In the definition of the **class clockType**, all data members are **private** and all function members are **public**. However, a function member can also be **private**. For example, if a member function is used only to implement other member functions of the class, and the user does not need to access this function, you make it **private**. Similarly, a data member of a class can also be **public**.

Note that we have not yet written the definitions of the function members of the class. You will learn how to write them shortly.

The function **setTime** sets the three data members—**hr**, **min**, and **sec**—to a given value. The given values are passed as parameters to the function **setTime**. The function **printTime** prints the time, that is, the values of **hr**, **min**, and **sec**. The function **incrementSeconds** increments the time by one second, the function **incrementMinutes** increments the time by one minute, the function **incrementHours** increments the time by one hour, and the function **equalTime** compares two times for equality.

Note that the function **equalTime** has only one parameter, although you need two things to make a comparison. We will explain this point with the help of an example in the section "Implementation of Member Functions" later in this chapter.

Variable (Object) Declaration

Once a class is defined, you can declare variables of that type. In C++ terminology, a class variable is called a **class object** or **class instance**. To help you become familiar with this terminology, from now on we will use the term **class object**, or simply **object**, for a class variable.

The syntax for declaring a class object is the same as that for declaring any other variable. The following statements declare two objects of the type **`clockType`**:

```
clockType    myClock;
clockType    yourClock;
```

Each object has 10 members: seven function members and three data members. Each object has separate memory allocated for **`hr`**, **`min`**, and **`sec`**.

In actuality, memory is allocated only for the data members of each class object. The C++ compiler generates only one physical copy of a function member of a class, and each class object executes the same copy of the member function. Therefore, whenever we draw the figure of a class, we will usually show all of its members. However, whenever we draw the figure of a class object, we will show only the data members. As an example, Figure 13-2 shows the objects **`myClock`** and **`yourClock`** with values in their data members.

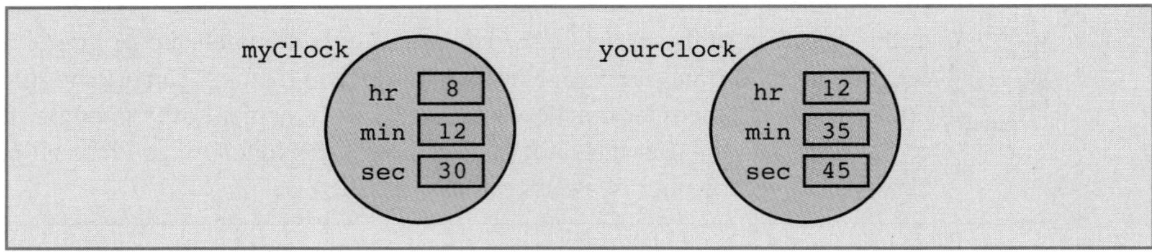

Figure 13-2 Objects `myClock` and `yourClock`

Accessing Class Members

Once an object is declared, it can access the **`public`** members of a class. The general syntax to access the member of a class is

```
classObjectName.memberName
```

Recall that in C++, the dot, **`.`** (period), is an operator called the **member access operator**.

Example 13-1 illustrates how to access the members of a class.

Example 13-1

Consider the following statements:

```
myClock.setTime(5,2,30);
myClock.printTime();
yourClock.setTime(x,y,z);        //Assume x, y, and z are
                                 //variables of the type int

if(myClock.equalTime(yourClock))
   .
   .
   .
```

These statements are legal; that is, they are syntactically correct.

In the first statement, `myClock.setTime(5,2,30);`, the function member `setTime` is executed. The values `5`, `2`, and `30` are passed as parameters to the function `setTime`, and the function uses the values to set the values of the three data members `hr`, `min`, and `sec` of `myClock` to `5`, `2`, and `30`, respectively. Similarly, the second statement executes the member function `printTime` and outputs the contents of the three data members of `myClock`. In the third statement, the values of the variables `x`, `y`, and `z` are used to set the values of the three data members of `yourClock`.

In the fourth statement, the member function `equalTime` executes and compares the three data members of `myClock` to the corresponding data members of `yourClock`. Because in this statement `equalTime` is a member of the object `myClock`, it has direct access to the three data members of `myClock`. So it needs one more object, which in this case, is `yourClock`, to compare. This explains why the function `equalTime` has only one parameter.

13

A class object can access only **`public`** members of the class. Thus, the following statements are illegal, because `hr` and `min` are **`private`** members of the **`class`** `clockType` and, therefore, cannot be accessed by the objects `myClock` and `yourClock`:

```
myClock.hr = 10;                 //illegal
myClock.min = yourClock.min;     //illegal
```

Built-In Operations on Classes

Most of C++'s built-in operations do not apply to classes. You cannot use arithmetic operators to perform arithmetic operations on class variables (unless they are overloaded; see Chapter 16). For example, you cannot use the operator + to add two class variables of, say, the type `clockType`. Also, you cannot use relational operators to compare two class variables for equality (unless they are overloaded; see Chapter 16).

The two built-in operations that are valid for class objects are member access (`.`) and assignment (=). You have seen how to access an individual member of a class by using the name of the class object, then a dot, and then the member name.

We now show how an assignment statement works with the help of an example.

The Assignment Operator and Classes

Suppose that **myClock** and **yourClock** are variables of the type **clockType** as defined previously. Furthermore, suppose that the values of **myClock** and **yourClock** are as shown in Figure 13-3.

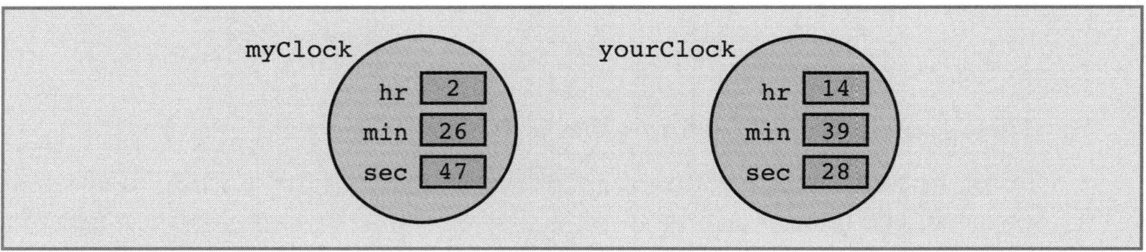

Figure 13-3 Objects myClock and yourClock

The statement

```
myClock = yourClock;            //Line A
```

copies the value of **yourClock** into **myClock**. That is,

1. The value of **yourClock.hr** is copied into **myClock.hr**,
2. The value of **yourClock.min** is copied into **myClock.min**, and
3. The value of **yourClock.sec** is copied into **myClock.sec**.

In other words, the values of the three data members of **yourClock** are copied into the corresponding data members of **myClock**. Therefore, an assignment statement performs a member-wise copy. After the statement in Line **A** executes, the values of **myClock** and **yourClock** are as shown in Figure 13-4.

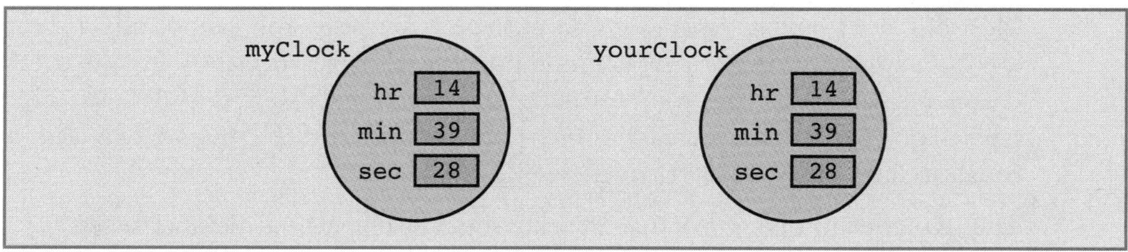

Figure 13-4 Objects myClock and yourClock after the assignment statement myClock = yourClock; executes

Class Scope

A **class** object can be either automatic (that is, created each time the control reaches its declaration and destroyed when the control exits the surrounding block) or static (that is, created once, when the control reaches its declaration and destroyed when the program terminates). Also, you can declare an array of **class** objects. A **class** object has the same scope as other variables. A member of a **class** has the same scope as a member of a **struct**. That is, a member of a **class** is local to the **class**. You access a **class** member outside the **class** by using the **class** object name and the member access operator (**.**).

Functions and Classes

The following rules describe the relationship between functions and classes:

- Class objects can be passed as parameters to functions and returned as function values.
- As parameters to functions, classes can be passed either by value or by reference.
- If a class object is passed by value, the contents of the data members of the actual parameter are copied into the corresponding data members of the formal parameter.

Reference Parameters and Class Objects (Variables)

Recall that when a variable is passed by value, the formal parameter copies the value of the actual parameter. That is, memory is allocated to copy the value of the actual parameter for the formal parameter. As a parameter, a class object can be passed by value.

Suppose that a class has several data members requiring a large amount of memory to store data, and you need to pass a variable by value. The corresponding formal parameter then receives a copy of the data of the variable. That is, the compiler must allocate memory for the formal parameter so as to copy the value of the data members of the actual parameter. This operation might require, in addition to a large amount of storage space, a considerable amount of computer time to copy the value of the actual parameter into the formal parameter.

On the other hand, if a variable is passed by reference, the formal parameter receives only the address of the actual parameter. Therefore, an efficient way to pass a variable as a parameter is by reference. If a variable is passed by reference, then when the formal parameter changes, the actual parameter also changes. Sometimes, however, you do not want the function to be able to change the values of the data members. In C++, you can pass a variable by reference and still prevent the function from changing its value, by using the keyword **const** in the formal parameter declaration. As an example, consider the following function definition:

```
void testTime(const clockType& otherClock)
{
      clockType dClock;
      ...
}
```

The function **testTime** contains a reference parameter, **otherClock**. The parameter **otherClock** is declared using the keyword **const**. Thus, in a call to the function **testTime**, the formal parameter **otherClock** receives the address of the actual parameter, but **otherClock** cannot modify the contents of the actual parameter. For example, after the following statement executes, the value of **myClock** will not be altered:

```
testTime(myClock);
```

Generally, if you want to declare a class object as a value parameter, you declare it as a reference parameter using the keyword **const** as described previously.

Recall that if a formal parameter is a value parameter, within the function definition you can change the value of the formal parameter. That is, you can use an assignment statement to change the value of the formal parameter (which, of course, would have no effect on the actual parameter). However, if a formal parameter is a constant reference parameter, you cannot use an assignment statement to change its value within the function, nor can you use any other function to change its value. Therefore, within the definition of the function **testTime**, you cannot alter the value of **otherClock**. For example, the following would be illegal in the definition of the function **testTime**:

```
otherClock.setTime(5, 34, 56); //illegal
otherClock = dClock;           //illegal
```

Implementation of Member Functions

When we defined the **class clockType**, for the function members, we included only the function prototype. For these functions to work properly, we must write the related algorithms. One way to implement these functions is to provide the function definition rather than the function prototype in the class itself. Unfortunately, the class definition would then be very long and difficult to comprehend. Another reason for providing function prototypes instead of function definitions relates to **information hiding**; that is, we want to hide the details of the operations on the data. We will discuss this issue later in this chapter (see the section "Information Hiding").

Next, let us write the definitions of the function members of the **class clockType**. That is, we will write the definitions of the functions **setTime**, **getTime**, **printTime**, **incrementSeconds**, **equalTime**, and so on. Because the identifiers **setTime**, **printTime**, and so forth are local to the class, we cannot reference them (directly) outside the class. In order to reference these identifiers, we use the **scope resolution operator**, **::** (double colon). In the function definition's heading, the name of the function is the name of the class, followed by the scope resolution operator, followed by the function name. For example, the definition of the function **setTime** is as follows:

```
void clockType::setTime(int hours, int minutes, int seconds)
{
      if(0 <= hours && hours < 24)
         hr = hours;
      else
         hr = 0;

      if(0 <= minutes && minutes < 60)
         min = minutes;
      else
         min = 0;

      if(0 <= seconds && seconds < 60)
         sec = seconds;
      else
         sec = 0;
}
```

Note that the definition of the function **setTime** checks for the valid values of **hours**, **minutes**, and **seconds**. If these values are out of range, the data members **hr**, **min**, and **sec** are initialized to 0. Let us now explain how the member function **setTime** works when accessed by an object of the type **clockType**.

The member function **setTime** is a **void** function and has three parameters. Therefore,

- A call to this function is a stand-alone statement.
- We must use three parameters in a call to this function.

Furthermore, recall that, because **setTime** is a member of the **class clockType**, it can directly access the data members **hr**, **min**, and **sec** as shown in the definition of **setTime**.

13

Suppose that **myClock** is an object of the type **clockType** (as declared previously). The object **myClock** has three data members, as shown in Figure 13-5.

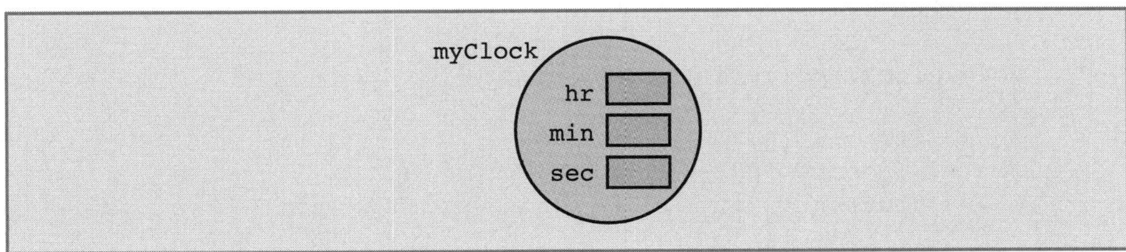

Figure 13-5 Object myClock

Consider the following statement:

```
myClock.setTime(3,48,52);
```

The object **myClock** accesses the member **setTime**. In the statement **myClock.setTime(3,48,52);**, **setTime** is accessed by the object **myClock**. Therefore, the three variables—**hr**, **min**, and **sec**—referred to in the body of the function **setTime** are the three data members of **myClock**. Thus, the values, **3**, **48**, and **52**, which are passed as parameters in the preceding statement, are assigned to the three data members of **myClock** by the function **setTime** (see the body of the function **setTime**). After the previous statement executes, the object **myClock** is as shown in Figure 13-6.

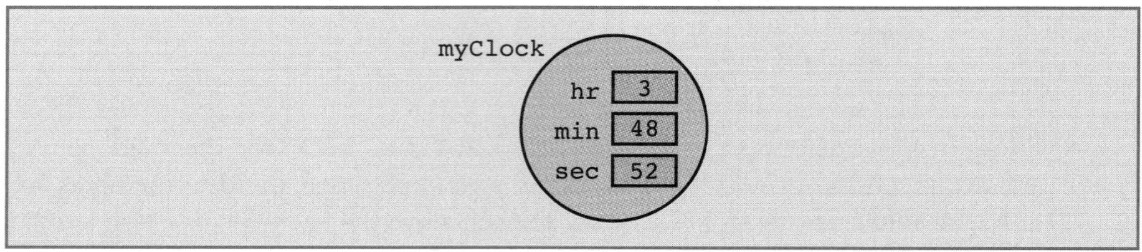

Figure 13-6 Object myClock after statement myClock.setTime(3,48,52); executes

Next, let us give the definitions of the other function members of the **class clockType**. The definitions of these functions are simple and easy to follow.

```
void clockType::getTime(int& hours, int& minutes, int& seconds)
{
       hours = hr;
       minutes = min;
       seconds = sec;
}

void clockType::printTime() const
{
       if(hr < 10)
          cout<<"0";
       cout<<hr<<":";

       if(min < 10)
          cout<<"0";
       cout<<min<<":";

       if(sec < 10)
          cout<<"0";
       cout<<sec;
}
```

```
void clockType::incrementHours()
{
      hr++;
      if(hr > 23)
         hr = 0;
}

void clockType::incrementMinutes()
{
      min++;
      if(min > 59)
      {
         min = 0;
         incrementHours();           //increment hours
      }
}

void clockType::incrementSeconds()
{
      sec++;
      if(sec > 59)
      {
         sec = 0;
         incrementMinutes();         //increment minutes
      }
}
```

From the definitions of the functions **incrementMinutes** and **incrementSeconds**, it is clear that a member function can call other member functions.

The function **equalTime** has the following definition:

```
bool clockType::equalTime(const clockType& otherClock) const
{
   return(hr == otherClock.hr
          && min == otherClock.min
          && sec == otherClock.sec);
}
```

Let us see how the member function **equalTime** works.

Suppose that **myClock** and **yourClock** are objects of the type **clockType**, as declared previously. Further suppose that we have **myClock** and **yourClock** as shown in Figure 13-7.

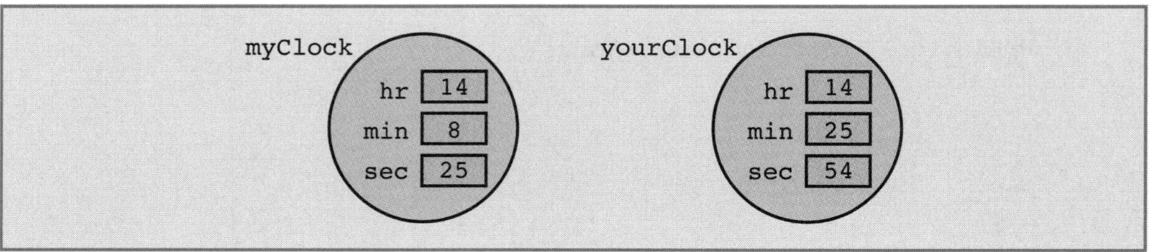

Figure 13-7 Objects `myClock` and `yourClock`

Consider the following statement:

```
if(myClock.equalTime(yourClock))
 .
 .
 .
```

In the expression

```
myClock.equalTime(yourClock)
```

the object **`myClock`** accesses the member function **`equalTime`**. The value of the parameter **`yourClock`** is passed to the formal parameter **`otherClock`**, as shown in Figure 13-8.

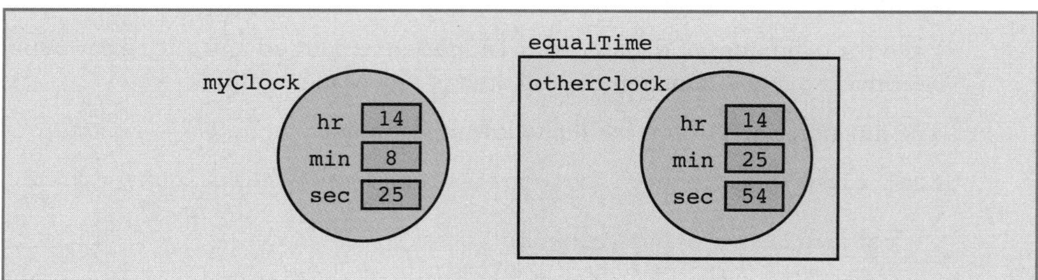

Figure 13-8 Object `myClock` and parameter `otherClock`

The data members **`hr`**, **`min`**, and **`sec`** of **`otherClock`** have the values `14`, `25`, and `54`, respectively. In other words, when the body of the function **`equalTime`** executes, the value of `otherClock.hr` is `14`, the value of `otherClock.min` is `25`, and the value of `otherClock.sec` is `54`. The function **`equalTime`** is a member of the function **`myClock`**. When the function **`equalTime`** executes, the variables **`hr`**, **`min`**, and **`sec`** in the body of the function **`equalTime`** are the data members of the variable **`myClock`**. Therefore, the member **`hr`** of **`myClock`** is compared with **`otherClock.hr`**, the member **`min`** of **`myClock`** is compared with **`otherClock.min`**, and the member **`sec`** of **`myClock`** is compared with `otherClock.sec`.

Once again, from the definition of the function **equalTime**, it is clear why it has only one parameter.

Now that you have seen how to define a class, how to access the members of a class, and how to implement the member functions, let us write a simple program that uses a class. We will write a simple function that uses the **class clockType**.

```
//Program that uses the class clockType

int main()
{
      clockType myClock;
      clockType yourClock;

      int hours;
      int minutes;
      int seconds;

      myClock.setTime(5,4,30);                          //Line 1
      cout<<"Line 2: myClock: ";                        //Line 2
      myClock.printTime();                              //Line 3
      cout<<endl;                                       //Line 4

      cout<<"Line 5: yourClock: ";                      //Line 5
      yourClock.printTime();                            //Line 6
      cout<<endl;                                       //Line 7

      yourClock.setTime(5,45,16);                       //Line 8

      cout<<"Line 9: After setting - yourClock: ";      //Line 9
      yourClock.printTime();                            //Line 10
      cout<<endl;                                       //Line 11

      if(myClock.equalTime(yourClock))                  //Line 12
         cout<<"Line 13: Both times are equal."
             <<endl;                                    //Line 13
      else                                              //Line 14
         cout<<"Line 15: The two times are not equal"
             <<endl;                                    //Line 15

      cout<<"Line 16: Enter hours, minutes, and "
          <<"seconds: ";                                //Line 16
      cin>>hours>>minutes>>seconds;                     //Line 17
      cout<<endl;                                       //Line 18

      myClock.setTime(hours,minutes,seconds);           //Line 19

      cout<<"Line 20: New myClock: ";                   //Line 20
      myClock.printTime();                              //Line 21
      cout<<endl;                                       //Line 22
```

```
        myClock.incrementSeconds();                        //Line 23

        cout<<"Line 24: After incrementing the clock by "
            <<"one second, myClock: ";                     //Line 24
        myClock.printTime();                               //Line 25
        cout<<endl;                                        //Line 26

        return 0;
}//end main
```

This function requires the user to input three numbers: the number of hours, minutes, and seconds. Suppose that the input is `5 23 59`.

A walk-through of this program produces the following output:

Output

```
Line 2: myClock: 05:04:30
Line 5: yourClock:        (The value of yourClock is undefined here).
Line 9: After setting - yourClock: 05:45:16
Line 15: The two times are not equal
Line 16: Enter hours, minutes, and seconds: 5 23 59

Line 20: New myClock: 05:23:59
Line 24: After incrementing the time by one second, myClock: 05:24:00
```

The user input is shaded.

We recommend that you do a walk-through of the execution of this function.

The next example combines the definition of the class, the definition of the function members, and the function **main** to create a complete program.

Example 13-2:

```
//The complete program listing of the program that defines
//and uses class clockType

#include <iostream>
using namespace std;

class clockType
{
public:
    void setTime(int, int, int);
    void getTime(int&, int&, int&);
    void printTime() const;
    void incrementSeconds();
    void incrementMinutes();
    void incrementHours();
    bool equalTime(const clockType&) const;
```

```
private:
    int hr;
    int min;
    int sec;
};

int main()
{
      clockType myClock;
      clockType yourClock;

      int hours;
      int minutes;
      int seconds;

      myClock.setTime(5,4,30);                          //Line 1
      cout<<"Line 2: myClock: ";                        //Line 2
      myClock.printTime();                              //Line 3
      cout<<endl;                                       //Line 4

      cout<<"Line 5: yourClock: ";                      //Line 5
      yourClock.printTime();                            //Line 6
      cout<<endl;                                       //Line 7

      yourClock.setTime(5,45,16);                       //Line 8

      cout<<"Line 9: After setting - yourClock: ";      //Line 9
      yourClock.printTime();                            //Line 10
      cout<<endl;                                       //Line 11

      if(myClock.equalTime(yourClock))                  //Line 12
         cout<<"Line 13: Both times are equal."
             <<endl;                                    //Line 13
      else                                              //Line 14
         cout<<"Line 15: The two times are not equal"
             <<endl;                                    //Line 15

      cout<<"Line 16: Enter hours, minutes, and "
          <<"seconds: ";                                //Line 16
      cin>>hours>>minutes>>seconds;                     //Line 17
      cout<<endl;                                       //Line 18

      myClock.setTime(hours,minutes,seconds);           //Line 19

      cout<<"Line 20: New myClock: ";                   //Line 20
      myClock.printTime();                              //Line 21
      cout<<endl;                                       //Line 22

      myClock.incrementSeconds();                       //Line 23
```

```
       cout<<"Line 24: After incrementing the clock by "
            <<"one second, myClock: ";                         //Line 24
       myClock.printTime();                                    //Line 25
       cout<<endl;                                             //Line 26

       return 0;
}//end main

void clockType::setTime(int hours, int minutes, int seconds)
{
       if(0 <= hours && hours < 24)
          hr = hours;
       else
          hr = 0;

       if(0 <= minutes && minutes < 60)
          min = minutes;
       else
          min = 0;

       if(0 <= seconds && seconds < 60)
          sec = seconds;
       else
          sec = 0;
}

void clockType::getTime(int& hours, int& minutes, int& seconds)
{
       hours = hr;
       minutes = min;
       seconds = sec;
}

void clockType::incrementHours()
{
       hr++;
       if(hr > 23)
           hr = 0;
}

void clockType::incrementMinutes()
{
       min++;
       if(min > 59)
       {
          min = 0;
          incrementHours();
       }
}
```

```
void clockType::incrementSeconds()
{
      sec++;

      if(sec > 59)
      {
         sec = 0;
         incrementMinutes();
      }
}

void clockType::printTime() const
{
      if(hr < 10)
         cout<<"0";
      cout<<hr<<":";

      if(min < 10)
         cout<<"0";
      cout<<min<<":";

      if(sec < 10)
         cout<<"0";
      cout<<sec;
}

bool clockType::equalTime(const clockType& otherClock) const
{
      return (hr == otherClock.hr
              && min == otherClock.min
              && sec == otherClock.sec);
}
```


Sample Run: In this sample run, the user input is shaded.

```
Line 2: myClock: 05:04:30
Line 5: yourClock: 0-858993460:0-858993460:0-858993460
Line 9: After setting - yourClock: 05:45:16
Line 15: The two times are not equal
Line 16: Enter hours, minutes, and seconds: 5 23 59

Line 20: New myClock: 05:23:59
Line 24: After incrementing the time by one second, myClock: 05:24:00
```

The value of `yourClock`, as printed in the second line of the output (Line 5:), is machine-dependent; you might get different values.

Order of `public` and `private` Members of a Class

C++ has no fixed order in which you declare **public** and **private** members; you can declare them in any order. The only thing you need to remember is that, by default, all members of a class are **private**. You must use the **public** label to make a member available for **public** access. If you decide to declare the **private** members after the **public** members (as is done in the case of `clockType`), you must use the **private** label to begin the declaration of the **private** members.

We can declare the **class** `clockType` in one of three ways, as shown in Examples 13-3 through 13-5.

Example 13-3

This declaration is the same as before. For the sake of completeness, we include the class definition.

```
class clockType
{
public:
    void setTime(int, int, int);
    void getTime(int&, int&, int&);
    void printTime() const;
    void incrementSeconds();
    void incrementMinutes();
    void incrementHours();
    bool equalTime(const clockType&) const;

private:
    int hr;
    int min;
    int sec;
};
```

Example 13-4

```
class clockType
{
private:
    int hr;
    int min;
    int sec;
```

```
public:
    void setTime(int, int, int);
    void getTime(int&, int&, int&);
    void printTime() const;
    void incrementSeconds();
    void incrementMinutes();
    void incrementHours();
    bool equalTime(const clockType&) const;
};
```

Example 13-5

```
class clockType
{
    int hr;
    int min;
    int sec;

public:
    void setTime(int, int, int);
    void getTime(int&, int&, int&);
    void printTime() const;
    void incrementSeconds();
    void incrementMinutes();
    void incrementHours();
    bool equalTime(const clockType&) const;
};
```

13

In Example 13-5, because the identifiers `hr`, `min`, and `sec` do not follow any member access specifier, they are `private`.

It is a common practice to list all of the `public` members first, and then the `private` members. This way, you can focus your attention on the `public` members.

Constructors

In the program in Example 13-2, when we printed the value of `yourClock` without calling the function `setTime`, the output was some strange numbers (that is, garbage; see the output of Line 5 in the sample run). This is due to the fact that C++ does not automatically initialize the variables. Because the `private` members of a class cannot be accessed outside the class (in our case, the data members), if the user forgets to initialize these variables by calling the function `setTime`, the program will produce erroneous results.

To guarantee that the data members of a class are initialized, you use constructors. There are two types of constructors: with parameters and without parameters. The constructor without parameters is called the **default constructor**.

Constructors have the following properties:

- The name of a constructor is the same as the name of the class.
- A constructor, even though it is a function, has no type. That is, it is neither a value-returning function nor a **void** function.
- A class can have more than one constructor. However, all constructors of a class have the same name.
- If a class has more than one constructor, they must have different sets of parameters.
- Constructors are automatically executed when a class object enters its scope. Because they have no types, they cannot be called like other functions.
- Which constructor executes depends on the type of values passed to the class object when the class object is declared.

Let us extend the definition of the **class clockType** by including two constructors.

```
class clockType
{
public:
    void setTime(int, int, int);
    void getTime(int&, int&, int&);
    void printTime() const;
    void incrementSeconds();
    void incrementMinutes();
    void incrementHours();
    bool equalTime(const clockType&) const;
    clockType(int, int, int);  //constructor with parameters
    clockType();  //default constructor

private:
    int hr;
    int min;
    int sec;
};
```

This definition of the **class clockType** includes two constructors: one with three parameters and one without any parameters. Let us now write the definitions of these constructors.

```
clockType::clockType(int hours, int minutes, int seconds)
{
      if(0 <= hours && hours < 24)
         hr = hours;
      else
         hr = 0;

      if(0 <= minutes && minutes < 60)
         min = minutes;
      else
         min = 0;
```

```
        if(0 <= seconds && seconds < 60)
            sec = seconds;
        else
            sec = 0;
}

clockType::clockType()  //default constructor
{
        hr = 0;
        min = 0;
        sec = 0;
}
```

From the definition of these constructors, it follows that the default constructor sets the three data members—**hr**, **min**, and **sec**—to 0. Also, the constructor with parameters sets the data members to whatever values are assigned to the formal parameters. Moreover, we can write the definition of the constructor with parameters by calling the function **setTime**, as follows:

```
clockType::clockType(int hours, int minutes, int seconds)
{
        setTime(hours, minutes, seconds);
}
```

Invoking a Constructor

Recall that, when a class object is declared, a constructor is automatically executed. Because a class might have more than one constructor, including the default constructor, next we discuss how to invoke a specific constructor.

Invoking the Default Constructor

13

Suppose that a class contains the default constructor. The syntax to invoke the default constructor is

```
className  classObjectName;
```

For example, the statement

```
clockType yourClock;
```

declares **yourClock** to be an object of the type **clockType**. In this case, the default constructor is executed and the data members of **yourClock** are initialized to 0.

If you declare an object and want the default constructor to be executed, the empty parentheses after the object name are not required in the object declaration statement. In fact, if you accidentally include the parentheses, the compiler generates a syntax error message. For example, the following statement is illegal:

```
clockType yourClock();  //illegal
```

Invoking a Constructor with Parameters

Suppose a class contains constructors with parameters. The syntax to invoke a constructor with a parameter is

```
className  classObjectName(argument1, argument2, ...);
```

where **argument1**, **argument2**, and so on, is either a variable or an expression.

Note the following:

- The number of arguments and their type should match the formal parameters (in the order given) of one of the constructors.
- If the type of the arguments does not match the formal parameters of any constructor (in the order given), C++ uses type conversion and looks for the best match. For example, an integer value might be converted to a floating-point value with a zero decimal part. Any ambiguity will result in a compile-time error.

Consider the statement

```
clockType myClock(5,12,40);
```

This statement declares an object **myClock** of the type **clockType**. Here we are passing three values of the type **int**, which matches the type of the formal parameters of the constructor with a parameter. Therefore, the constructor with parameters of the **class clockType** executes and the three data members of the object **myClock** are set to **5**, **12**, and **40**.

Example 13-6 further illustrates how constructors are executed.

Example 13-6

Consider the following class definition:

```
class testClass
{
public:
    void print();                    //Line a

    testClass();                     //Line b
    testClass(int, int);             //Line c
    testClass(int, double, int);     //Line d
    testClass(double, char);         //Line e
```

```
private:
    int x;
    int y;
    double z;
    char ch;
};
```

This class has five member functions, including four constructors. It also has four data members. Suppose that the definitions of the member functions of the `class testClass` are as follows:

```
void testClass::print()
{
      cout<<"x = "<<x<<", y = "<<y<<", z = "<<z
          <<", ch = "<<ch<<endl;
}

testClass::testClass()    //default constructor
{
      x = 0;
      y = 0;
      z = 0;
      ch = '*';
}

testClass::testClass(int a, int b)
{
      x = a;
      y = b;
      z = 0;
      ch = '*';
}

testClass::testClass(int a, double c, int b)
{
      x = a;
      y = b;
      z = c;
      ch = '*';
}

testClass::testClass(double c, char d)
{
      x = 0;
      y = 0;
      z = c;
      ch = d;
}
```

13

Consider the following declarations:

```
testClass  one;                 //Line 1
testClass  two(5,6);            //Line 2
testClass  three(5,4.5,7);      //Line 3
testClass  four(4,9,12);        //Line 4
testClass  five(3.4,'D');       //Line 5
```

For object `one` (declared at Line 1), the default constructor (at Line b) executes because no value is passed to this variable. Therefore, the data members `x`, `y`, `z`, and `ch` of `one` are initialized to `0`, `0`, `0`, and `'*'`, respectively. For object `two` (declared at Line 2), the constructor with `int` parameters at Line c executes because the arguments passed to object `two` are `5` and `6`, which are of the type `int`. Therefore, the data members `x`, `y`, `z`, and `ch` of `two` are initialized to `5`, `6`, `0`, and `'*'`, respectively (see the definition of the constructor at Line c).

The arguments passed to object `three` (declared at Line 3) are `5`, `4.5`, and `7`. These arguments match the parameters of the constructor at Line d. Therefore, to initialize the data members of object `three`, the constructor at Line d executes. From the definition of the constructor at Line d, it follows that the data members `x`, `y`, `z`, and `ch` of `three` are initialized to `5`, `7`, `4.5`, and `'*'`, respectively.

The arguments passed to object `four` are `4`, `9`, and `12`. The `class testClass` does not contain any constructor with three `int` parameters. However, it does contain a constructor with three parameters in the order `int`, `double`, and `int` (see the constructor at Line d). Because an `int` value can be converted to a `double` value with a zero decimal value, in the case of object `four`, the constructor at Line d executes. Thus, the data members `x`, `y`, `z`, and `ch` of `four` are initialized to `4`, `12`, `6.0`, and `'*'`, respectively (see the definition of the constructor at Line d).

The arguments passed to object `five` are `3.4` and `'D'`. These values match the parameters of the constructor at Line e. Therefore, to initialize the data members of object `five`, the constructor at Line e executes. From the definition of the constructor at Line e, it follows that the data members `x`, `y`, `z`, and `ch` of `five` are initialized to `0`, `0`, `3.4`, and `'D'`, respectively (see the definition of the constructor at Line e).

If the values passed to a class object do not match the parameters of any constructor, and if no type conversion is possible, a compile-time error will be generated.

The following program tests the previous class objects.

```
int main()
{
      testClass  one;                 //Line 1
      testClass  two(5,6);            //Line 2
      testClass  three(5,4.5,7);      //Line 3
      testClass  four(4,9,12);        //Line 4
      testClass  five(3.4,'D');       //Line 5
```

```
        one.print();                    //Line 6; output one
        two.print();                    //Line 7; output two
        three.print();                  //Line 8; output three
        four.print();                   //Line 9; output four
        five.print();                   //Line 10; output five

        return 0;
}
```

Output

```
x = 0, y = 0, z = 0, ch = *
x = 5, y = 6, z = 0, ch = *
x = 5, y = 7, z = 4.5, ch = *
x = 4, y = 12, z = 9, ch = *
x = 0, y = 0, z = 3.4, ch = D
```

As explained previously, the statements at Lines 1 through 5 declare and initialize objects `one`, `two`, `three`, `four`, and `five`. The statements at Lines 6 through 10 output the values of these objects—that is, the values of the data members of these objects.

Constructors and Default Parameters

A constructor can also have default parameters. In such cases, the rules for declaring formal parameters are the same as those for declaring default formal parameters in a function. Moreover, actual parameters to a constructor with default parameters are passed according to the rules for functions with default parameters. (Chapter 7 discusses functions with default parameters.) Using the rules for defining default parameters, in the definition of the class `clockType`, you can replace both constructors using the following statement. (Recall that in the function prototype, the name of a formal parameter is optional.)

13

```
clockType clockType(int = 0, int = 0, int = 0);
```

In the implementation file, the definition of this constructor is the same as the definition of the constructor with parameters.

Using these conventions, we can say that a constructor that has no parameters, or has all default parameters, is called the **default constructor**.

Example 13-7

Using default constructors, you can write the definition of the `class testClass` (defined previously) as follows:

```
class testClass
{
public:
    void print();

    testClass(int = 0, double = 0.0, int = 0, char = '*');
```

```
private:
    int x;
    int y;
    double z;
    char ch;
};
```

The definition of the constructor is as follows:

```
testClass::testClass(int a, double c, int  b, char d)
{
      x = a;
      y = b;
      z = c;
      ch = d;
}
```

You can now declare objects **one**, **two**, **three**, **four**, and **five** as follows:

```
testClass  one;
testClass  two(5,0.0,6);
testClass  three(5,4.5,7);
testClass  four(4,9,12);
testClass  five(0,3.4,0,'D');
```

In the declaration of object **two**, we want to use the default values of **z** and **ch**, and replace the default values of **x** and **y**. Because **z** is declared before **y**, to use the default value of **z** and replace the default value of **y**, we must specify the default value of **z** as shown in the declaration. Similarly, in the declaration of object **five**, we want to use the default values of **x** and **y**, and replace the default values of **z** and **ch**. Because **x** occurs before **z** and **ch**, and **y** occurs before **ch**, we must specify the default values of **x** and **y** as shown in the declaration.

Using default parameters simplifies the declarations and definitions of constructors. Thus, wherever possible (and when no confusion arises), we will effectively make use of constructors with parameters.

Arrays of Class Objects (Variables) and Constructors

If a class has constructors and you declare an array of class objects, the class must have the default constructor. The default constructor is used to initialize each (array) class object. If you declare, say, an array of 100 class objects, then it is not possible to specify different constructors for each component. With the previous definition of the **class clockType**, the statement

```
clockType clocks[100];
```

declares an array **clocks** of **100** components of the type **clockType**. (See Figure 13-9.)

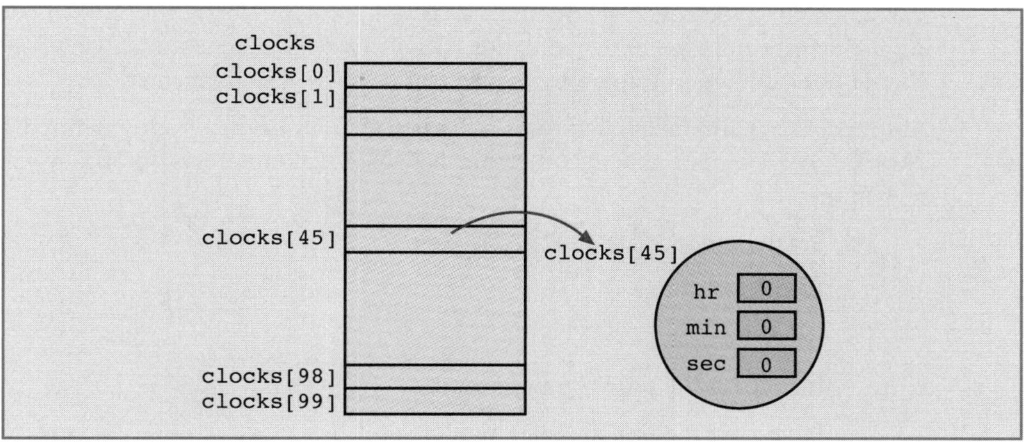

Figure 13-9 Array `clocks` of objects

The three data members of each array component are initialized to `0`.

Destructors

Like constructors, destructors are also functions. Moreover, like constructors, a destructor does not have a type; that is, it is neither a value-returning function nor a void function. However, a class can have only one destructor, and the destructor can have no parameters. The name of a destructor is the character `'~'`, followed by the name of the class. (The character `'~'` is called a *tilde*.) For example, the name of the destructor for the **`class`** `clockType` is

```
~clockType();
```

The destructor automatically executes when the class object goes out of scope. Ensuing chapters discuss the use of destructors.

DATA ABSTRACTION, CLASSES, AND ABSTRACT DATA TYPES

Have you ever wondered how the engine of your car works? Most of us want to know only how to start a car and drive it. Most people are not concerned with the complexity of how the engine works. By separating the design details of a car's engine from its use, the manufacturer helps the driver to focus on how to drive the car. Our daily life has other similar examples. For the most part, we are concerned with only how to use certain items, rather than how they work.

Separating the design details (that is, how the car's engine works) from its use is called **abstraction**. In other words, abstraction focuses on what the engine does and not on how it works. Thus, abstraction is the process of separating the logical properties from the implementation details. Driving the car is a logical property; the construction of the engine constitutes the implementation details. We have an abstract view of what the engine does, but are not interested in the engine's actual implementation.

Abstraction can also be applied to data. Earlier sections of this chapter defined a data type `clockType`. The data type `clockType` has three data members and the following basic operations:

1. Set the time.
2. Return the time.
3. Print the time.
4. Increment the time by one second.
5. Increment the time by one minute.
6. Increment the time by one hour.
7. Compare the two times to see whether they are equal.

The actual implementation of the operations on `clockType` was postponed. Data abstraction is defined as a process of separating the logical properties of the data from its implementation. The definition of `clockType` and its basic operations are the logical properties; the storing of `clockType` in the computer, and the algorithms to perform these operations, are the implementation details of `clockType`.

Abstract data type (ADT): A data type that specifies the logical properties without the implementation details.

Like any other data type, an ADT has three things associated with it: the name of the ADT, called the **type name**; the set of values belonging to the ADT, called the **domain**; and the set of **operations** on the data. Following these conventions, we can define the `clockType` ADT as follows:

```
dataTypeName
   clockType
domain
   Each clockType value is a time of day in the form of hours,
   minutes, and seconds.
operations
   Set the time.
   Return the time.
   Print the time.
   Increment the time by one second.
   Increment the time by one minute.
   Increment the time by one hour.
   Compare the two times to see whether they are equal.
```

Example 13-8

A list is defined as a set of values of the same type. Because all values in a list are of the same type, a convenient way to represent and process a list is to use an array. You can define a list as an ADT as follows:

```
dataTypeName
   listType
domain
   Every element of the type listType is a set of, say 1000 numbers.
operations
   Check to see if the list is empty.
   Check to see if the list is full.
   Search the list for a given item.
   Delete an item from the list.
   Insert an item in the list.
   Sort the list.
   Destroy the list.
   Print the list.
```

The next obvious question is how to implement an ADT in a program. To implement an ADT, you must represent the data and write algorithms to perform the operations.

The previous section used classes to group data and functions together. Furthermore, our definition of a class consisted only of the specifications of the operations; functions to implement the operations were written separately. Thus, we see that classes are a convenient way to implement an ADT. In fact, in C++ classes were specifically designed to handle an ADT.

The following **`class`**, `listType`, defines the list ADT. To be specific, suppose that the list is a set of elements of the type `int`. (See Figure 13-10.)

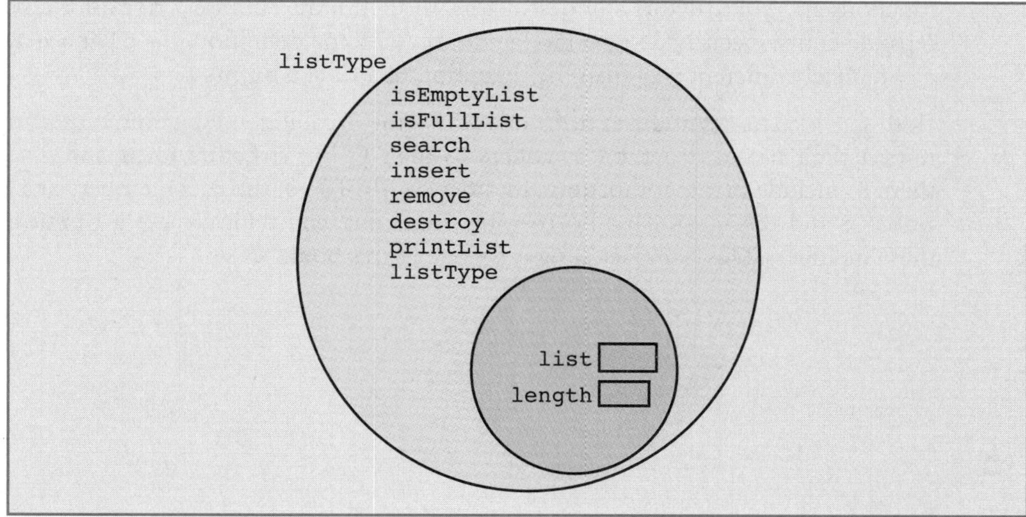

Figure 13-10 `class listType`

```
class listType
{
public:
    bool isEmptyList();
    bool isFullList();
    void search(int searchItem, int& found);
    void insert(int newElement);
    void remove(int removeElement);
    void destroyList();
    void printList();
    listType(); //constructor

private:
    int list[1000];
    int length;
};
```

A `struct` VERSUS A `class`

Chapter 12 defined a **`struct`** as a fixed collection of components, wherein the components can be of different types. This definition of components in a **`struct`** included only data members. However, a C++ **`struct`** is very similar to a C++ **`class`**. As with a **`class`**, members of a **`struct`** can also be functions, including constructors and a destructor. The only difference between a **`struct`** and a **`class`** is that, by default, all members of a **`struct`** are **`public`**, and all members of a **`class`** are **`private`**. You can use the label **`private`** in a **`struct`** to make a member **`private`**.

In C, the definition of a **`struct`** is similar to the definition of a **`struct`** in C++ as given in Chapter 12. Because C++ evolved from C, the standard **`C struct`**s are perfectly acceptable in C++. However, the definition of a **`struct`** in C++ was expanded to include member functions and constructors and destructors. In the future, because a **`class`** is a syntactically separate entity, specially designed to handle an ADT, the definition of a **`class`** may evolve in a completely different way than the definition of a C-like **`struct`**.

Both C++ **`class`**es and **`struct`**s have the same capabilities. However, most programmers restrict their use of structures to adhere to their C-like structure form, and so do not use them to include member functions. In other words, if all of the data members of a **`class`** are **`public`** and the **`class`** has no member functions, you typically use a **`struct`** to group these members. This is, in fact, how it is done in this book.

INFORMATION HIDING

The previous section defined the `class clockType` to implement the time in a program. We then wrote a program that used the `class clockType`. In fact, we combined the `class clockType` with the function definitions to implement the operations and the function `main` so as to complete the program. That is, the specification and implementation details of the `class clockType` were directly incorporated into the program.

Is it a good practice to include the specification and implementation details of an object in the program? Definitely not. There are several reasons for not doing so. First, the `private` data members of an object are no longer `private` to the object. The user has direct access to the data members through the functions that implement the operations on the data. Thus, the user can modify the operations in any way he or she pleases. If several programmers use the same object in a project, and if they have direct access to the internal parts of the object, there is no guarantee that every programmer will use the same object in exactly the same way. Thus, we must hide the implementation details. The user should know only what the object does, not how it does it. Hiding the implementation details frees the user from having to fit this extra piece of code in the program. Also, by hiding the details, we can ensure that an object will be used in exactly the same way throughout the project. Furthermore, once an object has been written, debugged, and tested properly, it becomes (and remains) error-free.

This section discusses how to hide the implementation details of an object. For illustration purposes, we will use the `class clockType`.

To implement `clockType` in a program, the user must declare objects of the type `clockType`, and know which operations are allowed and what the operations do. So the user must have access to the specification details. Because the user is not concerned with the implementation details, we must put those details in a separate file, called an **implementation file**. Also, because the specification details can be too long, we must free the user from having to include them directly in the program. However, the user must be able to look at the specification details so that he or she can correctly call the functions, and so forth. We must therefore put the specification details in a separate file. The file that contains the specification details is called the **header file** (or **interface file**).

The implementation file contains the definitions of the functions to implement the operations of an object. This file contains, among other things (such as the preprocessor directives), the C++ statements. Because a C++ program can have only one function, `main`, the implementation file does not contain the function `main`. Only the user program contains the function `main`. Because the implementation file does not contain the function `main`, we cannot produce the executable code from this file. In fact, we produce what is called the object code from the implementation file. The user then links the object code produced by the implementation file with the object code of the program that uses the class to create the final executable code.

Finally, the header file has an extension `h`, whereas the implementation file has an extension `cpp`. Suppose that the specification details of the `class clockType` are in a file called `clock`. The complete name of this file should then be `clock.h`. If the implementation details of the class `clockType` are in a file—say, `clockImp`—the name of this file must be `clockImp.cpp`.

The file `clockImp.cpp` contains only the definitions of the functions, not the definition of the class. Thus, to resolve the problem of an undeclared identifier (such as the function names and variables names), we include the header file `clock.h` in the file `clockImp.cpp` with the help of the `include` statement. The following `include` statement is required by any program that uses the `class clockType`, as well as by the implementation file that defines the operations for the `class clockType`:

```
#include "clock.h"
```

Note that the header file `clock.h` is enclosed in double quotation marks, not angular brackets. The header file `clock.h` is called the user-defined header file. All user-defined header files are enclosed in double quotation marks, whereas the system-provided header files (such as `iostream`) are enclosed between angular brackets.

Following are the specification and implementation files for the `class clockType`: (In the documentation, Post refers to the Post conditions that hold after the function executes.)

```
//clock.h, the header file for the class clockType

class clockType
{
public:
    void setTime(int hours, int minutes, int seconds);
      //Function to set the time
      //Post: The time is set according to the
      //parameters: hr = hours; min = minutes;
      //            sec = seconds;

    void getTime(int& hours, int& minutes, int& seconds)
      //Function to return the time
      //Post: hours = hr; minutes = min;
      //      seconds = sec;

    void printTime() const;
      //Function to print the time
      //Time is printed in the form hh:mm:ss

    void incrementSeconds();
      //Function to increment the time by one second
      //Post: The time is incremented by one second
      //If the before-increment time is 23:59:59, the time
      //is reset to 00:00:00
```

```
    void incrementMinutes();
      //Function to increment the time by one minute
      //Post: The time is incremented by one minute
      //If the before-increment time is 23:59:53, the time
      //is reset to 00:00:53

    void incrementHours();
      //Function to increment the time by one hour
      //Post: The time is incremented by one hour
      //If the before-increment time is 23:45:53, the time
      //is reset to 00:45:53

    bool equalTime(const clockType& otherClock) const;
      //Function to compare the two times
      //Function returns true if this time is equal to
      //otherClock, otherwise returns false

    clockType(int hours, int minutes, int seconds);
      //Constructor with parameters
      //Post: The time is set according to
      //      the parameters
      //     hr = hours; min = minutes; sec = seconds

    clockType();
      //Default constructor with parameters
      //Post: time is set to 00:00:00
      //     hr = 0; min = 0; sec = 0

private:
    int hr;  //store hours
    int min; //store minutes
    int sec; //store seconds
};


//clockImp.cpp, the implementation file
#include <iostream>
#include "clock.h"

using namespace std;
   .
   .
   .
//The definitions of the member functions of the class clockType go here
   .
   .
   .
```

Next, we describe the user file containing the program that uses the **class clockType**.

```
//TestClock.cpp. The user program that uses the class clockType

#include <iostream>
#include "clock.h"
using namespace std;
.
.
.
//Place the definitions of the function main and the other
//user-defined functions here
.
.
.
```

EXECUTABLE CODE

The previous section discussed how to hide the implementation details of a class. To use an object in a program, during execution the program must be able to access the implementation details of the object (that is, the algorithms to implement the operations on the object). This section discusses how a client's program obtains access to the implementation details of an object. For illustration purposes, we will use the **class clockType**.

As explained previously, to use the **class clockType**, the program must include the header file `clock.h` via the **include** statement. For example, the following program segment includes the header file `clock.h`:

```
//Program test.cpp
#include "clock.h"
.
.
.
int main()
{
   .
   .
   .
}
```

The program `test.cpp` must include only the header file, not the implementation file. To create the executable code to run the program `test.cpp`, the following steps are required:

1. We separately compile the file `clockImp.cpp` and create the object code file `clockImp.obj`. The object code file contains the machine language code, but the code is not in an executable form. Suppose that the command `cc` invokes the C++ compiler or linker, or both, on the computer's system command line. The command

   ```
   cc -c clockImp.cpp
   ```

   creates the object code file `clockImp.obj`.

2. To create the executable code for the source code file `test.cpp`, we compile the source code file `test.cpp`, create the object code file `test.obj`, and then link the files `test.obj` and `clockImp.obj` to create the executable file `test.exe`. The following command on the system command line creates the executable file `test.exe`:

```
cc test.cpp clockImp.obj
```

1. To create the object code file for any source code file, we use the command-line option `-c` on the system command line. For example, to create the object code file for the source code file, called `exercise.cpp`, we use the following command on the system command-line:

```
cc -c exercise.cpp
```

2. To link more than one object code file with a source code file, we list all of the object code files on the system command line. For example, to link `A.obj` and `B.obj` with the source code file `test.cpp`, we use the command

```
cc test.cpp A.obj B.obj
```

3. If a source code file is modified, it must be recompiled.
4. If modifications in one source file affect other files, the other files must be recompiled and relinked.
5. The user must have access to the header file and the object code file. Access to the header file is needed to see what the objects do and how to use them. Access to the object code file is needed so that the user can link the program with the object code to produce an executable code. The user does not need access to the source code file containing the implementation details.

As stated in Chapter 1, SDK's Visual C++, C++ Builder, and CodeWarrior put the editor, compiler, and linker all into one package. With one command, the program is compiled and linked with the other necessary files. These systems also manage multiple file programs in the form of a project. Thus, a project consists of several files, called the project files. These systems usually have a command, called **build, rebuild,** or **make**. (Check your system's documentation.) When the build, rebuild, or make command is applied to a project, the system automatically compiles and links all files required to create the executable code. When one or more files in the project change, you can use these commands to recompile and relink the files.

Example 13-9 further illustrates how classes are designed and implemented. The class `personType` that is designed in Example 13-9 is very useful; we will use this class in subsequent chapters.

Example 13-9

The most common attributes of a person are the person's first name and last name. The typical operations on a person's name are to set the name and print the name. The following statements define a class with these properties. (See Figure 13-11.)

```
class personType
{
public:
    void print() const;
      //Function to output the first name and last name
      //in the form firstName lastName

    void setName(string first, string last);
      //Function to set firstName and lastName according to
      //the parameters
      //Post: firstName = first; lastName = last;

    void getName(string& first, string& last);
      //Function to return firstName and lastName via the parameters
      //Post: first = firstName; last = lastName;

    personType(string first, string last);
      //constructor with parameters
      //Set firstName and lastName according to the parameters
      //Post: firstName = first; lastName = last;

    personType();
     //default constructor
     //Initialize firstName and lastName to empty string
     //Post: firstName = ""; lastName = "";

 private:
    string firstName; //store the first name
    string lastName;  //store the last name
};
```

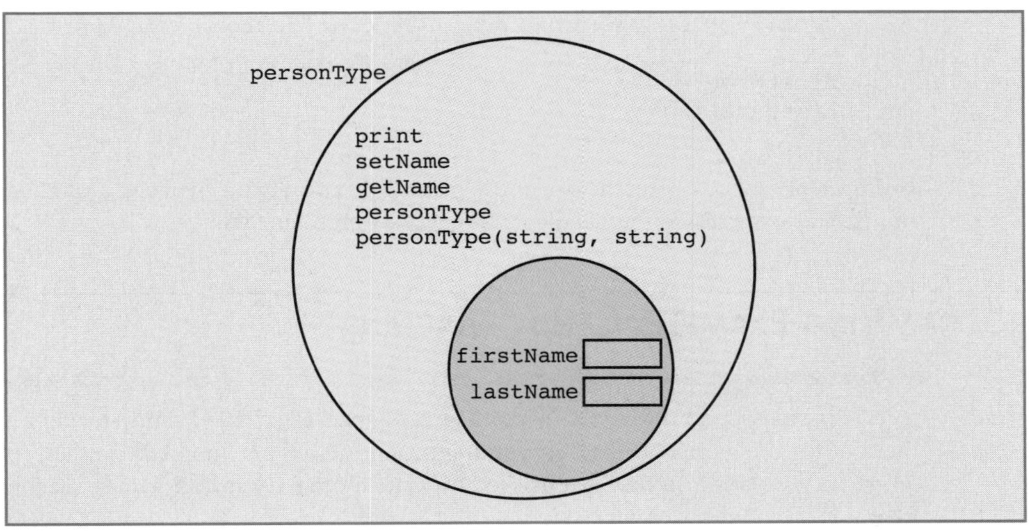

Figure 13-11 class personType

We now give the definitions of the function members of the class personType.

```
void personType::print() const
{
      cout<<firstName<<" "<<lastName;
}

void personType::setName(string first, string last)
{
      firstName = first;
      lastName = last;
}

void personType::getName(string& first, string& last)
{
      first = firstName;
      last = lastName;
}

            //constructor with parameters
personType::personType(string first, string last)

{
      firstName = first;
      lastName = last;
}
```

```
personType::personType()    //default constructor
{
      firstName = "";
      lastName = "";
}
```

You can replace both constructors of the **class personType** by using a single constructor with default parameters; the details are left as an exercise for you.

PROGRAMMING EXAMPLE: CANDY MACHINE

A common place to buy candy is from a candy machine. A new candy machine is bought for the gym, but it is not working properly. The machine sells candies, chips, gum, and cookies. You have been asked to write a program for this candy machine so that it can be put into operation.

The program should do the following:

1. Show the customer the different products sold by the candy machine.
2. Let the customer make the selection.
3. Show the customer the cost of the item selected.
4. Accept money from the customer.
5. Release the item.

Input The item selection and the cost of the item.

Output The selected item.

Problem Analysis and Algorithm Design

A candy machine has two main components: a built-in cash register and several dispensers to hold and release the products.

Cash Register Let us first discuss the properties of a cash register. The register has some cash on hand, it accepts the amount from the customer, and if the amount entered is more than the cost of the item, then—if possible—it returns the change. For simplicity, we assume that the user enters the exact amount for the product. The cash register should also be able to show to the candy machine's owner the amount of money in the register at any given time. The following class defines the properties of a cash register. (See Figure 13-12.)

```
class cashRegister
{
public:
    int currentBalance();
      //Function to show the current amount in the cash
      //register
      //Post: The value of the data member cashOnHand is returned
```

```
    void acceptAmount(int amountIn);
      //This function receives the amount deposited by
      //the customer and updates the amount in the register
      //Post: cashOnHand = cashOnHand + amountIn

    cashRegister(int cashIn = 500);
      //Constructor to set the cash in the register to a
      //specific amount
      //Post: cashOnHand = cashIn;
      //If no value is specified when the object is
      //declared, the default value assigned
      //to cashOnHand is 500

private:
     int cashOnHand;  //variable to store the cash
                      //in the register
};
```

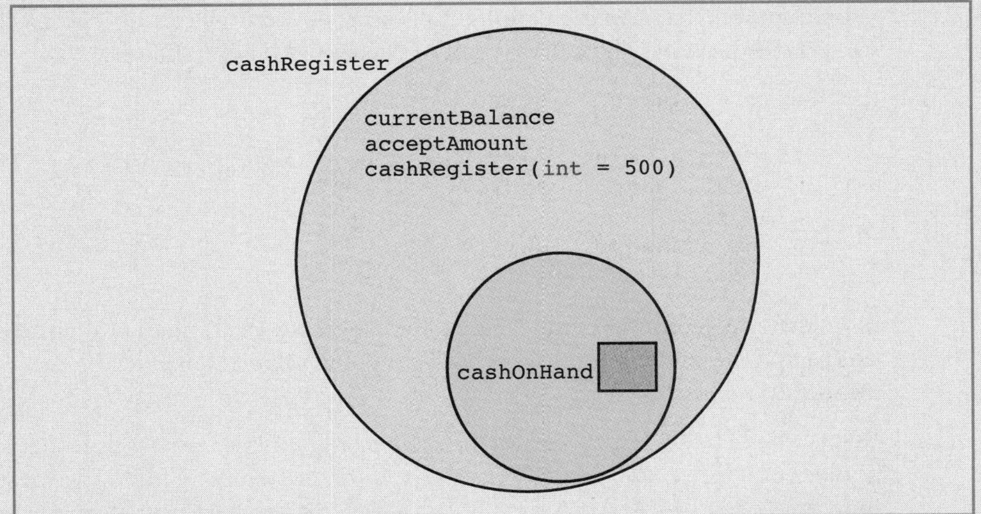

Figure 13-12 `class cashRegister`

Next, we give the definitions of the functions to implement the operations of the `class cashRegister`. The definitions of these functions are very simple and easy to follow.

The function `currentBalance` shows the current amount in the cash register. It returns the value of the `private` data member `cashOnHand`. So its definition is

```
int cashRegister::currentBalance()
{
      return cashOnHand;
}
```

The function `acceptAmount` accepts the amount entered by the customer. It updates the cash in the register by adding the amount entered by the customer to the previous amount in the cash register. Essentially, the definition of this function is

```
void cashRegister::acceptAmount(int amountIn)
{
      cashOnHand += amountIn;
}
```

In the definition of the `class cashRegister`, the constructor is declared with a default value. Therefore, if the user does not specify any value when the object is declared, the default value is used to initialize the data member `cashOnHand`. Recall that, because we have specified the default value for the constructor parameter in the definition of the class, in the definition of the constructor we do not specify the default value in the heading. The definition of the constructor is as follows:

```
cashRegister::cashRegister(int cashIn)
{
     if(cashIn >= 0)
        cashOnHand = cashIn;
     else
        cashOnHand = 500;
}
```

Note that the definition of the constructor checks for valid values of the parameter `cashIn`. If the value of `cashIn` is less than `0`, the value assigned to the data member `cashOnHand` is `500`.

Dispenser The dispenser releases the selected item if it is not empty. It should show the number of items in the dispenser and the cost of the item. The following class defines the properties of a dispenser. Let us call this `class dispenserType`. (See Figure 13-13.)

```
class dispenserType
{
public:
    int count();
      //Function to return the number of items in the machine
      //Post: The value of the data member numberOfProducts
              is returned
```

```
    int productCost();
      //Function to return the cost of the item
      //The value of the data member cost is returned

    void makeSale();
      //Function to reduce the number of items by 1
      //Post: numberOfProducts = numberOfProducts - 1;

    dispenserType(int setNoOfProducts = 50, int setCost = 50);
      //Constructor to set the cost and number of items
      //in the dispenser specified by the user
      //Post: numberOfProducts = setNoOfProducts;
      //                cost = setCost;
      //If no value is specified for either of the two
      //parameters, the default values are assigned to the
      //data members numberOfProducts and cost.

private:
    int numberOfProducts; //variable to store the number of
                          //items in the dispenser
    int cost;  //variable to store the cost of an item
};
```

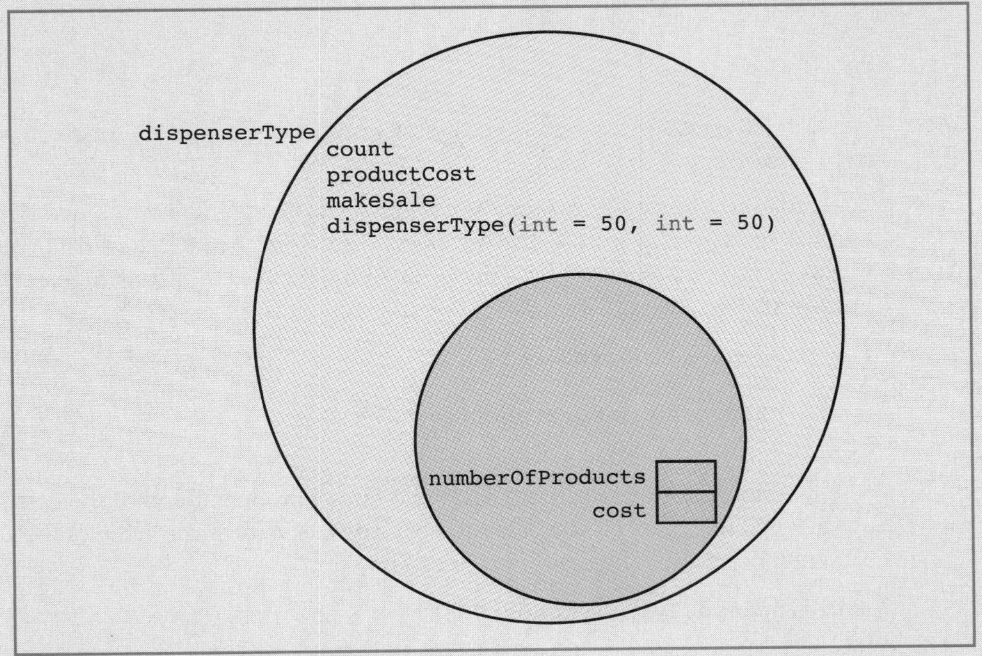

Figure 13-13 class dispenserType

Because the candy machine sells four types of items, we shall declare four objects of the type **dispenserType**. For example, the statement

```
dispenserType chips(100,65);
```

declares **chips** to be an object of the type **dispenserType**, and sets the number of chip bags in the dispenser to **100** and the cost of each chip bag to **65** cents. (See Figure 13-14.)

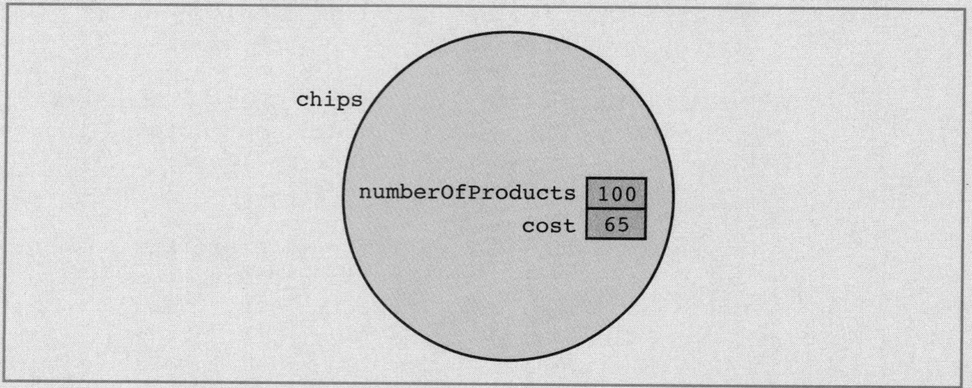

Figure 13-14 Object chips

Next, we discuss the definitions of the functions to implement the operations of the class **dispenserType**.

The function **count** returns the number of items of a particular product. Because the number of items currently in the dispenser is stored in the **private** data member **numberOfProducts**, it returns the value of the **private** data member **numberOfProducts**. The definition of this function is

```
int dispenserType::count()
{
      return numberOfProducts;
}
```

The function **productCost** returns the cost of a product. Because the cost of a product is stored in the **private** data member **cost**, it returns the value of the **private** data member **cost**. The definition of this function is

```
int dispenserType::productCost()
{
      return cost;
}
```

When a product is sold, the number of items in that dispenser is reduced by `1`. Therefore, the function `makeSale` reduces the number of items in the dispenser by `1`. That is, it decrements the value of the `private` data member `numberOfProducts` by `1`. The definition of this function is

```
void dispenserType::makeSale()
{
      numberOfProducts--;
}
```

The definition of the constructor checks for valid values of the parameters. If these values are less than `0`, the default values are assigned to the data members. The definition of the constructor is

```
           //constructor
dispenserType::dispenserType(int setNoOfProducts, int setCost)
{
      if(setNoOfProducts >= 0)
         numberOfProducts = setNoOfProducts;
      else
         numberOfProducts = 50;

      if(setCost >= 0)
         cost = setCost;
      else
         cost = 50;
}
```

Main Program

When the program executes, it must do the following:

1. Show the different products sold by the candy machine.
2. Show how to select a particular product.
3. Show how to terminate the program.

Furthermore, these instructions must be displayed after processing each selection (except exiting the program), so that the user need not remember what to do if he or she wants to buy two or more items. Once the user has made the appropriate selection, the candy machine must act accordingly. If the user has opted to buy a product and if that product is available, the candy machine should show the cost of the product and ask the user to deposit the money. If the money deposited is at least the cost of the item, the candy machine should sell the item and display an appropriate message.

This discussion translates into the following algorithm:

1. Show the selection to the customer.
2. Get the selection.

3. If the selection is valid and the dispenser corresponding to the selection is not empty, sell the product.

We divide this program into three functions—`showSelection`, `sellProduct`, and `main`.

`showSelection` This function displays the necessary information to help the user select and buy a product. Essentially, it contains the following output statements. (We assume that the candy machine sells four types of products.)

```
a. *** Welcome to Shelly's Candy Shop ***"
b. To select an item, enter
c. 1 for Candy
d. 2 for Chips
e. 3 for Gum
f. 4 for Cookies
g. 9 to exit
```

This definition of the function `showSelection` is

```
void showSelection()
{
      cout<<"*** Welcome to Shelly's Candy Shop ***"<<endl;
      cout<<"To select an item, enter "<<endl;
      cout<<"1 for Candy"<<endl;
      cout<<"2 for Chips"<<endl;
      cout<<"3 for Gum"<<endl;
      cout<<"4 for Cookies"<<endl;
      cout<<"9 to exit"<<endl;
}//end showSelection
```

`sellProduct` This function attempts to sell the product selected by the customer. Therefore, it must have access to the dispenser holding the product. The first thing that this function does is check whether the dispenser holding the product is empty. If the dispenser is empty, the function informs the customer that this product is sold out. If the dispenser is nonempty, it tells the user to deposit the necessary amount to buy the product.

If the user does not deposit enough money to buy the product, `sellProduct` tells the user how much additional money must be deposited. If the user fails to deposit enough money to buy the product, the function simply returns the money. If the money deposited by the user is sufficient, it accepts the money and sells the product. Selling the product means to decrement the number of items in the dispenser by `1`, and update the money in the cash register by adding the cost of the product. (Because this program does not return the extra money deposited by the customer, the cash register is updated by adding the money entered by the user.)

From this discussion, it is clear that the function `sellProduct` must have access to the dispenser holding the product (to decrement the number of items in the dispenser by `1` and to show the cost of the item) as well as the cash register (to update the cash). Therefore, this function has two parameters: one corresponding to the dispenser, and the other corresponding to the cash register. Furthermore, both parameters must be referenced.

In pseudocode, the algorithm for this function is

a. If the dispenser is nonempty
   i. Show and prompt the customer to enter the cost of the item.
   ii. Get the amount entered by the customer.
   iii. If the amount entered by the customer is less than the cost of the product
      1. Show and prompt the customer to enter the additional amount.
      2. Calculate the total amount entered by the customer.
   iv. If the amount entered by the customer is at least the cost of the product
      1. Update the amount in the cash register.
      2. Sell the product—that is, decrement the number of items in the dispenser by `1`.
      3. Display an appropriate message.
   v. If the amount entered by the user is less than the cost of the item, return the amount.

b. If the dispenser is empty, tell the user that this product is sold out.

This definition of the function `sellProduct` is

```
void sellProduct(dispenserType& product, cashRegister& pCounter)
{
    int amount;  //variable to hold the amount entered
    int amount2; //variable to hold the extra amount needed

    if(product.count() > 0)                              //Step a
    {
       cout<<"Please deposit "<<product.productCost()
           <<" cents"<<endl;                             //Step a.i
       cin>>amount;                                      //Step a.ii

       if(amount < product.productCost())                //Step a.iii
       {
           cout<<"Please deposit another "
               <<product.productCost() - amount          //Step a.iii.1
               <<" cents"<<endl;
           cin>>amount2;                                 //Step a.iii.2
           amount = amount + amount2;                    //Step a.iii.3
       }
```

```
        if(amount >= product.productCost())                 //Step a.iv
        {
           pCounter.acceptAmount(amount);                   //Step a.iv.1
           product.makeSale();                              //Step a.iv.2
           cout<<"Collect your item at the bottom"
               <<" and enjoy."<<endl;                       //Step a.iv.3
        }
        else
           cout<<"The amount is not enough. "
               <<"Collect what you deposited."<<endl;       //Step a.v
        cout<<"*-*-*-*-*-*-*-*-*-*-*-*-*-*-*-*-*-*-*-*-*"
            <<endl<<endl;
     }
     else
        cout<<"Sorry this item is sold out."<<endl;         //Step b
}//end sellProduct
```

Now that we have described the functions `showSelection` and `sellProduct`, the function `main` is described next.

`main`

The algorithm for the function `main` is as follows:

1. Create the cash register—that is, declare a variable of the type `cashRegister`.
2. Create four dispensers—that is, declare four objects of the type `dispenserType` and initialize these objects. For example, the statement

   `dispenserType candy(100, 50);`

   creates a dispenser object, `candy`, to hold the candies. The number of items in the dispenser is `100`, and the cost of an item is `50` cents.
3. Declare additional variables as necessary.
4. Show the selection; call the function `showSelection`.
5. Get the selection.
6. While not done (a selection of `9` exits the program).
   a. Sell the product; call the function `sellProduct`.
   b. Show the selection; call the function `showSelection`.
   c. Get the selection.

The definition of the function `main` is as follows:

```
int main()
{
     cashRegister counter;                                  //Step 1
     dispenserType candy(100,50);                           //Step 2
     dispenserType chips(100,65);                           //Step 2
     dispenserType gum(75,45);                              //Step 2
```

```
    dispenserType cookies(100,85);                      //Step 2

    int choice;                                         //Step 3

    showSelection();                                    //Step 4
    cin>>choice;                                        //Step 5

    while(choice != 9)                                  //Step 6
    {
          switch(choice)                                //Step 6a
          {
          case 1: sellProduct(candy, counter);
                  break;
          case 2: sellProduct(chips, counter);
                  break;
          case 3: sellProduct(gum, counter);
                  break;
          case 4: sellProduct(cookies, counter);
                  break;
          default: cout<<"Bad Selection"<<endl;
          }//end switch

     showSelection();                                   //Step 6b
     cin>>choice;                                       //Step 6c
     }//end while

     return 0;
}//end main
```

Complete Program Listing

```
//Candy Machine Header File

class cashRegister
{
public:
    int currentBalance();
      //Function to return the current amount in the cash
      //register
      //The value of the data member cashOnHand is returned

    void acceptAmount(int amountIn);
      //This function receives the amount deposited by
      //the customer and updates the amount in the register
      //Post: cashOnHand = cashOnHand + amountIn

    cashRegister(int cashIn = 500);
      //Constructor to set the cash in the register to a
      //specific amount
      //Post: cashOnHand = cashIn;
```

```
        //If no value is specified when the object is
        //declared, the default value assigned
        //to cashOnHand is 500

private:
    int cashOnHand;  //variable to store the cash
                     //in the register
};


class dispenserType
{
public:
    int count();
      //Function to return the number of items in the machine
      //The value of the data member numberOfProducts is returned

    int productCost();
      //Function to return the cost of the item
      //The value of the data member cost is returned

    void makeSale();
      //Function to reduce the number of items by 1
      //Post: numberOfProducts = numberOfProducts - 1;

    dispenserType(int setNoOfProducts = 50, int setCost = 50);
      //Constructor to set the cost and number of items
      //in the dispenser specified by the user
      //Post: numberOfProducts = setNoOfProducts;
      //      cost = setCost;
      //If no value is specified for either of the two
      //parameters, the default value is assigned to the
      //data members numberOfProducts and cost
private:
    int numberOfProducts; //variable to store the number of
                          //items in the dispenser
    int cost;  //variable to store the cost of an item
};


//Implementation file candyMachineImp.cpp
//This file contains the definitions of the functions
//to implement the operations of the classes
//cashRegister and dispenserType

#include <iostream>
#include "candyMachine.h"
using namespace std;
```

```
int cashRegister::currentBalance()
{
     return cashOnHand;
}

void cashRegister::acceptAmount(int amountIn)
{
      cashOnHand += amountIn;
}

cashRegister::cashRegister(int cashIn)
{
    if(cashIn >= 0)
       cashOnHand = cashIn;
    else
       cashOnHand = 500;
}

int dispenserType::count()
{
      return numberOfProducts;
}

int dispenserType::productCost()
{
      return cost;
}

void dispenserType::makeSale()
{
      numberOfProducts--;
}

dispenserType::dispenserType(int setNoOfProducts, int setCost)
{
    if(setNoOfProducts >= 0)
       numberOfProducts = setNoOfProducts;
    else
       numberOfProducts = 50;

    if(setCost >= 0)
       cost = setCost;
    else
       cost = 50;
}


//Main program:
#include <iostream>
#include "candyMachine.h"
```

```
using namespace std;

void showSelection();
void sellProduct(dispenserType& product,
                 cashRegister& pCounter);

int main()
{
      cashRegister  counter;
      dispenserType candy(100,50);
      dispenserType chips(100,65);
      dispenserType gum(75,45);
      dispenserType cookies(100,85);

      int choice;  //variable to hold the selection

      showSelection();
      cin>>choice;

      while(choice != 9)
      {
            switch(choice)
            {
            case 1: sellProduct(candy, counter);
                    break;
            case 2: sellProduct(chips, counter);
                    break;
            case 3: sellProduct(gum, counter);
                    break;
            case 4: sellProduct(cookies, counter);
                    break;
            default: cout<<"Bad Selection"<<endl;
            }//end switch
            showSelection();
            cin>>choice;
      }//end while

      return 0;
}//end main

void showSelection()
{
     cout<<"*** Welcome to Shelly's Candy Shop ***"<<endl;
     cout<<"To select an item, enter "<<endl;
     cout<<"1 for Candy"<<endl;
     cout<<"2 for Chips"<<endl;
     cout<<"3 for Gum"<<endl;
     cout<<"4 for Cookies"<<endl;
     cout<<"9 to exit"<<endl;
}//end showSelection
```

```
void sellProduct(dispenserType& product,
                 cashRegister& pCounter)
{
  int amount;  //variable to hold the amount entered
  int amount2; //variable to hold the extra amount needed

  if(product.count() > 0)  //if dispenser is not empty
  {
     cout<<"Please deposit "<<product.productCost()
         <<" cents"<<endl;
     cin>>amount;

     if(amount < product.productCost())
     {
        cout<<"Please deposit another "
            <<product.productCost() - amount
            <<" cents"<<endl;
        cin>>amount2;
        amount = amount + amount2;
     }

     if(amount >= product.productCost())
     {
        pCounter.acceptAmount(amount);
        product.makeSale();
        cout<<"Collect your item at the bottom and enjoy."<<endl;
     }
     else
        cout<<"The amount is not enough. "
            <<"Collect what you deposited."<<endl;

     cout<<"*-*-*-*-*-*-*-*-*-*-*-*-*-*-*-*-*-*-*-*"
         <<endl<<endl;
  }
  else
     cout<<"Sorry this item is sold out."<<endl;
}//end sellProduct
```

Sample Run: In this sample run, the user input is shaded.

```
*** Welcome to Shelly's Candy Shop ***
To select an item, enter
1 for Candy
2 for Chips
3 for Gum
4 for Cookies
9 to exit
```

```
1
Please deposit 50 cents
50
Collect your item at the bottom and enjoy
*-*-*-*-*-*-*-*-*-*-*-*-*-*-*-*-*-*-*-*-*

*** Welcome to Shelly's Candy Shop ***
To select an item, enter
1 for Candy
2 for Chips
3 for Gum
4 for Cookies
9 to exit
3
Please deposit 45 cents
45
Collect your item at the bottom and enjoy
*-*-*-*-*-*-*-*-*-*-*-*-*-*-*-*-*-*-*-*-*

*** Welcome to Shelly's Candy Shop ***
To select an item, enter
1 for Candy
2 for Chips
3 for Gum
4 for Cookies
9 to exit
9
```

QUICK REVIEW

1. A **class** is a collection of a fixed number of components.
2. Components of a **class** are called the members of the class.
3. Members of a **class** are accessed by name.
4. In C++, **class** is a reserved word.
5. Members of a class are classified into one of three categories: **private**, **protected**, and **public**.
6. The **private** members of a class are not accessible outside the class.
7. The **public** members of a class are accessible outside the class.
8. By default, all members of a class are **private**.
9. The **public** members are declared using the label **public:**.
10. The **private** members are declared using the label **private:**.
11. A member of a class can be a function or a variable (that is, data).

12. If any member of a class is a function, you usually use the function prototype to declare it.
13. If any member of a class is a variable, it is declared like any other variable.
14. In the definition of the class, you cannot initialize a variable when you declare it.
15. In C++, a `class` is a definition. No memory is allocated; memory is allocated for the class variables when you declare them.
16. In C++, class variables are called class objects or simply objects.
17. Any program (or software) that uses a class is called a client of the class.
18. A class member is accessed using the class variable name, followed by the dot operator (`.`), followed by the member name.
19. The only built-in operations on classes are the assignment and member selection.
20. As parameters to functions, classes can be passed either by value or by reference.
21. A function can return a value of the type `class`.
22. Constructors guarantee that the data members are initialized when an object is declared.
23. The name of a constructor is the same as the name of the class.
24. A class can have more than one constructor.
25. A constructor without parameters is called the default constructor.
26. Constructors automatically execute when a class object enters its scope.
27. Destructors automatically execute when a class object goes out of scope.
28. A class can have only one destructor and no parameters.
29. The name of a destructor is the tilde (~), followed by the class name (no spaces in between).
30. Constructors and destructors are functions without any type; that is, they are neither value-returning nor void. As a result, they cannot be called like other functions.
31. A data type that specifies the logical properties without the implementation details is called an abstract data type (ADT).
32. Classes were specifically designed in C++ to handle ADT.
33. To implement an ADT, you must represent the data and write related algorithms to implement the operations.

EXERCISES

1. Mark the following statements as true or false.
   a. The data members of a class must be of the same type.
   b. The function members of a class must be `public`.
   c. A class can have more than one constructor.
   d. A class can have more than one destructor.
   e. Both constructors and destructors can have parameters.

2. Find the syntax errors in the definitions of the following classes.

a.
```
class AA
{
 public:
        void print();
        int sum();
        AA();
        int AA(int , int);
 private :
        int x ;
        int y ;
} ;
```

b.
```
class BB
{
        int one ;
        int two;
public:
        bool equal();
        print();
        BB(int, int);
}
```

c.
```
class CC
{
public;
        void set(int, int);
        void print();
        CC();
        CC(int, int);
        bool CC(int, int);
private:
        int u;
        int v;
};
```

3. Consider the following declarations.

```
class xClass
{
 public:
      void func();
      void print() const;
      xClass ();
      xClass (int, double);
 private:
      int u;
      double w;
};

xClass x;
```

a. How many members does class **x** have?

b. How many **private** members does class **x** have?

c. How many constructors does class **x** have?

d. Write the definition of the member function **func** so that **u** is set to **10** and **w** is set to **15.3**.

e. Write the definition of the member function **print** that prints the contents of **u** and **w**.

f. Write the definition of the default constructor of the **class xClass** so that the **private** data members are initialized to **0**.

g. Write a C++ statement that prints the values of the data members of the object **x**.

h. Write a C++ statement that declares an object **t** of the type **xClass**, and initializes the data members of **t** to **20** and **35.0**, respectively.

4. Consider the definition of the following class:

```
class CC
{
public:
      CC();                   //Line 1
      CC(int);                //Line 2
      CC(int, int)            //Line 3
      CC(double, int)         //Line 4
          .
          .
          .
private:
      int u;
      double v;
};
```


a. Give the line number containing the constructor that is executed in each of the following declarations.

(i) `CC one;`

(ii)`CC two(5, 6);`

(iii)`CC three(3.5, 8);`

b. Write the definition of the constructor at Line 1 so that the **private** data members are initialized to **0**.

c. Write the definition of the constructor at Line 2 so that the **private** data member **u** is initialized according to the value of the parameter, and the **private** data member **v** is initialized to **0**.

d. Write the definition of the constructors at Lines 3 and 4 so that the **private** data members are initialized according to the values of the parameters.

5. Consider the definition of the following **class**:

```
class testClass
{
public:
    int sum();
       //return the sum of the private data members
    void print() const;
       //print the values of the private data members
    testClass();
       //default constructor
       //initialize the private data members to 0
    testClass(int a, int b);
       //constructors with parameters
       //initialize the private data members to the values
       //specified by the parameters
       //Post condition: x = a;    y = b;
private :
   int x;
   int y;
};
```

a. Write the definitions of the member functions as described in the definition of the **class testClass**.

b. Write a test program to test the various operations of the **class testClass**.

PROGRAMMING EXERCISES

1. Write a program that converts a number entered in Roman numerals to decimal. Your program should consist of a **class**, say **romanType**. An object of the type **romanType** should do the following:

   a. Store the number as a Roman numeral.

   b. Convert and store the number into decimal.

   c. Print the number as a Roman numeral or decimal number as requested by the user.

   The decimal values of the Roman numerals are:

   ```
   M   1000
   D    500
   C    100
   L     50
   X     10
   V      5
   I      1
   ```

   d. Test your program using the following Roman numerals: MCXIV, CCCLIX, MDCLXVI.

2. Design and implement a `class dayType` that implements the day of the week in a program. The `class dayType` should store the day, such as `Sun` for Sunday. The program should be able to perform the following operations on an object of the type `dayType`:
   a. Set the day.
   b. Print the day.
   c. Return the day.
   d. Return the next day.
   e. Return the previous day.
   f. Calculate and return the day by adding certain days to the current day. For example, if the current day is Monday and we add 4 days, the day to be returned is Friday. Similarly, if today is Tuesday and we add 13 days, the day to be returned is Monday.
   g. Add the appropriate constructors.
3. Write the definitions of the functions to implement the operations for the `class dayType` as defined in Programming Exercise 2.
4. Example 13-9 defined a `class personType` to store the name of a person. The member functions that we included merely print the name and set the name of a person. Redefine the `class personType` so that in addition to what the existing `class` does, you can:
   a. Set the last name only.
   b. Set the first name only.
   c. Store and set the middle name.
   d. Check whether a given last name is the same as the last name of this person.
   e. Check whether a given first name is the same as the first name of this person.

   Write the definitions of the member functions to implement the operations for this class.
5. a. Some of the characteristics of a book are the title, author(s), publisher, ISBN, price, and year of publication. Design a `class bookType` that defines the book as an ADT.
      i. Each object of the `class bookType` can hold the following information about a book: title, up to four authors, publisher, ISBN, price, and number of copies in stock. To keep track of the number of authors, add another data member.
      ii. Include the member functions to perform the various operations on objects of the type `bookType`. For example, the usual operations that can be performed on the title are to show the title, set the title, and check whether a title is the same as the actual title of the book. Similarly, the typical operations that can be performed on the number of copies in stock are to show the number of copies in stock, set the number of copies in stock, update the number of copies in stock, and return the number of copies in stock. Add similar operations for the publisher, ISBN, book price, and authors. Add the appropriate constructors and a destructor (if one is needed).

13

b. Write the definitions of the member functions of the `class bookType`.

c. Write a program that uses the `class bookType` and tests various operations on the objects of `class bookType`. Declare an array of 100 components of the type `bookType`. Some of the operations that you should perform are to search for a book by its title, search by ISBN, and update the number of copies of a book.

6. In this exercise, you will design a `class memberType`.

a. Each object of `memberType` can hold the name of a person, member ID, number of books bought, and amount spent.

b. Include the member functions to perform the various operations on the objects of `memberType`—for example, modify, set, and show a person's name. Similarly, update, modify, and show the number of books bought and the amount spent.

c. Add the appropriate constructors and a destructor (if one is needed).

d. Write the definitions of the member functions of `memberType`.

7. Using the classes designed in Programming Exercises 5 and 6, write a program to simulate a bookstore. The bookstore has two types of customers: those who are members of the bookstore and those who buy books from the bookstore only occasionally. Each member has to pay a $10 yearly membership fee and receives a 5% discount on each book bought.

For each member, the bookstore keeps track of the number of books bought and the total amount spent. For every eleventh book that a member buys, the bookstore takes the average of the total amount of the last 10 books bought, applies this amount as a discount, and then resets the total amount spent to `0`.

Write a program that can process up to 1000 book titles and 500 members. Your program should contain a menu that gives the user different choices to effectively run the program; in other words, your program should be self-driven.

CHAPTER

14

INHERITANCE AND COMPOSITION

In this chapter, you will:

- Learn about inheritance
- Learn about derived and base classes
- Explore how to redefine the member functions of a base class
- Examine how the constructors of base and derived classes work
- Learn how to construct the header file of a derived class
- Explore three types of inheritance: `public`, `protected`, and `private`
- Learn about composition
- Become familiar with the three basic principles of object-oriented design

Chapter 13 introduced classes, abstract data types (ADT), and ways to implement ADT in C++. By using classes, you can combine data and operations in a single unit. An object, therefore, becomes a self-contained entity. Operations can directly access the data, but the internal state of an object cannot be manipulated directly.

In addition to implementing ADT, classes have other features. For instance, classes can create new classes from existing classes. This important feature encourages code reuse. In C++, you can relate two or more classes in more than one way. Two common ways to relate classes in a meaningful way are

- **Inheritance** ("is-a" relationship), and
- **Composition** ("has-a" relationship).

INHERITANCE

Suppose that you want to design a `class`, `partTimeEmployee`, to implement and process the characteristics of a part-time employee. The main features associated with a part-time employee are the name, pay rate, and number of hours worked. In Example 13-9 (in Chapter 13), we designed a class to implement a person's name. Every part-time employee is a person. Therefore, rather than design the `class partTimeEmployee` from scratch, we want to be able to extend the definition of the `class personType` (from Example 13-9) by adding additional members (data and/or functions).

Of course, we do not want to make the necessary changes directly to the `class personType`—that is, edit the `class personType`, and add and/or delete members. In fact, we want to create the `class partTimeEmployee` without making any physical changes to the `class personType`, by adding only the members that are necessary. For example, because the `class personType` already has data members to store the first name and last name, we will not include any such members in the `class partTimeEmployee`. In fact, these data members will be inherited from the `class personType`. (We will design such a `class` in Example 14-1.)

In Chapter 13, we extensively studied and designed the `class clockType` to implement the time of day in a program. The `class clockType` has three data members, to store the hours, minutes, and seconds. Certain applications, in addition to the hours, minutes, and seconds, might also require us to store the time zone. In this case, we would like to extend the definition of the `class clockType` and create a `class`, `extClockType`, to accommodate this new information. That is, we want to derive the `class extClockType` by adding a data member—say, `timeZone`—and the necessary function members to manipulate the time (see Programming Exercise 1 at the end of this chapter). In C++, the mechanism that allows us to accomplish this task is the principle of **inheritance**. Inheritance is an "is-a" relationship; for instance, "every employee is a person."

Inheritance lets us create new classes from existing classes. The new classes that we create from the existing classes are called the **derived classes**; the existing classes are called the **base classes**. The derived classes inherit the properties of the base classes. So rather than create completely new classes from scratch, we can take advantage of inheritance and reduce software complexity.

Each derived class, in turn, becomes a base class for a future derived class. Inheritance can be either single inheritance or multiple inheritance. In **single inheritance**, the derived class is derived from a single base class; in **multiple inheritance**, the derived class is derived from more than one base class. This chapter concentrates on single inheritance.

Inheritance can be viewed as a tree-like, or hierarchical, structure wherein a base class is shown with its derived classes. Consider the tree diagram shown in Figure 14-1.

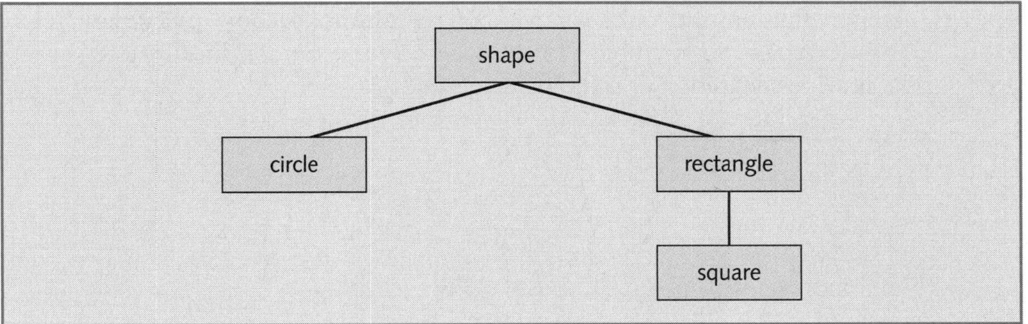

Figure 14-1 Inheritance hierarchy

In this diagram, `shape` is the base class. The `classes circle` and `rectangle` are derived from `shape`, and the `class square` is derived from `rectangle`. Every `circle` and every `rectangle` is a `shape`. Every `square` is a `rectangle`.

Suppose that we define a class called `shape`. To specify that the `class circle` is derived from `shape`, we typically use the following syntax:

```
class circle: public shape
{
    .
    .
    .
};
```

Recall that the word `public` in the heading is called the member access specifier. It specifies that all `public` members of the `class shape` are inherited as `public` members by the `class circle`. In other words, `public` members of the `class shape` become `public` members of the `class circle`.

On the other hand, consider the following definition of the `class circle`:

```
class circle: private shape
{
    .
    .
    .
};
```

In this definition, the **public** members of **shape** become **private** members of the **class circle**. So any object of the type **circle** cannot directly access these members. The previous definition of **circle** is equivalent to

```
class circle: shape
{
    .
    .
    .
};
```

That is, if we do not use either the **memberAccessSpecifier public** or **private**, the **public** members of a base class are inherited as **private** members.

The general syntax of a derived class is

```
class className: memberAccessSpecifier baseClassName
{
    member list
};
```

where **memberAccessSpecifier** is **public**, **protected**, or **private**. When no **memberAccessSpecifier** is specified, it is assumed to be a **private** inheritance. (We discuss **protected** inheritance later in this chapter.)

The following facts about the base and the derived classes should be kept in mind.

1. The **private** members of the base class are **private** to the base class; hence, the members of the derived class cannot directly access them. In other words, when you write the definitions of the member functions of the derived class, you cannot directly access the **private** members of the base class.
2. The **public** members of a base class can be inherited either as **public** members or as **private** members by the derived class. That is, the **public** members of the base class can become either **public** or **private** members of the derived class.
3. The derived class can include additional data and/or function members.
4. The derived class can redefine the **public** member functions of the base class. That is, in the derived class, you can have a function member with the same name, number, and types of parameters as a function in the base class. However, this redefinition applies only to the objects of the derived class, not to the objects of the base class.
5. All data members of the base class are also data members of the derived class. Similarly, the member functions of the base class (unless redefined) are also the member functions of the derived class. (Remember Rule 1 when accessing a member of the base class in the derived class.)

The next sections describe two important issues related to inheritance. The first issue is the redefinition of the member functions of the base class in the derived class. While discussing this issue, we will also address how to access the `private` (data) members of the base class in the derived class. The second key inheritance issue is related to the constructor. The constructor of a derived class cannot *directly* access the `private` data members of the base class. Thus, we need to ensure that the `private` data members that are inherited from the base class are initialized when a constructor of the derived class executes.

Redefining Member Functions of the Base Class

Suppose that a `class derivedClass` is derived from a `class baseClass`. Further assume that both `derivedClass` and `baseClass` have some data members. It then follows that the data members of the `class derivedClass` are its own data members, together with the data members of `baseClass`. Suppose that `baseClass` contains a function, `print`, that prints the values of the data members of `baseClass`. Now `derivedClass` contains data members in addition to the data members inherited from `baseClass`. Suppose that you want to include a function that prints the data members of `derivedClass`. You can give any name to this function. However, in the `class derivedClass`, you can also name this function as `print`, (the same name used by `baseClass`). This is called redefining the member function of the base class. Next we illustrate how to redefine the member functions of a base class with the help of an example.

To redefine a `public` member function of the base class in the derived class, the corresponding function in the derived class must have the same name, number, and types of parameters. In other words, the name of the function being redefined in the derived class must have the same name and the same set of parameters. If the corresponding functions in the base class and the derived class have the same name but different sets of parameters, then this is function overloading in the derived class, which is also allowed.

Consider the definition of the following class (see Figure 14-2):

```
class baseClass
{
public:
    void print() const;

private:
    int u;
    int v;
    char ch;
};
```

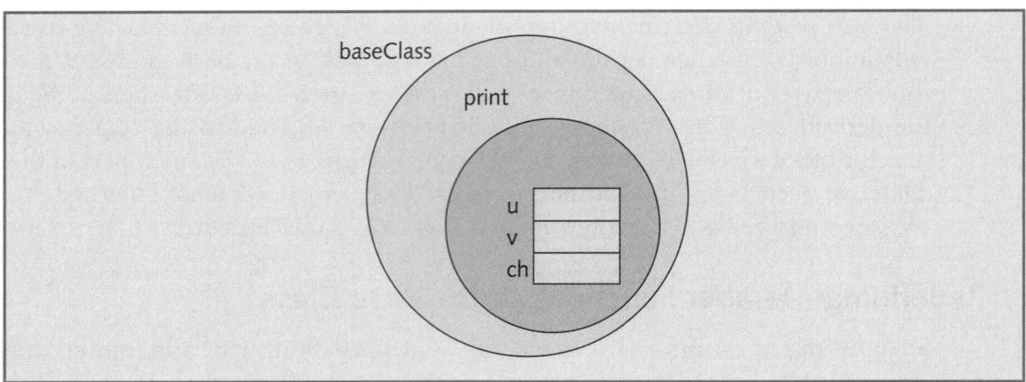

Figure 14-2 `class baseClass`

The **`class baseClass`** has four members. Suppose that the definition of the member function `print` of `baseClass` is

```
void baseClass::print() const
{
      cout<<"Base Class: u = "<<u<<", v = "<<v
          <<", ch = "<<ch<<endl;
}
```

Now consider the definition of the following class (see Figure 14-3):

```
class derivedClass: public baseClass
{
public:
    void print() const;

private:
    int first;
    double second;
};
```

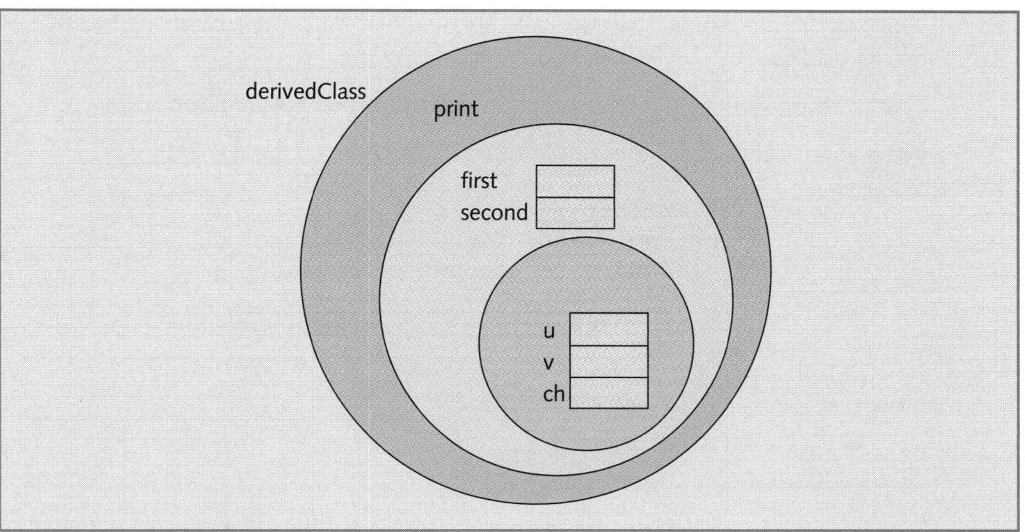

Figure 14-3 class derivedClass

From the definition of the class derivedClass, it is clear that the class derivedClass is derived from the class baseClass and it is a public inheritance. Therefore, all public members of baseClass are inherited as public members of derivedClass. The class derivedClass also overwrites the print function.

Next, let us write the definition of the member function print of derivedClass.

The class derivedClass has five data members: u, v, ch, first, and second. The print function of derivedClass prints the values of these data members. To write the definition of the member function print of derivedClass, keep the following in mind:

- The data members u, v, and ch are private members of the class baseClass and so cannot be directly accessed in the derivedClass. Therefore, when writing the definition of the function print of derivedClass, we cannot reference u, v, and ch directly.
- The data members u, v, and ch of the class baseClass are accessible in derivedClass through the public members of baseClass.

Therefore, when writing the definition of the function print of derivedClass, we first call the member function print of baseClass to print the values of u, v, and ch. After printing the values of u, v, and ch, we output the values of first and second.

To call the function print of baseClass in the definition of the function print of derivedClass, we must use the following statement:

```
baseClass::print();
```

This statement ensures that we call the member function **print** of **baseClass**, not of **derivedClass**.

The definition of the member function **print** of **derivedClass** is

```
void derivedClass::print() const
{
      baseClass::print();
      cout<<"Derived Class: first = "<<first
          <<", second = "<<second<<endl;
      cout<<"___________________________________"
          <<"________"<<endl;
}
```

Now consider the following statements:

```
baseClass         baseObject;
derivedClass      derivedObject;
```

The first statement declares **baseObject** to be an object of the type **baseClass**. Thus, the object **baseObject** has three data members: **u**, **v**, and **ch**. The second statement declares **derivedObject** to be an object of the type **derivedClass**. Thus, the object **derivedObject** has five data members: **u**, **v**, **ch**, **first**, and **second**. (See Figure 14-4.)

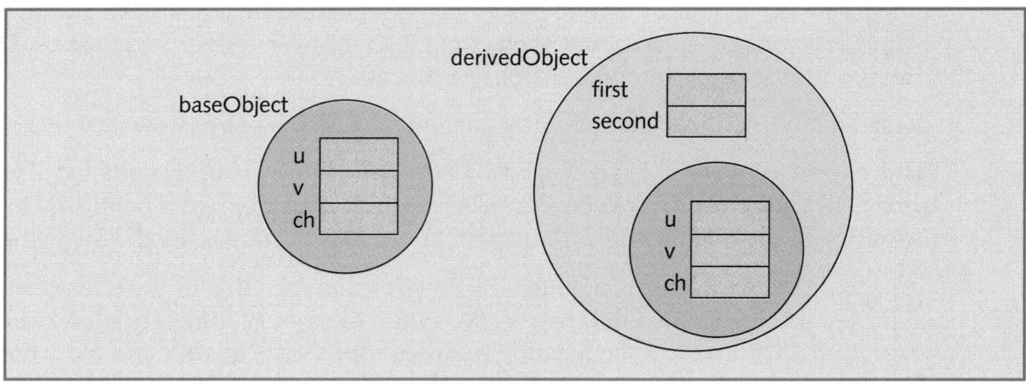

Figure 14-4 Objects baseObject and derivedObject

Suppose that the values of the data members **u**, **v**, and **ch** of **baseObject** are **5**, **6**, and *****, respectively. Further suppose that the values of the data members **u**, **v**, **ch**, **first**, and **second** of **derivedObject** are **12**, **76**, **&**, **32**, and **16.38**, respectively. (See Figure 14-5.)

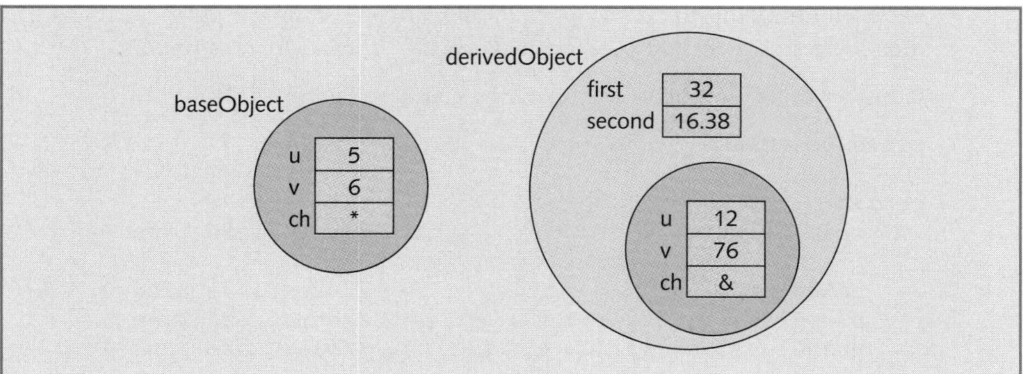

Figure 14-5 Objects `baseObject` and `derivedObject` with values

Consider the following statements:

```
baseObject.print();
derivedObject.print();
```

In the first statement, the function **print** of **baseClass** is executed; in the second statement, the function **print** associated with the **class derivedClass** is executed. Recall that, if a derived class redefines a member function of the base class, the redefinition applies only to the objects of the derived class. Thus, the output of the first statement is

```
Base Class: u = 5, v = 6, ch = *
```

The output of the second statement is

```
Base Class: u = 12, v = 76, ch = &
Derived Class: first = 32, second = 16.38
```

14

Constructors of Derived and Base Classes

A derived class can have its own **private** data members, and so a derived class can have its own constructors. A constructor typically serves to initialize the data members. When we declare a derived class object, this object inherits the members of the base class, but the derived class object cannot directly access the **private** (data) members of the base class. The same is true for the member functions of a derived class. That is, the member functions of the derived class cannot directly access the **private** members of the base class.

As a consequence, the constructors of the derived class can (directly) initialize only the **private** data members of the derived class. Thus, when a derived class object is declared, it must also automatically execute one of the constructors of the base class. Because constructors cannot be called like other functions, the execution of a derived class's constructor must trigger the execution of one of the base class's constructors. This is, in fact, what happens. Furthermore, a call to the base class's constructor is specified in the heading part of the derived class constructor's definition.

Let us illustrate this discussion with the help of an example. First we define a base class, and then we define a derived class. Both classes have their own constructors.

Consider the definition of the following class (see Figure 14-6):

```
class baseClass
{
public:
    void print();                       //baseClass Line 1

    baseClass();                        //baseClass Line 2
    baseClass(int x, int y);            //baseClass Line 3
    baseClass(int x, int y, char w); //baseClass Line 4

private:
    int u;
    int v;
    char ch;
};
```

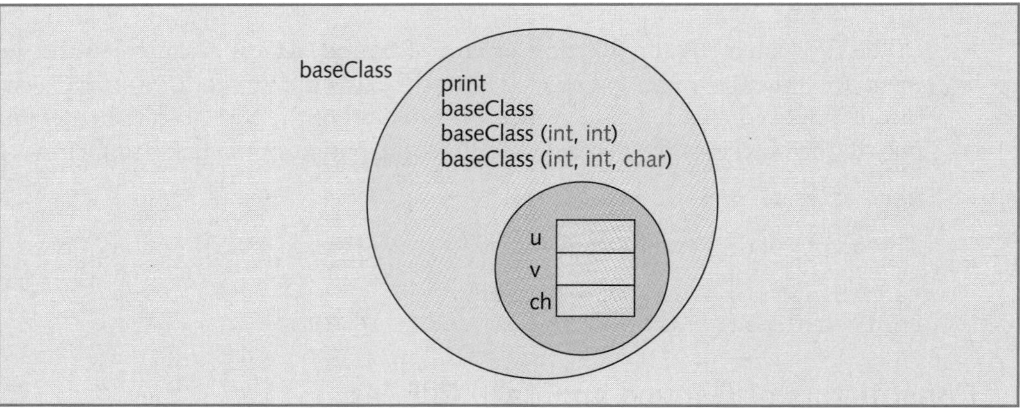

Figure 14-6 `class baseClass` with constructors

The **`class baseClass`** has three constructors, a member function **`print`**, and three data members. Suppose that the definitions of the member function and the constructors of **`baseClass`** are as follows:

```
void baseClass::print()
{
      cout<<"Base Class: u = "<<u<<", v = "<<v
          <<", ch = "<<ch<<endl;
}
```

```
      //default constructor; baseClass Line 2
baseClass::baseClass()
{
      u = 0;
      v = 0;
      ch = '*';
}

      //constructor; baseClass Line 3
baseClass::baseClass(int x, int y)
{
      u = x;
      v = y;
      ch = '*';
}

      //constructor; baseClass Line 4
baseClass::baseClass(int x, int y, char w)
{
      u = x;
      v = y;
      ch = w;
}
```

Now consider the definition of the following class (see Figure 14-7):

```
class derivedClass: public baseClass
{
public:
    void print();                        //derivedClass Line 1

    derivedClass();                      //derivedClass Line 2
    derivedClass(int x, int y,
                 int one, double two); //derivedClass Line 3
    derivedClass(int x, int y, char w,
                 int one, double two); //derivedClass Line 4

private:
    int first;
    double second;
};
```

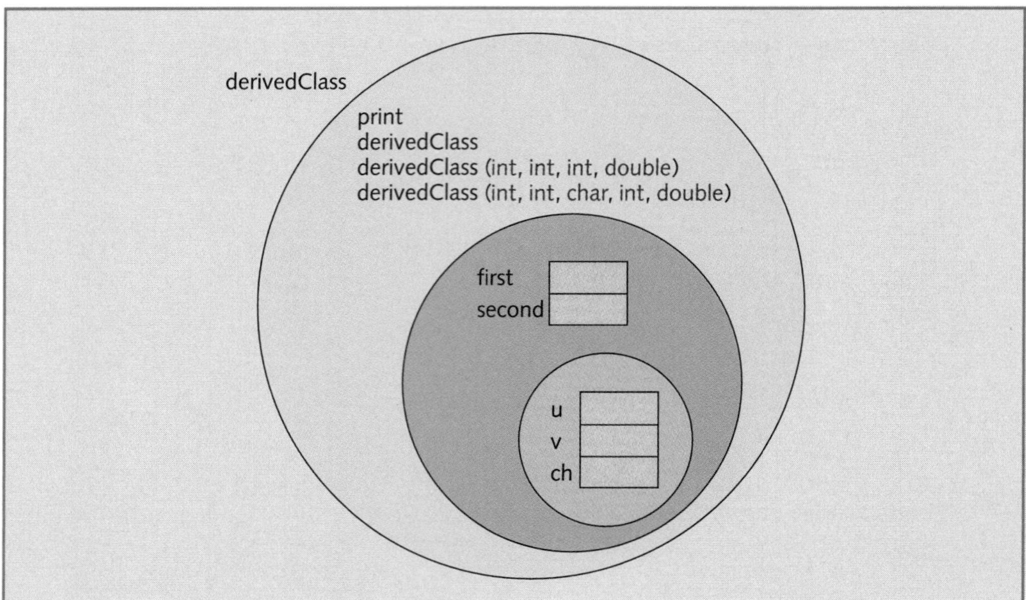

Figure 14-7 `class derivedClass` with constructors

The **`class derivedClass`** is derived from the **`class baseClass`**, and it is a **`public`** inheritance. The **`class derivedClass`** has five data members: `u`, `v`, `ch`, `first`, and `second`. The data members `u`, `v`, and `ch` are inherited from the **`class baseClass`**.

Let us first write the definition of the member function `print` of `derivedClass`.

```
void derivedClass::print()
{
      baseClass::print();
      cout<<"Derived Class: first = "<<first
          <<", second = "<<second<<endl;
      cout<<"__________________________________"
          <<"_________"<<endl;
}
```

We will now write the definitions of the constructors of `derivedClass`. Recall that a call to a base class's constructor is specified in the heading of the definition of the derived class's constructor.

First, let us write the definition of the default constructor of **derivedClass**. Recall that, if a class contains the default constructor and no values are specified during object declaration, the default constructor executes and initializes the object. Because the **class baseClass** contains the default constructor, when writing the definition of the default constructor of **derivedClass**, we do not specify any constructor of the base class.

```
derivedClass::derivedClass()     //default constructor
{
      first = 0;
      second = 0;
}
```

Next, we discuss how to write the definitions of constructors with parameters. To trigger the execution of a constructor (with parameters) of the base class, you specify the name of the constructor of the base class with the parameters in the heading of the definition of a constructor of the derived class.

Consider the following definition of the constructor of **derivedClass** (declared at the line **derivedClass**, Line 3):

```
            //derivedClass constructor Line 3
derivedClass::derivedClass(int x, int y, int one, double two)
       : baseClass(x,y)
{
      first = one;
      second = two;
}
```

In this definition, we specify the constructor of **baseClass** with two parameters (declared in the line **baseClass**, Line 3). When this constructor of **derivedClass** executes, it triggers the execution of the constructor with two **int** parameters (declared in the line **baseClass**, Line 3).

14

Next, consider the following definition of the constructor of **derivedClass** (declared in the line **derivedClass**, Line 4):

```
            //derivedClass; constructor Line 4
derivedClass::derivedClass(int x, int y, char w,
                           int one, double two)
      :baseClass(x,y,w)
{
      first = one;
      second = two;
}
```

In this definition, we specified the constructor of **baseClass** with three parameters (declared in the line **baseClass**, Line 4). When this constructor of **derivedClass** executes, it triggers the execution of the constructor with three parameters in the order **int**, **int**, **char** (declared in the line **baseClass**, Line 4).

The following program tests these concepts.

```
#include <iostream>
#include "baseClass.h"
#include "derivedClass.h"
using namespace std;

int main()
{
      baseClass baseObject1;
      baseClass baseObject2(5,6);
      baseClass baseObject3(4,8,'K');

      derivedClass derivedObject1;
      derivedClass derivedObject2(12,13,45,8.5);
      derivedClass derivedObject3(21,23,'Y',76,64.58);

      cout<<"Line 1: baseObject1: ";
      baseObject1.print();                          //main Line 1
      cout<<"Line 2: baseObject2: ";
      baseObject2.print();                          //main Line 2
      cout<<"Line 3: baseObject3: ";
      baseObject3.print();                          //main Line 3

      cout<<"Line 4: -*-*-*-*-*-*-*-*-*-*"
          <<"-*-*-*-*-*-*-*-*-*-*-*-*-"<<endl;      //main Line 4
      cout<<"Line 5: Derived Class Objects."
          <<endl;                                   //main Line 5
      cout<<endl;

      cout<<"Line 6: derivedObject1: "<<endl;
      derivedObject1.print();                       //main Line 6
      cout<<"Line 7: derivedObject2: "<<endl;
      derivedObject2.print();                       //main Line 7
      cout<<"Line 8: derivedObject3: "<<endl;
      derivedObject3.print();                       //main Line 8

      return  0;
}
```

Output

```
Line 1: baseObject1: Base Class: u = 0, v = 0, ch = *
Line 2: baseObject2: Base Class: u = 5, v = 6, ch = *
Line 3: baseObject3: Base Class: u = 4, v = 8, ch = K
Line 4: -*-*-*-*-*-*-*-*-*-*-*-*-*-*-*-*-*-*-*-*-*-*-
Line 5: Derived Class Objects.
```

```
Line 6: derivedObject1:
Base Class: u = 0, v = 0, ch = *
Derived Class: first = 0, second = 0
______________________________________________
Line 7: derivedObject2:
Base Class: u = 12, v = 13, ch = *
Derived Class: first = 45, second = 8.5
______________________________________________
Line 8: derivedObject3:
Base Class: u = 21, v = 23, ch = Y
Derived Class: first = 76, second = 64.58
______________________________________________
```

You are strongly encouraged to do a walk-through of the preceding program.

Suppose that a base **class**, **baseClass**, has *private* data members and constructors. Further suppose that the **class derivedClass** is derived from **baseClass**, and **derivedClass** has no data members. Therefore, the data members of **derivedClass** are the ones inherited from **baseClass**. A constructor cannot be called like other functions, and the data members of **baseClass** cannot be directly accessed by the member functions of **derivedClass**. To guarantee the initialization of the data members of an object of the type **derivedClass**, even though **derivedClass** has no data members, it must have the appropriate constructors. A constructor (with parameters) of **derivedClass** merely issues a call to a constructor (with parameters) of **baseClass**. Therefore, when you write the definition of the constructor (with parameters) of **derivedClass**, the heading of the definition of the constructor contains a call to an appropriate constructor (with parameters) of **derivedClass**, and the body of the constructor is empty—that is, it contains only the opening and closing braces.

Example 14-1

14

Suppose that you want to define a class to group the attributes of an employee. There are both full-time employees and part-time employees. Part-time employees are paid based on the number of hours worked and an hourly rate. Suppose that you want to define a class to keep track of a part-time employee's information such as **name**, **pay rate**, and **hours worked**. You can then print the employee's name together with his or her wages. Because every employee is a person, and Example 13-9 (Chapter 13) defined the **class personType** to store the first name and the last name together with the necessary operations on **name**, we can define a **class partTimeEmployee** based on the **class personType**. (See Figure 14-8.) You can also redefine the **print** function to print the appropriate information.

```
class partTimeEmployee: public personType
{
public:
    void print();
      //Function to output the first name, last name, and
      //the wages in the form:
      //firstName lastName wages are $$$$.$$
```

```
    double calculatePay();
      //Function to calculate and return the wages

    void setNameRateHours(string first, string last,
                          double rate, double hours);
      //Function to set the first name, last name, payRate,
      //and hoursWorked according to the parameters.
      //The parameters first and last are passed to the
      //base class. payRate = rate; hoursWorked = hours;

    partTimeEmployee(string first, string last,
                     double rate, double hours);
      //Constructor with parameters
      //Set the first name, last name, payRate, and
      //hoursWorked according to the parameters.
      //Parameters first and last are passed to the
      //base class. payRate = rate; hoursWorked = hours;

    partTimeEmployee();
      //default constructor
      //Set the first name, last name, payRate, and
      //hoursWorked to the default values.
      //The first name and last name are initialized to an empty
      //string by the default constructor of the base class.
      //payRate = 0; hoursWorked = 0;

private:
    double payRate;     //store the pay rate
    double hoursWorked; //store the hours worked
};
```

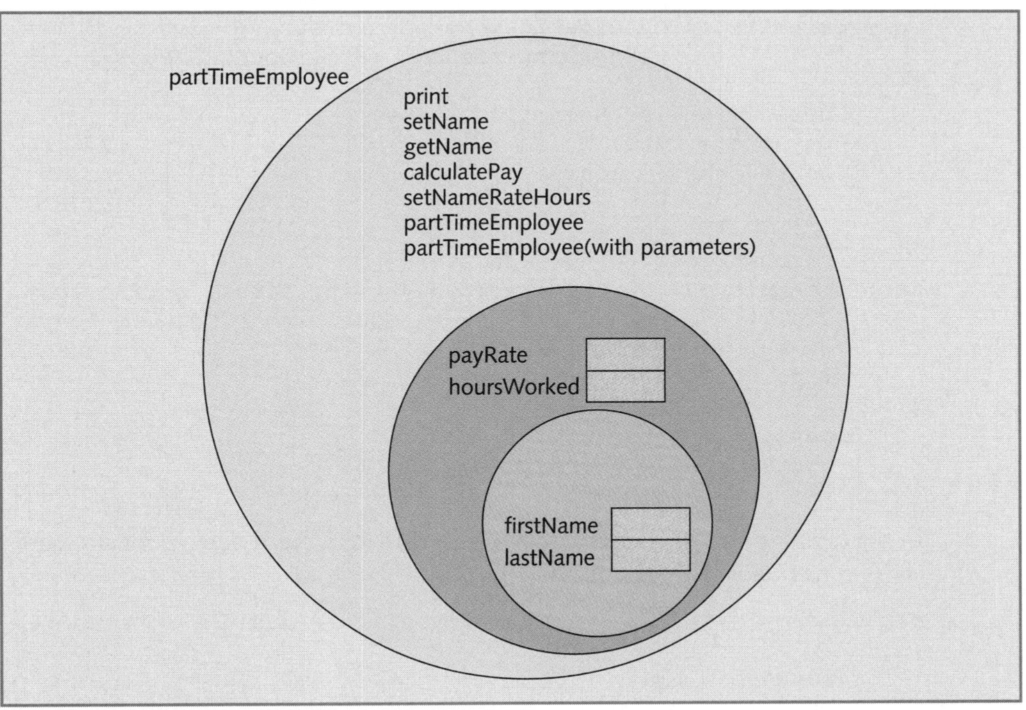

Figure 14-8 `class partTimeEmployee`

The **`class partTimeEmployee`** contains two constructors: the default constructor and a constructor with parameters. Both of these constructors can be replaced by one constructor with default parameters, the details of which are left as an exercise for you.

14

The definitions of the member functions of the **`class partTimeEmployee`** are as follows:

```
void partTimeEmployee::print()
{
      personType::print();      //print the name of the employee
      cout<<" wages are : "<<calculatePay()<<endl;
}

double partTimeEmployee::calculatePay()
{
      return (payRate * hoursWorked);
}
```

```
void partTimeEmployee::setNameRateHours(string first,
                string last, double rate, double hours)
{
      personType::setName(first,last);
      payRate = rate;
      hoursWorked = hours;
}

      //constructor with parameters
partTimeEmployee::partTimeEmployee(string first, string last,
                                   double rate, double hours)

      : personType(first, last)
{
      payRate = rate;
      hoursWorked = hours;
}
```

In the definition of the constructors with parameters, the heading contains a call to the base class's constructor with parameters.

```
partTimeEmployee:: partTimeEmployee()   //default constructor
{
      payRate = 0;
      hoursWorked = 0;
}
```

In the definition of the default constructor, because the heading contains no calls to the base class's constructor, the default constructor of the base class is executed.

Header File of a Derived Class

The previous section explained how to derive new classes from previously defined classes. To define new classes, you create new header files. The base classes are already defined, and header files contain their definitions. Thus, to create new classes based on the previously defined classes, the header files of the new classes contain commands that tell the computer where to look for the definitions of the base classes.

Suppose that the definition of the **class** `personType` is placed in the header file `person.h`. To create the definition of the **class** `partTimeEmployee`, the header file—say, `ptEmployee.h`—must contain the preprocessor directive

```
#include "person.h"
```

before the definition of the `class partTimeEmployee`. To be specific, the header file `ptEmployee.h` is

```
//Header file ptEmployee.h
#include "person.h"

class partTimeEmployee: public personType
{
public:
    void print() const;
    double calculatePay();
    void setNameRateHours(string, string, double, double);
    partTimeEmployee(string, string, double, double);
    partTimeEmployee();  //default constructor

private:
    double payRate;
    double hoursWorked;
};
```

The definitions of the member functions can be placed in a separate file. Recall that to include a system-provided header file, such as `iostream`, in a user program, you enclose the header file between angular brackets; to include a user-defined header file in a program, you enclose the header file between double quotation marks.

Multiple Inclusions of a Header File

The previous section discussed how to create the header file of a derived class. To include a header file in a program, you use the preprocessor command. Recall that before a program is compiled, the preprocessor first processes the program. Consider the following header file:

14

```
//Header file test.h
const int One = 1;
const int Two = 2;
```

Suppose that the header file `testA.h` includes the file `test.h` in order to use the identifiers `One` and `Two`. To be specific, suppose that the header file `testA.h` looks like

```
//Header file testA.h
#include "test.h"
.
.
.
```

Now consider the following program code:

```
//Program headerTest.cpp
#include "test.h"
#include "testA.h"
.
.
.
```

When the program **headerTest.cpp** is compiled, it is first processed by the preprocessor. The preprocessor includes first the header file **test.h** and then the header file **testA.h**. When the header file **testA.h** is included, because it contains the preprocessor directive **#include "test.h"**, the header file **test.h** is included twice in the program. The second inclusion of the header file **test.h** results in compile-time errors, such as the identifier **One** already being declared. This problem occurs because the first inclusion of the header file **test.h** has already defined the variables **One** and **Two**. To avoid multiple inclusion of a file in a program, we use certain preprocessor commands in the header file. Let us first rewrite the header file **test.h** using these preprocessor commands and then explain the meaning of these commands.

```
//Header file test.h

#ifndef H_test
#define H_test
const int One = 1;
const int Two = 2;
#endif
```

a. **#ifndef H_test** means "if not defined **H_test**"

b. **#define H_test** means "define **H_test**"

c. **#endif** means "**end if**"

Here **H_test** is a preprocessor identifier.

The effect of these commands is as follows: If the identifier **H_test** is not defined, we must define the identifier **H_test** and let the remaining statements between **#define** and **#endif** pass through the compiler. If the header file **test.h** is included the second time in the program, the statement **#ifndef** fails and all statements until **#endif** are skipped. In fact, all header files are written using similar preprocessor commands.

C++ Stream Classes

Chapter 3 described in detail how to perform input/output (I/O) using standard I/O devices and file I/O. In particular, you used the object **cin**, the extraction operator >>, and functions such as **get** and **ignore** to read data from the standard input device. You also used the object **cout** and the insertion operator << to send output to the standard output device. To use **cin** and **cout**, the programs included the header file **iostream**, which includes the definitions of the classes **istream** and **ostream**. Moreover, for file I/O, the programs included the header file **ifstream**, and they used objects of the type **ifstream** for file input, and objects of the type **ofstream** for file output. This section briefly describes how stream classes are related and implemented in C++.

In C++, stream classes are implemented using the inheritance mechanism, as shown in Figure 14-9.

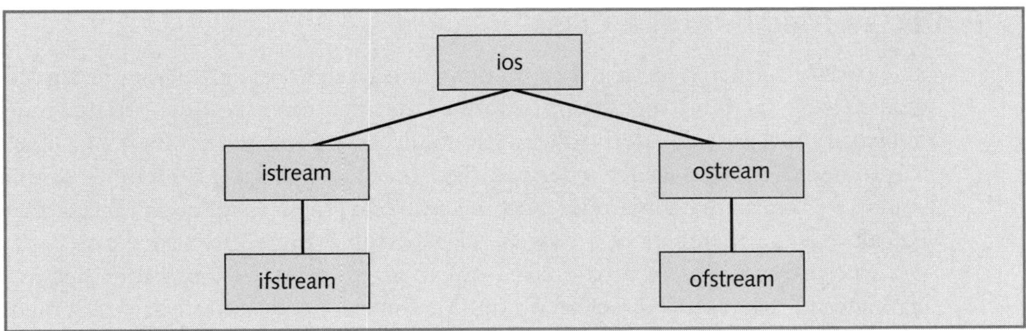

Figure 14-9 C++ stream classes hierarchy

Figure 14-9 shows the stream classes that we have encountered in previous chapters. From Figure 14-9, it follows that the **class ios** is the base class for all stream classes. Classes `istream` and `ostream` are directly derived from the **class ios**. The **class ifstream** is derived from the **class istream**, and the **class ofstream** is derived from the **class ostream**. Moreover, using the mechanism of multiple inheritance, the **class iostream** (not to be confused with the *header* file `iostream`—these are separate things) and the **class fstream** are derived from the **class iostream**. (The classes `iostream` and `fstream` are not discussed in this book.)

The **class ios** contains formatting flags and member functions to access and/or modify the setting of these flags. To identify the I/O status, the **class ios** contains an integer status word. This integer status word provides a continuous update reporting the status of the stream.

The **classes istream** and `ostream` are responsible for providing the operations for the data transfer between memory and devices. The **class istream** defines the extraction operator, >>, and functions such as `get` and `ignore`. The **class ostream** defines the insertion operator, <<, which is used by the object `cout`.

The **class ifstream** is derived from the **class istream** to provide the file input operations. Similarly, the **class ofstream** is derived from the **class ostream** to provide the file output operations. Objects of the type `ifstream` are used for file output; objects of the type `ofstream` are used for file output. The header file `fstream` contains the definition of the **classes ifstream** and `ofstream`.

14

Protected Members of a Class

The **private** members of a class are **private** to the class and cannot be directly accessed outside the class. Only member functions of that class can access the **private** members. As discussed previously, the derived class cannot access **private** members of a class. However, it is sometimes necessary for a derived class to access a **private** member of a base class. If you make a **private** member become **public**, then anyone can access that member. Recall that the members of a class are classified into three categories: **public**, **private**, and **protected**. So, for a base class to give access to a **private** member to its derived class and still prevent its direct access outside the class, you must declare that member under the memberAccessSpecifier **protected**. Thus, the accessibility of a **protected** member of a class is in between **public** and **private**. A derived class can directly access the **protected** members of a base class.

To summarize, if a member of a base class needs to be accessed by a derived class, that member is declared under the memberAccessSpecifier **protected**.

Inheritance as public, protected, or private

Suppose **class** B is derived from **class** A. Then B cannot directly access the **private** members of A. That is, the **private** members of A are hidden in B. What about the **public** and **protected** members of A? This section gives the rules that generally apply when accessing the members of a base class.

Consider the following statement:

```
class B: memberAccessSpecifier A
{
   .
   .
   .
};
```

In this statement, memberAccessSpecifier is either **public**, **protected**, or **private**.

1. If memberAccessSpecifier is **public**—that is, the inheritance is **public**—then
   a. The **public** members of A are **public** members of B. They can be directly accessed in **class** B.
   b. The **protected** members of A are **protected** members of B. They can be directly accessed by the member functions (and **friend** functions) of B.
   c. The **private** members of A are hidden in B. They can be accessed by the member functions (and **friend** functions) of B through the **public** or **protected** members of A.

2. If `memberAccessSpecifier` is `protected`—that is, the inheritance is `protected`—then
   a. The `public` members of `A` are `protected` members of `B`. They can be accessed by the member functions (and `friend` functions) of `B`.
   b. The `protected` members of `A` are `protected` members of `B`. They can be accessed by the member functions (and `friend` functions) of `B`.
   c. The `private` members of `A` are hidden in `B`. They can be accessed by the member functions (and `friend` functions) of `B` through the `public` or `protected` members of `A`.
3. If `memberAccessSpecifier` is `private`—that is, the inheritance is `private`—then
   a. The `public` members of `A` are `private` members of `B`. They can be accessed by the member functions (and `friend` functions) of `B`.
   b. The `protected` members of `A` are `private` members of `B`. They can be accessed by the member functions (and `friend` functions) of `B`.
   c. The `private` members of `A` are hidden in `B`. They can be accessed by the member functions (and `friend` functions) of `B` through the `public` or `protected` members of `A`.

Chapter 16 describes the `friend` functions.

Example 14-2 illustrates how the member functions of the derived class can directly access a `protected` member of the base class.

14

Example 14-2: (Accessing `protected` members in the derived class.)

Consider the following definition of the `class bClass`:

```
class bClass
{
public:
    void setData(double);
    void setData(char, double);
    void print() const;
    bClass(char = '*', double = 0.0);
protected:
    char bCh;

private:
    double bX;
};
```

The definition of the **class bClass** contains a **protected** data member **bCh** of the type **char**, and a **private** data member **bX** of the type **double**. It also contains an overloaded member function **setData**; one version is used to set both the data members, and the other version is used to set only the **private** data member. The class also has a constructor with default parameters. Suppose that the definitions of the member functions and the constructor are as follows:

```
void bClass::setData(double u)
{
        bX = u;
}

void bClass::setData(char ch, double u)

{
        bCh = ch;
        bX = u;
}

void bClass::print() const
{
    cout<<"Base class: bCh = "<<bCh<<", bX = "<<bX<<endl;
}

bClass::bClass(char ch, double u)
{
        bCh = ch;
        bX = u;
}
```

Next, we derive a **class dClass** from the **class bClass** using **public** inheritance as follows:

```
class dClass: public bClass
{
public:
    void setData(char, double, int);
    void print() const;

private:
    int dA;
};
```

The **class dClass** contains a **private** data member **dA** of the type **int**. It also contains a member function **setData**, with three parameters, and the function **print**.

Let us now write the definition of the function **setData**. Because **bCh** is a **protected** data member of the **class bClass**, it can be directly accessed in the definition of the function **setData**. However, because **bX** is a **private** data member of the **class bClass**, the function **setData** cannot directly access it. Thus, the function **setData** must set **bX** by using the function **setData** of the **class bClass**. The definition of the function **setData** of the **class dClass** can be written as follows:

```
void dClass::setData(char ch, double v, int a)
{
      bClass::setData(v);

      bCh = ch;       //initialize bCh using the assignment
                      //statement

      dA = a;
}
```

Note that the definition of the function **setData** calls the function **bClass::setData** with one parameter to set the data member **bX**, and then directly sets the value of **bCh**. Next, let us write the definition of the function **print** (of the **class dClass**).

The **class bClass** has only one function, **print** (that is, it is not overloaded like the function **setData**), and we do not want to print the value of **bCh** twice. For this reason, we first call the function **print** (of the **class bClass**) and then output only the value of **dA**. The definition of the function **print** is

```
void dClass::print() const

{
      bClass::print();

      cout<<"Derived class dA = "<<dA<<endl;
}
```

14

The following program illustrates how the objects of **bClass** and **dClass** work. We assume that the definition of the **class bClass** is in the header file **protectMembClass.h**, and the definition of the **class dClass** is in the header file **protectMembInDerivedCl.h**.

```
//Accessing protected members of a base class
//in the derived class

#include <iostream>
#include "protectMembClass.h"
#include "protectMembInDerivedCl.h"

using namespace std;
```

```
int main()
{
   bClass bObject;                                     //Line 1

   dClass dObject;                                     //Line 2

   bObject.print();                                    //Line 3

   cout<<endl;                                         //Line 4

   cout<<"*** Derived class object ***"<<endl;         //Line 5

   dObject.setData('&', 2.5, 7);                       //Line 6

   dObject.print();                                    //Line 7

   return 0;
}
```

Output

```
Base class: bCh = *, bX = 0

*** Derived class object ***
Base class: bCh = &, bX = 2.5
Derived class dA = 7
```

When you write the definitions of the member functions of the **class** **dClass**, the **protected** data member **bCh** can be accessed directly. However, **dClass** objects cannot directly access **bCh**. That is, the following statement is illegal (it is, in fact, a syntax error):

```
dObject.bCh = '&';     //Illegal
```

COMPOSITION

Composition is another way to relate two classes. In composition, one or more members of a class are objects of another class type. Composition is a "has-a" relation; for example, "every person has a date of birth."

Example 13-9, in Chapter 13, defined a class called **personType**. The **class personType** stores a person's first name and last name. Suppose we want to keep track of additional information for a person, such as a personal ID (*e.g.*, a Social Security number) and a date of birth. Because every person has a personal ID and a date of birth, we can define a new class, called **personalInfo**, in which one of the members is an object of the type **personType**. We can declare additional members to store the personal ID and date of birth for the **class personalInfo**.

First we define another **class**, **dateType**, to store only a person's date of birth. Then we construct the **class personalInfo** from the classes **personType** and **dateType**. This way, we can demonstrate how to define a new class using two classes.

To define the **class dateType**, we need three data members to store the month, day number, and year. Some of the operations that need to performed on a date are to set the date and to print the date. The following statements define the **class dateType** (see Figure 14-10):

```
class dateType
{
public:
    void setDate(int month, int day, int year);
      //Function to set the date
      //Data members dMonth, dDay, and dYear are set
      //according to the parameters
      //Post: dMonth = month; dDay = day;
      //               dYear = year;

    void getDate(int& month, int& day, int& year);
      //Function to return the date
      //Post: month = dMonth; day = dDay;
      //              year = dYear;

    void printDate() const;
      //Function to output the date in the form mm-dd-yyyy

    dateType(int month, int day, int year);
      //constructor to set the date
      //Data members dMonth, dDay, and dYear are set
      //according to the parameters
      //Post: dMonth = month; dDay = day;
      //      dYear = year;

    dateType();
      //default constructor
      //Data members dMonth, dDay, and dYear are set to
      //the default values
      //Post: dMonth = 1; dDay = 1; dYear = 1900;

private:
    int dMonth;       //variable to store the month
    int dDay;         //variable to store the day
    int dYear;        //variable to store the year
};
```

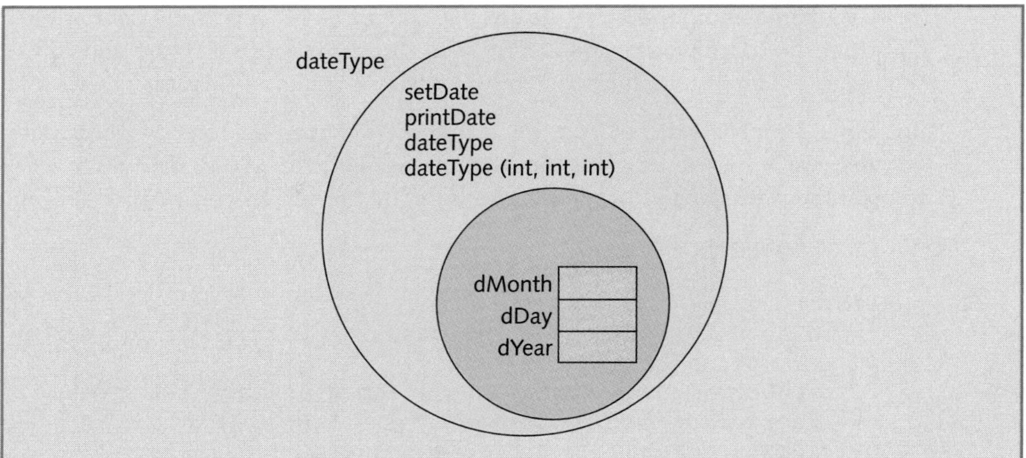

Figure 14-10 `class dateType`

The definition of the **`class dateType`** consists of two constructors: the default constructor and a constructor with parameters. Both of these constructors can be replaced by one constructor with default parameters. In Programming Exercise 2 at the end of this chapter, you are asked to do so.

The definitions of the member functions of the **`class dateType`** are as follows:

```
void dateType::setDate(int month, int day, int year)
{
      dMonth = month;
      dDay = day;
      dYear = year;
}
```

The definition of the function **`setDate`**, before storing the date into the data members, does not check whether the date is valid. That is, it does not confirm whether **`month`** is between `1` and `12`, **`year`** is greater than `0`, and **`day`** is valid (for example, for January, **`day`** should be between `1` and `31`). In Programming Exercise 2 at the end of this chapter, you are asked to rewrite the definition of the function **`setDate`** so that the date is validated before storing it in the data members. The definitions of the remaining member functions are as follows:

```
void dateType::getDate(int& month, int& day, int& year)
{
      month = dMonth;
      day = dDay;
      year = dYear;
}
```

```
void dateType::printDate() const
{
      cout<<dMonth<<"-"<<dDay<<"-"<<dYear;
}

                  //constructor with parameter
dateType:: dateType(int month, int day, int year)
{
      dMonth = month;
      dDay = day;
      dYear = year;
}
```

Just as in the case of **setDate**, in Programming Exercise 2, you are asked to rewrite the definition of the constructor so that it checks for valid values of **month**, **day**, and **year** before storing the date into data members.

```
dateType:: dateType()  //default parameter
{
      dMonth = 1;
      dDay = 1;
      dYear = 1900;
}
```

Next, we give the definition of the **class personalInfo** (see Figure 14-11):

```
class personalInfo
{
public:
    void setpersonalInfo(string first, string last, int month,
                         int day, int year, int ID);
      //Function to set the personal information
      //Data members are set according to the parameters
      //Post: firstName = first; lastName = last;
      //      dMonth = month; dDay = day; dYear = year;
      //      personID = ID;

    void printpersonalInfo () const;
      //Function to print personal information

    personalInfo(string first, string last, int month,
                 int day, int year, int ID);
      //constructor with parameters
      //Data members are set according to the parameters
      //Post: firstName = first; lastName = last;
      //      dMonth = month; dDay = day; dYear = year;
      //      personID = ID;
```

14

```
    personalInfo();
      //default constructor
      //Data members are set according to the default values
private:
    personType name;
    dateType bDay;
    int personID;
};
```

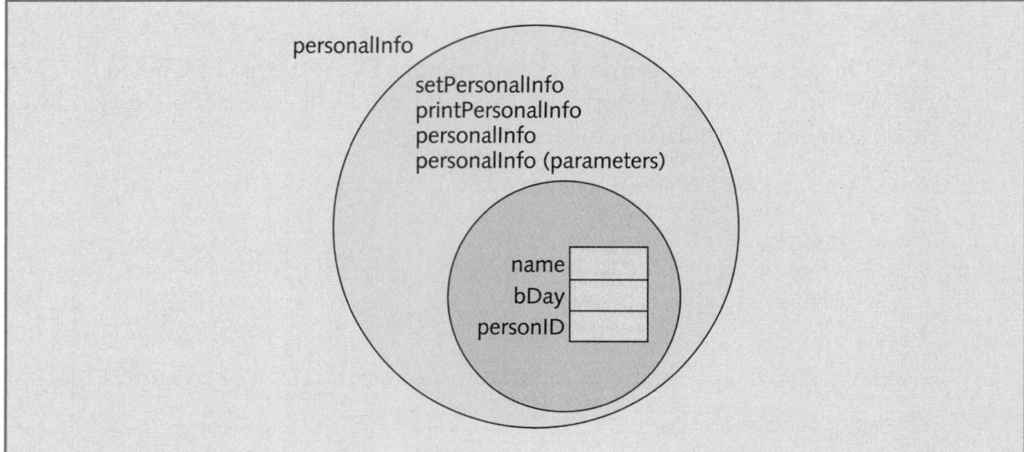

Figure 14-11 `class personalInfo`

Before we give the definition of the member functions of the **`class personalInfo`**, let us discuss how the constructors of the objects **`bDay`** and **`name`** are invoked.

Recall that a class constructor is automatically executed when a class object enters its scope. Suppose that we have the following statement:

```
personalInfo student;
```

When the object **`student`** enters its scope, the objects **`bDay`** and **`name`**, which are members of **`student`**, also enter their scopes; as a result, one of their constructors is executed. We therefore need to know how to pass arguments to the constructors of the member objects (that is, **`bDay`** and **`name`**), which occurs when we give the definitions of the constructors of the class. Recall that constructors do not have a type and so cannot be called like other functions. The arguments to the constructor of a member-object (such as **`bDay`**) are specified in the heading part of the definition of the constructor of the class. Furthermore, member-objects of a class are constructed (that is, initialized) in the order they are declared (not in the order they are listed in the constructor's member initialization list), and before the enclosing class objects are constructed. Thus, in our case, the object **`name`** is initialized first, then **`bDay`**, and finally **`student`**.

The following statements illustrate how to pass arguments to the constructors of the member objects:

```
personalInfo::personalInfo(string first, string last, int month,
                           int day, int year, int ID)
          :name(first,last), bDay(month,day,year)
{
   .
   .
   .
}
```

The definitions of the member functions of the `class personalInfo` are as follows:

```
void personalInfo::setpersonalInfo(string first, string last,
                              int month, int day, int year, int ID)
{
      name.setName(first,last);
      bDay.setDate(month,day,year);
      personID = ID;
}

void personalInfo::printpersonalInfo () const
{
      name.print();
      cout<<"'s date of birth is ";
      bDay.printDate();
      cout<<endl;
      cout<<"and personal ID is "<<personID;
}

personalInfo::personalInfo(string first, string last, int month,
                                 int day, int year, int ID)
          :name(first,last), bDay(month,day,year)
{
      personID = ID;
}

personalInfo::personalInfo() //default constructor
{
      personID = 0;
}
```

Because no arguments are passed to the member-objects in the heading of the default constructor, the default constructors of the member-objects `bDay` and `name` are executed.

In the case of inheritance, use the class name to invoke the base class's constructor. In the case of composition, use the member-object name to invoke its own constructor.

14

OBJECT-ORIENTED DESIGN (OOD) AND OBJECT-ORIENTED PROGRAMMING (OOP)

The first 11 chapters of this book used the top-down approach to programming, also called **structured programming**, to write programs. Problems were broken into modules, and each module solved a particular part of the problem. Data requirements were identified, and functions were written to manipulate the data. The functions and the data were kept separate, and the functions acted on the data in a passive way. Structured programming, therefore, has certain limitations. In structured programming, functions are dependent on the data, and functions are designed specifically to solve a particular problem. It is quite difficult, if not impossible, to reuse a function written for one program in another program. For some of these reasons, structured programming is not very efficient for large software development.

Chapter 13 began with the introduction of classes. We learned how classes are defined and used. Later in that chapter, we concentrated on the data requirements of a problem and the logical operations on that data. With the help of classes, we combined the data—and operations on that data—in a single unit. That is, the data and operations were encapsulated in a single unit. Also, with the help of classes, we were able to separate the data and the algorithms to manipulate that data. However, the functions to implement operations on the data had direct access to the data. This chapter explains how to create new classes from existing classes through inheritance (and also using composition). Furthermore, an object has the capability to hide the information details. These are some of the features of **object-oriented design (OOD)**.

The three basic principles of OOD are as follows:

- **Encapsulation**—The ability to combine data, and operations on that data, in a single unit.
- **Inheritance**—The ability to create new objects from existing objects.
- **Polymorphism**—The ability to use the same expression to denote different operations.

In OOD, an object is a fundamental entity; in structured programming, a function is a fundamental entity. In OOD, we debug objects; in structured programming, we debug functions. In OOD, a program is a collection of interacting objects; in structured programming, a program is a collection of interacting functions. Also, OOD encourages code reuse. Once an object becomes error-free, it can be reused in many programs because it is a self-contained entity. **Object-oriented programming (OOP)** implements OOD.

To create objects, we must know how to represent the data and write functions to manipulate that data. Thus, we must know everything that we have learned in Chapters 2 through 10. The first 10 chapters are essential for any type of programming, whether structured or object-oriented.

C++ supports OOP through the use of classes. We have already experienced the first two features of OOP, encapsulation and inheritance, in this chapter and Chapter 13. Chapter 16 discusses the third feature of OOD: polymorphism. A polymorphic function or operator has many forms.

In C++, a function name and the operators can be overloaded. An example of function overloading occurs when the function is called, and the operator is evaluated according to the arguments used. For instance, if both operands are integers, the division operator yields an integer result; otherwise, the division operator yields a decimal result. Suppose a class has constructors. If no arguments are passed to an object when it is declared, the default constructor is executed; otherwise, one of the constructors with parameters is executed. However, all constructors have the same name.

C++ also provides parametric polymorphism. In parametric polymorphism, the (data) type is left unspecified and then later instantiated. Templates (discussed in Chapter 16) provide parametric polymorphism. Also, C++ provides **virtual functions** as a means to implement polymorphism in an inheritance hierarchy, which allows the run-time selection of appropriate member functions. (Chapter 15 discusses virtual functions.)

There are several OOP languages in existence today, including Ada, Modula-2, Object Pascal, Turbo Pascal, Eiffel, C++, Java, and Smalltalk. The earliest OOP language was Simula, developed in 1967. The OOP terminology is influenced by the vocabulary of Smalltalk, the OOP language largely developed at a Xerox research center during the 1970s. An OOP language uses many "fancy" words, such as methods, message passing, and so forth.

OOP is a natural and intuitive way to view the programming process. When we view an object, we immediately think of what it can do. For example, when we think about a car, we also think about the operations on the car, such as starting the car and driving the car. When programmers think about a list, they also think about the operations on the list, such as searching, sorting, and inserting. OOP allows ADT to be created and used. In C++, we implement ADT through the use of classes.

Objects are created when class variables are declared. Objects interact with each other via function calls. Every object has an internal state and an external state. The **`private`** members form the internal state; the **`public`** members form the external state. Only the object can manipulate its internal state.

Identifying Classes, Objects, and Operations

In this book's first 12 chapters, in the problem analysis phase we analyzed the problem, identified the data, and outlined the algorithm. To reduce the complexity of the function `main`, we wrote functions to manipulate the data. In Chapter 13, we used the OOD technique and first identified the objects that made up the overall problem. The objects were designed and implemented independent of the main program. The hardest part in OOD is to identify the objects and classes. In this section, we describe a common and simple technique to identify classes and objects.

We begin with a description of the problem and then identify all of the nouns and verbs. From the list of nouns we choose our classes, and from the list of verbs we choose our operations.

For example, suppose that we want to write a program that calculates and prints the volume and surface area of a cylinder. We can state this problem as follows:

Write a **program** to *input* the **dimensions** of a **cylinder** and *calculate* and *print* the **surface area** and **volume**.

In this statement, the nouns are bold and the verbs are italic. From the list of nouns—**program**, **dimensions**, **cylinder**, **surface area**, and **volume**—we can easily visualize **cylinder** to be a class—say, `cylinderType`—from which we can create many cylinder objects of various dimensions. The nouns **dimensions**, **surface area**, and **volume** are characteristics of a **cylinder** and thus can hardly be considered classes.

After we identify a class, the next step is to determine three pieces of information:

- Operations that an object of that class type can perform
- Operations that can be performed on an object of that class type
- Information that an object of that class type must maintain

From the list of verbs identified in the problem description, we choose a list of possible operations that an object of that class can perform, or has performed, on itself. For example, from the list of verbs for the cylinder problem description—*write*, *input*, *calculate*, and *print*—the possible operations for a cylinder object are *input*, *calculate*, and *print*.

For the `class cylinderType`, the dimensions represent the data. The `center` of the base, `radius` of the base, and `height` of the cylinder are the characteristics of the dimensions. You can input data to the object either by a constructor or by a function.

The verb *calculate* applies to determining the volume and the surface area. From this you can deduce the operations: `cylinderVolume` and `cylinderSurfaceArea`. Similarly, the verb *print* applies to the display of the volume and the surface area on an output device. In Programming Exercise 5 at the end of this chapter, you are asked to design a class to implement the characteristics of a cylinder.

Identifying classes via the nouns and verbs from the descriptions to the problem is not the only technique possible. There are several other OOD techniques in the literature. However, this technique is sufficient for the programming exercises in this book.

PROGRAMMING EXAMPLE: GRADE REPORT

This programming example further illustrates the concepts of inheritance and composition.

The mid-semester point at your local university is approaching. The registrar's office wants to prepare the grade reports as soon as the students' grades are recorded. Some of the students enrolled have not yet paid their tuition, however.

1. If a student has paid the tuition, the grades are shown on the grade report together with the grade-point average (GPA).
2. If a student has not paid the tuition, the grades are not printed. For these students, the grade report contains a message indicating that the grades have been held for nonpayment of the tuition. The grade report also shows the billing amount.

The registrar's office and the business office want your help in writing a program that can analyze the students' data and print the appropriate grade reports. The data is stored in a file in the following form:

```
15000 345
studentName studentID isTuitionPaid numberOfCourses
courseName courseNumber creditHours grade
courseName courseNumber creditHours grade
.
.
.
studentName studentID isTuitionPaid numberOfCourses
courseName courseNumber creditHours grade
courseName courseNumber creditHours grade
.
.
.
```

The first line indicates the number of students enrolled and the tuition rate per credit hour. The students' data is given thereafter.

A sample input file follows:

```
3 345
Lisa Miller 890238 Y 4
Mathematics MTH345 4 A
Physics PHY357 3 B
ComputerSci CSC478 3 B
History HIS356 3 A
.
.
.
```

The first line indicates that 3 students are enrolled and the tuition rate is $345 per credit hour. Next, the course data for student `Lisa Miller` is given: Lisa Miller's ID is `890238`, she has paid the tuition, and is taking `4` courses. The course number for the mathematics class she is taking is `MTH345`, the course has `4` credit hours, her mid-semester grade is `A`, and so on.

The desired output for each student is of the following form:

```
Student Name: Lisa Miller
Student ID: 890238
Number of courses enrolled: 4

Course No  Course Name  Credits Grade
CSC478     ComputerSci       3      B
HIS356     History           3      A
MTH345     Mathematics       4      A
PHY357     Physics           3      B

Total number of credits: 13
Mid-Semester GPA: 3.54
```

It is clear from this output that the courses must be ordered according to the course number. To calculate the GPA, we assume that the grade `A` is equivalent to `4` points, `B` is equivalent to `3` points, `C` is equivalent to `2` points, `D` is equivalent to `1` point, and `F` is equivalent to `0` points.

Input A file containing the data in the form given previously. For easy reference in the rest of the discussion, let us assume that the name of the input file is `"a:stData.txt"`.

Output A file containing the output of the form given previously.

Problem Analysis and Algorithm Design

We must first identify the main components of the program. The university has students, and every student takes courses. Thus, the two main components are the student and the course.

Let us first describe the component course.

Course The main characteristics of a course are the course name, course number, and number of credit hours. Although the grade a student receives is not really a characteristic of a course, to simplify the program this component also includes the student's grade.

Some of the basic operations that need to be performed on an object of the course type follow:

1. Set the course information.
2. Print the course information.
3. Show the credit hours.
4. Show the course number.
5. Show the grade.

The following class defines the course as an ADT (see Figure 14-12):

```
class courseType
{
public:
    void setCourseInfo(string cName, string cNo,
                       char grade, int credits);
      //Function to set the course information
      //The course information is set according to the
      //incoming parameters.
      //Post: courseName = cName; courseNo = cNo;
      //     courseGrade = grade; courseCredits = credits;

    void print(bool isGrade);
      //Function to print the course information
      //This function prints the course information on the
      //screen. Furthermore, if the bool parameter isGrade is
      //true, the grade is shown; otherwise, three stars
      //are printed.

    void print(ofstream& outp, bool isGrade);
      //Function to print the course information
      //This function sends the course information to a file.
      //Furthermore, if the bool parameter isGrade is true,
      //the grade is shown; otherwise, three stars are printed.

    int getCredits();
      //Function to return the credit hours
      //The value of the private data member courseCredits
      //is returned.

    void getCourseNumber(string& cNo);
      //Function to return the course number
```

```
      //Post:  cNo = courseNo;

    char getGrade();
      //Function to return the grade for the course
      //The value of the private data member courseGrade
      //is returned.

    courseType(string cName = "", string cNo = "",
               char grade = '*', int credits = 0);
      //constructor
      //The object is initialized according to the
      //parameters.
      //Post: courseName = cName; courseNo = cNo;
      //      courseGrade = grade; courseCredits = credits;

private:
    string courseName;        //variable to store the course name
    string courseNo;          //variable to store the course number
    char courseGrade;         //variable to store the grade
    int courseCredits;        //variable to store the course credits
};
```

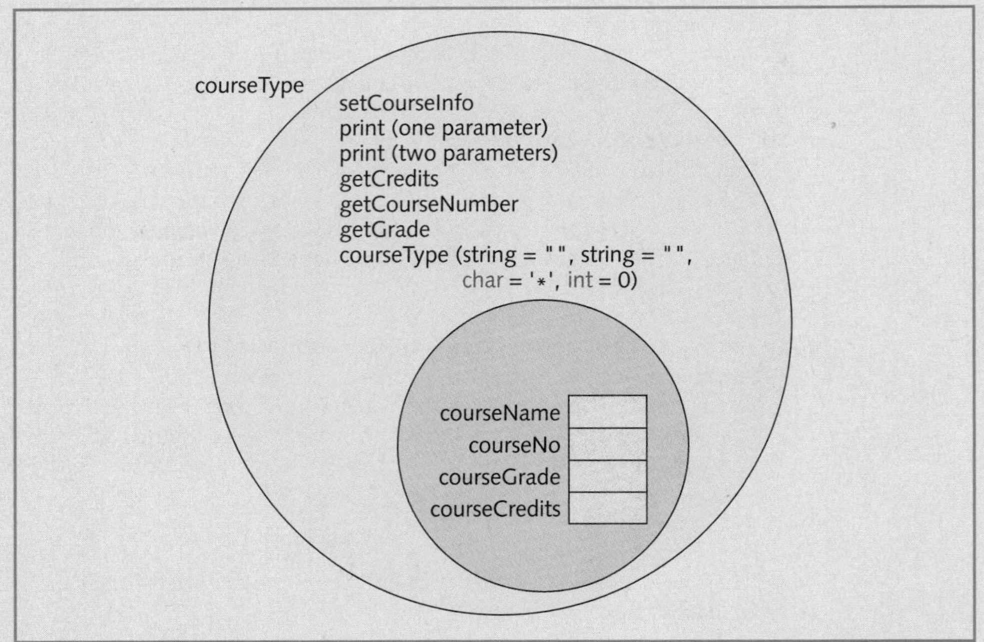

Figure 14-12 `class courseType`

Next, we discuss the definition of the functions to implement the operations of the `class courseType`. These definitions are quite straightforward and easy to follow.

The function `setCourseInfo` sets the values of the `private` data members according to the values of the parameters. Its definition is

```
void courseType::setCourseInfo(string cName, string cNo,
                               char grade, int credits)
{     courseName = cName;
      courseNo = cNo;
      courseGrade = grade;
      courseCredits = credits;
}
```

The function `print` with one parameter prints the course information on the screen. If the `bool` parameter `isGrade` is `true`, the grade is printed on the screen; otherwise, three stars are shown in place of the grade. Also, we print the course name and course number left-justified rather than right-justified (the default). Thus, we need to set the `left` manipulator. This manipulator will be unset before we print the grade and the credit hours. The following steps describe this function:

1. Set the `left` manipulator.
2. Print the course number.
3. Print the course name.
4. Unset the `left` manipulator.
5. Print the credit hours.
6. If `isGrade` is `true`
     Output the grade
   Else
     Output three stars.

The definition of the function `print` is

```
void courseType::print(bool isGrade)
{
      cout<<left;                                  //Step 1
      cout<<setw(8)<<courseNo<<"   ";              //Step 2
      cout<<setw(15)<<courseName;                  //Step 3
      cout.unsetf(ios::left);                      //Step 4
      cout<<setw(3)<<courseCredits<<"   ";         //Step 5

      if(isGrade)                                  //Step 6
         cout<<setw(4)<<courseGrade<<endl;
      else
         cout<<setw(4)<<"***"<<endl;
}
```

The function `print`, which has two parameters, sends the course information to a file. Other than sending the output to a file, which is passed as a parameter, this function has exactly the same definition as the definition of the previous `print` function. The definition of this function is

```
void courseType::print(ofstream& outp, bool isGrade)
{
      outp<<left;                                    //Step 1
      outp<<setw(8)<<courseNo<<"   ";                //Step 2
      outp<<setw(15)<<courseName;                    //Step 3
      outp.unsetf(ios::left);                        //Step 4
      outp<<setw(3)<<courseCredits<<"   ";           //Step 5

      if(isGrade)                                    //Step 6
         outp<<setw(4)<<courseGrade<<endl;
      else
         outp<<setw(4)<<"***"<<endl;
}
```

The constructor is declared with default values. If no values are specified when a `courseType` object is declared, the constructor uses the default to initialize the object. Using the default values, the object's data members are initialized as follows: `courseNo` to blank, `courseName` to blank, `courseGrade` to `*`, and `creditHours` to `0`. Otherwise, the values specified in the object declaration are used to initialize the object. Its definition is

```
courseType::courseType(string cName, string cNo,
                       char grade, int credits)
{
      courseName = cName;
      courseNo =  cNo;
      courseGrade = grade;
      courseCredits = credits;
}
```

The definitions of the remaining functions are straightforward.

```
int courseType::getCredits()
{
      return courseCredits;
}

char courseType::getGrade()
{
      return courseGrade;
}
```

```
void courseType::getCourseNumber(string& cNo)
{
      cNo = courseNo;
}
```

Next we discuss the component student.

Student The main characteristics of a student are the student name, student ID, number of courses in which enrolled, courses in which enrolled, and grade for each course. Because every student has to pay tuition, we also include a member to indicate whether the student has paid the tuition.

Every student is a person, and every student takes courses. We have already designed a `class personType` to process a person's first name and last name. We have also designed a class to process the information of a course. Thus, we see that we can derive the `class studentType` to keep track of a student's information from the `class personType`, and one member of this class is of the type `courseType`. We can add more members as needed.

The basic operations to be performed on an object of the type `studentType` are as follows:

1. Set the student information.
2. Print the student information.
3. Calculate the number of credit hours taken.
4. Calculate the GPA.
5. Calculate the billing amount.
6. Because the grade report will print the courses in ascending order, sort the courses according to the course number.

The following class defines `studentType` as an ADT. We assume that a student takes no more than six courses per semester (see Figure 14-13):

```
class studentType: public personType
{
public:
    void setInfo(string fname, string lName, int ID,
                 int nOfCourses, bool isTPaid,
                 courseType courses[]);
```

```
      //Function to set a student's information
      //The private data members are set according
      //to the parameters.

    void print(double tuitionRate);
      //Function to print a student's grade report

    void print(ofstream& out, double tuitionRate);
      //Function to print a student's grade report
      //The output is stored in a file specified by the
      //parameter out.

    studentType();
      //default constructor
      //The private data members are initialized.

    int getHoursEnrolled();
      //Function to return the credit hours in which a student
      //is enrolled

    double getGpa();
      //Function to return the grade-point average

    double billingAmount(double tuitionRate);
      //Function to return the tuition fees

private:
    void sortCourses();
      //Function to sort the courses
      //This function sorts the array coursesEnrolled.

    int sId;                //variable to store the student ID
    int numberOfCourses;    //variable to store the number
                            //of courses
    bool isTuitionPaid;   //variable to indicate if the tuition
                          //is paid
    courseType coursesEnrolled[6]; //array to store the courses
};
```

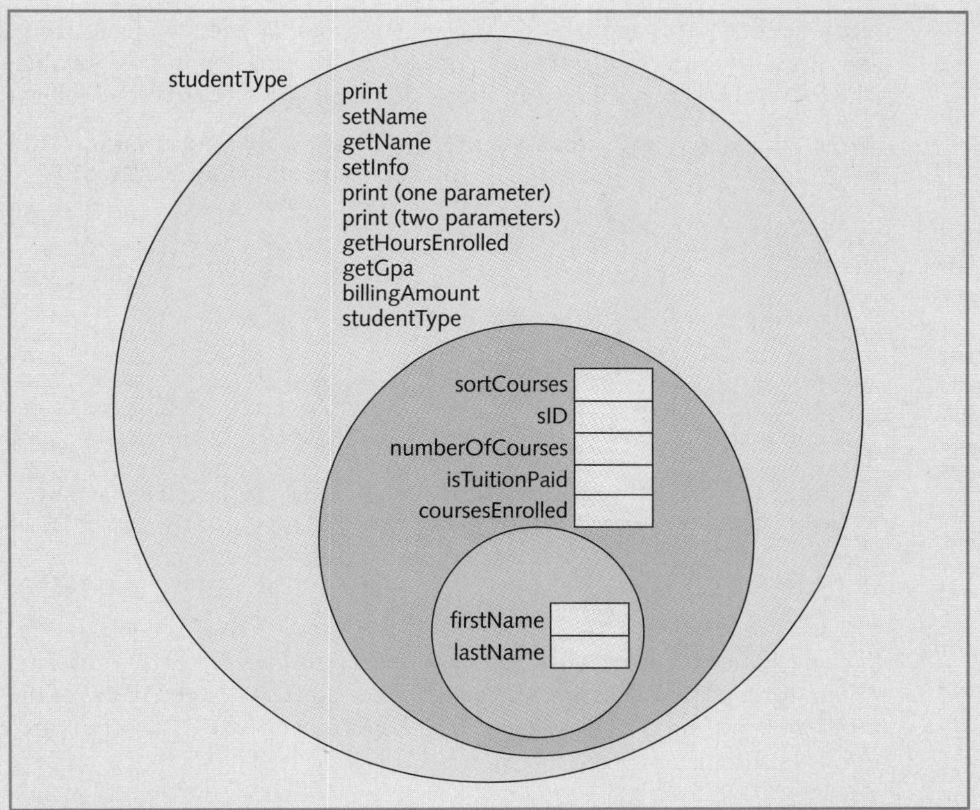

Figure 14-13 `class studentType`

Note that the function member `sortCourses` to sort the array `coursesEnrolled` is a `private` member of the `class studentType`. This is due to the fact that this function is needed for internal data manipulation and the user of the class does not need to access this member.

Next, we discuss the definitions of the functions to implement the operations of the `class studentType`.

The function `setInfo` first initializes the `private` data members according to the incoming parameters. This function then calls the function `sortCourses` to sort the array `coursesEnrolled` by course number. The `class studentType` is derived from the `class personType`, and the variables to store the first name and last name are **private** data members of that class. Therefore, we call the member function `setName` of the **class** `personType`, and we pass the appropriate variables to set the first and last names. The definition of the function `setInfo` is as follows:

```
void studentType::setInfo(string fName, string lName, int ID,
                          int nOfCourses, bool isTPaid,
                          courseType courses[])
{
   int i;

   personType::setName(fName,lName);      //set the name

   sId = ID;                              //set the student ID
   isTuitionPaid = isTPaid;          //set isTuitionPaid
   numberOfCourses = nOfCourses ;    //set the number of courses

   for(i = 0; i < numberOfCourses; i++)  //set the array
       coursesEnrolled[i] = courses[i];  //coursesEnrolled

   sortCourses();                //sort the array coursesEnrolled
}
```

The default constructor initializes the **private** data members to the default values. Note that because the **private** data member `coursesEnrolled` is of the type `courseType` and is an array, the default constructor of the **class** `courseType` executes automatically and the entire array is initialized.

```
studentType::studentType()
{
      numberOfCourses = 0;
      sId = 0;
      isTuitionPaid = false;
}
```

The function `print`, which has one parameter, prints the grade report on the screen. If the student has paid his or her tuition, the grades and the GPA are shown. Otherwise, three stars are printed in place of each grade, the GPA is not shown, a message indicates that the grades are being held for nonpayment of the tuition, and the amount due is shown. This function has the following steps:

1. Output the student's name.
2. Output the student's ID.
3. Output the number of courses in which the student is enrolled.

4. Output the heading: `CourseNo    CourseName    Credits    Grade`
5. Print each course's information.
6. Print the total credit hours.
7. To output the GPA and billing amount in a fixed decimal format with the decimal point and trailing zeroes, set the necessary flag. Also, set the precision to two decimal places.
8. `if isTuitionPaid` is `true`
   Output the GPA
   `else`
   Output the billing amount and a message about withholding the grades.

```
void studentType::print(double tuitionRate)
{
     int i;

     cout<<"Student Name: ";                            //Step 1
     personType::print();                               //Step 1
     cout<<endl;

     cout<<"Student ID: "<<sId<<endl;                   //Step 2

     cout<<"Number of courses enrolled: "
         <<numberOfCourses<<endl;                       //Step 3
     cout<<endl;

     cout<<left;        //set output left-justified
     cout<<"Course No"<<setw(15)<<"  Course Name"
         <<setw(8)<<"Credits"
         <<setw(6)<<"Grade"<<endl;                      //Step 4

     cout.unsetf(ios::left);

     for(i = 0; i < numberOfCourses; i++)               //Step 5
         coursesEnrolled[i].print(isTuitionPaid);
     cout<<endl;

     cout<<"Total number of credit hours: "
         <<getHoursEnrolled()<<endl;                    //Step 6

     cout<<fixed<<showpoint<<setprecision(2);           //Step 7

     if(isTuitionPaid)                                  //Step 8
        cout<<"Mid-Semester GPA: "<<getGpa()<<endl;
     else
     {
```

```
          cout<<"*** Grades are being held for not paying "
              <<"the tuition. ***"<<endl;
          cout<<"Amount Due: $"<<billingAmount(tuitionRate)
              <<endl;
      }

      cout<<"-*-*-*-*-*-*-*-*-*-*-*-*-*-*-*-*-*-*-*"
          <<"-*-*-*-*-*-*-"<<endl<<endl;
}
```

The function `print`, which has two parameters, sends the output to the screen. For the most part, its definition is the same as the other function `print`, which has one parameter. Because the `class personType` has no function to send the output to a file, we first use the member function `getName` of the `class personType` to retrieve the first and last names. We then print the first and last names. The definition of this function is now the same as the definition of the previous function `print`. The definition of this function is

```
void studentType::print(ofstream& outp, double tuitionRate)
{
      int i;
      string first;
      string last;

      personType::getName(first,last);

      outp<<"Student Name: "<<first<<" "<<last<<endl;

      outp<<"Student ID: "<<sId<<endl;

      outp<<"Number of courses enrolled: "
        <<numberOfCourses<<endl;
      outp<<endl;

      outp<<left;
      outp<<"Course No"<<setw(15)<<"  Course Name"
          <<setw(8)<<"Credits"
          <<setw(6)<<"Grade"<<endl;

      outp.unsetf(ios::left);

      for(i = 0; i < numberOfCourses; i++)
          coursesEnrolled[i].print(outp,isTuitionPaid);
      outp<<endl;

      outp<<"Total number of credit hours: "
```

```
        <<getHoursEnrolled()<<endl;

    outp<<fixed<<showpoint<<setprecision(2);

    if(isTuitionPaid)
        outp<<"Mid-Semester GPA: "<<getGpa()<<endl;
    else
    {
        outp<<"*** Grades are being held for not paying "
            <<"the tuition. ***"<<endl;
        outp<<"Amount Due: $"<<billingAmount(tuitionRate)
            <<endl;
    }

    outp<<"-*-*-*-*-*-*-*-*-*-*-*-*-*-*-*-*-*-*-*-*-*-*"
        <<"-*-*-*-*-"<<endl<<endl;
}
```

The function getHoursEnrolled calculates and returns the total credit hours that a student is taking. These credit hours are needed to calculate both the GPA and the billing amount. The total credit hours are calculated by adding the credit hours of each course in which the student is enrolled. Because the credit hours for a course are in the private data member of an object of the type courseType, we use the member function getCredits of the class courseType to retrieve the credit hours. The definition of this function is

```
int studentType::getHoursEnrolled()
{
    int totalCredits = 0;
    int i;

    for(i = 0; i < numberOfCourses; i++)
        totalCredits += coursesEnrolled[i].getCredits();

    return totalCredits;
}
```

If a student has not paid the tuition, the function billingAmount calculates and returns the amount due, based on the number of credit hours enrolled. The definition of this function is

```
double studentType::billingAmount(double tuitionRate)
{
    return tuitionRate * getHoursEnrolled();
}
```

We now discuss the function **getGpa**. This function calculates a student's GPA. To find the GPA, we find the equivalent points for each grade, add the points, and then divide the sum by the total credit hours the student is taking. The definition of this function is

```
double studentType::getGpa()
{
    int i;
    double sum = 0.0;

    for(i = 0; i < numberOfCourses; i++)
    {
        switch(coursesEnrolled[i].getGrade())
        {
        case 'A': sum += coursesEnrolled[i].getCredits() * 4;
                  break;
        case 'B': sum += coursesEnrolled[i].getCredits() * 3;
                  break;
        case 'C': sum += coursesEnrolled[i].getCredits() * 2;
                  break;
        case 'D': sum += coursesEnrolled[i].getCredits() * 1;
                  break;
        case 'F': sum += coursesEnrolled[i].getCredits() * 0;
                  break;
        default: cout<<"Invalid Course Grade"<<endl;
        }
    }

    return sum / getHoursEnrolled();
}
```

The function **sortCourses** sorts the array **coursesEnrolled** by course number. To sort the array, we use a selection sort algorithm. Because we will compare the course numbers, which are strings and the **private** data members of the **class courseType**, we first retrieve and store the course numbers in local variables.

```
void studentType::sortCourses()
{
    int i,j;
    int minIndex;
    courseType temp;       //variable to swap data
    string course1;
    string course2;
```

```
    for(i = 0; i < numberOfCourses - 1; i++)
    {
        minIndex = i;

        for(j = i + 1; j < numberOfCourses; j++)
        {
                //get course numbers
            coursesEnrolled[minIndex].getCourseNumber(course1);
            coursesEnrolled[j].getCourseNumber(course2);

            if(course1 < course2)
                minIndex = j;
        }//end for

        temp = coursesEnrolled[minIndex];
        coursesEnrolled[minIndex] = coursesEnrolled[i];
        coursesEnrolled[i] = temp;
    }//end for
}//end sortCourses
```

Main Program

Now that we have designed the classes `courseType` and `studentType`, we will use these classes to complete the program.

We will restrict our program to process a maximum of 10 students. Note that this program can easily be enhanced to process any number of students.

Because the `print` function of the class does the necessary computations to print the final grade report, the main program has very little work to do. In fact, all that is left for the main program is to declare the objects to hold the students' data, load the data into these objects, and then print the grade reports. Because the input is in a file and the output will be sent to a file, we declare stream variables to access the input and output files. Essentially, the main algorithm for the program is

1. Declare the variables.
2. Open the input file.
3. If the input file does not exist, exit the program.
4. Open the output file.
5. Get the number of students registered and the tuition rate.
6. Load the students' data.
7. Print the grade reports.

Variables

This program processes a maximum of 10 students. Therefore, we must declare an array of 10 components of the type `studentType` to hold the students' data. We also need to store the number of students registered and the tuition rate. Because the data will be read from a file, and because the output is sent to a file, we need two stream variables to access the input and output files. Thus, we need the following variables:

```
studentType studentList[maxNumberOfStudents]; //array to store
                                              //the students' data

int noOfStudents;         //variable to store the number of students
double tuitionRate;       //variable to store the tuition rate

ifstream infile;          //input stream variable
ofstream outfile;         //output stream variable
```

Function `getStudentData` This function has three parameters: a parameter to access the input file, a parameter to access the array `studentList`, and a parameter to know the number of students registered. In pseudocode, the definition of this function is as follows:

For each student in the university,

1. Get the first name, last name, student ID, and `isPaid`.
2. `if isPaid` is `'Y'`
   set `isTuitionPaid` to `true`
   `else`
   set `isTuitionPaid` to `false`
3. Get the number of courses the student is taking.
4. For each course
   Get the course name, course number, credit hours, and grade.
   Load the course information into a `courseType` object.
5. Load the data into a `studentType` object.

We need to declare several local variables to read and store the data. The definition of the function `getStudentData` is

```
void getStudentData(ifstream& infile,
                    studentType studentList[],
                    int numberOfStudents)
{
          //Local variable
   string fName;       //variable to store the first name
   string lName;       //variable to store the last name
   int ID;             //variable to store the student ID
   int noOfCourses;    //variable to store the number of courses
```

```
   char isPaid;        //variable to store Y/N; that is,
                       //is tuition paid?
   bool isTuitionPaid;  //variable to store true/false

   string cName;   //variable to store the course name
   string cNo;     //variable to store the course number
   int credits;    //variable to store the course credit hours
   char grade;     //variable to store the course grade

   int count;      //loop control variable
   int i;          //loop control variable

   courseType courses[6]; //array of objects to store the course
                          //information

   for(count = 0; count < numberOfStudents; count++)
   {
      infile<<fName<<lName<<ID<<isPaid;                //Step 1

      if(isPaid == 'Y')                                //Step 2
         isTuitionPaid = true;
      else
         isTuitionPaid = false;

      infile<<noOfCourses;                             //Step 3

      for(i = 0; i < noOfCourses; i++)                 //Step 4
      {
         infile<<cName<<cNo<<credits<<grade;           //Step 4.a
         courses[i].setCourseInfo(cName, cNo,
                                  credits, grade);     //Step 4.b
      }

      studentList[count].setInfo(fName, lName, ID,
                                 noOfCourses, isTuitionPaid,
                                 courses);             //Step 5
   }//end for
}
```

Function `printGradeReports` This function prints the grade reports. For each student, it calls the function print of the `class studentType` to print the grade report. The definition of the function `printGradeReports` is

```
void printGradeReports(ofstream& outfile,
                       studentType studentList[],
                       int numberOfStudents,
                       double tuitionRate)
{
```

```
    int count;

    for(count = 0; count < numberOfStudents; count++)
        studentList[count].print(outfile,tuitionRate);
}
```

Program Listing

```
//Header file courseType.h
#ifndef H_courseType
#define H_courseType

#include <fstream>
#include <string>
using namespace std;

//The definition of the class courseType goes here.
.
.
.
#endif




//Implementation file courseTypeImp.cpp
#include <iostream>
#include <fstream>
#include <string>
#include <iomanip>
#include "courseType.h"

using namespace std;
//The definitions of the member functions of the class
//courseType go here.
.
.
.


//Header file personType.h
#ifndef personType_H
#define personType_H

//The definition of the class personType goes here.
.
.
.
```

```
#endif


//Implementation File personTypeImp.cpp
#include <iostream>
#include <string>
#include "person.h"
using namespace std;

//The definitions of the member functions of the class
//personType go here.
.
.
.



//Header file studentType.h
#ifndef H_studentType
#define H_studentType

#include <fstream>
#include <string>
#include "person.h"
#include "courseType.h"

using namespace std;

//The definition of the class studentType goes here.
.
.
.

#endif



//Implementation file studentTypeImp.cpp
#include <iostream>
#include <iomanip>
#include <fstream>
#include <string>
#include "person.h"
#include "courseType.h"
#include "studentType.h"

using namespace std;
```

```
//The definitions of the member functions of the class
//studentType go here.
.
.
.

//Main program
#include <iostream>
#include <fstream>
#include <string>
#include "studentType.h"

using namespace std;

const int maxNumberOfStudents = 10;

void getStudentData(ifstream& infile,
                    studentType studentList[],
                    int numberOfStudents);

void printGradeReports(ofstream& outfile,
                       studentType studentList[],
                       int numberOfStudents,
                       double tuitionRate);

int main()
{
      studentType studentList[maxNumberOfStudents];

      int noOfStudents;
      double tuitionRate;

      ifstream infile;
      ofstream outfile;

      infile.open("a:stData.txt");

      if(!infile)
      {
         cout<<"Input file does not exist. "
             <<"Program terminates."<<endl;
         return 1;
      }

      outfile.open("a:sDataOut.txt");

      infile<<noOfStudents;        //get the number of students
```

```
    infile<<tuitionRate;        //get the tuition rate
    getStudentData(infile, studentList, noOfStudents);
    printGradeReports(outfile, studentList,
                      noOfStudents, tuitionRate);

    return 0;
}

void getStudentData(ifstream& infile,
                    studentType studentList[],
                    int numberOfStudents)
{
          //Local variable
   string fName;      //variable to store the first name
   string lName;      //variable to store the last name
   int ID;            //variable to store the student ID
   int noOfCourses;   //variable to store the number of courses
   char isPaid;       //variable to store Y/N; that is,
                      //is tuition paid?
   bool isTuitionPaid;  //variable to store true/false

   string cName;      //variable to store the course name
   string cNo;        //variable to store the course number
   int credits;       //variable to store the course credit hours
   char grade;        //variable to store the course grade

   int count;         //loop control variable
   int i;             //loop control variable

   courseType courses[6];  //array of objects to store the course
                           //information

   for(count = 0; count < numberOfStudents; count++)
   {
      infile<<fName<<lName<<ID<<isPaid;                //Step 1

      if(isPaid == 'Y')                                //Step 2
         isTuitionPaid = true;
      else
         isTuitionPaid = false;

      infile<<noOfCourses;                             //Step 3

      for(i = 0; i < noOfCourses; i++)                 //Step 4
      {
         infile<<cName<<cNo<<credits<<grade;           //Step 4.a
```

```
            courses[i].setCourseInfo(cName, cNo,
                                     grade, credits);      //Step 4.b
        }

        studentList[count].setInfo(fName, lName, ID,
                                   noOfCourses, isTuitionPaid,
                                   courses);               //Step 5
    }//end for
}

void printGradeReports(ofstream& outfile,
                       studentType studentList[],
                       int numberOfStudents,
                       double tuitionRate)
{
    int count;

    for(count = 0; count < numberOfStudents; count++)
        studentList[count].print(outfile,tuitionRate);
}
```

Sample Output

```
Student Name: Lisa Miller
Student ID: 890238
Number of courses enrolled: 4

Course No  Course Name  Credits Grade
CSC478     ComputerSci     3      B
HIS356     History         3      A
MTH345     Mathematics     4      A
PHY357     Physics         3      B

Total number of credit hours: 13
Mid-Semester GPA: 3.54
-*-*-*-*-*-*-*-*-*-*-*-*-*-*-*-*-*-*-*-*-*-*-*-*-

Student Name: Bill Wilton
Student ID: 798324
Number of courses enrolled: 5

Course No  Course Name  Credits Grade
BIO234     Biology         4     ***
CHM256     Chemistry       4     ***
ENG378     English         3     ***
MTH346     Mathematics     3     ***
```

```
PHL534     Philosophy       3    ***

Total number of credit hours: 17
*** Grades are being held for not paying the tuition. ***
Amount Due: $5865.00
-*-*-*-*-*-*-*-*-*-*-*-*-*-*-*-*-*-*-*-*-*-*-*-*-

Student Name: Dandy Goat
Student ID: 746333
Number of courses enrolled: 6

Course No  Course Name  Credits Grade
BUS128     Business         3      C
CHM348     Chemistry        4      B
CSC201     ComputerSci      3      B
ENG328     English          3      B
HIS101     History          3      A
MTH137     Mathematics      3      A

Total number of credit hours: 19
Mid-Semester GPA: 3.16
-*-*-*-*-*-*-*-*-*-*-*-*-*-*-*-*-*-*-*-*-*-*-*-*-
```

Input File

```
3 345
Lisa Miller 890238 Y 4
Mathematics MTH345 4 A
Physics PHY357 3 B
ComputerSci CSC478 3 B
History HIS356 3 A

Bill Wilton 798324 N 5
English ENG378 3 B
Philosophy PHL534 3 A
Chemistry CHM256 4 C
Biology BIO234 4 A
Mathematics MTH346 3 C

Dandy Goat 746333 Y 6
History HIS101 3 A
English ENG328 3 B
Mathematics MTH137 3 A
Chemistry CHM348 4 B
ComputerSci CSC201 3 B
Business BUS128 3 C
```

QUICK REVIEW

1. Inheritance and composition are meaningful ways to relate two or more classes.
2. Inheritance is an "is-a" relation.
3. Composition is a "has-a" relation.
4. In single inheritance, the derived class is derived only from one existing class, called the base class.
5. In multiple inheritance, a derived class is derived from more than one base class.
6. The **`private`** members of a base class are **`private`** to the base class. The derived class cannot directly access them.
7. The **`public`** members of a base class can be inherited either as **`public`** or **`private`** by the derived class.
8. A derived class can redefine the function members of a base class, but this redefinition applies only to the objects of the derived class.
9. A call to a base class's constructor is specified in the heading of the definition of the derived class's constructor.
10. When initializing the object of a derived class, the constructor of the base class is executed first.
11. Review the inheritance rules given in this chapter.
12. In composition, a member of a class is an object of another class.
13. In composition, a call to the constructor of member objects is specified in the heading of the definition of the class's constructor.
14. The three basic principles of OOD are encapsulation, inheritance, and polymorphism.
15. An easy way to identify classes, objects, and operations is to describe the problem in English and then identify all of the nouns and verbs. Choose your classes (objects) from the list of nouns and operations from the list of verbs.

EXERCISES

1. Mark the following statements as true or false.
   a. The constructor of a derived class specifies a call to the constructor of the base class in the heading of the function definition.
   b. The constructor of a derived class specifies a call to the constructor of the base class using the name of the class.
   c. Suppose that **`x`** and **`y`** are classes, one of the data members of **`x`** is an object of type **`y`**, and both classes have constructors. The constructor of **`x`** specifies a call to the constructor of **`y`** by using the object name of type **`y`**.
   d. A derived class must have a constructor.

2. Draw a class hierarchy in which several classes are derived from a single base class.
3. Suppose that a `class employeeType` is derived from the `class personType` (see Example 13-9, in Chapter 13). Give examples of data and function members that can be added to the `class employeeType`.
4. Explain the difference between the `private` and `protected` members of a class.
5. Consider the following class definition:

```
class aClass
{
public:
    void print() const;
    void set(int, int);
    aClass();
    aClass(int, int);

  private:
      int u;
      int v;
};
```

What is wrong with the following class definitions?

a.

```
class bClass public aClass
{
public:
    void print()
    void set(int, int, int);
private:
    int z;
}
```

b.

```
class cClass: public aClass
{
public:
    void print();
    int sum();
    cClass();
    cClass(int)
}
```

6. Consider the following statements:

```
class yClass
{
public:
    void one();
    void two(int, int);
    yClass();
private:
    int a;
    int b;
};

class xClass: public yClass
{
public:
    void one();
    xClass();
private:
    int z;
};

yClass y;
xClass x;
```

a. The `private` members of `yClass` are `public` members of `xClass`. True or False?

b. Mark the following statements as valid or invalid. If a statement is invalid, explain why.

(i)

```
void yClass::one()
{
        cout<<a+b<<endl;
}
```

(ii)

```
y.a = 15;
x.b = 30;
```

(iii)

```
void xClass::one()
{
        a = 10;
        b = 15;
        z = 30;
        cout<<a+b+z<<endl;
}
```

(iv)

```
cout<<y.a<<" "<<y.b<<" "<<x.z<<endl;
```

7. Assume the declaration of Exercise 6.
   a. Write the definition of the default constructor of `yClass` so that the `private` data members of `yClass` are initialized to `0`.
   b. Write the definition of the default constructor of `xClass` so that the `private` data members of `xClass` are initialized to `0`.
   c. Write the definition of the member function `two` of `yClass` so that the `private` data member `a` is initialized to the value of the first parameter of `two`, and the `private` data member `b` is initialized to the value of the second parameter of `two`.
8. What is wrong with the following code?

```
class classA
{
protected:
    void setX(int a);                        //Line 1
       //Post: x = a;                        //Line 2
private:                                     //Line 3
    int x;                                   //Line 4
};
 .
 .
 .
int main()
{
    classA aObject;                          //Line 5

    aObject.setX(4);                         //Line 6
    return 0;                                //Line 7
}
```

9. Consider the following code:

```
class one
{
public:
    void print() const;
      //Output the values of x and y
protected:
    void setData(int u, int v);
      //Post: x = u; y = v;
private:
    int x;
    int y;
};
```

```
class two: public one
{
public:
    void setData(int a, int b, int c);
      //Post: x = a; y = b; z = c;
    void print() const;
      //Output the values of x, y, and z
private:
    int z;
};
```

a. Write the definition of the function `setData` of the `class two`.

b. Write the definition of the function `print` of the `class two`.

10. What is the output of the following C++ program?

```
#include <iostream>
#include <string>

using namespace std;

class baseClass
{
public:
    void print() const;

    baseClass(string s = " ", int a = 0);
          //Post: str = s; x = a
protected:
    int x;

private:
    string str;
};

class derivedClass: public baseClass
{
public:
    void print() const;

    derivedClass(string s = "", int a = 0, int b = 0);
          //Post: str = s; x = a; y = b

private:
    int y;
};
```

```
int main()
{
   baseClass baseObject("This is base class", 2);
   derivedClass derivedObject("DDDDDD", 3, 7);

   baseObject.print();
   derivedObject.print();

   return 0;
}

void baseClass::print() const
{
       cout<<x<<" "<<str<<endl;
}

baseClass::baseClass(string s, int a)
{
   str = s;
   x = a;
}

void derivedClass::print() const
{
   cout<<"Derived class: "<<y<<endl;
   baseClass::print();
}

derivedClass::derivedClass(string s, int a, int b)
   :baseClass("Hello Base", a + b)
{
   y = b;
}
```


11. What is the output of the following program?

```
#include <iostream>

using namespace std;

class baseClass
{
public:
    void print() const;

    int getX();

    baseClass(int a = 0);

protected:
    int x;
};
```

```
class derivedClass: public baseClass
{
public:
    void print() const;

    int getResult();

    derivedClass(int a = 0, int b = 0);

private:
    int y;
};


int main()
{
   baseClass baseObject(7);
   derivedClass derivedObject(3,8);

   baseObject.print();
   derivedObject.print();

   cout<<"**** "<<baseObject.getX()<<endl;
   cout<<"#### "<<derivedObject.getResult()<<endl;

   return 0;
}

void baseClass::print() const
{
      cout<<"In base: x = "<<x<<endl;
}

baseClass::baseClass(int a)
{
   x = a;
}

int baseClass::getX()
{
   void  x;
}

void derivedClass::print() const
{
   cout<<"In derived: x = "<<x<<", y = "<<y<<"; x + y = "
       <<x + y<<endl;
}
```

```
int derivedClass::getResult()
{
   return x + y;
}

derivedClass::derivedClass(int a, int b)
   :baseClass(a)
{
   y = b;
}
```

PROGRAMMING EXERCISES

1. In Chapter 13, the `class clockType` was designed to implement the time of day in a program. Certain applications, in addition to hours, minutes, and seconds, might require you to store the time zone. Derive the `class extClockType` from the `class clockType` by adding a data member to store the time zone. Add the necessary member functions and constructors to make the class functional. Also, write the definitions of the member functions and the constructors. Finally, write a test program to test your `class`.
2. In this chapter, the `class dateType` was designed to implement the date in a program, but the member function `setDate` and the constructor with parameters do not check whether the date is valid before storing the date in the data members. Rewrite the definitions of the function `setDate` and the constructor so that the values for the month, day, and year are checked before storing the date into the data members. Also, replace the constructors, the default constructor, and the constructor with parameters with a single constructor with default arguments. Add a function member, `isLeapYear`, to check whether a year is a leap year. Moreover, write a test program to test your class.
3. A point in the *x*-*y* plane is represented by its *x*-coordinate and *y*-coordinate. Design a `class`, `pointType`, that can store and process a point in the *x*-*y* plane. You should then perform operations on a point, such as showing the point, setting the coordinates of the point, printing the coordinates of the point, returning the *x*-coordinate, and returning the *y*-coordinate. Also, write a test program to test the various operations on a point.
4. Every circle has a center and a radius. Given the radius, we can determine the circle's area and circumference. Given the center, we can determine its position in the *x*-*y* plane. The center of a circle is a point in the *x*-*y* plane. Design a `class`, `circleType`, that can store the radius and center of the circle. Because the center is a point in the *x*-*y* plane and you designed the class to capture the properties of a point in Programming Exercise 3, you must derive the `class circleType` from the `class pointType`. You should be able to perform the usual operations on a circle, such as setting the radius, printing the radius, calculating and printing the area and circumference, and carrying out the usual operations on the center.

5. Every cylinder has a base and height, where the base is a circle. Design a **class**, **cylinderType**, that can capture the properties of a cylinder and perform the usual operations on a cylinder. Derive this class from the **class circleType** designed in Programming Exercise 4. Some of the operations that can be performed on a cylinder are as follows: calculate and print the volume, calculate and print the surface area, set the height, set the radius of the base, and set the center of the base.

6. Using classes, design an online address book to keep track of the names, addresses, phone numbers, and dates of birth of family members, close friends, and certain business associates. Your program should be able to handle a maximum of 500 entries.

   a. Define a **class**, **addressType**, that can store a street address, city, state, and ZIP code. Use the appropriate functions to print and store the address. Also, use constructors to automatically initialize the data members.

   b. Define a **class extPersonType** using the **class personType** (as defined in Example 13-9, Chapter 13), the **class dateType** (as designed in this chapter's Programming Exercise 2), and the **class addressType**. Add a data member to this class to classify the person as a family member, friend, or business associate. Also, add a data member to store the phone number. Add (or override) the functions to print and store the appropriate information. Use constructors to automatically initialize the data members.

   c. Define the **class addressBookType** using the previously defined classes. An object of the type **addressBookType** should be able to process a maximum of 500 entries.

   The program should perform the following operations:

   (i) Load the data into the address book from a disk.

   (ii) Sort the address book by last name.

   (iii) Search for a person by last name.

   (iv) Print the address, phone number, and date of birth (if it exists) of a given person.

   (v) Print the names of the people whose birthdays are between two given dates.

   (vi) Print the names of all the people between two last names.

   (vii) Depending on the user's request, print the names of all family members, friends, or business associates.

7. In Programming Exercise 2, the `class dateType` was designed and implemented to keep track of a date, but it has very limited operations. Redefine the `class dateType` so that it can perform the following operations on a date in addition to the operations already defined:
   a. Set the month.
   b. Set the day.
   c. Set the year.
   d. Return the month.
   e. Return the day.
   f. Return the year.
   g. Test whether the year is a leap year.
   h. Return the number of days in the month. For example, if the date is 3-12-2002, the number of days to be returned is 31 because there are 31 days in March.
   i. Return the number of days passed in the year. For example, if the date is 3-18-2002, the number of days passed in the year is 77. Note that the number of days returned also includes the current day.
   j. Return the number of days remaining in the year. For example, if the date is 3-18-2002, the number of days remaining in the year is 288.
   k. Calculate the new date by adding a fixed number of days in the date. For example, if the date is 3-18-2002 and the days to be added are 25, the new date is 4-12-2002.
8. Write the definitions of the functions to implement the operations defined for the `class dateType` in Programming Exercise 7.
9. The `class dateType` defined in Programming Exercise 7 prints the date in numerical form. Some applications might require the date to be printed in another form, such as March 24, 2002. Derive the `class extDateType` so that the date can be printed in either form.

   Add a data member to the `class extDateType` so that the month can also be stored in string form. Add a function member to output the month in the string format followed by the year—for example, in the form March 2002.

   Write the definitions of the function to implement the operations for the `class extDateType`.
10. Using the classes `extDateType` (Programming Exercise 9) and `dayType` (Chapter 13, Programming Exercise 2), design the `class calendarType` so that, given the month and the year, we can print the calendar for that month. To print a monthly calendar, you must know the first day of the month and the number of days in that month. Thus, you must store the first day of the month, which is of the form `dayType`, and the month and the year of the calendar. Clearly, the month and the year can be stored in an object of the form `extDateType` by setting the day component of the date to `1`, and the month and year as specified by the user. Thus, the `class calendarType` has two data members: an object of the type `dayType`, and an object of the type `extDateType`.

Design the **class** `calendarType` so that the program can print a calendar for any month starting January 1, 1500. Note that the day for January 1 of the year 1500 is a Monday. To calculate the first day of a month, you can add the appropriate days to Monday of January 1, 1500.

For the **class** `calendarType`, include the following operations:

a. Determine the first day of the month for which the calendar will be printed. Call this operation `firstDayOfMonth`.

b. Set the month.

c. Set the year.

d. Return the month.

e. Return the year.

f. Print the calendar for the particular month.

g. Add the appropriate constructors to initialize the data members.

11. a. Write the definitions of the member functions of the **class** `calendarType` (designed in Programming Exercise 10) to implement the operations of the **class** `calendarType`.

    b. Write a test program to print the calendar for either a particular month or a particular year. For example, the calendar for September 2002 is

```
                      September 2002
  Sun     Mon     Tue     Wed     Thu     Fri     Sat
    1       2       3       4       5       6       7
    8       9      10      11      12      13      14
   15      16      17      18      19      20      21
   22      23      24      25      26      27      28
   29      30
```

CHAPTER

15

POINTERS, CLASSES, AND VIRTUAL FUNCTIONS

In this chapter, you will:

- Learn about the pointer data type and pointer variables
- Explore how to declare and manipulate pointer variables
- Learn about the address of operator and the dereferencing operator
- Discover dynamic variables
- Explore how to use the `new` and `delete` operators to manipulate dynamic variables
- Learn about pointer arithmetic
- Discover dynamic arrays
- Become aware of the shallow and deep copies of data
- Discover the peculiarities of classes with pointer data members
- Learn about virtual functions
- Examine the relationship between the address of operator and classes

In Chapter 2, you learned that C++'s data types are classified into three categories: simple, structured, and pointers. Until now, you have studied only the first two data types. This chapter discusses the third data type, called the pointer data type. You will first learn how to declare pointer variables (or pointers, for short) and manipulate the data to which they point. Later, you will use these concepts when you study dynamic arrays and linked lists. Linked lists are discussed in Chapter 17.

THE POINTER DATA TYPE AND POINTER VARIABLES

The values belonging to pointer data types are the memory addresses of your computer. As in many other languages, there is no name associated with the pointer data type in C++. Because the domain—that is, the values of a pointer data type—are the addresses (memory locations), a pointer variable is a variable whose content is an address, that is, a memory location.

Pointer variable: A variable whose content is an address (that is, a memory address).

Declaring Pointer Variables

Because no name is associated with pointer data types, pointer variables are not declared like other variables. When you declare a pointer variable, you also specify the data type of the value to be stored in the memory location pointed to by the pointer variable. In C++, you declare a pointer variable by using the asterisk symbol (`*`) between the data type and the variable name. The general syntax of declaring a pointer variable is

```
dataType *identifier;
```

As an example, consider the following statements:

```
int   *p;
char  *ch;
```

In these statements, both `p` and `ch` are pointer variables. The content of `p` (when properly assigned) points to a memory location of the type `int`, and the content of `ch` points to a memory location of the type `char`. Usually `p` is called a pointer variable of the type `int`, and `ch` is called a pointer variable of the type `char`.

Before discussing how pointers work, let us make the following observations. The statement

```
int   *p;
```

is equivalent to the statement

```
int*  p;
```

which is equivalent to the statement

```
int  * p;
```

Thus, the character `*` can appear anywhere between the data type name and the variable name.

Now consider the following statement:

```
int*   p, q;
```

In this statement, only `p` is the pointer variable, not `q`. Here `q` is an `int` variable. To avoid confusion, we prefer to attach the character `*` to the variable name. So the preceding statement is written as

```
int    *p, q;
```

Of course, the statement

```
int    *p, *q;
```

declares both `p` and `q` to be pointer variables of the type `int`.

Now that you know how to declare pointers, next we will discuss how to make a pointer point to a memory space and how to manipulate data stored in these memory locations.

Because the value of a pointer is a memory address, a pointer can store the address of a memory space of the designated type. For example, if `p` is a pointer of the type `int`, `p` can store the address of any memory space of the type `int`. C++ provides two operators—the address of operator (`&`) and the dereferencing operator (`*`)—to work with pointers. The next two sections describe these operators.

The Address of Operator (&)

In C++, the ampersand, `&`, called the **address of operator**, is a unary operator that returns the address of its operand. For example, given the statements

```
int  x;
int *p;
```

the statement

```
p = &x;
```

assigns the address of `x` to `p`. That is, `x` and the value of `p` refer to the same memory location.

15

The Dereferencing Operator (*)

Every chapter until now has used the asterisk character, `*`, as the binary multiplication operator. C++ also uses * as a unary operator. When used as a unary operator, `*`, commonly referred to as the **dereferencing operator** or **indirection operator**, refers to the object to which its operand (that is, a pointer) points. For example, given the statements

```
int  x = 25;
int *p;
p = &x;     //store the address of x in p
```

the statement

```
cout<<*p<<endl;
```

prints the value stored in the memory space pointed to by `p`, which is the value of `x`. Also, the statement

```
*p = 55;
```

stores `55` in the memory location pointed to by `p`—that is, in `x`.

Let us consider the following statements:

```
int *p;
int  num;
```

In these statements, `p` is a pointer variable of the type `int` and `num` is a variable of the type `int`. (See Figure 15-1.)

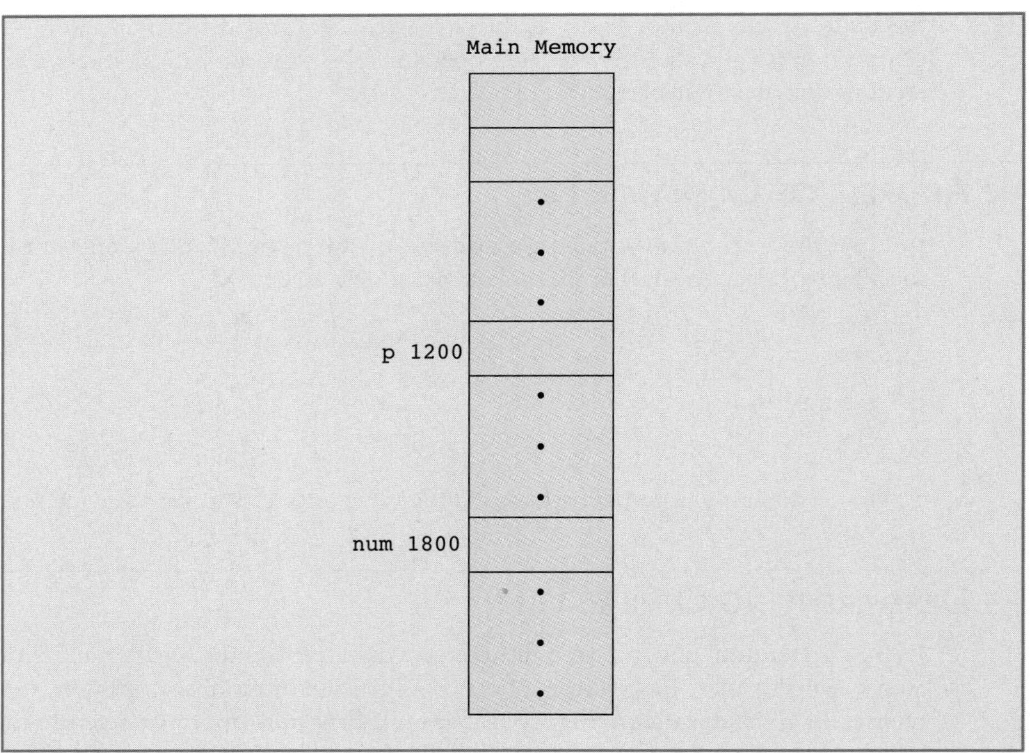

Figure 15-1 Main memory, `p`, and `num`

Let us assume that memory location `1200` is allocated for `p` and memory location `1800` is allocated for `num`. The statement

```
num = 78;
```

stores `78` in `num`—that is, in memory location `1800`. (See Figure 15-2.)

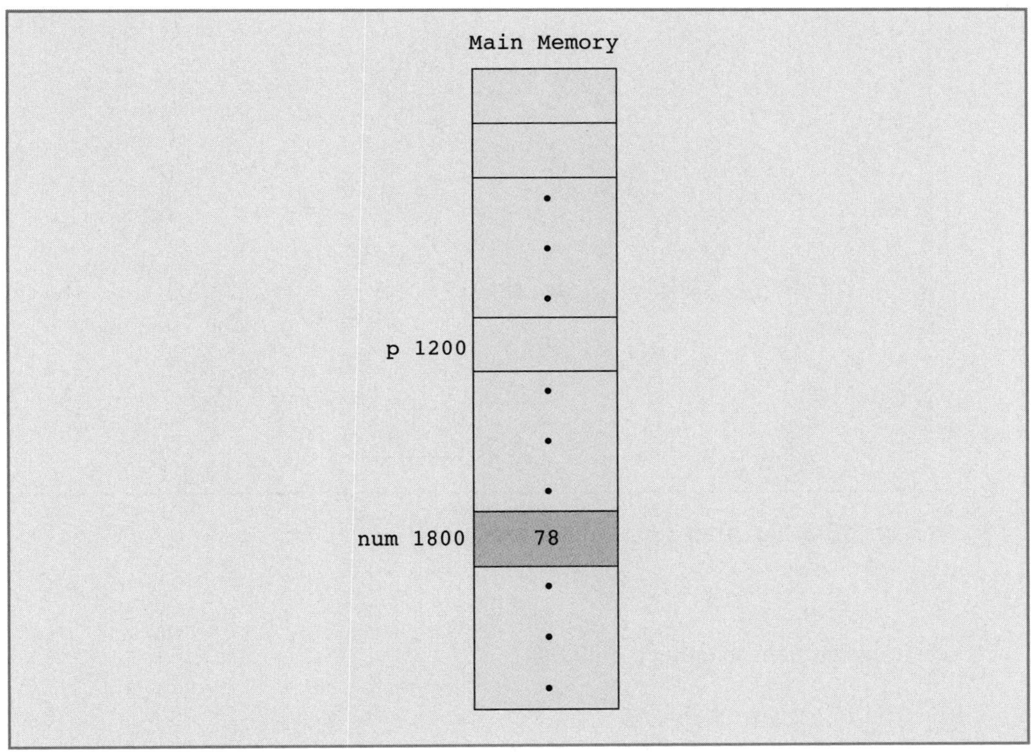

Figure 15-2 num after num =78; executes

The statement

```
p = &num;
```

stores the address—that is, `1800`—into `p`. After this statement executes, both `*p` and `num` refer to the content of memory location `1800`—that is, `num`. (See Figure 15-3.)

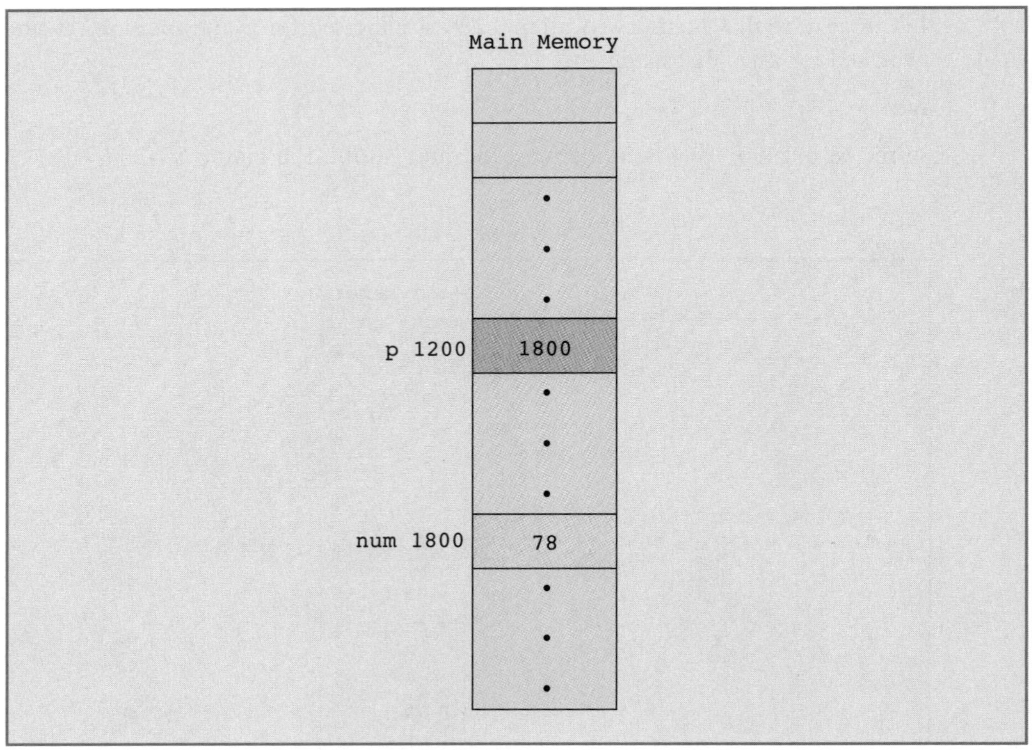

Figure 15-3 p after p = # executes

The assignment statement

```
*p = 24;
```

changes the content of memory location 1800 and thus also changes the content of **num**. (See Figure 15-4.)

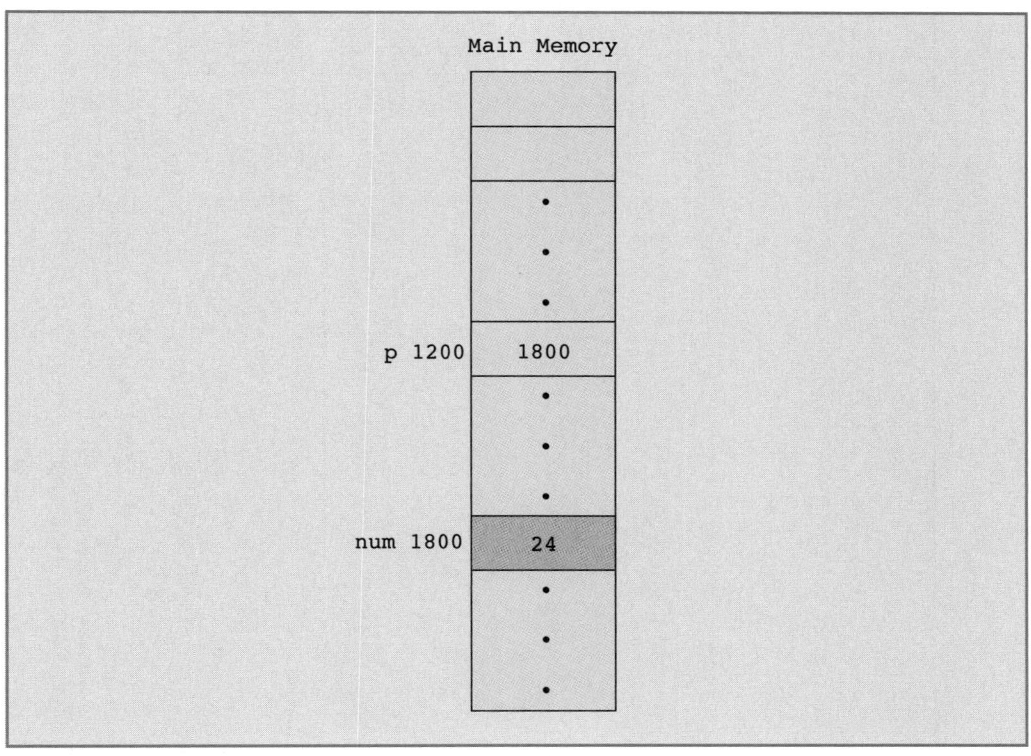

Figure 15-4 `*p` and `num` after `*p = 24;` executes

Let us summarize the preceding discussion.

1. `&p`, `p`, and `*p` all have different meanings.
2. `&p` means the address of `p`—that is, `1200` (in Figure 15-4).
3. `p` means the content of `p` (`1800` in Figure 15-4).
4. `*p` means the content (`24` in Figure 15-4) of the memory location (`1800` in Figure 15-4) pointed to by `p` (that is, pointed to by the content of memory location `1200`).

Example 15-1

Consider the following statements:

```
int *p;
int  x;
```

Suppose that we have the memory allocation for `p` and `x` as shown in Figure 15-5.

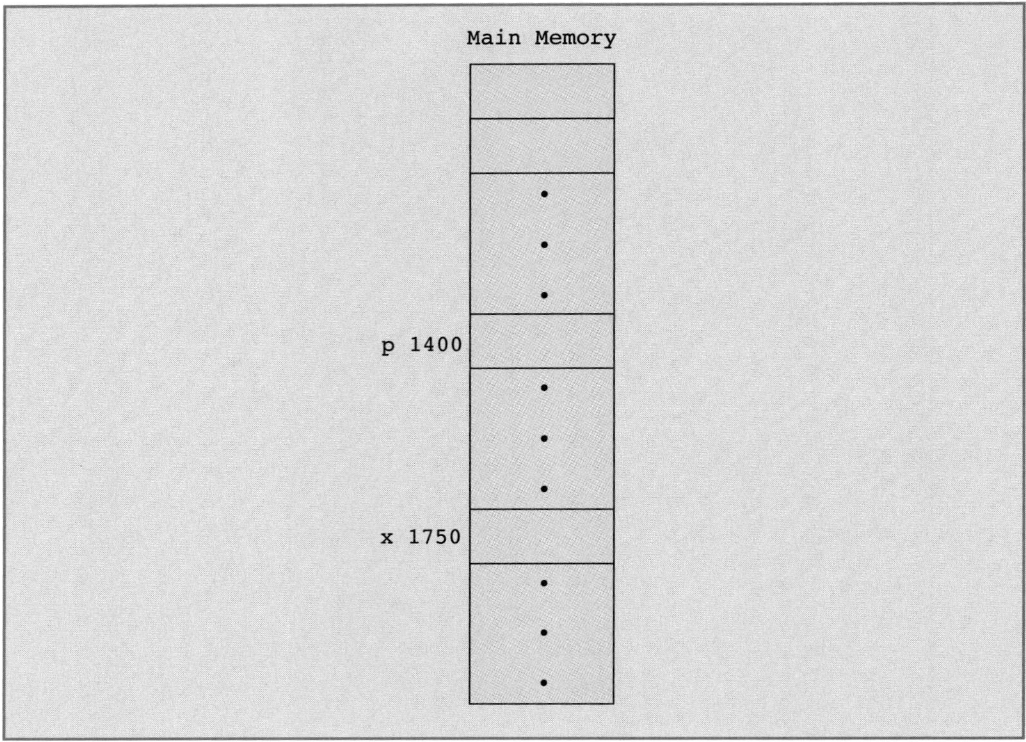

Figure 15-5 Main memory, p, and x

The values of &p, p, *p, &x, and x are as follows:

	Value
&p	1400
p	??? (unknown)
*p	Does not exist (undefined)
&x	1750
x	??? (unknown)

Suppose that the following statements are executed in the order given:

```
x = 50;
p = &x;
*p = 38;
```

The values of &p, p, *p, &x, and x are shown after each of these statements executes. After the statement:

```
x  = 50;
```

executes, the values of &p, p, *p, &x, and x are as follows:

	Value
&p	1400
p	??? (unknown)
*p	does not exist (undefined)
&x	1750
x	50

After the statement:

```
p = &x;
```

executes, the values of &p, p, *p, &x, and x are as follows:

	Value
&p	1400
p	1750
*p	50
&x	1750
x	50

Note that after the statement `p = &x;` executes, p contains the address of x, and so *p and x refer to the same memory space, which is x. Therefore, the value of *p is 50.

After the statement:

```
*p = 38;
```

executes, the values of &p, p, *p, &x, and x are as follows. (Because *p and x refer to the same memory space, the value of x is also changed to 38.)

	Value
`&p`	`1400`
`p`	`1750`
`*p`	`38`
`&x`	`1750`
`x`	`38`

Let us note the following from Example 15-1:

1. A declaration such as

   ```
   int *p;
   ```

   allocates memory for `p` only, not for `*p`. Later, you will learn how to allocate memory for `*p`.

2. Assume the following:

   ```
   int *p;
   int x;
   ```

   Then,

   a. `p` is a pointer variable.

   b. The content of `p` points only to a memory location of the type `int`.

   c. Memory location `x` exists and is of the type `int`. Therefore, the assignment statement

      ```
      p = &x;
      ```

      is legal. After this assignment statement executes, `*p` is valid and meaningful.

Example 15-2

The following program illustrates how pointer variables work:

```
//Chapter 15: Example 15-2

#include <iostream>

using namespace std;

int main()
{
   int *p;
   int x = 37;
```

```
    cout<<"Line 1: x = "<<x<<endl;                     //Line 1

    p = &x;                                             //Line 2

    cout<<"Line 3: *p = "<<*p
        <<", x = "<<x<<endl;                            //Line 3

    *p = 58;                                            //Line 4

    cout<<"Line 5: *p = "<<*p
        <<", x = "<<x<<endl;                            //Line 5

    cout<<"Line 6: Address of p = "<<&p<<endl;          //Line 6

    cout<<"Line 7: Value of p = "<<p<<endl;             //Line 7

    cout<<"Line 8: Value of the memory location "
        <<"pointed to by *p = "<<*p<<endl;              //Line 8
    cout<<"Line 9: Address of x = "<<&x<<endl;          //Line 9
    cout<<"Line 10: Value of x = "<<x<<endl;            //Line 10

    return 0;
}
```

Sample Run

```
Line 1: x = 37
Line 3: *p = 37, x = 37
Line 5: *p = 58, x = 58
Line 6: Address of p = 006BFDF4
Line 7: Value of p = 006BFDF0
Line 8: Value of the memory location pointed to by *p = 58
Line 9: Address of x = 006BFDF0
Line 10: Value of x = 58
```


The preceding program works as follows. The statement in Line 1 outputs the value of **x**, and the statement in Line 2 stores the address of **x** into **p**. The statement in Line 3 outputs the values of ***p** and **x**. Because **p** contains the address of **p**, the values of ***p** and **x** are the same, as shown by the output of Line 3. The statement in Line 4 changes the value of ***p** to **58**, and the statement in Line 5 outputs the values of ***p** and **x**, which are again the same. The statements between Lines 6 and 10 output the address of **p**, the value of **p**, the value of ***p**, the address of **x**, and the value of **x**. Note that the value of **p** and the address of **x** are the same because the address of **x** is stored in **p** by the statement in Line 2. (Note that the address of **p**, the value of **p**, and the address of **x** as shown by the outputs of Lines 6, 7, and 9, respectively, are machine dependent. When you run this program on your machine, you are likely to get different values.)

CLASSES, STRUCTS, AND POINTER VARIABLES

In the previous section, you learned how to declare and manipulate pointers of simple data types such as **int** and **char**. You can also declare pointers to other data types, such as classes. You will now learn how to declare and manipulate pointers to classes and structs. (Recall that both classes and structs have the same capabilities. The only difference between classes and structs is that by default all members of a class are **private**, and by default all members of a struct are **public**. Therefore, the following discussion applies to both.)

Consider the following declaration of a **struct**:

```
struct studentType
{
    char name[26];
    double gpa;
    int sID;
    char grade;
};

studentType     student;
studentType*    studentPtr;
```

In the preceding declaration, **student** is an object of the type **studentType**, and **studentPtr** is a pointer variable of the type **studentType**. The following statement stores the address of **student** in **studentPtr**:

```
studentPtr = &student;
```

The following statement stores **3.9** in the component **gpa** of the object **student**:

```
(*studentPtr).gpa = 3.9;
```

The expression **(*studentPtr).gpa** is a mixture of pointer dereferencing and the class component selection. In C++, the dot operator, **.**, has a higher precedence than the dereferencing operator. Because of this fact, the parentheses are important. To simplify the accessing of class components via a pointer, C++ provides another operator, called the **member access operator arrow**, **->**. The operator **->** consists of two consecutive symbols: a hyphen and the "greater than" symbol.

The syntax for accessing a **class** (**struct**) member using the operator **->** is

```
pointerVariableName->classMemberName
```

Thus, the statement

```
(*studentPtr).gpa = 3.9;
```

is equivalent to the statement

```
studentPtr->gpa = 3.9;
```

Accessing **class** (**struct**) components via pointers using the operator **->** thus eliminates the use of both parentheses and the dereferencing operator. Because typos are unavoidable and missing parentheses can result in either an abnormal program termination or erroneous results, when accessing **class** (**struct**) components via pointers, this book uses the arrow notation.

Example 15-3 illustrates how pointers work with class member functions.

Example 15-3

Consider the following class:

```
class classExample
{
public:
    void setX(int a);
      //Function to set the value of the data member x
      //Post condition: x = a;
    void print() const;
      //Function to output the value of x

private:
    int x;
};
```

The definition of the member function is as follows:

```
void classExample::setX(int a)
{
      x = a;
}

void classExample::print() const
{
      cout<<"x = "<<x<<endl;
}
```


Consider the following function **main**:

```
int main()
{
      classExample *cExpPtr;          //Line 1
      classExample cExpObject;        //Line 2

      cExpPtr = &cExpObject;          //Line 3

      cExpPtr->setX(5);               //Line 4
      cExpPtr->print();               //Line 5

      return 0;
}
```

Output

```
x = 5
```

In the function `main`, the statement in Line 1 declares `cExpPtr` to be a pointer of the type `classExample`, and the statement in Line 2 declares `cExpObject` to be an object of the type `classExample`. The statement in Line 3 stores the address of `cExpObject` into `cExpPtr`. (See Figure 15-6.)

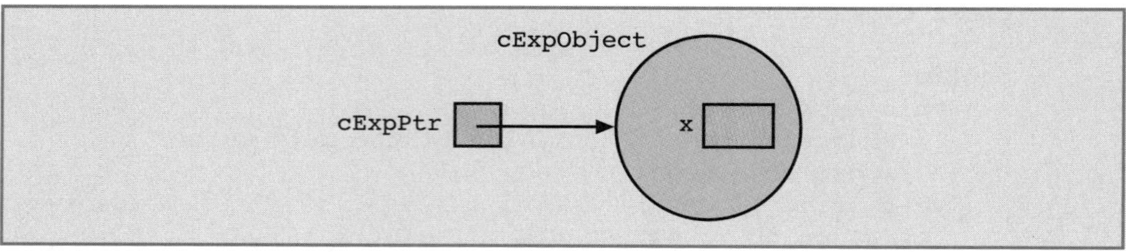

Figure 15-6 `cExpObject` and `cExpPtr` after `cExpPtr = &cExpObject;` executes

In the statement in Line 4, the pointer `cExpPtr` accesses the member function `setX` to set the value of the data member `x` (see Figure 15-7).

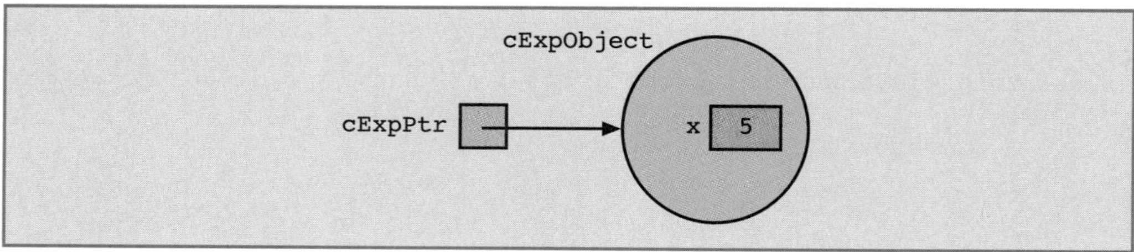

Figure 15-7 `cExpObject` and `cExpPtr` after `cExpPtr->setX(5);` executes

In the statement in Line 5, the pointer `cExpPtr` accesses the member function `print` to print the value of `x`, as shown above.

INITIALIZING POINTER VARIABLES

Because C++ does not automatically initialize variables, pointer variables must be initialized if you do not want them to point to anything. Pointer variables are initialized using the constant value `0`, called the **null pointer**. Thus, the statement `p = 0;` stores the null pointer in `p`; that is, `p` points to nothing. Some programmers use the named constant `NULL` to initialize pointer variables. The following two statements are equivalent:

```
p = NULL;

p = 0;
```

The number `0` is the only number that can be directly assigned to a pointer variable.

DYNAMIC VARIABLES

In the previous sections, you learned how to declare pointer variables, how to store the address of a variable into a pointer variable of the same type as the variable, and how to manipulate data using pointers. However, you learned how to use pointers to manipulate data only into memory spaces that were created using other variables. In other words, pointers manipulated data into existing memory spaces. So what is the big deal about using pointers? You can access these memory spaces by working with the variables that were used to create them. In this section, you will learn about the power behind pointers. In particular, you will learn how to allocate and deallocate memory during program execution using pointers.

Variables that are created during program execution are called **dynamic variables**. With the help of pointers, C++ creates dynamic variables. C++ provides two operators, **`new`** and **`delete`**, to create and destroy dynamic variables, respectively. When a program requires a new variable, the operator **`new`** is used; when a program no longer needs a dynamic variable, the operator **`delete`** is used.

15

In C++, **`new`** and **`delete`** are reserved words.

The operator **`new`** has two forms: one to allocate a single variable, and another to allocate an array of variables. The syntax to use the operator **`new`** is

```
new dataType;              //to allocate a single variable
new dataType[intExp];      //to allocate an array of variables
```

where `intExp` is any expression evaluating to a positive integer.

The operator **`new`** allocates memory (a variable) of the designated type and returns a pointer to it—that is, the address of this allocated memory. Moreover, the allocated memory is uninitialized.

Consider the following declaration:

```
int  *p;
char *q;
int  x;
```

The statement

```
p = &x;
```

stores the address of **x** in **p**. However, no new memory is allocated. On the other hand, consider the following statement:

```
p = new int;
```

This statement creates a variable during program execution somewhere in memory, and stores the address of the allocated memory in **p**. The allocated memory is accessed via pointer dereferencing—namely, ***p**. Similarly, the statement

```
q = new char[16];
```

creates an array of **16** components of the type **char** and stores the base address of the array in **q**.

Because a dynamic variable is unnamed, it cannot be accessed directly. It is accessed indirectly by the pointer returned by **new**. The following statements illustrate this concept:

```
int  *p;           //p is a pointer of the type int
char *name;        //name is a pointer of the type char
string *str;       //str is a pointer of the type string

p = new int;       //allocates memory of the type int
                   //and stores the address of the
                   //allocated memory in p
*p = 28;           //stores 28 in the allocated memory

name = new char[5];     //allocates memory for an array of
                        //five components of the type char and
                        //stores the base address of the array
                        //in name
strcpy(name, "John");   //stores John in name

str = new string; //allocates memory of the type string
                  //and stores the address of the
                  //allocated memory in str
*str = "Sunny Day";     //stores the string "Sunny Day" in
                        //the memory pointed to by str
```

When a dynamic variable is no longer needed, it can be destroyed; that is, the memory can be deallocated. The C++ operator **delete** is used to destroy dynamic variables. The syntax to use the operator **delete** has two forms:

```
delete pointervariable;    //to destroy a single dynamic variable
delete [] pointervariable; //to destroy a dynamically created array
```

Thus, the statements

```
delete p;
delete [] name;
```

deallocate the memory referenced by the pointers p and name.

Operations on Pointer Variables

The operations that are allowed on pointer variables are the assignment and relational operations and some limited arithmetic operations. The value of one pointer variable can be assigned to another pointer variable of the same type. Two pointer variables of the same type can be compared for equality, and so on. Integer values can be added and subtracted from a pointer variable. The value of one pointer variable can be subtracted from another pointer variable.

For example, suppose that we have the following statements:

```
int *p, *q;
```

The statement

```
p = q;
```

copies the value of q into p. After this statement executes, both p and q point to the same memory location. Any changes made to *p automatically change the value of *q, and vice versa.

The expression

```
p == q
```

evaluates to **true** if p and q have the same value—that is, if they point to the same memory location. Similarly, the expression

```
p != q
```

evaluates to **true** if p and q point to different memory locations.

The arithmetic operations that are allowed differ from the arithmetic operations on numbers. First, let us use the following statements to explain the increment and decrement operations on pointer variables:

```
int *p;
double *q;
char *chPtr;
studentType *stdPtr;    //studentType data type is as defined before
```

Recall that the size of the memory allocated for an **int** variable is 4 bytes, a **double** variable is 8 bytes, and a **char** variable is 1 byte. The memory allocated for a variable of the type **studentType** is then 39 bytes.

The statement

```
p++;      or      p = p + 1;
```

increments the value of **p** by 4 bytes since **p** is a pointer of the type **int**. Similarly, the statements

```
q++;
chPtr++;
```

increment the value of **q** by 8 bytes and the value of **chPtr** by 1 byte, respectively. The statement

```
stdPtr++;
```

increments the value of **stdPtr** by 39 bytes.

The increment operator increments the value of a pointer variable by the size of the memory to which it is pointing. Similarly, the decrement operator decrements the value of a pointer variable by the size of the memory to which it is pointing.

Moreover, the statement

```
p = p + 2;
```

increments the value of **p** by 8 bytes.

Thus, when an integer is added to a pointer variable, the value of the pointer variable is incremented by the integer times the size of the memory that the pointer is pointing to. Similarly, when an integer is subtracted from a pointer variable, the value of the pointer variable is decremented by the integer times the size of the memory to which the pointer is pointing.

Pointer arithmetic can be very dangerous. Using pointer arithmetic, the program can accidentally access the memory locations of other variables and change their content without warning, leaving the programmer in a state of disbelief and trying to find out what went wrong. If a pointer variable tries to access either the memory spaces of other variables or an illegal memory space, some systems might terminate the program with an appropriate error message. Always exercise extra care when doing pointer arithmetic.

DYNAMIC ARRAYS

In Chapter 9, you learned how to declare and process arrays. The arrays discussed in Chapter 9 are called static arrays because their size was fixed at compile time. One of the limitations of a static array is that every time you execute the program, the size of the array is fixed, so it might not be possible to use the same array to process different data sets of the same type. One way to handle this limitation is to declare an array that is large enough to process a variety of data sets. However, if the array is very big and the data set is small, such a declaration would result in memory waste. On the other hand, it would be extremely helpful if, during program execution, you could prompt the user to enter the size of the array and then create an array of the appropriate size. This approach is especially helpful if you cannot even guess the array size. In this section, you will learn how to create arrays during program execution and process such arrays.

An array created during the execution of a program is called a **dynamic array**. To create a dynamic array, we use the second form of the **new** operator.

The statement

```
int *p;
```

declares p to be a pointer variable of the type int. The statement

```
p = new int[10];
```

allocates 10 contiguous memory locations, each of the type int, and stores the address of the first memory location into p. In other words, the operator **new** creates an array of 10 components of the type int, it returns the base address of the array, and the assignment operator stores the base address of the array into p. Thus, the statement

```
*p = 25;
```

stores 25 into the first memory location and the statements

```
p++;        //p points to the next array component
*p = 35;
```


store 35 into the second memory location. Thus, by using the increment and decrement operations, you can access the components of the array. Of course, after performing a few increment operations, it is possible to lose track of the first array component. C++ allows us to use array notation to access these memory locations. For example, the statements

```
p[0] = 25;
p[1] = 35;
```

store 25 and 35 into the first and second array components, respectively. That is, p[0] refers to the first array component, p[1] refers to the second array component, and so on. In general, p[i] refers to the (i + 1)th array component. After the preceding statements execute, p still points to the first array component. Moreover, the following **for** loop initializes each array component to 0:

```
for(j = 0; j < 10; j++)
    p[j] = 0;
```

where j is an int variable.

When the array notation is used to process the array pointed to by p, p stays fixed at the first memory location. Moreover, p is an array created during program execution, called a **dynamic array**.

The statement

```
int list[10];
```

declares list to be an array of 10 components. Now list itself is a variable and the value stored in list is the base address of the array—that is, the address of the first array component. Because it contains a value of the type pointer, list is a pointer variable. However, the increment and decrement operations cannot be applied to list because we want list to always point to the first array component. Any attempt to use the increment or decrement operation on list results in a compile-time error. Furthermore, if p is a pointer variable of the type int, then the statement

```
p = list;
```

copies the value of list into p. We are allowed to perform increment and decrement operations on p.

An array name is a constant pointer.

Example 15-4

The following program illustrates how to obtain a user's response to get the array size and create a dynamic array during program execution. Consider the following statements:

```
int *intList;                       //Line 1
int arraySize;                      //Line 2

cout<<"Enter array size: ";         //Line 3
cin>>arraySize;                     //Line 4
cout<<endl;                         //Line 5

intList = new int[arraySize];       //Line 6
```

The statement in Line 1 declares intList to be a pointer of the type int, and the statement in Line 2 declares arraySize to be an int variable. The statement in Line 3 prompts the user to enter the size of the array, and the statement in Line 4 inputs the array size into the variable arraySize. The statement in Line 6 creates an array of the size specified by arraySize, and the base address of the array is stored in intList. From this point on, you can treat intList just like any other array. For example, you can use the array notation to process the elements of intList and pass intList as a parameter to the function.

Functions and Pointers

A pointer variable can be passed as a parameter to a function either by value or by reference. To declare a pointer as a value parameter in a function heading, you use the same mechanism as you use to declare a variable. To make a formal parameter be a reference parameter, you use & when you declare the formal parameter in the function heading. Therefore, to declare a formal parameter as a reference parameter, you must use &. Between the data type name and the identifier name, you must include * to make the identifier a pointer and & to make it a reference parameter. The obvious question is, In what order should & and * appear between the data type name and the identifier to declare a pointer as a reference parameter? In C++, to make a pointer a reference parameter in a function heading, * appears before the & between the data type name and the identifier. The following example illustrates this concept:

```
void example(int* &p, double *q)
{
        .
        .
        .
}
```

In this example, both p and q are pointers. The parameter p is a reference parameter; the parameter q is a value parameter.

Pointers and Function Return Value

In C++, a function can return a value of the type pointer. For example, the return type of the function

```
int* testExp(...)
{
        .
        .
        .
}
```

is a pointer of the type int.

15

SHALLOW VERSUS DEEP COPY AND POINTERS

In an earlier section, we discussed pointer arithmetic and explained that if we are not careful, one pointer might access the data of another (completely unrelated) pointer. This event might result in unsuspected or erroneous results. Here, we discuss another peculiarity of pointers. To facilitate the discussion, we will use pictorial diagrams to show pointers and their related memory.

Consider the following statements:

```
int *p;

p = new int;
```

The first statement declares `p` to be a pointer variable of the type `int`. The second statement allocates memory of the type `int`, and the address of the allocated memory is stored in `p`. We use a figure like Figure 15-8 to illustrate this situation.

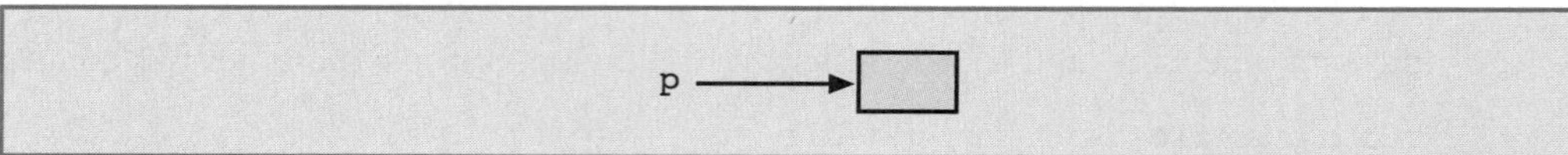

Figure 15-8 Pointer `p` and the memory to which it points

The box indicates the allocated memory (in this case, of the type `int`) and `p` together with the arrow, indicates that `p` points to the allocated memory. Now consider the following statement:

```
*p = 87;
```

This statement stores `87` in the memory pointed to by `p`. We use figures like Figure 15-9 to illustrate this situation.

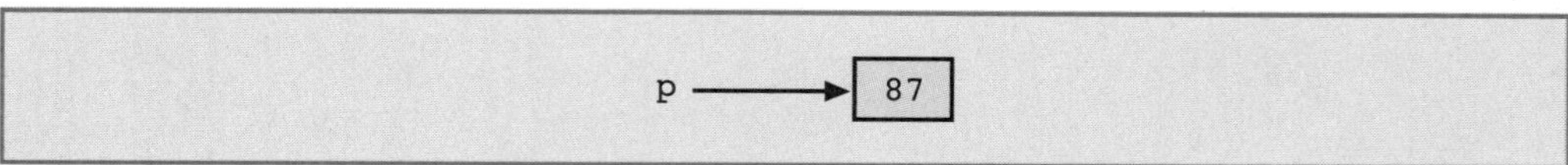

Figure 15-9 Pointer `p` with `87` in the memory to which it points

Consider the following statements:

```
int *first;
int *second;

first = new int[10];
```

The first two statements declare **first** and **second** pointer variables of the type **int**. The third statement creates an array of **10** components, and the base address of the array is stored into **first**. (See Figure 15-10.)

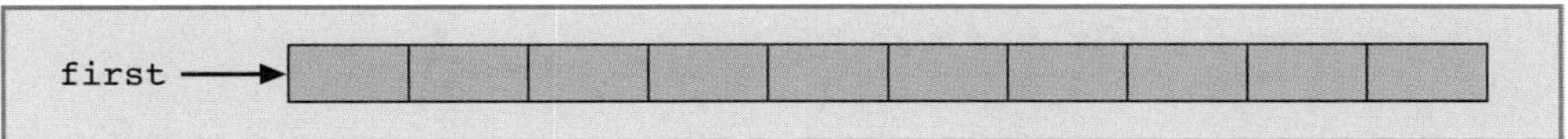

Figure 15-10 Pointer **first** and the array to which it points

Suppose that some meaningful data is stored in the array pointed to by **first**. To be specific, suppose that this array is as shown in Figure 15-11.

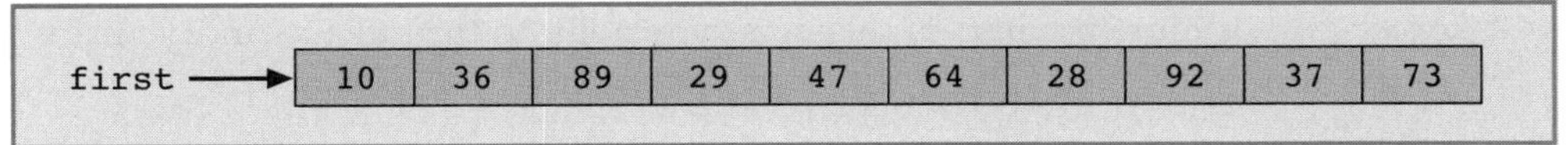

Figure 15-11 Pointer **first** and its array

Next, consider the following statement:

```
second = first;              //Line A
```

This statement copies the value of **first** into **second**. After this statement executes, both **first** and **second** point to the same array, as shown in Figure 15-12.

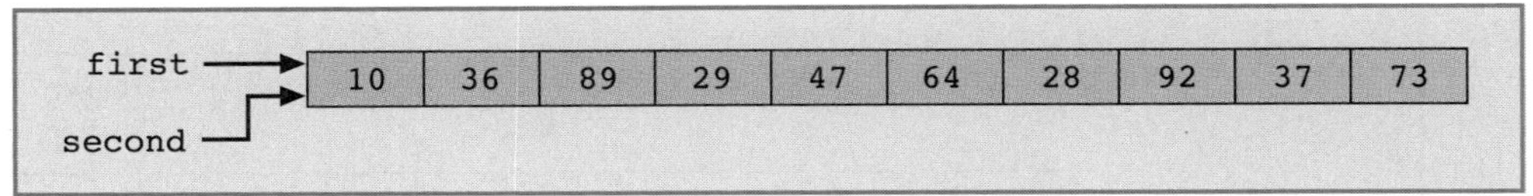

Figure 15-12 **first** and **second** after **second = first;** executes

15

Let us next execute the following statement:

```
delete [] second;
```

After this statement executes, the array pointed to by **second** is deleted. This action results in Figure 15-13.

Figure 15-13 **first** and **second** after **delete [] second;** executes

Because **first** and **second** pointed to the same array, after the statement

```
delete [] second;
```

executes, **first** becomes invalid. Therefore, if the program later tries to access the memory pointed to by **first**, either the program will access the wrong memory or it will terminate in an error. This case is an example of a shallow copy. More formally, in a **shallow copy**, two or more pointers of the same type point to the same memory; that is, they point to the same data.

On the other hand, suppose that we have the following statements instead of the earlier statement, **second = first;**, (in Line **A**):

```
second = new int[10];

for(int j = 0; j < 10; j++)
    second[j] = first[j];
```

The first statement creates an array of **10** components of the type **int**, and the base address of the array is stored in **second**. The second statement copies the array pointed to by **first** into the array pointed to by **second**. (See Figure 15-14.)

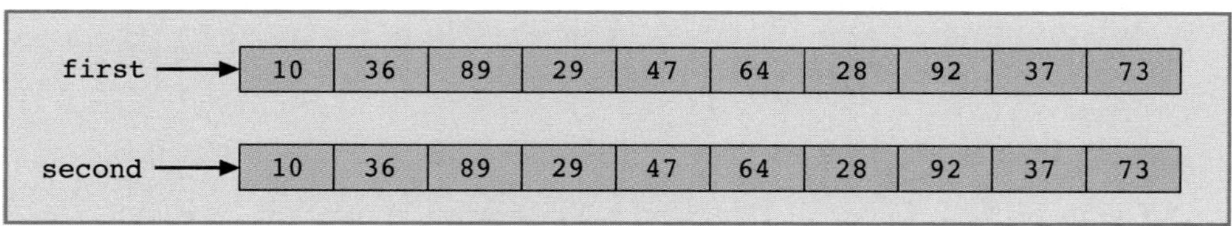

Figure 15-14 **first** and **second** both pointing to their own data

Both `first` and `second` now point to their own data. If `second` deletes its memory, there is no effect on `first`. This case is an example of a deep copy. More formally, in a **deep copy**, two or more pointers have their own data.

From the preceding discussion, it follows that you must know when to use a shallow copy and when to use a deep copy.

Classes and Pointers: Some Peculiarities

If a pointer variable is of a class type, we discussed—in the previous section—how to access class members via the pointer by using the arrow notation. Because a class can have pointer data members, this section discusses some peculiarities of such classes. To facilitate the discussion, we will use the following class:

```
class pointerDataClass
{
public:
    ...

private:
    int x;
    int lenP;
    int *p;
};
```

Also consider the following statements (see Figure 15-15):

```
pointerDataClass objectOne;
pointerDataClass objectTwo;
```

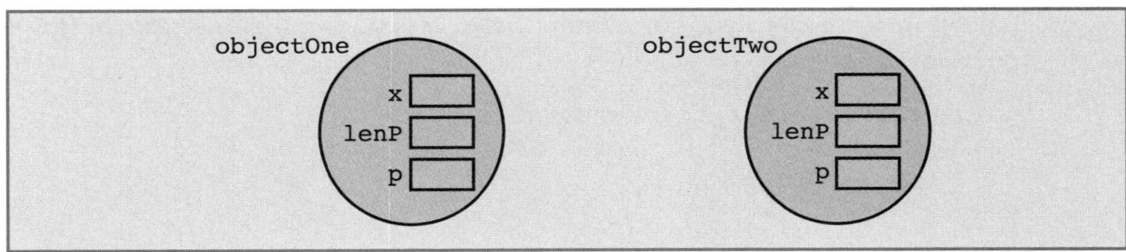

Figure 15-15 Objects `objectOne` and `objectTwo`

15

The Destructor

The object `objectOne` has a pointer data member `p`. Suppose that during program execution the pointer `p` creates a dynamic array. When `objectOne` goes out of scope, all data members of `objectOne` are destroyed. However, `p` created a dynamic array, and dynamic memory must be deallocated using the operator **`delete`**. Thus, if the pointer `p` does not use the **`delete`** operator to deallocate the dynamic array, the memory space of the dynamic array would stay marked as allocated, even though no one can access it. How do we ensure that when `p` is destroyed, the dynamic memory created by p is also destroyed? Suppose that `objectOne` is as shown in Figure 15-16.

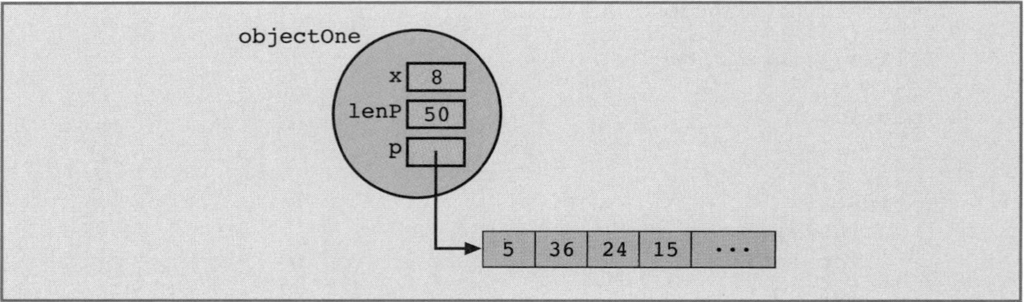

Figure 15-16 Objects `objectOne` and its data

Recall that if a class has a destructor, the destructor automatically executes whenever a class object goes out of scope (see Chapter 13). Therefore, we can put the necessary code in the destructor to ensure that when `objectOne` goes out of scope, the memory created by the pointer `p` is deallocated. For example, the definition of the destructor for the **`class`** `pointerDataClass` is

```
pointerDataClass::~pointerDataClass()
{
      delete [] p;
}
```

Of course, you must include the destructor as a member of the class in its definition. Let us extend the definition of the `class pointerDataClass` by including the destructor. Moreover, the remainder of this section assumes that the definition of the destructor is as given above—that is, the destructor deallocates the memory space pointed to by `p`.

```
class pointerDataClass
{
public:
    ~pointerDataClass();
      ...

private:
    int x;
    int lenP;
    int *p;
};
```

For the destructor to work properly, the pointer `p` must have a valid value. If `p` is not properly initialized (that is, if the value of `p` is garbage) and the destructor executes, either the program terminates with an error message or the destructor deallocates an unrelated memory space. For this reason, you should exercise extra caution while working with pointers.

The Assignment Operator

This section describes the limitations of the built-in assignment operators for classes with pointer data members. Suppose that `objectOne` and `objectTwo` are as shown in Figure 15-17.

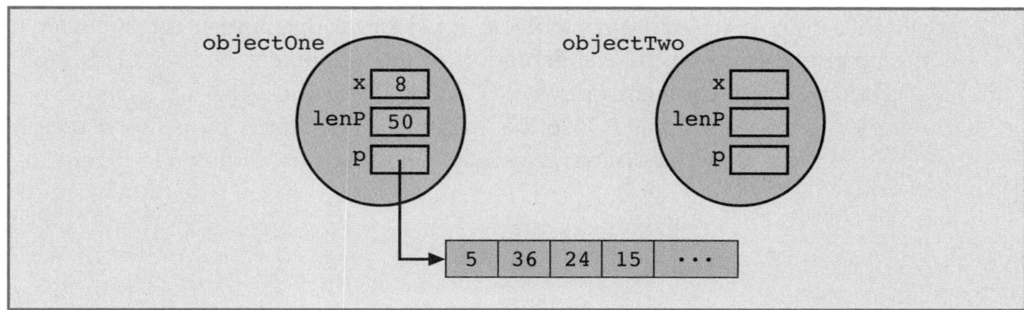

Figure 15-17 Objects `objectOne` and `objectTwo`

15

Recall that one of the built-in operations on classes is the assignment operator. For example, the statement

```
objectTwo = objectOne;
```

copies the data members of `objectOne` into `objectTwo`. That is, the value of `objectOne.x` is copied into `objectTwo.x`, and the value of `objectOne.p` is copied into `objectTwo.p`. Because `p` is a pointer, this member-wise copying of data would lead to a shallow copying of data. That is, both `objectTwo.p` and `objectOne.p` would point to the same memory space, as shown in Figure 15-18.

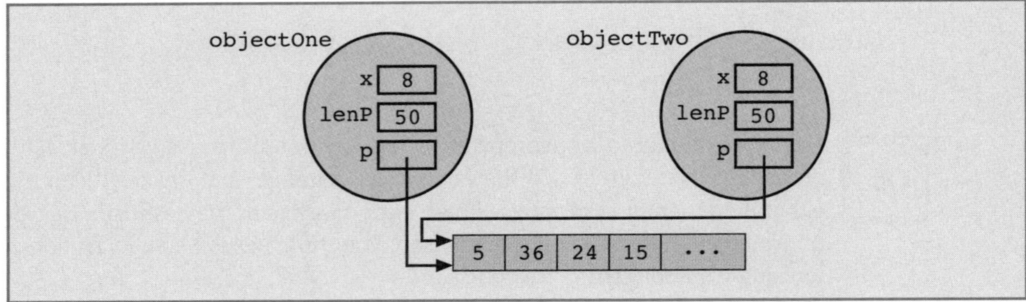

Figure 15-18 Objects `objectOne` and `objectTwo` after `objectTwo = objectOne;` executes

Now if `objectTwo.p` deallocates the memory space to which it points, `objectOne.p` would become invalid. This situation could very well happen, if the **`class`** `pointerDataClass` has a destructor that deallocates the memory space pointed to by `p` when an object of the type `pointerDataClass` goes out of scope. It suggests that there must be a way to avoid this pitfall. To avoid this shallow copying of data for classes with a pointer data member, C++ allows the programmer to extend the definition of the assignment operator. This process is called overloading the assignment operator. Chapter 16 explains how to accomplish this task by using operator overloading. Once the assignment operator is properly overloaded, both the objects `objectOne` and `objectTwo` have their own data, as shown in Figure 15-19.

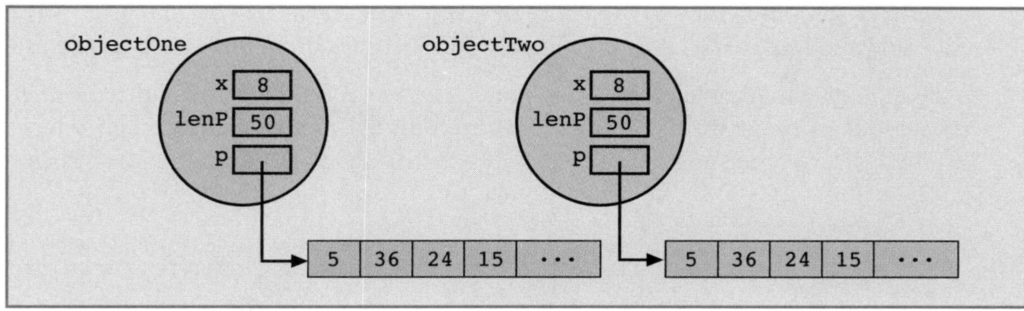

Figure 15-19 Objects `objectOne` and `objectTwo`

The Copy Constructor

When declaring a class object, you can initialize it by using the value of an existing object of the same type. For example, consider the following statement:

```
pointerDataClass objectThree(objectOne);
```

The object `objectThree` is being declared and is also being initialized by using the value of `objectOne`. That is, the values of the data members of `objectOne` are copied into the corresponding data members of `objectThree`. This initialization is called the default member-wise initialization. The default member-wise initialization is due to the constructor, called the **copy constructor** (provided by the compiler.) Just as in the case of the assignment operator, because the `class pointerDataClass` has pointer data members, this default initialization would lead to a shallow copying of the data as shown in Figure 15-20. (Assume that `objectOne` is given as before.)

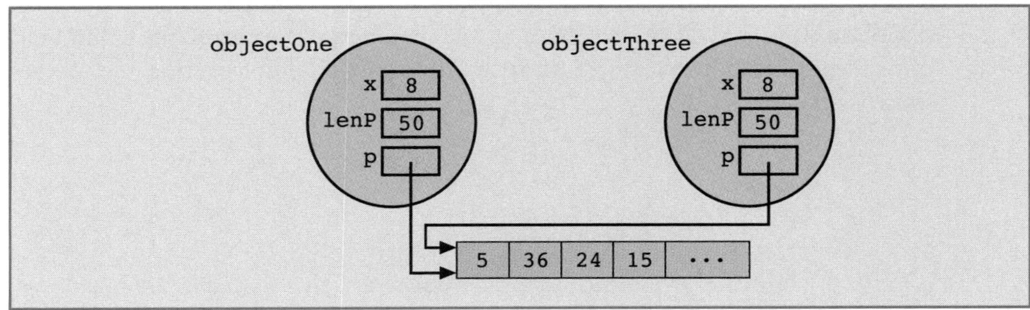

Figure 15-20 Objects `objectOne` and `objectThree`

Before describing how to overcome this deficiency, let us describe one more situation, which could also lead to a shallow copying of data. The solution to both these problems is the same.

Recall that, as parameters to a function, class objects can be passed either by reference or by value. Remember that the **class pointerDataClass** has the destructor, which deallocates the memory space pointed to by **p**. Suppose that **objectOne** is as shown in Figure 15-21.

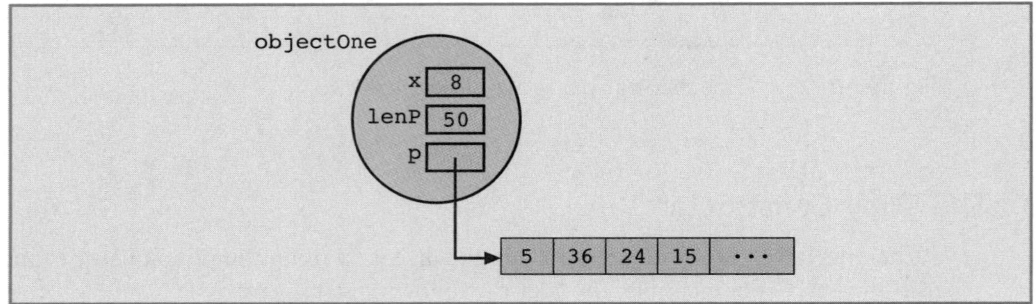

Figure 15-21 Object **objectOne**

Let us consider the following function prototype:

```
void destroyList(pointerDataClass  paramObject);
```

The function **pointerDataClass** has a formal value parameter, **paramObject**. Now consider the following statement:

```
destroyList(objectOne);
```

In this statement, **objectOne** is passed as a parameter to the function **destroyList**. Because **paramObject** is a value parameter, the copy constructor copies the data members of **objectOne** into the corresponding data members of **paramObject**. Just as in the previous case, **paramObject.p** and **objectOne.p** would point to the same memory space, as shown in Figure 15-22.

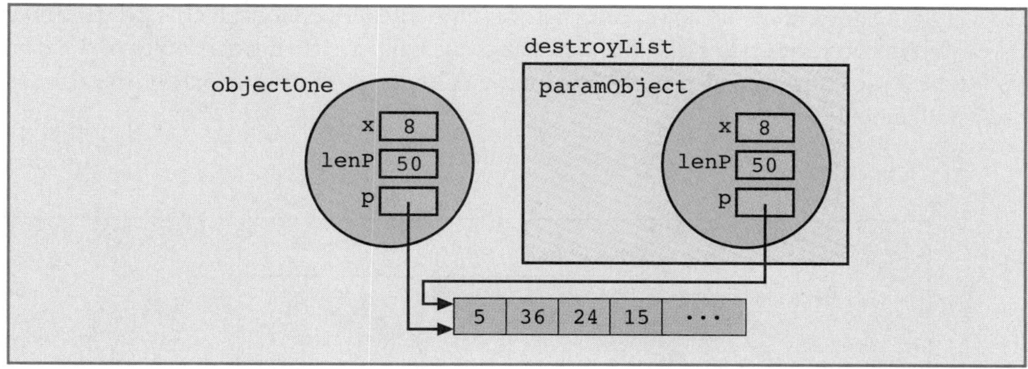

Figure 15-22 Pointer data members of objects `objectOne` and `paramObject` pointing to the same array

Because **`objectOne`** is passed by value, the data members of **`paramObject`** should have their own copy of the data. In particular, **`paramObject.p`** should have its own memory space. How do we ensure that this is, in fact, the case?

If a class has pointer data members:

- During object declaration, the initialization of one object using the value of another object would lead to a shallow copying of the data if the default member-wise copying of data is allowed.
- If, as a parameter, an object is passed by value and the default member-wise copying of data is allowed, it would lead to a shallow copying of the data.

In both cases, to force each object to have its own copy of the data, we must override the definition of the copy constructor provided by the compiler, that is, we must provide our own definition of the copy constructor. This is usually done by putting a statement that includes the copy constructor in the definition of the class, and then writing the definition of the copy constructor. Then, whenever the copy constructor needs to be executed, the system would execute the definition of the copy constructor provided by us, not the one provided by the compiler. Therefore, for the **`class pointerDataClass`**, we can overcome this shallow copying of data problem by including the copy constructor in the **`class pointerDataClass`**. Example 15-5 illustrates this.

The copy constructor automatically executes in two situations (as described in the previous list):

- When an object is declared and initialized by using the value of another object
- When, as a parameter, an object is passed by value

Therefore, once the copy constructor is properly defined for the class `pointerDataClass`, both `objectOne.p` and `objectThree.p` will have their own copies of the data. Similarly, `objectOne.p` and `paramObject.p` will have their own copies of the data, as shown in Figure 15-23.

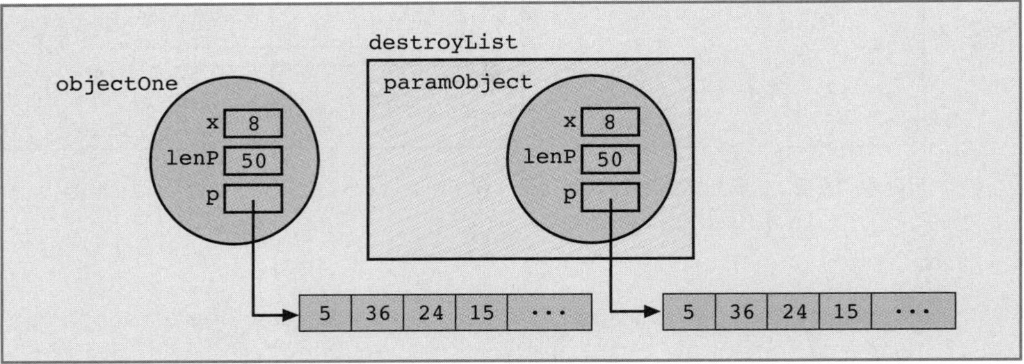

Figure 15-23 Pointer data members of objects `objectOne` and `paramObject` with their own data

When the function `destroyList` exits, the formal parameter `paramObject` goes out of scope, and the destructor for the object `paramObject` deallocates the memory space pointed to by `paramObject.p`. However, this deallocation has no effect on `objectOne`.

The general syntax to include the copy constructor in the definition of a class is

```
className(const className& otherObject);
```

Example 15-5 illustrates how to include the copy constructor in a class and how it works.

Example 15-5

Consider the following class:

```
class pointerDataClass
{
public:
    void print() const;
      //Function to output the value of x and
      //the value of the array p
    void setData();
      //Function to input data into x and
      //into the array p
```

```
    void destroyP();
      //Function to deallocates the memory space
      //occupied by the array p

    pointerDataClass(int sizeP = 10);
      //constructor
      //Creates an array of the size specified by the
      //parameter sizeP; the default array size is 10

    ~pointerDataClass();
      //destructor
      //deallocates the memory space occupied by the array p

    pointerDataClass (const pointerDataClass& otherObject);
      //copy constructor

private:
    int x;
    int lenP;
    int *p;       //pointer to an int array
};
```

Suppose that the definitions of the members of the `class pointerDataClass` are as follows:

```
void pointerDataClass::print() const
{
      cout<<"x = "<<x<<endl;

      cout<<"p = ";

      for(int i = 0; i < lenP; i++)
          cout<<p[i]<<" ";
      cout<<endl;
}

void pointerDataClass::setData()
{
      cout<<"Enter an integer for x: ";
      cin>>x;
      cout<<endl;

      cout<<"Enter "<<lenP<<" numbers: ";

      for(int i = 0; i < lenP; i++)
          cin>>p[i];

      cout<<endl;
}
```

```
void pointerDataClass::destroyP()
{
      lenP = 0;
      delete [] p;
      p = NULL;
}

pointerDataClass::pointerDataClass(int sizeP)
{
      x = 0;

      if(sizeP <= 0)
      {
         cout<<"Array size must be positive"<<endl;
         cout<<"Creating an array of size 10"<<endl;

         lenP = 10;
      }
      else
         lenP = sizeP;

      p = new int[lenP];
}

pointerDataClass::~pointerDataClass()
{
      delete [] p;
}

         //copy constructor
pointerDataClass::pointerDataClass
                  (const pointerDataClass& otherObject)
{
      x = otherObject.x;

      lenP = otherObject.lenP;
      p = new int[lenP];

      for(int i = 0; i < lenP; i++)
          p[i] = otherObject.p[i];

}
```

Consider the following function **main**. (We assume that the definition of the **class** **pointerDataClass** is in the header file **ptrDataClass.h**.)

```
#include <iostream>
#include "ptrDataClass.h"

using namespace std;
```

```
void testCopyConst(pointerDataClass temp);

int main()
{
      pointerDataClass one(5);                          //Line 1

      one.setData();                                    //Line 2
      cout<<"Line 3: ###Object one's data###"<<endl;    //Line 3
      one.print();                                      //Line 4
      cout<<"Line 5:______________________________"
         <<"______________"<<endl;                      //Line 5

      pointerDataClass two(one);                        //Line 6

      cout<<"Line 7: ^^^Object two's data^^^"<<endl;    //Line 7
      two.print();                                      //Line 8
      cout<<"Line 9:______________________________"
         <<"______________"<<endl;                      //Line 9

      two.destroyP();                                   //Line 10

      cout<<"Line 11: ~~~ Object one's data after "
         <<"destroying object two.p ~~~"<<endl;         //Line 11
      one.print();                                      //Line 12
      cout<<"Line 13:______________________________"
         <<"______________"<<endl;                      //Line 13

      cout<<"Line 14: Calling the function testCopyConst"
         <<endl;                                        //Line 14

      testCopyConst(one);                               //Line 15

      cout<<"Line 16:______________________________"
         <<"______________"<<endl;                      //Line 16

      cout<<"Line 17: After a call to the function "
         <<"testCopyConst, object one is:"<<endl;       //Line 17

      one.print();                                      //Line 18

      return 0;                                         //Line 19
}

void testCopyConst(pointerDataClass temp)
{
      cout<<"Line 20: *** Inside function "
         <<"testCopyConst ***"<<endl;                   //Line 20

      cout<<"Line 21: Object temp data:"<<endl;         //Line 21
      temp.print();                                     //Line 22
```

```
        temp.setData();                                    //Line 23
        cout<<"Line 24: After changing the object "
            <<"temp, its data is: "<<endl;                 //Line 24
        temp.print();                                      //Line 25

        cout<<"Line 26: *** Exiting function "
            <<"testCopyConst ***"<<endl;                   //Line 26
}
```

Sample Run: In this sample run, the user input is shaded.

```
Enter an integer for x: 28

Enter 5 numbers: 2 4 6 8 10

Line 3: ###Object one's data###
x = 28
p = 2 4 6 8 10
Line 5:______________________________________________
Line 7: ^^^Object two's data^^^
x = 28
p = 2 4 6 8 10
Line 9:______________________________________________
Line 11: ~~~ Object one's data after destroying object two.p ~~~
x = 28
p = 2 4 6 8 10
Line 13:_____________________________________________
Line 14: Calling the function testCopyConst
Line 20: *** Inside function testCopyConst ***
Line 21: Object temp data:
x = 28
p = 2 4 6 8 10
Enter an integer for x: 65

Enter 5 numbers: 1 3 5 7 9

Line 24: After changing the object temp, its data is:
x = 65
p = 1 3 5 7 9
Line 26: *** Exiting function testCopyConst ***
Line 16:_____________________________________________
Line 17: After a call to the function testCopyConst, object one is:
x = 28
p = 2 4 6 8 10
```

This is how the function `main` works. The statement in Line 1 creates an object `one` of the type `pointerDataClass`. This statement also creates an array of size `5` and stores the base address of the array into `one.p`, that is, `one.p` points to the array. The statements in Lines 2 through 5 input the data into `one` and also output the data of `one`. The statement in Line 6 creates the object `two` and also initializes `two` using the value of `one`. The copy constructor copies `one.x` into `two.x`, creates an array of size `5` and stores the base address of the array into `two.p` and then copies the array `one.p` into `two.p`. That is, both `one.p` and `two.p` have their own copy of the data. The statements in Lines 8 through 13 illustrate this. For example, the statement in Line 8 outputs the data of `two`, the statement in Line 11 deallocates the memory space pointed to by `two.p`, and the statement in Line 12 outputs the value of `one`. Similarly, the statements in Lines 15 through 19 illustrate that when object `one` is passed as a parameter by value to the function `testCopyConst`, the copy constructor provides the formal parameter `test` with its own copy of the data. Within the definition of the function `testCopyConst`, the value of `temp` is changed, which has no effect on `one`. Moreover, when the function `testCopyConst` terminates, the destructor of the `class` `pointerDataClass` deallocates the memory space occupied by `temp.p`, which has no effect on `one.p`.

For classes with pointer data members, three things are normally done:

1. Include the destructor in the class.
2. Overload the assignment operator for the class.
3. Include the copy constructor.

Chapter 16 discusses the overloading of the assignment operator. Until then, whenever we discuss classes with pointer data members, out of the three items in the previous list, we will implement only the destructor and the copy constructor.

INHERITANCE, POINTERS, AND VIRTUAL FUNCTIONS

15

This section can be skipped without experiencing any discontinuation.

Recall that, as a parameter, a class object can be passed either by value or by reference. Earlier chapters also said that the types of the actual and formal parameters must match. However, in the case of classes, C++ allows the user to pass an object of a derived class to a formal parameter of the base class type.

First, let us discuss the case when the formal parameter is either a reference parameter or a pointer. To be specific, let us consider the following classes:

```
class baseClass
{
public:
    void print();
    baseClass(int u = 0);

private:
    int x;
};

class derivedClass: public baseClass
{
public:
    void print();
    derivedClass(int u = 0, int v = 0);

private:
    int a;
};
```

The `class baseClass` is a class that has three members. The `class derivedClass` is derived from the `class baseClass` and it also has three members of its own. Both classes have a member function `print`. Suppose that the definitions of the member functions of both classes are as follows:

```
void baseClass::print()
{
      cout<<"In baseClass x = "<<x<<endl;
}

baseClass::baseClass(int u)
{
      x = u;
}

void derivedClass::print()
{
      cout<<"In derivedClass ***: ";
      baseClass::print();
      cout<<"In derivedClass a = "<<a<<endl;
}

derivedClass::derivedClass(int u, int v)
                : baseClass(u)
{
    a = v;
}
```

Consider the following function:

```
void callPrint(baseClass& p)
{
      p.print();
}
```

The function `callPrint` has a formal parameter `p` of the type `baseClass`. You can call the function `callPrint` by using an object of either the type `baseClass` or the type `derivedClass` as a parameter. Moreover, the body of the function `callPrint` calls the member function `print`. Consider the following function `main`:

```
int main()
{
   baseClass one(5);                          //Line 1
   derivedClass two(3, 15);                   //Line 2

   one.print();                               //Line 3
   two.print();                               //Line 4

   cout<<"*** Calling the function callPrint  ***"
       <<endl;                                //Line 5
   callPrint(one);                            //Line 6
   callPrint(two);                            //Line 7

   return 0;
}
```

Output

```
In baseClass x = 5
In derivedClass ***: In baseClass x = 3
In derivedClass a = 15
*** Calling the function callPrint  ***
In baseClass x = 5
In baseClass x = 3
```


The statements in Lines 1 through 5 are quite straightforward. Let us look at the statements in Lines 6 and 7. The statement in Line 6 calls the function `callPrint` and passes the object `one` as the parameter; it generates the fifth line of the output. The statement in Line 7 also calls the function `callPrint`, but passes the object `two` as the parameter; it generates the sixth line of the output. The output generated by the statements in Lines 6 and 7 shows only the value of `x`, even though each time a different class type object was passed as a parameter. (Because in Line 7 object `two` is passed as a parameter to the function `callPrint`, the output generated by the statement in Line 7 should be the same as the second and third lines of the output.) This is because for both statements (Lines 6 and 7), the member function `print` of the `class baseClass` is executed. This is due to the fact that the binding of the member function `print`, in the body of the function `callPrint`, occurred at compile time. Because the formal parameter `p` of the function `callPrint` is of the type `baseClass`, for the statement `p.print();`, the compiler associates the function `print` of the `class baseClass`. More specifically, in **compile-time binding**, the necessary code to call a specific function is generated by the compiler. (Compile-time binding is also known as **static binding**.)

For the statement in Line 7, the actual parameter is of the type `derivedClass`. Thus, when the body of function `two` executes, logically the `print` function of object `two` should execute, which is not the case. So, during program execution, how does C++ correct this problem of making the call to the appropriate function? C++ corrects this problem by providing the mechanism of **virtual functions**. The binding of virtual functions occurs at program execution time, not at compile time. This kind of binding is called the **run-time binding**. More formally, in run-time binding, the compiler does not generate the code to call a specific function; instead, it generates enough information to enable the run-time system to generate the specific code for the appropriate function call. Run-time binding is also known as **dynamic binding**.

In C++, virtual functions are declared using the reserved word `virtual`. Let us redefine the previous classes using this feature:

```
class baseClass
{
public:
    virtual void print();            //virtual function
    baseClass(int u = 0);

private:
    int x;
};

class derivedClass: public baseClass
{
public:
    void print();
    derivedClass(int u = 0, int v = 0);

private:
    int a;
};
```

Note that we need to declare a `virtual` function only in the base `class`.

The definition of the member function `print` is the same as before. If we execute the previous program with these modifications, the output is as follows.

Output

```
In baseClass x = 5
In derivedClass ***: In baseClass x = 3
In derivedClass a = 15
*** Calling the function callPrint  ***
In baseClass x = 5
In derivedClass ***: In baseClass x = 3
In derivedClass a = 15
```

This output shows that for the statement in Line 7, the `print` function of `derivedClass` is executed (see the last two lines of the output).

The previous discussion also applies when a formal parameter is a pointer to a class, and a pointer of the derived class is passed as an actual parameter. To illustrate this feature, suppose we have the above classes. (We assume that the definition of the `class baseClass` is in the header file `baseClass.h`, and the definition of the `class derivedClass` is in the header file `derivedClass.h`.) Consider the following program:

```
//Chapter 15: Virtual Functions

#include <iostream>

#include "derivedClass.h"

using namespace std;

void callPrint(baseClass *p);

int main()
{
   baseClass *q;                                   //Line 1
   derivedClass *r;                                //Line 2

   q = new baseClass(5);                           //Line 3
   r = new derivedClass(3,15);                     //Line 4

   q->print();                                     //Line 5
   r->print();                                     //Line 6

   cout<<"*** Calling the function callPrint  ***"
       <<endl;                                     //Line 7
   callPrint(q);                                   //Line 8
   callPrint(r);                                   //Line 9

   return 0;
}

void callPrint(baseClass *p)
{
      p->print();
}
```

Output

```
In baseClass x = 5
In derivedClass ***: In baseClass x = 3
In derivedClass a = 15
*** Calling the function callPrint  ***
In baseClass x = 5
In derivedClass ***: In baseClass x = 3
In derivedClass a = 15
```

The preceding examples show that if a formal parameter, say **p** of a class type is either a reference parameter or a pointer and **p** uses a virtual function of the base class, we can effectively pass a derived class object as an actual parameter to **p**. However, if **p** is a value parameter, then this mechanism of passing a derived class object as an actual parameter to **p** does not work even if **p** uses a virtual function. Recall that, if a formal parameter is a value parameter, the value of the actual parameter is copied into the formal parameter. Therefore, if a formal parameter is of the type **class**, the data members of the actual object are copied into the corresponding data members of the formal parameter.

Suppose that we have the above classes—that is, **baseClass** and **derivedClass**. Consider the following function definition:

```
void callPrint(baseClass p)   //p is a value parameter
{
      p.print();
}
```

Further suppose that we have the following declaration:

```
derivedClass two;
```

The object **two** has two data members, **x** and **a**. The data member **x** is inherited from the base class. Consider the following function call:

```
callPrint(two);
```

In this statement, because the formal parameter **p** is a value parameter, the data members of **two** are copied into the data members of **p**. However, because **p** is an object of the type **baseClass**, it has only one data member. Consequently, only the data member **x** of **two** will be copied into the data member **x** of **p**. Also, the statement

```
p.print();
```

in the body of the function will result in executing the member function **print** of the **class baseClass**.

The output of the following program further illustrates this concept. (As before, we assume that the definition of the `class baseClass` is in the header file `baseClass.h`, and the definition of the `class derivedClass` is in the header file `derivedClass.h`.)

```
//Chapter 15: Virtual functions and value parameters

#include <iostream>

#include "derivedClass.h"

using namespace std;

void callPrint(baseClass p);

int main()
{
   baseClass one(5);                            //Line 1
   derivedClass two(3, 15);                     //Line 2

   one.print();                                 //Line 3
   two.print();                                 //Line 4

   cout<<"*** Calling the function callPrint  ***"
       <<endl;                                  //Line 5
   callPrint(one);                              //Line 6
   callPrint(two);                              //Line 7

   return 0;
}

void callPrint(baseClass p) //p is a value parameter
{
      p.print();
}
```

Output

```
In baseClass x = 5
In derivedClass ***: In baseClass x = 3
In derivedClass a = 15
*** Calling the function callPrint  ***
In baseClass x = 5
In baseClass x = 3
```

Look closely at the output of the statements in Lines 6 and 7 (the last two lines of output). In Line 7, because the formal parameter `p` is a value parameter, the data members of `two` are copied into the data members of `p`. However, because `p` is an object of the type `baseClass`, it has only one data member. Consequently, only the data member `x` of `two` is copied into the data member `x` of `p`. Moreover, the statement `p.print();` in the function `callPrint` executes the function `print` of the `class baseClass`, not the `class derivedClass`. Therefore, the last line of output shows only the value of `x` (the data member of `two`).

An object of the base class type cannot be passed to a formal parameter of the derived class type.

Classes and Virtual Destructors

One thing recommended for classes with pointer data members is that these classes must have the destructor. The destructor is automatically executed when the class object goes out of scope. Thus, if the object creates dynamic objects, the destructor can be designed to deallocate the storage for them. If a derived class object is passed to a formal parameter of the base class type, the destructor of the base class executes regardless of whether the derived class object is passed by reference or by value. Logically, however, the destructor of the derived class should be executed when the derived class object goes out of scope.

To correct this problem, the destructor of the base class must be virtual. The **virtual destructor** of a base class automatically makes the destructor of a derived class be virtual. When a derived class object is passed to a formal parameter of the base class type, then when the object goes out of scope, the destructor of the derived class executes. After executing the destructor of the derived class, the destructor of the base class executes. Therefore, when the derived class object is destroyed, the base class part (that is, the members inherited from the base class) of the derived class object are also destroyed.

If a base class contains virtual functions, make the destructor of the base class virtual.

THE ADDRESS OF OPERATOR AND CLASSES

This chapter has used the address of operator, `&`, to store the address of a variable into a pointer variable. The address of operator is also used to create aliases to an object. Consider the following statements:

```
int x;
int &y = x;
```

The first statement declares `x` to be an `int` variable, and the second statement declares `y` to be an alias of `x`. That is, both `x` and `y` refer to the same memory location. Thus, `y` is like a constant pointer variable. The statement

```
y = 25;
```

sets the value of **y** (and hence) the value of **x** to 25. Similarly, the statement

```
x = 2 * x + 30;
```

updates the value of **x** (and hence) the value of **y**.

The address of operator can also be used to return the address of a **private** data member of a class. However, if you are not careful, this operation can result in serious errors in the program. The following example helps illustrate this idea.

Consider the following class definition:

```
//header file testadd.h
#ifndef H_testAdd
#define H_testAdd

class testAddress
{
public:
    void setX(int);

    void printX() const;
    int& addressOfX();    //this function returns the
                          //address of the private data member

private:
    int x;
};

#endif
```

The definitions of the functions to implement the member functions are as follows:

```
//Implementation file testAdd.cpp
#include <iostream>
#include "testAdd.h"
using namespace std;

void testAddress::setX(int inX)
{
      x = inX;
}

void testAddress::printX() const
{
     cout<<x;
}

int& testAddress::addressOfX()
{
   return x;
}
```

Because the return type of the function **addressOfX** is an address to an **int** memory location, the statement

```
return x;
```

returns the address of **x**.

Next, let us write a simple program that uses the **class testAddress** and illustrates what can go wrong. Later, we will show how to fix the problem.

```
//Test program
#include <iostream>
#include "testAdd.h"
using namespace std;

int main()
{
        testAddress a;
        int &y = a.addressOfX();

        a.setX(50);
        cout<<"x in class testAddress = ";
        a.printX();
        cout<<endl;

        y = 25;
        cout<<"After y = 25, x in class testAddress = ";
        a.printX();
        cout<<endl;

        return 0;
}
```

Output

```
x in class testAddress = 50
After y = 25, x in class testAddress = 25
```

In the preceding program, after the statement:

```
int &y = a.addressOfX();
```

executes, **y** becomes an alias of the **private** data member **x** of the object **a**. Thus, the statement

```
y = 25;
```

changes the value of **x**.

Chapter 13 said that **private** data members are not accessible outside the class. However, by returning their addresses, the programmer can manipulate them. One way to resolve this problem is to never provide the user of the class with the addresses of the **private** data members. Sometimes, however, it is necessary to return the address of a **private** data member, as we will see in the next chapter. How can we prevent the program from directly manipulating the **private** data members? To fix this problem, we use the word **const** before the return type of the function. This way, we can still return the addresses of the **private** data members, but at the same time prevent the programmer from directly manipulating the **private** data members. Let us rewrite the **class testAddress** using this feature.

```
#ifndef H_testAdd
#define H_testAdd

class testAddress
{
public:
    void setX(int);
    void printX() const;
    const int& addressOfX(); //this function returns the
                             //address of the private data
                             //member
private:
    int x;
};
#endif
```

The definition of the function **addressOfX** in the implementation file is

```
const int& testAddress::addressOfX()
{
   return x;
}
```

The same program will now generate a compile-time error.

QUICK REVIEW

1. Pointer variables contain the addresses of other variables as their values.
2. In C++, no name is associated with the pointer data type.
3. A pointer variable is declared using an asterisk, `*`, between the data type and the variable. For example, the statements

   ```
   int *p;
   char *ch;
   ```

   declare `p` and `ch` to be pointer variables. The value of `p` points to a memory space of the type `int`, and the value of `ch` points to a memory space of the type `char`. Usually, `p` is called a pointer variable of the type `int`, and `ch` is called a pointer variable of the type `char`.
4. In C++, `&` is called the address of operator.
5. The address of operator returns the address of its operand. For example, if `p` is a pointer variable of the type `int` and `num` is an `int` variable, the statement

   ```
   p = &num;
   ```

   sets the value of `p` to the address of `num`.
6. When used as a unary operator, `*` is called the dereferencing operator.
7. The memory location indicated by the value of a pointer variable is accessed by using the dereferencing operator, `*`. For example, if `p` is a pointer variable of the type `int`, the statement

   ```
   *p = 25;
   ```

   sets the value of the memory location indicated by the value of `p` to `25`.
8. You can use the member access operator arrow, `->`, to access the component of an object pointed to by a pointer.
9. Pointer variables are initialized using either `0` (the integer zero), `NULL`, or the address of a variable of the same type.
10. The only number that can be directly assigned to a pointer variable is `0`.
11. The only arithmetic operations allowed on pointer variables are increment (`++`), decrement (`--`), addition of an integer to a pointer variable, subtraction of an integer from a pointer variable, and subtraction of a pointer from another pointer.
12. Pointer arithmetic is different from ordinary arithmetic. When an integer is added to a pointer, the value added to the value of the pointer variable is the integer times the size of the object to which the pointer is pointing. Similarly, when an integer is subtracted from a pointer, the value subtracted from the value of the pointer variable is the integer times the size of the object to which the pointer is pointing.
13. Pointer variables can be compared using relational operators. (It makes sense to compare pointers of the same type.)

14. The value of one pointer variable can be assigned to another pointer variable of the same type.
15. A variable created during program execution is called a dynamic variable.
16. The operator `new` is used to create a dynamic variable.
17. The operator `delete` is used to deallocate the memory occupied by a dynamic variable.
18. In C++, both `new` and `delete` are reserved words.
19. The operator `new` has two forms: one to create a single dynamic variable, and another to create an array of dynamic variables.
20. If `p` is a pointer of the type `int`, the statement

    ```
    p = new int;
    ```

    allocates storage of the type `int` somewhere in memory and stores the address of the allocated storage in `p`.
21. The operator `delete` has two forms: one to deallocate the memory occupied by a single dynamic variable, and another to deallocate the memory occupied by an array of dynamic variables.
22. If `p` is a pointer of the type `int`, the statement

    ```
    delete p;
    ```

    deallocates the memory pointed to by `p`.
23. The array name is a constant pointer. It always points to the same memory location, which is the location of the first array component.
24. To create a dynamic array, the form of the `new` operator that creates an array of dynamic variables is used. For example, if `p` is a pointer of the type `int`, the statement

    ```
    p = new int[10];
    ```

    creates an array of `10` components of the type `int`. The base address of the array is stored in `p`. We call `p` a dynamic array.
25. Array notation can be used to access the components of a dynamic array. For example, suppose `p` is a dynamic array of 10 components. Then `p[0]` refers to the first array component, `p[1]` refers to the second array component, and so on. In particular, `p[i]` refers to the `(i + 1)`th component of the array.
26. An array created during program execution is called a dynamic array.
27. If `p` is a dynamic array, then the statement

    ```
    delete [] p;
    ```

    deallocates the memory occupied by `p`—that is, the components of `p`.
28. In a shallow copy, two or more pointers of the same type point to the same memory space; that is, they point to the same data.
29. In a deep copy, two or more pointers of the same type have their own copies of the data.

30. If a class has a destructor, the destructor is automatically executed whenever a class object goes out of scope.
31. If a class has pointer data members, the built-in assignment operators provide a shallow copy of the data.
32. A copy constructor executes when an object is declared and initialized by using the value of another object, and when an object is passed by value as a parameter.
33. C++ allows a user to pass an object of a derived class to a formal parameter of the base class type.
34. The binding of virtual functions occurs at execution time, not at compile time, and is called dynamic or run-time binding.
35. In C++, virtual functions are declared using the reserved word `virtual`.
36. The address of operator can be used to return the address of a `private` data member of a class.

EXERCISES

1. Mark the following statements as true or false.
   a. In C++, `pointer` is a reserved word.
   b. In C++, pointer variables are declared using the reserved word `pointer`.
   c. The statement `delete p;` deallocates the variable pointer `p`.
   d. The statement `delete p;` deallocates the dynamic variable that is pointed to by `p`.
   e. Given the declaration

      ```
      int list[10];
      int *p;
      ```

      the statement

      ```
      p = list;
      ```

      is valid in C++.
   f. Given the declaration

      ```
      int *p;
      ```

      the statement

      ```
      p = new int[50];
      ```

      dynamically allocates an array of `50` components of the type `int`, and `p` contains the base address of the array.
   g. The address of operator returns the address and value of its operand.
   h. If `p` is a pointer variable, then the statement `p = p * 2;` is valid in C++.

2. Given the declaration

```
int x;
int *p;
int *q;
```

Mark the following statements as valid or invalid. If a statement is invalid, explain why.

a. `p = q;`

b. `*p = 56;`

c. `p = x;`

d. `*p = *q;`

e. `q = &x;`

f. `*p = q;`

3. What is the output of the following C++ code?

```
int x;
int y;
int *p = &x;
int *q = &y;
*p = 35;
*q = 98;
*p = *q;
cout<<x<<"  "<<y<<endl;
cout<<*p<<"  "<<*q<<endl;
```

4. What is the output of the following C++ code?

```
int x;
int y;
int *p = &x;
int *q = &y;
x = 35;  y = 46;
p = q;
*p = 78;
cout<<x<<"  "<<y<<endl;
cout<<*p<<"  "<<*q<<endl;
```

5. Given the declaration

```
int num = 6;
int *p = &num;
```

which of the following statement(s) increment the value of num?

a. `p++;`

b. `(*p)++;`

c. `num++`

d. `(*num)++;`

6. What is the output of the following code?

```
int *p;
int *q;
p = new int;
q = p;
*p = 46;
*q = 39;
cout<<*p<<" "<<*q<<endl;
```

7. What is the output of the following code?

```
int *p;
int *q;
p = new int;
*p = 43;
q = p;
*q = 52;
p = new int;
*p = 78;
q = new int;
*q = *p;
cout<<*p<<" "<<*q<<endl;
```

8. What is wrong with the following code ?

```
int *p;                          //Line 1
int *q;                          //Line 2

p = new int;                     //Line 3
*p = 43;                         //Line 4

q = p;                           //Line 5
*q = 52;                         //Line 6

delete q;                        //Line 7

cout<<*p<<" "<<*q<<endl;         //Line 8
```

9. What is the output of the following code?

```
int x ;
int *p ;
int *q ;
p = new int[10] ;
q = p ;
*p = 4 ;
```

```
for(int j = 0; j < 10; j++)
{
    x = *p ;
    p++;
    *p = x + j ;
}

for(int k = 0; k < 10; k++)
{
    cout<<*q<<" ";
    q++;
}
cout<<endl;
```

10. What is the output of the following code?

```
int *secret;
int j;

secret = new int[10] ;
secret[0] = 10 ;
for(j = 1; j < 10; j++)
  secret[j] = secret[j -1] + 5 ;
for(j = 0; j < 10; j++)
  cout<<secret[j]<<" ";
cout<<endl;
```

11. Explain the difference between a shallow copy and a deep copy of data.

12. What is wrong with the following code?

```
int *p;                          //Line 1
int *q;                          //Line 2

p = new int [5];                 //Line 3
*p = 2;                          //Line 4

for(int i = 1; i < 5; i++)       //Line 5
     p[i] = p[i-1] + i;          //Line 6

q = p;                           //Line 6

delete [] p;                     //Line 7

for(int j = 0; j < 5; j++)       //Line 8
     cout<<q[j]<<" ";            //Line 9

cout<<endl;                      //Line 10
```

13. What is the output of the following code?

```
int *p;
int *q;
int i;

p = new int [5];
p[0] = 5;

for(i = 1; i < 5; i++)
   p[i] = p[i-1] + 2 * i;

cout<<"Array p: ";
for(i = 0; i < 5; i++)
   cout<<p[i]<<" ";
cout<<endl;

q = new int[5];

for(i = 0; i < 5; i++)
   q[i] = p[4 - i];

cout<<"Array q: ";
for(i = 0; i < 5; i++)
   cout<<q[i]<<" ";

cout<<endl;
```

14. What is the purpose of a copy constructor?
15. Name two situations when a copy constructor executes.
16. Name three things that you should do for classes with pointer data members.
17. Suppose that you have the following classes, `classA` and `classB`:

```
class classA
{
public:
    virtual void print() const;
    void doubleNum();
    classA(int a = 0);
private:
    int x;
};

void classA::print() const
{
    cout<<"ClassA x: "<<x<<endl;
}
```

```
void classA::doubleNum()
{
    x = 2 * x;
}

classA::classA(int a)
{
    x = a;
}

class classB: public classA
{
public:
    void print() const;
    void doubleNum();
    classB(int a = 0, int b = 0);
private:
    int y;
};

void classB::print() const
{
    classA::print();
    cout<<"ClassB y: "<<y<<endl;
}

void classB::doubleNum()
{
    classA::doubleNum();

    y = 2 * y;
}

classB::classB(int a, int b)
        : classA(a)
{
    y = b;
}
```

What is the output of the following function **main**?

```
int main()
{
    classA *ptrA;
    classA objectA(2);

    classB objectB(3,5);

    ptrA = &objectA;
    ptrA->doubleNum();
    ptrA->print();
    cout<<endl;

    ptrA = &objectB;

    ptrA->doubleNum();
    ptrA->print();
    cout<<endl;

    return 0;
}
```

18. What is the output of the function **main** of Exercise 17, if the definition of **classA** is replaced by the following definition:

```
class classA
{
public:
    virtual void print() const;
    virtual void doubleNum();
    classA(int a = 0);
private:
    int x;
};
```

19. What is the difference between compile-time binding and run-time binding?

PROGRAMMING EXERCISES

1. Redo Programming Exercise 5 of Chapter 9 using dynamic arrays.
2. Redo Programming Exercise 6 of Chapter 9 using dynamic arrays.
3. Redo Programming Exercise 7 of Chapter 9 using dynamic arrays. You must ask the user for the number of candidates, and then create the appropriate arrays to hold the data.

CHAPTER

16

OVERLOADING AND TEMPLATES

In this chapter, you will:

- Learn about overloading
- Become aware of the restrictions on operator overloading
- Examine the pointer `this`
- Learn about `friend` functions
- Explore the members and nonmembers of a class
- Discover how to overload various operators
- Learn about templates
- Explore how to construct function templates and class templates

In Chapter 13, you learned how classes in C++ are used to combine data, and operations on that data, in a single entity. The ability to combine data, and operations on that data, is called encapsulation. It is the first principle of object-oriented design (OOD). Chapter 13 defined the abstract data type (ADT) and described how classes in C++ implement ADT. Chapter 14 discussed how new classes can be derived from existing classes through the mechanism of inheritance. Inheritance, the second principle of OOD, encourages code reuse.

This chapter's first topic is **operator overloading**; its second subject is **templates**. Templates enable the programmer to write generic codes for related functions and classes. We will simplify function overloading through the use of templates, called **function templates**.

Why Operator Overloading Is Needed

Chapter 13 defined and implemented the `class clockType`. It also showed how you can use the `class clockType` to represent the time of day in a program. Let us review some of the characteristics of the `class clockType`.

Consider the following statements:

```
clockType myClock(8,23,34);
clockType yourClock(4,5,30);
```

The first statement declares `myClock` to be an object of the type `clockType` and initializes the data members `hr`, `min`, and `sec` of `myClock` to `8`, `23`, and `34`, respectively. The second statement declares `yourClock` to be an object of the type `clockType` and initializes the data members `hr`, `min`, and `sec` of `yourClock` to `4`, `5`, and `30`, respectively.

Now consider the following statements:

```
myClock.printTime();
myClock.incrementSeconds();
if(myClock.equalTime(yourClock))
.
.
.
```

The first statement prints the value of `myClock` in the form `hr:min:sec`. The second statement increments the value of `myClock` by one second. The third statement checks whether the value of `myClock` is the same as the value of `yourClock`.

These statements do their job. However, if we can use the insertion operator << to output the value of `myClock`, the increment operator ++ to increment the value of `myClock` by one second, and relational operators for comparison, we can enhance the flexibility of C++ considerably. More specifically, we prefer to use the following statements instead of the previous statements:

```
cout<<myClock;
myClock++;
```

```
if(myClock == yourClock)
   .
   .
   .
```

Recall that the only built-in operations on classes are the assignment operator and the member selection operator. Therefore, other operators cannot be directly applied to class objects. However, C++ allows the programmer to extend the definitions of most of the operators so that operators—such as relational operators, arithmetic operators, the insertion operator for data output, and the extraction operator for data input—can be applied to classes. In C++ terminology, this is called **operator overloading**. In addition to operator overloading, this chapter will discuss function overloading, which Chapter 7 briefly introduced.

OPERATOR OVERLOADING

Recall how the arithmetic operator / works. If both operands of / are integers, the result is an integer; otherwise, the result is a floating-point number. Similarly, the stream insertion operator << and the stream extraction operator >> are overloaded. The operator >> is used as both a stream extraction operator and a right shift operator. The operator << is used as both a stream insertion operator and a left shift operator. These are examples of operator overloading.

Other examples of overloaded operators are + and -. The results of + and - are different for integer arithmetic, floating-point arithmetic, and pointer arithmetic.

C++ allows the user to overload most of the operators so that the operators can work effectively in a specific application. It does not allow the user to create new operators. Most of the existing operators can be overloaded to manipulate class objects.

In order to overload an operator, you must write functions (that is, the header and body). The name of the function that overloads an operator is the reserved word `operator` followed by the operator to be overloaded. For example, the name of the function to overload the operator >= is

```
operator>=
```

Operator function: The function that overloads an operator.

16

Syntax for Operator Functions

The result of an operation is a value; therefore, the operator function is a value-returning function.

The syntax of the heading for an operator function is

```
returnType  operator operatorSymbol(formal parameter list)
```

In C++, `operator` is a reserved word.

Recall that the only built-in operations on classes are assignment (=) and member selection. To use other operators on class objects, they must be explicitly overloaded. Operator overloading provides the same concise expressions for user-defined data types as it does for built-in data types.

To overload an operator for a class:

1. Include the statement to declare the function to overload the operator (that is, the operator function) in the definition of the class.
2. Write the definition of the operator function.

Certain rules must be followed when you include an operator function in a class definition. These rules are described in the section, "Operator Functions as Member Functions and Nonmember Functions" later in this chapter.

Overloading an Operator: Some Restrictions

When overloading an operator, keep the following in mind:

1. You cannot change the precedence of an operator.
2. The associativity cannot be changed. (For example, the associativity of the arithmetic operator addition is from left to right and it cannot be changed.)
3. Default arguments cannot be used with an overloaded operator.
4. You cannot change the number of arguments an operator takes.
5. You cannot create new operators. Only existing operators can be overloaded. The operators that cannot be overloaded are

   `.    .*    ::    ?:    sizeof`

6. The meaning of how an operator works with built-in types, such as `int`, remains the same.
7. Operators can be overloaded either for objects of the user-defined types, or for a combination of objects of the user-defined type and objects of the built-in type.

The Pointer `this`

A member function of a class can (directly) access the data members of that class for a given object. Sometimes it is necessary for a function member to refer to the object as a whole, rather than the object's individual data members. How do you refer to the object as a whole (that is, as a single unit) in the definition of the member function, especially when the object is not passed as a parameter? Every object of a class maintains a (hidden) pointer to itself, and the name of this pointer is `this`. In C++, `this` is a reserved word. The pointer `this` is available for you to use. When an object invokes a member function, the member function references the pointer `this` of the object. For example, suppose that `test` is a class and has a member function called `one`. Further suppose that the definition of `one` looks like the following:

```
test test::one()
{
    .
    .
    .
    return *this;
}
```

If `x` and `y` are objects of the type `test`, then the statement

```
y = x.one();
```

copies the value of the object `x` into object `y`; that is, the data members of `x` are copied into the corresponding data members of `y`. When the object `x` invokes the function `one`, the pointer `this` in the definition of the member function `one` refers to the object `x`, and so `this` means the address of `x` and `*this` means the value of `x`.

The following example illustrates how the pointer `this` works.

Example 16-1

Consider the following class:

```
class thisPointerClass
{
public:
    void set(int a, int b, int c);
    void print() const;

    thisPointerClass updateXYZ();
        //Post: x = 2 * x; y = y + 2;
        //      z = z * z;

    thisPointerClass(int a = 0, int b = 0, int c = 0);

private:
    int x;
    int y;
    int z;
};
```

16

Suppose that the definitions of the member functions of the **class** thisPointerClass are as follows:

```
void thisPointerClass::set(int a, int b, int c)
{
      x = a;
      y = b;
      z = z;
}

void thisPointerClass::print() const
{
      cout<<"x = "<<x
          <<", y = "<<y
          <<", z = "<<z<<endl;
}

thisPointerClass thisPointerClass::updateXYZ()
{
      x = 2 * x;
      y = y + 2;
      z = z * z;

      return *this;
}
```

The definition of the function updateXYZ updates the values of x, y, and z. Using the pointer **this** returns the value of the entire object; that is, the values of the data members x, y, and z are returned.

```
thisPointerClass::thisPointerClass(int a, int b, int c)
{
      x = a;
      y = b;
      z = c;
}
```

Consider the following function main:

```
int main()
{
      thisPointerClass object1(3, 5, 7);          //Line 1
      thisPointerClass object2;                   //Line 2

      cout<<"Object 1: ";                         //Line 3
      object1.print();                            //Line 4

      object2 = object1.updateXYZ();              //Line 5

      cout<<"After updating object1: ";           //Line 6
      object1.print();                            //Line 7
```

```
    cout<<"Object 2: ";                         //Line 8
    object2.print();                            //Line 9

    return 0;
}
```

Output

```
Object 1: x = 3, y = 5, z = 7
After updating object1: x = 6, y = 7, z = 49
Object 2: x = 6, y = 7, z = 49
```

For the most part, the output is self-explanatory. The statement in Line 5 evaluates the expression `object1.updateXYZ()`, which updates the values of the data members of the object `object1`. The value of `object1` is then returned by the pointer `this`, as shown in the definition of the function `updateXYZ`. The assignment operator then copies the value into `object2`.

The following example also shows how the pointer `this` works.

Example 16-2

In Example 13-9 in (Chapter 13), we designed a class to implement a person's name in a program. Here, we extend the definition of the `class personType` to individually set a person's first name and last name, and then return the entire object. The extended definition of the `class personType` is

```
class personType
{
public:
    void print() const;
        //Function to output the first name and last name
        //Post: The name is printed in the form firstName lastName

    void setName(string first, string last);
        //Function to set firstName and lastName according to
        //the parameters
        //Post: firstName = first; lastName = last;

    personType& setLastName(string last);
        //Function to set the last name
        //Post: lastName = last;
        //After setting the last name, a reference
        //to the object, that is, the address of the
        //object, is returned
```

```
    personType& setFirstName(string first);
        //Function to set the first name
        //Post: firstName = first;
        //After setting the first name, a reference
        //to the object, that is, the address of the
        //object, is returned


    void getName(string& first, string& last);
        //Function to return firstName and lastName via
        //the parameters
        //Post: first = firstName; last = lastName;


    personType(string first = "", string last = "");
        //Constructor with parameters
        //Set firstName and lastName according to the parameters
        //Post: firstName = first; lastName = last;

 private:
    string firstName; //store the first name
    string lastName;  //store the last name
};
```

Notice that in this definition of the `class personType`, we replace the default constructor and the constructor with parameters by one constructor with default parameters.

The definitions of the functions `print`, `setTime`, `getName`, and the constructor is the same as before (see Example 13-9). The definitions of the functions `setFirstName` and `setLastName` are as follows:

```
personType& personType::setLastName(string last)
{
      lastName = last;

      return *this;
}

personType& personType::setFirstName(string first)
{
      firstName = first;

      return *this;
}
```

Consider the following function **main**:

```
int main()
{
   personType student1("Angela", "Clodfelter");          //Line 1

   personType student2;                                   //Line 2

   personType student3;                                   //Line 3

   cout<<"Line 4 -- Student 1: ";                         //Line 4
   student1.print();                                      //Line 5
   cout<<endl;                                            //Line 6

   student2.setFirstName("Shelly").setLastName("Malik"); //Line 7

   cout<<"Line 8 -- Student 2: ";                         //Line 8
   student2.print();                                      //Line 9
   cout<<endl;                                            //Line 10

   student3.setFirstName("Chelsea");                      //Line 11

   cout<<"Line 12 -- Student 3: ";                        //Line 12
   student3.print();                                      //Line 13
   cout<<endl;                                            //Line 14

   student3.setLastName("Tomek");                         //Line 15

   cout<<"Line 16 -- Student 3: ";                        //Line 16
   student3.print);                                       //Line 17
   cout<<endl;                                            //Line 18

   return 0;
}
```

Output

```
Line 4 -- Student 1: Angela Clodfelter
Line 8 -- Student 2: Shelly Malik
Line 12 -- Student 3: Chelsea
Line 16 -- Student 3: Chelsea Tomek
```


The statements in Lines 1, 2, and 3 declare and initialize the objects **student1**, **student2**, and **student3**, respectively. The objects **student2** and **student3** are initialized to empty strings. The statement in Line 5 outputs the value of **student1** (see Line 4 in the output, which contains the output of Lines 4, 5, and 6). The statement in Line 7 works as follows. In the statement

```
student2.setFirstName("Shelly").setLastName("Malik");
```

first the expression

```
student2.setFirstName("Shelly")
```

is executed because the associativity of the dot operator is from left to right. This expression sets the first name to `"Shelly"` and returns a reference of the object, which is `student2`. Thus, the next expression executed is

```
student2.setLastName("Malik")
```

which sets the last name of `student2` to `"Malik"`. The statement in Line 9 outputs the value of `student2`. The statement in Line 11 sets the first name of the object `student3` to `"Chelsea"`, and the statement in Line 13 outputs the value of `student3`. Notice the output in Line 12. The output shows only the first name, not the last name, because we have not yet set the last name of `student3`. The last name of `student3` is still empty, which was set by the statement in Line 3 when `student3` is declared. Next, the statement in Line 15 sets the last name of `student3`, and the statement in Line 16 outputs the value of `student3`.

Friend Functions of Classes

A function that is defined outside the scope of a class is called a **friend function** of the class. A friend function is a **nonmember function** of the class, but has access to the `private` data members of the class. To make a function be a friend to a class, the reserved word `friend` precedes the function prototype (in the class definition). (The word `friend` appears only in the function prototype in the class definition, not in the definition of the friend function.)

Consider the following statements:

```
class classIllusFriend
{
   friend void two(...);
        .
        .
        .
};
```

In the definition of the `class classIllusFriend`, `two` is declared as a `friend` of the `class classIllusFriend`; that is, it is a nonmember function of the `class classIllusFriend`. When you write the definition of the function `two`, any object of the type `classIllusFriend`—which is either a local variable of `two` or a formal parameter of `two`—can access its `private` members within the definition of the function `two`. (Example 16-3 illustrates this concept.) Moreover, because a `friend` function is not a member of a class, its declaration can be placed within the `private`, `protected`, or `public` part of the class.

Definition of a friend Function

When writing the definition of a **friend** function, the name of the class and the scope resolution operator do not precede the name of the **friend** function in the function heading. Also, recall that the word **friend** does not appear in the heading of the **friend** function's definition. Thus, the definition of the function **two** in the previous **class classIllusFriend** is

```
void two(...)
{
    .
    .
    .
}
```

Of course, we will place the definition of the **friend** function in the implementation file.

The next section illustrates the difference between a member function and a nonmember function (**friend** function), when we overload some of the operators for a specific class.

The following example shows how a **friend** function accesses the **private** members of a class.

Example 16-3

Consider the following class:

```
class classIllusFriend
{
    friend void two(classIllusFriend cLFObject);

public:
    void print();
    void setx(int a);

private:
    int x;
};
```

In the definition of the **class classIllusFriend**, **two** is declared as a **friend** function. Suppose that the definitions of the member functions of the **class classIllusFriend** are as follows: 16

```
void classIllusFriend::print()
{
      cout<<"In class classIllusFriend: x = "<<x<<endl;
}

void classIllusFriend::setx(int a)
{
      x = a;
}
```

Now consider the following definition of the function `two`:

```
void two(classIllusFriend cLFObject)                        //Line 1
{
    classIllusFriend localTwoObject;                        //Line 2

    localTwoObject.x = 45;                                  //Line 3

    localTwoObject.print();                                 //Line 4
    cout<<endl;                                             //Line 5
    cout<<"Line 6: In Friend Function two accessing "
        <<"private data member x "
        <<localTwoObject.x<<endl;                           //Line 6

    cLFObject.x = 88;                                       //Line 7

    cLFObject.print();                                      //Line 8
    cout<<endl;                                             //Line 9
    cout<<"Line 10: In Friend Function two accessing "
        <<"private data member x "
        <<cLFObject.x<<endl;                                //Line 10
}
```

The function `two` contains a formal parameter `cLFObject` and a local variable `localTwoObject`, both of the type `classIllusFriend`. In the statement in Line 3, the object `localTwoObject` accesses its `private` data member `x` and sets its value to `45`. If `two` is not declared as a `friend` function of the `class classIllusFriend`, then this statement would result in a syntax error because an object cannot directly access its `private` members. Similarly, in the statement in Line 7, the formal parameter `cLFObject` accesses its `private` data member `x` and sets its value to `88`. Once again, this statement would result in a syntax error if `two` is not declared a `friend` function of the `class classIllusFriend`. The statement in Line 6 outputs the value of the `private` data member `x` of `localTwoObject` by directly accessing `x`. Similarly, the statement in Line 10 outputs the value of `x` of `cLFObject` by directly accessing it. The function `two` also prints the value of `x` by using the function `print` (see the statements in Lines 4 and 8).

Now consider the definition of the following function `main`:

```
int main()
{
     classIllusFriend aObject;                              //Line 11

     aObject.setx(32);                                      //Line 12

     cout<<"Line 13: aObject.x: ";                          //Line 13
     aObject.print();                                       //Line 14
     cout<<endl;                                            //Line 15
```

```
        cout<<"*~*~*~*~*~* Testing Friend Function "
            <<"two *~*~*~*~*~*"<<endl<<endl;                //Line 16

        two(aObject);                                       //Line 17

        return 0;
}
```

Output

```
Line 13: aObject.x: In class classIllusFriend: x = 32

*~*~*~*~*~* Testing Friend Function two *~*~*~*~*~*

In class classIllusFriend: x = 45

Line 6: In Friend Function two accessing private data member x 45
In class classIllusFriend: x = 88

Line 10: In Friend Function two accessing private data member x 88
```

For the most part, the output is self-explanatory. The statement in Line 17 calls the function `two` (a `friend` function of the `class classIllusFriend`) and passes the object `aObject` as an actual parameter. Notice that the function `two` generates the last six lines of the output, including the two blank lines.

Operator Functions as Member Functions and Nonmember Functions

At the beginning of this chapter, we stated that certain rules must be followed when you include an operator function in the definition of a class. This section describes these rules.

Most operator functions can be either member functions or nonmember functions—that is, `friend` functions of a class. To make an operator function be a member or nonmember of a class, keep the following in mind:

1. The function that overloads any of the operators `()`, `[]`, `->`, or = for a class must be declared as a member of the class.

2. Suppose that an operator `op` is overloaded for a class—say, `OpOverClass`.
   a. If the leftmost operand of `op` is an object of a different type (that is, not of the type `OpOverClass`), the function that overloads the operator `op` for `OpOverClass` must be a nonmember—that is, a friend of the `class OpOverClass`.
   b. If the operator function that overloads the operator `op` for the `class OpOverClass` is a member of the `class OpOverClass`, then when applying `op` on objects of the type `OpOverClass`, the leftmost operand of `op` must be of the type `OpOverClass`.

You must follow these rules when including an operator function in a class definition.

You will see later in this chapter that functions that overload the insertion operator, <<, and the extraction operator, >>, for a class must be nonmembers—that is, **friend** functions of the class.

Except for certain operators noted previously, operators can be overloaded either as member functions or as nonmember functions. The following discussion shows the difference between these two types of functions.

To facilitate the discussion, we will use the following class to illustrate operator overloading:

```
class OpOverClass
{
        .
        .
        .
private:
   int a;
   int b;
};
```

The **class** OpOverClass has two **private** data members, a and b, of the type **int**. We will add operator functions to the **class** OpOverClass as we overload operators.

Also, suppose that you have the following statements:

```
OpOverClass x;
OpOverClass y;
OpOverClass z;
```

That is, x, y, and z are objects of the type OpOverClass.

Overloading Binary Operators

C++ consists of both binary and unary operators. It also has a ternary operator. This section and the next few sections discuss how to overload various binary and unary operators. We begin by describing how to overload binary operators.

Suppose that the binary operator + is to be overloaded for the **class** OpOverClass. This operator can be overloaded as either a member function of the class or as a **friend** function. We will describe both ways to overload this operator.

Overloading + as a Member Function

Suppose that + is overloaded as a member function of the **class** OpOverClass. The name of the function to overload + for the **class** OpOverClass is

```
operator+
```

Because x and y are objects of the type OpOverClass, you can perform the operation

```
x + y
```

The compiler translates this expression into the following expression:

```
x.operator+(y)
```

In this expression, you can clearly see that the function **operator+** has only one argument, which is **y**.

Because **operator+** is a member of the **class OpOverClass** and **x** is an object of the type **OpOverClass**, in the previous statement, **operator+** has direct access to the **private** members of object **x**. Thus, the first argument to **operator+** is the object that is invoking the function **operator+**, and the second argument is passed as a parameter to this function.

Suppose that **operator+** adds the corresponding data members of the objects. Thus, the result of the expression

```
x + y
```

is an object of the type **OpOverClass**. Therefore, the return type of the operator function **operator+** is of the type **OpOverClass**.

Next, we describe the function prototype and the definition of the function to overload the operator + for the **class OpOverClass**.

The function prototype of **operator+** in the definition of the **class OpOverClass** is

```
OpOverClass operator+(const OpOverClass&) const;
```

We now discuss how to write the definition of the function **operator+** for the **class OpOverClass**.

The function **operator+** adds the corresponding data members of the objects. For example, in the expression

```
x + y
```

the data member **a** of **x** is added with the data member **a** of **y**, and the data member **b** of **x** is added with the data member **b** of **y**.

Because **operator+** is a member of the **class OpOverClass**, when writing the definition of the function **operator+**, the name of the class—that is, **OpOverClass**—and the scope resolution operator **::** must appear in the function heading. The definition of the function **operator+** for the **class OpOverClass** is

16

```
OpOverClass OpOverClass::operator+
                        (const OpOverClass& otherObject) const
{
      OpOverClass temp;

      temp.a = a + otherObject.a;
      temp.b = b + otherObject.b;

      return temp;
}
```

In this function definition, we add the data members of the object with the corresponding data members of `otherObject`. The result is stored in the local variable `temp`. Finally, the value of the object `temp` is returned. Note that the return type of the function `operator+` is `OpOverClass`.

Similarly, we can overload other binary arithmetic operators.

General Syntax to Overload Binary (Arithmetic) Operators as Member Functions

The general form of the functions to overload binary operators as member functions of a class is described here.

Function Prototype (to be included in the definition of the class):

```
returnType operator op(const className&) const;
```

where `op` stands for the binary operator to be overloaded, `returnType` is the type of value returned by the function, and `className` is the name of the class for which the operator is being overloaded.

Function Definition:

```
returnType className::operator op
                     (const className& otherObject) const
{
    //algorithm to perform the operation

    return (value);
}
```

The following example illustrates how to overload and use binary arithmetic.

Example 16-4

Let us overload `+` and `*` for the `class OpOverClass`. These operators are overloaded as member functions.

```
class OpOverClass
{
public:
    void print() const;

          //Overload the arithmetic operators
    OpOverClass operator+(const OpOverClass&) const;
    OpOverClass operator*(const OpOverClass&) const;
```

```
    OpOverClass(int i = 0, int j = 0);

private:
    int a;
    int b;
};
```

The definitions of the functions `print`, `operator+`, `operator*`, and the constructor are

```
void OpOverClass::print() const
{
      cout<<"("<<a<<", "<<b<<")";
}

OpOverClass::OpOverClass(int i, int j)
{
      a = i;
      b = j;
}


OpOverClass OpOverClass::operator+
                        (const OpOverClass& right) const
{
      OpOverClass temp;

      temp.a = a + right.a;
      temp.b = b + right.b;

      return temp;
}

OpOverClass OpOverClass::operator*
                        (const OpOverClass& right) const
{
      OpOverClass temp;

      temp.a = a * right.a;
      temp.b = b * right.b;

      return temp;
}
```

Consider the following function main:

```
int main()
{
      OpOverClass u(23, 45);          //Line 1
      OpOverClass v(12, 10);          //Line 2
      OpOverClass w1;                 //Line 3
      OpOverClass w2;                 //Line 4

      cout<<"Line 5: u = ";           //Line 5
      u.print();                      //Line 6; output u
      cout<<endl;                     //Line 7

      cout<<"Line 8: v = ";           //Line 8
      v.print();                      //Line 9; output v
      cout<<endl;                     //Line 10

      w1 = u + v;                     //Line 11; add u and v

      cout<<"Line 12: w1 = ";         //Line 12
      w1.print();                     //Line 13; output w1
      cout<<endl;                     //Line 14

      w2 = u * v;                     //Line 15; multiply u and v

      cout<<"Line 16: w2 = ";         //Line 16
      w2.print();                     //Line 17; output w2
      cout<<endl;                     //Line 18

      return 0;
}
```

Output

```
Line 5: u = (23, 45)
Line 8: v = (12, 10)
Line 12: w1 = (35, 55)
Line 16: w2 = (276, 450)
```

The function main is self-explanatory, and you are encouraged to walk through it. For example, the statement in Line 6 outputs the value of u. See the output of the statement marked Line 5, which contains the output of the statements in Line 5, 6, and 7. Similarly, the statement in Line 9 outputs the value of v. The statement in Line 11 adds u and v and assigns the result to w1. Similarly, the statement in Line 15 multiplies u and v and assigns the result to w2.

Overloading Relational Operators as Member Functions

We now illustrate how to overload relational operators as member functions for a class. To be specific, let us overload the equality operator, ==, for the class OpOverClass.

Because the result of a relational operator is either **true** or **false**, the **returnType** of the function **operator==** is Boolean.

The syntax of the function prototype to be included in the definition of the **class OpOverClass** is

```
bool operator==(const OpOverClass&) const;
```

Two objects (of the same type) are usually the same if their corresponding data members are the same. Therefore, the definition of the function **operator==** for the **class OpOverClass** is

```
bool OpOverClass ::operator==
          (const OpOverClass& right) const
{
    return(a == right.a && b == right.b);
}
```

General Syntax to Overload Binary Relational Operators as Member Functions

The general form of the functions to overload binary operations as member functions of a class is described here.

Function Prototype (to be included in the definition of the class):

```
bool operator op(const className&) const;
```

where **op** is the relational operator that is being overloaded, and **className** is the name of the class for the operator **op** that is being overloaded.

Function Definition:

```
bool className::operator op(const className& right) const
{
      //Compare and return the value
}
```

16

The following example illustrates the overloading and use of relational operators.

Example 16-5

In this example, we overload the operators **==** and **!=** for the **class OpOverClass** as member functions.

The definition of the **class OpOverClass** and the definitions of the functions are

```
class OpOverClass
{
public:
    void print() const;
```

```
            //Overload the relational operators
    bool operator==(const OpOverClass&) const;
    bool operator!=(const OpOverClass&) const;

    OpOverClass(int i = 0, int j = 0);

private:
    int a;
    int b;
};

      //The definitions of the function print and the constructor
      //are the same as in Example 16-4
bool OpOverClass::operator==(const OpOverClass& right) const
{
      return(a == right.a && b == right.b);
}

bool OpOverClass::operator!=(const OpOverClass& right) const
{
      return(a != right.a || b != right.b);
}
```

The following program tests the operators `==` and `!=`:

```
int main()
{
   OpOverClass u(23, 45);                                //Line 1
   OpOverClass v(12, 10);                                //Line 2
   OpOverClass w(23, 45);                                //Line 3

   if(u == v)                                            //Line 4
      cout<<"Line 5: u and v are equal"<<endl;           //Line 5
   else                                                  //Line 6
      cout<<"Line 7: u and v are not equal"<<endl;       //Line 7

   if(u == w)                                            //Line 8
      cout<<"Line 9: u and w are equal"<<endl;           //Line 9
   else                                                  //Line 10
      cout<<"Line 11: u and w are not equal"<<endl;      //Line 11

   return 0;
}
```

Output

```
Line 7: u and v are not equal
Line 9: u and w are equal
```

Binary Operators as Nonmember Functions

Suppose that + is overloaded as a nonmember function of the `class OpOverClass`.

Further suppose that the following operation is to be performed:

```
x + y
```

In this case, the expression is compiled as

```
operator+(x,y)
```

Here we see that the function `operator+` has two arguments. It is also clear that in this expression, the function `operator+` is neither a member of the object `x` nor a member of the object `y`. The objects to be added are passed as arguments to the function `operator+`.

To include the operator function `operator+` as a nonmember of the class in the definition of the class, the reserved word `friend` must appear before the function heading. Also, the function `operator+` must have two arguments.

Thus, to include `operator+` as a nonmember in the definition of the `class OpOverClass`, its prototype in the definition of `OpOverClass` is

```
friend OpOverClass operator+(const OpOverClass&,
                             const OpOverClass&);
```

The definition of the function `operator+` is as follows:

```
OpOverClass operator+(const OpOverClass& firstObject,
                      const OpOverClass& secondObject)
{
     OpOverClass temp;

     temp.a = firstObject.a + secondObject.a;
     temp.b = firstObject.b + secondObject.b;

     return temp;
}
```

In the previous definition, the corresponding data members of `firstObject` and `secondObject` are added and the result is stored in `temp`. Recall that the `private` members of a class are local to the class and therefore cannot be accessed outside the class. If we follow this rule, then because `operator+` is not a member of the `class OpOverClass`. In the definition of the function `operator+`, expressions such as `firstObject.a` must be illegal because `a` is a `private` member of `firstObject`. However, because `operator+` was declared as a `friend` function of the `class OpOverClass`, an object of the type `OpOverClass` can access its `private` members in the definition of `operator+`. Also, note that in the function heading, the name of the class—that is, `OpOverClass`—and the scope resolution operator *are not included* before the name of the function `operator+` because the function `operator+` is not a member of the class.

General Syntax to Overload Binary (Arithmetic) Operators as Nonmember Functions

The general form of the functions to overload binary operators as nonmember functions of a class is described here.

a. **Function Prototype** (to be included in the definition of the class):

```
friend returnType operator op(const className&,
                              const className&);
```

where op stands for the binary operator to be overloaded, returnType is the type of value returned by the function, and className is the name of the class for which the operator is being overloaded.

b. **Function Definition:**

```
returnType operator op(const className& firstObject,
                       const className& secondObject)
{
   //algorithm to perform the operation
   return (value);
}
```

Overloading Relational Operators as Nonmember Functions

We now illustrate how to overload relational operators as nonmember functions for a class. To be specific, let us overload the equality operator, ==, for the class OpOverClass.

Clearly, the return type of the function operator== is Boolean.

Function Prototype (to be included in the definition of the class OpOverClass):

```
friend bool operator==(const OpOverClass&,
                       const OpOverClass&);
```

Function Definition of operator== for the class OpOverClass:

```
bool operator==(const OpOverClass& firstObject,
                const OpOverClass& secondObject)
{
      return(firstObject.a == secondObject.a &&
             firstObject.b == secondObject.b);
}
```

General Syntax to Overload Binary Relational Operators as Nonmember Functions

The general form of the functions to overload binary relational operators as nonmember functions of a class is described here.

Function Prototype (to be included in the definition of the class):

```
friend bool operator op(const className&, const className&);
```

where op is the relational operator that is being overloaded, and className is the name of the class for which the operator op is being overloaded.

Function Definition:

```
bool operator op (const className& firstObject,
                  const className& secondObject)
{
      //Compare and return the value
}
```

Overloading Stream Insertion (<<) and Extraction (>>) Operators

The operator function that overloads the insertion operator << or the extraction operator >> for a class must be a nonmember of that class for the following reason.

Consider the following expression:

cin>>x

In this expression, the leftmost operand of >> (that is, cin) is an object of the type istream, not an object of the type OpOverClass. Because the leftmost operand of >> is not an object of the type OpOverClass, the operator function that overloads the extraction operator for OpOverClass must be a nonmember of the class OpOverClass.

Similarly, the operator function that overloads the stream insertion operator for OpOverClass must be a nonmember function of OpOverClass.

Overloading the Stream Insertion Operator (<<)

The general syntax to overload the stream insertion operator << for a class is described next.

Function Prototype (to be included in the definition of the class):

```
friend ostream& operator<<(ostream&, const className&);
```

16

Function Definition:

```
ostream& operator<<(ostream& osObject, const className&  cObject)
{
       //local declaration if any
       //Output members of cObject
       //osObject<<. . .

       //return stream object
     return osObject;
}
```

In the preceding function definition:

- Both parameters are reference parameters.
- The first parameter—that is, `osObject`— is a reference to an `ostream` object.
- The second parameter is usually a `const` reference to a particular class, because (recall from Chapter 13) the most effective way to pass an object as a parameter to a class is by reference. In this case, the formal parameter does not need to copy the data members of the actual parameter. In the previous definition, the word `const` appears before the class name because we want to only print the data members of the object. That is, the function should not modify the data members of the object.
- The function return type is a reference to an `ostream` object.

The return type of the function to overload the operator << must be a reference to an `ostream` object for the following reasons.

Suppose that the operator << is overloaded for the `class OpOverClass`. The statement

```
cout<<x;
```

is equivalent to the statement

```
operator<<(cout,x);
```

This is a perfectly legal statement because both of the actual parameters are objects, not the value of the objects. The first argument, `cout`, is of the type `ostream`; the second argument, `x`, is of the type `OpOverClass`.

Now consider the following statement:

```
cout<<x<<y;
```

This statement is equivalent to the statement

```
operator<<(operator<<(cout,x),y);            //Line A
```

because the associativity of the operator << is from left to right.

To execute the previous statement, you must first execute the expression

```
cout<<x
```

that is, the expression

```
operator<<(cout,x)
```

After executing this expression, which outputs the value of `x`, whatever is returned by the function `operator<<` will become the left-side argument of the operator << (that is, the first parameter of the function `operator<<`) so as to output the value of the object `y` (see the statement in Line `A`). Because the left-side argument of the operator << must be an object of the `ostream` type, the expression

```
cout<<x
```

must return the object `cout` (not its value) so as to output the value of `y`.

Therefore, the return type of the function `operator<<` must be a reference to an object of the `ostream` type.

Overloading the Stream Extraction Operator (>>)

The general syntax to overload the stream extraction operator >> for a class is described next.

Function Prototype (to be included in the definition of the class):

```
friend istream& operator>>(istream&, className&);
```

Function Definition:

```
istream& operator>>(istream& isObject, className&  cObject)
{
       //local declaration if any
       //Read data into cObject
       //isObject>>. . .

       //return stream object
      return isObject;
}
```

In the preceding function definition:

- Both parameters are reference parameters.
- The first argument—that is, `isObject`—is a reference to an `istream` object.
- The second argument is usually a reference to a particular class. The data read will be stored in the object.
- The function return type is a reference to an `istream` object.

For the same reasons as explained previously (when we overloaded the insertion operator `<<`), the return type of the function `operator>>` must be a reference to an `istream` object. We can then successfully execute statements of the following type:

```
cin>>x>>y;
```

The next example illustrates the overloading of the stream insertion and extraction operators for the `class OpOverClass`.

16

Example 16-6

The definition of the `class OpOverClass` and the definitions of the operator functions are

```
class OpOverClass
{
            //overload the stream insertion and extraction operators
    friend ostream& operator<<(ostream&, const OpOverClass&);
    friend istream& operator>>(istream&, OpOverClass&);

public:
            //overload the arithmetic operators
    OpOverClass operator+(const OpOverClass&) const;
    OpOverClass operator*(const OpOverClass&) const;

    OpOverClass(int i = 0, int j = 0);

private:
    int a;
    int b;
};

      //The definitions of the functions operator+, operator*,
      //and the constructor are the same as in Example 16-4

ostream& operator<<(ostream& osObject, const OpOverClass& right)
{
      osObject<<"("<<right.a<<", "<<right.b<<")";

      return osObject;
}

istream& operator>>(istream& isObject, OpOverClass& right)
{
      isObject>>right.a>>right.b;

      return isObject;
}
```

Consider the following function `main`:

```
int main()
{
      OpOverClass u(23, 45);                       //Line 1
      OpOverClass v;                               //Line 2

      cout<<"Line 3: u : "<<u<<endl;               //Line 3

      cout<<"Line 4: Enter two integers: ";        //Line 4
      cin>>v;                                      //Line 5
```

```
        cout<<endl;                                    //Line 6
        cout<<"Line 7: v : "<<v<<endl;                 //Line 7

        cout<<"Line 8: u + v : "<<u + v<<endl;         //Line 8
        cout<<"Line 9: u * v : "<<u * v<<endl;         //Line 9

        return 0;
}
```

Sample Run: In this sample run, the user input is shaded.

```
Line 3: u = (23, 45)
Line 4: Enter two integers: 5 6

Line 7: v = (5, 6)
Line 8: u + v = (28, 51)
Line 9: u * v = (115, 270)
```

The statements in Lines 1 and 2 declare and initialize `u` and `v` to be objects of the type `OpOverClass`. The statement in Line 3 outputs the value of `u` using `cout` and the insertion operator. The statement in Line 5 inputs data into `v` using `cin` and the extraction operator. The statement in Line 7 outputs the value of `v` using `cout` and the insertion operator. The `cout` statement in Line 8 adds `u` and `v` and outputs the result. Similarly, the `cout` statement in Line 9 multiplies `u` and `v` and outputs the result. The output shows that both the stream insertion and stream extraction operators were overloaded successfully.

Overloading the Assignment Operator (=)

One of the allowable operations on classes is the assignment operation. The assignment operator causes a member-wise copy of the data members of the class. For example, the statement

```
x = y;
```

is equivalent to the statements

```
x.a = y.a;
x.b = y.b;
```


From Chapter 15, recall that the built-in assignment operator works well for classes that do not have pointer data members. Therefore, to avoid the shallow copy of data for classes with pointer data members, we must explicitly overload the assignment operator.

Recall that to overload the assignment operator = for a class, the operator function `operator=` must be a member of that class.

General Syntax to Overload the Assignment Operator = for a Class

The general syntax to overload the assignment operator = for a class is described next.

Function Prototype (to be included in the definition of the class):

```
const className& operator=(const className&);
```

Function Definition:

```
const className& className::operator=(const className& rightObject)
{
      //local declaration, if any

      if(this != &rightObject)  //avoid self-assignment
      {
         //algorithm to copy rightObject into this object
      }

      //return the object assigned
      return *this;
}
```

In the definition of the function `operator=`:

- There is only one formal parameter.
- The formal parameter is usually a `const` reference to a particular class.
- The function return type is a constant reference to a particular class.

We now explain why the return type of the function `operator=` must be a reference of the class type.

Suppose that the assignment operator = is overloaded for the `class OpOverClass`. The statement

```
x = y;
```

is equivalent to the statement

```
x.operator=(y);
```

That is, the object `y` becomes the actual parameter to the function `operator=`.

Now consider the statement

```
x = y = z;
```

Because the associativity of the operator = is from right to left, this statement is equivalent to the statement

```
x.operator=(y.operator=(z));               //Line B
```

Clearly, we must first execute the expression

```
y.operator=(z)
```

that is, the expression

```
y = z
```

The value returned by the expression

```
y.operator=(z)
```

will become the parameter to the function **operator=** so as to assign a value to the object **x** (see the statement in Line **B**). Because the formal parameter to the function **operator=** is a reference parameter, the expression

```
y.operator=(z)
```

must return a reference to the object, rather than its value. That is, it must return a reference to the object **y**, not the value of **y**. For this reason, the return type of the function to overload the assignment operator = for a class must be a reference of the class type.

Now consider the statement

```
x = x;
```

Here we are trying to copy the value of **x** into **x**; that is, this statement is a self-assignment. We must prevent such statements because they waste computer time.

The body of the function **operator=** does prevent such assignments. Let us see how.

Consider the **if** statement in the body of the operator function **operator=**:

```
if(this != &rightObject)   //avoid self-assignment
{
        //algorithm to copy rightObject into this object
}
```

Now the statement

```
x = x;
```

is compiled into the statement

```
x.operator=(x);
```

Because the function **operator=** is invoked by the object **x**, the pointer **this** in the body of the function **operator=** refers to the object **x**. Furthermore, because **x** is also a parameter to the function **operator=**, the formal parameter **rightObject** also refers to the object **x**. Therefore, in the expression

```
this != &rightObject
```

this means the address of **x**, and **&rightObject** also means the address of **x**. Thus, the expression will evaluate to **false** and, therefore, the body of the **if** statement will be skipped.

The following example illustrates how to overload the assignment operator.

Example 16-7

Consider the following class:

```
class cAssignmentOprOverload
{
public:
    const cAssignmentOprOverload&
            operator=(const cAssignmentOprOverload& otherList);
              //Overload the assignment operator

    void print() const;
      //Function to print the list

    void insertEnd(int item);
      //Function to insert an item at the end of the list
      //Post: if the list is not full, length++;
      //         list[length] = item
      //      if the list is full
      //         output an appropriate message

    void destroyList();
      //Function to destroy the list
      //Post: length = 0; maxSize = 0;
      //      list = NULL

    cAssignmentOprOverload(int size = 0);
      //constructor
      //Post: length = 0; maxSize = size;
      //      list is an array of size maxSize

private:
    int maxSize;
    int length;
    int *list;
};
```

The definitions of the member functions of the `class cAssignmentOprOverload` are

```
void cAssignmentOprOverload::print() const
{
      if(length == 0)
            cout<<"List is empty"<<endl;
      else
      {
            for(int i = 0; i < length; i++)
                  cout<<list[i]<<" ";
            cout<<endl;
       }
}
```

```
void cAssignmentOprOverload::insertEnd(int item)
{
      if(length == maxSize)
         cout<<"List is full"<<endl;
      else
         list[length++] = item;
}

void cAssignmentOprOverload::destroyList()
{
      delete [] list;
      list = NULL;
      length = 0;
      maxSize = 0;
}

cAssignmentOprOverload::cAssignmentOprOverload(int size)
{
      maxSize = size;
      length = 0;
      if(maxSize == 0)
         list = NULL;
      else
         list = new int[maxSize];
}


const cAssignmentOprOverload& cAssignmentOprOverload::operator=
                   (const cAssignmentOprOverload& otherList)
{
    if(this != &otherList)  //avoid self-assignment; Line 1
    {
        if(list != NULL)                                  //Line 2
            destroyList();                                //Line 3
        maxSize = otherList.maxSize;                      //Line 4
        length = otherList.length;                        //Line 5

        if(maxSize != 0)                                  //Line 6
        {
           list = new int[maxSize];                       //Line 7

           if(length != 0)                                //Line 8
              for(int i = 0; i < length; i++)             //Line 9
                  list[i] = otherList.list[i];            //Line 10
        }
        else                                              //Line 11
            list = NULL;                                  //Line 12
    }

    return *this;                                         //Line 13
}
```

The function to overload the assignment operator works as follows. The statement in Line 1 checks whether an object is copying itself. The statement in Line 2 checks whether `list` is nonempty. If it is nonempty, then `list` is destroyed by deallocating the memory occupied by `list`. The statements in Lines 4 and 5 copy the values of the data members `maxSize` and `length` of `otherList` into `maxSize` and `length` of `list`, respectively. If `otherList` is not `NULL` and not empty, the statements between Lines 6 and 10 create the array `list` and copy `otherList` into `list`. If `otherList` is `NULL`, `list` is initialized to `NULL`. The statement in Line 13 returns the address of this list because the return type of the function `operator=` is a reference type.

The following function tests the `class cAssignmentOprOverload`:

```
int main()
{
      cAssignmentOprOverload intList1(10);        //Line 14
      cAssignmentOprOverload intList2;            //Line 15
      cAssignmentOprOverload intList3;            //Line 16

      int i;                                      //Line 17
      int number;                                 //Line 18

      cout<<"Line 19: Enter 5 integers: ";        //Line 19

      for(i = 0; i < 5; i++)                      //Line 20
      {
          cin>>number;                            //Line 21
          intList1.insertEnd(number);             //Line 22
      }

      cout<<endl<<"Line 23: intList1: ";          //Line 23
      intList1.print();                           //Line 24

      intList3 = intList2 = intList1;             //Line 25

      cout<<"Line 26: intList2: ";                //Line 26
      intList2.print();                           //Line 27

      intList2.destroyList();                     //Line 28

      cout<<endl;                                 //Line 29
      cout<<"Line 30: intList2: ";                //Line 30
      intList2.print();                           //Line 31

      cout<<"Line 32: After destroying intList2, "
          <<"intList1: ";                         //Line 32
      intList1.print();                           //Line 33
```

```
        cout<<"Line 34: After destroying intList2, "
            <<"intList3: ";                          //Line 34
        intList3.print();                            //Line 35
        cout<<endl;                                  //Line 36

        return 0;
}
```

Sample Run: In this sample run, the output is shaded.

```
Line 19: Enter 5 integers: 8 5 3 7 2

Line 23: intList1: 8 5 3 7 2
Line 26: intList2: 8 5 3 7 2

Line 30: intList2: List is empty
Line 32: After destroying intList2, intList1: 8 5 3 7 2
Line 34: After destroying intList2, intList3: 8 5 3 7 2
```

The statement in Line 14 creates `intList1` of size `10`; the statements in Lines 15 and 16 create `intList2` and `intList3` of (default) size `50`. The statements in Lines 20–22 input data into `intList1`, and the statement in Line 24 outputs `intList1`. The statement in Line 25 first copies `intList1` into `intList2`, and then copies `intList2` into `intList3`. The statement in Line 27 outputs `intList2` (see Line 26 in the Sample Run, which contains the output of Lines 26 and 27). The statement in Line 28 destroys `intList2`. The statement in Line 31 outputs `intList2`, which is empty (see Line 30 in the Sample Run, which contains the output of Lines 30 and 31). After destroying `intList2`, the program outputs the contents of `intList1` and `intList3` (see Lines 32 and 34 in the Sample Run). It is clear from the Sample Run that the destruction of `intList2` does not affect `intList1` and `intList3`, because `intList1` and `intList3` have their own data.

Overloading Unary Operators

The process of overloading unary operators is similar to the process of overloading binary operators. The only difference is that in the case of binary operators, the operator has two operands; in the case of unary operators, the operator has only one argument. Therefore, to overload a unary operator for a class:

1. If the operator function is a member of the class, it has no parameters.
2. If the operator function is a nonmember—that is, a `friend` function of the class—it has one parameter.

Next, we describe how to overload the increment and decrement operators.

Overloading the Increment (++) and Decrement (--) Operators

The increment operator has two forms: pre-increment (++u) and post-increment (u++), where u is a variable, say of the type **int**. In the case of pre-increment, ++u, the value of the variable, u, is incremented by 1 before the value of u is used in an expression; in the case of post-increment, the value of u is used in the expression before it is incremented by 1.

Overloading the Pre-Increment Operator

Overloading the pre-increment operator is quite straightforward. In the function definition, first we increment the value of the object and then use the pointer **this** to return the object's value. For example, suppose that we overload the pre-increment operator for the **class** OpOverClass. Also, suppose that the operator function **operator**++ is a member of the **class** OpOverClass. The operator function **operator**++ then has no arguments. Because the operator function **operator**++ has no arguments, we use the pointer **this** to return the incremented value of the object. (For illustration purposes, we assume that the increment operator increments the value of the data members a and b of the **class** OpOverClass by 1.)

```
OpOverClass OpOverClass::operator++()
{
        //increment the object
    ++a;
    ++b;

   return *this;     //return the incremented value of the object
}
```

Because x is an object of the type OpOverClass, the statement

```
++x;
```

increments the value of x by 1, and the pointer **this** associated with x returns the incremented value of x. Also, because ++x does not appear in an expression, the value returned by ***this** is lost. Now y is also an object of the type OpOverClass and so the statement

```
y = ++x;
```

increments the value of x by 1, and the pointer **this** associated with x returns the incremented value of x, which is stored in y.

General Syntax to Overload the Pre-Increment Operator ++ as a Member Function

The general syntax to overload the pre-increment operator ++ as a member function is described next.

Function Prototype (to be included in the definition of the class):

```
className operator++();
```

Function Definition:

```
className className::operator++()
{
     //increment the value of the object by 1
   return *this;
}
```

The operator function to overload the pre-increment operator can also be a nonmember of the `class OpOverClass`, which we describe next.

Because the operator function `operator++` is a nonmember of the `class OpOverClass`, it has one parameter, which is an object of the type `OpOverClass`. (For illustration purposes, we assume that the increment operator increments the value of the data members `a` and `b` of the `class OpOverClass` by 1.)

```
OpOverClass operator++(OpOverClass& incObj)
{
      //increment the object
   (incObj.a)++;
   (incObj.b)++;

   return incObj;    //return the incremented value of the object
}
```

General Syntax to Overload the Pre-Increment Operator ++ as a Nonmember Function The general syntax to overload the pre-increment operator ++ as a nonmember function is described next.

Function Prototype (to be included in the definition of the class):

```
friend className operator++(className&);
```

Function Definition:

```
className operator++(className& incObj)
{
     //increment incObj by 1
   return incObj;
}
```

Overloading the Post-Increment Operator

We now discuss how to overload the post-increment operator. As in the case of the pre-increment operator, we first describe the overloading of this operator as a member of a class.

Let us overload the post-increment operator for the **class OpOverClass**. In both cases, pre- and post-increment, the name of the operator function is the same—**operator++**. To distinguish between pre- and post-increment operator overloading, we use a dummy parameter (of the type **int**) in the function heading of the operator function. Thus, the function prototype for the post-increment operator for the **class OpOverClass** is

```
OpOverClass operator++(int);
```

The statement

```
x++;
```

is compiled by the compiler in the statement

```
x.operator++(0);
```

and so the function **operator++** with a parameter executes. The parameter `0` is used merely to distinguish between the pre- and post-increment operator functions.

The post-increment operator first uses the value of the object in the expression, and then increments the value of the object. So the steps required to implement this function are:

1. Save the value of the object—say, in `temp`.
2. Increment the value of the object.
3. Return the value that was saved in `temp`.

The function definition of the post-increment operator for the **class OpOverClass** is

```
OpOverClass OpOverClass::operator++(int u)
{
   OpOverClass temp = *this;  //use this pointer to copy
                              //the value of the object
     //increment the object
   a++;
   b++;

   return temp;     //return the old value of the object
}
```

General Syntax to Overload the Post-Increment Operator ++ as a Member Function

The general syntax to overload the post-increment operator ++ as a member function is described next.

Function Prototype (to be included in the definition of the class):

```
className  operator++(int);
```

Function Definition:

```
className className::operator++(int u)
{
   className temp = *this;      //use this pointer to copy
                                //the value of the object
      //increment the object

   return temp;    //return the old value of the object

}
```

The post-increment operator can also be overloaded as a nonmember function of the class. In this situation, the operator function `operator++` has two parameters. The definition of the function to overload the post-increment operator for the `class OpOverClass` as a nonmember is

```
OpOverClass operator++(OpOverClass& incObj, int u)
{
   OpOverClass temp = incObj;  //copy incObj into temp

      //increment incObj
   (incObj.a)++;
   (incObj.b)++;

   return temp;    //return the old value of the object
}
```

General Syntax to Overload the Post-Increment Operator ++ as a Nonmember Function The general syntax to overload the post-increment operator ++ as a nonmember function is described next.

Function Prototype (to be included in the definition of the class):

```
friend className operator++(className&, int);
```

Function Definition:

```
className operator++(className& incObj, int u)
{
   className temp = incObj;  //copy incObj into temp

      //increment incObj

   return temp;    //return the old value of the object

}
```

16

The decrement operators can be overloaded in a similar way, the details of which are left as an exercise for you.

Let us now write the definition of the **class OpOverClass** and show how the operator functions appear in the class definition. Because certain operators can be overloaded as either member or nonmember functions, we give two equivalent definitions of the **class OpOverClass**. In the first definition, the increment, decrement, arithmetic, and relational operators are overloaded as member functions. In the second definition, the increment, decrement, arithmetic, and relational operators are overloaded as nonmember functions.

The definition of the **class OpOverClass** is as follows:

```
//Definition of the class OpOverClass
//The increment, decrement, arithmetic, and relational
//operator functions are members of the class.

class OpOverClass
{
      //overload the stream insertion and extraction operators
   friend ostream& operator<<(ostream&, const OpOverClass&);
   friend istream& operator>>(istream&, OpOverClass&);

public:
         //overload the arithmetic operators
   OpOverClass operator+(const OpOverClass&) const;
   OpOverClass operator-(const OpOverClass&) const;
   OpOverClass operator*(const OpOverClass&) const;
   OpOverClass operator/(const OpOverClass&) const;

      //overload the increment and decrement operators
   OpOverClass operator++();          //pre-increment
   OpOverClass operator++(int);       //post-increment
   OpOverClass operator--();          //pre-decrement
   OpOverClass operator--(int);       //post-decrement

      //overload the relational operators
   bool operator==(const OpOverClass&) const;
   bool operator!=(const OpOverClass&) const;
   bool operator<=(const OpOverClass&) const;
   bool operator<(const OpOverClass&) const;
   bool operator>=(const OpOverClass&) const;
   bool operator>(const OpOverClass&) const;

            //constructors
   OpOverClass();
   OpOverClass(int i, int j);

      //include other functions as needed
```

```
private:
      int a;
      int b;
};
```

Following is the definition of the **class OpOverClass** in which the arithmetic, increment, decrement, and relational operators are overloaded as nonmembers.

```
//Definition of the class OpOverClass
//The increment, decrement, arithmetic, and relational
//operator functions are nonmembers of the class.

class OpOverClass
{
         //overload the stream insertion and extraction operators
   friend ostream& operator<<(ostream&, const OpOverClass&);
   friend istream& operator>>(istream&, OpOverClass&);

                  //overload the arithmetic operators
   friend OpOverClass operator+(const OpOverClass&,
                                const OpOverClass&);
   friend OpOverClass operator-(const OpOverClass&,
                                const OpOverClass&);
   friend OpOverClass operator*(const OpOverClass&,
                                const OpOverClass&);
   friend OpOverClass operator/(const OpOverClass&,
                                const OpOverClass&);

             //overload the increment and decrement operators
   friend OpOverClass operator++(OpOverClass&);
      //pre-increment
   friend OpOverClass operator++(OpOverClass&, int);
      //post-increment
   friend OpOverClass operator--(OpOverClass&);
      //pre-decrement
   friend OpOverClass operator--(OpOverClass&, int);
      //post-decrement

         //overload the relational operators
   friend bool operator==(const OpOverClass&,
                          const OpOverClass&);
   friend bool operator!=(const OpOverClass&,
                          const OpOverClass&);
   friend bool operator<=(const OpOverClass&,
                          const OpOverClass&);
   friend bool operator<(const OpOverClass&,
                         const OpOverClass&);
   friend bool operator>=(const OpOverClass&,
                          const OpOverClass&);
   friend bool operator>(const OpOverClass&,
                         const OpOverClass&);
```

16

```
public:
            //constructors
    OpOverClass();
    OpOverClass(int i, int j);

      //include other functions as needed

private:
      int a;
      int b;
};
```

The definitions of the functions to overload the operators for the **class** OpOverClass are left as an exercise for you. (See Programming Exercises 1 and 2 at the end of this chapter.)

Operator Overloading: Member Versus Nonmember

The preceding sections discussed and illustrated how to overload operators. Certain operators must be overloaded as member functions of the class, and some must be overloaded as nonmember (**friend**) functions. What about the ones that can be overloaded as either member functions or nonmember functions? For example, the binary arithmetic operator + can be overloaded as a member function or a nonmember function. If you overload + as a member function, then the operator + has direct access to the data members of one of the objects, and you need to pass only one object as a parameter. On the other hand, if you overload + as a nonmember function, then you must pass both objects as parameters. Therefore, overloading + as a nonmember could require additional memory and computer time to make a local copy of the data. Thus, for efficiency purposes, wherever possible, you should overload operators as member functions.

Classes and Pointer Data Members (Revisited)

Chapter 15 described the peculiarities of classes with pointer data members. Now that we have discussed how to overload various operators, let us review the peculiarities of classes with pointer data members, for the sake of completeness, and how to avoid them.

Recall that the only built-in operations on classes are assignment and member selection. The assignment operator provides a member-wise copy of the data; that is, the data members of an object are copied into the corresponding data members of another object of the same type. We have seen that this member-wise copy does not work well for classes with pointer data members. Other problems that may arise with classes with pointer data members relate to deallocating dynamic memory when an object goes out of scope and passing a class object as a parameter by value. To resolve these problems, classes with pointer data members must:

1. Explicitly overload the assignment operator
2. Include the copy constructor
3. Include the destructor

Operator Overloading: One Final Word

Next, we look at three examples that illustrate operator overloading. Before delving into these examples, you must remember the following: Suppose that an operator **op** is overloaded for a **class**—say, **OpOverClass**. Whenever we use the operator **op** on the objects of the type **OpOverClass**, the body of the function that overloads the operator **op** for the **class OpOverClass** executes. Therefore, whatever code you put in the body of the function executes.

PROGRAMMING EXAMPLE: CLOCKTYPE

Chapter 13 defined a **class clockType** to implement the time of day in a program. We implemented the operations print time, increment time, and compare two times for equality using functions. This example redefines the **class clockType**. It also overloads the stream insertion and extraction operators for easy input and output, relational operators for comparisons, and the increment operator to increment the time by one second. The program that uses the **class clockType** requires the user to input the time in the form **hr:min:sec**.

The modified definition of the **class clockType** is as follows:

```
//Header file newClock.h

#ifndef H_newClock
#define H_newClock

#include <iostream>
using namespace std;

class clockType
{
    friend ostream& operator<< (ostream&, const clockType&);
    friend istream& operator>> (istream&, clockType&);

public:
   void setTime(int hours, int minutes, int seconds);
      //Function to set the private data members
      //hr, min, and sec
      //Post: hr = hours; min = minutes; sec = seconds

   void getTime(int& hours, int& minutes, int& seconds);
      //Function to return the time
      //Post: hours = hr; minutes = min; seconds = sec;

   clockType operator++();
      //Overload the pre-increment operator
      //Post: Time is incremented by one second
```

```
    bool operator==(const clockType& otherClock) const;
       //Overload the equality operator
       //Function returns true if the time is equal
       //to otherTime, otherwise it returns the value false

    bool operator<=(const clockType& otherClock) const;
       //Overload the less than or equal to operator
       //Function returns true if the time is less
       //than or equal to otherTime, otherwise it returns the
       //value false

    clockType(int hours = 0, int minutes = 0, int seconds = 0);
       //Constructor to initialize the object with the values
       //specified by the user. If no values are specified,
       //the default values are assumed.
       //Post: hr = hours; min = minutes; sec = seconds

private:
    int hr;  //variable to store the hours
    int min; //variable to store the minutes
    int sec; //variable to store the seconds
};

#endif
```

Let us now write the definitions of the functions to implement the operations of the `class clockType`. Notice that the `class clockType` overloads only the pre-increment operator. For consistency, however, the class should also overload the post-increment operator. This step is left as an exercise for you (see Programming Exercise 3 at the end of this chapter.)

First, we write the definition of the function `operator++`. The algorithm to increment the time by one second is as follows:

- a. Increment the seconds by 1.
- b. If seconds > 59
  - b.1. Set the seconds to 0.
  - b.2. Increment the minutes by 1.
  - b.3. If minutes > 59
    - b.3.1. Set the minutes to 0.
    - b.3.2. Increment the hours by 1.
    - b.3.3. If hours > 23
      - b.3.3.1 Set the hours to 0.
- c. Return the incremented value of the object.

The definition of the function **operator++** is

```
      //overload the pre-increment operator
clockType clockType::operator++()
{
          sec++;                     //Step a

      if(sec > 59)                   //Step b
      {
         sec = 0;                    //Step b.1

         min++;                      //Step b.2

         if(min > 59)                //Step b.3
         {
            min = 0;                 //Step b.3.1

            hr++;                    //Step b.3.2

            if(hr > 23)              //Step b.3.3
               hr = 0;               //Step b.3.3.1
         }
      }

      return *this;                  //Step c
}
```

The definition of the function **operator==** is quite simple. The two times are the same if they have the same hours, minutes, and seconds. Therefore, the definition of the function **operator==** is

```
     //overload the equality operator
bool clockType::operator==(const clockType& otherClock) const
{
      return(hr == otherClock.hr && min == otherClock.min
             && sec == otherClock.sec);
}
```

The definition of the function **operator<=** is given next. The first time is less than or equal to the second time if

1. The hours of the first time are less than the hours of the second time, or
2. The hours of the first time and the second time are the same, but the minutes of the first time are less than the minutes of the second time, or
3. The hours and minutes of the first time and the second time are the same, but the seconds of the first time are less than or equal to the seconds of the second time.

The definition of the function **operator<=** is

```
    //overload the less than or equal to operator
bool clockType::operator<=(const clockType& otherClock) const
{
   return((hr < otherClock.hr) ||
          (hr == otherClock.hr && min < otherClock.min) ||
          (hr == otherClock.hr && min == otherClock.min &&
             sec <= otherClock.sec));
}
```

The definitions of the constructors and the function **setTime** are the same as given in Chapter 13. They are included here for the sake of completeness.

```
      //constructor with parameters
clockType::clockType(int hours, int minutes, int seconds)
{
      if(0 <= hours && hours < 24)
         hr = hours;
      else
         hr = 0;

      if(0 <= minutes && minutes < 60)
         min = minutes;
      else
         min = 0;

      if(0 <= seconds && seconds < 60)
         sec = seconds;
      else
         sec = 0;
}

void clockType::setTime(int hours, int minutes, int seconds)
{
      if(0 <= hours && hours < 24)
         hr = hours;
      else
         hr = 0;

      if(0 <= minutes && minutes < 60)
         min = minutes;
      else
         min = 0;

      if(0 <= seconds && seconds < 60)
         sec = seconds;
      else
         sec = 0;
}
```

```
void clockType::getTime(int& hours, int& minutes, int& seconds)
{
      hours = hr;
      minutes = min;
      seconds = sec;
}
```

We now discuss the definition of the function `operator<<`. The time must be output in the form

```
hh:mm:ss
```

The algorithm to output the time in this format is the same as the body of the `printTime` function of `clockType` given in Chapter 13. Here, after printing the time in the previous format, we must return the `ostream` object. Therefore, the definition of the function `operator<<` is

```
      //overload the stream insertion operator
ostream& operator<< (ostream& osObject, const clockType& timeOut)
{
      if(timeOut.hr < 10)
         osObject<<'0';
      osObject<<timeOut.hr<<':';

      if(timeOut.min < 10)
         osObject<<'0';
      osObject<<timeOut.min<<':';

      if(timeOut.sec < 10)
         osObject<<'0';
      osObject<<timeOut.sec;

      return osObject;       //return the ostream object
}
```

Let us now discuss the definition of the function `operator>>`. The input to the program is of the form

```
hh:mm:ss
```

That is, the input is the hours followed by a colon, followed by the minutes, followed by a colon, followed by the seconds. Clearly, the algorithm to input the time is

a. Get the input, which is a number, and store it in the data member `hr`.
b. Get the next input, which is a colon, and discard it.
c. Get the next input, which is a number, and store it in the data member `min`.
d. Get the next input, which is a colon, and discard it.
e. Get the next input, which is a number, and store it in the data member `sec`.
f. Return the `istream` object.

Clearly, we need a local variable of the type **char** to read the colon.

The definition of the function **operator>>** is

```
      //overload the stream extraction operator
istream& operator>> (istream& isObject, clockType& timeIn)
{
      char ch;

      isObject>>timeIn.hr;        //Step a
      isObject.get(ch);           //Step b; read and discard :
      isObject>>timeIn.min;       //Step c
      isObject.get(ch);           //Step d; read and discard :
      isObject>>timeIn.sec;       //Step e

      return isObject;            //Step f
}
```

The following test program uses the **class clockType**:

```
//Program that uses the class clockType

#include <iostream>
#include "newClock.h"

using namespace std;

int main()
{
      clockType myClock(5,6,23);                          //Line 1
      clockType yourClock;                                //Line 2

      cout<<"Line 3: myClock = "<<myClock<<endl;          //Line 3
      cout<<"Line 4: yourClock = "<<yourClock<<endl;      //Line 4

      cout<<"Line 5: Enter the time in the form "
          <<"hr:min:sec ";                                //Line 5
      cin>>myClock;                                       //Line 6
      cout<<"Line 7: The new time of myClock = "
          <<myClock<<endl;                                //Line 7

      ++myClock;                                          //Line 8

      cout<<"Line 9: After incrementing the time, myClock = "
          <<myClock<<endl;                                //Line 9

      yourClock.setTime(13,35,38);                        //Line 10
      cout<<"Line 11: After setting the time, yourClock = "
          <<yourClock<<endl;                              //Line 11
```

```
    if(myClock == yourClock)                              //Line 12
       cout<<"Line 13: The times of myClock and "
           <<"yourClock are equal"<<endl;                 //Line 13
    else                                                  //Line 14
       cout<<"Line 15: The times of myClock and "
           <<"yourClock are not equal"<<endl;             //Line 15

    if(myClock <= yourClock)                              //Line 16
       cout<<"Line 17: The time of myClock is less "
           <<"than or equal to "<<endl
           <<"the time of yourClock"<<endl;               //Line 17
    else                                                  //Line 18
       cout<<"Line 19: The time of myClock is "
           <<"greater than the time of yourClock"
           <<endl;                                        //Line 19

    return 0;
}
```

Sample Run: In this sample run, the user input is shaded.

```
Line 3: myClock = 05:06:23
Line 4: yourClock = 00:00:00
Line 5: Enter the time in the form hr:min:sec 4:50:59
Line 7: The new time of myClock = 04:50:59
Line 9: After incrementing the time, myClock = 04:51:00
Line 11: After setting the time, yourClock = 13:35:38
Line 15: The times of myClock and yourClock are not equal
Line 17: The time of myClock is less than or equal to
the time of yourClock
```

PROGRAMMING EXAMPLE: COMPLEX NUMBERS

A number of the form $a + ib$, where $i^2 = -1$, and a and b are real numbers, is called a complex number. We call a the real part and b the imaginary part of $a + ib$. Complex numbers can also be represented as ordered pairs (a, b). The addition and multiplication of complex numbers is defined by the following rules:

$$(a + ib) + (c + id) = (a + c) + i(b + d)$$

$$(a + ib) * (c + id) = (ac - bd) + i(ad + bc)$$

Using the ordered pair notation, these rules are written as

$(a, b) + (c, d) = ((a + c), (b + d))$

$(a, b) * (c, d) = ((ac - bd), (ad + bc))$

C++ has no built-in data type that allows us to manipulate complex numbers. In this example, we will construct a data type, `complexNumber`, that can be used to process complex numbers. We will overload the stream insertion and stream extraction operators for easy input and output. We will also overload the operators + and * to perform addition and multiplication of complex numbers. If x and y are complex numbers, we can evaluate expressions such as $x + y$ and $x * y$.

```
//Specification file complexType.h
#ifndef H_complexNumber
#define H_complexNumber

class complexType
{
        //overload the stream insertion and extraction operators
    friend ostream& operator<< (ostream&, const complexType&);
    friend istream& operator>> (istream&, complexType&);

public:
    void setComplex(const double& real, const double& imag);
      //Set the complex number according to the parameters
      //Post: realPart = real; imaginaryPart = imag

    complexType(double real = 0, double imag = 0);
      //constructor
      //Initialize the complex number according to the parameters
      //Post: realPart = real; imaginaryPart = imag

    complexType operator+(const complexType& otherComplex) const;
      //overload +
    complexType operator*(const complexType& otherComplex) const;
      //overload *
    bool operator==(const complexType& otherComplex) const;
     //overload ==

private:
    double realPart;       //variable to store the real part
    double imaginaryPart; //variable to store
                           //the imaginary part
};
#endif
```

We will now write the definitions of the functions to implement the various operations of the `class complexType`.

The definitions of most functions are quite simple and straightforward. We will discuss only the definitions of the functions to overload the stream insertion operator, <<, and the stream extraction operator, >>.

To output the complex number in the form

```
(a, b)
```

where `a` is the real part and `b` is the imaginary part, clearly the algorithm is

a. Output the left parenthesis, `(`.
b. Output the real part.
c. Output the comma.
d. Output the imaginary part.
e. Output the right parenthesis, `)`.

Therefore, the definition of the function `operator<<` is

```
ostream& operator<<(ostream& osObject, const complexType& complex)

{
    osObject<<"(";                          //Step a
    osObject<<complex.realPart;             //Step b
    osObject<<", ";                         //Step c
    osObject<<complex.imaginaryPart;        //Step d
    osObject<<")";                          //Step e

    return osObject;                        //Return the ostream object
}
```

Next, we discuss the definition of the function to overload the stream extraction operator, >>.

The input is of the form

```
(3, 5)
```

In this input, the real part of the complex number is `3` and the imaginary part is `5`. Clearly, the algorithm to read the complex number is

a. Read and discard the left parenthesis.
b. Read and store the real part.
c. Read and discard the comma.
d. Read and store the imaginary part.
e. Read and discard the right parenthesis.

Following these steps, the definition of the function `operator>>` is

```
istream& operator>> (istream& isObject, complexType& complex)
{
      char ch;

      isObject>>ch;                       //Step a
      isObject>>complex.realPart;         //Step b
      isObject>>ch;                       //Step c
      isObject>>complex.imaginaryPart;    //Step d
      isObject>>ch;                       //Step e

      return isObject;                    //Return the istream object
}
```

The definitions of the other functions are as follows:

```
bool complexType::operator==(const complexType& otherComplex) const
{
      return(realPart == otherComplex.realPart &&
               imaginaryPart == otherComplex.imaginaryPart);
}

      //constructor
complexType::complexType(double real, double imag)
{
      realPart = real;
      imaginaryPart = imag;
}

void complexType::setComplex(const double& real, const double& imag)
{
      realPart = real;
      imaginaryPart = imag;
}

      //overload the operator +
complexType complexType::operator+
                       (const complexType& otherComplex) const
{
      complexType temp;

      temp.realPart = realPart + otherComplex.realPart;
      temp.imaginaryPart = imaginaryPart
                           + otherComplex.imaginaryPart;

      return temp;
}
```

```
        //overload the operator *
complexType complexType::operator*
                       (const complexType& otherComplex) const
{
  complexType temp;

  temp.realPart = (realPart * otherComplex.realPart) -
                 (imaginaryPart * otherComplex.imaginaryPart);
  temp.imaginaryPart = (realPart * otherComplex.imaginaryPart) +
                    (imaginaryPart * otherComplex.realPart);
  return temp;
}
```

The following program illustrates the use of the **class** complexType:

```
//Program that uses the class complexType

#include <iostream>
#include "complexType.h"

using namespace std;

int main()
{
      complexType num1(23,34);                          //Line 1
      complexType num2;                                 //Line 2
      complexType num3;                                 //Line 3

      cout<<"Line 4: Num1 = "<<num1<<endl;              //Line 4
      cout<<"Line 5: Num2 = "<<num2<<endl;              //Line 5

      cout<<"Line 6: Enter the complex number "
          <<"in the form (a,b) ";                       //Line 6
      cin>>num2;                                        //Line 7
      cout<<endl;                                       //Line 8

      cout<<"Line 9: New value of num2 = "
          <<num2<<endl;                                 //Line 9

      num3 = num1 + num2;                               //Line 10

      cout<<"Line 11: Num3 = "<<num3<<endl;             //Line 11
      cout<<"Line 12: "<<num1<<" + "<<num2
          <<" = "<<num1 + num2<<endl;                   //Line 12
      cout<<"Line 13: "<<num1<<" * "<<num2
          <<" = "<<num1 * num2<<endl;                   //Line 13

      return 0;
}
```

Sample Run: In this sample run, the user input is shaded.

```
Line 4: Num1 = (23, 34)
Line 5: Num2 = (0, 0)
Line 6: Enter the complex number in the form (a,b) (3,4)

Line 9: New value of num2 = (3, 4)
Line 11: Num3 = (26, 38)
Line 12: (23, 34) + (3, 4) = (26, 38)
Line 13: (23, 34) * (3, 4) = (-67, 194)
```

You can extend this data type to perform subtraction and division on complex numbers.

Next, we will define a class, called `newString`, and overload the assignment and relational operators. That is, when we declare a variable of the type `newString`, we will be able to use the assignment operator to copy one string into another, and relational operators to compare two strings.

Before discussing the `class newString`, however, we examine the overloading of the operator `[]`. Recall that we have used the operator `[]` to access the components of an array. To access individual characters in a string of the type `newString`, we have to overload the operator `[]` for the `class newString`.

Overloading the Array Index (Subscript) Operator ([ ])

Recall that the function to overload the operator `[]` for a class must be a member of the class. Furthermore, because an array can be declared as constant or nonconstant, we need to overload the operator `[]` to handle both the cases.

The syntax to declare the operator function `operator[]` as a member of a class for nonconstant arrays is

```
Type& operator[](int index);
```

The syntax to declare the operator function `operator[]` as a member of a class for constant arrays is

```
const Type& operator[](int index) const;
```

where `Type` is the data type of the array elements.

Suppose that `classTest` is a class that has an array data member. The definition of `classTest` to overload the operator function operator `[]` is

```
class classTest
{
public:
    Type& operator[](int index);
        //overload the operator for nonconstant arrays
    const Type& operator[](int index) const;
        //overload the operator for constant arrays
      .
      .
      .
private:
    Type *list;  //pointer to the array
    int   arraySize;
};
```

where `Type` is the data type of the array elements.

The definitions of the functions to overload the operator `[]` for `classTest` are

```
   //overload the operator [] for nonconstant arrays
Type& classTest::operator[](int index)
{
   assert(0 <= index && index < arraySize);
   return(list[index]);   //return a pointer of the
                          //array component
}

      //overload the operator [] for constant arrays
const Type& classTest::operator[](int index) const
{
   assert(0 <= index && index < arraySize);
   return(list[index]);   //return a pointer of the
                          //array component
}
```

Consider the following statements:

```
classTest list1;
classTest list2;
const classTest list3;
```


In the case of the statement

```
list1[2] = list2[3];
```

the body of the operator function `operator[]` for nonconstant arrays is executed. In the case of the statement

```
list1[2] = list3[5];
```

first the body of the operator function `operator[]` for constant arrays is executed because `list3` is a constant array. Next, the body of the operator function `operator[]` for non-constant arrays is executed to complete the execution of the assignment statement.

PROGRAMMING EXAMPLE: NEWSTRING

Chapter 9 discussed C-strings. Recall that

1. A C-string is a sequence of one or more characters
2. C-strings are enclosed in double quotation marks
3. C-strings are null terminated
4. C-strings are stored in character arrays.

In this example, by a string we mean a C-string.

The only aggregate operations allowed on strings are input and output. To use other operations, the programmer needs to include the header file `cstring`, which contains the specification of many functions for string manipulation.

Initially, C++ did not provide any built-in data types to handle strings. More recent versions of C++, however, provide a string class to handle strings and operations on strings.

Our objective in this example is to define our own class for string manipulation and, at the same time, to further illustrate operator overloading. More specifically, we overload the assignment operator, the relational operators, and the stream insertion and extraction operators for easy input and output. Let us call this `class newString`. First we give the definition of the `class newString`:

```
//Header file myString.h
#ifndef H_myString
#define H_myString
#include <iostream>
using namespace std;

class newString
{
        //overload the stream insertion and extraction operators
    friend ostream& operator<<(ostream&, const newString&);
    friend istream& operator>>(istream&, newString&);

public:
    const newString& operator=(const newString&);
      //overload the assignment operator
    newString(const char *);
      //constructor; conversion from the char string
    newString();
      //default constructor to initialize the string to null
    newString(const newString&);
      //copy constructor
    ~newString();
      //destructor
```

```
    char &operator[] (int);
    const char &operator[](int) const;
          //overload the relational operators
    bool operator==(const newString&) const;
    bool operator!=(const newString&) const;
    bool operator<=(const newString&) const;
    bool operator<(const newString&)  const;
    bool operator>=(const newString&) const;
    bool operator>(const newString&)  const;

private:
    char *strPtr;   //pointer to the char array
                    //that holds the string
    int strLength;  //data member to store the length
                    //of the string
};
#endif
```

The `class` `newString` has two `private` data members: one to store the string and one to store the length of the string.

Next, we give the definitions of the functions to implement the `newString` operations. The implementation file includes the header file `cassert` because we are using the function `assert`. For an explanation of the function `assert`, see Chapter 4 or the header file `cassert` in Appendix F.

```
//Implementation file myString.cpp
#include <iostream>
#include <iomanip>
#include <cstring>
#include <cassert>
#include "myString.h"

using namespace std;


  //constructor: conversion from the char string to newString
newString::newString(const char *str)
{
   strLength = strlen(str);
   strPtr = new char[strLength+1];     //allocate memory to store
                                       //the char string

   assert(strPtr != NULL);
   strcpy(strPtr,str);  //copy string into strPtr
}
```

```
//default constructor to store the null string
newString::newString()
{
      strLength = 0;
      strPtr = new char[1];
      assert(strPtr != NULL);
      strcpy(strPtr,"");
}

newString::newString(const newString& rightStr)//copy constructor
{
      strLength = rightStr.strLength;
      strPtr = new char[strLength + 1];
      assert(strPtr != NULL);
      strcpy(strPtr, rightStr.strPtr);
}

newString::~newString()  //destructor
{
      delete [] strPtr;
}

        //overload the assignment operator
const newString& newString::operator=(const newString& rightStr)
{
      if(this != &rightStr) //avoid self-copy
      {
         delete [] strPtr;
         strLength = rightStr.strLength;
         strPtr = new char[strLength + 1];
         assert(strPtr != NULL);
         strcpy(strPtr, rightStr.strPtr);
      }
      return *this;
}

char& newString::operator[] (int index)
{
      assert(0 <= index && index < strLength);
      return strPtr[index];
}

const char& newString::operator[](int index) const
{
      assert(0 <= index && index < strLength);
      return strPtr[index];
}
```

```
	//overload the relational operators
bool newString::operator==(const newString& rightStr) const
{
	return(strcmp(strPtr, rightStr.strPtr) == 0);
}

bool newString::operator<(const newString& rightStr) const
{
	return(strcmp(strPtr, rightStr.strPtr) < 0);
}

bool newString::operator<=(const newString& rightStr) const
{
	return(strcmp(strPtr, rightStr.strPtr) <= 0);
}

bool newString::operator>(const newString& rightStr) const
{
	return(strcmp(strPtr, rightStr.strPtr) > 0);
}

bool newString::operator>=(const newString& rightStr) const
{
	return(strcmp(strPtr, rightStr.strPtr) >= 0);
}

bool newString::operator!=(const newString& rightStr) const
{
	return(strcmp(strPtr, rightStr.strPtr) != 0);
}

	//overload the stream insertion operator <<
ostream& operator<<(ostream& osObject, const newString& str)
{
	osObject<<str.strPtr;
	return osObject;
}

	//overload the stream extraction operator >>
istream& operator>>(istream& isObject, newString& str)
{
	char temp[81];

	isObject>>setw(81)>>temp;
	str = temp;
	return isObject;
}
```

Consider the statement

```
is>>setw(81)>>temp;
```

in the definition of the function `operator>>`. Because `temp` is declared to be an array of size `81`, the largest string that can be stored into `temp` is of length `80`. The manipulator `setw` in this statement (that is, in the input statement) ensures that no more than `80` characters are read into `temp`.

Most of these functions are quite straightforward. Let us explain the functions that overload the conversion constructor, the assignment operator, and the copy constructor.

The **conversion constructor** is a single-parameter function that converts its argument to the object of the constructor's class. In our case, the conversion constructor converts a string to an object of the `newString` type.

Note that the assignment operator is explicitly overloaded only for objects of the `newString` type. However, the overloaded assignment operator also works if we want to store a character string into a `newString` object. Consider the declaration

```
newString str;
```

and the statement

```
str = "Hello there";
```

The compiler translates this statement into

```
str.operator=("Hello there");
```

1. First, the compiler automatically invokes the conversion constructor to create an object of the `newString` type to temporarily store the string `"Hello there"`.
2. Second, the compiler invokes the overloaded assignment operator to assign the temporary `newString` object to the object `str`.

Hence, it is not necessary to explicitly overload the assignment operator to store a character string into an object of the type `newString`.

Next, we write a C++ program that tests some of the operations of the `class newString`.

```
//Test Program
#include <iostream>
#include "myString.h"

using namespace std;

int main()
{
   newString str1 = "Sunny";          //initialize str1 using
                                      //the assignment operator
   const newString str2("Warm");      //initialize str2 using
                                      //the conversion constructor
```

```
newString str3;  //initialize str3 to null
newString str4;  //initialize str4 to null

cout<<"Line 1: "<<str1<<"    "<<str2<<"  ***"
    <<str3<<"###."<<endl;                              //Line 1

if(str1 <= str2)             //compare str1 and str2; Line 2
   cout<<"Line 3: "<<str1<<" is less than "<<str2
       <<endl;                                         //Line 3
else                                                   //Line 4
   cout<<"Line 5: "<<str2<<" is less than "
       <<str1<<endl;                                   //Line 5

cout<<"Line 6: Enter a string with a length "
    <<"of at least 7 –> ";                             //Line 6
cin>>str1;                         //input str1;         Line 7
cout<<endl<<"Line 8: The new value of str1 = "
    <<str1<<endl;                                      //Line 8

str4 = str3 = "Birth Day";                             //Line 9
cout<<"Line 10: str3 = "<<str3<<", str4 = "
    <<str4<<endl;                                      //Line 10

str3 = str1;                                           //Line 11
cout<<"Line 12: The new value of str3 = "<<str3<<endl; //Line 12

str1 = "Bright Sky";                                   //Line 13

str3[1] = str1[5];                                     //Line 14
cout<<"Line 15: After replacing the second character "
    <<"of str3 = "<<str3<<endl;                        //Line 15

str3[2] = str2[0];                                     //Line 16
cout<<"Line 17: After replacing the third character "
    <<"of str3 = "<<str3<<endl;                        //Line 17

str3[5] = 'g';                                         //Line 18
cout<<"Line 19: After replacing the sixth character "
    <<"of str3 = "<<str3<<endl;                        //Line 19

return 0;
```

Sample Run: In this sample run, the user input is shaded.

```
Line 1: Sunny    Warm  ***###.
Line 3: Sunny is less than Warm
Line 6: Enter a string with a length of at least 7 --> 123456789

Line 8: The new value of str1 = 123456789
```

```
Line 10: str3 = Birth Day, str4 = Birth Day
Line 12: New value of str3 = 123456789
Line 15: After replacing the second character of str3 = 1t3456789
Line 17: After replacing the third character of str3 = 1tW456789
Line 19: After replacing the sixth character of str3 = 1tW45g789
```

The preceding program works as follows. The statement in Line 1 outputs the values of `str1`, `str2`, and `str3`. Notice that the value of `str3` is to be printed between *** and ###. Because `str3` is empty, nothing is printed between *** and ###, see the output marked Line 1. The statement in Line 2-5 compares `str1` and `str2` and outputs the result. The statement in Line 7 inputs a string with a length of at least 7 into `str1`, and the statement in Line 8 outputs the new value of `str1`. Note that in the statement (see Line 9)

```
str4 = str3 = "Birth Day";
```

because the associativity of the assignment operator is from right to left, first the statement `str3 = "Birth Day";` executes and then the statement `str4 = str3;` executes. The statement in Line 10 outputs the values of `str3` and `str4`. The statements in Lines 14, 16, and 18 use the array subscripting operator `[]` to individually manipulate the characters of `str3`. The meanings of the remaining statements are straightforward.

FUNCTION OVERLOADING

The previous section discussed operator overloading. Operator overloading provides the programmer with the same concise notation for user-defined data types as the operator has with built-in types. The types of arguments used with an operator determine the action to take. Similar to operator overloading, C++ allows the programmer to overload a function name. Chapter 7 introduced function overloading. For easy reference in the following discussion, let us review this concept.

Recall that a class can have more than one constructor, but all constructors of a class have the same name, which is the name of the class. This case is an example of overloading a function. Further recall that overloading a function refers to having several functions with the same name, but different parameters. The types of parameters determine which function will execute.

For function overloading to work, we must give the definition of each function. The next section teaches you how to overload functions with a single code segment and leave the job of generating code for separate functions for the compiler.

TEMPLATES

Templates are a very powerful feature of C++. They allow you to write a single code segment for a set of related functions, called a **function template**, and for a set of related classes, called a **class template**. The syntax we use for templates is

```
template <class Type>
   declaration;
```

where `Type` is the type of data, and `declaration` is either a function declaration or a class declaration. In C++, `template` is a reserved word. The word `class` in the heading refers to any user-defined type or built-in type. `Type` is referred to as a formal parameter to the template.

Similar to variables being parameters to functions, types (that is, data types) are parameters to templates.

Function Templates

In Chapter 7, when we introduced function overloading, the function `larger` was overloaded to find the larger of two integers, characters, floating-point numbers, or strings. To implement the function `larger`, we need to write four function definitions for the data type: one for `int`, one for `char`, one for `double`, and one for `string`. However, the body of each function is similar. C++ simplifies the process of overloading functions by providing function templates.

The syntax of the function template is

```
template <class Type>
function definition;
```

where `Type` is referred to as a formal parameter of the template. It is used to specify the type of parameters to the function and the return type of the function, and to declare variables within the function.

The statements

```
template <class Type>
Type larger(Type x, Type y)
{
   if(x >= y)
      return x;
   else
      return y;
}
```

define a function template **larger**, which returns the larger of two items. In the function heading, the type of the formal parameters **x** and **y** is **Type**, which will be specified by the type of the actual parameters when the function is called. The statement

```
cout<<larger(5,6)<<endl;
```

is a call to the function template **larger**. Because **5** and **6** are of the type **int**, the data type **int** is substituted for **Type** and the compiler generates the appropriate code.

If we omit the body of the function in the function template definition, the function template, as usual, is the prototype.

The following example illustrates the use of function templates.

Example 16-8

In this example, we use the function template **larger** to determine the larger of the two items.

```
#include <iostream>
#include "myString.h"
using namespace std;

template <class Type>
Type larger(Type x, Type y);

int main()
{
      cout<<"Line 1: Larger of 5 and 6 = "
          <<larger(5,6)<<endl;                    //Line 1

      cout<<"Line 2: Larger of A and B = "
          <<larger('A','B')<<endl;                //Line 2

      cout<<"Line 3: Larger of 5.6 and 3.2 = "
          <<larger(5.6,3.2)<<endl;                //Line 3

      newString str1 = "Hello";                   //Line 4
      newString str2 = "Happy";                   //Line 5

      cout<<"Line 6: Larger of "<<str1<<" and "
          <<str2<<" = "<<larger(str1,str2)
          <<endl;                                 //Line 6

      return 0;
}
```

```
template<class Type>
Type larger(Type x, Type y)
{
      if(x >= y)
            return x;
      else
            return y;
}
```

Output

```
Line 1: Larger of 5 and 6 = 6
Line 2: Larger of A and B = B
Line 3: Larger of 5.6 and 3.2 = 5.6
Line 6: Larger of Hello and Happy = Hello
```

Class Templates

Like function templates, class templates are used to write a single code segment for a set of related classes. For example, in Chapter 13, we defined a list as an ADT; our list element type there was `int`. If the list element type changes from `int` to, say, `char`, `double`, or `string`, we need to write separate classes for each element type. For the most part, the operations on the list and the algorithms to implement those operations remain the same. Using class templates, we can create a generic class `listType`, and the compiler can generate the appropriate source code for a specific implementation.

The syntax we use for a class template is

```
template<class Type>
class declaration
```

Class templates are called **parameterized types** because, based on the parameter type, a specific class is generated.

The following statements define `listType` to be a class template.


```
template<class elemType>
class listType
{
public:
    bool isEmpty();
        //Function returns true if the list is empty;
        //otherwise, it returns false.
    bool isFull();
        //Function returns true if the list is full,
        //otherwise, it returns false.
    void search(const elemType& searchItem, bool& found);
        //Search the list for searchItem
        //Post: found is set to true if the
```

```
        //searchItem is found in the list; otherwise, found
        //is set to false.
    void insert(const elemType& newElement);
        //Insert newElement in the list
        //Prior to insertion, the list must not be full
        //Post: the list is an old list plus the
        //newElement
    void remove(const elemType& removeElement);
        //If removeElement is found in the list, it is deleted
        //If the list is empty, output the message "Cannot delete
        //from the empty list"
        //Post: the list is an old list minus
        //removeElement if removeElement is found in the list
    void destroyList();
        //Post: length = 0
    void printList();
        //Output the elements of the list
    listType();
        //default constructor
        //Set the length of the list to 0
        //Post: length = 0
protected:
    elemType list[100];     //array to hold the list elements
    int length;             //variable to store the number of
                            //elements in the list
};
```

This definition of the class template `listType` is a generic definition and includes only the basic operations on a list. To derive a specific list from this list and to add or rewrite the operations, we declare the array containing the list elements and the length of the list as `protected`.

Next, we describe a specific list. Suppose that you want to create a list to process integer data. The statement

```
listType<int> intList;         //Line 1
```

declares `intList` to be a list of `100` components, with each component being of the type `int`. Similarly, the statement

```
listType<newString> stringList;         //Line 2
```

declares `stringList` to be a list of `100` components, with each component being of the type `newString`.

In the statements in Lines 1 and 2, `listType<int>` and `listType<newString>` are referred to as **template instantiations** or **instantiations** of the class template `listType<elemType>`, where `elemType` is the class parameter in the template header. A template instantiation can be created with either a built-in or user-defined type.

The function members of a class template are considered function templates. Thus, when giving the definitions of function members of a class template, we must follow the definition of the function template. For example, the definition of the member **insert** of the **class listType** is

```
template<class elemType>
void listType<elemType>::insert(elemType newElement)
{
   .
   .
   .
}
```

In the heading of the member function's definition, the name of the class is specified with the parameter **elemType**.

The statement in Line 1 declares **intList** to be a list of 100 components. When the compiler generates the code for **intList**, it replaces the word **elemType** with **int** in the definition of the **class listType**. The template parameter in the definitions of the member functions (for example, **elemType** in the definition of **insert**) of the **class listType** is also replaced by **int**.

Header File and Implementation File of a Class Template

Until now, we have placed the definition of the class (in the header file) and the definition of the member functions (in the implementation file) in separate files. The object code was generated from the implementation file and linked with the user code. However, this mechanism of separating the class definition and the definitions of the member functions does not work with class templates. Passing parameters to a function has an effect at run time, whereas passing a parameter to a class template has an effect at compile time. Because the actual parameter to a class is specified in the user code, and because the compiler cannot instantiate a function template without the actual parameter to the template, we can no longer compile the implementation file independently of the user code.

This problem has several possible solutions. We could put the class definition and the definitions of the function templates directly in the client code, or we could put the class definition and the definitions of the function templates together in the same header file. Another alternative is to put the class definition and the definitions of the functions in separate files (as usual), but include a directive to the implementation file at the end of the header file. In either case, the function definitions and the client code are compiled together. For illustrative purposes, we will put the class definition and the function definitions in the same header file.

The following example demonstrates the use of class templates.

Example 16-9

In this example, we will write a program that uses the **class listType**. Some of the operations included are as follows: check whether the list is empty, check whether the list is full, sort the list, and print the list. Because we can dynamically allocate arrays, the user will have the option to specify the size of the array. The default array size is `50`. We will manipulate a list of integers and a list of strings. Because the `class newString` that we defined earlier allows us to use relational operators for comparison and the assignment operator for assignment, we will use the `class newString` to declare strings.

The definition of the `class listType` is

```
//Header file listType.h

#ifndef H_listType
#define H_listType

#include <iostream>
#include <cassert>
using namespace std;

template <class elemType>
class listType
{
public:
    bool isEmpty();
        //Returns true if the list is empty, false otherwise
    bool isFull();
        //Returns true if the list is full, false otherwise
    int getLength();
        //Returns the length of the list, which is the number of
        //elements currently in the list
    int getMaxSize();
        //Returns the maximum number of elements that can
        //be stored in the list
    void sort();
        //Sorts the list
        //Post: the list elements are in ascending order
    void print() const;
        //Outputs the elements of the list
    void insertAt(const elemType& item, int position);
        //Post: list[position] = item; length++;
        //If the position is out of range, the program is aborted

    listType(int listSize = 50);
        //constructor
        //Creates an array of the size specified by the
        //parameter listSize; the default array size is 50
        //Post: list contains the base
        //          address of the array, length = 0 and
        //          maxsize = listSize

    ~listType();
        //destructor
        //Delete all elements of the list
        //Post: the array list is deleted
```

```
private:
    int maxSize; //maximum number that can be
                 //stored in the list
    int length;  //number of elements in the list
    elemType *list; //pointer to the array that holds the
                    //list elements
};


template<class elemType>
bool listType<elemType>::isEmpty()
{
      return (length == 0)
}

template<class elemType>
bool listType<elemType>::isFull()
{
      return (length == maxSize);
}

template<class elemType>
int listType<elemType>::getLength()
{
      return length;
}

template<class elemType>
int listType<elemType>::getMaxSize()
{
      return maxSize;
}

   //constructor; the default array size is 50
template<class elemType>
listType<elemType>::listType(int listSize)
{
      maxSize = listSize;
      length = 0;
      list = new elemType[maxSize];
}

template<class elemType>
listType<elemType>::~listType()  //destructor
{
      delete [] list;
}
```

```
template<class elemType>
void listType<elemType>::sort()   //selection sort
{
      int i, j;
      int min;
      elemType  temp;

      for(i = 0; i <length; i++)
      {
           min = i;
           for(j = i+1; j < length; ++j)
              if(list[j] < list[min])
                 min = j;
           temp = list[i];
           list[i] = list[min];
           list[min] = temp;
      }//end for
}//end sort

template<class elemType>
void listType<elemType>::print() const
{
      int i;
      for(i = 0; i < length; ++i)
           cout<<list[i]<<"  ";
      cout<<endl;
}//end print


template<class elemType>
void listType<elemType>::insertAt(const elemType& item,
                                  int position)
{
      assert(position >= 0 && position < maxSize);
      list[position] = item;
      length++;
}

#endif


//Program to test the class listType

#include <iostream>
#include "listType.h"
#include "myString.h"
using namespace std;
```

```
int main()
{
   listType<int> intList(100);                         //Line 1
   listType<newString> stringList;                    //Line 2

   int counter;                                        //Line 3
   int number;                                         //Line 4

   cout<<"List 5: Processing the integer list"
       <<endl;                                         //Line 5
   cout<<"List 6: Enter 5 integers: ";                 //Line 6

   for(counter = 0; counter < 5; counter++)            //Line 7
   {
       cin>>number;                                    //Line 8
       intList.insertAt(number,counter);               //Line 9
   }

   cout<<endl;                                         //Line 10
   cout<<"List 11: The list you entered is: ";         //Line 11
   intList.print();                                    //Line 12
   cout<<endl;                                         //Line 13
   cout<<"Line 14: After sorting, the list is: ";      //Line 14
   intList.sort();                                     //Line 15
   intList.print();                                    //Line 16
   cout<<endl;                                         //Line 17

   newString str;                                      //Line 18

   cout<<"Line 19: Processing the string list"
       <<endl;                                         //Line 19

   cout<<"Line 20: Enter 5 strings: ";                 //Line 20

   for(counter = 0; counter < 5; counter++)            //Line 21
   {
      cin>>str;                                        //Line 22
      stringList.insertAt(str,counter);                //Line 23
   }

   cout<<endl;                                         //Line 24
   cout<<"Line 25: The list you entered is: "
       <<endl;                                         //Line 25
   stringList.print();                                 //Line 26
   cout<<endl;                                         //Line 27
   cout<<"Line 28: After sorting, the list is: "
       <<endl;                                         //Line 28
   stringList.sort();                                  //Line 29
   stringList.print();                                 //Line 30
   cout<<endl;                                         //Line 31
```

```
    int intListSize;                                   //Line 32

    cout<<"Line 33: Enter the size of the integer "
        <<list: ";                                     //Line 33
    cin>>intListSize;                                  //Line 34

    listType<int> intList2(intListSize);               //Line 35

    cout<<"Line 36: Processing the integer list"
        <<endl;                                        //Line 36
    cout<<"Line 37: Enter "<<intListSize
        <<" integers: ";                               //Line 37

    for(counter = 0; counter < intListSize; counter++)//Line 38
    {
       cin>>number;                                    //Line 39
       intList2.insertAt(number,counter);              //Line 40
    }

    cout<<endl;                                        //Line 41
    cout<<"Line 42: The list you entered is: "<<endl; //Line 42
    intList2.print();                                  //Line 43
    cout<<endl;                                        //Line 44
    cout<<"Line 45: After sorting, the list is: "
        <<endl;                                        //Line 45
    intList2.sort();                                   //Line 46
    intList2.print();                                  //Line 47
    cout<<endl;                                        //Line 48
    cout<<"Line 49: Length of the list = "
        <<intList2.getLength()<<endl;                  //Line 49
    cout<<"Line 50: Maximum size of the list = "
        <<intList2.getMaxSize()<<endl;                 //Line 50

     return 0;
}
```

Sample Run: In this sample run, the user input is shaded.

```
List 5: Processing the integer list
List 6: Enter 5 integers: 19 15 66 24 34

List 11: The list you entered is: 19  15  66  24  34

Line 14: After sorting, the list is: 15  19  24  34  66

Line 19: Processing the string list
Line 20: Enter 5 strings: summer cold winter warm sunny

Line 25: The list you entered is:
summer  cold  winter  warm  sunny
```

```
Line 28: After sorting, the list is:
cold  summer  sunny  warm  winter

Line 33: Enter the size of the integer list: 10
Line 36: Processing the integer list
Line 37: Enter 10 integers: 23 65 34 8 11 5 3 16 45 2

Line 42: The list you entered is:
23  65  34  8  11  5  3  16  45  2

Line 45: After sorting, the list is:
2  3  5  8  11  16  23  34  45  65

Line 49: Length of the list = 10
Line 50: Maximum size of the list = 10
```

QUICK REVIEW

1. An operator that has different meanings with different data types is said to be overloaded.
2. In C++, >> is used as a stream extraction operator and as a right shift operator. Similarly, << is used as a stream insertion operator and as a left shift operator. Both are examples of operator overloading.
3. The function that overloads an operator is called an operator function.
4. The syntax of the heading of the operator function is

   `returnType operator operatorSymbol(parameters)`
5. In C++, `operator` is a reserved word.
6. Operator functions are value-returning functions.
7. Except for the assignment operator and the member selection operator, to use an operator on class objects, that operator must be overloaded. The assignment operator performs a default member-wise copy.
8. For classes with pointer data members, the assignment operator must be explicitly overloaded.
9. Operator overloading provides the same concise notation for user-defined data types as is available with built-in data types.
10. When an operator is overloaded, its precedence cannot be changed, its associativity cannot be changed, default arguments cannot be used with an overloaded operator, the number of arguments that the operator takes cannot be changed, and the meaning of how an operator works with built-in data types remains the same.
11. It is not possible to create new operators. Only existing operators can be overloaded.
12. Most C++ operators can be overloaded.

13. The operators that cannot be overloaded are `.`, `.*`, `::`, `?:`, and `sizeof`.
14. The pointer `this` refers to the object as a whole.
15. The operator function that overloads the operator `()`, `[]`, `->`, or `=` must be a member of a class.
16. A friend function is a nonmember of a class.
17. The heading of a friend function is preceded by the word `friend`.
18. In C++, `friend` is a reserved word.
19. If an operator function is a member of a class, the leftmost operand of the operator must be a class object (or a reference to a class object) of that operator's class.
20. The binary operator function as a member of a class has only one parameter; as a nonmember of a class, it has two parameters.
21. The operator functions that overload the stream insertion operator, <<, and the stream extraction operator, >>, for a class must be friend functions of that class.
22. To overload the pre-increment (++) operator for a class if the operator function is a member of that class, it must have no parameters. Similarly, to overload the pre-decrement (--) operator for a class if the operator function is member of that class, it must have no parameters.
23. To overload the post-increment (++) operator for a class if the operator function is a member of that class, it must have one parameter, of the type `int`. The user does not specify any value for the parameter. The dummy parameter in the function heading helps the compiler generate the correct code. The post-decrement operator has similar conventions.
24. A copy constructor initializes an object with the value of another object of the same class. The object that is being copied must be passed as a reference parameter.
25. When a formal parameter is a value parameter, the copy constructor is executed to pass the value of the actual parameter to the formal parameter.
26. A conversion constructor is a single-parameter function.
27. A conversion constructor converts its argument to an object of the constructor's class. The compiler implicitly calls such constructors.
28. Classes with pointer data members must overload the assignment operator and include both the copy constructor and the destructor.
29. In C++, a function name can be overloaded.
30. Every instance of an overloaded function has different sets of parameters.
31. In C++, `template` is a reserved word.
32. Using templates, you can write a single code segment for a set of related functions—called the function template.
33. Using templates, you can write a single code segment for a set of related classes—called the class template.

34. The syntax of a template is

```
template <class Type>
declaration;
```

where **Type** is a user-defined identifier, which is used to pass types (that is, data types) as parameters, and **declaration** is either a function or a class. The word **class** in the heading refers to any user-defined data type or built-in data type.

35. Class templates are called parameterized types.

36. In a class template, the parameter **Type** specifies how a generic class template is to be customized to form a specific template class.

37. The parameter **Type** is mentioned in every class header and member function definition.

38. Suppose **cType** is a class template and **func** is a member function of **cType**. The heading of the function definition of **func** is

```
template <class Type>
funcType cType<Type>::func(parameters)
```

where **funcType** is the type of the function, such as **void**.

39. Suppose **cType** is a class template, which can take **int** as a parameter. The statement

```
cType<int> x;
```

declares **x** to be an object of the type **cType**, and the type passed to the **class cType** is **int**.

EXERCISES

1. Mark the following statements as true or false.
   a. In C++, all operators can be overloaded for user-defined data types.
   b. In C++, operators cannot be redefined for built-in types.
   c. The function that overloads an operator is called the operator function.
   d. C++ allows users to create their own operators.
   e. The precedence of an operator cannot be changed, but its associativity can be changed.
   f. Every instance of an overloaded function has the same number of parameters.
   g. It is not necessary to overload relational operators for classes that have only **int** data members.
   h. The member function of a **class** template is a function template.

i. When writing the definition of a **`friend`** function, the keyword **`friend`** must appear in the function heading.

j. Templates provide the capability for software reuse.

k. The function heading of the operator function to overload the pre-increment operator `(++)` and the post-increment operator `(++)` is the same because both operators have the same symbols.

2. What is a **`friend`** function?
3. Suppose that the operator << is to be overloaded for a user-defined **`class`** **`mystery`**. Why must << be overloaded as a **`friend`** function?
4. Suppose that the binary operator + is overloaded as a member function for a **`class`** **`strange`**. How many parameters does the function **`operator+`** have?
5. When should a class overload the assignment operator and define the copy constructor?
6. Consider the following declaration:

```
class strange
{
   .
   .
   .
};
```

   a. Write a statement that shows the declaration in the **`class strange`** to overload the operator >>.

   b. Write a statement that shows the declaration in the **`class strange`** to overload the operator =.

   c. Write a statement that shows the declaration in the **`class strange`** to overload the binary operator + as a member function.

   d. Write a statement that shows the declaration in the **`class strange`** to overload the operator == as a member function.

   e. Write a statement that shows the declaration in the **`class strange`** to overload the post-increment operator ++ as a member function.

7. Assume the declaration of Exercise 6.

   a. Write a statement that shows the declaration in the **`class strange`** to overload the binary operator + as a **`friend`** function.

   b. Write a statement that shows the declaration in the **`class strange`** to overload the operator == as a **`friend`** function.

   c. Write a statement that shows the declaration in the **`class strange`** to overload the post-increment operator ++ as a **`friend`** function.

8. Find the error(s) in the following code:

```
class mystery                          //Line 1
{
    ...
    bool operator <= (mystery);        //Line 2
    ...
};

bool mystery::<=(mystery rightObj)     //Line 3
{
    ...
}
```

9. Find the error(s) in the following code:

```
class mystery                                 //Line 1
{
    ...
    bool operator <= (mystery, mystery);      //Line 2
    ...
};
```

10. Find the error(s) in the following code:

```
class mystery                          //Line 1
{
    ...
    friend operator+ (mystery);        //Line 2
      //overload binary +
    ...
};
```

11. How many parameters are required to overload the pre-increment operator for a class as a member function?

12. How many parameters are required to overload the pre-increment operator for a class as a **friend** function?

13. How many parameters are required to overload the post-increment operator for a class as a member function?

14. How many parameters are required to overload the post-increment operator for a class as a **friend** function?

15. Let $a + ib$ be a complex number. The conjugate of $a + ib$ is $a - ib$ and the absolute value of $a + ib$ is $\sqrt{a^2 + b^2}$. Extend the definition of the **class complexType** of the Programming Example: Complex Numbers by overloading the operators ~ and **!** as member functions so that ~ returns the conjugate of a complex number and **!** returns the absolute value. Write the definitions of these operator functions.

16. Redo Exercise 15 so that the operators ~ and **!** are overloaded as nonmember functions.

17. Find the error(s) in the following code:

```
template <class type>        //Line 1
class strange                //Line 2
{
    ...
};

strange<int> s1;            //Line 3
strange<type> s2;           //Line 4
```

18. Consider the following declaration:

```
template <class type>
class strange
{
   ...
private:
    Type a;
    Type b;
};
```

a. Write a statement that declares `sObj` to be an object of the type `strange` such that the `private` data members `a` and `b` are of the type `int`.

b. Write a statement that shows the declaration in the `class strange` to overload the operator == as a member function.

c. Assume that two objects of the type `strange` are equal if their corresponding data members are equal. Write the definition of the function `operator==` for the `class strange`, which is overloaded as a member function.

19. Consider the definition of the following function template:

```
template <class Type>
Type surprise(Type x, Type y)
{
    return x + y ;
}
```

What is the output of the following statements?

a. `cout<<surprise(5,7)<<endl;`

b.
```
string str1 = "Sunny";
string str2 = " Day";
cout<<surprise(str1, str2)<<endl;
```

20. Consider the definition of the following function template:

```
Template <class Type>
Type funcExp(Type list[], int size)
{
    int j;
    Type x = list[0];
    Type y = list[size – 1];
```

```
    for(j = 1; j < (size - 1)/2; j++)
    {
         if(x < list[j])
              x = list[j];
         if(y > list[size - 1 -j])
              y = list[size - 1 -j];
    }

    return x + y;
}
```

Further suppose that you have the following declarations:

```
int list[10] = {5,3,2,10,4,19,45,13,61,11};
string strList[] = {"One", "Hello", "Four", "Three", "How", "Six"};
```

What is the output of the following statements?

a. `cout<<funExp(list,10);`

b. `cout<<funExp(strList,6)<<endl;`

21. Write the definition of the function template that swaps the contents of two variables.

22. a. Overload the operator + for the `class newString` to perform string concatenation. For example, if `s1` is `"Hello "` and `s2` is `"there"`, the statement

    ```
    s3 = s1 + s2;
    ```

    should assign `"Hello there"` to `s3`, where `s1`, `s2`, and `s3` are `newString` objects.

    b. Overload the operator `+=` for the `class newString` to perform the following string concatenation: Suppose that `s1` is `"Hello "` and `s2` is `"there"`. Then the statement

    ```
    s1 += s2;
    ```

    should assign `"Hello there"` to `s1`, where `s1` and `s2` are `newString` objects.

PROGRAMMING EXERCISES

16

1. a. Write the definitions of the functions to overload the increment, decrement, arithmetic, and relational operators as members of the `class opOverClass`.

   b. Write a test program that tests the various operations on the `class opOverClass`.

2. a. Write the definitions of the functions to overload the increment, decrement, arithmetic, and relational operators as nonmembers of the `class opOverClass`.

   b. Write a test program that tests the various operations on the `class opOverClass`.

3. a. Extend the definition of the `class clockType` by overloading the post-increment operator function as a member of the `class clockType`.

b. Write the definition of the function to overload the post-increment operator for the `class clockType` as defined in part a.

4. a. The increment and relational operators in the `class clockType` are overloaded as member functions. Rewrite the definition of the `class clockType` so that these operators are overloaded as nonmember functions. Also, overload the post-increment operator for the `class clockType` as a nonmember.

b. Write the definitions of the member functions of the `class clockType` as designed in part a.

c. Write a test program that tests the various operations on the class as designed in parts a and b.

5. a. Extend the definition of the `class complexType` so that it performs the subtraction and division operations. Overload the operators subtraction and division for this class as member functions.

If (a, b) and (c, d) are complex numbers,

$(a, b) - (c, d) = (a - c, b - d)$.

If (c, d) is nonzero,

$(a, b) / (c, d) = ((ac + bd) / (c^2 + d^2), (-ad + bc) / (c^2 + d^2))$.

b. Write the definitions of the functions to overload the operators – and / as defined in part a.

c. Write a test program that tests various operations on the `class complexType`. Format your answer with two decimal places.

6. a. Rewrite the definition of the `class complexType` so that the arithmetic and relational operators are overloaded as nonmember functions.

b. Write the definitions of the member functions of the `class complexType` as designed in part a.

c. Write a test program that tests the various operations on the `class complexType` as designed in parts a and b. Format your answer with two decimal places.

7. a. Extend the definition of the `class newString` as follows:

i. Overload the operators + and += to perform the string concatenation operations.

ii. Add the function `length` to return the length of the string.

b. Write the definition of the function to implement the operations defined in part a.

c. Write a test program to test the various operations on the `newString` objects.

8. a. Rewrite the definition of the `class newString` as defined and extended in Programming Exercise 7, so that the relational operators are overloaded as nonmember functions.

b. Write the definition of the `class newString` as designed in a.

c. Write a test program that tests the various operations on the `class newString`.

9. Rational fractions are of the form $a\ /\ b$, where a and b are integers and $b \neq 0$. In this exercise, by "fractions" we mean rational fractions. Suppose $a\ /\ b$ and $c\ /\ d$ are fractions. Arithmetic operations on fractions are defined by the following rules:

   $a\ /\ b + c\ /\ d = (ad + bc)\ /\ bd$
   $a\ /\ b - c\ /\ d = (ad - bc)/bd$
   $a\ /\ b \times c\ /\ d = ac\ /\ bd$
   $(a\ /\ b)\ /\ (c\ /\ d) = ad\ /\ bc$, where $c\ /\ d \neq 0$.

   Fractions are compared as follows: $a\ /\ b\ \ op\ \ c\ /\ d$ if $ad\ \ op\ \ bc$, where op is any of the relational operations. For example, $a\ /\ b\ <\ c\ /\ d$ if $ad < bc$.

   Design a **class**—say, **fraction**—that performs the arithmetic and relational operations on fractions. Overload the arithmetic and relational operators so that the appropriate symbols can be used to perform the operation. Also, overload the stream insertion and stream extraction operators for easy input and output.

   Write a C++ program that, using the **class fraction**, performs operations on fractions.

   Among other things, test the following. Suppose **x**, **y**, and **z** are objects of the type **fraction**. If the input is 2/3, the statement

   ```
   cin>>x;
   ```

   should store 2/3 in **x**. The statement

   ```
   cout<<x+y<<endl;
   ```

   should output the value of **x + y** in fraction form. The statement

   ```
   z = x + y;
   ```

   should store the sum of **x** and **y** in **z** in fraction form. Your answer need not be in the lowest terms.

10. Recall that in C++ there is no check on the array index out of bound. However, during program execution, an array index out of bound can cause serious problems. Also, in C++ the array index starts at 0.

    Design and implement the **class myArray** that solves the array index out of bound problem, and also allows the user to begin the array index starting at any integer, positive or negative. Every object of the type **myArray** is an array of the type **int**. During execution, when accessing an array component, if the index is out of bounds, the program must terminate with an appropriate error message. Consider the following statements.


    ```
    myArray<int> list(5);                //Line 1
    myArray<int> myList(2,13);           //Line 2
    myArray<int> yourList(-5,9);         //Line 3
    ```

    The statement in Line 1 declares **list** to be an array of 5 components, the component type is **int**, and the components are: list[0], list[1], ..., list[4]; the statement in Line 2 declares **myList** to be an array of 11 components, the component type is **int**, and the components are: myList[2], myList[3], ..., myList[12]; the statement in Line 3 declares **yourList** to be an array of 14 components, the component type is **int**, and the components are: yourList[-5], yourlist[-4], ..., yourList[0], ..., yourList[8]. Write a program to test the **class myArray**.

11. Programming Exercise 10 processes only **int** arrays. Redesign the **class myArray** using class templates so that the **class** can be used in any application that requires arrays to process data.

12. Design a class to perform the various matrix operations. A matrix is a set of numbers arranged in rows and columns. Therefore, every element of a matrix has a row position and a column position. If A is a matrix of 5 rows and 6 columns, we say that the matrix A is of the size 5×6 and sometimes denote it as $A_{5\times 6}$. Clearly, a convenient place to store a matrix is in a two-dimensional array. Two matrices can be added and subtracted if they have the same size. Suppose $A = [a_{ij}]$ and $B = [b_{ij}]$ are two matrices of the size $m \times n$, where a_{ij} denotes the element of A in the ith row and the jth column, and so on. The sum and difference of A and B is given by

$$A + B = [a_{ij} + b_{ij}]$$
$$A - B = [a_{ij} - b_{ij}]$$

The multiplication of A and B ($A * B$) is defined only if the number of columns of A are the same as the number of rows of B. If A is of the size $m \times n$ and B is of the size $n \times t$, then $A * B = [c_{ik}]$ is of the size $m \times t$ and the element c_{ik} is given by the formula

$$c_{ik} = a_{i1}b_{1k} + a_{i2}b_{2k} + \dots + a_{in}b_{nk}$$

Design and implement a **class matrixType** that can store a matrix of any size. Overload the operators +, -, and * to perform the addition, subtraction, and multiplication operations, respectively, and overload the operator << to output a matrix. Also, write a test program to test the various operations on the matrices.

13. a. In Programming Exercise 1 in Chapter 13, we defined a **class romanType** to implement Roman numbers in a program. In that exercise, we also implemented a function, `romanToDecimal`, to convert a Roman number into its equivalent decimal number.

    Modify the definition of the **class romanType** so that the data members are declared as **protected**. Use the **class newString**, as designed in Programming Exercise 7, to manipulate strings. Furthermore, overload the stream insertion and stream extraction operators for easy input and output. The stream insertion operator outputs the Roman number in the Roman format.

    Also, include a member function, `decimalToRoman`, that converts the decimal number (the decimal number must be a positive integer) to an equivalent Roman number format. Write the definition of the member function `decimalToRoman`.

    For simplicity, we assume that only the letter `I` can appear in front of another letter and that it appears only in front of the letters `V` and `X`. For example, 4 is represented as `IV`, 9 is represented as `IX`, 39 is represented as `XXXIX`, and 49 is represented as `XXXXIX`. Also, 40 will be represented as `XXXX`, 190 will be represented as `CLXXXX`, and so on.

    b. Derive a **class extRomanType** from the **class romanType** to do the following. In the **class extRomanType**, overload the arithmetic operators +, -, *, and / so that arithmetic operations can be performed on Roman numbers. Also, overload the pre- and post-increment and decrement operators as member functions of the **class extRomanType**.

To add (subtract, multiply, or divide) Roman numbers, add (subtract, multiply, or divide, respectively) their decimal representations and then convert the result to the Roman number format. For subtraction, if the first number is smaller than the second number, output a message saying that, "`Because the first number is smaller than the second, the numbers cannot be subtracted`". Similarly, for division, the numerator must be larger than the denominator. Use similar conventions for the increment and decrement operators.

c. Write the definitions of the functions to overload the operators described in part b.

d. Test your **`class`** `extRomanType` on the following program. (Include the appropriate header files.)

```
int main()
{
    extRomanType num1("XXXIV");
    extRomanType num2("XV");
    extRomanType num3;

    cout<<"Num1 = "<<num1<<endl;
    cout<<"Num2 = "<<num2<<endl;
    cout<<"Num1 + Num2 = "<<num1+num2<<endl;
    cout<<"Num1 * Num2 = "<<num1*num2<<endl;

    cout<<"Enter two numbers in Roman format: ";
    cin>>num1>>num2;
    cout<<endl;

    cout<<"Num1 = "<<num1<<endl;
    cout<<"Num2 = "<<num2<<endl;

    num3 = num2 * num1;
    cout<<"Num3 = "<<num3<<endl;

    cout<<"--num3: "<<--num3<<endl;
    cout<<"++num3: "<<++num3<<endl;

    return 0;
}
```

16

14. In Example 16-9, the class template `listType` is designed to implement a list in a program. For illustration purposes, that example included only the sorting operation. Extend the definition of the class template to include the remove and search operations. Write the definitions of the member functions to implement the class template `listType`. Also, write a test program to test the various operations on a list.

15. **(Stock Market)** Write a program to help a local stock trading company automate its systems. The company invests only in the stock market. At the end of each trading day, the company would like to generate and post the listing of its stocks so that investors can see how their holdings performed that day. We assume that the company invests in, say, 10 different stocks. The desired output is to produce two listings, one sorted by stock symbol and another sorted by percent gain from highest to lowest.

The input data is provided in a file in the following format:

```
symbol openingPrice closingPrice todayHigh todayLow prevClose volume
```

For example, the sample data is

```
MSMT 112.50 115.75 116.50 111.75 113.50 6723823
CBA 67.50 75.50 78.75 67.50 65.75 378233
.
.
.
```

The first line indicates that the stock symbol is **MSMT**, today's opening price was 112.50, the closing price was 115.75, today's high price was 116.50, today's low price was 111.75, yesterday's closing price was 113.50, and the number of shares currently being held is 6723823.

The listing sorted by stock symbols must be of the following form:

```
*********  First Investor's Heaven  **********
*********     Financial Report        **********
Stock               Today                     Previous  Percent
Symbol  Open    Close   High    Low     Close     Gain            Volume
------  -----   -----   -----   -----   --------  -------         ------
   ABC  123.45  130.95  132.00  125.00  120.50      8.67%          10000
  AOLK   80.00   75.00   82.00   74.00   83.00     -9.64%           5000
  CSCO  100.00  102.00  105.00   98.00  101.00      0.99%          25000
   IBD   68.00   71.00   72.00   67.00   75.00     -5.33%          15000
  MSET  120.00  140.00  145.00  140.00  115.00     21.74%          30920
Closing Assets: $9628300.00
-*-*-*-*-*-*-*-*-*-*-*-*-*-*-*-*-*-*-*-*-*-*-*
```

Develop this programming exercise in two steps. In the first step (part a), design and implement a stock object. In the second step (part b), design and implement an object to maintain a list of stocks.

a. **(Stock Object)** Design and implement the stock object. Call the class that captures the various characteristics of a stock object **stockType**.

   The main components of a stock are the stock symbol, stock price, and number of shares. Moreover, we need to output the opening price, high price, low price, previous price, and the percent gain/loss for the day. These are also all the characteristics of a stock. Therefore, the stock object should store all this information.

   Perform the following operations on each stock object:

   i. Set the stock information.

   ii. Print the stock information.

   iii. Show the different prices.

   iv. Calculate and print the percent gain/loss.

   v. Show the number of shares.

a.1. The natural ordering of the stock list is by stock symbol. Overload the relational operators to compare two stock objects by their symbols.

a.2. Overload the insertion operator, <<, for easy output.

a.3. Because data is stored in a file, overload the stream extraction operator, >>, for easy input.

For example, suppose `infile` is an `ifstream` object and the input file was opened using the object `infile`. Further suppose that `myStock` is a stock object. Then, the statement

```
infile>>myStock;
```

reads data from the input file and stores it in the object `myStock`. (Note that this statement reads and stores data in relevant components of `myStock`.)

b. Now that you have designed and implemented the `class stockType` to implement a stock object in a program, it is time to create a list of stock objects.

Let us call the class to implement a list of stock objects `stockListType`.

The `class stockListType` must be derived from the `class listType`, which you designed and implemented in the previous exercise. However, the `class stockListType` is a very specific class, designed to create a list of stock objects. Therefore, the `class stockListType` is no longer a template.

Add and/or overwrite the operations of the `class listType` to implement the necessary operations on a stock list.

The following statement derives the `class stockListType` from the `class listType`:

```
class stockListType: public listType<stockType>
{
    member list
};
```

The data members to hold the list elements, the length of the list, and the `max listSize` were declared as `protected` in the `class listType`. Therefore, these members can be directly accessed in the `class stockListType`.

Because the company also requires you to produce the list ordered by the percent gain/loss, you need to sort the stock list by this component. However, you are not to physically sort the list by the component percent gain/loss. Instead, you will provide a logical ordering with respect to this component.

To do so, add a data member, an array, to hold the indices of the stock list ordered by the component percent gain/loss. Call this array `sortIndicesGainLoss`. When printing the list ordered by the component percent gain/loss, use the array `sortIndicesGainLoss` to print the list. The elements of the array `sortIndicesGainLoss` will tell which component of the stock list to print next.

c. Write a program that uses these two classes to automate the company's analysis of stock data.

CHAPTER

17

LINKED LISTS

In this chapter, you will:

- Learn about linked lists
- Become aware of the basic properties of linked lists
- Explore the insertion and deletion operations on linked lists
- Discover how to build and manipulate a linked list
- Learn how to construct a doubly linked list

You have already seen how data is organized and processed sequentially using an array, called a *sequential list*. You have performed several operations on sequential lists, such as sorting, inserting, deleting, and searching. You also found that if data is not sorted, then searching for an item in the list can be very time-consuming, especially with large lists. Once the data is sorted, you can use a binary search and improve the search algorithm. However, in this case, insertion and deletion become time-consuming, especially with large lists, because these operations require data movement. Also, because the array size must be fixed during execution, new items can be added only if there is room. Thus, there are limitations when you organize data in an array.

This chapter helps you to overcome some of these problems. Chapter 15 showed how memory (variables) can be dynamically allocated and deallocated using pointers. This chapter uses pointers to organize and process data in lists, called **linked lists**. Recall that when data is stored in an array, memory for the components of the array is contiguous—that is, the blocks are allocated one after the other.

LINKED LISTS

A linked list is a collection of components, called **nodes.** Every node (except the last node) contains the address of the next node. Thus, every node in a linked list has two components: one to store the relevant information (that is, data), and one to store the address, called the **link**, of the next node in the list. The address of the first node in the list is stored in a separate location, called the **head** or **first**. Figure 17-1 is a pictorial representation of a node.

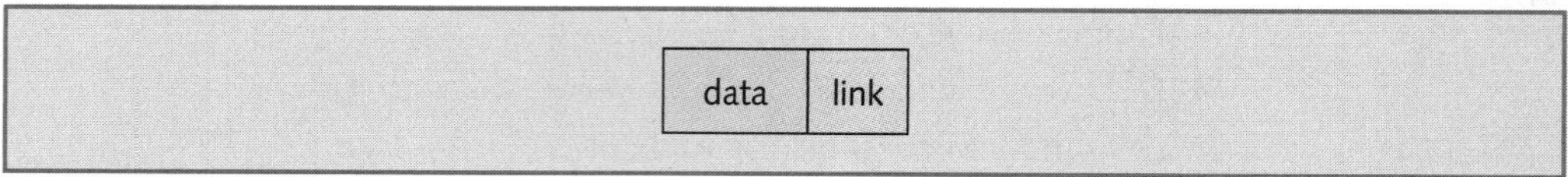

Figure 17-1 Structure of a node

Linked list: A list of items, called **nodes**, in which the order of the nodes is determined by the address, called the **link**, stored in each node.

The list in Figure 17-2 is an example of a linked list.

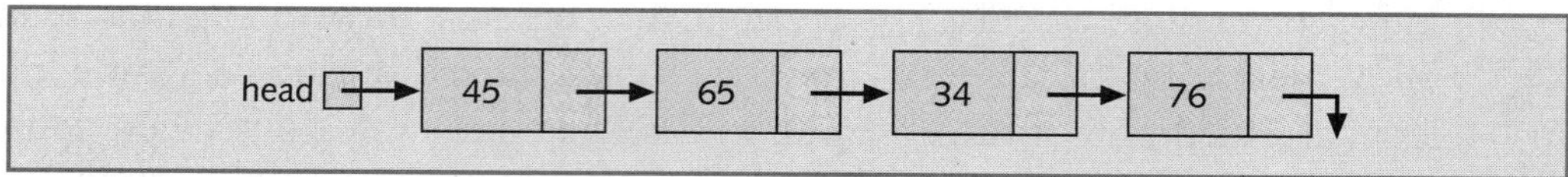

Figure 17-2 Linked list

The down arrow in the last node indicates that this link field is `NULL`. The arrow in each node indicates that the address of the node to which it is pointing is stored in that node. For a better understanding of this notation, suppose that the first node is at memory location `1200`, and the second node is at memory location `1575`. We thus have Figure 17-3.

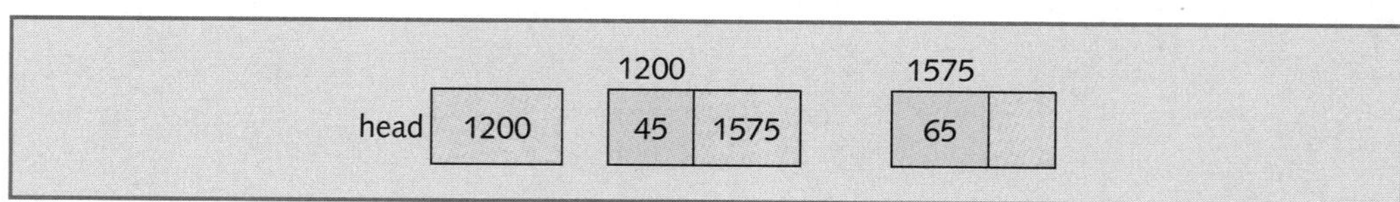

Figure 17-3 Linked list and values of the links

The value of the head is `1200`, the data part of the first node is `45`, and the link component of the first node contains `1575`, the address of the second node. If no confusion arises, then we will use the arrow notation whenever we draw the figure of a linked list.

Because each node of a linked list has two components, we need to declare each node as a **`class`** or **`struct`**. The data type of each node depends on the specific application—that is, what kind of data is being processed; however, the link component of each node is a pointer. The data type of this pointer variable is the node type itself. For the previous linked list, the definition of the node is as follows. (Suppose that the data type is **`int`**.)

```
struct nodeType
{
      int  info;
      nodeType *link;
};
```

The variable declaration is

```
nodeType  *head;
```

Linked Lists: Some Properties

To help you better understand the concept of a linked list and a node, some important properties of linked lists are described next.

Consider the linked list in Figure 17-4.

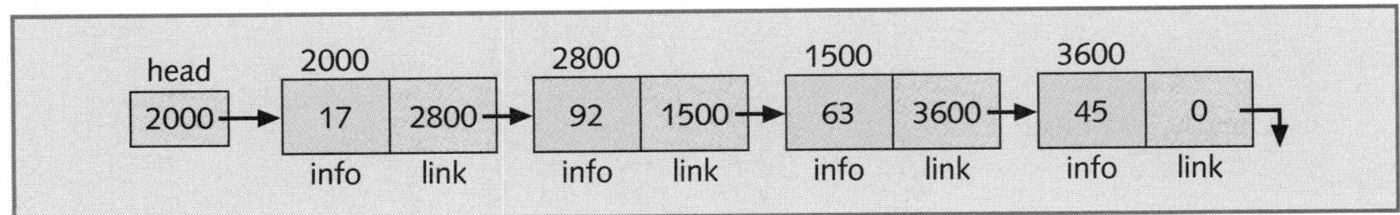

Figure 17-4 Linked list with four nodes

This linked list has four nodes. The address of the first node is stored in the pointer **`head`**. Each node has two components: **`info`**, to store the info, and **`link`**, to store the address of the next node. For simplicity, we assume that **`info`** is of the type **`int`**.

Suppose that the first node is at location `2000`, the second node is at location `2800`, the third node is at location `1500`, and the fourth node is at location `3600`. Therefore, the value of **`head`** is `2000`, the value of the component **`link`** of the first node is `2800`, the value of the component **`link`** of the second node is `1500`, and so on. Also, the value `0` in the component link of the last node means that this value is `NULL`, which we indicate by drawing a down arrow. The number at the top of each node is the address of the node. The following table shows that in this list.

	Value	
head	2000	
head->info	17	Because head is 2000 and the info of the node at location 2000 is 17
head->link	2800	
head->link->info	92	Because head->link is 2800 and the info of the node at location 2800 is 92

Suppose that **current** is a pointer of the same type as the pointer **head**. Then the statement

```
current = head;
```

copies the value of **head** into **current**. (See Figure 17-5.)

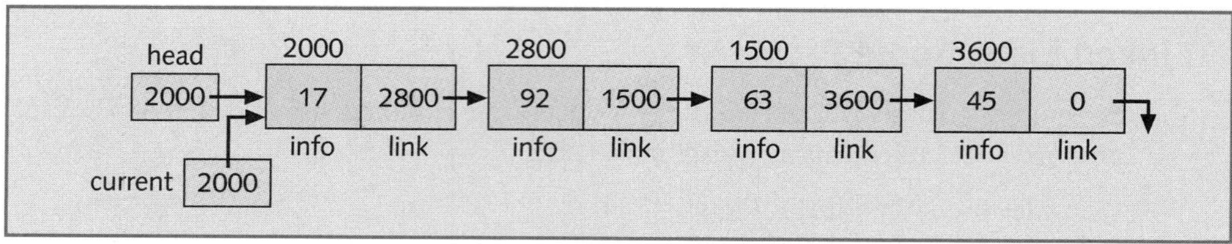

Figure 17-5 Linked list after current = head; executes

Clearly, in Figure 17-5,

	Value
current	2000
current->info	17
current->link	2800
current->link->info	92

Now consider the statement:

```
current = current->link;
```

This statement copies the value of `current->link`, which is `2800`, into `current`. Therefore, after this statement executes, `current` points to the second node in the list. (When working with linked lists, we typically use these types of statements to advance a pointer to the next node in the list.) See Figure 17-6.

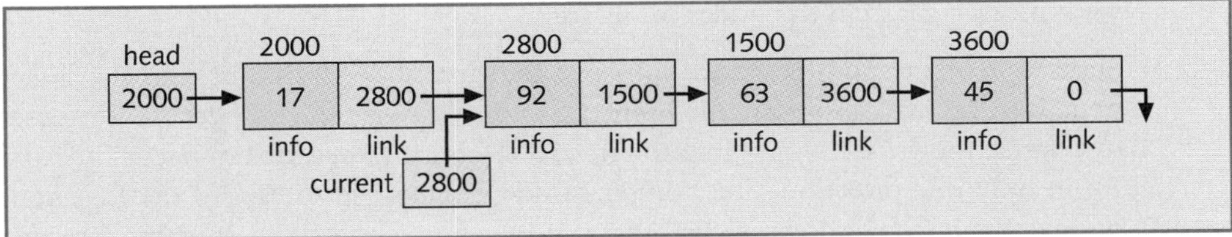

Figure 17-6 List after `current = current->link;` executes

In Figure 17-6,

	Value
`current`	`2800`
`current->info`	`92`
`current->link`	`1500`
`current->link->info`	`63`

Finally, note that in Figure 17-6,

	Value
`head->link->link`	`1500`
`head->link->link->info`	`63`
`head->link->link->link`	`3600`
`head->link->link->link->info`	`45`
`current->link->link`	`3600`
`current->link->link->info`	`45`
`current->link->link->link`	`0` (that is, `NULL`)
`current->link->link->link->info`	Does not exist

17

From now on, when working with linked lists, we will use only the arrow notation.

Traversing a Linked List

The basic operations of a linked list are as follows: search the list to determine whether a particular item is in the list, insert an item in the list, and delete an item from the list. These operations require the list to be traversed. That is, given a pointer to the first node of the list, we must step through the nodes of the list.

Suppose that the pointer **head** points to the first node in the list, and the link of the last node is **NULL**. We cannot use the pointer **head** to traverse the list because if we use the **head** to traverse the list we would lose the nodes of the list. This problem occurs because the links are in only one direction. The pointer **head** contains the address of the first node, the first node contains the address of the second node, the second node contains the address of the third node, and so on. If we move **head** to the second node, the first node is lost (unless we save the pointer to this node). If we keep advancing **head** to the next node, we will lose all the nodes of the list (unless we save the pointer to each node before advancing **head**, which is impractical because it would require additional computer time and memory space to maintain the list).

Therefore, we always want **head** to point to the first node. It now follows that we must traverse the list using another pointer of the same type. Suppose that **current** is a pointer of the same type as **head**. The following code traverses the list:

```
current = head;
while(current != NULL)
{
        //Process current
        current = current->link;
}
```

For example, suppose that **head** points to a linked list of numbers. The following code outputs the data stored in each node:

```
current = head;
while(current != NULL)
{
        cout<<current->info<<" ";
        current = current->link;
}
```

Item Insertion and Deletion

This section discusses how to insert an item in, and delete an item from, a linked list. Consider the following definition of a node. (For simplicity, we assume that the **info** type is **int**. The next section, which discusses linked lists as an abstract data type (ADT) using templates, uses the generic definition of a node.)

```
struct nodeType
{
      int  info;
      nodeType *link;
};
```

We will use the following variable declaration:

```
nodeType  *head, *p, *q, *newNode;
```

Insertion

Consider the linked list shown in Figure 17-7.

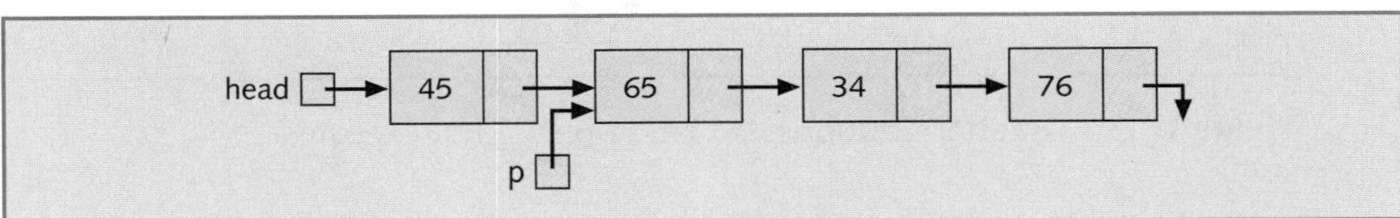

Figure 17-7 Linked list before item insertion

Suppose that `p` points to the node with `info 65`, and a new node with `info 50` is to be created and inserted after `p`. The following statements create and store `50` in the `info` field of a new node:

```
newNode = new nodeType;   //create newNode
newNode->info = 50;       //store 50 in the new node
```

The first statement (that is, `newNode = new nodeType;`) creates a node somewhere in memory and stores the address of the newly created node in `newNode`. The second statement (that is, `newNode->info = 50;`) stores `50` in the `info` field of the new node. (See Figure 17-8.)

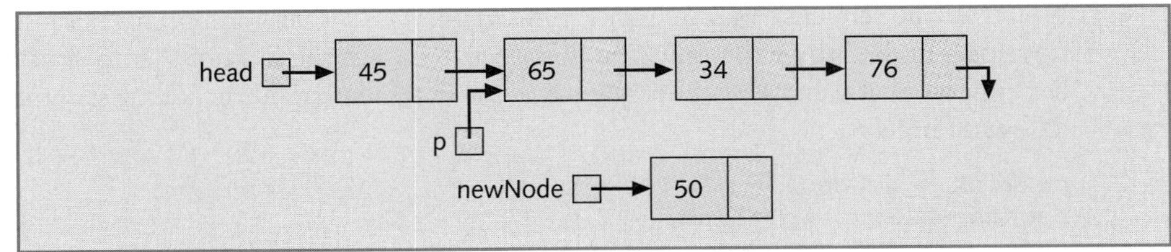

Figure 17-8 Create `newNode` and store `50` in it

17

The following statements insert the node in the linked list at the required place:

```
newNode->link = p->link;
p->link = newNode;
```

After the first statement (that is, `newNode->link = p->link;`) executes, the resulting list is as shown in Figure 17-9.

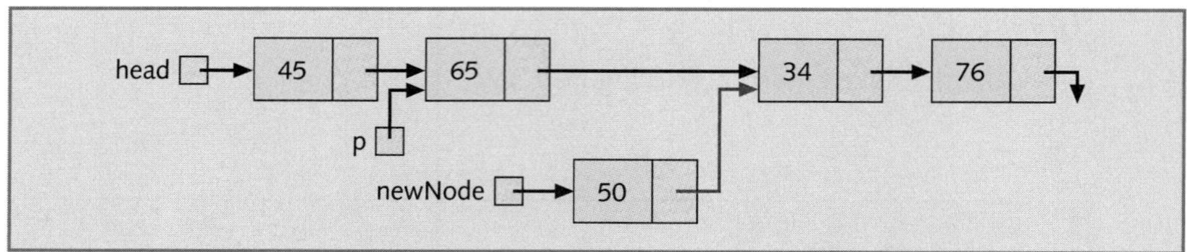

Figure 17-9 List after `newNode->link = p->link;` executes

After the second statement (that is, `p->link = newNode;`) executes, the resulting list is as shown in Figure 17-10.

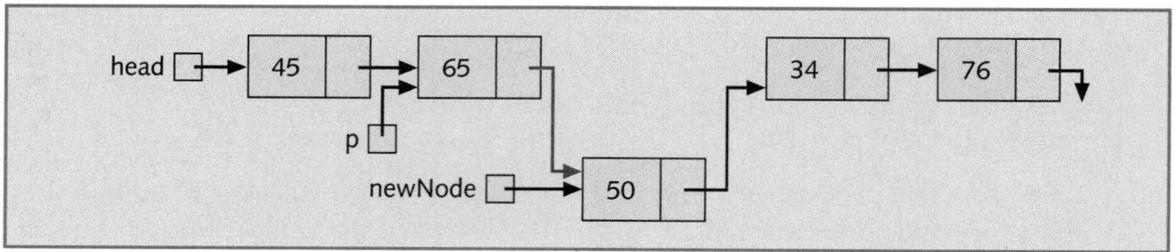

Figure 17-10 List after `p->link = newNode;` executes

Note that the sequence of statements to insert the node is very important because to insert **newNode** in the list we use only one pointer, **p**, to adjust the links of the node of the linked list. Suppose that we reverse the sequence of the statements and execute the statements in the following order:

```
p->link = newNode;
newNode->link = p->link;
```

Figure 17-11 shows the resulting list after these statements execute.

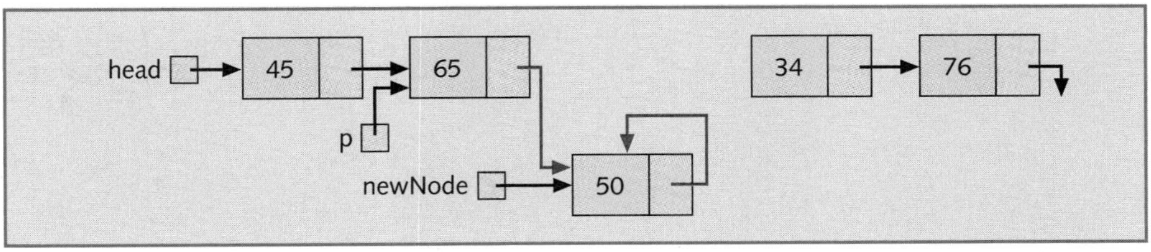

Figure 17-11 List after execution of `p->link = newNode;` followed by execution of `newNode->link = p->link;`

From Figure 17-11, it is clear that **newNode** points back to itself and the remainder of the list is lost.

Using two pointers, we can simplify the insertion code somewhat. Suppose **q** points to the node with **info 34**. (See Figure 17-12.)

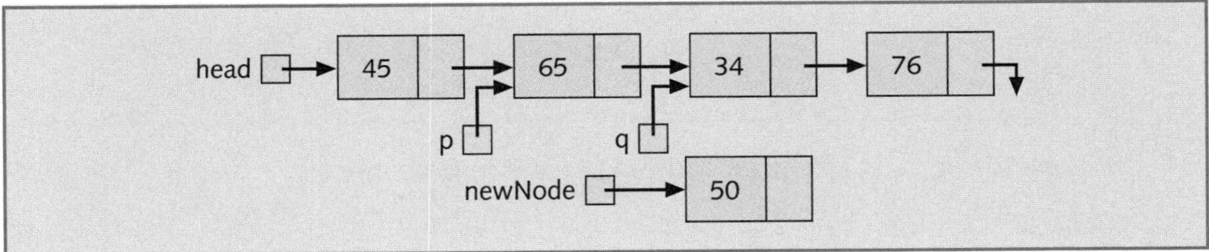

Figure 17-12 List with pointers p and q

The following statements insert **newNode** between **p** and **q**:

```
newNode->link = q;
p->link = newNode;
```

The order in which these statements execute does not matter. To illustrate this, suppose that we execute the statements in the following order:

```
p->link = newNode;
newNode->link = q;
```

After the statement **p->link = newNode;** executes, the resulting list is as shown in Figure 17-13.

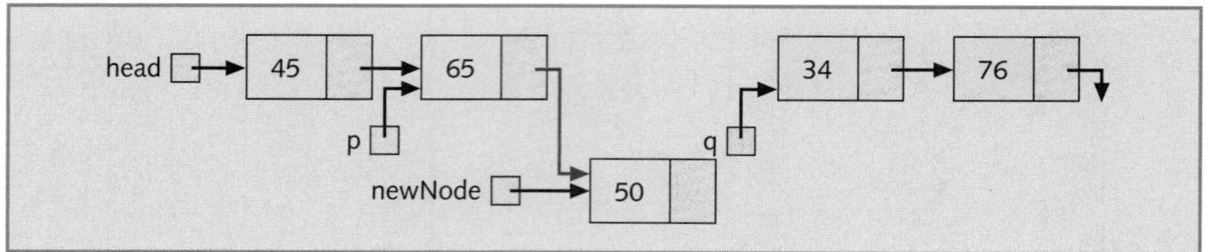

Figure 17-13 List after `p->link = newNode;` executes

Because we have a pointer, **q**, pointing to the remaining list, the remaining list is not lost. After the statement `newNode->link = q;` executes, the list is as shown in Figure 17-14.

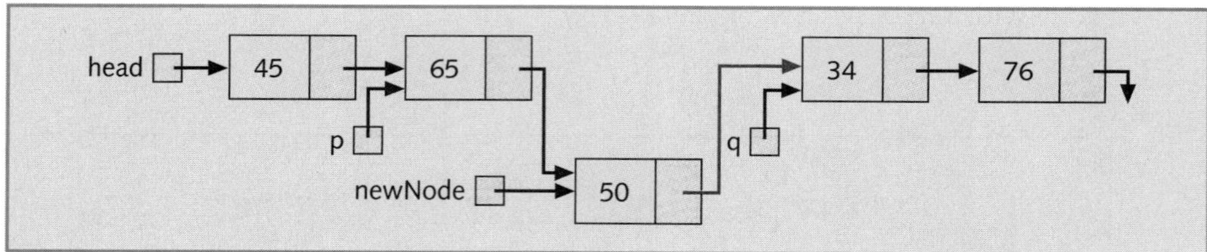

Figure 17-14 List after `newNode->link = q;` executes

Deletion

Consider the linked list shown in Figure 17-15.

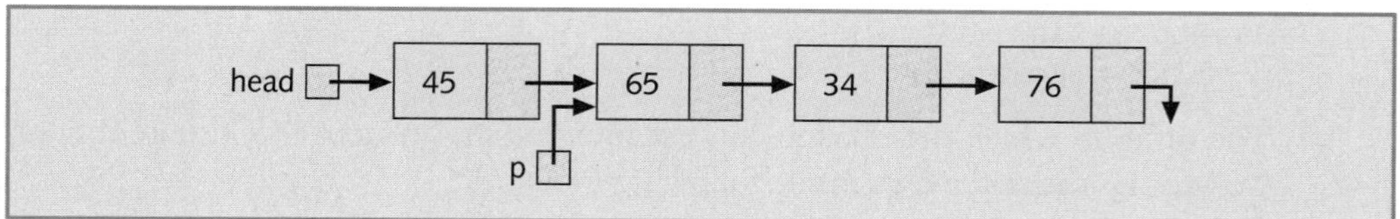

Figure 17-15 Node to be deleted is with `info 34`

Suppose that the node with `info 34` is to be deleted from the list. The following statement removes the node from the list:

```
p->link = p->link->link;
```

Figure 17-16 shows the resulting list after the preceding statement executes.

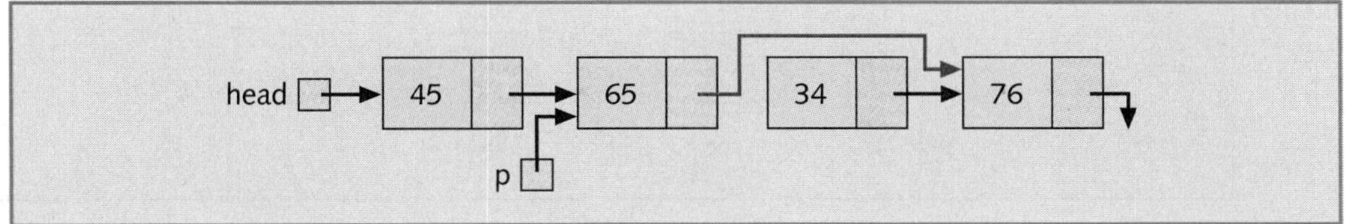

Figure 17-16 List after `p->link = p->link->link;` executes

From Figure 17-16, it clear that the node with `info 34` is removed from the list. However, the memory is still occupied by this node; that is, this node is dangling. To deallocate the memory, we need a pointer to this node. The following statements delete the node from the list and deallocate the memory occupied by this node:

```
q = p->link;
p->link = q->link;
delete q;
```

After statement `q = p->link;` executes, the list is as shown in Figure 17-17.

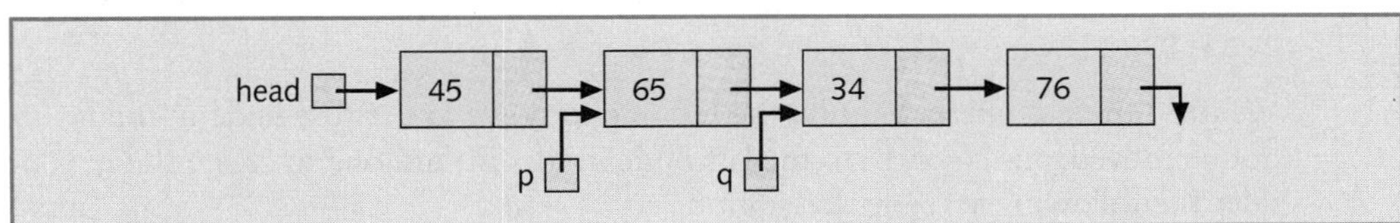

Figure 17-17 List after `q = p->link;` executes

After the statement `p->link = q->link;` executes, the resulting list is as shown in Figure 17-18.

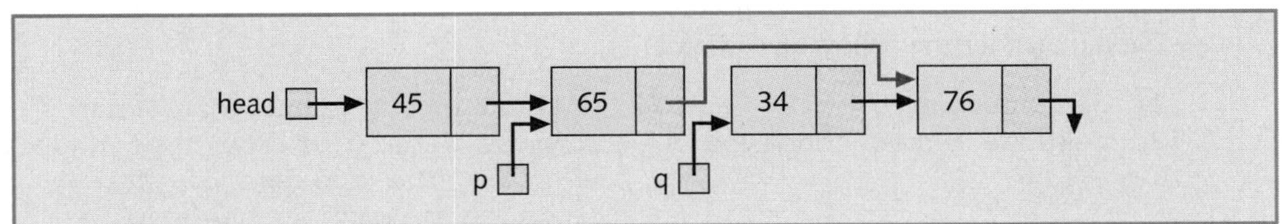

Figure 17-18 List after `p->link = q->link;` executes

After the statement `delete q;` executes, the list is as shown in Figure 17-19.

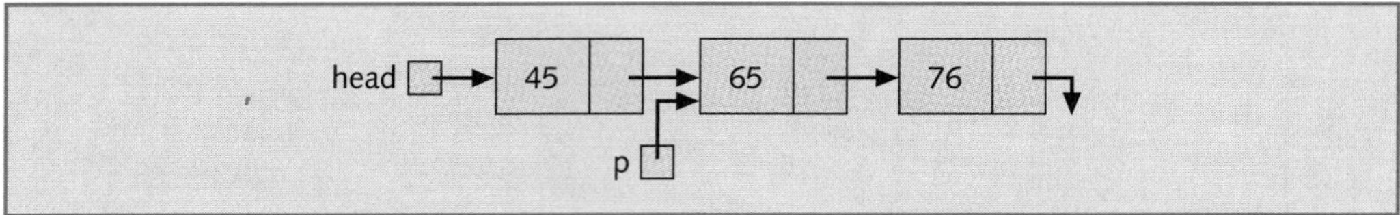

Figure 17-19 List after `delete q;` executes

Building a Linked List

Now that we know how to insert a node in a linked list, let us see how to build a linked list. First, we consider a linked list in general. If the data we read is unsorted, the linked list will be unsorted. Such a list can be built in two ways: in the forward manner and in the backward manner. In the forward manner, a new node is always inserted at the end of the linked list; in the backward manner, a new node is always inserted at the beginning of the list. We will consider both cases.

Building a Linked List Forward

Suppose that the nodes are in the usual `info-link` form and `info` is of the type `int`. Let us assume that we process the following data:

```
2 15 8 24 34
```

We need three pointers to build the list: one to point to the first node in the list, which cannot be moved; one to point to the last node in the list; and one to create the new node. Consider the following variable declaration:

```
nodeType  *first, *last, *newNode;
int    num;
```

Suppose that `first` points to the first node in the list. Initially, the list is empty, so both `first` and `last` are `NULL`. Thus, we must have the statements

```
first = NULL;
last = NULL;
```

to initialize `first` and `last` to `NULL`.

Next, consider the following statements:

```
1  cin>>num;                  //read and store a number in num
2  newNode = new nodeType;    //allocate memory of the type nodeType
                              //and store the address of the
                              //allocated memory in newNode
3  newNode->info = num;       //copy the value of num into the
                              //info field of newNode
4  newNode->link = NULL;      //initialize the link field of
                              //newNode to NULL
```

```
5  if (first == NULL)       //if first is NULL, the list is empty;
                            //make first and last point to newNode
   {
5a    first = newNode;
5b    last = newNode;
   }
6  else                     //list is not empty
   {
6a    last->link = newNode; //insert newNode at the end of the list
6b    last = newNode;        //set last so that it points to the
                             //actual last node in the list
   }
```

Let us now execute these statements. Initially, both `first` and `last` are `NULL`. Therefore we have the list as shown in Figure 17-20.

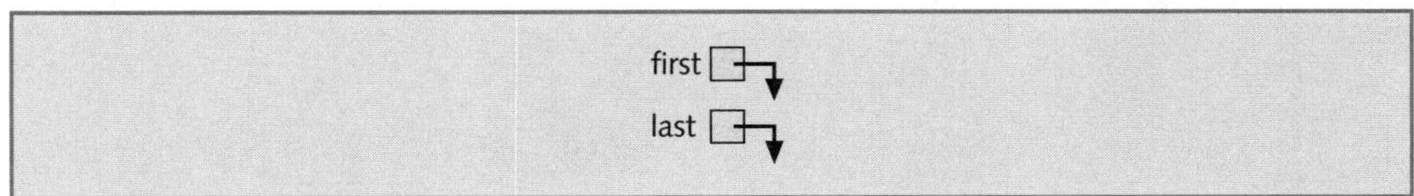

Figure 17-20 Empty list

After statement 1 executes, `num` is `2`. Statement 2 creates a node and stores the address of that node in `newNode`. Statement 3 stores `2` in the `info` field of `newNode`, and statement 4 stores `NULL` in the `link` field of `newNode` (see Figure 17-21.)

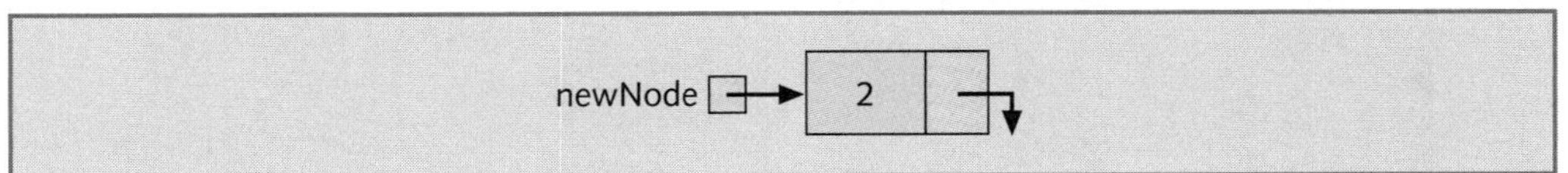

Figure 17-21 `newNode` with `info 2`

Because `first` is `NULL`, we execute statements 5a and 5b. Figure 17-22 shows the resulting list.

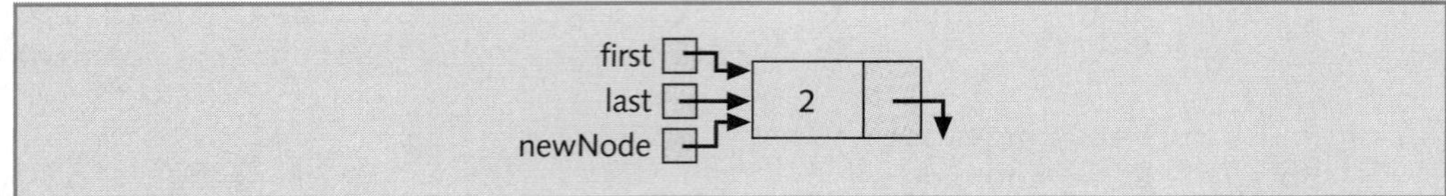

Figure 17-22 List after inserting `newNode` in it

We now repeat statements 1 through 6b. After statement 1 executes, **`num`** is **`15`**. Statement 2 creates a node and stores the address of the node in **`newNode`**. Statement 3 stores **`15`** in the **`info`** field of **`newNode`**, and statement 4 stores **`NULL`** in the link field of **`newNode`**. (See Figure 17-23.)

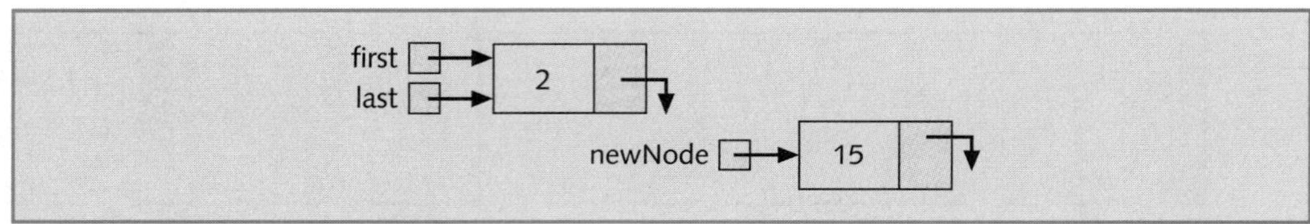

Figure 17-23 List and `newNode` with `info 15`

Because **`first`** is not **`NULL`**, we execute statements 6a and 6b. Figure 17-24 shows the resulting list.

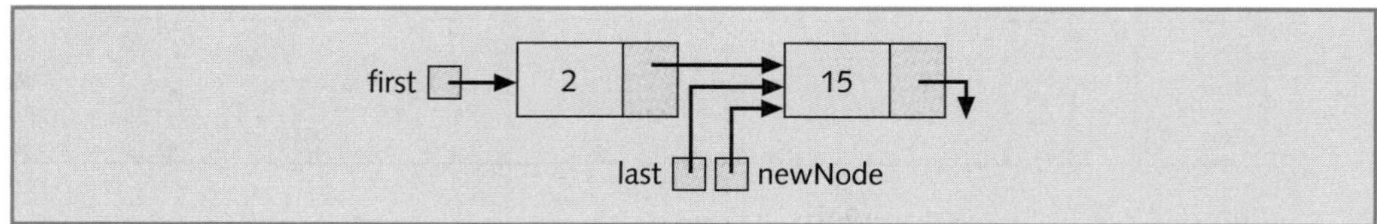

Figure 17-24 List after inserting `newNode` at the end

We now repeat statements 1 through 6b three more times. Figure 17-25 shows the resulting list.

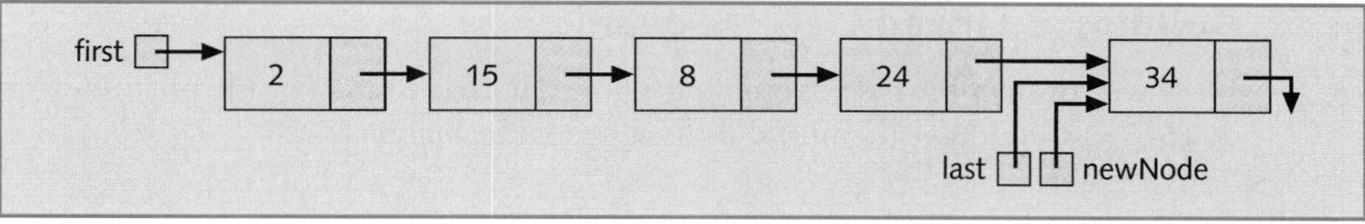

Figure 17-25 List after inserting 8, 24, and 34

We can put the previous statements in a loop, and execute the loop until certain conditions are met, to build the linked list. We can, in fact, write a C++ function to build a linked list.

Suppose that we read a list of integers ending with -999. The following function, **buildListForward**, builds a linked list (in a forward manner) and returns the pointer of the built list:

```
nodeType* buildListForward()
{
    nodeType   *first, *newNode,  *last;
    int num;

    cout<<"Enter a list of integers ending with -999.\n";
    cin>>num;
    first = NULL;

    while (num != -999)
    {
       newNode = new nodeType;
       newNode->info = num;
       newNode->link = NULL;

       if (first == NULL)
       {
           first = newNode;
           last = newNode;
       }
       else
       {
           last->link = newNode;
           last = newNode;
       }
       cin>>num;
   }//end while

   return first;
}//end buildListForward
```

Building a Linked List Backward

Now we consider the case of building a linked list backward. For the previously given data—`2, 15, 8, 24,` and `34`—the linked list is as shown in Figure 17-26.

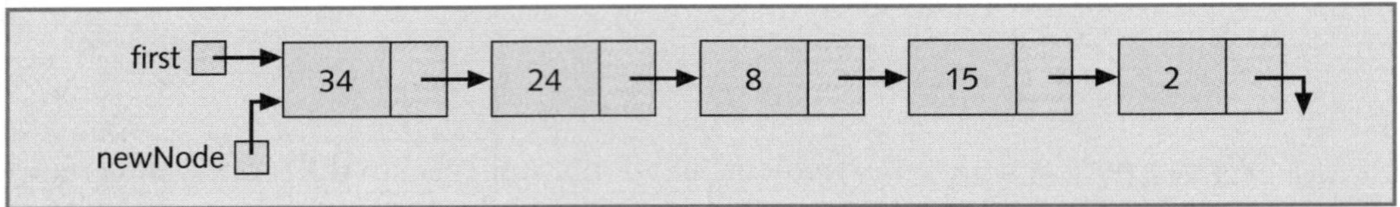

Figure 17-26 List after building it backward

Because the new node is always inserted at the beginning of the list, we do not need to know the end of the list, so the pointer `last` is not needed. Also, after inserting the new node at the beginning, the new node becomes the first node in the list. Thus, we need to update the value of the pointer `first` to correctly point to the first node in the list. We see, then, that we need only two pointers to build the linked list: one to point to the list, and one to create the new node. Because initially the list is empty, the pointer `first` must be initialized to `NULL`. In pseudocode, the algorithm is

1. Initialize `first` to `NULL`.
2. For each item in the list,
    a. Create the new node, `newNode`.
    b. Store the item in `newNode`.
    c. Insert `newNode` before `first`.
    d. Update the value of the pointer `first`.

The following C++ function builds the linked list backward and returns the pointer of the built list:

```
nodeType* buildListBackward()
{
    nodeType  *first, *newNode;
    int num;

    cout<<"Enter a list of integers ending with -999.\n";
    cin>>num;
    first = NULL;
```

```
    while (num != -999)
    {
        newNode = new nodeType; //create a node
        newNode->info = num;    //store the data in newNode
        newNode->link = first;  //put newNode at the beginning of
                                //the list
        first = newNode;        //update the head pointer of the
                                //list, that is, first
        cin>>num;               //read the next number
    }

   return first;
}//end buildListBackward
```

Linked List as an ADT

The previous sections taught you the basic properties of linked lists and how to construct and manipulate linked lists. Because a linked list is a very important data structure, rather than discuss specific lists such as a list of integers or a list of strings, this section discusses linked lists as an abstract data type (ADT). Using templates, this section gives a generic definition of linked lists, which is then used in the next section and later in this book. The programming example at the end of this chapter also uses this generic definition of linked lists.

The basic operations on linked lists are

1. Initialize the list.
2. Check whether the list is empty.
3. Check whether the list is full.
4. Print the list.
5. Find the length of the list.
6. Destroy the list.
7. Search the list for a given item.
8. Insert an item in the list.
9. Delete an item from the list.

The following operation on linked lists is also included. It is helpful if you want to check the first node's information.

10. Retrieve the `info` contained in the first node.

First, we discuss these operations on arbitrary lists—that is, lists that may be sorted or unsorted. The next section discusses sorted linked lists.

If a list is arbitrary, then we can insert a new item at either the end or the beginning. Furthermore, such a list may initially be built in either a forward manner or a backward manner. The function **buildListForward** requires the new item to be inserted at the end, whereas the function **buildListBackward** requires the new item to be inserted at the beginning. To accommodate both operations, we will write two functions: **insertFirst**, to insert the **newitem** at the beginning of the list, and **insertLast**, to insert the **newitem** at the end of the list. Also, to make the algorithms somewhat efficient, we will maintain two pointers in the list: `first`, pointing to the first node in the list, and `last`, pointing to the last node in the list.

The following class defines the linked list as an ADT:

```
//Definition of the node

template<class Type>
struct nodeType
{
      Type info;
      nodeType<Type> *link;
};


template<class Type>
class linkedListType
{
public:
    const linkedListType<Type>& operator=
                                (const linkedListType<Type>&);
      //Overload the assignment operator
    void initializeList();
      //Initialize the list to an empty state
      //Post: first = NULL, last = NULL
    bool isEmptyList();
      //Function returns true if the list is empty;
      //otherwise, it returns false
    bool isFullList();
      //Function returns true if the list is full;
      //otherwise, it returns false
    void print();
      //Output the data contained in each node
      //Post: None
    int length();
      //Return the number of elements in the list
    void destroyList();
      //Delete all nodes from the list
      //Post: first = NULL, last = NULL
```

```
    void retrieveFirst(Type& firstElement);
      //Return the data contained in the first node of the list
      //Post: firstElement = first element of the list
    void search(const Type& searchItem);
      //Outputs "Item is found in the list" if searchItem is in
      //the list; otherwise, outputs "Item is not in the list"
    void insertFirst(const Type& newItem);
      //newItem is inserted in the list
      //Post: first points to the new list and
      //     newItem is inserted at the beginning of the list
    void insertLast(const Type& newItem);
      //newItem is inserted in the list
      //Post: first points to the new list,
      //     newItem is inserted at the end of the list, and
      //     last points to the last node in the list
    void deleteNode(const Type& deleteItem);
      //If found, the node containing deleteItem is deleted
      //from the list
      //Post: first points to the first node and
      //     last points to the last node of the updated list
    linkedListType();
      //default constructor
      //Initializes the list to an empty state
      //Post: first = NULL, last = NULL
    linkedListType(const linkedListType<Type>& otherList);
         //copy constructor
    ~linkedListType();
      //destructor
      //Deletes all nodes from the list
      //Post: list object is destroyed

protected:
    nodeType<Type> *first; //pointer to the first node of the list
    nodeType<Type> *last;  //pointer to the last node of the list
};
```

Note that the data members of the **class linkedListType** are **protected**, not **private**, because we will derive other classes from this class. This class is referred to in the section "Ordered Linked Lists" later in this chapter and in Chapter 18.

17

The definition of the **class linkedListType** includes a member function to overload the assignment operator. For classes that include pointer data members, the assignment operator must be explicitly overloaded (see Chapters 15 and 16). For the same reason, the definition of the class also includes a copy constructor. Next, we discuss the implementation of the member functions.

The member functions `isEmptyList` and `isFullList` are quite straightforward. The list is empty if `first` is `NULL`. Because the memory to store the data is allocated dynamically, (logically) the list is never full. (The list is full only if we run out of memory space.) As a consequence, the function `isFullList` always returns `false`. The definitions of the functions to implement these operations are as follows:

```
template<class Type>
bool linkedListType<Type>::isEmptyList()
{
      return(first == NULL);
}

template<class Type>
bool linkedListType<Type>::isFullList()
{
      return false;
}
```

Default Constructor

The default constructor, `linkedListType`, is quite straightforward. It simply initializes the list to an empty state. Recall that when an object of the `linkedListType` type is declared and no value is passed, the default constructor is executed automatically.

```
template<class Type>
linkedListType<Type>::linkedListType() //default constructor
{
      first = NULL;
      last = NULL;
}
```

Destroy List

The function `destroyList` deallocates the memory occupied by each node. We traverse the list starting from the first node and deallocate the memory by calling the operator `delete`. We need a temporary pointer to deallocate the memory. Once the entire list is destroyed, we must set the pointers `first` and `last` to `NULL`.

```
template<class Type>
void linkedListType<Type>::destroyList()
{
      nodeType<Type> *temp;    //pointer to deallocate the memory
                               //occupied by the node
      while(first != NULL)     //while there are nodes in the list
      {
         temp = first;         //set temp to the current node
         first = first->link;  //advance first to the next node
         delete temp;         //deallocate the memory occupied by temp
      }
      last = NULL;    //initialize last to NULL; first has already
                      //been set to NULL by the while loop
}
```

Initialize List

The function `initializeList` initializes the list to an empty state. Note that the default constructor or the copy constructor has already initialized the list when the list object was declared. This operation, in fact, reinitializes the list to an empty state, and so it must delete the nodes (if any) from the list. This task can be accomplished by using the `destroyList` operation, which also resets the pointers `first` and `last` to `NULL`.

```
template<class Type>
void linkedListType<Type>::initializeList()
{
      destroyList(); //if the list has any nodes, delete them
}
```

Print List

The member function `print` prints the data contained in each node. To print the data contained in each node, we must traverse the list starting at the first node. Because the pointer `first` always points to the first node in the list, we need another pointer to traverse the list. (If we use `first` to traverse the list, the entire list will be lost.)

```
template<class Type>
void linkedListType<Type>::print()
{
      nodeType<Type> *current; //pointer to traverse the list

      current = first;  //set current so that it points to
                        //the first node
      while(current != NULL) //while there is more data to print
      {
         cout<<current->info<<" ";
         current = current->link;
      }
}//end print
```

Length of the List

To find the length of the linked list (that is, how many nodes are in the list), we set a counter (initialized to 0) and traverse the list, incrementing the counter by 1 for each node.

17

```
template<class Type>
int linkedListType<Type>::length()
{
      int count = 0;
      nodeType<Type> *current; //pointer to traverse the list

      current = first;
```

```
    while (current!= NULL)
    {
       count++;
       current = current->link;
    }

    return count;
} //end length
```

Retrieve Data of the First Node

The function `retrieveFirst` returns the `info` contained in the first node and its definition is straightforward.

```
template<class Type>
void linkedListType<Type>::retrieveFirst(Type& firstElement)
{
    firstElement = first->info; //copy the info of the first node
}//end retrieveFirst
```

Search List

The member function `search` searches the list for a given item. If the item is found, it outputs "Item is found in the list"; otherwise, it outputs "Item is not in the list." Because a linked list is not a random access data structure, we must sequentially search the list starting from the first node.

The following steps describe this function:

1. Compare the search item with the current node in the list. If the `info` of the current node is the same as the search item, stop the search; otherwise, make the next node the current node.
2. Repeat Step 1 until either the item is found or no more data is left in the list to compare with the search item.

```
template<class Type>
void linkedListType<Type>::search(const Type& item)
{
   nodeType<Type> *current; //pointer to traverse the list
   bool found;

   if(first == NULL)  //list is empty
      cout<<"Cannot search an empty list. "<<endl;
   else
   {
      current = first; //set current to point to the first
                       //node in the list
      found = false;   //set found to false
```

```
      while(!found && current != NULL) //search the list
        if(current->info == item)      //item is found
            found = true;
        else
            current = current->link; //make current point to
                                     //the next node

      if(found)
         cout<<"Item is found in the list."<<endl;
      else
         cout<<"Item is not in the list."<<endl;
   } //end else
}//end search
```

Insert First Node

The function `insertFirst` inserts the new item at the beginning of the list—that is, before the node pointed to by `first`. To implement this function, the following steps are needed:

1. Create a new node.
2. Store the new item in the new node.
3. Insert the node before `first`.

```
template<class Type>
void linkedListType<Type>::insertFirst(const Type& newItem)
{
   nodeType<Type> *newNode; //pointer to create the new node

   newNode = new nodeType<Type>;  //create the new node
   newNode->info = newItem;       //store the new item in the node
   newNode->link = first;         //insert newNode before first
   first = newNode;               //make first point to the
                                  //actual first node

   if(last == NULL)    //if the list was empty, newNode is also
                       //the last node in the list
      last = newNode;
}
```


Insert Last Node

The definition of the member function `insertLast` is similar to the definition of the member function `insertFirst`. Here we insert the new node after `last`. Essentially the function `insertLast` is

```
template<class Type>
void linkedListType<Type>::insertLast(const Type& newItem)
{
   nodeType<Type> *newNode; //pointer to create the new node
```

```
    newNode = new nodeType<Type>; //create the new node
    newNode->info = newItem;      //store the new item in the node
    newNode->link = NULL;         //set the link field of newNode
                                  //to NULL

    if(first == NULL)  //if the list is empty, newNode is
                       //both the first and last node
    {
       first = newNode;
       last = newNode;
    }
    else     //the list is not empty, insert newNode after last
    {
       last->link = newNode; //insert newNode after last
       last = newNode; //make last point to the actual last node
    }
 }//end insertLast
```

Delete Node

Next, we discuss the implementation of the member function **deleteNode**, which deletes a node from the list with a given **info**. We need to consider several cases:

1. The list is empty.
2. The first node is the node with the given **info**. In this case, we need to adjust the pointer **first**.
3. The node with the given **info** is somewhere in the list. If the node to be deleted is the last node, then we must adjust the pointer **last**.
4. The list does not contain the node with the given **info**.

If **list** is empty, we can simply print a message indicating that the list is empty. If **list** is not empty, we search the list for the node with the given **info** and, if such a node is found, we delete this node. In pseudocode, the algorithm is

```
if list is empty
   Output(cannot delete from an empty list);
else
{
   if the first node is the node with the given info,
       adjust the head pointer, that is, first, and deallocate
       the memory;
   else
   {
       search the list for the node with the given info;
       if such a node is found, delete it
   }
}
```

Case 1: The list is empty.

If the list is empty, output an error message as shown in the pseudocode.

Case 2: The list is not empty. The node to be deleted is the first node.

This case has two scenarios: `list` has only one node, and `list` has more than one node. Consider the list with one node, as shown in Figure 17-27.

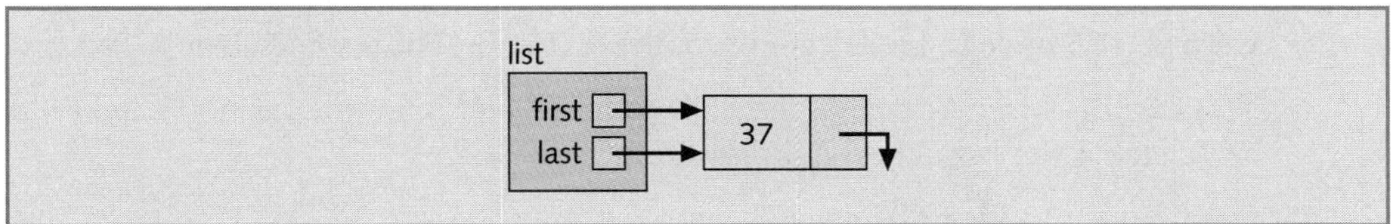

Figure 17-27 `list` with one node

Suppose that we want to delete `37`. After deletion, the list becomes empty. Therefore, after deletion, both `first` and `last` are set to `NULL`.

Now consider the list of more than one node, as shown in Figure 17-28.

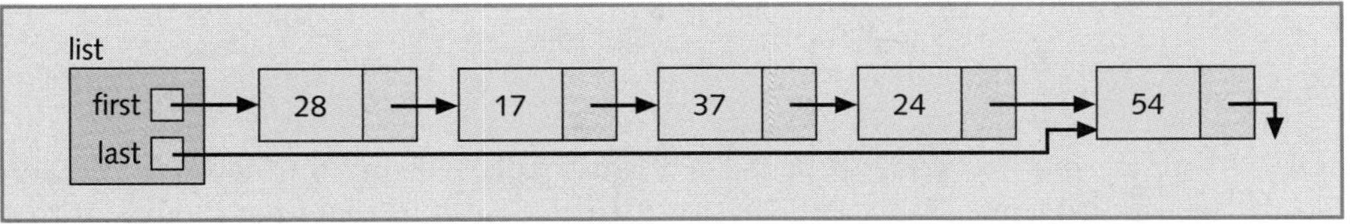

Figure 17-28 `list` with more than one node

Suppose that the node to be deleted is `28`. After deleting this node, the second node becomes the first node. Therefore, after deleting this node the value of the pointer `first` changes; that is, after deletion, `first` contains the address of the node with `info 17`. Figure 17-29 shows the list after deleting `28`.

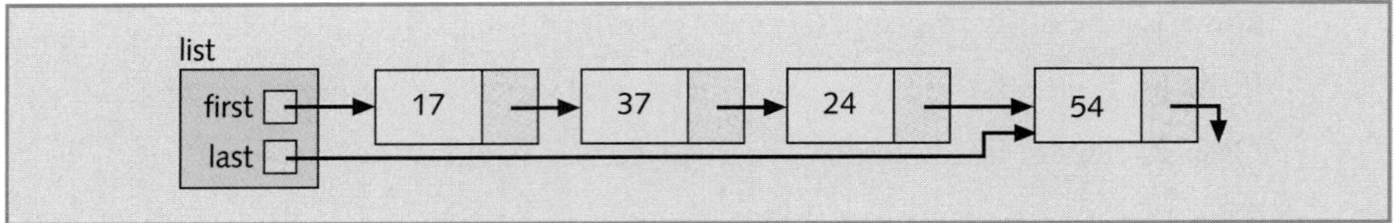

Figure 17-29 `list` after deleting node with `info` 28

Case 3: The node to be deleted is not the first node, but is somewhere in this list.

This case has two subcases: (a) the node to be deleted is not the last node, and (b) the node to be deleted is the last node. Let us illustrate both cases.

Case 3a: The node to be deleted is not the last node.

Consider the list shown in Figure 17-30.

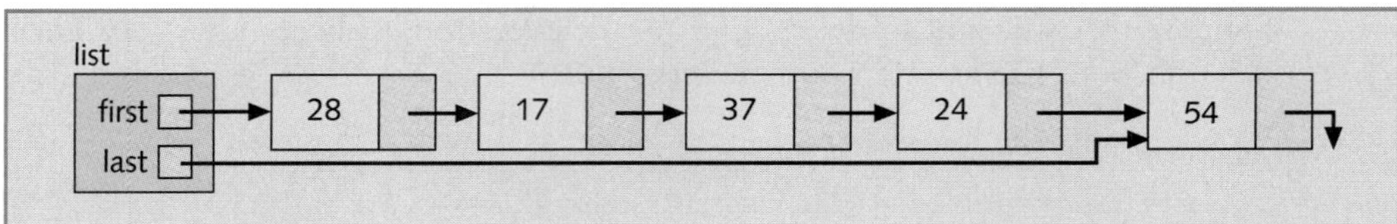

Figure 17-30 `list` before deleting 37

Suppose that the node to be deleted is `37`. After deleting this node, the resulting list is as shown in Figure 17-31. (Notice that the deletion of `37` does not require us to change the values of **`first`** and **`last`**. The link field of the previous node—that is, `17`—changes. After deletion, the node with **`info 17`** contains the address of the node with `24`.)

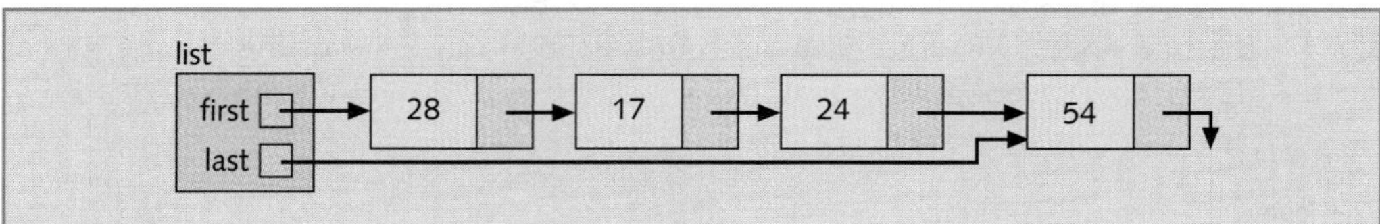

Figure 17-31 `list` after deleting 37

Case 3b: The node to be deleted is the last node.

Consider the list shown in Figure 17-32. Suppose that the node to be deleted is `54`.

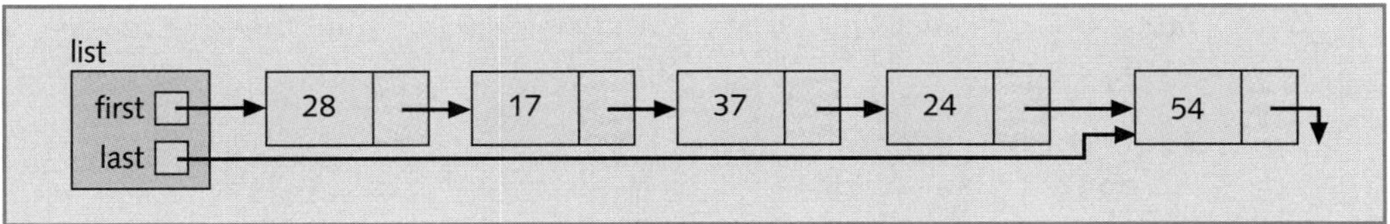

Figure 17-32 `list` before deleting `54`

After deleting `54`, the node with `info 24` becomes the last node. Therefore, the deletion of `54` requires us to change the value of the pointer `last`. After deleting `54`, `last` contains the address of the node with `info 24`. Figure 17-33 shows the resulting list.

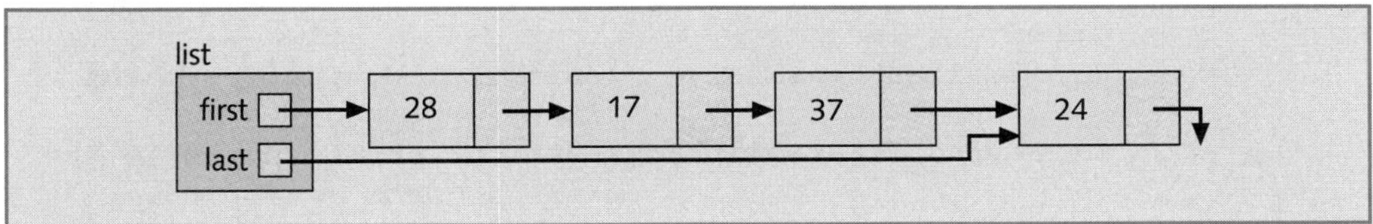

Figure 17-33 `list` after deleting `54`

Case 4: The node to be deleted is not in the list. In this case, the list requires no adjustment. We simply output an error message, indicating that the item to be deleted is not in the list.

From cases 2, 3, and 4, it follows that the deletion of a node requires us to traverse the list. Because a linked list is not a random access data structure, we must sequentially search the list. We will handle case 1 separately, because it does not require us to traverse the list. We sequentially search the list starting at the second node. If the node to be deleted is in the middle of the list, we need to adjust the link field of the node just before the node to be deleted. Thus, we will need a pointer to the previous node. When we search the list for the given `info`, we use two pointers: one to check the `info` of the current node, and one to keep track of the node just before the current node. If the node to be deleted is the last node, we must adjust the pointer `last`.

17

The definition of the function **deleteNode** is

```
template<class Type>
void linkedListType<Type>::deleteNode(const Type& deleteItem)
{
   nodeType<Type> *current; //pointer to traverse the list
   nodeType<Type> *trailCurrent; //pointer just before current
   bool found;

   if(first == NULL)    //Case 1: list is empty
      cout<<"Cannot delete from an empty list.\n";
   else
   {
    if(first->info == deleteItem) //Case 2
    {
       current = first;
       first = first->link;
       if(first == NULL)    //list had only one node
          last = NULL;
       delete current;
    }
    else  //search the list for the node with the given info
    {
       found = false;
       trailCurrent = first;   //set trailCurrent to point to
                               //the first node
       current = first->link;  //set current to point to the
                               //second node

       while((!found) && (current != NULL))
       {
          if(current->info != deleteItem)
          {
             trailCurrent = current;
             current = current->link;
          }
          else
             found = true;
       } // end while

       if(found) //Case 3: if found, delete the node
       {
          trailCurrent->link = current->link;

          if(last == current)       //node to be deleted was
                                    //the last node
             last = trailCurrent;  //update the value of last
          delete current;  //delete the node from the list
       }
```

```
        else
           cout<<"Item to be deleted is not in the list."<<endl;
     } //end else
   } //end else
} //end deleteNode
```

Destructor

Before we give the definition of the copy constructor, let us consider the destructor. The purpose of the destructor is to deallocate the memory occupied by the nodes of a list when the class object goes out of scope. Because memory is allocated dynamically, resetting the pointers **first** and **last** does not deallocate the memory occupied by the nodes in the list. We must traverse the list, starting at the first node and delete each node in the list. It is now clear that the definition of the function to implement the destructor is similar to the definition of the function **destroyList**. We give its definition here for the sake of completeness. Recall that the destructor is executed automatically when the class object goes out of scope.

```
template<class Type>
linkedListType<Type>::~linkedListType() //destructor
{
   nodeType<Type> *temp;

   while(first != NULL)  //while there are nodes left in the list
   {
      temp = first;           //set temp to point to the current node
      first = first->link;    //advance first to the next node
      delete temp;            //deallocate memory occupied by temp
   }//end while

   last = NULL; //initialize last to NULL; first is already NULL
}//end destructor
```

Copy Constructor

Because the **class linkedListType** contains pointer data members, the definition of this class contains the copy constructor. Recall that, if a formal parameter is a value parameter, the copy constructor provides the formal parameter with its own copy of the data. The copy constructor also executes when an object is declared and initialized using another object. (For more information, see Chapter 15.)

17

The copy constructor makes an identical copy of the linked list. Therefore, we traverse the list to be copied starting at the first node. Corresponding to each node in the original list, we

1. Create a node, and call it **newNode**.
2. Copy the **info** of the node (in the original list) into **newNode**.
3. Insert **newNode** at the end of the list being created.

The definition of the copy constructor is as follows:

```
template<class Type>
linkedListType<Type>::linkedListType
                        (const linkedListType<Type>& otherList)
{
   nodeType<Type> *newNode; //pointer to create a node
   nodeType<Type> *current; //pointer to traverse the list

   if(otherList.first == NULL) //otherList is empty
   {
      first = NULL;
      last = NULL;
   }
   else
   {
      current = otherList.first;   //current points to the
                                   //list to be copied

        //copy the first node
      first = new nodeType<Type>;  //create the node
      first->info = current->info; //copy the info
      first->link = NULL;          //set the link field of
                                   //the node to NULL
      last = first;                //make last point to the
                                   //first node
      current = current->link;     //make current point to the
                                   //next node

       //copy the remaining list
      while(current != NULL)
      {
            newNode = new nodeType<Type>;  //create a node
            newNode->info = current->info; //copy the info
            newNode->link = NULL;          //set the link of
                                           //newNode to NULL
            last->link = newNode;      //attach newNode after last
            last = newNode;            //make last point to
                                       //the actual last node
            current = current->link;   //make current point to
                                       //the next node
      }//end while
   }//end else
}//end copy constructor
```

Overloading the Assignment Operator

The definition of the function to overload the assignment operator for the **class linkedListType** is very similar to the definition of the copy constructor. We give its definition for the sake of completeness.

```
template<class Type>
const linkedListType<Type>& linkedListType<Type>::operator=
                        (const linkedListType<Type>& otherList)
{
   nodeType<Type> *newNode; //pointer to create a node
   nodeType<Type> *current; //pointer to traverse the list

   if(this != &otherList) //avoid self-copy
   {
      if(first != NULL)  //if the list is not empty, destroy the list
         destroyList();

      if(otherList.first == NULL) //otherList is empty
      {
         first = NULL;
         last = NULL;
      }
      else
      {
         current = otherList.first; //current points to the
                                    //list to be copied

                 //copy the first element
         first = new nodeType<Type>;    //create the node
         first->info = current->info;  //copy the info
         first->link = NULL;            //set the link field of
                                        //the node to NULL
         last = first;             //make last point to the first node
         current = current->link; //make current point to the next
                                  //node of the list being copied

            //copy the remaining list
         while(current != NULL)
         {
             newNode = new nodeType<Type>;
             newNode->info = current->info;
             newNode->link = NULL;
             last->link = newNode;
             last = newNode;
             current = current->link;
         }//end while
      }//end else
   }//end else

   return *this;
}
```

17

Ordered Linked Lists

Now that you have some idea how pointer variables are used in C++ to dynamically allocate and deallocate memory and how to build and process linked lists, this section discusses how to build ordered linked lists and describes various operations on these lists. The following operations are usually performed on a (ordered) list:

1. Initialize the list.
2. Check whether the list is empty.
3. Check whether the list is full.
4. Print the list.
5. Print the list in reverse order.
6. Destroy the list.
7. Search the list for a given item.
8. Insert an item in the list.
9. Delete an item from the list.
10. Find the length of the list.
11. Make a copy of the list.

Many of the operations on ordered linked lists are similar to the operations on general lists discussed in the last section. Because the list is ordered, we need to modify only the algorithms to implement the search, insert, and delete operations. Thus, the definition of the class defining the ordered linked list as an ADT is derived from the `class linkedListType`.

```
template<class Type>
class orderedLinkedListType: public linkedListType<Type>
{
public:
    void search(const Type& item);
        //Outputs "Item is found in the list" if searchItem is in
        //the list; otherwise, outputs "Item is not in the list"
    void insertNode(const Type& newItem);
        //newItem is inserted in the list
        //Post: first points to the new list and
        //      newItem is inserted at the proper place in the list
    void deleteNode(const Type& deleteItem);
        //If found, the node containing deleteItem is deleted
        //from the list
        //Post: first points to the first node of the
        //      new list
    void printListReverse() const;
        //This function prints the list in reverse order
        //Because the original list is in ascending order, the
        //elements will be printed in descending order
```

```
private:
    void reversePrint(nodeType<Type> *current) const;
        //This function is called by the public member
        //function to print the list in reverse order
};
```

Here the pointer `last` does not play any role. We will ignore this pointer.

Search List

First, we discuss the search operation. The algorithm to implement the search operation is similar to the search algorithm for general lists discussed earlier. Here, because the list is sorted, we can improve the search algorithm somewhat. As before, we start the search at the first node in the list. We stop the search as soon as we find a node in the list with `info` greater than or equal to the search item, or we have searched the entire list.

The following steps describe this algorithm:

1. Compare the search item with the current node in the list. If the `info` of the current node is greater than or equal to the search item, stop the search; otherwise, make the next node the current node.
2. Repeat Step 1 until either an item in the list that is greater than or equal to the search item is found, or no more data is left in the list to compare with the search item.

Note that the loop does not explicitly check whether the search item is equal to an item in the list. Thus, after the loop executes, we must check whether the search item is equal to the item in the list.

```
template<class Type>
void orderedLinkedListType<Type>::search(const Type& item)
{
   bool found;
   nodeType<Type> *current; //pointer to traverse the list

   found = false;     //initialize found to false
   current = first;  //start the search at the first node

   if(first == NULL)
      cout<<"Cannot search an empty list."<<endl;
   else
   {
       while(current != NULL && !found)
         if(current->info >= item)
           found = true;
         else
           current = current->link;
```

17

```
        if(current == NULL)           //item is not in the list
           cout<<"Item is not in the list"<<endl;
        else
           if(current->info == item) //test for equality
              cout<<"Item is found in the list"<<endl;
           else
              cout<<"Item is not in the list"<<endl;
    }//end else
}//end search
```

Insert Node

To insert an item in an ordered linked list, we first find the place where the new item is supposed to go, then we insert the item in the list. To find the place for the new item in the list, as before, we search the list. Here we use two pointers, **current** and **trailCurrent**, to search the list. The pointer **current** points to the node whose **info** is being compared with the item to be inserted, and **trailCurrent** points to the node just before **current**. Because the list is in order, the search algorithm is the same as before. The following cases arise:

1. The list is initially empty. The node containing the new item is the only node and thus the first node in the list.
2. The new item is smaller than the smallest item in the list. The new item goes at the beginning of the list. In this case, we need to adjust the list's head pointer—that is, **first**.
3. The item is to be inserted somewhere in the list.

   3a. The new item is larger than all items in the list. In this case, the new item is inserted at the end of the list. Thus, the value of **current** is **NULL** and the new item is inserted after **trailCurrent**.

   3b. The new item is to be inserted somewhere in the middle of the list. In this case, the new item is inserted between **trailCurrent** and **current**.

The following statements can accomplish both cases 3a and 3b. Assume **newNode** points to the new node.

```
trailCurrent->link = newNode;
newNode->link = current;
```

Let us next illustrate these cases.

Case 1: The list is empty.

Consider the list shown in Figure 17-34.

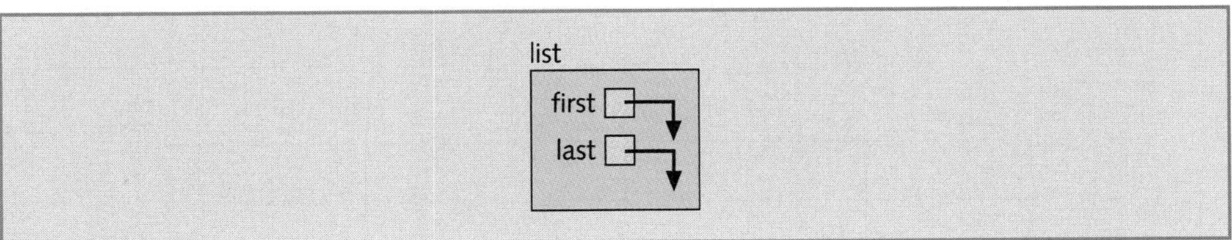

Figure 17-34 Empty `list`

Suppose that we want to insert `27` in the list. To accomplish this task, we create a node, copy `27` into the node, set the link of the node to `NULL`, and make `first` and `last` point to the node. Figure 17-35 shows the resulting list.

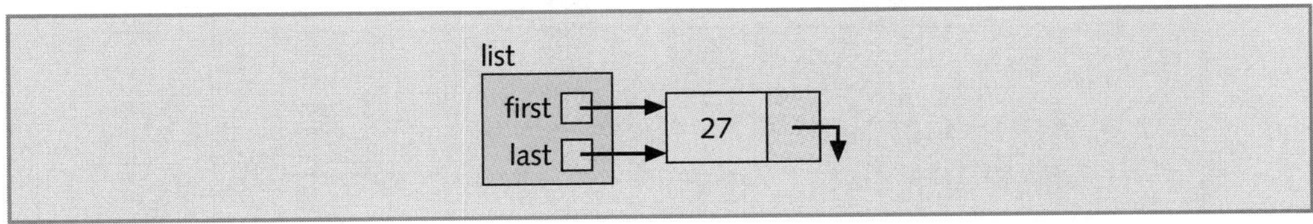

Figure 17-35 `list` after inserting `27`

Notice that, after inserting `27`, the values of both `first` and `last` change.

Case 2: The list is not empty, and the item to be inserted is smaller than the smallest item in the list. Consider the list shown in Figure 17-36.

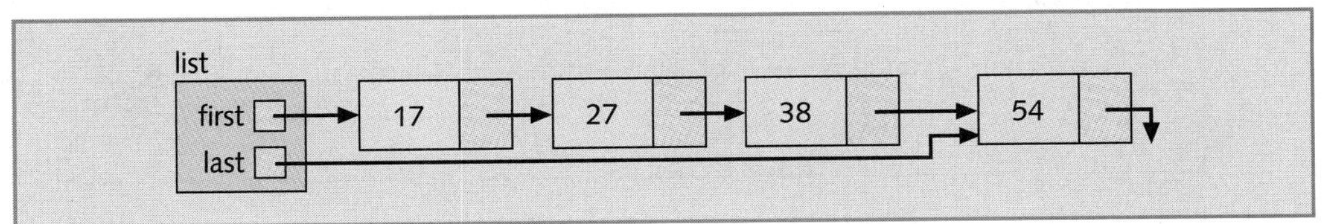

Figure 17-36 Nonempty `list` before inserting `10`

Suppose that `10` is to be inserted. After inserting `10` in the list, the node with `info 10` becomes the first node of `list`. This requires us to change the value of `first`. Figure 17-37 shows the resulting list.

17

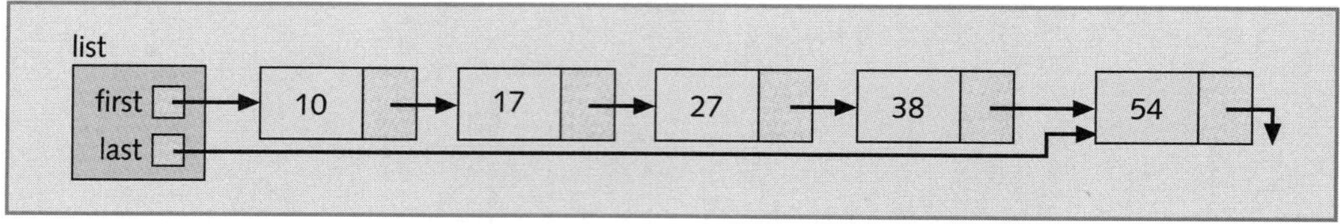

Figure 17-37 `list` after inserting `10`

Case 3: The list is not empty, and the item to be inserted is larger than the first item in the list. As indicated previously, this case has two scenarios.

Case 3a: The item to be inserted is larger than the largest item in the list; that is, it goes at the end of the list. Consider the list shown in Figure 17-38.

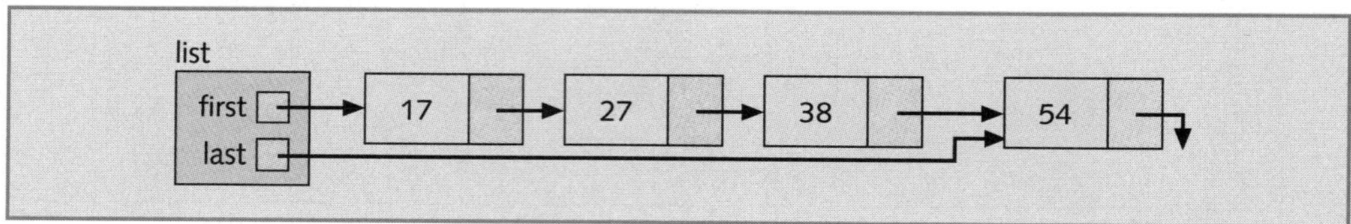

Figure 17-38 `list` before inserting `65`

Suppose that we want to insert `65` in the list. After inserting `65`, the resulting list is as shown in Figure 17-39. (Notice that insertion of `65` requires us to change the value of `last`.)

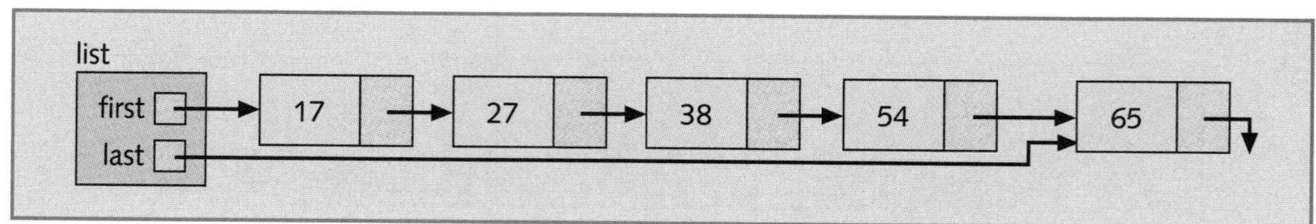

Figure 17-39 `list` after inserting `65`

Case 3b: The item to be inserted goes somewhere in the middle of the list. Consider the list shown in Figure 17-40.

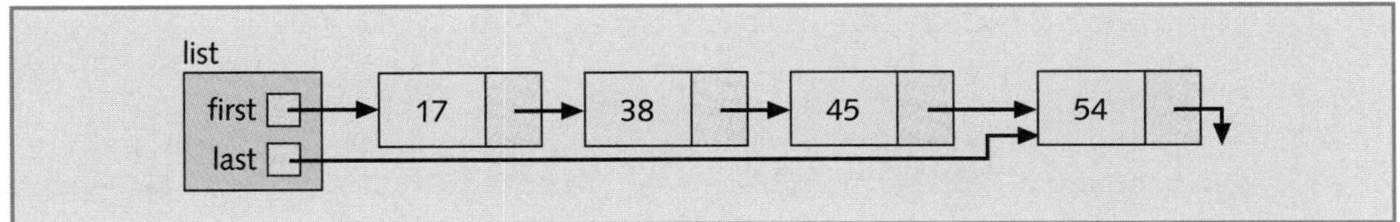

Figure 17-40 `list` before inserting `27`

Suppose that we want to insert `27` in this list. Clearly, `27` goes between `17` and `38`, which would require the link of the node with `info 17` to be changed. After inserting `27`, the resulting list is as shown in Figure 17-41.

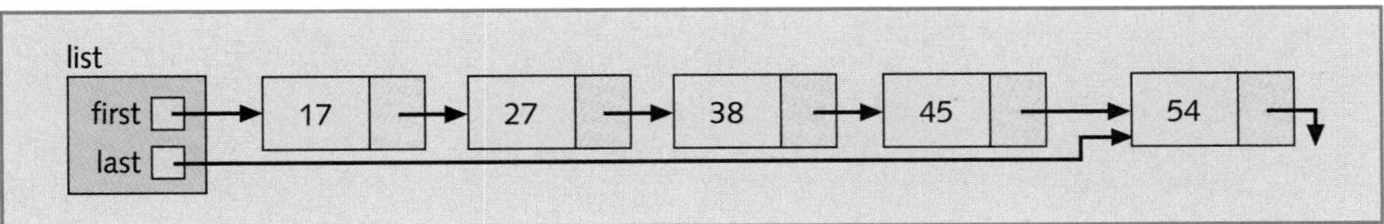

Figure 17-41 `list` after inserting `27`

From case 3, it follows that we must first traverse the list to find the place where the new item is to be inserted. It also follows that we must traverse the list with two pointers—say, `current` and `trailCurrent`. The pointer `current` is used to traverse the list and compare the `info` of the node in the list with the item to be inserted. The pointer `trailCurrent` points to the node just before `current`. For example, in case 3b, when the search stops, `trailCurrent` points to node `17` and `current` points to node `38`. The item is inserted after `trailCurrent`. In case 3a, after searching the list to find the place for `65`, `trailCurrent` points to node `54` and `current` is `NULL`.

Essentially, the function `insertNode` is as follows:

17

```
template<class Type>
void orderedLinkedListType<Type>::insertNode(const Type& newitem)
{
      nodeType<Type> *current; //pointer to traverse the list
      nodeType<Type> *trailCurrent; //pointer just before current
      nodeType<Type> *newNode;  //pointer to create a node
```

```
    bool  found;

    newNode = new nodeType<Type>; //create the node
    newNode->info = newitem;   //store newitem in the node
    newNode->link = NULL;      //set the link field of the node
                               //to NULL

    if(first == NULL)  //Case 1
       first = newNode;
    else
    {
       current = first;
       found = false;

       while(current != NULL && !found) //search the list
           if(current->info >= newitem)
               found = true;
           else
           {
               trailCurrent = current;
               current = current->link;
           }

       if(current == first)      //Case 2
       {
          newNode->link = first;
          first = newNode;
       }
       else                   //Case 3
       {
           trailCurrent->link = newNode;
           newNode->link = current;
       }
   }//end else
}//end insertNode
```

Delete Node

To delete a given item from an ordered linked list, first we search the list to see whether the item to be deleted is in the list. The function to implement this operation is the same as the delete operation on general linked lists. Here, because the list is sorted, we can somewhat improve the algorithm for ordered linked lists.

As in the case of `insertNode`, we search the list with two pointers, `current` and `trailCurrent`. Similar to the operation `insertNode`, several cases arise:

1. The list is initially empty. We have an error. We cannot delete from an empty list.
2. The item to be deleted is contained in the first node of the list. We must adjust the head pointer of the list—that is, `first`.
3. The item to be deleted is somewhere in the list. In this case, `current` points to the node containing the item to be deleted, and `trailCurrent` points to the node just before the node pointed to by `current`.
4. The list is not empty, but the item to be deleted is not in the list.

The definition of the function `deleteNode` is

```
template<class Type>
void orderedLinkedListType<Type>::deleteNode(const Type& deleteItem)
{
   nodeType<Type> *current; //pointer to traverse the list
   nodeType<Type> *trailCurrent; //pointer just before current
   bool found;

   if(first == NULL) //Case 1
      cout<<"Cannot delete from an empty list."<<endl;
   else
   {
      current = first;
      found = false;

      while(current != NULL && !found)  //search the list
        if(current->info >= deleteItem)
           found = true;
        else
        {
           trailCurrent = current;
           current = current->link;
        }

      if(current == NULL)   //Case 4
         cout<<"Item to be deleted is not in the list."<<endl;
      else
         if(current->info == deleteItem) //item to be deleted is
                                         //in the list
         {
           if(first == current)          //Case 2
           {
              first = first->link;
              delete current;
           }
```

```
            else                            //Case 3
            {
               trailCurrent->link = current->link;
               delete current;
            }
        }
        else                            //Case 4
          cout<<"Item to be deleted is not in the list."<<endl;
    }
} //end deleteNode
```

Print List in Reverse Order (Recursion Revisited)

The nodes of an ordered list (as constructed previously) are in ascending order. Certain applications, however, might require the data to be printed in descending order, which means that we must print the list backward. We now discuss the function **reversePrint**. Given a pointer to a list, this function prints the elements of the list in reverse order.

Consider the linked list shown in Figure 17-42.

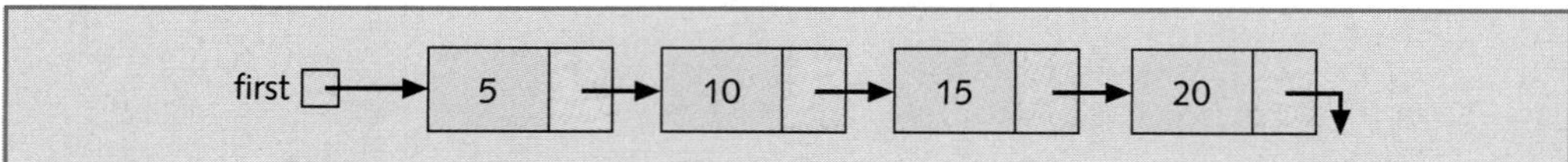

Figure 17-42 Linked list

For the list in Figure 17-42, the output should be in the following form:

```
20 15 10 5
```

Because the links are in only one direction, we cannot traverse the list backward starting from the last node. Let us see how we can effectively use recursion to print the list in reverse order.

Let us think in terms of recursion. We cannot print the **info** of the first node until we have printed the remainder of the list (that is, the tail of the first node). Similarly, we cannot print the **info** of the second node until we have printed the tail of the second node, and so on. Every time we consider the tail of a node, we reduce the size of the list by 1. Eventually the size of the list will be reduced to zero, in which case the recursion will stop. Let us first write the algorithm in pseudocode. (Suppose that **current** is a pointer to a linked list.)

```
if(current != NULL)
{
   reversePrint(current->link);  //print the tail
   cout<<current->info<<endl;    //print the node
}
```

Here, we do not see the base case; it is hidden. The list is printed only if the pointer to the list is not `NULL`. Also, inside the `if` statement the recursive call is on the tail of the list. Because eventually the tail of the list will be empty, the `if` statement in the next call will fail and the recursion will stop. Also, note that statements (for example, printing the `info` of the node) appear after the recursive call; thus, when the transfer comes back to the calling function, we must execute the remaining statements. Recall that the function exits only after the last statement executes. (By the "last statement" we do not mean the physical last statement, but rather the logical last statement.)

Let us write the previous function in C++ and then apply it to a list.

```
template<class Type>
void orderedLinkedListType<Type>::reversePrint
                              (nodeType<Type> *current) const
{
      if(current != NULL)
      {
            reversePrint(current->link);     //print the tail
            cout<<current->info<<" ";        //print the node
      }
}
```

Consider the statement

```
reversePrint(first);
```

where `first` is a pointer of the type `nodeType<Type>`.

Let us trace the execution of this statement, which is a function call, for the list shown in Figure 17-42. Because the formal parameter is a value parameter, the value of the actual parameter is passed to the formal parameter. See Figure 17-43.

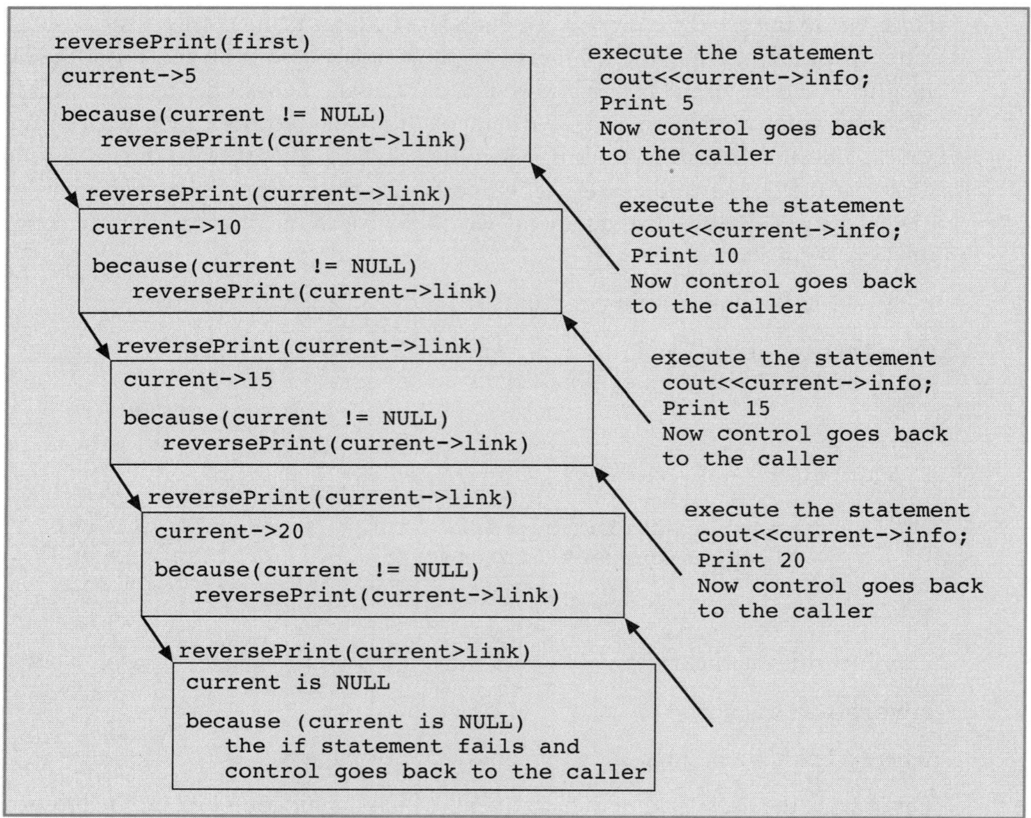

Figure 17-43 Execution of the statement `reversePrint(first);`

printListReverse

Now that we have written the function **reversePrint**, we can write the definition of the function **printListReverse**. Its definition is

```
template<class Type>
void orderedLinkedListType<Type>::printListReverse() const
{
      reversePrint(first);
      cout<<endl;
}
```

Header File of the Ordered Linked List

For the sake of completeness, we will show how to create the header file that defines the `class orderedListType` and the operations on such lists. (We assume that the definition of the `class linkedListType` and the definitions of the functions to implement the operations are in the header file `linkedlist.h`.)

```
//Ordered linked list derived from general linked list
//Header File: orderedList.h

#ifndef H_orderedListType
#define H_orderedListType

#include <iostream>
#include "linkedlist.h"

using namespace std;

template<class Type>
class orderedLinkedListType: public linkedListType<Type>
{
public:
    void search(Type item);
    void insertNode(Type newitem);
    void deleteNode(Type deleteitem);
    void printListReverse() const;

private:
    void reversePrint(nodeType<Type> *current) const;
};

//Definitions of the functions search, insertNode,
//deleteNode, printListReverse, and reversePrint go here
.
.
.
#endif
```

The following program tests the various operations on an ordered linked list:

```
//Program to test the various operations on an ordered linked list

#include <iostream>
#include "orderedList.h"

using namespace std;
```

```
int main()
{
      orderedLinkedListType<int> list1, list2;            //Line 1
      int num;                                            //Line 2

      cout<<"Line 3: Enter integers ending with -999"
          <<endl;                                         //Line 3
      cin>>num;                                           //Line 4

      while(num != -999)                                  //Line 5
      {
            list1.insertNode(num);                        //Line 6
            cin>>num;                                     //Line 7
      }

      cout<<endl;                                         //Line 8

      cout<<"Line 9: List 1: ";                           //Line 9
      list1.print();                                      //Line 10
      cout<<endl;                                         //Line 11

      cout<<"Line 12: List 1 in the reverse order: "
          <<endl;                                         //Line 12
      list1.printListReverse();                           //Line 13
      cout<<endl;                                         //Line 14

      list2 = list1;     //test the assignment operator Line 15

      cout<<"Line 16: List 2: ";                          //Line 16
      list2.print();                                      //Line 17
      cout<<endl;                                         //Line 18

      cout<<"Line 19: Enter the number to be "
          <<"deleted: ";                                  //Line 19
      cin>>num;                                           //Line 20
      cout<<endl;                                         //Line 21

      list2.deleteNode(num);                              //Line 22

      cout<<"Line 23: After deleting the node, "
          <<"List 2: "<<endl;                             //Line 23
      list2.print();                                      //Line 24
      cout<<endl;                                         //Line 25

      return 0;
}
```

Sample Run: In this sample run, the user input is shaded.

```
Line 3: Enter integers ending with -999
23 65 34 72 12 82 36 55 29 -999

Line 9: List 1: 12 23 29 34 36 55 65 72 82
Line 12: List 1 in the reverse order:
82 72 65 55 36 34 29 23 12

Line 16: List 2: 12 23 29 34 36 55 65 72 82
Line 19: Enter the number to be deleted: 36

Line 23: After deleting the node, List 2:
12 23 29 34 55 65 72 82
```

The preceding output is self-explanatory. The details are left as an exercise for you.

Doubly Linked Lists

A doubly linked list is a linked list in which every node has a next pointer and a back pointer. In other words, every node contains the address of the next node (except the last node), and every node contains the address of the previous node (except the first node). (See Figure 17-44.)

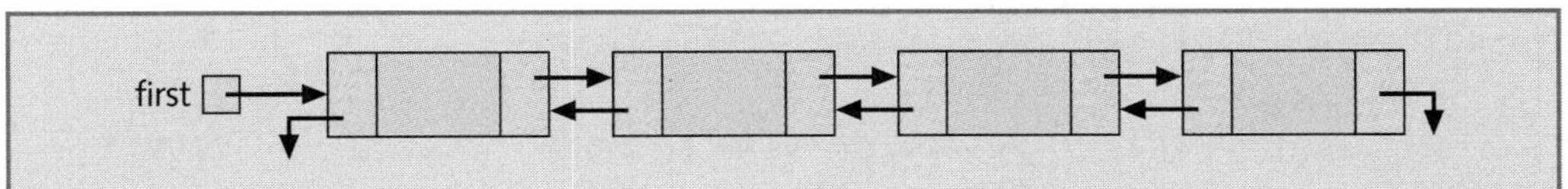

Figure 17-44 Doubly linked list

A doubly linked list can be traversed in either direction. That is, we can traverse the list starting at the first node or, if a pointer to the last node is given, we can traverse the list starting at the last node.

17

The basic operations on a doubly linked list are

1. Initialize the list.
2. Destroy the list.
3. Check whether the list is empty.
4. Check whether the list is full.
5. Search the list for a given item.

6. Insert an item in the list.
7. Delete an item from the list.
8. Find the length of the list.
9. Print the list.

Next, we describe these operations for an ordered doubly linked list. The following class defines a doubly linked list as an ATD:

```
//Definition of the node
template <class Type>
struct  nodeType
{
      Type info;
      nodeType<Type> *next;
      nodeType<Type> *back;
};

template <class Type>
class doublyLinkedList
{
public:
    const doublyLinkedList<Type>& operator=
                        (const doublyLinkedList<Type> &);
       //overload the assignment operator
    void initializeList();
        //Initialize the list to an empty state
        //Post: first = NULL
    bool isEmptyList();
        //This function returns true if the list is empty;
        //otherwise, it returns false
    void destroy();
        //Delete all nodes from the list
        //Post: first = NULL
    void print();
        //Output the info contained in each node
    int length();
        //This function returns the number of nodes in the list
    void search(const Type& searchItem);
        //Outputs "Item is found in the list" if searchItem
        //is in the list; otherwise, outputs "Item not in the list"
    void insertNode(const Type& insertItem);
        //newItem is inserted in the list
        //Post: first points to the new list and the
        //     newItem is inserted at the proper place in the list
    void deleteNode(const Type& deleteItem);
        //If found, the node containing the deleteItem is deleted
        //from the list
        //Post: first points to the first node of the
        //     new list
```

```
    doublyLinkedList();
        //default constructor
        //Initialize the list to an empty state
        //Post: first = NULL
    doublyLinkedList(const doublyLinkedList<Type>& otherList);
       //copy constructor
    ~doublyLinkedList();
        //destructor
        //Post: the list object is destroyed
private:
    nodeType<Type> *first;  //pointer to the list
};
```

The functions to implement the operations of a doubly linked list are similar to the ones discussed earlier. Here, because every node has two pointers, **back** and **next**, some of the operations require the adjustment of two pointers in each node. For the insert and delete operations, because we can traverse the list in either direction, we use only one pointer to traverse the list. Let us call this pointer **current**. We can set the value of **trailCurrent** by using both the **current** pointer and the **back** pointer of the node pointed to by **current**. We will give the definition of each function here, with two exceptions. Definitions of the copy constructor and overloading the assignment operator are left as exercises for you.

Default Constructor

The default constructor initializes the doubly linked list to an empty state. It sets **first** to NULL.

```
template<class Type>
doublyLinkedList<Type>::doublyLinkedList()
{
      first= NULL;
}
```

isEmptyList

This operation returns **true** if the list is empty; otherwise, it returns **false**. The list is empty if the pointer **first** is NULL.

```
template<class Type>
bool doublyLinkedList<Type>::isEmptyList()
{
    return(first == NULL);
}
```

17

Destroy List

This operation deletes all nodes in the list, leaving the list in an empty state. We traverse the list starting at the first node and then delete each node.

```
template<class Type>
void doublyLinkedList<Type>::destroy()
{
	nodeType<Type>  *temp; //pointer to delete the node

	while(first != NULL)
	{
		temp = first;
		first = first->next;
		delete temp;
	}
}
```

Initialize List

This operation reinitializes the doubly linked list to an empty state. This task can be accomplished by using the operation **destroy**. The definition of the function **initializeList** is

```
template<class Type>
void doublyLinkedList<Type>:: initializeList()
{
   destroy();
}
```

Length of List

The length of a list is the number of nodes in the list. This operation counts the number of nodes in the list and then returns the count.

```
template<class Type>
int doublyLinkedList<Type>::length()
{
   int length = 0;
   nodeType<Type> *current; //pointer to traverse the list

   current = first;  //set current to point to the first node

   while(current != NULL)
   {
      length++;   //increment the length
      current = current->next; //advance current
   }

   return length;
}
```

Print List

This function outputs the `info` contained in each node. We traverse the list starting from the first node.

```
template<class Type>
void doublyLinkedList<Type>::print()
{
    nodeType<Type> *current; //pointer to traverse the list

    current = first;  //set current to point to the first node

    while(current != NULL)
    {
       cout<<current->info<<"  ";  //output info
       current = current->next;
    }//end while
}//end print
```

Search List

The function `search` outputs "Item is found in the list" if the `searchItem` is in the list; otherwise, it outputs "Item not in the list." The search algorithm is exactly the same as the search algorithm for an ordered linked list.

```
template<class Type>
void doublyLinkedList<Type>::search(const Type& searchItem)
{
   bool found;
   nodeType<Type> *current; //pointer to traverse the list

   if(first == NULL)
      cout<<"Cannot search an empty list"<<endl;
   else
   {
      found = false;
      current = first;

      while(current != NULL && !found)
         if(current->info >= searchItem)
            found = true;
         else
            current = current->next;

      if(current == NULL)
           cout<<"Item not in the list"<<endl;
```

```
        else
            if(current->info == searchItem) //test for equality
                cout<<"Item is found in the list"<<endl;
            else
                cout<<"Item not in the list"<<endl;
    }//end else
}//end search
```

Insert Node

Because we are inserting an item in a doubly linked list, the insertion of a node in the list requires the adjustment of two pointers in certain nodes. As before, we find the place where the new item is supposed to be inserted, create the node, store the new item, and adjust the link fields of the new node and other particular nodes in the list. There are four cases:

1. Insertion in an empty list
2. Insertion at the beginning of a nonempty list
3. Insertion at the end of a nonempty list
4. Insertion somewhere in a nonempty list

Both cases 1 and 2 require us to change the value of the pointer `first`. Cases 3 and 4 are similar. Next, we show case 4.

Consider the double linked list shown in Figure 17-45.

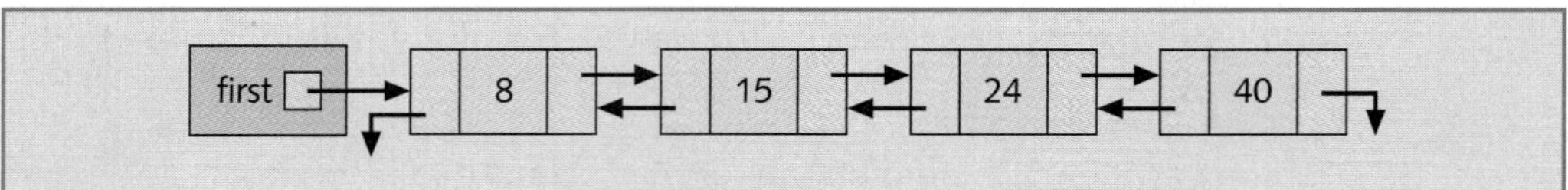

Figure 17-45 Doubly linked list before inserting `20`

Suppose that `20` is to be inserted in the list. After inserting `20`, the resulting list is as shown in Figure 17-46.

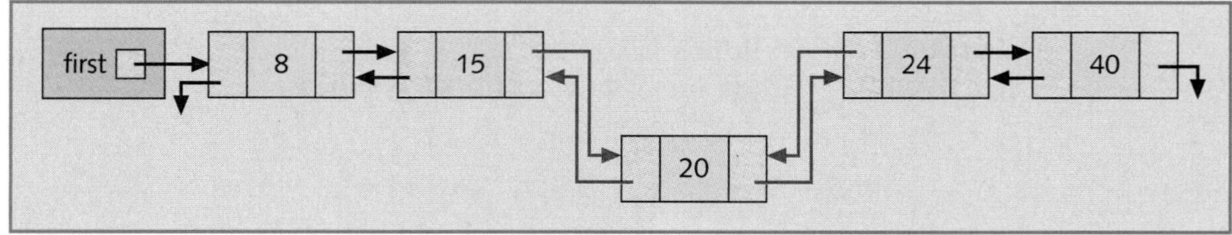

Figure 17-46 Doubly linked list after inserting `20`

From Figure 17-46, it follows that the `next` pointer of node `15`, the `back` pointer of node `24`, and both the `next` and `back` pointers of node `20` need to be adjusted.

The definition of the function `insertNode` is

```
template<class Type>
void doublyLinkedList<Type>::insertNode(const Type& insertItem)
{
    nodeType<Type> *current; //pointer to traverse the list
    nodeType<Type> *trailCurrent; //pointer just before current
    nodeType<Type> *newNode;  //pointer to create a node
    bool found;

    newNode = new nodeType<Type>; //create the node
    newNode->info = insertItem;   //store the new item in the node
    newNode->next = NULL;
    newNode->back = NULL;

    if(first == NULL) //if the list is empty, newNode is the only node
        first = newNode;
    else
    {
      found = false;
      current = first;

      while(current != NULL && !found) //search the list
          if(current->info >= insertItem)
             found = true;
          else
          {
              trailCurrent = current;
              current = current->next;
          }

      if(current == first) //insert newNode before the first node
      {
          first->back = newNode;
          newNode->next = first;
          first = newNode;
      }
      else
      {
            //insert newNode between trailCurrent and current
          if(current != NULL)
          {
              trailCurrent->next = newNode;
              newNode->back = trailCurrent;
              newNode->next = current;
              current->back = newNode;
          }
```

```
            else
            {
                trailCurrent->next = newNode;
                newNode->back = trailCurrent;
            }
        }//end else
    }//end else
}//end insertNode
```

Delete Node

This operation deletes a given item (if found) from the doubly linked list. As before, we first search the list to see whether the item to be deleted is in the list. The search algorithm is the same as before. Similar to the `insertNode` operation, this operation (if the item to be deleted is in the list) requires the adjustment of two pointers in certain nodes. The delete operation has several cases:

1. The list is empty.
2. The item to be deleted is in the first node of the list, which would require us to change the value of the pointer `first`.
3. The item to be deleted is somewhere in the list.
4. The item to be deleted is not in the list.

Let us demonstrate case 3. Consider the list shown in Figure 17-47.

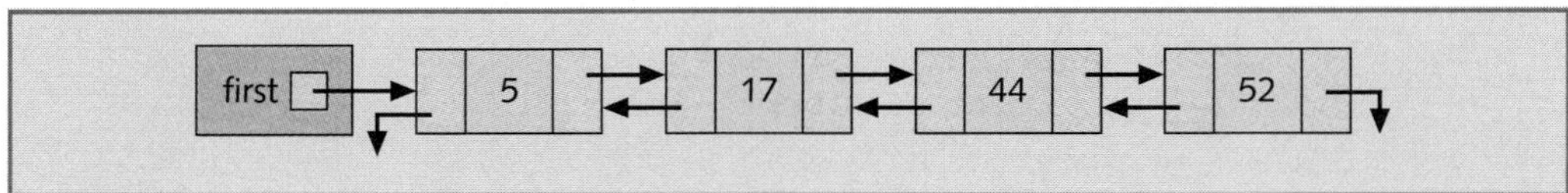

Figure 17-47 Doubly linked list before deleting 17

Suppose that the item is to be deleted is `17`. First we search the list with two pointers and find the node with `info 17`, and then we adjust the link field of the affected nodes. (See Figure 17-48.)

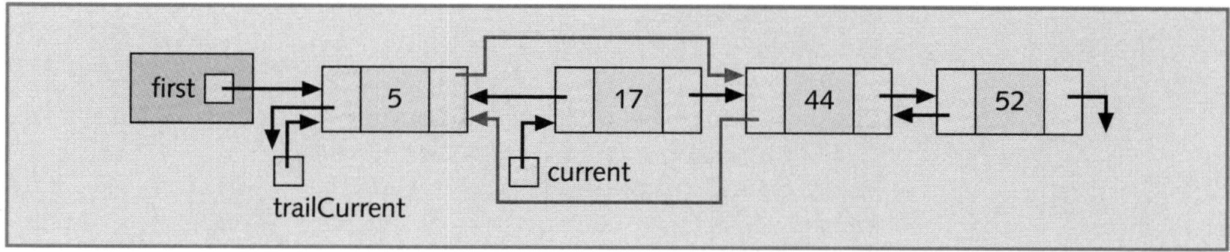

Figure 17-48 List after adjusting the links of the nodes before and after the node with `info` 17

Next, we delete the node pointed to by **current**. (See Figure 17-49.)

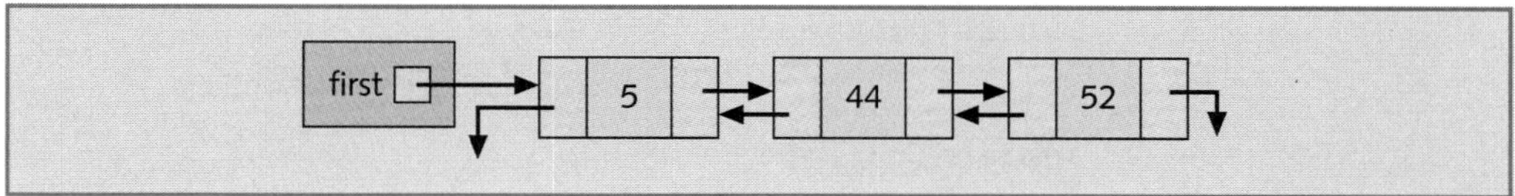

Figure 17-49 List after deleting the node with `info` 17

The definition of the function **deleteNode** is

```
template<class Type>
void doublyLinkedList<Type>::deleteNode(const Type& deleteItem)
{
   nodeType<Type> *current; //pointer to traverse the list
   nodeType<Type> *trailCurrent; //pointer just before current

   bool found;

   if(first == NULL)
      cout<<"Cannot delete from an empty list"<<endl;
   else
      if(first->info == deleteItem) //node to be deleted is the
                                    //first node
      {
        current = first;
        first = first->next;

        if(first != NULL)
           first->back = NULL;

        delete current;
      }
      else
      {
```

17

```
            found = false;
            current = first;

            while(current != NULL && !found)  //search the list
                 if(current->info >= deleteItem)
                    found = true;
               else
                current = current->next;

            if(current == NULL)
               cout<<"Item to be deleted is not in the list"<<endl;
            else
               if(current->info == deleteItem) //check for equality
               {
                   trailCurrent = current->back;
                   trailCurrent->next = current->next;

               if(current->next != NULL)
                  current->next->back = trailCurrent;

               delete current;
            }
            else
               cout<<"Item to be deleted is not in the list."<<endl;
      }//end else
}//end deleteNode
```

PROGRAMMING EXAMPLE: VIDEO STORE

For a family or an individual, a favorite place to go on weekends or holidays is to a video store to rent movies. A new video store in your neighborhood is about to open. However, it does not have a program to keep track of its videos and customers. The store managers want someone to write a program for their system so that the video store can function. The program should be able to perform the following operations:

1. Rent a video; that is, check out a video.
2. Return, or check in, a video.
3. Create a list of videos owned by the store.
4. Show the details of a particular video.
5. Print a list of all videos in the store.
6. Check whether a particular video is in the store.
7. Maintain a customer database.
8. Print a list of all the videos rented by each customer.

Let us write a program for the video store. This example further illustrates the object-oriented design methodology and, in particular, inheritance and overloading.

The programming requirement tells us that the video store has two major components: videos and customers. We will describe these two components in detail. We also need to maintain two lists:

1. A list of all the videos in the store
2. A list of all the store customers

We will develop the program in two parts. In part 1, we design, implement, and test the video component. In part 2, we design and implement the customer component, which is then added to the video component developed in part 1. That is, after completing parts 1 and 2, we can perform all the operations listed previously.

Part 1: The Video Component

The Video Object This is the first stage, wherein we discuss the video component. The common things associated with a video are the (see Figure 17-50)

1. Name of the movie
2. Names of the stars
3. Name of the producer
4. Name of the director
5. Name of the production company
6. Number of copies in the store

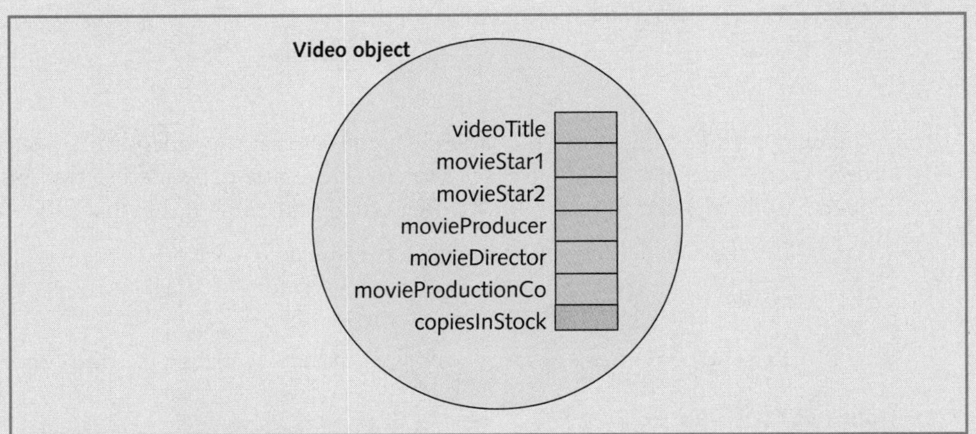

Figure 17-50 Data components of a video

From this list, we see that some of the operations to be performed on the video object are (see Figure 17-51)

a. Set the video information—that is, the title, stars, production company, and so on.
b. Show the details of a particular video.
c. Check the number of copies in the store.
d. Check out (that is, rent) the video. In other words, if the number of copies is greater than zero, decrement the number of copies by one.
e. Check in (that is, return) the video. To check in a video, first we must check whether the store owns such a video and, if it does, increment the number of copies by one.
f. Check whether a particular video is available—that is, the number of copies currently in the store is greater than zero.

1. Set a video info
2. Retrieve the number of copies in stock
3. Check in a video
4. Check out the video
5. Print the title of a video
6. Check the title of a video
7. Check whether two videos are the same
8. Update the number of copies in stock
9. Set the number of copies in stock

Figure 17-51 Operations on a video object

The deletion of a video from the video list requires that the video list be searched for the video to be deleted. Thus, we need to check the title of a video to find out which video is to be deleted from the list. Two videos are the same if they have the same title.

The following class defines the video object as an ADT:

```
class videoType
{
      friend ostream& operator<<(ostream&, const videoType&);

public:
    void setVideoInfo(newString title, newString star1,
                      newString star2, newString producer,
                      newString director, newString productionCo,
                      int setInStock);
        //This function sets the details of a video
        //Private data members are set according to the parameters.
```

```
    //Post: videoTitle = title; movieStar1 = star1;
    //      movieStar2 = star2; movieProducer = producer;
    //      movieDirector = director;
    //      movieProductionCo = productionCo;
    //      copiesInStock = setInStock;
int getNoOfCopiesInStock() const;
    //This function checks the number of copies in stock
    //The value of the data member copiesInStock is returned.
void checkOut();
    //This function rents a video.
    //The number of copies in stock is decremented by one.
void checkIn();
    //This function checks in a video.
    //The number of copies in stock is incremented by one.
void printTitle() const;
    //This function prints the title of a movie
void printInfo() const;
    //This function prints the details of a video
    //The title of the movie, stars, director, and so on are
    //displayed on the screen.
bool checkTitle(newString title);
    //This function checks whether the title is the same as the
    //title of the video
    //Returns the value true if the title is the same as the
    //title of the video, false otherwise.
void updateInStock(int num);
    //This function increments the number of copies in stock by
    //adding the value of the parameter num
    //Post: copiesInStock = copiesInStock  + num;
void setCopiesInStock(int num);
    //This function sets the number of copies in stock
    //Post: copiesInStock = num;

newString getTitle();
    //Returns the title of the video

videoType(newString title = "", newString star1 = "",
          newString star2 = "", newString producer = "",
          newString director = "", newString productionCo = "",
          int setInStock = 0);
    //constructor
    //The private data members are set according to the
    //incoming parameters. If no values are specified, the
    //default values are assigned.
    //Post: videoTitle = title; movieStar1 = star1;
    //      movieStar2 = star2; movieProducer = producer;
    //      movieDirector = director;
    //      movieProductionCo = productionCo;
    //      copiesInStock = setInStock;
```

```
    bool operator==(videoType);
    bool operator!=(videoType);

private:
    newString videoTitle;  //variable to store the name
                           //of the movie
    newString movieStar1;  //variable to store the name
                           //of the star
    newString movieStar2;  //variable to store the name
                           //of the star
    newString movieProducer; //variable to store the name
                             //of the producer
    newString movieDirector; //variable to store the name
                             //of the director
    newString movieProductionCo; //variable to store the name
                                 //of the production company
    int copiesInStock;  //variable to store the number of
                        //copies in stock
};
```

For easy output, we will overload the output stream insertion operator, <<, for the `class videoType`. Notice that the `class videoType` uses the `class newString`, designed in Chapter 16, to manipulate strings.

Next, we write the definitions of each function in the `class videoType`. The definitions of these functions, as given below, are quite straightforward and easy to follow.

```
void videoType::setVideoInfo(newString title, newString star1,
                        newString star2, newString producer,
                        newString director, newString productionCo,
                        int setInStock)
{
    videoTitle = title;
    movieStar1 = star1;
    movieStar2 = star2;
    movieProducer = producer;
    movieDirector = director;
    movieProductionCo = productionCo;
    copiesInStock = setInStock;
}

void videoType::checkOut()
{
      if(getNoOfCopiesInStock() > 0)
            copiesInStock--;
      else
            cout<<"Currently out of Stock"<<endl;
}
```

```
void videoType::checkIn()
{
      copiesInStock++;
}

int videoType::getNoOfCopiesInStock() const
{
      return copiesInStock;
}

void videoType::printTitle() const
{
      cout<<"Video Title: "<<videoTitle<<endl;
}

void videoType::printInfo() const
{
      cout<<"Video Title: "<<videoTitle<<endl;
      cout<<"Stars: "<<movieStar1<<" and "<<movieStar2<<endl;
      cout<<"Producer: "<<movieProducer<<endl;
      cout<<"Director: "<<movieDirector<<endl;
      cout<<"Production Company: "<<movieProductionCo<<endl;
      cout<<"Copies in stock: "<<copiesInStock<<endl;
}

bool videoType::checkTitle(newString title)
{
      return(videoTitle == title);
}

void videoType::updateInStock(int num)
{
      copiesInStock += num;
}

void videoType::setCopiesInStock(int num)
{
      copiesInStock = num;
}

newString videoType::getTitle()
{
      return videoTitle;
}
```

```
videoType::videoType(newString title, newString star1,
                     newString star2, newString producer,
                     newString director,
                     newString productionCo, int setInStock)
{
      videoTitle = title;
      movieStar1 = star1;
      movieStar2 = star2;
      movieProducer = producer;
      movieDirector = director;
      movieProductionCo = productionCo;
      copiesInStock = setInStock;
}

videoType::videoType()
{
      copiesInStock = 0;
}

bool videoType::operator==(videoType other)
{
      return (videoTitle == other.videoTitle);
}

bool videoType::operator!=(videoType other)
{
      return (videoTitle != other.videoTitle);
}

ostream& operator<<(ostream& osObject, const videoType &video)
{
      osObject<<endl;
      osObject<<"Video Title: "<<video.videoTitle<<endl;
      osObject<<"Stars: "<<video.movieStar1<<" and "
              <<video.movieStar2<<endl;
      osObject<<"Producer: "<<video.movieProducer<<endl;
      osObject<<"Director: "<<video.movieDirector<<endl;
      osObject<<"Production Company: "<<video.movieProductionCo
              <<endl;
      osObject<<"Copies in stock: "<<video.copiesInStock<<endl;
      osObject<<"_____________________________________"<<endl;
      return osObject;
}
```

Video List This program requires us to maintain a list of all the videos in the store, and we should be able to add a new video to our list. In general, we would not know how many videos are in the store, and adding or deleting a video from the store would change the number of videos in the store. Therefore, we will use a linked list to create a list of videos. (See Figure 17-52.)

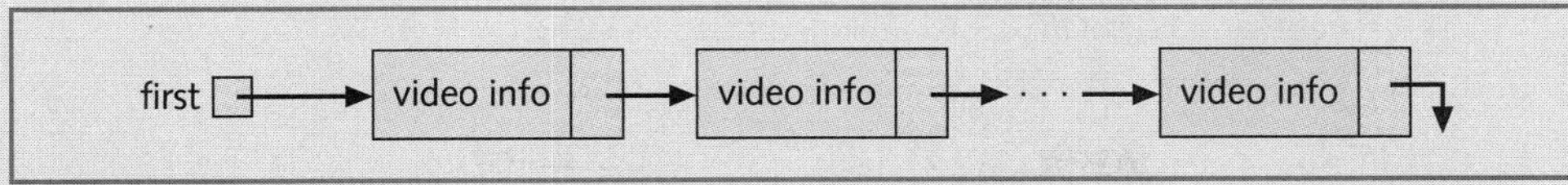

Figure 17-52 videoList

Earlier in this chapter, we defined the **class** linkedListType to create a linked list of objects. We also defined the basic operations such as insertion and deletion of a video in the list. However, some operations are very specific to the video list, such as check out a video, check in a video, set the number of copies of a video, and so on. These operations are not available in the **class** linkedListType. We will therefore derive a **class** videoListType from the **class** linkedListType and add these operations. (See Figure 17-53.)

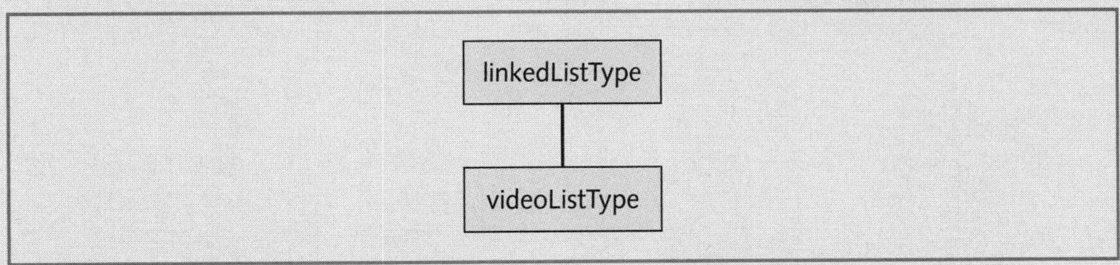

Figure 17-53 videoListType derived from linkedListType

The definition of the **class** videoListType is

```
class videoListType:public linkedListType<videoType>
{
public:
    bool videoSearch(newString title);
        //This function searches the list to see whether a
        //particular title, specified by the parameter title,
        //is in the store.
        //Returns true if the title is found, false otherwise.
    bool isVideoAvailable(newString title);
        //This function returns true if at least one copy of a
        //particular video is in the store.
    void videoCheckOut(newString title);
        //This function checks out a video, that is,
        //rents a video.
        //Post: copiesInStock is decremented by one.
```

```
    void videoCheckIn(newString title);
        //This function checks in a video returned by a customer.
        //Post: copiesInstock is incremented by one.
    bool videoCheckTitle(newString title);
        //This function returns true if a particular video is
        //in the store.
    void videoUpdateInStock(newString title, int num);
        //This function updates the number of copies of a video
        //by adding the value of the parameter num. The
        //parameter title specifies the name of the video for
        //which the number of copies is to be updated.
        //Post: copiesInStock = copiesInStock + num;
    void videoSetCopiesInStock(newString title, int num);
        //This function resets the number of copies of a video.
        //The parameter title specifies the name of the video
        //for which the number of copies is to be reset, and the
        //parameter num specifies the number of copies.
        //Post: copiesInStock = num;
    void videoPrintTitle();
        //This function prints the titles of all the videos in
        //the store.

private:
    void searchVideoList(newString title, bool& found,
                         nodeType<videoType>* &current);
        //This function searches the video list for a
        //particular video, specified by the parameter title.
        //If the video is found, the parameter found is set to
        //true; it is set to false otherwise. The parameter
        //current points to the node containing the video.
};
```

Note that the `class videoListType` is derived from the `class linkedListType` via a public inheritance. Furthermore, `linkedListType` is a class template and we have passed the `class videoType` as a parameter to this class. That is, the `class videoListType` is not a template. Because we are now dealing with a very specific data type, the `class videoListType` is no longer needed to be a template. Thus, the `info` type of each node in the linked list is now `videoType`. Through the member functions of the `class videoType`, certain members—such as `videoTitle` and `copiesInStock` of an object of the type `videoType`—can now be accessed.

The definitions of the functions to implement the operations of the `class videoListType` are given next.

The primary operations on the video list are to check in a video and to check out a video. Both operations require the list to be searched and the location of the video being checked in or checked out to be found in the video list. Other operations such as seeing whether a particular video is in the store, updating the number of copies of a video, and so on also require the video list to be searched. To simplify the search process, we will write a function that searches the video list for a particular video. If the video is found, it sets a parameter `found` to `true` and returns a pointer to the video so that check-in, check-out, and other operations on the video object can be performed. Note that the function `searchVideoList` is a `private` data member of the `class videoListType` because it is used only for internal manipulation. First, we describe the search procedure.

Consider the node of the video list shown in Figure 17-54.

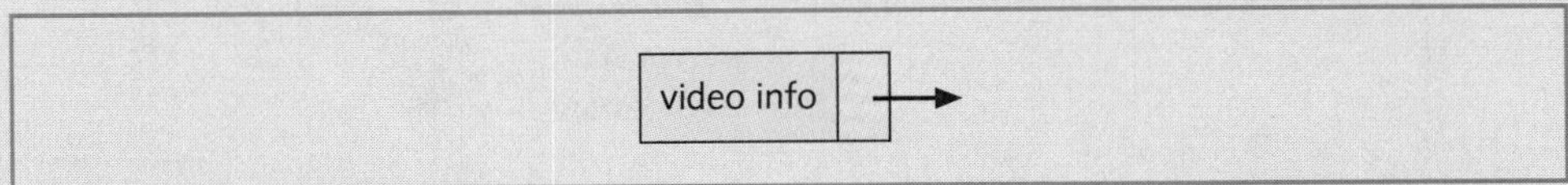

Figure 17-54 Node of a video list

The component `info` is of the type `videoType` and contains the necessary information about a video. In fact, the component `info` of the node has seven members: `videoTitle`, `movieStar1`, `movieStar2`, `movieProducer`, `movieDirector`, `movieProductionCo`, and `copiesInStock`. (See the definition of the `class videoType`.) Therefore, the node of a video list has the form shown in Figure 17-55.

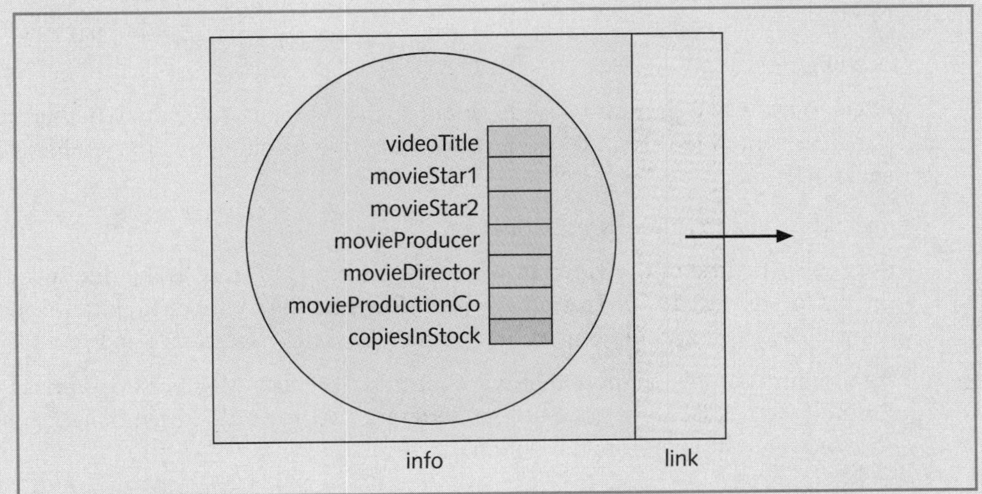

Figure 17-55 Video list node showing components of `info`

These data members are all **private** and cannot be accessed directly. The member functions of the **class videoType** will help us in checking and/or setting the value of a particular component.

Suppose a pointer—say, **current**—points to a node in the video list. (See Figure 17-56.)

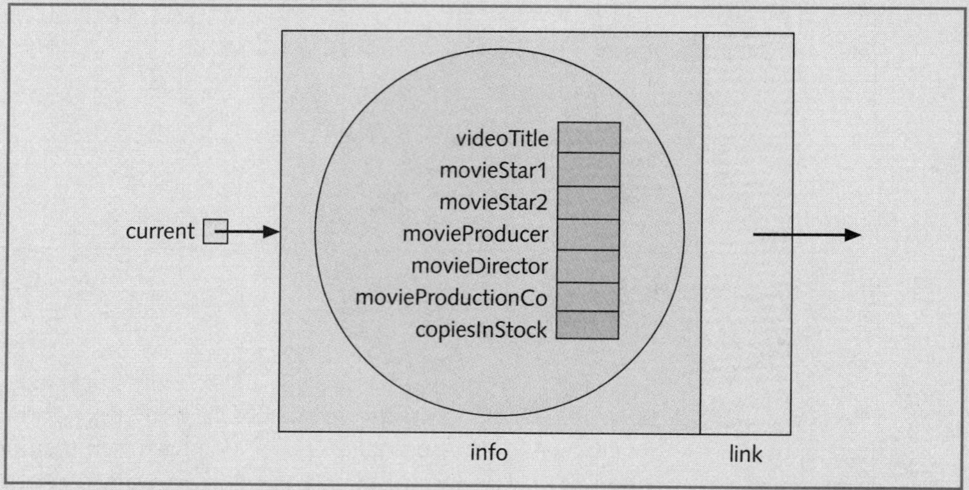

Figure 17-56 Pointer **current** and the video list node

Now

```
current->info
```

refers to the **info** part of the node. Suppose that we want to know whether the title of the video stored in this node is the same as the title specified by the variable **title**. The expression

```
current->info.checkTitle(title)
```

is **true** if the title of the video stored in this node is the same as the title specified by the parameter **title**, **false** otherwise. (Note that the member function **checkTitle** is a value-returning function. See its declaration in the **class videoType**.)

As another example, suppose that we want to set the data member **copiesInStock** of this node to 25. Because **copiesInStock** is a **private** data member, it cannot be accessed directly. Therefore the statement

```
current->info.copiesInStock = 10;   //illegal
```

is incorrect and will generate a compile-time error. We have to use the member function `setCopiesInStock` as follows:

```
current->info.setCopiesInStock(10);
```

Now that we know how to access a data member of a video stored in a node, let us describe the algorithm to search the video list.

```
if video list is empty
      Error
else
      while (not found)
        if the title of the current video is the same as the
           desired title
           stop search
        else
           check the next node
```

The following function definition performs the desired search:

```
void videoListType:: searchVideoList(newString title, bool& found,
                                     nodeType<videoType>* &current)
{
   found = false;    //set found to false

   if(first == NULL)  //list is empty
      cout<<"Cannot search an empty list. "<<endl;
   else
   {
    current = first; //set current to point to the first node
                     //in the list
    found = false;     //set found to false

    while(!found && current != NULL)       //search the list
       if(current->info.checkTitle(title)) //item is found
          found = true;
       else
          current = current->link; //advance current to
                                   //the next node
    } //end else
}//end searchVideoList
```

If the search is successful, the parameter `found` is set to `true` and the parameter `current` points to the node containing the video `info`. If it is unsuccessful, `found` is set to `false` and `current` will be `NULL`.

The definitions of the other functions of the `class videoListType` follow:

```
bool videoListType::isVideoAvailable(newString title)
{
      bool found;
      nodeType<videoType> *location;

      searchVideoList(title, found, location);

      if(found)
          found =(location->info.getNoOfCopiesInStock() > 0);
      else
          found = false;

      return found;
}

void videoListType::videoCheckIn(newString title)
{
      bool found = false;
      nodeType<videoType> *location;

      searchVideoList(title, found, location);  //search the list

      if(found)
          location->info.checkIn();
      else
          cout<<"Video not in stock "<<endl;
}

void videoListType::videoCheckOut(newString title)
{
      bool found = false;
      nodeType<videoType> *location;

      searchVideoList(title, found, location);  //search the list

      if(found)
          location->info.checkOut();
      else
          cout<<"Video not in stock "<<endl;
}
```

```
bool videoListType::videoCheckTitle(newString title)
{
      bool found = false;
      nodeType<videoType> *location;

      searchVideoList(title, found, location); //search the list

      return found;
}

void videoListType::videoUpdateInStock(newString title, int num)
{
      bool found = false;
      nodeType<videoType> *location;

      searchVideoList(title, found, location); //search the list

      if(found)
          location->info.updateInStock(num);
      else
          cout<<"Video not in stock "<<endl;
}

void videoListType::videoSetCopiesInStock(newString title, int num)
{
      bool found = false;
      nodeType<videoType> *location;

      searchVideoList(title, found, location);

      if(found)
          location->info.setCopiesInStock(num);
      else
          cout<<"Video not in stock "<<endl;
}

bool videoListType::videoSearch(newString title)
{
      bool found = false;
      nodeType<videoType> *location;

      searchVideoList(title, found, location);
```

```
    return found;
}

void videoListType::videoPrintTitle()
{
    nodeType<videoType>* current;

    current = first;
    while(current != NULL)
    {
        current->info.printTitle();
        current = current->link;
    }
}
```

Part 2: The Customer Component

The Customer Object The customer object stores information about a customer, such as the first name, last name, account number, and a list of videos rented by the customer. Thus, our video store program has two components:

1. A video object that contains the necessary information about a video as described previously
2. A customer object that contains the necessary information about a customer, which will be described soon

We will create two lists that correspond to these two objects:

a. A list of all videos in the store (as described earlier)
b. A list of all customers

Next, we describe the customer object.

The primary characteristics of a customer are:

1. The customer's first name
2. The customer's last name
3. The customer's account number
4. The list of rented videos

Every customer is a person. We have already designed the **`class personType`** in Example 13-9 (Chapter 13) and described the necessary operations on the name of a person. Therefore, we can derive the **`class customerType`** from the **`class personType`** and add the additional members that we need (see Figure 17-57). First, however, we redefine the **`class personType`** to take advantage of the new features of object-oriented design that you have learned, such as operator overloading, and then derive the **`class customerType`**.

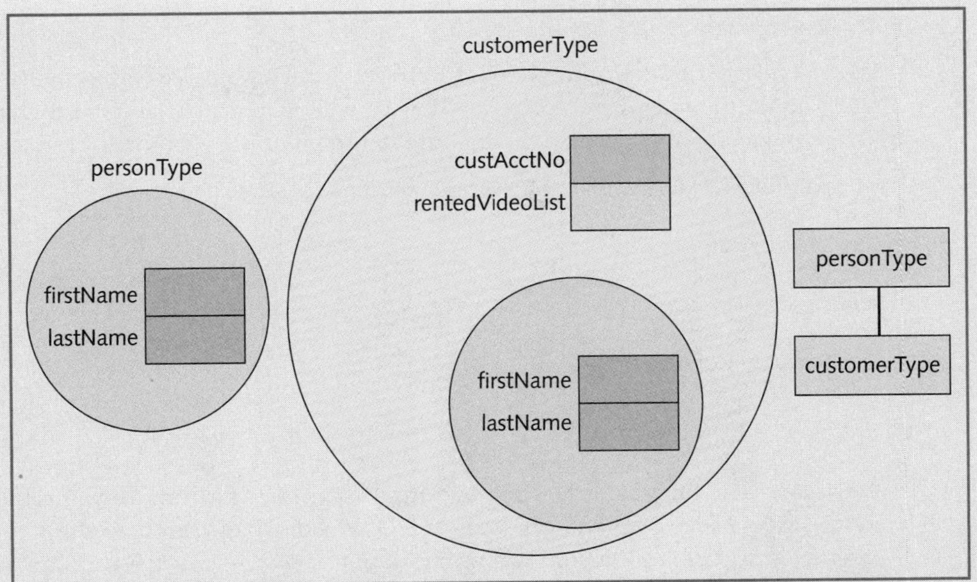

Figure 17-57 Classes `personType` and `customerType` with data members

The basic operations on an object of the type `personType` are

1. Print the name
2. Set the name
3. Show the first name
4. Show the last name

Similarly, the basic operations on an object of the type `customerType` are

1. Print the name, account number, and the list of rented videos
2. Set the name and the account number
3. Rent a video; that is, add the rented video to the list
4. Return a video; that is, delete the rented video from the list
5. Show the account number

The details of implementing the customer component are left as an exercise for you. (See Programming Exercise 5 at the end of this chapter.)

Main Program

We will now write the main program to test the video object. We assume that the necessary data for the videos are stored in a file. We will open the file and create the list of videos owned by the video store. The data in the input file is in the following form:

```
video title (that is, the name of the movie)
movie star1
movie star2
movie producer
movie director
movie production co.
number of copies
.
.
.
```

We will write a function, `createVideoList`, to read data from the input file and create the list of videos. We will also write a function, `displayMenu`, to show the different choices—such as check in a movie or check out a movie—that the user can make. The algorithm of the function `main` is

1. Open the input file
   If the input file does not exist, exit the program.
2. Create the list of videos (`createVideoList`).
3. Show the menu (`displayMenu`).
4. While not done
   Perform the various operations.

Opening the input file is straightforward. Let us describe Steps 2 and 3, which are accomplished by writing two separate functions: `createVideoList` and `displayMenu`.

`createVideoList`

This function reads the data from the input file and creates a linked list of videos. Because the data will be read from a file and the input file was opened in the function `main`, we pass the input file pointer to this function. We also pass the video list pointer, declared in the function `main`, to this function. Both parameters are reference parameters. Next, we read the data for each video and then insert the video in the list. The general algorithm is

```
a.   Read the data and store it in a video object.
b.   Insert the video in the list.
c.   Repeat steps a and b for each video's data in the file.
```

`displayMenu`

This function informs the user what to do. It contains the following output statements:

```
a. Select one of the following
b. 1: To check whether a particular video is in the store
c. 2: To check out a video
d. 3: To check in a video
e. 4: To check whether a particular video is in the store
f. 5: To print the titles of all the videos
g. 6: To print a list of all the videos
h. 9: To exit
```

In pseudocode, Step 4 is

```
a. get choice
b. while (choice != 9)
   {
      switch(choice)
      {
      case 1:  a. get the movie name
               b. search the video list
               c. if found report success
                  else report "failure"
      case 2:  a. get the movie name
               b. search the video list
               c. if found check out the video
                  else report "failure"
      case 3:  a. get the movie name
               b. search the video list
               c. if found check in video
                  else report "failure"
      case 4:  a. get the movie name
               b. search the video list
               c. if found
                    if number of copies > 0
                           report "success"
                    else
                           report "currently out of stock"
                    else report "failure"
      case 5: print the titles of the videos
      case 6: print all the videos in the store
      default: bad selection
     }//end switch

     displayMenu();
     get choice;
}//end while
```

Main Program Listing

```
#include <iostream>
#include <fstream>
#include "myString.h"
#include "linkedList.h"
#include "videoType.h"
#include "videoLinkedListType.h"

using namespace std;

void createVideoList(ifstream& infile, videoListType& videoList);
void displayMenu();

int main()
{
   videoListType  videoList;
   int choice;
   char ch;
   char title[50];

   ifstream infile;

      //open input file
   infile.open("a:videoDat.txt");
   if(!infile)
   {
      cout<<"Input file does not exist"<<endl;
      return 1;
   }
      //create video list
   createVideoList(infile, videoList);
   infile.close();

      //show menu
   displayMenu();
   cout<<"Enter choice: ";
   cin>>choice;        //get request
   cout<<endl;

      //process requests
   while(choice != 9)
   {
      switch(choice)
      {
      case 1: cout<<"Enter Title: ";
              cin.get(ch);
              cin.get(title,50);
              cout<<endl;
```

```
        if(videoList.videoSearch(title))
            cout<<"Title found"<<endl;
        else
            cout<<"Video not in store"<<endl;

        break;

case 2: cout<<"Enter Title: ";
        cin.get(ch);
        cin.get(title,50);
        cout<<endl;

        if(videoList.videoSearch(title))
        {
          if(videoList.isVideoAvailable(title))
          {
             videoList.videoCheckOut(title);
             cout<<"Enjoy your movie: "<<title<<endl;
          }
          else
             cout<<"Currently "<<title
                  <<" is out of stock."<<endl;
        }
        else
            cout<<"Video not in store"<<endl;

        break;

case 3: cout<<"Enter title: ";
        cin.get(ch);
        cin.get(title,50);
        cout<<endl;

        if(videoList.videoSearch(title))
        {
           videoList.videoCheckIn(title);
           cout<<"Thanks for returning "<<title<<endl;
        }
        else
           cout<<"This video is not from our store"<<endl;

        break;

case 4: cout<<"Enter title: ";
        cin.get(ch);
        cin.get(title,50);
        cout<<endl;
```

```
            if(videoList.videoSearch(title))
            {
               if(videoList.isVideoAvailable(title))
                  cout<<"Currently in stock"<<endl;
               else
                  cout<<"Out of stock"<<endl;
            }
            else
               cout<<"Video not in store "<<endl;

            break;

      case 5: videoList.videoPrintTitle();
            break;

      case 6: videoList.print();
            break;

      default: cout<<"Bad Selection"<<endl;
      }//end switch

      displayMenu();          //display menu

      cout<<"Enter choice: ";
      cin>>choice;          //get the next request
      cout<<endl;
   }//end while

   return 0;
}

void createVideoList(ifstream& infile, videoListType& videoList)
{
    char  Title[50];
    char  Star1[50];
    char  Star2[50];
    char  Producer[50];
    char  Director[50];
    char  ProductionCo[70];
    char  ch;
    int   InStock;

    videoType newVideo;

    infile.get(Title,50);
    infile.get(ch);
```

```
    while(infile)
    {
      infile.get(Star1,50);
      infile.get(ch);
      infile.get(Star2,50);
      infile.get(ch);
      infile.get(Producer,50);
      infile.get(ch);
      infile.get(Director,50);
      infile.get(ch);
      infile.get(ProductionCo,70);
      infile.get(ch);
      infile>>InStock;
      infile.get(ch);
      newVideo.setVideoInfo(Title,Star1,Star2,Producer,
                            Director,ProductionCo,InStock);
      videoList.insertFirst(newVideo);

      infile.get(Title,50);
      infile.get(ch);
    }//end while
}//end createVideoList

void displayMenu()
{
    cout<<"Select one of the following "<<endl;
    cout<<"1: To check whether a particular video is in the store"
        <<endl;
    cout<<"2: To check out a video"<<endl;
    cout<<"3: To check in a video"<<endl;
    cout<<"4: To check whether a particular video is in the store"
        <<endl;
    cout<<"5: To print the titles of all the videos"<<endl;
    cout<<"6: To print a list of all the videos"<<endl;
    cout<<"9: To exit"<<endl;
}
```

Quick Review

1. A linked list is a list of items, called nodes, in which the order of the nodes is determined by the address, called a link, stored in each node.
2. The pointer to a linked list—that is, the pointer to the first node in the list—is stored in a separate location, called the head or first.
3. A linked list is a dynamic data structure.

4. The length of a linked list is the number of nodes in the list.
5. Item insertion and deletion from a linked list does not require data movement; only the pointers are adjusted.
6. A (single) linked list is traversed in only one direction.
7. The search on a linked list is sequential.
8. The first (or head) pointer of the linked list is always fixed, pointing to the first node in the list.
9. To traverse a linked list, the program must use a pointer different than the head pointer of the list, initialized to the first node in the list.
10. When a class object is passed by value, the copy constructor copies the value of the actual object into the formal parameter.
11. A linked list with header and trailer nodes simplifies the insertion and deletion operations.
12. The header and trailer nodes are not part of the actual list. The actual list elements are between the header and trailer nodes.
13. A linked list with header and trailer nodes is empty if the only nodes in the list are the header and the trailer.
14. In a doubly linked list, every node has two links: one points to the next node, and one points to the previous node.
15. A doubly linked list can be traversed in either direction.
16. In a doubly linked list, item insertion and deletion requires the adjustment of two pointers in a node.

EXERCISES

1. Mark the following statements as true or false.
   a. In a linked list, the order of the elements is determined by the order in which the nodes were created to store the elements.
   b. In a linked list, memory allocated for the nodes is sequential.
   c. A single linked list can be traversed in either direction.
   d. In a linked list, nodes are always inserted either in the beginning or the end because a linked link is not a random access data structure.
   e. Item insertion (and deletion) in a linked list with header and trailer nodes is simpler than in an ordinary linked list because the former list has no special cases.
   f. The head pointer of a linked list cannot be used to traverse the list.

   Consider the linked list shown in Figure 17-58. Assume that the nodes are in the usual `info-link` form. Use this list to answer Exercises 2–7. If necessary, declare additional variables. (Assume that `List`, `p`, `s`, `A`, and `B` are pointers of the type `nodeType`.)

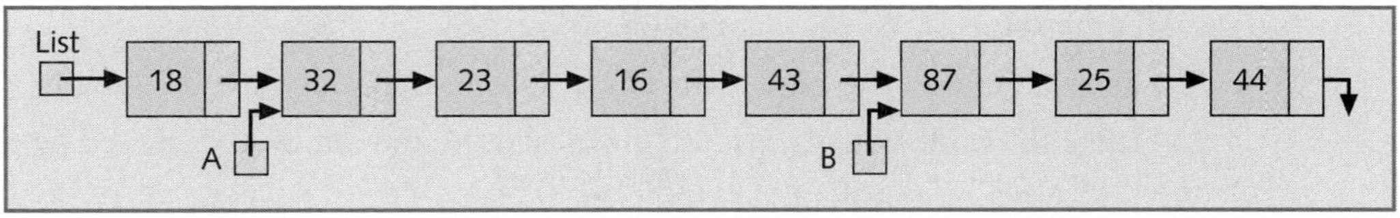

Figure 17-58 Linked list for Exercises 2–7

2. What is the output of the following C++ statements?
   a. `cout<<List->info;`
   b. `cout<<A->info;`
   c. `cout<<B->link->info;`
   d. `cout<<List->link->link->info`
3. What is the value of the following relational expressions?
   a. `List->info >= 18`
   b. `List->link == A`
   c. `A->link->info == 16`
   d. `B->link == NULL`
   e. `List->info == 18`
4. Mark each of the following statements as valid or invalid. If a statement is invalid, explain why.
   a. `A = B;`
   b. `List->link = A->link;`
   c. `List->link->info = 45;`
   d. `*List = B;`
   e. `*A = *B;`
   f. `B = A->link->info;`
   g. `A->info = B->info;`
   h. `List = B->link->link;`
   i. `B = B->link->link->link;`
5. Write C++ statements to do the following.
   a. Make `A` point to the node containing `info 23`.
   b. Make `List` point to the node containing `16`.
   c. Make `B` point to the last node in the list.
   d. Make `List` point to an empty list.

e. Set the value of the node containing `25` to `35`.

f. Create and insert the node with `info 10` after the node pointed to by `A`.

g. Delete the node with `info 23`. Also, deallocate the memory occupied by this node.

6. What is the output of the following C++ code?

```
p = List;

while(p != NULL)
  cout<<p->info<<" ";
  p = p->link;
cout<<endl;
```

7. If the following C++ code is valid, show the output. If it is invalid, explain why.

a.
```
s = A;
p = B;
s->info = B;
p = p->link;
cout<<s->info<<" "<<p->info<<endl;
```

b.
```
p = A;
p = p->link;
s = p;
p->link = NULL;
s = s->link;
cout<<p->info<<" "<<s->info<<endl;
```

8. Show what is produced by the following C++ code. Assume the node is in the usual `info-link` form with `info` of the type `int`. (`List` and `ptr` are pointers of the type `nodeType`.)

a.
```
List = new nodeType;
List->info = 10;
ptr = new nodeType;
ptr->info = 13;
ptr->link = NULL;
List->link = ptr;
ptr = new nodeType;
ptr->info = 18;
ptr->link = List->link;
List->link = ptr;
cout<<List->info<<"  "<<ptr->info<<" ";
ptr = ptr->link;
cout<<ptr->info<<endl;
```

b.
```
List = new nodeType;
List->info = 20;
ptr = new nodeType;
ptr->info = 28;
ptr->link = NULL;
List->link = ptr;
ptr = new nodeType;
```

```
ptr->info = 30;
ptr->link = List;
List = ptr;
ptr = new nodeType;
ptr->info = 42;
ptr->link = List->link;
List->link = ptr;
ptr = List;
while(ptr != NULL)
{
   cout<<ptr->info<<endl;
   ptr = ptr->link;
}
```

9. Consider the following C++ statements. (The **class linkedListType** is as defined in this chapter.)

```
linkedListType<int> list;

list.insertFirst(15);
list.insertLast(28);
list.insertFirst(30);
list.insertFirst(2);
list.insertLast(45);
list.insertFirst(38);
list.insertLast(25);
list.deleteNode(30);
list.insertFirst(18);
list.deleteNode(28);
list.deleteNode(12);
list.print();
```

What is the output of this program segment?

10. Suppose the input is

`18 30 4 32 45 36 78 19 48 75 –999`

What is the output of the following C++ code? (The **class linkedListType** is as defined in this chapter.)

```
linkedListType<int> list;
linkedListType<int> copyList;
int num;

cin>>num;
while(num != -999)
{
   if(num % 5 == 0 || num % 5 == 3)
      list.insertFirst(num);
   else
      list.insertLast(num);
   cin>>num;
}
```

```
list.print();
cout<<endl;

copyList = list;

copyList.deleteNode(78);
copyList.deleteNode(35);

cout<<"Copy List = ";
copyList.print();
cout<<endl;
```

PROGRAMMING EXERCISES

1. (Online Address Book Revisited) Programming Exercise 6 in Chapter 14 could handle a maximum of only 500 entries. Using linked lists, redo the program to handle as many entries as required. Add the following operations to your program:
   a. Add or delete a new entry to the address book.
   b. When the program terminates, write the data in the address book to a disk.
2. Extend the **class linkedListType** by adding the following operations:
   a. Find and delete the node with the smallest `info` in the list. (Delete only the first occurrence. Traverse the list only once.)
   b. Find and delete all occurrences of a given `info` from the list. (Traverse the list only once.)
3. Some other operations that are usually performed on linked lists are **divideMid** and `divideAt`.
   a. **divideMid**: This operation splits the given list into two sublists of (almost) equal size.

      For example, suppose that the given list is `13 72 89 65 34`. Then the two sublists are `13 72 89` and `65 34`. Similarly, if the original list is `12 67 34 65`, the two sublists are `12 67` and `34 65`.

      i. Add the operation **divideMid** to the **class linkedListType** as follows:

```
void divideMid(linkedListType<Type> &sublist);
   //This operation divides the given list into two sublists of
   //(almost) equal size.
   //Post: first points to the first node and last
   //      points to the last node of the first sublist.
   //      sublist.first points to the first node and
   //      sublist.last points to the last node of the
   //      second sublist.
```

Consider the following statements:

```
linkedListType<int> myList;
linkedListType<int> subList;
```

Suppose myList points to the list with elements 34 65 27 89 12 (in this order). The statement

```
myList.divideMid(subList);
```

divides myList into two sublists: myList points to the list with elements 34 65 27, and subList points to the sublist with elements 89 12.

ii. Write the definition of the function template to implement the operation divideMid.

b. divideAt: This operation divides a given list at a node whose info is given.

Suppose oldList points to a list with the elements

10 18 34 6 28 92 56 48

and the list is to divide at the node whose info is 6. Then the two sublists are

10 18 34 and 6 28 92 56 48

i. Add the following operation to the class linkedListType:

```
void divideAt(linkedListType &secondList, Type item);
  //Divide the list at the node with the info item into two
  //sublists.
  //Post: first and last point to the first and
  //      last nodes of the first sublist.
  //      secondList.first and secondList.last point to the
  //      first and last nodes of the second sublist.
```

Consider the following statements:

```
linkedListType<int> myList;
linkedListType<int> otherList;
```

Suppose myList points to the list with the elements 34 65 18 39 27 89 12 (in this order). The statement

```
myList.divideAt(otherList,18);
```

divides myList into two sublists: myList points to the list with the elements 34 65, and otherList points to the sublist with the elements 18 39 27 89 12.

ii. Write the definition of the function template to implement the operation divideAt.

4. a. Add the following operation to the **class** orderedLinkedListType:

```
void mergeLists(orderedLinkedListType<Type> &list1,
                             orderedLinkedListType<Type> &list2);

   //This operation creates a new list by merging the elements
   //of list1 and list2.
   //Post: first points to the merged list
   //list1 and list2 are empty
```

Example: Consider the following statements:

```
orderedLinkedListType<int> newList;
orderedLinkedListType<int> list1;
orderedLinkedListType<int> list2;
```

Suppose `list1` points to the list with the elements `2 6 7` and `list2` points to the list with the elements `3 5 8`. The statement

```
newList.mergeLists(list1,list2);
```

creates a new linked list with the elements in the order `2 3 5 6 7 8` and the object `newList` points to this list. Also, after the preceding statement executes, `list1` and `list2` are empty.

b. Write the definition of the function template `mergeLists` to implement the operation `mergeLists`.

5. (Programming Example Video Store)

   a. Complete the design and implementation of the **class** customerType defined in the Programming Example, Video Store.

   b. Design and implement the **class** customerListType to create and maintain a list of customers for the video store.

6. (Programming Example Video Store) Complete the design and implementation of the video store program.

CHAPTER

18

STACKS AND QUEUES

In this chapter, you will:

- Learn about stacks
- Examine various stack operations
- Learn how to implement a stack as an array
- Learn how to implement a stack as a linked list
- Discover stack applications
- Learn how to use a stack to remove recursion
- Learn about queues
- Examine various queue operations
- Learn how to implement a queue as an array
- Learn how to implement a queue as a linked list
- Discover queue applications

This chapter discusses two very useful data structures, stacks and queues. Both stacks and queues have numerous applications in computer science.

STACKS

Suppose that you have a program with several functions. To be specific, suppose that you have the functions A, B, C, and D in your program. Now suppose that function A calls function B, function B calls function C, and function C calls function D. When function D terminates, control goes back to function C; when function C terminates, control goes back to function B; and when function B terminates, control goes back to function A. During program execution, how do you think the computer keeps track of the function calls? What about recursive functions? How does the computer keep track of recursive calls? In Chapter 17, we designed a recursive function to print a linked list backward. What if you want to write a nonrecursive algorithm to print a linked list backward?

This section discusses the data structure called the **stack**, which the computer uses to implement function calls. You can also use stacks to convert recursive algorithms into nonrecursive algorithms, especially recursive algorithms that are not tail recursive. Stacks have numerous other applications in computer science. After developing the tools necessary to implement a stack, we will examine some applications of stacks.

A stack is a list of homogenous elements, wherein the addition and deletion of elements occurs only at one end, called the **top** of the stack. For example, in a cafeteria, the second tray in a stack of trays can be removed only if the first tray has been removed. For another example, to get to your favorite computer science book, which is underneath your math and history books, you must first remove the math and history books. After removing these books, the computer science book becomes the top book—that is, the top element of the stack. Figure 18-1 shows some examples of stacks.

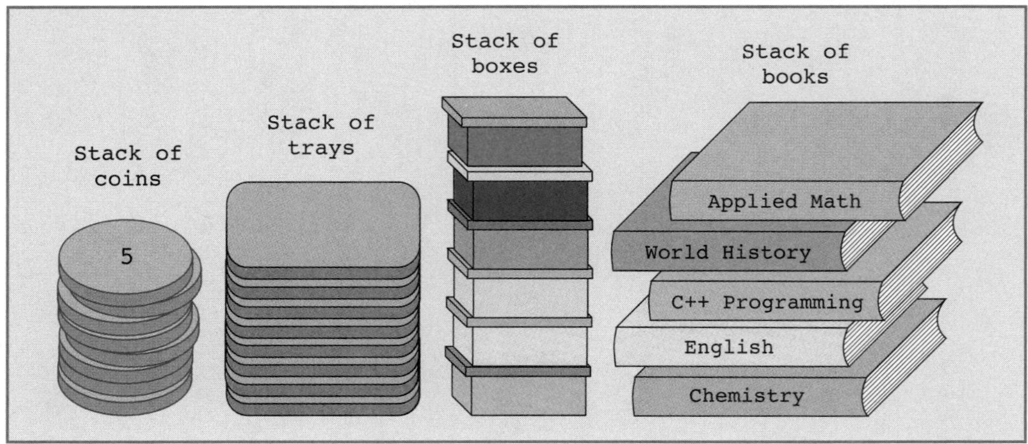

Figure 18-1 Various types of stacks

The elements at the bottom of the stack have been in the stack the longest. The top element of the stack is the last element added to the stack. Because elements are added and removed from one end (that is, the top), it follows that the item that is added last will be removed first. For this reason, a stack is also called a **Last In First Out (LIFO)** data structure.

Stack: A data structure in which the elements are added and removed from one end only; a Last In First Out (LIFO) data structure.

Now that you know what a stack is, let us see what kinds of operations can be performed on a stack. Because new items can be added to the stack, we can perform the add operation, called **push**, to add an element onto the stack. Similarly, because the top item can be removed from the stack, we can perform the remove operation, called **pop**, to remove an element from the stack. Figures 18-2 through 18-7 illustrate the push and pop operations.

The push and pop operations work as follows: Suppose there are boxes lying on the floor that need to be stacked on a table. Initially, all of the boxes are on the floor and the stack is empty. (See Figure 18-2.)

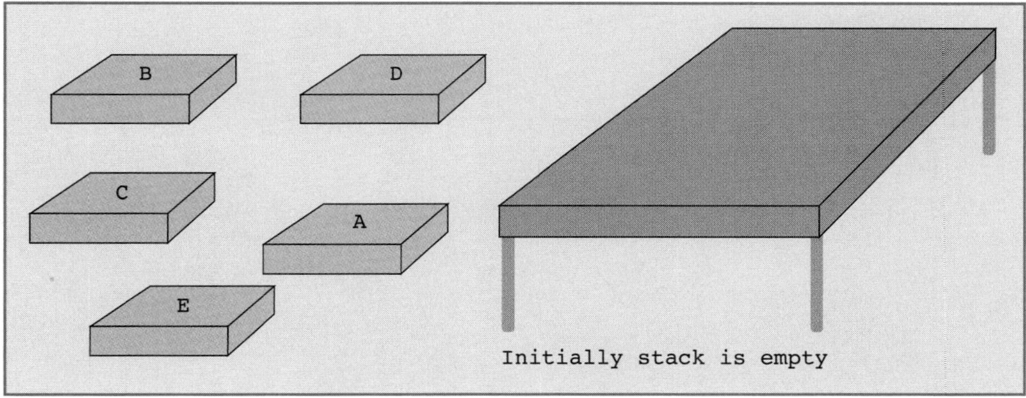

Figure 18-2 Empty stack

First we push box `A` onto the stack. After the push operation, the stack is as shown in Figure 18-3.

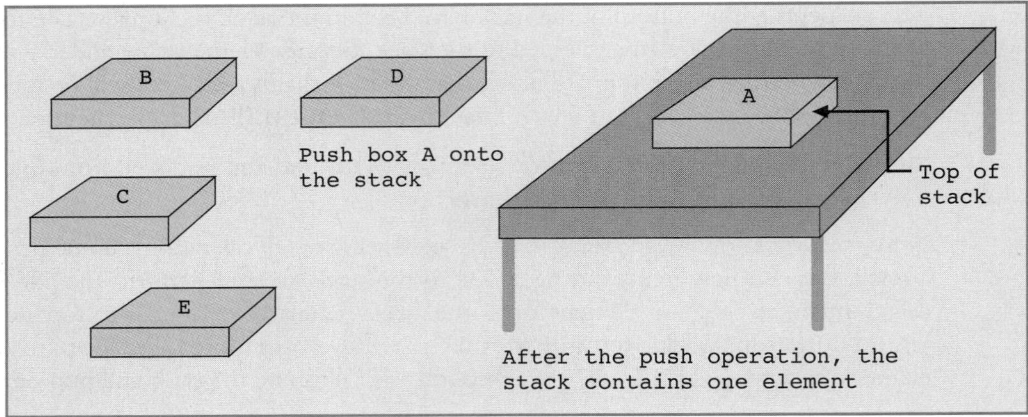

Figure 18-3 Stack after pushing box A

We then push box B onto the stack. After the push operation, the stack is as shown in Figure 18-4.

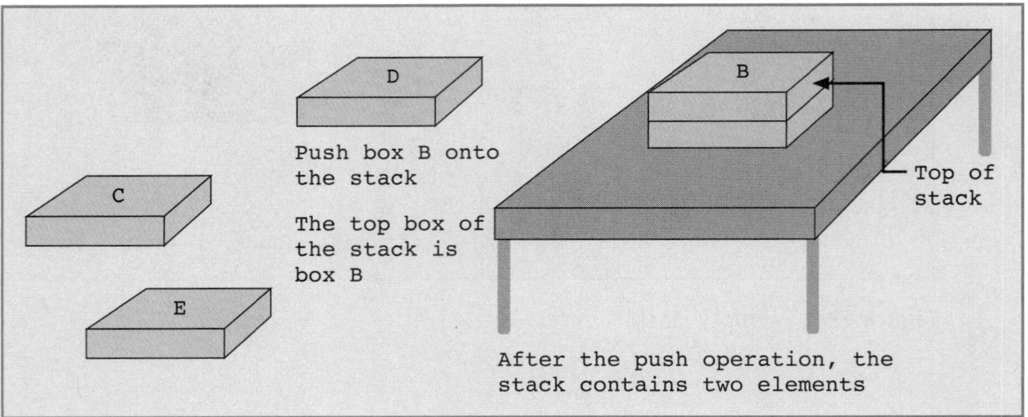

Figure 18-4 Stack after pushing box B

Next, we push box C onto the stack. After the push operation, the stack is as shown in Figure 18-5.

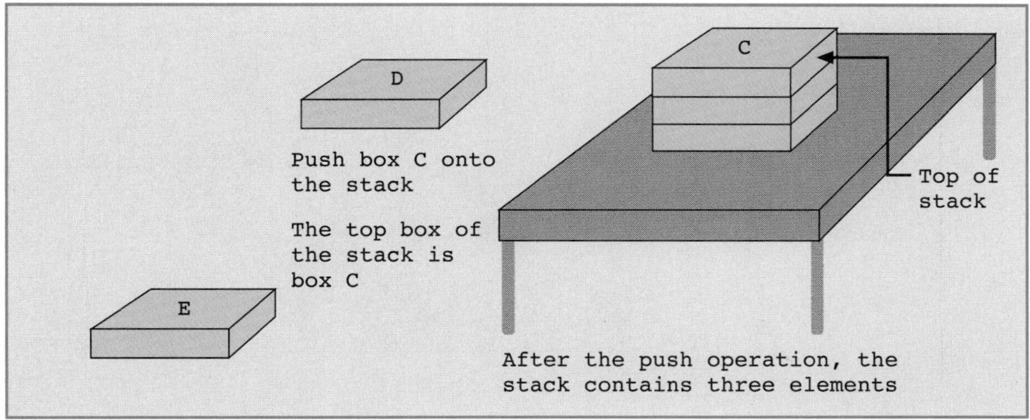

Figure 18-5 Stack after pushing box C

We then push box D onto the stack. After the push operation, the stack is as shown in Figure 18-6.

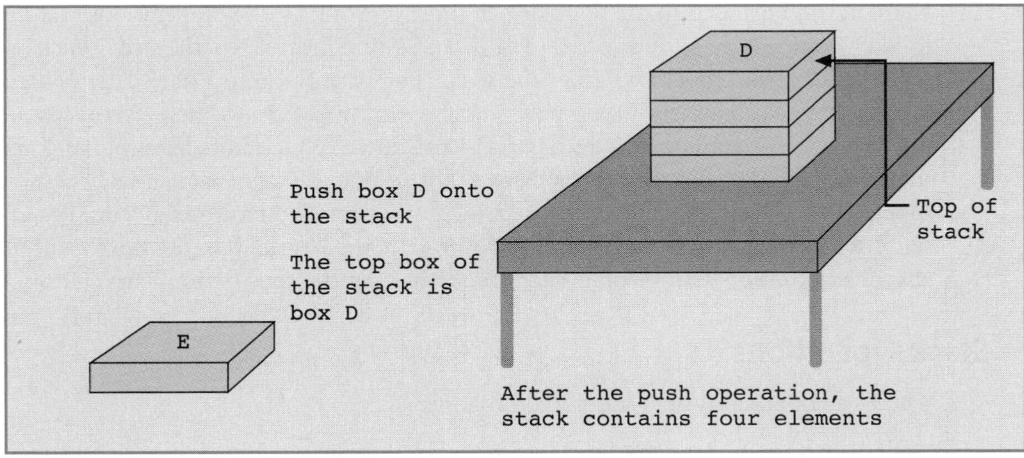

Figure 18-6 Stack after pushing box D

Next, we pop the stack. After the pop operation, the stack is as shown in Figure 18-7.

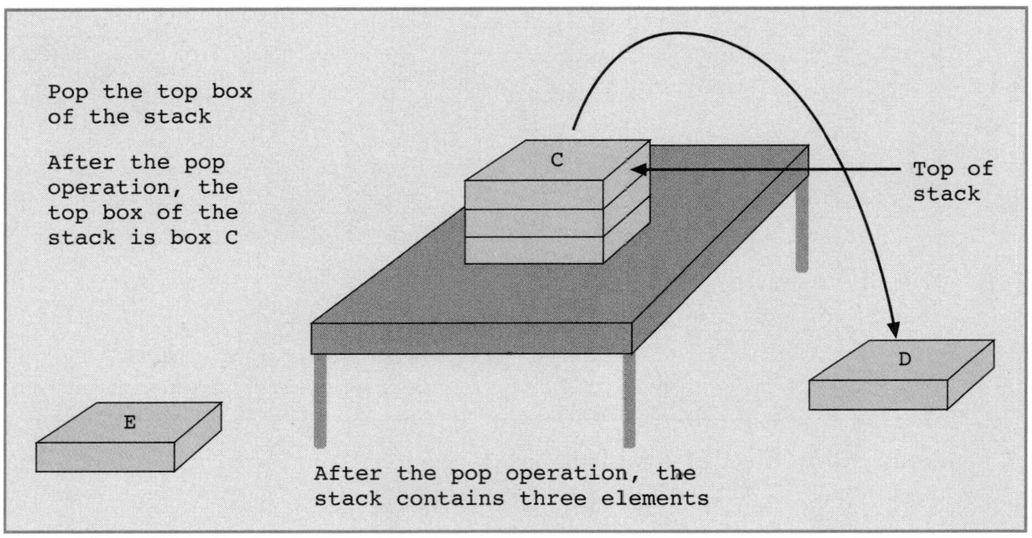

Figure 18-7 Stack after the pop operation

An element can be removed from the stack only if there is something in the stack, and an element can be added to the stack only if there is room. The two operations that immediately follow from **push** and **pop** are **isFullStack** (checks whether the stack is full) and **isEmptyStack** (checks whether the stack is empty). Because a stack keeps changing as we add and remove elements, the stack must be empty before we first start using it. Thus, we need another operation, called **initializeStack**, which initializes the stack to an empty state. Another useful operation is **destroyStack**. This operation usually removes all elements from a stack, leaving the stack in an empty state. Therefore, to successfully implement a stack, we need at least these six operations, which are described in the next section. We might also need other operations on a stack, depending on the specific implementation.

Stack Operations

The basic operations on a stack are as follows:

1. **InitializeStack**: This operation initializes the stack to an empty state.
2. **DestroyStack**: This operation removes all the elements from the stack, leaving the stack empty.
3. **isEmptyStack**: This operation checks whether the stack is empty. If the stack is empty, it returns the value `true`; otherwise, it returns the value `false`.
4. **isFullStack**: This operation checks whether the stack is full. If the stack is full, it returns the value `true`; otherwise, it returns the value `false`.

5. **push**: This operation adds a new element to the top of the stack. Input to this operation consists of the stack and the new element. Prior to this operation, the stack must exist and must not be full.
6. **pop**: This operation removes the top element of the stack and stores the top element into a location called **poppedElement**. Input to this function consists of the stack and the location where the top element will be stored. Prior to this operation, the stack must exist and must not be empty.

We now consider the implementation of our abstract stack data structure. Functions such as **push** and **pop** that are required to implement a stack are not available to C++ programmers. We must write the functions to implement the stack operations.

Because all the elements of a stack are of the same type, a stack can be implemented as either an array or a linked structure. Both implementations are useful and are discussed in this chapter.

THE IMPLEMENTATION OF STACKS AS ARRAYS

Because all the elements of a stack are of the same type, you can use an array to implement a stack. The first element of the stack can be put in the first array slot, the second element of the stack in the second array slot, and so on. The top of the stack is the index of the last element added to the stack.

In this implementation of a stack, stack elements are stored in an array, and an array is a random access data structure; that is, you can directly access any element of the array. However, by definition, a stack is a data structure in which the elements are accessed (popped or pushed) at only one end—that is, a Last In First Out data structure. Thus, a stack element is accessed only through the top, not through the bottom or middle. This feature of a stack is extremely important and must be recognized in the beginning.

To keep track of the top position of the array, we can simply declare another variable, called **top**.

The following **class**, **stackType**, defines a stack as an abstract data type (ADT). By using a pointer, we can dynamically allocate arrays, so we will leave it for the user to specify the size of the array (that is, the stack size). We assume that the default stack size is 100. Because the **class stackType** has a pointer data member (the pointer to the array to store the stack elements), we must overload the assignment operator and include the copy constructor and destructor. Moreover, we give a generic definition of the stack. Depending on the specific application, we can pass the stack element type when we declare a stack object.

```
template<class Type>
class stackType
{
public:
    const stackType<Type>& operator=(const stackType<Type>&);
        //overload the assignment operator
    void initializeStack();
        //Initialize the stack to an empty state
        //Post: top = 0
    bool isEmptyStack();
        //This function returns true if the stack is empty;
        //otherwise, it returns false.
    bool isFullStack();
        //This function returns true if the stack is full;
        //otherwise, it returns false.
    void destroyStack();
        //Remove all elements from the stack
        //Post: top = 0
    void push(const Type& newItem);
        //Add newItem to the stack
        //Post: stack is changed and the newItem
        //      is added to the top of stack
    void pop(Type& poppedItem);
        //Remove the top element of the stack
        //Post: the stack is changed and the top element
        //      is removed from the stack. The top element
        //      of the stack is saved in poppedItem.
    stackType(int stackSize = 100);
        //constructor
        //Create an array of size stackSize to hold the
        //stack elements. The default stack size is 100.
        //Post: the variable list contains the base
        //      address of the array, top = 0 and
        //      maxStackSize = stackSize
    stackType(const stackType<Type>& otherStack);
        //copy constructor
    ~stackType();
        //destructor
        //Remove all the elements from the stack
        //Post: the array (list) holding the stack
        //      elements is deleted

private:
    int maxStackSize; //variable to store the maximum stack size
    int top;          //variable to point to the top of the stack
    Type *list;       //pointer to the array that holds
                      //the stack elements
};
```

Because C++ arrays begin with the index `0`, we need to distinguish between the value of `top` and the array position indicated by `top`. If `top` is `0`, the stack is empty; if `top` is nonzero, then the stack is nonempty and the top element of the stack is given by `top-1`.

Figure 18-8 shows this data structure, wherein **`stack`** is an object of the type **`stackType`**. Note that **`top`** can range from `0` to **`maxStackSize`**. If **`top`** is nonzero, then **`top-1`** is the index of the **`top`** element of the stack. Suppose that **`maxStackSize = 100`**.

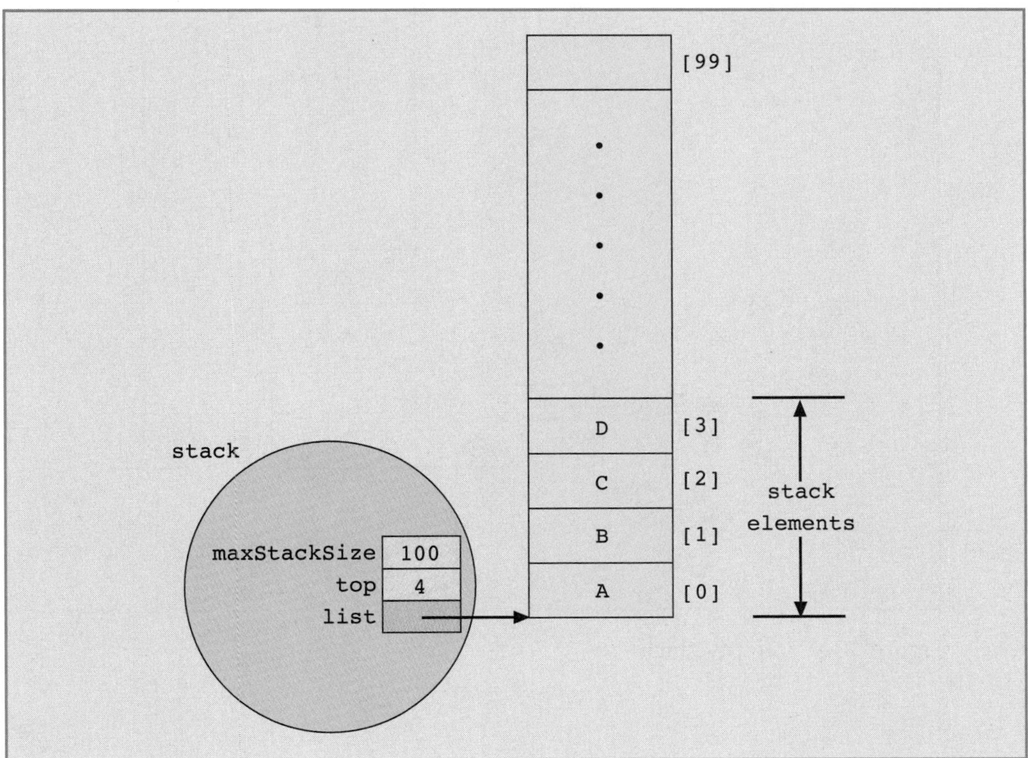

Figure 18-8 Example of a stack

Note that the pointer **`list`** contains the base address of the array (holding the stack elements)—that is, the address of the first array component. The next nine sections define the member functions of the **`class stackType`** to implement the stack operations.

Initialize Stack

Let us consider the **initializeStack** operation. Because the value of **top** indicates whether the stack is empty, we can simply set **top** to **0** to initialize the stack. (See Figure 18-9.)

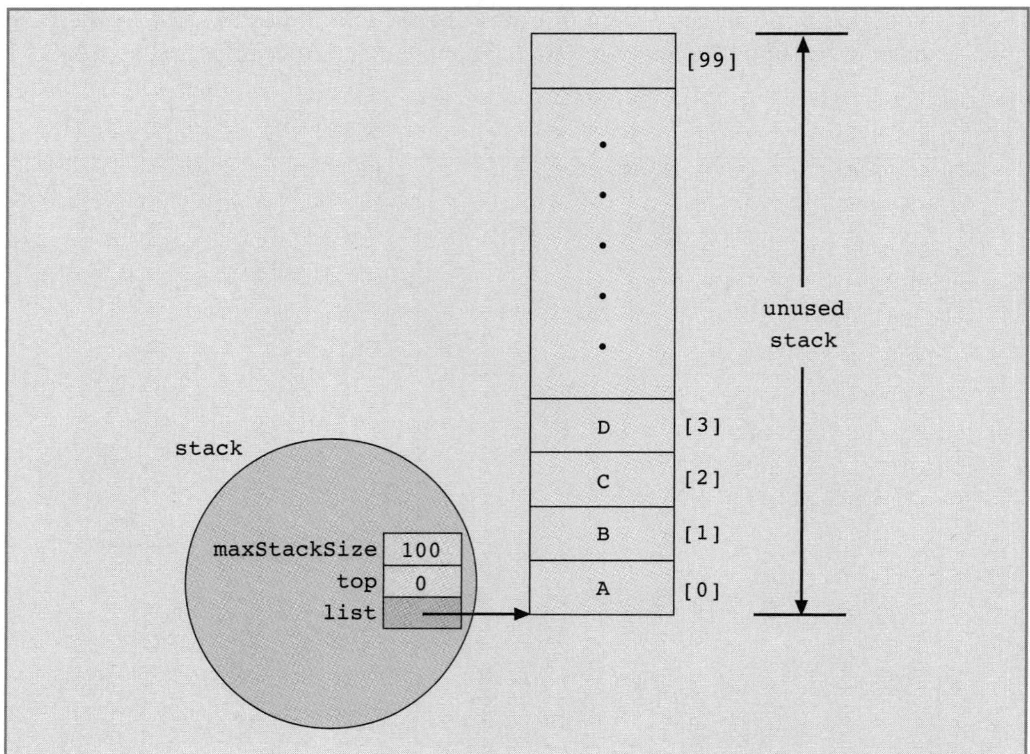

Figure 18-9 Empty stack

The definition of the function **initializeStack** is

```
template<class Type>
void stackType<Type>::initializeStack()
{
      top = 0;
}//end initializeStack
```

Destroy Stack

In the array implementation of a stack, the **destroyStack** operation is similar to the **initializeStack** operation. If we set the value of **top** to **0**, then all elements of the stack are destroyed. Even though the elements are still in the stack (they are treated as garbage), the value of **top** indicates whether the stack is empty.

```
template<class Type>
void stackType<Type>::destroyStack()
{
      top = 0;
}//end destroyStack
```

Empty Stack

We have seen that the value of **top** indicates whether the stack is empty. If **top** is **0**, the stack is empty; otherwise, the stack is not empty. The definition of the function **isEmptyStack** is

```
template<class Type>
bool stackType<Type>::isEmptyStack()
{
      return(top == 0);
}//end isEmptyStack
```

Full Stack

Next, we consider the operation **isFullStack**. It follows that the stack is full if **top** is equal to **maxStackSize**. The definition of the function **isFullStack** is

```
template<class Type>
bool stackType<Type>::isFullStack()
{
      return(top == maxStackSize);
} //end isFullStack
```

Constructors and Destructors

The functions to implement the constructors and the destructor are straightforward. The constructor with parameters sets the stack size to the size specified by the user, and sets **top** to **0**, and creates an appropriate array in which to store the stack elements. If the user does not specify the size of the array in which to store the stack elements, the constructor uses the default value, which is **100**, to create an array of size **100**. The destructor simply deallocates the memory occupied by the array (that is, the stack) and sets **top** to 0. The definitions of the constructor and destructor are

```
      //constructor
template<class Type>
stackType<Type>::stackType(int stackSize)
{
   if(stackSize <= 0)
   {
      cout<<"The size of the array to hold the stack must "
          <<"be positive."<<endl;
      cout<<"Creating an array of size 100."<<endl;

      maxStackSize = 100;
   }
   else
      maxStackSize = stackSize;  //set the stack size to
                                 //the value specified by
                                 //the parameter stackSize
   top = 0;                      //set top to 0
   list = new Type[maxStackSize]; //create the array to
                                  //hold the stack elements
}//end constructor

template<class Type>
stackType<Type>::~stackType() //destructor
{
   delete [] list; //deallocate the memory occupied by the array
}//end destructor
```

Copy Constructor

The copy constructor is called when a stack object is passed as a (value) parameter to a function. It copies the data members of the actual parameter into the corresponding data members of the formal parameter. Its definition is

```
template<class Type>
stackType<Type>::stackType(const stackType<Type>& otherStack)
{
   int j;

   maxStackSize = otherStack.maxStackSize;
   top = otherStack.top;
   list = new Type[maxStackSize]; //create the array

   if(top != 0)                   //if otherStack is not empty
    for(j = 0; j < top; j++)      //copy other stack onto this stack
        list[j] = otherStack.list[j];
}//end copy constructor
```

Overloading the Assignment Operator (=)

Recall that for classes that have pointer data members, the assignment operator must be explicitly overloaded. The definition of the function to overload the assignment operator for the `class stackType` is

```
template<class Type>
const stackType<Type>& stackType<Type>::operator=
                              (const stackType<Type>& otherStack)
{
   int j;

   if(this != &otherStack) //avoid self-copy
   {
     if(maxStackSize != otherStack.maxStackSize)
         cout<<"Cannot copy. The two stacks are of "
             <<"different sizes"<<endl;
     else
     {
       top = otherStack.top;

       if(top != 0) //if the otherStack is not empty
          for(j = 0; j < top; j++)  //copy the otherStack
                                    //onto this stack
             list[j] = otherStack.list[j];
     } //end else
   } //end if

     return *this;
} //end operator=
```

Push

Adding, or pushing, an element onto the stack is a two-step process. Recall that the value of `top` indicates the number of elements in the stack, and `top-1` gives the position of the `top` element of the stack. Therefore, the push operation is as follows:

1. Store the `newItem` in the array component indicated by `top`.
2. Increment `top`.

Figures 18-10 and 18-11 illustrate the push operation.

(a) Suppose that before the push operation, the stack is as shown in Figure 18-10.

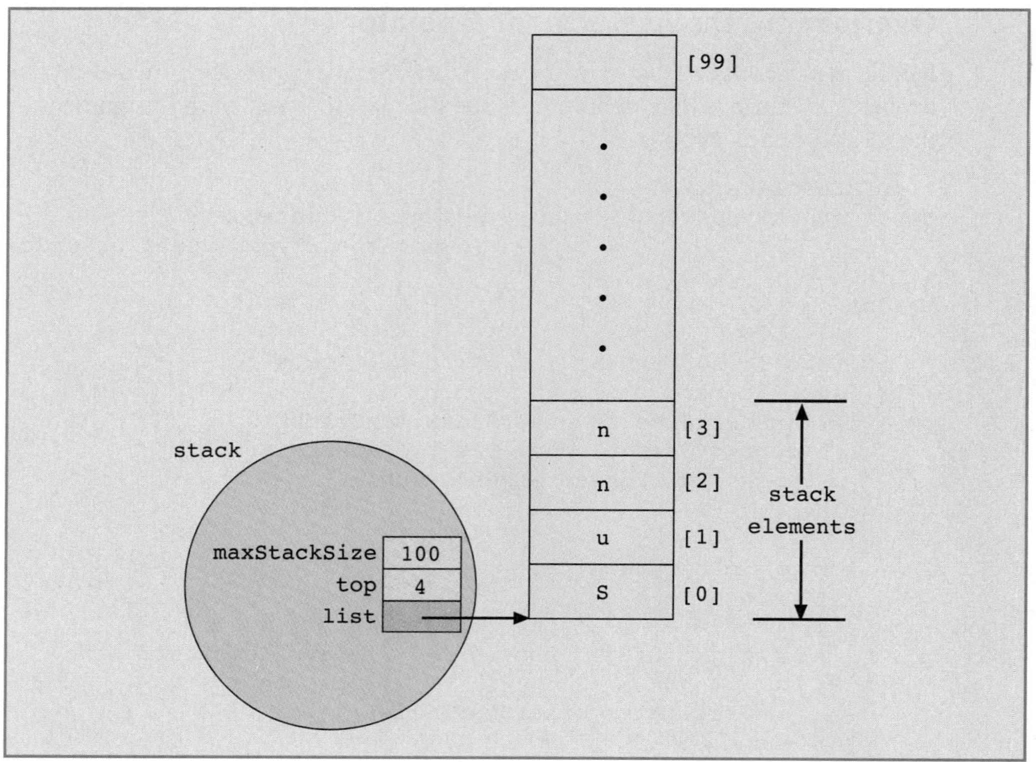

Figure 18-10 Stack before pushing `y`

(b) Assume `newItem` is `'y'`. After the push operation, the stack is as shown in Figure 18-11.

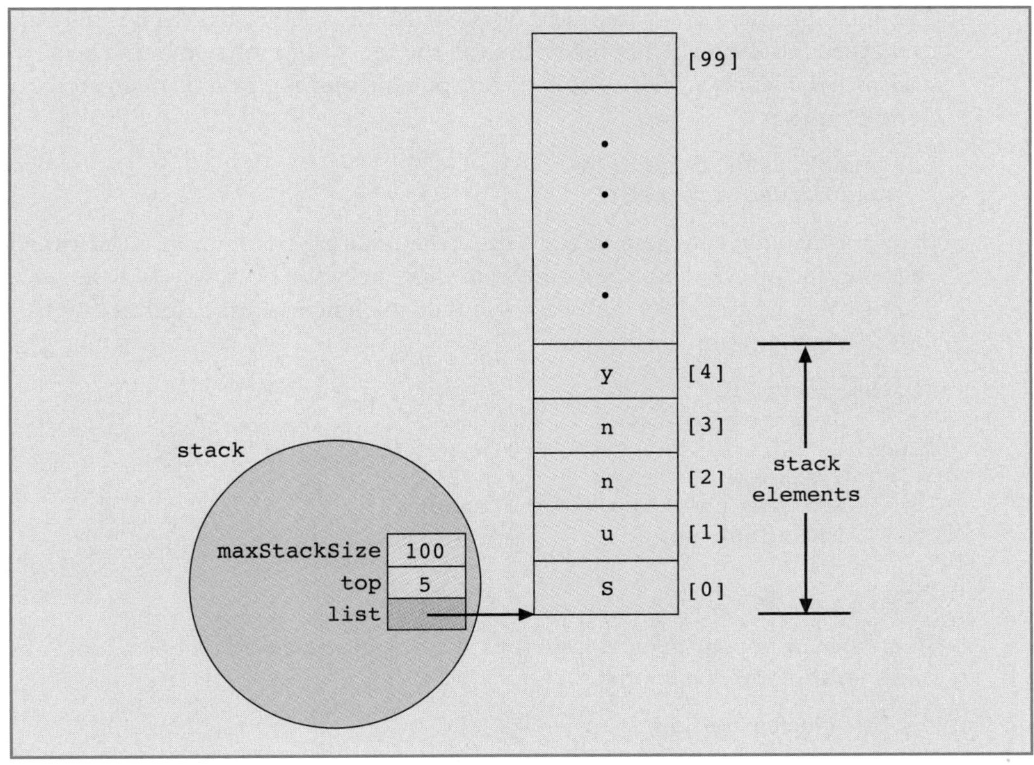

Figure 18-11 Stack after pushing y

Using the previous algorithm, the definition of the function **push** is

```
template<class Type>
void stackType<Type>::push(const Type& newItem)
{
      list[top] = newItem; //add newItem at the top of the stack
      top++;    //increment top
}//end push
```

18

The function **push** as written here does not check whether the stack is full before storing **newItem** in the stack. Thus, before we call the function **push**, we must check whether the stack is full. Hence, a call to the function **push** (assuming **stack** is an object of the type **stackType**) is

```
if(!stack.isFullStack())
   stack.push(newItem);
```

If we try to add a new item to a full stack, the resulting condition is called **overflow**. Error checking for overflow can be handled in different ways. One way is as shown previously. Alternatively, we can check for overflow inside the function **push**. In this case, the algorithm for the function **push** is as follows:

```
If the stack is full
      Overflow is true
Else
      Overflow is false
      Add the new item to the stack
      Increment top
```

Pop

To remove, or pop, an element from the stack, we reverse the **push** operation. Thus, the algorithm for the **pop** operation is

1. Decrement **top**.
2. Assign the value of the top element of the stack to the memory location **poppedItem**.

   Figures 18-12 and 18-13 illustrate the **pop** operation.

   (a) Suppose that before the **pop** operation, the stack is as shown in Figure 18-12.

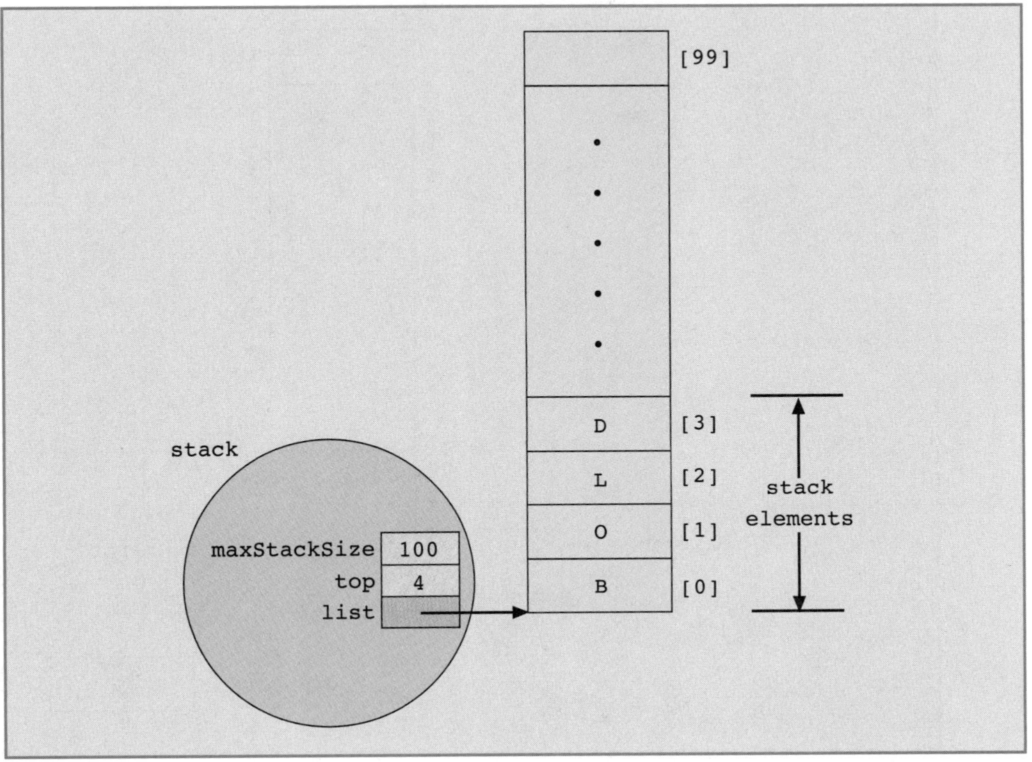

Figure 18-12 Stack before popping D

(b) After the pop operation, the stack is as shown in Figure 18-13.

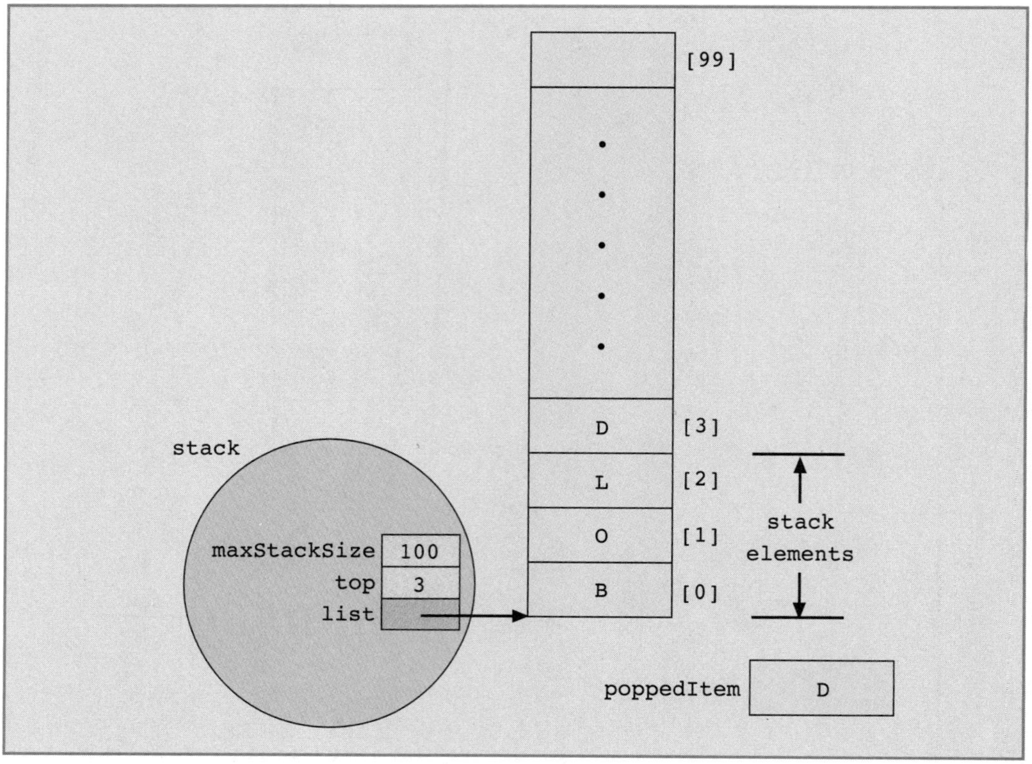

Figure 18-13 Stack after popping D

Using the previous algorithm, the definition of the function **pop** is

```
template<class Type>
void stackType<Type>::pop(Type& poppedItem)
{
      top--;                        //decrement top
      poppedItem = list[top];       //copy the top element of
                                    //the stack onto poppedItem
}//end pop
```

As in the case of the function **push**, we must test whether the stack is empty before we call the function **pop**. (Suppose **stack** is an object of the type **stackType**.)

```
if(!stack.isEmptyStack())
   stack.pop(poppedItem);
```

Popping, or removing, an element from an empty stack is called **underflow**. As in the case of **push**, error checking for **pop** can be handled in different ways. If we check the underflow inside the function **pop**, the algorithm, in pseudocode, for the function **pop** is

```
If the stack is empty
      Underflow is true
Else
      Underflow is false
      Decrement top
      Assign the top element of the stack to poppedItem
```

Stack Header File

Now that you know how to implement the stack operations, you can put the definitions of the class, and the functions to implement the stack operations, together to create the stack header file. For the sake of completeness, we next describe the header file. (To save space, only the definition of the class is shown; no documentation is provided.) Suppose that the name of the header file containing the definition of the **class stackType** is **myStack.h**. We will refer to this header file in any program that uses a stack.

```
//Header file: myStack.h

#ifndef H_StackType
#define H_StackType

template<class Type>
class stackType
{
 public:
   const stackType<Type>& operator=(const stackType<Type>&);
       //overload the assignment operator
   void initializeStack();
   bool isEmptyStack();
   bool isFullStack();
   void destroyStack();
   void push(const Type& newItem);
   void pop(Type& poppedItem);
   stackType(int stackSize = 100);
      //constructor to specify the size of the stack
   stackType(const stackType<Type>& otherStack);
      //copy constructor
   ~stackType(); //destructor

private:
   int maxStackSize;
   int top;
   Type *list;
};

template<class Type>
void stackType<Type>::initializeStack()
{
      top = 0;
}
```

18

```
template<class Type>
bool stackType<Type>::isEmptyStack()
{
      return(top == 0);
}

template<class Type>
bool stackType<Type>::isFullStack()
{
      return(top == maxStackSize);
}

template<class Type>
void stackType<Type>::destroyStack()
{
      top = 0;
}

template<class Type>
void stackType<Type>::push(const Type& newItem)
{
      list[top] = newItem;
      top++;
}

template<class Type>
void stackType<Type>::pop(Type& poppedItem)
{
      top--;
      poppedItem = list[top];
}

template<class Type>
stackType<Type>::stackType(int stackSize)
{
     if(stackSize <= 0)
     {
        cout<<"The size of the array to hold the stack must "
            <<"be positive."<<endl;
        cout<<"Creating an array of size 100."<<endl;

        maxStackSize = 100;
     }
     else
        maxStackSize = stackSize;
     top = 0;
     list = new Type[maxStackSize];
  }//end constructor
```

```
template<class Type>
stackType<Type>::~stackType() //destructor
{
      top = 0;
      delete [] list;
}

template<class Type>
const stackType<Type>& stackType<Type>::operator=
                        (const stackType<Type>& otherStack)
{
   int j;

   if(this != &otherStack) //avoid self-copy
   {
      if(maxStackSize != otherStack.maxStackSize)
         cout<<"Cannot copy. The two stacks are of "
             <<"different sizes."<<endl;
       else
       {
          top = otherStack.top;

          if(top != 0)
             for(j = 0; j < top; j++)
                 list[j] = otherStack.list[j];
      }
   }

  return *this;
}

template<class Type>  //copy constructor
stackType<Type>::stackType(const stackType<Type>& otherStack)
{
   int j;

   maxStackSize = otherStack.maxStackSize;
   top = otherStack.top;
   list = new Type[maxStackSize];

   if(top != 0)
      for(j = 0; j < top; j++)
          list[j] = otherStack.list[j];
}

#endif
```

Example 18-1

Before we give a programming example, let us first write a simple program that uses the **class stackType** and tests some of the stack operations. Among others, we will test the assignment operator and the copy constructor. The program and its output are as follows:

```
//Program to test the various operations of a stack
#include <iostream>
#include "myStack.h"

using namespace std;

void testCopyConstructor(stackType<int> otherStack);

int main()
{
      stackType<int> stack(50);
      stackType<int> copyStack(50);
      stackType<int> dummyStack(100);
      int x;

      stack.initializeStack();
      stack.push(23);
      stack.push(45);
      stack.push(38);
      copyStack = stack;  //copy stack into copyStack

      while(!copyStack.isEmptyStack())  //print copyStack
      {
         copyStack.pop(x);
         cout<<"Inside copyStack "<<x<<endl;
      }

      copyStack = stack;
      testCopyConstructor(stack);  //test the copy constructor

      if(!stack.isEmptyStack())
      {
         cout<<"Original stack is not empty"<<endl;
         stack.pop(x);
         cout<<"Top element of the original stack: "<<x<<endl;
      }

      dummyStack = stack;  //copy stack into dummyStack

      return 0;
}
```

```
void testCopyConstructor(stackType<int> otherStack)
{
      int x;

      if(!otherStack.isEmptyStack())
      {
         cout<<"Other stack is not empty"<<endl;
         otherStack.pop(x);
         cout<<"Top element of the other stack: "<<x<<endl;
      }
}
```

Output

```
Inside copyStack 38
Inside copyStack 45
Inside copyStack 23
Other stack is not empty
Top element of the other stack: 38
Original stack is not empty
Top element of the original stack: 38
Cannot copy. The two stacks are of different sizes.
```

It is recommended that you do a walk-through of this program.

PROGRAMMING EXAMPLE: HIGHEST GPA

In this example, we write a C++ program that reads a data file consisting of each student's GPA followed by the student's name. The program then prints the highest GPA and the names of all students who received that GPA. The program scans the input file only once.

Input The program reads an input file consisting of each student's GPA, followed by the student's name. Sample data is

```
3.5 Bill
3.6 John
2.7 Lisa
3.9 Kathy
3.4 Jason
3.9 David
3.4 Jack
```

Output The highest GPA and all names associated with the highest GPA. For example, for the above data, the highest GPA is 3.9 and the students with that GPA are Kathy and David.

Program Analysis and Algorithm Design

We read the first GPA and the name of the student. Because this data is the first item read, it is the highest GPA so far. Next, we read the second GPA and the name of the student. We then compare this (second) GPA with the highest GPA so far. Three cases arise:

1. The new GPA is greater than the highest GPA so far. In this case, we
   (a) Update the value of the highest GPA so far.
   (b) Destroy the stack—that is, remove the names of the students from the stack.
   (c) Save the name of the student having the highest GPA so far in the stack.
2. The new GPA is equal to the highest GPA so far. In this case, we add the name of the new student to the stack.
3. The new GPA is smaller than the highest GPA so far. In this case, we discard the name of the student having this grade.

We then read the next GPA and the name of the student, and repeat Steps 1 through 3. We continue this process until we reach the end of file.

From this discussion, it is clear that we need the following variables:

```
double GPA;             //variable to hold the current GPA
double highestGPA;  //variable to hold the highest GPA
newString  name;    //variable to hold the name of the student
stackType<newString> stack; //object to implement the stack
```

Note that we use the **class** newString that we designed in Chapter 16 for the student name. We can use the assignment operator to store a name in a variable of the newString type.

The preceding discussion translates into the following algorithm:

1. Declare the variables.
2. Open the input file.
3. If the input file does not exist, exit the program.
4. Set the output of the floating-point numbers in a fixed decimal format with a decimal point and trailing zeroes. Also, set the precision to two decimal places.
5. Read the GPA and student name.
6. `highestGPA = GPA;`
7. Initialize the stack.
8. **while** (not end of file)

```
{
8.1 if (GPA > highestGPA)
    {
    8.1.1 clearstack(stack);
    8.1.2 push(stack, student name);
    8.1.3 highestGPA = GPA;
    }
```

8.2 else
    if(GPA is equal to highestGPA)
        push(stack, student name);

8.3 Read the GPA and student name;

}

9. Output the highest GPA.
10. Output the names of the students having the highest GPA.

Complete Program Listing

```
//Program Highest GPA

#include <iostream>
#include <iomanip>
#include <fstream>
#include "myString.h"
#include "myStack.h"

using namespace std;

int main()
{
            //Step 1
   double GPA;
   double highestGPA;
   newString name;
   stackType<newString> stack(100);
   ifstream infile;


   infile.open("a:Ch18_HighestGPAData.txt");         //Step 2

   if(!infile)                                        //Step 3
   {
      cout<<"Input file does not exist. "
          <<"Program terminates!"<<endl;
      return 1;
   }

   cout<<fixed<<showpoint;                            //Step 4
   cout<<setprecision(2);                             //Step 4

   infile>>GPA>>name;                                 //Step 5

   highestGPA = GPA;                                  //Step 6

   stack.initializeStack();                           //Step 7
```

```
   while(infile)                                          //Step 8
   {
      if(GPA > highestGPA)                                //Step 8.1
      {
         stack.destroyStack();                            //Step 8.1.1

         if(!stack.isFullStack())                         //Step 8.1.2
         stack.push(name);

         highestGPA = GPA;                                //Step 8.1.3
      }
      else
         if(GPA == highestGPA)                            //Step 8.2
           if(!stack.isFullStack())
               stack.push(name);
           else
           {
               cout<<"Stack overflow. Program terminates."<<endl;
               return 1;  //exit program
           }
      infile>>GPA>>name;                                  //Step 8.3
   }

   cout<<"Highest GPA = "<<highestGPA<<endl;          //Step 9
   cout<<"Students holding the highest GPA are:"
       <<endl;

   while(!stack.isEmptyStack())                           //Step 10
   {
      stack.pop(name);
      cout<<name<<endl;
   }

   cout<<endl;
   return 0;
}
```

Sample Run

Input File (a:Ch18_HighestGPAData.txt)

```
3.4 Holt
3.2 Bolt
2.5 Colt
3.4 Tom
3.8 Ron
3.8 Mickey
3.6 Pluto
3.5 Donald
```

```
3.8 Cindy
3.7 Dome
3.9 Andy
3.8 Fox
3.9 Minne
2.7 Goofy
3.9 Doc
3.4 Danny
```

Output

```
Highest GPA = 3.90
Students holding the highest GPA are:
Doc
Minne
Andy
```

LINKED IMPLEMENTATION OF STACKS

Because an array size is fixed, in the array (linear) representation of a stack, only a fixed number of elements can be pushed onto the stack. If in a program the number of elements to be pushed exceeds the size of the array, the program may terminate in an error. We must overcome these problems.

We have seen that by using pointer variables we can dynamically allocate and deallocate memory, and by using linked lists we can dynamically organize data (such as an ordered list). Next, we will use these concepts to implement a stack dynamically.

Recall that in the linear representation of a stack, the value of `top` indicates the number of elements in the stack, and the value of `top-1` points to the top item in the stack. With the help of `top`, we can do several things: find the top element, check whether the stack is empty, and so on.

Similar to the linear representation, in a linked representation `top` is used to locate the top element in the stack. However, there is a slight difference. In the former case, `top` gives the index of the array; in the latter case, `top` gives the address (memory location) of the top element of the stack.

The following statements define a linked stack as an ADT:

```
//Definition of the node
template <class Type>
struct nodeType
{
      Type info;
      nodeType<Type> *link;
};
```

```
template<class Type>
class linkedStackType
{
public:
    const linkedStackType<Type>& operator=
                                (const linkedStackType<Type>&);
        //overload the assignment operator
    void initializeStack();
        //Initialize the stack to an empty state
        //Post: stack elements are removed; top = NULL
    bool isEmptyStack();
        //This function returns true if the stack is empty;
        //otherwise, it returns false
    bool isFullStack();
        //This function returns true if the stack is full;
        //otherwise, it returns false
    void push(const Type& newItem);
        //Add newItem to the stack.
        //Post: the stack is changed and the newItem
        //     is added to the top of stack. top points to
        //     the updated stack.
    void pop(Type& poppedElement);
        //Remove the top element of the stack.
        //Post: the stack is changed and the top
        //     element is removed from the stack. The top
        //     element of the stack is saved in poppedElement.
    void destroyStack();
        //Remove all elements of the stack, leaving the
        //stack in an empty state.
        //Post: top = NULL
    linkedStackType();
        //default constructor
        //Post: top = NULL
    linkedStackType(const linkedStackType<Type>& otherStack);
        //copy constructor
    ~linkedStackType();
        //destructor
        //All elements of the stack are removed from the stack

private:
    nodeType<Type> *top; //pointer to the stack
};
```

The following example shows how both empty and nonempty linked stacks appear.

Example 18-2

(a) Empty stack: Suppose that `stack` is an object of the type `linkedStackType`. (See Figure 18-14.)

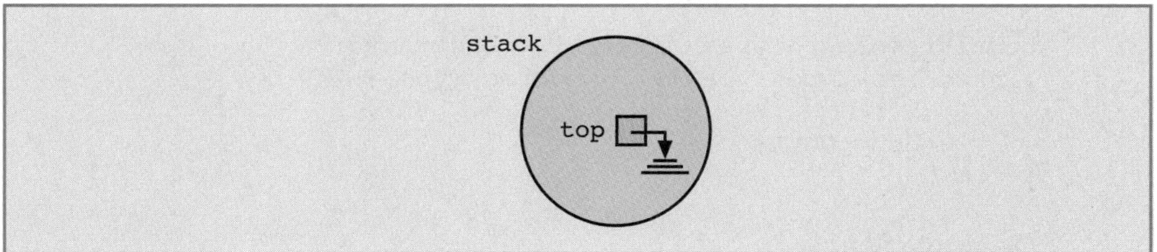

Figure 18-14 Empty linked stack

(b) Nonempty stack (see Figure 18-15).

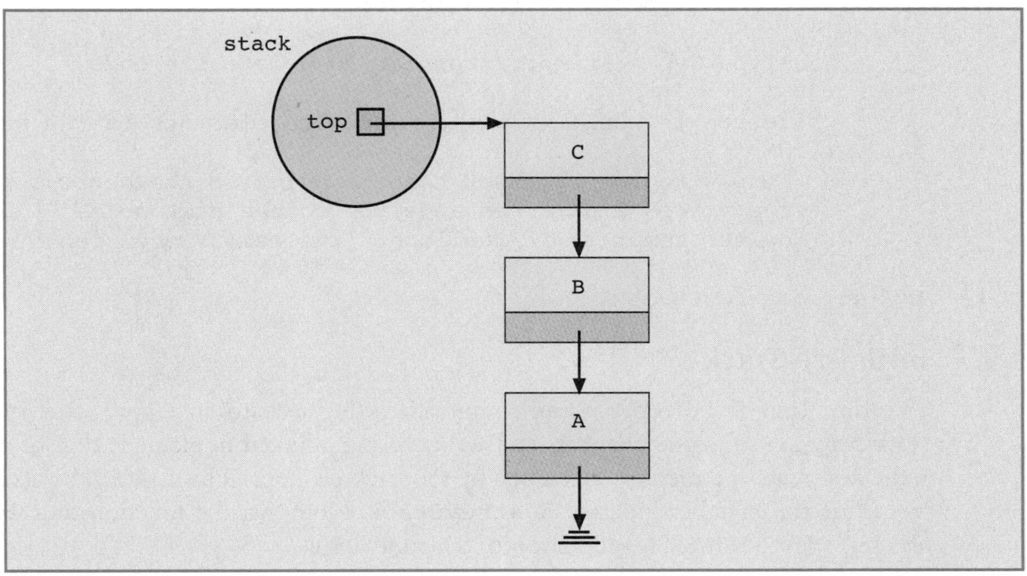

Figure 18-15 Nonempty linked stack

In Figure 18-15, the top element of the stack is `C`; that is, the last element pushed onto the stack is `C`.

Next, we discuss the definitions of the functions to implement the operations of a linked stack.

Default Constructor

The first operation that we consider is the default constructor. The default constructor initializes the stack to an empty state when a stack object is declared. Thus, this function sets **top** to **NULL**. The definition of this function is

```
template<class Type> //default constructor
linkedStackType<Type>::linkedStackType()
{
      top = NULL;
}
```

Destroy Stack

In a linked representation, the function **destroyStack** does more work than it does in the linear representation. In the array representation, the stack is destroyed simply by setting **top** to 0. In the linked representation, memory for the stack elements is allocated dynamically. Thus, we need to set **top** to **NULL**, and we must deallocate the memory occupied by the stack elements.

```
template<class Type>
void linkedStackType<Type>::destroyStack()
{
      nodeType<Type> *temp; //pointer to delete the node

      while(top != NULL)  //while there are elements in the stack
      {
         temp = top;      //set temp to point to the current node
         top = top->link; //advance top to the next node
         delete temp;     //deallocate the memory occupied by temp
      }
}// end destroyStack
```

Initialize Stack

The operation **initializeStack** reinitializes the stack to an empty state. Because the stack may contain some elements and we are using a linked implementation of a stack, we must deallocate the memory occupied by the stack elements. This task can be accomplished by calling the member function **destroyStack**. Note that the function **destroyStack** also sets **top** to **NULL**. The definition of this function is

```
template<class Type>
void linkedStackType<Type>:: initializeStack()
{
    destroyStack();
}
```

Empty Stack and Full Stack

The operations `isEmptyStack` and `isFullStack` are quite straightforward. The stack is empty if `top` is `NULL`. Also, because the memory for a stack element is allocated and deallocated dynamically, the stack is never full. (The stack is full if we run out of memory.) Thus, the function `isFullStack` always returns the value `false`. The definitions of the functions to implement these operations are

```
template<class Type>
bool linkedStackType<Type>::isEmptyStack()
{
      return(top == NULL);
}

template<class Type>
bool linkedStackType<Type>:: isFullStack()
{
    return false;
}
```

Next, we consider the `push` and `pop` operations. From Figure 18-15, it is clear that the `newElement` will be added (in the case of `push`) at the beginning of the linked list pointed to by `top`. In the case of `pop`, the node pointed to by `top` will be removed. In both cases, the value of the pointer `top` is updated.

push

Consider the stack shown in Figure 18-16.

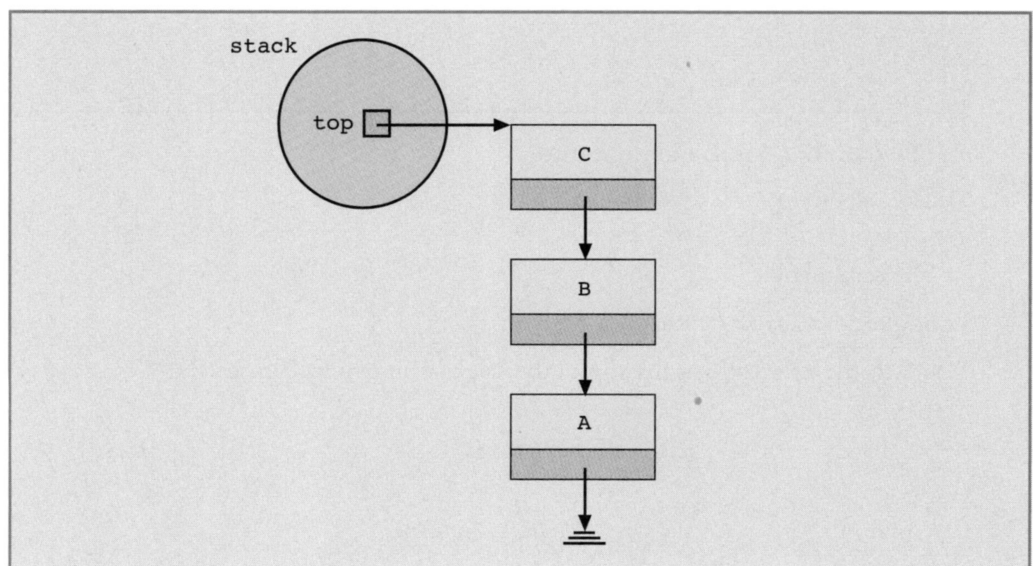

Figure 18-16 Stack before `push` operation

Assume that the new element to be pushed is `'D'`. First, we allocate memory for the new node. We then store `'D'` in the new node and insert the new node at the beginning of the list. Finally, we update the value of **top**. The statements

```
newNode = new nodeType<Type>; //create the new node
newNode->info = newElement;
```

create a node, store the address of the node into the variable **newNode**, and store **newElement** into the **info** field of **newNode**. Thus, we have the situation shown in Figure 18-17.

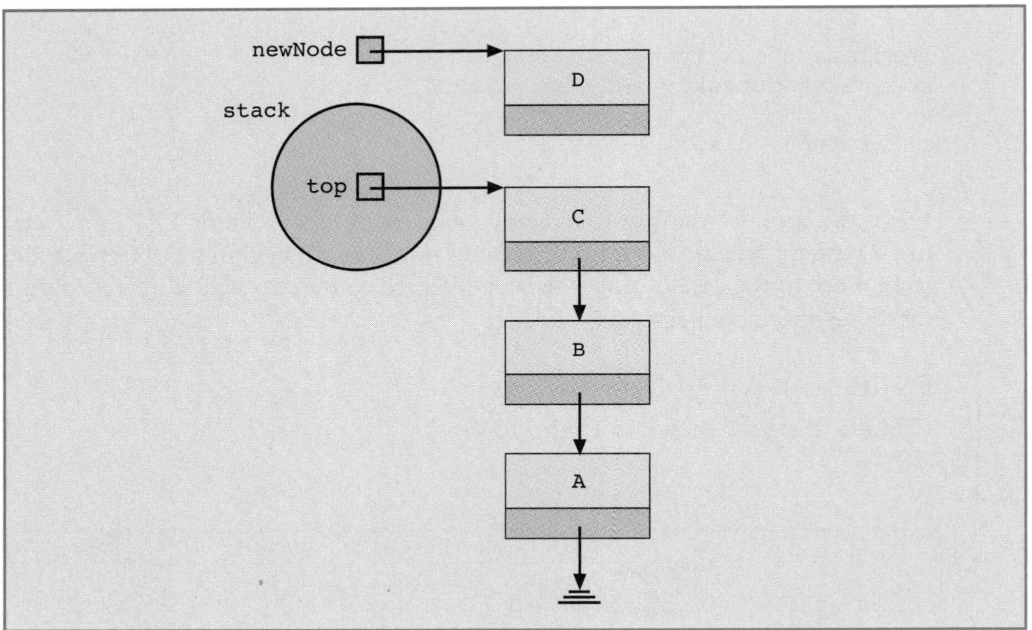

Figure 18-17 Stack and newNode

The statement

```
newNode->link = top;
```

inserts the **newNode** at the top of the stack, as shown in Figure 18-18.

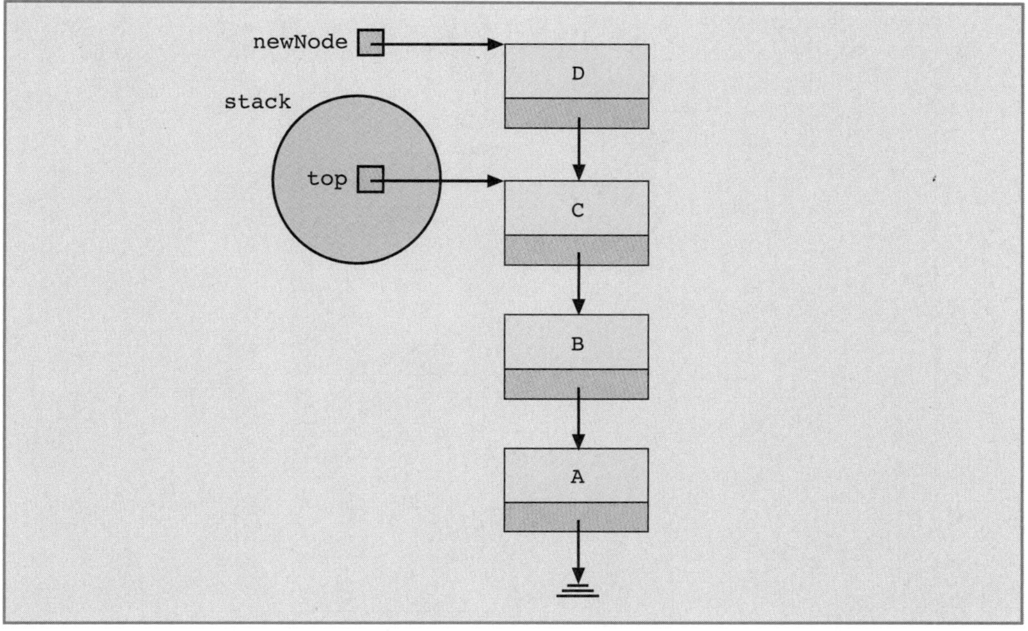

Figure 18-18 Stack after statement `newNode->link = top;` executes

Finally the statement

```
top = newNode;
```

updates the value of `top`, which results in Figure 18-19.

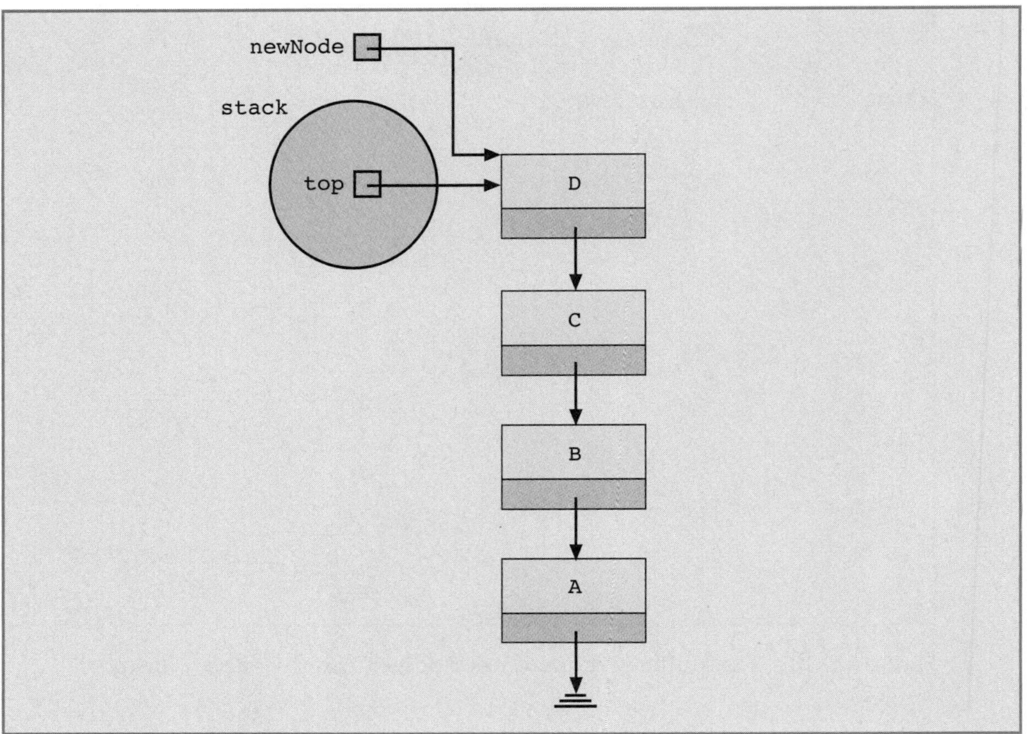

Figure 18-19 Stack after statement `top = newNode;` executes

The definition of the function **push** is

```
template<class Type>
void linkedStackType<Type>::push(const Type& newElement)
{
   nodeType<Type> *newNode; //pointer to create the new node

   newNode = new nodeType<Type>; //create the node
   newNode->info = newElement;    //store newElement in the node
   newNode->link = top;           //insert newNode before top
   top = newnode;                 //set top to point to the top node
} //end push
```

We do not need to check whether the stack is full before we push an element onto the stack because in this implementation, logically, the stack is never full.

pop

Now we consider the **pop** operation, which is the reverse of the **push** operation. Consider the stack shown in Figure 18-20.

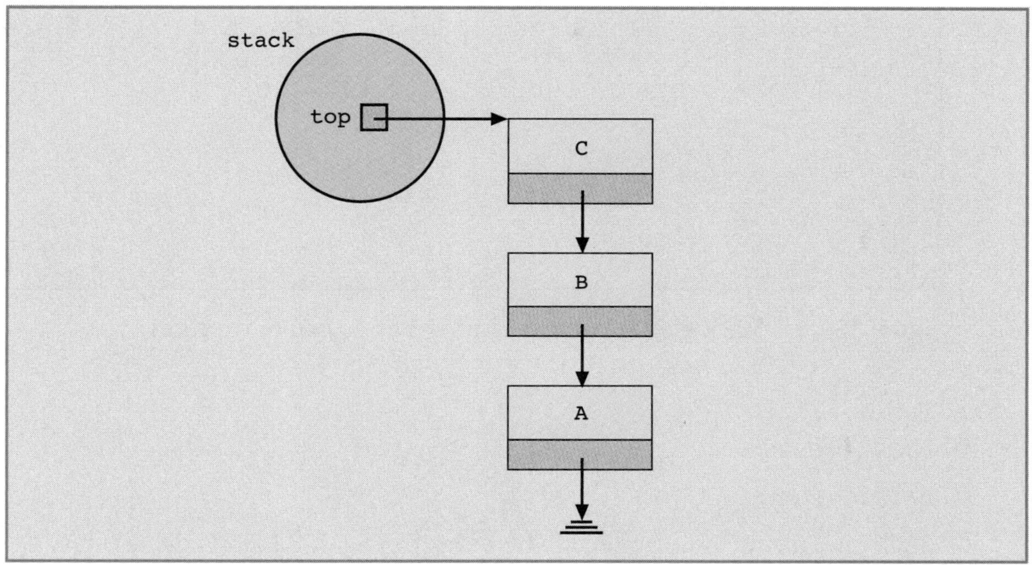

Figure 18-20 Stack before pop operation

Suppose that the top element is to be saved in the location **poppedElement**. The statement

```
poppedElement = top->info;
```

copies the top element of the stack into **poppedElement**. The statement

```
temp = top;
```

makes **temp** point to the top of the stack, and the statement

```
top = top->link;
```

makes the second element of the stack become the top element of the stack. We then have the situation shown in Figure 18-21.

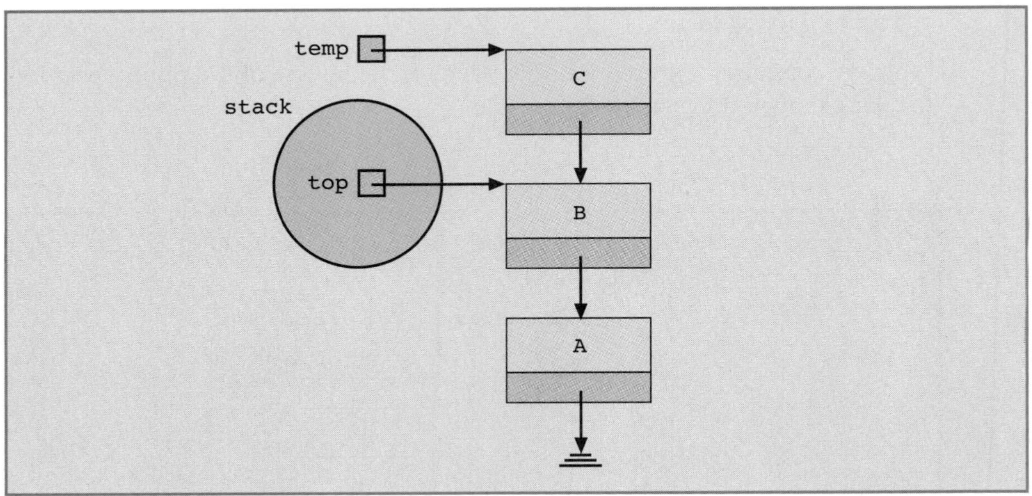

Figure 18-21 Stack after statement `top = top->link;` executes

Finally, the statement

```
delete temp;
```

deallocates the memory pointed to by `temp`. Figure 18-22 shows the resulting stack.

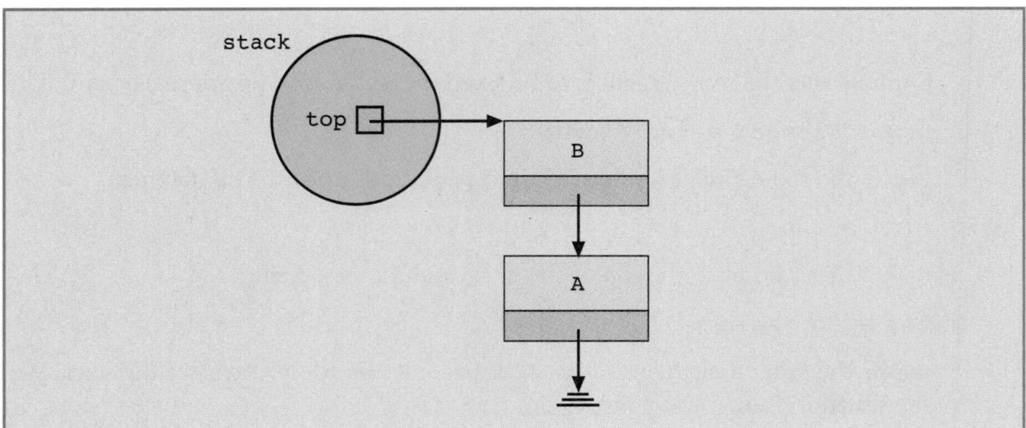

Figure 18-22 Stack after statement `delete temp;` executes

The definition of the function **pop** is

```
template<class Type>
void linkedStackType<Type>::pop(Type& poppedElement)
{
   nodeType<Type> *temp;       //pointer to deallocate memory

   poppedElement = top->info; //copy the top element into
                              //poppedElement
   temp = top;                //set temp to point to the top node
   top = top->link;           //advance top to the next node
   delete temp;               //delete the top node
}//end pop
```

As in the array representation of stacks, we must check whether the stack is empty before popping an element from the stack. Thus, the function **isEmptyStack** should be called before the function **pop**. So a call to the function **pop** (assuming that **stack** is an object of the type **linkedStackType**) is

```
if(!stack.isEmptyStack())
    stack.pop(poppedElement);
```

Constructors and Destructors

We have already discussed the default constructor. To complete the implementation of the stack operations, next we give the definitions of the functions to implement the copy constructor and the destructor, and to overload the assignment operator. (These functions are similar to those discussed for linked lists in Chapter 17.)

```
template<class Type>   //copy constructor
linkedStackType<Type>::linkedStackType(const linkedStackType<Type>&
otherStack)
{
   nodeType<Type> *newNode, *current, *last;

   if(otherStack.top == NULL)
      top = NULL;
   else
   {
      current = otherStack.top;  //set current to point to the
                                 //stack to be copied

         //copy the top element of the stack
    top = new nodeType<Type>;   //create the node
    top->info = current->info;  //copy the info
    top->link = NULL;           //set the link field of the
                                //node to null
    last = top;                 //set last to point to the node
    current = current->link;    //set current to point to the
                                //next node
```

18

```
        //copy the remaining stack
    while(current != NULL)
    {
       newNode = new nodeType<Type>;
       newNode->info = current->info;
       newNode->link = NULL;
       last->link = newNode;
       last = newNode;
       current = current->link;
    }//end while
   }//end else
}//end copy constructor

template<class Type> //destructor
linkedStackType<Type>::~linkedStackType()
{
   nodeType<Type> *temp;

   while(top != NULL)      //while there are elements in the stack
   {
      temp = top;          //set temp to point to the current node
      top = top->link;     //advance first to the next node
      delete temp;         //deallocate the memory occupied by temp
   }//end while
}//end destructor
```

Overloading the Assignment Operator (=)

The definition of the function to overload the assignment operator for the **class** `linkedStackType` is

```
template<class Type>   //overloading the assignment operator
const linkedStackType<Type>& linkedStackType<Type>::operator=
                    (const linkedStackType<Type>& otherStack)
{
   nodeType<Type> *newNode, *current, *last;

   if(this != &otherStack) //avoid self-copy
   {
      if(top != NULL)  //if the stack is not empty, destroy it
          destroyStack();

      if(otherStack.top == NULL)
          top = NULL;
      else
      {
          current = otherStack.top;  //set current to point to
                                     //the stack to be copied
```

```
            //copy the top element of otherStack
        top = new nodeType<Type>;  //create the node
        top->info = current->info; //copy the info
        top->link = NULL;          //set the link field of the
                                   //node to null
        last = top;                //make last point to the node
        current = current->link;   //make current point to
                                   //the next node

             //copy the remaining elements of the stack
        while(current != NULL)
        {
           newNode = new nodeType<Type>;
           newNode->info = current->info;
           newNode->link = NULL;
           last->link = newNode;
           last = newNode;
           current = current->link;
        }//end while
     }//end else
  }//end if
  return *this;
}//end operator=
```

The definition of a stack, and the functions to implement the stack operations discussed previously, are generic. Also, as in the case of an array representation of a stack, in the linked representation of a stack we must put the definition of the stack, and the functions to implement the stack operations, together in a (header) file. A client's program can include this header file via the `include` statement. Also, when we declare a stack object, we must pass the type of stack element as a parameter to the type (name) `linkedStackType`. For example, the statement

```
linkedStackType<int> stack;
```

declares `stack` to be an object of the type `linkedStackType`, and the stack element type is `int`. Similarly, the statement

```
linkedStackType<newString> stringStack;
```

declares `stringStack` to be an object of the type `linkedStackType` and the stack element type is `newString`.

To check the various operations of a linked stack, in Example 18-3 we will write a short program. You are encouraged to do a walk-through of this program.

Example 18-3

We assume that the definition of the **class linkedStackType**, and the functions to implement the stack operations, are included in the header file "linkedStack.h".

```
//This program tests the various operations of a linked stack

#include <iostream>
#include "linkedStack.h"

using namespace std;

void testCopy(linkedStackType<int> OStack);

int main()
{
      linkedStackType<int> stack;
      linkedStackType<int> otherStack;
      linkedStackType<int> newStack;
      int num;

      stack.push(34);
      stack.push(43);
      stack.push(27);
      newStack = stack;

      cout<<"After the assignment operator, newStack: "<<endl;

      while(!newStack.isEmptyStack())
      {
            newStack.pop(num);
            cout<<num<<endl;
      }

      otherStack = stack;

      cout<<"Testing the copy constructor"<<endl;

      testCopy(otherStack);

      cout<<"After the copy constructor, otherStack: "<<endl;

      while(!otherStack.isEmptyStack())
      {
            otherStack.pop(num);
            cout<<num<<endl;
      }

      return 0;
}
```

```
void testCopy(linkedStackType<int> OStack) //function to test the
                                      //copy constructor
{
      int num;

      cout<<"Stack in the function testCopy:"<<endl;

      while(!OStack.isEmptyStack())
      {
            OStack.pop(num);
            cout<<num<<endl;
      }
}
```

Output

```
After the assignment operator, newStack:
27
43
34
Testing the copy constructor
Stack in the function testCopy:
27
43
34
After the copy constructor, otherStack:
27
43
34
```

Stack as Derived from the `class linkedListType`

If we compare the **push** function of the stack with the **insertFirst** function discussed for general lists in Chapter 17, we see that the algorithms to implement these operations are similar. A comparison of other functions, such as **initializeStack** and **initializeList**, **isEmptyList** and **isEmptyStack**, and so on, suggests that the **class linkedStackType** can be derived from the **class linkedListType**. Moreover, the **pop** function can be implemented as in the previous section.

Next, we define the **class linkedStackType** that is derived from the **class linkedListType**. The definitions of the functions to implement the stack operations are also given.

18

```
#ifndef H_derivedLinkedStack
#define H_derivedLinkedStack
#include <iostream>
#include "linkedList.h"
```

```
using namespace std;

template<class Type>
class linkedStackType: public linkedListType<Type>
{
      public:
      void initializeStack();
      bool isEmptyStack();
      bool isFullStack();
      void push(const Type& newItem);
      void pop(Type& poppedElement);
      void destroyStack();
};

template<class Type>
void linkedStackType<Type>:: initializeStack()
{
      linkedListType<Type>::initializeList();
}

template<class Type>
bool linkedStackType<Type>::isEmptyStack()
{
      return linkedListType<Type>::isEmptyList();
}

template<class Type>
bool linkedStackType<Type>::isFullStack()
{
      return linkedListType<Type>::isFullList();
}

template<class Type>
void linkedStackType<Type>::destroyStack()
{
      linkedListType<Type>::destroyList();
}

template<class Type>
void linkedStackType<Type>::push(const Type& newElement)
{
      linkedListType<Type>::insertFirst(newElement);
}
```

```
template<class Type>
void linkedStackType<Type>::pop(Type& poppedElement)
{
      nodeType<Type> *temp;

      poppedElement = first->info;
      temp = first;
      first = first->link;
      delete temp;
}
#endif
```

APPLICATION OF STACKS: POSTFIX EXPRESSIONS CALCULATOR

The usual notation for writing arithmetic expressions (the notation we learned in elementary school) is called **infix** notation, in which the operator is written between the operands. For example, in the expression $a + b$, the operator + is between the operands a and b. In infix notation, the operators have precedence. That is, we must evaluate expressions from left to right, and multiplication and division have higher precedence than do addition and subtraction. If we want to evaluate the expression in a different order, we must include parentheses. For example, in the expression $a + b * c$, we first evaluate * using the operands b and c, and then we evaluate + using the operand a and the result of $b * c$.

In the early 1950s, the Polish mathematician Lukasiewicz discovered that if operators were written before the operands (**prefix** or **Polish** notation; for example, $+ \ a \ b$) or after the operands (**suffix**, **postfix**, or **reverse Polish** notation; for example, $a \ b \ +$), the parentheses can be omitted. For example, the expression

$a + b * c$

in a postfix expression is

$a \ b \ c * +$

The following example shows infix expressions and their equivalent postfix expressions.

Example 18-4

Infix Expression	Equivalent Postfix Expression
a + b	a b +
a + b * c	a b c * +
a * b + c	a b * c +
(a + b) * c	a b + c *
(a - b) * (c + d)	a b - c d + *
(a + b) * (c - d / e) + f	a b + c d e / - * f +

18

Shortly after Lukasiewicz's discovery, it was realized that postfix notation had important applications in computer science. In fact, many compilers now first translate arithmetic expressions into some form of postfix notation and then translate this postfix expression into machine code. Postfix expressions can be evaluated using the following algorithm:

Scan the expression from left to right. When an operator is found, back up to get the required number of operands, perform the operation, and continue.

Consider the following postfix expression:

```
6 3 + 2 * =
```

Let us evaluate this expression using a stack and the above algorithm.

1. Read the first symbol, `6`, which is a number. Push that number onto the stack (see Figure 18-23).

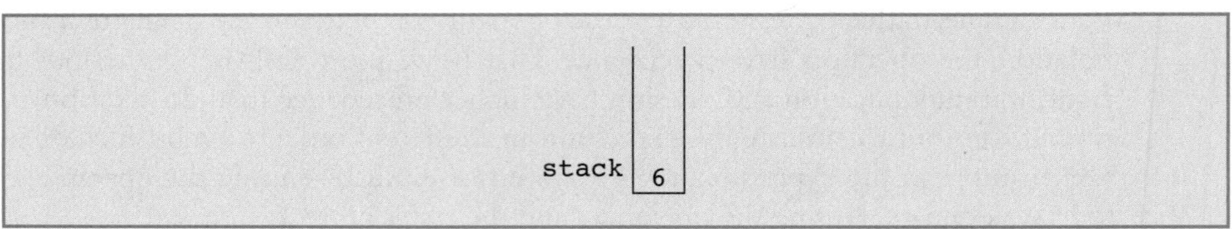

Figure 18-23 Stack after pushing `6`

2. Read the next symbol, `3`, which is a number. Push that number onto the stack (see Figure 18-24).

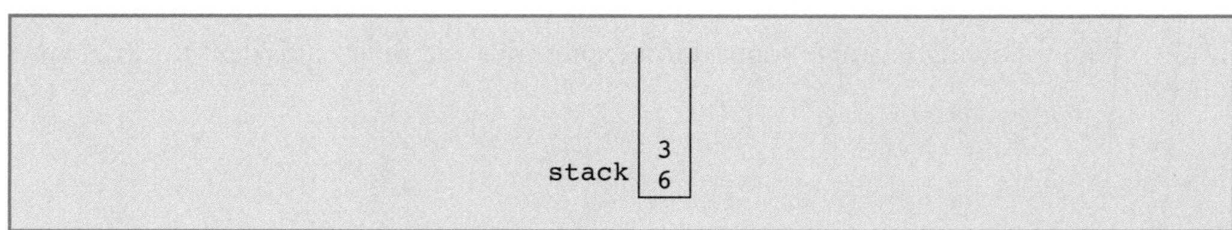

Figure 18-24 Stack after pushing `3`

3. Read the next symbol, `+`, which is an operator. Because an operator requires two operands to be evaluated, pop the stack twice. Perform the operation and put the result back onto the stack (see Figure 18-25).

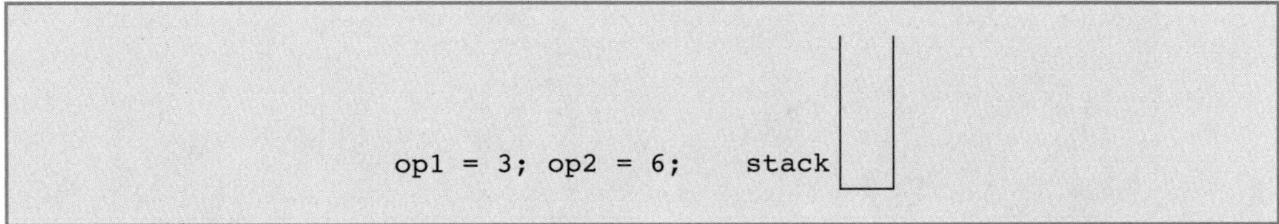

Figure 18-25 Stack after popping twice

Perform the operation: `op2 + op1 = 6 + 3 = 9`.

Push the result onto the stack (see Figure 18-26).

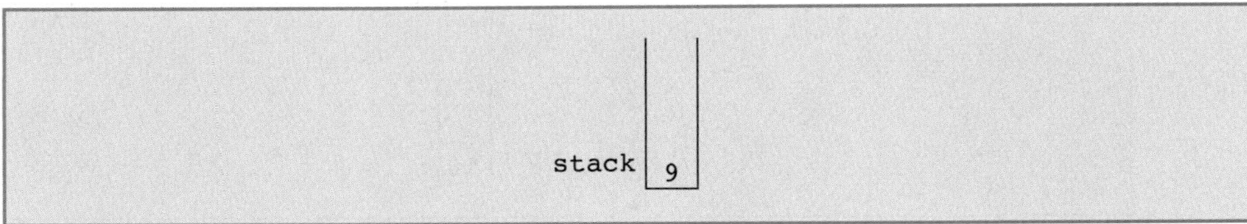

Figure 18-26 Stack after pushing result of `op2 + op1`, which is 9

4. Read the next symbol, `2`, which is a number. Push that number onto the stack (see Figure 18-27).

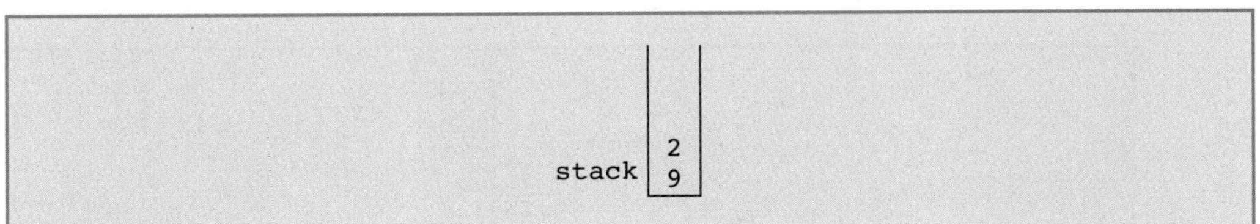

Figure 18-27 Stack after pushing 2

5. Read the next symbol, `*`, which is an operator. Because an operator requires two operands to be evaluated, pop the stack twice. Perform the operation and put the result back onto the stack (see Figures 18-28 and 18-29).

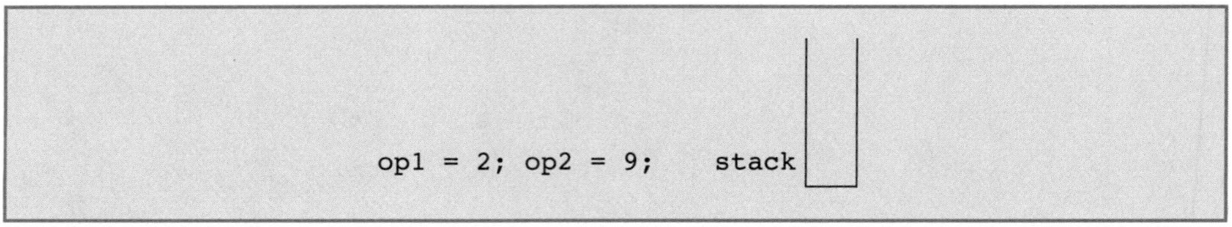

op1 = 2; op2 = 9; stack

Figure 18-28 Stack after popping twice

Perform the operation: `op2 * op1 = 9 * 2 = 18`.

Push the result onto the stack (see Figure 18-29).

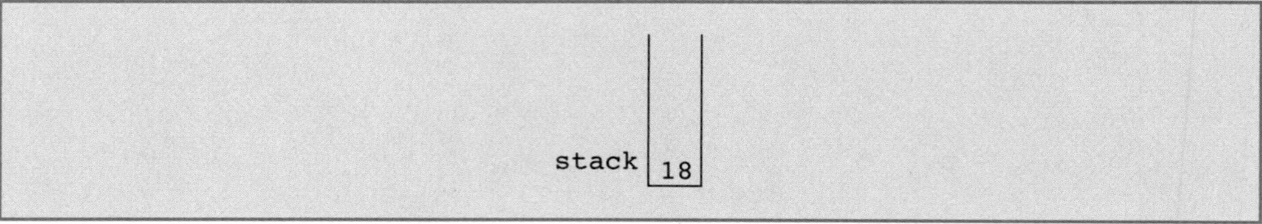

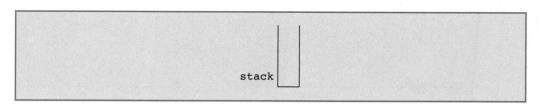

Figure 18-29 Stack after pushing result of `op2 * op1`, which is `18`

6. Scan the next symbol, =, which is the equal sign, indicating the end of the expression. Therefore, we print the result. The result of the expression is in the stack, so pop and print are as shown in Figure 18-30.

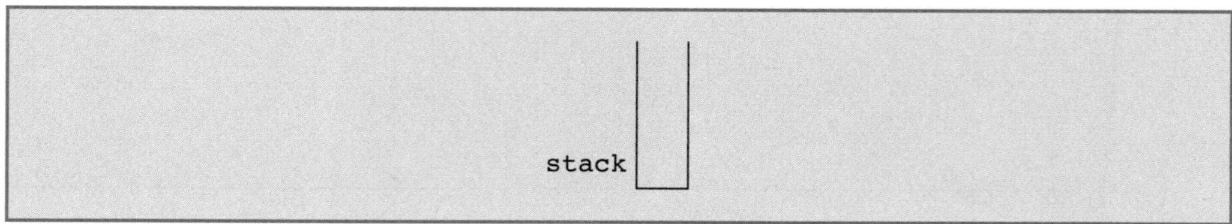

Figure 18-30 Stack after popping the element

The value of the expression `6 3 + 2 * = 18`.

From this discussion, it is clear that when we read a symbol other than a number, the following cases arise:

1. The symbol we read is one of the following: +, -, /, *, or =.
   a. If the symbol is +, -, *, or /, the symbol is an operator and so we must evaluate it. Because an operator requires two operands, the stack must have at least two elements; otherwise, the expression has an error.
   b. If the symbol is = (an equal sign), the expression ends and we must print the answer. At this step the stack must contain exactly one element; otherwise, the expression has an error.
2. The symbol we read is something other than +, -, /, *, or =. In this case, the expression contains an illegal operator.

It is also clear that when an operand (number) is encountered in an expression, it is pushed onto the stack because the operator comes after the operands.

Consider the following expressions:

(i) `7 6 + 3 ; 6 - =`

(ii) `14 + 2 3 * =`

(iii) `14 2 3 + =`

Expression (i) has an illegal operator, expression (ii) does not have enough operands for +, and expression (iii) has too many operands. In the case of expression (iii), when we encounter the equal sign (=), the stack will have two elements and this error cannot be discovered until we are ready to print the value of the expression.

To make the input easier to read, we assume that the postfix expressions are in the following form:

`#6 #3 + #2 * =`

The symbol # precedes each number in the expression. If the symbol scanned is #, then the next input is a number (that is, an operand). If the symbol scanned is not #, then it is either an operator (may be illegal) or an equal sign (indicating the end of the expression). Furthermore, we assume that each expression contains only the +, -, *, and / operators.

This program outputs the entire postfix expression together with the answer. If the expression has an error, the expression is discarded. In this case, the program outputs the expression together with an appropriate error message. Because an expression may contain an error, we must clear the stack before processing the next expression. Also, the stack must be initialized; that is, the stack must be empty.

Main Algorithm

Pursuant to the previous discussion, the main algorithm in pseudocode is

```
read the first ch;
while more data to process
{
   clear stack;
   output ch;

   while (ch is not = '=') //process each expression
                           //= marks the end of an expression
   {
      switch(ch)
      {
         case '#': read a number
                   output the number;
                   push the number onto the stack;
                   break;
         default: Assume that ch is an operation
                  evaluate the operation;
      } //end switch

      if no error was found, then
      {
         read next ch;
         output ch;
      }
    }   //end while

   if the expression did not contain any error(s), then
      output the result;
   else
     discard the result;

   start processing the next expression;
}
```

Evaluate: This function (if possible) evaluates an expression. Two operands are needed to evaluate an operation and operands are saved in the stack. Therefore, the stack must contain at least two numbers. If the stack contains fewer than two numbers, then the expression has an error. In this case, the entire expression is discarded and an appropriate message is printed. This function also checks for any illegal operations. In pseudocode, this function is

```
if stack is empty
{
  error in the expression
  set expressionOk to false
}
else
{
  pop stack, op1  //get the first number from the stack
  if stack is empty
  {
    error in the expression
    set expressionOk to false
  }
  else
  {
    pop stack, op2 //get the second number

        //if the operation is legal, perform the
        //operation and push the result onto the stack
    switch(ch)
    {
    case '+': //perform the operation and push the result
              //onto the stack
              stack.push(op2+op1);
    case '-': //perform the operation and push the result
              //onto the stack
              stack.push(op2-op1);
    case '*': //perform the operation and push the result
              //onto onto the stack
              stack.push(op2*op1);
    case '/': //perform the operation and push the result
              //onto the stack
              stack.push(op2/op1);
    otherwise operation is illegal
       {
          output an appropriate message;
          set expressionOk to false
       }
    } //end switch
}
```

Discard: This function is called whenever an error is discovered in the expression. It reads and writes the input data only until the input is `'='`, the end of the expression.

18

```
while(ch != '=')
{
  read ch;
  output ch;
}
```

Complete Program Listing

```
//Postfix Calculator
#include <iostream>
#include <iomanip>
#include <fstream>
#include "mystack.h"

using namespace std;

void evaluate(ofstream& out,stackType<double>& stack,
              char& ch, bool& expressionOk);
void discard(ifstream& in, ofstream& out, char& ch);

int main()
{
   double num, result;
   bool expressionOk;
   char ch;
   stackType<double> stack(100);
   ifstream infile;
   ofstream outfile;

   infile.open("a:Ch18_RpnData.txt");

   if(!infile)
   {
      cout<<"Cannot open input file. Program terminates!"<<endl;
      return 1;
   }

   outfile.open("a:Ch18_RpnOutput.txt");

   outfile<<fixed<<showpoint;
   outfile<<setprecision(2);

   infile>>ch;
   while(infile)
   {
      stack.initializeStack();
      expressionOk = true;
      outfile<<ch;

      while(ch != '=')
      {
         switch(ch)
         {
         case '#': infile>>num;
                   outfile<<num<<" ";
```

```
                if(!stack.isFullStack())
                     stack.push(num);
                else
                {
                     cout<<"Stack overflow. "
                         <<"Program terminates!"<<endl;
                     return 1;
                }

                break;
         default: evaluate(outfile, stack, ch, expressionOk);

         }//end switch

         if(expressionOk) //if no error
         {
            infile>>ch;
            outfile<<ch;
            if(ch != '#')
                  outfile<<" ";
         }
         else
            discard(infile,outfile,ch);
    }//end while (!= '=')

    if(expressionOk) //if no error, print the result
    {
         if(!stack.isEmptyStack())
         {
             stack.pop(result);

             if(stack.isEmptyStack())
                 outfile<<result<<endl;
             else
                 outfile<<" (Error: Too many operands)"<<endl;
         }//end if
         else
       outfile<<" (Error in the expression)"<<endl;
  }
  else
       outfile<<" (Error in the expression)"<<endl;

  outfile<<"_________________________________"<<endl<<endl;

  infile>>ch; //begin processing the next expression
}//end while

infile.close();
outfile.close();
```

```
 return 0;

}//end main

void evaluate(ofstream& out, stackType<double>& stack,
              char& ch, bool& expressionOk)
{
   double op1, op2;

   if(stack.isEmptyStack())
   {
      out<<" (Not enough operands)";
      expressionOk = false;
   }
   else
   {
      stack.pop(op1);

      if(stack.isEmptyStack())
      {
           out<<" (Not enough operands)";
           expressionOk = false;
      }
      else
      {
            stack.pop(op2);
            switch(ch)
            {
            case '+': stack.push(op2 + op1);
                break;
            case '-': stack.push(op2 - op1);
                break;
            case '*': stack.push(op2 * op1);
                break;
            case '/': stack.push(op2 / op1);
                break;
            default:  out<<" (Illegal operator)";
                      expressionOk = false;
            }//end switch
      }//end else
   }//end else
}//end evaluate

void discard(ifstream& in, ofstream& out, char& ch)
{
   while(ch != '=')
   {
      in.get(ch);
      out<<ch;
   }
}//end discard
```

Sample Run

Input File

```
#35 #27 + #3 * =
#26 #28 + #32 #2 ; - #5 / =
#23 #30 #15 * / =
#2 #3 #4 + =
#20 #29 #9 * ; =
#25 #23 - + =
#34 #24 #12 #7 / * + #23 - =
```

Output

```
#35.00 #27.00 + #3.00 * = 186.00
_________________________________

#26.00 #28.00 + #32.00 #2.00 ;  (Illegal operator) - #5 / = (Error in the
expression)
_________________________________

#23.00 #30.00 #15.00 * / = 0.05
_________________________________

#2.00 #3.00 #4.00 + =  (Error: Too many operands)
_________________________________

#20.00 #29.00 #9.00 * ;  (Illegal operator) = (Error in the expression)
_________________________________

#25.00 #23.00 - +  (Not enough operands) = (Error in the expression)
_________________________________

#34.00 #24.00 #12.00 #7.00 / * + #23.00 - = 52.14
_________________________________
```

Removing Recursion: Nonrecursive Algorithm to Print a Linked List Backward

In Chapter 17, we used recursion to print a linked list backward. In this section, you will learn how a stack can be used to design a nonrecursive algorithm to print a linked list backward. 18

Consider the linked list shown in Figure 18-31.

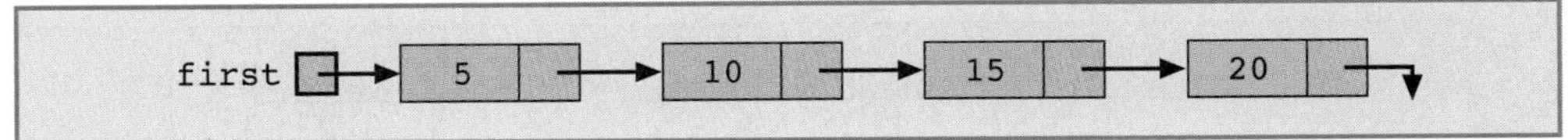

Figure 18-31 Linked list

To print the list backward, first we need to get to the last node of the list, which we can do by traversing the linked list starting at the first node. However, once we are at the last node, how do we get back to the previous node, especially given that links go in only one direction? You can again traverse the linked list with the appropriate loop termination condition, but this approach might waste a considerable amount of computer time, especially if the list is very large. Moreover, if we do this for every node in the list, the program might execute very slowly. Next, we show how to use a stack effectively to print the list backward.

After printing the `info` of a particular node, we need to move to the node immediately behind this node. For example, after printing `20`, we need to move to the node with `info 15`. Thus, while initially traversing the list to move to the last node, we must save a pointer to each node. For example, for the list in Figure 18-31, we must save a pointer to each of the nodes with `info 5`, `10`, and `15`. After printing `20`, we go back to the node with `info 15`; after printing `15`, we go back to the node with `info 10`, and so on. From this, it follows that we must save pointers to each node in a stack, so as to implement the Last In First Out principle.

Because the number of nodes in a linked list is usually not known, we will use the linked implementation of a stack. Suppose that `stack` is an object of the type `linkedListType`, and `current` is a pointer of the same type as the pointer `first`. Consider the following statements:

```
current = first;                    //Line 1

while(current != NULL)              //Line 2
{
      stack.push(current);          //Line 3
      current = current->link;      //Line 4
}
```

After the statement in Line 1 executes, `current` points to the first node (see Figure 18-32).

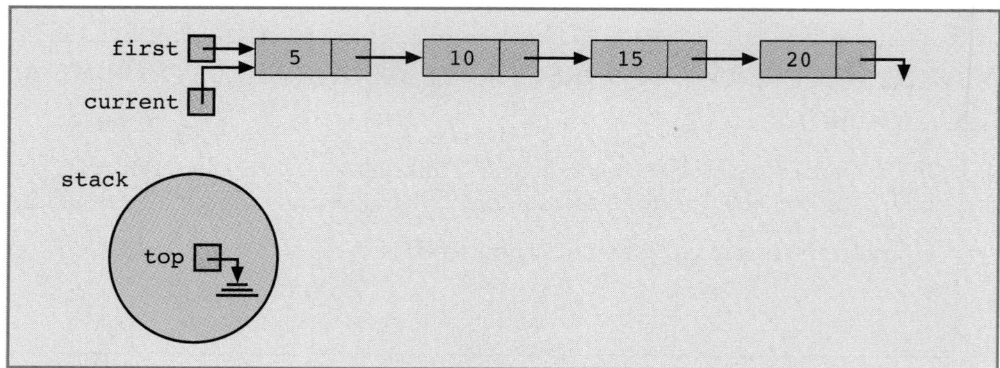

Figure 18-32 List after statement `current = first;` executes

Because `current` is not `NULL`, the statements in Lines 3 and 4 execute (see Figure 18-33).

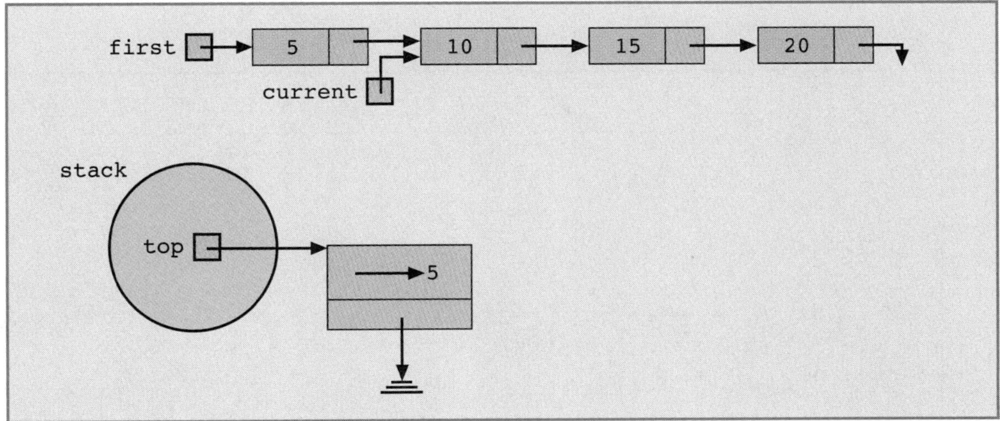

Figure 18-33 List and stack after statements `stack.push(current);` and `current = current->link;` execute

After the statement in Line 4 executes, the loop condition, in Line 2, is re-evaluated. Because `current` is not `NULL`, the loop condition evaluates to `true` and so the statements in Line 3 and 4 execute (see Figure 18-34).

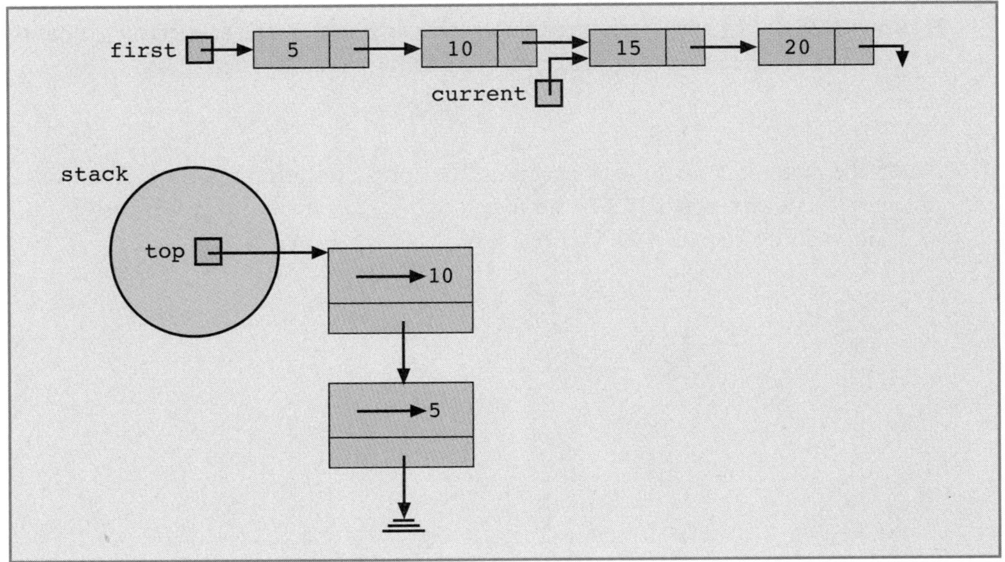

Figure 18-34 List and stack after statements `stack.push(current);` and `current = current->link;` execute

After the statement in Line 4 executes, the loop condition, in Line 2, is evaluated again. Because `current` is not `NULL`, the loop condition evaluates to `true` and so the statements in Lines 3 and 4 execute (see Figure 18-35).

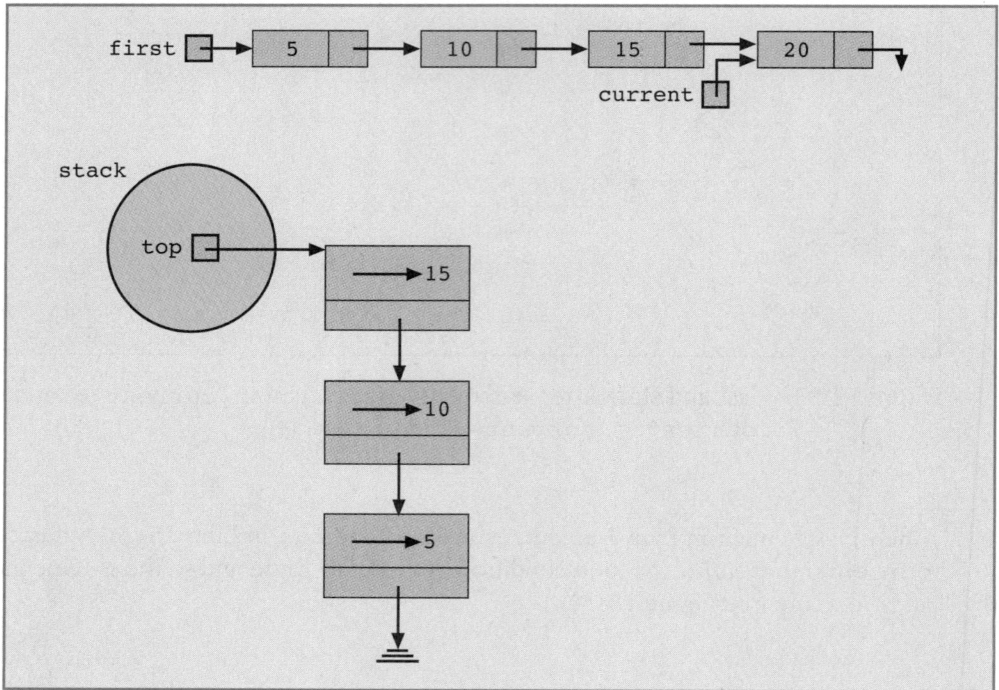

Figure 18-35 List and stack after statements `stack.push(current);` and `current = current->link;` execute

After the statement in Line 4 executes, the loop condition, in Line 2, is evaluated again. Because `current` is not `NULL`, the loop condition evaluates to `true` and so the statements in Lines 3 and 4 execute (see Figure 18-36).

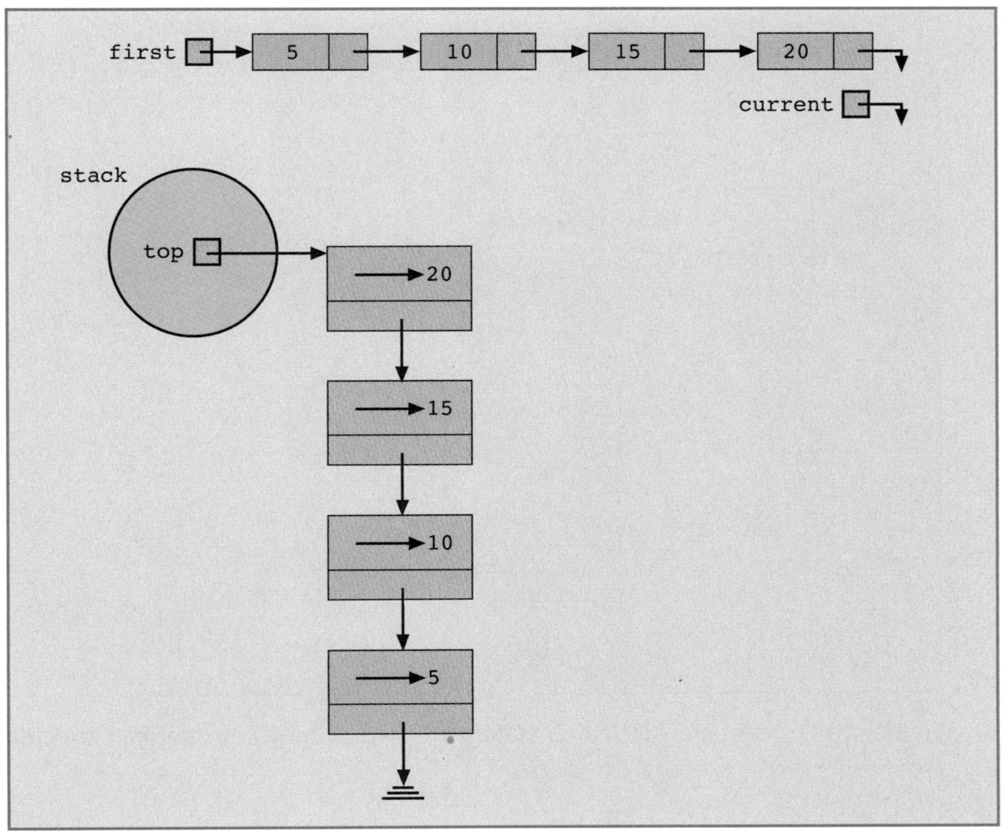

Figure 18-36 List and stack after statements `stack.push(current);` and `current = current->link;` execute

After the statement in Line 4 executes, the loop condition, in Line 2, is evaluated again. Because **current** is **NULL**, the loop condition evaluates to **false** and the **while** loop, in Line 2, terminates. From Figure 18-36, it follows that a pointer to each node in the linked list is saved in the stack. The top element of the stack contains a pointer to the last node in the list, and so on. Let us now execute the following statements:

```
while(!stack.isEmptyStack())        //Line 5
{
      stack.pop(current);           //Line 6
      cout<<current->info<<" ";     //Line 7
}
```

The loop condition in Line 5 evaluates to **true** because the stack is nonempty. Therefore, the statements in Lines 6 and 7 execute. After the statement in Line 6 executes, **current** points to the last node (see Figure 18-37).

18

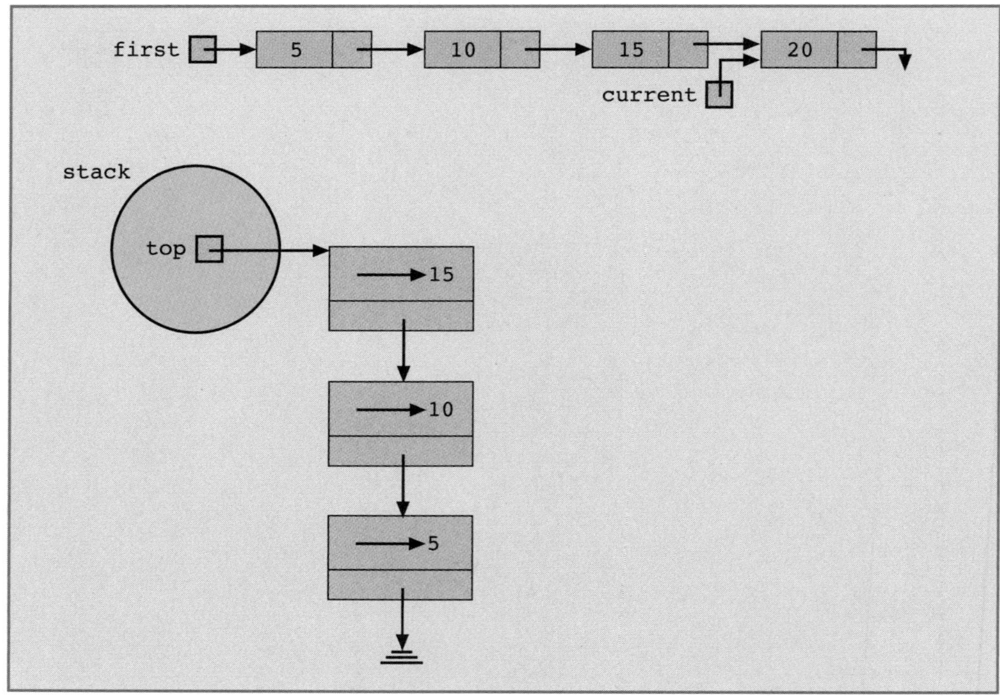

Figure 18-37 List and stack after statement `stack.pop(current);` executes

The statement in Line 7 outputs `current->info`, which is `20`. Next, the loop condition in Line 5 is evaluated. Because the loop condition evaluates to **`true`**, the statements in Lines 6 and 7 execute. After the statement in Line 6 executes, Figure 18-38 results.

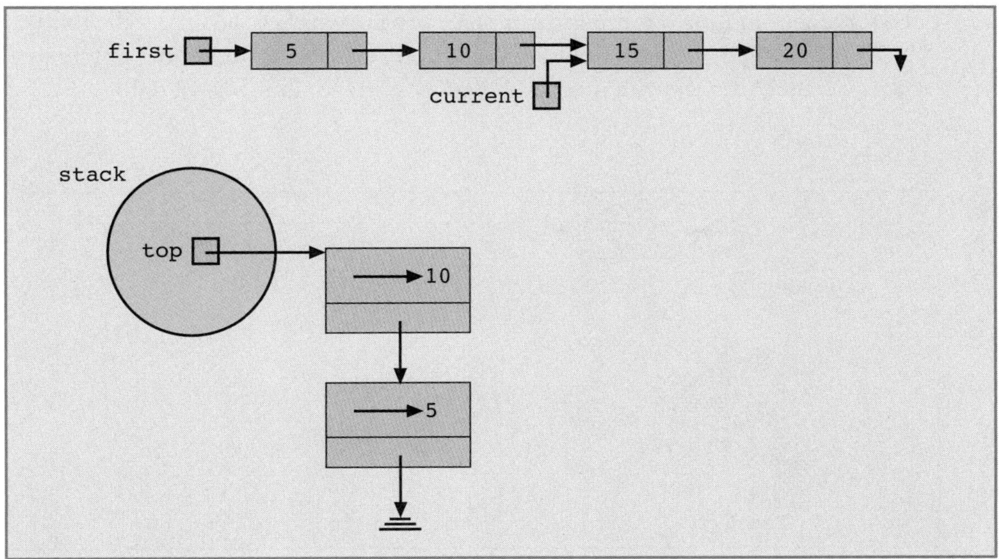

Figure 18-38 List and stack after statement `stack.pop(current);` executes

The statement in Line 7 outputs `current->info`, which is `15`. Next, the loop condition in Line 5 is evaluated. Because the loop condition evaluates to **`true`**, the statements in Lines 6 and 7 execute. After the statement in Line 6 executes, Figure 18-39 results.

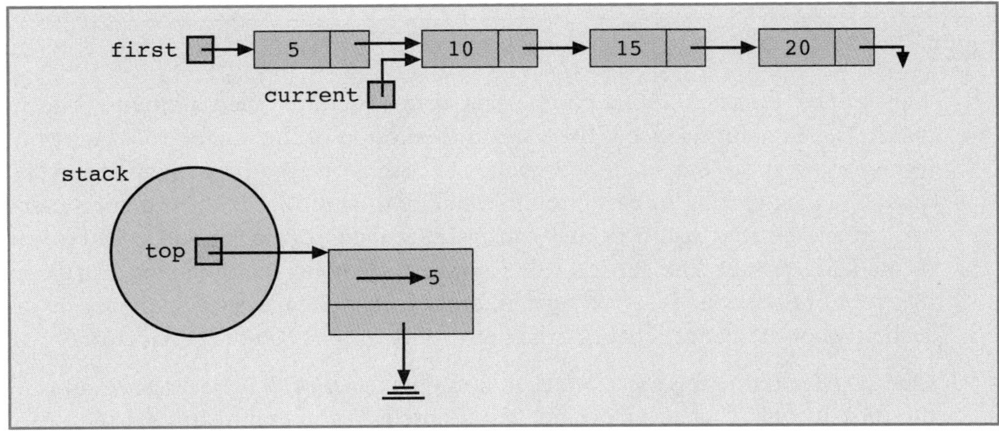

Figure 18-39 List and stack after statement `stack.pop(current);` executes

The statement in Line 7 outputs **current->info**, which is **10**. Next, the loop condition in Line 5 is evaluated. Because the loop condition evaluates to **true**, the statements in Lines 6 and 7 execute. After the statement in Line 6 executes, Figure 18-40 results.

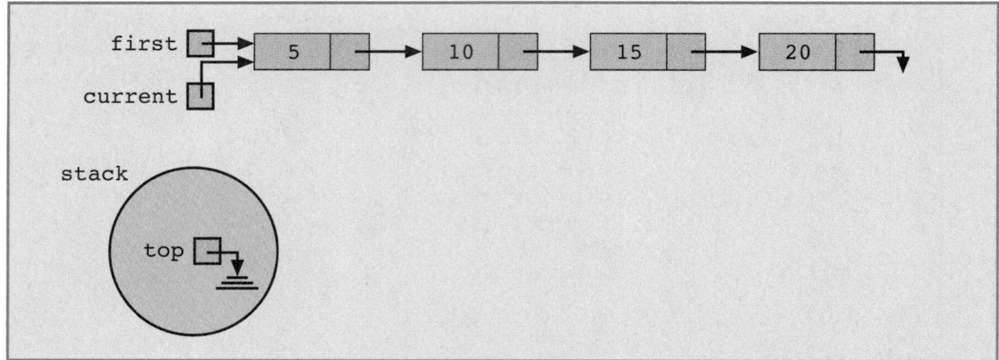

Figure 18-40 List and stack after statement `stack.pop(current);` executes

The statement in Line 7 outputs **current->info**, which is **5**. Next, the loop condition in Line 5 is evaluated. Because the loop condition evaluates to **false**, the **while** loop terminates. The **while** loop in Line 5 produces the following output:

```
20 15 10 5
```

QUEUES

This section discusses another important data structure, called a **queue**. The notion of a queue in computer science is the same as the notion of the queues to which you are accustomed in everyday life. There are queues of customers in a bank or in a grocery store, and queues of cars waiting to pass through a tollbooth. Similarly, because a computer can send a print request faster than a printer can print, a queue of documents is often waiting to be printed at a printer. The general rule to process elements in a queue is that the customer at the front of the queue is served next and that when a new customer arrives, he or she stands at the end of the queue. That is, a queue is a First In First Out data structure.

Queues have numerous applications in computer science. Whenever a system is modeled on the First In First Out principle, queues are used. At the end of this section, we will discuss one of the most widely used applications of queues, computer simulation. First, however, we need to develop the tools necessary to implement a queue. The next few sections discuss how to design classes to implement queues as an ADT.

A queue is a set of elements of the same type in which the elements are added at one end, called the **back** or **rear**, and deleted from the other end, called the **front**. For example, consider a line of customers in a bank, wherein the customers are waiting to withdraw/deposit money or to conduct some other business. Each new customer gets in the line at the rear. Whenever a teller is ready for a new customer, the customer at the front of the line is served.

The rear of the queue is accessed whenever a new element is added to the queue, and the front of the queue is accessed whenever an element is deleted from the queue. As in a stack, the middle elements of the queue are inaccessible, even if the queue elements are stored in an array.

Queue: A data structure in which the elements are added at one end, called the rear, and deleted from the other end, called the front; a First In First Out (FIFO) data structure.

Queue Operations

From the definition of queues, we see that the two key operations are add and delete. We call the add operation **`addQueue`** and the delete operation **`deQueue`**. Because elements can be neither deleted from an empty queue nor added to a full queue, we need two more operations to successfully implement the `addQueue` and `deQueue` operations: **`isEmptyQueue`** (checks whether the queue is empty) and **`isFullQueue`** (checks whether a queue is full).

We also need an operation, **`initializeQueue`**, to initialize the queue to an empty state, and—similar to stacks—we need an operation **`destroyQueue`** to destroy the queue, leaving it empty. Thus, some of the queue operations are as follows:

1. **`initializeQueue`**: This operation initializes the queue to an empty state.
2. **`destroyQueue`**: This operation removes all elements from the queue, leaving the queue empty.
3. **`isEmptyQueue`**: This operation checks whether the queue is empty. If the queue is empty, it returns the value **`true`**; otherwise, it returns the value **`false`**.
4. **`isFullQueue`**: This operation checks whether the queue is full. If the queue is full, it returns the value **`true`**; otherwise, it returns the value **`false`**.
5. **`addQueue`**: This operation adds a new element to the rear of queue. Input to this operation consists of the queue and the new element. Prior to this operation, the queue must exist and must not be full.
6. **`deQueue`**: This operation removes the front element from the queue and stores the front element into a location called **`deqElement`**. Input to this function consists of the queue and the location where the front element will be stored. Prior to this operation, the queue must exist and must not be empty.

As in the case of a stack, a queue can be stored in an array or in a linked structure. We will consider both implementations. Because elements are added at one end and removed from the other end, we need two pointers to keep track of the front and rear of the queue, called **`front`** and **`rear`**.

The Implementation of Queues as Arrays

Before giving the definition of the class to implement a queue as an ADT, we need to decide how many data members are needed to implement the queue. Of course, we need an array to store the queue elements, the variables `front` and `rear` to keep track of the first and last elements of the queue, and the variable `maxQueueSize` to specify the maximum size of the queue. Thus, we need at least four data members.

Before writing the algorithms to implement the queue operations, we need to decide how to use `front` and `rear` to access the queue elements. How do `front` and `rear` indicate that the queue is empty or full? Suppose that `front` gives the index of the first element of the queue, and `rear` gives the index of the last element of the queue. To add an element to the queue, first we advance `rear` to the next array position and then add the element to the position that `rear` is pointing to. To delete an element from the queue, first we retrieve the element that `front` is pointing to and then advance `front` to the next element of the queue. Thus, `front` will change after each `deQueue` operation and `rear` will change after each `addQueue` operation.

Let us see what happens when `front` changes after a `deQueue` operation and `rear` changes after an `addQueue` operation. Assume that the array to hold the queue elements is of size 100.

Initially, the queue is empty. After the operation

```
addQueue(Queue,'A');
```

the array is as shown in Figure 18-41.

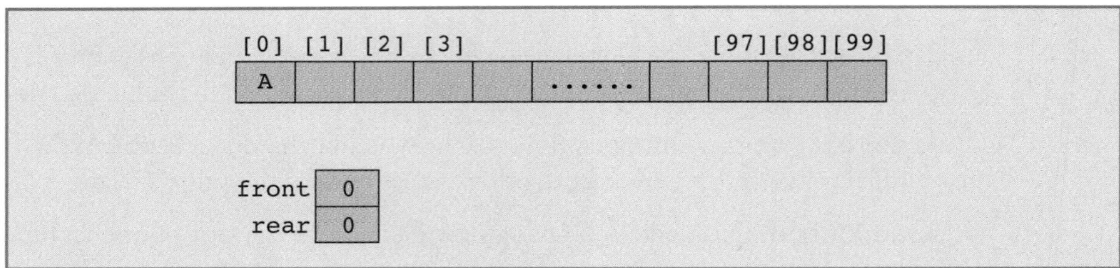

Figure 18-41 Queue after first `addQueue` operation

After two more `addQueue` operations,

```
addQueue(Queue,'B');
addQueue(Queue,'C');
```

the array is as shown in Figure 18-42.

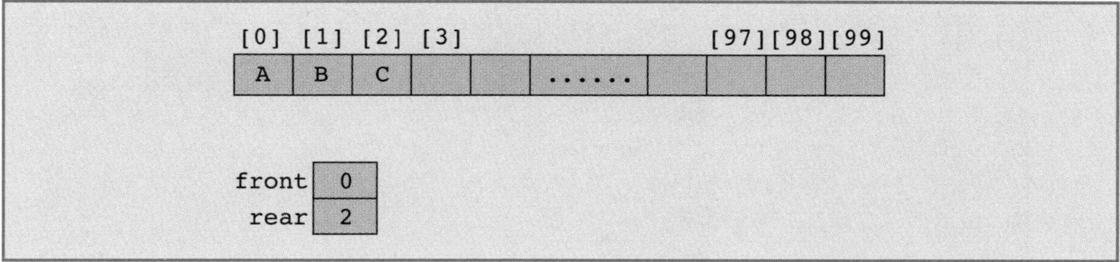

Figure 18-42 Queue after two more `addQueue` operations

Now consider the `deQueue` operation

```
deQueue(Queue,deqElement);
```

After this operation, the array containing the queue is as shown in Figure 18-43.

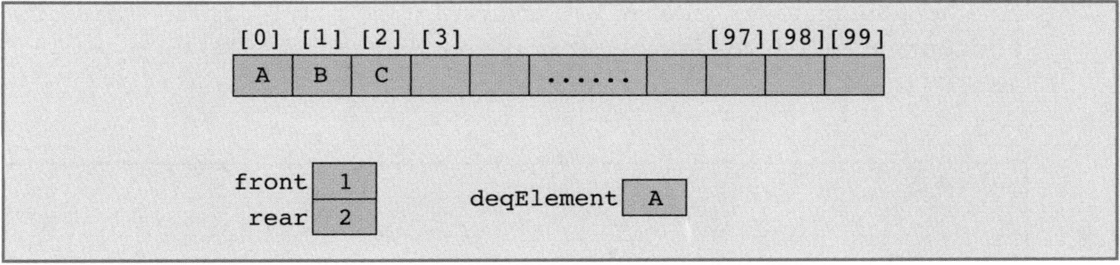

Figure 18-43 Queue after `deQueue` operation

Will this queue design work? Suppose `A` stands for adding (that is, `addQueue`) an element to the queue, and `D` stands for deleting (that is, `deQueue`) an element from the queue. Consider the following sequence of operations:

```
AAADADADADADADADA...
```

This sequence of operations would eventually set the index `rear` to point to the last array position, giving the impression that the queue is full. However, the queue has only two or three elements and the front of the array is empty (see Figure 18-44).

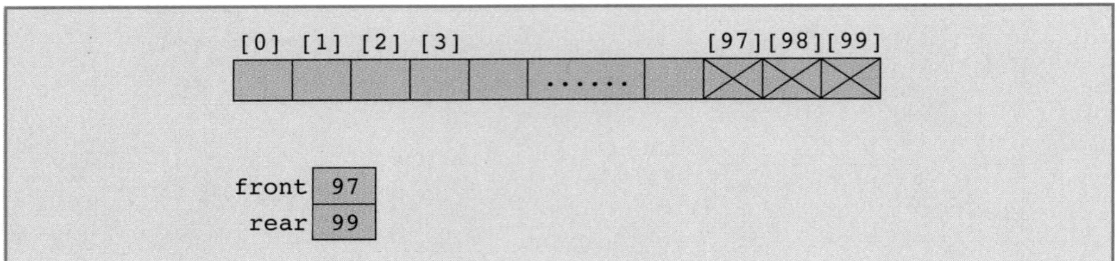

Figure 18-44 Queue after sequence of operations `AAADADADADADA...`

One solution to this problem is that when the queue overflows to the rear (that is, `rear` points to the last array position), we can check the value of the index `front`. If the value of `front` indicates that there is room in the front of the array, then when the rear gets to the last array position, we can slide all of the queue elements toward the first array position. This solution is good if the queue size is very small; otherwise, the program may execute more slowly.

Another solution to this problem is to assume that the array is circular—that is, the first array position immediately follows the last array position (see Figure 18-45).

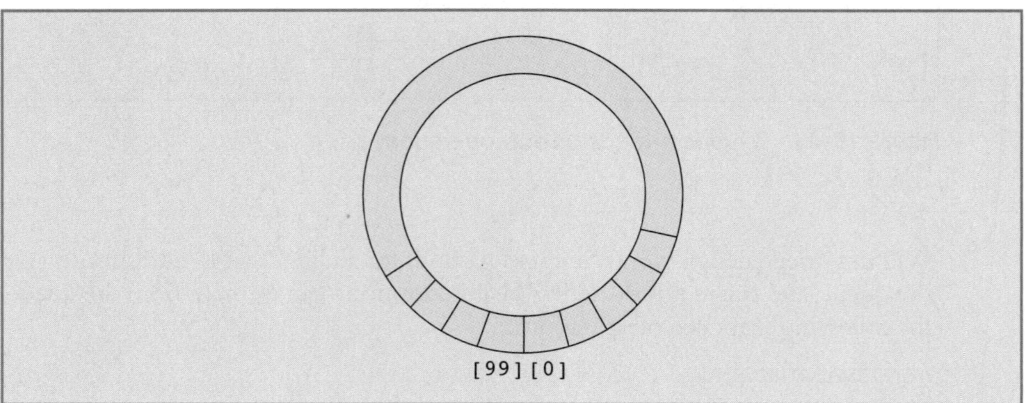

Figure 18-45 Circular queue

We will consider the array containing the queue to be circular, although we will draw the figures of the array holding the queue elements as before.

Suppose that we have the queue as shown in Figure 18-46.

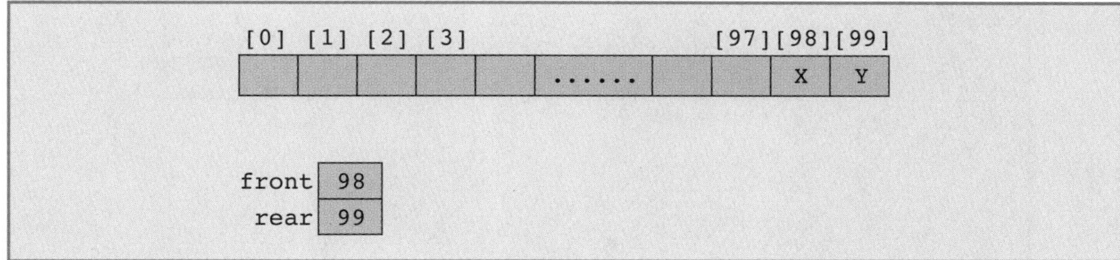

Figure 18-46 Queue with two elements at positions 98 and 99

After the operation

```
addQueue(Queue,'Z');
```

the queue is as shown in Figure 18-47.

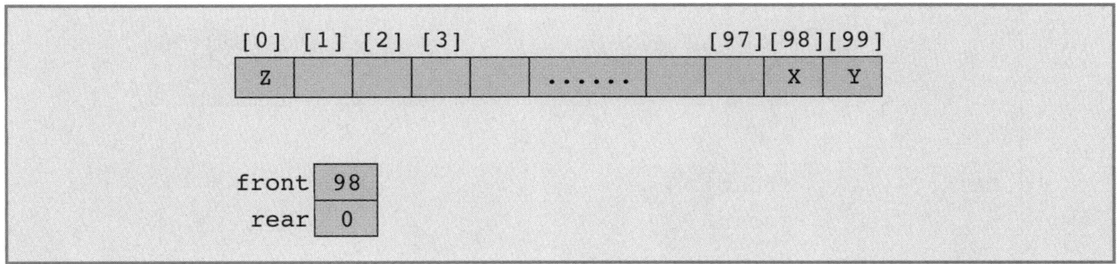

Figure 18-47 Queue after one more `addQueue` operation

Because the array containing the queue is circular, we can use the following statement to advance `rear` (`front`) to the next array position:

```
rear = (rear + 1) % maxQueue;
```

If `rear < maxQueue - 1`, then `rear + 1 <= maxQueue - 1` and so `(rear + 1) % maxQueue = rear + 1`. If `rear == maxQueue - 1` (that is, `rear` points to the last array position), `rear + 1 == maxQueue` and so `(rear + 1) % maxQueue == 0`. In this case, `rear` will be set to `0`, which is the first array position.

This queue design seems to work well. Before we write the algorithms to implement the queue operations, consider the following two cases.

Case 1: Suppose that after certain operations, the array containing the queue is as shown in Figure 18-48.

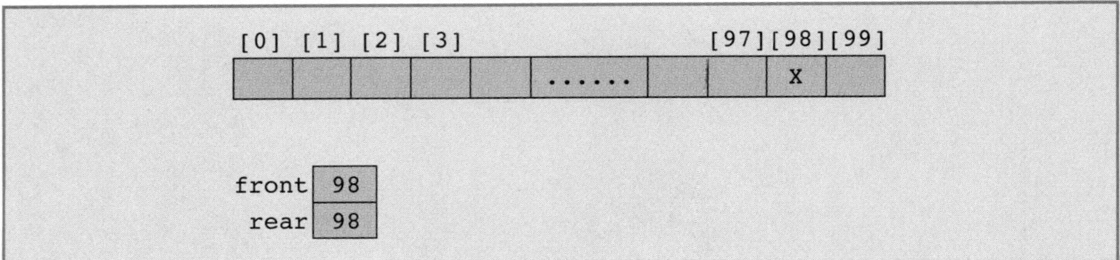

Figure 18-48 Queue with one element

After the operation

```
deQueue(Queue,deqElement);
```

the resulting array is as shown in Figure 18-49.

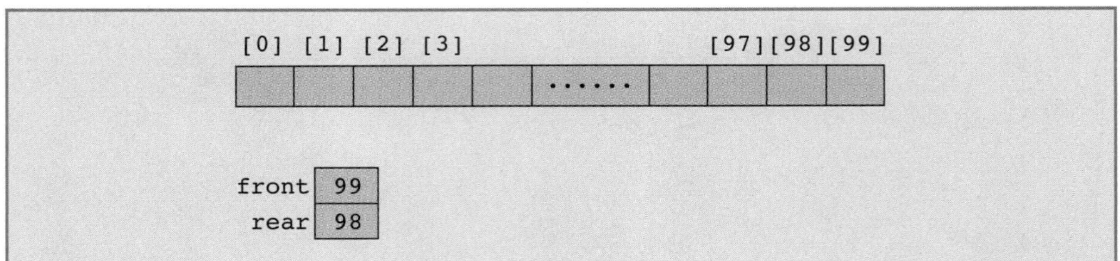

Figure 18-49 Queue after `deQueue` operation

Case 2: Let us now consider the queue shown in Figure 18-50.

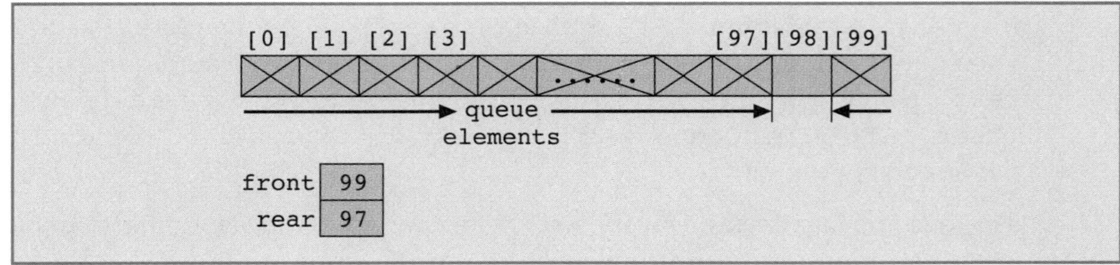

Figure 18-50 Queue with 99 elements

After the operation

```
addQueue(Queue,'Z');
```

the resulting array is as shown in Figure 18-51.

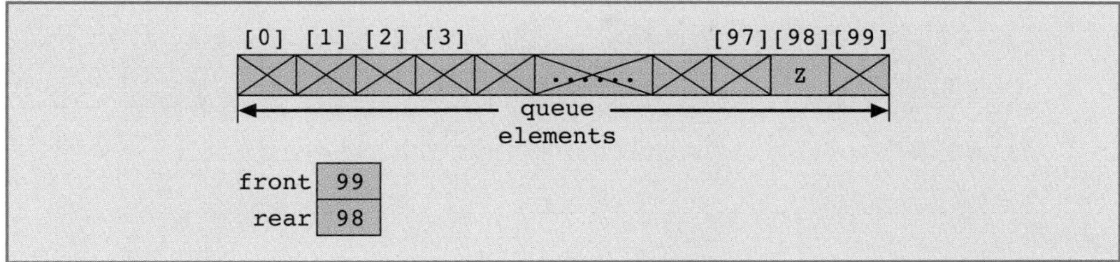

Figure 18-51 Queue after `addQueue` operation; it is full

The arrays in Figures 18-49 and 18-51 have identical values for `front` and `rear`. However, the resulting array in Figure 18-49 represents an empty queue, whereas the resulting array in Figure 18-51 represents a full queue. This latest queue design has brought up another problem of distinguishing between an empty and a full queue.

This problem has several solutions. One solution is to keep a count. In addition to the data members' `front` and `rear` pointers, we need another variable, `count`, to implement the queue. The value of `count` is incremented whenever a new element is added to the queue, and it is decremented whenever an element is removed from the queue. In this case, the functions `initializeQueue` and `destroyQueue` initialize `count` to `0`. This solution is very useful if the user of the queue frequently needs to know the number of elements in the queue.

Another solution is to let `front` indicate the index of the array position *preceding* the first element of the queue, rather than the index of the (actual) first element itself. In this case, assuming `rear` still indicates the index of the last element in the queue, the queue is empty if `front == rear`. In this solution, the slot indicated by the index `front` (that is, the slot preceding the first true element) is reserved. The queue will be full if the next available space is the special reserved slot indicated by `front`. Finally, because the array position indicated by `front` is to be kept empty, if the array size is, say, `100`, then 99 elements can be stored in the queue (see Figure 18-52).

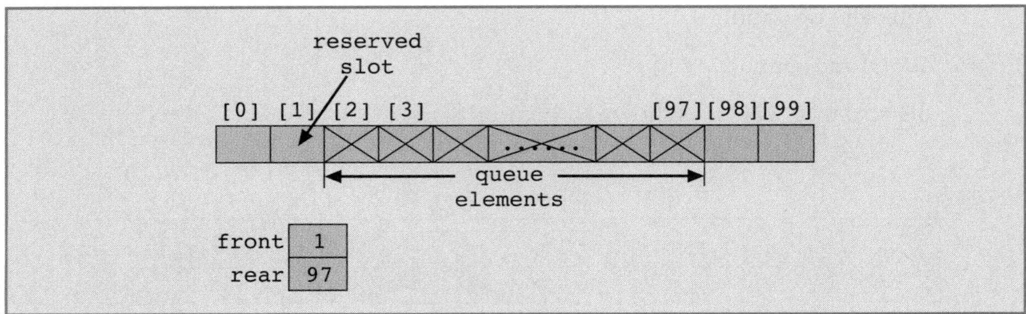

Figure 18-52 Array to store queue elements with a reserved slot

Let us implement the queue using the first solution. That is, we use a variable **count** to indicate whether the queue is empty or full.

The following class defines the queue as an ADT. Because arrays can be allocated dynamically, we will leave it for the user to specify the size of the array to implement the queue. The default size of the array is `100`.

We give only the definition of the queue and leave the documentation as an exercise for you. The documentation of the queue operations in the definition of the class is similar to the documentation of the stack class.

```
template<class Type>
class queueType
{
public:
    const queueType<Type>& operator=(const queueType<Type>&);
              //overload the assignment operator
    void initializeQueue();
    void destroyQueue();
    int isEmptyQueue();
    int isFullQueue();
    void addQueue(Type queueElement);
    void deQueue(Type& deqElement);

    queueType(int queueSize = 100);
    queueType(const queueType<Type>& otherQueue);
      //copy constructor
    ~queueType();
      //destructor
```

```
private:
    int maxQueueSize;
    int count;
    int front;
    int rear;
    Type *list;       //pointer to the array that holds
                      //the queue elements
};
```

Next, we consider the implementation of the queue operations.

Initialize Queue

The first operation that we consider is **initializeQueue**. This operation initializes a queue to an empty state. The first element is added at the first array position. Therefore, we initialize **front** to `0`, **rear** to **maxQueueSize-1**, and **count** to `0`. See Figure 18-53.

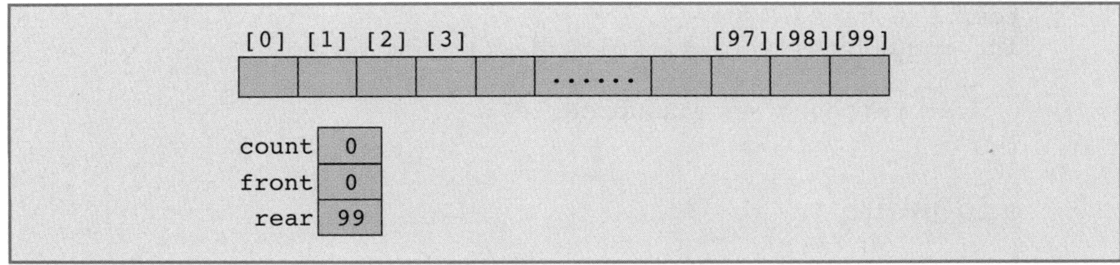

Figure 18-53 Empty queue

```
template<class Type>
void queueType<Type>::initializeQueue()
{
      front = 0;
      rear = maxQueueSize - 1;
      count = 0;
}
```

Destroy Queue

18

The **destroyQueue** operation removes all the elements from the queue, leaving the queue in an empty state. Because the queue is stored in an array, we can remove all the elements from the queue simply by resetting **front**, **rear**, and **count**. So in this implementation of the queue, the **destroyQueue** operation is the same as the **initializeQueue** operation.

```
template<class Type>
void queueType<Type>::destroyQueue()
{
      front = 0;
      rear = maxQueueSize - 1;
      count = 0;
}
```

Empty Queue and Full Queue

As discussed earlier, the queue is empty if `count == 0`, and the queue is full if `count == maxQueueSize`. So the functions to implement these operations are:

```
template<class Type>
int queueType<Type>::isEmptyQueue()
{
   return(count == 0);
}

template<class Type>
int queueType<Type>::isFullQueue()
{
   return(count == maxQueueSize);
}
```

addQueue

Next we implement the **addQueue** operation. Because **rear** points directly to the last element of the queue, to add a new element to the queue we first advance **rear** to the next array position and then add the new element to the array position indicated by **rear**. We also increment `count` by `1`. So the function **addQueue** is

```
template<class Type>
void queueType<Type>::addQueue(Type newElement)
{
   rear = (rear + 1) % maxQueueSize; //use the mod operator to
                                     //advance rear because
                                     //the array is circular
   count++;
   list[rear] = newElement;
}
```

Because the function **addQueue** does not check whether or not the queue is full before adding the new element, we must call the function **isFullQueue** to check whether or not the queue is full before calling the function **addQueue**. Suppose that **queue** is an object of the type **queueType**. Then a call to the function **addQueue** is

```
if(!queue.isFullQueue())
   queue.addQueue(newElement);
```

deQueue

To implement the deQueue operation, we access the index front. Because front points to the array position containing the first element of the queue, in order to remove the first element of the queue we access the queue element indicated by front, decrement count by 1, and advance front to the next queue element. So the function deQueue is

```
template<class Type>
void queueType<Type>::deQueue(Type& deqElement)
{
   deqElement = list[front];
   count--;
   front = (front + 1) % maxQueueSize; //use the mod operator to
                                        //advance front because
                                        //the array is circular
}
```

The function deQueue does not check whether or not the queue is empty before removing an element from the queue. Therefore, we must call the function isEmptyQueue to check whether the queue is empty before calling the function deQueue. So a call to the function deQueue is

```
if(!queue.isEmptyQueue())
   queue.deQueue(deqElement);
```

Constructors and Destructors

To complete the implementation of the queue operations, we next consider the implementation of the constructor and the destructor. The constructor gets the maxQueueSize from the user, sets the variable maxQueueSize to the value specified by the user, and creates the array of size maxQueueSize. If the user does not specify the queue size, the constructor uses the default value, which is 100, to create an array of size 100. The constructor also initializes front and rear to indicate that the queue is empty. The definition of the function to implement the constructor is

```
      //constructor
template<class Type>
queueType<Type>::queueType(int queueSize)   //constructor
{
    if(queueSize <= 0)
    {
       cout<<"The size of the array to hold the queue must "
           <<"be positive."<<endl;
       cout<<"Creating an array of size 100."<<endl;

       maxQueueSize = 100;
    }
```

```
    else
       maxQueueSize = queueSize;  //set maxQueueSize to queueSize

    front = 0;                    //initialize front
    rear = maxQueueSize - 1;      //initialize rear
    count = 0;
    list = new Type[maxQueueSize];  //create the array to
                                    //hold the queue elements
}
```

The array to store the queue elements is created dynamically. Therefore, when the queue object goes out of scope, the destructor simply deallocates the memory occupied by the array that stores the queue elements. The definition of the function to implement the destructor is

```
template<class Type>
queueType<Type>::~queueType()   //destructor
{
   delete [] list;
}
```

The implementation of the copy constructor and overloading the assignment operator are left as exercises for you. (The definitions of these functions are similar to those discussed for linked lists and stacks.)

Linked Implementation of Queues

Because the size of the array to store the queue elements is fixed, only a finite number of queue elements can be stored in the array. Also, the array implementation of the queue requires the array to be treated in a special way together with the values of the indices **front** and **rear**. The linked implementation of a queue simplifies many of the special cases of the array implementation and, because the memory to store a queue element is allocated dynamically, the queue is never full. This section discusses the linked implementation of a queue.

Because elements are added at one end, **rear**, and removed from the other end, **front**, we need to know the front of the queue and the rear of the queue. Thus, we need two pointers, **front** and **rear**, to maintain the queue. The following class defines the linked queue as an ADT.

Only the definition of the queue is provided; the documentation is left as an exercise for you.

```
//Definition of the node
template <class Type>
struct nodeType
{
      Type info;
      nodeType<Type> *link;
};
```

```
template<class Type>
class linkedQueueType
{
public:
    const linkedQueueType<Type>& operator=
                                (const linkedQueueType<Type>&);
              //overload the assignment operator
    bool isEmptyQueue();
    bool isFullQueue();
    void destroyQueue();
    void initializeQueue();
    void addQueue(const Type& newElement);
    void deQueue(Type& deqElement);
    linkedQueueType(); //default constructor
    linkedQueueType(const linkedQueueType<Type>& otherQueue);
             //copy constructor
    ~linkedQueueType(); //destructor
private:
    nodeType<Type> *front; //pointer to the front of the queue
    nodeType<Type> *rear;  //pointer to the rear of the queue
};
```

The definitions of the functions to implement the queue operations are quite straightforward. The queue is empty if **front** is **NULL**. Memory to store the queue elements is allocated dynamically. Therefore, the queue is never full and so the function to implement the **isFullQueue** operation returns the value **false**. (The queue is full only if we run out of memory.)

The operation **destroyQueue** removes all the elements of the queue, leaving the queue in an empty state. Memory to store the queue elements is allocated dynamically. Therefore, this operation traverses the list containing the queue starting at the first node, and it deallocates the memory occupied by the queue elements.

The definitions of the functions to implement the operations **isEmptyQueue**, **isFullQueue**, and **destroyQueue** are given next.

```
template<class Type>
bool linkedQueueType<Type>::isEmptyQueue()
{
      return(front == NULL);
}

template<class Type>
bool linkedQueueType<Type>::isFullQueue()
{
      return false;
}
```

```
template<class Type>
void linkedQueueType<Type>::destroyQueue()
{
      nodeType<Type> *temp;

      while(front != NULL)  //while there are elements left
                            //in the queue
      {
         temp = front;    //set temp to point to the current node
         front = front->link;  //advance first to the next node
         delete temp;       //deallocate memory occupied by temp
      }
      rear = NULL;  //set rear to NULL
}
```

The operation `initializeQueue` initializes the queue to an empty state. The queue is empty if there are no elements in the queue. As in the case of stacks, the `initializeQueue` operation reinitializes the queue to an empty state. Note that the constructor initializes the queue when the queue object is declared. So this operation must remove all the elements from the queue. This task can be accomplished by calling the function `destroyQueue`.

```
template<class Type>
void linkedQueueType<Type>::initializeQueue()
{
  destroyQueue();
}
```

addQueue and deQueue Operations

The `addQueue` operation adds a new element at the end of the queue. To implement this operation, we access the pointer `rear`. Similarly, the operation `deQueue` removes the first element of the queue, so we access the pointer `front`. The definitions of the functions to implement these operations are

```
template<class Type>
void linkedQueueType<Type>::addQueue(const Type& newElement)
{
     nodeType<Type> *newNode;

     newNode = new nodeType<Type>;  //create the node
     newNode->info = newElement;    //store the info
     newNode->link = NULL;   //initialize the link field to NULL

     if(front == NULL)        //if initially the queue is empty
     {
        front = newNode;
        rear = newNode;
     }
```

```
    else                  //add newNode at the end
    {
        rear->link = newNode;
        rear = rear->link;
    }
}//end addQueue

template<class Type>
void linkedQueueType<Type>::deQueue(Type& deqElement)
{
    nodeType<Type> *temp;

    deqElement = front->info;   //copy the info of the first element
    temp = front;               //make temp point to the first node
    front = front->link;        //advance front to the next node
    delete temp;                //delete the first node

    if(front == NULL)        //if after deletion the queue is empty,
       rear = NULL;          //set rear to NULL
}//end deQueue
```

The function **deQueue** does not check whether the queue is empty. Therefore, we must call the function **isEmptyQueue** to check whether the queue is empty before calling the function **deQueue**. Thus, a call to the function **deQueue** is

```
if(!queue.isEmptyQueue())
   queue.deQueue(deqElement);
```

The definition of the function to implement the default constructor is similar to the definition of the function **initializeQueue**. When the queue object goes out of scope, the destructor destroys the queue; that is, it deallocates the memory occupied by the elements of the queue. The definition of the function to implement the destructor is similar to the definition of the function **destroyQueue**. Also, the functions to implement the copy constructor and overload the assignment operators are similar to the corresponding functions for stacks. Implementing these operations is left as an exercise for you.

A Queue Derived from the class linkedListType

From the definitions of the functions to implement the queue operations, it is clear that the linked implementation of the queue is similar to the implementation of a linked list created in a forward manner (see Chapter 17). The **addQueue** operation is similar to the operation **insertFirst**. Likewise, the operations **initializeQueue** and **initializeList**, **isEmptyQueue** and **isEmptyList**, and **destroyQueue** and **destroyList** are similar. The **deQueue** operation can be implemented as before. The pointer **front** is the same as the pointer **first**, and the pointer **rear** is the same as the pointer **last**. This correspondence suggests that we can derive the class to implement the queue from the **class linkedListType** (see Chapter 17).

Next, we derive the **class linkedQueueType** from the **class linkedListType**, and we implement the queue operations using the operations defined for linked lists.

```
//Queue derived from the class linkedListType
//Header file: queueLinked.h
#ifndef H_QueueType
#define H_QueueType

#include <iostream>
#include "linkedList.h"

using namespace std;

template<class Type>
class linkedQueueType: public linkedListType<Type>
{
public:
    bool isEmptyQueue();
    bool isFullQueue();
    void destroyQueue();
    void initializeQueue();
    void addQueue(const Type& newElement);
    void deqQueue(Type& deqElement);
};

template<class Type>
void linkedQueueType<Type>::initializeQueue()
{
      linkedListType<Type>::initializeList();
}

template<class Type>
void linkedQueueType<Type>::destroyQueue()
{
      linkedListType<Type>::destroyList();
}

template<class Type>
bool linkedQueueType<Type>::isEmptyQueue()
{
      return linkedListType<Type>::isEmptyList();
}

template<class Type>
bool linkedQueueType<Type>::isFullQueue()
{
      return linkedListType<Type>::isFullList();
}
```

```
template<class Type>
void linkedQueueType<Type>::addQueue(const Type& newElement)
{
      linkedListType<Type>::insertLast(newElement);
}

template<class Type>
void linkedQueueType<Type>::deqQueue(Type& deqElement)
{
   nodeType<Type> *temp;

   deqElement = first->info; //copy the info of the first element
   temp = first;             //make temp point to the first node
   first = first->link;      //advance front to the next node
   delete temp;              //delete the first node
   if(first == NULL)         //if after deletion the queue is empty,
      last = NULL;           //set last to NULL
}

#endif
```

Example 18-5

The following program tests the various operations on a queue. It uses the linked version of the queue derived from the `class linkedListType`.

```
//Program to test the queue operations: QueueTest.cpp
#include <iostream>
#include "linkedList.h"
#include "queueLinked.h"

using namespace std;

int main()
{
      linkedQueueType<int> queue;
      linkedQueueType<int> copyQueue;

      int num;

      cout<<"Queue Operations"<<endl;
      cout<<"Enter numbers ending with -999"<<endl;
      cin>>num;

      while(num != -999)
      {
         queue.addQueue(num); //add an element to the queue
         cin>>num;
      }
```

```
    copyQueue = queue;  //copy the queue into copyQueue

    cout<<"Queue contains: ";
    while(!copyQueue.isEmptyQueue())
    {
       copyQueue.deqQueue(num);  //remove an element from
                                 //the queue
       cout<<num<<" ";
    }

    cout<<endl;

    return 0;
}
```

Sample Run (In this sample run, the user input is shaded.)

```
Queue Operations
Enter numbers ending with -999
23 76 64 56 28 91 21 11 82 -999
Queue contains: 23 76 64 56 28 91 21 11 82
```

APPLICATION OF QUEUES: SIMULATION

A technique in which one system models the behavior of another system is called **simulation**. For example, physical simulators include wind tunnels used to experiment with the design of car bodies and flight simulators used to train airline pilots. Simulation techniques are used when it is too expensive or dangerous to experiment with real systems. You can also design computer models to study the behavior of real systems. (We will describe some real systems modeled by computers shortly.) Simulating the behavior of an expensive or dangerous experiment using a computer model is usually less expensive than using the real system, and a good way to gain insight without putting human life in danger. Moreover, computer simulations are particularly useful for complex systems where it is difficult to construct a mathematical model. For such systems, computer models can retain descriptive accuracy. In mathematical simulations, the steps of a program are used to model the behavior of a real system. Let us consider one such problem.

The manager of a local movie theater is hearing complaints from customers about the time they have to wait in line to buy tickets. The theater currently has only one cashier. Another theater is preparing to open in the neighborhood and the manager is afraid of losing customers. The manager wants to hire enough cashiers so that a customer does not have to wait too long to buy a ticket, but does not want to hire extra cashiers on a trial basis and potentially waste time and money. One thing that the manager would like to know is the average time a customer has to wait for service. The manager wants someone to write a program to simulate the behavior of the theater.

In computer simulation, the objects being studied are usually represented as data. For the theater problem, some of the objects are the customers and the cashier. The cashier serves the customers and we want to determine a customer's average waiting time. Actions are implemented by writing algorithms, which in a programming language are implemented with the help of functions. Thus, functions are used to implement the actions of the objects. In C++, we can combine the data and the operations on that data into a single unit with the help of classes. Thus, objects can be represented as classes. The data members of the class describe the properties of the objects, and the function members describe the actions on that data. This change in simulation results can also occur if we change the values of the data or modify the definitions of the functions (that is, modify the algorithms implementing the actions). The main goal of a computer simulation is to either generate results showing the performance of an existing system or predict the performance of a proposed system.

In the theater problem, when the cashier is serving a customer, the other customers must wait. Because customers are served on a first come, first served basis and queues are an effective way to implement a First In First Out system, queues are important data structures for use in computer simulations. This section examines computer simulations in which queues are the basic data structure. These simulations model the behavior of systems, called **queuing systems**, in which queues of objects are waiting to be served by various servers. In other words, a queuing system consists of servers and queues of objects waiting to be served. We deal with a variety of queuing systems on a daily basis. For example, a grocery store and a banking system are both queuing systems. Furthermore, when you send a print request to a networked printer that is shared by many people, your print request goes in a queue. Print requests that arrived before your print request are usually completed before yours. Thus, the printer acts as the server when a queue of documents is waiting to be printed.

Next, we describe a queuing system that can be used in a variety of applications, such as a bank, grocery store, movie theater, printer, or a mainframe environment in which several people are trying to use the same processors to execute their programs. To describe a queuing system, we use the term **server** for the object that provides the service. For example, in a bank, a teller is a server; in a grocery store or movie theater, a cashier is a server. We will call the object receiving the service the **customer**, and the service time—the time it takes to serve a customer—the **transaction time**.

Because a queuing system consists of servers and a queue of waiting objects, we will model a system that consists of a list of servers and a waiting queue holding the customers to be served. The customer at the front of the queue waits for the next available server. When a server becomes free, the customer at the front of the queue moves to the free server to be served.

When the first customer arrives, all servers are free and the customer moves to the first server. When the next customer arrives, if a server is available, the customer immediately moves to the available server; otherwise, the customer waits in the queue. To model a queuing system, we need to know the number of servers, the expected arrival time of a customer, the time between the arrivals of customers, and the number of events affecting the system.

Let us again consider the movie theater system. Suppose that the number of servers is 1, on average it takes 6 minutes to serve a customer, and on average a new customer arrives every 4 minutes. The performance of the system depends on how many servers are available, how long it takes to serve a customer, and how often a customer arrives. If it takes too long to serve a customer and customers arrive frequently, then more servers are needed. This system can be modeled as a time-driven simulation. In a **time-driven simulation**, the clock is implemented as a counter and the passage of, say, 1 minute can be implemented by incrementing the counter by 1. The simulation is run for a fixed amount of time. If the simulations need to be run for 100 minutes, the counter starts at 1 and goes up to 100, which can be implemented by using a loop.

In the simulation described in this section, among others, we want to determine the average wait time for a customer. To calculate the average wait time for a customer, we need to add the waiting time of each customer; the sum is then divided by the number of customers who have arrived. When a customer arrives, he or she goes to the end of the queue and the customer's waiting time starts. If the queue is empty and a server is free, the customer is served immediately and so this customer's waiting time is zero. On the other hand, if when the customer arrives and either the queue is nonempty or all servers are busy, the customer must wait for the next available server and, therefore, this customer's waiting time starts. We can keep track of the customer's waiting time by using a timer for each customer. When a customer arrives, its timer is set to 0, which is incremented after each clock unit.

Suppose that, on average, it takes five minutes for a server to serve a customer. When a server becomes free and the waiting customer's queue is nonempty, the customer at the front of the queue proceeds to begin the transaction. Thus, we must keep track of the time a customer is with a server. When the customer arrives at a server, the transaction time is set to five and is decremented after each clock unit. When the transaction time becomes zero, the server is marked free. Hence, the two objects needed to implement a time-driven computer simulation of a queuing system are the customer and the server.

Next, before designing the main algorithm to implement the simulation, we design classes to implement each of the two objects: *customer* and *server*.

Customer

Every customer has a customer number, arrival time, waiting time, transaction time, and departure time. If we know the arrival and departure times, we can determine the departure time by adding the arrival time, waiting time, and transaction time. Let us call the class to implement the customer object `customerType`. It follows that the **`class`** `customerType` has four data members: the `customerNumber`, `arrivalTime`, `waitingTime`, and `transactionTime`, each of the data type `int`. The basic operations that must be performed on an object of the type `customerType` are as follows: set the customer's number, arrival, and waiting time; increment the waiting time by one clock unit; return the waiting time; return the arrival time; return the transaction time; and return the customer number. The following **`class`**, `customerType`, implements the customer as an ADT (see also Figure 18-54):

```
class customerType
{
public:
    customerType(int cN = 0, int arrvTime = 0, int wTime = 0,
                 int tTime = 0);
        //constructor to initialize the data members
        //according to the parameters
        //In the object declaration if no value is specified,
        //the default is assigned
        //Post: customerNumber = cN;
        //      arrivalTime.clock = arrvTime;
        //      waitingTime.clock = wTime;
        //      transactionTime.clock = tTime;
    void setCustomerInfo(int customerN = 0, int inTime = 0,
                         int wTime = 0, int tTime = 0);
        //Data members are set according to the parameters
        //Post: customerNumber = customerN;
        //      arrivalTime.clock = arrvTime;
        //      waitingTime.clock = wTime;
        //      transactionTime.clock = tTime;
    int getWaitingTime() const;
        //Return the value of the data member waitingTime

    void setWaitingTime(int time);
        //The waiting time is set according to the parameter
        //Post: waitingTime = time
    void incrementWaitingTime();
        //The value of the data member waitingTime is
        //incremented by one time unit
        //Post: waitingTime++
    int getArrivalTime();
        //Return the value of the data member arrivalTime
    int getTransactionTime();
        //Return the value of the data member transactionTime
    int getCustomerNumber();
        //Return the value of the data member customerNumber
private:
    int customerNumber;
    int arrivalTime;
    int waitingTime;
    int transactionTime;
};
```

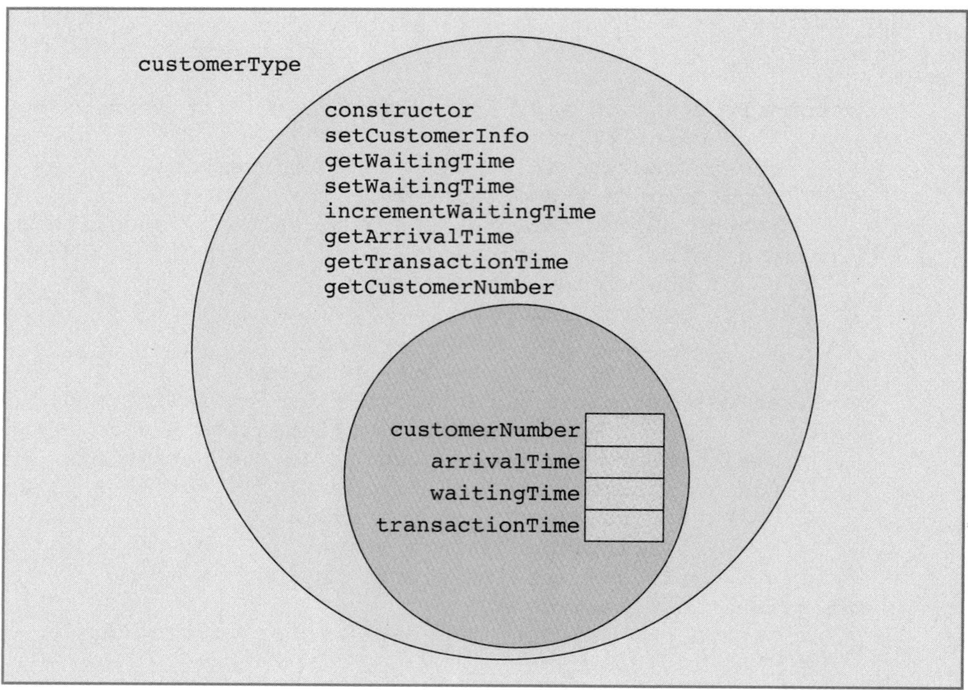

Figure 18-54 `class customerType`

The definitions of the member functions of the `class customerType` follow easily from their descriptions. Next, we give the definitions of the member functions of the `class customerType`.

The constructor uses the values of the parameters to initialize `customerNumber`, `arrivalTime`, `waitingTime`, and `transactionTime`. Its definition is

```
customerType::customerType(int cN, int arrvTime, int wTime,
                           int tTime)
{
      customerNumber = cN;
      arrivalTime = arrvTime;
      waitingTime = wTime;
      transactionTime = tTime;
}
```

The definition of the function **setCustomerInfo** is similar to that of the constructor just described. Its definition is

```
void customerType::setCustomerInfo(int customerN, int inTime,
                                   int wTime, int tTime)
{
      customerNumber = customerN;
      arrivalTime = inTime;
      waitingTime = wTime;
      transactionTime = tTime;
}
```

The function **getWaitingTime** returns the current waiting time. The definition of the function **getWaitingTime** is

```
int customerType::getWaitingTime() const
{
    return waitingTime;
}
```

The function **incrementWaitingTime** increments the value of **waitingTime**. Its definition is

```
void customerType::incrementWaitingTime()
{
    waitingTime++;
}
```

The definitions of the functions **setWaitingTime**, **getArrivalTime**, and **getTransactionTime** are similar to the definition of **incrementWaitingTime**:

```
void customerType::setWaitingTime(int time)
{
    waitingTime = time;
}


int customerType::getArrivalTime()
{
    return arrivalTime;
}

int customerType::getTransactionTime()
{
    return transactionTime;
}
```

18

The function **getCustomerNumber** returns the customer number; that is, it returns the value of the data member **customerNumber**.

```
int customerType::getCustomerNumber()
{
      return customerNumber;
}
```

Server

At any given time unit, the server either is busy serving a customer or is free. We use a string variable to set the status of the server. Every server has a timer, and, because the program might need to know which customer is served by which server, the server also stores the information of the customer being served. Thus, three data members are associated with a server: the **status**, the **transactionTime**, and the **currentCustomer**. Some of the basic operations that must be performed on a server are as follows: check whether the server is free; set the server as free; set the server as busy; set the transaction time (that is, how long it takes to serve the customer); return the remaining transaction time (to determine whether the server should be set to free); if the server is busy after each time unit, decrement the transaction time by one time unit; and so on. The following **class**, **serverType**, implements the server as an ADT (see also Figure 18-55):

```
class serverType
{
public:
    serverType();
        //default constructor
        //Sets the values of the data members to their
        //default values
        //Post: currentCustomer is initialized by its
        //      default constructor
        //      status = "free"
        //      transaction time is initialized to 0
    bool isFree() const;
        //Returns true if the server is free; false otherwise
    void setBusy();
        //Set the status of the server to busy
        //Post: status = "busy";
    void setFree();
        //Set the status of the server to free
        //Post: status = "free";
    void setTransactionTime(int t);
        //Set the transaction time according to the parameter t
        //Post: transactionTime = t;
    void setTransactionTime();
        //Set the transaction time according to the current
        //customer's transaction time
        //Post: transactionTime = currentCustomer.transactionTime;
    int getRemainingTransactionTime();
        //Returns the remaining transaction time value of the
        //data member transactionTime is returned
    void decreaseTransactionTime();
        //Decrease the transactionTime by 1
        //Post: transactionTime--;
    void setCurrentCustomer(customerType cCustomer);
        //Set the info of the current customer according to the
        //parameter cCustomer
        //Post: currentCustomer = cCustomer;
```

```
    int getCurrentCustomerNumber();
        //Returns the customer number of the current customer
    int getCurrentCustomerArrivalTime();
        //Returns the arrival time of the current customer
        //The value of the data member arrivalTime of
        //currentCustomer is returned
    int getCurrentCustomerWaitingTime();
        //Returns the current waiting time of the current customer
        //The value of the data member transactionTime is returned
    int getCurrentCustomerTransactionTime();
        //Returns the current customer's transaction time
        //The value of the data member clock of transactionTime of
        //the current customer is returned

private:
    customerType currentCustomer;
    string status;
    int transactionTime;
};
```

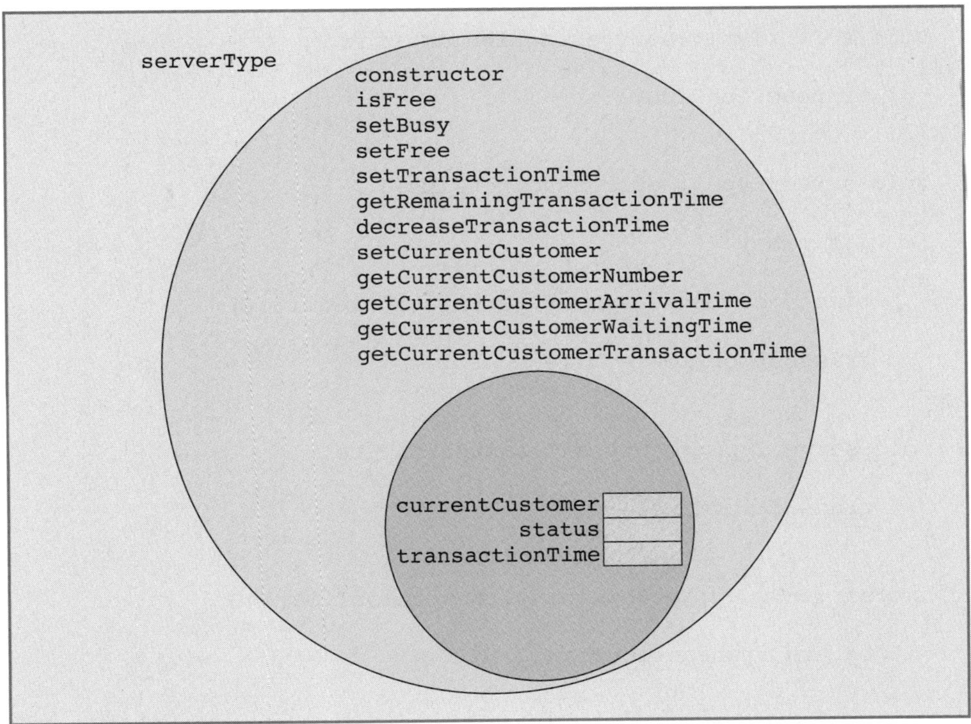

Figure 18-55 class serverType

The definitions of the member functions of the **class serverType** are straightforward.

```
serverType::serverType()
{
    status = "free";
    transactionTime = 0;
}

bool serverType::isFree() const
{
    return (status == "free");
}

void serverType::setBusy()
{
    status = "busy";
}

void serverType::setFree()
{
    status = "free";
}

void serverType::setTransactionTime(int t)
{
    transactionTime = t;
}

void serverType::setTransactionTime()
{
    int time;

    time = currentCustomer.getTransactionTime();

    transactionTime = time;
}

void serverType::decreaseTransactionTime()
{
    transactionTime--;
}

int serverType::getRemainingTransactionTime()
{
    return transactionTime;
}

void serverType::setCurrentCustomer(customerType cCustomer)
{
    currentCustomer = cCustomer;
}
```

```
int serverType::getCurrentCustomerNumber()
{
      return currentCustomer.getCustomerNumber();
}

int serverType::getCurrentCustomerArrivalTime()
{
      return currentCustomer.getArrivalTime();
}

int serverType::getCurrentCustomerWaitingTime()
{
      return currentCustomer.getWaitingTime();
}

int serverType::getCurrentCustomerTransactionTime()
{
      return currentCustomer.getTransactionTime();
}
```

Because we are designing a simulation program that can be used in a variety of applications, we need to design two more classes: a class to create and process a list of servers, and a class to create and process a queue of waiting customers. The next two sections describe each of these classes.

Server List

A server list is a set of servers. At any given time, a server is either free or busy. For the customer at the front of the queue, we need to find a server in the list that is free. If all the servers are busy, then the customer must wait until one of the servers becomes free. Thus, the class that implements a list of servers has two data members: one to store the number of servers and one to maintain a list of servers. Using dynamic arrays, depending on the number of servers specified by the user, a list of servers is created during program execution. Some of the operations that must be performed on a server list are as follows: return the server number of a free server; when a customer gets ready to do business and a server is available, set the server to busy; when the simulation ends, some of the servers might still be busy, so return the number of busy servers; after each time unit, reduce the `transactionTime` of each busy server by one time unit; and if the `transactionTime` of a server becomes zero, set the server to free. The following **`class`**, `serverListType`, implements the list of servers as an ADT (see also Figure 18-56):


```
class serverListType
{
public:
   serverListType(int num = 1);
      //constructor to initialize a list of servers
      //Post: numOfServers = num
      //      A list of servers, specified by num, is
      //      created and each server is initialized to free.
```

```
    ~serverListType();
       //destructor
       //Post: the list of servers is destroyed.
    int getFreeServerID();
       //Search the list of servers.
       //If a free server is found, return its ID;
       //otherwise, return -1.
    int getNumberOfBusyServers();
       //Returns the number of busy servers
    void setServerBusy(int serverID, customerType cCustomer,
                       int tTime);
       //Set the server specified by serverID to busy.
       //To serve the customer specified by cCustomer, the
       //transaction time is set according to the
       //parameter tTime.
    void setServerBusy(int serverID, customerType cCustomer);
       //Set the server specified by serverID to busy.
       //To serve the customer specified by cCustomer, the
       //transaction time is set according to the
       //customer's transaction time
    void updateServers();
       //The transaction time of each busy server is decremented
       //by one unit. If the transaction time of a busy server
       //is reduced to zero, the server is set to free and a
       //message indicating which customer is served, together
       //with the customer's departing time, is printed on
       //the screen.
    void updateServers(ofstream& outFile);
       //The transaction time of each busy server is decremented
       //by one unit. If the transaction time of a busy server
       //is reduced to zero, the server is set to free and a
       //message indicating which customer is served, together
       //with the customer's departing time, is sent to a file.

private:
     int numOfServers;
     serverType *servers;
};
```

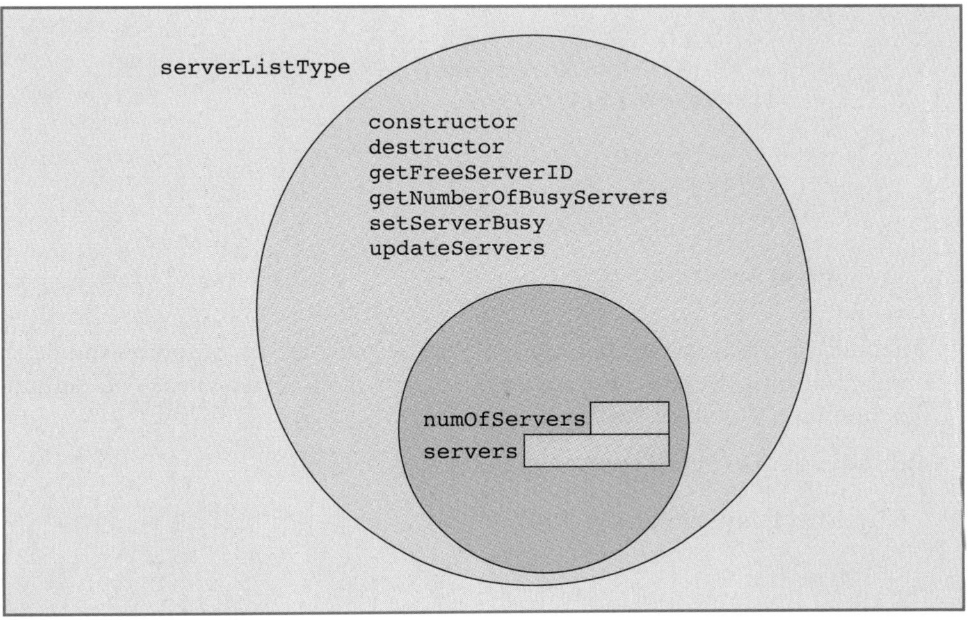

Figure 18-56 `class serverListType`

Following are the definitions of the member functions of the `class serverListType`. The definitions of the constructor and destructor are straightforward.

```
serverListType::serverListType(int num)
{
      numOfServers = num;
      servers = new serverType[num]; //create a list of servers

      for(int i = 0; i < num; i++)
          servers[i].setFree();     //initialize each server to free
}

serverListType::~serverListType()
{
      delete [] servers;
}
```


The function `getFreeServerID` searches the list of servers. If a free server is found, it returns the server's ID; otherwise, the value `-1` is returned, which indicates that all the servers are busy. The definition of this function is

```
int serverListType::getFreeServerID()
{
      int serverID = -1;
```

```
        int i;

        for(i = 0; i < numOfServers; i++)
            if(servers[i].isFree())
            {
                serverID = i;
                break;
            }

        return serverID;
}
```

The function getNumberOfBusyServers searches the list of servers and determines the number of busy servers. The number of busy servers is returned. The definition of this function is

```
int serverListType::getNumberOfBusyServers()
{
        int busyServers = 0;

        int i;

        for(i = 0; i < numOfServers; i++)
            if(!servers[i].isFree())
                busyServers++;

        return busyServers;
}
```

The function setServerBusy sets a server to busy. This function is overloaded. The serverID of the server that is set to busy is passed as a parameter to this function. One function sets the server's transaction time according to the parameter tTime, and the other function sets it by using the transaction time stored in the object cCustomer. The transaction time is later needed to determine the average wait time. The definitions of these functions are

```
void serverListType::setServerBusy(int serverID,
                                   customerType cCustomer,
                                   int tTime)
{
   servers[serverID].setBusy();
   servers[serverID].setTransactionTime(tTime);
   servers[serverID].setCurrentCustomer(cCustomer);
}
```

```
void serverListType::setServerBusy(int serverID,
                                   customerType cCustomer)
{
      int time;

      time = cCustomer.getTransactionTime();

      servers[serverID].setBusy();
      servers[serverID].setTransactionTime(time);
      servers[serverID].setCurrentCustomer(cCustomer);

}
```

The definition of the function **updateServers** is quite straightforward. Starting at the first server, it searches the list of servers for busy servers. When a busy server is found, its **transactionTime** is decremented by 1. If the **transactionTime** reduces to zero, the server is set to free. If the **transactionTime** of a busy server reduces to zero, then the transaction of the customer being served by the server is complete. A message indicating the customer's server number, customer number, and departure time is then printed. The function **updateServers** is overloaded. One function sends the output to the screen; the other sends the output to a file. The definitions of these functions are as follows:

```
void serverListType::updateServers()
{
   int i;

   for(i = 0; i < numOfServers; i++)
      if(!servers[i].isFree())
      {
         servers[i].decreaseTransactionTime();

         if(servers[i].getRemainingTransactionTime() == 0)
         {
            cout<<"Server No: "<<(i+1)<<" Customer number "
                <<servers[i].getCurrentCustomerNumber()
                <<" departed at "<<endl
                <<"                clock unit "
                <<servers[i].getCurrentCustomerArrivalTime()
                  + servers[i].getCurrentCustomerWaitingTime()
                  + servers[i].getCurrentCustomerTransactionTime()
                <<endl;
            servers[i].setFree();
         }
      }
}
```

```
void serverListType::updateServers(ofstream& outFile)
{
   int i;

   for(i = 0; i < numOfServers; i++)
      if(!servers[i].isFree())
      {
         servers[i].decreaseTransactionTime();

         if(servers[i].getRemainingTransactionTime() == 0)
         {
            outFile<<"Server No: "<<(i+1)<<" Customer number "
                   <<servers[i].getCurrentCustomerNumber()
                   <<" departed at "<<endl
                   <<"                clock unit "
                   <<servers[i].getCurrentCustomerArrivalTime()
                    + servers[i].getCurrentCustomerWaitingTime()
                    + servers[i].getCurrentCustomerTransactionTime()
                   <<endl;
            servers[i].setFree();
         }
      }
}
```

Waiting Customers Queue

When a customer arrives, he or she goes to the end of the queue. When a server becomes available, the customer at the front of the queue leaves to conduct the transaction. After each time unit, the waiting time of each customer in the queue is incremented by 1. The ADT `queueType` designed in this chapter has all the operations needed to implement a queue, except the operation of incrementing the waiting time of each customer in the queue by one time unit. We will derive a **class**, `waitingCustomerQueueType`, from the **class** `queueType` and add the additional operations to implement the customer queue. The definition of the **class** `waitingCustomerQueueType` is as follows:

```
class waitingCustomerQueueType: public queueType<customerType>
{
public:
    waitingCustomerQueueType(int size = 100);
        //The queue is initialized according to the
        //parameter size
        //The value of the size is passed to the constructor
        //of queueType
    ~waitingCustomerQueueType();
        //The queue is destroyed
    void updateWaitingQueue();
        //Increment the waiting time of each customer in the
        //queue by one time unit
};
```

The definitions of the member functions are given next. The definitions of the constructor and the destructor are as follows:

```
waitingCustomerQueueType::waitingCustomerQueueType(int size)
                          :queueType<customerType>(size)
{
}

waitingCustomerQueueType::~waitingCustomerQueueType()
{
}
```

The function `updateWaitingQueue` increments the waiting time of each customer in the queue by one time unit. The `class waitingCustomerQueueType` is derived from the `class queueType`. Because the data members of `queueType` are `private`, the function `updateWaitingQueue` cannot directly access the elements of the queue. The only way to access the elements of the queue is to use the `deQueue` operation. After incrementing the waiting time, the element can be put back into the queue by using the `addQueue` operation.

The `addQueue` operation inserts the element at the end of the queue. If we perform the `deQueue` operation followed by the `addQueue` operation for each element of the queue, then eventually the front element again becomes the front element. Given that each `deQueue` operation is followed by an `addQueue` operation, how do we determine that all the elements of the queue have been processed? We cannot use the `isEmptyQueue` or `isFullQueue` operation on the queue, because the queue will never be empty or full.

One solution to this problem is to create a temporary queue. Every element of the original queue is removed, processed, and inserted into the temporary queue. When the original queue becomes empty, all of the elements in the queue are processed. We can then copy the elements from the temporary queue back into the original queue. However, this solution requires us to use extra memory space, which could be significant. Also, if the queue is large, extra computer time is needed to copy the elements from the temporary queue back into the original queue. Let us look into another solution.

In the second solution, before starting to update the elements of the queue, we can insert a dummy customer with a waiting time of, say, `-1`. During the update process, when we arrive at the customer with the waiting time of `-1`, we can stop the update process without processing the customer with the waiting time of `-1`. If we do not process the customer with the waiting time `-1`, this customer is removed from the queue and, after processing all the elements of the queue, the queue will contain no extra elements. This solution does not require us to create a temporary queue, so we do not need extra computer time to copy the elements back into the original queue. We will use this solution to update the queue. Therefore, the definition of the function `updateWaitingQueue` is 18

```
void waitingCustomerQueueType::updateWaitingQueue()
{
      customerType cust;
```

```
        cust.setWaitingTime(-1);
        int wTime = 0;

        addQueue(cust);

        while(wTime != -1)
        {
              deQueue(cust);
              wTime = cust.getWaitingTime();

              if(wTime == -1)
                    break;

              cust.incrementWaitingTime();
              addQueue(cust);
        }
}
```

Main Program

To run the simulation, we first need to get the following information:

- The number of time units the simulation should run. Assume that each time unit is one minute.
- The number of servers.
- The amount of time it takes to serve a customer—that is, the transaction time.
- The approximate time between customer arrivals.

These pieces of information are called simulation parameters. By changing the values of these parameters, we can observe the changes in the performance of the system. We can write a function, `setSimulationParameters`, to prompt the user to specify these values. The definition of this function is

```
void setSimulationParameters(int& sTime, int& numOfServers,
                             int& transTime,
                             int& tBetweenCArrival)
{
      cout<<"Enter simulation time: "<<flush;
      cin>>sTime;
      cout<<endl;

      cout<<"Enter number of servers: "<<flush;
      cin>>numOfServers;
      cout<<endl;

      cout<<"Enter transaction time: "<<flush;
      cin>>transTime;
      cout<<endl;
```

```
        cout<<"Enter time between customer arrivals: "<<flush;
        cin>>tBetweenCArrival;
        cout<<endl;
}
```

When a server becomes free and the customer queue is nonempty, we can move the customer at the front of the queue to the free server to be served. Moreover, when a customer starts the transaction, the waiting time ends. The waiting time of the customer is added to the total waiting time. The general algorithm to start the transaction (supposing that **serverID** denotes the ID of the free server) is

1. Remove the customer from the front of the queue.

   ```
   customerQueue.addQueue(customer);
   ```

2. Update the total waiting time by adding the current customer's waiting time to the previous total waiting time.

   ```
   totalWait = totalWait + customer.getWaitingTime();
   ```

3. Set the free server to begin the transaction.

   ```
   serverList.setServerBusy(serverID, customer, transTime);
   ```

To run the simulation, we need to know the number of customers arriving at a given time unit and how long it takes to serve the customer. We use the Poisson distribution from statistics, which says that the probability of occurring y events at a given time is given by the formula:

$$P(y) = \frac{\lambda^y e^{-\lambda}}{y!}, \quad y = 0, 1, 2, ...,$$

where λ is the expected value that y events occur at that time. Suppose that, on average, a customer arrives every four minutes. During this four-minute period, the customer can arrive at any one of the four minutes. Assuming an equally likelihood of each of the four minutes, the expected value that a customer arrives in each of the four minutes is, therefore, $1/4 = .25$. Next, we need to determine whether or not the customer actually arrives at a given minute.

Now $P(0) = e^{-\lambda}$ is the probability that no event occurs at a given time. One of the basic assumptions of the Poisson distribution is that more than one outcome will occur in a short time interval is negligible. For simplicity, we assume that only one customer arrives at a given time unit. Thus, we use $e^{-\lambda}$ as the cutoff point to determine whether a customer arrives at a given time unit. Suppose that, on average, a customer arrives every four minutes. Then $\lambda = 0.25$. We can use an algorithm to generate a number between 0 and 1. If the value of the number generated is $> e^{-0.25}$, we can assume that the customer arrived at a particular time unit. For example, suppose that *rNum* is a random number such that $0 \leq rNum \leq 1$. If $rNum > e^{-0.25}$, the customer arrived at given time unit.

We now describe the function `runSimulation` to implement the simulation. Suppose that we run the simulation for 100 time units and customers arrive at time units 93, 96, and 100. The average transaction time is 5 minutes—that is, 5 time units. For simplicity, assume that we have only one server and the server becomes free at time unit 97, and that all customers arriving before time unit 93 have been served. When the server becomes free at time unit 97, the customer arriving at time unit 93 starts the transaction. Because the transaction of the customer arriving at time unit 93 starts at time unit 97 and it takes 5 minutes to complete a transaction, when the simulation loop ends, the customer arriving at time unit 93 is still at the server. Moreover, customers arriving at time units 96 and 100 are in the queue. For simplicity, we assume that when the simulation loop ends, the customers at the servers are considered served. The general algorithm for this function is

1. Declare and initialize the variables such as the simulation parameters, customer number, clock, total and average waiting times, number of customers arrived, number of customers served, number of customers left in the waiting queue, number of customers left with the servers, `waitingCustomersQueue`, and a list of servers.
2. The main loop is

   ```
   for(clock = 1; clock <= simulationTime; clock++)
   {
   ```

   2.1 Update the server list to decrement the transaction time of each busy server by one time unit.

   2.2 If the customer's queue is nonempty, increment the waiting time of each customer by one time unit.

   2.3 If a customer arrives, increment the number of customers by 1 and add the new customer to the queue.

   2.4 If a server is free and the customer's queue is nonempty, remove a customer from the front of the queue and send the customer to the free server.

   ```
   }
   ```
3. Print the appropriate results. Your results must include the number of customers left in the queue, the number of customers still with servers, the number of customers arrived, and the number of customers who actually completed a transaction.

Once you have designed the function `runSimulation`, the definition of the function `main` is simple and straightforward because the function `main` calls only the function `runSimulation`.

When we tested our version of the simulation program, we generated the following results. We assumed that the average transaction time is 5 minutes and that on average a customer arrives every 3 minutes, and we used a random number generator to generate a number between `0` and `1` to decide whether a customer arrived at a given time unit.

Sample Runs:

Sample Run 1:

```
Customer number 1 arrived at time unit 4
Customer number 2 arrived at time unit 8
Server No: 1 Customer number 1 departed at
             clock unit 9
Customer number 3 arrived at time unit 9
Customer number 4 arrived at time unit 12
Server No: 1 Customer number 2 departed at
             clock unit 14
Server No: 1 Customer number 3 departed at
             clock unit 19
Customer number 5 arrived at time unit 21
Server No: 1 Customer number 4 departed at
             clock unit 24
Server No: 1 Customer number 5 departed at
             clock unit 29
Customer number 6 arrived at time unit 37
Customer number 7 arrived at time unit 38
Customer number 8 arrived at time unit 41
Server No: 1 Customer number 6 departed at
             clock unit 42
Customer number 9 arrived at time unit 43
Customer number 10 arrived at time unit 44
Server No: 1 Customer number 7 departed at
             clock unit 47
Customer number 11 arrived at time unit 49
Customer number 12 arrived at time unit 51
Server No: 1 Customer number 8 departed at
             clock unit 52
Customer number 13 arrived at time unit 52
Customer number 14 arrived at time unit 53
Customer number 15 arrived at time unit 54
Server No: 1 Customer number 9 departed at
             clock unit 57
Customer number 16 arrived at time unit 59
Server No: 1 Customer number 10 departed at
             clock unit 62
Customer number 17 arrived at time unit 66
Server No: 1 Customer number 11 departed at
             clock unit 67
Customer number 18 arrived at time unit 71
Server No: 1 Customer number 12 departed at
             clock unit 72
Server No: 1 Customer number 13 departed at
             clock unit 77
Customer number 19 arrived at time unit 78
Server No: 1 Customer number 14 departed at
             clock unit 82
```

```
Server No: 1 Customer number 15 departed at
             clock unit 87
Customer number 20 arrived at time unit 90
Server No: 1 Customer number 16 departed at
             clock unit 92
Customer number 21 arrived at time unit 92
Server No: 1 Customer number 17 departed at
             clock unit 97

Simulation ran for 100 time units
Number of servers: 1
Average transaction time: 5
Average arrival time difference between customers: 4
Total wait time: 269
Number of customers completed transaction: 17
Number of customers left in servers: 1
Customers left in queue: 3
Average wait time: 12.81
************** END SIMULATION *************
```

Sample Run 2:

```
Customer number 1 arrived at time unit 4
Customer number 2 arrived at time unit 8
Server No: 1 Customer number 1 departed at
             clock unit 9
Customer number 3 arrived at time unit 9
Customer number 4 arrived at time unit 12
Server No: 2 Customer number 2 departed at
             clock unit 13
Server No: 1 Customer number 3 departed at
             clock unit 14
Server No: 2 Customer number 4 departed at
             clock unit 18
Customer number 5 arrived at time unit 21
Server No: 1 Customer number 5 departed at
             clock unit 26
Customer number 6 arrived at time unit 37
Customer number 7 arrived at time unit 38
Customer number 8 arrived at time unit 41
Server No: 1 Customer number 6 departed at
             clock unit 42
Server No: 2 Customer number 7 departed at
             clock unit 43
Customer number 9 arrived at time unit 43
Customer number 10 arrived at time unit 44
Server No: 1 Customer number 8 departed at
             clock unit 47
Server No: 2 Customer number 9 departed at
             clock unit 48
```

```
Customer number 11 arrived at time unit 49
Customer number 12 arrived at time unit 51
Server No: 1 Customer number 10 departed at
             clock unit 52
Customer number 13 arrived at time unit 52
Customer number 14 arrived at time unit 53
Server No: 2 Customer number 11 departed at
             clock unit 54
Customer number 15 arrived at time unit 54
Server No: 1 Customer number 12 departed at
             clock unit 57
Server No: 2 Customer number 13 departed at
             clock unit 59
Customer number 16 arrived at time unit 59
Server No: 1 Customer number 14 departed at
             clock unit 62
Server No: 2 Customer number 15 departed at
             clock unit 64
Customer number 17 arrived at time unit 66
Server No: 1 Customer number 16 departed at
             clock unit 67
Server No: 2 Customer number 17 departed at
             clock unit 71
Customer number 18 arrived at time unit 71
Server No: 1 Customer number 18 departed at
             clock unit 76
Customer number 19 arrived at time unit 78
Server No: 1 Customer number 19 departed at
             clock unit 83
Customer number 20 arrived at time unit 90
Customer number 21 arrived at time unit 92
Server No: 1 Customer number 20 departed at
             clock unit 95
Server No: 2 Customer number 21 departed at
             clock unit 97

Simulation ran for 100 time units
Number of servers: 2
Average transaction time: 5
Average arrival time difference between customers: 4
Total wait time: 20
Number of customers completed transaction: 21
Number of customers left in servers: 0
Customers left in queue: 0
Average wait time: 0.95
************** END SIMULATION *************
```

Sample Run 3: (In this output, to save space, the details of the output of the customers' arrival and departure times are omitted.)

```
Customer number 1 arrived at time unit 4
Customer number 2 arrived at time unit 8
Server No: 1 Customer number 1 departed at
             clock unit 9
Customer number 3 arrived at time unit 9
Customer number 4 arrived at time unit 12
Server No: 1 Customer number 2 departed at
             clock unit 14
Server No: 1 Customer number 3 departed at
             clock unit 19
Customer number 5 arrived at time unit 21
Server No: 1 Customer number 4 departed at
             clock unit 24
Server No: 1 Customer number 5 departed at
             clock unit 29
Customer number 6 arrived at time unit 37
Customer number 7 arrived at time unit 38
Customer number 8 arrived at time unit 41
Server No: 1 Customer number 6 departed at
             clock unit 42
Customer number 9 arrived at time unit 43
Customer number 10 arrived at time unit 44
...

Simulation ran for 1000 time units
Number of servers: 1
Average transaction time: 5
Average arrival time difference between customers: 4
Total wait time: 8008
Number of customers completed transaction: 197
Number of customers left in servers: 1
Customers left in queue: 15
Average wait time: 37.60
************** END SIMULATION *************
```

Sample Run 4: (In this output, to save space, the details of the output of the customers' arrival and departure times are omitted.)

```
Customer number 1 arrived at time unit 4
Customer number 2 arrived at time unit 8
Server No: 1 Customer number 1 departed at
             clock unit 9
Customer number 3 arrived at time unit 9
Customer number 4 arrived at time unit 12
```

```
Server No: 2 Customer number 2 departed at
             clock unit 13
Server No: 1 Customer number 3 departed at
             clock unit 14
Server No: 3 Customer number 4 departed at
             clock unit 17
Customer number 5 arrived at time unit 21
Server No: 1 Customer number 5 departed at
             clock unit 26
Customer number 6 arrived at time unit 37
Customer number 7 arrived at time unit 38
Customer number 8 arrived at time unit 41
Server No: 1 Customer number 6 departed at
             clock unit 42
Server No: 2 Customer number 7 departed at
             clock unit 43
Customer number 9 arrived at time unit 43
Customer number 10 arrived at time unit 44
Server No: 3 Customer number 8 departed at
             clock unit 46

...

Simulation ran for 1000 time units
Number of servers: 3
Average transaction time: 5
Average arrival time difference between customers: 4
Total wait time: 13
Number of customers completed transaction: 212
Number of customers left in servers: 1
Customers left in queue: 0
Average wait time: 0.06
************** END SIMULATION *************
```

Quick Review

1. A stack is a data structure wherein the items are added and deleted from one end only.
2. A stack is a Last In First Out (LIFO) data structure.
3. The basic operations on a stack are as follows: push an item onto the stack, pop an item from the stack, initialize the stack, destroy the stack, check whether the stack is empty, and check whether the stack is full.
4. A stack can be implemented as an array or a linked list.
5. The middle elements of a stack should not be accessed directly.

6. To inspect the top element of a stack, it must first be removed from the stack.
7. Stacks are restricted versions of arrays and linked lists.
8. The postfix notation does not require the use of parentheses to enforce operator precedence.
9. In postfix notation, operators are written after the operands.
10. Postfix expressions are evaluated according to the following rules:
    a. Scan the expression from left to right.
    b. If an operator is found, back up to get the required number of operands, evaluate the operator, and continue.
11. A queue is a data structure wherein the items are added at one end and removed from the other end.
12. A queue is a First In First Out (FIFO) data structure.
13. The basic operations on a queue are as follows: add an item to the queue, remove an item from the queue, initialize the queue, destroy the queue, check whether the queue is empty, and check whether the queue is full.
14. A queue can be implemented as an array or a linked list.
15. The middle elements of a queue should not be accessed directly.
16. To inspect the front element of a queue, it must first be removed from the queue.
17. Queues are restricted versions of arrays and linked lists.

EXERCISES

1. Consider the following statements.

```
stackType<int> stack;
int x, y;
```

Show what is output by the following segment of code.

```
stack.initializeStack();

x = 4;
y = 6;
stack.push(7);
stack.push(x);
stack.push(x + 5);
stack.pop(y);
stack.push(x + y);
stack.push(y - 2);
```

```
stack.push(3);
stack.pop(x);
cout<<"x = "<<x<<endl;
cout<<"y = "<<y<<endl;
while(!stack.isEmptyStack())
{
  stack.pop(y);
  cout<<y<<endl;
}
```

2. Consider the following statements.

```
stackType<int> stack;
int x, y;
```

Suppose that the input is

```
14 45 34 23 10 5 -999
```

Show what is output by the following segment of code.

```
stack.initializeStack();

stack.push(5);
cin>>x;
while (x != -999)
{
   if(x % 2 == 0)
   {
        if(!stack.fullStack())
          stack.push(x);
   }
   else
        cout<<"x = "<<x<<endl;
   cin>>x;
}

cout<<"Stack Elements: ";

while(!stack.isEmptyStack())
{
   stack.pop(y);
   cout<<" "<<y;
}
cout<<endl;
```

3. Evaluate the following postfix expressions.

   a. `8 2 + 3 * 16 4 / - =`

   b. `12 25 5 1 / / * 8 7 + - =`

   c. `70 14 4 5 15 3 / * - - / 6 + =`

   d. `3 5 6 * + 13 - 18 2 / + =`

18

4. Convert the following infix expressions to postfix notations.

   a. `(A + B ) * (C + D) - E`

   b. `A - (B + C) * D + E / F`

   c. `((A + B) / (C - D) + E) * F - G`

   d. `A + B * ( C + D ) - E / F * G + H`

5. Consider the following statements.

```
stackType<int> stack;
queueType<int> queue;
int x, y;
```

   Show what is output by the following segment of code.

```
queue.initializeQueue();
x = 4;
y = 5;
queue.addQueue(x);
queue.addQueue(y);
queue.deQueue(x);
queue.addQueue(x + 5);
queue.addQueue(16);
queue.addQueue(x);
queue.addQueue(y - 3);

cout<<"Queue Elements: ";
while(!queue.isEmptyQueue())
{
  queue.deQueue(y);
  cout<<" "<<y;
}
```

6. Consider the following statements.

```
stackType<int> stack;
queueType<int> queue;
int x, y;
```

   Suppose the input is

```
15 28 14 22 64 35 19 32 7 11 13 30 -999
```

   Show what is written by the following segment of code.

```
stack.initializeStack()
queue.initializeQueue();
stack.push(0);
queue.addQueue (0);
cin>>x;
```

```
while(x != -999)
{
    switch(x % 4)
    {
    case 0: stack.push(x);
            break;
    case 1: if(!stack.isEmptyStack())
            {
                stack.pop(y);
                cout<<"Stack Element = "<<y<<endl;
            }
            else
                cout<<"Sorry stack is empty"<<endl;
            break;
    case 2: queue.addQueue(x);
            break;
    case 3: if(!queue.isEmptyQueue())
            {
                queue.deQueue(y);
                cout<<"Queue Element = "<<y<<endl;
            }
            else
                cout<<"Sorry queue is empty"<<endl;
            break;
   }//end switch

   cin>>x;
}//end while

cout<<"Stack Elements: ";
while(!stack.isEmptyStack())
 {
    stack.pop(x);
    cout<<x<<" ";
 }

cout<<endl;
cout<<"Queue Elements: ";
while(!queue.isEmptyQueue())
{
    queue.deQueue(x);
    cout<<x<<" ";
}
      cout<<endl;
```

7. Write a function template, `reverseStack`, that takes as a parameter a stack object and a queue object whose elements are of the same type. The function `reverseStack` uses the queue to reverse the elements of the stack.

8. Write a function template, `reverseQueue`, that takes as a parameter a stack object and a queue object whose elements are of the same type. The function `reverseQueue` uses the stack to reverse the elements of the queue.
9. Write the definition of the function template, `printListReverse`, that uses a stack to print a linked list in reverse order. Assume that this function is a member of the `class linkedListType`, designed in Chapter 17.
10. Add the operation `queueCount` to the `class queueType` (the array implementation of queues), which returns the number of elements in the queue. Write the definition of the function template to implement this operation.

PROGRAMMING EXERCISES

1. Two stacks of the same type are the same if they have the same size and their elements at the corresponding positions are the same. Overload the relational operator == for the `class stackType` that returns `true` if two stacks of the same type are same; `false` otherwise. Also, write the definition of the function template to overload this operator.
2. Repeat Exercise 1 for the `class linkedStackType`.
3. a. Add the following operation to the `class stackType`

   ```
   void reverseStack(stackType<Type> &otherStack);
   ```

   This operation copies the elements of a stack in reverse order onto another stack.

   Consider the following statements.

   ```
   stackType<int> stack1;
   stackType<int> stack2;
   ```

   The statement

   ```
   stack1.reverseStack(stack2);
   ```

   copies the elements of `stack1` onto `stack2` in reverse order. That is, the top element of `stack1` is the bottom element of `stack2`, and so on. The old contents of `stack2` are destroyed and `stack1` is unchanged.

   b. Write the definition of the function `template` to implement the operation `reverseStack`.
4. Repeat Exercises 3a and 3b for the `class linkedStackType`.
5. Write a program that outputs an appropriate message of grouping symbols, such as parentheses and braces, if an arithmetic expression matches. For example, the expression `{25 + ( 3 - 6) * 8}` contains matching grouping symbols.
6. Write a program that uses a stack to print the prime factors of a positive integer in descending order.

7. The Programming Example, Converting a Number from Binary to Decimal, in Chapter 11, uses recursion to convert a binary number into an equivalent decimal number. Write a program that uses a stack to convert a binary number into an equivalent decimal number.
8. The Programming Example, Converting a Number from Decimal to Binary, in Chapter 11, contains a program that uses recursion to convert a decimal number into an equivalent binary number. Write a program that uses a stack to convert a decimal number into an equivalent binary number.
9. **(Infix to Postfix)** Write a program that converts an infix expression into an equivalent postfix expression.

   The rules to convert an infix expression into an equivalent postfix expression are as follows:

   Suppose `infx` represents the infix expression and `pfx` represents the postfix expression. The rules to convert `infx` into `pfx` are as follows:

   a. Initialize `pfx` to an empty expression and also initialize the stack.

   b. Get the next symbol, `sym`, from `infx`.

      b.1. If `sym` is an operand, append `sym` to `pfx`.

      b.2. If `sym` is `(`, push `sym` into the stack.

      b.3. If `sym` is `)`, pop and append all the symbols from the stack until the most recent left parentheses. Pop and discard the left parentheses.

      b.4 If `sym` is an operator:

         b.4.1 Pop and append all the operators from the stack to `pfx` that are above the most recent left parentheses and have precedence greater than or equal to `sym`.

         b.4.2 Push `sym` into the stack.

   c. After processing `infx`, some operators might be left in the stack. Pop and append to `pfx` everything from the stack.

   In this program, you will consider the following (binary) arithmetic operators: `+`, `-`, `*`, and `/`. You may assume that the expressions you will process are error-free.

   Design a class that stores the infix and postfix strings. The class must include the following operations:

   1. **`getInfix`**: Stores the infix expression.
   2. **`showInfix`**: Outputs the infix expression.
   3. **`showPostfix`**: Outputs the postfix expression.

      Some other operations that you might need are the following:

   4. **`convertToPostfix`**: Converts the infix expression into a postfix expression. The resulting postfix expression is stored in `postfixString`.

5. `precedence`: Determines the precedence between two operators. If the first operator is of higher or equal precedence than the second operator, it returns the value `true`; otherwise, it returns the value `false`.

   Include the constructors and destructors for automatic initialization and dynamic memory deallocation.

   Test your program on the following expressions:

   1. `A + B - C;`
   2. `(A + B ) * C;`
   3. `(A + B) * (C - D);`
   4. `A + ((B + C) * ( E - F) - G) / (H - I);`
   5. `A + B * ( C + D ) - E / F * G + H;`

   For each expression, your answer must be in the following form:

   ```
   Infix Expression: A + B - C;
   Postfix Expression: AB+C-
   ```

10. Write the definitions of the functions to overload the assignment operator and copy constructor for the `class queueType`. Also, write a program to test these operations.
11. Write the definitions of the functions to overload the assignment operator and copy constructor for the `class linkedQueueType`. Also, write a program to test these operations.
12. This chapter described the array implementation of queues that use a special array slot, called the reserved slot, to distinguish between an empty and a full queue. Write the definition of the class and the definitions of the function members of this queue design. Also, write a test program to test the various operations on a queue.
13. Write the definition of the function `runSimulation` to complete the design of the computer simulation program (see the section, "Application of Queues: Simulation"). Test run your program for a variety of data. In this exercise, use a random number generator to decide whether a customer arrived at a given time unit.

APPENDIX

RESERVED WORDS

and	and_eq	asm	auto
bitand	bitor	bool	break
case	catch	char	class
compl	const	const_cast	continue
default	delete	do	double
dynamic_cast	else	enum	explicit
export	extern	false	float
for	friend	goto	if
inline	int	long	mutable
namespace	new	not	not_eq
operator	or	or_eq	private
protected	public	register	signed
reinterpret_cast	return	short	struct
sizeof	static	static_cast	throw
switch	template	this	typeid
true	try	typedef	using
typename	union	unsigned	wchar_t
virtual	void	volatile	
while	xor	xor_eq	

APPENDIX

B

OPERATOR PRECEDENCE

Precedence (highest to lowest)

The following table shows the precedence (highest to lowest) and associativity of the operators in C++.

Operator	Associativity
:: (binary scope resolution)	Left to right
:: (unary scope resolution)	Right to left
()	Left to right
[] -> .	Left to right
++ -- (as postfix operators)	Right to left
typeid dynamic_cast	Right to left
static_cast const_cast	Right to left
reinterpret_cast	Right to left
++ -- (as prefix operators) ! + (unary) - (unary)	Right to left
~ & (address of) * (dereference)	Right to left
new delete sizeof	Right to left
->* -- .*	Left to right
* / %	Left to right
+ -	Left to right
<< >>	Left to right
< <= > >=	Left to right
== !=	Left to right
&	Left to right
^	Left to right
|	Left to right
&&	Left to right

Operator	Associativity
`||`	Left to right
`?:`	Right to left
`=   +=   -=   *=   /=   %=`	Right to left
`<<=   >>=   &=   |=   ^=`	Right to left
`throw`	Right to left
`,` (the sequencing operator)	Left to right

APPENDIX

C

CHARACTER SETS

ASCII (American Standard Code for Information Interchange)

The following table shows the ASCII character set.

	ASCII									
	0	1	2	3	4	5	6	7	8	9
0	nul	soh	stx	etx	eot	enq	ack	bel	bs	ht
1	lf	vt	ff	cr	so	si	del	dc1	dc2	dc3
2	dc4	nak	syn	etb	can	em	sub	esc	fs	gs
3	rs	us	b	!	"	#	$	%	&	'
4	(	)	*	+	,	-	.	/	0	1
5	2	3	4	5	6	7	8	9	:	;
6	<	=	>	?	@	A	B	C	D	E
7	F	G	H	I	J	K	L	M	N	O
8	P	Q	R	S	T	U	V	W	X	Y
9	Z	[	\	]	^	_	`	a	b	c
10	d	e	f	g	h	i	j	k	l	m
11	n	o	p	q	r	s	t	u	v	w
12	x	y	z	{	|	}	~	del		

The numbers 0–12 in the first column specify the left digit(s), and the numbers 0–9 in the second row specify the right digit of each character in the ASCII data set. For example, the character in the row marked 6 (the number in the first column) and the column marked 5 (the number in the second row) is A. Therefore, the character at position 65 (which is the 66th character) is A. Moreover, the character b at position 32 represents the space character.

The first 32 characters, that is, the characters at positions 00–31 and at position 127 are nonprintable characters. The following table shows the abbreviations and meanings of these characters.

`nul`	null character
`soh`	start of header
`stx`	start of text
`etx`	end of text
`eot`	end of transmission
`enq`	enquiry
`ack`	acknowledge
`bel`	bell
`bs`	back space
`ht`	horizontal tab
`lf`	line feed
`vt`	vertical tab
`ff`	form feed
`cr`	carriage return
`so`	shift out
`si`	shift in
`del`	data link escape
`dc1`	device control 1
`dc2`	device control 2
`dc3`	device control 3
`dc4`	device control 4
`nak`	negative acknowledge
`syn`	synchronous idle
`etb`	end of transmitted block
`can`	cancel
`em`	end of medium
`sub`	substitute
`esc`	escape
`fs`	file separator
`gs`	group separator
`rs`	record separator
`us`	unit separator
`b`	space
`del`	delete

C

EBCDIC (Extended Binary Coded Decimal Interchange Code)

The following table shows some of the characters in the EBCDIC character set.

	EBCDIC									
	0	1	2	3	4	5	6	7	8	9
6					b					
7						.	<	(	+	|
8	&									
9	!	$	*	)	;	¬	-	/		
10							^	,	%	_
11	>	?								
12		`	:	#	@	'	=	"		a
13	b	c	d	e	f	g	h	i		
14						j	k	l	m	n
15	o	p	q	r						
16		~	s	t	u	v	w	x	y	z
17								\	{	}
18	[	]								
19				A	B	C	D	E	F	G
20	H	I								J
21	K	L	M	N	O	P	Q	R		
22							S	T	U	V
23	W	X	Y	Z						
24	0	1	2	3	4	5	6	7	8	9

The numbers 6-24 in the first column specify the left digit(s), and the numbers 0-9 in the second row specify the right digits of the characters in the EBCDIC data set. For example, the character in the row marked 19 (the number in the first column) and the column marked 3 (the number in the second row) is `A`. Therefore, the character at position 193 (which is the 194th character) is `A`. Moreover, the character `b` at position 64 represents the space character. The preceding table does not show all the characters in the EBCDIC character set. In fact, the characters at positions 00-63 and 250-255 are nonprintable control characters.

APPENDIX

D

OPERATOR OVERLOADING

The following table lists the operators that can be overloaded.

<table>
<tr><th colspan="8">Operators that can be overloaded</th></tr>
<tr><td>+</td><td>-</td><td>*</td><td>/</td><td>%</td><td>^</td><td>&</td><td>|</td></tr>
<tr><td>!</td><td>&&</td><td>||</td><td>=</td><td>==</td><td><</td><td><=</td><td>></td></tr>
<tr><td>>=</td><td>!=</td><td>+=</td><td>-=</td><td>*=</td><td>/=</td><td>%=</td><td>^=</td></tr>
<tr><td>|=</td><td>&=</td><td><<</td><td>>></td><td>>>=</td><td><<=</td><td>++</td><td>—</td></tr>
<tr><td>->*</td><td>,</td><td>-></td><td>[]</td><td>()</td><td>~</td><td>new</td><td>delete</td></tr>
</table>

The following table lists the operators that cannot be overloaded.

Operators that cannot be overloaded				
.	.*	::	?:	sizeof

APPENDIX

E

NAMING CONVENTIONS OF HEADER FILES IN ANSI/ISO STANDARD C++ AND STANDARD C++

The programs in this book are written using ANSI/ISO Standard C++ while simultaneously indicating (in the earlier chapters) how to write the same program using Standard C++. From the programs in this book it is clear that the header files in Standard CPP have the extension `.h`, while the header files in ANSI/ISO Standard CPP have no extension. Moreover, the names of certain header files, such as `math.h`, in ANSI/ISO Standard C++ start with the letter `c`. The language C++ evolved from C. Therefore, certain header files—such as `math.h`, `stdlib.h`, and `string.h`—were brought from C into C++. The header files_such as `iostream.h`, `iomanip.h`, and `fstream.h`—were specially designed for C++. Recall that when a header file is included in a program, the global identifiers of the header file also become the global identifiers of the program. In ANSI/ISO Standard C++, to take advantage of the `namespace` mechanism, all of the header files were modified so that the identifiers are declared within a `namespace`. Recall that the name of this `namespace` is `std`. In ANSI/ISO Standard C++, the extension `.h` of the header files that were specially designed for C++ was dropped. For the header files that were brought from C into C++, the extension `.h` was dropped and the names of these header files started with the letter `c`. Following are the names of the most commonly used header files in Standard C++ and ANSI/ISO Standard C++:

Standard CPP Header File Name	ANSI/ISO Standard CPP Header File Name
assert.h	cassert
ctype.h	cctype
float.h	cfloat
fstream.h	fstream
iostream.h	iostream
iomanip.h	iomanip
limits.h	climits
math.h	cmath
stdlib.h	cstdlib
string.h	cstring

To include the header file, say **iostream**, the following statement is required:

```
#include <iostream>
```

Furthermore, to use identifiers, such as **cin**, **cout**, **endl**, and so on, the program should use either the statement

```
using namespace std;
```

or the prefix **std::** before the identifier.

APPENDIX

F

HEADER FILES

The C++ standard library contains many predefined functions, named constants, and specialized data types. This appendix discusses some of the most widely used library routines (and several named constants). For additional explanation and information on functions, named constants, and so on, check your system documentation. The names of the Standard C++ header files are shown in parentheses.

Header File `cassert` (`assert.h`)

The following table describes the function **`assert`**. Its specification is contained in the header file **`cassert`** (**`assert.h`**).

`assert(expression)`	`expression` is any `int expression;` `expression` is usually a logical expression	• If the value of the `expression` is nonzero (`true`), the program continues to execute. • If the value of the `expression` is 0 (`false`), execution of the program terminates immediately. The expression, the name of the file containing the source code, and the line number in the source code are displayed.

To disable all the `assert` statements, place the preprocessor directive **`#define`** `NDEBUG` before the directive **`#include`** `<cassert>`.

Header File `cctype` (`ctype.h`)

The following table shows various functions from the header file **`cctype`** (**`ctype.h`**).

Function Name and Parameters	Parameter(s) Types	Function Return Value
`isalnum(ch)`	`ch` is a `char` value	Function returns an `int` value as follows: • If `ch` is a letter or a digit character, that is (`'A'-'Z'`, `'a'-'z'`, `'0'-'9'`), it returns a nonzero value (`true`) • `0` (`false`), otherwise
`iscntrl(ch)`	`ch` is a `char` value	Function returns an `int` value as follows: • If `ch` is a control character (in ASCII, a character value `0-31` or `127`), it returns a nonzero value (`true`) • `0` (`false`), otherwise
`isdigit(ch)`	`ch` is a `char` value	Function returns an `int` value as follows: • If `ch` is a digit (`'0'-'9'`), it returns a nonzero value (`true`) • `0` (`false`), otherwise
`islower(ch)`	`ch` is a `char` value	Function returns an `int` value as follows: • If `ch` is lowercase (`'a'-'z'`), it returns a nonzero value (`true`) • `0` (`false`), otherwise
`isprint(ch)`	`ch` is a `char` value	Function returns an `int` value as follows: • If `ch` is a printable character, including blank (in `ASCII`, `' '` through `'~'`), it returns a nonzero value (`true`) • `0` (`false`), otherwise
`ispunct(ch)`	`ch` is a `char` value	Function returns an `int` value as follows: • If `ch` is a punctuation character, it returns a nonzero value (`false`) • `0` (`true`), otherwise
`isspace(ch)`	`ch` is a `char` value	Function returns an `int` value as follows: • If `ch` is a whitespace character (blank, newline, tab, carriage return, form feed), it returns a nonzero value (`true`) • `0` (`false`), otherwise
`isupper(ch)`	`ch` is a `char` value	Function returns an `int` value as follows: • If `ch` is an uppercase letter (`'A'-'Z'`), it returns a nonzero value (`true`) • `0` (`false`), otherwise
`tolower(ch)`	`ch` is a `char` value	Function returns a `char` value as follows: • If `ch` is an uppercase letter, it returns the lowercase equivalent of `ch` • `ch`, otherwise
`toupper(ch)`	`ch` is a `char` value	Function returns a `char` value as follows: • If `ch` is a lowercase letter, it returns the uppercase equivalent of `ch` • `ch`, otherwise

Header File cfloat (float.h)

In Chapter 2, we listed the largest and smallest values belonging to the floating-point data types. We also remarked that these values are system-dependent. These largest and smallest values are stored in named constants. The header file **cfloat** contains many such named constants. The following table lists some of these constants.

Named Constant	Description
FLT_DIG	Approximate number of significant digits in a **float** value
FLT_MAX	Maximum positive **float** value
FLT_MIN	Minimum positive **float** value
DBL_DIG	Approximate number of significant digits in a **double** value
DBL_MAX	Maximum positive **double** value
DBL_MIN	Minimum positive **double** value
LDBL_DIG	Approximate number of significant digits in a **long double** value
LDBL_MAX	Maximum positive **long double** value
LDBL_MIN	Minimum positive **long double** value

A program similar to the following can print the values of these named constants on your system.

```
#include <iostream>
#include <cfloat>

using namespace std;

int main()
{
    cout<<"Approximate number of significant digits "
        <<"in a float value "<<FLT_DIG<<endl;
    cout<<"Maximum positive float value "<<FLT_MAX<<endl;
    cout<<"Minimum positive float value "<<FLT_MIN<<endl;
    cout<<"Approximate number of significant digits "
        <<"in a double value "<<DBL_DIG<<endl;
    cout<<"Maximum positive double value "<<DBL_MAX<<endl;
    cout<<"Minimum positive double value "<<DBL_MIN<<endl;
    cout<<"Approximate number of significant digits "
        <<"in a long double value "<<LDBL_DIG<<endl;
    cout<<"Maximum positive long double value "<<LDBL_MAX
        <<endl;
```

```
    cout<<"Minimum positive long double value "<<LDBL_MIN
        <<endl;

    return 0;
}
```

In the previous program, to use Standard C++ header files, replace the statements

```
#include <iostream>
#include <cfloat>
using namespace std;
```

with the statements

```
#include <iostream.h>
#include <float.h>
```

Header File `climits` (`limits.h`)

In Chapter 2, we listed the largest and smallest values belonging to the integral data types. We also remarked that these values are system-dependent. These largest and smallest values are stored in named constants. The header file **`climits`** contains many such named constants. The following table lists some of these constants.

3Named Constant	Description
`CHAR_BIT`	Number of bits in a byte
`CHAR_MAX`	Maximum **`char`** value
`CHAR_MIN`	Minimum **`char`** value
`SHRT_MAX`	Maximum **`short`** value
`SHRT_MIN`	Minimum **`short`** value
`INT_MAX`	Maximum **`int`** value
`INT_MIN`	Minimum **`int`** value
`LONG_MAX`	Maximum **`long`** value
`LONG_MIN`	Minimum **`long`** value
`UCHAR_MAX`	Maximum **`unsigned char`** value
`USHRT_MAX`	Maximum **`unsigned short`** value
`UINT_MAX`	Maximum **`unsigned int`** value
`ULONG_MAX`	Maximum **`unsigned long`** value

A program similar to the following can print the values of these named constants on your system.

```
#include <iostream>
#include <climits>

using namespace std;

int main()
{
     cout<<"Number of bits in a byte "<<CHAR_BIT<<endl;
     cout<<"Maximum char value "<<CHAR_MAX<<endl;
     cout<<"Minimum char value "<<CHAR_MIN<<endl;
     cout<<"Maximum short value "<<SHRT_MAX<<endl;
     cout<<"Minimum short value "<<SHRT_MIN<<endl;
     cout<<"Maximum int value "<<INT_MAX<<endl;
     cout<<"Minimum int value "<<INT_MIN<<endl;
     cout<<"Maximum long value "<<LONG_MAX<<endl;
     cout<<"Minimum long value "<<LONG_MIN<<endl;
     cout<<"Maximum unsigned char value "<<UCHAR_MAX<<endl;
     cout<<"Maximum unsigned short value "<<USHRT_MAX<<endl;
     cout<<"Maximum unsigned int value "<<UINT_MAX<<endl;
     cout<<"Maximum unsigned long value "<<ULONG_MAX<<endl;

     return 0;
}
```

In the above program, to use the Standard C++ header files, replace the statements

```
#include <iostream>
#include <climits>
using namespace std;
```

with the statements

```
#include <iostream.h>
#include <limits.h>
```

Header File `cmath` (`math.h`)

The following table shows various math functions.

Function Name and Parameters	Parameter(s) Type	Function Return Value
`acos(x)`	x is a floating-point expression, $-1.0 \le x \le 1.0$	Arc cosine of x, a value between 0.0 and π
`asin(x)`	x is a floating-point expression, $-1.0 \le x \le 1.0$	Arc sine of x, a value between $-\pi/2$ and $\pi/2$
`atan(x)`	x is a floating-point expression	Arc tan of x, a value between $-\pi/2$ and $\pi/2$
`ceil(x)`	x is a floating-point expression	The smallest whole number $\ge$ x ("ceiling" of x)

Function Name and Parameters	Parameter(s) Type	Function Return Value
`cos(x)`	`x` is a floating-point expression, `x` is measured in radians	Trigonometric cosine of the angle; for example, if `x = 90`, `cos(x)` is 0
`cosh(x)`	`x` is a floating-point expression	Hyperbolic cosine of `x`
`exp(x)`	`x` is a floating-point expression	The value `e` raised to the power of `x`; (`e = 2.718...`)
`fabs(x)`	`x` is a floating-point expression	Absolute value of `x`
`floor(x)`	x is a floating-point expression	The largest whole number ≤ `x`; ("floor" of x)
`log(x)`	`x` is a floating-point expression where `x > 0.0`	Natural logarithm (base `e`) of `x`
`log10(x)`	`x` is a floating-point expression where `x > 0.0`	Common logarithm (base `10`) of `x`
`pow(x,y)`	`x` and `y` are floating-point expressions. If `x = 0.0`, `y` must be positive; if `x ≤ 0.0`, `y` must be a whole number.	`x` raised to the power of `y`
`sin(x)`	`x` is a floating-point expression; `x` is measured in radians	Trigonometric sine of the angle; for example, if `x = 90, sin(x)` is 1
`sinh(x)`	`x` is a floating-point expression	Hyperbolic sine of `x`
`sqrt(x)`	`x` is a floating-point expression; where `x ≥ 0.0`	Square root of `x`
`tan(x)`	`x` is a floating-point expression; `x` is measured in radians	Trigonometric tangent of the angle; for example, if `x = 45, tax(x)` is 1
`tanh(x)`	`x` is a floating-point expression	Hyperbolic tangent of `x`

Header File `cstddef (stddef.h)`

Among others, this header file contains the definition of the following symbolic constant:

`NULL`: The system-dependent null pointer (usually 0)

Header File `cstring (string.h)`

The following table shows various string functions.

Function Name and Parameters	Parameter(s) Type	Function Return Value
`strcat(destStr, srcStr)`	`destStr` and `srcStr` are null-terminated `char` arrays; `destStr` must be large enough to hold the result	The base address of `destStr` is returned; `srcStr`, including the null character is concatenated to the end of `destStr`

Function Name and Parameters	Parameter(s) Type	Function Return Value
`strcmp(str1, str2)`	`str1` and `str2` are null-terminated `char` arrays	The returned value is as follows: • An `int` value < `0`, if `str1 < str2` • An `int` value `0`, if `str1 = str2` • An `int` value > `0`, if `str1 > str2`
`strcpy(destStr, srcStr)`	`destStr` and `srcStr` are null-terminated `char` arrays	The base address of `destStr` is returned; `srcStr` is copied into `destStr`
`strlen(str)`	`str` is a null-terminated `char` array	An `int` value ≥ `0` specifying the length of the `str` (excluding the `'\0'`) is returned

F

Header File `string`

This header file—not to be confused with the header file `cstring`—supplies a programmer-defined data type named `string`. Associated with the `string` type are a data type `string::size_type` and a named constant `string::npos`. These are defined as follows:

```
string::size_type      An unsigned integer type
string::npos           The maximum value of type string::size_type
```

Several functions are associated with the `string` type. The following table shows some of these functions. Unless stated otherwise, `str`, `str1`, and `str2` are variables (objects) of the type `string`. The position of the first character in a `string` variable (such as `str`) is `0`, the second character is `1`, and so on.

Function Name and Parameters	Arguments	Effect and Function Return Value
`str.c_str()`	None	The base address of a null-terminated C-string corresponding to the characters in `str`.
`getline(istreamVar, str)`	`istreamVar` is an input stream variable (of the type `istream` or `ifstream`). `str` is a `string` object (variable).	Characters until the newline character are input from `istreamVar` and stored into `str`. (The newline character is read but not stored into `str`.) The value returned by this function is usually ignored.
`str.empty()`	None	Returns `true` if `str` is empty, that is, the number of characters in `str` is zero, `false` otherwise.
`str.length()`	None	A value of the type `string::size_type`, giving the number of characters in the string.

Function Name and Parameters	Arguments	Effect and Function Return Value
`str.size()`	None	A value of the type `string::size_type`, giving the number of characters in the string.
`str.find(strExp)`	`str` is a string object and `strExp` is a string expression evaluating to a string. The string expression, `strExp`, can also be a character.	The `find` function searches `str` to find the first occurrence of the string or the character specified by `strExp`. If the search is successful, the function `find` returns the position in `str` where the match begins. If the search is unsuccessful, the function returns the special value `string::npos`
`str.substr(pos, len)`	Two unsigned integers, `pos` and `len.pos`, represent the starting position (of the substring in `str`), and `len` represents the length (of the substring). The value of `pos` must be less than `str.length()`.	A temporary string object that holds a substring of `str` starting at `pos`. The length of the substring is at most `len` characters. If `len` to too large, it means "to the end" of the string in `str`.
`str1.swap(str2);`	One parameter of the type `string`. `str1` and `str2` are objects of the type `string`.	The contents of `str1` and `str2` are swapped.
`str.clear();`	None	Removes all characters from `str`.
`str.erase();`	None	Removes all characters from `str`.
`str.erase(m);`	One parameter of the type `string::size_type`.	Removes all characters from `str` starting at the index `m`.
`str.erase(m, n);`	Two parameters of the type `int`.	Starting at the index `m`, removes the next `n` characters from `str`. If `n` > length of `str`, removes all characters starting at the `m`th.
`str.insert(m, c);`	Parameter `m` and `n` are of the type `string::size_type`; `c` is a character.	Inserts the character `c` at the index `m` into `str`.
`str.insert(m, n, c);`	Parameter `m` is of the type `string::size_type`;	Inserts `n` occurrences of the character `c` at the index `m` into `str`.
`str1.insert(m, str2);`	Parameter `m` is of the type `string::size_type`;	Inserts all characters of `str2` at the index `m` into `str1`.
`str1.replace(m, n, str2);`	Parameters `m` and `n` are of the type `string::size_type`.	Starting at the index `m`, replaces the next `n` characters of `str1` with all the characters of `str2`. If `n` > length of `str1`, then all characters until the end of `str1` are replaced.

APPENDIX

G

MEMORY SIZE ON A SYSTEM

A program similar to the following prints the memory size for the built-in data types on your system. (The output of the program shows the size of the built-in data type on which this program was run.)

```
#include <iostream>
using namespace std;

int main()
{
   cout<<"Size of char = "<<sizeof(char)
       <<endl;
   cout<<"Size of int = "<<sizeof(int)
       <<endl;
   cout<<"Size of short = "<<sizeof(short)
       <<endl;
   cout<<"Size of unsigned int = "<<sizeof(unsigned int)
       <<endl;
   cout<<"Size of long = "<<sizeof(long)
       <<endl;
   cout<<"Size of bool = "<<sizeof(bool)
       <<endl;
   cout<<"Size of float = "<<sizeof(float)
       <<endl;
   cout<<"Size of double = "<<sizeof(double)
       <<endl;
   cout<<"Size of long double = "<<sizeof(long double)
       <<endl;
   cout<<"Size of unsigned short = "<<sizeof(unsigned short)
       <<endl;
   cout<<"Size of unsigned long = "<<sizeof(unsigned long)
       <<endl;

   return 0;
}
```

Output:

```
Size of char = 1
Size of int = 4
Size of short = 2
Size of unsigned int = 4
Size of long = 4
Size of bool = 1
Size of float = 4
Size of double = 8
Size of long double = 8
Size of unsigned short = 2
Size of unsigned long = 4
```

APPENDIX

H

ANSWERS TO SELECTED EXERCISES

Chapter 1

1. a. True; b. False; c. False; d. False; e. False; f; False; g. False; h. True; i. True; j. True
2. Control unit, instruction register, program counter, arithmetic logic unit, and accumulator.
4. Keyboard and mouse.
5. Screen and printer.
8. Instructions in a high-level language are closer to a natural language, such as English, and therefore, are easier to understand and learn than the machine language.

Chapter 2

1. a. False; b. False; c. False; d. True; e. True; f. False; g. True; h. True; i. False; j. True; k. False
3. a, b
5. a. `3`; b. not possible; c. not possible; d. `38.5`; e. `1`; f. `2`; g. `2`; h. `420.0`
8. Only the variable declaration **`double x, y, z;`** is correct
9. `a` and `c` are valid
12. `x = 5`

    `y = 2`

    `z = 3`

    `w = 9`
14. a. `x = 2, y = 5, z = 6`

    b. `x + y = 7`

    c. `Sum of 2 and 6 is 8`

    d. `z / x = 3`

    e. `2 times 2 = 4`
17. `a` and `c` are correct
20. a. `x = x + 5 - z;`

    b. `y = y * (2 * x + 5 - z);`

    c. `w = w + 2 * z + 4;`

    d. `x = x - (z + y - t);`

    e. `sum = sum + num;`

22.

	a	b	c	sum
`sum = a + b + c;`	3	5	14.1	22
`c /= a;`	3	5	4.7	22
`b += c - a;`	3	6	4.7	22
`a *= 2 * b + c;`	50	6	4.7	22

Chapter 3

1. a. True; b. True; c. False; d. False; e. True; f. True
2. a. `x = 5, y = 28, ch = '3'`

   b. `x = 28, y = 36, ch = '5'`

   c. `x = 5, y = 8, ch = '2'`

   d `x = 5, y = 28, ch = ' '`
5. `cout<<setfill('*')<<setw(35)<<'*'<<endl;`
7. a. Invalid data may cause the input stream to enter the fail state.

   b. When an input stream enters the fail state, all further inputs associated with that input stream are ignored. The program continues to execute with whatever values the variables have.

Chapter 4

1. a. False; b. False; c. False; d. True; e. False; f. False; g. False; h. False; i. False; j. True
2. a. i; b. i; c. ii; d. i; e. iii.
5. Omit the semicolon after **else**. The correct statement is

```
if(score >= 60)
   cout<<"You pass."<<endl;
else
   cout<<"You fail."<<endl;
```

7. `15`
9. `96`

10.

```
#include <iostream>
using namespace std;

int main ()
{
       int a, b, c found;
       cout<<"Enter two integers: ";
       cin>>a>>b;

       if(a > a*b  &&  10 < b)
              found = 2* a > b;
       else
       {
              found = 2 * a < b;
              if(found)
                 a = 3;
              c = 15;
              if(b)
              {
                     b = 0;
                     a = 1;
              }
       }
       return 0;
}
```

Chapter 5

1. a. False; b. True; c. False; d. True; e. True; f. True; g. True
2. `y = 1 and count = 100`
3. `5`
5. `if ch > 'Z' or ch < 'A'`
6. `Sum = 112`
8. `Sum = 157`
12. `8  23  21  0  23  0  12  1  20`
14. `0 10 30 60`
15. `2 7 17 37 77 157`
17. a. `*`
    b. Infinite loop
    c. Infinite loop
    d. `****`
    e. `******`
    f. `***`

20. `11 19 30 49`

26.

a.

```
cin>>number;
while(number != -1)
{
     total =  total + number;
     cin>>number;
}
cout<<endl;
cout<<total;
```

27. a.

```
number = 1;
while(number <= 10)
{
    cout<<setw(3)<<number;
    number++;
}
```

30.

a.

```
1  2  3  4  5
2  4  6  8 10
3  6  9 12 15
4  8 12 16 20
5 10 15 20 25
```

b.

```
1  1  1  1  1
2  2  2  2  2
3  3  3  3  3
4  4  4  4  4
5  5  5  5  5
```

Chapter 6

1. a. False; b. True; c. True; d. True; e. False
3. a. Invalid; the function return type is missing.
   b. Valid.
   c. Invalid; the data type for the parameter `b` is missing.
   d. Invalid; the parentheses after the function name are missing.
5. a. `4`
   b. `26`
   c. `10 4 0`
   d. `0`

8. a. (i) 125; (ii) 432
   b. The function computes x^3, where **x** is the argument of the function.

Chapter 7

1. a. True; b. False; c. True; d. False; e. True; f. False; g. False; h. False; i. True
5.

```
3  4  20  78
7  3  20  4
7  5  6   2
```

8.

```
10 20
5 20
```

9.

```
Line 4: In main: num1 = 10, num2 = 20, and t = 15
Line 11: In funOne: a = 10, x = 15, z = 25, and t = 15
Line 13: In funOne: a = 10, x = 20, z = 25, and t = 20
line 15: In funOne: a = 22, x = 20, z = 25, and t = 20
Line 17: In funOne: a = 22, x = 33, z = 25, and t = 33
Line 6: In main after funOne: num1 = 22, num2 = 20, and t = 33
Line 19: In funTwo: u = 20, v = 22, aTwo = 20, and t = 33
Line 11: In funOne: a = 20, x = 20, z = 40, and t = 33
Line 13: In funOne: a = 20, x = 25, z = 40, and t = 33
line 15: In funOne: a = 32, x = 25, z = 40, and t = 33
Line 17: In funOne: a = 32, x = 25, z = 40, and t = 46
Line 21: In funTwo after funOne: u = 25, v = 22, aTwo = 32, and t = 46
Line 23: In funTwo: u = 38, v = 22, aTwo = 32, and t = 46
Line 25: In funTwo: u = 38, v = 22, aTwo = 32, and t = 92
Line 8: In main after funTwo: num1 = 22, num2 = 38, and t = 92
```

11. (i), (ii), and (iv) are correct.

Chapter 8

1. a. True; b. False; c. True; d. False; e. False; f. True; g. True; h. True; i. False; j. True; k. False
4. a. true; b. false; c. true; d. false
6. The namespace mechanism cannot be used with Standard C++ style header files, that is, header files that end with **.h**. Therefore, remove **.h** at Line 1.
8. The keyword **namespace** in Line 3 is missing.

Chapter 9

1. a. True; b. True; c. False; d. False; e. True; f. False; g. False; h. False; i. True; j. False; k. False

2. a. Valid
   b. Valid
   c. Invalid; the assignment operator is not defined for C-strings.
   d. Valid
   e. Valid
   f. Invalid; relational operators are not defined for C-strings.
   g. Valid.
5.
   a. `strcpy(str1, "Sunny Day");`
   b. `length = strlen(str1);`
   c. `strcpy(str2, name);`
   d.

```
if(strcmp(str1,str2)<= 0)
   cout<<str1;
else
  cout<<str2;
```

7.
   a. `funcOne(list,50);`
   d. `funcTwo(list,Alist);`
9. a. Valid
   b. Valid
   c. Valid
   d. Invalid; the assignment operator is not defined for C-strings.
   e. Invalid; the relational and assignment operators are not defined for C-strings.
   f. Valid
   g. Valid
   h. Valid
11. List elements: `11 16 21 26 30`

Chapter 10

1. a. False; b. True; c. False; d. False; e. False
2. a. 8
   b. 6
   c. 1
   d. 8

4.

a.

Iteration	first	last	mid	list[mid]	No of comparisons
1	0	10	5	55	2
2	0	4	2	17	2
3	0	1	0	2	2
4	1	1	1	10	2
5	2	1	the loop stops		

This is an unsuccessful search. The total number of comparisons is 8.

5. a. 30

   b. 5

   e. column

6. a. `int alpha[10][20];`

   b.

```
for(j = 0; j < 10; j++)
  for(k = 0; k < 20; k++)
      alpha[j][k] = 0;
```

   e.

```
for(j = 0; j < 10; j++)
{
   for(k = 0; k < 20; k++)
      cout<<alpha[j][k]<<" ";
  cout<<endl;
 }
```

7. a. `beta is initialized to zero.`

   d.

```
First row of beta:  0 2 0
Second row of beta: 2 0 2
Third row of beta:  0 2 0
```

Chapter 11

1. a. True; b. True; c. False; d. False; e. False

2. a. Base case:

```
if(u == 0)
   cout<<v;
else if(u == 1)
     cout<<static_cast<char>(static_cast<int>(v) + 1);
```

H

b. Recursive case: `funcRec(u - 1, v);`

c. B

Chapter 12

1. a. False; b. False; c. True; d. True; e. True; f. True; g. False
3. a. Invalid; the member `name` of `newEmployee` is a `struct`. Specify the member of `name` to store the value `"John Smith"`. For example,

```
newEmployee.name.first = "John";
newEmployee.name.first = "Smith";
```

   b. Invalid; the member `name` of `newEmployee` is a `struct`. There are no aggregate input operations on structs. The correct statements are

```
cin>>newEmployee.name.first;
cin>>newEmployee.name.last;
```

   c. Valid

   d. Valid

   e. Invalid; `employees` is an array. There is no aggregate assignment operation on arrays.

Chapter 13

1. a. False ; b. False; c. True; d. False; e. False
4. a. (i) Constructor in Line 1.

   (ii) Constructor in Line 3.

   (iii) Constructor in Line 4.

   b.

```
CC::CC()
{
  u = 0;
  v = 0;
}
```

   c.

```
CC::CC(int x)
{
  u = x;
  v = 0;
}
```

Chapter 14

1. a. True; b. True; c. True; d. False

4. The private members of a class are **private**; they cannot be directly accessed by the member functions of the derived class. The **protected** members of the base class can be directly accessed by the member functions of the derived class.

5. a. The statement

```
class bClass public aClass
```

should be

```
class bClass: public aClass
```

b. The semicolon after } is missing.

7.

a.

```
yClass::yClass()
{
    a = 0;
    b = 0;
}
```

b.

```
xClass::xClass()
{
    z = 0;
}
```

c.

```
void yClass::two(int u, int v)
{
    a = u;
    b = v;
}
```

11.

```
In base: x = 7
In derived: x = 3, y = 8; x + y = 11
**** 7
#### 11
```

Chapter 15

1. a. False; b. False; c. False; d. True; e. True; f. True; g False; h. False

2. a. Valid

   b. Valid

   c. Invalid; **p** is a pointer variable and **x** is an **int** variable. The value of **x** cannot be assigned to **p**.

   d. Valid

H

e. Valid

f. Invalid; `*p` is an `int` variable and `q` is a pointer variable. The value of `q` cannot be assigned to `*p`.

5. b and c
7. `78 78`
8. The statement in Line 5 copies the value of `p` into `q`. After this statement executes, both `p` and `q` point to the same memory location. The statement in Line 7 deallocates the memory space pointed to by `q`, which in turn invalidates both `p` and `q`. Therefore, the values printed by the statement in Line 8 are unpredictable.
9. `4 4 5 7 10 14 19 25 32 40`
12. The statement in Line 6 copies the value of `p` into `q`. After this statement executes, both `p` and `q` point to the same array. The statement in Line 7 deallocates the memory space, which is an array, pointed to by `p`, which in turns invalidates `q`. Therefore, the values printed by the statement in Line 9 are unpredictable.
16. Classes with pointer data members should include the destructor, overload the assignment operator, and explicitly provide the copy constructor by including it in the class definition and providing its definition.
17.

```
ClassA x: 4

ClassA x: 6
ClassB y: 5
```

19. In compile-time binding, the compiler generates the necessary code to call a function. In run-time binding, the run-time system generates the necessary code to make the appropriate function call.

Chapter 16

1. a. False; b. True; c. True; d. False; e. False; f. True; g. False; h. True; i. False; j. True; k. False
5. When the class has pointer data members.
7.

a. `friend strange operator+(const strange&, const strange&);`

b. `friend bool operator==(const strange&, const strange&);`

c. `friend strange operator++(strange&, int);`

9. In Line 2, the word `friend` before the word `bool` is missing. The correct statement is:

```
friend  bool operator <= (mystery, mystery);     //Line 2
```

11. None.
14. Two.
17. Error in Line 4. A template instantiation can be for only a built-in type or a user-defined type. The word "type" between the angular brackets must be replaced either with a built-in type or a user-defined type.

19. a. `12` b. `Sunny Day`

20. a. `21` b. `OneHow`

21.

```
template <class Type>
void swap(Type &x, Type &y)
{
   Type temp;
   temp = x;
   x = y;
   y = temp;
}
```

Chapter 17

1. a. False; b. False; c. False; d. False; e. True; f. True
3. a. True; b. True; c. False; d. False; e. True
4.
   a. Valid
   b. Valid
   c. Valid
   d. Invalid; `B` is a pointer while `*List` is a `struct`.
   e. Valid
   f. Invalid; `B` is a pointer while `A->link->info` is of the type `int`.
   g. Valid
   h. Valid
   i. Valid
6. This is an infinite loop, continuously printing `18`.
7. a. This is an invalid code. The statement `s->info = B;` is invalid because `B` is a pointer and `s->info` is an `int`.

   b. This is an invalid code. After the statement `s = s->link;` executes, `s` is `NULL` and so `s->info` does not exist.

Chapter 18

1.

```
x = 3
y = 9
7
13
4
7
```

2.

```
x = 45
x = 23
x = 5
Stack Elements: 10 34 14 5
```

4. a. AB+CD+*E-

b. ABC+D*-EF/+

c. AB+CD-/E+F*G-

d. ABCD+*+EF/G*-H+

6.

```
Queue Element = 0
Queue Element = 14
Queue Element = 22
Sorry queue is empty
Sorry queue is empty
Stack Element = 32
Stack Elements: 64 28 0
Queue Elements: 30
```

8.

```
template <class Type>
void reverseQueue(queueType<Type> &q, stackType<Type> &s)
{
   Type elem;

   while(!q.isEmptyQueue())
   {
       q.deQueue(elem);
       s.push(elem);
   }

   while(!s.isEmptyStack())
   {
       s.pop(elem);
       q.addQueue(elem);
   }
}
```

Index

Note:

- Page numbers followed by *def* indicate definitions and accompanying descriptions.
- Page numbers followed by *tbl* indicate tables.

Symbols

Numbers

A

D

F

G

H

N

O

Q

S

T

Malik